Fodor's 2011

SPAIN

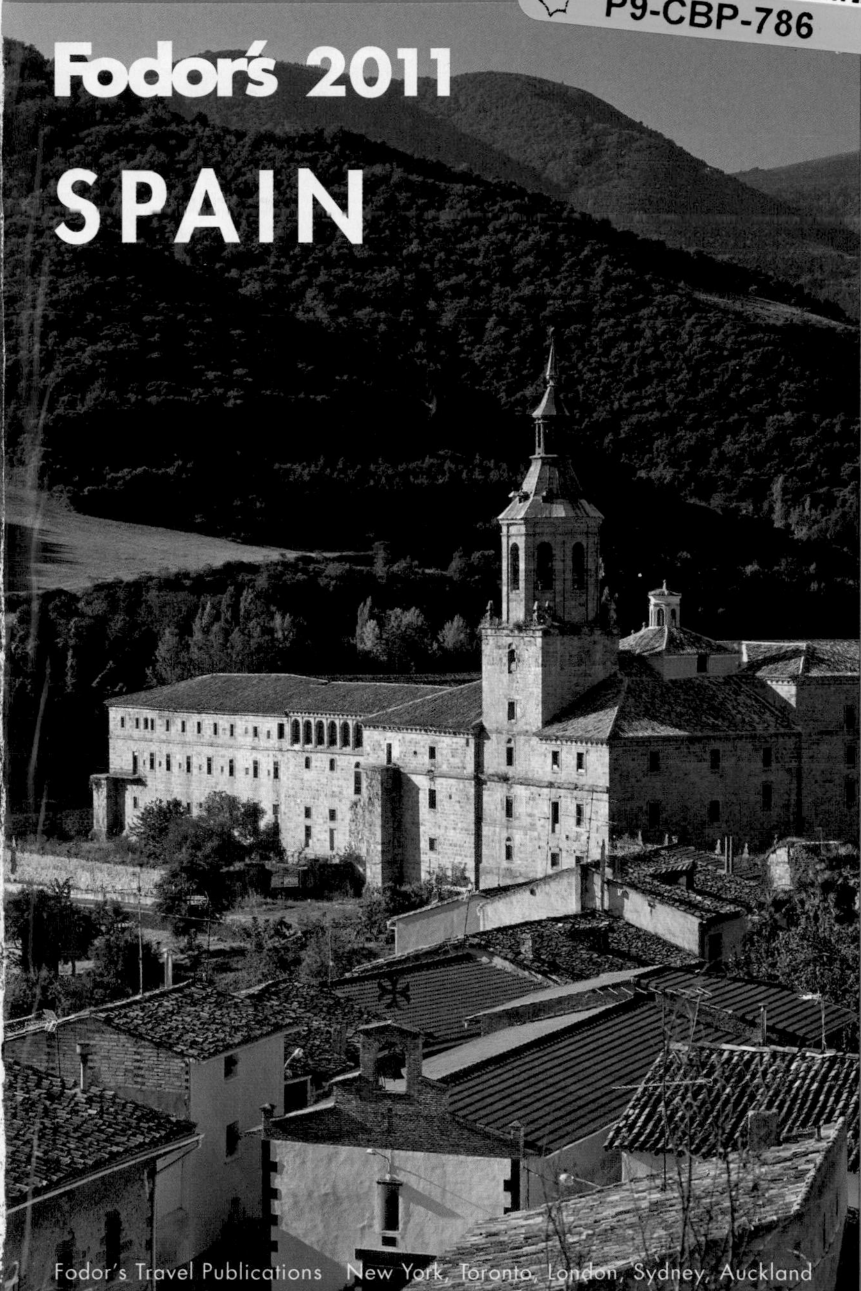

Fodor's Travel Publications New York, Toronto, London, Sydney, Auckland

www.fodors.com

Dalí

Be a Fodor's Correspondent

Your opinion matters. It matters to us. It matters to your fellow Fodor's travelers, too. And we'd like to hear it. In fact, we need to hear it.

When you share your experiences and opinions, you become an active member of the Fodor's community. That means we'll not only use your feedback to make our books better, but we'll publish your names and comments whenever possible. Throughout our guides, look for "Word of Mouth," excerpts of your unvarnished feedback.

Here's how you can help improve Fodor's for all of us.

Tell us when we're right. We rely on local writers to give you an insider's perspective. But our writers and staff editors—who are the best in the business—depend on you. Your positive feedback is a vote to renew our recommendations for the next edition.

Tell us when we're wrong. We're proud that we update most of our guides every year. But we're not perfect. Things change. Hotels cut services. Museums change hours. Charming cafés lose charm. If our writer didn't quite capture the essence of a place, tell us how you'd do it differently. If any of our descriptions are inaccurate or inadequate, we'll incorporate your changes in the next edition and will correct factual errors at fodors.com immediately.

Tell us what to include. You probably have had fantastic travel experiences that aren't yet in Fodor's. Why not share them with a community of like-minded travelers? Maybe you chanced upon a beach or bistro or B&B that you don't want to keep to yourself. Tell us why we should include it. And share your discoveries and experiences with everyone directly at fodors.com. Your input may lead us to add a new listing or highlight a place we cover with a "Highly Recommended" star or with our highest rating, "Fodor's Choice."

Give us your opinion instantly at our feedback center at www.fodors.com/feedback. You may also e-mail editors@fodors.com with the subject line "Spain Editor." Or send your nominations, comments, and complaints by mail to Spain Editor, Fodor's, 1745 Broadway, New York NY 10019.

You and travelers like you are the heart of the Fodor's community. Make our community richer by sharing your experiences. Be a Fodor's correspondent.

Tim Jarrell, Publisher

FODOR'S SPAIN 2011
Editor: Caroline Trefler

Editorial Contributors: Paul Cannon, K. Aleisha Fetters, Ignacio Gómez, Kati Krause, Jared Lubarsky, George Semler

Production Editor: Jennifer DePrima
Maps & Illustrations: Mark Stroud and David Lindroth, *cartographers;* Bob Blake, Rebecca Baer, *map editors;* William Wu, *information graphics*
Design: Fabrizio La Rocca, *creative director*; Guido Caroti, Siobhan O'Hare, *art directors*; Tina Malaney, Chie Ushio, Ann McBride, Jessica Walsh, *designers*; Melanie Marin, *senior picture editor*
Cover Photo: (Albarracín, Aragón) Ripani Massimo/eStock Photo
Production Manager: Angela L. McLean

ISBN 978-1-4000-0481-2

ISSN 0071-6545

SPECIAL SALES
This book is available at special discounts for bulk purchases for sales promotions or premiums. Special editions, including personalized covers, excerpts of existing books, and corporate imprints, can be created in large quantities for special needs. For more information, write to Special Markets/Premium Sales, 1745 Broadway, MD 6-2, New York, New York 10019, or e-mail specialmarkets@randomhouse.com.

AN IMPORTANT TIP & AN INVITATION
Although all prices, opening times, and other details in this book are based on information supplied to us at press time, changes occur all the time in the travel world, and Fodor's cannot accept responsibility for facts that become outdated or for inadvertent errors or omissions. So **always confirm information when it matters,** especially if you're making a detour to visit a specific place. Your experiences—positive and negative—matter to us. If we have missed or misstated something, **please write to us.** We follow up on all suggestions. Contact the Spain editor at editors@fodors.com or c/o Fodor's at 1745 Broadway, New York, NY 10019.

PRINTED IN CHINA

10 9 8 7 6 5 4 3 2 1

CONTENTS

Fodor's Features

MAPS

ABOUT THIS BOOK

Our Ratings

Sometimes you find terrific travel experiences, and sometimes they just find you. But usually the burden is on you to select the right combination of experiences. That's where our ratings come in.

As travelers we've all discovered a place so wonderful that its worthiness is obvious. And sometimes that place is so experiential that superlatives don't do it justice: you just have to be there to know. These sights, properties, and experiences get our highest rating, **Fodor's Choice,** indicated by orange stars throughout this book.

Black stars highlight sights and properties we deem **Highly Recommended,** places that our writers, editors, and readers praise again and again for consistency and excellence.

By default, there's another category: any place we include in this book is by definition worth your time, unless we say otherwise. And we will.

Disagree with any of our choices? Care to nominate a place or suggest that we rate one more highly? Visit our feedback center at www.fodors.com/feedback.

Budget Well

Hotel and restaurant price categories from ¢ to $$$$ are defined in the opening pages of each chapter. For attractions, we always give standard adult admission fees; reductions are usually available for children, students, and senior citizens. Want to pay with plastic? **AE, D, DC, MC, V** after restaurant and hotel listings indicate if American Express, Discover, Diners Club, MasterCard, and Visa are accepted.

Restaurants

Unless we state otherwise, restaurants are open for lunch and dinner daily. We mention dress only when there's a specific requirement and reservations only when they're essential or not accepted—it's always best to book ahead.

Hotels

Hotels have private bath, phone, TV, and air-conditioning and operate on the European Plan (aka EP, meaning without meals), unless we specify that they use the Continental Plan (CP, with a continental breakfast), Breakfast Plan (BP, with a full breakfast), or Modified American Plan (MAP, with breakfast and dinner) or are all-inclusive (including all meals and most activities). We always list facilities but not whether you'll be charged an extra fee to use them, so when pricing accommodations, find out what's included.

Listings

- ★ Fodor's Choice
- ★ Highly recommended
- ✉ Physical address
- ✣ Directions or Map coordinates
- Mailing address
- Telephone
- Fax
- On the Web
- E-mail
- Admission fee
- Open/closed times
- Ⓜ Metro stations
- Credit cards

Hotels & Restaurants

- Hotel
- Number of rooms
- Facilities
- Meal plans
- ✕ Restaurant
- Reservations
- Dress code
- Smoking
- BYOB

Outdoors

- Golf
- Camping

Other

- Family-friendly
- ⇨ See also
- Branch address
- ☞ Take note

Experience Spain

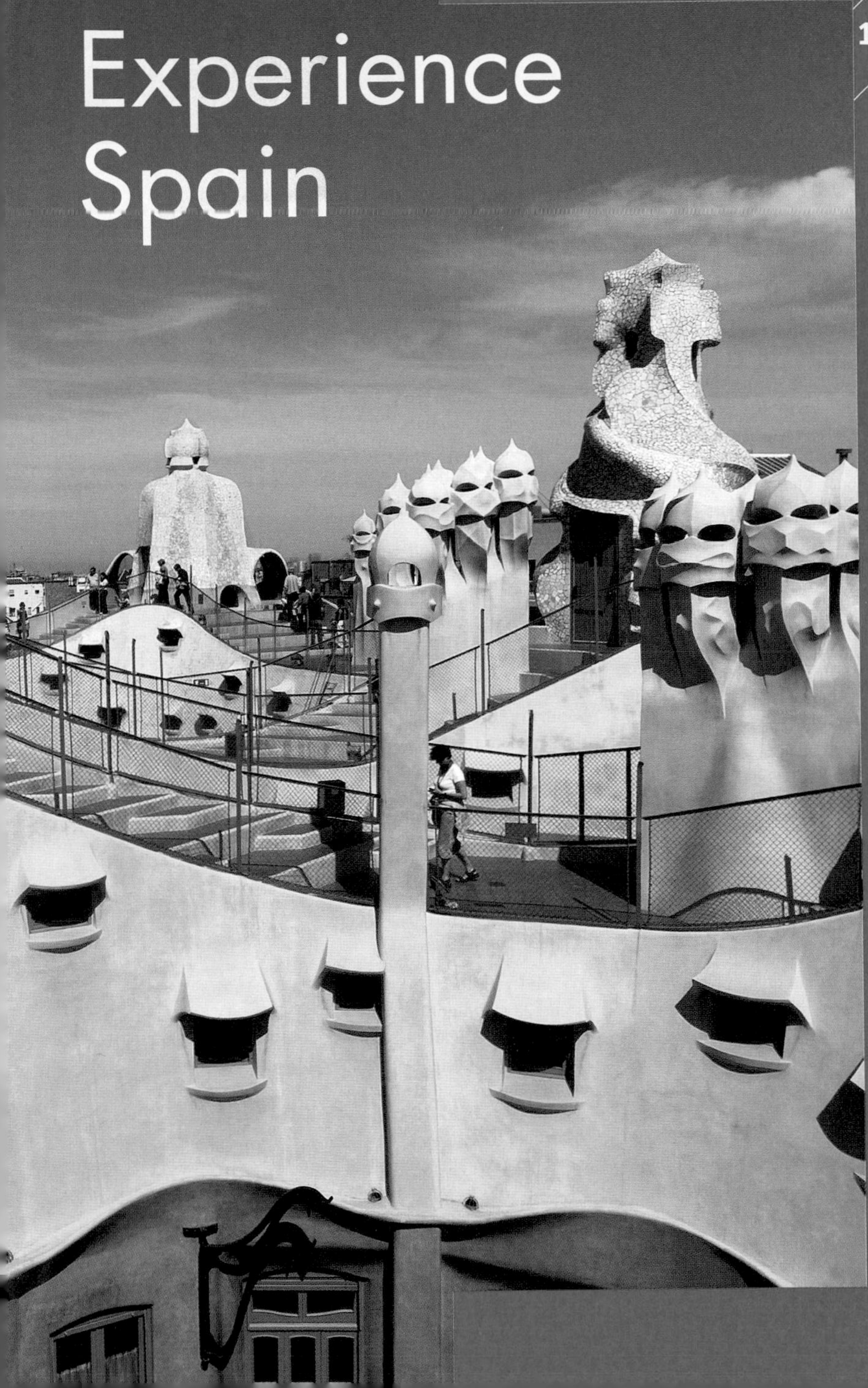

WHAT'S WHERE

Numbers refer to chapters.

2 Madrid. Its boundless energy makes sights and sounds larger than life. The Prado, Reina Sofía, and Thyssen-Bornemisza museums comprise one of the greatest repositories of Western art in the world. The cafés in the Plaza Mayor and the wine bars in the nearby Cava Baja buzz, and nightlife stretches into the wee hours around Plaza Santa Ana. Sunday's crowded flea market in El Rastro is thick with overpriced oddities.

3 Toledo and Trips from Madrid. From Madrid there are several important excursions, notably Toledo, as well as Segovia and Salamanca. Other cities in Castile–La Mancha and Castile–León worth checking out if you're traveling include León, Burgos, Soria, Sigüenza, and Cuenca. Extremadura, Spain's remote borderland with Portugal, is often overlooked, but has some intriguing places to discover. Highlights include prosperous Cáceres, packed with medieval and Renaissance churches and palaces; Trujillo, lined with mansions of Spain's imperial age; ancient Mérida, Spain's richest trove of Roman remains; and the Jerte Valley, which turns white in late March with the blossoming of its 1 million cherry trees.

4 Galicia and Asturias. On the way to Santiago de Compostela to pay homage to St. James, Christian pilgrims once crossed Europe to a corner of Spain so remote it was called *finis terrae* (end of the earth). Santiago still resonates with mystic importance. In the more mountainous Asturias, picturesque towns nestle in green highlands, and sandy beaches stretch out along the Atlantic. Farther east, in Cantabria, is the Belle Epoque beach resort of Santander.

5 Bilbao and the Basque Country. Greener and cloudier than the rest of Spain, and stubbornly independent in spirit, the Basque region is a country within a country, proud of its own language and culture as well as its coastline along the Bay of Biscay—one of the peninsula's wildest and most dramatic.

6 The Pyrenees. Cut by some 23 steep north–south valleys on the Spanish side alone, with four independent geographical entities—the valleys of Camprodón, Cerdanya, Aran, and Baztán—the Pyrenees has a wealth of areas to explore, with a dozen highland cultures and languages to match.

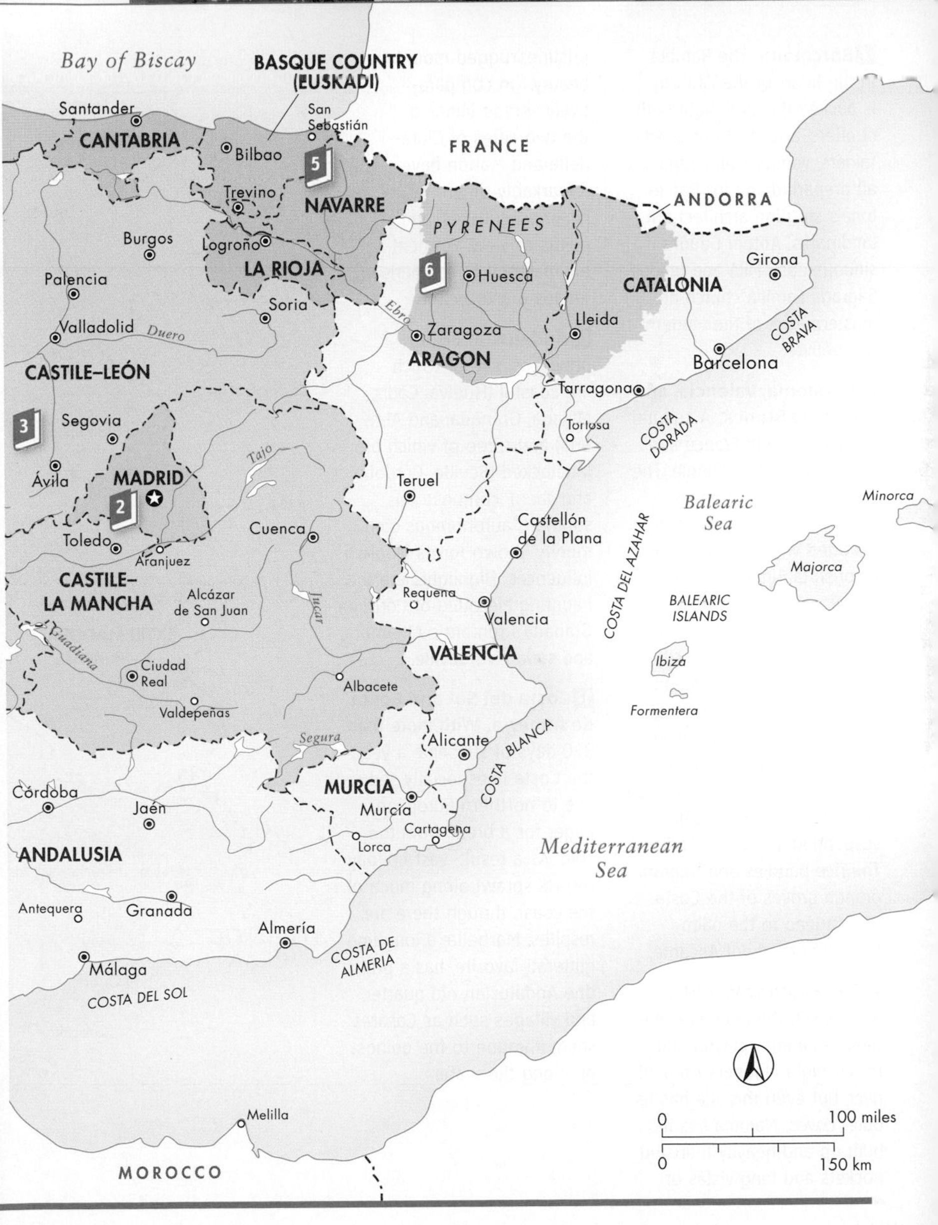
Bay of Biscay
BASQUE COUNTRY
(EUSKADI)
Santander
San Sebastián
CANTABRIA
Bilbao
5
FRANCE
Trevino
NAVARRE
ANDORRA
PYRENEES
Burgos
Logroño
LA RIOJA
6
Huesca
Girona
Palencia
CATALONIA
Soria
Ebro
Lleida
Valladolid
Duero
Zaragoza
COSTA BRAVA
Barcelona
CASTILE–LEÓN
ARAGON
Tarragona
3
Segovia
Tortosa
Tajo
COSTA DORADA
Ávila
MADRID
2
Teruel
Minorca
Balearic Sea
Toledo
Cuenca
Castellón de la Plana
Aranjuez
Majorca
CASTILE–LA MANCHA
Alcázar de San Juan
Requena
Jucar
Valencia
COSTA DEL AZAHAR
BALEARIC ISLANDS
Guadiana
VALENCIA
Ciudad Real
Ibiza
Albacete
Valdepeñas
Formentera
Segura
Alicante
COSTA BLANCA
Córdoba
MURCIA
Jaén
Murcia
Cartagena
Lorca
ANDALUSIA
Mediterranean Sea
Antequera
Granada
Almería
Málaga
COSTA DE ALMERIA
COSTA DEL SOL
Melilla
0
100 miles
0
150 km
MOROCCO

WHAT'S WHERE

7 Barcelona. The Rambla in the heart of the Old City is packed day and night with strollers, artists, street entertainers, vendors, and vamps, all preparing you for Barcelona's startling architectural landmarks. Antoni Gaudí's sinuous Casa Milà and unique Sagrada Família church are masterpieces of the Moderniste oeuvre.

8 Catalonia, Valencia, and the Costa Blanca. A cultural connection with France and Europe defines Catalonia. The citrus-scented, mountain-backed plain of the Levante is dotted with Christian and Moorish landmarks and extensive Roman ruins. Valencia's signature dish, *paella*, fortifies visitors touring the city's medieval masterpieces and exuberant modern architecture. The Costa Blanca has party-'til-dawn resort towns like Benidorm as well as small villages where time seems suspended in the last century. The rice paddies and fragrant orange groves of the Costa Blanca lead to the palm-fringed port city of Alicante.

9 The Balearic Islands. Ibiza is still the famous—infamous—summer playground for all-night clubbers from all over, but even this isle has its quiet coves. Majorca has its built-up and heavily touristed pockets and long vistas of pristine, rugged mountain beauty. On comparatively serene Minorca, the two cities of Ciutadella and Mahón have remarkably different histories, cultures, and points of view. Formentera, pastoral in comparison, retains a wild beauty.

10 Andalusia. Eight provinces, five of which are coastal (Huelva, Cádiz, Málaga, Granada, and Almería) and three of which are landlocked (Seville, Córdoba, and Jaén), compose this southern autonomous community known for its Moorish influences. Highlights are the haunting Mezquita of Córdoba, Granada's romantic Alhambra, and seductive Seville.

11 Costa del Sol and Costa de Almería. With more than 320 days of sunshine a year, the Costa is especially seductive to northern Europeans eager for a break from the cold. As a result, vast holiday resorts sprawl along much of the coast, though there are respites: Marbella, a longtime glitterati favorite, has a pristine Andalusian old quarter, and villages such as Casares seem immune to the goings-on along the water.

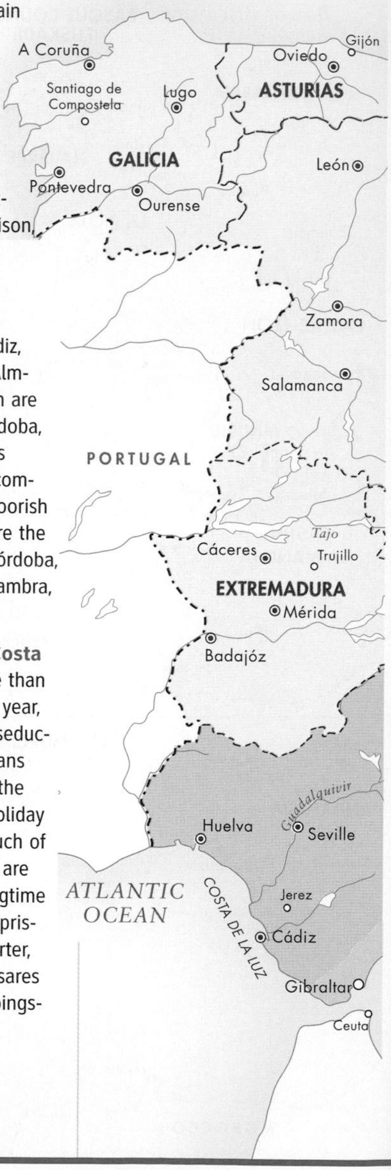

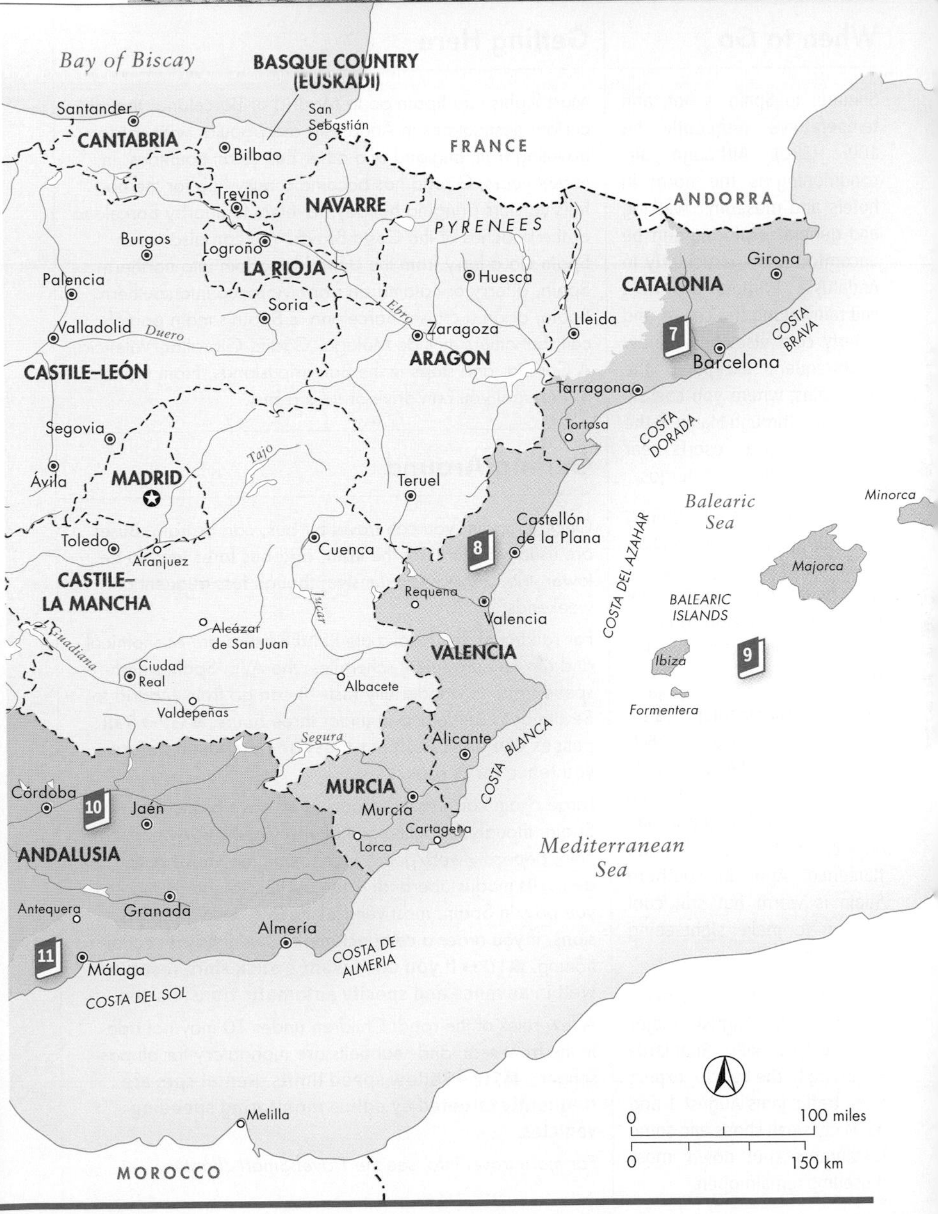

Bay of Biscay
BASQUE COUNTRY (EUSKADI)
Santander
San Sebastián
CANTABRIA
Bilbao
FRANCE
ANDORRA
Trevino
NAVARRE
PYRENEES
Burgos
Logroño
LA RIOJA
Palencia
Huesca
Girona
CATALONIA
Soria
Ebro
Lleida
Valladolid
Duero
Zaragoza
ARAGON
COSTA BRAVA
7
Barcelona
CASTILE–LEÓN
Tarragona
Tortosa
COSTA DORADA
Segovia
Tajo
Ávila
MADRID
Teruel
Balearic Sea
Minorca
Castellón de la Plana
Toledo
Aranjuez
Cuenca
8
COSTA DEL AZAHAR
Majorca
CASTILE–LA MANCHA
Requena
Valencia
BALEARIC ISLANDS
Júcar
Alcázar de San Juan
Guadiana
VALENCIA
Ibiza
9
Ciudad Real
Albacete
Valdepeñas
Formentera
Segura
Alicante
COSTA BLANCA
Córdoba
10
Jaén
MURCIA
Murcia
Cartagena
Lorca
ANDALUSIA
Mediterranean Sea
Antequera
Granada
Almería
COSTA DE ALMERIA
11
Málaga
COSTA DEL SOL
0
100 miles
Melilla
0
150 km
MOROCCO

SPAIN PLANNER

When to Go

Summer in Spain is hot, and temperatures frequently hit 100F (38C). Although air-conditioning is the norm in hotels and museums, walking and general exploring can be uncomfortable—particularly in Andalusia. Winters are mild and rainy along the coasts and bitterly cold elsewhere. Snow is infrequent except in the mountains, where you can ski December through March in the Pyrenees and at resorts near Granada, Madrid, and Burgos.

May and October are optimal for visiting Spain as it's generally warm and dry. May has more hours of daylight; October is the harvest season, which is especially colorful in the wine regions.

April has spectacular fiestas, particularly Valencia's Las Fallas and Seville's Semana Santa (Holy Week), which is followed by the *Feria de Abril* (April Fair), showcasing horses, bulls, and flamenco. April in southern Spain is warm but still cool enough to make sightseeing comfortable.

July and August mean crowds and heat. In August, major cities empty, with Spaniards migrating to the beach—expect huge traffic jams August 1 and 31. Many small shops and some restaurants shut down; most museums remain open.

Getting Here

Most flights into Spain go to Madrid or Barcelona, though certain destinations in Andalusia are popular with carriers traveling from England and other European countries; in recent years, Girona has become a busy hub for the no-frills carriers bringing holiday travelers to nearby Barcelona or the beaches of the Costa Brava. You can also reach Spain via a ferry from the United Kingdom into northern Spain, a ferry or catamaran from Morocco into southern Spain, or on a cruise: Barcelona is Spain's main port-of-call, but others include Málaga, Cádiz, Gibraltar, Valencia, A Coruña, and stops in the Balearic Islands. From France or Portugal you can drive or take a bus.

Getting Around

Once in Spain, you can travel by bus, car, or train. Buses are usually faster than the train, and bus fares tend to be lower, too. Service is extensive, though less frequent on weekends.

For rail travel, the local-route RENFE trains are economical and run on convenient schedules; the AVE, Spain's high-speed train, is wonderfully fast—it can go from Madrid to Seville or to Barcelona in under three hours. ■ **TIP→ Rail passes like the Eurailpass must be purchased before you leave for Europe.**

Large chain car rental companies all have branches in Spain, though the online outfit Pepe Car (🌐 *www.pepecar.com/pepecar/web/guest/index.html*) may have better deals. Its modus operandi is the earlier you book, the less you pay. In Spain, most vehicles have manual transmissions; if you order a compact, make sure it has air-conditioning. ■ **TIP→ If you don't want a stick shift, reserve well in advance and specify automatic transmission.**

A few rules of the road: Children under 10 may not ride in the front seat, and seat belts are mandatory for all passengers. ■ **TIP→ Follow speed limits. Rental cars are frequently targeted by police monitoring speeding vehicles.**

For more travel info, see the Travel Smart chapter.

Restaurant Basics

Most restaurants in Spain don't serve breakfast (*desayuno*); for coffee and carbs, head to a bar or *cafetería*. Outside major hotels, which serve morning buffets, breakfast in Spain is usually limited to coffee and toast or a roll. Lunch (*comida* or *almuerzo*) traditionally consists of an appetizer, a main course, and dessert, followed by coffee and perhaps a liqueur. Between lunch and dinner the best way to snack is to sample a variety of *tapas* (appetizers) at a bar. Dinner (*cena*) is somewhat lighter than lunch, with perhaps only one course. In addition to an à la carte menu, most restaurants offer a daily fixed-price menu (*menú del día*), including two courses, wine, and dessert at an attractive price. It's traditionally a lunch thing but is increasingly offered at dinner in popular tourist destinations.

Hotel Basics

There are many types of lodgings in Spain, from youth hostels (different from a hostal, which is a budget hotel) to boutique hotels and modern high-rises and various options in between. One of the most popular types of lodgings in Spain are the *paradors*—government-run, upmarket hotels, many of them in historic buildings or visit-worthy locations. Rates are reasonable, considering that most *paradors* have four- or five-star amenities, including a restaurant serving regional specialties. (⇨ *See the "A Night with History" Infocus feature for more information.)*

Do I Have to Eat So Late?

Many of the misunderstandings for visitors to Spain concern meal times. The Spanish eat no earlier than 1:30 PM for lunch, preferably after 2, and not before 9 PM for dinner. Dining out on the weekend can begin at 10 PM or even later. In areas with heavy tourist traffic, some restaurants open a bit earlier.

Siesta?

Dining is not the only part of Spanish life with a bizarre timetable. Outside of major cities most shops shut in the afternoons from 2 to 5, when shopkeepers go home to eat the main meal of the day and perhaps snooze for a while. It's best to work this into your plans on an "if you can't beat them, join them" basis, taking a quick siesta after lunch in preparation for a long night out on the town.

Smoking?

One of the major drawbacks of drinking and eating in Spanish bars and restaurants used to be the amount of cigarette smoke. Antismoking laws introduced in 2006, however, require bars and clubs with 100 square meters of space or more to provide a nonsmoking section; in most of the better restaurants, smoking is not allowed at all.

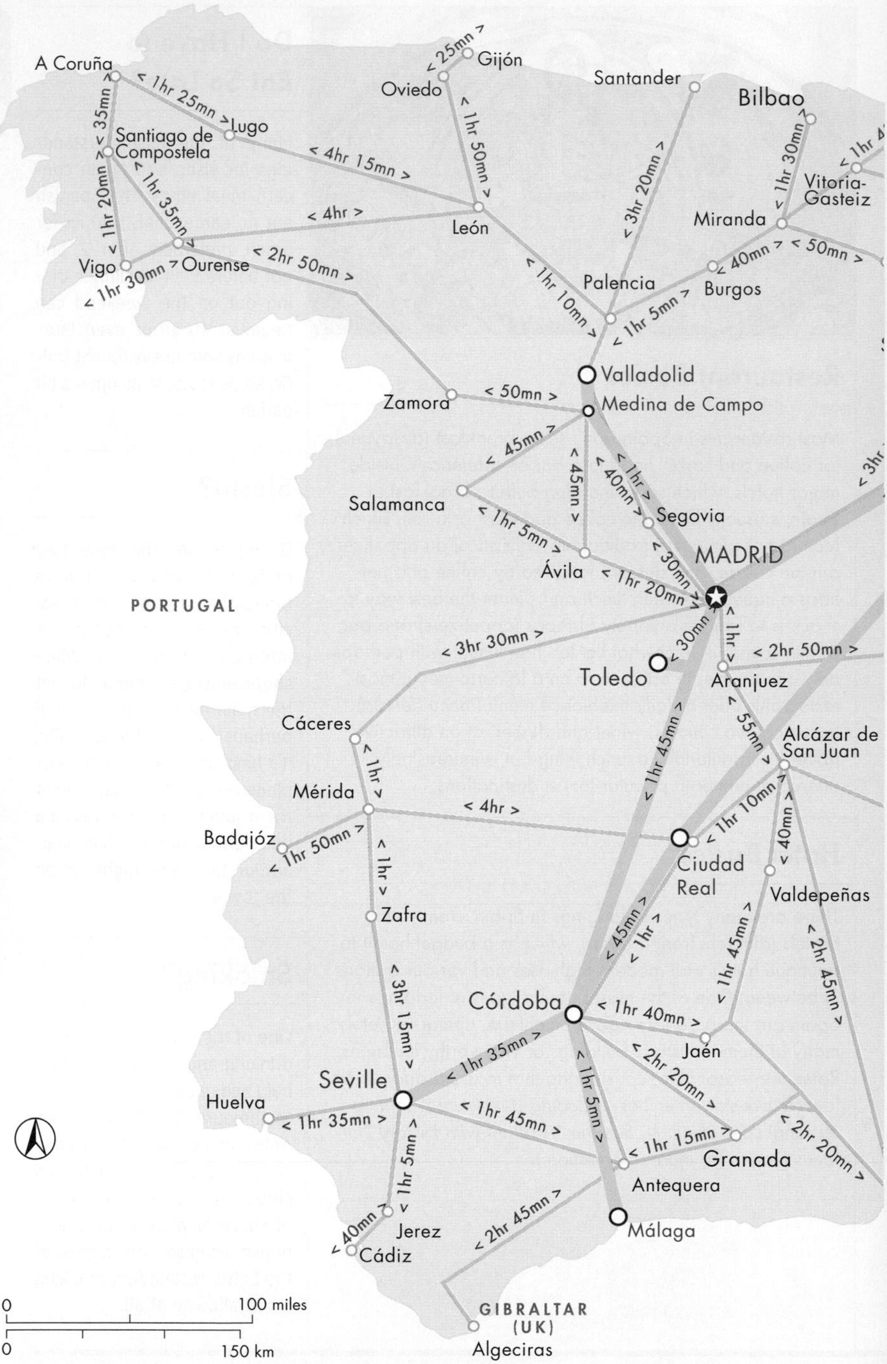
A Coruña
Gijón
Oviedo
Santander
Bilbao
Lugo
Santiago de Compostela
León
Vitoria-Gasteiz
Miranda
Vigo
Ourense
Palencia
Burgos
Valladolid
Zamora
Medina de Campo
Salamanca
Segovia
Ávila
MADRID
PORTUGAL
Toledo
Aranjuez
Cáceres
Alcázar de San Juan
Mérida
Badajóz
Ciudad Real
Valdepeñas
Zafra
Córdoba
Jaén
Seville
Huelva
Granada
Antequera
Jerez
Málaga
Cádiz
GIBRALTAR (UK)
Algeciras
< 25mn >
< 1hr 25mn >
< 35mn >
< 1hr 50mn >
< 4hr 15mn >
< 3hr 20mn >
< 1hr 30mn >
< 1hr 35mn >
< 1hr 20mn >
< 4hr >
< 2hr 50mn >
< 1hr 30mn >
< 1hr 10mn >
< 40mn >
< 50mn >
< 1hr 5mn >
< 50mn >
< 45mn >
< 45mn >
< 1hr >
< 40mn >
< 1hr 5mn >
< 30mn >
< 1hr 20mn >
< 3hr 30mn >
< 30mn >
< 1hr >
< 2hr 50mn >
< 1hr 45mn >
< 55mn >
< 1hr >
< 4hr >
< 1hr 10mn >
< 1hr 50mn >
< 1hr >
< 40mn >
< 45mn >
< 1hr >
< 1hr 45mn >
< 2hr 45mn >
< 3hr 15mn >
< 1hr 40mn >
< 1hr 35mn >
< 1hr 5mn >
< 2hr 20mn >
< 1hr 45mn >
< 1hr 35mn >
< 1hr 15mn >
< 2hr 20mn >
< 1hr 5mn >
< 40mn >
< 2hr 45mn >
0
100 miles
0
150 km

Travel Times by Train

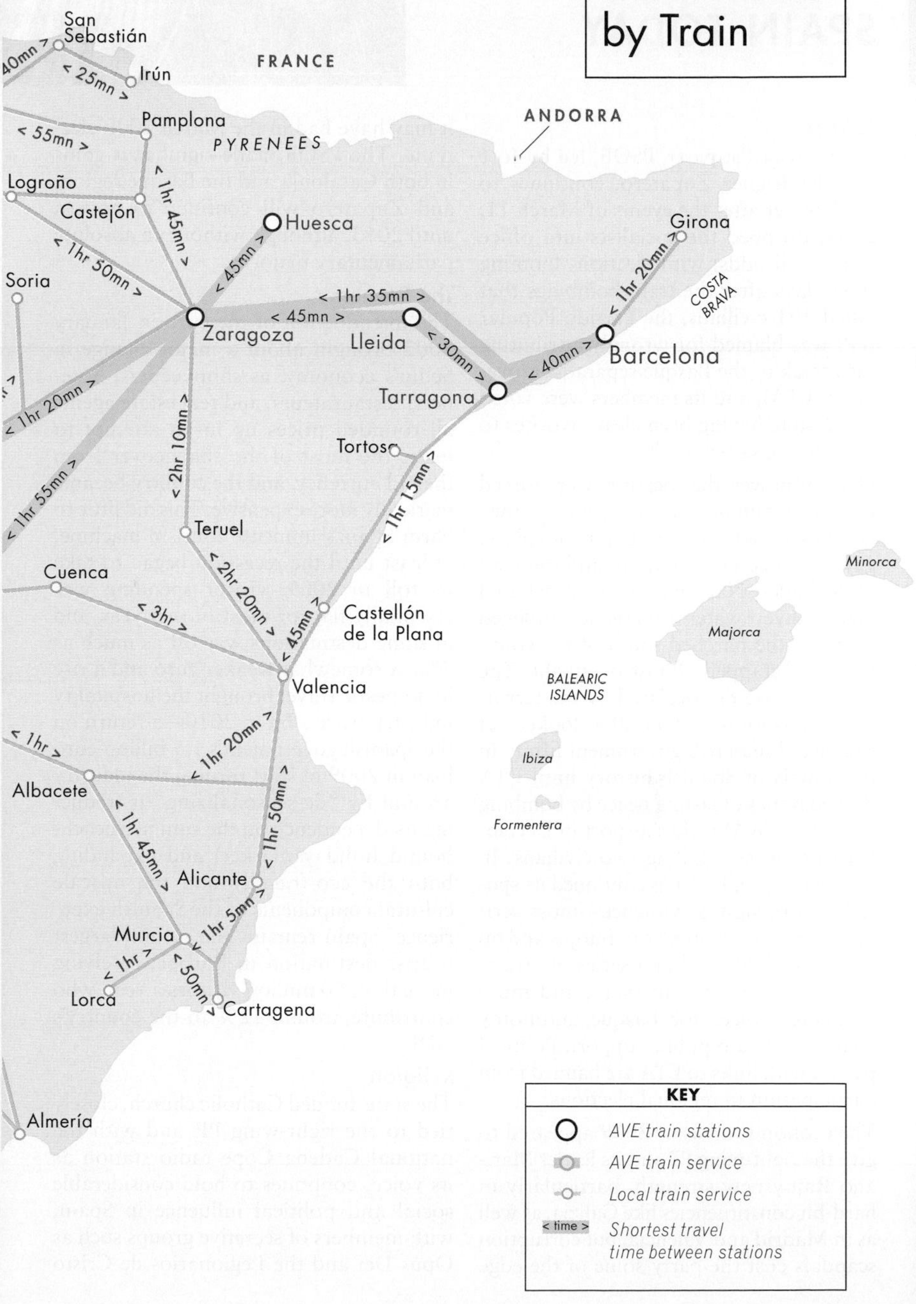

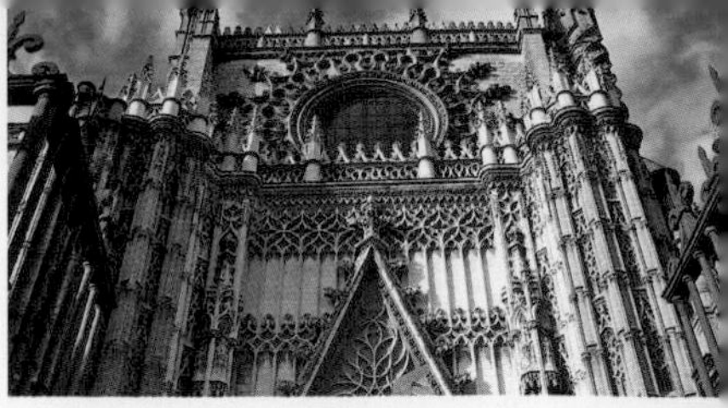

SPAIN TODAY

Politics

Spain's socialist party, PSOE, led by José Luis Rodriguez Zapatero, continues to hold power after the events of March 11, 2004, dropped the socialists into office against all odds: with elections looming three days after the train bombings that killed 191 civilians, the Partido Popular (PP) was blamed for wrongly attributing the attack to the Basque separatist movement (ETA), and its members were voted out despite having been clear favorites to win only days before.

Once in power, the socialists were forced to keep certain pre-electoral promises they never expected to be able to put into place: gay marriage became legal, and the Plan Hidrológico Nacional, a much-debated plan to divert water from the waterlogged north to the parched south of the country, was scrapped almost overnight. The historic cease-fire declared by the terrorist organization ETA in 2006 looked set to place Zapatero's government firmly in the annals of Spanish history until ETA dashed hopes of lasting peace by bombing a car park in Madrid's airport in December of that year, killing two civilians. In the years since, ETA has continued its sporadic campaign of violence—most seriously with bomb attacks in Burgos and on Majorca in 2009—but a series of arrests has weakened its leadership, and more moderate voices for Basque autonomy continue to gain public support. Political parties with links to ETA are banned from participation in regional elections.

The economic crisis of 2009 appeared to give the right-wing PP and its leader Mariano Rajoy new strength, particularly in hard-hit constituencies like Galicia, as well as in Madrid and Valencia, but corruption scandals cost the party some of the edge it may have had in the March 2009 elections. The PSOE made significant gains in both Catalonia and the Basque region, and Zapatero will continue to govern until 2013, although without an absolute parliamentary majority.

The Economy

The introduction of the euro in January 2002 brought about a major change in Spain's economy, as shopkeepers, hoteliers, restaurateurs, and real estate agents all rounded prices up in an attempt to make the most of the changeover from the old currency, and the country became markedly more expensive. This did little to harm Spain's immense tourism machine, at least until the recession began to take its toll in 2009; visitor spending was essentially flat for most of that year, and in some destinations was off as much as 7%. A somewhat weaker euro and a rise in domestic travel brought the hospitality industry back a bit in 2010—a return on the Spanish government's 1.5-billion-euro loan in 2009 to start turning the industry around by "de-seasonalizing" it (reducing its dependence on the summer beach-bound holiday market) and expanding both the eco-friendly and the upscale cultural components of the Spanish experience. Spain remains the second largest tourist destination in Europe, receiving more than 50 million visitors a year, who contribute around 12% to the country's GDP.

Religion

The state-funded Catholic church, closely tied to the right-wing PP, and with the national Cadena Cope radio station as its voice, continues to hold considerable social and political influence in Spain, with members of secretive groups such as Opus Dei and the Legionarios de Cristo

holding key government and industry positions.

Despite the church's influence, at street level, Spain has become a distinctly secular country, as demonstrated by the fact that 70% of Spaniards supported the decidedly un-Catholic 2005 law allowing gay marriage. And although more than 75% of the population claims to be Catholic, less than 20% go to church on a regular basis.

More than 1 million Muslims reside in Spain, making Islam the country's second-largest religion. Meanwhile, attendances at mass have been greatly bolstered over the last decade by strongly Catholic South American and Eastern European immigrants.

The Arts

Spain's devotion to the arts is clearly shown by the attention, both national and international, paid to its annual Principe de Asturias prize, where Prince Felipe hands out accolades to international high achievers such as Woody Allen and homegrown talent such as the architect/sculptor Santiago Calatrava and filmmaker Pedro Almodóvar. While Calatrava takes the world of architecture by storm (he designed the yet-to-be-completed World Trade Center PATH station at Ground Zero in New York), Almodóvar and his muse Penelope Cruz continue to flourish at home and abroad with movies such as *Volver.* With Spanish household names such as Paz Vega and Javier Bardem also making a splash in Hollywood, film is without doubt at the forefront of the Spanish arts scene.

In contrast, Spanish music continues to be a rather local affair, though the summer festival scene, including the Festival Internacional de Benicàssim and WOMAD (World of Music and Dance), serves up top names to revelers who come from all over Europe to soak up music in the sun.

While authors such as Miguel Delibes, Rosa Montero, and Maruja Torres flourish in Spain, very few break onto the international scene, with the exception of Arturo Pérez Reverte, whose books include *Captain Alatriste* and *The Fencing Master,* and Carlos Ruiz Zafón, author of the internationally acclaimed *Shadow of the Wind.* Spain's contribution to the fine arts is still dominated by two names: the Majorcan-born artist Miquel Barceló and the Basque sculptor Eduardo Chillida, who died in 2002 and whose work can be seen at the Chillida-Leku museum close to San Sebastián.

Sports

You'd probably have to be hidden in a cave somewhere not to have heard the *vuvuzela* horns of the 2010 World Cup, and the news that Spain finally won the world cup. *Fútbol* has long been the nation's favorite sport but this world cup victory is even more special because the winning team was an amalgam of La Liga's two top clubs, FC Barcelona Real Madrid, who have long been bitter rivals. After fútbol, what rivets the Spanish fan's attention are cycling, basketball, and tennis. Alberto Contador won the 2009 Tour de France and was fighting the good fight in 2010 as this book went to press; Rafael Nadal, the first tennis player to hold Grand Slam titles on clay, grass, and hardcourt, regained his No. 1 ranking in mid–2010 after winning Wimbledon; and Pau Gasol, who plays for the Los Angeles Lakers, are national heroes.

WHAT'S NEW IN SPAIN

In the decades following Franco's dictatorship, Spain quickly earned a reputation as a travel destination, largely on the strength of its holiday beach resorts. Since the 1990s, the country has proven to have far more to offer: it's a land of cutting-edge cuisine and exceptional wines, it's a showcase of historical and modern architecture, and it's a force to reckon with in art and film and fashion. Here's some of what's new this year.

Kicks

In 2009 FC Barcelona—the beloved *Barça*—finished the season holding every trophy possible for a Spanish soccer club to acquire: the *Liga*, the King's Cup, the UEFA European Champions League, the Spanish *Supercopa*, the UEFA Super Cup, and the FIFA Club World Cup. All the marbles. A repeat of that double hat trick eluded *Barça* in 2010, but they remained the acknowledged best *fútbol* team in the world, and again dominated the *Liga* and again denying the title to star-studded archrival Real Madrid by a mere one-point margin. The contention of these two great clubs is sure to light up the 2011–12 season as well.

Flix

Hoping to reverse the 2010 decline in tourism, many of Spain's local governments have been promoting their cities as film locations. The Tom Cruise–Cameron Diaz 2010 action movie *Knight and Day* was partially shot in Cadiz and Seville; *The Way,* also released in 2010, takes Martin Sheen on a pilgrimage across northern Spain's celebrated *Camino de Santiago*; there's also talk of a remake of the Steve McQueen–Dustin Hoffman 1973 escape classic *Papillon,* to be filmed in the Canary Islands.

Getting Around

In-country connections are better than ever. In the air, Madrid and Barcelona bristle with connections to more than 20 regional cities—but Madrid-Barcelona commuter flights face stiff competition on the ground from the national railway's high-speed AVE trains: prices are about the same, but at two hours and 40 minutes the AVE is the fastest and most comfortable center-city to center-city connection. A new portion of the AVE system was inaugurated in 2010, connecting Madrid with Valencia; Spain now has more high-speed track in service or under construction than any other country in Europe. *See the Travel Smart chapter for details.*

No Bull?

In 2010, the Catalan Parliament narrowly approved a bill to ban bullfighting in the region (a similar ban has been in force on the Canary Islands since 1991); the more conservative regions of Madrid, Valencia, and Murcia reacted with proposals to give the "sport" the legal status of a protected cultural heritage. Like anything else that even remotely touches on the question of Spanish identity, this is a politically hot issue; animal rights activists have an uphill battle ahead.

Holy Ground

A work in progress since 1882, Gaudí's Sagrada Familia church in Barcelona was formally consecreated on November 7, 2010, by Pope Benedict XVI. Still a long way from a fully functioning house of worship—construction is expected to take at least another 30 years—the church remains a major tourist attraction (see Chapter 7) but rules of decorum are likely to stiffen, so expect less tolerance for bare arms and legs.

MAKING THE MOST OF YOUR EUROS

Way back when, people would travel to Europe because it was relatively cheap. Not so today; a weak dollar and a strong euro are making trips to Europe more and more daunting, but we don't think that should stop you from going—you just need to think more creatively about how to spend your money. Where better to get tips on beating the euro in Spain than from the Fodor's forums at www.fodors.com.

Sightsee, Don't Sight-Spend

"We planned our museum visits to coincide with the free admission days, which was especially easy to do in Madrid since they aren't all on the same day. In Barcelona, we bought the Articket, which more than paid for itself after visiting three of the seven featured attractions."
—misty_in_stl

". . . the Prado is free from 6 PM onward every day (Sundays from 5). Strangely enough, it's not really crowded at that time, and you can have a very enjoyable evening." —cova

Travel Wisely

"I agree that travel by bus (rather than train) is a great way to save some money. Yes, it takes a bit longer, but you can use that time to catch up on your sleep, read, etc." —AJMelheim

"RENFE has discounted tickets if bought in advance. WEB fares are 60% off and ESTRELLA fares are 40% off. Good deal if your itinerary is set in stone." —yk

Think with Your Stomach

"Food: avoid touristy places (on Barcelona's Ramblas, for example) and go where locals are. Eat your main meal at lunchtime when 'Menu del Dia' is available: 3 courses with drink starting from 6 to 10 euro. Tapas are a pleasant way to eat but watch what you are ordering. Cost can mount up. Put together a picnic from local market or shops. Instead of often poor-value hotel breakfast, get coffee and toast in a local bar for a few euro." —Alec

"In Barcelona the Boqueria Market is ideal not only for the experience of browsing but for picking up a great picnic lunch. Lots of fresh salads, fresh-pressed juices etc. Walk a few minutes down to the port for a great setting." —grimy

"In cafés, eat/drink at the bar on a stool, which is cheaper than an inside table, which is cheaper than an outdoor terrace table (in most cases) . . . and remember beer costs less than soft drinks many a time!" —lincasanova

Bargains for Lodgings

"I think the best bargain are the *paradors*, but they're mostly located outside of cities. They are a fantastic experience. One tip I can add is to become an 'amigo,' which can be done on their Web site, and you can get notices for specials. The five-day or seven-day cards are truly terrific bargains. We've done this on our last two trips and all I can say is that I've never stayed in a *parador* I didn't like!"
—artlover

"The single place you can save the most money is by choosing a less expensive place to stay." —suze

SPAIN'S TOP ATTRACTIONS

La Alhambra, Granada

(A) Nothing can prepare you for the Moorish grandeur of Andalusia's greatest monument. The palace is set around sumptuous courtyards and gardens complete with bubbling fountains and magnificent statues. *(⇨ Chapter 10.)*

Toledo

(B) Toledo—El Greco's city—an hour southwest of Madrid, is often described as Spain's spiritual capital, and past inhabitants—including Jews, Romans, and Muslims—have all felt its spiritual pull. This open-air museum of a city on a ridge high above the Río Tajo is an architectural tapestry of medieval buildings, churches, mosques, and synagogues threaded by narrow, cobbled streets and squares. *(⇨ Chapter 3.)*

La Sagrada Família, Barcelona

(C) *The* symbol of Barcelona, Antoni Gaudí's extraordinary unfinished cathedral should be on everyone's must-see list. The pointed spires, with organic shapes that resemble honeycombed stalagmites, give the whole city a fairy-tale quality. *(⇨ Chapter 7.)*

Guggenheim, Bilbao

(D) All swooping curves and rippling forms, the architecturally innovative museum—one of Frank Gehry's most breathtaking projects—was built on the site of the city's former shipyards and inspired by the shape of a ship's hull. The Guggenheim's cachet is its huge spaces: there's room to stand back and admire works in the permanent collection such as Richard Serra's monumental steel forms; sculpture by Miquel Barceló and Eduardo Chillida; and paintings by Anselm Kiefer, Willem de Kooning, Mark Rothko, and Jim Dine. *(⇨ Chapter 5.)*

Museo del Prado, Madrid

(E) One of the world's greatest museums, the Prado holds masterpieces by Italian and Flemish painters but its jewels are the

works of Spaniards: Goya, Velázquez, and El Greco. *(⇨ Chapter 2.)*

Mérida's Roman Ruins

(F) You may be tempted to rub your eyes in disbelief: in the center of a somewhat drab modern town is the largest Roman city on the Iberian Peninsula. Ogle the fabulously preserved Roman amphitheater with its columns, statues, and tiered seating, or the humbler, yet equally beguiling, 2nd-century house with mosaics and frescoes. *(⇨ Chapter 3.)*

Cuenca's Hanging Houses

(G) The old town of Cuenca is all honey-color buildings, handsome mansions, ancient churches, and earthy local bars. Seek out the famous Casas Colgadas, or "Hanging Houses," with their facades dipping precipitously over a steep ravine. Dating from the 15th century, the balconies appear as an extension of the rock face. *(⇨ Chapter 3.)*

San Lorenzo de El Escorial

(H) Seriously over the top, this giant palace-monastery (with no less than 2,673 windows), built by the megalomaniac Felipe II, makes visitors stop in their tracks. The exterior is austere, but inside, the Bourbon apartments and library are lush with rich, colorful tapestries, ornate frescoes, and paintings by such masters as El Greco, Titian, and José de Ribera. *(⇨ Chapter 2.)*

Mezquita, Córdoba

An extraordinary mosque, the Mezquita is famed for its thicket of red-and-white striped columns resembling a palm grove oasis interspersed with arches and traditional Moorish embellishments. It's a fabulous, massive monument that comprises a whole block in the center of Córdoba's tangle of ancient streets and squares. *(⇨ See Chapter 10.)*

SPAIN'S TOP EXPERIENCES

Get Festive

Plan your visit, if you can, to coincide with one of the Spain's virtually countless fairs and festivals. With the possible exception of the Italians, nobody does annual celebrations like the Spanish: fireworks, solemn processions, historical reenactments, pageants in costume, and street carnivals of every description fill the calendar. The most famous fair of all is Seville's **Feria de Abril** (April Fair), when sultry señoritas dance in traditional flamenco garb, and the cream of society parade through the streets in horse-drawn carriages. Second only to Rio in terms of revelry and costumes, Spain's pre-Lenten **Carnaval** inspires serious partying: Santa Cruz de Tenerife, in the Canary Islands, is legendary for its annual extravaganza of drinking, dancing, and dressing up—the more outrageous the better—but Cadíz, on the Atlantic coast, and Sitges, south of Barcelona, have blow-outs nearly as good; celebrations typically carry on for 10 days. For Barcelona's **Festa de Sant Jordi**, honoring St. George, the city's patron saint, tradition dictates that men buy their true love a rose, and women reciprocate by buying their beau a book; on that day (April 23) the city streets are filled with impromptu book and flower stalls. In the **Semana Santa** (Holy Week: end of March to mid-April), the events of the Passion are recalled in elaborate processions of hooded and gowned religious brotherhoods carrying elaborate floats through the streets from local churches to cathedrals in cities all over Spain; the most impressive take place in Seville, Valencia, and Cartagena in Murcia. And did we mention fireworks? The fiesta of **Las Fallas de San José**, in Valencia (mid-March), is a week of rockets, firecrackers, pinwheels, and processions in traditional costume, culminating on the *Nit del Foc* (Night of the Fire), when hundreds of huge papier-mâché figures are dispatched in a spectacular pyrotechnic finale.

Dance 'til Dawn

A large part of experiencing Spain doesn't begin until the sun sets, or end until it rises again. The Spaniards know how to party and nightlife is, well, an essential part of life. If you really want to experience the ultimate party, head to the island of Ibiza in the summer, but otherwise, any of the big cities can pretty much guarantee late night fun.

Play the Market

Markets (*mercados*) are the key to delicious local cuisine and represent an essential part of Spanish life, largely unaffected by competition from supermarkets and hypermarkets. You'll find fabulous produce sold according to whatever is in season: counters neatly piled with shiny purple eggplants, blood-red peppers, brilliant orange cantaloupes, fresh figs, and cornucopias of mushrooms and olives. While cities and most large towns have daily fruit and vegetable markets from Monday through Saturday, Barcelona might be the best city for market browsers, with its famed Boqueria as well as smaller *mercados* in lovingly restored Moderniste buildings, with wrought-iron girders and stained-glass windows, all over the city. Take the opportunity to get a culinary education. Vendors are authorities on their offerings and only too happy to share their secrets.

Get Outdoors

Crisscrossed with mountain ranges, Spain has regions that are ideal for walking, mountain biking, and backpacking, and mountain streams throughout the country offer trout- and salmon-fishing

opportunities. Perhaps the best thing about exploring Spain's great outdoors is that it often brings you nearer to some of the finest architecture and cuisine in Iberia. The 57,000-acre Parque Nacional de Ordesa y Monte Perdido, in the Pyrenees, is Spain's version of the Grand Canyon, with waterfalls, caves, forests, meadows, and more. The Sierra de Gredos,, west of Madrid, in Castile and León, bordering Extremadura, is a popular destination for climbing and trekking. Hiking is excellent in the interior of Spain, in the Alpujarras Mountains southeast of Granada and in the Picos de Europa. The pilgrimage road to Santiago de Compostela, known as El Camino de Santiago, is still in vogue after hundreds of years; it traverses the north of Spain from either Roncesvalles in Navarra or the Aragonese Pyrenees to Galicia. The Doñana National Park, in Andalusia, is one of Europe's last tracts of true wilderness, with wetlands, beaches, sand dunes, marshes, 150 species of rare birds, and countless kinds of wildlife, including the endangered imperial eagle and lynx.

Drink Like a Madrileño

To experience Madrid like a local, you have to eat and drink like a local, and in the capital an aperitif is a crucial part of daily life. In fact, there are more bars per square mile here than in any other capital in Europe, so finding a venue poses no great challenge. Go the traditional route and try a *vermut* (vermouth) on tap, typically served with a squirt of soda. Or try a glass of ice-cold *fino* (dry sherry) with its common *tapas* accompaniment of a couple of *gambas* (prawns). Beer houses (*cervecerías*) typically specialize in local varieties on tap; in Madrid's Plaza Santa Ana some of the best-loved *cervecerías* line the pretty central square.

Lordly Lodgings

A quintessential experience for visitors to Spain is spending a night, or several, in one of the government-run hotels called *paradors*. The settings are unique—perhaps a restored castle, a citadel, a monastery, or a ducal palace, and most are furnished in the style of the region. Every *parador* has a restaurant that serves local specialties. The *paradors* attract Spanish and international travelers alike and receive almost consistently rave reviews.

Hit the Beach

Virtually surrounded by bays, oceans, gulfs, straits, and seas, Spain is a beach-lover's dream as well as an increasingly popular destination for water-sports enthusiasts. Oceanfront—8,000 km (5,000 mi) of it, not counting the islands—is Spain's most important hospitality asset, and sun worshippers can choose from long sweeps of beach on sheltered bays to tiny crescents of sand in rocky inlets that only boats can reach. There are 12 *costas* (designated coastal areas) along the Mediterranean, and seven more along the Atlantic from Portugal around to France. One of the great things about Spanish sands is that some of the best are literally extensions of the cities you otherwise come to Spain for—so you can spend a morning in the surf and sun, then steep yourself in history or art for an afternoon, and finish the day with a great meal and an evening of music. Among the best city beaches are La Concha (San Sebastian), Playa de la Victoria (Cadiz). Barcelona's string of beaches, Playa de los Peligros (Santander), and El Cabanyal (Valencia).

SPAIN'S TOP MUSEUMS

In the Golden Age of Empire (1580–1680), Spanish monarchs used Madrid's wealth not only to finance wars and civil projects, but to underscore their own grandeur by collecting and commissioning great works of art. That national patrimony makes Spain a museum lover's paradise—all the more so for the masterworks of modern painting and sculpture that have been added since, and for the museum buildings themselves, many of them architecturally stunning. This list of must-sees will help you plan your trip.

Madrid

Centro de Arte Reina Sofía, Madrid. The modern collection focuses on Spain's three great modern masters: Picasso, Dalí, and Miró. The centerpiece is Picasso's monumental *Guernica*. *(⇨ Ch. 2.)*

Museo del Prado, Madrid. In a magnificent neoclassical building on one of Madrid's most elegant boulevards, the Prado, with its collection of Spanish and European masterpieces, is frequently compared to the Louvre. *(⇨ Ch. 2.)*

Museo Thyssen-Bornemisza, Madrid. This mass of artwork was purchased by the Spanish government in 1993 from the Baron Thyssen-Bornemisza. Among the some 1,600 paintings in the collection are works by Dürer, Rembrandt, Titian, and Caravaggio—and important pieces from the Impressionist and early modern periods. *(⇨ Ch. 2.)*

Catalonia and Valencia

Museo Picasso, Barcelona. Five elegant Medieval and early Renaissance palaces in the Gothic Quarter house this collection of some 3,600 works by Picasso, who spent the early years of his career (1895–1904) in Barcelona. *(⇨ Ch. 7.)*

Museu Nacional d'Art de Catalunya, Barcelona. MNAC has the finest collection of Romanesque frescoes and devotional sculpture in the world, most rescued from abandoned chapels in the Pyrenees. Taking the fragile frescoes off crumbling walls, building supports for them in the same intricate shapes as the spaces they came from (vaults, arches, windows), and rehanging them was an astonishing feat of restoration. *(⇨ Ch. 7.)*

Fundació Miró, Barcelona. Designed by Miró's friend and collaborator, architect Lluís Sert, this museum was the artist's gift to the city that shaped his career. It houses some 11,000 of Miró's works: oils, sculpture, textiles, drawings, and prints. *(⇨ Ch. 7.)*

Museo de Bellas Artes, Valencia. At the edge of the city's Royal Gardens, the MBA is one of the finest smaller collections in Spain. It houses masterworks by Ribalta, Velázquez, Ribera, and Goya, and a gallery devoted to the 19th-century Valencian painter Joaquin Sorolla. *(⇨ Ch. 8.)*

Northern Spain

Museo Guggenheim, Bilbao. Frank Gehry's striking museum has generated controversy, but many art critics hail it as the first great building of the 21st century. Inside, the large spaces showcase international and Spanish artwork from the 20th century. It's easy to combine a several-day visit to Bilbao with a trip to Barcelona. *(⇨ Ch. 5.)*

Southern Spain

Museo de Bellas Artes, Seville. Rivaled only by the Prado in Madrid, the MBA collection includes works by Murillo, Zurbarán, and El Greco, and Gothic art, baroque religious sculpture, and Sevillian art from the 19th and 20th centuries. From Madrid, the fast train makes the trip to Seville in less than three hours. *(⇨ Ch. 10.)*

FAQ

What are my lodging options in Spain? For a slice of Spanish culture, stay in a *parador*; to indulge your pastoral fantasies, try a *casa rural* (country house), Spain's version of a bed-and-breakfast. On the other end of the spectrum are luxurious high-rise hotels along the coastline and chain hotels in the major cities. Traveling with your family? Consider renting an apartment.

Do I need to book hotels beforehand, or can I just improvise once I'm in Spain? In big cities or popular tourist areas it's best to reserve well ahead. In smaller towns and rural areas you can usually find something on the spot, except when local fiestas are on—for those dates you may have to book months in advance.

How can I avoid looking like a tourist in Spain? Ditch the white tennis shoes and shorts for a start, and try to avoid baseball caps. A fanny pack will betray you instantly; a *mochila*—an all-purpose cloth or leather bag with a long shoulder strap, bought locally, will serve you better.

Do shops really close for siesta? In general, shops close from 2 PM to 5 PM, particularly in small towns and villages. The exceptions are supermarkets and large department stores, which tend to be open from 9 AM to 9 PM in the center of Madrid and Barcelona, and at major resorts stores often stay open all day.

How much should I tip at a restaurant? You won't find a service charge on the bill, but the tip is included. For stellar service, leave a small sum in addition to the bill, but not more than 10%. If you're indulging in *tapas*, just round the bill to the nearest euro. For cocktails, tip about €0.50 a drink.

If I only have time for one city, should I choose Barcelona or Madrid? It depends on what you're looking for. Madrid will give you world-class art and much more of a sense of a workaday Spanish city, while cosmopolitan Barcelona has Gaudí, Catalan cuisine, and its special Mediterranean atmosphere.

Can I get dinner at 7, or do I really have to wait until the Spanish eat at 9? If you really can't wait, head for the most touristy part of town; there you should be able to find bars and cafés that will serve meals at any time of day. But it won't be nearly as good as the food the Spaniards are eating a couple of hours later. You might be better off just dining on *tapas*.

How easy is it to cross the border from Spain into neighboring countries? Spain, Portugal, and France are members of the EU, so borders are open. Good trains connect Madrid and Lisbon (about €59), and Madrid and Paris (about €166). U.S. citizens need only a valid passport to enter Morocco; ferries run regularly to Tangier from Tarifa (about €37 one-way, €88 with a car) and Gibraltar (€75).

Can I bring home the famous ibérico ham, Spanish olives, almonds, or baby eels? Products you can legally bring into the United States include olive oil, cheese, olives, almonds, wood-smoked paprika, and saffron. Ibérico ham, even vacuum-sealed, is not legal, so you may not get past customs agents and their canine associates. If caught, you risk confiscation and fines. And don't even think about trying to bring back *angulas* (eels).

For more help on trip planning, see the Travel Smart chapter.

QUINTESSENTIAL SPAIN

La Siesta

The unabashed Spanish pursuit of pleasure and the unswerving devotion to establishing a healthy balance between work and play is nowhere more apparent than in the midday shutdown. In the two-salary, 21st-century Spanish family, few people still observe the custom of going home for lunch, and fewer still take the classic midday snooze—described by novelist Camilo José Cela as "*de padrenuestro y pijama*" (with a prayer and pajamas). The fact remains, however, that most stores and businesses close from about 1:30 to 4:30.

El Fútbol and the Tortilla de Patata

The Spanish National Fútbol (soccer) League and the *tortilla de patata* (potato omelet) have been described as the only widely shared phenomena that bind the nation together. Often referred to as *tortilla española* to distinguish it from the French omelet or the flat, all-dough Mexican tortilla, the Spanish potato omelet is a thick mold of potatoes and onions bound with egg, ideal for breakfast, snacks, or *tapas*. In the right chef's hands, it can be elevated to a gourmet delicacy, but even at a hole-in-the-wall spot, you can't go too far wrong. In the case of the soccer league, the tie that binds has often resembled tribal warfare, as bitter rivalries centuries old are played out on the field. Some, like the Real Sociedad (San Sebastián)–Athletic de Bilbao feud, are fraternal in nature, brother Basques battling for boasting rights, but others, like the Madrid–Barcelona face-offs, are as basic to Spanish history as the battle between the Moors and the Christians. The *fútbol* team that won the 2010 World Cup, however, was an incredible force of unification, with players players from teams Real Madrid and FC Barcelona, with represenatives from Basque Country, Catalonia, and Madrid. Who knows, this might take the edge of some of these

If you want to get a sense of Spanish culture and indulge in some of its pleasures, start by familiarizing yourself with the rituals of Spanish life. These are a few things you can take part in with relative ease.

heretofore bitter rivalries. But don't count on it. At any rate, the fact still stands that while the beauty of the game is best appreciated in the stadiums, local sports bars, many of them official fan clubs of local teams, are where you'll see *fútbol* passions at their wildest.

El Paseo

One of the most delightful Spanish customs is *el paseo* (the stroll), which traditionally takes place during the early evening and is common throughout the country but particularly in *pueblos* and towns. Given the modern hamster-wheel pace of life, there is something appealingly old-fashioned about families and friends walking around at a leisurely pace with no real destination or purpose. Dress is usually formal or fashionable: elderly señoras with their boxy tweed suits, men with jackets slung, capelike, round the shoulders, teenagers in their latest Zara gear, and younger children in their Sunday best. *El paseo* provides everyone with an opportunity to participate in a lively slice of street theater.

Sunday Lunch

The Spanish love to eat out, especially on Sunday, the traditional day when families make an excursion of a long leisurely lunch—often, depending on the time of year, at an informal seaside restaurant or a rural *venta*. The latter came into being in bygone days when much of the seasonal work, particularly in southern Spain, was done by itinerant labor. Cheap, hearty meals were much in demand, and some enterprising country housewife saw the opportunity to provide *ventas* (meals for sale); the idea soon spread. *Ventas* are still a wonderfully good value today, not just for the food but also for the atmosphere: long, scrubbed wooden tables; large, noisy Spanish families; and a convivial informality. Sunday can be slow. So relax, and remember that all good things are worth waiting for.

GREAT ITINERARIES

MADRID AND THE SOUTH

Days 1–3: Welcome to Madrid

The elegant Plaza Mayor is the perfect jumping-off point for a tour of the Spanish capital. To the west, see the Plaza de la Villa, Palacio Real (the Royal Palace), Teatro Real (Royal Theater), and the royal convents; to the south, wander around the maze of streets of La Latina and the Rastro and indulge yourself in local *tapas*. Start or end the day with a visit to the Prado, the Museo Thyssen-Bornemisza, or the Centro de Arte Reina Sofía.

On Day 2, visit the sprawling Barrio de las Letras, centered on the Plaza de Santa Ana. This was the favorite neighborhood of writers during the Spanish golden literary age in the 17th century, and it's still crammed with theaters, cafés, and good tapas bars. It borders the Paseo del Prado on the east, allowing you to comfortably walk to any of the art museums in the area. If the weather is pleasant, take an afternoon stroll in the Parque del Buen Retiro.

For your third day in the capital, wander in Chueca and Malasaña, the two neighborhoods most favored by young Madrileños. Fuencarral, a landmark street that serves as the border between the two, is one of the city's trendiest shopping enclaves. From there you can walk to the Parque del Oeste and the Templo de Debod—the best spot from which to see the city's sunset. Among the lesser-known museums, consider visiting the captivating Museo Sorolla, Goya's frescoes and tomb at the Ermita de San Antonio de la Florida, or the Real Academia de Bellas Artes de San Fernando for classic painting. People-watch at any of the terrace bars in either Plaza de Chueca or Plaza 2 de Mayo in Malasaña. ⇨ *See Chapter 2 for details on Madrid.*

Logistics: If you're traveling light, the subway (Metro) or the bus will take you from the airport to the city for €1–€1.25. A taxi will do the same for around €25–€30. Once in the center consider walking or taking the subway rather than cabbing it in gridlock traffic.

Days 4 and 5: Castilian Charmers

There are several excellent options for half- or full-day side trips from Madrid to occupy Days 4 and 5. Toledo and Segovia are two of the oldest Castilian cities—both have delightful old quarters dating back to the Romans. There's also El Escorial, which houses the massive monastery built by Felipe II. Two other nearby towns also worth visiting are Aranjuez and Alcalá de Henares. ⇨ *See Chapter 3 for details on these Castilian cities.*

Logistics: In 2007, Toledo and Segovia became stops on the high-speed train line (AVE), so you can get to either of them in a half hour from Madrid. To reach the old quarters of both cities take a bus or cab from the train station or take the bus from Madrid; bus is also the best way to get to El Escorial. Reach Aranjuez and Alcalá de Henares via the intercity train system.

Day 6: Córdoba and Its Mosque or Extremadura

Córdoba, the capital of both Roman and Moorish Spain, was the center of Western art and culture between the 8th and 11th centuries. The city's breathtaking mosque (now a cathedral) and the medieval Jewish Quarter bear witness to the city's brilliant past. From Madrid you could also rent a car and visit the lesser-known cities north of Extremadura, such as Guadalupe, Trujillo, and Cáceres, overnighting

in Cáceres, a UNESCO World Cultural Heritage city, and returning to Madrid the next day. ⇨ *See Chapter 10 for Córdoba and Chapter 3 for Extremadura.*

Logistics: The AVE train will take you to Córdoba from Madrid in under two hours. A good alternative is to sleep over in Toledo, also on the route heading south, and then head to Córdoba the next day. Once in Córdoba, take a taxi for a visit out to the summer palace at Medina Azahara.

Days 7 and 8: Seville

Seville's Giralda tower, cathedral, bullring, and Barrio de Santa Cruz are visual feasts. Forty minutes south you can sip the world-famous sherries of Jerez de la Frontera, then munch jumbo shrimp on the beach at Sanlúcar de Barrameda. *For more on Seville,* ⇨ *see Chapter 10.*

Logistics: From Seville's AVE station, take a taxi to your hotel. After that, walking and hailing the occasional taxi are the best ways to explore the city.

Days 9 and 10: Granada

The hilltop Alhambra palace, Spain's most visited attraction, was conceived by the Moorish caliphs as heaven on earth. Try any of the city's famous *tapas* bars and tea shops, and make sure to roam the magical, steep streets of the Albayzín, the ancient Moorish quarter. *For more on Andalusia,* ⇨ *see Chapter 10.*

Logistics: The Seville–Granada leg of this trip is best accomplished by renting a car. However, the Seville-to-Granada trains (four daily, just over three hours, costing less than €24) are an alternative. Another idea is to head first from Madrid to Granada, and then from Granada via Córdoba to Seville.

> **TIP**
>
> Spain's modern freeways and tollways are as good as any in the world—with the exception of the signs, which are often hard to decipher as you sweep past them at the routine speed of 120 km/hr (74 mph).

GREAT ITINERARIES

BARCELONA AND THE NORTH

Days 1–3: Welcome to Barcelona

To get a feel for Barcelona, begin with the Rambla and Boquería market. Then set off for the Gothic Quarter to see the Catedral de la Seu, Plaça del Rei, and the Catalan and Barcelona government palaces in Plaça Sant Jaume. Next, cross Via Laietana to the Born-Ribera (waterfront neighborhood) for the Gothic Santa Maria del Mar and nearby Museu Picasso.

Make Day 2 a Gaudí day: Visit the Temple Expiatori de la Sagrada Família, then Park Güell. In the afternoon see the Casa Milà and Casa Batlló, part of the Manzana de la Discòrdia on Passeig de Gràcia. Palau Güell, off the lower Rambla, is probably too much Gaudí for one day, but don't miss it. *(Learn more in the In-focus feature "Gaudí: Architecture Through the Looking Glass" in Chapter 7.)*

On Day 3, climb Montjuïc for the Museu Nacional d'Art de Catalunya, in the hulking Palau Nacional. Investigate the Fundació Miró, Estadi Olímpic, the Mies van der Rohe Pavilion, and CaixaForum exhibition center. At lunchtime, take the cable car across the port for seafood in Barceloneta. ⇨ *See Chapter 7 for more on Barcelona.*

Logistics: In Barcelona, walking or taking the subway is better than cabbing it.

Days 3 and 4: San Sebastián

San Sebastián is one of Spain's most beautiful—and delicious—cities. Belle Epoque buildings nearly encircle the tiny bay, and *tapas* bars flourish in the old quarter. Not far from San Sebastián is historic Pasajes de San Juan. *For more on San Sebastián,* ⇨ *see Chapter 5.*

Logistics: You don't need a car in San Sebastián proper, but visits to cider houses in Astigarraga, Chillida Leku on the outskirts of town, and many of the finest restaurants around San Sebastián are possible only with your own transportation or a taxi (the latter with the advantage that you won't get lost). The freeway west to Bilbao is beautiful and fast, but the coastal road is recommended at least as far as Zumaia.

Days 5 and 6: The Basque Coast

The Basque coast between San Sebastián and Bilbao has a succession of fine beaches, rocky cliffs, and picture-perfect fishing ports. The wide beach at Zarautz, the fishermen's village of Getaria, the Zuloaga Museum in Zumaia, and Bermeo's port and fishing museum should all be near the top of your list. ⇨ *See Chapter 5 for information on the Basque country.*

Days 7 and 8: Bilbao

Bilbao's Guggenheim Museum is worth a trip for the building itself, and the Museum of Fine Arts has an impressive collection of Basque and Spanish paintings. Restaurants and *tapas* bars are famously good in Bilbao. ⇨ *See Chapter 5 for more details on Bilbao.*

Logistics: In Bilbao, use the subway or the Euskotram, which runs up and down the Nervión estuary.

Days 9 and 10: Santander and Cantabria

The elegant beach town of Santander has an excellent summer music festival every August. Nearby, Santillana del Mar is one of Spain's best Renaissance towns, and the museum of the Altamira Caves displays reproductions of the famous underground Neolithic rock paintings discovered here. Exploring the Picos de Europa will take

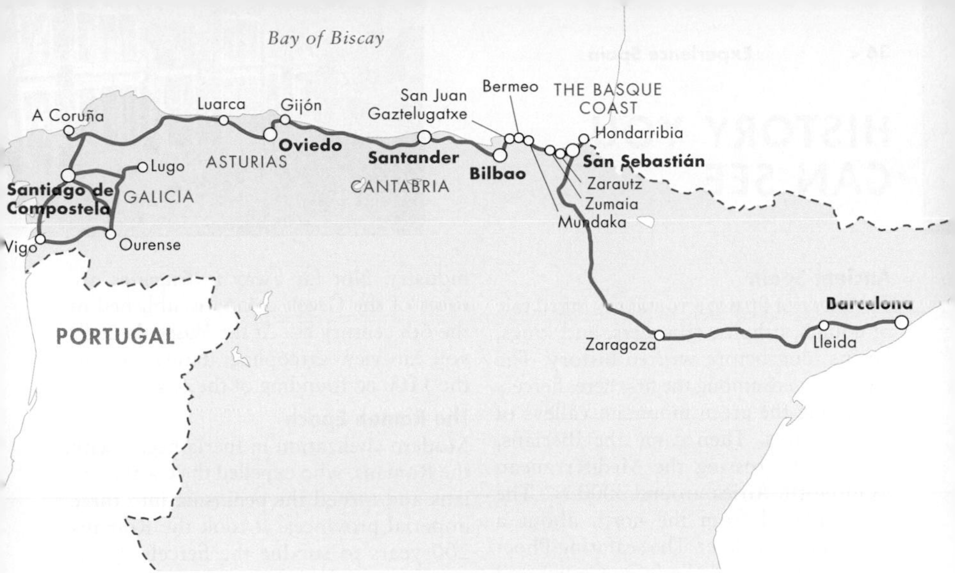

you through some of the peninsula's wildest reaches, and the port towns along the coast provide some of Spain's most pristine beaches. ⇨ *See Chapter 4 for more on Santander and other Cantabria destinations.*

Days 11–13: Oviedo and Asturias

The coast road through Ribadesella and the cider capital Villaviciosa to Oviedo is scenic and punctuated with tempting beaches. Oviedo, its cathedral, and its pre-Romanesque churches are worlds away from Córdoba's Mezquita and Granada's Alhambra. ⇨ *See Chapter 4 for details on Asturias.*

Logistics: The A8 coastal freeway gets you quickly and comfortably to Oviedo and just beyond. From there, go west into Galicia via the two-lane N634 or the coastal N632—slow but scenic routes to Santiago.

Days 14–16: Santiago de Compostela and Galicia

Spain's northwest corner, with Santiago de Compostela at its spiritual and geographic center, is a green land of bagpipes and apple orchards. The Albariño wine country, along the Río Miño border with Portugal, and the *rías* (estuaries), full of delicious seafood, will keep you steeped in *enxebre*—Gallego for "local specialties and atmosphere." ⇨ *See Chapter 4 for more on Galicia.*

Logistics: The four-lane freeways AP9 and A6 whisk you from Lugo and Castro to Santiago de Compostela and to the Rías Baixas. By car is the only way to tour Galicia. The AC552 route around the upper northwest corner and the Rías Altas turns into the AC550 coming back into Santiago.

> **TIP**
>
> Be prepared for bilingual traffic signs and local spellings that do not match your map, which probably adheres to the "traditional" Castilian spelling.

HISTORY YOU CAN SEE

Ancient Spain

The story of Spain, a romance-tinged tale of counts, caliphs, crusaders, and kings, begins long before written history. The Basques were among the first here, fiercely defending the green mountain valleys of the Pyrenees. Then came the Iberians, apparently crossing the Mediterranean from North Africa around 3000 BC. The Celts arrived from the north about a thousand years later. The seafaring Phoenicians founded Gadir (now Cádiz) and several coastal cities in the south three millennia ago. The parade continued with the Greeks, who settled parts of the east coast, and then the Carthaginians, who founded Cartagena around 225 BC and dubbed the then-wild, forested and game-rich country Ispania, after their word for rabbit: *span*.

What to See: Near Barcelona, on the Costa Brava, rocket yourself back almost 3,000 years at **Ullastret**, a settlement occupied by an Iberian people known as the Indiketas. On a tour, actors guide groups through the homes and fortifications of some of the peninsula's earliest inhabitants, the defensive walls attesting to the constant threat of attack and the bits of pottery evidence of the settlement's early ceramic industry. Not far away in **Empúries** are ruins of the Greek colony established in the 6th century BC. At the **Museo de Cádiz** you can view sarcophagi dating back to the 1100 BC founding of the city.

The Roman Epoch

Modern civilization in Iberia began with the Romans, who expelled the Carthaginians and turned the peninsula into three imperial provinces. It took the Romans 200 years to subdue the fiercely resisting Iberians, but their influence is seen today in the fortifications, amphitheaters, aqueducts, and other ruins in cities across Spain, as well as in the country's legal system and in the Latin base of Spain's Romance languages and dialects.

What to See: Segovia's nearly 3,000-foot-long **Acueducto Romano** is a marvel of Roman engineering. Mérida's Roman ruins are some of Spain's finest, including its **bridge, theater,** and **outdoor amphitheater.** Tarragona was Rome's most important city in Catalonia, as the **walls, circus,** and **amphitheater** bear witness, while Zaragoza boasts a **Roman amphitheater** and a **Roman fluvial port** that dispatched flat-bottomed riverboats loaded with wine and olive oil down the Ebro.

1100 BC	Earliest Phoenician colonies are formed, including Cádiz, Villaricos, Almuñecar, and Málaga. Natives include Basques in the Pyrenees, Iberians in the south, and Celts in the northwest.
237 BC	Carthaginians land in Spain.
206 BC	Romans expel Carthaginians from Spain and gradually conquer peninsula.
AD 74	Roman citizenship extended to all Spaniards.
419	Visigothic kingdom established in northern Spain, with capital at Toledo.
711–12	Visigothic kingdom overthrown by invading Muslims (Moors), who create an emirate, with the capital at Córdoba.
813	Discovery of remains of St. James; the cathedral of Santiago de Compostela is built and becomes a major pilgrimage site.
1085–1270	Main years of the Reconquest.

The Visigoths and Moors

In the early 5th century, invading tribes crossed the Pyrenees to attack the weakening Roman empire. The Visigoths became the dominant force in northern Spain by 419, establishing their kingdom at Toledo and eventually adopting Christianity. But the Visigoths, too, were to fall before a wave of invaders. The Moors, an Arab-led Berber force, crossed the Strait of Gibraltar in 711 and swept through Spain in an astonishingly short time, launching almost eight centuries of Muslim rule. The Moors brought with them citrus fruits, rice, cotton, sugar, palm trees, glassmaking, and the complex irrigation system still used around Valencia. The influence of Arabic in modern Spanish includes words beginning with "al," such as *albóndiga* (meatball), *alcalde* (mayor), *almohada* (pillow), and *alcázar* (fortress), as well as prominent phonetic characteristics ranging from the fricative "j" to, in all probability, the lisping "c" (before "e" and "i") and "z." The Moorish and Mudejar (Moorish decorative details) architecture found throughout most of Spain tells much about the splendor of the Islamic culture that flourished here.

What to See: Moorish culture is most spectacularly evident in Andalusia, derived from the Arabic name for the Moorish reign on the Iberian Peninsula, al-Andalus, which meant "western lands." The fairytale **Alhambra** palace overlooking Granada captures the refinement of the Moorish aesthetic, while the earlier **9th-century mesquite** (mosque) at Córdoba bears witness to the power of Islam in al-Andalus.

Spain's Golden Age

By 1085, Alfonso VI of Castile had captured Toledo, giving the Christians a firm grip on the north. In the 13th century, Valencia, Seville, and finally Córdoba—the capital of the Muslim caliphate in Spain—fell to Christian forces, leaving only Granada in Moorish hands. Nearly 200 years later, the so-called Catholic Monarchs—Ferdinand of Aragón and Isabella of Castile—were joined in a marriage that would change the world. Finally, on January 2, 1492, 244 years after the fall of Córdoba, Granada surrendered and the Moorish reign was over.

The year 1492 was the beginning of the nation's political golden age: Christian forces conquered Granada and unified all of current-day Spain as a single kingdom;

1478	Spanish Inquisition begins.
1479–1504	Isabella and Ferdinand rule jointly.
1492	Granada, the last Moorish outpost, falls. Christopher Columbus, under Isabella's sponsorship, discovers the islands of the Caribbean, setting off a wave of Spanish exploration. Ferdinand and Isabella expel Jews and Muslims from Spain.
1516	Ferdinand dies. His grandson Charles I inaugurates the Hapsburg dynasty.
1519–22	First circumnavigation of the world by Ferdinand Magellan's ships.
ca. 1520–1700	Spain's Golden Age.
1605	Miguel de Cervantes publishes the first part of *Don Quixote de la Mancha*.

in what was, at the time, viewed as a measure promoting national unity, Jews and Muslims who did not convert to Christianity were expelled from the country. The departure of educated Muslims and Jews was a blow to the nation's agriculture, science, and economy from which it would take nearly 500 years to recover. The Catholic monarchs and their centralizing successors maintained Spain's unity, but they sacrificed the spirit of international free trade that was bringing prosperity to other parts of Europe. Carlos V weakened Spain with his penchant for waging war, and his son, Felipe II (Phillip II), followed in the same expensive path, defeating the Turks in 1571 but losing the "Invincible Spanish Armada" in the English Channel in 1588.

What to See: Celebrate Columbus's voyage to America with **festivities in Seville, Huelva, Granada, Cádiz, and Barcelona,** all of which display venues where "The Discoverer" was commissioned, was confirmed, set out from, returned to, or was buried. Wander through the somber **El Escorial,** a monastery northwest of Madrid whose construction Felipe II oversaw and which is the resting place of Carlos V.

War of the Spanish Succession

The 1700–14 War of the Spanish Succession ended with the fall of Barcelona, which sided with the Hapsburg Archduke Carlos against the Bourbon Prince Felipe V. El Born market, completed in 1876, covered the buried remains of the Ribera neighborhood where the decisive battle took place. Ribera citizens were required to tear down a thousand houses to clear space for the Ciutadella fortress, from which fields of fire were directed, quite naturally, toward the city the Spanish and French forces had taken a year to subdue. The leveled neighborhood, then about a third of Barcelona, was plowed under and forgotten by the victors, though never by Barcelonins.

What to See: In Barcelona, the **Fossar de les Moreres cemetery,** next to the Santa María del Mar basilica, remains a powerful symbol for Catalan nationalists who gather there every September 11, Catalonia's National Day, to commemorate the fall of the city in 1714.

Spanish Civil War

Spain's early-19th-century War of Independence required five years of bitter guerrilla fighting to rid the peninsula

1618–1648	Thirty Years' War: a dynastic struggle between Hapsburgs and Bourbons.
1701–14	War of the Spanish Succession. Claimants to the throne are Louis XIV of France, Holy Roman Emperor Leopold I, and electoral prince Joseph Ferdinand of Bavaria.
1756–63	Seven Years' War: Spain and France versus Great Britain.
1808	Napoleon takes Madrid.
1809–14	The Spanish War of Independence: Napoleonic armies thrown out of Spain.
1834–39	First Carlist War: Don Carlos contests the crown; an era of upheaval begins.
1873	First Spanish Republic declared. Three-year Second Carlist War begins.

of Napoleonic troops. Later, the Carlist wars set the stage for the Spanish civil war (1936–39), in which more than half a million people died. Intellectuals and leftists sympathized with the elected government; the International Brigades, with many American, British, and Canadian volunteers, took part in some of the worst fighting, including the storied defense of Madrid. But General Francisco Franco, backed by the Catholic Church, got far more help from Nazi Germany, whose Condor legions destroyed the Basque town of Gernika (in a horror made infamous by Picasso's monumental painting *Guernica*), and from Fascist Italy. For three years, European governments stood quietly by as Franco's armies ground their way to victory. After the fall of Barcelona in January 1939, the Republican cause became hopeless, and Franco's Nationalist forces entered Madrid on March 27, 1939.

What to See: Snap a shot of **Madrid's Plaza Dos de Mayo,** in the Malasaña neighborhood; it is the site of the heroic stand of officers Daoiz and Velarde against vastly superior French forces at the start of the popular uprising against Napoleon. The archway in the square is all that remains of the armory Daoiz and Velarde defended to the death. Trace the shrapnel marks on the wall of the **Sant Felip Neri church** in Barcelona, material evidence of the 1938 bombing of the city by Italian warplanes under Franco's orders. East of Zaragoza, the town of **Belchite** was the scene of bloody fighting during the decisive Battle of the Ebro. The town has been left exactly as it appeared on September 7, 1937, the day the battle ended.

HIDDEN MEANINGS

What's *not* there in Spain can be just as revealing as what is. For example, there are no Roman ruins in Madrid, as it was founded as a Moorish outpost in the late 10th century and was not the capital of Spain until 1560, a recent date in Spanish history. Likewise, Barcelona has no Moorish architecture—the Moors sacked Barcelona but never established themselves there, testifying to Catalonia's medieval past as part of Charlemagne's Frankish empire. Al-Andalus, the 781-year Moorish sojourn on the peninsula, was farther south and west.

1898	Spanish-American War: Spain loses Cuba, Puerto Rico, and the Philippines.
1936–39	Spanish civil war; more than 600,000 die. General Francisco Franco wins and rules Spain for the next 36 years.
1977–78	First democratic election in 40 years; new constitution restores civil liberties and freedom of the press.
1992	Olympic Games held in Barcelona.
2000	Juan Carlos celebrates 25 years as Spain's king.
2004	Terrorist bombs on Madrid trains claim almost 200 lives.

LANGUAGES OF SPAIN

Spanish

One of the questions you might be asking yourself as you plan your trip to a non-English-speaking country is how useful your high school Spanish will be. Well, you don't need to be fluent to make yourself understood pretty much anywhere in Spain. With immigrants in substantial numbers, many from Latin America, people in Spain are generally quite tolerant of variations on the "standard" language known as *castellano,* or Castilian Spanish—the official language of the country, by royal decree, since 1714. The Spanish you learned in school is a Romance language descended from Latin, with considerable Arabic influence—the result of the nearly eight centuries of Moorish presence on the Iberian Pensinsula. The first recorded use of Spanish dates to the 13th century; in the 15th century, Antonio de Nebrija's famous grammar helped spread Spanish throughout the empire's sprawling global possessions. Pick up a Spanish phrase book, dust off that Spanish accent your high school language instructor taught you, and most Spaniards will understand your earnest request for directions to the subway—and so will some 400 million other Spanish speakers around the world.

Spain's Other Languages

What Spaniards speak among themselves is another matter. The country has a number of other significant language populations, most of which predate Castilian Spanish. These include the Romance languages Catalan and Gallego (or Galician-Portuguese) and the non–Indo-European Basque language, Euskera. A third tier of local dialects include Asturiano (or Bable); Aranés; the variations of Fabla Aragonesa (the languages of the north-central community of Aragón); and, in Extremadura, the provincial dialect, Extremaduran.

Catalan is spoken in Barcelona, in Spain's northeastern autonomous community of Catalonia, in southern France's Roussillon region, in the city of L'Alguer on the Italian island of Sardinia, and in Andorra (where it is the national language). It is derived from Provençal French and is closer to Langue d'Oc and Occitan than to Spanish. Both **Valenciano** and **Mallorquín,** spoken respectively in the Valencia region and in the Balearic Islands, in the Mediterranean east of Barcelona, are considered dialects of Catalan.

Gallego is spoken in Galicia in Spain's northwestern corner and more closely resembles Portuguese than Spanish.

Euskera, the Basque language, is Spain's greatest linguistic mystery. Links to Japanese, Sanskrit, Finnish, Gaelic, and the language of the lost city of Atlantis have proven to be false leads or pure mythology. The most accepted theory on Euskera suggests that it evolved from a language spoken by the aboriginal inhabitants of the Iberian Peninsula and survived in isolation in the remote hills of the Basque Country. Euskera is presently spoken by about a million inhabitants of the Spanish and French Basque provinces.

Asturiano (or Bable) is a Romance language (sometimes called a dialect) spoken in Asturias and in parts of León, Zamora, Salamanca, Cantabria, and Extremadura by some 700,000 people.

Aranés (or Occitan), derived from Gascon French, is spoken in Catalonia's westernmost valley, the Vall d'Arán.

Fabla aragonesa is the collective term for all of Aragón's mountain dialects—some 15 of them in active use and all more closely related to Gascon French and Occitan than to Spanish.

Extremaduran, a Spanish dialect, is spoken in Extremadura.

Gain access to the inner chambers of paradors in Santiago de Compostela (left) and Sigüenza (above).

A NIGHT WITH HISTORY

Spain's nearly 100 paradors all have one thing in common: heritage status. More often than not they also have killer views. Plan a trip with stays at a number of paradors, and you'll have the chance to experience an authentic slice of Spanish culture around the country. Spaniards themselves love the paradors and make up about 70 percent of visitors.

Parador accommodations come in all manner of distinguished settings, including former castles, convents, and Arab fortresses—soon, in Madrid, you'll even be able to check into a former women's prison. Talk about ex-cell-ent sleeping. . . .

Even if you find yourself in a parador that's a (ho-hum) stately historic home, you'll most likely be perched above, or nestled in, some lovely surroundings—from the *pueblos blancos* (whitewashed villages) and verdant golf courses of Andalusia to the rolling fields, mountains, and beaches of northern Spain.

THE PARADOR'S TRUE CHARM: PAY LESS, GET MORE

Why pay top-euro prices when you can get top-notch quality for considerably less? In most cases, the accommodations, interior decor, and cuisine at paradors are just as good and, in many cases, vastly superior to that of four- and five-star hotels—usually at reasonable prices. And most paradors have magnficent settings: depending on where you stay, for instance, you might have a balcony with views of the Alhambra, or perhaps you'll be able to see snow-peaked mountains or vistas of the sweeping Spanish plains from your bedroom.

FROM ROYAL HUNTING LODGE TO FIRST PARADOR

An advocate for Spanish tourism in the early 20th century, King Alfonso XIII was eager to develop a countrywide hotel infrastructure that would cater to local and overseas travelers. He directed the Spanish government to set up the Royal Tourist Commission to mull it over, and in 1926, commissioner Marquis de la Vega Inclán came up with the parador ("stopping place") idea and searched for where to build the first such inn. His goal was to find a setting that would reflect both the beauty of Spain and its cultural heritage. He nominated the wild Gredos Mountains, where royalty came to hunt and relax, a few hours west of Madrid.

King Alfonso XIII

By October of 1928, the Parador de Gredos opened at a spot chosen by King Alfonso himself, amid pine groves, rocks, and the clear waters of Avilá. In 1937, this parador is where the fascist Falange party was established, and a few decades later, in 1978, it's where national leaders drafted the Spanish Constitution.

SPAIN'S PARADOR CHAIN

When Alfonso gave his blessing to the establishment of Spain's first parador, he probably didn't realize that he was sitting on a financial, cultural, and historical gold mine. But after it opened, the Board of Paradors and Inns of Spain was formed and focused its energies on harnessing historical, artistic, and cultural monuments with lovely landscapes into a chain—an effort that has continued to this day.

The number of state-run paradors today approaches nearly 100, with the latest two being the Parador La Granja on the grounds of the royal summer home of Carlos III and Isabel de Farnesio in Segovia, and the Parador de Gran Canaria in Cruz in Tejeda in the Canary Islands.

PILLOW TALK

Grace Kelly

Given that many paradors were once homes and residences to noble families and royalty, it's no surprise that they've continued to attract the rich and famous. Italian actress Sophia Loren stayed at the Parador de Hondarribia, as did distinguished Spanish writer José Cela, and Cardona's castle and fortress was the backdrop for the Orson Welles movie *Falstaff.*

Topping the list, though, may be the Parador de Granada: President Johnson, Queen Elizabeth, actress Rita Hayworth, and even Franco himself all stayed here. Additionally, Grace Kelly celebrated some of her honeymoon trip with Prince Rainier of Monaco in these hallowed halls, and many a Spanish intellectual and artist have also gotten cozy in this charming, sophisticated abode.

WHAT TO EXPECT

Walk where famous people have walked in the Parador de Granada's courtyard.

Paradors have been restored to provide modern amenities, within their classic settings, so you can count on some luxuries. Some have swimming pools, while others have fitness rooms and/or saunas. Most paradors have access to cable TV, though English channels may be limited to the basics; movies may be available via a pay-per-view service. Laundry facilities are available at almost all of the paradors, but Internet access tends to be limited.

As with most lodgings, it's always advised to reserve in advance.

Lodging at the paradors is generally equivalent to a four-star hotel and occasionally a five-star. The dining is another feature, though, that sets the paradors apart. The food is generally very good and traditionally inspired—you'd pay considerably more to eat the quality of food they serve at the same caliber restaurant elsewhere.

Cost: Prices at the paradors vary, depending on location and time of year. In general, one-night stays range from €95 to €200, though the Parador de Granada will hit your wallet for at least 60 euros more per night. July through September and Easter Week tend to be the most expensive times.

GREAT FOR DAY VISITS, TOO

While paradors are a great means of accommodation, they also attract huge numbers of day visitors. The reasons for this are twofold. First, the buildings are often spectacular and historically significant and many contain great views. Second, the restaurants are consistently excellent but reasonably priced. Each parador strives to use local produce and reproduce the traditional gastronomy found in its region.

PARADORES WORTH VISITING

With its Spanish plateresque façade, the Parador de León adorns the Plaza de San Marcos.

PARADOR DE CANGAS DE ONIS, *Chapter 4*. This beautiful former monastery is in the mountains of Picos de Europa.

PARADOR DE GRANADA, *Chapter 10*. Within the walls of Alhambra, this former monastery is Spain's most popular, and most expensive, parador.

PARADOR DE HONDARRIBIA, *Chapter 5*. This 10th-century castle-cum-fortress in the heart of Hondarribia looks severe from the outside but is elegant and lovely inside, with sweeping views of the French coastline.

PARADOR HOSTAL SAN MARCOS, *Chapter 3*. Pure luxury sums up this five-star monastery, with arguably the best restaurant in the parador network.

PARADOR DE PLASENCIA, *Chapter 3*. This Gothic convent lies in the heart of Plasencia's beautiful old quarters.

PARADOR DE SANTILLANA GIL BLAS, *Chapter 4*. Santillana de Mar may be one of the most beautiful villages in Spain; this parador in the mountains is perfect for peace and quiet.

PARADOR DE SIGÜENZA, *Chapter 3*. This sprawling 12th-century Moorish citadel is arguably the finest architectural example of all the parador castles.

PARADOR DE SANTIAGO DE CAMPOSTELA, *Chapter 4*. This 15th-century hospital is one of the most luxurious and beautiful of the parador chain.

TIP→ If you plan to spend at least five nights in the paradors, the "five-night card" offers excellent savings. You can purchase and use the card at any parador but in most, discounted nights aren't available in June, July, and August, and are offered only Sunday through Thursday in spring. Note that the card does not guarantee a room; you must make reservations in advance.

PARADOR INFORMATION

For more information about paradors, consult the official parador Web site, www.paradores.es/english, or call 34 902/547979.

Madrid

WORD OF MOUTH

"[With three days in Madrid] I would go to the Prado one day, the Reina Sofia one day, and the Thyssen Bornemisza one day. I would hang out in the Plaza Santa Ana having tapas and enjoying the late night atmosphere."

—Nikki

WELCOME TO MADRID

TOP REASONS TO GO

★ **Hitting the Centro Histórico:** The Plaza Mayor on any late night when it's almost empty is the place that best evokes the glory of Spain's golden age.

★ **Strolling Down Museum Row:** Find a pleasant mix of art and architecture in the Prado, the Reina Sofía, and the Thyssen, all of which display extensive and impressive collections.

★ **Nibbling Tapas into the Night:** Indulge in a *madrileño* way of socializing. Learn about the art of tapas and sample local wines while wandering among the bars of Cava Baja.

★ **Relaxing in the Retiro Gardens:** Visit on a Sunday morning, when it's at its most boisterous, to unwind and take in the sun and merrymaking.

★ **Burning the Midnight Oil:** When other cities turn off their lights, *madrileños* swarm to the bars of the liveliest neighborhoods—Malasaña, Chueca, Lavapiés, and more—and stretch the party out until dawn.

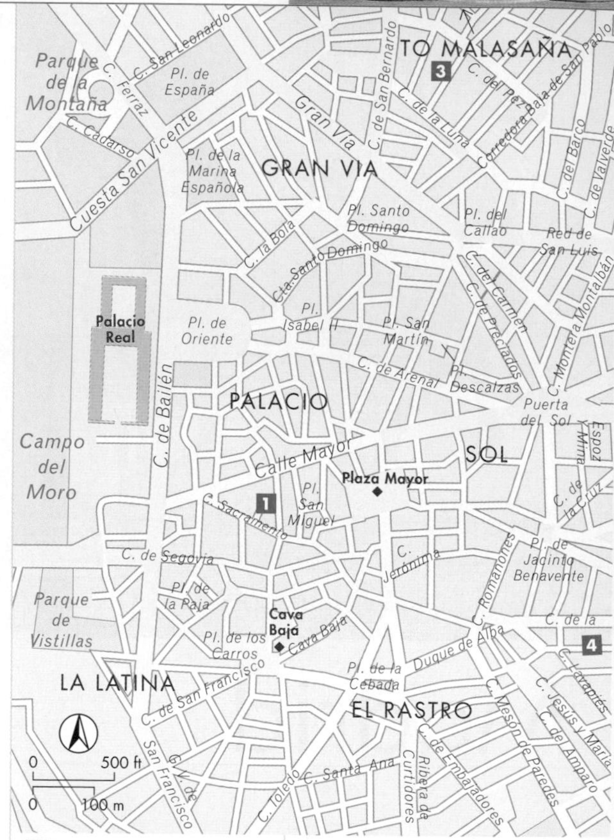

1 Old Madrid. This area comprises the three present-day neighborhoods of Sol, Palacio, and La Latina. The latter two have the city's highest concentration of aristocratic buildings and elegant yet affordable bars and restaurants, and Sol has some of the city's busiest streets and oldest shops.

2 Barrio de las Letras. This area, home to the city's first open-air theaters in the late 16th century, is where all the major Spanish writers eventually settled. There's still a bohemian spirit here, good nightlife, and some of the city's trendiest hotels.

3 Chueca and Malasaña. These neighborhoods offer eclectic, hip restaurants, shops run by young

proprietors selling a unique variety of goods, and landmark cafés where young people sip cappuccinos, read books, and surf the Web.

4 Rastro and Lavapiés. Tracing back to the 16th century, these two areas are full of winding streets. The Rastro thrives every Sunday with the flea market; Lavapiés is the city's multicultural beacon, with plenty of low-budget African and Asian restaurants.

5 Salamanca and Retiro. Salamanca has long been the upper middle class's favorite enclave and has great designer shops and sophisticated and expensive restaurants. Retiro, so called for its proximity to the park of the same name, holds some of the city's most expensive buildings.

GETTING ORIENTED

Madrid is composed of 21 districts, each broken down into several neighborhoods. The most central district is called just that, Centro. Within this district you'll find all of Madrid's oldest neighborhoods: Palacio, Sol, La Latina, Lavapiés, Barrio de las Letras, Malasaña, and Chueca. Other well-known districts, which we'll call neighborhoods in this chapter for the sake of convenience, are Salamanca, Retiro, Chamberí (north of Centro), Moncloa (east of Chamberí), and Chamartín. The city of Madrid dates back to the 9th century, but its perimeter wasn't enlarged by much until the mid-19th century, when an urban planner knocked down the wall built in 1625 and penciled new neighborhoods in what were formerly the outskirts. This means that even though there are now more than 3.3 million people living in a sprawling metropolitan area, the almond-shaped historic center is a concentrated area that can pleasantly be covered on foot.

MADRID PLANNER

When to Go

Madrid is hot and dry in summer—with temperatures reaching 95°F to 105°F in July and August—and chilly in winter, with minimum temperatures in the low 30s or slightly below in January and February, though snow in the city is rare. **The most pleasant time to visit is spring, especially May,** when the city honors its patron saint and bullfighting season begins. June, and September through December are also good.

The Festival de Otoño (Autumn Festival), from late September to late November, blankets the city with pop concerts, poetry readings, flamenco, and ballet and theater from world-renowned companies.

If you can, avoid Madrid in July and August—especially August, even though fares are better and there are plenty of concerts and open-air activities; many locals flee to the coast or to the mountains, so many restaurants, bars, and shops are closed.

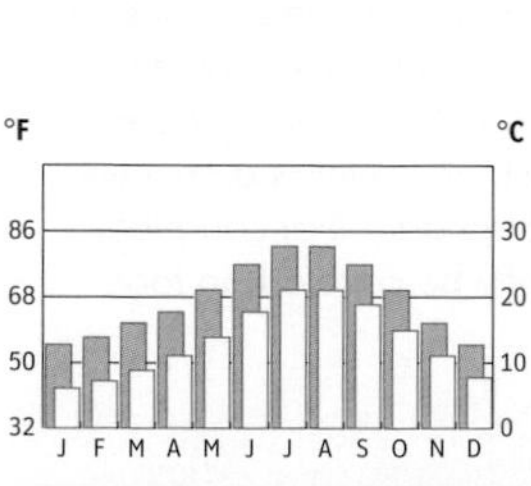

Planning Your Time

Madrid's most valuable art treasures are all on display within a few blocks of Paseo del Prado. This area is home to the Prado Museum, with its astounding selection of masterworks by Diego Velázquez, Francisco de Goya y Lucientes, El Greco, and others; the Centro de Arte Reina Sofía, with an excellent collection of contemporary art; and the Thyssen Museum, with a singular collection that stretches from the Renaissance to the 21st century. Each can take a number of hours to explore, so it's best to alternate museum visits with less overwhelming attractions. If you're running short on time and want to pack everything in, replenish your energy at any of the tapas bars or restaurants in the Barrio de las Letras (behind the Paseo del Prado, across from the Prado Museum).

Any visit to Madrid should include a walk in the old area between Puerta del Sol and the Royal Palace. Leave the map in your back pocket as you come across the Plaza Mayor, the Plaza de la Villa, and the Plaza de Oriente, and let the streets guide you to some of the oldest churches and convents standing. The Royal Palace makes a good start/end point.

Side Trips

Madrid is in the geographical center of Spain, and it's an excellent jumping-off point for exploring other historically significant sites. The massive monastery of El Escorial is probably the best destination if you want to stick close to Madrid, but the high-speed train makes it easy to venture farther, to two destinations that should be on everybody's list, Toledo and Segovia. Other options worth exploring are Ávila (1½ hours away by AVE) and Salamanca (2½ hours away by AVE). Any of these four destinations (all detailed in Chapter 3) make great day trips, except for Salamanca, which you really need an overnight to experience fully; Toledo would optimally get an overnight, as well, but you can do it a day if time is limited.

About the Hotels

Most hotels offer special weekend plans and discount prices during the month of August. Prices fluctuate, even with hotels of the same category belonging to the same chain, so it's best to shop around. Hostal rooms found on the upper floors of apartment buildings often go for €50 or less. These cheap lodgings are frequently full, especially on the weekends, and sometimes don't take reservations, so you simply have to try your luck door-to-door. Many are in the old city, in the trapezoid between the Puerta del Sol, the Atocha Station, the Basílica de San Francisco on Calle Bailén, and the Royal Palace; start your quest around Plaza Santa Ana or on the streets that are behind Puerta de Sol, near Plaza Mayor and Calle Atocha.

Mealtimes

Madrileños tend to eat their meals even later than people in other parts of Spain, and that's saying something. Restaurants open for lunch at 1:30 and fill up by 3. Dinnertime begins at 9, but reservations for 11 are common, and meals can be lengthy—up to three hours. If you face hunger meltdown several hours before Madrid dinner, make the most of the early-evening tapas hour.

WHAT IT COSTS IN EUROS

	¢	$	$$	$$$	$$$$
Restaurants	under €10	€10–€15	€16–€22	€23–€29	over €29
Hotels	under €75	€75–€124	€125–€174	€175–€225	over €225

Restaurant prices are per person for a main course at dinner. Hotel prices are for two people in a standard double room in high season, excluding tax.

Bike Tours

Although biking in the city can be risky because of the heavy traffic and madrileños' disregard for regulations, the city parks and the surroundings towns are good for enjoyable rides. There are several bike-rental outlets by Retiro Park, including **By Bike** (€8 for 2 hours). **Bravo Bike** organizes one-day or multiday biking tours around Madrid (Toledo, Aranjuez, Chinchón, Segovia) and Spain (the pilgrimage to Santiago, the Andalucía route, and others). They have a guided Madrid tour (€25), and also rent bikes (€15 a day or less if you rent for a few days). **Bike Spain** also rents bikes and organizes guided tours (in Madrid and all over Spain); it's €10–€15 for half-day and one-day bike rentals and €75 for a one-day guided trip to El Escorial. Bike Spain also organizes **Discover Madrid** bike tours, which take place every Saturday (10 AM) and Sunday afternoon (4 PM) in English (in Spanish they take place Saturday afternoon and Sunday morning).

Contact Information Bravo Bike (🌐 *www.bravobike.com*). **Bike Spain** (☎ *91/559–0653; 677/356586 ask for Pablo* 🌐 *www.bikespain.info*). **Discover Madrid** (☎ *91/588–2906 Patronato de Turismo*)

GETTING HERE AND AROUND

By Air

Madrid's Barajas Airport is Europe's fourth-largest. Terminal 4 (T-4) handles flights from 32 carriers, including American Airlines, British Airways, and Iberia. All other U.S. airlines use Terminal 1.

Airport terminals are connected by a bus service and also to the metro (*Línea 8*) and take you to the city center in 30 to 45 minutes for €2 (€1 plus a €1 airport supplement). For €1 there's also a convenient bus to Avenida de América, where you can catch the subway or a taxi to your hotel.

By Taxi

Taxis work under three different tariff schemes. Tariff 1 is for the city center from 6 AM to 9 PM; meters start at €2.05. Supplements include €5.50 to or from the airport and €2.95 to or from bus and train stations. Tariff 2 is from 9 PM to 6 AM in the city center (and 6 AM to 10 PM in the suburbs); the meter runs faster and charges more per km. Tariff 3 runs at night beyond the city limits. All tariffs are listed on taxi windows.

Taxi Services Radio Taxi Gremial (☎ *91/447–5180*). **Radioteléfono Taxi** (☎ *91/547–8200*). **Tele-Taxi** (☎ *91/371–2131*).

Tours

Madrid's **city hall (Plaza Mayor tourist office)** runs popular bus, cycling, and walking tours called "Descubre Madrid/Discover Madrid"—there are tours in English every day, with various departure points (€3.90–€12.95). Also popular are **Madrid Vision** tourist buses, which make two different 1½-hour circuits of the city (Historic Madrid and Modern Madrid) with recorded English commentary. No reservation is needed; check the Web site for departure points. One-day or two-day passes allow you to get on and off at various attractions (€17 or €21, less if you buy through the Web site).

The **Asociación Profesional de Guías de Turismo** has custom-made history and art walks. **Carpetania Madrid** also does custom tours, as well as literary walks on the life and works and life of some of Spain's classical and contemporary authors. **Julià Tours** has half- and one-day trips to sites outside Madrid, including Toledo, El Escorial, and Segovia.

Contact Information Asociación Profesional de Guías de Turismo (☎ *91/542–1214* 🌐 *www.apit.es*). **Carpetania Madrid** (☎ *91/531–1418 or 657/847685* 🌐 *www.carpetaniamadrid.com*). **Julià Tours** (☎ *91/559–9605* 🌐 *www.juliatours.es*). **Madrid Visión** (☎ *91/765–1016* 🌐 *www.madridvision.es*). **Plaza Mayor tourist office** (☎ *91/588–2906 wwww.esmadrid.com*).

By Bus

Buses are generally less popular than trains, though they're sometimes faster. Madrid has no central bus station: most of southern and eastern Spain (including Toledo) is served by the Estación del Sur. Estación de Avenida de América and Estación del Sur have subway stops (Avenida de América and Méndez Álvaro).

Red city buses (€1) run from about 6 AM to 11:30 PM.

Bus Stations Estación del Avenida de América (✉ *Av. de América 9, Salamanca* Ⓜ *Av. de América*). **Estación del Sur** (✉ *Méndez Álvaro s/n, Atocha* 🌐 *www.estaciondeautobuses.com* Ⓜ *Méndez Álvaro*). **Intercambiador de Moncloa** (✉ *Princesa 89* Ⓜ *Moncloa*).

By Subway

The metro costs €1; you can also buy a cheaper 10-ride Metrobus ticket or a daily ticket for €9 that can also be used on buses. The **Abono Turístico** (Tourist Pass) allows unlimited use of public buses and the subway for one to seven days. Buy it at tourist offices, metro stations, or select newsstands. The metro runs from 6 AM to 1:30 AM, though a few entrances close earlier. *There is a metro map on the inside front book cover.*

Metro Madrid (☎ *902/444403* 🌐 *www.metromadrid.es*).

By Train

Madrid is the geographical center of Spain, and all major train lines depart from one of its two main train stations (Chamartín and Atocha) or pass through Madrid (the third train station, Norte, is primarily for commuter trains). Though train travel is comfortable, for some destinations buses run more frequently and make fewer stops; this is true for Segovia and Toledo, unless you take the more expensive high-speed train.

Commuter trains to El Escorial, Aranjuez, and Alcalá de Henares run frequently. The best way to get a ticket for such trains is to use one of the automated reservation terminals at the station (they're in the *cercanías* area), but you can buy tickets online for the high-speed AVE regional lines. You can reach Segovia from the Atocha station in a half hour, the same time it takes you to get to Toledo. If you return the same day, the ticket may cost less than €18. The AVE stations in Toledo and Segovia are outside the city, meaning once there you'll have to take either a bus or a taxi to get to their old quarters.

The AVE line can get you to Barcelona in less than three hours. If you buy the ticket more than two weeks ahead and are lucky enough to find a Web fare, you'll pay less than €50 each way. Otherwise expect to pay between €115 and €135 each way—the more expensive being the AVE +, which is nonstop. ⇨ *For more information about buying train tickets, see the Travel Smart chapter.*

Train Information Estación de Atocha (✉ *Glorieta del Emperador Carlos V, Atocha* ☎ *91/528–4630* Ⓜ *Atocha*). **Estación Chamartín** (✉ *Calle Agustín de Foxá s/n, Chamartín* ☎ *91/315–9976* Ⓜ *Chamartín*). **Estación de Príncipe Pío (Norte)** (✉ *Paseo de la Florida s/n, Moncloa* ☎ *902/240202 RENFE* Ⓜ *Príncipe Pío*).

By Car

Driving in Madrid is best avoided because parking and traffic are nightmares, but many of the nation's highways radiate from Madrid, including the A6 (Segovia, Salamanca, Galicia); A1 (Burgos and the Basque Country); the A2 (Guadalajara, Barcelona, France); the A3 (Cuenca, Valencia, the Mediterranean coast); the A4 (Aranjuez, La Mancha, Granada, Seville); the A42 (Toledo); and the A5 (Talavera de la Reina, Portugal). The city is surrounded by ring roads (M30, M40, and M50), from which most of these highways are easily picked up. There are also toll highways (marked R2, R3, R4, and R5) that bypass major highways, and the A41, a toll highway connecting Madrid and Toledo.

Discounts and Deals

For €47, €60, or €74 (one, two, or three days, respectively) you can get the **Madrid Card,** which gives you entry to 40 museums and monuments, the tourist bus Madrid Visión, all the guided visits in the Discover Madrid program (🌐 *www.esmadrid.com*), and admission to the Faunia biological park and the zoo. It's available at 🌐 *www.madridcard.com,* at tourist offices, on Madrid Visión buses, at the kiosk next to the Prado Museum on Felipe IV, and at Atocha and Chamartín train stations.

EATING AND DRINKING WELL IN MADRID

Spain's capital draws the finest cuisine, from seafood to rice dishes, from all over the Iberian Peninsula but Madrid's most authentic local fare is based on the roasts and stews of Castile, Spain's mountain-studded central tableland.

Top left: A selection of tapas, including smoked ham and roasted peppers. Top right: A hearty meat soup. Bottom left: Ingredients for a classic *cocido madrileño* stew.

With a climate sometimes described as *nueves meses de invierno y tres de infierno* (nine months of winter and three of hell) it's no surprise that classic Madrid cuisine is winter fare. Garlic soup, partridge stew, and roast suckling pig and lamb are standard components of Madrid feasts, as are baby goat and chunks of beef from Ávila and the Sierra de Guadarrama. *Cocido madrileño* (a powerful winter stew) and callos a la madrileña (stewed tripe) are favored local specialties, while *jamón ibérico de bellota* (acorn-fed Ibérico ham)—a specialty from *la dehesa*, the rolling oak parks of Extremadura and Andalusia—has become a Madrid staple. Summer fare borrows heavily from Andalusian cuisine while minimalist contemporary cooking offers lighter postmodern alternatives based on traditional ingredients and recipes.

TAPAS

Itinerant grazing from tavern to tavern is especially important in Madrid, beneficiary of tapas traditions from every corner of Spain. The areas around Plaza Santa Ana, Plaza Mayor, and Cava Baja buzz with excitement as groups arrive for a glass of wine or two accompanied by anything from *boquerones* (pickled anchovies) or *aceitunas* (olives) to *raciones* (small plates) of *calamares* (squid) or *albóndigas* (meat balls).

SOUPS

Sopa de ajo, garlic soup, also known as *sopa castellana,* is cooked with *pimentón* (paprika), a laurel leaf, stale bread, and an egg or two for flavor and texture. A warming start to a winter meal, bits of ham or chorizo may be added, while a last-minute visit to the oven crisps the surface sprinkling of manchego cheese. Often eaten during Lent as an ascetic but energizing fasting dish, garlic soup appears in slightly different versions all over Spain. *Caldo* (chicken or beef broth), a Madrid favorite on wet winter days, is often offered free of charge in traditional bars and cafés with an order of anything else.

STEWS

Cocido madrileño is a Madrid classic, a winter favorite of broth, garbanzo beans, vegetables, potatoes, sausage, pork, and hen simmered in earthenware crocks over coals. *Estofado de perdiz* is a red leg partridge stewed slowly with garlic, onions, carrots, asparagus, and snow peas before being served in an earthenware casserole that keeps the stew piping hot. *Estofado de judiones de La Granja* (broad-bean stew) is another Madrid favorite: pork, quail, clams, or ham stewed with onions, tomato, carrots, laurel, thyme and broadbeans from the Segovian town of La Granja de San Ildefonso.

ROASTS

Asadores (restaurants specializing roasts) are an institution in and around Madrid, where the *cochinillo asado,* roast piglet, is the most iconic specialty. From Casa Botín in Madrid to Mesün de Cándido in Segovia and Toledo's Asador Adolfo (see chapter 3), madrileños love their roasts. Using milk-fed piglets not more than 21 days old, oak-burning wood ovens turn out crisp roasts tender enough to cut up using the edge of a plate. Close behind is the *lechazo* or milk-fed lamb that emerges from wood ovens accompanied by the aromas of oak and Castile's wide meseta: thyme, rosemary, and thistle.

WINES

The traditional Madrid house wine, a simple Valdepeñas from La Mancha south of the capital, is giving way to designer wines from Castilla-La Mancha, El Bierzo, Ribera de Duero, and new wine-growing regions popping up all over the peninsula. Traditional light red wines lack the character to properly accompany a *cocido* or a roast, whereas many of these new wines combine power and an earthy complexity capable of matching central Spain's harsh continental climate and hearty cuisine.

Updated by Ignacio Gómez

Swashbuckling Madrid—the Spanish capital since 1561—celebrates itself and life in general around the clock. A vibrant crossroads, Madrid has an infectious appetite for art, music, and epicurean pleasure, and it's turned into a cosmopolitan, modern urban center while fiercely preserving its traditions.

The modern city spreads east into the 19th-century grid of the Barrio de Salamanca and sprawls north through the neighborhoods of Chamberí and Chamartín. But the Madrid you should explore thoroughly on foot is right in the center, in Madrid's oldest quarters, between the Royal Palace and the midtown forest, the Parque del Buen Retiro. Wandering around the sprawling conglomeration of residential buildings with ancient red-tile rooftops punctuated by redbrick Mudejar churches and grand buildings with gray-slate roofs and spires left by the Hapsburg monarchs, you're more likely to grasp what is probably the city's major highlight: the buzzing bustle of people who are elated when they're outdoors.

And then there are the paintings, the artistic legacy of one of the greatest global empires ever assembled. King Carlos I (1500–58), who later became Emperor Carlos V, made sure the early masters of all European schools found their way to Spain's palaces. The collection was eventually placed in the Prado Museum. Among the Prado, the contemporary Reina Sofía museum, the eclectic Thyssen-Bornemisza collection, and Madrid's smaller artistic repositories—the Real Academia de Bellas Artes de San Fernando, the Convento de las Descalzas Reales, the Sorolla Museum, the Lázaro Galdiano Museum, and the CaixaForum—there are more paintings than anyone can admire in a lifetime.

But the attractions go beyond the well-known baroque landmarks. Now in the middle of an expansion plan, Madrid has made sure some of the world's best architects leave their imprint on the city. This is the case with Jacques Herzog and Pierre de Meuron, who are responsible for a new arts center, CaixaForum, opened in 2008 across from the Botanical Garden. Major renovations of the Museo del Prado and the

Centro Reina Sofía are by Rafael Moneo and Jean Nouvel, respectively. Looming towers by Norman Foster and César Pelli have changed the city's northern landscape. Other projects include the daring renovation project of the whole area of Paseo del Prado that's been entrusted to Portuguese architect Alvaro Siza, which is unfortunately stalled for the time being.

EXPLORING MADRID

The real Madrid is not to be found along major arteries like the Gran Vía and the Paseo de la Castellana. To find the quiet, intimate streets and squares that give the city its true character, duck into the warren of villagelike byways in the downtown area that extends 2 km (1 mi) from the Royal Palace to the Parque del Buen Retiro and from Plaza de Lavapiés to the Glorieta de Bilbao. Broad *avenidas,* twisting medieval alleys, grand museums, stately gardens, and tiny, tile taverns are all jumbled together, creating an urban texture so rich that walking is really the only way to soak it in.

■ TIP→ Petty street crime is a serious problem in Madrid, and tourists are frequent targets. Be on your guard, and try to blend in by keeping cameras concealed, avoiding obvious map reading, and securing bags and purses, especially on buses and subways and outside restaurants.

Numbers in the text correspond to numbers in the margin and on chapter maps.

OLD MADRID

The narrow streets of Madrid's old section, which includes the Palacio, La Latina, and Sol neighborhoods—part of Madrid's greater Centro district—wind back through the city's history to its beginnings as an Arab fortress. As elsewhere in Madrid, there is a mix of old buildings and new ones: the neighborhoods here might not be as uniformly ancient as those in the nearby cities of Toledo and Segovia (or as grand), but the quiet alleys make for wonderful exploring.

Beyond the most central neighborhoods, Madrid also has several other sites of interest scattered around the city. Moncloa and Casa de Campo are the neighborhoods to the north and east of Palacio—that is, you can easily walk to the Templo de Debod or visit Goya's tomb if you're in the vicinity of the Royal Palace.

TOP ATTRACTIONS

3 ★ **Cava Baja.** The epicenter of the fashionable and historic La Latina neighborhood—a maze of narrow streets that extend south of Plaza Mayor and across Calle Segovia—Cava Baja is a diagonal street crowded with excellent tapas bars and traditional restaurants. Its lively atmosphere spills over into nearby streets and squares, including Almendro, Cava Alta, Plaza del Humilladero, and Plaza de la Paja. ✉ *Cava Baja, La Latina* Ⓜ *La Latina.*

20 **Monasterio de la Encarnación** *(Monastery of the Incarnation).* Once connected to the Royal Palace by an underground passageway, this

CLOSE UP

A Good Walk: Old Madrid

Stroll around Puerta del Sol for a look at Madrid's oldest buildings, bustling taverns, and quiet cobblestone alleys. Budget about two hours, more if you visit the Palacio Real or Monasterio de la Encarnación.

Begin at the **Puerta del Sol** ❶, the center of Madrid and a major social and transportation hub, then take Calle Mayor to the **Plaza Mayor** ❷. Inaugurated in 1620 on the site of a thriving street market, this is Madrid's main square, where you'll find the Casa de la Panadería (Bakery House)—an imposing building with mythological figures painted on its facade, home of the main tourist office.

Exit Plaza Mayor through the arch (Arco de Cuchilleros) and go down the stairs: to the right is Calle Cava de San Miguel—a stretch of colorful taverns going uphill to the posh Mercado de San Miguel and Calle Mayor; to the left is Calle Cuchilleros (knife-sellers street), which leads to the Plaza de Puerta Cerrada, or "Closed Gate," named for the city gate that once stood here. The mural up to your right reads "*Fui sobre agua edificada; mis muros de fuego son*" ("I was built on water; my walls are made of fire"), a reference to the city's origins as a fortress with abundant springs and its ramparts, made of spark-making flint. Cross the street to Calle **Cava Baja** ❸, packed with taverns and restaurants this. At Plaza del Humilladero, walk past Plaza de San Andrés and take Costanilla de San Andrés from Plaza Puerta de Moros, down to **Plaza de la Paja** ❺. The **Capilla del Obispo** (Bishop's Chapel), on the south edge of the plaza, completed in 1535, houses one of Spain's most magnificent Renaissance altarpieces. Look right on narrow Calle Príncipe Anglona—at it's end you'll see a tall redbrick Mudejar tower, the only original element belonging to San Pedro el Real (St. Peter the Royal), one of Madrid's oldest churches.

Cross Calle Segovia to Plaza de la Cruz Verde, take the stairs (Calle del Rollo) to your right, go straight to Calle Cordón, then turn left. Walk up the stairs, and cross the Plaza del Cordón and Calle Sacramento to get to **Plaza de la Villa** ❻; noteworthy buildings here are (west) the former City Hall main office, finished in 1692; (east) the Casa and Torre de los Lujanes, the oldest civil building in Madrid, dating to the mid-15th century; and (south) the Casa Cisneros, from the 16th century. Turn left on Calle Mayor and walk to Calle San Nicolás; on the corner is the Palacio del Duque de Uceda, a residential building from the 17th century now used as military headquarters. Turn right onto Calle San Nicolás (San Nicolás de los Servitas is Madrid's oldest standing church, with a Mudejar tower dating to the 17th century) and walk to Plaza de Ramales, where you'll find a display of a ruined section of the foundation of the medieval Iglesia de San Juan, demolished in the 19th century. Take Calle San Nicolas until it becomes Calle de Lepanto, which leads to the **Plaza de Oriente** ㉑. The equestrian statue of Felipe IV was sculpted from a drawing by Velázquez, who worked and died in what is now a residential building on the east side of the plaza. Lounge in the plaza, then visit the **Palacio Real** ⓫, stroll in the palace gardens, or visit nearby **Monasterio de la Encarnación** ⓴.

Augustinian convent now houses less than a dozen nuns. Founded in 1611 by Queen Margarita de Austria, the wife of Felipe III, it has several artistic treasures, including a reliquary where a vial with the dried blood of St. Pantaleón is said to liquefy every July 27. The ornate church has superb acoustics for medieval and Renaissance choral concerts. ✉ *Pl. de la Encarnación 1, Palacio* ☎ *91/454–8800 tourist information office* 🎫 *€3.60, €6 combined ticket with Convento de las Descalzas Reales, free Wed.* ⏲ *Tues.–Thurs. and Sat. 10:30–12:45 and 4–5:45, Fri. 10:30–12:45, Sun. 11–1:45* Ⓜ *Ópera.*

23 **Monasterio de las Descalzas Reales** *(Monastery of the Royal Discalced, or Barefoot, Nuns).* This 16th-century building was restricted for 200 years to women of royal blood. Its plain, brick-and-stone facade hides paintings by Francisco de Zurbarán, Titian, and Pieter Brueghel the Elder—all part of the dowry the novices had to provide when they joined the monastery—as well as a hall of sumptuous tapestries crafted from drawings by Peter Paul Rubens. The convent was founded in 1559 by Juana of Austria, one of Felipe II's sisters, who ruled Spain while he was in England and the Netherlands. It houses 33 different chapels—the age of Christ when he died and the maximum number of nuns allowed to live at the monastery at the same time—and more than 100 sculptures of Jesus as a baby. About 30 nuns (not necessarily of royal blood) still live here, cultivating their own vegetables in the convent's garden. **TIP→ You must take a tour in order to visit the convent; it's conducted in Spanish only.** ✉ *Pl. de las Descalzas Reales 3, Palacio* ☎ *91/454–8800* 🎫 *€5, €6 combined ticket with Convento de la Encarnación, free Wed.* ⏲ *Tues.–Thurs. and Sat. 10:30–12:30 and 4–5:30, Fri. 10:30–12:30, Sun. 11–1:30* Ⓜ *Sol.*

RAINY-DAY TREAT

Despite what the ads say, Madrid is not always sunny. If you hit a rainy or a chilly day, walk along the western side of the Convento de las Descalzas Reales until you see, on your left, the Chocolatería Valor (✉ *Calle Postigo de San Martín 7, Centro* Ⓜ *Callao*) ; there you'll find the thick Spanish version of hot chocolate, perfect for dipping crispy churros.

11 **Palacio Real.** Emblematic of the oldest part of the city and intimately related to the origins of Madrid—it rests on the terrain where the Muslims built their defensive fortress in the 9th century—the Royal Palace awes visitors with its sheer size and monumental presence that unmistakably stands out against the city's silhouetted background. The palace was commissioned in the early 18th century by the first of Spain's Bourbon rulers, Felipe V. Outside, you can see the classical French architecture on the graceful **Patio de Armas:** Felipe was obviously inspired by his childhood days at Versailles with his grandfather Louis XIV. Look for the stone statues of Inca prince Atahualpa and Aztec king Montezuma, perhaps the only tributes in Spain to these pre-Columbian American rulers. Notice how the steep bluff drops west to the Manzanares River—on a clear day, this vantage point commands a view of the mountain passes leading into Madrid from Old Castile; it's easy to see why the Moors picked this spot for a fortress.

Fodor's Choice ★

Inside, 2,800 rooms compete with each other for over-the-top opulence. A two-hour guided tour in English winds a mile-long path through the palace; highlights include the **Salón de Gasparini,** King Carlos III's private apartments, with swirling, inlaid floors and curlicued stucco wall and ceiling decoration, all glistening in the light of a 2-ton crystal chandelier; the **Salón del Trono,** a grand throne room with the royal seats of King Juan Carlos and Queen Sofía; and the **banquet hall,** the palace's largest room, which seats up to 140 people for state dinners. No monarch has lived here since 1931, when Alfonso XIII was deposed after a Republican electoral victory. The current king and queen live in the far simpler Zarzuela Palace on the outskirts of Madrid; this palace is used only for official occasions.

Also worth visiting are the **Museo de Música** (Music Museum), where five stringed instruments by Antonio Stradivari form the world's largest such collection; the **Painting Gallery,** which displays works by Spanish, Flemish, and Italian artists from the 15th century on; the **Armería Real** (Royal Armory), with historic suits of armor and frightening medieval torture implements; and the **Real Oficina de Farmacía** (Royal Pharmacy), with vials and flasks used to mix the king's medicines. ✉ *Calle Bailén s/n, Palacio* ☎ *91/454–8800* 🎫 *€8, guided tour €10; Royal Armory only €3.40; Painting Gallery only €2* ⏱ *Apr.–Sept., Mon.–Sat. 9–6, Sun. 9–3; Oct.–Mar., Mon.–Sat. 9:30–5, Sun. 9–2* Ⓜ *Ópera.*

5 **Plaza de la Paja**. At the top of the hill, on Costanilla San Andrés, the Plaza de la Paja was the most important square in medieval Madrid. The plaza's jewel is the **Capilla del Obispo** (Bishop's Chapel), built between 1520 and 1530; this was where peasants deposited their tithes, called *diezmas*—literally, one-tenth of their crop. The stacks of wheat on the chapel's ceramic tiles refer to this tradition. Architecturally, the chapel marks a transition from the blocky Gothic period, which gave the structure its basic shape, to the Renaissance, the source of the decorations. It houses an intricately carved polychrome altarpiece by Francisco Giralta, with scenes from the life of Christ. It's part of the complex of the domed church of **San Andrés,** one of Madrid's oldest, which for centuries held the remains of Madrid's male patron saint, San Isidro Labrador (they are now with his wife's remains, at the Real Colegiata de San Isidro, on nearby Calle Toledo). The church was severely damaged during the civil war. St. Isidore the Laborer was a peasant who worked fields belonging to the Vargas family. The 16th-century **Vargas Palace** forms the eastern side of the Plaza de la Paja. According to legend, St. Isidro worked little but had the best-tended fields thanks to many hours of prayer. When Señor Vargas came out to investigate the phenomenon, Isidro made a spring of sweet water spurt from the ground to quench his master's thirst. A hermitage (Ermita de San Isidro), now on Paseo de la Ermita del Santo, west of the Manzanares River, was built next to the spring in 1528. Every May 15 there's a procession followed by festivities in the meadow next to the hermitage. (In olden days, the saint's remains were traditionally paraded through the city in times of drought.) ✉ *Plaza de la Paja, La Latina* Ⓜ *La Latina.*

DID YOU KNOW?

The Casa de la Panadería (Bakery House), on the left side of this photo of the Plaza Mayor, is the oldest building in the plaza and was originally a bread shop. It's recognizable by the colorfully painted facade.

6 **Plaza de la Villa**. Madrid's town council used to meet in this medieval-looking complex starting in the Middle Ages, though in 2009 it moved to the new city hall headquarters in the post-office building at Plaza Cibeles, leaving the space to house city hall offices. The oldest building is the **Casa de los Lujanes,** on the east side—it's the one with the Mudejar tower. Built as a private home in the late 15th century, the house carries the Lujanes crest over the main doorway. Also on the plaza's east end is the brick-and-stone **Casa de la Villa,** built in 1629, a classic example of Madrid design, with clean lines and spire-topped corner towers. Connected by an overhead walkway, the **Casa de Cisneros** was commissioned in 1537 by the nephew of Cardinal Cisneros. It's one of Madrid's rare examples of the flamboyant plateresque style, which has been likened to splashed water. ✉ *Mayor, Palacio* ⏲ *Closed to public except for free guided tour in Spanish Mon. at 5* Ⓜ *Sol, Ópera.*

21 **Plaza de Oriente**. The stately plaza in front of the Royal Palace is surrounded by massive stone statues of Spanish monarchs. These sculptures were meant to be mounted on the railing on top of the palace, but Queen Isabel of Farnesio, one of the first royals to live in the palace, had them removed because she was afraid their enormous weight would bring the roof down. (Well, that's the *official* reason; according to palace insiders, the queen wanted the statues removed because her own likeness had not been placed front and center.) A Velázquez drawing of King Felipe IV is the inspiration for the statue in the plaza's center. It's the first equestrian bronze ever cast with a rearing horse. The sculptor, Italian artist Pietro de Tacca, enlisted Galileo Galilei's help in configuring the statue's weight so it wouldn't tip over. ✉ *Plaza de Oriente, Palacio* Ⓜ *Ópera.*

2 **Plaza Mayor**. Austere, grand, and often surprisingly quiet compared with the rest of Madrid, this 360- by-300-foot public square—finished in 1620 under Felipe III, whose equestrian statue stands in the center—is one of the largest in Europe. It's seen it all: autos-da-fé (trials of faith, i.e., public burnings of heretics); the canonization of saints; criminal executions; royal marriages, such as that of Princess María and the King of Hungary in 1629; bullfights (until 1847); masked balls; and all manner of other events. Special events still take place here.

This space was once occupied by a city market, and many of the surrounding streets retain the charming names of the trades and foods once headquartered there. Nearby are Calle de Cuchilleros (Knifemakers' Street), Calle de Lechuga (Lettuce Street), Calle de Fresa (Strawberry Street), and Calle de Botoneros (Buttonmakers' Street). The plaza's oldest building is the one with the brightly painted murals and the gray spires, called Casa de la Panadería (Bakery House) in honor of the bread shop over which it was built; it is now the tourist office. Opposite is the Casa de la Carnicería (Butcher Shop), now a police station.

The plaza is closed to motorized traffic, making it a pleasant place to sit at one of the sidewalk cafés, watching alfresco artists, street musicians, and madrileños from all walks of life. Sunday morning brings a stamp and coin market. Around Christmas the plaza fills with stalls selling trees, ornaments, and nativity scenes. ✉ *Pl. Mayor, Sol* Ⓜ *Sol.*

QUICK BITES

Near the Plaza Mayor, the most exciting, and interactive, addition to the Madrid tapas scene is the old market, Mercado de San Miguel (✉ *Pl. de San Miguel s/n* 🌐 *www.mercadodesanmiguel.es* ⏲ *Mon.–Wed. and Sun. 10 AM–midnight; Thurs., Fri., and Sat., 10–2 AM* Ⓜ *Ópera, Sol*), which has been converted into a gourmet nirvana. Open till the wee hours of the night, the swanky, bustling stalls are usually filled with a mix of madrileños and tourists sampling plates of Manchego cheese with a good Rioja or Rivera de Duero red wine, or perhaps less traditional fare such as oysters with champagne, Austrian pastries, crackers topped with Russian caviar, Andalusian shrimp paired with sherry, and much more.

❶ **Puerta del Sol.** Crowded with people and exhaust—and now made even more chaotic by the construction of a massive underground station that has been delayed several times due to the discovery of archaeological remains—Sol is the nerve center of Madrid's traffic. The city's main subway interchange is below, and buses fan out from here. A brass plaque in the sidewalk on the south side of the plaza marks Kilometer 0, the spot from which all distances in Spain are measured. The restored 1756 French-neoclassical building near the marker now houses the offices of the regional government, but during Franco's reign it was the headquarters of his secret police, and it's still known folklorically as the Casa de los Gritos (House of Screams). Across the square are a bronze statue of Madrid's official symbol, a bear with a *madroño* (strawberry tree), and a statue of King-Mayor Carlos III on horseback. ✉ *Puerta del Sol, Sol* Ⓜ *Sol.*

㉔ **Real Academia de Bellas Artes de San Fernando** *(St. Ferdinand Royal Academy of Fine Arts).* Designed by José Churriguera in the waning baroque years of the early 18th century, this museum showcases 500 years of Spanish painting, from José Ribera and Bartolomé Esteban Murillo to Joaquín Sorolla and Ignacio Zuloaga. The tapestries along the stairways are stunning. Because of a lack of personnel, only the first floor is now open, displaying paintings up to the 18th century, including some by Goya. The same building houses the **Instituto de Calcografía** (Prints Institute), which sells limited-edition prints from original plates engraved by Spanish artists. Check listings for classical and contemporary concerts in the small upstairs hall. ✉ *Alcalá 13, Sol* ☎ *91/524–0864* 🎟 *€5, free Wed.* ⏲ *Tues.–Fri. 9–7, Sat. 9–2:30 and 4–7, Sun. and Mon. 9–2:30; free guided tour Wed. 5–7* Ⓜ *Sol.*

WORTH NOTING

❽ **Arab Wall.** The remains of the Moorish military outpost that became the city of Madrid are visible on Calle Cuesta de la Vega. The sections of wall here protected a fortress built in the 9th century by Emir Mohammed I. In addition to being an excellent defensive position, the site had plentiful water and was called *Mayrit,* Arabic for "source of life" (this is the likely origin of the city's name). All that remains of the *medina*—the old Arab city that formed within the walls of the fortress—is the neighborhood's crazy quilt of streets and plazas, which probably follow the same layout they did more than 1,100 years ago. ✉ *Cuesta de la Vega, Palacio* Ⓜ *Ópera.*

The Puerta del Sol, Madrid's central transportation hub, is sure to be passed through by every visitor to the city.

4 **Basílica de San Francisco el Grande.** In 1760 Carlos III built this impressive basilica on the site of a Franciscan convent, allegedly founded by St. Francis of Assisi in 1217. The dome, 108 feet in diameter, is the largest in Spain, even larger than that of St. Paul's in London. The seven main doors were carved of American walnut by Casa Juan Guas. Three chapels adjoin the circular church, the most famous being that of **San Bernardino de Siena,** which contains a Goya masterpiece depicting a preaching San Bernardino. The figure standing on the right, not looking up, is a self-portrait of Goya. The 16th-century Gothic choir stalls came from La Cartuja del Paular, in rural Segovia Province. ✉ *Pl. de San Francisco, La Latina* ☎ *91/365–3800* 💳 *€3 guided tour* ⏲ *Oct.–May, Tues.–Fri. 10:30–12:30 and 4–6; June–Sept., Tues.–Fri. 10:30–12:30 and 5–7* Ⓜ *Puerta de Toledo, La Latina.*

10 **Campo del Moro** *(Moors' Field).* Below the Sabatini Gardens, but accessible only by an entrance on the far side, is the Campo del Moro. Enjoy the clusters of shady trees, winding paths, and lawn leading up to the Royal Palace. Inside the gardens is a **Museo de Carruajes** (Carriage Museum), displaying royal carriages and equestrian paraphernalia from the 16th through 20th century. ✉ *Paseo Virgen del Puerto s/n, Palacio.* Ⓜ *Príncipe Pío.*

9 **Catedral de la Almudena.** The first stone of the cathedral (which adjoins the Royal Palace) was laid in 1883 by King Alfonso XII, and the result was consecrated by Pope John Paul II in 1993. Built on the site of the old church of Santa María de la Almudena (thought to be the city's main mosque during Arab rule), the new cathedral was intended to be Gothic in style, with needles and spires; funds ran low, so the design

was simplified into the existing, more austere classical form. The cathedral has a wooden statue of Madrid's female patron saint, the Virgin of Almudena, reportedly discovered after the Christian Reconquest of Madrid. Legend has it that when the Arabs invaded Spain, the local Christian population hid the statue of the Virgin in a vault carved in the old Roman wall that encircled the city. When the Christians reconquered Madrid in 1085, they looked for it, and after nine days of intensive praying—others say it was after a procession honoring the Virgin—the wall opened up to show the statue framed by two lighted candles. Its name is derived from the place where it was found: the wall of the old citadel (in Arabic, *al mudeyna*). ✉ *Bailén 10, Palacio* ☎ *91/542–2200* 🎟 *Free* 🕐 *Daily 9–9* Ⓜ *Ópera.*

⓭ **Ermita de San Antonio de la Florida (Goya's tomb).** Built from 1792 to 1798 by the Italian architect Francisco Fontana, this neoclassical church was financed by King Carlos IV, who also commissioned Goya to paint the vaults and the main dome: he took 120 days to complete his assignment, painting alone except for a little boy who stirred his pigments. This gave him absolute freedom to depict events of the 13th century (St. Anthony of Padua resurrecting a dead man) as if they had happened five centuries later with naturalistic images never used before to paint religious scenes. Opposite the image of the frightening dead man on the main dome, Goya painted himself as a man covered with a black cloak. The frescoes' third-restoration phase ended in 2005, and visitors can now admire them in their full splendor. Goya, who died in Bordeaux in 1828, is buried here (without his head, since it was stolen in France), under an unadorned gravestone. ✉ *Glorieta de San Antonio de la Florida 5, Príncipe Pío* ☎ *91/542–0722* 🎟 *Free* 🕐 *Tues.–Fri. 9:30–8, weekends 10–2* Ⓜ *Príncipe Pío.*

⓬ **Jardines de Sabatini** *(Sabatini Gardens).* The formal gardens to the north of the Royal Palace are crawling with stray cats but are still a pleasant place to rest or watch the sun set. ✉ *Bailén s/n, Palacio* Ⓜ *Príncipe Pío, Plaza de España.*

⓱ **Museo del Traje** *(Costume Museum).* This museum traces the evolution of dress in Spain from the old burial garments worn by kings and nobles (very few of which remain) and the introduction of French fashion by Felipe V to the 20th-century creations of couturiers such as Balenciaga and Pertegaz. The 18th century claims the largest number of pieces. Explanatory notes are in English, and the museum has a superb restaurant. To get here, from Moncloa take Bus 46 or walk along the northeastern edge of Parque del Oeste. ✉ *Av. Juan de Herrera 2, Ciudad Universitaria* ☎ *91/549–7150* 🌐 *museodeltraje.mcu.es* 🎟 *€3, free Sat. after 2 and Sun.* 🕐 *Tues.–Sat. 9:30–7, Sun. 10–3* Ⓜ *Ciudad Universitaria.*

❼ **San Nicolás de los Servitas** *(Church of St. Nicholas of the Servitas).* This church tower is one of the oldest buildings in Madrid. There's some debate over whether it once formed part of an Arab mosque. It was more likely built after the Christian Reconquest of Madrid in 1085, but the brickwork and the horseshoe arches are evidence that it was crafted by either Mudejars (Moorish workers) or Spaniards well versed

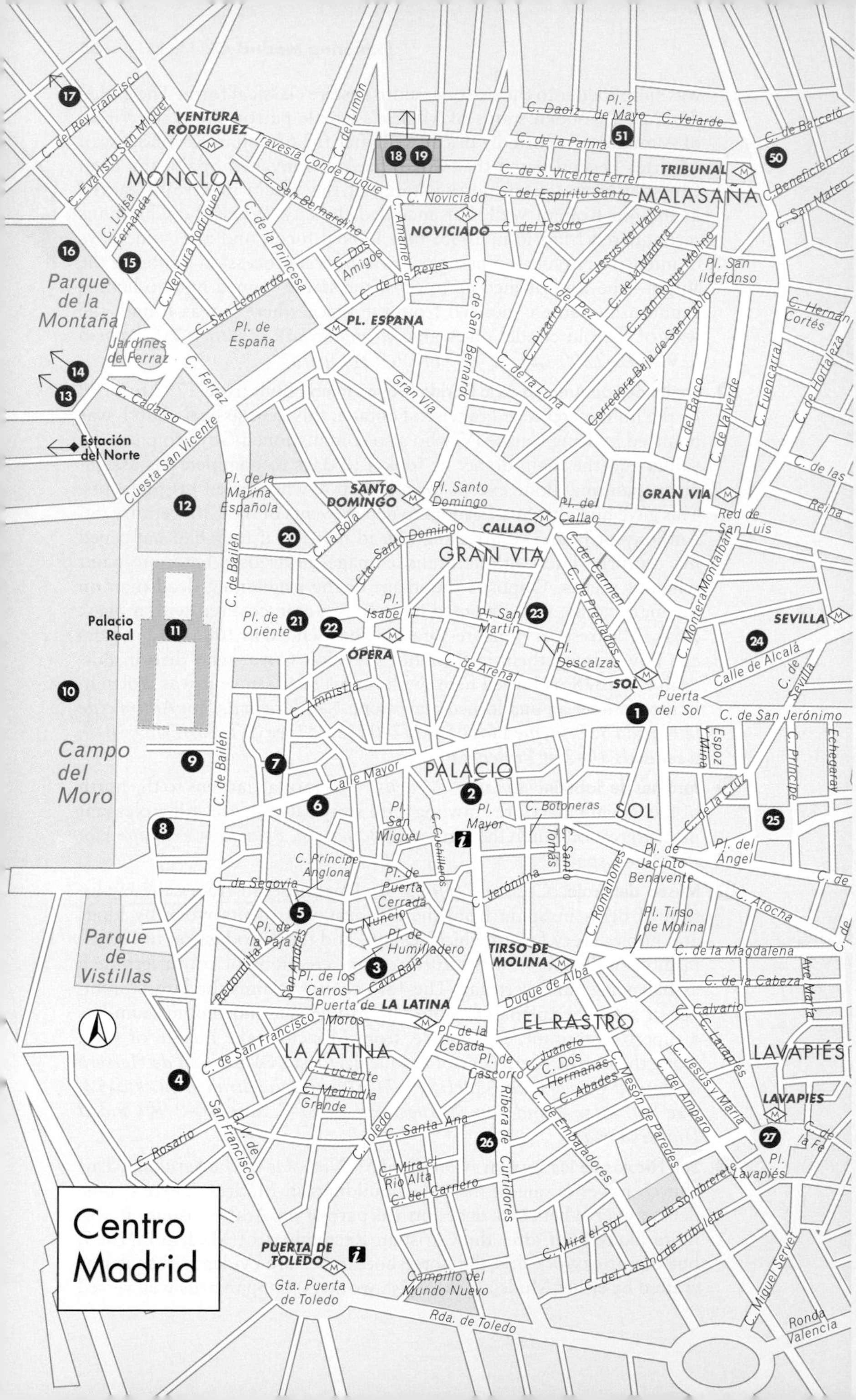
Centro Madrid
MONCLOA
MALASAÑA
GRAN VIA
PALACIO
SOL
EL RASTRO
LA LATINA
LAVAPIÉS
VENTURA RODRIGUEZ
NOVICIADO
TRIBUNAL
PL. ESPANA
SANTO DOMINGO
CALLAO
GRAN VIA
SEVILLA
SOL
ÓPERA
TIRSO DE MOLINA
LA LATINA
LAVAPIES
PUERTA DE TOLEDO
Parque de la Montaña
Jardines de Ferraz
Estación del Norte
Palacio Real
Campo del Moro
Parque de Vistillas
C. del Rey Francisco
C. Evaristo San Miguel
C. Luisa Fernanda
C. Ventura Rodriguez
C. de la Princesa
C. San Leonardo
Travesía Conde Duque
C. San Bernardino
C. de Limón
C. Amaniel
C. Dos Amigos
C. de los Reyes
C. Noviciado
C. Daoiz
Pl. 2 de Mayo
C. Velarde
C. de la Palma
C. de S. Vicente Ferrer
C. del Espiritu Santo
C. del Tesoro
C. de Barceló
C. Beneficencia
C. San Mateo
C. Jesus del Valle
C. de la Madera
C. San Roque Molino
Pl. San Ildefonso
C. Pizarro
C. de Pez
C. de San Bernardo
C. de la Luna
Corredora Baja de San Pablo
C. Hernán Cortés
C. de Hortaleza
C. Fuencarral
C. de Valverde
C. del Barco
C. de las Reina
Pl. de España
C. Ferraz
C. Cadarso
Cuesta San Vicente
Gran Vía
Pl. de la Marina Española
Pl. Santo Domingo
Pl. del Callao
Red de San Luis
C. la Bola
Cta. Santo Domingo
C. de Bailén
C. del Carmen
C. de Preciados
C. Montera
Montalbán
Pl. Isabel II
Pl. San Martín
Pl. de Oriente
Pl. Descalzas
C. de Arenal
Puerta del Sol
Calle de Alcalá
C. de Sevilla
C. de San Jerónimo
C. Amnistía
Calle Mayor
Espoz Y Mina
C. Príncipe
Echegaray
C. Botoneras
Pl. Mayor
Pl. San Miguel
C. Cuchilleros
C. Santo Tomás
C. de la Cruz
Pl. de Jacinto Benavente
Pl. del Ángel
C. Príncipe Anglona
C. de Segovia
Pl. de Puerta Cerrada
C. Jerónima
C. Romanones
C. Atocha
Pl. Tirso de Molina
C. Nuncio
Pl. de Humilladero
Pl. de la Paja
Redondilla
San Andrés
Pl. de los Carros
Cava Baja
Puerta de Moros
C. de la Magdalena
Duque de Alba
C. de la Cabeza
Ave María
C. Calvario
C. Lavapiés
C. de San Francisco
Pl. de la Cebada
Pl. de Cascorro
C. Juanelo
C. Dos Hermanas
C. Abades
C. Mesón de Paredes
C. del Amparo
C. Jesús y María
C. Luciente
C. Mediodia Grande
G. V. de San Francisco
C. Rosario
C. Toledo
C. Santa Ana
Ribera de Curtidores
C. de Embajadores
C. de la Fe
Pl. Lavapiés
C. Mira el Río Alta
C. del Carnero
C. de Sombrerete
C. Mira el Sol
C. del Casino
de Tribulete
C. Miguel Servet
Gta. Puerta de Toledo
Campillo del Mundo Nuevo
Rda. de Toledo
Ronda Valencia
1
2
3
4
5
6
7
8
9
10
11
12
13
14
15
16
17
18
19
20
21
22
23
24
25
26
27
50
51

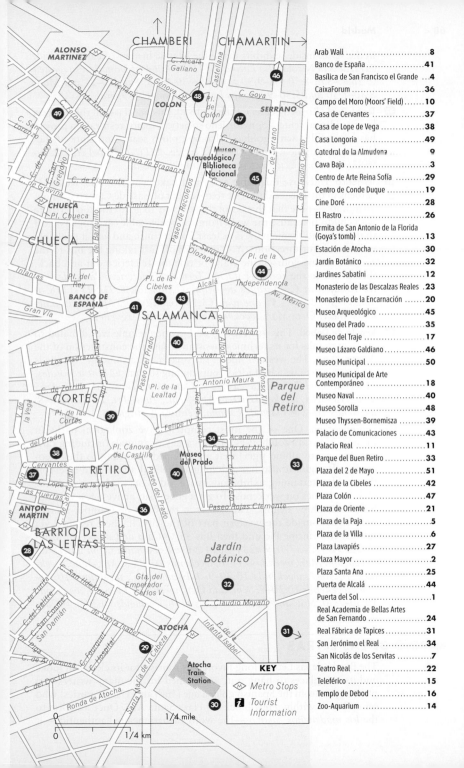

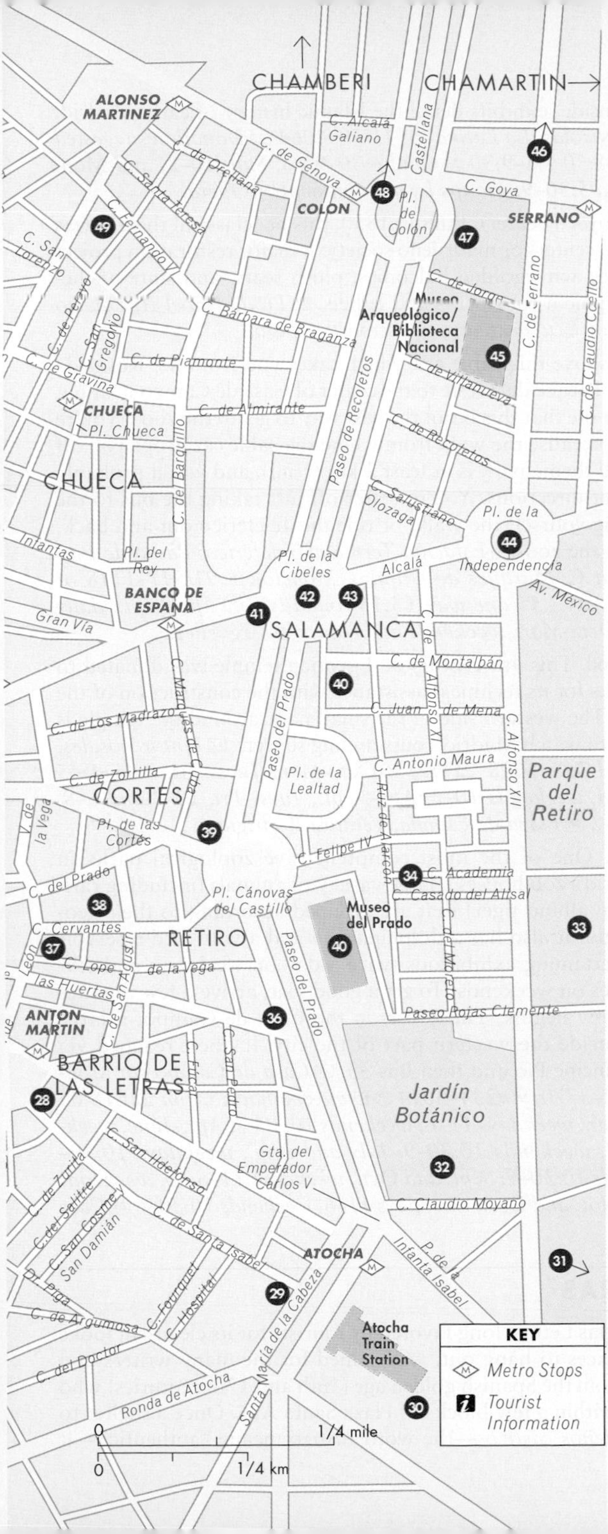

Arab Wall 8
Banco de España 41
Basílica de San Francisco el Grande ... 4
CaixaForum 36
Campo del Moro (Moors' Field) 10
Casa de Cervantes 37
Casa de Lope de Vega 38
Casa Longoria 49
Catedral de la Almudena 9
Cava Baja 3
Centro de Arte Reina Sofía 29
Centro de Conde Duque 19
Cine Doré 28
El Rastro 26
Ermita de San Antonio de la Florida (Goya's tomb) 13
Estación de Atocha 30
Jardín Botánico 32
Jardines Sabatini 12
Monasterio de las Descalzas Reales 23
Monasterio de la Encarnación 20
Museo Arqueológico 45
Museo del Prado 35
Museo del Traje 17
Museo Lázaro Galdiano 46
Museo Municipal 50
Museo Municipal de Arte Contemporáneo 18
Museo Naval 40
Museo Sorolla 48
Museo Thyssen-Bornemisza 39
Palacio de Comunicaciones 43
Palacio Real 11
Parque del Buen Retiro 33
Plaza del 2 de Mayo 51
Plaza de la Cibeles 42
Plaza Colón 47
Plaza de Oriente 21
Plaza de la Paja 5
Plaza de la Villa 6
Plaza Lavapiés 27
Plaza Mayor 2
Plaza Santa Ana 25
Puerta de Alcalá 44
Puerta del Sol 1
Real Academia de Bellas Artes de San Fernando 24
Real Fábrica de Tapices 31
San Jerónimo el Real 34
San Nicolás de los Servitas 7
Teatro Real 22
Teleférico 15
Templo de Debod 16
Zoo-Aquarium 14

in the style. Inside, exhibits detail the Islamic history of early Madrid. ✉ *Pl. de San Nicolás, La Latina* ☎ *91/559–4064* 🎫 *Donation suggested* ⏲ *Tues.–Sat. 8:30* AM*–9:30* AM *and 6:30–9* PM, *Sun. 10–2, and Mon. 8:30–1:30 and 5:30–9; groups by appointment* Ⓜ *Ópera.*

22 **Teatro Real** *(Royal Theater).* Built in 1850, this neoclassical theater was long a cultural center for madrileño society. A major restoration project has left it filled with golden balconies, plush seats, and state-of-the-art stage equipment for operas and ballets. ✉ *Pl. de Isabel II, Palacio* ☎ *91/516–0660* 🌐 *www.teatro-real.com* Ⓜ *Ópera.*

11 **Teleférico.** Kids love this cable car, which takes you from the Rosaleda gardens in the Parque del Oeste to the center of Casa de Campo in about 10 minutes—note that this is not the best way to get to the zoo if you're with children because the walk from where the cable car drops you off to the zoo and theme park is at least 2 km (1 mi), and you'll probably have to ask for directions. You're better off just taking the bus to the zoo and saving yourself the walk, or ride the Teleferico out and back, then bus it to the zoo. ✉ *Estación Terminal Teleférico, Paseo de Pintor Rosales, at C. Marques de Urquijo, Moncloa* ☎ *91/541–1118 or 90/234–5012* 🎫 *€3.55 one-way, €5.15 round-trip* ⏲ *Apr.–Sept., daily noon–dusk; Oct.–Mar., weekends noon–dusk* Ⓜ *Arguelles.*

16 **Templo de Debod.** This 4th-century BC Egyptian temple was donated to Spain in thanks for its technical assistance with the construction of the Aswan Dam. The western side of the small park around the temple is the best place to watch Madrid's outstanding sunsets. ✉ *Pintor Rosales, Moncloa* ☎ *91/765–1008* 🎫 *Free* ⏲ *Oct.–Mar., Tues.–Fri. 9:45–1:45 and 4:15–6:15, weekends 10–2; Apr.–Sept., Tues.–Fri. 10–2 and 6–8, weekends 10–2* Ⓜ *Plaza de España, Ventura Rodríguez.*

14 **Zoo-Aquarium.** One of the most comprehensive zoological parks in Europe, Madrid's zoo houses a large variety of animals (including rarities such as an albino tiger) that are grouped according to their geographical origin. It also has a dolphinarium and a wild bird reservoir that hold entertaining exhibitions twice a day on weekdays and several more times on weekends. To get a good seat, arrive a few minutes before the show begins. The zoo is in the Casa de Campo, a large park right outside the western part of the city. It's best reached via subway to Príncipe Pío and then Bus 33. ✉ *Casa de Campo s/n Moncloa* ☎ *91/512–3770, 90/234–5014* 🌐 *www.zoomadrid.com* 🎫 *€18.65* ⏲ *Feb. and Mar., weekdays 11–6, weekends 10:30–7; Apr.–June, weekdays 10:30–7, weekends 10:30–9; July and Aug., weekdays 10:30–7:30, weekends 10:30–9; Sept. and Oct., weekdays 11–6:30, weekends 10:30–7:30; Nov. and Dec., weekdays 11–6, weekends 10:30–6* Ⓜ *Casa de Campo.*

BARRIO DE LAS LETRAS

The Barrio de las Letras, long favored by tourists for its clean-cut looks and its fun places to hang out, was named for the many writers and playwrights from the Spanish golden age (16th and 17th centuries) who set up house within a few blocks of Plaza Santa Ana. Once a shelter to the *los madrileños castizos*—the word *castizo* means "authentic"—it

The vertical outdoor garden is a stunning element of the CaixaForum cultural center. The sculpture in front of the building is changed periodically.

is fast becoming one of the favored living areas of Spanish and foreign professionals affluent enough to pay the soaring real estate prices and willing to withstand the chaos of living within these lively and creative enclaves. Calle de las Huertas (full of bars and clubs), is pedestrian only, making the neighborhood even more attractive for walking around and socializing.

TOP ATTRACTIONS

36 ★ **CaixaForum.** Swiss architects Jacques Herzog and Pierre de Meuron—who transformed a factory into London's Tate Modern—took this early-20th-century power station and turned it into a stunning arts complex fit to be considered the fourth point in Madrid's former triangle of great art institutions—the Prado, the Reina Sofía, and the Thyssen-Bornemisza museums. The Caixa belongs to one of the country's wealthiest foundations (La Caixa) and seems to float on a newly created, sloped public plaza, with a tall vertical garden designed by French botanist Patrick Blanc on its northern side contrasting with a geometric rust-color roof. Inside, the huge exhibition halls display ancient as well as contemporary art, including a sample of La Caixa's own collection. There's a cafeteria on the fourth floor that has good views. ✉ *Paseo del Prado 36, Cortes* ☎ *91/330–7300* 🌐 *obrasocial.lacaixa.es/centros/caixaforummadrid_es.html* 🎟 *Free* 🕓 *Daily 10–8* Ⓜ *Atocha.*

29 Fodor's Choice ★ **Centro de Arte Reina Sofía** *(Queen Sofía Art Center).* Madrid's museum of modern art was once a hospital, but today the classical granite austerity of the space is somewhat relieved (or ruined, depending on your point of view) by the playful pair of glass elevator shafts on its facade. Three separate buildings joined by a common vault were added to the

original complex in a renovation that was completed at the end of 2005. The first contains an art bookshop and a public library, the second a center for contemporary exhibitions, and the third an auditorium and restaurant/cafeteria managed by Sergi Arola, of the restaurant Gastro. The latter, although expensive, makes an excellent stop for refreshment, be it a cup of tea or coffee, a snack, or even a cocktail.

The permanent art collection was reorganized in mid-2009. It now features 1,000 works on four floors (the second and fourth floor of the Sabatini building and the ground and first floor of the Nouvel annex) and, despite concentrating on painting, puts a much higher emphasis on other art forms such as photography and cinema. The new collection breaks from the traditional habit of grouping works by major artistic movement and individual artist: instead, the current director has chosen to contextualize the works of the great modern masters—Picasso, Miró, and Salvador Dalí—and of other big local names, such as Juan Gris, Jorge Oteiza, Pablo Gargallo, Julio Gonzalez, Eduardo Chillida, and Antoni Tàpies, into broader narratives that attempt to explain better the evolution of modern art. This means, for instance, that in the first room of the collection (201), you'll find a selection of Goya's Disasters of War engravings (the proto-romantic and proto-surrealist great master serving as a precursor of the avante-garde movements of the 20th century) next to one of the first movies ever made, "Employees leaving the Lumière family," by the Lumière brothers, and that you won't find the Picassos or Dalís all displayed together in a single room, but scattered around the 38 rooms of the permanent collection.

The museum's showpiece is Picasso's *Guernica,* in room 206 on the second floor. The huge black-and-white canvas—now displayed in better lighting and without distracting barriers—depicts the horror of the Nazi Condor Legion's bombing of the ancient Basque town of Gernika in 1937, during the Spanish civil war. The work, something of a national shrine, was commissioned from Picasso by the Republican government for the Spanish pavilion at the 1937 World's Fair in an attempt to gather sympathy for the Republican side during the civil war—the museum rooms adjacent to *Guernica*'s now reconstruct the artistic significance of the Spanish participation in the World's Fair, with works from other artists such as Miró, Josep María Sert, and Alexander Calder. *Guernica* did not reach Madrid until 1981, as Picasso had stipulated in his will that the painting return to Spain only after democracy was restored.

The fourth floor in the Sabatini building is devoted to art created after the Second World War, and the Nouvel annex displays paintings, sculptures, photos, videos, and installations from the last quarter of the 20th century. ✉ *Santa Isabel 52, Lavapiés* ☎ *91/467–5062* 🌐 *museoreinasofia.mcu.es* 🎫 *€6, free Mon. and Wed.–Fri. after 7, Sat. after 2:30, and all day Sun.; €17.60 combined Paseo del Arte (Art Walk) ticket for the Prado, Reina Sofia, and Thyssen-Bornemisza* ⏲ *Mon. and Wed.–Sat. 10–9, Sun. 10–2:30* Ⓜ *Atocha.*

See "The Art Walk" box for how to include the Centro de Arte Reina Sofía as part of an art-theme Paseo del Arte excursion.

39 **Museo Thyssen-Bornemisza.** The newest of Madrid's "big three" art centers (not including CaixaForum), the Thyssen opened in 1992 and occupies spacious galleries filled with natural light in the late-18th-century Villahermosa Palace, finished in 1771. This ambitious collection of almost 1,000 paintings traces the history of Western art with examples from every important movement, from the 13th-century Italian Gothic through 20th-century American pop art. The works were gathered from the 1920s to the 1980s by Swiss industrialist Baron Hans Heinrich Thyssen-Bornemisza and his father. At the urging of his wife, the baron donated the entire collection to Spain in 1993, and a renovation in 2004 increased the number of paintings on display to include the baron's wife's personal collection (considered of lesser quality). Critics have described the museum's paintings as the minor works of major artists and the major works of minor artists, but the collection still traces the development of Western humanism as no other in the world.

Fodor's Choice ★

One of the high points is Hans Holbein's *Portrait of Henry VIII* (purchased from the late Princess Diana's grandfather, who used the money to buy a Bugatti sports car). American artists are also well represented; look for the Gilbert Stuart portrait of George Washington's cook, and note how closely the composition and rendering resemble the artist's famous painting of the Founding Father. Two halls are devoted to the Impressionists and post-Impressionists, including many works by Camille Pissarro and a few each by Pierre-Auguste Renoir, Claude Monet, Edgar Degas, Vincent Van Gogh, and Paul Cézanne. Find Pissarro's *Saint-Honoré Street in the Afternoon, Effect of Rain* for a jolt of mortality, or Renoir's *Woman with a Parasol in a Garden* for a sense of bucolic beauty lost.

Within 20th-century art, the collection is strong on dynamic German expressionism, with some works by Georgia O'Keeffe and Andrew Wyeth along with Edward Hoppers, Francis Bacons, Robert Rauschenbergs, and Roy Lichtensteins. The temporary exhibits can be fascinating and in summer are sometimes open until 11 PM. A rooftop restaurant serving tapas and drinks is open in the summer until past midnight. You can buy tickets in advance online. ✉ *Paseo del Prado 8, Cortes* ☎ *91/369–0151* 🌐 *www.museothyssen.org* 🎫 *Permanent collection €8, temporary exhibition €8, combined €13; €17.60 combined Paseo del Arte (Art Walk) ticket for the Prado, Reina Sofia, and Thyssen-Bornemisza* 🕓 *Tues.–Sun. 10–7* Ⓜ *Banco de España.*

See "The Art Walk" box for how to include the Museo Thyssen-Bornemisza as part of an art-theme Paseo del Arte excursion.

25 **Plaza Santa Ana.** This plaza was the heart of the theater district in the 17th century—the Golden Age of Spanish literature—and is now the center of Madrid's thumping nightlife. A statue of 17th-century playwright Pedro Calderón de la Barca faces the **Teatro Español,** where playwrights such as Félix Lope de Vega, Tirso de Molina, Pedro Calderón de la Barca, and Ramón del Valle-Inclán released some of their plays. (Opposite the theater and off to the side of a hotel is the diminutive **Plaza del Ángel,** with one of Madrid's best jazz clubs, the **Café Central.**) One of Madrid's most famous cafés, **Cervecería Alemana,** is

CLOSE UP

The Art Walk (Paseo del Prado)

Picasso's Guernica, at the Centro de Arte Reina Sofia, almost always has a crowd of onlookers.

Any visit to Madrid should include a stroll along Paseo del Prado, lined with some world-class museums (whose architecture as well as art are worth admiring), and some wandering in the adjoining Barrio de las Letras, the old literary neighborhood that is now a happening area full of restaurants. You can tour the area in about two hours, longer if visit the Prado, lounge in any of the Barrio de las Letras's charming tapas bars, or take a stroll in Retiro Park.

■ TIP→ The *Paseo del Arte* (Art Walk) pass allows you to visit the Prado, the Reina Sofía, and the Thyssen-Bornemisza for €17.60. You can buy it at any of the three museums, and you don't have to visit all of them on the same day.

The Paseo del Prado stretches from the Plaza de la Cibeles to Plaza del Emperador Carlos V (also known as Plaza Atocha) and is home to Madrid's three main art museums—the Prado, the Reina Sofía, and the Thyssen-Bornemisza—as well as the CaixaForum, an art institution with fabulous temporary exhibitions. In earlier times the Paseo marked the eastern boundary of the city, and in the 17th century it was given a cleaner neoclassical look. A century later, King Carlos III designed a leafy nature walk with glorious fountains and a botanical garden to provide respite to madrileños during the scorching summers.

The stretch of the Paseo del Prado from Plaza Cánovas del Castillo north to Cibeles houses some notable buildings, but it's the southern end of the Paseo that shouldn't be missed. Start your walk on Plaza Cánovas del Castillo, with its Fuente de Neptuno (Fountain of Neptune); on the northwestern corner is the **Museo Thyssen-Bornemisza** ㊴. To your left, across from the plaza, is the elegant Ritz hotel, alongside the obelisk dedicated to all those who have died for Spain, and across it on the right is the **Museo del Prado** ㉟, the best example of neoclassical architecture in the city and one of the world's best-known museums. It was enlarged in 2007 with the addition of what's widely known as "Moneo's cube," architect Rafael Moneo's steel and glass building that now encloses the cloister of the old Monasterio de los Jerónimos. The monastery, of which now only the church stands, is easily dwarfed by the museum, but this is by far the oldest building in this part of the city, dating to 1503, and was at one time the core of the old **Parque del Buen Retiro** 33 (the park stretched as far as the Paseo del Prado until the 19th century, when Queen Isabel II sold a third of its terrains to the State) and the reason for the park's name: the monastery is where the Hapsburg kings would temporarily "retire" from their mundane yet overwhelming state affairs. The park, always bustling, especially on the weekends, is a great place to finish off a day or to unwind after some intense sightseeing.

To the right of the Prado, across from the Murillo Gate, is the **Jardín Botánico** 32, also a wonderful place to relax with a book or to sketch under the shelter of a leafy exotic tree. Across the street is the sloping plaza that leads to the **CaixaForum** 36, a free, impressive arts exhibition center.

The Paseo del Prado ends on the Glorieta (roundabout) del Emperador Carlos V, where you'll find the **Estación de Atocha** 30, a railway station resembling the overturned hull of a ship, and, to the west of the Plaza, across from Calle Atocha, in the building with the exterior glass elevators, the **Centro de Arte Reina Sofía** 29, Madrid's modern art museum and the current home of Picasso's *Guernica*.

West of the Paseo del Prado is the lively Barrio de las Letras neighborhood, full of charming and historic streets and popular bars for a snack or a sit-down meal after museum sightseeing—from the Paseo del Prado, just take Calle Huertas, Calle Lope de Vega, or any of the other cross streets from Calle Alameda or Calle San Pedro. Along Calle Lope de Vega are the excellent tapas bars La Dolores and El Cervantes. Near here, at the corner of Calle León and Calle Cervantes is the Casa de Cervantes, where, as the plaque on the wall attests, the author of *Don Quijote* died on April 23, 1616 (he was buried in the convent and church of the Trinitarias Descalzas, also on Calle Lope de Vega, but his remains were misplaced in the 17th century). Down the street, at No. 11, is the Casa de Lope de Vega, where the "Spanish Shakespeare," Fray Lope Félix de la Vega Carpio, lived and worked. Walk Calle León until it merges with Calle Prado, then make a left and end your tour of this neighborhood at Plaza de Santa Ana, the Barrio de las Letras's lively main square, also crowded with bars, including the Cervecería Alemana, one of Ernest Hemingway's favorite hangouts while he was in Madrid (it's a fine place to sip a beer, but for eating we suggest checking our Tapas and Restaurant reviews later in the chapter).

If you feel the need to wear out your walking shoes a little more, take Calle Príncipe and then Calle Sevilla to Calle Alcalá, make a right, and head down until you reach **Plaza de la Cibeles** 42, then walk up to the **Puerta de Alcalá** 44 and enter the **Parque del Buen Retiro** 33 through the entrance on that square.

on Plaza Santa Ana and is still catnip to writers and poets; it's a good spot for a beer but for eating check out our listings for Tapas Bars and Where to Eat. ✉ *Pl. Santa Ana s/n, Barrio de las Letras* Ⓜ *Sevilla.*

WORTH NOTING

41 **Banco de España.** This massive 1884 building, Spain's central bank, takes up an entire block. It's said that part of the nation's gold reserves are held in vaults that stretch under the Plaza de la Cibeles traffic circle all the way to the fountain. (Some reserves are also stored in Fort Knox, in the United States.) The bank is not open to visitors, but the architecture is worth viewing. ✉ *Paseo del Prado s/n, at Pl. de la Cibeles, Cortes* Ⓜ *Banco de España.*

37 **Casa de Cervantes.** A plaque marks the private home where Miguel de Cervantes Saavedra, author of *Don Quijote de la Mancha,* committed his final words to paper: "*Puesto ya el pie en el estribo, con ansias de la muerte*" ("One foot already in the stirrup and yearning for death"). The Western world's first runaway best seller and still one of the most widely translated and read books in the world, Cervantes's spoof of a knightly novel playfully but profoundly satirized Spain's rise and decline while portraying man's dual nature in the pragmatic Sancho Panza and the idealistic Don Quijote, ever in search of wrongs to right. ✉ *C. Cervantes and C. León, Barrio de las Letras* Ⓜ *Sevilla.*

38 **Casa de Lope de Vega.** Considered the Shakespeare of Spanish literature, Fray Lope Félix de la Vega Carpio (1562–1635) is best known as Lope de Vega. A contemporary and adversary of Cervantes, he wrote some 1,800 plays and enjoyed great success during his lifetime. His former home is now a museum with an intimate look into a bygone era: everything from the whale-oil lamps and candles to the well in the tiny garden and the pans used to warm the bedsheets brings you closer to the great dramatist. The space was enlarged in 2008 and now accommodates poetry readings and workshops. There is a 45-minute guided tour in English starting every half hour (reservations are necessary) that runs through the playwright's professional and personal life—including his intense love life—and also touching on 17th-century traditions. Don't miss the Latin inscription over the door: PARVA PROPIA MAGNA / MAGNA ALIENA PARVA (small but mine big / big but someone else's small). ✉ *C. Cervantes 11, Barrio de las Letras* ☎ *91/429–9216* 🎫 *Free* ⏲ *Tues.–Sun. 10–3* Ⓜ *Sevilla.*

49 **Casa Longoria.** A Moderniste palace commissioned in 1902 by the businessman and politician Javier González Longoria, the Casa Longoria was built by a disciple of Gaudí. The winding shapes, the plant motifs, and the wrought-iron balconies are reminiscent of Gaudí's works in Barcelona. The building's jewel is its main iron, bronze, and marble staircase, which is unfortunately off-limits to tourists because the building is now in private hands. ✉ *Fernando VI 4, Chueca* Ⓜ *Alonso Martínez, Chueca.*

CHUECA AND MALASAÑA

Once known primarily for thumping nightlife and dodgy streets, these two Madrid neighborhoods have changed significantly in the past decade. Money from City Hall and from private investors was used to renovate buildings and public zones, thereby drawing prosperous businesses and many professional and young inhabitants. Chueca, especially, has been completely transformed by the gay community. Noisy bars and overcrowded nightclubs are still trademarks of both areas, but they now also make for pleasant daytime walks and have many inexpensive restaurants, hip shops, great cultural life, and inviting summer terraces. Chamberí is a large area to the north of Chueca and Malasaña. It's mostly residential but has a few lively spots, especially the streets around Plaza de Olavide.

TOP ATTRACTIONS

19 **Centro de Conde Duque.** Built by Pedro de Ribera in 1717–30 to accommodate the Regiment of the Royal Guard, this imposing building has gigantic proportions (the facade is 250 yards long) and was used as a military academy and an astronomical observatory in the 19th century. A fire damaged the upper floors in 1869, and after some decay it was partially renovated and turned into a cultural and arts center, with temporary art exhibitions in some of its spaces, including the public and historical libraries. In summer, outdoor concerts are held in the main plaza. ✉ *Conde Duque 9 and 11, Malasaña* ⏲ *Tues.–Sat. 10–2 and 6–9, Sun. 10:30–2 exhibitions only* Ⓜ *San Bernardo.*

QUICK BITES

Walking past the Cisne Azul (✉ *Gravina 19, Chueca* Ⓜ *Chueca* ☎ *91/521–3799*) you may wonder why such a bland-looking bar is crowded with locals in a neighborhood that's obsessed with style. The reason is simple: wild mushrooms. In Spain there are more than 2,000 different species, and here they bring the best from the province of León, grill them on the spot with a bit of olive oil and serve them in a variety of ways: with a fried egg yolk, scallops, *foie (liver)*, and so on. We suggest you elbow yourself up to the bar and order the popular *mezcla de setas* (mushroom sampler) with a fried egg yolk.

WORTH NOTING

50 **Museo Municipal.** Founded in 1929 on what was formerly a hospice from the 17th century, this museum displays paintings, drawings, pictures, ceramics, furniture, and other objects explaining Madrid's history. There is a good exhibition on Madrid that will be best enjoyed by those who speak Spanish and already know a bit about the city's history, but the ornamented facade—a baroque jewel by Pedro de Ribera—and the painstakingly precise, nearly 18-foot model of Madrid, a project coordinated by León Gil de Palacio in 1830, are two exhibits anyone can appreciate. As of the time of writing, the museum is temporarily closed for some major renovations, scheduled to reopen sometime in late 2010. ✉ *Fuencarral 78, Malasaña* ☎ *91/701–1863* 🎫 *Free* ⏲ *Tues.–Fri. 9:30–8, weekends 10–2* Ⓜ *Tribunal.*

QUICK BITES

For an inexpensive lunch on a pleasant day, stop at La vita e'bella (✉ *Calle Espíritu Santo 13 or Plaza de San Ildefonso 5, Malasaña* Ⓜ *Tribunal, Noviciado* ☎ *91/521–4108*) for any of its savory take-away dishes (strombolis, calzones, pizzas, arancini [fried rice balls coated with bread crumbs], or pastas), and enjoy your meal with other young madrileños while sitting on a bench at the nearby and bustling Plaza de San Ildefonso or Plaza de Juan Pujol.

18 **Museo Municipal de Arte Contemporáneo.** To reach this museum inside the Centro de Conde Duque, take the door to your right after the entrance and walk up the stairs. Founded in 2001, the museum displays 200 modern artworks acquired by City Hall since 1980. The paintings, graphic art, sculpture, and photography are mostly by local artists. ✉ *Conde Duque 9 and 11, Malasaña* ☎ *91/588–5928* *Free* *Tues.–Sat. 10–2 and 5:30–9, Sun. 10:30–2:30* Ⓜ *San Bernardo.*

48 **Museo Sorolla.** See the world through the exceptional eye of Spain's most famous Impressionist painter, Joaquín Sorolla (1863–1923), who lived and worked most of his life at the home and garden he designed. Entering this diminutive but cozy domain is a little like stepping into a Sorolla painting because it's filled with the artist's best-known works, most of which shimmer with the bright Mediterranean light and color of his native Valencia. ✉ *General Martinez Campos 37, Chamberí* ☎ *91/310–1584* *museosorolla.mcu.es* *€3, free Sun.* *Tues.–Sat. 9:30–8, Sun. 10–3* Ⓜ *Rubén Darío, Gregorio Marañón.*

51 **Plaza del 2 de Mayo.** On this unassuming square stood the Monteleón Artillery barracks, where some brave Spanish soldiers and citizens fought Napoléon's invading troops on May 2, 1808. The arch that now stands in the middle of the plaza was once at the entrance of the old barracks, and the sculpture under the arch represents captains Daoiz and Velarde. All the surrounding streets carry the names of that day's heroes. The plaza, now filled with spring and summer terraces, makes a good place to stop for a drink. One of the most popular cafés, Pepe Botella, carries the demeaning nickname the people of Madrid gave to Joseph Bonaparte, Napoléon's brother, who ruled Spain from 1808 to 1813: Botella ("bottle" in English) is a reference to his falsely alleged fondness for drink. ✉ *Pl. del 2 de Mayo, Malasaña* Ⓜ *Noviciado, Tribunal.*

RASTRO AND LAVAPIÉS

Bordering the old city wall (torn down by the mid-19th century) to the south, Rastro and Lavapiés were Madrid's industrial areas in the 17th and 18th centuries. The old slaughterhouses in the Rastro area (and all of the other businesses related to that trade) are the origins of today's flea market, which spreads all over the neighborhood on Sundays. Lavapiés has the highest concentration of immigrants—mostly Chinese, Indian, and North African—in Madrid, and as a result the area has plenty of ethnic markets and inexpensive restaurants as well as bustling crowds, especially at the Plaza de Lavapíes. Purse snatching and petty crime are not uncommon in these two areas, so be alert.

You can rent rowboats at the lake in the Parque del Buen Retiro: a great way to cool off in the summer.

TOP ATTRACTIONS

33 **El Rastro.** Named for the *arrastre* (dragging) of animals in and out of the slaughterhouse that once stood here and, specifically, the *rastro* (blood trail) left behind, this site explodes into a rollicking flea market every Sunday from 10 to 2, with dozens and dozens of street vendors with truly bizarre bric-a-brac ranging from stolen earrings to sent postcards to thrown-out love letters. There are also more formal shops where it's easy to turn up treasures such as old iron grillwork, a marble tabletop, or a gilt picture frame. The shops (not the vendors) are also open during the week, allowing for quieter and more serious bargaining. Even so, people-watching on Sunday is the best part: for serious browsing and bargaining, any *other* morning is a better time to turn up treasures. ✉ *Ribera de los Curtidores s/n, Rastro* Ⓜ *La Latina, Puerta de Toledo.*

WORTH NOTING

28 **Cine Doré.** A rare example of Art Nouveau architecture in Madrid, the hip Cine Doré shows movies from the Spanish National Film Archives and eclectic foreign films for €2.50 per session. Showtimes are listed in newspapers under "Filmoteca." The pink neon–trimmed lobby has a sleek café-bar and a bookshop. ✉ *Santa Isabel 3, Lavapiés* ☎ *91/369–1125* ⏲ *Tues.–Sun.; 4–5 shows daily, starting at 5:30* PM Ⓜ *Antón Martín.*

27 **Plaza Lavapiés.** The heart of the historic Jewish barrio, this plaza remains a neighborhood hub. To the east is the Calle de la Fe (Street of Faith), which was called Calle Sinagoga until the expulsion of the Jews in 1492. The church of **San Lorenzo** at the end was built on the site of the razed synagogue. Legend says Jews and Moors who chose baptism over exile

CLOSE UP

The Events of May 2

In 1808 Spain was ruled by Carlos IV, a king more interested in hunting than in the duties attached to government. The king delegated power to his wife, María Luisa, and she to the chief minister, Manuel de Godoy, one of the country's most despised statesmen of all time. Godoy succeeded in tripling the country's debt in 20 years, and signed the secret Convention of Fontainebleau with Napoléon, which allowed the French troops to cross Spain freely on their way to Portugal. Napoléon's plans were different—he intended to use the convention as an excuse to annex Spain to his vast domains. While the French troops entered Spain, the Spanish people, tired of the inept king and the greedy Godoy, revolted against the French in Aranjuez on March 17, 1808, hoping Napoléon would hand the throne over to the king's elder son, Prince Ferdinand. In the following days Carlos IV abdicated, and his son was proclaimed the new king, Fernando VII. Napoléon had already chosen a person for that job, though—one of his brothers, José Bonaparte. The shrewd French emperor managed to attract the Spanish royal family to France and had Carlos IV, his wife, and Ferdinand VII imprisoned in Bayonne, France, and his brother placed on the Spanish throne.

When the French general Joachim Murat arrived in Madrid on March 23 with 10,000 men (leaving 20,000 more camped outside the city), following Napoléon's orders, Madrid's Captain General Francisco Javier Negrete ordered the Spanish troops to remain in their military quarters, arguing that resistance was futile. On the morning of May 2, a group of civilians revolted in front of the Palacio Real, fearing the French troops intended to send Francisco de Paula, King Carlos IV's youngest son, to Bayonne with his brother and father. Gunfire ensued, and word of the events spread all over the city. The people rose up, fighting the mightier French troops with whatever they could use as weapons. Two captains, Luis Daoiz and Pedro Velarde, and a lieutenant, Jacinto Ruiz, disobeyed Negrete's orders and quartered at the Monteleón Artillery barracks, which stretched from what is now Plaza de 2 de mayo to Calle Carranza. Helped by a small group of soldiers and some brave citizens who had marched to the barracks from the Royal Palace, the group resisted the French for three hours, doing so with very little ammunition, as they couldn't access the armory.

Daoiz and Velarde died in the bloody fight. Ruiz managed to escape, only to die from his wounds later. Murat's forces executed soldiers and civilians throughout the city, including in the Casa de Campo and what's now the Parque del Oeste, captured by Goya in one of his two famous paintings of the executions—both restored in 2008 to celebrate the bicentennial of the events. The events marked the beginning of the five-year War of Independence against the French. The remains of the three military heroes, together with those who were executed at Paseo del Prado, are now held in an obelisk/mausoleum at Plaza de la Lealtad.

Paradoxically, José Bonaparte proved to be a good ruler, implementing wise renovations in the then congested and unhygienic city. He built new squares, enlarged key streets, and moved some cemeteries outside the city.

had to walk up this street barefoot to the ceremony to demonstrate their new faith. ✉ *Top of Calle de la Fe, Lavapiés* Ⓜ *Lavapiés.*

SALAMANCA AND RETIRO

By the mid-19th century, city officials decided to expand Madrid beyond the 1625 wall erected by Felipe IV. The result was a handful of new, well-laid-out neighborhoods. Salamanca became a home to the working classes, though today it draws a more mixed crowd and houses most of the city's expensive restaurants and shops. The Retiro holds the city's best-known park. The area between the western side of the park and the Paseo del Prado showcases some of the city's most exclusive, expensive, and sought-after real estate.

TOP ATTRACTIONS

45 **Museo Arqueológico** *(Museum of Archaeology).* The biggest attraction here is a replica of the early cave paintings in Altamira. (Access to the real thing, in Cantabria Province, is highly restricted.) Also here, look for *La Dama de Elche,* a bust of a wealthy, 5th-century BC Iberian woman, and notice that her headgear is a rough precursor to the mantillas and hair combs still associated with traditional Spanish dress. The ancient Visigothic votive crowns are another highlight; discovered in 1859 near Toledo, they are believed to date back to the 8th century. The museum—now under renovation—shares its neoclassical building with the **Biblioteca Nacional** (National Library). ✉ *Calle Serrano 13, Salamanca* ☎ *91/577–7912, 91/580–7823 library* 🌐 *man.mcu.es* 💵 *Free (while the renovations last)* ⏲ *Museum Tues.–Sat. 9:30–8, Sun. 9:30–3; library (now closed for renovations) weekdays 9–9, Sat. 9–2* Ⓜ *Colón.*

35 ★ **Museo del Prado** *(Prado Museum). See the In-focus feature "El Prado: Madrid's Brush with Greatness." See "The Art Walk" box for how to include the Centro de Arte Reina Sofía as part of an art-theme Paseo del Arte excursion.* A combined ticket for the Prado, Reina Sofia, and Thyssen-Bornemisza costs €17.60. Ⓜ *Banco de España, Atocha.*

QUICK BITES

La Dolores (✉ *Plaza de Jesús 4, Barrio de las Letras* ☎ *91/429–2243*) is an atmospheric ceramic-tile bar that's the perfect place for a beer or glass of wine and a plate of olives. It's a great alternative to the Prado's basement cafeteria and is just across the Paseo and one block up, on Calle Lope de Vega Ⓜ *Antón Martín.*

46 Fodor's Choice ★ **Parque del Buen Retiro** *(The Retreat).* Once the private playground of royalty, Madrid's crowning park is a vast expanse of green encompassing formal gardens, fountains, lakes, exhibition halls, children's play areas, outdoor cafés, and a **Puppet Theater** featuring free slapstick routines that even non–Spanish speakers will enjoy. Shows take place on Saturday at 1 and on Sunday at 1, 6, and 7. The park is especially lively on weekends, when it fills with street musicians, jugglers, clowns, gypsy fortune-tellers, and sidewalk painters, along with hundreds of Spanish families out for a walk. The park holds a book fair in May and occasional flamenco concerts in summer. From the entrance at the Puerta de Alcalá, head straight toward the center and you can find the **Estanque**

Continued on page 89

EL PRADO: MADRID'S BRUSH WITH GREATNESS

One of the world's top museums, the Prado is to Madrid what the Louvre is to Paris, or the Uffizi to Florence: a majestic city landmark and premiere art institution that merits the attention of every traveler who visits the city.

Approaching its 200th anniversary, the Prado, with its unparalleled collection of Spanish paintings, is one of the most visited museums in the world. Foreign artists are also well represented—the collection includes masterpieces of European painting such as Hieronymus Bosch's *Garden of Earthly Delights*, *The Annunciation* by Fra Angelico, *Christ Washing the Disciples' Feet* by Tintoretto, and *The Three Graces* by Rubens—but the Prado is best known as home to more paintings by Diego Velázquez and Francisco de Goya than anywhere else.

Originally meant by King Charles III to become a museum of natural history, the Prado nevertheless opened, in 1819, as a sculpture and painting museum under the patronage of his grandchild, King Philip VII. For the first bewildered *madrileños* who crossed the museum's entrance back then, there were only about 300 paintings on display. Today there are more than 2.7 million visitors a year and, since the 2007 opening of the gleaming new addition by Spanish architect Rafael Moneo, known as the Jerónimos building, the displayed collection is 2,000-plus paintings, and still growing (the whole collection is estimated at about 8,000 canvases, plus 1,000 sculptures).

WHEN TO GO
The best time to visit the Prado is early in the morning, when the museum first opens, to beat the rush.

HUNGRY?
If your stomach rumbles during your visit, check out the café/restaurant in the foyer of the new building.

CONTACT INFORMATION
✉ Paseo del Prado s/n, 28014 Madrid
☎ (+34) 91 330 2800.
www.museodelprado.es

HOURS OF OPERATION
9 AM to 8 PM, Tues. to Sun.
Closed Monday, New Year's Day, Good Friday, Fiesta del Trabajo (May 1), and Christmas.

ADMISSION
€8. Free Tues. to Sat. 6 PM–8 PM, Sun. 5AM–8PM. To avoid lines, buy tickets in advance online.

The Trinity by El Greco, 1577. Oil on canvas.

THE COLLECTION

(top) A Velázquez statue graces the museum's old entrance. (bottom) Visitors now enter via a new $202 million wing, designed by Rafael Moneo.

With works from the Middle Ages to the 19th century, the Prado's painting collection—though smaller than that of the Louvre and St. Petersburg's Hermitage—may arguably be the world's most captivating for the quality of the masterworks it features.

The Prado's origins can be traced back to the royal collections put together by the successive Hapsburg kings, who were not all equally adept at governing but who all had a penchant for the arts. Throughout the 16th and 17th centuries they amassed troves of paintings from Spanish and foreign painters and spread them among their many palaces. This meant that the bulk of the Prado's collection grew out of the rulers' whim and therefore doesn't offer, like some of its peers, an uninterrupted vision of the history of painting. This shortcoming turned into a blessing, though, as the kings' artistic "obsessions" are the reason you'll find such extensive collections of paintings by Velázquez, Titian, and Rubens (in the latter case, it was Phillip IV who, when Rubens died, sent representatives to Antwerp to bid for the artist's best works).

The collection starts with the Spanish Romanesque (12th and 13th century), and features important Italian (Veronese, Tintoretto, Titian), Flemish (Van Dyck, Rubens), and Dutch (Bosch, Rembrandt) collections, as well as scores of works by the great Spanish masters (Velázquez, Goya, Ribera, Zurbarán, Murillo, and others). The new Jerónimos building made it possible to add some new works from 19th-century Spanish painters (Rosales, Fortuny, Madrazo, and more).

GETTING IN

The museum has two ticket-selling points and four entrance points. **The best thing to do is buy your tickets online:** you'll avoid the usually long lines and save a euro per ticket; you can also reserve an audio guide (pick it up in the main foyer in the Jerónimos building) at the same time. If you don't buy tickets online, **another time-saving option is the two vending machines** outside the Goya entrance.

All in-person ticket sales are at the Goya entrance, on the north side of the museum, either at the main entrance at street level, or on the upper level: street level is ticket sales for temporary exhibitions and where you collect tickets bought online if you didn't print them out at home; the upper level gives access to the permanent collection. If you've purchased tickets for the temporary exhibition, you must access the museum through the Jerónimos entrance. **With online tickets printed at home, or a Museum Pass, you can enter at any entrance.**

HOW TO SEE THE ESSENTIALS

Inside the Jerónimos cloister.

Don't let the Prado's immense size intimidate you. You can't see it all in a day, but if you zero in on some of the museum's masterpieces, you can have a rich experience without collapsing.

With 2,000 paintings distributed among dozens of galleries, the question immediately arises: What should I see? Let's face it: While the Prado has sculptures, drawings, and other treasures spanning centuries, its "why-go"—its "must-go"—is its paintings. Most of the attention, all of it deserved, goes to the Spanish historical headliners: Diego Velázquez, El Greco, and Francisco de Goya, and on a lesser scale, Pedro Ribera, Bartolomé Murillo, and Francisco de Zurbarán. Most of these artists' works are on display on the first floor of the Villanueva building.

A QUICK TOUR

If you want to focus on the essentials—which will take about an hour and a half—enter the museum through the Goya entrance on the upper level: to the left and right, after you enter, are the galleries devoted to Renaissance and Baroque Italian painting (Titian, Tintoretto, Veronés, and Caravaggio). From there move onto Rubens (gallery 24), then on to the long spinal gallery (rooms 25 to 29) that accommodates the works of Ribera and Murillo. Make a required detour to the adjacent

THE JERÓNIMOS CLOISTER

On the second floor of the new addition is the restored cloister of San Jerónimo el Real, the medieval church now adjacent to the museum. There, in one of the quietest corners of the Prado, you'll find a collection of 16th-century sculptures by Milanese bronze artists Leone and Pompeo Leoni. While you take it all in, ponder the fact that during Moneo's expansion, the 3,000 blocks of stone that make up this cloister had to be dismantled, restored, and reassembled in their original positions.

galleries (rooms 9A-10A) on the east side to admire the elongated spiritual figures of El Greco, and the folkloric characters and penetrating self-portraits of Rembrandt (room 7). Head back to the main corridor, where you'll find 46 of Velázquez's masterful works, and which will also take you past Gallery 12, home to the museum's most famous canvas: Velázquez's *Las Meninas*. Make sure, also, to see Goya's two "Majas"—one fully dressed, the other nude—displayed next to each other in Gallery 36, and his famous subtle royal composition "The family of Charles IV" (Gallery 32). Then head down to the ground floor to see some of Goya's best known works ("Second of May, 1808" and "Third of May 1808", as well as "Saturn devouring his child," and the gory Black Paintings (all in rooms 64-67).

Once you exit the Goya galleries downstairs you'll be facing the 12 new galleries (60 to 75) devoted to the 19th-century Spanish painters: if you're curious about Joaquín Sorolla and haven't had a chance to visit the museum dedicated to his work, stop at galleries 60 and 60A to see some of his colorful art. Otherwise, cross the main foyer and stop at gallery 56 to take in Hieronymus Bosch's triptych *The Garden of Earthly Delights,* before heading toward the Velázquez exit or toward the Jerónimos new building and its small but bustling café/restaurant for a well-deserved break.

THE PRADO ONLINE

The Prado has followed the example many other big-name museums and enhanced its Web site in an attempt to make the collection more accessible, even if you can't be there in person. The site includes an online gallery of more than 1,000 paintings (3,000 if you speak Spanish), and offers audio commentary and in-depth analysis of some paintings, among other things. If you're hungry for more, check the 14 paintings (including Bosch's The Garden of Earthly Delights, Las Meninas by Velázquez, or Third of May 1808 by Goya) scanned and displayed in super-high definition on Google Earth—search for Prado 3D, activate the tag "3D Buildings," and enjoy the technological feat!

The airy upper-level galleries.

MONEO'S DAZZLING EXPANSION

In 2007 Spanish architect Rafael Moneo's gleaming new addition to the Prado opened, bringing the museum into a new era. Moneo's red stucco "cube" envelopes the Cloister of the Jerónimos behind the old Villanueva building, but the bulk of the new premises are under the street in a vast steel-and-glass wedge-shape foyer that houses the temporary exhibitions plus some state-of-the-art add-ons: a café/restaurant, a bookshop with print-on-demand services, and a 400-seat auditorium. The new building has enabled the Prado to double its exhibition space to a total of 16,000 square meters (52,800 square feet) and to showcase more than 400 hundred new paintings—mostly from the Romanesque and the 19th century—that until the addition had laid hidden on huge steel shelves in the museum's underground vaults.

THREE GREAT MASTERS

Francisco de Goya

FRANCISCO DE GOYA 1746–1828
Goya's work spans a staggering range of tone, from bucolic to horrific, his idyllic paintings of Spaniards at play and portraits of the family of King Carlos IV contrasting with his dark, disturbing "black paintings." Goya's attraction to the macabre assured him a place in posterity, an ironic statement at the end of a long career in which he served as the official court painter to a succession of Spanish kings, bringing the art of royal portraiture to unknown heights.

Goya found fame in his day as a portraitist, but he is admired by modern audiences for his depictions of the bizarre and the morbid. Beginning as a painter of decorative Rococo figures, he evolved into an artist of great depth in the employ of King Charles IV. The push-pull between Goya's love for his country and his disdain for the enemies of Spain yielded such masterpieces as *Third of May 1808,* painted after the French occupation ended. In the early 19th century, Goya's scandalous *The Naked Maja* brought him before the Spanish Inquisition, whose judgment was to end his tenure as a court painter.

Diego Velázquez

DIEGO VELÁZQUEZ 1599–1660
A native of Seville, Velázquez gained fame at age 24 as court painter to King Philip IV. He developed a lifelike approach to religious art in which both saints and sinners were specific people rather than generic types. The supple brushwork of his ambitious history paintings and portraits was unsurpassed. Several visits to Rome, and his friendship with Rubens, made him the quintessential baroque painter with an international purview.

Domenikos Theotokopoulos

DOMENIKOS THEOTOKOPOULOS (AKA "EL GRECO") 1541–1614
El Greco's art was one of rapture and devotion, but beyond that his style is almost impossible to categorize. "The Greek" found his way from his native Crete to Spain through Venice; he spent most of his life in Toledo. His twisted, elongated figures imbue both his religious subjects and portraits with a sense of otherworldliness. While his palette and brushstrokes were inspired by Italian Mannerism, his approach to painting was uniquely his own. His inimitable style left few followers.

SIX PAINTINGS TO SEE

SATURN DEVOURING ONE OF HIS SONS (1819)
FRANCISCO DE GOYA Y LUCIENTES
In one of fourteen nightmarish "Black Paintings" executed by Goya to decorate the walls of his home in the later years of his life, the mythological God Kronos, or Saturn, cannibalizes one of his children in order to derail a prophecy that one of them would take over his throne. *Mural transferred to canvas.*

Saturn Devouring One of His Sons

THE GARDEN OF DELIGHTS OR LA PINTURA DEL MADROÑO (1500)
HIËRONYMUS BOSCH
Very little about the small-town environment of the Low Countries where the Roman Catholic Bosch lived in the late Middle Ages can explain his thought-provoking, and downright bizarre, paintings. His depictions of mankind's sins and virtues, and the heavenly rewards or demonic punishments that await us all, have fascinated many generations of viewers, who have called the devout painter a "heretic," and most recently compared him to Salvador Dalí for his disturbingly twisted renderings. In this three-panel painting, Adam and Eve are created, mankind celebrates its humanity, and hell awaits the wicked, all within a journey of 152 inches! *Wooden Triptych.*

The Garden of Delights

LAS MENINAS (THE MAIDS OF HONOR) (1656-57)
DIEGO VELÁZQUEZ DE SILVA
Velázquez's masterpiece of spatial perspective occupies pride-of-place in the center of the Spanish baroque galleries. In this complex visual game, *you* are the king and queen of Spain, reflected in a distant hazy mirror as the court painter (Velázquez) pauses in front of his easel to observe your features. The actual subject is the Princess Margarita, heir to the throne in 1656. *Oil on canvas.*

Las Meninas

STILL LIFE (17th Century; no date)
FRANCISCO DE ZURBARÁN
Best known as a painter of contemplative saints, Zurbarán, a native of Extremadura who found success working with Velázquez in Seville, was a peerless observer of beauty in the everyday. His rendering of the surfaces of these homely objects elevates them to the stature of holy relics, urging the viewer to touch them. But the overriding mood is one of serenity and order. *Oil on canvas.*

Still Life

DAVID VICTORIOUS OVER GOLIATH (1599)
MICHELANGELO MERISI (CARAVAGGIO)
Caravaggio used intense contrasts between his dark and light passages (called *chiaroscuro* in Italian) to create drama in his bold baroque paintings. Here, a surprisingly childlike David calmly ties up the severed head of the giant Philistine Goliath, gruesomely featured in the foreground plane of the picture. The astonishing realism of the Italian painter, who was as well known for his tempestuous personal life as for his deftness with a paint brush, had a profound influence on 17th century Spanish art. *Oil on canvas.*

David Victorious over Goliath

THE TRINITY (1577)
DOMENIKOS THEOTOKOPOULOS (EL GRECO)
Soon after arriving in Spain, Domenikos Theotokopoulos created this view of Christ ascending into heaven supported by angels, God the Father, and the Holy Spirit. It was commissioned for the altar of a convent in Toledo. The acid colors recall the Mannerist paintings of Venice, where El Greco was trained, and the distortions of the upward-floating bodies show more gracefulness than the anatomical contortions that characterize his later works. *Oil on canvas.*

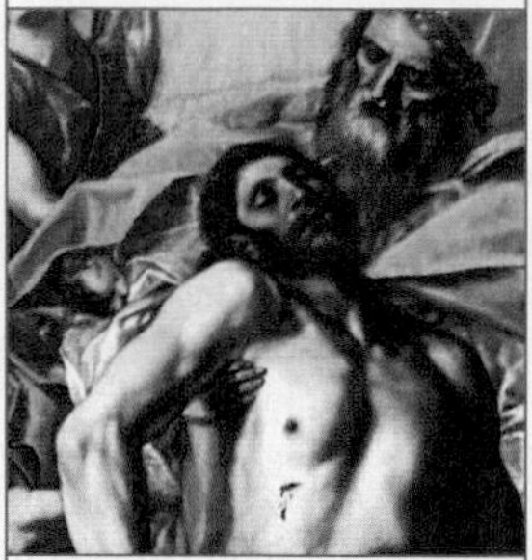
The Trinity

PICASSO AND THE PRADO

The Prado contains no modern art, but one of the greatest artists of the 20th century had an important history with the museum. **Pablo Picasso** (1891–1973) served as the director of the Prado during the Spanish civil war, from 1936 to 1939. The Prado was a "phantom museum" in that period, Picasso once noted, since it was closed for most of the war and its collections hidden elsewhere for safety.

Later that century, the abstract artist's enormous *El Guernica* hung briefly on the Prado's walls, returning to Spain from the Museum of Modern Art in 1981. Picasso had stipulated that MoMA give up his anti-war masterpiece after the death of fascist dictator Francisco Franco, and it was displayed at the Prado and the Casón del Buen Retiro until the nearby Reina Sofia was built to house it in 1992.

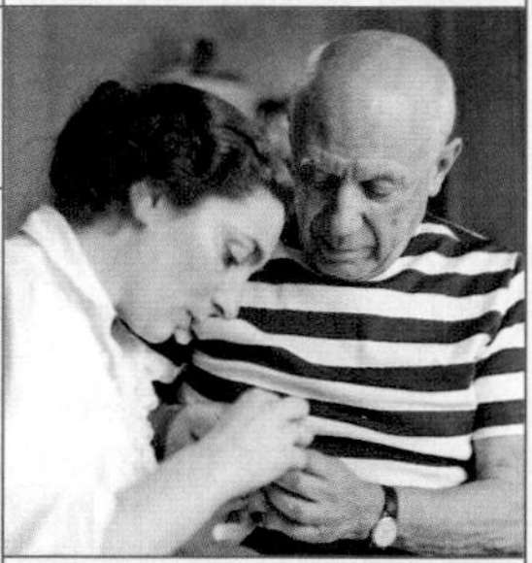
Picasso with his wife Jacqueline Roque

Picasso in his atelier

(lake), presided over by a grandiose equestrian statue of King Alfonso XII, erected by his mother. Just behind the lake, north of the statue, is one of the best of the park's many cafés.

The 19th-century **Palacio de Cristal** (Crystal Palace), southeast of the Estanque, was built to house exotic plants from the Philippines, a Spanish possession at the time. This airy marvel of steel and glass sits on a base of decorative tile. Next door is a small lake with ducks and swans. Along the Paseo del Uruguay at the park's south end is the **Rosaleda** (Rose Garden), bursting with color and heavy with floral scents for most of the summer. West of the Rosaleda, look for a statue called the **Ángel Caído** (Fallen Angel), which madrileños claim is the only one in the world depicting the prince of darkness before (during, actually) his fall from grace. ✉ *Puerta de Alcalá, Retiro* 🎫 *Free* Ⓜ *Retiro.*

WORTH NOTING

30 **Estación de Atocha.** A steel-and-glass hangar, Madrid's main railroad station was built in the late 19th century by Alberto Palacio Elissague, the architect who became famous for his work with Ricardo Velázquez in the creation of the Palacio de Cristal (Crystal Palace) in Madrid's Retiro Park. Closed for years, and nearly torn down, Atocha was restored and refurbished by Spain's internationally acclaimed architect Rafael Moneo. ✉ *Paseo de Atocha s/n, Retiro* ☎ *91/420–9875* Ⓜ *Atocha.*

32 **Jardín Botánico** *(Botanical Garden).* Just south of the Prado, the gardens provide a pleasant place to stroll or sit under the trees. True to the wishes of King Carlos III, they hold many plants, flowers, and cacti from around the world. ✉ *Pl. de Murillo 2, Retiro* ☎ *91/420–3017* 🌐 *www.rjb.csic.es* 🎫 *€2.50* ⏲ *Nov.–Feb., daily 10–6; Mar. and Oct., daily 10–7; Apr. and Sept., daily 10–8; May–Aug., daily 10–9* Ⓜ *Atocha.*

46 **Museo Lázaro Galdiano.** This stately mansion of writer and editor José Lázaro Galdiano (1862–1947), a 10-minute walk across the Castellana from the Museo Sorolla, has decorative items and paintings by Bosch, El Greco, Murillo, and Goya, among others. The remarkable collection comprises five centuries of Spanish, Flemish, English, and Italian art. Bosch's *St. John the Baptist* and the many Goyas are the stars of the show, with El Greco's *San Francisco de Assisi* and Zurbarán's *San Diego de Alcalá* close behind. ✉ *Calle Serrano 122, Salamanca* ☎ *91/561–6084* 🌐 *www.flg.es* 🎫 *€4, free Sun.* ⏲ *Wed.–Mon. 10–4:30* Ⓜ *Gregorio Marañón.*

40 **Museo Naval.** Anyone interested in Patrick O'Brian's painstakingly detailed naval novels or in old vessels and war ships will be bouncing off the walls experiencing the 500 years of Spanish naval history displayed in this museum. The collection, which includes documents, maps, weaponry, paintings, and hundreds of ship models of different sizes, is best enjoyed by those who speak some Spanish. Beginning with Queen Isabella and King Ferdinand's reign and the expeditions led by Christopher Columbus and the conquistadors, exhibits also reveal how Spain built a naval empire that battled Turkish, Algerian, French, Portuguese, and English armies and commanded the oceans and the shipping routes for a century and a half. Moving to the present day, the museum covers Spain's more recent shipyard and naval construction accomplishments.

✉ *Paseo del Prado 5, Retiro* ☎ *91/523–8789* 🌐 *www.armada.mde.es* 🎟 *Free* 🕙 *Tues.–Sun. 10–2. Guided tour, in Spanish only, weekends at 11:30* Ⓜ *Banco de España.*

43 **Palacio de Comunicaciones.** This ornate building on the southeast side of Plaza de la Cibeles, built at the start of the 20th century, is a massive stone compound of French, Viennese, and traditional Spanish influences. It now houses the office of the mayor of Madrid and still functions as the main post office. ✉ *Pl. de Cibeles, Retiro* ☎ *902/197197* 🕙 *Weekdays 8:30* AM*–9:30* PM*, Sat. 8:30–2* Ⓜ *Banco de España.*

47 **Plaza Colón.** Named for Christopher Columbus, this plaza has a statue of the explorer (identical to the one in Barcelona's port) looking west from a high tower in the middle of the square. Behind Plaza Colón is **Calle Serrano,** the city's premier shopping street (think Gucci, Prada, and Loewe). Stroll in either direction on Serrano for some window-shopping. ✉ *Pl. Colón, Salamanca* Ⓜ *Colón.*

42 **Plaza de la Cibeles.** A tree-lined walkway runs down the center of Paseo del Prado to the grand Plaza de la Cibeles, where the famous Fuente de la Cibeles (Fountain of Cybele) depicts the nature goddess driving a chariot drawn by lions. Even more than the officially designated bear and arbutus tree of Madrid's coat of arms, this monument, beautifully lighted at night, has come to symbolize Madrid—so much so that during the civil war, patriotic madrileños risked life and limb to sandbag it as Nationalist aircraft bombed the city. ✉ *Pl. de la Cibeles, Cortes* Ⓜ *Banco de España.*

44 **Puerta de Alcalá.** This triumphal arch was built by Carlos III in 1778 to mark the site of one of the ancient city gates. You can still see the bomb damage inflicted on it during the civil war. ✉ *C. de Alcalá s/n, Retiro* Ⓜ *Retiro.*

31 **Real Fábrica de Tapices.** Tired of the previous monarchs' dependency on the Belgian and Flemish thread mills and craftsmen, King Felipe V decided to establish the Royal Tapestry Factory in Madrid in 1721. It was originally housed near Alonso Martínez, and moved to its current location in 1889. Some of Europe's best artists collaborated in the factory's tapestry designs. The most famous was Goya, who produced 63 cartoons (rough plans), some of which can be seen at the Prado. It's said that he put so much detail into them that the craftsmen complained he'd made their work miserable. The factory, still in operation, applies traditional weaving techniques from the 18th and 19th centuries to modern and classic designs—including Goya's. Textiles are available for sale (you can suggest your own design) at skyrocketing prices: €1,000 a square meter (10¾ square feet) for carpets, €9,000–€12,000 a square meter for tapestries. The factory also runs a training center that teaches traditional weaving techniques to unemployed teenagers, who later become craftspeople. ✉ *Fuenterrabía 2, Retiro* ☎ *91/434–0550* 🌐 *www.realfabricadetapices.com* 🎟 *€4* 🕙 *Weekdays 10–2; guided tour every 30 min starting at 10* Ⓜ *Atocha.*

(34) **San Jerónimo el Real.** Ferdinand and Isabella used this church and cloister as a *retiro,* or place of meditation—hence the name of the nearby park. The building was devastated in the Napoleonic Wars, then rebuilt in the late 19th century. ✉ *Moreto 4, behind Prado Museum, Retiro* ☎ *91/420–3578* ⏲ *Daily 10–1 and 5–8:30* Ⓜ *Banco de España, Atocha.*

TAPAS BARS AND CAFÉS

Use the coordinate (✣ B2) at the end of each listing to locate a site on the corresponding map.

The best tapas areas in Madrid are in the Chueca, La Latina, Sol, Santa Ana, Salamanca, and Lavapiés neighborhoods. Trendy La Latina has a concentration of good tapas bars in Plaza de la Paja and on Cava Baja, Cava Alta, and Almendro streets. Chueca is colorful and lively, and the tapas bars there reflect this casual and cheerful spirit in the food and decor. The bars around Sol are quite traditional (many haven't changed in decades), but the constant foot traffic guarantees customers (and means they don't always have to strive for better food and service). In touristy Santa Ana, avoid the crowded and usually pricey tapas bars in the main plaza and go instead to the ones on the side streets. The tapas bars in the Salamanca neighborhood are more sober and traditional, but the food is often excellent. In Lavapiés, the neighborhood with the highest concentration of immigrants, there are plenty of tapas bars serving Moroccan, African, and Asian-inspired food.

Most of the commendable cafés you'll find in Madrid can be classified into two main groups. The ones that have been around for many years (Café del Círculo, Café de Oriente), where writers, singers, poets, and discussion groups still meet and where conversations are usually more important than the coffee itself; and the new ones (Faborit, Diurno, Delic, Anglona), which are tailored to hip and hurried urbanites and tend to have a wider product selection, modern decor, and Wi-Fi.

TAPAS BARS

CHUECA

✕ **El Bocaíto.** This spot has three dining areas and more than 130 tapas on the menu, including 15 to 20 types of *tostas* (toast topped with prawns, egg and garlic, pâté with caviar, cockles, and so on), and surely the best *pescaito frito* (deep-fried whitebait) in the city. ✉ *Libertad 6, Chueca* ☎ *91/532–1219* ⏲ *Closed Sun. and Aug.* Ⓜ *Chueca* ✣ *F3.*

✕ **La Bardemcilla.** Candid photos of Javier Bardem on the wall tip you off to the fact that this homey bar belongs to the actor's family. There are plenty of tables, and a good selection of wines and tapas. Highlights include the grilled vegetables, *huevos estrellados* (fried eggs with potatoes and sausage), and the *croquetas* (béchamel and meat—usually chicken or ham—with a fried bread-crumb crust). There's a fixed-price lunch for less than €10. ✉ *Augusto Figueroa 47, Chueca* ☎ *91/521–4256* ⏲ *Closed Sun. No lunch Sat.* Ⓜ *Chueca* ✣ *F2.*

CLOSE UP

Tapas: A Moveable Feast

Originally a lid used to *tapar* (cover or close) a glass of wine, a *tapa* is a kind of hors d'oeuvre that sometimes comes free with a drink: the term supposedly came from pieces of ham or cheese laid across glasses of wine to keep flies out and to keep stagecoach drivers sober. The history of tapas goes back to the 7th- to 15th-century Moorish presence on the Iberian Peninsula. The Moors brought with them exotic ingredients, such as saffron, almonds, and peppers, and a taste for small delicacies that eventually became Spain's best-known culinary innovation.

Often miniature versions of classic Spanish dishes, the individual *pinchos* or tapas, or the larger *raciones*, which usually feed a few, allow you to sample different kinds of food and wine with minimal alcohol poisoning, especially on a *tapeo*, the Spanish version of a pub crawl: you walk off your wine and tapas as you move from bar to bar. In the tapas bars you can test the food without committing to a sit-down meal. Here are a few standards to watch for: *croquetas* (béchamel and meat with a fried bread-crumb crust), *tortilla de patata* (Spanish potato omelet), chorizo (hard pork sausage), *gambas* (shrimp grilled or cooked in parsley, oil, and garlic), *patatas bravas* (potatoes in spicy sauce), and *boquerones en vinagre* (fresh anchovies marinated in salt and vinegar).

For more on tapas, see the in-focus feature in Chapter 5.

LA LATINA

✕ **Casa Lucas.** Some of the favorites at this small, cozy bar with a short but creative selection of homemade tapas include the *Carinena* (grilled pork sirloin with caramelized onion), *Madrid* (scrambled eggs with onion, *morcilla* [blood pudding], and pine nuts in a tomato base), and *huevos a la Macarena* (eggs in puff pastry with mushrooms, fried artichokes, fried ham, béchamel, and pine nuts). ✉ *Cava Baja 30, La Latina* ☎ *91/365–0804* ⏲ *No lunch Wed.* Ⓜ *La Latina* ✣ *C5.*

✕ **El Almendro.** Getting a weekend seat in this rustic old favorite is quite a feat, but drop by any other time and you'll be served great *roscas* (round hot bread filled with various types of cured meats), *huevos rotos* (fried eggs with potatoes), *pistos* (sautéed vegetables with a tomato base), or *revueltos* (scrambled eggs; a favorite preparation is the *habanero*, with fava beans and blood pudding). Note that drinks and food need to be ordered separately (a bell rings when your food is ready). ✉ *Almendro 13, La Latina* ☎ *91/365–4252* Ⓜ *La Latina* ✣ *C5.*

✕ **Juana la Loca.** This tempting spot serves sophisticated and unusual tapas that can be as pricey as they are delightful (don't miss the *tortilla de patatas*—it's made with caramelized onions and is sweeter and juicier than the ones you might find elsewhere). If you drop by the bar during the weekend, go early, when the tapas are freshest. On weekdays, order from the menu. ✉ *Pl. Puerta de Moros 4, La Latina* ☎ *91/364–0525* ⏲ *Closed Mon.* Ⓜ *La Latina* ✣ *B5.*

✕ **Txirimiri.** It's easy to spot this Basque tapas place by the crush of people that gather at its door, which may make it uncomfortable at times, but the food is worth being jostled a bit. Among the highlights, try the Unai hamburger (fried in tempura with foie) or the Spanish omelet, one of the city's best. Show up early and you may be lucky enough to get one of the tables in the back. ✉ *Humilladero 6, La Latina* ☎ *91/364–1196* ⏲ *No lunch Mon, and Tues.* Ⓜ *La Latina* ✥ *C5.*

LAVAPIÉS

✕ **La Bodega de Lete.** The laid-back spirit of the neighborhood is represented here in bold colors and unassuming decor, but it's the simple yet superb *raciones* (large portions for sharing) that keep the six tables in high demand. Split an *entraña* (a cut of grilled beef), the *patatas chimichurri* (potatoes with a garlic, oregano, and parsley sauce), or the Atlantic salad—all with the young house Rioja. Your smile won't fade when the tab comes. ✉ *Buenavista 42, Lavapiés* ☎ *91/530–0259* ⏲ *Closed Mon. No dinner Sun. No lunch Tues.–Sat.* Ⓜ *Lavapiés* ✥ *E6.*

MALASAÑA

✕ **Bodega de la Ardosa.** Big wooden barrels serve as tables at this charming tavern with more than 100 years of history. There's great vermouth and draft beer, along with specialties such as *salmorejo* (a thick, cold tomato soup similar to gazpacho), a juicy *tortilla de patatas* (Spanish omelet) made by the owner's mother, and *croquetas,* including varieties with béchamel and prawns (*carabineros*) as well as aromatic cheese (*Cabrales*). Expect to hear a good selection of jazz. ✉ *Colón 13, Malasaña* ☎ *91/521–4979* Ⓜ *Tribunal* ✥ *E2.*

PALACIO

✕ **Taberneros.** This museumlike wine bar has wine racks and decanters exhibited all around, and a menu that includes local specialties (*croquetas,* grilled mussels, duck sirloin, fresh liver) as well as Asian-inspired ones (tuna burger, sirloin in soy sauce). A tapas sampler and a weekly lunch menu are also available. Show up early or prepare to wait a while. ✉ *Santiago 9, Palacio* ☎ *91/542–2460* ⏲ *No lunch Mon.* Ⓜ *Ópera* ✥ *C4.*

RETIRO

✕ **Arzábal.** The eastern side of Retiro Park hides some of the best tapas bars in the city, and this sleek one just a block from the park has a small counter, which is great for a cold beer or a good Rioja or Ribera wine with some ham, mushroom croquetas, or a bowl of salmorejo (a garlicky, thick version of gazpacho). The handful of tables, where you can indulge in more sophisticated fare—think sautéed rice with truffle and wild mushroom, quails with sautéed onions, or a tomato and white tuna belly salad—are usually in high demand. ✉ *Doctor Castelo 2, Retiro* ☎ *91/557–2691* ⏲ *Closed Mon. No dinner Sun.* Ⓜ *Príncipe de Vergara* ✥ *H3.*

SALAMANCA

✕ **Estay.** A two-story bar and restaurant with austere furnishings, this spot has quickly become a landmark among the city's posh crowd for outstanding food. The tapas menu is plentiful and diverse, with specialties like the *tortilla española con atún y lechuga* (Spanish omelet with tuna and lettuce) and *rabas* (fried calamari). There is a dish of the day for €12, and a few tapas samplers. ✉ *Hermosilla 46, Salamanca* ☎ *91/578–0470* ⏲ *Closed Sun.* Ⓜ *Velázquez* ✣ *H1.*

✕ **Jurucha.** If you're shopping in the Serrano area, this is the place to go for a quick bite. There's a long bar with all the food on display; tapas highlights include the *gambas con allioli* (prawns with a garlic-mayo sauce), fried *empanadillas* (small empanadas), and Spanish omelets. A small seating space has wooden stools, and there are tables at the back. ✉ *Ayala 19, Salamanca* ☎ *91/575–0098* ⏲ *Closed Sun and Aug.* Ⓜ *Serrano* ✣ *H1.*

BARRIO DE LAS LETRAS

✕ **El Cervantes.** Clean, elegant and very popular among locals, this spot serves plenty of hot and cold tapas and one of the best and most refreshing draft beers in the city. Good choices are the *pulpo a la gallega* (octopus with potatoes, olive oil, and paprika), any of the *tostas* (toast topped with mushroom, shrimp, etc.), or the tapas sampler. ✉ *Pl. de Jesús 7, Barrio de las Letrasa* ☎ *91/429–6093* Ⓜ *Antón Martín* ✣ *F4.*

✕ **Estado Puro.** At this hypersleek dining space (with a great summer terrace) cooking wizard Paco Roncero reinvents popular dishes such as the *patatas bravas* or the *pepito de ternera* (a beef sandwich that resembles a kebab). Don't skip dessert: this version of the almond-based Tarta de Santiago is highly recommended. ✉ *Pl. Cánovas del Castillo 4, Barrio de las Letras* ☎ *91/330–2400* ⏲ *No dinner Sun.* Ⓜ *Banco de España* ✣ *F4.*)

✕ **La Dolores.** Usually crowded and noisy, this bar serves one of the best draft beers in Madrid. It also has a decent, though pricey, selection of tapas, which you can enjoy at one of the few tables in the back. ✉ *Pl. de Jesús 4, Barrio de las Letras* ☎ *91/429–2243* Ⓜ *Antón Martín* ✣ *F5.*

CAFÉS

SOL

✕ **Café del Círculo** *(La Pecera).* Spacious and elegant, with large velvet curtains, marble columns, hardwood floors, painted ceilings, and sculptures scattered throughout, this eatery inside the famous art center Círculo de Bellas Artes feels more like a private club than a café. Expect a bustling, intellectual crowd. ✉ *Marqués de Casa Riera 2, Sol* ☎ *91/522–5092* Ⓜ *Banco de España, Sevilla* ✣ *F3.*

✕ **Chocolatería San Ginés.** Gastronomical historians suggest that the practice of dipping explains Spaniards' lasting fondness for superthick hot chocolate. Only a few of the old places where this hot drink was served exclusively (with crispy churros), such as this *chocolatería,* remain standing. Gastronomical historians suggest that the practice of dipping explains Spaniards' lasting fondness for superthick hot chocolate. Only a few of the old places where this hot drink was served exclusively (with crispy churros), such as this *chocolatería,* remain standing. It's open virtually 24 hours a day (9:30 AM to 7 AM weekdays; 9 AM to 7 AM, weekends) and is the last stop for many a bleary-eyed soul after a night out. ✉ *Pasadizo de San Ginés, enter by Arenal 11, Sol* ☎ *91/365–6546* Ⓜ *Sol* ✣ *C4.*

A typical evening scene: beer and tapas on the terrace of one of Madrid's many tapas bars.

✕ **Faborit**. A chain spot bold enough to open next door to Starbucks had better serve some great coffee, and for less money; Faborit does, and offers a warm, high-tech environment to boot. Whether your feet hurt and the sun is blazing, or it's chilly out and you're tired of shivering, indulge in a mug of cappuccino with cream or a chai cappuccino. The main café is two blocks from the Puerta del Sol, but there are also now branches on Paseo del Prado, near the CaixaForum, across from the Palace Hotel, and on San Bernardo, just a block off Gran Vía. ✉ *Alcalá 21, Sol* ☎ *91/521–8616* Ⓜ *Sevilla* ✣ *E3.*

PALACIO

✕ **Café de Oriente**. This landmark spot has a magnificent view of the Royal Palace and its front yard. Inside, the café is divided into two sections—the left one serves tapas and raciones; the right serves more elaborate food. The café also has a splendid terrace that's open when the sun is out. ✉ *Pl. de Oriente 2, Palacio* ☎ *91/547–1564* Ⓜ *Ópera* ✣ *B3.*

MALASAÑA

✕ **Lolina Café**. Diverging in its spirit and decor (think vintage furniture and pop art wallpaper) from the classier baroque cafés of the neighborhood, this hectic spot attracts the young and techno-savvy with its free Wi-Fi and good assortment of teas, chocolates, cakes, and drinks. ✉ *Espíritu Santo 9, Malasaña* ☎ *667/201169* Ⓜ *Tribunal* ✣ *D1.*

CHUECA

✕ **Diurno**. A Chueca landmark, this café, DVD rental stop, and take-out spot is spacious, with large windows facing the street, sleek white chairs and couches, and lots of plants. Diurno serves healthy snacks and sandwiches along with some indulgent desserts. ✉ *San Marcos 37, Chueca* ☎ *91/522–0009* Ⓜ *Chueca* ⊕ *F3.*

LA LATINA

✕ **Anglona**. A good option if you're in La Latina, this small café serves a variety of hot chocolates (with cognac, caramel, mint, and more) and imported teas, as well as some sweets, including chocolate cake, carrot cake, and custard crème mille-feuille. At night, sip *mojitos* or caipirinhas and take in the scene-setting jazz or bossa nova. ✉ *Príncipe de Anglona 3, La Latina* ☎ *91/365–0587* ⏲ *Closed Mon.* Ⓜ *La Latina* ⊕ *B5.*

✕ **Delic**. This warm, inviting café is a hangout for Madrid's trendy crowd. Besides the *patatitas con mousse de parmesano* (potatoes with a Parmesan mousse) and zucchini cake, homesick travelers will find carrot cake, brownies, and pumpkin pie among the offerings. ✉ *Costanilla de San Andrés 14, Pl. de la Paja, La Latina* ☎ *91/364–5450* ⏲ *Closed Mon. and Aug. 1–15* Ⓜ *La Latina* ⊕ *B5.*

LAVAPIÉS

✕ **Gaudeamus Café**. Along with the theater on the neighborhood's main plaza, the reconstruction of the Escuelas Pías—an 18th-century religious school burnt down during the Spanish civil war and now turned into a university center—is one of Lavapiés's modern highlights. The rooftop has a hidden café: the large terrace is open all year round and has great views for enjoying the wide selection of tea and coffee. It opens at 3:30 PM on weekdays and at 8 PM on Saturday. ✉ *Tribulete 14, 4th fl., Lavapiés* ☎ *91/528–2594* ⏲ *Closed Sun.* Ⓜ *Lavapiés* ⊕ *D6.*

WHERE TO EAT

Spain in general has become a popular foodie pilgrimage, and Madrid showcases its strengths with a cornucopia of cuisine, cutting-edge decor, and celebrated chefs who put the city on par with Europe's celebrated dining capitals.

Top Spanish chefs fearlessly borrow from other cuisines and reinvent traditional dishes. The younger crowd, as well as movie stars and artists, flock to the casual Malasaña, Chueca, and La Latina neighborhoods for the affordable restaurants and the tapas bars with truly scintillating small creations. When modern cuisine gets tiresome, seek out such local enclaves as Casa Ciriaco, Casa Botín, and Casa Paco for unpretentious and hearty home cooking.

The house wine in basic Madrid restaurants is often a sturdy, uncomplicated Valdepeñas from La Mancha. Serious dining is normally accompanied by a Rioja or a more powerful, complex Ribera de Duero, the latter from northern Castile. Ask your waiter's advice; a smooth Rioja, for example, may not be up to the task of accompanying a *cocido* or roast suckling pig. After dinner, try the anise-flavor liqueur (*anís*) produced outside the nearby village of Chinchón. *Use the coordinate (⊕ B2) at the end of each listing to locate a site on the corresponding map.*

BARRIO DE LAS LETRAS AND LAVAPIÉS

$$ MEDITERRANEAN ✕ **Arrocería Gala.** Hidden on a back street not far from Calle Atocha and the Reina Sofía museum, this cheerful Mediterranean restaurant is usually packed, thanks to the choice of paellas, *fideuás* (paellas with noodles instead of rice), risottos, and hearty meat and potato stews—all served with salad, dessert, and a wine jar. Everyone at tables of four or fewer must order the same type of rice. The front dining area is modern and festive; the back room incorporates trees and plants in a glassed-in patio. ✉ *Moratín 22, Barrio de las Letras* ☎ *91/429–2562* ✍ *Reservations essential* ▭ *No credit cards* ⊙ *Closed Mon.* Ⓜ *Antón Martín* ⊕ *F5.*

$$$ SPANISH ✕ **Asador Frontón I.** Uptown's Asador Frontón II is swankier, but this downtown original is more charming, and fine meat and fish are the headliners on the menu. Appetizers include *anchoas frescas* (fresh grilled anchovies) and *pimientos rellenos con bacalao* (peppers stuffed with cod). The huge *chuletón* (T-bone steak), seared over charcoal and sprinkled with sea salt, is for two or more; order *cogollo de lechuga* (lettuce hearts) as an accompaniment. The *cogotes de merluza* (hake jowls) are light and aromatic. ✉ *Tirso de Molina 7, entrance on Jesus y Maria 1, Lavapiés* ☎ *91/369–1617* ✍ *Reservations essential* ▭ *AE, DC, MC, V* ⊙ *Closed 1 wk in Aug. and Easter wk. No dinner Sun.* Ⓜ *Tirso de Molina* ⊕ *D5.*

$$ SPANISH ✕ **Casa Lastra.** Established in 1926, this Asturian tavern is popular with Lavapiés locals. The rustic, half-tile walls are strung with relics from the Asturian countryside, including wooden clogs, cowbells, sausages, and garlic. Specialties include *fabada* (Asturian white beans stewed with sausage), *fabes con almejas* (white beans with clams), and *queso de cabrales,* aromatic cheese made in the Picos de Europa. Great hunks of bread and Asturian hard cider complement the hearty meals; desserts include tangy baked apples. There's an inexpensive fixed-price lunch menu on weekdays. ✉ *Olivar 3, Lavapiés* ☎ *91/369–0837* ▭ *MC, V* ⊙ *Closed Wed. and July. No dinner Sun.* Ⓜ *Tirso de Molina, Antón Martín* ⊕ *E5.*

$$–$$$ ITALIAN ✕ **Come Prima.** There are fancier and more expensive Italian restaurants in the city but none as warm or authentic as this one. Decorated with black-and-white photos of Italian actors and stills from movies, the interior is divided into three areas; the bistrolike front, with green-and-white checkered tablecloths, is the most charming. Portions are large, eye-catching, and tastefully presented. The risottos are popular, especially the Milanesa with lobster and the porcini. The menu also offers fresh pasta dishes, with surprises such as liver- or pumpkin-filled ravioli, and the timbale *come prima* (a molded pasta cake filled with vegetables). ✉ *C. Echegaray 27, Barrio de las Letras* ☎ *91/420–3042* ✍ *Reservations essential* ▭ *MC, V* ⊙ *No lunch Sun. and Mon.* Ⓜ *Antón Martín* ⊕ *E5.*

$$ MEDITERRANEAN ✕ **El Cenador del Prado.** The name means "The Prado Dining Room," and the space includes a boldly painted dining room as well as a plant-filled

BEST BETS FOR MADRID DINING

Need a cheat sheet for Madrid's restaurants? Fodor's writers have selected their favorites by price, cuisine, and experience. Details are in the full reviews. ¡Buen provecho!

Fodor's Choice ★

Asiana, $$$$, p. 107
Casa Paco, $$–$$$, p. 109
DiverXo, $$$, p. 102
Gastro, $$$$, p. 103
Goizeko Wellington, $$$, p. 103
La Terraza—Casino, $$$$, p. 110
Las Tortillas de Gabino, $–$$, p. 105
Mercado de la Reina, $–$$, p. 108
Santceloni, $$$$, p. 106
Sudestada, $$, p. 102
Zalacaín, $$$$, p. 106

By Price

¢

Arabia, p. 106
Bazaar, p. 107
Nueva Galicia, p. 111

$

Casa Ciriaco, p. 108
Home Burger, p. 107
La Musa, p. 107
Las Tortillas de Gabino, p. 105
Mercado de la Reina, p. 108
Puerto Lagasca, p. 105
Pulcinella, p. 108
Taberna Bilbao, p. 109

$$

Arrocería Gala, p. 97
La Castela, p. 105
La Gamella, p. 105
La Gastroteca de Santiago, p. 110
Le Petit Bistrot, p. 99
Sacha, p. 102
Sudestada, p. 102

$$$

Espacio Alboroque, p. 99
Goizeko Wellington, p. 103
Viridiana, p. 106

$$$$

DiverXo, p. 102
La Terraza—Casino, p. 110

By Cuisine

CONTEMPORARY SPANISH

DiverXo, p. 102
Espacio Alboroque, $$$, p. 99
Estado Puro*, p. 94
Goizeko Wellington, $$$, p. 103
La Gastroteca de Santiago, $$, p. 110
Sacha, $$, p. 102
Zalacaín, $$$$, p. 106

PAELLA-RICE

Arrocería Gala, $$, p. 97
Casa Benigna, $$, p. 102

SEAFOOD

Goizeko Wellington, $$$, p. 103
La Trainera, $$$, p. 105

STEAK HOUSE

Asador Frontón I, $$$, p. 97
Casa Paco, $$–$$$, p. 109

TAPAS

Arzábal, p. 93
El Bocaíto*, p. 91
Estay*, p. 93
Juana la Loca*, p. 92
Taberna Bilbao, $, p. 109
Taberneros*, p. 93
Txirimiri*, p. 92

TRADITIONAL SPANISH

Casa Botín, $$$, p. 108
Casa Ciriaco, $–$$, p. 108
El Landó, $$$, p. 109
La Bola, $$, p. 110
La Castela, $$, p. 105
La Trucha, $, p. 99
Las Tortillas de Gabino, $–$$, p. 105
Mercado de la Reina, $, p. 108
Puerto Lagasca, $, p. 105
Taberna Bilbao, $, p. 109

Tapas bars are marked with *

conservatory, which is also used for dining (there's a baroque salon, too, usually for large groups). The innovative menu has French and Asian touches as well as exotic Spanish dishes, and the house specialty is *patatas a la importancia* (sliced potatoes fried in a sauce of garlic, parsley, and clams); other recommended options include black rice with baby squid and prawns and sirloin on a pear pastry puff. For dessert try the *bartolillos* (custard-filled pastries). ✉ *C. del Prado 4, Barrio de las Letras* ☎ *91/429–1561* ▭ *DC, V* ⏲ *Closed 1 wk in Aug. No dinner Sun.* Ⓜ *Antón Martín, Sevilla* ✣ *E4.*

$$$–$$$$ MEDITERRANEAN ✕ **Espacio Alboroque.** Chefs Alberto Gómez and Etienne Bastiats unleash their creativity here, on the bottom floor of a completely rehabilitated 19th-century mansion. The dining rooms are vast gallerylike spaces with lots of natural light. The food is based on seasonal market findings and menu items focus on the nitty-gritty of Mediterranean cooking with hints of sophistication: look for smoked rice with *zambouriñas* (a type of scallop), cured ham and fennel, the *urta* (a kind of snapper) with spicy mussels and couscous, or the artichokes with peanut *turrón*. There are two sampler menus (€35 and €50), and two wine pairing options (€10 and (€20). ✉ *Calle Atocha 34, Barrio de las Letras* ☎ *91/389–6570* ▭ *AE, DC, MC, V* ⏲ *Closed Sun. No lunch Sat.* Ⓜ *Antón Martín* ✣ *E5.*

$$ SPANISH ✕ **La Ancha.** The traditional Spanish menu here includes some of the best lentils, meat cutlets, and croquettes in Madrid, as well as more elaborate dishes, such as the juicy *tortilla con almejas* (Spanish omelet with clams). Both locations of the restaurant belong to the same family and are unpretentious inside but known for the outstanding quality of their food. The original Príncipe de Vergara location has a covered patio for the summer; the newer one, behind the Congress, is often filled with politicians. ✉ *Zorrilla 7, Barrio de las Letras* ☎ *91/429–8186* ⏲ *Closed Sun. and 1 wk in Aug., Zorrilla branch closed 3 wks in Aug.* Ⓜ *Sevilla* ✣ *F4* ✉ *Príncipe de Vergara 204, Chamartín* ☎ *91/563–8977* ▭ *AE, DC, MC, V* ⏲ Ⓜ *Concha Espina*

$ SPANISH ✕ **La Trucha.** This Andalusian tavern, decorated with hanging hams, ceramic plates, and garlic, is one of the happiest places in Madrid. The staff is jovial, and the house specialty, *trucha a la truchana* (trout stuffed with ham and garlic), is a work of art. Other star entrées are *chopitos* (baby squid), *pollo al ajillo* (chunks of chicken in crisped garlic), fried fish, and *espárragos trigueros* (wild asparagus). *Jarras* (pitchers) of chilled Valdepeñas seem to act like laughing gas on the guests. The Nuñez de Arce branch, near the Hotel Reina Victoria, is usually less crowded. ✉ *Manuel Fernandez y Gonzalez 3, Barrio de las Letras* ☎ *91/429–5833* Ⓜ *Sevilla, Sol* ✣ *E4* ✉ *Nuñez de Arce 6, Barrio de las Letras* ☎ *91/532–0890* ▭ *AE, MC, V* ⏲ *Nuñez de Arce branch closed Sun., Mon., and Aug.* Ⓜ *Sol* ✣ *E4*

$$ FRENCH ✕ **Le Petit Bistrot.** After more than a decade of working in French restaurants and hotels in different parts of the world, Carlos Campillo and his wife Frédérique Sévèque took on a challenge converting what was once a bullfighting-themed tavern into a Parisian bistro. Though some elements, such as the long brass-topped bar, hint at its *castizo* (authentic) origins, there's much that's truly French here in addition to the food,

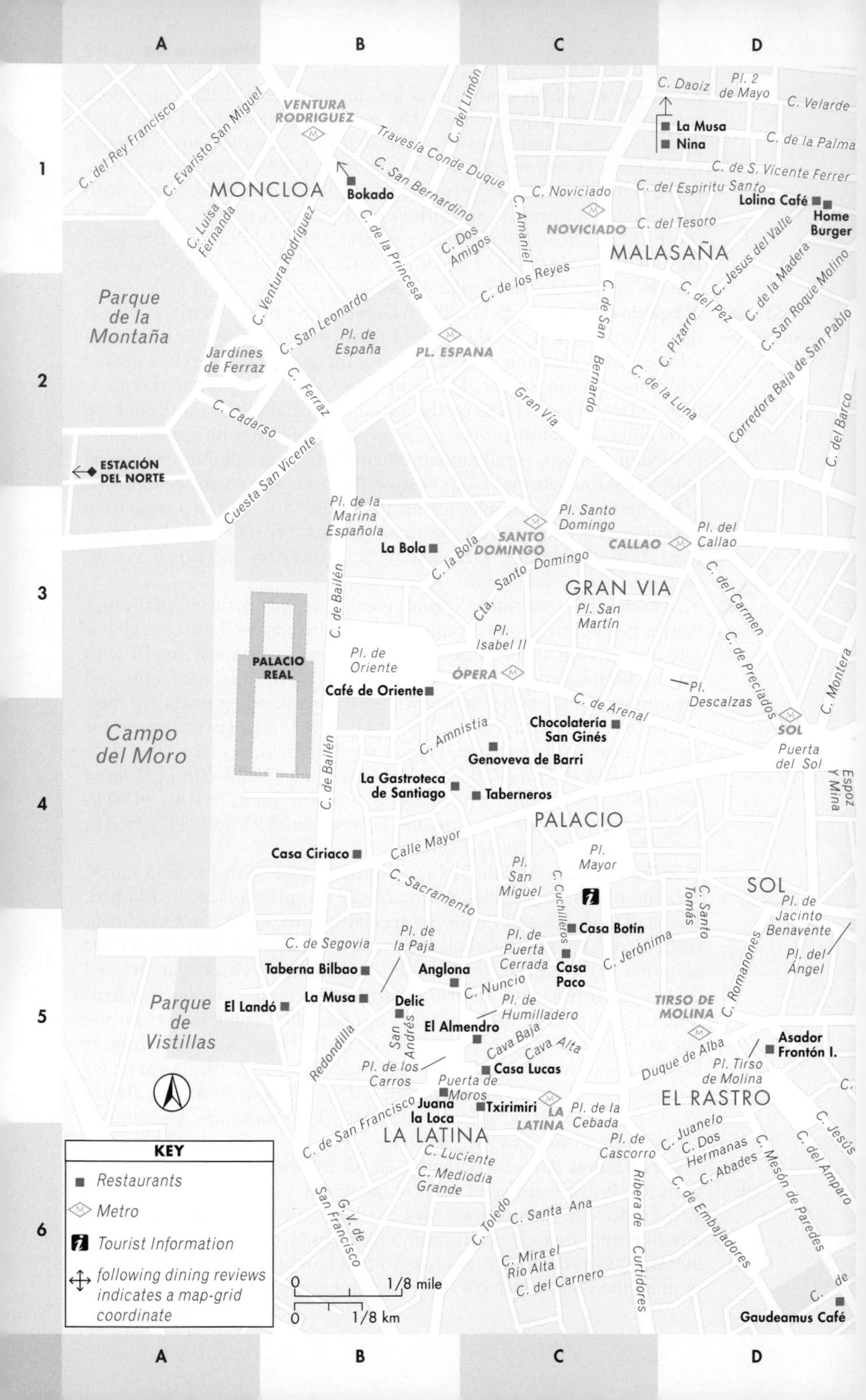
A
B
C
D
1
2
3
4
5
6
MONCLOA
MALASAÑA
GRAN VIA
PALACIO
SOL
EL RASTRO
LA LATINA
VENTURA RODRIGUEZ
NOVICIADO
PL. ESPANA
SANTO DOMINGO
CALLAO
ÓPERA
SOL
TIRSO DE MOLINA
LA LATINA
Parque de la Montaña
Jardines de Ferraz
Campo del Moro
Parque de Vistillas
PALACIO REAL
ESTACIÓN DEL NORTE
C. del Rey Francisco
C. Evaristo San Miguel
C. Luisa Fernanda
C. Ventura Rodríguez
C. San Leonardo
C. Ferraz
C. Cadarso
Cuesta San Vicente
Travesía Conde Duque
C. San Bernardino
C. del Limón
C. de la Princesa
C. Dos Amigos
C. Amaniel
C. Noviciado
C. de los Reyes
Pl. de España
C. Daoiz
Pl. 2 de Mayo
C. Velarde
C. de la Palma
C. de S. Vicente Ferrer
C. del Espiritu Santo
C. del Tesoro
C. de San Bernardo
C. Jesus del Valle
C. del Pez
C. de la Madera
C. San Roque Molino
C. Pizarro
C. de la Luna
Corredora Baja de San Pablo
C. del Barco
Gran Vía
Pl. de la Marina Española
Pl. Santo Domingo
Pl. del Callao
C. la Bola
Cta. Santo Domingo
Pl. San Martín
C. del Carmen
C. de Preciados
C. Montera
Pl. Isabel II
Pl. de Oriente
C. de Bailén
Pl. Descalzas
C. de Arenal
C. Amnistia
Puerta del Sol
Espoz Y Mina
Calle Mayor
Pl. Mayor
Pl. San Miguel
C. Cuchilleros
C. Santo Tomás
C. Sacramento
Pl. de Jacinto Benavente
Pl. del Ángel
C. de Segovia
Pl. de la Paja
Pl. de Puerta Cerrada
C. Jerónima
C. Romanones
C. Nuncio
Pl. de Humilladero
Redondilla
San Andrés
Cava Baja
Cava Alta
Duque de Alba
Pl. de los Carros
Puerta de Moros
Pl. Tirso de Molina
C. de San Francisco
Pl. de la Cebada
Pl. de Cascorro
C. Juanelo
C. Dos Hermanas
C. Abades
C. Mesón de Paredes
C. Jesús
C. del Amparo
C. Luciente
C. Mediodia Grande
G. V. de San Francisco
C. Toledo
C. Santa Ana
Ribera de Curtidores
C. de Embajadores
C. Mira el Rio Alta
C. del Carnero
C. de
La Musa
Nina
Bokado
Lolina Café
Home Burger
La Bola
Café de Oriente
Chocolatería San Ginés
Genoveva de Barri
La Gastroteca de Santiago
Taberneros
Casa Ciriaco
Casa Botín
Taberna Bilbao
Anglona
Casa Paco
La Musa
El Landó
Delic
El Almendro
Asador Frontón I.
Casa Lucas
Juana la Loca
Txirimiri
Gaudeamus Café
0
1/8 mile
0
1/8 km
KEY
Restaurants
Metro
Tourist Information
following dining reviews indicates a map-grid coordinate

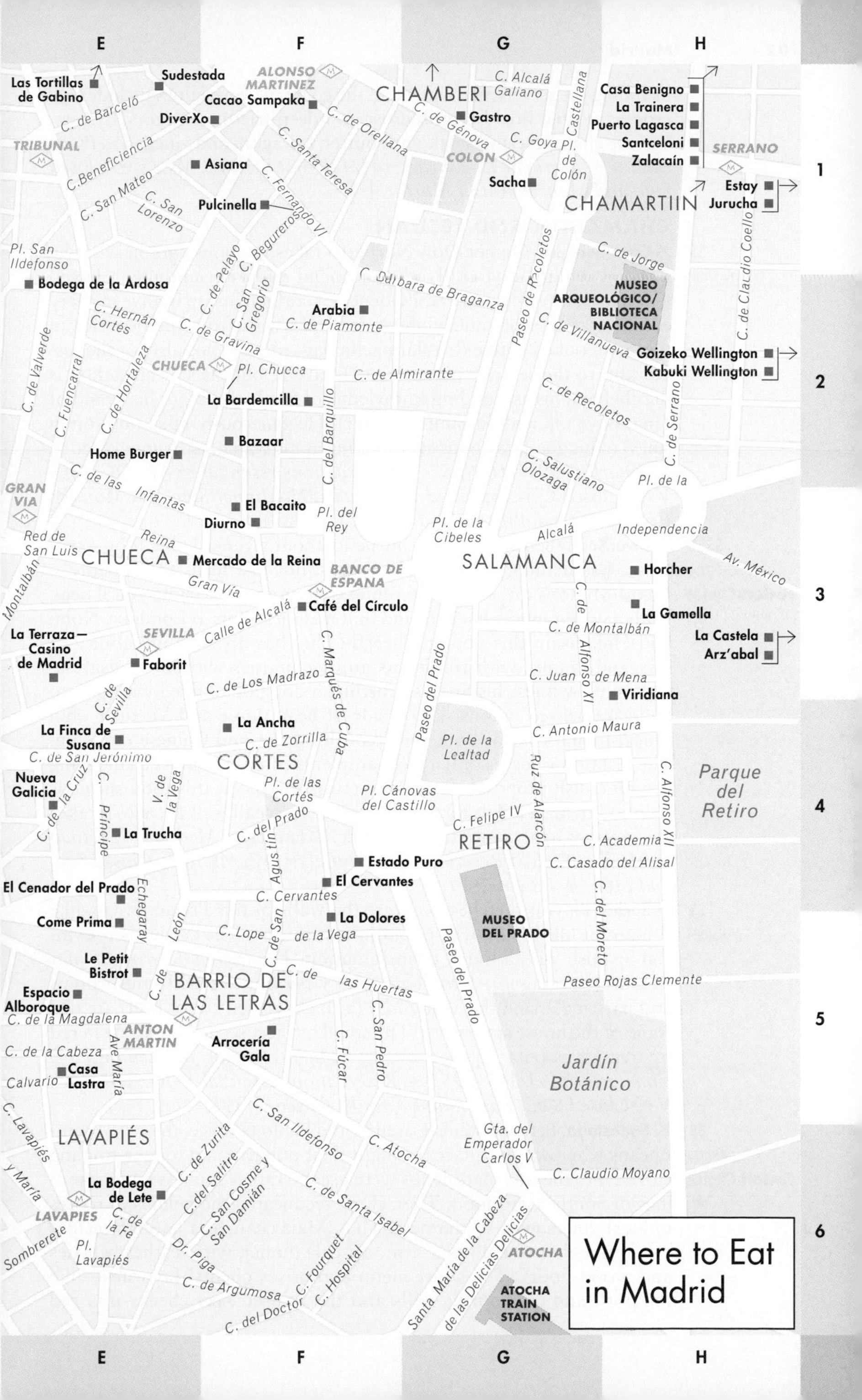

E
F
G
H
1
2
3
4
5
6
Las Tortillas de Gabino
Sudestada
ALONSO MARTINEZ
Cacao Sampaka
DiverXo
CHAMBERI
C. Alcalá Galiano
Castellana
Casa Benigno
La Trainera
Puerto Lagasca
Santceloni
Zalacaín
SERRANO
Estay
Jurucha
Gastro
C. de Génova
C. Goya
Pl. de Colón
COLON
Sacha
CHAMARTIIN
C. de Barceló
TRIBUNAL
C. Beneficiencia
C. San Mateo
C. San Lorenzo
Asiana
Pulcinella
C. Fernando VI
C. de Orellana
C. Santa Teresa
C. Beguerero
C. de Pelayo
Pl. San Ildefonso
Bodega de la Ardosa
C. Hernán Cortés
C. San Gregorio
C. de Gravina
C. Bárbara de Braganza
Arabia
C. de Piamonte
Paseo de Recoletos
C. de Jorge
MUSEO ARQUEOLÓGICO/ BIBLIOTECA NACIONAL
C. de Villanueva
Goizeko Wellington
Kabuki Wellington
C. de Claudio Coello
C. de Valverde
C. Fuencarral
C. de Hortaleza
CHUECA
Pl. Chueca
La Bardemcilla
C. de Almirante
C. de Recoletos
C. de Serrano
Bazaar
Home Burger
C. del Barquillo
C. Salustiano Olozaga
Pl. de la Independencia
GRAN VIA
C. de las Infantas
El Bacaito
Diurno
Pl. del Rey
Pl. de la Cibeles
Alcalá
Red de San Luis
Reina
CHUECA
Mercado de la Reina
BANCO DE ESPANA
SALAMANCA
Horcher
Av. México
Montalbán
Gran Vía
Café del Círculo
C. de Alfonso XI
La Gamella
C. de Montalbán
La Terraza—Casino de Madrid
SEVILLA
Calle de Alcalá
Faborit
C. Marqués de Cuba
Paseo del Prado
La Castela
Arz'abal
C. de Los Madrazo
C. Juan de Mena
Viridiana
C. de Sevilla
La Ancha
C. de Zorrilla
La Finca de Susana
C. de San Jerónimo
CORTES
Pl. de la Lealtad
C. Antonio Maura
Ruz de Alarcón
C. Alfonso XII
Parque del Retiro
Nueva Galicia
C. de la Cruz
C. Príncipe
V. de la Vega
Pl. de las Cortés
Pl. Cánovas del Castillo
C. Felipe IV
La Trucha
C. del Prado
RETIRO
C. Academia
C. San Agustín
Estado Puro
C. Casado del Alisal
El Cervantes
El Cenador del Prado
Echegaray
C. Cervantes
C. del Moreto
Come Prima
La Dolores
León
C. Lope de la Vega
MUSEO DEL PRADO
Le Petit Bistrot
C. de León
BARRIO DE LAS LETRAS
C. de las Huertas
Paseo Rojas Clemente
Espacio Alboroque
C. de la Magdalena
ANTON MARTIN
Arrocería Gala
C. San Pedro
C. Fúcar
C. de la Cabeza
Ave María
Casa Lastra
Calvario
Jardín Botánico
C. Lavapiés
LAVAPIÉS
C. San Ildefonso
C. Atocha
Gta. del Emperador Carlos V
C. de Zurita
C. del Salitre
C. San Cosme y San Damián
C. de Santa Isabel
C. Claudio Moyano
y María
La Bodega de Lete
LAVAPIES
C. de la Fe
Sombrerete
Pl. Lavapiés
Dr. Piga
C. de Argumosa
C. Fourquet
C. Hospital
C. del Doctor
Santa María de la Cabeza
de las Delicias Delicias
ATOCHA
ATOCHA TRAIN STATION
Where to Eat in Madrid

including the servers, the wine, and the cocktails. Specialties include Brie *croquetas* (in a bread-crumb crust and deep-fried), escargots, oysters, and the chateaubriand steak with butter, tarragon, and vinegar. ✉ *Pl. de Matute 5, Barrio de las Letras* ☎ *91/429–6265* ▭ *AE, MC, V* ⏲ *Closed Sun. and Mon.* Ⓜ *Anton Martín* ✥ *E5.*

CHAMARTÍN AND TETUÁN

$$ SPANISH

✕ **Casa Benigna.** Owner Don Norberto takes gracious care in what he does, providing a carefully chosen menu and painstakingly selected wines to devoted customers. Evidence of craftsmanship is alive in every corner of the casual and understated hideaway, from the best rice in the city (cooked with extra-flat paella pans made especially for the restaurant) to the ceramic plates from Talavera, but the star attraction is the chef and his astounding knowledge of food (check out his brand of tuna, olive oil, and balsamic vinegar). He generously talks (and often sings) to his guests without ever looking at his watch. ✉ *Benigno Soto 9, Chamartín* ☎ *91/416–9357* ✍ *Reservations essential* ▭ *AE, DC, MC, V* ⏲ *Closed Christmas and Easter wks. No dinner Sun. and Mon.* Ⓜ *Concha Espina, Prosperidad* ✥ *H1.*

$$$$ ECLECTIC Fodor's Choice ★

✕ **DiverXo.** When you ask a madrileño about a remarkable food experience—something that stirs the senses, not just feeds the appetite—David Muñoz's rather austere venue is often the first name you'll hear. With a wide-ranging background that includes stints at London's Nobu and Hakkasan, this young, cheerful chef has an uncanny ability to mix and tamper with traditions and techniques without transgressing them—witness his Spanish tortilla: a dough ball filled with potato and caramelized onions with a side of bean purée and Mexican chili sauce, reminiscent of both the Spanish omelet and Chinese dim sum. The restaurant serves only three sampler menus—the most challenging is a nine-dish proposal, for €72. Getting a table at this food shrine is akin to buying a ticket for the Super Bowl, so call well ahead—it takes reservations up to a month in advance. ✉ *Francisco Medrano 5, Tetuán* ☎ *91/570–0766* ✍ *Reservations essential* ▭ *DC, MC, V* ⏲ *Closed Sun. and Mon.* Ⓜ *Tetúan* ✥ *F1.*

$$ SPANISH

✕ **Sacha.** Playful sketches decorate the walls of this French bistro–like restaurant filled with oversize antique furniture. The cuisine is provincial Spanish with a touch of imagination. The *lasaña de erizo de mar* (sea urchin lasagna), *arroz con setas y perdiz* (rice with mushrooms and partridge), and the *Villagodio* (a thick, grilled cut of beef) are just some of the house specialties. The small terrace, secluded and sheltered by trees, is popular in the summer. ✉ *Juan Hurtado de Mendoza 11, Chamartín* ☎ *91/345–5952* ✍ *Reservations essential* ▭ *AE, DC, MC, V* ⏲ *Closed Sun., Easter, and Aug.* Ⓜ *Cuzco* ✥ *G1.*

$$ ASIAN Fodor's Choice ★

✕ **Sudestada.** Before Estanis Carenzo and Pablo Giudice, the two Argentineans who own this place, brought their pungent and tongue-tingling curries into the city, madrileños were used to rather soulless understandings of South Asian food. They alone reeducated the palates of scores of local diners with Vietnamese, Thai, Malaysian, and Laotian recipes in a venue that resembles a neat, upscale dinner, with leather benches and wood floors. The short menu comprises clients' favorites—like the pork and crab spring rolls and the braised beef cheeks in a red curry sauce—to which they add some daily specials. Try a Tom Collins with lychee syrup to accompany your meal. ✉ *Ponzano 85, Tetuán* ☎ *91/533–4154* ▭ *DC, MC, V* ⊗ *Closed Sun.* Ⓜ *Ríos Rosas* ⊕ *E1*

CHAMBERÍ, RETIRO, AND SALAMANCA

$$$$ LA NUEVA COCINA Fodor's Choice ★

✕ **Gastro.** At the end of 2007, celebrity chef Sergi Arola—Ferran Adrià's most popular disciple—left La Broche, the restaurant where he vaulted to the top of the Madrid dining scene, to go solo. The result is a smaller, less minimalist though equally modern bistro space crafted to enhance the dining experience, 30 customers at a time. At the height of his career and surrounded by an impeccable team—which now also includes a talented and talkative bartender in the lounge—Arola offers three sampler menus (no à la carte) ranging from seven courses (€105) to more than a dozen in the namesake "Gastro" menu (€160). The latter includes some of the chef's classic surf-and-turf dishes (such as rabbit filled with giant scarlet shrimp) and nods to his Catalonian roots (sautéed broad beans and peas with blood sausage). The wine list has more than 600 different wines, mostly from small producers, all available by the glass. ✉ *Zurbano 31, Chamberí* ☎ *91/310–2169* ✍ *Reservations essential* ▭ *AE, DC, MC, V* Ⓜ *Alonso Martínez* ⊕ *G1.*

$$$ SPANISH Fodor's Choice ★

✕ **Goizeko Wellington.** Aware of the more sophisticated palate of Spain's new generation of diners, the owners of the traditional madrileño dreamland that is Goizeko Kabi opened another restaurant that shares the virtues of its kin but none of its stuffiness. The menu delivers the same quality northern white fishes, house staples such as the *kokotxas de merluza* (hake jowls), and the *chipirones en su tinta* (line-caught calamari cooked in its own ink), as well as pastas, risottos, and hearty bean stews. The interior is warm and modern with citrus-yellow walls, lattices, and screens. ✉ *Villanueva 34, in Hotel Wellington, Salamanca* ☎ *91/577–6026* ✍ *Reservations essential* ▭ *AE, DC, MC, V* ⊗ *Closed Sun. No lunch Sat. July and Aug.* Ⓜ *Retiro, Príncipe de Vergara* ⊕ *H2.*

$$$$ GERMAN

✕ **Horcher.** The faithful continue to fill this traditional shrine to fine dining, once considered Madrid's best restaurant and still worth seeking out. Wild boar, venison, hare, partridge, and wild duck, as well as unique burgers (ostrich and turkey, monkfish, and swordfish) are standard options. Ox stroganoff with noodles and a Pommery mustard sauce, pork chops with sauerkraut, and *baumkuchen* (a chocolate-covered fruit-and-cake dessert) reflect the restaurant's Germanic roots. The dining room is decorated with brocade and antique Austrian porcelain; an ample selection of French and German wines rounds out the menu. ✉ *Alfonso XII 6, Retiro* ☎ *91/522–0731* ✍ *Reservations essential; jacket and tie* ▭ *AE, DC, MC, V* ⊗ *Closed Sun., Easter wk, and Aug. No lunch Sat.* Ⓜ *Retiro* ⊕ *H3.*

$$$–$$$$ JAPANESE

✕ **Kabuki Wellington.** This elegant Japanese dining spot serves the kind of superbly fresh sushi and sashimi you'll find in other parts of the world, but where it excels most is in chef Ricardo Sanz's Spanish-based combinations. Examples of such dishes are the raw calamari or sardine carpaccios (*usuzukuri)* with tempura crumbs, a tribute to two Spanish staples, fried calamari and the sardine sandwich; the beef bone marrow nigiri sushi (honoring another classic, the *madrileño cocido*); and

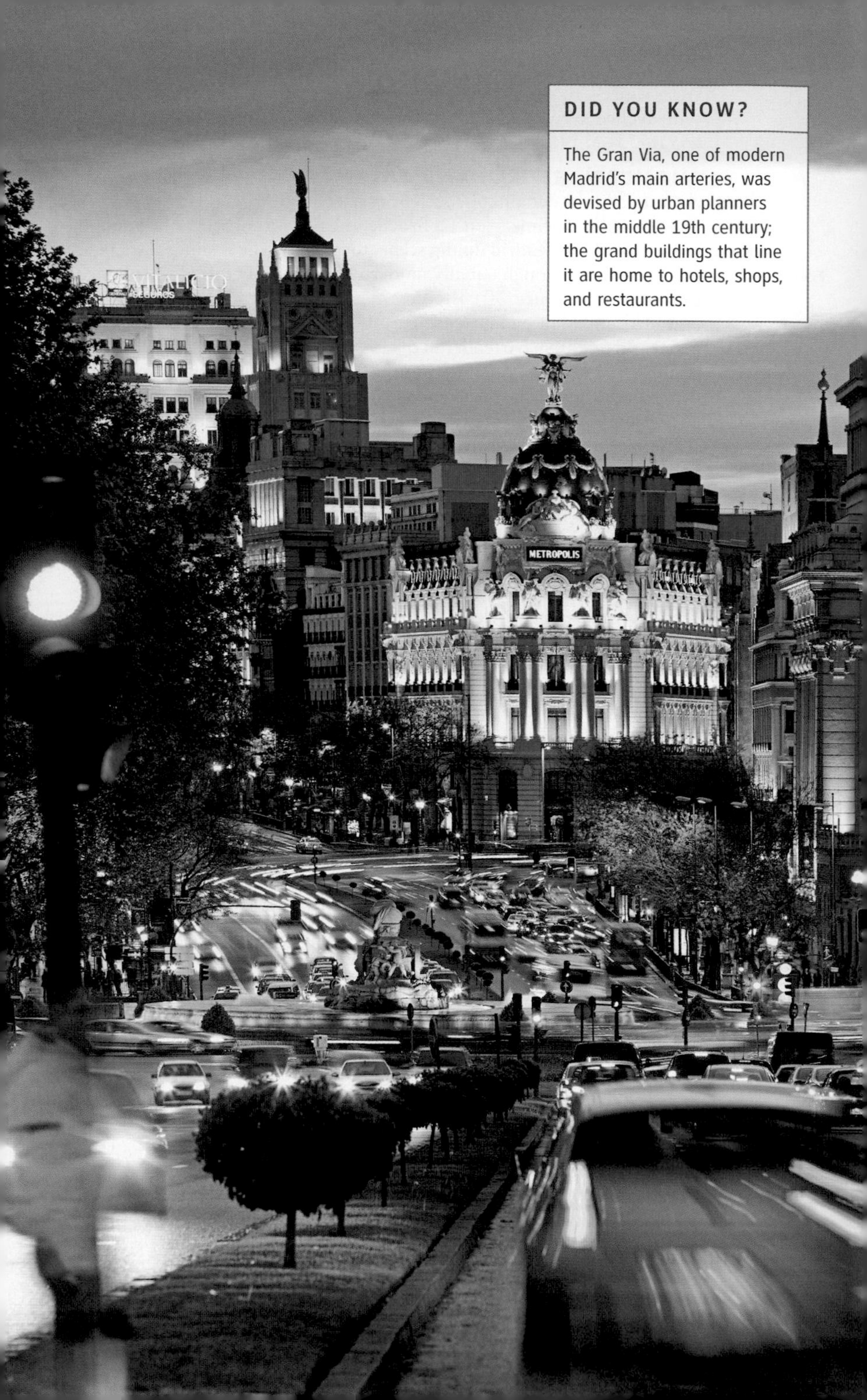

DID YOU KNOW?

The Gran Via, one of modern Madrid's main arteries, was devised by urban planners in the middle 19th century; the grand buildings that line it are home to hotels, shops, and restaurants.

the oxtail with teriyaki sauce. For dessert, don't miss the reinvented hot chocolate with crispy *churros*. ✉ *Velázquez 6, in Hotel Wellington Salamanca* ☎ *91/575–4400* ▭ *AE, DC, MC, V* ⏲ *Closed Sun. No lunch Sat.* Ⓜ *Retiro, Príncipe de Vergara* ✥ *H2.*

$–$$ SPANISH ✕ **La Castela.** Traditional taverns with tin-top bars, beer and vermouth cooled with stainless-steel coils, and uberefficient waiters are a dying breed in Madrid, but this one, just a couple of blocks from the Retiro park, is one of the best, always busy with locals clamoring over plates of sautéed wild mushrooms, fresh salty anchovies served with a cucumber and tomato salad (*pipirrana*), or clams in an Andalusian white wine sauce. You can stop for a quick bite at the bar—they'll serve you a free tapa with every drink—or enjoy heartier choices—such as the chickpea and king prawn stew—in the homey dining room at the back. *Doctor Castelo 22, Retiro* ☎ *91/574–0015* *Reservations essential* ▭ *DC, MC, V* ⏲ *Closed Sun.* Ⓜ *Ibiza* ✥ *H3.*

$$ MEDITERRANEAN ✕ **La Gamella.** Classic American dishes—Caesar salad, hamburger, steak tartare—as well as fusion Mediterranean and American options are the heart of the reasonably priced menu at this perennially popular dinner spot. The sophisticated rust-red dining room, batik tablecloths, and oversize plates are complemented by attentive service. The lunchtime *menú del día* (fixed menu) is a great value, as is the Sunday American-style brunch. ✉ *Alfonso XII 4, Retiro* ☎ *91/532–4509* ▭ *AE, DC, MC, V* ⏲ *No dinner weekends* Ⓜ *Retiro* ✥ *H3.*

$$$ SEAFOOD ✕ **La Trainera.** With its nautical theme and maze of little dining rooms, this informal restaurant is all about fresh seafood—the best that money can buy. Crab, lobster, shrimp, mussels, and a dozen other types of shellfish are served by weight in *raciones* (large portions). Many Spanish diners share several plates of these shellfish as their entire meal, but the grilled hake, sole, or turbot makes an unbeatable second course. To accompany the legendary *carabineros* (giant scarlet shrimp), skip the listless house wine and go for a bottle of Albariño, from the southern Galician coast. ✉ *Lagasca 60, Salamanca* ☎ *91/576–8035* ▭ *AE, DC, MC, V* ⏲ *Closed Sun. and Aug.* Ⓜ *Serrano* ✥ *H1.*

$–$$ SPANISH Fodor's Choice ★ ✕ **Las Tortillas de Gabino.** Few national dishes raise more intense debates among Spaniards than the *tortilla de patata* (Spanish omelet). A deceivingly simple dish, it has many variations: some like it soft with the eggs runny, others prefer a spongy, evenly cooked result. At this lively restaurant you'll find crowds of Spaniards gobbling up one of the city's finest traditional versions of the tortilla, as well as some unconventional ones—potatoes with octopus, potato chips with *salmorejo* (a gazpacho-like soup), tortillas with garlic soup, with codfish and leek stew, with truffles (when available), and with a potato mousse, just to name a few—that are best enjoyed when shared by everyone at the table. The menu includes plenty of equally succulent non-egg choices and a green-apple sorbet that shouldn't be missed. ✉ *Rafael Calvo 20, Chamberí* ☎ *91/319–7505* ▭ *MC, V* ⏲ *Closed Sun. No lunch Sat.* Ⓜ *Rubén Darío* ✥ *E1.*

$ SPANISH ✕ **Puerto Lagasca.** Old-style tapas bars, with floors littered with prawn tails and cigarette butts, are still a majority of what you'll find in the city, but there's a new breed that has more in common with the city's upscale restaurants, though with menus that don't leave you gasping for air when the check arrives. Puerto Lagasca, with dishes based on what's in season, is one of the best tapas bars in its league, where diners can share traditional appetizers like *salmorejo*, roasted peppers, fresh anchovies, a tomato and tuna salad, and good assortment of meat and fish options—among the latter, a good pick is the fried-fish sampler. Note that it also serves half portions. ✉ *Lagasca 81, Salamanca* ☎ *91/576–4111* ▭ *MC, V* ⏲ *No dinner Sun.* Ⓜ *Nuñez de Balboa* ✣ *H1.*

$$$$ MEDITERRANEAN Fodor's Choice ★ ✕ **Santceloni.** Santi Santamaría's Madrid branch of his Racó de Can Fabes (near Barcelona) proved to be an immediate and major success in the Spanish capital. One of the reigning group of top Spanish chefs, Santamaría works in a sophisticated environment, where the service is as impeccable as the food, and the exquisite combinations of Mediterranean ingredients are accompanied by a comprehensive and daring wine list. Go with an appetite and lots of time (a minimum of three hours) because a meal here is ceremonious. If you're a meat lover, don't leave without trying the *jarrete* (veal shank). And if you love cheese you'll swoon for the cheese sampler offered before dessert. ✉ *Paseo de la Castellana 57, Chamberí* ☎ *91/210–8840* ✍ *Reservations essential* ▭ *AE, DC, MC, V* ⏲ *Closed Sun., Easter wk, and Aug. No lunch Sat.* Ⓜ *Gregorio Marañón* ✣ *H1.*

$$$–$$$$ ECLECTIC ✕ **Viridiana.** A black-and-white color scheme punctuated with prints from Luis Buñuel's classic film, the restaurant's namesake, is the hallmark of this relaxed, somewhat cramped bistro. Iconoclast chef Abraham Garcia says "market-based" is too narrow a description for his creative menu, which changes every two weeks: standards include *foie de pato con chutney de frutas* (duck liver with fruit chutney) and *huevos sobre mousse de hongos* (eggs on a mushroom mousse). The wine choices can be overwhelming, so ask for help, and save room to try one of the creative desserts such as the sour chocolate tamale wrapped in banana leaves. ✉ *Juan de Mena 14, Retiro* ☎ *91/531–1039* ✍ *Reservations essential* ▭ *AE, MC, V* ⏲ *Closed Sun. and Easter* Ⓜ *Retiro* ✣ *H3.*

$$$$ BASQUE Fodor's Choice ★ ✕ **Zalacaín.** This restaurant decorated in dramatic dark wood, gleaming silver, and apricot hues introduced nouvelle Basque cuisine to Spain in the 1970s and has since become a Madrid classic. It's particularly known for using the best and freshest seasonal products available as well as for having the best service in town. Making use of ingredients such as various fungi, game, and hard-to-find seafood, the food here tends to be unusual—it's not one of those places where they cook with liquid nitrogen, yet you won't find these dishes elsewhere. ✉ *Alvarez de Baena 4, Salamanca* ☎ *91/561–4840* ✍ *Reservations essential; jacket and tie* ▭ *AE, DC, V* ⏲ *Closed Sun., Aug., and Easter wk. No lunch Sat.* Ⓜ *Gregorio Marañón* ✣ *H1.*

CHUECA AND MALASAÑA

¢ MOROCCAN ✕ **Arabia.** Pass through the heavy wool rug hanging at the entrance and you may feel as if you've entered Aladdin's cave, decorated as this restaurant is with adobe, wood, brass, whitewashed walls, and lavish palms. Full of young, boisterous madrileños, this is a great place to try elaborate Moroccan dishes like stewed lamb with honey and dry fruits or vegetarian favorites such as couscous with milk and pumpkin. To start, order the best falafel outside of Morocco or the yogurt cucumber salad. Reservations are essential on the weekend. ✉ *Piamonte 12, Chueca* ☎ *91/532–5321* ⏲ *Closed Mon. No lunch Tues.–Fri.* Ⓜ *Chueca* ⊕ *F2.*

$$$$ ECLECTIC Fodor's Choice ★ ✕ **Asiana.** Young chef Jaime Renedo surprises even the most jaded palates in this unique setting—his mother's Asian antiques furniture store, which used to be a ham-drying shed: seats are amid a Vietnamese bed, a life-size Buddha, and other merchandise for sale. Renedo brings to his job a contagious enthusiasm for cooking and experimentation as well as painstaking attention to detail, and the eclectic 16-dish fixed menu perfectly balances Spanish, East Asian, Peruvian, and Japanese cooking traditions. If you're willing to forfeit exclusiveness but want to indulge in a milder version of the chef's creations, try the adjacent and much more affordable Asiana Next Door. ✉ *Travesía de San Mateo 4, Chueca* ☎ *91/310–4020 or 91/310–0965* ✍ *Reservations essential* ▭ *AE, MC, V* ⏲ *Closed Sun., Mon., and Aug. No lunch* Ⓜ *Tribunal* ⊕ *E1.*

¢ MEDITERRANEAN ✕ **Bazaar.** The owners of the successful central restaurant La Finca de Susana expanded their repertoire and opened this Chueca spot, which resembles an old-fashioned convenience store. Done in tones of white, Bazaar serves low-priced, creative Mediterranean food of reasonable quality in a trendy environment. The square-shaped upper floor has large windows facing the street, high ceilings, and hardwood floors; the downstairs is larger but less interesting. Standout dishes include the tuna *rosbif* (roasted and sliced thinly, like beef) with mango chutney and the tender ox with Parmesan and arugula. For dessert, a popular choice is the *chocolatísimo* (chocolate soufflé). To get a table, arrive by 1 for lunch and by 8:30 for dinner. ✉ *C. Libertad 21, Chueca* ☎ *91/523–3905* ✍ *Reservations not accepted* ▭ *MC, V* Ⓜ *Chueca* ⊕ *F2.*

$ AMERICAN ✕ **Home Burger.** If you're getting nostalgic after days of traveling across Spain, don't miss out on this mishmash of two deeply ingrained American concepts—the hamburger and the diner—with a European twist. The result is a very affordable menu, favored by Chueca and Malasaña hipsters, that includes your traditional beef hamburgers but also plenty of unusual offerings, such the Tandoori burger; the Mexican, with chicken, avocado, and a salsa made with red chiles; the *Caprichosa*, with Brie and onion jam; or the vegetarian options with falafel or Indian pakoras. ✉ *San Marcos 26, Chueca* ☎ *91/522–9728* Ⓜ *Chueca* ✉ *Espíritu Santo 12, Malasaña* ☎ *91/521–8531* ✍ *Reservations essential* ▭ *MC, V* Ⓜ *Tribunal* ⊕ *D1, E2.*

$ MEDITERRANEAN ✕ **La Musa.** The trendy, elegant vibe and creative menu of unique salads and tapas (try the *bomba,* a potato filled with meat or vegetables in a spinach sauce, or the huge marinated venison brochette) draw a stylish young crowd. Breakfast is served during the week, and there's a good fixed-price lunch menu. The second, bigger location in Plaza de la Paja in La Latina has a larger menu and an expensive ($$$) and even trendier adjunct speakeasy/restaurant in the basement called Junk Club—it has vintage decor and über-sophisticated dishes such as the ribs Cuba Libre (in a rum and Coke sauce) and a reinvented chocolate con churros, served here in a cup with foie and mascarpone cream, with churros on the side. Show up early or expect to wait. ✉ *Manuela Malasaña 18, Malasaña* ☎ *91/448–7558* Ⓜ *Bilbao* 🌐 *www.lamusalatina.*

com ⚠ *Reservations not accepted* ✉ *Costanilla de San Andrés 12, Pl. de la Paja, La Latina* ☎ *91/354–0255* ▭ *DC, MC, V* Ⓜ *La Latinao* ✣ *D1, B5.*

$–$$ SPANISH Fodor's Choice ★ ✕ **Mercado de la Reina.** Plentiful and inexpensive tapas and succulent larger portions—scrambled eggs with a variety of meats and vegetables, tasty local cheeses, and salads—make this large, tastefully decorated bar/restaurant a handy stop for people who want to refuel without having to sit through a long meal. And where else can you sip a beer standing next to an olive tree? There's also a more formal dining area with long tables where groups can share some of the more elaborate meat and fish options and an outdoor terrace. A lounge downstairs—with an extensive gin menu—accommodates those who want to keep the night rolling. ✉ *Gran Vía 12, Chueca* ☎ *91/521–3198* ▭ *AE, MC, V* Ⓜ *Banco de España* ✣ *E3.*

$ MEDITERRANEAN ✕ **Nína.** One of the first restaurants to bring sophistication and refinement to a neighborhood best known for its wild and unrestricted spirit, Nina has an airy loftlike interior with high ceilings, exposed brick-and-alabaster walls, and dark hardwood floors. Waiters dressed in black serve the creative Mediterranean cuisine with an Eastern touch to a mostly young, hip crowd. Highlights include goat cheese *milhojas* (pastry puffs), glazed codfish with honey sauce, and venison and mango in a mushroom sauce. There is a good weekday fixed-price lunch menu, and brunch is served on weekends. ✉ *Manuela Malasaña 10, Malasaña* ☎ *91/591–0046* ▭ *AE, DC, MC, V* Ⓜ *Bilbao* ✣ *D1.*

$ ITALIAN ✕ **Pulcinella.** Tired of not being able to find a true Italian restaurant in the city, owner Enrico opened this homey trattoria filled with memorabilia of Italian artists. Always bustling and frequented by families and young couples, it seems like a direct transplant from Naples. Superb fresh pastas; the best pizzas and focaccias in the city, cooked in a brick oven; and the homemade tiramisu are the standout dishes. The branch across the street, Cantina di Pulcinella, serves the same food but permits smoking. ✉ *Regueros 7, Chueca* ☎ *91/319–7363* ⚠ *Reservations essential* ▭ *AE, DC, MC, V* Ⓜ *Chueca* ✣ *F1.*

LA LATINA

$$$ SPANISH ✕ **Casa Botín.** The *Guinness Book of Records* calls this the world's oldest restaurant (est. 1725), and Hemingway called it the best. The latter claim may be a bit over the top, but the restaurant *is* excellent and extremely charming (and so successful that the owners opened a "branch" in Miami, Florida). There are four floors of tile and wood-beam dining rooms, and, if you're seated upstairs, you'll pass centuries-old ovens. Musical groups called *tunas* (mostly made up of students dressed in medieval costumes) often come by to perform. The specialties are *cochinillo* (roast pig) and *cordero* (roast lamb). It's rumored Goya washed dishes here before he made it as a painter. ✉ *Cuchilleros 17, off Pl. Mayor, La Latina* ☎ *91/366–4217* ▭ *AE, DC, MC, V* Ⓜ *Tirso de Molina* ✣ *C5.*

$–$$ SPANISH ✕ **Casa Ciriaco.** One of Madrid's most traditional restaurants—host to a long list of Spain's who's who, from royalty to philosophers, painters, and bullfighters—serves up simple home cooking in an unpretentious environment. You can get a carafe of Valdepeñas or a split of

Rioja reserve to accompany the *perdiz con judiones* (partridge with broad beans). The *pepitoria de gallina* (hen in an almond sauce) is another favorite. ✉ *C. Mayor 84, La Latina* ☎ *91/559–5066* ▬ *DC, MC, V* ⏲ *Closed Wed. and Aug.* Ⓜ *Ópera* ✥ *B4.*

> **DEALS AND DISCOUNTS**
>
> Most restaurants offer a fixed *menú del día* for lunch that includes a starter, main course, dessert, wine, and coffee.

2

$$–$$$ STEAK Fodor's Choice ★ **Casa Paco.** This Castilian tavern wouldn't have looked out of place two or three centuries ago, and today you can still squeeze past the old, zinc-top bar, crowded with madrileños downing Valdepeñas red wine, and into the tiled dining rooms. Feast on thick slabs of red meat, sizzling on plates so hot the meat continues to cook at your table. The Spanish consider overcooking a sin, so expect looks of dismay if you ask for your meat well done (*bien hecho*). You order by weight, so remember that a *medio kilo* is more than a pound. To start, try the *pisto manchego* (La Mancha version of ratatouille) or the Castilian *sopa de ajo* (garlic soup). ✉ *Puerta Cerrada 11, La Latina* ☎ *91/366–3166* ✍ *Reservations essential* ▬ *DC, MC, V* ⏲ *Closed Sun. and Aug.* Ⓜ *Tirso de Molina* ✥ *C5.*

$$$ SPANISH **El Landó.** This *castizo* (authentic or highly traditional) restaurant with dark wood-paneled walls lined with bottles of wine serves classic Spanish food. Specialties of the house are *huevos estrellados* (fried eggs with potatoes and sausage), grilled meats, a good selection of fish (sea bass, haddock, grouper) with many different sauces, and steak tartare. As you sit down for your meal, you'll immediately be served a plate of bread with tomato, a salad, and Spanish ham. Check out the pictures of famous celebrities who've eaten at this typically noisy landmark; they line the staircase that leads to the main dining area. ✉ *Pl. Gabriel Miró 8, La Latina* ☎ *91/366–7681* ✍ *Reservations essential* ▬ *AE, DC, MC, V* ⏲ *Closed Sun., Easter, and Aug.* Ⓜ *La Latina* ✥ *B5.*

$ BASQUE **Taberna Bilbao.** This popular tavern is somewhere between a tapas bar and a restaurant. It has three small dining areas, floor and walls of red Italian marble, plain wooden furniture, and a menu that focuses on Basque cuisine. Try any of the fish or mushroom *revueltos* (scrambled eggs), the *habas* (fava beans), or the *bacalao* (cod), and order a glass of *txakolí* (tart, young Basque white wine). ✉ *Costanilla de San Andrés 8, Pl. de la Paja, La Latina* ☎ *91/365–6125* ▬ *DC, MC, V* ⏲ *No lunch Mon.* Ⓜ *La Latina* ✥ *B5.*

MONCLOA

$$$$ BASQUE **Bokado.** Chefs Mikel and Jesús Santamaría, best known for breaking ground in the world of tapas in both Navarra and the Basque Country, have brought their talent to Madrid. Away from the bustling city center and five minutes from Moncloa, the restaurant, a spacious, elegant, and design-rich setting, is part of the Museo del Traje's building. The menu includes sophisticated interpretations of oyster, monkfish, haddock, stews, mushroom delicacies, and savory game dishes. The terrace is one of the city's best choices for summer dining. If you're not feeling flush, try the more affordable tapas menu in the adjacent cafeteria. ✉ *Av. Juan*

de Herrera 2, Moncloa ☎ 91/549–0041 ▭ AE, MC, V ⏲ Closed Sun. and Mon. Ⓜ *Ciudad Universitaria ✣ B1.*

SOL AND PALACIO

$$ MEDITERRANEAN ✕ **Genoveva de Barri**. A few blocks from Palacio Real, this charming restaurant is on a *callejuela* (small street) that's easy to miss. The diminutive space is the playground of young chef and sommelier Gonzalo Lara; inside, a handful of tables are accented with a few baroque touches: white-and-gold wallpaper, fringed mirrors, and a hanging crystal lamp. The short menu is full of surprises such as duck tartare; scrambled eggs with lobster, asparagus, and mushrooms; and an unconventional, although expert, selection of wines. ✉ *Espejo 10, Palacio ☎ 91/547–8014 ✍ Reservations essential ▭ AE, V ⏲ Closed Sun. No lunch Sat. and Mon.* Ⓜ *Ópera ✣ C4.*

$$ SPANISH ✕ **La Bola**. First opened as a *botellería* (wine shop) in 1802, La Bola slowly developed into a tapas bar and then into a full-fledged restaurant. The traditional setting is the draw: the bar is original, and the dining nooks, decorated with polished wood, Spanish tile, and lace curtains, are charming. Amazingly, the restaurant belongs to its founding family, with the seventh generation currently in training. Try the house specialty: *cocido a la madrileña* (a hearty meal of broth, garbanzo beans, vegetables, potatoes, and pork). ✉ *Bola 5, Palacio ☎ 91/547–6930 ▭ No credit cards ⏲ No dinner Sun., and Sat. in Aug. Closed Sun. in Aug.* Ⓜ *Ópera ✣ B3.*

¢–$ MEDITERRANEAN ✕ **La Finca de Susana**. A diverse crowd is drawn to this loftlike space for the grilled vegetables, oven-cooked *bacalao* (salt cod) with spinach, and the caramelized duck with plums and couscous. Not irrelevant is the fact that it is also one of the best bargains in the city. The hardwood floor is offset by warm colors, and one end of the dining room has a huge bookcase lined with wine bottles. Arrive by 1 for lunch and 8:30 for dinner or be prepared to wait. ✉ *C. Arlabán 4, Cortes ☎ 91/369–3557 ✍ Reservations not accepted ▭ MC, V* Ⓜ *Sevilla ✣ E4.*

$$ MEDITERRANEAN ✕ **La Gastroteca de Santiago**. Among the trendy restaurants with talented chefs, this one offers good value, with a short and creative menu (barely a dozen dishes) that changes monthly and expert wine advice. It's an excellent place to see where contemporary creative Spanish cuisine is heading without having to guess what's on your plate. The restaurant seats only 16, and the open kitchen is as big as the dining area. If you feel adventurous, ask for the €60 sampler menu (€20 more if you get the wine to partner), or show up for its Sunday-only special rice dishes. ✉ *Pl. de Santiago 1, Palacio ☎ 91/548–0707 ✍ Reservations essential ▭ AE, MC, V ⏲ Closed Mon. No lunch Sun.* Ⓜ *Ópera ✣ B4.*

$$$$ LA NUEVA COCINA Fodor's Choice ★ ✕ **La Terraza—Casino de Madrid**. This rooftop terrace just off Puerta del Sol is in one of Madrid's oldest, most exclusive clubs (the *casino* is a club for gentlemen, not gamblers; it's members only, but the restaurant is open to all). When it opened the food was inspired and overseen by celebrity chef Ferran Adriá, but as the years have gone by, chef Francisco Roncero has built a reputation of his own. Try any of the light and tasty mousses, foams, and liquid jellies, or indulge in the unique tapas—experiments of flavor, texture, and temperature, such as the salmon *ventresca* in miso with radish ice cream or the spherified sea

The dishes at La Terraza are as enchanting to look at as the patrons at this classy restaurant.

urchin. There's also a sampler menu. ✉ *Alcalá 15, Sol* ☎ *91/521–8700* ✍ *Reservations essential* ▭ *AE, DC, MC, V* ⏲ *Closed Sun. and Aug. No lunch Sat.* Ⓜ *Sol* ✥ *E3.*

¢ SPANISH

✕ **Nueva Galicia.** This small family-run bar and restaurant has long been one of the best values in the center of Madrid—it's two blocks from the Puerta del Sol—and you can eat inside or, during summer, at tables on the pedestrian-only side street. It's usually noisy and serves simple food, but a starter, main course, dessert, and a full bottle of wine can be consumed for a ridiculously low €8.50, or you can choose to share some of the larger portions (*raciones*) of octopus, cuttlefish, *lacón* (cooked ham with Galician potatoes), or *pisto* (a Spanish ratatouille). If you're heading out, get a sandwich to go. ✉ *Cruz 6, Sol* ☎ *91/522–5289* ▭ *No credit cards* ⏲ *Closed Sun. and Aug.* Ⓜ *Sevilla* ✥ *E4.*

WHERE TO STAY

Madrid kicked off the new millennium with a hotel boom, and the last decade has seen its number of hotel rooms nearly double. From 2009 to 2010 alone, the number of hotel rooms available increased by 4,000, and hotels in construction will add another 4,000.

Plenty of the new arrivals are medium-price chain hotels that try to combine striking design with affordable prices. A step higher is the handful of new hotels that lure the hip crowd with top-notch design and superb food and nightlife. These have caused quite a stir in the five-star range and forced some of the more traditional hotels—long favored by dignitaries, star athletes, and artists—to enhance their food and service.

BEST BETS FOR MADRID LODGING

Having trouble deciding where to stay in Madrid? Fodor's writers have selected some of their favorites in the lists below. Details are in the full reviews.

Fodor's Choice ★

AC Palacio del Retiro, $$$$, p. 119

De las Letras, $$$–$$$$, p. 123

Hostal Adriano, ¢, p. 123

Hotel Intur Palacio San Martín, $$$–$$$$, p. 124

Hotel Urban, $$$$, p. 116

Room Mate Alicia, $, p. 117

Room Mate Óscar, $, p. 122

By Price

¢

Hostal Adriano, ¢, p. 123

$

Abalú, $, p. 122

Chic & Basic Mayerling, $, p. 123

Inglés, $, p. 116

Room Mate Alicia, $, p. 117

Room Mate Óscar, $, p. 122

$$

Hotel Preciados, $–$$, p. 124

$$$

Hotel Catalonia Las Cortes, $$–$$$, p. 116

Radisson Blu, $$–$$$, p. 117

$$$$

AC Santo Mauro, $$$$, p. 120

Hospes Madrid, $$$–$$$$, p. 120

Hotel NH Paseo del Prado, $$$–$$$$, p. 120

Hotel Urban, $$$$, p. 116

ME Reina Victoria, $$$$, p. 117

Orfila, $$$$, p. 121

Silken Puerta de América, $$$$, p. 121

Westin Palace, $$$$, p. 122

By Experience

MOST CHARMING

Abalú, $, p. 122

AC Santo Mauro, $$$$, p. 120

Hospes Madrid, $$$–$$$$, p. 120

Hostal Adriano, ¢, p. 123

Hotel Intur Palacio San Martín, $$$–$$$$, p. 124

Orfila, $$$$, p. 121

Quo Puerta del Sol, $$–$$$, p. 124

Room Mate Alicia, $, p. 117

Room Mate Laura, $, p. 124

MOST HISTORIC

Hotel Intur Palacio San Martín, $$$–$$$$, p. 124

Ritz, $$$$, p. 121

Tryp Ambassador, $$–$$$, p. 125

Westin Palace, $$$$, p. 122

BEST DESIGN

Abalú, $, p. 122

De las Letras, $$$–$$$$, p. 123

Hotel Urban, $$$$, p. 116

ME Reina Victoria, $$$$, p. 117

Room Mate Alicia, $, p. 117

Room Mate Laura, $, p. 124

Room Mate Óscar, $, p. 122

Silken Puerta de America, $$$$, p. 121

Vincci Soho, $$$–$$$$, p. 119

BEST FOR FAMILIES

Jardín de Recoletos, $$$, p. 121

Suite Prado, $$, p. 119

MOST CENTRAL

Hotel Intur Palacio San Martín, $$$–$$$$, p. 124

Hotel Urban, $$$$, p. 116

Radisson Blu, $$–$$$, p. 117

Ritz, $$$$, p. 121

Room Mate Alicia, $, p. 117

Room Mate Laura, $, p. 124

Westin Palace, $$$$, p. 122

BEST FOR HIPSTERS

Abalú, $, p. 122

Chic & Basic Mayerling, $, p. 123

De las Letras, $$$–$$$$, p. 123

Hostal Adriano, ¢, p. 123

Hotel Urban, $$$$, p. 116

ME Reina Victoria, $$$$, p. 117

Room Mate Alicia, $, p. 117

Room Mate Laura, $, p. 124

Room Mate Óscar, $, p. 122

WHERE SHOULD I STAY?

	Neighborhood Vibe	Pros	Cons
Barrio de las Letras (including Carrera de San Jerónimo and Paseo del Prado)	A magnet for tourists, this classic literary nest has several pedestrian-only streets. Most of the exciting new hotel openings are here.	Renovated Plaza Santa Ana and Plaza del Ángel; the emergence of posh hotels and restaurants; conveniently between the oldest part of the city and all the major art museums.	Noisy, especially around Plaza Santa Ana; some bars and restaurants overpriced due to the tourists.
Chamberí, Retiro, and Salamanca	Swanky, posh, and safe, these are the neighborhoods many high-end hotels and restaurants call home.	Quiet at day's end; plenty of good restaurants; home to the upscale shopping (Salamanca) and residential (Salamanca and the eastern side of Retiro) areas.	Blander and with less character (except for the expensive area of Retiro, which is also less lively) than other districts; expensive.
Chueca and Malasaña	Vibrant and bustling, this is where you want to be if you're past your twenties but still don't want to be in bed before midnight.	These barrios burst with a bit of everything: busy nightlife, alternative shops, charming cafés, and fancy and inexpensive local and international restaurants.	Extremely loud, especially on the weekends; dirtier than most other neighborhoods.
Palacio and Sol	Anchored by the locally flavored Plaza Mayor, this historic quarter is full of narrow streets and taverns.	Has the most traditional feel of Madrid neighborhoods; lodging and dining of all sorts, including many inexpensive (though usually undistinguished) hostels and old-flavor taverns.	Can be tough to navigate; many tourist traps.

Meanwhile, hostals and small hotels have shown that low prices can walk hand in hand with good taste and friendly service.

The Gran Vía, a big commercial street, cuts through many neighborhoods. During the day it has a good feel of Madrid's hustle and bustle and nightlife energy but it does lose a bit of its charm when the stores are closed.

Use the coordinate (⊕ B2) at the end of each listing to locate a site on the corresponding map.

BARRIO DE LAS LETRAS

$$–$$$ **Catalonia Moratín**. The regal corridor leading to the reception desk, the atrium with walls made partly of original granite blocks, and the magnificent main wooden staircase presided over by a lion statue best reveal this building's 18th-century origins. The other common areas, including the restaurant and a reading room with a small library, have less character. Guest rooms are comfortable, with functional wooden furniture and striped curtains and bedspreads. **Pros:** grand, quiet building; spacious rooms. **Cons:** street looks a bit scruffy. ✉ *Calle Atocha 23,*

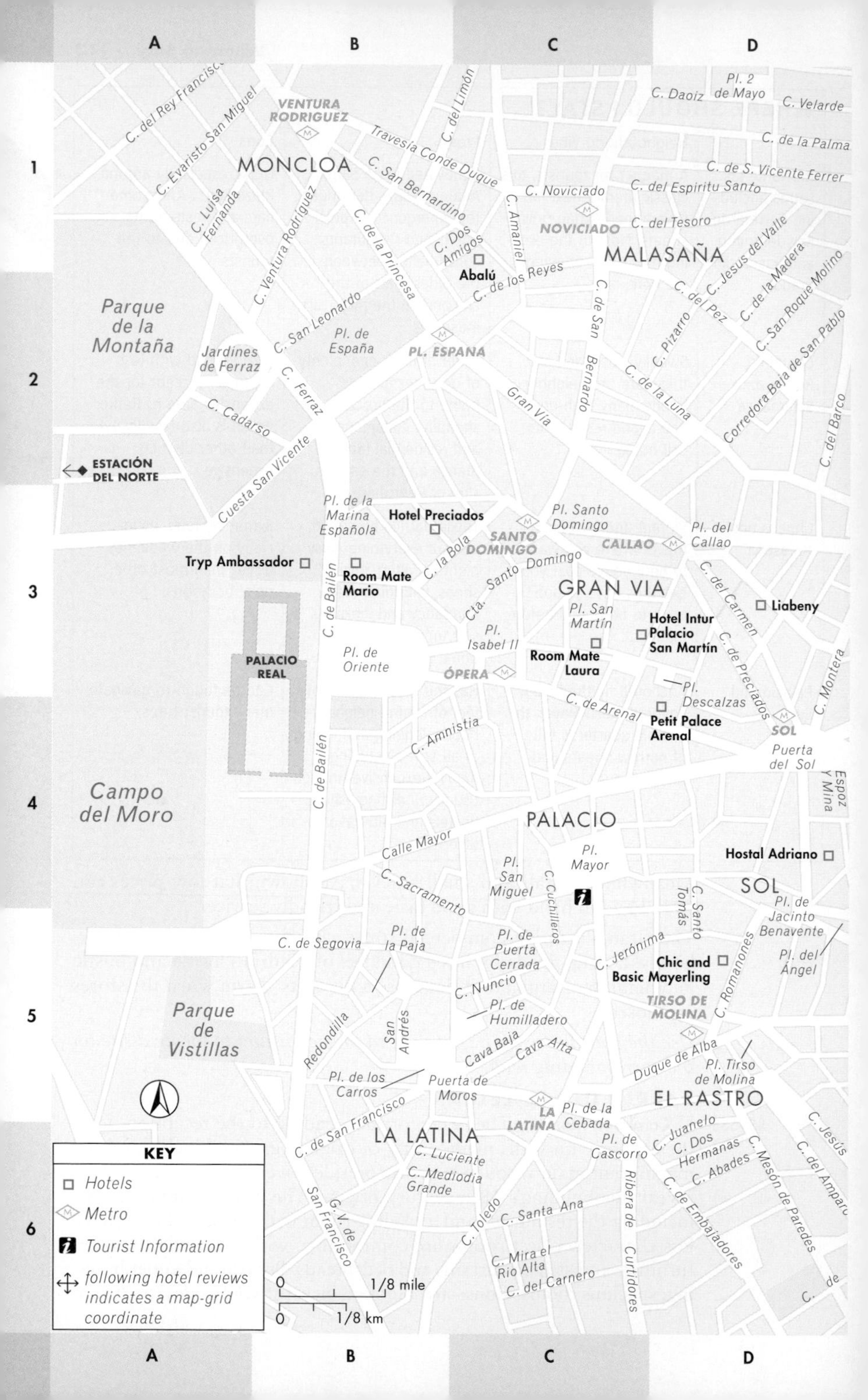

A
B
C
D
1
2
3
4
5
6
MONCLOA
MALASAÑA
GRAN VIA
PALACIO
SOL
EL RASTRO
LA LATINA
VENTURA RODRIGUEZ
NOVICIADO
PL. ESPANA
SANTO DOMINGO
CALLAO
ÓPERA
SOL
TIRSO DE MOLINA
LA LATINA
C. del Rey Francisco
C. Evaristo San Miguel
C. Luisa Fernanda
C. Ventura Rodriguez
C. de la Princesa
C. San Bernardino
Travesía Conde Duque
C. del Limón
C. Amaniel
C. Dos Amigos
C. de los Reyes
C. Noviciado
C. del Espiritu Santo
C. del Tesoro
C. Daoiz
Pl. 2 de Mayo
C. Velarde
C. de la Palma
C. de S. Vicente Ferrer
C. Jesus del Valle
C. de la Madera
C. San Roque Molino
C. del Pez
C. Pizarro
C. de San Bernardo
C. de la Luna
Corredora Baja de San Pablo
C. del Barco
Gran Vía
Parque de la Montaña
Jardines de Ferraz
C. San Leonardo
Pl. de España
C. Ferraz
C. Cadarso
Cuesta San Vicente
ESTACIÓN DEL NORTE
Pl. de la Marina Española
Hotel Preciados
Tryp Ambassador
Room Mate Mario
C. la Bola
Cta. Santo Domingo
Pl. Santo Domingo
Pl. del Callao
C. del Carmen
Liabeny
Pl. San Martín
Hotel Intur Palacio San Martín
Room Mate Laura
Pl. Isabel II
C. de Bailén
PALACIO REAL
Pl. de Oriente
Pl. Descalzas
C. de Arenal
Petit Palace Arenal
C. de Preciados
C. Montera
Puerta del Sol
Espoz y Mina
C. Amnistia
Campo del Moro
Calle Mayor
Pl. Mayor
Hostal Adriano
C. Sacramento
Pl. San Miguel
C. Cuchilleros
C. Santo Tomás
Pl. de Jacinto Benavente
Pl. del Ángel
C. de Segovia
Pl. de la Paja
Pl. de Puerta Cerrada
C. Jerónima
Chic and Basic Mayerling
C. Romanones
C. Nuncio
Pl. de Humilladero
Parque de Vistillas
Redondilla
San Andrés
Cava Baja
Cava Alta
Duque de Alba
Pl. Tirso de Molina
Pl. de los Carros
Puerta de Moros
Pl. de la Cebada
C. de San Francisco
C. Luciente
C. Mediodia Grande
Pl. de Cascorro
C. Juanelo
C. Dos Hermanas
C. Abades
C. Mesón de Paredes
C. Jesús
C. del Amparo
C. de Embajadores
Ribera de Curtidores
C. Toledo
C. Santa Ana
G. V. de San Francisco
C. Mira el Rio Alta
C. del Carnero
C. de
KEY
Hotels
Metro
Tourist Information
following hotel reviews indicates a map-grid coordinate
0
1/8 mile
0
1/8 km

E
F
G
H
1
2
3
4
5
6
Where to Stay in Madrid
ALONSO MARTINEZ
TRIBUNAL
COLON
SERRANO
CHUECA
GRAN VIA
BANCO DE ESPANA
SEVILLA
ANTON MARTIN
LAVAPIES
ATOCHA
CHAMBERI
CHAMARTIN
CHUECA
SALAMANCA
CORTES
RETIRO
BARRIO DE LAS LETRAS
LAVAPIÉS
AC Santo Mauro
Orfila
Gran Meliá Fénix
Silken Puerta de América
MUSEO ARQUEOLÓGICO/ BIBLIOTECA NACIONAL
Jardín de Recoletos
Hospes Madrid
Room Mate Oscar
De Las Letras
Ateneo Hotel
AC Palacio del Retiro
Quo Puerta del Sol
Hotel Urban
Inglés
Suite Prado
Ritz
Westin Palace
Vincci Soho
ME Reina Victoria
Hotel Catalonia Las Cortes
Room Mate Alicia
Hotel NH Paseo del Prado
MUSEO DEL PRADO
Catalonia Moratín
Radisson Blue
Chic and Basic Atocha
ATOCHA TRAIN STATION
Parque del Retiro
Jardín Botánico
C. de Barceló
C. Beneficiencia
C. San Mateo
C. San Lorenzo
Pl. San Ildefonso
C. de Orellana
C. Santa Teresa
C. Fernando VI
C. Alcalá Galiano
C. de Génova
Castellana
Pl. de Colón
C. Goya
C. Bárbara de Braganza
C. Beguerero
C. de Pelayo
C. San Gregorio
C. Hernán Cortés
C. de Gravina
C. de Piamonte
Paseo de Recoletos
C. de Jorge
C. de Villanueva
C. de Serrano
C. de Claudio Coello
C. de Valverde
C. Fuencarral
C. de Hortaleza
Pl. Chueca
C. de Almirante
C. del Barquillo
C. de Recoletos
C. Salustiano Olozaga
Pl. de la Independencia
C. de las Infantas
Pl. del Rey
Pl. de la Cibeles
Alcalá
Red de San Luis
Reina
Gran Vía
Av. México
Montalbán
Calle de Alcalá
C. Marqués de Cuba
Paseo del Prado
C. de Alfonso XI
C. de Montalbán
C. Juan de Mena
C. de Los Madrazo
C. de Sevilla
C. de Zorrilla
Pl. de la Lealtad
C. Antonio Maura
C. de San Jerónimo
C. de la Cruz
C. Príncipe
V. de la Vega
Pl. de las Cortés
Pl. Cánovas del Castillo
C. Felipe IV
Ruz de Alarcón
C. Alfonso XII
C. del Prado
C. Academia
C. Casado del Alisal
Echegaray
León
C. de San Agustín
C. Cervantes
C. del Moreto
C. Lope de la Vega
C. de las Huertas
Paseo Rojas Clemente
C. de Moratín
C. San Pedro
C. Fúcar
C. de la Magdalena
Ave María
C. de la Cabeza
C. Calvario
C. Lavapiés
C. San Ildefonso
C. Atocha
Gta. del Emperador Carlos V
C. Claudio Moyano
C. de Zurita
C. del Salitre
C. San Cosme y San Damián
C. de Santa Isabel
y María
C. de la Fe
Sombrerete
Pl. Lavapiés
Dr. Piga
C. de Argumosa
C. del Doctor
C. Fourquet
C. Hospital
Santa María de la Cabeza
de las Delicias Delicias

Barrio de las Letras ☎ *91/369–7171* 🌐 *www.hoteles-catalonia.es* *63 rooms* *In-room: safe, Wi-Fi. In-hotel: restaurant, bar, Wi-Fi hotspot* *AE, DC, MC, V* Ⓜ *Tirso de Molina* ✥ *E5.*

$ **Chic & Basic Atocha.** This is the latest addition (summer 2009) of the chain that competes with Room Mate for the young urban traveler who doesn't mind sacrificing some services—for instance, there's no bar or restaurant, but you get a breakfast of fruit, juice, and a croissant in a recyclable paper bag delivered every morning and a small lounge area with free coffee and tea by the reception desk—in exchange for lower prices. Rooms are not large, with stark white furnishings and bright color accents. Bathrooms are small. Staff is generally friendly, and there's a nice deck with a view on the top floor, but be aware lodgings are distinctly not fancy. **Pros:** great location between Lavapiés and the Barrio de las Letras and a stone's throw from the Reina Sofía; free Wi-Fi. **Cons:** bare services; the fact that there's no separation between the toilet and the shower may be off-putting for some; exterior rooms facing Calle Atocha are a bit more expensive. ✉ *Atocha 113, Barrio de las Letras* ☎ *91/369–2895* 🌐 *www.chicandbasic.com* *36 rooms* *In-room: Wi-Fi. In-hotel: Wi-Fi hotspot* *AE, D, DC, MC, V* *CP* Ⓜ *Atocha* ✥ *F5.*

$$–$$$ **Hotel Catalonia Las Cortes.** A late-18th-century palace formerly owned by the duke of Noblejas, this hotel retains a good part of its aristocratic past: a gorgeous wooden staircase, some of the old moldings, and stained-glass windows. It has a classic feel without being ostentatious or overwhelming. Rooms are elegant, and bathrooms are quite decent in size for Madrid. Better still, the hotel is a few yards from Plaza Santa Ana. **Pros:** tasteful room decor; big walk-in shower; triple rooms available; great location. **Cons:** common areas are rather dull. ✉ *Prado 6, Barrio de las Letras* ☎ *91/389–6051* 🌐 *www.hoteles-catalonia.com* *65 rooms, 8 junior suites, 2 suites* *In-room: safe, Wi-Fi. In-hotel: restaurant, bar, laundry facilities, Wi-Fi hotspot* *AE, DC, MC, V* Ⓜ *Sevilla, Antón Martín* ✥ *E4.*

$$$$ Fodor's Choice ★ **Hotel Urban.** With a stylish mix of the ancient (New Guinean carvings in the lobby, a small Egyptian museum, and antique Chinese or Burmese statues in every room, all belonging to the owner, a renowned art collector) and daring sophistication (the tall alabaster column in the lobby's atrium, the tiled and gold-inlay wall on the main staircase, and the sleek cocktail bar), this is the hotel that best conveys Madrid's new cosmopolitan spirit. Rooms, done in dark hues, are less flamboyant, and some are small. There's a great restaurant and an ultrachic bar on the roof, where the glamorous gather on summer nights to enjoy the views and sip champagne cocktails. **Pros:** excellent restaurant and happening bar; rooftop swimming pool. **Cons:** rooms near the elevator can be noisy. ✉ *Carrera de San Jerónimo 34, Barrio de las Letras* ☎ *91/787–7770* 🌐 *www.derbyhotels.com* *96 rooms, 3 junior suites, 4 suites* *In-room: safe, Wi-Fi. In-hotel: 2 restaurants, bar, pool, gym, parking (paid)* *AE, DC, MC, V* Ⓜ *Sevilla* ✥ *E4.*

$ **Inglés.** Virginia Woolf was among the first luminaries to discover this hotel in the middle of the old city's bar-and-restaurant district. Since then, it has attracted more than its share of less-celebrated artists and

2

writers. Half of the rooms were tiled and painted in 2005, and new bathrooms were installed, but the decor still resembles the ornate and outdated lobby. You get twice the space for what you'd pay for a standard double elsewhere, and if your room faces Calle Echegaray, you can get an unusual aerial view of the medieval quarter, which is all red tiles and ramshackle gables. Suites, which are double rooms with a salon, are a bargain. **Pros:** huge rooms by local standards; centrally located. **Cons:** outdated decor; noisy street; standoffish staff. ✉ *Echegaray 8, Barrio de las Letras* ☎ *91/429–6551* *58 rooms* *In-room: no a/c (some). In-hotel: restaurant, bar, gym, parking (paid)* *AE, DC, MC, V* Ⓜ *Sevilla* ✣ *E4.*

$$$$ **ME Reina Victoria.** A few bulls' heads hanging in the lounge and some abstract pictures of bullfighting scattered around this ultramodern hotel are all that remain to remind visitors that it was once where bullfighters convened before heading off to Las Ventas. The old flair has been superseded by cutting-edge amenties like a USB port for recharging iPods, MP3 players, and the like; a large flat-screen TV with surround sound; an advanced memory-foam mattress; and a minibar that's double the usual size. The hotel has a good restaurant, and two of the city's fanciest and busiest bars are here, including one on the roof with a 360-degree panoramic view of the city. **Pros:** unbeatable location; modern vibe; trendy bars and restaurant. **Cons:** rooms are a bit small. ✉ *Pl. Santa Ana 14, Barrio de las Letras* ☎ *91/531–4500* 🌐 *www.solmelia.com* *182 rooms, 9 suites* *In-room: safe, DVD, Wi-Fi. In-hotel: restaurant, bars, laundry facilities, Wi-Fi hotspot, parking (paid), some pets allowed* *AE, DC, MC, V* Ⓜ *Sol* ✣ *E4.*

$$$–$$$$ **Radisson Blu.** The Radisson chain may not be Scandinavian anymore, but this outpost across from the Prado Museum retains the austere lines of its lineage: the lobby and guest rooms are decorated in black and gray tones, and only slight orange and purple splashes (in the bar/lounge sitting area and on the pillows and bedspreads in the rooms) remind you of the zest of the Mediterranean. The counterbalance is painstaking attention to detail: bulletproof sound insulation in an otherwise noisy neighborhood and eye-catching details such as the headboards printed with screens of emblematic Madrid buildings, roomy beds, towel heaters, an antifog mirror in the bathroom, and free fancy Nespresso machine coffee. The hotel also has a small pool and spa area to help you unwind on hot summer days. **Pros:** terrific location; wide array of services. **Cons:** some standard rooms are rather small; pricey breakfast. ✉ *Moratín 52, Barrio de las Letras* ☎ *91/524–2626* 🌐 *www.radissonblu.com/pradohotel-madrid* *54 rooms, 6 suites* *In-room: safe, Wi-Fi. In-hotel: restaurant, bar, spa* *AE, DC, MC, V* Ⓜ *Atocha* ✣ *G5.*

$$ **Room Mate Alicia.** The all-white lobby with curving walls, ceiling,
Fodor's Choice ★
and lamps sets the mood for the mostly young urban visitors to this former trench coat factory. Carpeted rooms, though not large, are very modern; the black-slate bathrooms, all with showers (no tubs), are in the bedroom, separated only by a glass door. For just a few more euros you can upgrade to an executive room with a terrace or a minisuite with large windows overlooking Plaza Santa Ana. **Pros:** great value;

Hotel Urban

Hostel Adriano

Palacio del Retiro

chic design; laid-back atmosphere; unbeatable location. **Cons:** standard rooms are small; some might not like that bathrooms are not in a separate space. ✉ *Prado 2, Barrio de las Letras* ☎ *91/389–6095* 🌐 *www.room-matehoteles.com* ⇨ *31 rooms, 3 suites* ☝ *In-room: Wi-Fi. In-hotel: bar, Wi-Fi hotspot, parking (paid)* ▭ *AE, DC, MC, V* Ⓜ *Sevilla* ✣ *E4.*

> **ROOM MATES**
>
> The Room Mate chain has hit on a winning combination: great design and limited services at a low price. They all have free Wi-Fi, and breakfast is served until noon. Room Mate Mario was the first of the now worldwide chain and has since been joined in Madrid by Laura, Alicia, and Oscar. Full reviews are in the neighborhoods. 🌐 *www.room-matehoteles.com.*

$–$$ **Suite Prado.** Popular with Americans, this stylish apartment hotel is near the Prado, the Thyssen-Bornemisza, and the Plaza Santa Ana tapas area. The attractive attic studios on the fourth floor have sloped ceilings with wood beams; there are larger suites downstairs. All apartments are brightly decorated and have marble baths and basic kitchens. The property has an agreement with the nearby Hotel Prado for breakfast, which can also be ordered as room service. Triples and quadruples are a great deal. **Pros:** large rooms; great for families and longer stays. **Cons:** a bit noisy; kitchens not always available for use. ✉ *Manuel Fernández y González 10, Barrio de las Letras* ☎ *91/420–2318* 🌐 *www.suiteprado.com* ⇨ *18 suites* ☝ *In-room: safe, kitchen, Wi-Fi* ▭ *AE, DC, MC, V* Ⓜ *Sevilla* ✣ *F4.*

$$$–$$$$ **Vincci Soho.** Faithful to its surname, this hotel seems as if it has been transplanted from London or New York into one of Madrid's busiest neighborhoods. Everything on the ground floor—the lamps, the mustard-color circular divan in front of the reception desk, the meeting lounges with velvet armchairs and silk screens, the steel butterfly cutouts on the restaurant walls—emphasizes urban elegance and imagination. No two rooms are alike in shape—the hotel is made of five old private houses—but they're all comfortable and bright, even the interior ones, thanks to a large open courtyard that keeps the street noise out and lets the sun in. **Pros:** stylish; central location; great breakfast buffet. **Cons:** standard rooms are rather small and some can be noisy. ✉ *Prado 18, Barrio de las Letras* ☎ *91/141–4100* 🌐 *www.vinccihoteles.com* ⇨ *167 rooms* ☝ *In-room: safe, Wi-Fi. In-hotel: restaurant, bar, Wi-Fi hotspot, parking (paid)* ▭ *AE, DC, MC, V* Ⓜ *Sevilla, Antón Martín* ✣ *F4.*

CHAMBERÍ, RETIRO, AND SALAMANCA

$$$$ Fodor's Choice ★ **AC Palacio del Retiro.** An early-20th-century restored palatial building owned by a noble family with extravagant habits (the elevator carried the horses up and down from the exercise ring on the roof), this spectacular hotel closely follows the path of the first AC Santo Mauro with its tasteful, modern decor in a historical building. The Palacio preserves pieces of its grandiose past: baseboards and fountains covered with ceramics from Talavera, Parisian stained-glass windows, marble floors and columns, and original moldings. All rooms have superb views of the nearby Retiro Park. Bathroom doors in the double superior rooms are full-size Lichtenstein silk-screen prints. **Pros:** spacious, stylish rooms;

within walking distance of the Prado; bathrooms stocked with all sorts of complimentary products. **Cons:** pricey; lower rooms facing the park can get noisy. ✉ *Alfonso XII 14, Retiro* ☎ *91/523–7460* 🌐 *www.ac-hotels.com* *50 rooms, 8 suites* *In-room: safe, DVD, Wi-Fi. In-hotel: restaurant, bar, gym, spa, Wi-Fi hotspot, parking (paid)* *AE, DC, MC, V* Ⓜ *Retiro* ✥ *H3.*

$$$$ **AC Santo Mauro.** Once the Canadian embassy, this turn-of-the-20th-century mansion is now an intimate luxury hotel, an oasis of calm a short walk from the city center. The neoclassical architecture is accented by contemporary furniture in white, gray, aubergine, and black. Some of the rooms in the main building still maintain the original details and fixtures, and the top-notch restaurant is in what used to be the mansion's library. Views vary; request a room with a terrace overlooking the gardens. **Pros:** quite private; sizable rooms with comfortable beds; good restaurant. **Cons:** pricey; not in the historic center. ✉ *Zurbano 36, Chamberí* ☎ *91/319–6900* 🌐 *www.ac-hotels.com* *51 rooms* *In-room: DVD, Wi-Fi. In-hotel: restaurant, bar, pool, gym, Wi-Fi hotspot, parking (paid)* *AE, DC, MC, V* Ⓜ *Alonso Martínez, Rubén Darío* ✥ *F1.*

$$$$ **Gran Meliá Fénix.** An impressive lobby with marble floors, antique furniture, and a stained-glass dome ceiling define the style of this refurbished Madrid institution. Overlooking Plaza de Colón on the Castellana, the hotel is a mere hop from the posh shops of Calle Serrano. Spacious rooms are decorated in reds and golds and are amply furnished; flowers abound. Ask for a room facing the Plaza de Colón; otherwise, the view is rather dreary. **Pros:** close to shopping; great breakfast buffet. **Cons:** rather small bathrooms; below-average restaurant. ✉ *Hermosilla 2, Salamanca* ☎ *91/431–6700* 🌐 *www.solmelia.com* *214 rooms, 11 suites* *In-room: Internet. In-hotel: 2 restaurants, bar, gym, spa, Wi-Fi hotspot, parking (paid)* *AE, DC, MC, V* Ⓜ *Colón* ✥ *H1.*

$$$–$$$$ **Hospes Madrid.** One of the newest five-star additions to the city center, the Hospes has all the right ingredients for meeting the demands of today's discerning travelers: a historic 19th-century building facing Retiro Park; stylish design that isn't overwhelming; an interior patio turned into a deck; a good restaurant with an emerging and innovative young chef; and a spa with a two-page service list. **Pros:** intimate and quiet; right next to Madrid's version of Central Park. **Cons:** some rooms have a shower but no bathtub; standard rooms don't face the park. ✉ *Pl. de la Independencia 3, Retiro* ☎ *91/432–2911* 🌐 *www.hospes.com* *41 rooms, 6 suites* *In-room: DVD, Internet, Wi-Fi. In-hotel: 2 restaurants, gym, spa* *AE, DC, MC, V* Ⓜ *Retiro* ✥ *H2.*

$$$–$$$$ **Hotel NH Paseo del Prado.** Once the residence of a count, this hotel a block from the Prado is a reasonable yet luxurious alternative to the five-star establishments that populate the area. The common areas feature odd combinations, like period chairs around a brown leather couch, but guest rooms are spacious and more stylish, with hand-painted Canarian motifs, bold-colored carpets from the Royal Factory of Tapestries, and wooden furniture. The tapas bar, open to the public, is overseen by one of the city's best chefs and is a magnet for peckish passersby. **Pros:** sizable and elegant bathrooms; good location. **Cons:**

you'll have to upgrade if you want good views; extra fee for Wi-Fi. ✉ *Pl. Cánovas del Castillo 4, Retiro* ☎ *91/330–2400* 🌐 *www.nh-hoteles.es* *114 rooms, 5 suites* *In-room: safe, Wi-Fi. In-hotel: restaurant, Wi-Fi hotspot* *AE, DC, MC, V* Ⓜ *Banco de España* ✣ *F4.*

$$$ **Jardín de Recoletos.** This apartment hotel offers great value on a quiet street close to Plaza Colón and upmarket Calle Serrano. The large lobby has marble floors and a stained-glass ceiling and adjoins a café, restaurant, and the hotel's restful private garden. The large rooms, with light wood trim and beige-and-yellow furnishings, include sitting and dining areas. "Superior" rooms and suites have hydromassage baths and large terraces. Book well in advance. **Pros:** spacious rooms with kitchens; good for families. **Cons:** bland decor. ✉ *Gil de Santivañes 6, Salamanca* ☎ *91/781–1640* 🌐 *www.vphoteles.com* *36 rooms, 7 suites* *In-room: kitchen, Internet, Wi-Fi. In-hotel: restaurant, room service, Wi-Fi hotspot, parking (paid)* *AE, DC, MC, V* Ⓜ *Colón* ✣ *H2.*

$$$$ **Orfila.** This elegant 1886 town house, hidden away on a leafy little residential street not far from Plaza Colón, has every comfort of a larger hotel but in more intimate surroundings. Originally the in-town residence of the literary and aristocratic Gomez-Acebo family, Orfila 6 was an address famous for theater performances in the late 19th and early 20th centuries. The restaurant, garden (superb for summer dining), and tearoom have period furniture; guest rooms are draped with striped and floral silks. **Pros:** quiet street; refined decor; attentive service. **Cons:** no gym (though the Orfila has an agreement with one nearby that guests can use for a fee); pricey breakfast. ✉ *Orfila 6, Chamberí* ☎ *91/702–7770* 🌐 *www.hotelorfila.com* *20 rooms, 12 suites* *In-room: Internet, Wi-Fi. In-hotel: restaurant, bar, Wi-Fi hotspot, parking (paid)* *AE, DC, MC, V* Ⓜ *Alonso Martínez* ✣ *G1.*

$$$$ **Ritz.** Alfonso XIII, about to marry Queen Victoria's granddaughter, encouraged the construction of this hotel, the most exclusive in Spain, for his royal guests. Opened in 1910 by the king (who also personally supervised construction), the Ritz is a monument to the Belle Epoque, its salons furnished with rare antiques, hand-embroidered linens, and handwoven carpets. All rooms (which are slowly being revamped) have canopy beds; some have views of the Prado. The famous and pricey restaurant, Goya, serves a Sunday brunch feast that's accompanied by the soothing strains of harp music; from February to May, you can enjoy chamber music during weekend tea and supper. **Pros:** old-world flair; lovely tearoom and summer terrace; excellent location. **Cons:** what's classic for some may feel stuffy and outdated to others. ✉ *Pl. de la Lealtad 5, Retiro* ☎ *91/701–6767* 🌐 *www.ritzmadrid.com* *167 rooms* *In-room: Internet, Wi-Fi. In-hotel: restaurant, bar, gym, spa, Wi-Fi hotspot, parking (paid)* *AE, DC, MC, V* Ⓜ *Banco de España* ✣ *G4.*

$$$$ **Silken Puerta de América.** Inspired by Paul Eluard's *La Liberté* (whose verses are written across the facade), the owners of this hotel granted an unlimited budget to 19 of the world's top architects and designers. The result: 12 hotels in one, with floors by Zaha Hadid, Norman Foster, Jean Nouvel, David Chipperfield, and more. You can pick the floor of your choice online; most popular are the futuristic all-white layout by

Hadid, the elegant black wood and white leather proposal by Foster, and the imaginative re-creation of space by Ron Arad. There's also a well-reputed restaurant and two bars (one on the rooftop), which are all just as impressive in design. The only snag: you'll need a taxi or the subway to get to the city center. **Pros:** an architect's dreamland; top-notch restaurant and bars. **Cons:** less than convenient location; the distinctive decor doesn't always get the required maintenance. ✉ *Av. de América 41, Salamanca* ☎ *91/744–5400* 🌐 *www.hotelpuertamerica.com* *282 rooms, 21 junior suites, 12 suites* *In-room: safe, Wi-Fi. In-hotel: 2 restaurants, bars, pool, gym, Wi-Fi hotspot, parking (paid)* *AE, DC, MC, V* Ⓜ *Avenida de América* ✥ *G1.*

$$$$ **Westin Palace.** Built in 1912, Madrid's most famous grand hotel is a Belle Epoque creation of Alfonso XIII and has hosted the likes of Salvador Dalí, Marlon Brando, Rita Hayworth, and Madonna. Guest rooms are high-tech and generally impeccable; banquet halls and lobbies have been beautified, and the facade has been restored. The Art Nouveau stained-glass dome over the lounge remains exquisitely original, and guest-room windows are double-glazed against street noise. The hotel also houses the well-known Asia Gallery restaurant ($$$). **Pros:** grand hotel with tons of history; weekend brunch with opera performances. **Cons:** fourth floor has not been renovated yet; standard rooms face a back street. ✉ *Pl. de las Cortés 7, Retiro* ☎ *91/360–8000* 🌐 *www.palacemadrid.com* *465 rooms, 45 suites* *In-room: Internet, Wi-Fi. In-hotel: 2 restaurants, bar, gym, Wi-Fi hotspot, parking (paid)* *AE, DC, MC, V* Ⓜ *Banco de España, Sevilla* ✥ *F4.*

CHUECA AND MALASAÑA

$ **Abalú.** Each of the 17 rooms in this hotel at the heart of one of the city's youngest and liveliest neighborhoods is a small oasis of singular design. Designer Luis Delgado's mission is to make each room special, with a hodgepodge of one-of-a-kind accents, such as the black stenciled butterflies scattered along the walls of the White Room. If you're interested in feeling Malasaña's vibe and are not easily daunted by noise, ask for one of the three rooms facing the street, or, for a little more, one of the junior suites with a Jacuzzi. **Pros:** unique room decor; very charming cafeteria. **Cons:** rooms smaller than average; scruffy neighborhood may turn some people off. ✉ *Pez 19, Malasaña* ☎ *91/531–4744* 🌐 *www.hotelabalu.com* *15 rooms, 2 suites* *In-room: safe, DVD, Wi-Fi* *AE, MC, V* *CP* Ⓜ *Noviciado* ✥ *C1.*

$ **Room Mate Óscar.** Bold, bright, and modern, the flagship Room Mate is undeniably hip and glamorous. It has sizable rooms decorated with graffiti art, a lively restaurant, a trendy bar that stays opens late every night with largely gay clientele, and a year-round roof terrace that's the envy of the city. The location, just off the Gran Vía, bustles but is excellent for getting around. **Pros:** friendly staff; hip guests; fashionable facilities. **Cons:** noisy street; may be *too* happening for some. ✉ *Pl. Vázquez de Mella 12, Chueca* ☎ *91/701–1173* 🌐 *www.room-matehoteles.com* *69 rooms, 6 suites* *In-room: Wi-Fi. In-hotel: restaurant, bar, pool, laundry facilities, Wi-Fi hotspot* *AE, DC, MC, V* *CP* Ⓜ *Chueca* ✥ *E2.*

Fodor's Choice ★

2

PALACIO AND SOL

$ **Ateneo Hotel.** This hotel is in the restored 18th-century building that once housed the Ateneo, a club founded in 1835 to promote freedom of thought. The spacious rooms are done in cream and light wood tones with parquet flooring and red-and-gold-striped bedspreads. Exterior rooms have balconies overlooking the crowded street, except those on the fourth floor, which have sloped ceilings and skylights above the beds. **Pros:** sizeable rooms. **Cons:** though now pedestrianized and safe thanks to the police station, the street still attracts some sketchy characters; noisy area. ✉ *Montera 22, Sol* ☎ *91/521–2012* 🌐 *www.hotel-ateneo.com* *38 rooms, 6 junior suites* *In-room: Internet* *AE, DC, MC, V* *BP* Ⓜ *Gran Vía, Sol* ✣ *E3.*

$ **Chic & Basic Mayerling.** What once was a textile wholesaler is now a small boutique hotel just a few blocks off Plaza Mayor and Plaza Santa Ana that lives up to the franchise name, offering sleek minimalism at just the right value. Rooms, which come in two sizes (large and extra-large, the latter for just a few more euros) are decorated in white, with colorful headboards, a small open closet, and LED-lit showers separated by a glass wall. Though it has no restaurant, there is a common help-yourself area where you can grab breakfast and free juice, yogurt, and fruit throughout the day. **Pros:** some rooms accommodate up to three people; nice terrace; free Wi-Fi; comfortable beds; great location. **Cons:** rooms are smallish by U.S. standards; white walls show dirt; services are spartan. ✉ *Conde de Romanones 6, Sol* ☎ *91/420–1580* 🌐 *www.chicandbasic.com* *22 rooms* *In-room: Wi-Fi* *DC, MC, V* *CP* Ⓜ *Tirso de Molina* ✣ *D5.*

$$$–$$$$ Fodor's Choice ★ **De Las Letras.** This hotel is a seamless mix of modern-pop interior design that respects and accents the original details of the 1917 structure (glazed tiles, canopies, original wood-and-iron elevator, wooden staircase, stone carvings). Rooms are painted in tones of ocher, orange, or burgundy and have high ceilings, wooden floors, indirect lighting, and over-the-top modern bathrooms; each junior suite has a terrace with a whirlpool bath. There is also a charming rooftop terrace bar open to the public. Enjoying a meal or a cocktail in the restaurant-lounge on the street level, you would never think you're around the corner from the bustling Gran Vía. **Pros:** young vibe; charming spa; happening rooftop bar. **Cons:** small gym. ✉ *Gran Vía 11, Sol* ☎ *91/523–7980* 🌐 *www.hoteldelasletras.com* *103 rooms, 1 suite, 6 junior suites* *In-room: DVD, Wi-Fi. In-hotel: restaurant, bar, gym, spa, Wi-Fi hotspot, parking (paid)* *AE, DC, MC, V* Ⓜ *Banco de España* ✣ *E3.*

¢ Fodor's Choice ★ **Hostal Adriano.** Tucked away on a street with dozens of bland competitors a couple of blocks from Sol, this hotel stands out for its price and quality. The rooms, though not especially big, are charming and far from the standard hostal fare. They're thoughtfully decorated with bright-color walls and bedspreads and furniture and accessories collected over the years by the two friendly Argentine owners. The best of the lot has been wallpapered with some old María Callas pictures and the musical score from *Tosca*. In case it's fully booked, note that the owners have another small (10 rooms, 1 quadruple) and equally welcoming hostal (Adria Santa Ana), with no elevator, on nearby Nuñez de Arce 15. **Pros:** friendly service; great value; charming touches. **Cons:** short on facilities. ✉ *De la Cruz 26, 4th fl., Sol* ☎ *91/521–1339* 🌐 *www.hostaladriano.com* *22 rooms* *In-room: safe. In-hotel: Wi-Fi hotspot* ▭ *MC, V* Ⓜ *Sol* ✥ *D4.*

$$–$$$ Fodor's Choice ★ **Hotel Intur Palacio San Martín.** In an unbeatable location across from one of Madrid's most celebrated monuments (the Convent of Descalzas), this hotel, once the old U.S. embassy and later a luxurious residential building crowded with noblemen, still exudes a kind of glory. The entrance leads to a glass-dome atrium that serves as a tranquil sitting area, there's an antique elevator, and many of the ceilings are carved and ornate. Rooms are spacious and carpeted; the five at street level have a much more modern decor, with stenciled headboards and ceramic floors; request one facing the big plaza. **Pros:** charming location; spacious rooms. **Cons:** no restaurant. ✉ *Pl. de San Martín 5, Palacio* ☎ *91/701–5000* 🌐 *www.intur.com* *94 rooms, 8 suites* *In-room: safe, Wi-Fi. In-hotel: gym, Wi-Fi hotspot, parking (paid)* ▭ *AE, DC, MC, V* Ⓜ *Ópera, Callao* ✥ *C3.*

$$ **Hotel Preciados.** In a 19th-century building on the quieter edge of one of Madrid's main shopping areas, this hotel is both charming and convenient. Rooms are modern and sophisticated, with hardwood floors and opaque glass closets. Some of the "double superiors" (slightly more expensive) have skylights in the bathrooms. **Pros:** conveniently located; good-size bathrooms; free Wi-Fi. **Cons:** expensive breakfast; bustling area. ✉ *C. Preciados 37, Sol* ☎ *91/454–4400* 🌐 *www.preciadoshotel.com* *74 rooms, 6 suites* *In-room: Wi-Fi. In-hotel: restaurant, bar, gym, Wi-Fi hotspot, parking (paid)* ▭ *AE, DC, MC, V* Ⓜ *Callao* ✥ *B3.*

$$–$$$ **Quo Puerta del Sol.** The rooms in this modern, design-oriented boutique hotel between Santa Ana and Sol have views of the city center and are equipped with cutting-edge technology, dark hardwood floors, and modern touches such as the stainless-steel-and-glass sinks in the bathrooms. Common areas may not be ample in size but are charming, trendy, and full of character. **Pros:** good design; centrally located. **Cons:** small lobby; no restaurant. ✉ *C. Sevilla 4, Sol* ☎ *91/532–9049* 🌐 *www.hotelesquo.com* *61 rooms, 1 junior suite* *In-room: Wi-Fi. In-hotel: Wi-Fi hotspot, parking (paid)* ▭ *AE, DC, MC, V* Ⓜ *Sevilla* ✥ *E4.*

$ **Room Mate Laura.** On Plaza de las Descalzas, this Room Mate is in an old apartment building refurbished following the company's mantra of good design, distinctiveness (all rooms, many duplex, have different layouts), and friendly service—without burning a hole in the customer's pocket. **Pros:** kitchenettes for long stays; rooms are large enough to fit three people comfortably. **Cons:** only the best rooms have views of the convent; no restaurant; some bathrooms need to be revamped. ✉ *Travesía de Trujillos 3, Palacio* ☎ *91/701–1670* 🌐 *www.room-matehotels.com* *36 rooms* *In-room: kitchen, DVD, Wi-Fi. In-hotel: restaurant, Wi-Fi hotspot* ▭ *AE, DC, MC, V* Ⓜ *Ópera* ✥ *C3.*

$ **Room Mate Mario.** In the city center, just steps from the major sights and nightlife, Mario is small and limited in services, but its bold modern style—original silk-print headboards and combinations of white, gray, and black tones—and friendly service are a welcome alternative to Madrid's traditional hotel options. There's a great breakfast, but no restaurant. **Pros:** unusual decor; centrally located; great breakfast; convivial staff; it's the cheapest of the chain. **Cons:** no restaurant; its rooms are slightly smaller and offer fewer external views than the other Room Mate hotels. ✉ *Campomanes 4, Palacio* ☏ *91/548–8548* 🌐 *www.room-matehoteles.com* ⇆ *54 rooms, 3 suites* *In-room: Wi-Fi. In-hotel: laundry facilities, Wi-Fi hotspot* ▭ *AE, DC, MC, V* 🍴 *CP* Ⓜ *Ópera* ✣ *B3.*

$$–$$$ **Tryp Ambassador.** On an old street between Gran Vía and the Royal Palace, the Ambassador occupies the renovated 19th-century palace of the dukes of Granada. The facade (restored in 2007), a magnificent front door, and a graceful three-story staircase recall the building's aristocratic past. The rest has been transformed into the elegant, though somewhat soulless type of lodgings favored by executives. Large guest rooms have sitting areas, wooden floors, and mahogany furnishings. The greenhouse restaurant, filled with plants and songbirds, is especially pleasant on cold days. **Pros:** grand building; central location; better rooms have big balconies with good views. **Cons:** some worn-out rooms need to be revamped. ✉ *Cuesta Santo Domingo 5 and 7, Palacio* ☏ *91/541–6700* 🌐 *www.solmelia.com* ⇆ *183 rooms, 25 suites* *In-room: Wi-Fi. In-hotel: restaurant, bar, Wi-Fi hotspot, parking (paid)* ▭ *AE, DC, MC, V* Ⓜ *Ópera* ✣ *B3.*

NIGHTLIFE AND THE ARTS

THE ARTS

As Madrid's reputation as a vibrant, contemporary arts center has grown, artists and performers have been arriving in droves. Consult the daily listings and Friday city-guide supplements in any of the leading newspapers—*El País, El Mundo,* or *ABC,* all of which are fairly easy to understand even if you don't read much Spanish. Seats for the classical performing arts can usually be purchased through your hotel concierge, on the Internet, or at the venue itself. **El Corte Inglés** (☏ *902/400222* 🌐 *www.elcorteingles.es/entradas*) sells tickets for major concerts. **FNAC** (✉ *Preciados 28, Sol* ☏ *91/595–6100* 🌐 *www.fnac.es*), a large retail media store, also sells tickets to musical events. **Ticket brokers** to try are **Tel-Entrada** (☏ *902/101212* 🌐 *www.telentrada.com*) and **Entradas.com** (☏ *902/221622*).

DANCE AND MUSIC PERFORMANCES

In addition to concert halls listed below, the Convento de la Encarnación and the Real Academia de Bellas Artes de San Fernando museum (⇨ *Exploring Madrid*) hold concerts.

The modern **Auditorio Nacional de Música** (✉ *Príncipe de Vergara 146, Salamanca* ☏ *91/337–0100* 🌐 *www.auditorionacional.mcu.es*) is Madrid's main concert hall, with spaces for both symphonic and chamber music. The **Centro de Conde Duque** (✉ *Conde Duque 11, Centro* ☏ *91/588–5834*) is best known for its summer live-music concerts (flamenco, jazz, pop), but it also has free and often interesting exhibitions. The **Círculo de**

CLOSE UP

Summer Terraces

Madrid is blazing hot in the late spring and summer, but madrileños have a relentless yearning for nightlife. As a result, the city allows nearly 2,000 bars and restaurants to create outdoor spaces for enjoying the cooler, dry summer nighttime air.

For formal summer dining, we recommend some of the many lovely hotel restaurants, most of which have private and peaceful gardens or roof terraces. Try the Ritz hotel, La Biblioteca del Santo Mauro (at Hotel Santo Mauro), El Jardín de Orfila (at Hotel Orfila), and La Terraza del Casino.

Three mid-range restaurants with good terraces are Sacha, Bokado, and Mercado de la Reina.

If you just want a bite or an early-evening drink, drop by the La Latina neighborhood, especially Plaza de la Paja or Plaza de San Andrés, across from the Church of San Andrés, or the terraces at Plaza de Olavide, near Malasaña and the Bilbao subway stop.

Plaza Santa Ana is a pricier, more touristy alternative. Plaza Chueca in the neighborhood of the same name, the Mercado de Fuencarral (halfway between Gran Vía and Tribunal), the Plaza de 2 de Mayo, and the Plaza de las Comendadoras in Malasaña are always bustling and crowded with younger people.

The best nightlife is along the terraces on Castellana, at Terraza Atenas on Calle Segovia, and at the hotel rooftop bars that have spread out in the last few years: Hotel Urban, ME Reina Victoria, Silken Puerta de América, De las Letras, and Room Mate Óscar.

Bellas Artes (✉ *Marqués de Casa Riera 2, Centro* ☎ *902/422442* 🌐 *www.circulobellasartes.com*) has concerts, theater, dance performances, art exhibitions, and other arts events. **La Casa Encendida** (✉ *Ronda de Valencia 2, Lavapiés* ☎ *91/506–3875* 🌐 *www.lacasaencendida.com*) is an exhibition space with movie festivals, art shows, dance performances, and weekend events for children. The **Matadero Madrid** (✉ *Paseo de la Chopera 14, Legazpi* ☎ *91/517–7309*) is the city's newest and biggest arts center. It's in the city's old slaughterhouse—a massive early-20th-century *neomudejar* compound of 13 buildings—and has a theater, multiple exhibition spaces, workshops, and a lively bar. It's so large, it won't be completely finished until 2011, but some of the exhibition spaces and the theater are open during construction. The resplendent **Teatro Real** (✉ *Pl. de Isabel II, Palacio* ☎ *91/516–0660* 🌐 *www.teatro-real.com*) is the site of opera and dance performances.

FILM

Of Madrid's 60 movie theaters, only 12 show foreign films, generally in English, with original soundtracks and Spanish subtitles. These are listed in newspapers under "v.o."—*versión original,* that is, undubbed. Your best bet for catching a new release is the **Ideal Yelmo Cineplex** (✉ *Doctor Cortezo 6, Centro* ☎ *902/220922*). The excellent, classic v.o. films at the **Filmoteca Cine Doré** (✉ *Santa Isabel 3, Lavapiés* ☎ *91/369–1125*) change daily.

Continued on page 132

THE ART OF BULLFIGHTING

Whether you attend is your choice, but love it or hate it, you can't ignore it: bullfighting in Spain is big. For all the animal-rights protests, attempted bans, failed censures, and general worldwide antipathy, there are an astounding number of fans crowding Spain's bullrings between March and October.

CONTROVERSIAL ENTERTAINMENT

SPORT VS. ART

Its opponents call it a blood sport, its admirers—Hemingway, Picasso, and Goya among them—an art form. And the latter wins when it comes to media placement: you won't find tales of a star matador's latest conquest in the newspaper with car racing stories; you'll spy bullfighting news alongside theater and film reviews. This is perhaps the secret to understanding bullfighting's powerful cultural significance and why its popularity has risen over the past decade.

Bullfighting is making certain people very, very rich, via million-dollar TV rights, fight broadcasts, and the 300-plus bull-breeding farms. The owners of these farms comprise a powerful lobby that receives subsidies from the EU and exemption from a 1998 amendment to the Treaty of Rome that covers animal welfare. The Spanish Ministry of Culture also provides considerable money to support bullfighting, as do local and regional governments.

The Spanish media thrive on it, too. The matador is perhaps Spain's last remaining stereotypical hombre, whose popularity outside the ring in the celebrity press is often dramatically disproportionate to what he achieves inside it.

SOME HISTORY

How bullfighting came to Spain isn't completely clear. It may have been introduced by the Moors in the 11th century or via ancient Rome, where human vs. animal events were warm-ups for the gladiators.

Historically, the bull was fought from horseback with a javelin, to train and prepare for war, like hunting and jousting. Religious festivities and royal weddings were celebrated by fights in the local plaza, where noblemen would compete for royal favor, with the populace enjoying the excitement. In the 18th century, the Spanish introduced the practice of fighting on foot. As bullfighting developed, men started using capes to aid the horsemen in positioning the bulls. This type of fighting drew more attention from the crowds, thus the modern *corrida,* or bullfight, took root.

THE CASE AGAINST BULLFIGHTING

Animal welfare activists aggressively protest bullfighting: they argue that the bulls die a cruel death, essentially being butchered alive, and that the horses used as shields sometimes die or are injured.

Activists have had little success in banning bullfights on a national level, and the sport is as popular as ever in the south of Spain and Madrid. In Catalonia, however, a final vote was cast in 2010 that will outlaw bullfighting in Barcelona and the rest of Catalonia as of 2010.

SUITING UP

Matadors are easily distinguished by their spectacular and quite costly *traje de luces* (suit of lights), inspired by 18th-century Andalusian clothing. This ensemble can run several thousand dollars, and a good matador uses at least six of them each season. The matador's team covers the cost.

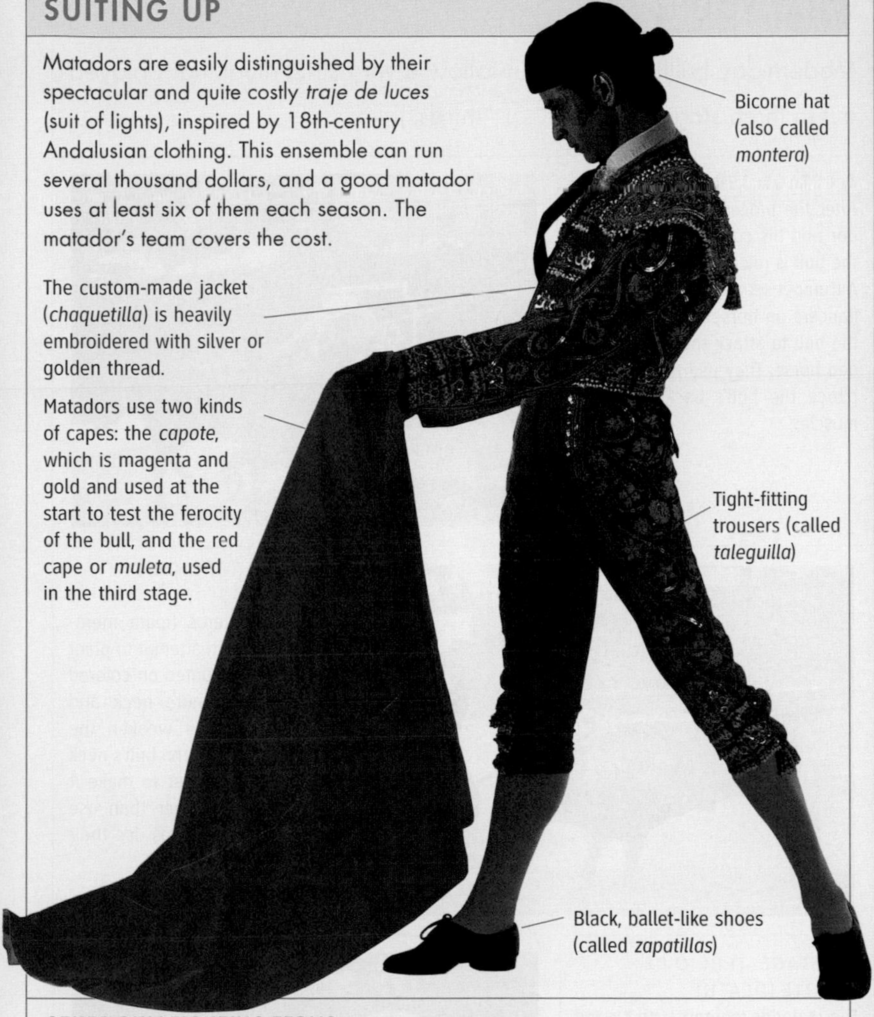
Bicorne hat (also called *montera*)
The custom-made jacket (*chaquetilla*) is heavily embroidered with silver or golden thread.
Matadors use two kinds of capes: the *capote*, which is magenta and gold and used at the start to test the ferocity of the bull, and the red cape or *muleta*, used in the third stage.
Tight-fitting trousers (called *taleguilla*)
Black, ballet-like shoes (called *zapatillas*)

OTHER BULLFIGHTING TERMS

Alguacilillo—the title given to the two men in the arena who represent the presiding dignitary and apply his orders.

Banderilleros—the torero's team members who place a set of banderillas (barbed sticks mounted on colored shafts) into the bull's neck.

Corrida de toros—bullfight (literally, running of the bulls); sometimes just referred to as *corrida*.

Cuadrilla the matador's team of three *banderilleros* and two *picadors*.

Matador—matador literally means "killer."

Paseíllo—the parade that the participants make when they enter the bullring.

Picador—lancers mounted on horseback.

Presidente—the presiding dignitary.

Varas—lances.

WHAT YOU'LL SEE

Modern-day bullfights in Spain follow a very strict ritual that's played out in three stages ("*tercios*" or "thirds").

1st STAGE: TERCIO DE VARAS

After the procession of the matador and his cuadrilla (entourage), the bull is released into the arena. A trumpet sounds and the picadors (lancers on horseback) encourage the bull to attack the heavily padded horse. They use the lances to pierce the bull's back and neck muscles.

2nd STAGE: TERCIO DE BANDERILLAS

Three banderilleros (team members) on foot each attempt to plant barbed sticks mounted on colored shafts into the bull's neck and back. These further weaken the enormous ridges of the bull's neck and shoulder in order to make it lower its head. Rather than use capes, the banderilleros use their bodies to attract the bull.

3rd STAGE: TERCIO DE MUERTE (DEATH)

The matador reenters with his red cape and, if he so chooses, dedicates the bull to an individual, or to the audience. The faena (work), which is the entire performance with the muleta (cape), ends with a series of passes in which the matador attempts to maneuver the bull into a position so he can drive his sword between the shoulder blades and through the heart.

Lancers astride heavily padded horses parade around the bullring near the beginning of a fight.

HOW TO BEHAVE

The consummate bullfighting fan is both passionate and knowledgeable. Audiences are in fact part of the spectacle, and their responses during the event is often an indicator of the quality of the corrida. For instance, during the tercio de varas, or first third of the fight, when the matador performs with art and courage, he will be rewarded with an ovation. If a picador is overzealous in stabbing the bull and leaves it too weak to fight, the crowd will boo him with whistles.

Similarly, the estocada, the act of thrusting the sword by the matador, can generate disaproval from the crowd if it's done clumsily and doesn't achieve a quick and clean death. A trofeo (literally a "trophy" but in practical terms the ear of a bull) is the usual indicator of a job well done. When the records of bullfights are kept, trofeos earned by the matador are always mentioned. If the crowd demands, the matador takes a lap of victory around the ring. If more than or about half the spectators petition the presidente by waving handkerchiefs, the presidente is obliged to award the matador one bull's ear. The best trofeo is the two ears and the tail of a single bull, awarded only on memorable days.

■ TIP→ When buying tickets for a bullfight, it's usually worth the extra cost for seats in the shade (*sombra*) rather than the cheaper one in the sun (*sol*) because bullfighting season coincides with summer. Seats in areas that get sun and then shade are called *sol y sombra*. Take a cushion with you, or rent one for €1, so you're not sitting on the hard concrete. Buy your tickets well in advance—call go online to 🌐 www.taquillatoros.com.

STARGAZING

It's not uncommon for local Spanish celebrities to attend bullfights, and during the most prestigious summer carnival, the San Isidro in Madrid, King Juan Carlos often makes an appearance.

FLAMENCO

> **BEST BETS FOR ENTERTAINMENT**
>
> ■ **Best flamenco:** Café de Chinitas
>
> ■ **Best jazz venue:** Café Central
>
> ■ **Best salsa:** Azúcar

Although the best place in Spain to find flamenco is Andalusia, there are a few venues in Madrid. Note that *tablaos* (flamenco venues) charge around €30–€40 for the show only (with a complimentary drink included), so save money by dining elsewhere. If you want to dine at the *tablaos* anyway, note that three of them, Carboneras, Corral de la Moreriá, and Café de Chinitas, also offer a show-plus-fixed-menu option that's worth considering.

Café de Chinitas. It's expensive, but the flamenco is the best in Madrid. Make reservations because shows often sell out. The restaurant opens at 8 and there are performances at 8:30 and 10:30 Monday through Saturday. ✉ *Torija 7, Palacio* ☎ *91/559–5135.*

Casa Patas. Along with tapas, this well-known space offers good, relatively authentic (according to the performers) flamenco. Prices are more reasonable than elsewhere. Shows are at 10:30 Monday through Thursday and at 9 and midnight on Friday and Saturday. ✉ *Canizares 10, Lavapiés* ☎ *91/369–0496.*

Corral de la Morería. Dinner à la carte and well-known visiting flamenco stars accompany the resident dance troupe here. Since Morería opened its doors in 1956, celebrities such as Frank Sinatra and Ava Gardner have left their autographed photos for the walls. Shows are nightly at 10 and midnight. ✉ *Morería 17, on C. Bailén; cross bridge over C. Segovia and turn right, Centro* ☎ *91/365–8446.*

Las Carboneras. A prime flamenco showcase, this venue rivals Casa Patas as the best option in terms of quality and price. Performers here are both the young, less commercial artists and the more established stars on tour. The nightly show is staged at 10:30 Monday through Thursday and at 8:30 and 11 Friday and Saturday. ✉ *Pl. del Conde de Miranda 1, Centro* ☎ *91/542–8677.*

NIGHTLIFE

Nightlife—or *la marcha*—reaches legendary heights in Madrid. It's been said that madrileños rarely sleep, largely because they spend so much time in bars, socializing in the easy, sophisticated way that's unique to this city. This is true of young and old alike, and it's not uncommon for children to play on the sidewalks past midnight while multigenerational families and friends convene over coffee or cocktails at an outdoor café. For those in their thirties, forties, and up who don't plan on staying out until sunrise, the best options are the bars along the Cava Alta and Cava Baja, Calle Huertas near Plaza Santa Ana, and Moratín near Antón Martín. Younger people who want to stay out till the wee hours have more options: Calle Príncipe and Calle De la Cruz—also in Santa Ana—and the Plaza de Anton Martín, especially the scruffier streets that lead onto Plaza Lavapiés. The biggest night scene—with a mixed crowd—happens in Malasaña, which has plenty of trendy hangouts on both sides of Calle San Vicente Ferrer, on Calle La Palma, and on the streets that come out onto Plaza 2 de Mayo. Also big is nearby Chueca, where tattoo parlors and street-chic boutiques break up the endless alleys of gay and lesbian bars, techno discos, and after-hours clubs.

BARS AND NIGHTCLUBS

Jazz, rock, classical, and flamenco music are all popular in Madrid's many clubs.

Bar Cock. Resembling a room at a very exclusive club (with all the waiters in suits), this bar with a dark wood interior and cathedral-like ceilings serves about 20 different cocktails (hence the name). It caters to an older, more classic crowd. ✉ *Reina 16, Chueca* ☎ *91/532–2826.*

Café Belén. The handful of tables here are rarely empty on weekends, thanks to the candlelit, cozy atmosphere—it attracts a young, mixed, postdinner crowd. Weekdays are mellower. ✉ *Belén 5, Chueca* ☎ *91/308–2747.*

Café Central. Madrid's best-known jazz venue is chic, and the musicians are often internationally known. Performances are usually from 10 to midnight. ✉ *Pl. de Ángel 10, Santa Ana* ☎ *91/369–4143.*

Café la Palma. There are four different spaces here: a bar in front, a music venue for intimate concerts, a chill-out room in the back, and a café in the center room. Don't miss it if you're in Malasaña. ✉ *La Palma 62, Malasaña* ☎ *91/522–5031.*

Coquette. Come here to check out the most authentic blues bar in the city, with live music Tuesday to Thurday at 11, smoke-filled air, barmen with jeans and leather jackets, and bohemian executives who've left their suits at home and parked their Harley-Davidsons at the door. ✉ *Torrecilla del Leal 18, Lavapiés* ☎ *91/530–8095.*

Costello. A multispace that combines a café and a lounge, Costello caters to a relaxed, conversational crowd; the bottom floor is suited to partygoers, with the latest in live and club music. On weekdays, it also features theater and stand-up comedy. ✉ *Caballero de Gracia 10, Sol* ☎ *91/522–1815.*

Del Diego. Arguably Madrid's trendiest cocktail bar, this place is frequented by a variety of crowds from movie directors to moviegoers. ✉ *Calle de la Reina 12, Centro* ☎ *91/523–3106* ⏲ *Closed Sun.*

El Clandestino. This bar-café is a hidden hot spot with a local following. Jam sessions on the bottom floor (Thursday through Saturday) alternate mellow jazz with house and ambient music. ✉ *Barquillo 34, Centro* ☎ *91/521–5563* ⏲ *Closed Sun.*

El Viajero. You can get food here, but this place is best known among the madrileños who swarm La Latina on the weekends for its middle-floor bar, which is usually filled by those looking for a drink between lunch and dinner. The fabulous terrace tends to be packed. ✉ *Pl. de la Cebada 11, La Latina* ☎ *91/366–9064* ⏲ *Closed Sun. night and Mon.*

Glass Bar. The hip, happening bar in the Hotel Urban, styled as Madrid's only oyster bar, attracts the stylish international set for excellent cocktails to accompany those oysters and other, mostly Japanesese-style, bites. ✉ *Carrera de San Jerónimo 34, Barrio de las Letras* ☎ *91/787–7770.*

La Piola. With a truly bohemian spirit and a shabby-chic decor—a secondhand couch, a handful of tables, and a brass bar—this small place, which serves a great Spanish omelet during the day and cocktails at night, is a magnet for people who want to get away from the bustle of the Santa Ana area. ✉ *León 9, Barrio de las Letras* ☎ *679/744898* ⏲ *Closed Sun.*

Maluca. Reasonable prices and soft jazz and soul music draw a crowd in its forties to this cocktail bar/lounge. Besides the mojitos, martinis, and negronis, you'll find creative concoctions such as the wasabi daiquiri and the sweet mustard *kaipiroska*. ✉ *Calatrava 13, La Latina* ☎ *91/365–0996* ⏲ *Closed Mon.*

Marula Café. Popular for its quiet summer terrace under the Puente de Segovia arches, its unbeatable electro-funk mixes, and for staying open into the wee hours, this is a cleverly designed narrow space with lots of illuminated wall art. ✉ *C. Caños Viejos 3, Palacio* ☎ *91/366–1596.*

Midnight Rose and the Penthouse. This is two different spaces connected by an elevator that could easily be confused for a dance floor. The bottom lounge takes up most of the ground floor of the chic ME Reina Victoria, including the reception area; the rooftop terrace in the same hotel offers an unbeatable view of the city. ✉ *Covarrubias 24, Chamberí* ☎ *91/445–6886.*

Museo Chicote. This landmark cocktail bar–lounge is said to have been one of Hemingway's haunts. Much of the interior decor can be traced back to the 1930s but modern elements, like the in-house DJ, keep this spot firmly in the present. ✉ *Gran Vía 12, Centro* ☎ *91/532–6737* ⏲ *Closed Sun.*

Ramsés. A multispace venue across from Retiro Park designed by Philippe Starck with two restaurants, a club in the basement, and a bar at street level, this spot is perfect for an early though expensive cocktail, before or after dinner, preferably during the week. Order a Ramsés (black vodka, absinthe, and cranberry juice) and enjoy the parade of the glamorous see-and-be-seen set. ✉ *Pl. de la Independencia 4, Retiro* ☎ *91/435–1666.*

Zombie Bar. The Zombie Kids, the trio who also run two of the more popular music sessions at Charada, have opened their own bar to continue exploring their creative mantra of bringing back trends that you thought were dead. The decor is mostly recycled material and concepts. ✉ *Pez 7, Malasaña* ☎ *91/435–1666.*

DISCOS

Five minutes from Plaza de Castilla, **69 Pétalos** (✉ *Alberto Alcocer, 32, Chamartín* ☎ *No phone* ⏲ *Closed Sun.–Wed.*) is a popular disco among people in their thirties; there's an eclectic music vibe—pop, hip-hop, swing, electronic—and on-stage performances by actors, go-go dancers, and musicians. Dizzingly colorful **Adraba** (✉ *Alcalá 20, Sol* ☎ *91/445–7938* ⏲ *Closed Mon.–Wed.*) has a large dance floor, a bar specializing in fancy cocktails, and four different house music sessions—the one on Thurday, called "Vanité," caters to the city's most glamorous and refined.

DID YOU KNOW?

In 1997 the Teatro Real returned to its intended use as a dedicated opera house—it was a major European opera venue when it was first opened in 1850, but in the interim years it was also used as a parliamentary debate chamber, a dance hall, a temporary war barracks, and even as a gunpowder storage facility.

Salsa has become a fixture in Madrid; check out the most spectacular moves at **Azúcar** (✉ *Paseo Reina Cristina 7, Atocha* ☎ *91/501–6107*). A few blocks from the Royal Palace, **Charada** (✉ *Calle de la Bola 13, Palacio* ☎ *91/541–9291* ⏲ *Closed Mon.–Thurs.*) is one of the sleekest clubs in the city, with a huge LED screen on the ceiling, professional barmen serving cocktails until 6 AM, lots of house and funk music, and a crowd mostly in its late thirties. **Clamores** (✉ *Albuquerque 14, Chamberí* ☎ *91/445–7938* ⏲ *Closes at 11* PM *Sun.*) has good jazz concerts and a superb soul and groove disco session ("Supafly") every Saturday night. An indie, hip crowd flocks to **Elástico** (✉ *Aduana 21, Sol*), the Saturday-night (from 1 AM to 6 AM) pop and indie session at Moon club; it has two different spaces and a good selection of guest DJs. Madrid's oldest disco, and one of the hippest clubs for all-night dancing to an international music mix, is **El Sol** (✉ *Jardines 3, Centro* ☎ *91/532–6490*), open until 5:30 AM. There's live music starting at around midnight, Thursday through Saturday.

Golden Boite (✉ *Duque de Sesto 54, Retiro* ☎ *91/573–8775*) is always hot from midnight on. **Joy Eslava** (✉ *Arenal 11, Sol* ☎ *91/366–3733*), a downtown disco in a converted theater, is an old standby. At the popular **New Garamond** (✉ *Rosario Pino 20, Castillejos*) you'll find plenty of space to dance (under the gaze of the go-go girls) but also quieter nooks where you can chat and sip a drink. **Pachá** (✉ *Barceló 11, Centro* ☎ *91/447–0128* ⏲ *Closed Mon.–Wed.*) is always energetic. Magical and chameleonlike thanks to the use of LED lighting and the undulating shapes of the columns and walls, **Reina Bruja** (✉ *Jacometrezo 6, Palacio* ☎ *91/445–6886* ⏲ *Closed Sun.–Wed.*) is the place to go if you want a late-night drink—it opens at 11 and closes at 5:30 AM—without the thunder of a full-blown disco. For funky rhythms, try **Stella** (✉ *Arlabán 7, Centro* ☎ *91/531–6378* ⏲ *Closed Sun.–Wed.*). On Thursday and Friday it houses the famous Mondo session (electronic, house, and Afro music). Show up late.

SPORTS AND THE OUTDOORS

HIKING

The region north of Madrid, into some parts of Ávila and Segovia, is taken up by the Sierra de Guadarrama mountain range, which is fast becoming Spain's 14th national park. Long favored by naturalists, writers (including John Dos Passos), painters, poets, and historians, it also attracts sporty madrileños looking to get away from the chaos of the capital. The Sierra's eastern border lies at Puerto de Somosierra, west of the A1 highway heading to Burgos; the little town of Robledo de Chavela, southwest of El Escorial, marks the park's western edge. Near the middle of this long stretch sprouts another branch to the northeast, giving the Sierra de Guadarrama the shape of a fork, with the Valle de Lozoya in its tines. Hiking options are nearly limitless, but two destinations stand out for their geological importance: the Parque de la Pedriza, a massive, orangish, fancifully shaped granite landscape in the Cuenca Alta del Manzanares, and the Peñalara's alpine *cirques* (basins) and lakes.

The **Arawak Viajes Madrid** (✉ *Peñuelas 12, Atocha* ☎ *91/474–2524* 🌐 *www.arawakviajes.com*) travel agency offers three or four different one-day trips every weekend to different spots in the Madrid Sierra (and to Guadalajara or Sierra de Gredos), plus a weekend trek every month. Prices to the Sierra de Guadarrama are usually around €20–€25. You must reserve in advance and pay within one day of making the reservation. Buses depart from Estación de Autobuses Ruiz on Ronda de Atocha 12.

RUNNING

Madrid's best running spots are the Parque del Buen Retiro, where the main path circles the park and others weave under trees and through gardens, and the Parque del Oeste, with more uneven terrain but fewer people. The Casa de Campo is crisscrossed by numerous, sunnier trails.

SOCCER

Fútbol is Spain's number-one sport, and Madrid has four teams, Real Madrid, Atlético Madrid, Rayo Vallecano, and Getafe. The two major teams are Real Madrid and Atlético Madrid. For tickets, either call a week in advance to reserve and pick them up at the stadium or stand in line at the stadium of your choice. The **Estadio Santiago Bernabeu** (✉ *Paseo de la Castellana 140, Chamartín* ☎ *91/398–4300* 🌐 *www.realmadrid.es*), which seats 75,000, is home to Real Madrid, winner of a staggering nine European Champions Cups. Atlético Madrid plays at the **Estadio Vicente Calderón** (✉ *Virgen del Puerto 67, Arganzuela* ☎ *91/366–4707 or 91/364–0888* 🌐 *www.clubatleticodemadrid.com*), on the edge of the Manzanares River south of town.

SHOPPING

Spain has become one of the world's design centers. You'll have no trouble finding traditional crafts, such as ceramics, guitars, and leather goods, albeit not at countryside prices (think Rodeo Drive, not outlet mall). Known for contemporary furniture and decorative items as well as chic clothing, shoes, and jewelry, Spain's capital has become stiff competition for Barcelona. Keep in mind that many shops, especially those that are small and family-run, close during lunch hours, on Sunday, and on Saturday afternoon. Shops generally accept most major credit cards.

DEPARTMENT STORES

El Corte Inglés. Spain's largest department store carries the best selection of everything, from auto parts to groceries, electronics, lingerie, and designer fashions. It also sells tickets for major sports and arts events and has its own travel agency, a restaurant (usually the building's top floor), and a great gourmet store. Madrid's biggest branch is the one on the corner of Calle Raimundo Fernández Villaverde and Castellana, which is not a central location. Try instead the one at Sol-Callao (split into three separate buildings), or the ones at Serrano or Goya (each of these has two independent buildings). ✉ *Preciados 1, 2, and 3, Sol* ☎ *91/379–8000, 901/122122 general information, 902/400222 ticket sales* 🌐 *www.elcorteingles.es* ✉ *Callao 2, Centro* ☎ *91/379–8000* ✉ *Calle Goya 76 and 85, Salamanca* ☎ *91/432–9300* ✉ *Princesa 41, 47, and 56, Centro* ☎ *91/454–6000* ✉ *Calle Serrano 47 and 52, Salamanca* ☎ *91/432–5490* ✉ *Raimundo Fernández Villaverde 79, Chamartín* ☎ *91/418–8800.*

SHOPPING DISTRICTS

Madrid has three main shopping areas. The first, the area that stretches from Callao to Puerta del Sol (Calle Preciados, Gran Vía on both sides of Callao, and the streets around the Puerta del Sol), includes the major department stores (El Corte Inglés and the French music-and-book chain FNAC) and popular brands such as H&M and Zara.

The second area, far more elegant and expensive, is in the eastern Salamanca district, bounded roughly by Serrano, Juan Bravo, Jorge Juan (and its blind alleys), and Velázquez; the shops on Goya extend as far as Alcalá. The streets just off the Plaza de Colón, particularly Calle Serrano and Calle Ortega y Gasset, have the widest selection of designer goods—think Prada, Loewe, Armani, and Louis Vuitton—as well as other mainstream and popular local designers (Purificación García, Pedro del Hierro, Adolfo Domínguez, or Roberto Verino). Hidden within Calle Jorge Juan, Calle Lagasca, and Calle Claudio Coello is the widest selection of smart boutiques from renowned young Spanish designers, such as Sybilla, Josep Font, Amaya Arzuaga, and Victorio & Lucchino.

Finally, for hipper clothes, Chueca, Malasaña, and what's now called the Triball (the triangle formed by Fuencarral, Gran Vía, and Corredera Baja, with Calle Ballesta in the middle) are your best bets. Calle Fuencarral, from Gran Vía to Tribunal, is the street with the most shops in this area. On Fuencarral you can find name brands such as Diesel, Gas, and Billabong, but also local brands such as Homeless, Adolfo Domínguez U (selling the Galician designer's younger collection), and Custo, as well as some makeup stores (Madame B and M.A.C). Less mainstream and sometimes more exciting is the selection you can find on nearby Calles Hortaleza, Almirante, and Piamonte and in the Triball area.

FLEA MARKET

On Sunday morning, Calle de Ribera de Curtidores is closed to traffic and jammed with outdoor booths selling everything under the sun—this is its weekly transformation into the **El Rastro** flea market. Crowds get so thick that it takes a while just to advance a few feet amid the hawkers and gawkers. Be careful: pickpockets abound here, so hang on to your purse and wallet, and be especially careful if you bring a camera. The flea market sprawls into most of the surrounding streets, with certain areas specializing in particular products. Many of the goods are wildly overpriced. But what goods! The Rastro has everything from antique furniture to exotic parrots and cuddly puppies, pirated cassette tapes of flamenco music, and key chains emblazoned with symbols of the CNT, Spain's old anarchist trade union. Practice your Spanish by bargaining with the vendors over paintings, colorful Gypsy oxen yokes, heraldic iron gates, new and used clothes, and even hashish pipes. They may not lower their prices, but sometimes they'll throw in a handmade bracelet or a stack of postcards to sweeten the deal. Plaza General Vara del Rey has some of the Rastro's best antiques, and the streets beyond—Calles Mira el Río Alta and Mira el Río Baja—have some truly magnificent junk and bric-a-brac. The market shuts down shortly after 2 PM, in time for a street party to start in the area known as La Latina, centered on the bar El Viajero in Plaza Humilladero. Off the Ribera are two *galerías*, courtyards with higher-quality, higher-price antiques shops. All the shops (except for the street vendors) are open during the week.

SPECIALTY STORES

BOOKS

Casa del Libro (✉ *Maestro Victoria 3, Centro* ☎ *91/521–4898*), not far from the Puerta del Sol, has an impressive collection of English-language books, including translated Spanish classics. It's also a good source for maps. Its discount store around the corner, on Calle Salud 17, sells English classics. **Booksellers** (✉ *Pl. de Olavide 10, Chamberí* ☎ *91/702–7944*), just off the upper Castellana near the Hotel Miguel Ángel, has a large selection of books in English. **J&J** (✉ *Espíritu Santo 47, Centro* ☎ *91/521–8576*), a block off San Bernardo, is a charming café and bookstore run by a woman from Alabama and her Spanish husband. The store stocks a good selection of used books in English. stablished in 1950, **La Tienda Verde** (✉ *Maudes 23 and 38, Chamberí* ☎ *91/535–3810*) is perfect for outdoor enthusiasts planning hikes, mountain-climbing expeditions, spelunking trips, and so forth; it has detailed maps and Spanish-language guidebooks.

BOUTIQUES AND FASHION

Chueca shelters some local name brands (Hoss, Adolfo Domínguez, and Mango) on Calle Fuencarral and has a multifloor and multistore market (Mercado de Fuencarral) selling modern outfits for younger crowds at No. 45 on the same street.

CHUECA AND MALASAÑA

Brothers Custodio and David Dalmau are the creative force behind the success of **Custo** (✉ *Mayor 37, Sol* ☎ *91/354–0099* ✉ *Fuencarral 29, Chueca* ☎ *91/360–4636* ✉ *Gran Vía 26, Chueca* ☎ *91/521–4895*), whose eye-catching T-shirts can be found in the closets of such stars as Madonna and Julia Roberts. They have expanded their collection to incorporate pants, dresses, and accessories, never relinquishing the traits that have made them famous: bold colors and striking graphic designs.

Chueca's trademark is its multibrand boutiques and small multibrand fashion shops, often managed by eccentric and outspoken characters. A good example of this is **H.A.N.D** (✉ *Hortaleza 26, Chueca* ☎ *91/521–5152*), a cozy, tasteful store owned by two Frenchmen: Stephan and

The bustling El Rastro flea market takes place every Sunday from 10 to 2; you never know what kind of treasures you might find.

Thierry. They specialize in feminine, colorful, and young French prêt-à-porter designers (Stella Forest, La Petite, Tara Jarmon). Prominent designer **Jesús del Pozo** (✉ *Almirante 9, Chueca* ☎ *91/531–3646*) has clothes for both sexes. It's an excellent, if pricey, place to try on some classic Spanish style. **L'Habilleur** (✉ *Pl. de Chueca 8, Chueca* ☎ *91/531–3222*) is a fancy outlet selling samples and end-of-season designer clothes at a large discount.

Mango. The Turkish brothers Isaac and Nahman Andic opened their first store in Barcelona in 1984. Two decades later Mango has stores all over the world, and the brand rivals Zara as Spain's most successful fashion venture. Mango's target customer is the young, modern, and urban woman. In comparison with Zara, Mango has fewer formal options and favors bohemian sundresses, sandals, and embellished T-shirts. ✉ *Fuencarral 70, Malasaña* ☎ *91/523–0412* 🌐 *www.mango.com* ✉ *Fuencarral 140, Bilbao* ☎ *91/445–7811* ✉ *Calle Goya 83, Salamanca* ☎ *91/435–3958* ✉ *Hermosilla 22, Salamanca* ☎ *91/576–8303.*

A favorite among fashion-magazine editors, **Pez** (✉ *Regueros 15, Chueca* ☎ *91/308–6677*), on the corner of Calle Fernando VI, features a very chic and seductive European collection—especially Parisian and Scandinavian. The highly energetic owner of **Próxima Parada** (✉ *Piamonte 25, Chueca* ☎ *91/310–3421*) enthusiastically digs into racks looking for daring garments from Spanish designers in her quest to redefine quickly and modernize her customers' look. The store also sells some original clothespins made by art school students. **Uno de 50** (✉ *Fuencarral 25, Malasaña* ☎ *91/523–9975* ✉ *Jorge Juan 17, Salamanca* ☎ *91/308–2953*) carries original, youngish, and inexpensive (all pieces less than €200) costume jewelry (mostly made in leather and a silver-plated tin alloy) and accessories by Spanish designer Concha Díaz del Río.

SALAMANCA Salamanca is the area with the most concentrated local fashion offering, especially on Calles Claudio Coello, Lagasca, and the first few blocks of Serrano. You'll find a good mix of mainstream designers, small-scale exclusive boutiques, and multibrand stores. Most mainstream designer stores are on Calle Serrano.

The top stores for non-Spanish fashions are mostly scattered along Ortega y Gasset, between Nuñez de Balboa and Serrano, but if you want the more exclusive local brands, head to the smaller designer shops unfolding along Calles Claudio Coello, Jorge Juan, and Lagasca. Start on Calle Jorge Juan and its alleys, and then move north along Claudio Coello and Lagasca toward the core of the Salamanca district.

A quemarropa (✉ *Lagasca 58, Salamanca* ☎ *91/435–7264*) sells very informal clothes for young and modern women from French and Italian designers such as Patrizia Pepe or Et-Vous and from some Spanish ones such as Masscob. **Adolfo Domínguez** (✉ *Calle Serrano 18 and 96, Salamanca* ☎ *91/576–7053*) is a Galician designer with simple, sober, and elegant lines for both men and women. Of his eight other locations in the city, the one at Calle Fuencarral 5, a block away from Gran Vía, is geared toward a younger crowd, with more affordable and colorful clothes. **Alma Aguilar** (✉ *Jorge Juan 12, Salamanca* ☎ *91/577–6698*) is known for using natural and luxe fabrics (silks, cashmere, wool, crepe) for her sundresses and romantic and feminine coats. Drapes, lines, ribbons, and polka dots are some of the trademarks of **Amaya Arzuaga** (✉ *Lagasca 50, Salamanca* ☎ *91/426–2815*) and its elaborate—yet simple-looking—glamorous party dresses. A men's collection is downstairs. For shoes to excite even the most jaded shopper, drop by the small **Columela** (✉ *Columela 6, Salamanca* ☎ *91/435–1925*). You won't find Jimmy Choos or Manolo Blahniks, but rather a more personal selection: Italy's Trans-parents and Costume National, France's L'Autre Chose, American Marc Jacobs, local brands such as Juan Antonio López, and shoes made in Italy expressly for the store.

The three young female designers working for **Hoss** (✉ *Calle Serrano 16, Salamanca* ☎ *91/781–0612* ✉ *Fuencarral 16, Chueca* ☎ *91/524–1728*) and their hip and fashionable clothes are gaining a growing acceptance with younger crowds. Next to Sybilla is **Jocomomola** (✉ *Jorge Juan 12, Salamanca* ☎ *91/575–0005*), Sybilla's younger and more affordable second brand. Here you'll find plenty of informal and provocative, colorful pieces, as well as some accessories. Young and highly praised Catalonian designer **Josep Font** (✉ *Don Ramón de la Cruz 51, Salamanca* ☎ *91/575–9716*) sells his seductive clothes a few blocks from the customary shopping route in the Salamanca neighborhood. Worth the detour, his clothes are distinctive and colorful, with original shapes and small, subtle touches such as ribbons or flounces that act as the designer's signature. If you're on a tight schedule, dropping by some of the multibrand fashion shops in the neighborhood may save you a headache. Posh **Loewe** (✉ *Calle Serrano 26 and 34, Salamanca* ☎ *91/577–6056* ✉ *Gran Vía 8, Centro* ☎ *91/532–7024*) carries high-quality designer purses, accessories, and clothing made of butter-soft leather in gorgeous jewel-like colors. The store on Serrano 26 displays the women's collection; ment's items are a block away, on Serrano 34. Prices can hit the stratosphere.

Nac (✉ *Génova 17, Chamberí* ☎ *91/310–6050* ✉ *Conde de Aranda 6, Salamanca* ☎ *91/431–2515*) has a good selection of Spanish designer brands (Antonio Miró, Hoss, Josep Font, Jocomomola, and Ailanto). The store on Calle Génova is the biggest of the four in Madrid. Also popular is the madrileño designer **Pedro del Hierro** (✉ *Calle Serrano 24 and 63, Salamanca* ☎ *91/575–6906*), who has built himself a good reputation for his sophisticated but uncomplicated clothes for both sexes. **Purificación García** (✉ *Calle Serrano 28 and 92, Salamanca* ☎ *91/435–8013*) is a good choice for women searching for contemporary all-day wear. **Roberto Torretta** (✉ *Jorge Juan 12, at end of one of two cul-de-sacs, Salamanca* ☎ *91/435–7989*) is another designer with a celebrity following and elegant, sophisticated clothes for the urban woman.

Sybilla (✉ *Jorge Juan 12, at end of one of two cul-de-sacs, Salamanca* ☎ *91/578–1322*) is the studio of Spain's best-known female designer. Her fluid dresses and hand-knit sweaters have made her a favorite with Danish former supermodel and now editor and designer Helena Christensen.

At **Victorio & Lucchino** (✉ *Lagasca 75, Salamanca* ☎ *91/431–8786*) you can find sophisticated party dresses (many with characteristic Spanish features) in materials such as gauze, silk, and velvet, as well as more casual wear and a popular line of jewelry and accessories. Young professionals who want the latest look without the sticker shock hit **Zara** for hip clothes that won't last more than a season or two. The store's minimalist window displays are hard to miss; inside you'll find the latest looks for men, women, and children. Zara is self-made entrepreneur Amancio Ortega's textile empire flagship, and you will find locations all over the city. Its clothes are considerably cheaper in Spain than in the United States or the United Kingdom. There are also two outlet stores in Madrid—in the Gran Vía store and in Calle Carretas—both called Lefties. If you choose to try your luck at the outlets, keep in mind that Monday and Thursday are when new deliveries arrive. ✉ *Centro Comercial ABC, Calle Serrano 61, Salamanca* ☎ *91/575–6334* ✉ *Gran Vía 34, Centro* ☎ *91/521–1283* ✉ *Velázquez 49, Salamanca* ☎ *91/575–1476* ✉ *Carretas 6, Sol* ☎ *91/522–6945* ✉ *Princesa 63, Centro* ☎ *91/543–2415* ✉ *Conde de Peñalver 4, Salamanca* ☎ *91/435–4135.*

SOL The area around Sol is more mainstream, with big names such as Zara and H&M, and retail media and department stores (e.g., FNAC, El Corte Inglés), but there are some interesting isolated stops such as **Seseña** (✉ *De la Cruz 23, Sol* ☎ *91/531–6840*), which since the turn of the 20th century has outfitted international celebrities in wool and velvet capes, some lined with red satin.

2

CERAMICS

Antigua Casa Talavera (✉ *Isabel la Católica 2, Centro* ☎ *91/547–3417*) is the best of Madrid's many ceramics shops. Despite the name, the finest wares sold here are from Manises, near Valencia, but the blue-and-yellow Talavera ceramics are also excellent. **Cántaro** (✉ *Flor Baja 8, Centro* ☎ *91/547–9514*) sells traditional handmade ceramics and pottery. **Cerámica El Alfar** (✉ *Claudio Coello 112, Salamanca* ☎ *91/411–3587*) has pottery from around Spain. **Sagardelos** (✉ *Zurbano 46, Chamberí* ☎ *91/310–4830*), specializing in modern Spanish ceramics from Galicia, has breakfast sets, coffeepots, and objets d'arts.

FOOD AND WINE

SALAMANCA **Lavinia** (✉ *José Ortega y Gasset 16, Salamanca* ☎ *91/426–0604*) claims to be the largest wine store in Europe. It has a large selection of bottles, books, and bar accessories and a restaurant where you can sample its products. n the middle of Salamanca's shopping area is **Mantequerías Bravo** (✉ *Ayala 24, Salamanca* ☎ *91/576–7641*), which sells Spanish wines, olive oils, cheeses, and hams. You can find more than 120 different cheeses from all over Spain as well as almost 300 others from nearby countries such as France, Portugal, Italy, and Holland at **Poncelet** (✉ *Argensola 27, Alonso Martínez* ☎ *91/308–0221*). Marmalades, wines, and items to help you savor your cheese are also available.

SANTA ANA Named after the current owner, the liquor store **David Cabello** (✉ *Cervantes 6, Barrio de las Letras* ☎ *91/429–5230*) has been in the family for more than 100 years. It's rustic and a bit dusty and looks like a warehouse rather than a shop, but David knows what he's selling. Head here for a good selection of Rioja wines (some dating as far back as 1920) and local liqueurs, including anisettes and *pacharan,* a fruity liquor made with sloes (wild European plums).The traditional food store **González** (✉ *León 12, Barrio de las Letras* ☎ *91/429–5618*) has a secret in back—a cozy and well-hidden bar where you can sample most of its fare: canned asparagus; olive oil; honey; cold cuts; smoked anchovies, salmon, and other fish; and a good selection of Spanish cheeses and local wines. It also serves good, inexpensive breakfasts. Just across from Los Gabrieles, behind Plaza Santa Ana, **Mariano Aguado** (✉ *Echegaray 19, Barrio de las Letras* ☎ *91/429–6088*) is a charming 150-year-old wine store with a broad range of wines and fine spirits.

MUSIC

José Ramírez (✉ *Calle de la Paz 8, Centro* ☎ *91/531–4229*) has provided Spain and the rest of the world with guitars since 1882, and his store includes a museum of antique instruments. Prices for new ones range from €120 to €225 for children and €150 to €2,200 for adults, though some of the top concert models easily break the €10,000 mark. **Percusión Campos** (✉ *Olivar 36, Lavapiés* ☎ *91/539–2178*) is an easy-to-miss percussion shop-workshop where the young Canarian Pedro Navarro crafts his own *cajones flamencos,* or flamenco box drums, that are greatly appreciated among professionals. Prices range between €120 and €250 and vary according to the quality of woods used. **Musical Ópera** (✉ *Carlos III 1, Centro* ☎ *91/540–1672*), around the corner from the Teatro Real, is a music lover's dream, with books, CDs, sheet music, memorabilia, guitars, and a knowledgeable staff.

SIDE TRIP FROM MADRID

EL ESCORIAL

50 km (31 mi) northwest of Madrid.

Outside Madrid in the foothills of the Sierra de Guadarrama, the **Real Monasterio de San Lorenzo de El Escorial** *(Royal Monastery of St. Lawrence of Escorial)* is severe, rectilinear, and unforgiving—one of the most gigantic yet simple architectural monuments on the Iberian Peninsula. Felipe II was one of history's most deeply religious and forbidding monarchs—not to mention one of its most powerful—and the great granite monastery that he had constructed in a remarkable 21 years (1563–84) is an enduring testament to his character.

Felipe built the monastery in the village of San Lorenzo de El Escorial to commemorate Spain's crushing victory over the French at Saint-Quentin on August 10, 1557, and as a final resting place for his all-powerful father, the Holy Roman Emperor Carlos V. He filled the place with treasures as he ruled the largest empire the world had ever seen, knowing all the while that a marble coffin awaited him in the pantheon below. The building's vast rectangle, encompassing 16 courts, is modeled on the red-hot grille upon which St. Lawrence was martyred—appropriately, as August 10 is that saint's day. (It's also said that Felipe's troops accidentally destroyed a church dedicated to St. Lawrence during the battle and sought to make amends.)

The building and its adjuncts—a palace, museum, church, and more—can take hours or even days to tour. Easter Sunday's candlelight midnight mass draws crowds, as does the summer tourist season.

The monastery was begun by the architect Juan Bautista de Toledo but finished in 1584 by Juan de Herrera, who would eventually give his name to a major Spanish architectural school. It was completed just in time for Felipe to die here, gangrenous and tortured by the gout that had plagued him for years, in the tiny, sparsely furnished bedroom that resembled a monk's cell more than the resting place of a great monarch. It's in this bedroom—which looks out, through a private entrance, into the royal chapel—that you most appreciate the man's spartan nature. Spain's later Bourbon kings, such as Carlos III and Carlos IV, had clearly different tastes, and their apartments, connected to Felipe's by the Hall of Battles, and which can be visited only by appointment, are far more luxurious.

GETTING HERE AND AROUND

El Escorial is easily reached by car, train, bus, or organized tour from Madrid. If you plan on taking public transportation, the bus is probably the best option. Herranz's Lines 661 (through Galapagar) and 664 (through Guadarrama) depart a few times every hour (less frequently on the weekends) from bay 30 at the *intercambiador* (station) at Moncloa.

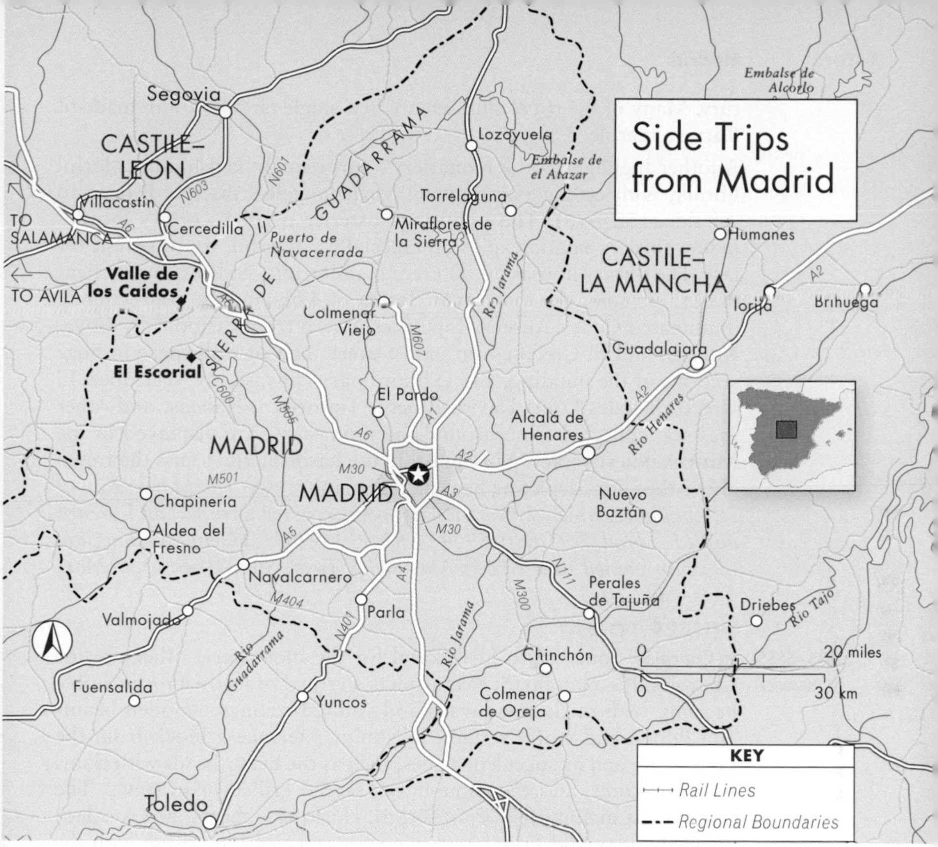

The 50-minute ride leaves you within a five-minute walk of the monastery. You can also take the *cercanías C-8a* (commuter train C-8a) from either Atocha or Chamartín, but it runs less frequently than the buses and stops at the town of El Escorial, from which you must either take Bus L-4 (also run by Herranz) to San Lorenzo de El Escorial (where the monastery is) or a strenuous, long walk uphill. To get to the **local tourist office** (☒ *Calle Grimaldi 4* ☎ *91/890–5313*), cross the arch that's across from the visitors' entrance to the monastery.

EXPLORING

Perhaps the most interesting part of the entire Escorial is the **Panteón de los Reyes** (Royal Pantheon), a baroque construction room from the 17th century that contains the body of every king since Carlos I except three—Felipe V (buried at La Granja), Ferdinand VI (in Madrid), and Amadeus of Savoy (in Italy). The body of Alfonso XIII, who died in Rome in 1941, was brought to El Escorial in January 1980. The rulers' bodies lie in 26 sumptuous marble-and-bronze sarcophagi that line the walls (three of which are empty, awaiting future rulers). Only those queens who bore sons later crowned lie in the same crypt; the others, along with royal sons and daughters who never ruled, lie nearby, in the **Panteón de los Infantes,** built in the latter part of the 19th century. Many of the royal children are in a single circular tomb made of Carrara marble.

Another highlight is the monastery's surprisingly lavish and colorful **library,** with ceiling paintings by Michelangelo's disciple Pellegrino Tibaldi (1527–96). The imposing austerity of El Escorial's facades makes this chromatic explosion especially powerful; try to save it for last. The library houses 50,000 rare manuscripts, codices, and ancient books, including the diary of St. Teresa of Ávila and the gold-lettered, illuminated Codex Aureus. Tapestries woven from cartoons by Goya, Rubens, and El Greco cover almost every inch of wall space in huge sections of the building, and extraordinary canvases by Velázquez, El Greco, Jacques-Louis David, Ribera, Tintoretto, Rubens, and other masters, collected from around the monastery, are displayed in the **Museos Nuevos** (New Museums). In the **basilica,** don't miss the fresco above the choir, depicting heaven, or Titian's fresco *The Martyrdom of St. Lawrence,* which shows the saint being roasted alive. ✉ *San Lorenzo de El Escorial* ☎ *91/890–5904 or 91/890–5905* 🎫 *General admission €8; with guided tour €10* ⏲ *Apr.–Sept., Tues.–Sun. 10–6; Oct.–Mar., Tues.–Sun. 10–5.*

WHERE TO EAT

$$$–$$$$ SPANISH

✕ **Charolés.** Some go to El Escorial for the monastery; others go for Charolés. It's a landmark that attracts a crowd of its own for its noble bearing, with thick stone walls and vaulted ceilings, wooden beams and floors, and stuffy service; its summer terrace a block from the monastery; and its succulent dishes, such as the heavy beans with clams or mushrooms, and the game meats served grilled or in stews. The four-course mammoth *cocido* (broth, chickpeas, meats, and a salad) on Wednesday and Friday tests the endurance of even those with the heartiest appetites. ✉ *Calle Floridablanca 24* ☎ *91/890–5975* 💳 *DC, MC, V.*

$$ SPANISH

✕ **La Horizontal.** Away from town and surrounded by trees in what used to be a mountain cabin, this family-oriented restaurant is coveted by madrileños, who come here to enjoy the terrace in summer and the cozy bar area with a fireplace in winter. It has a good selection of fish and rice dishes, but the meats and seasonal plates are what draw the large following. Take Paseo Juan de Borbón, which surrounds the monastery, exit through the arches and pass the *casita del infante* (Prince's Quarters) on your way up to the Monte Abantos, or get a cab at the taxi station on Calle Floridablanca. ✉ *C. Horizontal s/n* ☎ *91/890–3811* 💳 *AE, MC, V* ⏲ *No dinner Mon.–Wed. Nov.–Mar.*

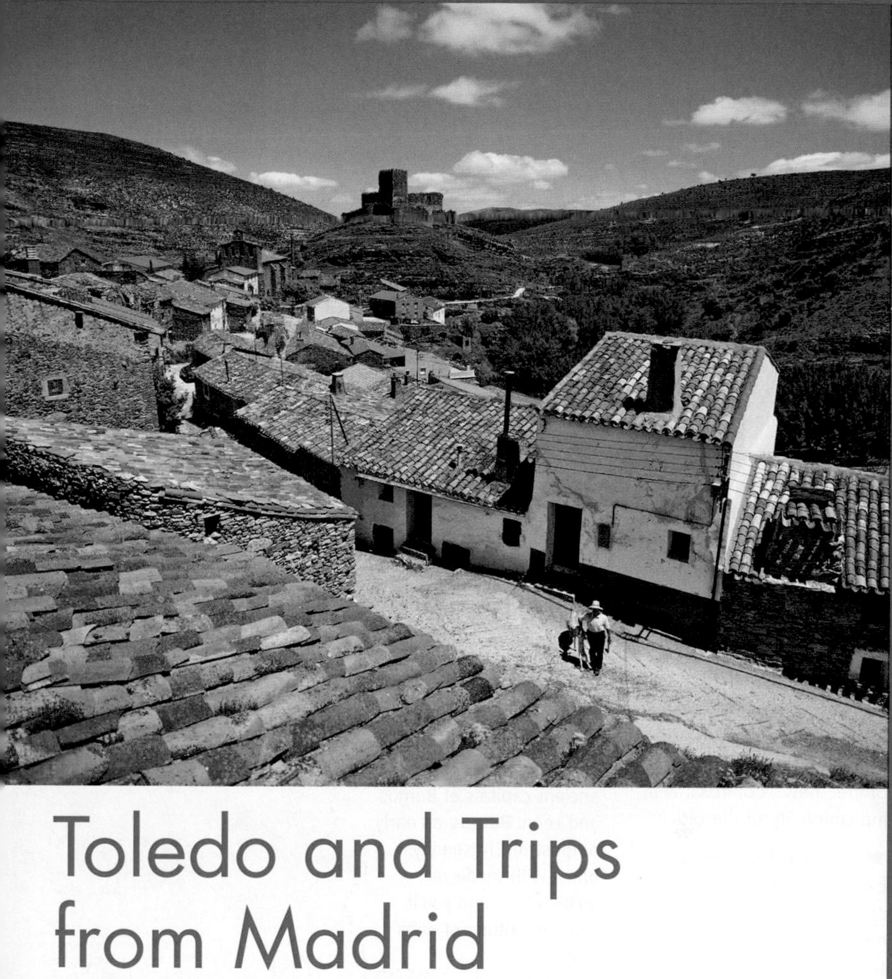

3

Toledo and Trips from Madrid

WORD OF MOUTH

"Our day in Toledo was magical. The cathedral is indeed stunning and awe-inspiring and the buildings that used to be synagogues are worth the visit as well. If you are a lover of marzipan DO NOT MISS the Santo Tome store, on the main Plaza Zocodover, and you cannot miss it."

—Flame123

WELCOME TO TOLEDO

TOP REASONS TO GO

★ **El Greco's Toledo:** You can't help but get lost in Toledo's labyrinthine streets, but make an effort to find some of El Greco's famous paintings.

★ **Cuenca's "Hanging Houses":** Las Casas Colgadas, suspended over the cliff, seems to defy gravity; stop in at the excellent Museo de Arte Abstracto, inside.

★ **Salamanca's Old and New Cathedrals:** These adjacent cathedrals are a fascinating dichotomy: the intricate detail of the of the "new" contrasts with the simplicity of the old.

★ **Medieval Musing:** Explore León's Gothic cathedral, with its mesmerizing, kaleidoscopic windows.

★ **Segovia's Aqueduct:** The sight of this amazingly preserved, still-functioning 2,000-year-old aqueduct is unforgettable.

★ **Get Stuck in a Time Warp:** The walled city of Cáceres is especially evocative at dusk, with its skyline of ancient spires, towers, and cupolas.

1 Castile–La Mancha. Toledo, once home to Spain's famous artist El Greco, is a major destination outside Madrid. Other highlights of the area include lovely Cuenca with its "hanging houses" architecture; Almagro with its splendid parador; and Alarcón.

2 Castile–León. There are several worthy destinations in the northern Castile, including medieval Segovia, with its famed Roman aqueduct and Alcázar palace; and the walled city of Ávila. Farther north is Salamanca, dominated by luminescent sandstone buildings, and the ancient capitals of Burgos and León: Burgos, an early outpost of Christianity, brims with medieval architecture, and you'll see a multitude of nuns roaming its streets; León is a fun university town with some of its Roman walls still in place.

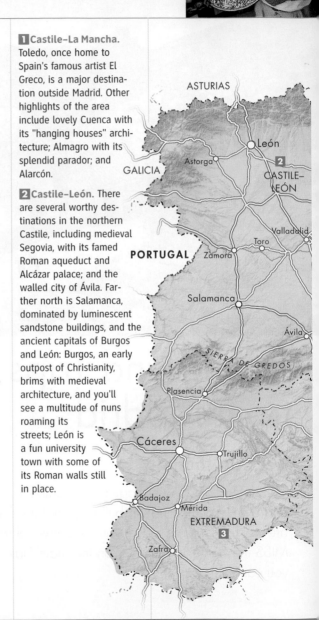

3 Extremadura. Green valleys and pristine mountain villages, along with the cities of Cáceres, and Trujillo are the main attractions in upper Extremadura, while the Jerte Valley has stunning natural settings with remote villages that the 20th century seems to have skipped entirely. Southern Extremadura shows the pull of Portugal and Andalusia, and the early Roman capital of Lusitania at Mérida is Iberia's finest compendium of Roman ruins. The *dehesa*, southwestern Spain's rolling oak forest and meadowland, is prime habitat for the semiwild Iberian pig and covers much of southern Extremadura.

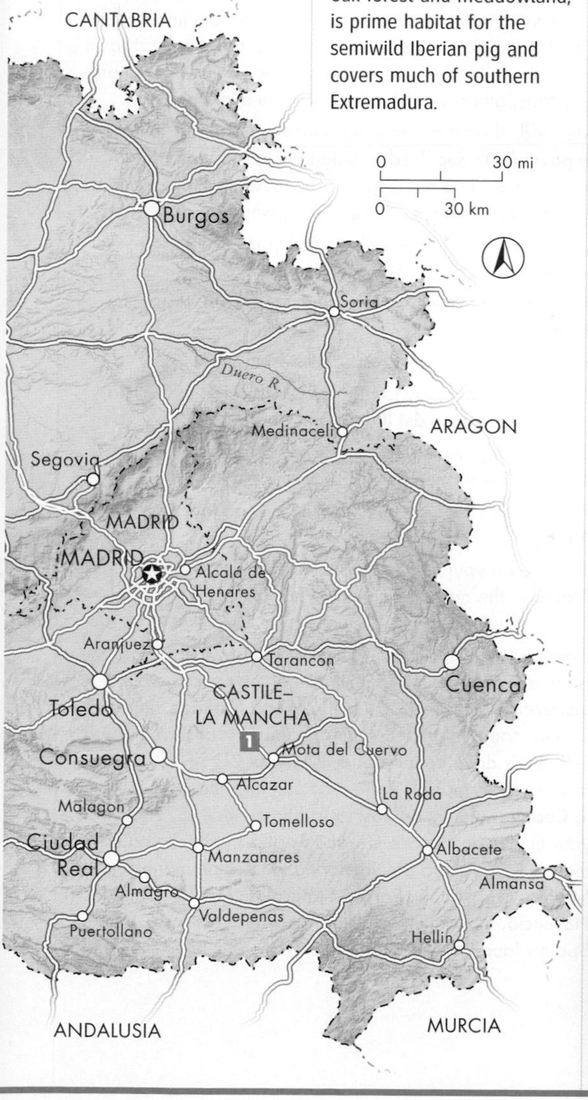

GETTING ORIENTED

Castile–La Mancha and Castile–León are like parentheses around Madrid, one north and one south. The name Castilla refers to the great east–west line of castles and fortified towns built in the 12th century between Salamanca and Soria. Segovia's Alcázar, Ávila's fully intact city walls, and other bastions are among Castile's greatest monuments. Extremadura, just west of Madrid, covers an area of 41,602 square km (16,063 square mi) and consists of two provinces: Cáceres to the north and Badajoz to the south, divided by the Toledo Mountains. To the west, this region borders Portugal; to the south, Andalusia; and to the east, Castile–La Mancha.

TOLEDO PLANNER

When to Go

July and August can be brutally hot; November through February can get bitterly cold, especially in the Sierra de Guadarrama. May and October, when the weather is sunny but relatively cool, are the two best months to visit central Spain.

Cuenca's Easter celebration and Toledo's Corpus Christi draw people from all over Spain. During the pre-Lenten carnival, León and nearby La Bañeza are popular party centers. Expect crowds and book accommodations months in advance if going then.

Spring in Extremadura is ideal season, especially in the countryside when the valleys and hills are covered with a dazzle of wildflowers. If you can time it right, the stunning spectacle of cherry-blossom season in the Jerte Valley and La Vera takes place around mid-March. Fall is also a good time for Extremadura, though there may be rain starting in late October.

Planning Your Time

Madrid is an excellent hub for venturing farther into Spain, but with so many choices, we've divided them into must-see stand-alone destinations, and those that are worthy stops if you're traveling on to other parts of the country. Some are day trips; others are best done with an overnight.

Must-see, short-trip destinations from Madrid are **Toledo**, **Segovia** (with **Sepúlveda**), **Salamanca**, and **Ávila**. Salamanca should be an overnight, because it's farther, and it also has fun nightlife, unlike Toledo, which is rather staid.

Otherwise, if you're traveling to other areas in Spain, we suggest the following stopover destinations:

If you're on your way to Santander or Bilbao, stop in **Burgos.**

If you're on your way to Asturias stop in **León.**

If you're on your way to Lugo and A Coruña, in Galicia, stop in **Villafranca del Bierzo** or **Astorga.**

If you're on your way to Zaragoza or Barcelona (by car; the AVE doesn't stop here) visit **Siguenza**.

If you're on your way to Cordoba or Granada, stop in **Almagro**.

If you're on your way to.Valencia, detour to **Cuenca** (and **Alarcón**); the new high-speed AVE to Valencia will go through Cuenca.

Extremadura is a neglected destination, even for Spanish tourists, but it's a beautiful part of the country, with fasincating cities like Cáceres (a World Heritage site) and Trujillo. You can get a lightning impression of Extremadura in a day's drive from Madrid. It's about 2½ hours from Madrid to **Jerte**; from there, you can take the A66 south to **Cáceres,** then head east to **Trujillo** on the N521. Split your time evenly between Cáceres and Trujillo. If you have more time, spend a day exploring the Roman monuments in Mérida, and visit the **Parque Natural de Monfragüe,** near **Plasencia.** If you can, visit the **Monasterio de Yuste,** where Spain's founding emperor Carlos V died in 1558.

Tours

In summer the tourist offices of Segovia, Toledo, and Aranjuez organize Trénes Turísticos (miniature tourist trains) that glide past all the major sights; contact the local tourist office for schedules, or call *925/142274* for information. **Equiberia** leads horseback tours ranging from 1 to 10 days, a unique way to experience the gorges, fields, and forests of the Sierra de Guadarrama.

A great way to really get to know Extremadura is by bike, and you can cut down on the map-reading by following the ancient Roman Ruta Vía de la Plata: it runs through Extremadura from north to south along A66, dividing it in two, and passes by such villages as Plasencia, Cáceres, Mérida, and Zafra. Parts of the Ruta Vía are still preserved and bicycleable. Note that the region north of the province of Cáceres, including the Jerte Valley, La Vera, and the area surrounding Guadalupe, is mountainous and uneven. If you attempt it, be prepared for a bumpy and exhausting ride. The regional government has opened a Vía Verde, which goes from Logrosán (a couple of miles southwest of Guadalupe) to Villanueva de la Serena (east of Mérida and near Don Benito). This path is a roughly cleared track, more like a nature trail for hikers and bikers, and closed to motor vehicles.

Horseback riding tours are also an option in Extremadura, and **Hidden Trails**, based in Vancouver, Canada, offers weeklong riding tours of the Gredo Mountains on the border of Cáceres province. **Valle Aventura** organizes hiking, horseback-riding, cycling, and kayaking trips in the Jerte Valley.

Contacts Equiberia (☏ *920/348338* 🌐 *www.equiberia.com*). **EuroAdventures Vacations** (🌐 *www.euroadventures.net*). **Hidden Trails** (☏ *604/323–1141* 🌐 *www.hiddentrails.com*). **Valle Aventura** (☏ *927/472196* 🌐 *www.valleaventura.com*).

WHAT IT COSTS (IN EUROS)

	¢	$	$$	$$$	$$$$
Restaurants	under €8	€8–€12	€13–€17	€18–€22	over €22
Hotels	under €60	€60–€90	€91–€125	€126–€180	over €180

Prices are per person for a main course at dinner, and for two people in a standard double room in high season, excluding tax.

About the Hotels

Most of the oldest and most attractive paradores in Castile are in quieter towns such as Almagro, Ávila, Cuenca, León, and Sigüenza. Those in Toledo, Segovia, and Salamanca are modern buildings with magnificent views and, in the case of Segovia, have wonderful indoor and outdoor swimming pools. There are plenty of pleasant alternatives to paradors, too, such as Segovia's Infanta Isabel, Salamanca's Hotel Rector, and Cuenca's Posada San José, a 16th-century convent.

Extremadura's paradors are remarkable, occupying buildings of great historic or architectural interest in all major tourist areas. The Extremaduran government runs a few *hospederías,* a sort of regional version of the parador chain; some have historic quarters in scenic areas. Most other high-end hotels, with a few exceptions, are modern boxes with little character. Throughout Extremadura's countryside are a number of charming bed-and-breakfast inns (*hoteles rurales*) and 135 guesthouses (*casas rurales*).

GETTING HERE AND AROUND

By Air

The only international airport in Castile is Madrid's Barajas; Salamanca, León, and Valladolid have domestic airports. Extremadura's only airport is Badajoz, which receives domestic flights from Madrid, Barcelona, and Bilbao. The nearest international airports are Madrid and Seville.

By Train

All of the main towns in Castile–León and Castile–La Mancha are accessible by fast train from Madrid, for about €10. Several make feasible day trips: there are commuter trains from Madrid to Segovia (30 minutes), Guadalajara (30 minutes), and Toledo (30 minutes). Trains to Toledo depart from Madrid's Atocha station; trains to Salamanca, Burgos, and León depart from Chamartín; and both stations serve Ávila, Segovia, El Escorial, and Sigüenza, though Chamartín may have more frequent service. The one important town that's accessible only by train (and not bus) is Sigüenza. Trains from Segovia go only to Madrid, but you can change at Villalba for Ávila and Salamanca.

For Extremadura, trains from Madrid stop at Monfragüe, Plasencia, Cáceres, Mérida, Zafra, and Badajoz, running as often as six times daily. The journey from Madrid to Cáceres takes about 4 hours. Within the province there are services from Badajoz to Cáceres (3 daily, 1 hour 55 minutes), to Mérida (5 daily, 40 minutes), and to Plasencia (2 daily, 2 hours 40 minutes); from Cáceres to Badajoz (3 daily, 1 hour 55 minutes), to Mérida (5 daily, 1 hour), to Plasencia (4 daily, 1 hour 10 minutes), and to Zafra (2 daily, 2 hours 10 minutes); from Plasencia to Badajoz (2 daily, 3 hours), to Cáceres (4 daily, 1 hour 10 minutes), and to Mérida (4 daily, 2 hours 10 minutes). Note that train stations in Extremadura are often far from town centers.

By Car

Major divided highways—the A1 through A6—radiate out from Madrid, making Spain's farthest corners no more than five- to six-hour drives, and the capital's outlying towns are only minutes away. If possible, avoid returning to Madrid on major highways at the end of a weekend or a holiday. The beginning and end of August are notorious for traffic jams, as is Semana Santa (Holy Week), which starts on Palm Sunday and ends on Easter Sunday. Side roads vary in quality but provide one of the great pleasures of driving around the Castilian countryside: surprise encounters with historical monuments and spectacular vistas.

If you're heading from Madrid to Extremadura by car, the main gateway, the four-lane NV, moves quickly. The N630, or Vía de la Plata, which crosses Extremadura from north to south, is also effective. The fastest way heading from Portugal is the A6 from Lisbon to Badajoz. If you're in a hurry, driving is the most feasible way to get around Extremadura. The main roads are well surfaced and not too congested. Side roads—particularly those that cross the wilder mountainous districts, such as the Sierra de Guadalupe—can be both poorly paved and marked, but afford some of the most spectacular vistas in Extremadura. For some of the best views, head north of Guadalupe on EX118, toward the village of Navalmoral. Continue northwest from here on the EX102 at Cañamero and on to the main Navalmoral–Trujillo road near the Puerto de Miravete, where you can enjoy a fabulous lookout point with sweeping views of Trujillo in the distance.

Mileage between destinations:

Madrid to Burgos is 237 km (147 mi).

Madrid to Caceres is 297 km (184 mi).

Madrid to Cuenca is167 km (104 mi).

Madrid to Granada is 434 km (270 mi).

Madrid to Léon is 333 km (207 mi).

Madrid to Salamanca is 212 km (44 mi).

Madrid to Segovia is 87 km (54 mi).

Madrid to Toledo is 71 km (44 mi).

Madrid to Avila is 115 km (71 mi).

The Travel Smart chapter has contact info for major car rental agencies.

By Bus

Bus connections between Madrid and Castile are excellent. There are several stations and stops in Madrid; buses to Toledo (1 hour) leave every half hour from the Estación del Sur, and buses to Segovia (1¼ hours) leave every hour from La Sepulvedana's headquarters, near Príncipe Pío. Larrea sends buses to Ávila (1¾ hours) from the Estación del Sur. Alsa and Movelia have service to León (4½ hours). Auto Res serves Cuenca (2¾ hours) and Salamanca (3 hours). Buses to Burgos (2½ hours) are run by Continental Auto.

From Burgos, buses head north to the Basque Country; from León, you can press on to Asturias. Service between towns is not as frequent as it is to and from Madrid, so you may find it quicker to return to Madrid and make your way from there. Reservations are rarely necessary.

Buses to Extremadura's main cities can be reached from Madrid and are reliable. The first bus of the day on lesser routes often sets off early in the morning, so plan carefully to avoid getting stranded. Some examples of destinations from Madrid are: Cáceras (7 daily), Guadalupe (2 daily), Trujillo (12 daily), and Mérida (8 daily). For schedules and prices, check the tourist offices or contact the Auto Res bus line. Note that it's best to avoid taking the bus at rush hour, as journeys can be delayed by more than an hour.

EATING AND DRINKING WELL IN CASTILE AND EXTREMADURA

Spain's central *meseta* is an arid, high plateau where peasant cooking evolved to provide comfort and energy. Roast lamb and goat are staples, as are soups, stews, and dishes made from scraps, such as the classic *migas de pastor,* shepherd's breadcrumbs.

Top left: Roast lamb with potatoes. Top right: A simple dish of migas is an excellent way to use up leftover bread or tortillas. Bottom left: The pisto manchego incorporates a variety of stewed vegetables.

Classic Castilian dishes are *cordero* (lamb) and *cochinillo* (suckling pig) roasted in wood ovens, and other prized entrées include *perdiz en escabeche (*marinated partridge), and *perdices a la Toledana (*stewed partridge). Broadbean dishes are specialties in the areas around Ávila and La Granja (Segovia), while *trucha* (trout) and *cangrejos de río* (river crayfish) are Guadalajara specialties. Some of Castile's most exotic cuisine is found in Cuenca, where a Moorish influence appears in such dishes as *gazpacho pastor* (shepherd's stew), a stew made with an assortment of meats. Wild mushrooms are used to enhance aromas in meat dishes and stews, or are served on their own in earthenware dishes. *Níscalos estofados* (stewed saffron milk cap mushrooms) or *setas a la segoviana,* a fragrant stew of king trumpet mushrooms.

DON QUIJOTE FOOD

Cervantine menus are favorites at taverns and inns throughout Quijote country southeast of Madrid. *Gachas manchegas,* a thick peasant porridge based on fried legume flour and pork, is mentioned in the Miguel de Cervantes masterpiece *Don Quijote de la Mancha* along with *duelos y quebrantos* (scrambled eggs and bacon) as typical offerings on late 15th-century rural menus.

LAMB

Roast lamb, *cordero asado,* is a favorite dish throughout Castile. A *lechazo* or milk-fed lamb should be two to three weeks old, and have been carefully protected from bumps and bruises by his shepherd. It's handled with great delicacy all the way to the wood oven where it's roasted slowly on low heat. The forward quarter is considered better than the hindquarters, and the left side is more tender, as lambs tend to lie on their right sides, which toughens the meat.

PARTRIDGE

Perdices a la Toledana, partridge prepared in the Toledo way, is one of Castilla–La Mancha's most sought after gastronomical delicacies. Toledo partridges are neither *estofadas* (stewed) nor *escabechadas* (marinated) but, rather, cooked on low heat in wine with vinegar. Up to a dozen wild partridges stew for hours with white wine, olive oil, onions, garlic, and laurel leaves until the sauce has nearly evaporated. October to February are the hunting months for partridge and the best time to try this local favorite with fresh-killed birds.

VEGETABLE STEW

La Mancha, the arid and windswept area southeast of Madrid, has its moist vegetable-growing pockets along the Tajo river. *Pisto Manchego* is the classic vegetable stew, with ham and chorizo added for protein and flavor. Onions, green peppers, eggplants, ripe tomatoes, olive oil, chorizo, and ham are the ingredients in this Castilian favorite typically served in an earthenware vessel.

MIGAS DE PASTOR

Translated as "shepherd's breadcrumbs," this dish is made with hardened bread that's been softened with water, then broken up and fried in olive oil with garlic and eggs, as well as bacon, chorizo, peppers, sardines, or squash if available.

GAZPACHO PASTOR (SHEPHERD'S STEW)

Andalusian gazpacho is a cold soup but in La Mancha, especially in and around Cuenca, gazpacho is a thick stew made of virtually everything in the barnyard, and served very hot. Partridge, hare, rabbit, hen, peppers, paprika and *tortas gazpacheras,* flatbread made especially for this dish, complete the stew.

CASTILIAN WINES

In Toledo, Carlos Falcó (aka Marqués de Griñón) has developed excellent Dominio de Valdepusa wines using Petit Verdot and Syrah grapes. In Ribera de Duero, winemakers from Pingus and Protos to Pago de Carraovejas offer full-bodied wines using Tempranillo grapes, while El Bierzo northwest of León has good values and earthy wines made with the local Mencía grape.

Updated by Aleisha K. Fetters

Madrid, in the geographical center of Spain, is an excellent jumping-off point for exploring other historically significant areas of Spain, and the high-speed train makes many destinations easily within reach. The Castiles, which bracket Madrid to the east and west, and Extremadura, bordering Portugal, are filled with compelling destinations.

For all the variety in the towns and countryside around Madrid, there's something of an underlying unity in Castile—the high, wide meseta (plain) of gray, bronze, and (briefly) green. This central Spanish steppe is divided into what was historically known as Old and New Castile, the former north of Madrid, the latter south (known as "New" because it was captured from the Moors a bit later). No Spaniard refers to either as "Old" or "New" anymore, preferring instead Castilla y León or Castile–León for the area north of Madrid and Castilla y La Mancha or Castile–La Mancha for the area to the south. Stone, a dominant element in the Castilian countryside, provides the region much of its intense character. Gaunt mountain ranges frame the horizons; gorges and rocky outcrops break up flat expanses; and the fields around Ávila and Segovia are littered with giant boulders. Castilian villages are built predominantly of granite, and their solid, formidable look contrasts markedly with the whitewashed walls of most of southern Spain. Over the centuries, poets—most notably Antonio Machado, whose experiences at Soria in the early 20th century inspired his haunting *Campos de Castilla* (Fields of Castile)—and others have characterized Castile as austere and melancholy. There is a distinct, chilly beauty in the stark lines and soothing colors of these expanses.

The very name Extremadura, widely accepted as "the far end of the Duero," as in the Duero River, expresses the wild, remote, isolated, and end-of-the-line character of this haunting region. With its poor soil and minimal industry, Extremadura never experienced the kind of modern economic development typical of other parts of Spain, but no other place in Spain has as many Roman monuments as Mérida, capital of the vast Roman province of Lusitania, which included most of the western half of the Iberian Peninsula. Mérida guarded the Vía de la Plata, the major Roman highway that crossed Extremadura from north to south, connecting Gijón with Seville. The economy and the arts declined after the Romans left, but the region revived in the 16th century, when explorers and conquerors of the New World—from Francisco Pizarro and Hernán Cortés to Francisco de Orellana, first navigator of the Amazon—returned to their birthplace. These men built the magnificent palaces that now glorify towns such as Cáceres and Trujillo, and they turned the remote monastery of Guadalupe into one of the great artistic repositories of Spain.

CASTILE–LA MANCHA

TOLEDO

Fodor's Choice ★ *71 km (44 mi) southwest of Madrid.*

Long the spiritual capital of Spain, Toledo is perched atop a rocky mount with steep golden hills rising on either side, and is bound on three sides by the Río Tajo (Tagus River). When the Romans arrived here in 192 BC, they built their fortress, the Alcázar, on the highest point of the rock. Later, the Visigoths remodeled the stronghold.

In the 8th century, the Moors arrived and strengthened Toledo's reputation as a center of religion and learning. Unusual tolerance was extended to those who practiced Christianity (the Mozarabs) and to the city's exceptionally large Jewish population. Today, the Moorish legacy is evident in Toledo's strong crafts tradition, the mazelike streets, and the predominance of brick (rather than the stone of many of Spain's historical cities). For the Moors, beauty was to be savored from within rather than displayed on the surface. Even Toledo's cathedral—one of the most richly endowed in Spain—is hard to see from the outside, largely obscured by the warren of houses around it.

Alfonso VI, aided by El Cid ("Lord Conqueror"), captured the city in 1085 and dubbed himself emperor of Toledo. Under the Christians, the town's strong intellectual life was maintained, and Toledo became famous for its school of translators, who taught Arab medicine, law, culture, and philosophy. Religious tolerance continued, and during the rule of Peter the Cruel (so named because he allegedly had members of his own family murdered to advance his position), a Jewish banker, Samuel Levi, became the royal treasurer and one of the wealthiest men in the booming city. By the early 1600s, however, hostility toward Jews and Arabs had grown as Toledo developed into a bastion of the Catholic Church.

Under Toledo's long line of cardinals—most notably Mendoza, Tavera, and Cisneros—Renaissance Toledo emerged as a center of the humanities. Economically and politically, however, Toledo began to decline at the end of the 15th century. The expulsion of the Jews from Spain in 1492, as part of the Spanish Inquisition, eroded Toledo's economic prowess. When Madrid became the permanent center of the Spanish court in 1561, Toledo lost its political importance, and the expulsion from Spain of the converted Arabs (Moriscos) in 1601 meant the departure of most of the city's artisan community. The years the painter El Greco spent in Toledo—from 1572 to his death in 1614—were those of the city's decline, which is greatly reflected in his works. In the late 19th century, after hundreds of years of neglect, the works of El Greco came to be widely appreciated, and Toledo was transformed into a major tourist destination. Today, Toledo is conservative, prosperous, and expensive.

Its winding streets and steep hills can be exasperating, especially when you're searching for a specific sight. Take the entire day to absorb the town's medieval trappings and expect to get a little lost.

GETTING HERE AND AROUND

The best way to get to Toledo from Madrid is the high-speed AVE train. The AVE leaves from Madrid at minimum 9 times daily from Atocha station and gets you there in 30 minutes. Buses leave every half hour from Plaza Elíptica and take 1¼ hours.

If you're with children, check out the **Zocotren Imperial** (☎ *925/220300* *€4.25* *Daily 11–7*) a tourist train that chugs past many of the main sights. It departs every hour on the hour from the Plaza de Zocodover.

ESSENTIALS

Visitor Information Toledo (✉ *Pl. del Consistorio 1* ☎ *925/254030* *www.toledo-turismo.com*).

TOP ATTRACTIONS

5 **Alcázar.** Expected to reopen in mid-2010 after years of renovations, the Alcázar ("fortress" in Arabic), originally a Moorish citadel occupied from the 10th century to the Reconquest, is rich in both beauty and history. The south facade—the building's most severe—is the work of Juan de Herrera, of El Escorial fame, while the east facade incorporates a large section of battlements. The finest facade is the northern, one of many Toledan works by Covarrubias, who did more than any other architect to introduce the Renaissance style here. It is also the new site for the Museo del Ejército (Military Museum), which was formerly in Madrid. The Alcázar's architectural highlight is Covarrubias's Italianate courtyard, which, like most other parts of the building, was largely rebuilt after the civil war, when the Alcázar was besieged by the Republicans. Though the Nationalists' ranks were depleted, they held on to the building. General Francisco Franco later turned the Alcázar into a monument to Nationalist bravery. More cheerful is a ground-floor room full of beautifully crafted swords, a Toledo specialty introduced by Moorish silversmiths. At the top of the grand staircase are rooms displaying a vast collection of toy soldiers. ✉ *C. Cuesta del Alcázar s/n* ☎ *925/238800* *€5* *Tues.–Sun. 9:30–2:30*.

11 **Casa y Museo de El Greco** *(El Greco House and Museum)*. This house on the property that once belonged to Peter the Cruel's treasurer, Samuel Levi, is said to have been El Greco's home. Although it is known he once lived in a house owned by Levi, the claim that it was here is pure conjecture. The interior, decorated in the late 19th century to resemble a "typical" house of El Greco's time, is fake, albeit pleasant. The museum

3

A GOOD WALK

The eastern end of the Tagus gorge, along Calle de Circunvalación, is a good place to park your car and look down over historic Toledo. If you want to be closer to the city, park next to the Alcázar. The streets in Toledo are steep and winding, making it hard to find sights. To avoid frustration, you might prefer to visit only some of these sights or spread your tour over several days.

A complete tour starts at the **Puente de Alcántara** ❶. If you skirt the city walls traveling northwest, a long walk past the Puerta de Bisagra on Calle Cardenal Tavera brings you to the **Hospital de Tavera** ❷. If, instead, you enter the city wall, walk west and pass the **Museo de la Santa Cruz** ❸ to emerge in the **Plaza de Zocodover** ❹. Due south, on Calle Cuesta de Carlos V, is the **Alcázar** ❺; a short walk northwest on Calle Nueva brings you to the **Mezquita del Cristo de la Luz** ❻. From the southwestern corner of the Alcázar, a series of alleys descends to the **catedral** ❼. Make your way around the southern side of the building, passing the mid-15th-century Puerta de los Leones. On the small plaza in front of the cathedral's west facade, you'll see the stately *ayuntamiento* (town hall).

Near the Museo de los Concilios, on Calle de San Clemente, take in the Convento de San Clemente's richly sculpted portal by Alonso de Covarrubias. Across the street is the church of **San Román** ❽. Almost every wall in this part of town belongs to a convent, and the empty streets make for contemplative walks. This was a district loved by the Romantic poet Gustavo Adolfo Bécquer, author of *Rimas* (*Rhymes*), once the most popular collection of Spanish verse. Bécquer's favorite corner of Toledo was the tiny square in front of the 16th-century convent church of **Santo Domingo** ❾, a few minutes' walk north of San Román, below the Plazuela de Padilla.

Backtrack, following Calle de San Clemente through Plaza de Valdecaleros to Calle de Santo Tomé, to get to the church of **Santo Tomé** ❿. Downhill from Santo Tomé, off Calle de San Juan de Díos, is the **Casa y Museo de El Greco** ⓫ (follow the signs, as it's a bit of a labyrinth). Next to the Casa de El Greco is the 14th-century **Sinagoga del Tránsito** ⓬, financed by Samuel Levi, and the accompanying Museo Sefardí. From the synagogue, turn right up Calle de Reyes Católicos. A few steps past the town's other synagogue, **Santa María la Blanca** ⓭, is the late-15th-century church of **San Juan de los Reyes** ⓮. The town's western extremity is the **Puente de San Martín** ⓯.

next door has a few of El Greco's paintings, including a panorama of Toledo with the Hospital of Tavera in the foreground. As of this writing the museum was closed for renovations so call for more details ✉ *C. Samuel Levi s/n* ☎ *925/224046* 🎟 *€2.50, free Sat. afternoon and Sun. morning* ⏲ *Tues.–Sat. 10–2 and 4–9, Sun. 10–2.*

❼ **Cathedral.** The cathedral owes its impressive Mozarabic chapel, with an elongated dome crowning the west facade, to Jorge Manuel Theotokópoulos. The rest of the facade, however, is mainly early 15th

Alcázar **5**
Casa y Museo del Greco **11**
Cathedral **7**
Hospital de Tavera **2**
Mezquita del Cristo de la Luz **6**
Museo de la Santa Cruz **3**
Plaza de Zocodover **4**
Puente de Alcántara **1**
Puente de San Martín **15**
San Juan de los Reyes **14**
San Román **8**
Santa María la Blanca **13**
Santo Domingo **9**
Santo Tomé **10**
Sinagoga del Tránsito **12**

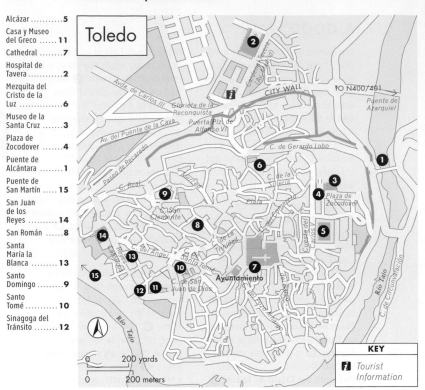

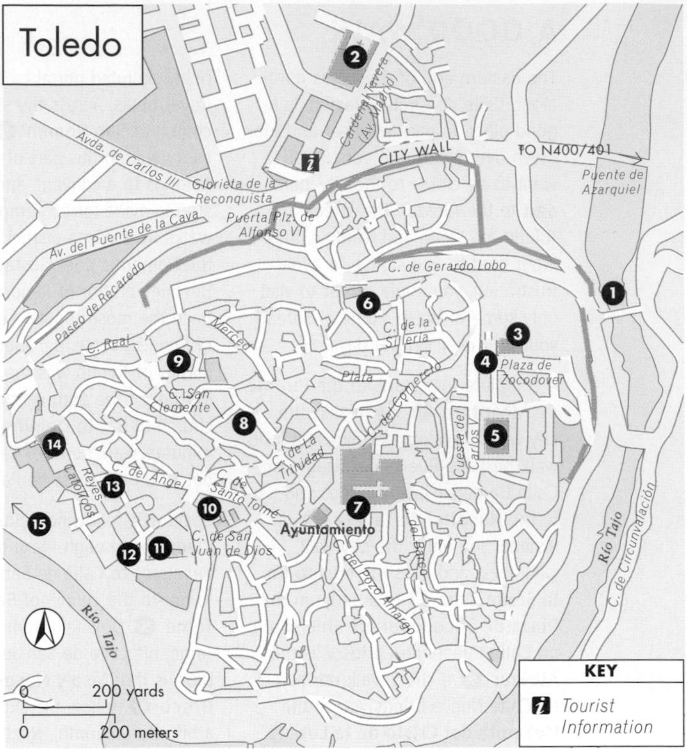

century; it features a depiction of Mary presenting her robe to Toledo's patron saint, the Visigothic Ildefonsus. Chartres and other Gothic cathedrals in France inspired the cathedral's 13th-century architecture, but the squat proportions give it a Spanish feel, as do the weight of the furnishings and the elaborate choir in the center of the nave. Immediately to your right as you enter the building is a beautifully carved plateresque doorway by Covarrubias, marking the entrance to the Treasury. The latter houses a small Crucifixion by the Italian painter Cimabue and an extraordinarily intricate late-15th-century monstrance by Juan del Arfe, a silversmith of German descent; the ceiling is an excellent example of Mudejar (11th- to 16th-century Moorish-influenced) workmanship.

From here, walk around to the ambulatory; off to the right side is a chapter house with a strange mixture of Italianate frescoes by Juan de Borgoña. In the middle of the ambulatory is an exemplary baroque illusionism by Narciso Tomé known as the *Transparente,* a blend of painting, stucco, and sculpture. Finally, off the northern end of the ambulatory, you'll come to the sacristy and several El Grecos, including one version of *El Espolio* (Christ Being Stripped of His Raiment), the first recorded instance of the painter in Spain. Before leaving the sacristy, look up at the colorful and spirited late-baroque ceiling painting

CLOSE UP

El Greco: the Titan of Toledo

"Crete gave him his life, and brushes; Toledo, a better land, where he begins with Death to attain Eternity." With these words, the Toledan poet Fray Hortensio Paravicino paid homage to his friend El Greco—and to the symbiotic connection between El Greco and his adopted city of Toledo. El Greco's intensely individual and expressionist style—elongated and sometimes distorted figures, charged colors, and a haunting mysticism—was seen as strange and disturbing, and his work remained largely neglected until the late 19th century, when he found wide acclaim and joined the ranks of Velazquez and Goya as a master of Spanish painting.

Born Domenikos Theotokópoulos on the island of Crete, El Greco ("The Greek") received his artistic education and training in Italy, then moved to Spain around 1577, lured in part by the prospect of painting frescoes for the royal monastery of El Escorial. King Felipe II, however, rejected El Greco's work for being too unusual. It was in Toledo that El Greco came into his own, creating many of his greatest works and honing his singular style and unique vision. He remained here until his death in 1614.

The master painter immortalized the city and its citizens. His masterpiece *The Burial of Count Orgaz,* which hangs in Toledo's Chapel of Santo Tomé, pays tribute to Toledan society. Perhaps the most famous rendering of Toledo is El Greco's dramatic *View of Toledo* (which hangs in the Metropolitan Museum of Art, in New York City), in which the cityscape crackles with a sinister energy underneath a stormy sky—El Greco's other famous landscape, *View and Plan of Toledo,* can be seen at Toledo's Casa y Museo de El Greco.

3

by the Italian Luca Giordano. ✉ *C. Cardenal Cisneros 1* ☎ *925/222241* 🎟 *€7* ⏲ *Mon.–Sat. 10–6:30, Sun. 2–6:30.*

❷ **Hospital de Tavera.** Architect Alonso de Covarrubias's last work, this hospital lies outside the city walls beyond Toledo's main northern gate. Unfinished and slightly dilapidated, it is nonetheless full of character and has the evocatively ramshackle **Museo de Duque de Lema** in its southern wing. The most important work in the museum's miscellaneous collection is a painting by the 17th-century artist José Ribera. The hospital's monumental chapel holds El Greco's *Baptism of Christ* and the exquisitely carved marble tomb of Cardinal Tavera, the last work of Alonso de Berruguete. Descend into the crypt to experience some bizarre acoustical effects. ✉ *C. Duque de Lerma 2* ☎ *925/220451* 🎟 *€4.50* ⏲ *Mon.–Sat. 10–1:30 and 3–5:30, closed Sun. afternoon.*

❸ **Museo de Santa Cruz.** Housed in a beautiful Renaissance hospital with a stunning classical-plateresque facade, this museum is open all day without a break (unlike many of Toledo's other sights). The light and elegant interior has changed little since the 16th century, apart from works of art having replaced the hospital beds; among the displays is El Greco's *Assumption* of 1613, the artist's last known work. A small **Museo de Arqueología** (Museum of Archaeology) is in and around the

DID YOU KNOW?

An anecdote of Nationalist lore purports that Nationalist Colonel Moscardó was defending Toledo's alcazar against the Republicans during the Spanish civil war, when they took his son hostage and demanded the fortress be surrendered. Ever the loyal nationalist, Moscardo refused, telling his son to "commend his soul to God and die like a hero."

hospital's delightful cloister. ✉ *C. Cervantes s/n* ☎ *925/221036* 🎫 *Free* 🕑 *Mon.–Sat. 10–6:30, Sun. 10–2.*

4 **Plaza de Zocodover.** Toledo's main square was built in the early 17th century as part of an unsuccessful attempt to impose a rigid geometry on the chaotic Moorish streets. This tiny plaza is also home to the largest and oldest marzipan store in town, Santo Tomé, as well as Toledo's only McDonald's. You can catch inner-city buses here, and the tourist office is just around the corner. Nearby, you can find **Calle del Comercio,** the town's narrow and lively pedestrian thoroughfare, lined with bars and shops and shaded in summer by awnings.

10 **Santo Tomé.** Topped with a Mudejar tower, this chapel was specially built to house El Greco's most famous painting, *The Burial of Count Orgaz,* and remains devoted to that purpose. The painting portrays the benefactor of the church being buried with the posthumous assistance of St. Augustine and St. Stephen, who have appeared at the funeral to thank the count for his donations to religious institutions named after the two saints. Though the count's burial took place in the 14th century, El Greco painted the onlookers in contemporary 16th-century costumes and included people he knew; the boy in the foreground is one of El Greco's sons, and the sixth figure on the left is said to be the artist himself. To avoid crowds in summer, come as soon as the building opens. ✉ *Pl. del Conde 4* ☎ *925/256098* 🌐 *www.santotome.org* 🎫 *€2.30* 🕑 *Mar.–mid-Oct., daily 10–6:45; mid-Oct.–Feb., daily 10–5:45.*

Fodor's Choice ★

12 **Sinagoga del Tránsito.** Financed by Samuel Levi, this 14th-century rectangular synagogue is plain on the outside, but the inside walls are embellished with intricate Mudejar decoration, as well as Hebraic inscriptions glorifying God, Peter the Cruel, and Levi himself. It's said that Levi imported cedars from Lebanon for the building's construction, à la Solomon when he built the First Temple in Jerusalem. Adjoining the main hall is the **Museo Sefardí,** a small museum of Jewish culture in Spain. ✉ *C. Samuel Levi s/n* ☎ *925/223665* 🎫 *€3, free Sat. afternoon and Sun.* 🕑 *Mar.–Oct., Tues.–Sat. 9:30–7, Sun. 10–2; Nov.–Feb., Tues.–Sat. 9:30–6, Sun. 10–2.*

WORTH NOTING

6 **Mezquita del Cristo de la Luz** *(Mosque of Christ of the Light).* In a park above the ramparts, a gardener will show you around this mosque-chapel; if one's not around, ask for a guide at the house opposite the mosque. Originally a tiny Visigothic church, the chapel was transformed into a mosque during the Moorish occupation. The Islamic arches and vaulting survived, making this the most important relic of Moorish Toledo. The chapel got its name when Alfonso VI's horse, striding triumphantly into Toledo in 1085, fell to its knees out front (a white stone marks the spot). It was then discovered that a candle had burned continuously behind the masonry the whole time the Muslims had been in power. Allegedly, the first Mass of the Reconquest was held here, and later a Mudejar apse was added. ✉ *C. Cuesta de los Carmelitas Descalzas 10* ☎ *925/254191* 🎫 *€2.30* 🕑 *Oct. 16–Feb. 28, weekdays 10–2 and 3:30–5:45, weekends 10–5:45; Mar. 1–Oct. 15, weekdays 10–2 and 3:30–6:45, weekends 10–6:45.*

1 **Puente de Alcántara.** Roman in origin, this is the city's oldest bridge. Next to it is a heavily restored castle built after the Christian capture of 1085 and, above this, a vast and depressingly severe military academy, a typical example of fascist architecture under Franco.

15 **Puente de San Martín.** This pedestrian bridge on the western edge of the town dates from 1203 and has splendid horseshoe arches.

14 **San Juan de los Reyes.** This convent church in western Toledo was erected by Ferdinand and Isabella to commemorate their victory at the Battle of Toro in 1476 and was intended to be their burial place. (The tomb of the Catholic Monarchs is in Granada's Capilla Real). The building is largely the work of architect Juan Guas, who considered it his masterpiece and asked to be buried here himself. In true plateresque fashion, the white interior is covered with inscriptions and heraldic motifs. ✉ *C. de los Reyes Católicos 17* ☎ *925/223802* 🎫 *€2.30* ⏲ *Oct. 1–Mar. 1, daily 10–6; Mar. 2–Sept. 30, daily 10–7.*

QUICK BITES

If the maze of Toledo's streets exhausts you, unwind at Dar Al-Chai (✉ *Pl. Barrio Nuevo 5*). Just south of San Juan de los Reyes on Calle de los Reyes Católicos, this Arabian café-bar has plush couches, low tables, and colorful tapestries. The selection of common teas is delightful, but why not try one from the special list: mixed and brewed in-house, they feature a blend of flowers, dried fruit, and spices such as cardamom.

8 **San Román.** Hidden in a virtually unspoiled part of Toledo, this early-13th-century Mudejar church is now the **Museo de los Concilios y de la Cultura Visigótica,** with exhibits of statuary, manuscript illustrations, jewelry, and an extensive collection of frescoes. ✉ *San Román s/n* ☎ *925/227872* 🎫 *Free* ⏲ *Tues.–Sat. 10–2 and 4–6:30, Sun. 10–2.*

13 **Santa María la Blanca.** Founded in 1203, Toledo's second synagogue is nearly two centuries older than the more elaborate Tránsito. The white interior has a forest of columns supporting capitals of enchanting filigree workmanship. ✉ *Calle de Reyes Católicos 21* ☎ *925/227257* 🎫 *€2.30* ⏲ *Apr.–Sept., daily 10–7; Oct.–Mar., daily 10–6.*

9 **Santo Domingo el Antiguo.** A few minutes' walk north of San Román is this 16th-century convent church, where you'll find the earliest of El Greco's Toledo paintings as well as the crypt where the artist is believed to be buried. The friendly nuns at the convent will show you around its odd little museum that includes documents bearing El Greco's signature. ✉ *Pl. Santo Domingo el Antiguo s/n* ☎ *925/222930* 🎫 *€2* ⏲ *Mon.–Sat. 11–1:30 and 4–7, Sun. 4–7.*

WHERE TO EAT AND STAY

$$–$$$ SPANISH

✕ **Asador Adolfo.** Steps from the cathedral but discreetly hidden, this restaurant has an intimate interior with a coffered ceiling that was painted in the 14th century. From the entryway you can see game, fresh produce, and traditional Toledan recipes being prepared in the kitchen, combining local tastes with Nueva Cocina tendencies. The *tempura de flor de calabacín* (tempura-battered zucchini blossoms in a saffron sauce) makes for a tasty starter; King Juan Carlos I has declared Adolfo's partridge stew the best in Spain. Finish with a Toledan specialty, *delicias de*

Toledo's Santa María la Blanca synagogue is a fascinating symbol of cultural cooperation: built by Islamic architects, in a Christian land, for Jewish use.

mazapán (marzipan sweets). ✉ *C. del Hombre de Palo 7* ☎ *925/227321* 🌐 *www.adolforestaurante.com* ✍ *Reservations essential* 💳 *AE, DC, MC, V* ⏲ *Closed Mon. No dinner Sun.*

¢–$$ SPANISH ✕ **Bar Ludeña**. Down a couple steps from the Zocodover square, locals and visitors come together at this bar to have a beer and share the typical Toledan *caramusas,* a meat stew with peas and tomatoes served in a hot dish. ✉ *Pl. de la Madalena 10* ☎ *925/223384* 💳 *AE, DC, MC, V.*

$$–$$$$ SPANISH ✕ **Casón Lopez de Toledo**. A vaulted foyer leads to a patio with marble statues, twittering caged birds, a fountain, and abstract religious paintings; in the dining room, carved wood abounds. The menu outlines an appetizer list for two, a fresh market entrée selection, and a variety of fish and meat specialties. It includes ravioli filled with truffle and bull tail, venison cooked in a truffled dried-fruit oil, braised rabbit with sesame sauce and mashed potatoes, and cod with Manchego cheese. Try the *mazapán* (marzipan) cake topped with cream cheese. ✉ *C. Sillería 3* ☎ *902/198344* 🌐 *www.casontoledo.com* ✍ *Reservations essential* 💳 *AE, DC, MC, V* ⏲ *No dinner Sun.*

$–$$ ★ **Hotel del Cardenal**. Built in the 18th century (restored in 1972) as a summer palace for Cardinal Lorenzana, this quiet and beautiful hotel is fully outfitted with antique furniture. Some rooms overlook the hotel's enchanting wooded garden, which lies at the foot of the town's walls. The restaurant, popular with tourists, has a long-standing reputation; dishes are mainly local, and in season you can find delicious asparagus and strawberries from Aranjuez. **If you have a car, reserve a parking spot when you book your room, or you may not be guaranteed a space.** **Pros:** lovely courtyard; convenient parking. **Cons:** restaurant often full and somewhat pricey. ✉ *Paseo de Recaredo 24* ☎ *925/224900* 🌐 *www.hostaldelcardenal.com* 27 *rooms* *In-room: Wi-Fi. In-hotel: restaurant, laundry service, parking (free), some pets allowed* ▭ *AE, DC, MC, V.*

$$–$$$ **Hotel Pintor El Greco Sercotel.** Next door to the painter's house, this friendly hotel occupies what was once a 17th-century bakery. Restored to a chic contemporary look punctuated with ancient stones, the modern interior is warm and elegant, with tawny colors and antique touches. An exposed-brick vaulting pulls your imagination back to El Greco's time. **Pros:** parking garage adjacent. **Cons:** street noise in most rooms; elevator goes to the second floor only. ✉ *Alamillos del Tránsito 13* ☎ *925/285191* 🌐 *www.hotel-pintorelgreco.com* *61 rooms* *In-room: Wi-Fi. In-hotel: laundry service, parking (paid)* ▭ *AE, DC, MC, V.*

$$–$$$ **Parador de Toledo.** This modern building with Mudejar-style touches on Toledo's outskirts has an unbeatable panorama of the town from the rooms' terraces, where you can sit and watch the sunset. Architecture and furnishings nod to traditional style, emphasizing brick and wood. The restaurant ($$$–$$$$) is stately and traditional, with top-quality regional wines and products. **Pros:** outdoor swimming pool. **Cons:** austere setting can be dark. ✉ *Calle Cerro del Emperador s/n* ☎ *925/221850* 🌐 *www.parador.es* *80 rooms* *In-room: Wi-Fi. In-hotel: restaurant, pool* ▭ *AE, DC, MC, V.*

SHOPPING

The Moors established silver work, damascene (metalwork inlaid with gold or silver), pottery, embroidery, and marzipan traditions here, and next to San Juan de los Reyes a turn-of-the-20th-century art school keeps these crafts alive. For inexpensive pottery, stop at the large emporia on the outskirts of town, on the main road to Madrid. Most of the region's pottery is made in Talavera la Reina, 76 km (47 mi) west of Toledo. At **Museo Cerámica Ruiz de Luna** (✉ *C. San Augustín de Viejo 13* ☎ *925/800149* *Museum €0.60, weekends free* *Tues.–Sat. 10–2 and 4–6:30, Sun. 10–2*) watch artisans throw local clay, then trace the development of Talavera's world-famous ceramics, chronicled through about 1,500 tiles, bowls, vases, and plates dating back to the 15th century.

ALMAGRO

215 km (134 mi) south of Madrid.

The center of this noble town contains the only preserved medieval theater in Europe, which stands beside the ancient Plaza Mayor, where 85 Roman columns form two colonnades supporting green-frame, 16th-century buildings. Near the plaza are granite mansions embellished with the heraldic shields of their former owners and a splendid parador in a restored 17th-century convent.

ESSENTIALS

Visitor Information Almagro (✉ *Pl. Mayor 1* ☎ *926/860717* 🌐 *www.ciudad-almagro.com*).

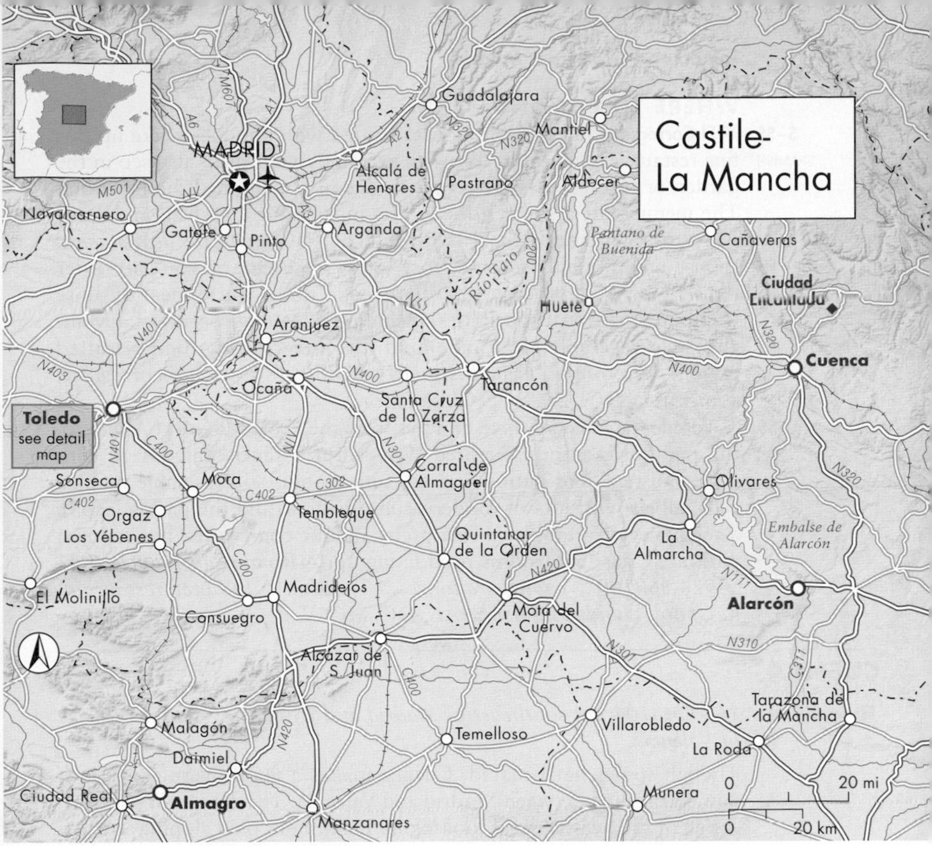

EXPLORING

★ The **Corral de Comedias** theater stands almost as it did in the 16th century, when it was built, with wooden balconies on four sides and the stage at one end of the open patio. During the golden age of Spanish theater—the time of playwrights Pedro Calderón de la Barca, Cervantes, and Lope de Vega—touring actors came to Almagro, which prospered from mercury mines and lace making. The Corral is the site of an international theater festival each July. Festival tickets may be purchased with a credit card through Tele-Entrada (☎ 926/882458) or with cash (after mid-May only) at Palacio de los Medrano on San Agustín 7. ✉ *Pl. Mayor 18* ☎ *926/861539* 🎫 *Audio tour €2.50 individuals, €2 for group members; dramatized tour €3 individuals, €3 for group members* ⏲ *Apr.–June, Aug., and Sept., daily 10–2 and 5–8; July, daily 10–2 and 6–9; Oct.–Mar., daily 10–2 and 4–7.*

The **Museo Nacional del Teatro** displays models of the Roman amphitheaters in Mérida (Extremadura) and Sagunto (near Valencia), both still in use, as well as costumes, pictures, and documents relating to the history of Spanish theater. ✉ *C. del Gran Maestre 2* ☎ *926/261014* 🌐 *museoteatro.mcu.es* 🎫 *€3 individuals, free Sat. afternoon and Sun.* ⏲ *Tues.–Fri. 10–2 and 4–7 (4–6 July), Sat. 11–2 and 4–6, Sun. 11–2.*

WHERE TO EAT AND STAY

$–$$ SPANISH **El Corregidor**. Several old houses stuffed with antiques make up this fine restaurant and tapas bar. You can enjoy your meal alfresco in the garden or terrace, or take refuge in the air-conditioned dining room. The menu centers on rich local fare, including game, fish, and spicy Almagro eggplant, a local delicacy. The €50 *menú de degustación* (house menu) yields seven savory tapas (courses), or you can order the €30 *menu Manchego gastronómico*, a three-course meal of more traditional, regional specialties, including *pisto manchego* (a La Mancha–style vegetable ratatouille) and *ravioli de cordero* (lamb-stuffed ravioli). *Jerónimo Ceballos s/n 926/860648 www.elcorregidor.com AE, DC, MC, V Closed Mon.*

$$$ ★ **Parador de Almagro**. Five minutes from the Plaza Mayor of Almagro, this parador is a finely restored 17th-century Franciscan convent with cells, cloisters, and patios. Indeed, some rooms still resemble monks' cells, albeit with lots of modern conveniences, and the patios inspire a meditative tranquility. **Pros:** pretty indoor courtyards; has its own parking. **Cons:** bathrooms need fixing up. *Ronda San Francisco 31 926/860100 www.parador.es 54 rooms In-hotel: restaurant, bar, pool, laundry service AE, DC, MC, V.*

CUENCA

Fodor's Choice ★ *167 km (104 mi) southeast of Madrid and 150 km (93 mi) northwest of Valencia.*

Though somewhat isolated, Cuenca makes a good overnight stop if you're traveling between Madrid and Valencia. The delightful old town is one of the most surreal looking in Spain, built on a sloping, curling finger of rock whose precipitous sides plunge down to the gorges of the Huécar and Júcar rivers. Because the town ran out of room to expand, some medieval houses dangle right over the abyss and are now a unique architectural attraction: the Casas Colgadas (Hanging Houses). The old town's dramatic setting grants spectacular gorge views, and its cobblestone streets, cathedral, churches, bars, and taverns contrast starkly with the modern town, which sprawls beyond the river gorges.

GETTING HERE AND AROUND

From Madrid, buses leave for Cuenca about every two hours from Conde de Casal. From Valencia, four buses leave every four to six hours, starting at 8:30 AM. Trains stop in Cuenca from either Madrid or Valencia twice a day, but this is not recommended as the train is bumpy, makes many stops, and is much slower than the bus.

ESSENTIALS

Visitor Information Cuenca (*Av. Cruz Roja 1 969/241050 turismo.cuenca.es*).

EXPLORING

Cuenca has 14 churches and two cathedrals—but, unfortunately, visitors are allowed inside only about half of them. The best views of the city are from the square in front of a small palace at the very top of Cuenca, where the town tapers out to the narrowest of ledges. Here, gorges are on either side of the precipice, and old houses sweep down toward a distant plateau in front. The lower half of the old town is a maze of tiny streets, any of which will take you up to the Plaza del Carmen. From here the town narrows and a single street, Calle Alfonso VIII, continues the ascent to the Plaza Mayor, which passes under the arch of the town hall. Calle San Pedro shoots off from the northern side of Plaza Mayor; just off Calle San Pedro, clinging to the western edge of Cuenca, is the tiny **Plaza San Nicolás**, a pleasingly dilapidated square. Nearby, the unpaved Ronda del Júcar hovers over the Júcar gorge and commands remarkable views.

Santa María de Gracia Cathedral looms large and casts an enormous shadow in the evening throughout the adjacent Plaza Mayor. Built during the Gothic era in the 12th century, the cathedral's massive triptych facade has lost all its Gothic origins thanks to the Renaissance. Inside are the tombs of the cathedral's founding bishops, an impressive portico of the Apostles, and a Byzantine reliquary. ✉ *Pl. Mayor s/n* ☎ *969/224626* 🎫 *€2.80* ⏲ *Daily 10:30–1:30 and 4–6 (4–7 Aug. and Sept.).*

The **Museo Diocesano de Arte Sacro** *(Diocesan Museum of Sacred Art)* is in what were once the cellars of the Bishop's Palace. The beautiful collection includes a jewel-encrusted, Byzantine diptych of the 13th century; a Crucifixion by the 15th-century Flemish artist Gerard David; and two small El Grecos. From the Plaza Mayor, follow the signs on Calle del Obispo Valero toward the Casas Colgadas. ✉ *C. del Obispo Valero 1* ☎ *969/224210* 🎫 *€2* ⏲ *Oct.–May, Tues.–Sat. 11–2 and 4–6, Sun. 11–2; June–Sept., Tues.–Sat. 11–2 and 5–7, Sun. 11–2.*

★ As if Cuenca's famous **Casas Colgadas** *(Hanging Houses)* suspended impossibly over the cliffs below were not eye-popping enough, they also house one of Spain's finest and most curious museums, the **Museo de Arte Abstracto Español** (Museum of Spanish Abstract Art)—not to be confused with the Museo Municipal de Arte Moderno, which is next to the Casas Colgadas. Projecting over the town's eastern precipice, these houses originally formed a 15th-century palace, which later served as a town hall before falling into disrepair in the 19th century. In 1927 the cantilevered balconies that had once hung over the gorge were rebuilt, and in 1966 the painter Fernando Zóbel decided to create (inside the houses) the world's first museum devoted exclusively to abstract art. The works he gathered are almost all by the remarkable generation of Spanish artists who grew up in the 1950s and were forced to live abroad during the Franco regime. The major names include Carlos Saura, Eduardo Chillida, Lucio Muñoz, Manuel Millares, Antoni Tàpies, and Zóbel himself. ✉ *C. de los Canónigos s/n* ☎ *969/212983* 🌐 *www.march.es/arte/cuenca/index.asp* 🎫 *€3* ⏲ *Tues.–Fri. 11–2 and 4–6, Sat. 11–2 and 4–8, Sun. 11–2:30.*

★ The **Puente de San Pablo**, an iron footbridge over the Huécar gorge, was built in 1903 for the convenience of the Dominican monks of San Pablo, who lived on the other side. If you don't have a fear of heights, cross the narrow bridge to take in the vertiginous view of the river below and the equally thrilling panorama of the Casas Colgadas. It's by far

Cuenca's precarious *Casas Colgadas* (Hanging Houses) are also home to the well-regarded Museum of Abstract Art.

the best view of the city. A path from the bridge descends to the bottom of the gorge, landing you by the bridge that you crossed to enter the old town.

WHERE TO EAT AND STAY

Much of Cuenca's cuisine is based on wild game: partridge, lamb, rabbit, and hen. Trout, from the adjacent river, is the fish of choice and is featured in many main courses and soups. In almost every town restaurant, you can find Cuenca's pâté, *morterualo,* a mixture of wild boar, rabbit, partridge, hen, liver, pork loin, and spices, as well as *galianos,* a thick stew served on wheat cake. For dessert, try almond-based confections called *alajú,* which are enriched with honey, nuts, and lemon, and *torrijas,* made of bread dipped in milk, fried, and decorated with confectioner's sugar.

$$–$$$ SPANISH ★ **El Figón de Huécar.** Mercedes Torres Ortega, the daughter of revered restaurateur Pedro Torres, runs this intimate restaurant. Specialty dishes include *pichón* (dove) stuffed with a basket of quail eggs; old wine veal with potatoes *al montón* (fried with garlic); Huecar cold vegetable mousse; or fish "melodies" with potato confit and vegetables. ✉ *Julián Romero 6* ☎ *969/240062* 🌐 *www.figondelhuecar.com* 💳 *AE, DC, MC, V* ⏲ *Closed Mon. No dinner Sun.*

$–$$ SPANISH **La Ponderosa.** Famous all over Spain for Cuenca's finest tapas and *raciones*, this popular place on the town's liveliest tippling and tapeo street is always filled and buzzing. *Chuletillas de lechal* (suckling lamb chops), *huevos fritos con pócima secreta* (fried eggs with a "secret potion"), *setas* (wild mushrooms), *mollejas* (sweetbreads), and a carefully selected list of wines all add up to a superior tapas experience. It's a standing-room-only joint, so if you want to sit, you'll have to come early and sit on the terrace. ✉ *C. de San Francisco 20* ☎ *969/213214* ▭ *DC, MC, V* ⏲ *Closed Sun. and June and July.*

$–$$$$ SPANISH ✕ **Mesón Casas Colgadas.** Run by Pedro Torres Pacheco, the celebrated restaurateur who has done much to promote Cuenca's cuisine, this restaurant offers local produce, fish, and a variety of game during hunting season, all with an upscale vibe. The sleek and modern white dining room is next to the Museum of Abstract Art in one of the iconic, gravity-defying Casas Colgadas. There are fantastic views of the hanging houses and the plunging gorge below—not for the acrophobic! ✉ *C. de los Canónigos s/n* ☎ *969/223509* ⌂ *Reservations essential* ▭ *AE, DC, MC, V* ⏲ *No dinner Mon. Closed Tues.*

¢ **Hostal Cánovas.** Near Plaza España, in the heart of the new town, this is one of Cuenca's best bargains. The lobby's not impressive, but the inviting rooms more than compensate with hardwood floors, gold-trimmed burgundy fabrics, and decorative white moldings. Brothers Edilio and Paulino, the owners, spent more than two years restoring the run-down 1878 building before they opened the hostal in 1998. **Pros:** low prices even during the high season. **Cons:** can be noisy; old, bulky furniture makes rooms feel cramped. ✉ *C. Fray Luis de León 38* ☎ *969/213973* ⊕ *www.hostalcanovas.com* *17 rooms* ▭ *AE, MC, V.*

$–$$$ ★ **Posada San José.** In a 17th- to 18th-century convent, formerly the San José choir school, this posada (inn) clings to the top of the Huécar gorge in Cuenca's old town. Intimate and personal touches, like a leafy garden and cozy nooks distributed around the public spaces, give the inn its charm. Most rooms have balconies or terraces over the river. Furnishings are traditional, but the mood is informal and friendly. Of the 31 rooms, 22 have their own bathrooms. **Pros:** cozy rooms; stunning views of gorge. **Cons:** difficult to reach by car; not recommended for anyone with vertigo. ✉ *C. Julián Romero 4* ☎ *969/211300* ⊕ *www.posadasanjose.com* *31 rooms* *In-room: no a/c, no TV (some). In-hotel: restaurant, bar* ▭ *AE, DC, MC, V.*

OFF THE BEATEN PATH

Ciudad Encantada *(Enchanted City).* Not really a city at all, the Ciudad Encantada (35 km [22 mi] north of Cuenca) is a series of large and fantastic mushroomlike rock formations erupting in a landscape of pines. This commanding spectacle, deemed a "site of national interest," was formed over thousands of years by the forces of water and wind on limestone rocks. Of the ones with names, the most notable are Cara (Face), Puente (Bridge), Amantes (Lovers), and Olas en el Mar (Waves in the Sea). You can stroll through this enchanted city in less than two hours.

ALARCÓN

69 km (43 mi) south of Cuenca.

This fortified village on the edge of the great plains of La Mancha stands on a high spit of land encircled almost entirely by a bend of the Júcar River.

ESSENTIALS

Visitor Information Alarcón (✉ *Posada 6* ☎ *969/330301* ⊕ *aytoalarcon.org*).

EXPLORING

Alarcón's **castle** (✉ *Av. Amigos de los Castillos 3*) dates from the 8th century, and in the 14th century it came into the hands of the *infante* (child prince) Don Juan Manuel, who wrote a collection of classic moral tales. Today the castle is one of Spain's finest paradors. If you're not driving, a bus to Motilla will leave you a short taxi ride away (call ☎ *969/331797* for a cab).

WHERE TO EAT AND STAY

$$$$ ★ **Parador de Alarcón.** This 8th- to 12th-century gorge-top castle is in a fairytale setting: a fortress of Moorish origin decorated in a military motif. The turret room is the best and biggest; the rooms in the corner towers have arrow-slit windows, and others have window niches where women used to do needlework. Dinner ($$$–$$$$) is served in an arched baronial hall complete with shields, armor, and a gigantic fireplace. **Pros:** worth the price; ambience to spare; good for a romantic getaway. **Cons:** after 11 PM, room service prices jump 25%. ✉ *Av. Amigos de los Castillos 3* ☎ *969/330315* 🌐 *www.parador.es* *14 rooms* *In-hotel: restaurant, bar, laundry service* *AE, DC, MC, V.*

CASTILE–LEÓN

SIGÜENZA

136 km (85 mi) northeast of Madrid.

Sigüenza has splendid architecture and one of the most beautifully preserved cathedrals in Castile.

ESSENTIALS

Visitor Information Sigüenza (✉ *C. Serrano Sanz 9* ☎ *949/347007* 🌐 *www.siguenza.es*).

EXPLORING

An enchanting **castle**, overlooking wild, hilly countryside from above Sigüenza, is now a parador. Founded by the Romans but rebuilt at various later periods, most of the structure went up in the 14th century, when it became a residence for the queen of Castile, Doña Blanca de Borbón, who was banished here by her husband, Peter the Cruel.

Begun around 1150 and not completed until the early 16th century, Sigüenza's remarkable **cathedral** combines Spanish architecture dating from the Romanesque period all the way to the Renaissance. The sturdy western front is forbidding but houses a wealth of ornamental and artistic masterpieces. Go directly to the sacristan, the officer in charge of the care of the sacristy, which holds sacred vestments. From there (the sacristy is at the north end of the ambulatory), you can go on a guided tour, which is a must. The late-Gothic cloister leads to a room lined with 17th-century Flemish tapestries. In the north transept is the late-15th-century plateresque sepulchre of Dom Fadrique of Portugal. The Chapel of the Doncel (to the right of the sanctuary) contains Don Martín Vázquez de Arca's tomb, commissioned by Queen Isabella, to whom Don Martín served as *doncel* (page) before dying young (at 25)

Castile-León

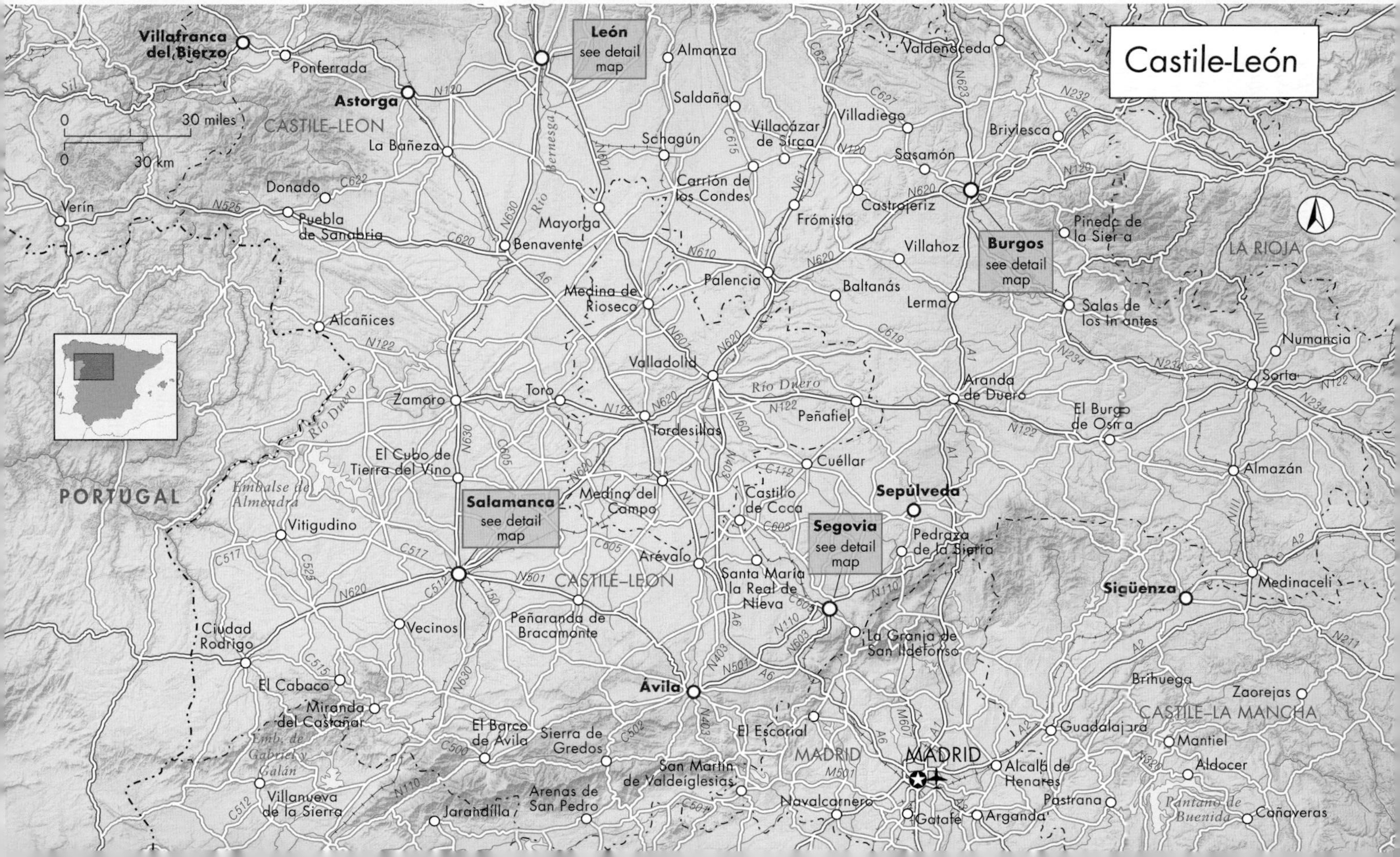

at the gates of Granada in 1486. ✉ *C. Serrano Sanz 2* 🎫 *Entry free; guided tour €3* ⏲ *Daily 9:30–2 and 4:30–8. Guided tours Tues.–Sun. at noon, 1, 4:30, and 5:30* ☎ *619/362715 to set up tours, as schedules can be erratic.*

In a refurbished early-19th-century house next to the cathedral's west facade, the **Museo Diocesano de Arte Sacro** *(Diocesan Museum of Sacred Art)* contains a prehistoric section and much religious art from the 12th to 18th centuries. ✉ *Pl. Mayor* ☎ *949/391023* 🎫 *€3* ⏲ *Oct.–May, Tues.–Sat. 11–2 and 4–7, Sun. 11–2; June–Sept., Tues.–Sat. 11–2 and 5–8, Sun. 11–2.*

WHERE TO EAT AND STAY

$$–$$$ ★ **Parador de Sigüenza.** This mighty 12th-century fortress has hosted royalty for centuries, from Ferdinand and Isabella right up to Spain's present king, Juan Carlos I. Some rooms have four-poster beds and balconies overlooking the wild landscape. The excellent dining room ($$$–$$$$) makes for a leisurely lunch, an essential part of the experience here; your choices might include roast goat, pheasant, or cod with truffles and cheese. **Pros:** excellent breakfast buffet. **Cons:** much of this fantastical castle, though still beautiful, is a neo-medieval replica. ✉ *Pl. del Castillo s/n* ☎ *949/390100* 🌐 *www.parador.es* *81 rooms* *In-hotel: restaurant, parking (paid)* 💳 *AE, DC, MC, V.*

SEGOVIA

Fodor's Choice ★

87 km (54 mi) north of Madrid.

Breathtaking Segovia—on a ridge in the middle of a gorgeously stark, undulating plain—is defined by its Roman and medieval monuments, its excellent cuisine, its embroideries and textiles, and its sense of well-being. An important military town in Roman times, Segovia was later established by the Moors as a major textile center. Captured by the Christians in 1085, it was enriched by a royal residence, and in 1474 the half-sister of Henry IV, Isabella the Catholic (married to Ferdinand of Aragón), was crowned queen of Castile here. By that time Segovia was a bustling city of about 60,000 (its population is about 50,000 today), but its importance soon diminished as a result of its taking the losing side of the Comuneros in the popular revolt against the emperor Carlos V. Though the construction of a royal palace in nearby La Granja in the 18th century somewhat revived Segovia's fortunes, it never recovered its former vitality. Early in the 20th century, Segovia's sleepy charm came to be appreciated by artists and writers, among them painter Ignacio Zuloaga and poet Antonio Machado. Today the streets swarm with tourists from Madrid—if you can, visit sometime other than in summer.

If you approach Segovia on N603, the first building you see is the cathedral, which seems to rise directly from the fields. Between you lies a steep and narrow valley, which shields the old town from view. Only once you descend into the valley do you begin to see the old town's spectacular position, rising on top of a narrow rock ledge shaped like a ship. As soon as you reach the modern outskirts, turn left onto the

Paseo E. González and follow the road marked **Ruta Panorámica**—you'll soon descend on the narrow and winding Cuesta de los Hoyos, which takes you to the bottom of the wooded valley that dips to the south of the old town. Above, you can see the Romanesque church of San Martín to the right, the cathedral in the middle, and on the far left, where the rock ledge tapers, the turrets, spires, and battlements of Segovia's castle, known as the Alcázar.

Tourists on a day trip from Madrid generally hit the triumvirate of basic sights: the aqueduct, the Alcázar, and the cathedral.

GETTING HERE AND AROUND

Urbanos de Segovia operates 13 inner-city bus lines and one tourist line. (☎ *902/330080* ⊕ *www.urbanosdesegovia.com*).

ESSENTIALS

Visitor Information Segovia (✉ *Pl. Mayor 9* ☎ *921/466070* ⊕ *www.turismodesegovia.com*).

EXPLORING

2 Fodor's Choice ★ **Acueducto Romano.** Segovia's Roman aqueduct ranks with the Pont du Gard in France as one of the greatest surviving examples of Roman engineering, and it's the city's main event, sightseeing-wise. If you take the AVE in from Madrid on a day trip, the inner-city bus drops you right there. Stretching from the walls of the old town to the lower slopes of the Sierra de Guadarrama, it's about 2,952 feet long and rises in two tiers—above what is now the Plaza del Azoguejo, whose name means "highest point"—to a height of 115 feet. The raised section of stonework in the center originally carried an inscription, of which only the holes for the bronze letters remain. Neither mortar nor clamps hold the massive granite blocks together, but the aqueduct has been standing since the end of the 1st century AD. Its only damage is from the demolition of 35 of its arches by the Moors, later replaced on the orders of Ferdinand and Isabella. Steps at the side of the aqueduct lead up to the walls of the old town. ✉ *Pl. del Azoguejo.*

7 **Alcázar.** Possibly dating from Roman times, this castle was considerably expanded in the 14th century, remodeled in the 15th, altered again toward the end of the 16th, and completely remodeled after being gutted by a fire in 1862, when it was used as an artillery school. The exterior, especially when seen below from the Ruta Panorámica, is certainly imposing, and striking murals and stained-glass windows pepper the interior. Crowned by crenellated towers that seem to have been carved out of icing (it's widely believed that the Walt Disney logo is modeled after this castle's silhouette), the rampart can be climbed for superb views. The claustrophobia-inducing winding tower is worth the knee-wobbling climb and small extra fee, though the views of the green hillside from below the tower are excellent as well. ✉ *Pl. de la Reina Victoria s/n* ☎ *921/460759* ⊕ *www.alcazardesegovia.com* 🎫 *€4 individual entrance fee, €2 to climb the tower, €1 to see the Segovianos, €1 for a guided tour* ⏲ *Apr.–Sept., daily 10–7; Oct.–Mar., Mon.–Thurs. 10–6, Fri.–Sun. 10–7.*

9 **Casa de la Moneda** *(Mint).* All Spanish coinage was struck here from 1455 to 1730. The mint, scheduled for reconstruction work, offers tours

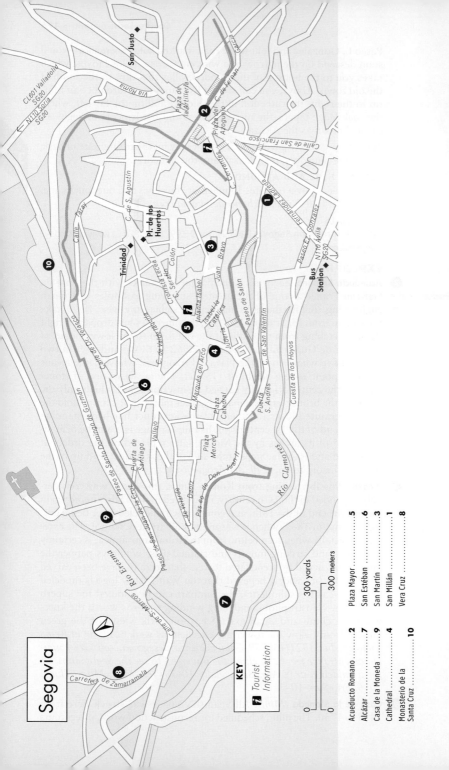

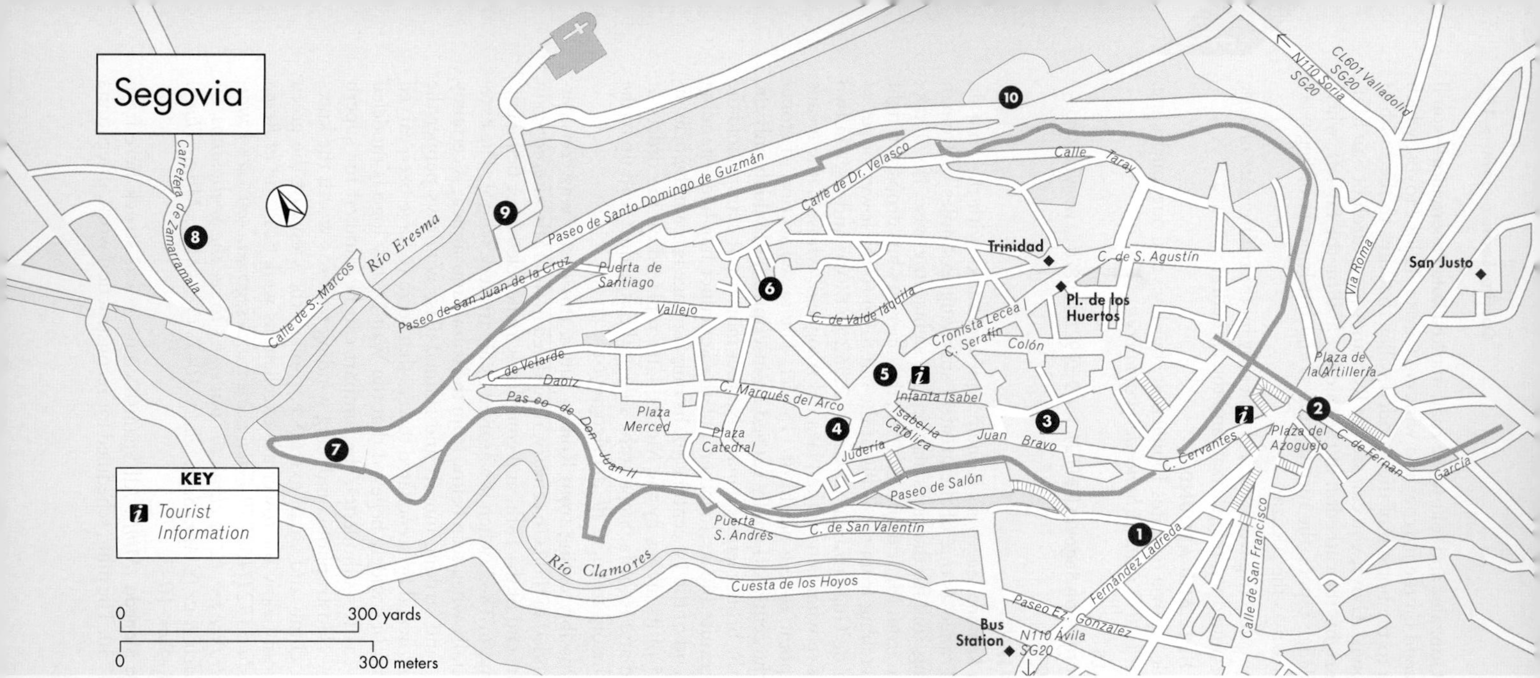

Acueducto Romano 2
Alcázar 7
Casa de la Moneda 9
Cathedral 4
Monasterio de la Santa Cruz 10
Plaza Mayor 5
San Estéban 6
San Martín 3
San Millán 1
Vera Cruz 8

every first and third Saturday of the month, with English-language guides available by prior arrangement. Call or e-mail (✉ *info£segoviamint.org*) to reserve a tour. ✉ *C. de la Moneda, just south of Eresma River* ☎ *921/420921* 🌐 *www.segoviamint.org* 💳 *Free.*

❹ **Cathedral.** Begun in 1525 and completed 65 years later, Segovia's cathedral was built to replace an earlier one destroyed during the revolt of the Comuneros against Carlos V. It's one of the country's last great examples of the Gothic style. The designs were drawn up by the leading late-Gothicist Juan Gil de Hontañón but executed by his son Rodrigo, in whose work you can see a transition from the Gothic to the Renaissance style. The interior, illuminated by 16th-century Flemish windows, is light and uncluttered, the one distracting detail being the wooden, neoclassical choir. Enter through the north transept, which is marked MUSEO; turn right, and the first chapel on your right has a lamentation group carved in wood by the baroque sculptor Gregorio Fernández. Across from the entrance, on the southern transept, is a door opening into the late-Gothic cloister—both the cloister and the elaborate door leading into it were transported from the old cathedral and are the work of architect Juan Guas. Under the pavement immediately inside the cloister are the tombs of Juan and Rodrigo Gil de Hontañón; that these two lie in a space designed by Guas is appropriate, as the three men together dominated the last phase of the Gothic style in Spain. Off the cloister, a small museum of religious art, installed partly in the 1st-floor chapter house, has a white-and-gold 17th-century ceiling, a late example of Mudejar *artesonado* work. At night the cathedral is lit up with lovely amber lights. **■TIP→ Watch your purse as you enter: There are usually at least half a dozen beggars at the door of the church.** ✉ *Pl. Mayor s/n* ☎ *921/462205* 💳 *Cathedral cloister and museum €3* ⏲ *Apr.–Oct., Mon.–Sat. 9:30–6:30, Sun. 9:30–2:30; Nov.–Mar., Mon.–Sat. 9:30–5:30, Sun. 9:30–2:30.*

❿ **Monasterio de la Santa Cruz la Real.** Built in the 13th century, this church was established by St. Dominic of Guzmán, founder of the Dominican order, and rebuilt in the 15th century by Ferdinand and Isabella. Now it's the private IE (Instituto de Impresa) University, and during the academic year you can see the Gothic interior with plateresque and Renaissance touches. ✉ *C. Cardenal Zúñiga 12* ☎ *921/412410.*

❺ **Plaza Mayor.** In front of the cathedral, you can sit in a charming gazebo and watch the world go by. There are plenty of cafés around the perimeter. ✉ *Pl. Mayor.*

❻ **San Estéban.** Though the interior has a baroque facing, the exterior has kept some splendid capitals, as well as an exceptional tower. Due east of the church square is the **Capilla de San Juan de Dios,** next to which is the former pension where the poet Antonio Machado spent his last years in Spain. The family who looked after Machado still owns the building and will show you the poet's room on request, with its kerosene stove, iron bed, and round table. ✉ *Pl. de San Estéban*

❸ **San Martín.** This elevated Romanesque church is on the main street between the aqueduct and cathedral, in a small plaza of the same name. It's open for Mass only. ✉ *Pl. San Martín.*

7 **San Millán.** A perfect example of the Segovian Romanesque style, this 12th-century church is perhaps the finest in town apart from the cathedral. The exterior is notable for its arcaded porch, where church meetings were once held. The virtually untouched interior is dominated by massive columns, whose capitals carry such carved scenes as the Flight into Egypt and the Adoration of the Magi. The vaulting on the crossing shows the Moorish influence on Spanish medieval architecture. It's open for Mass only. ✉ *Av. Fernández Ladreda 26, 5-min walk outside town walls* ⏲ *Apr.–Oct., weekdays 11* AM *and 8* PM, *Sun. 10* AM *and 11* AM; *Nov.–Mar., weekdays 11:30* AM, *Sun. 9:30* AM *and noon.*

8 **Vera Cruz.** Made of the local warm-orange stone, this isolated Romanesque church was built in 1208 for the Knights Templar. Like other buildings associated with this order, it has 12 sides, inspired by the Church of the Holy Sepulchre in Jerusalem. The trek out here pays off in full when you climb the bell tower and see all of Segovia profiled against the Sierra de Guadarrama. ✉ *Ctra. de Zamarramia s/n, on northern outskirts of town, off Cuesta de los Hoyos* ☎ *921/431475* 🎫 *€1.75; free Tues. afternoons* ⏲ *Wed.–Sun., 10:30–1:30 and 4–6; Tues. 4–6.*

WHERE TO EAT AND STAY

$$–$$$$ SPANISH

✕ **Casa Duque.** Founded in 1895 and still run by the same family, this restaurant, the oldest in Segovia, has an intimate interior, with handsome wood beams and a plethora of fascinating bric-a-brac from wood carvings to coats of armor stashed in every nook and cranny. Roasts and meats are the main specialty here, but the *judiones de La Granja Duque*—enormous white beans from the family farm stewed with sausages or partridge—are also excellent. The local Ribera de Duero wines hold up well with roasts, while *setas* (wild mushrooms) from the Sierra de Guadarrama add a forest fragrance. Be prepared for wedding parties; if you're lucky, you might get included. ✉ *C. Cervantes 12* ☎ *921/462487* 🌐 *www.restauranteduque.es* ✍ *Reservations essential* 💳 *AE, DC, MC, V.*

$$–$$$$ SPANISH ★

✕ **Mesón de Cándido.** Cándido began life as an inn near the end of the 18th century and was declared a national monument in 1941. Tucked beside the aqueduct, it has a medley of small, irregular dining rooms decorated with a hodgepodge of memorabilia. Amid the dark-wood beams and Castilian knickknacks hang photos of celebrities who have dined here, from Ernest Hemingway to Princess Grace. The original owner's son now runs the place. If it's your first time here, the *cochinillo* (piglet), roasted in a wood-fire oven, is a great choice. The partridge stew and roast lamb are also memorable, especially on cold winter afternoons. Ask for a table near a window so you can take in the view of the aqueduct just a few feet away. ✉ *Pl. de Azoguejo 5* ☎ *921/428103* ✍ *Reservations essential* 💳 *AE, DC, MC, V.*

$$$–$$$$ SPANISH Fodor's Choice ★

✕ **Mesón de José María.** With a boisterous bar setting the tone and decibel level, this *mesón* (traditional tavern-restaurant) is hospitable, and the owner is devoted to maintaining traditional Castilian specialties while concocting innovations of his own, changing dishes with the seasons. The large, old-style, brightly lighted dining room is often packed, and the waiters are uncommonly friendly. Although it's a bit touristy, it's equally popular with locals, and the *cochinillo* (suckling

Segovia's Roman aqueduct, built about 2,000 years ago, is remarkably well preserved.

pig) is delicious in any company. ✉ *C. Cronista Lecea 11* ☎ *921/461111* 🌐 *www.rtejosemaria.com* 💳 *AE, DC, MC, V.*

\$–\$\$\$ 🏨 **Infanta Isabel.** You'll get great views of the cathedral from this 19th-century town house perched on the corner of Plaza Mayor—with an entrance on a charming, albeit congested, pedestrian shopping street. Rooms are true to the name "Princess Isabel," with light and feminine furnishings like wrought-iron beds and little round tables; those on the plaza have floor-length shutters and small verandas. **Pros:** boutiquey in design; central location; some rooms have balconies overlooking the plaza. **Cons:** some rooms are oddly shaped and small. ✉ *Pl. Mayor 12* ☎ *921/461300* 🌐 *www.hotelinfantaisabel.com* *37 rooms* *In-room: Wi-Fi. In-hotel: restaurant, parking (paid)* 💳 *AE, DC, MC, V.*

\$–\$\$\$ 🏨 **La Casa Mudejar Hospedería.** Built in the 15th century as a Mudejar palace, this historical property is the site of Segovia's largest Roman-constructed well, which has been turned into a lounge, as well as other Roman ruins; free Sunday-morning tours are open to the public. The rooms are spacious, and many have comfortable seating areas. Ask for a room with a view of the Sierra de Guadarrama. The hotel's restaurant, El Fogón Sefardí, features delicious dishes made from recipes that have been handed down from ancestors who were expelled from Spain during the Reconquest. **Pros:** great location; historic building. **Cons:** decor leans to the tacky side. ✉ *C. Isabel la Católica 8* ☎ *921/466250* 🌐 *www.lacasamudejar.com* *40 rooms* *In-room: Wi-Fi. In-hotel: restaurant, spa, parking (paid)* 💳 *AE, DC, MC, V.*

\$\$\$ 🏨 **Parador de Segovia.** Architecturally one of the most interesting of Spain's modern paradors (if you like naked concrete), this low building is set on a hill overlooking the city. The rooms are cold in appearance, but from the large windows the panorama of Segovia and its aqueduct are spectacular. (The ground floors have views of hedges, so request a room with a view if you want one.) The restaurant ($$$$) serves Segovian and international dishes, such as *lomo de merluza al aroma de estragón* (hake fillet with tarragon and shrimp). **Pros:** beautiful views of the city. **Cons:** need a car to get here; rooms not as elegant as in some other paradors. ✉ *Ctra. de Valladolid s/n, 2 km (1 mi) from Segovia* ☎ *921/443737* 🌐 *www.parador.es* *113 rooms* *In-room: Wi-Fi. In-hotel: restaurant, pools, gym, parking (paid)* ▭ *AE, DC, MC, V.*

OFF THE BEATEN PATH

Fodor's Choice ★ While in the Segovia area, don't miss the **Palacio Real de La Granja (Royal Palace of La Granja)** in the town of La Granja de San Ildefonso, about 11 km (7 mi) southeast of Segovia (on N601) on the northern slopes of the Sierra de Guadarrama. The palace site was once occupied by a hunting lodge and a shrine to San Ildefonso, administered by Hieronymite monks from the Segovian monastery of El Parral. Commissioned by the Bourbon king Felipe V in 1719, the palace has been described as the first great building of the Spanish Bourbon dynasty. The Italian architects Juvarra and Sachetti, who finished it in 1739, were responsible for the imposing garden facade, a late-baroque masterpiece anchored throughout its length by a giant order of columns. The interior has been badly gutted by fire, but the collection of 15th- to 18th-century tapestries warrants a visit. Even if you don't go into the palace, walking through the gardens is magnificent: terraces, ornamental ponds, lakes, classical statuary, woods, and baroque fountains dot the mountainside. On Wednesday, Saturday, and Sunday evenings in the summer (May–September, 6–7 PM), the fountains are turned on, one by one, creating an effect to rival that of Versailles. The starting time has been known to change on a whim, so call ahead. ☎ *921/470020* 🌐 *www.patrimonionacional.es* *Palace €5, gardens free* ⏲ *Palace Oct.–Mar., Tues.–Sat. 10–1:30 and 3–5, Sun. 10–2; Apr.–Sept., Tues.–Sun. 10–6. Gardens daily 10–sunset.*

SHOPPING

After Toledo, the province of Segovia is Castile's most important for crafts. Glass and crystal are specialties of La Granja, and ironwork, lace, and embroidery are famous in Segovia itself. You can buy good lace from the Gypsies in Segovia's Plaza del Alcázar, but be prepared for some strenuous bargaining, and never offer more than half the opening price. For genuine crafts, go to **San Martín 4** (✉ *Pl. San Martín 4*), an excellent antiques shop. **Calle Daoíz**, leading to the Alcázar, overflows with touristy ceramic, textile, and gift shops.

OFF THE BEATEN PATH

Tucked away amid the tourist ceramics shops in Segovia is a witchcraft museum, **El Antiguo Museo de Brujería**. The eight-room creep show of spells, artifacts, and jarred curiosities features standouts like the shrunken head of supposed vampire Oktavius von Bergengruen, as well as torture instruments from the Inquisition. ✉ *C. Daoíz 9* ☎ *921/460443* 🌐 *www.seamp.net/museobrujeriasegovia.htm* *€4.*

SEPÚLVEDA

60 km (37 mi) northeast of Segovia.

ESSENTIALS

Visitor Information Sepúlveda (✉ *Pl. del Trigo 6* ☎ *921/540237* 🌐 *www.sepulveda.es*).

EXPLORING

A walled village with a commanding position, Sepúlveda has a charming main square, but its major attraction is the 11th-century **El Salvador**, the oldest Romanesque church in Segovia's province. The carvings on its capitals, probably by a Moorish convert, are quite fantastical. ✉ *C. Subida a El Salvador 10.*

OFF THE BEATEN PATH

Perhaps the most famous medieval sight near Segovia—worth a detour between Segovia and Ávila or Valladolid—is the **Castillo de Coca**, 52 km (32 mi) northwest of the city. Built in the 15th century for Archbishop Alonso de Fonseca I, the castle is a turreted structure of plaster and red brick, surrounded by a deep moat. It looks like a stage set for a fairy tale, and, indeed, it was intended not as a fortress but as a place for the notoriously pleasure-loving archbishop to hold riotous parties. The interior, now occupied by a forestry school, has been modernized, with only fragments of the original decoration preserved. Note that hours are erratic; call ahead if possible. ☎ *921/586622* 🎫 *€2.70* ⏲ *May–Aug., weekdays 11–1 and 4–7, weekends 11–1 and 4–6; Sept.–Apr., weekdays 10:30–1 and 4:30–6, weekends 11–1 and 4–6. Closed 1st Tues. of every month.*

ÁVILA

107 km (66 mi) northwest of Madrid.

In the middle of a windy plateau littered with giant boulders, with the Sierra de Gredos in the background, Ávila can look wild and sinister. Modern development on the outskirts of town partially obscures Ávila's **walls**, which, restored in parts, look as they did in the Middle Ages. Begun in 1090, shortly after the town was reclaimed from the Moors, the walls were completed in only nine years—thanks to the daily employment of an estimated 1,900 men. The walls have nine gates and 88 cylindrical towers bunched together, making them unique to Spain in form—they're quite unlike the Moorish defense architecture that the Christians adapted elsewhere. They're also most striking when seen from outside town; for the best view on foot, cross the Adaja River, turn right on the Carretera de Salamanca, and walk uphill about 250 yards to a monument of four pilasters surrounding a cross.

The walls reflect Ávila's importance during the Middle Ages. Populated during the reign of Alfonso VI by Christians, many of who were nobles, the town came to be known as Ávila of the Knights. Decline set in at the beginning of the 15th century, with the gradual departure of the nobility to the court of Carlos V in Toledo. Ávila's fame later on was largely because of St. Teresa. Born here in 1515 to a noble family of Jewish origin, Teresa spent much of her life in Ávila, leaving a legacy of

Ávila's city walls, which still encircle the old city, have a perimeter of about two and a half kilometers.

convents and the ubiquitous *yemas* (candied egg yolks), originally distributed free to the poor but now sold for high prices to tourists. Ávila is well preserved, but the mood is slightly sad, austere, and desolate. It has a sense of quiet beauty, but the silence is dispelled during Fiestas de la Santa Teresa in October; the weeklong celebration includes lighted decorations, parades, singing in the streets, and religious observances.

GETTING HERE AND AROUND

Avilabus (🌐 *www.avilabus.com*) serves the city of Ávila and surrounding villages, though the city itself is easily manageable on foot.

ESSENTIALS

Visitor Information **Ávila** (✉ *Av. De Madrid 39* ☎ *920/225969* 🌐 *www.avila-turismo.com*).

EXPLORING

Cathedral. Its battlement apse forms the most impressive part of Ávila's walls. Entering the town gate to the right of the apse, you can reach the sculpted north portal (originally the west portal, until it was moved in 1455 by the architect Juan Guas) by turning left and walking a few steps. The present west portal, flanked by 18th-century towers, is notable for the crude carvings of hairy male figures on each side. Known as "wild men," these figures appear in many Castilian palaces of this period. The Transitional Gothic interior, with its granite nave, is heavy and severe. The Lisbon earthquake of 1755 deprived the building of its Flemish stained glass, so the main note of color appears in the beautiful mottled stone in the apse, tinted yellow and red. Elaborate, plateresque choir stalls built in 1547 complement the powerful high altar of circa 1504 by painters Juan de Borgoña and Pedro Berruguete. On the wall of the ambulatory, look for the early-16th-century marble sepulchre of Bishop Alonso de Madrigal, a remarkably lifelike representation of the bishop seated at his writing table. Known as "El Tostado" (the Toasted One) for his swarthy complexion, the bishop was a tiny man of enormous intellect, the author of 54 books. When on one occasion Pope Eugenius IV ordered him to stand—mistakenly thinking him to still be on his knees—the bishop pointed to the space between his eyebrows and hairline, and retorted, "A man's stature is to be measured from here to here!" ✉ *Pl. de la Catedral 8* ☎ *920/211641* 🎫 *€4* ⏲ *June–Oct., Mon.–Sat. 10–7, Sun. 11–6; Nov.–Mar., weekdays 10–5, Sat. 10–6, Sun. 11–5; Apr. and May, weekdays 10–6, Sat. 10–7, Sun. 11–5.*

The 15th-century **Mansión de los Deanes** *(Deans' Mansion)* houses the cheerful **Museo Provincial de Ávila,** a provincial museum full of local archaeology and folklore. It's adjacent to the old Romanesque temple of San Tomé el Viejo, a few minutes' walk east of the cathedral apse. ✉ *Pl. de Nalvillos 3* ☎ *920/211003* 🎫 *€1.20, weekends free* ⏲ *July–Sept., Tues.–Sat. 10–2 and 5–8, Sun. 10–2; Oct.–June, Tues.–Sat. 10–2 and 4–7, Sun. 10–2.*

In the **Convento de San José** *(de Las Madres)*, four blocks east of the cathedral is the **Museo Teresiano,** with musical instruments used by St. Teresa and her nuns (Teresa specialized in percussion). ✉ *C. de las Madres 4* ☎ *920/222127* 🎫 *€1.20* ⏲ *Apr.–Oct., daily 10–1:30 and 4–7; Nov.–Mar., daily 10–1:30 and 3–6.*

North of Ávila's cathedral, on Plaza de San Vincente, is the much-venerated Romanesque **Basílica de San Vicente** *(Basilica of St. Vincent)*, founded on the supposed site where St. Vincent was martyred in 303 with his sisters, Sts. Sabina and Cristeta. The west front, shielded by a vestibule, has damaged but expressive Romanesque carvings depicting the death of Lazarus and the parable of the rich man's table. The sarcophagus of St. Vincent forms the centerpiece of the basilica's Romanesque interior. The extraordinary, Asian-looking canopy above the sarcophagus is a 15th-century addition. ✉ *Pl. de San Vicente 1* ☎ *920/255230* 🌐 *www.basilicasanvicente.com* 🎫 *€1.40* ⏲ *Daily 10–1:30 and 4–6:30.*

Renaissance stained glass by Nicolás de Holanda illuminates the elegant chapel of **Mosen Rubi** (circa 1516). Try to persuade the nuns in the adjoining convent to let you inside. ✉ *C. de Lopez Nuñez.*

At the west end of the town walls, next to the river in a farmyard largely hidden by poplars, is the small Romanesque **Ermita de San Segundo** *(Hermitage of St. Secundus)*. Founded on the site where the remains of St. Secundus (a follower of St. Peter) were reputedly discovered, the hermitage has a realistic marble monument to the saint, carved by Juan de Juni. You may have to ask for the key in the adjoining house. ✉ *Pl. de San Segundo s/n* ☎ *920/353900* 🎫 *€0.60* ⏲ *July–Sept., daily 10–1 and 3:30–6; Oct.–June, daily 11–1 and 4–5.*

Inside the south wall on the corner of Calle Dama and Plaza de la Santa, the **Convento de Santa Teresa** was founded in the 17th century on the site of the saint's birthplace. Teresa's famous written account of an ecstatic vision in which an angel pierced her heart inspired many baroque artists, most famously the Italian sculptor Giovanni Bernini. The convent has a small museum with relics, including one of Teresa's fingers. You can also see the small and rather gloomy garden where she played as a child. The restaurant is closed Monday from October through Easter. ✉ *Pl. de la Santa 2* ☎ *920/211030* 🎫 *Museum €2* ⏲ *Museum May–Sept., Tues.–Sun. 9:30–1 and 3:30–7; Apr.–Oct., Tues.–Fri. and Sun. 10–2 and 4–7, Sat. 10–1 and 4–7.*

On the south side of the city sits the **Santuario de Nuestra Señora de Sonsoles**, built over the Ermita de los Santos Justo y Pastor in 1509 and currently a small church. The surrounding gardens are lovely, with benches, fountains, and statues, and a good view of the city. Inside is a taxidermied crocodile brought back from the Americas by a Spanish explorer. Prime Minister José Luis Rodríguez Zapatero and his wife, who is from Ávila, were married here. There is a very pleasant restaurant on the property featuring traditional Spanish fare such as roasted meats, fish, and paella. It's sometimes in use for wedding receptions but is also available for lunch and dinner reservations. ✉ *Cta. de Toledo, Km 4.8* ☎ *920/223367* 🎫 *Free* ⏲ *Restaurant closed Tues. Nov.–Mar.*

The **Museo del Convento de la Encarnación** is the convent where St. Teresa first took orders and was based for almost 40 years. Its Museo Teresiano has an interesting drawing of the Crucifixion by her teacher St. John of the Cross, as well as a reconstruction of the cell she used when she was a prioress here. The convent is outside the walls in the northern part of town. ✉ *Paseo de la Encarnación s/n* ☎ *920/211212* 🎫 *€1.05* ⏲ *May–Oct., weekdays 9:30–1 and 4–7, weekends 10–1 and 4–6; Nov.–Apr., weekdays 9:30–1:30 and 3:30–6, weekends 10–1 and 4–6.*

The most interesting architectural monument on Ávila's outskirts is the **Monasterio de Santo Tomás**. A good 10-minute walk from the walls among housing projects, it's not where you would expect to find one of the most important religious institutions in Castile. The monastery was founded by Ferdinand and Isabella with the financial assistance of the notorious Inquisitor-General Tomás de Torquemada, who is buried in the sacristy. Further funds were provided by the confiscated property of converted Jews who ran afoul of the Inquisition. Three decorated cloisters lead to the church; inside, a masterly high altar (circa 1506) by Pedro Berruguete overlooks a serene marble tomb by the Italian artist Domenico Fancelli. One of the earliest examples of the Italian Renaissance style in Spain, this influential work was built for Prince Juan, the only son of Ferdinand and Isabella, who died at 19 while a student at the University of Salamanca. After Juan's burial here, his heartbroken parents found themselves unable to return; in happier times they had often attended Mass here, seated in the upper choir behind a balustrade exquisitely carved with their coats of arms. ✉ *Pl. de Granada 1* ☎ *920/220400* 🌐 *www.monasteriosantotomas.com* 🎫 *€3* ⏲ *Monastery Mon.–Sat. 10–1 and 4–8, Sun. 10–2. Museum closed Mon.*

WHERE TO EAT AND STAY

$–$$$ SPANISH ★ ✕ **El Molino de la Losa.** Sitting at the edge of the serene Adaja River, Molino boasts one of the best views of the town walls. The building is a 15th-century mill, the working mechanism of which has been well preserved and provides much distraction for those seated in the animated bar. Lamb is roasted in a medieval wood oven, and the beans from nearby El Barco (*judías de El Barco*) are famous. The garden has a small playground for children. ✉ *C. Bajada de la Losa 12* ☎ *920/211101 or 920/211102* 🌐 *www.elmolinodelalosa.com* ▭ *AE, MC, V* ⊗ *Closed Mon.*

$–$$$ **SPANISH** ✗ **Las Cancelas.** Locals flock to this little tavern for the ample selection of tapas, but you can also push your way through the loud bar area to the dining room. There, wooden tables are heaped with combination platters of roast chicken, french fries, fried eggs, and chunks of home-baked bread. The classic T-bone steak, *chuletón de Ávila,* is enormous and offers good value at €20. The succulent *cochinillo* (roast piglet) bursts with flavor. There are 14 hotel rooms available, too; simple, slightly ramshackle arrangements at moderate prices ($). ✉ *C. Cruz Vieja 6* ☎ *920/212249* ▭ *AE, DC, MC, V* ⊗ *Closed Jan. 7–Feb. 1.*

$–$$ ★ **Palacio de los Velada.** Ávila's top hotel occupies a beautifully restored 16th-century palace in the heart of the city next to the cathedral, an ideal spot if you like to relax between sightseeing jaunts. Upscale locals like to gather in the bar and the lovely interior patio at Ávila's vortex. Rooms are elegantly decorated, modern, and comfortable. **Pros:** gorgeous glass-covered patio; quality service that alone is worth the price. **Cons:** some rooms don't have views because the windows are so high. ✉ *Pl. de la Catedral 10* ☎ *920/255100* 🌐 *www.veladahoteles.com* *145 rooms* *In-hotel: restaurant, bar* ▭ *AE, DC, MC, V.*

$$ **Parador de Ávila.** A largely rebuilt 16th-century medieval castle attached to the massive town walls, Ávila's parador has the advantage of a lush garden. The interior is unusually warm, done mostly in tawny tones, and the common rooms, elegantly decorated, if somewhat formal, are convivial places to meet for a beverage. Guest rooms have terra-cotta tile floors and clubby leather chairs. **Pros:** central location. **Cons:** staff isn't overly friendly; limited parking; run-down here and there with a few well-worn carpets. ✉ *C. Marqués de Canales de Chozas 2* ☎ *920/211340* 🌐 *www.parador.es* *61 rooms* *In-hotel: restaurant, bar* ▭ *AE, DC, MC, V.*

SALAMANCA

Fodor's Choice ★ *205 km (127 mi) northwest of Madrid.*

Salamanca's radiant sandstone buildings, immense Plaza Mayor, and hilltop riverside perch make it one of the most attractive and beloved cities in Spain. Today, as it did centuries ago, the university predominates, providing an intellectual flavor, a stimulating arts scene, and nightlife—best experienced on the weekend—to match.

If you approach from Madrid or Ávila, your first glimpse of Salamanca will be of it rising on the northern banks of the wide and winding River Tormes. In the foreground of the city is its sturdy, 15-arch Roman bridge, above which soars the combined bulk of the old and new cathedrals. Piercing the skyline to the right is the Renaissance monastery and church of San Estéban. Behind San Estéban and the cathedrals, and largely out of sight from the river, extends a stunning series of palaces, convents, and university buildings that culminates in Plaza

Mayor. Despite considerable damage over the centuries, Salamanca remains one of Spain's greatest cities architecturally, a showpiece of the Spanish Renaissance.

FONSECA'S MARK

Nearly all of Salamanca's outstanding Renaissance buildings bear the five-star crest of the all-powerful and ostentatious Fonseca family. The most famous Fonseca, Alonso de Fonseca I, was the archbishop of Santiago and then of Seville; he was also a notorious womanizer and a patron of the Spanish Renaissance.

GETTING HERE AND AROUND

Salamanca de Transportes (☎ *923/190545*) runs 64 municipal buses equipped with lifts for disabled passengers throughout the city of Salamanca. The main destinations requiring bus travel are the train and bus stations on the outskirts of the city.

ESSENTIALS

There are two tourist offices in town.

Visitor Information Salamanca Municipal Tourist Office (✉ *Pl. Mayor 32* ☎ *923/218342*). **Salamanca Casa de las Conchas** (✉ *C. Rúa Mayor s/n* ☎ *923/268571*).

EXPLORING

6 **Casa de Las Conchas** *(House of Shells)*. This house was built around 1500 for Dr. Rodrigo Maldonado de Talavera, a professor of medicine at the university and a doctor at the court of Isabella. The scallop motif was a reference to Talavera's status as chancellor of the Order of St. James (Santiago), the symbol of which is the shell. Among the playful plateresque details are the lions over the main entrance, engaged in a fearful tug-of-war with the Talavera crest. The interior has been converted into a public library. Duck into the charming courtyard, which has an intricately carved upper balustrade that imitates basketwork. ✉ *C. Compañía 2* ☎ *923/269317* *Free* *Mon.–Sat. noon–2 and 6–9, Sun. noon–2.*

10 **Casa de Las Muertes** *(House of the Dead)*. Built in about 1513 for the majordomo of Alonso de Fonseca II, the house takes its name from the four tiny skulls that adorn its top two windows. Alonso de Fonseca II commissioned the construction to commemorate his deceased uncle, the licentious archbishop who lies in the Convento de Las Ursulas, across the street. For the same reason, the facade also bears the archbishop's portrait. The small square in front of the house was a favorite haunt of the poet, philosopher, and university rector Miguel de Unamuno, whose statue stands here. Unamuno supported the Nationalists under Franco at the outbreak of the civil war, but he later turned against them. Placed under virtual house arrest, Unamuno died in the house next door in 1938. During the Franco period, students often daubed his statue red to suggest that his heart still bled for Spain. ✉ *C. de los Bordadores 6.*

3 Fodor's Choice ★ For a complete exterior tour of the old and new **cathedrals**, take a 10-minute walk around the complex, circling counterclockwise. Nearest the river stands the **Catedral Vieja** (Old Cathedral), built in the late 12th century, one of the most interesting examples of the Spanish Romanesque. Because the dome of the crossing tower has strange,

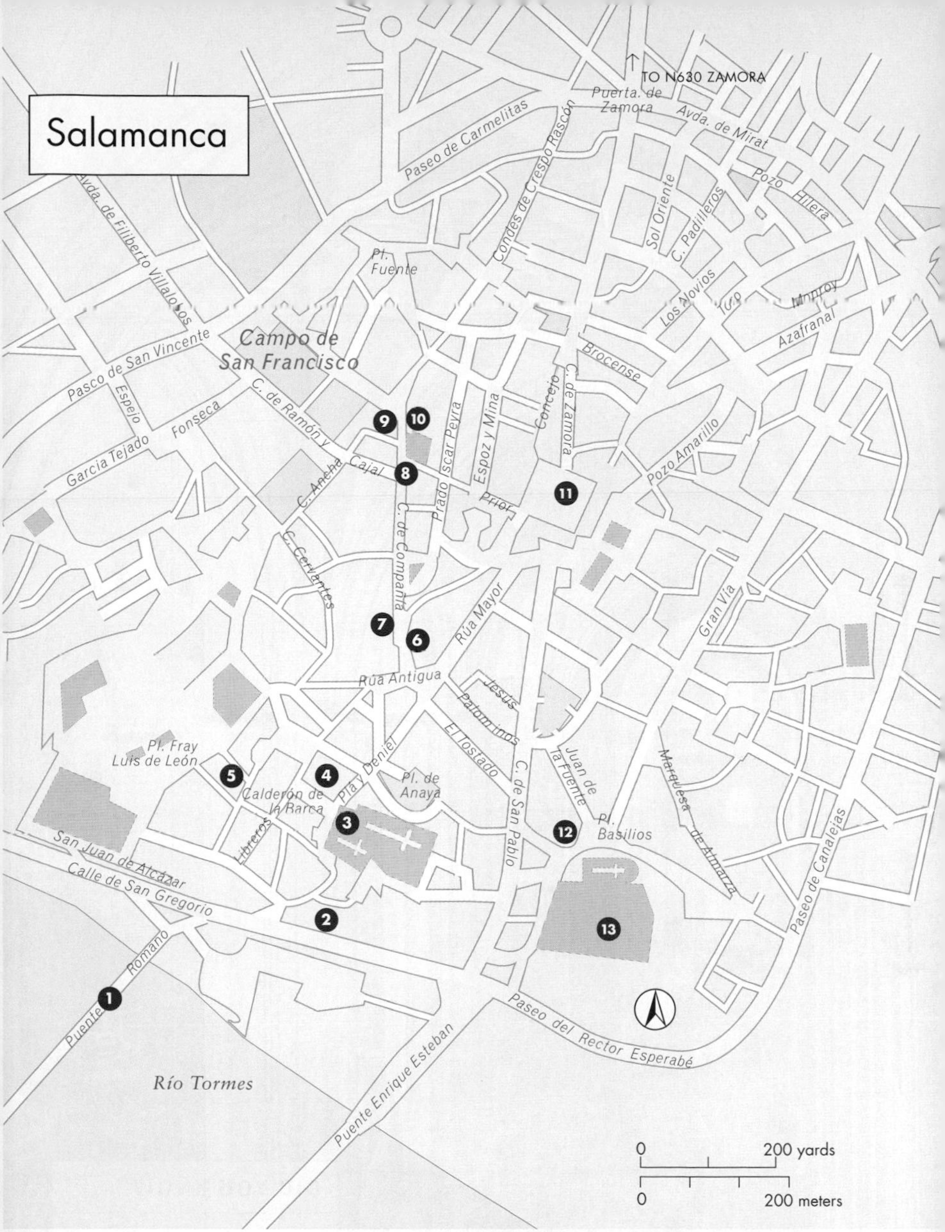
Salamanca
TO N630 ZAMORA
Puerta de Zamora
Avda. de Mirat
Paseo de Carmelitas
Condes de Crespo Rascón
Sol Oriente
C. Padilleros
Pozo Hilera
Avda. de Filiberto Villalobos
Pl. Fuente
Los Novios
Toro
Azafranal
Campo de San Francisco
Brocense
Pasco de San Vincente
Espejo
C. de Ramón y Cajal
Prado
Iscar Peyra
Espoz y Mina
Concejo
C. de Zamora
Pozo Amarillo
Garcia Tejado
Fonseca
C. Ancha
Prior
C. de Compañía
C. Cervantes
Rúa Mayor
Gran Vía
Rúa Antigua
Jesús
Palominos
El Tostado
Pl. Fray Luis de León
Calderón de la Barca
Pla y Deniel
Pl. de Anaya
C. de San Pablo
Juan de la Fuente
Marquesa de Almarza
Pl. Basilios
Libreros
San Juan de Alcázar
Calle de San Gregorio
Paseo de Canalejas
Puente Romano
Paseo del Rector Esperabé
Río Tormes
Puente Enrique Esteban
0
200 yards
0
200 meters

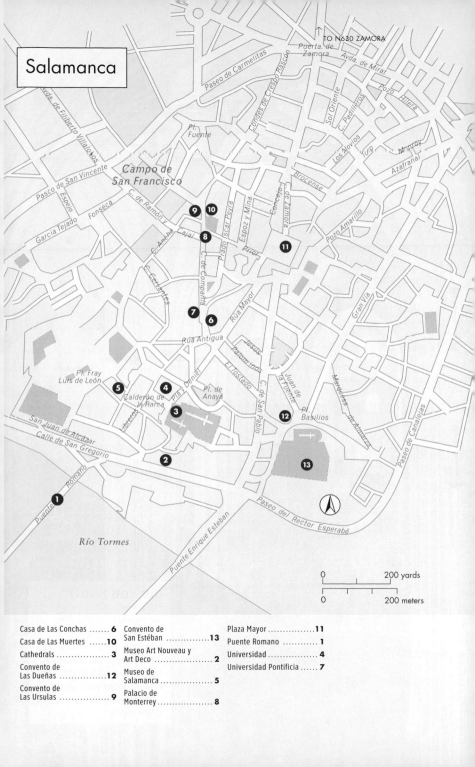

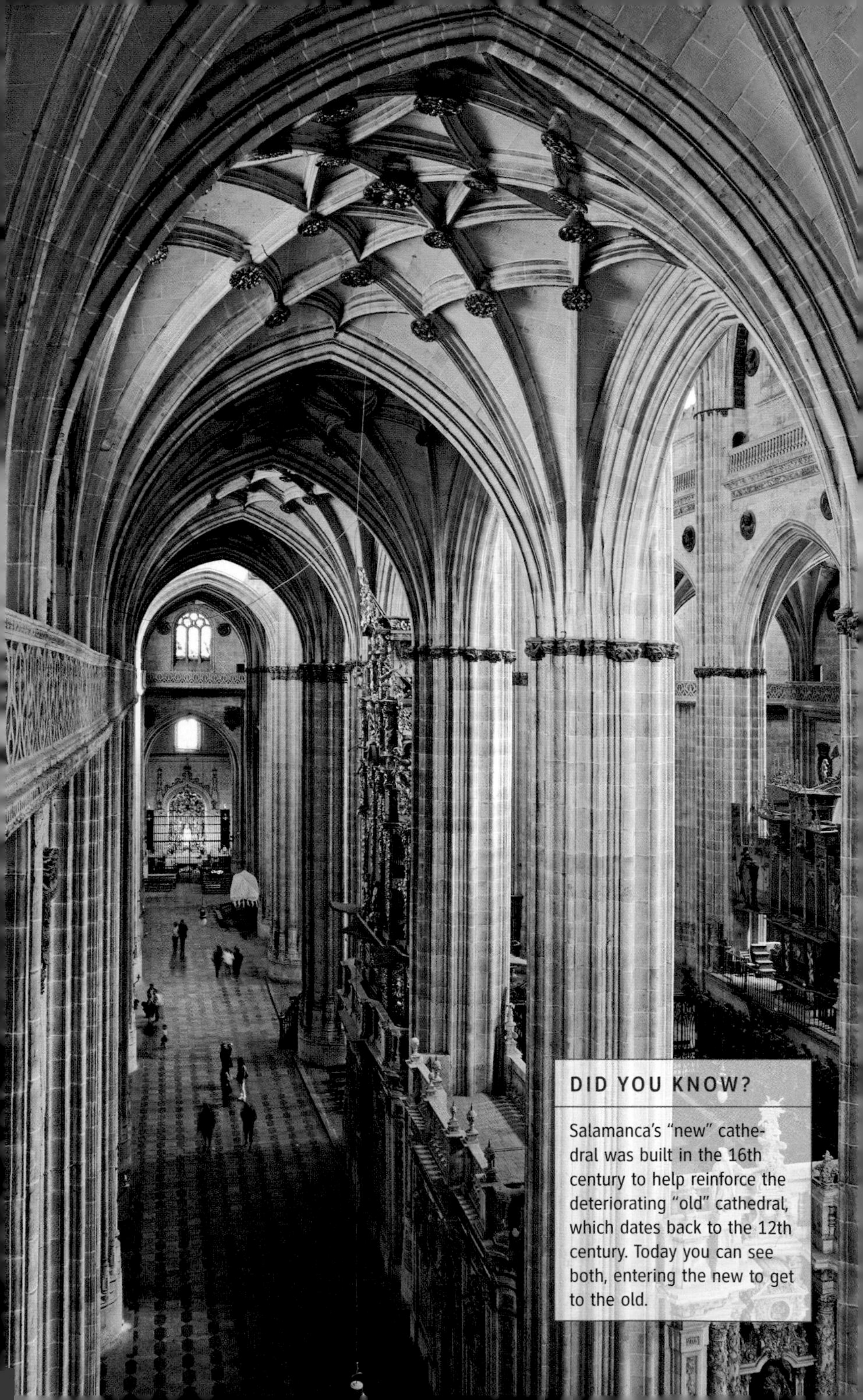

DID YOU KNOW?

Salamanca's "new" cathedral was built in the 16th century to help reinforce the deteriorating "old" cathedral, which dates back to the 12th century. Today you can see both, entering the new to get to the old.

plume-like ribbing, it's known as the Torre del Gallo (Rooster's Tower). The two cathedrals are all part of the same complex, though they have different visiting hours, and you need to enter the Old Cathedral to get to the new one.

The much larger **Catedral Nueva** (New Cathedral) dates mainly from the 16th century, though some parts, including the dome over the crossing and the bell tower attached to the west facade, had to be rebuilt after the Lisbon earthquake of 1755. Work began in 1513 under the direction of the distinguished late-Gothic architect Juan Gil de Hontañón, and, as at Segovia's cathedral, Juan's son Rodrigo took over the work after his father's death in 1526. The New Cathedral's north facade (which contains the main entrance) is ornamental enough, but the west facade is dazzling in its sculptural complexity. Try to visit in late afternoon, when the sun beams off of its surface.

The interior of the New Cathedral is as light and harmonious as that of Segovia's cathedral but larger. It's a triumphant baroque effusion designed by the Churriguera family. The wooden choir seems almost alive with cherubim and saints. From a door in the south aisle, steps descend into the Old Cathedral, where boldly carved capitals supporting the vaulting are accented by foliage, strange animals, and touches of pure fantasy. Then comes the dome, which seems to owe much to Byzantine architecture; it's a remarkably light structure raised on two tiers of arcaded openings. Not the least of the Old Cathedral's attractions are its furnishings, including sepulchres from the 12th and 13th centuries and a curved high altar comprising 53 colorful and delicate scenes by the mid-15th-century artist Nicolás Florentino. In the apse above, Florentino painted an astonishingly fresh Last Judgment fresco.

From the south transept of the Old Cathedral, a door leads into the cloister, which was begun in 1177. From about 1230 until the construction of the main university building in the early 15th century, the chapels around the cloister served as classrooms for university students. In the Chapel of St. Barbara, on the eastern side, theology students answered the grueling questions meted out by their doctoral examiners. The chair in which they sat is still there, in front of a recumbent effigy of Bishop Juan Lucero, on whose head the students would place their feet for inspiration. Also attached to the cloister is a small cathedral museum with a 15th-century triptych of St. Catherine by Salamanca's greatest native artist, Fernando Gallego. ✉ *C. Cardenal Plá y Deniel s/n* ☎ *923/217476* 🌐 *www.catedralsalamanca.org* 💰 *New Cathedral free. Old Cathedral €4.75, free Tues. 10–noon* ⏰ *New Cathedral, Apr.–Sept., daily 9–2 and 4–8; Oct.–Mar., daily 9–1 and 4–6; Old Cathedral, Apr.–Sept., daily 10–1:30 and 4–7:30; Oct.–Mar., daily 10–12:30 and 4–5:30. Nov.–Feb., both cathedrals close on Sun. afternoon.*

12 **Convento de Las Dueñas** *(Convent of the Dames)*. Founded in 1419, this convent hides a 16th-century cloister that is the most fantastically decorated in Salamanca, if not in all of Spain. The capitals of its two superimposed Salmantine arcades are crowded with a baffling profusion of grotesques that can absorb you for hours. As you're wandering through, take a moment to look down. The interlocking diamond pattern on

the ground floor of the cloister is decorated with the knobby vertebrae of goats and sheep. It's an eerie yet perfect accompaniment to all the grinning, disfigured heads sprouting from the capitals looming above you. Don't leave without buying some sweets; the nuns are excellent bakers. ✉ *Pl. del Concilio de Trento s/n* ☎ *923/215442* 🎟 *€2* ⏲ *Apr.–Oct., Mon.–Sat. 11–1 and 4–6:30; Nov.–Mar., Mon.–Sat. 11–12:45 and 4–5:30.*

9 **Convento de Las Úrsulas** *(Convent of the Ursulines).* Archbishop Alonso de Fonseca I lies here, in a splendid marble tomb created by Diego de Siloe during the early 1500s. ✉ *C. Las Úrsulas 2* ☎ *923/219877* 🎟 *€2* ⏲ *Tues.–Sun. 10:30–1:30 and 4:30–7:30. Closed last Sun. of every month.*

13 **Convento de San Esteban** *(Convent of St. Stephen).* The convent's monks, among the most enlightened teachers at the university, were the first to take Columbus's ideas seriously and helped him gain his introduction to Isabella (hence his statue in the nearby Plaza de Colón, back toward Calle de San Pablo). The complex was designed by one of San Esteban's monks, Juan de Alava. The massive west facade, a thrilling plateresque work in which sculpted figures and ornamentation are piled up to a height of more than 98 feet, is a gathering spot for tired tourists and picnicking locals. The door to the right of the west facade leads you into a golden sandstone cloister with Gothic arcading, interrupted by tall, spindly columns adorned with classical motifs. The church, unified and uncluttered but also dark and severe, allows the one note of color provided by the ornate and gilded high altar of 1692. An awe-inspiring baroque masterpiece by José Churriguera, it deserves five minutes from you to just sit and stare. ✉ *Pl. Concilio de Trento s/n* ☎ *923/215000* 🎟 *€3* ⏲ *Apr.–Sept., daily 10–2 and 4–8; Oct.–Mar., daily 10–2 and 4–7.*

2 **Museo Art Nouveau y Art Deco.** The museum is in the Casa Lis, a Modерniste building from the end of the 19th century. On display are 19th-century paintings and glass, French and German china dolls, Viennese bronze statues, furniture, jewelry, enamels, and jars. ✉ *C. El Expolio 14* ☎ *923/121425* 🌐 *www.museocasalis.org* 🎟 *€3* ⏲ *Apr.–Oct. 15, Tues.–Fri. 11–2 and 5–9, weekends and holidays 11–9; Oct. 16–Mar., Tues.–Fri. 11–2 and 4–7, weekends and holidays 11–8.*

5 **Museum of Salamanca.** Consisting mainly of minor 17th- and 18th-century paintings, this museum, also known as the Museo de Bellas Artes (Museum of Fine Arts), is interesting for its 15th-century building, which belonged to Isabella's physician, Alvárez Abarca. ✉ *Patio de Escuelas Menores 2* ☎ *923/212235* 🎟 *€1.20, free weekends* ⏲ *Oct.–June, Tues.–Sat. 10–2 and 4–7, Sun. 10–2; July–Sept., Tues.–Sat. 10–2 and 5–8, Sun. 10–2.*

8 **Palacio de Monterrey.** Built after 1538 by Rodrigo Gil de Hontañón, the Monterrey Palace was meant for an illegitimate son of Alonso de Fonseca I. As in Rodrigo's other local palaces, the building is flanked by towers and has an open arcaded gallery running the length of the upper level. Such galleries—which in Italy you would expect to see on the ground floor—are common in Spanish Renaissance palaces and were

Salamanca's central plaza mayor was once the venue for the city's bullfights.

intended to provide privacy for the women of the house and cool the floor below during the summer. Privately owned, the palace is not open to visitors, but you can stroll its grounds. ✉ *Pl. de las Agustinas*.

11 **Plaza Mayor**. Built in the 1730s by Alberto and Nicolás Churriguera, Salamanca's Plaza Mayor is one of the largest—and most beautiful—squares in Spain. The lavishly elegant, pinkish **ayuntamiento** (city hall) dominates its northern side. The square and its arcades are popular gathering spots for most of Salmantino society, and the many surrounding cafés make this the perfect spot for a coffee break. At night, the plaza swarms with students meeting "under the clock" on the plaza's north side. *Tunas* (strolling musicians in traditional garb) often meander among the cafés and crowds, playing for smiles and applause rather than tips.

Fodor's Choice ★

QUICK BITES

Unwind at La Regenta (✉ *C. Espoz y Mina 19–20* ☎ *923/123230* 🌐 *www.cafelaregenta.com*), a plush, baroque-style café-bar warms the thronged heart of town. Heavy pink-and-purple curtains block most of the street noise, making the Plaza Mayor, a half block away, a distant memory. Try a *café al caramelo* (coffee with caramel). In the evening you can order potent cocktails with names like Kiss Me Boy and Sangre del Toro (Bull's Blood).

1 **Puente Romano** *(Roman Bridge)*. Next to the bridge is an Iberian stone bull, and opposite the bull is a statue commemorating Lazarillo de Tormes, the young hero of the eponymous (but anonymous) 16th-century work that is one of the masterpieces of Spanish literature.

4 **Universidad**. Parts of the university's walls, like those of the cathedral and other structures in Salamanca, are covered with large ocher lettering recording the names of famous university graduates. The earliest names are said to have been written in the blood of the bulls killed to celebrate the successful completion of a doctorate. The **Escuelas Mayores** (Upper Schools) dates to 1415, but it was not until more than 100 years later that an unknown architect created its elaborate facade. Above the main door is the famous double portrait of Isabella and Ferdinand, surrounded by ornamentation that plays on the yoke-and-arrow heraldic motifs of the two monarchs. The double-eagle crest of Carlos V, flanked by portraits of the emperor and empress in classical guise, dominates the middle layer of the frontispiece.

Perhaps the most famous rite of passage for new students is to find the single carved frog on the facade. Legend has it that if you spot the frog on your first try, you'll pass all your exams and have a successful university career; for this reason, it's affectionately called *la rana de la suerte* (the lucky frog). It can be hard to spot the elusive amphibian, but the ticket booth has posted a clue. The crowd of pointing tourists helps, too. You can then see the beloved frog all over town, on sweatshirts, magnets, pins, jewelry, and postcards.

The interior of the Escuelas Mayores, drastically restored in parts, comes as a slight disappointment after the splendor of the facade. But the *aula* (lecture hall) of Fray Luis de León, where Cervantes, Pedro Calderón de la Barca, and numerous other luminaries of Spain's golden age once sat, is of particular interest. Cervantes carved his name on one of the wooden pews up front. After five years' imprisonment for having translated the *Song of Songs* into Spanish, Fray Luis returned to this hall and began his lecture, "As I was saying yesterday." The Escuelas Menores (Lower Schools) wraps around the patio in front of the Escuelas Mayores. Duck into its courtyard for a serene treat. ✉ *C. Libreros s/n* ☎ *923/294400* 🌐 *www.usal.es* 🎫 *€4* ⏲ *Weekdays 9:30–1:30 and 4–7:30, Sat. 9:30–1:30 and 4–7, Sun. 10–1:30.*

7 **Universidad Pontificia.** The ornate, towering complex of the university features a lovely baroque courtyard, but the highlight here is the early-16th-century Escalara Noble (Noble Staircase), which was modeled after San Esteban's Escalera Soto (Grove Staircase) but is larger, taller, and much more stunning. The bottom of each flight is decorated with myriad scenes including games, tournaments, and bullfighting on horseback. From below, it provides one of the best architectural views in Salamanca. Founded in the 13th century as part of the University of Salamanca, the Universidad Pontificia was closed in 1854 after the Spanish government dissolved the University of Salamanca's faculties of theology and canon law in 1854. Reopened in the 1940s, the university continues to teach theology, philosophy, and canon law. Also, from both within and outside the university, take note of the chapel's slightly crocked dome; the Lisbon earthquake of 1755 is to thank. ✉ *C. Compañía 5* ☎ 923/277100 🎫 *Guided tours €3* ⏲ *Guided tours every ½ hr Apr.–Oct., Tues.–Fri. 10:30–12:45 and 5–6:30, Sat. 10–1 and 5–7:15, Sun. 10–1; Nov.–Mar., Wed.–Fri. 10:30–12:45 and 4–5:30, Sat. 10–1 and 5–7:15, Sun. 10–1*

Continued on page 200

Vineyard in Rioja.

THE WINES OF SPAIN

After years of being in the shadows of other European wines, Spanish wines are finally gunning for the spotlight—and what has taken place is nothing short of a revolution. The wines of Spain, like its cuisine, are currently experiencing a firecracker explosion of both quality and variety that has brought a new level of interest, awareness, and recognition throughout the world, propelling them to superstar status. A generation of young, ambitious winemakers has jolted dormant areas awake, rediscovered long-forgotten local grapes, and introduced top international varieties. Even the most established regions have undergone makeovers in order to keep up with these dramatic changes and to compete in the global market.

THE ROAD TO GREAT WINE

Frank Gehry designed the visitor center for the Marqués de Riscal winery in Rioja.

Spain has a long wine history dating back to the time when the Phoenicians introduced viticulture, over 3,000 years ago. Some of the country's wines achieved fame in Roman times, and the Visigoths enacted early wine laws. But in the regions under Muslim rule, winemaking slowed down for centuries. Starting in the 16th century, wine trade expanded along with the Spanish Empire, and by the 18th and 19th centuries the Sherry region *bodegas* (wineries) were already established.

In the middle of the 19th century, seeds of change blossomed throughout the Spanish wine industry. In 1846, the estate that was to become Vega Sicilia, Spain's most revered winery, was set up in Castile. Three years later the famous Tío Pepe brand was established to produce the excellent dry fino wines. Marqués de Murrieta and the Marqués de Riscal wineries opened in the 1860s creating the modern Rioja region and clearing the way for many centenary wineries. *Cava*—Spain's white or pink sparkling wine—was created the following decade in Catalonia.

After this flurry of activity, Spanish wines languished for almost a century. Vines were hit hard by phylloxera, and then a civil war and a long dictatorship left the country stagnant and isolated. Just 30 short years ago, Spain's wines were split between the same dominant trio of Sherry, Rioja, and cava, and loads of cheap, watered-down wines made by local cooperatives with little gumption to improve and even less expertise.

Starting in the 1970s, however, a wave of innovation crashed through Rioja and emergent regions like Ribera del Duero and Penedés. In the 1990s, it turned into a revolution that spread all over the landscape—and is still going strong. Today, Spain is the third largest wine producer in the world and makes enticing wines at all price ranges, in never before seen quality and variety. As a result, in 2006 Spain became the second largest wine exporting country by volume, beating out France and trailing just behind Italy.

SPANISH WINE CATEGORIES BY AGE

A unique feature of Spanish wines is their indication of aging process on wine labels. DO wines (see "A *Vino* Primer" on following page) show this on mandatory back panels. Aging requirements are longer for reds, but also apply to white, rosé, and sparkling wines. For reds, the rules are as follows:

Vino Joven
A young wine that may or may not have spent some time aging in oak barrels before it was bottled. Some winemakers have begun to shun traditional regulations to produce cutting-edge wines in this category. An elevated price distinguishes the ambitious new reds from the easy-drinking *jóvenes.*

Crianza
A wine aged for at least 24 months, six of which are in barrels (12 in Rioja, Ribera del Duero, and Navarra). A great bargain in top vintages from the most reliable wineries and regions.

Reserva
A wine aged for a minimum of 36 months, at least 12 of which are in oak.

Gran Reserva
Traditionally the top of the Spanish wine hierarchy, and the pride of the historic Rioja wineries. A red wine aged for at least 24 months in oak, followed by 36 months in the bottle before release.

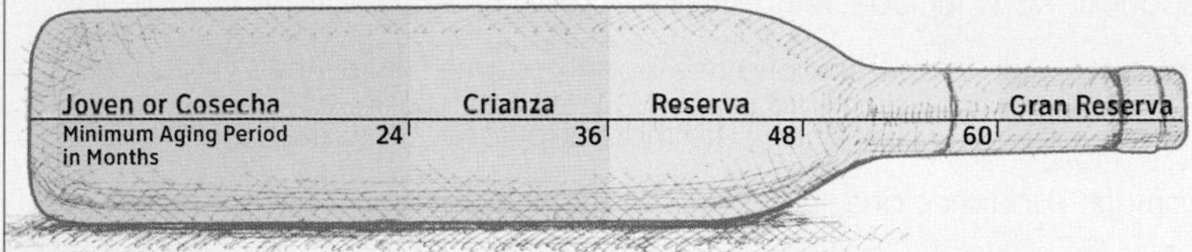

READING LABELS LIKE A PRO

A *VINO* PRIMER

Spain offers a daunting assortment of wine styles, regions, and varietals. But don't worry: a few pointers will help you understand unfamiliar names and terms. Most of Spain's quality wines come from designated regions called *Denominaciones de Origen* (Appellations of Origin), often abbreviated as DO. Spain has more than 60 of these areas, which are tightly regulated to protect the integrity and characteristics of the wines produced there. Beyond international varieties like Cabernet Sauvignon and Chardonnay, the country is home to several high-quality varietals, both indigenous and imported. Reds include Tempranillo, an early-ripening grape that blends and ages well, and Garnacha (the Spanish name for France's Grenache), a spicy, full-bodied red wine. The most popular white wines are the light, aromatic Albariño, and the full-bodied Malvasia.

Rioja wines

❶ The green and more humid areas of the Northwest deliver crisp, floral white albariños in Galicia's **Rías Biaxas.** In the **Bierzo** DO, the Mencía grape distills the essence of the schist slopes, where it grows into minerally infused red wines.

❷ Moving east, in the iron-rich riverbanks of the Duero, Tempranillo grapes, here called "Tinto Fino," produce complex and age-worthy **Ribera del Duero** reds and hefty **Toro** wines. Close by, the **Rueda** DO adds aromatic and grassy whites from local Verdejo and adopted Sauvignon Blanc.

❸ The **Rioja** region is a winemaker's paradise. Here a mild, nearly perfect vine-growing climate marries limestone and clay soils with Tempranillo, Spain's most noble grape, to deliver wines that possess the two main features of every great region: personality and quality. Tempranillo-based Riojas evolve from a young cherry color and aromas of strawberries and red fruits, to a brick hue, infused with scents of tobacco and leather. Whether medium or full-bodied, tannic or velvety, these reds are some of the most versatile and food-friendly wines, and have set the standard for the country for over a century.

Nearby, **Navarra** and three small DO's in Aragón deliver great wines made with the local Garnacha, Tempranillo, and international grape varieties.

❹ Southwest of Barcelona is the region of **Catalonia,** which encompasses the areas of Penedès and Priorat. Catalonia is best known as the heartland of *cava,*

Chardonnay vines in Navarra.

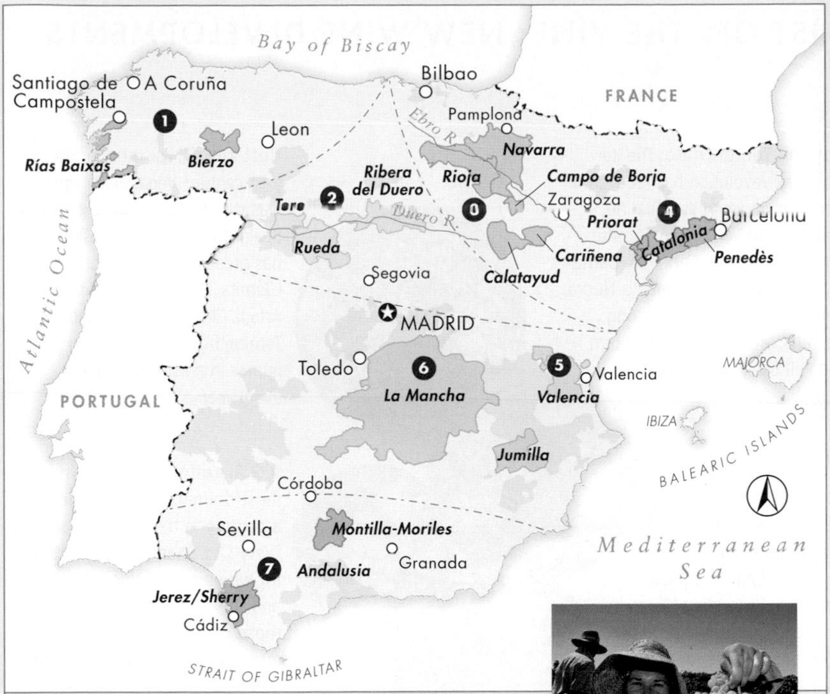

the typically dry, sparkling wine made from three indigenous Spanish varietals: Parellada, Xarel-lo, and Macabeo. The climatically varied Penedès—just an hour south of Barcelona—produces full-bodied reds like Garnacha on coastal plains, and cool-climate varietals like Riesling and Sauvignon Blanc in the mountains. Priorat is a region that has emerged into the international spotlight during the past decade, as innovative winemakers have transformed winemaking practices there. Now, traditional grapes like Garnacha and Cariñena are blended with Cabernet Sauvignon and Syrah to produce rich, concentrated reds with powerful tannins.

❺ The region of **Valencia** is south of Catalonia on the Mediterranean coast. The wines of this area have improved markedly in recent years, with red wines from Jumilla and other appellations finding their way onto the international market. Tempranillo and Monastrell (France's Mourvèdre) are the most common reds. A local specialty of the area is Moscatel de Valencia, a highly aromatic sweet white wine.

❻ In the **central plateau south of Madrid**, rapid investment, modernization, and replanting is resulting in medium bodied, easy drinking, and fairly priced wines made with Tempranillo (here called "Cencíbel"), Cabernet, Syrah, and even Petit Verdot, that are opening the doors to more ambitious endeavors.

Grapes harvested for Sherry

❼ In sun-drenched Andalusia, where the white albariza limestone soils reflect the powerful sunlight while trapping the scant humidity, the fortified **Jerez** (Sherry) and **Montilla** emerge. In all their different incarnations, from dry finos, Manzanillas, amontillados, palo cortados, and olorosos, to sweet creams and Pedro Ximénez, they are the most original wines of Spain.

JUST OFF THE VINE: NEW WINE DEVELOPMENTS

Beyond Tempranillo: The current wine revolution has recovered many native varieties. Albariño, Godello, and Verdejo among the whites, and Callet, Cariñena, Garnacha, Graciano, Mandó, Manto Negro, Mencía, and Monastrell among the reds, are gaining momentum and will likely become more recognized.

Vinos de Pagos: *Pago,* a word meaning plot or vineyard, is the new legal term chosen to create Spain's equivalent of a *Grand Cru* hierarchy, by protecting quality oriented wine producers that make wine from their own estates.

Petit Verdot: Winemakers in Spain are discovering that Petit Verdot, the "little green" grape of Bordeaux, ripens much easier in warmer climates than in its birthplace. This is contributing to the rise of Petit Verdot in red blends, and even to the production of single varietal wines.

Andalusia's New Wines: For centuries, scorching southern Andalusia has offered world-class Sherry and Montilla wines. Now trailblazing winemakers are making serious inroads in the production of quality white, red, and new dessert wines, something deemed impossible a few years back.

Cult Wines: For most of the past century, Vega Sicilia Unico was the only true cult wine from Spain. The current explosion has greatly expanded the roster: L'Ermita, Pingus, Clos Erasmus, Artadi, Cirsion, Terreus, and Termanthia are the leading names in a list that grows every year.

V.O.S. and V.O.R.S: Sherry's most dramatic change in over a century is the creation of the "Very Old Sherry" designation for wines over 20 years of age, and the addition of "Rare" for those over 30, to easier distinguish the best, oldest, and most complex wines.

Innovative New Blends: A few wine regions have strict regulations concerning the varieties used in their wines, but most allow for experimentation. All over the country, *bodegas* are crafting wines with creative blends that involve local varieties, Tempranillo, and famous international grapes.

Island Wines: In both the Balearic and Canary Islands the strong tourist industry helped to revive local winemaking. Although hard to find, the best Callet and Manto Negro based red wines of Majorca, and the sweet *malvasías* of Lanzarote will reward the adventurous drinker.

SPAIN'S SUPERSTAR WINEMAKERS

Mariano García

Peter Sisseck

Alvaro Palacios

Josep Lluís Pérez

The current wine revolution has made superstars out of a group of dynamic, innovative, and visionary winemakers. Here are some of the top names:

Mariano García. His 30 years as winemaker of Vega Sicilia made him a legend. Now García displays his deft touch in the Ribera del Duero and Bierzo through his four wineries: Aalto, Mauro, San Román, and Paixar.

Peter Sisseck. A Dane educated in Bordeaux, Sisseck found his calling in the old Ribera del Duero vineyards, where he crafted Pingus, Spain's most coveted cult wine.

Alvaro Palacios. In Priorat, Palacios created L'Ermita, a Garnacha wine that is one of Spain's most remarkable bottlings. Palacios also is a champion of the Bierzo region, where he produces wines from the ancient Mencía varietal, known for their vibrant berry flavors and stony minerality.

Josep Lluís Pérez. From his base in Priorat and through his work as a winemaker, researcher, teacher, and consultant, Pérez (along with his daughter Sara Pérez) has become the main driving force in shaping the modern Mediterranean wines of Spain.

MATCHMAKING KNOW-HOW

A pairing of wine with *jamón* and Spanish olives.

Spain has a great array of regional products and cuisines, and its avant-garde chefs are culinary world leaders. As a general rule, you should match local food with local wines—but Spanish wines can be matched very well with some of the most unexpected dishes.

Albariños and the white wines of Galicia are ideal partners for seafood and fish. Dry sherries complement Serrano and Iberico hams, *lomo, chorizo,* and *salchichón* (white dry saugage), as well as olives and nuts. Pale, light, and dry finos and Manzanillas are the perfect aperitif wines, and the ideal companion for fried fish. Fuller bodied amontillados, palo cortados, and olorosos go well with hearty soups. Ribera del Duero reds are the perfect match for the outstanding local lamb. Try Priorat and other Mediterranean reds with strong cheeses and barbecue meats. Traditional Rioja harmonizes well with fowl and game. But also take an adventure off the beaten path: manzanilla and fino are great with sushi and sashimi; Rioja *reserva* fit tuna steaks; and cream sherry will not be out of place with chocolate. *¡Salud!*

WHERE TO EAT AND STAY

¢–$$ SPANISH ✕ **Bambú**. At peak times, it's standing room only in this jovial basement tapas bar catering to students. The floor may be littered with napkins, and you might have to shout to be heard, but it's the generous tapas and big, sloppy *bocadillos* (sandwiches) that draw the crowds. Although paella is usually the exclusive domain of pricey restaurants devoted to the specialty, you can enjoy a *ración* of paella during lunch here, ladled out from a large *caldero* (shallow pan). Another bonus: even if you just order a drink, you'll be served a liberal helping of the "tapa of the day." ✉ *C. Prior 4* ☎ *923/260092* ▭ *MC, V.*

$$–$$$$ SPANISH ✕ **El Candil Viejo**. Beloved by locals for its superb, no-nonsense Castilian fare, this tavern is an old favorite with professors in pinstripes and students on dates. Aside from a simple salad, the menu consists of meat, meat, and more meat, including pork, lamb, kid, sausage, and fantastic *marucha* (short ribs). The homemade pork sausages are especially good. For tapas, try the *farinato* sausage, made from pork, onion, eggs, and bread crumbs, or the *picadillo,* similar but spicier with pepper, garlic, and tomato. ✉ *C. Ventura Ruiz Aguilera 14–16* ☎ *923/217239* ▭ *AE, DC, MC, V* ⊙ *Closed 3 wks in Jan.*

$$–$$$$ SPANISH Fodor's Choice ★ ✕ **La Hoja 21**. Just off the Plaza Mayor, this restaurant has a glass facade, high ceilings, butter-yellow walls, and minimalist art—signs of an apart-from-the-usual Castilian dining experience. Young chef-owner Alberto López Oliva prepares an innovative menu of traditional fare with a twist, such as *manitas, manzana, y langostinas al aroma de Módena* (pig trotters with prawns and apple slices in Módena vinegar), and *perdiz al chocolate con berza* (partridge cooked in chocolate, served with cabbage). ✉ *C. San Pablo 21* ☎ *923/264028* ▭ *AE, MC, V* ⊙ *Closed Mon. and 2 wks in Aug. No dinner Sun.*

$$$–$$$$ 🏨 **Don Gregorio**. This upscale hotel, opened at the beginning of 2010, traces its history back to the 15th century, and has been used by the likes of the bishop of Salamanca as his private palace. More recently, the building was owned by Don Gregorio de Diego Curto, a prosperous businessman to whom the hotel owes its name. The rooms are spacious and contemporary but pay homage to the building's history with antiques that belonged to the original structure, the Don Gregorio family, and even the nearby cathedral. In-room massages are available, which will make it even harder to leave. **Pros:** chic, contemporary facilities. **Cons:** no restaurant. ✉ *C. San Pablo 80–82* ☎ *923/217015* 🌐 *www.hoteldongregorio.com* *17 rooms* *In-room: Wi-Fi. In-hotel: bar, laundry service, parking (paid)* ▭ *AE, DC, MC, V.*

$ 🏨 **Hostal Plaza Mayor**. You can't beat the location of this great little *hostal,* just steps from the Plaza Mayor. Rooms are small but modern. Reservations are advisable, as rooms fill up fast. **Pros:** good value; views of the plaza; international and polyglot staff. **Cons:** occasional noise on the street side; with porters few and far between and no elevator, hauling bags upstairs can be grueling. ✉ *Pl. del Corrillo 20* ☎ *923/262020* 🌐 *www.hostalplazamayor.es* *19 rooms* *In-hotel: restaurant* ▭ *MC, V.*

$$–$$$ ★ 🏨 **Hotel Rector**. From the stately entrance to the high-ceiling guest rooms, this lovely hotel is a true European experience. Rooms offer everything

from twice-daily maid service to complimentary Internet hookups, and double-glazed windows eliminate virtually all street noise. Mahogany antique furniture pieces and marble bathrooms add to the elegance. The sitting areas, hallways, and breakfast room are all spotless, spacious, warm, and quiet. Staff is helpful and can tell you all about Salamanca. **Pros:** terrific, personal service; good location. **Cons:** breakfast is an additional cost (€12 per person); no balconies. ✉ *Paseo Rector Esperabé 10* ☎ *923/218482* 🌐 *www.hotelrector.com* 13 *rooms* *In-hotel: bar* AE, DC, MC, V.

NIGHTLIFE

Particularly in summer, Salamanca sees the greatest influx of foreign students of any city in Spain—by day they study Spanish, and by night they fill Salamanca's bars and clubs to capacity. **Mesón Cervantes** (✉ *Entrance on southeast corner of Pl. Mayor*), an upstairs tapas bar, draws crowds to its balcony for a drink and unparalleled views of the action below. Bask in the romantic glow from stained-glass lamps in the **Posada de las Almas** (✉ *Pl. San Boal s/n*), the preferred cocktail-and-conversation nightspot for stylish students. Wrought-iron chandeliers hang from the high wood-beam ceilings, harp-strumming angels top elegant pillars, and one entire wall of shelves showcases colorful dollhouses.After 11, a well-dressed twenty- and thirtysomething crowd comes to dance at **Camelot** (✉ *C. de los Bordadores 3*), an ancient stone-wall warehouse in one corner of the 16th-century Convento de Las Ursulas. For good wine, heaping portions of tapas, and live music, try the **Café Principal** (✉ *C. Rúa Mayor 9*). After-hours types end (if not spend) the night at **Café Moderno** (✉ *Gran Vía 75*), snacking on *churros con chocolate* at daybreak.

SHOPPING

On Sunday, the **Rastro** flea market is held on Avenida de Aldehuela. Buses leave from Plaza de España.The husband-and-wife team in tiny **Artesanía Duende** (✉ *C. San Pablo 29–31* ☎ *923/213622*) have been creating and selling unique wooden crafts for decades. Their music boxes, thimbles, photo frames, and other items are beautifully carved or stenciled with local themes, from the *bailes charros,* Salamanca's regional dance, to the floral designs embroidered on the hems of provincial dresses.

BURGOS

240 km (149 mi) north of Madrid on A1.

On the banks of the Arlanzón River, this small city boasts some of Spain's most outstanding medieval architecture. If you approach on the A1 from Madrid, the spiky twin spires of Burgos's cathedral, rising above the main bridge, welcome you to the city. Burgos's second pride is its heritage as the city of El Cid, the part-historical, part-mythical hero of the Christian Reconquest of Spain. The city has been known for centuries as a center of both militarism and religion, and even today more nuns fill the streets than almost anywhere else in Spain. Burgos was born as a military camp—a fortress built in 884 on the orders of the Christian king Alfonso III, who was struggling to defend the upper reaches of Old

Castile from the constant forays of the Arabs. It quickly became vital in the defense of Christian Spain, and its reputation as an early outpost of Christianity was cemented with the founding of the Royal Convent of Las Huelgas, in 1187. Burgos also became a place of rest and sustenance for Christian pilgrims on the Camino de Santiago.

GETTING HERE AND AROUND

Burgos municipal buses cover 45 routes throughout the city, many of then originating in Plaza de España.

ESSENTIALS

Visitor Information Burgos (✉ *Pl. Alonso Martinez 7* ☎ *947/203125* 🌐 *www.turismoburgos.org*).

EXPLORING

2 ★ Start your tour of the city with the **cathedral**, which contains such a wealth of art and other treasures that the local burghers lynched their civil governor in 1869 for trying to take an inventory of it: the proud Burgalese feared that the man was plotting to steal their riches. Just as opulent is the sculpted Flamboyant Gothic facade of the cathedral. The cornerstone was laid in 1221, and the two 275-foot towers were completed by the middle of the 14th century, though the final chapel was not finished until 1731. There are 13 chapels, the most elaborate of which is the hexagonal Condestable Chapel. You'll find the **tomb of El Cid** (1026–99) and his wife, Ximena, under the transept. El Cid (whose real name was Rodrigo Díaz de Vivar) was a feudal warlord revered for his victories over the Moors; the medieval *Song of My Cid* transformed him into a Spanish national hero.

At the other end of the cathedral, high above the West Door, is the **Reloj de Papamoscas** (Flycatcher Clock), so named for the sculptured bird that opens its mouth as the hands mark each hour. The grilles around the choir have some of the finest wrought-iron work in central Spain, and the choir itself has 103 delicately carved walnut stalls, no two alike. The 13th-century stained-glass windows that once shed a beautiful, filtered light were destroyed in 1813, one of many cultural casualties of Napoléon's retreating troops. ✉ *Between Pl. del Rey San Fernando and Pl. de Santa María* ☎ *947/204712* 🌐 *www.catedraldeburgos.es* 🎫 *Museum and cloister €5* ⏱ *Mar. 19–Oct., daily 9:30–7:30 and 4–7; Nov.–Mar. 18, daily 10–7; last entry 1 hr prior to closing.*

3 Across the Plaza del Rey San Fernando from the cathedral is the city's main gate, the **Arco de Santa María**; walk through toward the river and look above the arch at the 16th-century statues of the first Castilian judges, El Cid, King Carlos I, and Spain's patron saint, James.

4 The Arco de Santa María frames the city's loveliest promenade, the **Espolón**. Shaded with black poplars, it follows the riverbank.

6 Founded in 1441, the **Cartuja de Miraflores** is an old Gothic monastery, the outside of which is rather plain. Inside, however, is a mass of rich decoration. The Isabelline church has an altarpiece by Gil de Siloe that is said to be gilded with the first gold brought back from the Americas. To get there, follow signs from the city's main gate. ✉ *Cta. Fuentes Blancas, 3 km (2 mi) east of Burgos, at end of a poplar- and elm-lined*

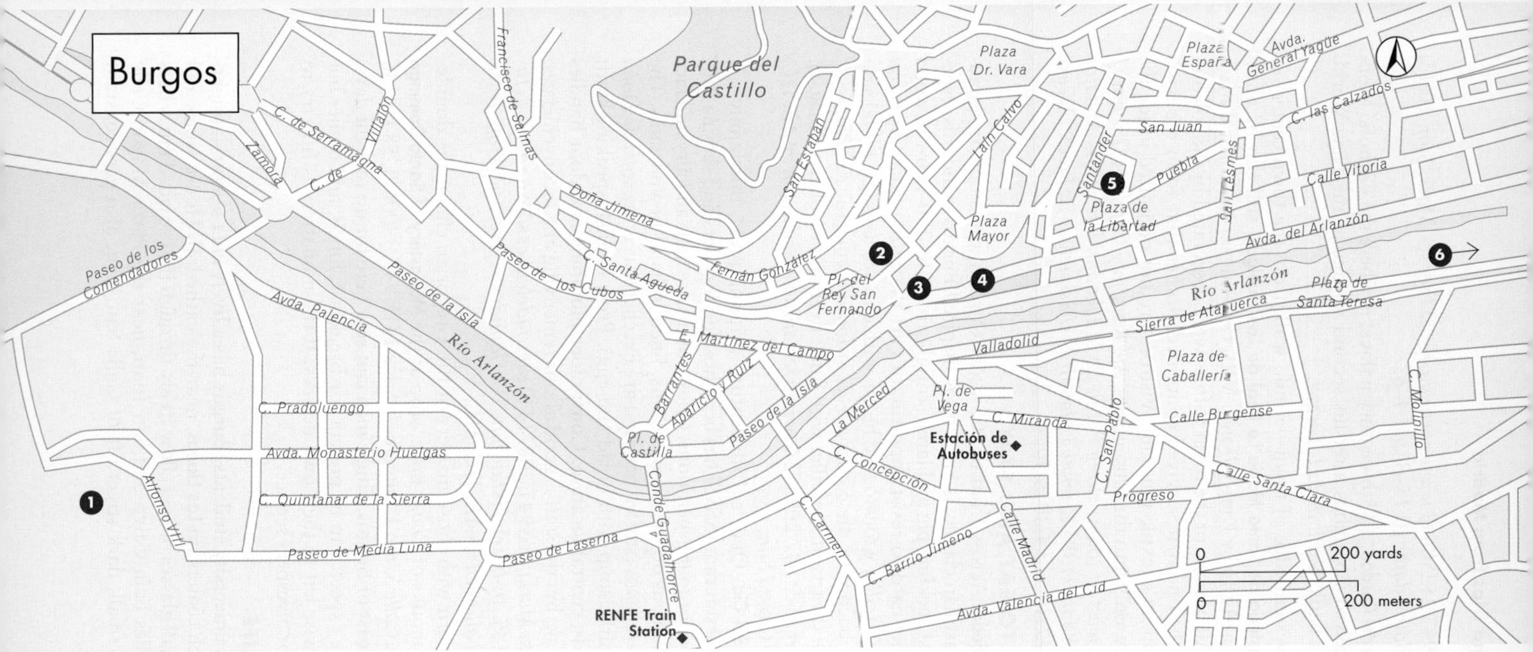

Arco de Santa María 3
Cartuja de Miraflores 6
Casa del Cordón 5
Cathedral 2
Espolón 4
Monasterio de las Huelgas Reales 1

road ☎ *947/252586* 🌐 *www.cartuja.org* 🎫 *Free* ⏲ *Mass, Sun. 10:15; main building daily 10:15–3 and 4–6.*

5 The **Casa del Cordón**, a 15th-century palace, is where the Catholic Monarchs received Columbus after his second voyage to the New World. It's now a bank. ✉ *Pl. de la Libertad.*

1 On the western edge of town—a mile walk from the town center—is the **Monasterio de Santa María La Real de Las Huelgas**, still run by nuns. Founded in 1187 by King Alfonso VIII, the convent has a royal mausoleum. All but one of the royal coffins were desecrated by Napoléon's soldiers; the one that survived contained clothes that form the basis of the convent's textile museum. Visitors are not permitted inside the monastery, only into the museum. ✉ *Av. Ramon y Cajal s/n, 1½ km (1 mi) southwest of town, along Paseo de la Isla and left across Malatos Bridge* ☎ *983/291395* 🌐 *www3.planalfa.es/lashuelgas* 🎫 *Free* ⏲ *Weekdays 10–12:30 and 4:30–6:30.*

WHERE TO EAT AND STAY

$$–$$$$ SPANISH ★ ✕ **Casa Ojeda.** Across from the Casa del Cordón, this popular restaurant, a Castilian classic, is known for inspired Burgos standards, especially roast suckling pig and lamb straight from the 200-year-old wood oven. Other hard-to-resist opportunities are the *alubias rojas ibeas con chorizo, morcilla, y tocino* (red beans with chorizo sausage, blood sausage, and bacon) or the *corazones de solomillo con foie al vinagre de frambuesa* (hearts of beef fillet with duck liver and raspberry vinegar). ✉ *C. Vitoria 5* ☎ *947/209052* 🌐 *www.restauranteojeda.com* 💳 *AE, DC, MC, V* ⏲ *Closed Sun.*

$$$ 🏨 **Mesón del Cid.** Once a 15th-century printing press, this family-run hotel and restaurant ($$$$) has been hosting travelers and serving Burgalese food for four generations. Guest rooms are light and airy and face the cathedral, as do the dining rooms, lined in hand-hewn beams. The *pimientos rellenos* (stuffed peppers) are excellent, as is the *sopa de Doña Jimena* (garlic soup with bread and egg). **Pros:** English-speaking staff; comfy beds; central location. **Cons:** older plumbing and door handles might break, but the staff is good about remedying any inconveniences. ✉ *Pl. Santa María 8* ☎ *947/208715* 🌐 *mesondelcid.es* 🛏 *56 rooms* 👍 *In-room: Wi-Fi. In-hotel: restaurant, bar, laundry service, parking (free), some pets allowed* 💳 *AE, DC, MC, V.*

EN ROUTE

For a sojourn with those masters of the Gregorian chant, the double-platinum monks of *Chant* fame, stop at the **Monastery of Santo Domingo de Silos** (✉ *Calle Santo Domingo de Silos 14* ☎ *947/390068*), 58 km (36 mi) southeast of Burgos. Single men can stay here for up to eight days. Guests are expected to be present for breakfast, lunch, and dinner but are otherwise left to their own devices. If the monastery is full, try to drop in for a vespers service.

NIGHTLIFE

Due to its university students, Burgos has a lively *vida nocturna* (nightlife), which centers on **Las Llanas,** near the cathedral. House wines and *cañas* (small glasses of beer) flow freely through the crowded tapas bars along Calles Laín Calvo and San Juan, near the Plaza Mayor. Calle Puebla, a small, dark street off of Calle San Juan, also gets constant revelers, who pop into Café Principal, La Rebotica, and Spils Cervecería for a quick drink and bite before moving on. When you order a drink at any Burgos bar, the bartender plunks down a free *pinchito* (small tapa)—a long-standing tradition.

SHOPPING

A good buy is a few bottles of local Ribera de Duero *tinto* wines, now strong rivals to those of Rioja-Alta. Burgos is also known for its cheeses. **Casa Quintanilla** (✉ *C. Paloma 17*) is a good spot to pick up some *queso de Burgos*, a fresh, ricotta-like cheese.

3

LEÓN

333 km (207 mi) northwest of Madrid, 216 km (134 mi) west of Burgos.

León, the ancient capital of Castile–León, sits on the banks of the Bernesga River in the high plains of Old Castile; today it's a wealthy provincial capital and prestigious university town. The wide avenues of western León are lined with boutiques, and the twisting alleys of the half-timbered old town hide the bars, bookstores, and *chocolaterías* most popular with students.

Historians say that the city was not named for the proud lion that has been its emblem for centuries; rather, they assert that the name is a corruption of the Roman word *legio* (legion), from the fact that the city was founded as a permanent camp for the Roman legions in AD 70. The capital of Christian Spain was moved here from Oviedo in 914 as the Reconquest spread south, and this was the city's richest era.

As you're wandering the old town, you can still see fragments of the 6-foot-thick ramparts that were once part of the Roman walls. Look down occasionally and you just might notice small brass scallop shells set into the street. The scallop is the symbol of St. James; the town government installed them to mark the path for modern-day pilgrims.

GETTING HERE AND AROUND

Alsa (🌐 *www.alsa.es*) runs 14 lines around León, but visitors to the city will rarely need them as the historic center is primarily composed of pedestrian-only streets. A Tren Turístico originating in front of Gaudí's Casa de Botines in Plaza San Marcelo operates during July and August.

ESSENTIALS

Visitor Information León (✉ *Pl. de la Regla 3* ☎ *987/237082* 🌐 *www.leon.es*).

EXPLORING

❹ ★ The pride of León is its soaring Gothic **catedral**, on the Plaza de Regla. Its upper reaches have more windows than stone. Flanked by two aggressively square towers, the facade has three arched, weatherworn doorways, the middle one adorned with slender statues of the apostles. Begun in 1205, the cathedral has 125 long, thin stained-glass windows, dozens of decorative small ones, and three giant rose windows. The windows depict abstract floral patterns as well as various biblical and medieval scenes; on sunny days, they cast bejeweled streams of light

Antiguo Convento de San Marcos **8**
Casa de Botines **5**
Cathedral **4**
Fundación Vela Zanetti **6**
MUSAC **9**
Museo de León **10**
Plaza Mayor **3**
Plaza San Martín **2**
Plaza de Santa María del Camino **1**
San Isidoro el Real **7**

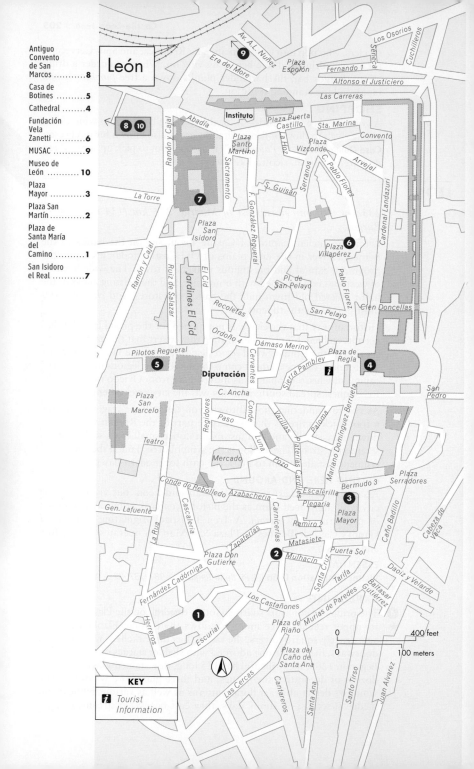

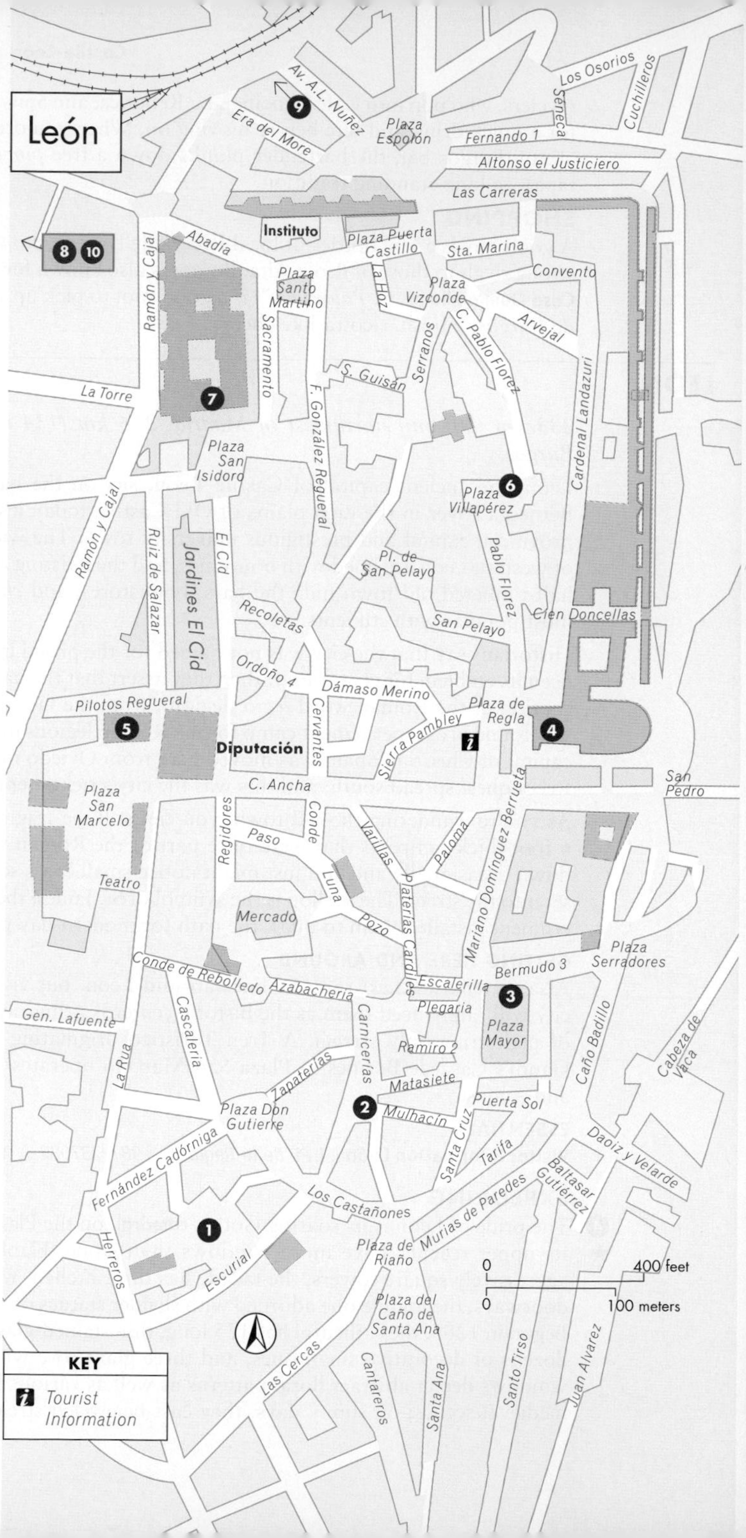

on the beautifully spare, pale sandstone interior. A glass door to the choir gives an unobstructed view of nave windows and the painted altarpiece, framed with gold leaf. The cathedral also contains the sculpted tomb of King Ordoño II, who moved the capital of Christian Spain to León. The **museum's collection boasts** giant medieval hymnals, textiles, sculptures, wood carvings, and paintings. Look for the carved-wood Mudejar archive, with a letter of the alphabet above each door; it's one of the world's oldest file cabinets. The partial museum visit excludes the museum's best and earliest works: the Romanesque, Gothic, and Renaissance ivory carvings and silversmithery, so opt for the full museum ticket. ✉ *Pl. de Regla s/n* ☎ *987/875770* 🌐 *www.catedraldeleon.org* 🎫 *Cathedral free (€1.70 with guide), full museum €4, partial museum €2, cloister only €1* ⏲ *Cathedral Oct.–May, weekdays 9:30–1:30 and 4–7, Sat. 9:30–1:30; July–Sept., Mon.–Sat. 8:30–1:30 and 4–8, Sun. 8:30–2:30 and 5–8. Museum Oct.–May, weekdays 9:30–1:30 and 4–7, Sat. 9:30–1:30; June–Sept., weekdays 9:30–2 and 4–7:30, Sat. 9:30–2 and 4–7.*

EL CAMINO

West of Burgos, the N120 to León crosses the ancient Way of St. James, revealing lovely old churches, tiny hermitages, ruined monasteries, and medieval villages across rolling fields. West of León, you can follow the well-worn Camino pilgrimage route as it approaches the giant cathedral in Santiago de Compostela. *See the El Camino de Santiago In Focus feature in Chapter 4 for more information about El Camino.*

6 Hidden away just north of the cathedral is the **Fundación Vela Zanetti**, a contemporary art museum made of minimalist wood beams and glass panels inside a 15th-century mansion. Zanetti was a 20th-century Castilian artist with a penchant for warm tones. Some of his portraits recall El Greco. Art lovers will find this widely unknown museum a pleasant surprise. ✉ *C. Pablo Flórez s/n* ☎ *987/244121* 🎫 *Free* ⏲ *Tues.–Sat. 10–1 and 5–8.*

3 The **Plaza Mayor** is the heart of the old town. On Wednesday and Saturday, the arcaded plaza bustles with farmers selling produce and cheeses. Many farmers still wear wooden shoes called *madreñas,* designed to walk on mud in this usually wet part of Spain; odd-looking, they're raised on three heels, two in front and one in back.

2 Most of León's tapas bars are in the 12th-century **Plaza San Martín**. This area is called the Barrio Húmedo, or Wet Neighborhood, because of the large amount of wine spilled here late at night.

1 Southwest of the Plaza San Martín is the **Plaza de Santa María del Camino**, which used to be called Plaza del Grano (Grain Square) because it hosted the city's corn and bread market. Also here is the church of **Santa María del Camino,** where pilgrims stop on their way west to Santiago de Compostela. The fountain in the middle of the plaza depicts two cherubs clutching a pillar, symbolizing León's two rivers and the capital.

7 ★ The sandstone basilica of **San Isidoro el Real**, on Calle Cid, was built into the side of the city wall in 1063 and rebuilt in the 12th century.

Adjoining the basilica, the **Panteón de los Reyes** (Royal Pantheon), which has earned the title of the Sistine Chapel of Romanesque art, has vibrant 12th-century frescoes on its pillars and ceiling. The pantheon was the first building in Spain to be decorated with scenes from the New Testament. Look for the agricultural calendar painted on one archway, showing which farming task should be performed each month. Twenty-three kings and queens were once buried here, but their tombs were destroyed by French troops during the Napoleonic Wars. Treasures in the adjacent **Museo de San Isidoro** include a jewel-encrusted agate chalice, a richly illustrated handwritten Bible, and many polychrome wood statues of the Virgin Mary. ✉ *Pl. de San Isidoro 4* ☎ *987/876161* 🌐 *www.sanisidorodeleon.net* 🎟 *Basilica free, Royal Pantheon and museum €4* ⏲ *July and Aug., Mon.–Sat. 9–8, Sun. 9–2; Sept.–June, Mon.–Sat. 10–1:30 and 4–6:30, Sun. 10–1:30.*

7 Just south of the old town is the **Casa de Botines**, a multigabled, turreted, granite behemoth designed in the late 1800s by the controversial Catalan Antoni Gaudí. It now houses a bank. ✉ *Pl. de Obispo Marcelo 5.*

8 Fronted by a large, airy pedestrian plaza, the sumptuous **Antiguo Convento de San Marcos** is now a luxury hotel, the Parador Hostal San Marcos. Originally a home for knights of the Order of St. James, who patrolled the Camino de Santiago, and a pit stop for weary pilgrims, the monastery you see today was begun in 1513 by the head of the order, King Ferdinand, who thought that knights deserved something better. Finished at the height of the Renaissance, the plateresque facade is a majestic swath of small, intricate sculptures (many depicting knights and lords) and ornamentation. Inside, the elegant staircase and a cloister full of medieval statues lead you to the bar, which still has the original defensive arrow slits as windows. As the Anexo Monumental del Museo de León, the convent also displays historic paintings and artifacts. ✉ *Pl. de San Marcos s/n* ☎ *987/245061* 🎟 *Museum inside parador €0.60* ⏲ *Museum, Oct.–June, Tues.–Sat. 10–2 and 4–7; Sun. 10–2; July–Sept., Tues.–Sat. 10–2 and 5–8, Sun. 10–2.*

9 ★ The inside of the **MUSAC (Museo de Arte Contemparáneo de Castilla y León)** *(Museum of Modern Art of Castillo y León)* reflects contemporary León, while the outside pays homage to the city's history with its own cluster of buildings whose exteriors are cascaded with rectangular stained glass, like its cathedral. This "Museum of the Present" brings art to the people by offering varied workshops and activities for children amid exhibiting modern creations from all over the globe. Films and concerts also show throughout the year. ✉ *Av. de Los Reyes Leoneses 24* ☎ *987/090000* 🌐 *www.musac.org.es* 🎟 *Free* ⏲ *Weekdays 10–3 and 5–8, weekends 11–3 and 5–9.*

10 **Museo de León** displays a comprehensive history of the city and region from prehistoric to contemporary times. Pride of place belongs to the Cristo Carrizo (Carrizo Crucifix), a small 11th-century Romanesque ivory carving distinguished by its lifelike expression and powerful presence. Notable are the figure's carefully coiffed hair and beard and the loincloth arranged in sumptuous Byzantine detail. ✉ *Pl. de Santo Domingo 8* ☎ *987/236405* 🌐 *www.museodeleon.com* 🎟 *€1.20*

The multicolored panels on León's MUSAC, the Museum of Contemporary Art, were inspired by the rose window of the city's Gothic cathedral.

Oct.–June, Tues.–Sat. 10–2 and 4–7, Sun. 10–2; July –Sept., Tues.–Sat. 10–2 and 4–7, Sun. 10–2.

WHERE TO EAT AND STAY

¢–$$ SPANISH **Bodega Regia**. Next to the cathedral, this charming and relaxed restaurant has a restored 14th-century garden patio with lovely stone arches, a great place to appreciate the good food. Desserts such as the *pastel de castañas con chocolate caliente* (chestnut cake with hot chocolate) are worth splurging on. *C. Regidores 9–11* *987/213173* *www.regialeon.com* *AE, DC, MC, V* *Closed Sun. and 15 days in Jan. and Sept.*

$$–$$$$ SPANISH **Nuevo Racimo de Oro**. Upstairs from a ramshackle 12th-century tavern in the heart of the old town, this rustic restaurant, once a hostel and hospital for weary pilgrims, now specializes in roast lamb cooked in a wood-burning clay oven. The spicy *sopa de ajo leonesa* (garlic soup) is a classic, and the *solomillo Racimo con micuit de foie al aceite de trufa* (veal fillet with duck liver and truffle oil) is criminally good. It's worth saving some room for the *Tarta de San Marcos,* a lemon cake served with whipped cream. *Pl. San Martín 8* *987/214767* *www.racimodeoro.com* *AE, DC, MC, V* *Closed Sun.*

$ **Hotel Paris**. This modest but elegant establishment managed by a group of brothers and sisters is both comfortable and conveniently located. The classic basement *mesón* (student tavern and restaurant) snuggles up against the 2,000-year-old stones of a Roman wall. The hotel is on the modern thoroughfare heading east from Plaza Santo Domingo, halfway between the cathedral and the new town. Rooms are classically designed and equipped with traditional furniture. **Pros:** great location; in-house spa. **Cons:** street noise; few staff members speak English. ✉ *C. Ancha 18* ☎ *987/238600* 🌐 *www.hotelparisleon.com* *61 rooms* *In-hotel: restaurant, bar, spa* *AE, DC, MC, V.*

$$–$$$ Fodor's Choice ★ **Parador Hostal San Marcos.** This magnificent parador occupies a restored 16th-century monastery built by King Ferdinand to shelter pilgrims walking the Camino de Santiago. Its plateresque facade also fronts a church and museum of archaeology. Hallways and guest rooms have antiques and high-quality reproductions paired with contemporary art. The modern wing has 175 standard rooms, and the original section of the hotel has all the luxury suites and superior rooms. The elegant dining room ($$$–$$$$) offers regional fare. **Pros:** among the most beautiful paradors in Spain; great restaurant. **Cons:** large disparity in quality between the most and least expensive rooms (this is the place to splurge for the good ones). ✉ *Pl. de San Marcos 7* ☎ *987/237300* 🌐 *www.parador.es* *186 rooms, 16 suites* *In-room: Wi-Fi. In-hotel: 2 restaurants, bar, pool, parking (paid)* *AE, DC, MC, V.*

NIGHTLIFE

Most of León's liveliest hangouts are clustered in Plaza Mayor and Plaza San Martín, with the former drawing couples and families and the latter a university crowd. The streets around these plazas (Calles Escalerilla, Plegaria, Ramiro 2, Matasiete, and Mulhacén) are packed with tapas bars. In the Plaza Mayor, you might want to start at **Universal, Mesón de Don Quixote, Casa Benito,** or **Bar La Plaza Mayor**. In the Plaza San Martín, the **Latino Bar at No. 10** serves a glass of house wine and your choice of one of four generous tapas.

SHOPPING

Tasty regional treats include roasted red peppers, potent brandy-soaked cherries, and candied chestnuts. You can buy these in food shops all over the city. **Cuesta Castañón** (✉ *C. Castoñones 2* ☎ *987/208070*), near Plaza San Martín, has a great selection of wines, cured meats, cookies, preserves, and bottled delicacies, not to mention books on related topics. Friendly owner José María González lets you sample the stock. At **Hojaldres Alonso** (✉ *C. Ancha 7* ☎ *987/252151*), near the cathedral, you can browse shelves of local goodies (candied nuts, preserves), all produced in nearby Astorga, and then head to the café in the back. The focus here is on the baked goods, particularly the *hojaldres* (puff pastries) and *torrijas,* a Castilian version of French toast. The café is a favorite among locals who come for their early evening *merienda* (usually between 6 and 8), Spain's answer to the afternoon tea. You can shop while having tapas at **Prada a Tope** (✉ *C. Alfonso IX 9* ☎ *987/257 221*), where they're packaged by the house.For fine, funky gifts, visit **Tricosis** (✉ *Cta. León-collanzo 54* ☎ *987/283574*) outside of town, a gallery opened by art students from the universities of León and Gijón. Colorful papier-mâché and experimental media form outstanding lamps, candleholders, vases, and frames.

ASTORGA

46 km (29 mi) southwest of León.

Astorga, where the pilgrimage roads from France and Portugal merge, once had 22 hospitals to lodge and care for ailing travelers. The only one left today is next to the cathedral, which is itself a huge 15th-century building with four statues of St. James.

ESSENTIALS

Tourist Information Astorga (⊠ *Pl. Eduardo de Castro 5* ☎ *987/618222*).

EXPLORING

The **Museo de la Catedral** displays 10th- and 12th-century chests, religious silverware, and paintings and sculptures by various Astorgans. ⊠ *Pl. de la Catedral* ☎ *987/615820* ☑ *€2.50* ☉ *Oct.–Feb., daily 11–2 and 4–6; Mar.–Sept., daily 10–2 and 4–8.*

Just opposite Astorga's cathedral is the fairy-tale, neo-Gothic **Palacio Episcopal** *(Archbishop's Palace)*, designed for a Catalan cleric by Antoni Gaudí in 1889. Visiting the palace during Astorga's Fiesta de Santa María, the last week of August, is a treat for the senses: fireworks explode in the sky, casting rainbows of light over Gaudí's ornate, mystical towers. It's also home of the **Museo de Los Caminos** (Museum of the Way), which boasts a large collection of folk items, such as the standard pilgrim costume—heavy black cloak, staff hung with gourds, and wide-brimmed hat bedecked with scallop shells—as well as contemporary Spanish art. ⊠ *Glorieta Eduardo de Castro s/n, adjacent to cathedral, on Pl. de la Catedral* ☎ *987/616882* ☑ *€2.50* ☉ *Mar. 20–Sept. 20, Tues.–Sat. 10–2 and 4–8, Sun. 10–2; Sept. 21–Mar. 19, Tues.–Sat. 11–2 and 4–6, Sun. 11–2.*

WHERE TO EAT AND STAY

$$–$$$ ✕ **Restaurante Serrano.** Popular with locals, and occasionally serving game, wild mushrooms, and pork during special gastronomic weeks, this *mesón* has both contemporary cuisine and traditional roasts of baby lamb. Monthly culinary themes vary from a celebration of game cuisine in December to *matanza del cerdo* (pig-killing) products in January to *cocina maragata* (regional specialties such as *cocido maragato*, a thick stew) in March and Astur-Roman dishes in July. Don't be surprised by imaginative contemporary adventures such as duck with chocolate and raspberry sauce. ⊠ *C. Portería 2* ☎ *987/617866* ☰ *AE, MC, V* ☉ *Closed last 2 wks in June. No dinner Mon.*

$–$$ ☷ **Astur Plaza.** This gleaming, well-run hotel is near Astorga's city hall. The yellow guest rooms have dark-brown furnishings, and ample light shines in from large windows. The lounge is glassed in; the large bar and Los Hornos restaurant have beam ceilings and exposed brick walls. ⊠ *Pl. de España 2–3* ☎ *987/618900* ⊕ *www.asturplaza.com* ☞ *32 rooms, 5 suites* ☖ *In-hotel: restaurant, bar, parking (paid)* ☰ *AE, MC, V.*

VILLAFRANCA DEL BIERZO

135 km (84 mi) west of León.

After crossing León's grape-growing region, where the complex and full-bodied Bierzo wines are produced, you'll arrive in this medieval village, dominated by a massive and still-inhabited feudal fortress. Villafranca was a destination in itself for some of Santiago's pilgrims. Visit the Romanesque church of Santiago to see the Puerta del Perdón (Door of Pardon), a sort of spiritual consolation prize for exhausted worshippers who couldn't make it over the mountains. Stroll the streets and seek out the onetime home of the infamous Grand Inquisitor Tomás de Torquemada. On the way out, you can buy wine at any of three local bodegas (wineries).

ESSENTIALS

Visitor Information Villafranca del Bierzo (✉ *Av. Bernardo Díaz Ovelar 10* ☎ *987/540028* 🌐 *www.villafrancadelbierzo.org*).

WHERE TO STAY

$$–$$$ **Parador de Villafranca del Bierzo.** This modern, two-story hotel overlooks the Bierzo valley. Rooms have heavy wood furniture, shuttered windows, and large baths. At the parador's restaurant ($$$$) you can dine on fresh Bierzo trout, *surtido de verduras naturales* (mixed fresh vegetables), or *tournedo con higos agridulces y setas* (a plump, juicy steak wrapped in bacon and served with marinated figs and wild mushrooms). Try the local Bierzo wine, made primarily from the Mencia grape. **Pros:** comfortable beds; quiet surroundings. **Cons:** pricey restaurant; not much to do near hotel; elevator goes only to the first floor. ✉ *Av. de Calvo Sotelo 28* ☎ *987/540175* 🌐 *www.parador.es* *38 rooms, 1 suite* *In-hotel: restaurant, bar* *AE, DC, MC, V.*

EXTREMADURA

Rugged Extremadura is a find for any lover of the outdoors. The lush Jerte Valley and the craggy peaks of the Sierra de Gredos mark Upper Extremadura's fertile landscape. South of the Jerte Valley is the historical town of Plasencia and the 15th-century Yuste Monastery. In Extremadura's central interior are the provincial capital of Cáceres and the Monfragüe Nature Park. Lower Extremadura's main towns—Mérida, Badajoz, Olivenza, and Zafra—bolstered by the sizable Portuguese population, have long exuded a Portuguese flavor.

ABOUT THE RESTAURANTS

Extremaduran food relies on peasant fare, with strong character and hearty flair. In addition to fresh produce, Extremadurans rely on pigs, of which they use every part, including the *criadillas* (testicles—don't confuse them with *criadillas de la tierra,* which are "earth testicles," also known as truffles). Meats are outstanding, most notably the complex and nutty *jamón ibérico de bellota* (ham from acorn-fed Iberian pigs) such as that from the Sierra de Montánchez north of Cáceres or the Dehesa de Extremadura from the southern oak parks around Zafra. Equally irresistible are the chorizo and *morcilla* (blood sausage), often

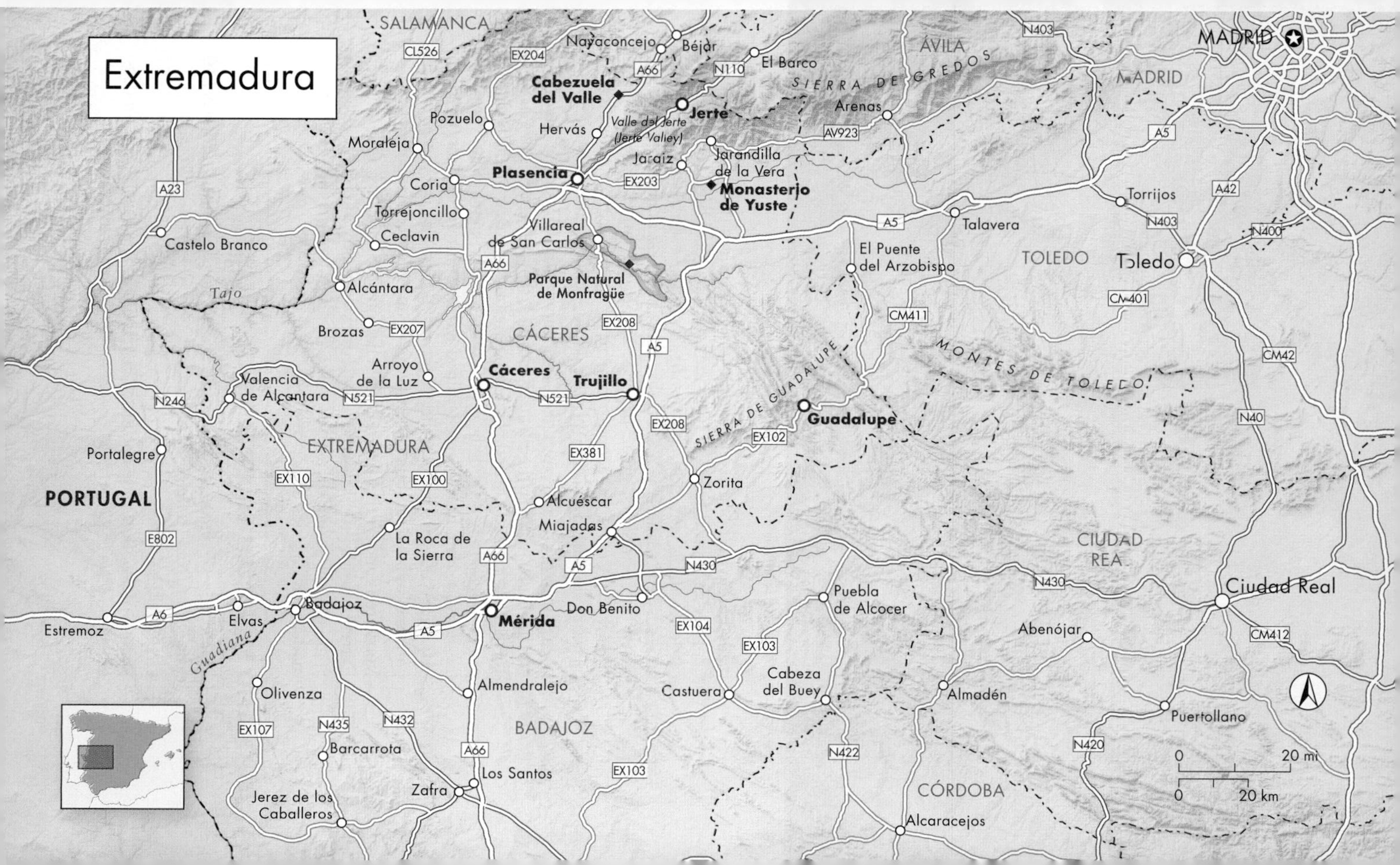
Extremadura
SALAMANCA
ÁVILA
MADRID
SIERRA DE GREDOS
TOLEDO
CÁCERES
EXTREMADURA
PORTUGAL
BADAJOZ
CIUDAD REAL
CÓRDOBA
MONTES DE TOLEDO
SIERRA DE GUADALUPE
Tajo
Guadiana
Navaconcejo
Béjar
El Barco
Cabezuela del Valle
Jerte
Valle del Jerte (Jerte Valley)
Arenas
Pozuelo
Hervás
Moraleja
Jaraiz
Jarandilla de la Vera
Plasencia
Monasterio de Yuste
Coria
Torrejoncillo
Ceclavin
Villareal de San Carlos
Parque Natural de Monfragüe
Castelo Branco
Alcántara
Brozas
Arroyo de la Luz
Cáceres
Trujillo
Valencia de Alcantara
Guadalupe
Portalegre
Zorita
Alcuéscar
Miajadas
La Roca de la Sierra
Badajoz
Elvas
Estremoz
Mérida
Don Benito
Olivenza
Almendralejo
Barcarrota
Los Santos
Zafra
Jerez de los Caballeros
Castuera
Cabeza del Buey
Puebla de Alcocer
Almadén
Alcaracejos
Abenójar
Puertollano
Ciudad Real
Toledo
Torrijos
Talavera
El Puente del Arzobispo
MADRID
CL526
EX204
A66
N110
N403
AV923
A5
A23
EX203
A42
N403
N400
CM401
CM411
EX208
A5
EX207
N521
N521
N246
EX208
EX102
CM42
N40
EX381
EX110
EX100
E802
A66
A5
N430
N430
A6
A5
EX104
EX103
CM412
EX107
N435
N432
A66
EX103
N422
N420
0
20 mi
0
20 km

Cherry trees in blossom in the Jerte Valley

made here with potatoes. The *caldereta de cordero* (lamb stew) is particularly tasty, as is the beef from the *retinto,* a local breed of longhorn cattle. Game is common, and *perdiz al modo de Alcántara* (partridge cooked with truffles) is a specialty. Extremadurans make a gazpacho based on cucumbers, green peppers, and broth rather than tomatoes and water. A common accompaniment is *migas,* bread crumbs soaked in water then fried in olive oil with garlic, peppers, and sausage.

Local sheep, goat, and cow cheeses are known for their strong flavors. If you have a chance, try the *tortas,* the round, semisoft cheeses of Cáceres: Torta de Casar and Torta de La Serena are frequent Best Spanish Cheese prizewinners. Pimentón de la Vera, a smoked paprika from the Vera Valley, has also long been a much-valued Extremaduran product. Favorite *extremeño* desserts include the *técula mécula* (an almond-flavor marzipan tart), which combines the flavors of Spain and Portugal.

Marketed under the generic appellation "Ribera del Guadiana," Extremadura's little-known fruity red wines are up and coming on the Spanish wine scene and a good value. Typical digestifs include liqueurs made from cherries or acorns.

JERTE AND EL VALLE DEL JERTE (JERTE VALLEY)

220 km (137 mi) west of Madrid. For a scenic route, follow N110 southwest from Ávila to Plasencia.

ESSENTIALS

Visitor Information Valle del Jerte (✉ *Paraje Virgen de Peñas Albas s/n Cabezuela del Valle* ☎ *927/472558* 🌐 *www.turismovalledeljerte.com*).

EXPLORING

There's no more striking introduction to Extremadura than the **Puerto de Tornavacas** *(Tornavacas Pass)*—literally, the "point where the cows turn back." Part of the N110 road northeast of Plasencia, the pass marks the border between Extremadura and the stark plateau of Castile. At 4,183 feet above sea level, it has a breathtaking view of the valley formed by the fast-flowing Jerte River. The valley's lower slopes are covered with a dense mantle of ash, chestnut, and cherry trees, whose richness contrasts with the granite cliffs of Castile's Sierra de Gredos. Cherries are the principal crop. To catch their brilliant blossoms, visit in spring. Camping is popular in this region, and even the most experienced hikers can find some challenging trails.

Cabezuela del Valle, full of half-timber stone houses, is one of the valley's best-preserved villages. Follow N110 to Plasencia, or, if you have a taste for mountain scenery, detour from the village of Jerte to Hervás, traveling a narrow road that winds 35 km (22 mi) through forests of low-growing oak trees and over the Honduras Pass.

WHERE TO EAT AND STAY

$–$$$ SPANISH ✕ **Valle del Jerte.** Service is always cheerful in this family-run restaurant (with five cozy rooms for overnights) just off the N110 in the village of Jerte. House specialties include gazpacho, *cabrito* (suckling goat), and local trout from the Jerte River. The homemade, regional desserts are outstanding, with many featuring the Jerte Valley's famed cherries; ask for the *tarta de cerezas* (cherry tart) or try the *queso fresco de cabra con miel de cerezo* (goat cheese topped with cherry-flavored honey). Ask to see the ancient and wonderful wine cellar. ✉ *Gargantilla 16, Jerte* ☎ *927/470052* 🌐 *www.donbellota.com* ▭ *MC, V.*

$–$$ 🏨 **Hotel Rural Finca El Carpintero.** In two adjacent stone buildings, this hotel has three types of rooms, the best of which has a fireplace, a sitting room (salon), and its own entrance. The simpler rooms are elegant and colorful and have canopy wrought-iron beds; all the bathrooms have hydromassage tubs. The restaurant has wood beams and a cozy rustic feel, as well as a reasonably priced set menu. **Pros:** cozy atmosphere inside; nice grounds outside; good value. **Cons:** large disparity in quality between rooms and suites. ✉ *N110, Km 360.5, Tornavacas* ☎ *927/177089* 🌐 *www.fincaelcarpintero.com* 🛏 *5 rooms, 3 suites* 👍 *In-hotel: restaurant, pool, Wi-Fi hotspot* ▭ *AE, D, MC, V.*

$–$$ 🏨 **La Casería.** This rambling home is on a 120-acre working farm, once a 16th-century Franciscan convent. One of Extremadura's first rural guesthouses, this is a place for animal lovers, as the household keeps lots of dogs and cats. Aside from the six rooms in the main lodge, there are three cottages. Activities such as horseback riding, mountain biking, and paragliding can be arranged. It's wise to reserve in advance, and the sign is easy to miss. **Pros:** privacy in the cottages; outdoor activities. **Cons:** main lodge often rented out to groups; a bit isolated. ✉ *N110, Km 378.5, Navaconcejo* ☎ *927/173141* 🌐 *www.lacaseria.net* 🛏 *6 rooms, 3 cottages* 👍 *In-room: no a/c, no TV, Wi-Fi. In-hotel: pool* ▭ *MC, V.*

PLASENCIA

255 km (160 mi) west of Madrid, 79 km (49 mi) north of Cáceres.

Rising dramatically from the banks of the narrow Jerte River and backed by the peaks of the Sierra de Gredos, this community was founded by Alfonso VIII in 1180, just after he captured the entire area from the Moors. The town's motto, *ut placeat Deo et hominibus* (To give pleasure to God and men), might well have been a ploy on Alfonso's part to attract settlers to this wild, isolated place on the southern border of the former kingdom of León. Partly destroyed during the Peninsular War of 1808, Plasencia retains far less of its medieval quarter than other Extremaduran towns, but it still has extensive remains of its early walls and a smattering of fine old buildings. In addition to being a site for visiting ruins, the city makes a good base for side trips to Hervás and the Jerte Valley, the Monasterio de Yuste and Monfragüe Nature Park, or, farther northwest, the wild Las Hurdes and Sierra de Gata.

ESSENTIALS

Visitor Information Plasencia (⊠ *Santa Clara 2* ☎ *927/423843* ⊕ *www.ayto-plasencia.es/Turismo*).

EXPLORING

Plasencia's **cathedral** was founded in 1189 and rebuilt after 1320 in an austere Gothic style that looks a bit incongruous looming over the town's red-tile roofs. In 1498 the great architect Enrique Egas designed a new structure, intending to complement or even overshadow the original, but despite the later efforts of other notable architects of the time, such as Juan de Alava and Francisco de Colonia, his plans were never fully realized. The entrance to this incomplete, curious, and not wholly satisfactory addition is through a door on the cathedral's ornate but somber north facade. The dark interior of the new cathedral is notable for the beauty of its pilasters, which sprout like trees into the ribs of the vaulting. You enter the old cathedral through the Gothic cloister, which has four enormous lemon trees. Off the cloister stands the building's oldest surviving section, a 13th-century chapter house (now the chapel of **San Pablo**)—a late-Romanesque structure with an idiosyncratic, Moorish-inspired dome. Inside are medieval hymnals and a 13th-century gilded wood sculpture of the Virgen del Perdón. The **museum** in the truncated nave of the old cathedral has ecclesiastical and archaeological antiques. ⊠ *Pl. de la Catedral* ☎ *927/4244062* 🎫 *Old cathedral €1.50* ⏲ *Oct.–Apr., Mon.–Sat. 9–1 and 4–6; May–Sept., Mon.–Sat. 9–1 and 5–7.*

The cloister of the elegant **Palacio Episcopal** (*Bishop's Palace* ⊠ *Pl. de la Catedral*) is open weekdays from 9 to 2.

Lined with orange trees, the narrow, carefully preserved **Plaza de San Vicente** is at the northwest end of the old medieval quarter. At one end is the 15th-century church of **San Vicente Ferrer,** with an adjoining convent that's now the Parador Plasencia. The north side of the square is dominated by the Renaissance **Palacio de Mirabel** (*Palace of the Marquis of Mirabel* ☎ *927/410701*) >—go through the central arch for a back view. The hours can be sporadic, but it's usually open daily 10–2 and 4–6; just knock on the door. Don't forget to tip the caretaker.

East of the Plaza de San Vicente, at the other end of the Rúa Zapatería, is the cheerful, arcaded square **Plaza Mayor.** The mechanical figure clinging to the town-hall clock tower depicts the clock maker and is called the **Mayorga** in honor of his Castilian hometown. Also east of the Plaza de San Vicente you can find a large section of the town's **medieval wall,** on the other side of which is a heavily restored Roman aqueduct. Walk southeast from the Plaza de San Vicente to the **Parque de los Pinos**, home to wildlife that includes peacocks, cranes, swans, pheasants, and monkeys.

3

WHERE TO EAT AND STAY

$–$$$ SPANISH ✕ **La Cocina del Alfonso VIII.** The hotel may be a few decades past its prime, but the restaurant here has long been regionally renowned for its excellent fare; the *ensalada de perdiz* (partridge salad) makes for a tasty starter. ✉ *Alfonso VIII 32* ☎ *927/410250* 🌐 *www.hotelalfonsoviii.com* 💳 *AE, DC, MC, V.*

$$$ 🏨 **Parador de Plasencia.** In a 15th-century Gothic convent, this parador cultivates a medieval environment. Common areas are majestic and somber; guest rooms are decorated with monastic motifs and heavy wood furniture. Rooms are spacious and comfortable with stylishly modern bathrooms; most have sitting rooms. The high-ceiling, stone-and-wood-beam restaurant—the former convent refectory—is almost intimidating in its architectural magnificence. Parking adds a hefty €14 nightly. **Pros:** successful fusion of old and new; good restaurant. **Cons:** free (legal) parking a long walk away. ✉ *Pl. de San Vicente Ferrer* ☎ *927/425870* 🌐 *www.parador.es* 🛏 *64 rooms, 2 suites* 👍 *In-room: Wi-Fi. In-hotel: restaurant, bar, pool, parking (paid)* 💳 *AE, D, MC, V.*

SHOPPING

If you're in Plasencia on Tuesday morning, head for the Plaza Mayor and do what the locals have been doing since the 12th century. Scout bargains in the weekly market. On the first Tuesday of August the market is even larger, with vendors from all over the region. For local art and crafts, try **Bámbara de Artesanía** (✉ *Sancho Polo 12* ☎ *927/411766*). Near the parador is **Artesanías Canillas** (✉ *C. San Vicente Ferrer s/n* ☎ *927/411668*), which sells regional costumes, pottery, and handmade straw hats. At **Casa del Jamón** (✉ *C. Sol 18, east of Pl. Mayor* ☎ *927/419328* ✉ *C. Zapatería 17, between Pl. Mayor and parador* ☎ *927/419328*), you can stock up on local charcuterie, sausages, *jamón ibérico*, cheeses, extremeño wines, and cherry liqueur.

LA VERA AND MONASTERIO DE YUSTE

45 km (28 mi) from Plasencia. Turn left off C501 at Cuacos and follow signs for the monastery (1 km [½ mi]).

ESSENTIALS

Visitor Information Jaraíz de la Vera (✉ *Av. de la Constitución 67* ☎ *927/170587*).

EXPLORING

In the heart of La Vera, a region of steep ravines (*gargantas*), rushing rivers, and villages (including the town of Jaraíz de la Vera), lies **Monasterio de Yuste** *(Yuste Monastery)*, founded by Hieronymite monks in the early 15th century. Badly damaged in the Peninsular War, it was left to decay after the suppression of Spain's monasteries in 1835, but it has since been restored and taken over once more by the Hieronymites. Carlos V (1500–58), founder of Spain's vast 16th-century empire, spent his last two years in the Royal Chambers, enabling the emperor to attend Mass within a short stumble of his bed. The required guided tour also covers the church, the crypt where Carlos V was buried before being moved to El Escorial (near Madrid), and a glimpse of the monastery's cloisters. ✉ *Cuacos de Yuste* ☎ *927/172197* 🎫 *€3* 🕑 *Tues.–Sun. 10–6:30.*

WHERE TO EAT AND STAY

$$ **Camino Real.** In a village in the highest valley of the Vera, this hotel was once a rural mansion. Rooms have exposed stone walls and wood-beam ceilings. There's a sitting room with fireplace, plus an outside hot tub. The room rate includes a lavish buffet breakfast. The owners organize local excursions and can arrange anything from equestrian outings to golf to guided fly-fishing expeditions. **Pros:** views over the valley; rough stone decor. **Cons:** can be windy and cold in the winter. ✉ *C. El Monje 27, Guijo de Santa Bárbara* ☎ *927/561119* 🌐 *www.casaruralcaminoreal.com* *10 rooms* *In-room: Wi-Fi. In-hotel: restaurant* *MC, V* *BP.*

SHOPPING

If you like to cook, pick up a tin or two of *pimentón de la Vera* (sweet paprika), made from the region's prized red peppers, at a deli or grocery shop in the area.

EN ROUTE

At the junction of the rivers Tiétar and Tajo, 20 km (12 mi) south of Plasencia on the EX208, is the **Parque Natural de Monfragüe.** This rocky, mountainous wilderness is known for its diverse plant and animal life, including lynx, boar, deer, fox, black storks, imperial eagles, and the world's largest colony of black vultures. Bring binoculars and find the lookout point called Salto del Gitano (Gypsy's Leap), on the C524 just south of the Tajo River—vultures can often be spotted wheeling in the dozens at close range. The park's visitor center and main entrance is in the hamlet of Villareal de San Carlos. ✉ *Villareal de San Carlos* ☎ *927/199134* 🕑 *Oct.–Apr., daily 9:30–6; audiovisual show every hr on ½ hr.*

CÁCERES

Fodor's Choice ★

307 km (190 mi) west of Madrid, 79 km (49 mi) south of Plasencia, 125 km (78 mi) southwest of Monasterio de Yuste, 90 km (55 mi) west of Monasterio de Guadalupe.

Cáceres, the provincial capital and one of Spain's oldest cities, is a prosperous agricultural town with a vibrant nightlife that draws villagers from the surrounding pueblos every weekend. The Roman colony

The San Mateo church, with the Torre de las Cigüeñas (Tower of the Storks) in the background

called Norba Caesarina was founded in 35 BC, but when the Moors took over in the 8th century, they named the city Quazris, which eventually morphed into the Spanish Cáceres. Ever since noble families helped Alfonso IX expel the Moors in 1229, the city has prospered. The pristine condition of the city's medieval and Renaissance quarter is the result of the families' continued occupancy of the palaces erected in the 15th century.

ESSENTIALS

Bus Station Cáceres (✉ *C. Túnez 1, Cáceres* ☎ *927/232550*).

Visitor Information Cáceres (✉ *Pl. Mayor 9* ☎ *927/010834* 🌐 *turismo.caceres.es*).

EXPLORING

Cáceres Viejo (Old Cáceres), which begins just east of Plaza San Juan, is the best part of town to stay in and explore. On the long, inclined, arcaded **Plaza Mayor**, you can find several outdoor cafés, tourist offices, and, on breezy summer nights, nearly everyone in town. In the middle of the arcade opposite the old quarter is the entrance to the lively Calle General Ezponda, lined with tapas bars, student hangouts, and discos that keep the neighborhood awake and moving until dawn. On high ground on the eastern side of the Plaza Mayor, pass through the gate of the town's wall, which surrounds one of the best-preserved medieval quarters in Spain. Packed with treasures, Cáceres's **Ciudad Monumental** (monumental city or old town, also called the *casco antiguo* or *Cáceres Viejo*) is a marvel: small, but without a single modern building to distract from its aura. The old town is virtually deserted in winter. Once you pass through the gate leading to the old quarter, note the **Palacio de los Golfines de Arriba** (✉ *C. Adarve de Santa Ana*), dominated by a soaring tower dating from 1515. The ground floor is a now stylish restaurant, but there are better dining options around.

STORKS DROPPING BY

Storks are common in the old quarter of Cáceres, and virtually every tower and spire is topped by nests of storks, considered since the Roman era to be sacred birds emblematic of home, the soul, maternity, spring, and well-being.

On the Plaza San Mateo is the **San Mateo church** (✉ *C. Ancha*). Built mainly in the 14th century but with a 16th-century choir, it has an austere interior, the main decorative notes being the baroque high altar and some heraldic crests.The battlement tower of the **Palacio del Capitán Diego de Cáceres** (✉ *Pl. San Mateo*) is also known as the Torre de las Cigüeñas (Tower of the Storks) for obvious reasons. It's now a military residence, but some rooms are occasionally opened up for exhibitions.

The **Casa de las Veletas** (House of the Weather Vanes) is a 12th-century Moorish mansion that is now the **Museo de Cáceres**. Filled with archaeological finds from the Paleolithic through the Visigothic periods, the art section includes medieval to contemporary painters from El Greco to Tàpies. A highlight is the superb Moorish cistern—the *aljibe*—with horseshoe arches supported by moldy stone pillars. ✉ *Pl. de las Veletas 1* ☎ *927/010877* 🌐 *www.museosextremadura.com/caceres* 🎫 *€1.20, free Sun. and for EU citizens* ⏲ *Oct.–Apr., Tues.–Sat. 9–2:30 and 4–7:15, Sun. 10–2:30; May–Sept., 9–2:30 and 5–8:15, Sun. 10–2:30.*

The stony severity of the **Palacio de los Golfines de Abajo** (✉ *Pl. de los Golfines s/n*) seems appropriate when you consider it was once the headquarters of General Franco. The exterior is somewhat relieved by elaborate Mudejar and Renaissance decorative motifs.

The Gothic church of **Santa María**, built mainly in the 16th century, is now the town cathedral. The elegantly carved high altar, dating from 1551, is barely visible in the gloom. A small museum displays religious artifacts. ✉ *Pl. de Santa María s/n* ☎ *927/215313* 🎫 *€2 for cathedral, tower, and museum* ⏲ *Mon.–Sat. 10–2 and 5–8, Sun. 9:30–2 and 5–7:30.*

Near the cathedral of Santa María is the elegant **Palacio de Carvajal**, Cáceres' only old palace you can tour besides the Casa de las Veletas (which houses the Museo de Cáceres). It has an imposing granite facade and an arched doorway, and the interior has been restored, with period furnishings and art, to look as it did when the Carvajal family lived here in the 16th century. ✉ *C. de la Amargura 1* ☎ *927/255597* 🎫 *Free* ⏲ *Weekdays 8 AM–9 PM, Sat. 10–2 and 5–8, Sun. 10–3.*

The chief building of interest outside the wall of the old town is the church of **Santiago de los Caballeros** (✉ *C. Villalobos*), rebuilt in the 16th century by Rodrigo Gil de Hontañón, Spain's last great Gothic architect. The easiest way to reach the church is by exiting the old town on the west side, through the Socorro gate.

Just up the hill behind Cáceres's Ciudad Monumental is the **Santuario de la Virgen de la Montaña** *(Sanctuary of the Virgin of the Mountain)*. Inside are a golden baroque altar and a statue of the patroness virgin, which is paraded through town each May. On a clear day the view of old Cáceres from the front of the building is spectacular, well worth the 15-minute drive up the hill. ✉ *Cta. Santuario Virgin de la Montaña s/n. Follow C. Cervantes until it becomes Ctra. Miajadas; the sanctuary is just off the town tourist map, which you can pick up from the local tourist office.* ☎ *927/220049* *Donation accepted* ⏲ *Daily 8:30–2 and 4–8.*

3

WHERE TO EAT AND STAY

$$$$ SPANISH Fodor's Choice ★ ✕ **Atrio.** Off Cáceres's main boulevard, this elegant restaurant is the best in Extremadura, possibly the best in Andalucía. Toño Pérez and his staff specialize in highly refined contemporary cooking, and the menu changes often, but you won't be disappointed with any of the selections, especially if they include venison, partridge, wild mushrooms, or truffles. *Vieiras asadas con trufa negra* (roast scallops with truffle) or *pichón asado* (roast wood pigeon) are two of the signature offerings. ✉ *Av. de España 30* ☎ *927/242928* ▭ *AE, DC, MC, V* ⏲ *No dinner Sun. Closed Mon.*

$$$–$$$$ SPANISH ✕ **El Figón de Eustaquio.** A fixture on the quiet and pleasant Plaza San Juan, across from the Melía hotel, this restaurant is always busy, especially at lunch. In its jumble of small, old-fashioned dining rooms with low-beamed ceilings, you'll be served mainly regional delicacies, including *venado de montería* (wild venison) or *perdiz estofada* (partridge stew). Fine Spanish wines are also available. ✉ *Pl. San Juan 14* ☎ *927/244362* *Reservations essential* ▭ *AE, MC, V.*

$–$$ **Antigua Casa del Heno.** This 150-year-old stone farmhouse is near a natural spring, with trout fishing nearby. With wood floors, stone walls, and sprightly fabrics, the rooms are cozy and cheerful; some have balconies or skylights, and all have unhindered views of the countryside. The inn is a favorite with stressed-out executives from Madrid, so reservations are essential. The restaurant, for guests only, serves Spanish dishes. Beware: The narrow, unpaved road uphill is challenging and remote. **Pros:** fresh, natural cuisine; lovely sylvan retreat. **Cons:** remote and isolated; rough access road. ✉ *Finca Valdepimienta s/n, follow signs from village, Losar de la Vera* ☎ *927/198077* 🌐 *www.antiguacasadelheno.com* *6 rooms, 1 suite* *In-room: no a/c, no TV. In-hotel: restaurant* ▭ *MC, V* *BP.*

$$$ **Parador de Cáceres.** This 14th-century palace provides a noble setting, decorated in soft cream tones offset by stone walls and heavy wood beams. Rooms are comfortable, and public spaces are elegant and filled with antiques. The restaurant, Torreorgaz ($$–$$$), with tables on the terrace in summer, offers *solomillo de ibérico a la Torta del Casar* (fillet of ibérico pig with creamy Torta del Casar sheep's cheese) or *cabrito asado al romero* (young goat roasted with rosemary). Friday to Sunday the parador's wine cellar, Enoteca Torreorgaz, holds wine tastings. **Pros:** good blend of tradition and comfort; fine cuisine and wines. **Cons:** some rooms are basic; old-town location can be confusing to reach by car. ✉ *C. Ancha 6* ☎ *927/211759* 🌐 *www.parador.es* *32*

rooms, 1 suite ♿ *In-room: Wi-Fi. In-hotel: restaurant, parking (paid)* ▭ *AE, DC, MC, V.*

NIGHTLIFE AND THE ARTS

Bars in Cáceres are lively until the wee hours. Nightlife centers on the **Plaza Mayor,** which fills after dinner with families out for a *paseo* (stroll) as well as students swigging *calimocho* (a mix of red wine and Coca-Cola) or *litronas* (liter bottles of beer). In the adjacent old town, you can take in live music at **El Corral de las Cigueñas** (✉ *Cuesta de Aldana* 6), which from October to April is open only Thursday to Sunday evenings. **Calle de Pizarro,** south of Plaza San Juan, is lined with cafés and bars.

TRUJILLO

★ *48 km (30 mi) east of Cáceres, 250 km (155 mi) southwest of Madrid.*

Trujillo rises up from the fertile fields like a great granite schooner under full sail. Up top, the rooftops and towers seem medieval. Down below, Renaissance architecture flourishes in squares such as the Plaza Mayor, with its elegant San Martín church. The storks' nests that top many towers in and around the old town have become a symbol of Trujillo. Dating back at least to Roman times, the city was captured from the Moors in 1232 and colonized by a number of leading military families.

GETTING HERE AND AROUND

It's best to see Trujillo on foot, as the streets are mostly cobbled or crudely paved with stone. The two main roads into Trujillo leave you at the town's unattractive bottom. Things get progressively older the farther you climb, but even on the lower slopes—where most of the shops are concentrated—you need walk only a few yards to step into what seems like the Middle Ages.

ESSENTIALS

Visitor Information Trujillo (✉ *Pl. Mayor s/n* ☎ *927/322677* 🌐 *www.trujillo.es*).

EXPLORING

Trujillo's large **Plaza Mayor**, one of the finest in Spain, is a superb Renaissance creation and the site of the local tourist office. At the foot of the stepped platform on the plaza's north side stands a large, bronze equestrian statue of Pizarro—the work, curiously, of an American sculptor, Charles Rumsey. Behind the Pizarro statue, the **Church of San Martín** is a Gothic structure from the early 16th century, with Renaissance tombs and an old organ. Three of Spanish history's most prominent kings prayed there: Carlos V, Felipe II, and Felipe V. ✉ *Pl. Mayor* 🎫 *€1.40* ⏲ *Mon.–Sat. 10–2 and 4–6:30, Sun. 10–12:30.*

The **Palacio de los Duques de San Carlos** *(Palace of the Dukes of San Carlos)* is next to the church of San Martín. The building is now a convent of Hieronymite nuns, who can occasionally be glimpsed on the balconies in full habit, hanging laundry or watering their flowers. To visit, ring the bell by pulling the chain in the foyer. The convent also produces and sells typical pastries, including *perrunillas* (almond cookies) and *tocinillos del cielo* (custardlike egg-yolk sweets). ✉ *Pl. Mayor* ☎ *927/320058* 🎟 *Free* ⏲ *Mon.–Sat. 10–1 and 4:30–6:30, Sun. 10–12:30.*

Trujillo's oldest area, known as **La Villa**, is entirely surrounded by its original, albeit much restored, walls. Follow them along Calle Almenas, which runs west from the Palacio de Orellana-Pizarro, beneath the **Alcázar de Los Chaves,** a castle-fortress that was converted into a guest lodge in the 15th century and hosted visiting dignitaries, includ ing Ferdinand and Isabella. Now a college, the building has seen better days. Passing the Alcázar, continue west along the wall to the **Puerta de San Andrés,** one of La Villa's four surviving gates (there were originally seven).

Attached to a Romanesque bell tower, the Gothic **Church of Santa María la Mayor** is occasionally used for masses, but its interior has been virtually untouched since the 16th century. The upper choir has an exquisitely carved balustrade; the coats of arms at each end indicate the seats Ferdinand and Isabella occupied when they attended Mass here. Note the high altar, circa 1480, adorned with great 15th-century Spanish paintings. To see it properly illuminated, place a coin in the box next to the church entrance. Climb the tower for stunning views of the town and vast plains stretching toward Cáceres and the Sierra de Gredos. ✉ *Pl. de Santa María* 🎟 *€1* ⏲ *Oct.–Apr., daily 10–2 and 4–7; May–Sept., daily 10–2 and 5–8.*

The Pizarro family home is now a modest museum, the **Casa Museo de Pizarro**, dedicated to the connection between Spain and Latin America. ✉ *Pl. de Santa María* 🎟 *€1* ⏲ *Oct.–Apr., daily 10–2 and 4–7; May–Sept., daily 10–2 and 5–8.*

Near the Puerta de la Coria, housed in a former Franciscan convent, is the **Museo de la Coria**. Its exhibits on the relationship between Spain and Latin America are similar to those in the Casa Museo de Pizarro (formerly the Pizarro family home) but more impressive, with an emphasis on the troops as well as other conquistadors who led missions across the water. ☎ *927/321898* 🎟 *Free* ⏲ *Weekends 11:30–2.*

For spectacular views, climb the fortress of Trujillo's large **castle**, or *castillo,* built by the Moors on Roman foundations. To the south are silos, warehouses, and residential neighborhoods. To the north are green fields and brilliant flowers, partitioned by a maze of nearly leveled Roman stone walls. 🎟 *€1* ⏲ *Oct.–Apr., daily 10–2 and 4–7; May–Sept., daily 10–2 and 5–8:30.*

WHERE TO EAT AND STAY

$–$$$ **SPANISH** ✕ **Mesón La Troya**. An institution in these parts, this restaurant has a noisy tapas bar papered with photos of celebrity diners happily posing with its late, great owner, Concha. The charismatic dining room has a barrel-vaulted brick ceiling. If you choose the €22 prix-fixe meal, you're served a starter of *tortilla de patatas* (potato omelet), *chorizo ibérico* (ibérico pork sausage), and a salad. Notable mains to watch for include the delicious *pruebas de cerdo* (ibérico pork casserole with garlic and spices). Arrive ravenous; portions are enormous. ✉ *Pl. Mayor 10* ☎ *927/321364* 💳 *V.*

$$–$$$$ SPANISH ★ **Pizarro.** On the main plaza in a small but quiet and elegant upstairs dining room, this friendly restaurant focuses on traditional Extremaduran home cooking. The two sisters who run it do nearly everything themselves. A long-revered house specialty is the *gallina trufada* (truffled hen), a sweet-salty recipe with Moorish roots that includes cognac, black truffles, and nutmeg—it was once a common Christmas dish in western Spain, but the Pizarro sisters are among the few restaurateurs who know how to prepare this recipe today. ☒ *Pl. Mayor 13* ☎ *927/320255* ▭ *MC, V* ⊙ *Closed Tues. Lunch only.*

$$$ ★ **Meliá Trujillo.** Once a 16th-century convent, this splendid hotel has a rusty red–ocher color scheme on its facade, in its cloisters, and in its courtyard, where there's a swimming pool (much appreciated in the heat of midsummer) surrounded by wrought-iron furniture. The restaurant in the former refectory serves regional dishes such as wild boar, free-range ibérico pork, and red-leg partridge stewed with broad beans during the October–January hunting season. **Pros:** aesthetically impeccable; friendly and efficient staff. **Cons:** small swimming pool; rooms vary in size. ☒ *Pl. del Campillo 1* ☎ *927/458900* ⊕ *www.solmelia.com* *74 rooms, 3 suites* *In-room: Internet. In-hotel: restaurant, bar, pool, Wi-Fi hotspot* ▭ *AE, DC, MC, V* *BP.*

$$–$$$ **Posada Dos Orillas.** In the historic center of town, this 16th-century former stagecoach inn has rooms individually decorated in traditional Spanish colonial style with lots of wrought iron and dark wood furniture. Guests can enjoy breakfast on the delightful patio with columns and leafy plants or at the hotel restaurant, which serves classic Extremaduran cuisine with contemporary innovations. **Pros:** pleasant decor; good location; good weekend values. **Cons:** food neither classical nor fully original; difficult to find parking in center of town. ☒ *C. de los Cambrones 6* ☎ *927/659079* ⊕ *www.dosorillas.com* *13 rooms* *In-room: Wi-Fi (some). In-hotel: restaurant* ▭ *MC, V* *BP.*

SHOPPING

Trujillo sells more folk art than almost any other place in Extremadura. The most attractive crafts are multicolor rugs, blankets, and embroideries. **Eduardo Pablos Mateos** (☒ *Plazuela de San Judas 12* ☎ *927/321066*) specializes in wood carvings, basketwork, and furniture. Several shops on the **Plaza Mayor** have enticing selections; the one just across from the tourist office displays a centuries-old loom along with the work of local craftswoman Maribel Vallar. Store hours are erratic.

GUADALUPE

★ *200 km (125 mi) southwest of Madrid, 96 km (60 mi) east of Trujillo.*

Guadalupe's monastery is one of the most inspiring sights in Extremadura. Whether you come from Madrid, Trujillo, or Cáceres, the last leg of your journey takes you through wild, astonishingly beautiful mountain scenery. The monastery clings to the slopes, forming a profile that echoes the gaunt wall of mountains behind it. The story of Guadalupe goes back to about 1300, when a local shepherd uncovered a statue of the virgin, supposedly carved by St. Luke. King Alfonso XI, who often

DID YOU KNOW?

The city of Guadalupe has been a tourist attraction—or pilgrimage destination—since the early 1300s, when a local man found a half-buried statue of the virgin Mary, rumored to have been carved by Saint Luke.

hunted here, had a church built to house the statue and later vowed to found a monastery should he defeat the Moors at the battle of Salado in 1340. After his victory, he kept his promise. The greatest period in the monastery's history was between the 15th and 18th centuries, when, under the rule of the Hieronymites, it was turned into a pilgrimage center rivaling Santiago de Compostela in importance. Pilgrims have been coming here since the 14th century, but for the past 10 years they have been joined by a growing number of tourists. Even so, the monastery's isolation—it's a good two-hour drive from the nearest town—has protected it from commercial excess. Documents authorizing Columbus's first voyage to the Western Hemisphere were signed here. The Virgin of Guadalupe became the patroness of Latin America, honored by the dedication of thousands of churches and towns in the New World. The monastery's decline coincided with Spain's loss of overseas territories in the 19th century. Abandoned for 70 years and left to decay, it was restored after the civil war.

ESSENTIALS

Visitor Information Guadalupe (✉ *Pl. Santa María de Guadalupe* ☎ *927/154128* 🌐 *www.puebladeguadalupe.net*).

EXPLORING

In the middle of the tiny, irregularly shaped **Plaza Mayor** (also known as the Plaza de Santa María de Guadalupe and transformed during festivals into a bullring) is a 15th-century **fountain,** where Columbus's two American Indian servants were baptized in 1496.

Real Monasterio de Santa María de Guadalupe (*Royal Monastery of Our Lady of Guadalupe*). Looming in the background of the Plaza Mayor is the late-Gothic facade of Guadalupe's **monastery church,** flanked by battlement towers. The entrance to the monastery is to the left of the church. From the large Mudejar cloister, the required guided tour progresses to the **chapter house,** with hymnals, vestments, and paintings, including a series of small panels by Zurbarán. The ornate 17th-century **sacristy** has a series of eight Zurbarán paintings of 1638–47. These austere representations of monks of the Hieronymite order and scenes from the life of St. Jerome are the artist's only significant paintings still in the setting for which they were intended. The tour concludes with the garish, late-baroque **Camarín,** the chapel where the famous *Virgen Morena* (*Black Virgin*) is housed. The dark, mysterious wooden figure hides under a heavy veil and mantle of red and gold; painted panels tell the virgin's life story. Each September 8, the virgin is brought down from the altarpiece and walked around the cloister in a procession with pilgrims following on their knees. Outside, the monastery's gardens have been restored to their original, geometric Moorish style. ✉ *Entrance on Pl. Mayor* ☎ *927/367000* 🌐 *www.monasterioguadalupe.com* 🎫 *€4* ⏲ *Daily 9:30–1 and 3:30–6:30, guided tours run continuously.*

WHERE TO EAT AND STAY

$–$$ SPANISH ✕ **El Mesón Extremeño.** For authentic flavors and a hearty meal, particularly if you're a fan of Spain's vast assortment of wild mushrooms, try this restaurant just down the road from the monastery. The menu *de la casa* (prix-fixe house menu) includes *migas de pastor* (bread crumbs cooked with garlic and bits of ham), *sopa de ajo* (garlic soup), *chuletillas de cerdo* (pork chops) with green beans, and *solomillo* (filet mignon) topped with aromatic *setas* (wild mushrooms) of different varieties according to the season. ✉ *Gregorio López 18* ☎ *927/367360.*

$$ **Hospedería del Real Monasterio.** An excellent and considerably cheaper alternative to the town parador, this inn was built around the 16th-century Gothic cloister of the monastery itself. The cloister's courtyard is also an outdoor café, open to all, from May to September. The simple, traditional rooms with wood-beam ceilings are handsome and comfortable. Fine local dishes at the restaurant ($–$$) include *caldereta de cabrito* (baby goat stew), *revuelto de cardillos* (scrambled eggs with thistle), and *morcilla de berza* (blood sausage with cabbage). **Pros:** excellent restaurant; helpful staff. **Cons:** bells around the clock. ✉ *Pl. Juan Carlos I s/n* ☎ *927/367000* 🌐 *www.monasterioguadalupe.com* *46 rooms, 1 suite* *In-hotel: restaurant, bar, Internet terminal* *MC, V* *Closed mid-Jan.–mid-Feb.*

Fodor's Choice ★

$$$ ★ **Parador de Guadalupe.** The first autopsy in Spain was performed in this building, a 15th-century hospital and then pilgrims' hostel. Despite its prior functions, the parador has an unusually luxurious feel, thanks to its Mudejar architecture, Moorish-style rooms, and exotic vegetation. The best rooms look out onto the monastery. The restaurant ($$–$$$) serves simple local dishes, such as *bacalao monacal* ("monastic codfish" with spinach and potatoes) and *frite de cordero* (lamb stew). **Pros:** authentic *extremeño* cooking; stunning architecture. **Cons:** tight parking; long hike from reception to farthest rooms. ✉ *C. Marqués de la Romana 12* ☎ *927/367075* 🌐 *www.parador.es* *41 rooms* *In-room: Wi-Fi. In-hotel: restaurant, bar, tennis court, pool* *AE, DC, MC, V.*

SHOPPING

On sale everywhere in Guadalupe is the town's famous copperware, crafted here since the 16th century.

MÉRIDA

70 km (43 mi) south of Cáceres, 250 km (155 mi) north of Seville, 347 km (216 mi) southwest of Madrid.

Mérida is the administrative capital of Extremadura. Founded by the Romans in 25 BC on the banks of the Río Guadiana, Mérida is strategically situated at the junction of major Roman roads from León to Seville and Toledo to Lisbon. Then named Augusta Emerita, it quickly became the capital of the vast Roman province of Lusitania. A bishopric in Visigothic times, Mérida never regained the importance that it had under the Romans, and it's now a rather plain large town with the exception of its Roman monuments; they pop up all over town, surrounded by thoroughly modern buildings.

The glass-and-steel bus station is in a modern district on the other side of the river from the town center. It commands a good view of the exceptionally long **Roman bridge,** which spans two forks of this sluggish river. On the farther bank is the Alcazaba fortress.

Mérida's excellently preserved Roman amphitheater is the site of a drama festival every July.

Some other Roman sites require a drive. Across the train tracks in a modern neighborhood is the **circo** (circus), where chariot races were held. Little remains of the grandstands, which seated 30,000, but the outline of the circus is clearly visible and impressive for its size: 1,312 feet long and 377 feet wide. Of the existing aqueduct remains, the most impressive is the **Acueducto de los Milagros** (Aqueduct of Miracles), north of the train station. It carried water from the Roman dam of Proserpina, which still stands, 5 km (3 mi) away.

GETTING HERE AND AROUND

Mérida is definitely walkable, but a small tourist train, the Tren Turístico, does a 35-minute circle past all of the sites for €3, starting from the tourist office.

ESSENTIALS

Tram Contact Tren Turístico (☎ *667/471907*).

Visitor Information Mérida (✉ *C. de Santa Eulalia 64* ☎ *924/330722* 🌐 *www.merida.es*).

EXPLORING

Fodor'sChoice ★

To reach Mérida's **Roman monuments**—the **teatro** (theater) and **anfiteatro** (amphitheater)—by car, follow signs to the MUSEO DE ARTE ROMANO. The sites are arranged in a verdant park, and the theater, the best preserved in Spain, is used for a classical drama festival each July; it seats 6,000. The amphitheater, which holds 15,000 spectators, opened in 8 BC for gladiatorial contests. Parking is usually easy to find. Next to the entrance to the Roman ruins is the **main tourist office,** where you can pick up maps and brochures. You can buy a ticket to see only the

Roman ruins or, for a slightly higher fee, an *entrada conjunta* (joint admission), which also grants access to the Basílica de Santa Eulalia and the Alcazaba. ✉ *C. Pedro Maria Plano s/n* ☎ *924/312530* 🎫 *Theater and amphitheater €8; combined admission to Roman sites, basilica, and Alcazaba €12* ⏲ *Oct.–Apr., daily 9:30–1:45 and 4–6:15; May–Sept., 9:30–1:45 and 5–7:15.*

★ Across the street from the entrance to the Roman sites and connected by an underground passageway is Mérida's superb, modern **Museo Nacional de Arte Romano** *(National Museum of Roman Art)*, in a monumental building designed by the renowned Spanish architect Rafael Moneo. You walk through a series of passageways to the luminous, cathedral-like main exhibition hall, which is supported by arches the same proportion and size (50 feet) as the Roman arch in the center of Mérida, the Arco de Trajano (Trajan's Arch). The exhibits include mosaics, frescoes, jewelry, statues, pottery, household utensils, and other Roman works. Visit the **crypt** beneath the museum—it houses the remains of several homes and a necropolis that were uncovered while the museum was built in 1981. ✉ *José Ramón Mélida 2* ☎ *924/311690* 🌐 *www.mnar.es* 🎫 *€3, free Sat. afternoon and Sun.* ⏲ *Oct.–Apr., Tues.–Sat. 10–2 and 4–6, Sun. 10–2; May–Sept., Tues.–Sat. 10–2 and 5–7, Sun. 10–2.*

Alcazaba *(fortress)*. To get to this sturdy square fortress, built by the Romans and strengthened by the Visigoths and Moors, continue west from the Museo Nacional de Arte Romano, down Suarez Somontes toward the river and the city center. Turn right at Calle Baños and you can see the towering columns of the **Templo de Diana**, the oldest of Mérida's Roman buildings. To enter the alcazaba, follow the fortress walls around to the side farthest from the river. Climb up to the battlements for sweeping river views. ☎ *924/317309* 🎫 *€4* ⏲ *Oct.–Apr., daily 10–2 and 4–6:30; May–Sept., daily 10–2 and 5–7:30.*

Mérida's main square, the **Plaza de España**, adjoins the northwestern corner of the Alcazaba and is highly animated both day and night. The plaza's oldest building is a 16th-century palace, now a Meliá hotel (there are more atmospheric places to stay). Behind the palace stretches Mérida's most charming area, with Andalusian-style white houses shaded by palms, in the midst of which stands the **Arco de Trajano**, part of a Roman city gate.

The **Basílica de Santa Eulalia**, originally a Visigothic structure, marks the site of a Roman temple as well as supposedly where the child martyr Eulalia was burned alive in AD 304 for spitting in the face of a Roman magistrate. In 1990, excavations surrounding the tomb of the famous saint revealed layer upon layer of Paleolithic, Visigothic, Byzantine, and Roman settlements. ✉ *Rambla Mártir Santa Eulalia* ☎ *924/303407* 🎫 *€4* ⏲ *Oct.–Apr., Mon.–Sat. 10–1:45 and 4–6:15; May–Sept., 10–1:15 and 5–7:15.*

WHERE TO EAT AND STAY

¢ SPANISH ✕ **Cervecería 100 Montaditos.** Don't be put off by the fact that this popular local tavern is part of a nationwide chain. It's still an excellent informal restaurant specializing in both classic and creative *montaditos* (canapés or open sandwiches)—at least a hundred of them, topped with anything from tortilla de patatas (potato omelet) to *jamón ibérico, mousse de pato* (duck pâté), salmon with julienned garlic and parsley, or wild mushrooms. With draft beer or a local wine, these light morsels are tasty and excellent value. ✉ *C. Félix Valverde Lillo 3* ☎ *924/318105* ▭ *AE, MC, V.*

$$–$$$$ **SPANISH** ✕ **Nicolás.** Mérida's best-known restaurant is in a distinctive house with yellow awnings, near the municipal market. There's a tavern serving tapas downstairs and a dining room upstairs. The regionally inspired food includes *perdiz en escabeche* (marinated partridge), lamb dishes, and frogs' legs. Desserts might include the traditional *tocino del cielo* (bacon from heaven) made with honey and egg yolks, or a superb and creamy (nearly soupy) sheeps' milk cheese from La Serena, usually served with a spoon, called Torta de la Serena. ✉ *Félix Valverde Lillo 13* ☎ *924/319610* ▭ *AE, DC, MC, V* ⊙ *No dinner Sun. and July 1–15.*

$$$ ★ **Parador de Mérida.** Built over the remains of a Roman temple that later became a baroque convent and then a prison, this spacious white-washed building exudes an Andalusian cheerfulness, with hints at its Roman and Moorish past. Also called Parador Vía de la Plata, the hotel has bright guest rooms with traditional dark wood furniture. The brilliant-white interior of the convent's former church has been turned into a restful lounge. Try the restaurant's ($$–$$$) *revuelto* (scrambled eggs) prepared in myriad ways, including *con aroma de pimentón* (in paprika sauce) and with *cabrito al ajillo* (baby goat fried with garlic). **Pros:** central location; dazzling light and decor. **Cons:** expensive parking; erratic Wi-Fi. ✉ *Pl. Constitución 3* ☎ *924/313800* 🌐 *www.parador.es* *80 rooms, 2 suites* *In-room: Wi-Fi. In-hotel: restaurant, bar, pool, gym, Wi-Fi hotspot, parking (paid)* ▭ *AE, DC, MC, V.*

NIGHTLIFE AND THE ARTS

The many cafés, tapas bars, and restaurants surrounding the Plaza España and in the Plaza de la Constitución fill with boisterous crowds late into the evening. Calle John Lennon, off the northwest corner of the plaza, is your best bet for late-night dance action, especially in summer. As you walk south on Santa Eulalia, the bars get cheaper and the music louder. Locals pack **Rafael II** (✉ *C. Santa Eulalia 13*) for ham, cheese, and sausages; there's also a small, cork-lined dining room in the back.

4

Galicia and Asturias

WITH CANTABRIA

WORD OF MOUTH

"I would stay at least 4 days in Santiago and from there do day trips to Coruña and Pontevedra . . . You could stay in Oviedo 2–3 days and from there visit Cudillero, Luarca, Gijon . . . In Cantabria I recommend staying in Santander. Very nice city with a gorgeous beach. From there I did day trips to Santillana del Mar, Fuente de, Potes, Liebana."

—cruiseluv

Join, Ask, Share. www.fodors.com/community/

WELCOME TO GALICIA AND ASTURIAS

TOP REASONS TO GO

★ **Experience Gourmet Heaven:** The beautiful Santiago de Compostela is said to contain more restaurants and bars per square mile than any other city in Spain.

★ **Sleep in a Luxurious Parador:** El Parador de Baiona is arguably Spain's most elegant parador.

★ **Rugged Hikes and Exploring:** Spend days in the spectacular Picos de Europa range getting lost in forgotten mountain villages.

★ **Get in on the Grapevine:** The Ribeira region yields Spain's—if not Europe's—finest white wines.

★ **Enjoy the Waterfront Activity:** Watch the oyster hawkers at work while dining on a fresh catch on Vigo's Rúa Pescadería.

★ **Discover Santander:** With its intoxicating schedule of live music, opera, and theater performances on the beach and in gardens and monasteries, the city's August festival of music and dance is the perfect backdrop for exploring this vibrant city.

1 Santiago de Compostela and Eastern Galicia. Books and movies have been written about it and millions have walked it, but you don't have to be a pilgrim to enjoy the journey of Camino de Santiago. At the end of the path is Santiago itself, a vibrant university town embedded in hills around the soaring spires of one of Spain's most emblematic cathedrals.

2 The Costa da Morte and Rías Baixas. From Fisterra (known as "world's end") down to Vigo and the Portuguese border, this area takes in the peaceful seaside towns of Cambados and Baiona, the exquisite beaches of Las Islas Cĕes, and the beautifully preserved medieval streets of Pontevedra.

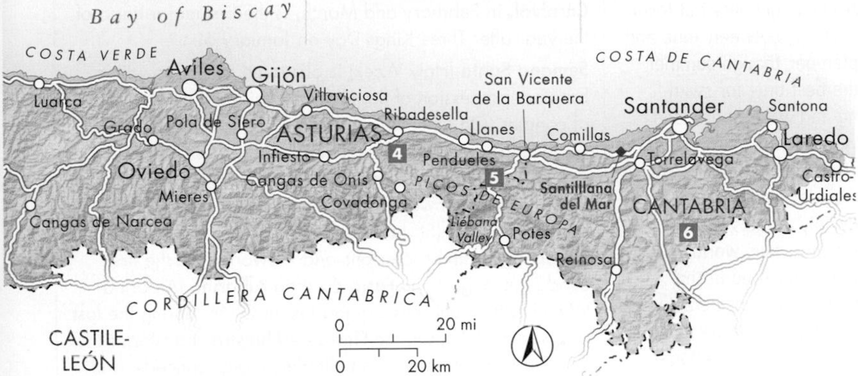

3 A Coruña and Rías Altas. Galicia has more coastline and unspoiled and untouristed beaches than anywhere else in the country. You can opt for vast expanses of sand facing the Atlantic Ocean or tiny, tucked-away coves, but take note: the water is colder than the Mediterranean, and the region's weather is more unreliable.

4 Asturias. Also known as the Costa Sendera (Coastal Way), this partly paved nature route between Pendueles and Llanes takes in some of Asturias's most spectacular coastal scenery, including noisy *bufones* (large waterspouts created naturally by erosion) and the Playa de Ballota.

5 Picos de Europa. One of Spain's best-kept secrets, the Peaks of Europe lie across Asturias, Cantabria, and León. In addition to 2,700-meter (8,910-foot) peaks, the area has deep caves, excellent mountain refuges, and interesting wildlife. This region is also known for its fine cheeses.

6 Cantabria. Santander's wide beaches and summer music and dance festival are highlights of this mountain and maritime community. The Liébana valley, the Renaissance town at Santillana del Mar, and ports and beaches such as San Vicente de la Barquera all rank among northern Spain's finest treasures.

GETTING ORIENTED

The bewitching provinces of Galicia and Asturias lie in Spain's northwest; these rugged Atlantic regions hide a corner of Spain so remote it was once called *finis terrae* (the end of the earth). Galicia is famous for Santiago de Compostela, to which Christian pilgrims travel to pay homage to St. James. Asturias attracts with its verdant hills, sandy beaches, and the massive Picos de Europa mountain range. To the east, Cantabria borders the Bay of Biscay.

4

GALICIA AND ASTURIAS PLANNER

When to Go

Galicia can get very hot (over 30°C/90°F) between June and September, though summer is the best time for swimming and water sports and for Celtic music festivals—the **Ortigueira Festival** (🌐 *www.festivaldeortigueira.com*) in early July attracts leading Celtic musicians worldwide. Asturias, being up in the mountains, is considerably cooler. Galicia can be rainy to the point of saturation—not for nothing is this region called Green Spain. Avoid traveling in the area in winter: the rain, wind, and freezing temperatures make driving an arduous experience. **Spring and fall may be the ideal time to explore, as the weather is reasonable and crowds are few.**

Discounts and Deals

Compostela 48 Horas (🌐 *www.santiagoturismo.com*) is a €15 visitor's card providing discounts or free entry to key Santiago sites.

Festivals

Carnival, in February and March, is the first major fiesta of the year after Three Kings Day on January 6.

Semana Santa (Holy Week) is observed in Viveiro with a barefoot procession of flagellants illuminated by hundreds of candles. On June 14, during the feast of **Corpus Christi,** Pontevedra celebrates flowers and the harvest. The **Rapa das Bestas** (Taming of the Beasts—the breaking of wild horses) is the first weekend of July in various locales. **El Día de Santiago** (St. James's Day), July 25, is celebrated in Santiago with processions and fireworks. On the first Sunday in August, the **Festa do Vino Albariño** (Albariño Wine Festival) enlivens Cambados. In Gijón, during the last two weeks of August, the **Fiesta de Muestras** transforms the city into a street party with bullfights, crafts, concerts, and all-night parties. On August 15, sailors and fishermen in Luarca celebrate **Nuestra Señora del Rosario** (Our Lady of the Rosary) by parading their boats through the harbor. The late September **Procesión de las Mortajas** (Procession of the Shrouded), in A Coruña, dating from the 15th century, carries survivors of illness, bad luck, or bad love around town in open coffins. At O Grove's **Festa do Marisco** (Seafood Festival), the second Sunday in October, crowds feast on delicacies from the sea. Santander's big event is the **Festival Internacional Santander** (🌐 *www.festivalsantander.com*) in August, which attracts top international music and dance artists.

There are also a number of festivals in towns that don't otherwise have much to offer the average traveler. The **Festa do Chourizo en Sant Anton de Abedes** (St. Anthony of Abedes Sausage Festival) on January 17 in Verin, honors the local patron saint through sausage appreciation and a parade. The **Procesión dos Fachós** (Procession of the Scarecrows, January 19), in Ourense, is a torchlight procession commemorating the village's survival of a 1753 cholera outbreak. On February 2, for **Fiesta del Gallo,** a ritual rooster slaughter celebrates Candlemas, the day Christ was first presented at the temple. The spectacle is not for the faint of heart—the cock is often buried alive or beaten to death with a club. The first week of March, the **Festa do Queixo** (Cheese Festival), in Arzúa near A Coruña, celebrates food and folklore.

Beaches and the Outdoors

Galician and Asturian beaches include urban strands with big-city amenities steps from the sand, as well as remote expanses that rarely become as crowded as the beaches of the Mediterranean. When the sun comes out, you can relax on the sand on the Asturian beaches of (from east to west) Llanes, Ribadesella, Cudillero, Santa Ana (by Cadavedo), Luarca, and Tapia de Casariego, among others. In Galicia, the beaches of Muros, Noya, O Grove, the Islas Cíes, Boa, and Testal are the top destinations. For surfers, Galicia's Montalvo, Foxos, and Canelas beaches, near Pontevedra, are tops. Others with good waves are Nerga and Punto de Couso, near Cangas, and, farther south, El Vilar, Balieros, Rio Sieira, and Os Castros. Santander has excellent sandy beaches.

For more about outdoor activities in the region, from ballooning to hiking, golf, and rafting, see the Sports and the Outdoors box in this chapter.

Tours

FEVE's Transcantábrico narrow-gauge train tour (🌐 *www.transcantabrico.feve.es*) is an eight-day, 1,000-km (600-mi) journey through the Basque country, Asturias, and Galicia. English-speaking guides narrate, and a private bus takes the group from train stations to natural attractions. Passengers sleep on the train in suites and dine on local specialties. Trains run May–October; the all-inclusive cost is €4,400 for two people in a suite.

WHAT IT COSTS (IN EUROS)

	¢	$	$$	$$$	$$$$
Restaurants	under €8	€8–€12	€13–€17	€18–€22	over €22
Hotels	under €60	€60–€90	€91–€125	€126–€180	over €180

Prices are per person for a main course at dinner, and for two people in a standard double room in high season, excluding tax.

Planning Your Time

You can fly into Santiago de Compostela, and a week should be long enough to cover the Santiago area and Galicia's south. From Santiago, you can drive down the C550 to Cambados, stopping on the way at fishing villages along the Ría de Arousa. If you take the coastal road to Pontevedra, you can spend time there exploring the medieval streets and tapas bars, then drive down to Vigo for a lunch of oysters on Rúa Pescadería. Continue south and arrive before dark at the Baiona parador. The more adventurous will want to explore the Camino villages of Samos, Sarria, Portomarín, and Vilar de Donas—they embody all that is spiritual about Galicia.

Alternatively, travel to A Coruña, and from there head north to some of Spain's loveliest beaches and Viveiro. From here cross into Asturias and spend time in Luarca or Gijón. Another attractive option is getting lost in a small village in the Picos de Europa.

Heading farther east, Santillana del Mar's Renaissance architecture, the Altamira Caves, and the Sardinero Beach at Santander are top spots, while the fishing villages and beaches around Llanes in eastern Asturias, and San Vicente de la Barquera in Cantabria have charming ports and inlets. If you want to get to grips with the Picos de Europa and the region's pretty coastline, Asturias and Cantabria merit more than a week's exploration.

4

GETTING HERE AND AROUND

By Air

The region's domestic airports are in Santander, A Coruña, Vigo, and near San Estéban de Pravia, 47 km (29 mi) north of Oviedo. Airport shuttles usually take the form of ALSA buses from the city bus station. Iberia sometimes runs a private shuttle from its office to the airport; inquire when you book your ticket.

By Bus

ALSA runs daily buses from Madrid to Galicia and Asturias. Once here, there is good bus service between the larger destinations in the area, like Santiago, Vigo, Pontevedra, Lugo, La Coruña, Gijón, Oviedo, and Santander, though train travel is generally smoother, faster, and easier.

Getting to the smaller towns by bus can be difficult, especially those that are inland.

By Bike

The official *El Camino de Santiago en Bicicleta* leaflet available from **Información Xacobeo** or from the Santiago tourist office warns that the approximately 800-km (525-mi) route from the French border to Santiago is a very tough bike trip—bridle paths, dirt tracks, rough stones, and mountain passes. The best time of year to tackle it is late spring or early autumn. Tourist offices in Asturias sell the booklet *Rutas de Montaña, Senderismo, Montañismo y Bicicleta de Montaña,* which outlines different routes, for about €1.20. Bici Total, in Santiago, rents bikes, as do some hotels.

Bike Routes **Información Xacobeo** (🌐 *www.xacobeo.es*). **Santiago bike route information** (🌐 *www.caminhodesantiago.com*).

By Car

A car is the best way to get around. The four-lane A6 expressway links the area with central Spain; it takes about five hours (650 km [403 mi]) to get from Madrid to Santiago, and from Madrid, it's 240 km (149 mi) on the N1 or the A1 toll road to Burgos, after which you can take the N623 to complete the 390 km (242 mi) to Santander.

The expressway north from León to Oviedo and Gijón is the fastest way to cross the Cantabrian mountains. The AP9 north–south Galician ("Atlantic") expressway links A Coruña, Santiago, Pontevedra, and Vigo, and the A8 in Asturias links Santander to Ribadeo. Local roads along the coast or through the hills are more scenic but slower.

By Train

RENFE runs several trains a day from Madrid to Santander (4½ hours), Oviedo (7 hours), and Gijón (8 hours), and a separate line serves Santiago (11 hours). Local RENFE trains connect the region's major cities with most of the surrounding small towns, but be prepared for dozens of stops. Narrow-gauge FEVE trains clatter slowly across northern Spain, connecting Galicia and Asturias with Santander, Bilbao, and Irún, on the French border.

DID YOU KNOW?

Hiking is a key activity in Galicia: all the better to work off some of those excellent meals.

EATING AND DRINKING WELL IN GALICIA AND ASTURIAS

Galicia, Asturias, and Cantabria are famous for seafood and fish so fresh that chefs frown on drowning the inherent flavors in sauces and seasonings. Inland, the Picos de Europa and the mountain meadows are rich in game, sheep, and beef.

Top left: A plethora of seafood delicacies. Top right: The classic octopus and potato combination. Bottom left: The hearty and fortifying *caldo gallego* stew.

The northern coast of Spain is justly famous for fish and seafood and specialties range from *merluza a la gallega* (steamed hake with paprika sauce) in Galicia, to *merluza a la sidra* (hake in a cider sauce) in Asturias. Look also for Galician seafood treasures such as vieiras (scallops) and *pulpo à feira* (octopus on potato slices). The rainy weather also means that bracing stews are a favorite form of sustenance, especially *fabada asturiana,* the Asturian bean-and-sausage stew, and Galicia's *caldo gallego* a thick soup of white beans, turnip greens, chickpeas, cabbage, and potatoes. Cantabria's cooking is part mountain fare, such as roast kid and lamb or *cocidos* (pork and bean stews) in the highlands, and, along the coast, seafood such as *sorropotún,* a bonito, potato, and vegetable stew.

CABRALES CHEESE

Asturias is known for having Spain's bluest and most aromatic cheese, the Cabrales, produced in the Picos de Europa mountains of eastern Asturias. Made of raw cow's milk (with goat curd added for a softer consistency), the secret is the quality of the cows' milk and the dry highland air used to cure the cheese. Cabrales is ideal melted over meat or for dessert with a sweet sherry.

BEANS AND LEGUMES

*Fabada Asturiana (*fava bean and sausage stew) is as well known throughout Spain as is Valencias's paella or Andalusia's gazpacho. A meal in itself, usually consumed in copious quantities, the secret to the fabada is slow simmering while adding small quantities of cold water, and crushing some of the beans so that the creamy paste becomes part of the sauce. Fatback, black sausage, chorizo, and pork chops are added to this powerful dose of protein and vitamin B, and it's cooked on low heat for at least two and half hours.

VEGETABLES

The turnip (*grelo* in Gallego) is a favorite vegetable in Galicia, celebrated in La Festa do Grelo during Carnavales in February. *Lacón con Grelos* is a classic Galician specialty combining cured pork shoulder, turnip stalks and greens, potatoes, and chorizo, all boiled for about four hours. The grelo's acidity and the pork shoulder's heavy fat content make the marriage of these two products an ideal union. Similarly, *caldo gallego* is a powerful mountain or seafarers stew, the whole garden in a pot—including *grelos* stalks and greens, *repollo* (cabbage), and *nabizas* (sprouting turnip leaves)—with pork for ballast and taste. Traditionally served in earthenware cups called cuncas, the diverse ingredients and the fat from the pork make this a fortifying

antidote to the bitter Atlantic climate of Spain's northwest corner.

PULPO À FEIRA

A typical Galician specialty, *pulpo à feira*, so-called because it was originally a festive dish reserved for ferias or fairs, consists of octopus that's been boiled, cut into slices, sprinkled with bittersweet paprika and served atop slices of boiled potato on a wooden plate. The texture of the potato slices balances the consistency of the octopus.

TO DRINK

The best Galician wine is the fresh, full-bodied, white Albariño from Rías Baixas, perfect with seafood. Ribeiro, traditionally sipped from shallow white ceramic cups or *tazas* in order allow aromas to expand, is lighter and fresher. Asturias is known for its *sidra* (hard cider), poured from overhead and quaffed in a single gulp for full enjoyment of its effervescent flavor. Brandy buffs should try Galicia's *queimada* (which superstitious locals claim is a witches' brew), made of potent, grappalike *orujo* mixed with lemon peel, coffee beans, and sugar in an earthenware bowl, then set aflame and stirred until the desired amount of alcohol is burned off.

Updated by
Paul Cannon

Spain's most Atlantic region is en route to nowhere, an end in itself. Though Galicia and Asturias are off the beaten track for many foreigners, they are not undiscovered. These magical, remote regions are sure to pull at your heartstrings, so be prepared to fall in love. In Gallego they call the feeling *morriña,* a powerful longing for a person or place you've left behind.

Stretching northwest from the lonesome Castilian plains to the rocky seacoast, Asturias and Galicia incorporate lush hills and vineyards, gorgeous *rías* (estuaries), and the country's wildest mountains, the Picos de Europa. Santander and the entire Cantabrian region are cool summer refuges with sandy beaches, high sierra (including part of the Picos de Europa), and tiny highland towns. Santander, once the main seaport for Old Castile on the Bay of Biscay, is in a mountainous zone wedged between the Basque Country and Asturias.

Northwestern Spain is a series of rainy landscapes, stretching from your feet to the horizon. Ancient granite buildings wear a blanket of moss, and even the stone *horreos* (granaries) are built on stilts above the damp ground. Swirling fog and heavy mist help keep local folktales of the supernatural alive. Rather than a guitar, you'll hear the *gaita* (bagpipe), legacy of the Celts' settlements here in the 5th and 6th centuries BC. Spanish families flock to these cool northern beaches and mountains each summer, and Santiago de Compostela, where a cathedral holds the remains of the apostle James, has drawn pilgrims for 900 years, leaving churches, shrines, and former hospitals in their path. Asturias, north of the main pilgrim trail, has always maintained a separate identity, isolated by the rocky Picos de Europa. This and the Basque Country are the only parts of Spain never conquered by the Moors, so Asturian architecture shows little Moorish influence. It was from a mountain base at Covadonga that the Christians won their first decisive battle against the Moors and launched the Reconquest of Spain. Despite being very much its own region, Cantabria is in spirit much closer to Asturias—with whom it shares the Picos de Europa, Castillian

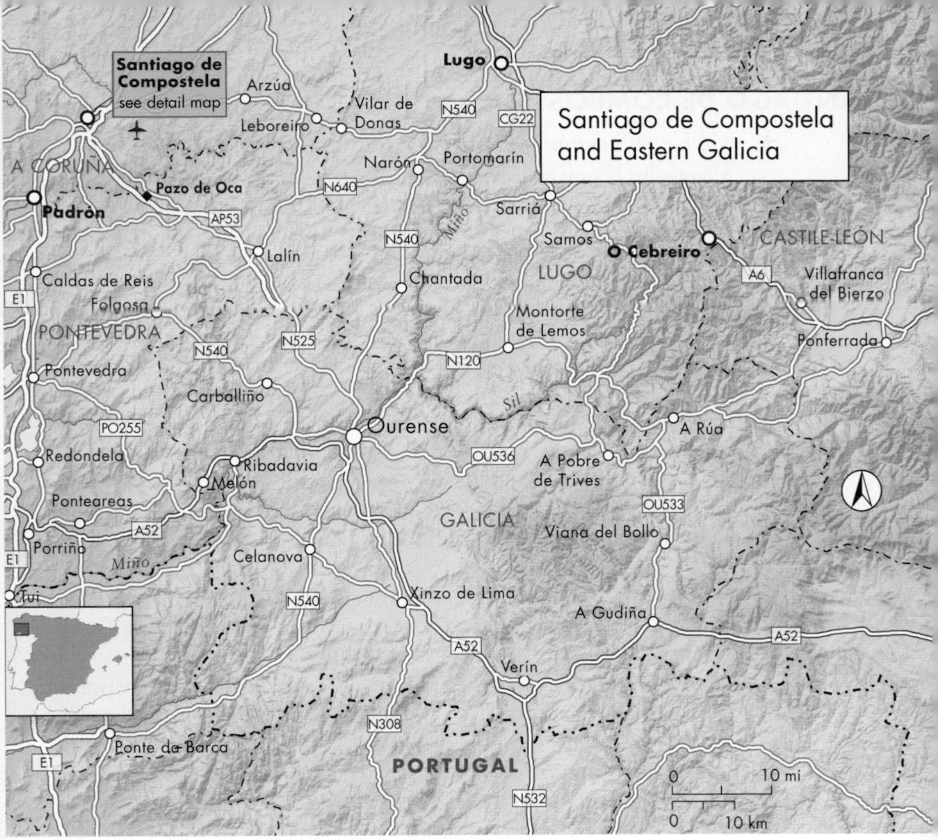

Spanish, and similar architecture—than its passionately independent neighbor, the Basque Country.

EXPLORING GALICIA AND ASTURIAS

Santiago de Compostela holds center stage in Spain's northwest corner, the final destination of the Camino de Santiago. To the south are the Rías Baixas, to the west the beaches along the Atlantic coast. Farther north is the thriving port of A Coruña; the Bay of Biscay lies east, along the coast of Asturias. Oviedo is just inland, backed by the Picos de Europa, with Cantabria to the east.

SANTIAGO DE COMPOSTELA AND EASTERN GALICIA

The main pilgrimage route of the Camino de Santiago, the *camino francés*, crosses the Pyrenees from France and heads west across northern Spain. If you drive into Galicia on the A6 expressway from Castile-León, you enter the homestretch, but many fly into Santiago de Compostela and start exploring from here.

SANTIAGO DE COMPOSTELA

★ *650 km (403 mi) northwest of Madrid.*

A large, lively university makes Santiago one of the most exciting cities in Spain, and its cathedral makes it one of the most impressive. The building is opulent and awesome, yet its towers create a sense of harmony as a benign St. James, dressed in pilgrim's costume, looks down from his perch. Santiago de Compostela welcomes more than 4.5 million visitors a year, with an extra million during Holy Years (the most recent was 2010), when St. James's Day, July 25, falls on a Sunday.

GETTING HERE AND AROUND

Santiago is connected to Pontevedra (61 km [38 mi]) and A Coruña (57 km [35 mi]) via the AP9 tollway. The N550 is free, but slower. Parking anywhere in the city center can be difficult unless you use one of the numerous car parks around its edges.

Bus service out of Santiago's Castromil Station is plentiful, with eight daily buses to Madrid (seven to nine hours) and hourly buses to A Coruña.

The fast train Talgo service to Madrid takes seven hours; there is daily service to Irún, on the French border, via León and Santander. Trains depart every hour for Galicia's other major towns.

Santiago's center is very pedestrian-friendly, and the distances between attractions are relatively short, so walking is the best and often the only way around town.

Santiago's association of well-informed guides, La Asociación de Guias de Galicia, part of the tourist office, can arrange private walking tours of the city or tours to any place in Galicia.

ESSENTIALS

Bike Rentals Bici Total (✉ *Av. de Lugo 221, Santiago de Compostela* ☎ *981/564562*).

Bus Station Santiago (✉ *Rúa de San Caetano s/n* ☎ *981/542416*).

Tour Information La Asociación de Guias de Galicia (☎ *981/569890* 🌐 *www.guisdegalicia.org*).

Visitor Information Santiago de Compostela (✉ *Rúa do Vilar 30–32* ☎ *981/555129*).

EXPLORING

For excellent views of the city, join a tour across the granite steps of the **cathedral roofs**. Pilgrims made the same 100-foot climb in medieval times to burn their travel-worn clothes below the Cruz dos Farrapos (Cross of Rags). ✉ *Pazo de Xelmírez, Praza do Obradoiro* ☎ *981/552985* 🎟 *€10* ⏲ *Tues.–Sun. 10–2 and 4–8.*

Santiago de Compostela's streets hold many old *pazos* (manor houses), convents, and churches that in most towns would receive headline attention. The best way to spend your time here is simply to walk around the *casco antiguo (*old town*)*, losing yourself in its maze of stone-paved narrow streets and little plazas. The most beautiful pedestrian thoroughfares are Rúa do Vilar, Rúa do Franco, and Rúa Nova—portions of which are covered by arcaded walkways called *soportales,* designed to keep walkers out of the rain.

3 From the Praza do Obradoiro, climb the two flights of stairs to the main entrance of Santiago's **cathedral**. Although the facade is baroque, the interior holds one of the finest Romanesque sculptures in the world, the **Pórtico de la Gloria.** Completed in 1188 by Maestro Mateo, this is the cathedral's original entrance, its three arches carved with figures from the apocalypse, the last judgment, and purgatory. Below Jesus is a serene St. James, poised on a carved column. Look carefully and you can see five smooth grooves, formed by the millions of pilgrims who have placed their hands here over the centuries. On the back of the pillar, people, especially students preparing for exams, lean forward to touch foreheads with the likeness of Maestro Mateo in the hope that his genius can be shared. In his bejeweled cloak, St. James presides over the **high altar.** The stairs behind it are the cathedral's focal point, surrounded by dazzling baroque decoration, sculpture, and drapery. Here, as the grand finale of their spiritual journey, pilgrims embrace St. James and kiss his cloak. In the crypt beneath the altar lie the remains of James and his disciples St. Theodore and St. Athenasius.

A pilgrims' mass is celebrated every day at noon. On special, somewhat unpredictable occasions, the *botafumeiro* (huge incense burner) is attached to the thick ropes hanging from the ceiling and prepared for a ritual at the end of the pilgrims' mass: as small flames burn inside, eight strong laymen move the ropes to swing the vessel in a massive semicircle across the apse. In earlier centuries, this rite served as an air freshener—by the time pilgrims reached Santiago, they smelled a bit, well, you can imagine. A *botafumeiro* and other cathedral treasures are on display in the **museums** downstairs and next door. On the right (south) side of the nave is the **Porta das Praterías** (Silversmiths' Door), the only purely Romanesque part of the cathedral's facade. The statues on the portal were cobbled together from parts of the cathedral. The double doorway opens onto the **Praza das Praterías,** named for the silversmiths' shops that used to line it. ✉ *Praza do Obradoiro* ☎ *981/560527 museum, 981/569327 cathedral* 🎫 *Cathedral free, combined museum ticket €5* ⏲ *Cathedral daily 7* AM*–9* PM*; museums June–Oct., Mon.–Sat. 10–2 and 4–8, Sun. 10–2; Nov.–May, Mon.–Sat. 10–1:30 and 4–6:30, Sun. 10–1:30.*

6 On the north side of town, off the Porta do Camino, the **Centro Galego de Arte Contemporánea** *(Galician Center for Contemporary Art)* is a stark but elegant modern building that contrasts Santiago's ancient feel. Portuguese designer Álvaro Siza built the museum of smooth, angled granite, which mirrors the medieval convent of San Domingos de Bonaval next door. Inside, a gleaming lobby of white Italian marble gives way to white-walled, high-ceiling exhibition halls flooded with light from massive windows and skylights. The museum has a good permanent collection and even better changing exhibits. ✉ *Rúa de Valle Inclán s/n* ☎ *981/546619* 🌐 *www.cgac.org* 🎫 *Free* ⏲ *Tues.–Sun. 11–8.*

1 The **Hostal dos Reis Católicos** *(Hostel of the Catholic Monarchs)*, facing the cathedral from the left, was built in 1499 by Ferdinand and Isabella

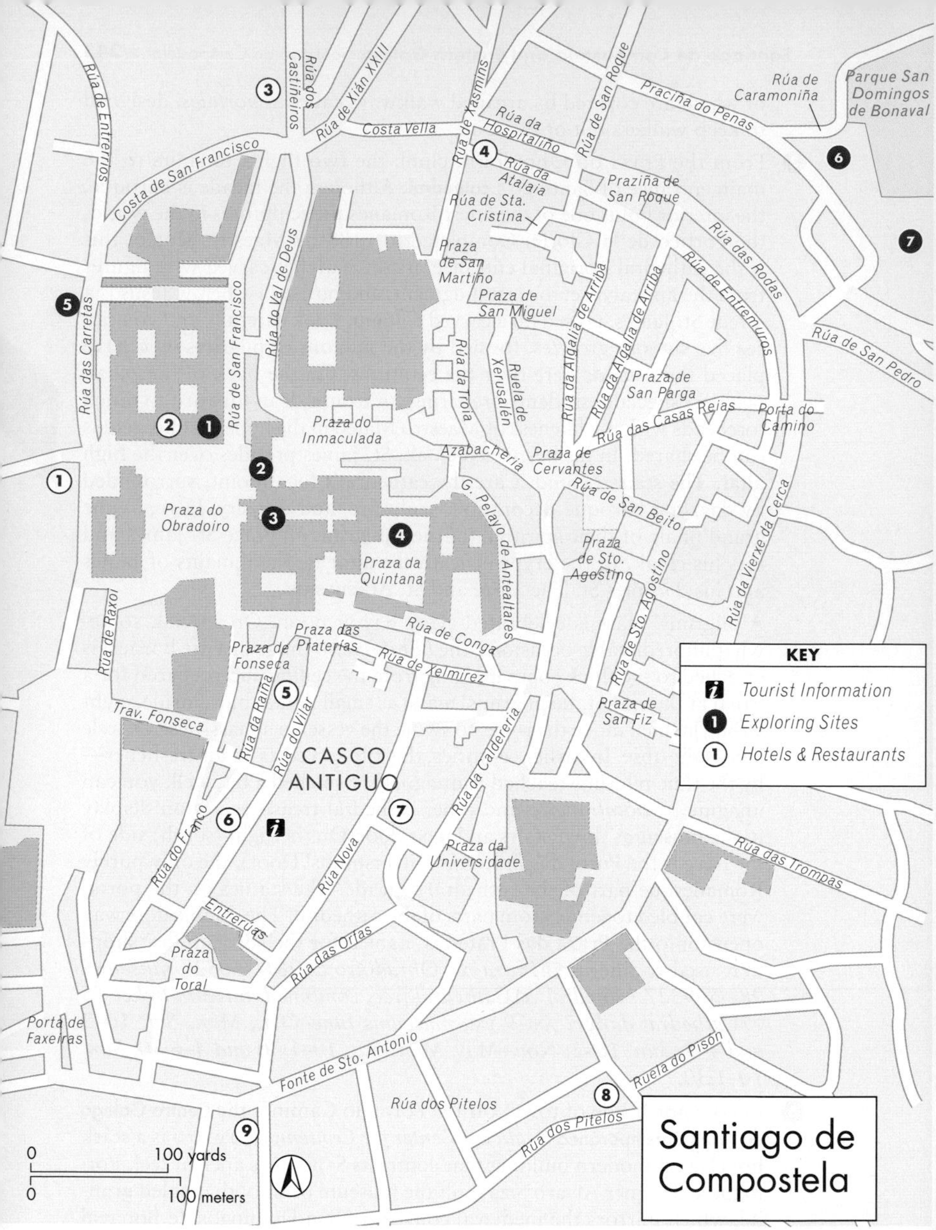

Exploring Sites

Cathedral **3**

Centro Galego de Arte Contemporánea **6**

Hostal de los Reyes Católicos **1**

Museo de las Peregrinaciones **5**

Museo do Pobo Galego **7**

Pazo de Xelmírez **2**

Praza da Quintana **4**

Hotels & Restaurants

A Barrola **6**

Carretas **5**

Casa Marcelo **1**

Don Gaiferos **7**

Hotel-Residencia Costa Vella **4**

Hotel Monumento San Francisco **3**

Moncho Vilas **9**

Parador de Santiago de Compostela: Hostal dos Reis Católicos **2**

Pazo Cibrán **10**

to house the pilgrims who slept on Santiago's streets every night. Having lodged and revived travelers for nearly 500 years, it's the oldest refuge in the world and was converted from a hospital to a parador in 1953. The facade bears a Castilian coat of arms along with Adam, Eve, and various saints; inside, the four arcaded patios have gargoyle rainspouts said to be caricatures of 16th-century townsfolk. There's a small art gallery behind the lobby. Walk-in spectators without room keys risk being asked to leave, but for a negotiable cost, as part of a city tour, you can visit in the company of an official guide from the tourist office. ✉ *Praza do Obradoiro 1* ☎ *981/582200 hostel, 981/555129 tourist office* 🌐 *www.parador.es* ⏲ *Daily 10–1 and 4–6.*

4

❷ Step into the rich 12th-century **Pazo de Xelmírez** (Palace of Archbishop Xelmírez), an unusual example of Romanesque civic architecture with a cool, clean, vaulted dining hall. The little figures carved on the corbels in this graceful, 100-foot-long space are lifelike, partaking of food, drink, and music with great medieval gusto. Each is different, so stroll around for a tableau of mealtime merriment. ✉ *Praza do Obradoiro* 🎫 *Combined ticket for Pazo and cathedral €5* ⏲ *Tues.–Sun. 10–2 and 4–8.*

❹ The wide **Praza da Quintana**, behind the Santiago cathedral, is the haunt of young travelers and folk musicians in summer.

❺ North of Azabachería (follow Ruela de Xerusalén) is the **Museo de las Peregrinaciones** (Pilgrimage Museum), with Camino de Santiago iconography from sculptures and carvings to *azabache* (compact black coal, or jet) items. For an overview of the history of the pilgrimage and the Camino's role in the development of the city itself, this is a key visit. ✉ *Rúa de San Miguel 4* ☎ *981/581558* 🎫 *€2.50* ⏲ *Tues.–Fri. 10–8, Sat. 10:30–1:30 and 5–8, Sun. 10:30–1:30.*

❼ Next door to the Center for Contemporary Art is the **Museo do Pobo Galego** (Galician Folk Museum), in the medieval convent of Santo Domingo de Bonaval. Photos, farm implements, and other displays illustrate aspects of traditional Galician life. The star attraction is the 13th-century self-supporting spiral granite staircase that still connects three floors. ✉ *Calle San Domingos de Bonaval* ☎ *981/583620* 🌐 *www.museodopobo.es* 🎫 *Free* ⏲ *Tues.–Sat. 10–2 and 4–8, Sun. 11–2.*

TAPAS BARS

A five-minute walk from the Colegio San Jerónimo, **Adega Abrigadoiro** serves one of the best selections of Galician delicacies in town. ✉ *Carreira do Conde 5* ☎ *981/563163*. Behind the cathedral, **Bierzo Enxebre** specializes in products from El Bierzo, either at the bar or in one of the dining rooms. ✉ *Rua La Troia 10* ☎ *981/581909*. **La Bodeguilla de San Roque**, one of Santiago's favorite spots for *tapeo* (tapas grazing) and *chiquiteo* (wine sampling), is a five-minute walk from the cathedral. ✉ *Rua San Roque 13* ☎ *981/564379*. Specialists in small servings of great products, **O Dezaseis**, near the town's center, is a must on any tapas crawl. ✉ *Rúa de San Pedro 16* ☎ *981/564880*.

CAFÉS

Santiago is a great city for European-style coffee nursing. Popular with students, **A Calderería** (✉ *Rua Calderería 26* ☎ *981/572045*) juxtaposes contemporary and traditional aesthetics. Try the Clip Nougat: ice cream with pistachios and toasted almonds. Once a gathering place for Galician poets, the **Cafe Bar Derby** (✉ *Rúa das Orfas 29* ☎ *981/586417*) remains a serene spot for coffee and pastries. ozy **Iacobus** (✉ *Rua Azibechería 5* ☎ *981/582804*✉ *Rua Caldererría 42* ☎ *981/583415*) blends stone walls with contemporary wood trim and light fixtures; there's a glass cache of coffee beans in the floor.

WHERE TO EAT

$$–$$$$ SPANISH ✕ **A Barrola.** Now one of a chain of four restaurants in the area, A Barrola has polished wooden floors and a lively terrace and is a favorite with the university faculty. The house salads, mussels with *santiagui-ños* (crabmeat), *arroz con bogavante* (rice with lobster), and seafood empanadas are superb. If options overwhelm and you can't decide, you might opt for the *parillada de pescados* (mixed seafood grill). Sister restaurants Casa Elisa, Xantares, and A Barrola II are all equally popular and within a stone's throw on the Rúa do Franco. ✉ *Rúa do Franco 29* ☎ *981/577999* ▭ *AE, MC, V* ⏲ *Closed Mon. and Jan.–Mar.*

$$–$$$$ SEAFOOD ✕ **Carretas.** This casual spot for fresh Galician seafood is around the corner from the Hostal dos Reis Católicos. Fish dishes abound, but the specialty here is shellfish. For the full experience, order the labor-intensive *variado de mariscos,* a comprehensive platter of langostinos, king prawns, crab, and "goose" barnacles, a white or gray crustacean found in deep waters. *Salpicón de mariscos* presents the same creatures helled. For dessert, there's the tastier-than-it-sounds fried milk pudding. ✉ *Rúa de Carretas 21* ☎ *981/563111* ▭ *AE, DC, MC, V* ⏲ *Closed Sun.*

$$$$ SPANISH ★ ✕ **Casa Marcelo.** Dining in this 18th-century building behind the Obradoiro Square is worth the splurge. Leek-and-potato soup with clams, scallops in cream of seaweed, tuna carpaccio with tomato jelly, and other refined dishes based on local ingredients are the rule. The €60 prix-fixe meal (there is no à la carte) consists of a selection of six main dishes and two desserts. For wine, try the Pedralonga, a white Albariño from the Rías Baixas, which is rare in restaurants. ✉ *Rúa Hortas 1* ☎ *981/558580* ▭ *AE, MC, V* ⏲ *Closed Sun.–Tues. and Feb.*

$$–$$$$ SEAFOOD ✕ **Don Gaiferos.** Tucked away behind the Rúa Nova's columned porticos is one of Santiago's most distinguished restaurants, equally popular with tourists and locals. The exposed stone walls and tile floors lend it a certain medieval charm, and the food is decidedly up to date: jumbo prawns stuffed with smoked salmon, exquisite baked scallops, and white Ribeiro and Albariño wines are among its many delights. The spicy fish stew is enough for two, and, should you still have room for dessert, the *tarta de almendra* (almond tart) and the bilberry cheesecake are irresistible. ✉ *Rúa Nova 23* ☎ *981/583894* ▭ *AE, DC, MC, V* ⏲ *Closed Sun. and Dec. 24–31.*

$$$ SPANISH ★ ✕ **Moncho Vilas.** The unassuming facade of this rustic tavern belies a formidable culinary reputation; indeed, the owner of the eponymous restaurant reached a zenith when he prepared a banquet for the late Pope John Paul II (the pontiff visited Santiago in 1989). Word on the streets says Moncho is in mild decline, but with specialties including salmon with clams and *merluza a la gallega* (hake with paprika sauce) or *a la vasca* (in a green sauce), it's still a Santiago classic. ✉ *Av. Villagarcia 21* ☎ *981/598637* ▭ *AE, DC, MC, V* ⏲ *Closed Mon. No dinner Sun.*

Santiago de Compostela's Obradoiro Square

WHERE TO STAY

$$$ ★ **Hotel Monumento San Francisco.** Contemporary stained-glass windows add a touch of pizzazz to the solemn interior of this converted 13th-century convent. Guest rooms are pious in nature, with Franciscan dark browns, wooden beams, and stone walls, but are enlivened by views of the cathedral or gardens. Adjoining the church of the same name, the San Francisco is run with monastic efficiency. **Pros:** superb location in tranquil corner of Santiago's old town; clean and tidy; easily accessible by car. **Cons:** cell-like rooms; a bit too quiet at times; mediocre food. *Campillo San Francisco 3 981/581634 www.sanfranciscohm.com 76 rooms In-hotel: restaurant, bar, pool, Wi-Fi hotspot, parking AE, DC, MC, V.*

$$ **Hotel-Residencia Costa Vella.** A classically Galician inn, this property has a cheerful interior awash in smooth blond wood and natural light from floor-to-ceiling windows—the better to behold the perfect little garden, red-tile rooftops, the baroque convent of San Francisco, and the green hills beyond (ask for a garden view). Enjoy nice vistas from the airy breakfast room and reading area. Owner José also offers rooms around the corner in the sleek, spotless, and highly recommended Hotel Altair. **Pros:** charming views; ideal location; accommodating staff. **Cons:** creaky floors; no elevator. *Rúa Porta da Pena 17 981/569530 www.costavella.com 14 rooms In-hotel: bar, Wi-Fi hotspot AE, DC, MC, V.*

$$$$ Fodor's Choice ★ **Parador de Santiago de Compostela: Hostal dos Reis Católicos.** One of the parador chain's most highly regarded hotels, this 15th-century masterpiece was originally built as a royal hospital for sick pilgrims. A mammoth baroque doorway gives way to austere courtyards of box hedge

and simple fountains, and to rooms furnished with antiques, some with canopy beds. Libredón, the restaurant ($$$–$$$$) in the grand, vaulted dining room, serves top-notch regional fare, including *lonchas de pulpo* (octopus with paprika and potato), foie gras, and *filloas de manzana y crema caramelizadas* (apple-and-caramel-cream pancakes). The tapas bar, Enxebre, is lively and informal. **Pros:** views of Obradoiro square; excellent cuisine; fascinating collection of antiques and paintings. **Cons:** confusing corridors; often filled with people on guided tours. ✉ *Praza do Obradoiro 1* ☎ *981/582200* 🌐 *www.parador.es* *137 rooms* *In-hotel: 2 restaurants, bar, parking (paid)* ▭ *AE, DC, MC, V.*

$$ **Pazo Cibrán.** This 18th-century Galician farm mansion is 7 km (4 mi) from Santiago de Compostela, and owner Mayka Iglesias maintains six rooms in the main house and five large rooms in the old stable. The antique-packed living room overlooks gardens with camellias, magnolias, palms, vines, and a bamboo walk. Breakfast is served in the *pazo* itself, with lunch and dinner available in the nearby Casa Roberto. To get here, take the N525 toward Ourense from Santiago and turn right at Km 11, after the gas station. **Pros:** personal hospitality; authentic character of a stately country home; delightful gardens. **Cons:** inaccessible without a car; poor local dining options. ✉ *Rua San Xulián de Sales* ☎ *981/511515* 🌐 *www.pazocibran.com* *11 rooms* *In-room: no a/c* ▭ *AE, DC, MC, V.*

NIGHTLIFE AND THE ARTS

Santiago's nightlife peaks on Thursday night because many students spend weekends at home with their families. For up-to-date info on concerts, films, and clubs, pick up the *Compostelan* magazine at newsstands or check the monthly *Compostela,* available at the main tourist office on Rúa do Vilar. Bars and seafood-theme tapas joints line the old streets south of the cathedral, particularly **Rúa do Franco, Rúa da Raiña,** and **Rúa do Vilar**. A great first stop, especially if you haven't eaten dinner, is **Rúa de San Clemente,** off the Praza do Obradoiro, where several bars offer two or three plates of tapas free with each drink.

Drink to Galicia's Celtic roots with live music at **Casa das Crechas** (✉ *Vía Sacra 3* ☎ *981/560751*), where Celtic wood carvings hang from thick stone walls and dolls of playful Galician witches ride their brooms above the bar. Galicia's oldest pub is also one of its most unusual: **Modus Vivendi** (✉ *Praza Feixóo 1*) is in a former stable. The old stone feeding trough is now a low table, and instead of stairs you walk on ridged stone inclines designed for the former occupants—horses and cattle. On weekends the bar hosts live music (jazz, ethnic, Celtic) and sometimes storytelling. **O Beiro** (✉ *Rúa da Raiña 3* ☎ *981/581370*) is a rustic wine bar with a laid-back professional crowd. **Retablo Concerto** (✉ *Rúa Nova 13* ☎ *981/564851*) is cozy and has live music on weekends.

SHOPPING

Galicia is known throughout Spain for its distinctive blue-and-white ceramics with bold modern designs, made in Sargadelos and O Castro. There is a wide selection at **Sargadelos** (✉ *Rúa Nova 16* ☎ *981/581905*).

SIDE TRIP FROM SANTIAGO: PADRÓN

20 km (12 mi) south of Santiago.

Padrón grew up beside the Roman port of Iría Flavia and is where the body of St. James is believed to have washed ashore after its miraculous maritime journey. The town is known for its *pimientos de Padrón,* tiny green peppers fried and sprinkled with sea salt. The fun in eating these is that about one in five is spicy-hot. Galicia's biggest **food market** is held here every Sunday.

Padrón was the birthplace of one of Galicia's heroines, the 19th-century poet Rosalía de Castro. The lovely **Casa-Museo Rosalía de Castro**, where she lived with her husband, a historian, now displays family memorabilia. ✉ *Ctra. de Herbón* ☎ *981/811204* 🌐 *www.rosaliadecastro.org* *€1.50* ⏲ *May–Sept., Tues.–Sat. 10–2 and 4–8, Sun. 10–1:30; Oct.–Apr., Tues.–Sat. 10–1:30 and 4–7, Sun. 10–1:30.*

4

WHERE TO STAY

$$ ★ **A Casa Antiga do Monte.** This graceful manor house combines modern comfort with vintage furniture and Asturian architecture. The crackling fire in the dining room and the 18th-century *horreo* (granary) in the yard add up to perfect rustic comfort, and there's a swimming pool for hot days. Meals ($) include local delights such as *fabada* (bean-and-sausage stew) and *chorizo a la sidra* (chorizo sausage soaked in cider). **Pros:** authentic rustic feel; genuine hospitality; very clean. **Cons:** bit of a walk from Padrón itself. ✉ *Boca do Monte-Lestrove, 1 km (1 mi) southwest of Padrón* ☎ *981/812400* 🌐 *www.susavilaocio.es* *16 rooms* *In-room: no a/c, Wi-Fi (some). In-hotel: restaurant, bar, pool, gym, parking (paid)* *AE, DC, MC, V.*

LUGO

102 km (63 mi) east of Santiago.

ESSENTIALS

Bus Station Lugo (✉ *Pl. de la Constitución s/n* ☎ *982/223985*).

Visitor Information Lugo (✉ *Praza Miño10-12* ☎ *982/231361*).

EXPLORING

Just off the A6 freeway, Galicia's oldest provincial capital is most notable for its 2-km (1½-mi) **Roman wall.** These beautifully preserved ramparts completely surround the hidden granite streets of the old town. The walkway on top has good views. The baroque *ayuntamiento* (city hall) has a magnificent rococo facade overlooking the tree-lined **Praza Maior** (Plaza Mayor). There's a good view of the Río Miño valley from the **Parque Rosalía de Castro,** outside the Roman walls near the cathedral, which is a mixture of Romanesque, Gothic, baroque, and neoclassical styles.

WHERE TO EAT AND STAY

$$–$$$$ SPANISH ✕ **Mesón de Alberto.** A hundred meters from the cathedral, this cozy venue has excellent Galician fare and professional service. The bar and adjoining bodega (winery) serve plenty of cheap *raciónes* (appetizers). The *surtido de quesos Gallegos* provides generous servings of four local

SPORTS AND THE OUTDOORS

With so much rugged wilderness, Spain's northwest has become the country's main outdoor-adventure region. The Picos de Europa and the green hills of Galicia beg to be hiked, trekked, climbed, or simply walked. Ribadesella is Spain's white-water capital, with an international kayak race held in August on the Sella River from Arriondas to Ribadesella.

BALLOONING

Stable weather conditions and outstanding mountain landscapes make the Picos de Europa ideal for year-round ballooning. Flights cost between €150 per person for a 30-minute introduction and €545 for a three-hour trip.

Contacts Globoastur (✉ *Gijón, Asturias* ☎ *985/355818* 🌐 *www.globoastur.com*).

GOLF

Asturias has golf courses in Gijón, Siero, and just outside of Llanes, atop a plateau 300 feet above sea level, where nine holes have views of the Asturian coastline, and the other nine face the towering Picos de Europa.

Galician courses include Monte la Zapateira, near A Coruña; Domaio, in Pontevedra province; La Toja, on the island of the same name near O Grove; and Padrón. Santiago's links are near the airport, at Labacolla. Call a day in advance to reserve equipment.

Contacts Campo de Golf del Aero Club Lavacolla (✉ *General Pardiñas 34, Lugar de Mourena* ☎ *981/888276*). **Campo Municipal de Golf de las Caldas** (✉ *Av. La Premaña s/n, Las Caldas, Oviedo* ☎ *985/798132*). **Campo Municipal la Llorea** (✉ *N632, Km 62, La Llorea, Gijón* ☎ *985/181030*). **Club de Golf de Castiello** (✉ *N632, 5 km [3 mi] from Gijón toward Santander* ☎ *985/366313*). **Club de Golf La Cuesta** (✉ *Ctra. N634, Km 298, Llanes* ✣ *3 km [2 mi] east of Llanes, near Cué* ☎ *985/403319* 🌐 *www.golflacuesta.com*). **Domaio** (✉ *San Lorenzo* ☎ *986/327051*). **La Barganiza** (✉ *San Martí de Anes-Siero, 12 km [7 mi] from Oviedo and 14 km [9 mi] from Gijón* 🖂 *La Barganiza 33192–Carretera Siero-Asturias* ☎ *985/742468*). **La Toja** (✉ *El Grove* ☎ *986/730158*). **Monte la Zapateira** (✉ *C. Zapateira s/n, A Coruña* ☎ *981/285200*).

HIKING

The tourist offices in Oviedo and Cangas de Onís can help you organize a Picos de Europa trek. The Picos visitor center in Cangas has general information, route maps, and a useful scale model of the range. In summer, another reception center opens between Lakes Enol and Ercina, on the mountain road from Covadonga. The Centro de Aventuro Monteverde can organize canoeing, canyon rappelling, spelunking, horseback riding, and jeep trips. Turismo y Aventura Viesca offers rafting, canoeing, jet skiing, climbing, trekking, bungee jumping, and archery. In A Coruña, Nortrek is a one-stop source for information and equipment pertaining to hiking, rock climbing, and skiing.

Contacts Centro de Aventura Monteverde (✉ *Calle Sargento Provisional 5, Cangas de Onís* ☎ *985/848079*) is closed November to March. **Nortrek** (✉ *Calle Inés de Castro 7, A Coruña* ☎ *981/151674*). **Picos de Europa visitor center** (✉ *Casa Dago, Av. Covadonga 43, Cangas de Onís* ☎ *985/848614*). **Turismo y Aventura Viesca** (✉ *Av. del Puente Romano 1, Cangas de Onís* ☎ *985/357369* 🌐 *www.aventuraviesca.com*).

HORSEBACK RIDING

Trastur leads wilderness trips on horseback through the remote valleys of western Asturias. The 5-to-10-day outings are designed for both beginners and experienced cowboys; mountain cabins provide shelter along the trail. Tours begin and end in Oviedo and cost about €108 a day, all-inclusive. The Centro Hípico de Turismo Ecuestre y de Aventuras / "Granjo O Castelo" conducts horseback rides along the pilgrimage routes to Santiago from O Cebreiro and Braga (Portugal). Federación Hípica Gallega has a list of all riding facilities in Galicia.

Contacts Centro Hípico de Turismo Ecuestre y de Aventuras / "Granja O Castelo" (✉ *Rúa Urzáiz 91–5D, Vigo* ☎ *986/425937* 🌐 *www.galicianet.com/castelo*). **Federación Hípica Gallega** (✉ *Fotografo Luis Ksado 17, Edificio Federaciones Deportivas, Vigo* ☎ *986/213800* 📠 *986/201461* 🌐 *www.fhgallega.com*). **Trastur** (✉ *Muñalen-Cal Teso, Tineo* ☎ *985/806036 or 985/806310*).

SKIING

The region's three small ski areas cater mostly to local families. The largest is San Isidro, in the Cantabrian Mountains, with four chairlifts, eight drag lifts, and more than 22 km (14 mi) of slopes. East of here is Valgrande Pajares, with two chairlifts, eight slopes, and cross country trails. West of Ourense, in Galicia, Mazaneda has two chairlifts, 17 slopes, and one cross-country trail.

Contacts Manzaneda (✉ *A Pobra de Trives* ☎ *988/309080*). **San Isidro** (✉ *Puerto San Isidro* ☎ *987/731115*). **Valgrande Pajares** (✉ *Brañillín* ☎ *985/496123 or 985/957123*).

WATER SPORTS

In Santiago, contact diving experts Turisnorte for information on scuba lessons, equipment rental, guided dives, windsurfing, and parasailing. Courageous and experienced sailors might find yachting a spectacular way to discover hidden coastal sights; Yatesport Coruña (also in Santiago) rents private yachts and can arrange sailing lessons.

Contacts Turisnorte (✉ *Raxoeira 14, Milladoiro, A Coruña* ☎ *981/530009 or 902/162172*). **Yatesport Coruña** (✉ *Puerto Deportivo, Marina Sada, Sada, A Coruña* ☎ *981/620732*).

cheeses; ask for some *membrillo* (quince jelly) to go with them and the brown, crusty corn bread. For dessert, try the *filloas flameadas con fresas* (flambéed pancakes with strawberries). The dining room upstairs has an inexpensive set menu. ✉ *Rúa da Cruz 4* ☎ *982/228310* 💳 *AE, DC, MC, V* ⏲ *Closed Sun.*

$$ **Gran Hotel Lugo**. In a garden near the Praza Maior but outside the city walls, this spacious modern hotel has comfortable rooms done in yellows and browns. Rooms overlook the garden swimming pool or a broad street. There's a spa, too, to soothe a weary travelers' limbs. **Pros:** very close to central monuments; spacious rooms; extensive spa facilities. **Cons:** the spa is costly and can get crowded; pricey parking. ✉ *Av. Ramón Ferreiro 21* ☎ *982/224152* 🌐 *www.gh-hoteles.com* *156 rooms, 11 suites* *In-hotel: restaurant, pool, spa, Wi-Fi hotspot, parking (paid)* 💳 *AE, DC, MC, V.*

O CEBREIRO

181 km (112 mi) southeast of Santiago; 82 km (51 mi) southeast of Lugo.

Deserted and haunting when it's not high season (and often fogged in or snowy to boot), O Cebreiro is a stark mountaintop hamlet built around a 9th-century church. Known for its round, thatched-roof stone huts called *pallozas*, the village has been perfectly preserved and is now an open-air museum showing what life was like in these mountains in the Middle Ages—indeed, up until a few decades ago. One hut is now a museum of the region's Celtic heritage. Higher up, at 3,648 feet, you can visit a rustic 9th-century sanctuary.

WHERE TO STAY

$ **Hostal San Giraldo de Aurillac**. This rural lodging surrounded by the distinctive, local, thatched *palloza* huts has been a fixture for weary pilgrims walking the Camino de Santiago since the 19th century. It's a good budget base for discovering the surrounding mountains, the kitchen turns out hearty home cooking, and there are lovely views of the mountains. The Santuario do Cebreiro next door is run by the same establishment. **Pros:** good food; cheap and cheerful; well located. **Cons:** spartan interior; only six rooms available; no elevator. ✉ *Calle O Cebreiro, O Cebreiro* ☎ *982/367125* 📠 *982/367115* *6 rooms* *In-room: no a/c. In-hotel: restaurant, bar* 💳 *MC, V.*

THE COSTA DA MORTE AND RÍAS BAIXAS

West of Santiago, scenic C543 leads to the coast. Straight west, the shore is windy, rocky, and treacherous—hence its name, the "Coast of Death." The series of wide, quiet estuaries south of here is called the Rías Baixas (Low Estuaries). The hilly drive takes you through a green countryside dappled with vineyards, tiny farms, and Galicia's trademark *horreos* (granaries), most with a cross at one or both ends.

Continued on page 260

Cathedral of Santiago de Compostela

EL CAMINO DE SANTIAGO

Traversing meadows, mountains, and villages across Spain, about 100,000 travelers embark each year on a pilgrimage to Galicia's Santiago de Compostela, the sacred city of St. James—they're not all deeply religious these days, though a spiritual quest is generally the motivation. The pilgrims follow one of seven main routes, logging about 19 miles a day in a nearly 500-mile journey. Along the way, they encounter incredible local hospitality and trade stories with fellow adventurers.

A SPIRITUAL JOURNEY

Puente la Reina, a town heavily influenced by the Pilgrim's Road to Santiago de Compostela, owes its foundation to the bridge that Queen Doña Mayor built over the Arga River.

The surge of spiritual seekers heading to Spain's northwest coast began as early as the 9th century, when news spread that the Apostle James's remains were there. By the middle of the 12th century, about 1 million pilgrims were arriving in Santiago each year. An entire industry of food hawkers, hoteliers, and trinket sellers awaited their arrival. They even had the world's first travel guide, the Codex Calixtinus (published in the 1130s), to help them on their way.

Some made the journey in response to their conscience, to do penance for their sins against God, while others were sentenced by law to make the long walk as payment for crimes against the state.

Legend claims that St. James's body was transported secretly to the area by boat after his martyrdom in Jerusalem in AD 44. The idea picked up steam in 814, when a hermit claimed to see miraculous lights in the sky, accompanied by the sound of angels singing, on a wooded hillside near Padrón. Human bones were quickly discovered at the site, and immediately—and perhaps somewhat conveniently—declared to be those of the apostle (the bones may actually have belonged to Priscillian, the leader of a 4th-century Christian sect).

Word of this important find quickly spread across a relic-hungry Europe. Within a couple of centuries, the road to Santiago had become as popular as the other two major medieval pilgrimages, to Rome and to Jerusalem.

After the 12th century, pilgrim numbers began to gradually decline, due to the dangers of robbery along the route, a growing scepticism about the genuineness of St. James's remains, and the popular rise of science in place of religion.

SCALLOP SHELLS

The scallop shell can be bought at most *albergues* along the route. After carrying it on the Camino, pilgrims take it home with them as a keepsake.

HOW MANY PILGRIMS TODAY?

By the late 1980s, there were only about 3,000 pilgrims a year, but in 1993 the Galician government launched an initiative called the *Xacobeo* (i.e., Jacobean; the name James comes from the Latin word "Jacob"), to increase the number of visitors to the region, and the popularity of the pilgrimage soared. Numbers increased exponentially, and there have been over 100,000 annually since 2006. In holy years, when St. James Day (July 25) falls on a Sunday the number of pilgrims usually doubles; the most recent holy year was 2010.

WHO WAS ST. JAMES?

After his martyrdom, the apostle James was revered even more by some and made a saint.

St. James the Great, brother of St. John the Evangelist (author of the Gospel of John and the Book of Revelation), was one of Jesus's first apostles. Sent by Jesus to preach that the kingdom of heaven had come, he crossed Europe and ended up in Spain. Along the way, he saved a knight from drowning in the sea. As legend goes, the knight resurfaced, covered in scallop shells: this is why Camino pilgrims carry this seashell on their journey.

Legend has it that St. James was beheaded by King Herod Agrippa on his return to Judea in AD 44, but that he was rescued by angels and transported in a rudderless boat back to Spain, where his lifeless body was encased in stone. James is said to have resurfaced to aid the Christians in the Reconquista Battle of Clavijo, gaining him the title of Matamoros, or Moor Killer.

When the body of St. James was found people came in droves to see his remains—the Spanish and Portuguese name for St. James is Santiago. The notion that sins would be cleansed developed as a kind of reward for walking so far, an idea no doubt encouraged by the church at the time.

THE PILGRIMAGE EXPERIENCE

A key Camino stop in La Rioja is the Romanesque-Gothic cathedral Santo Domingo de la Calzada, named for an 11th-century saint who had roads and bridges built along the route.

Not everyone does the route in one trip. Some split it into manageable chunks and take years to complete the whole course. Most, however, walk an average of 19 miles (30 kilometers) a day to arrive in Santiago after a month-long trek. Though not as obvious as Dorothy's yellow-brick road to Oz, the Camino path, which sometimes follows a mountain trail and other times goes through a village or across a field, is generally so well marked that most travelers claim not to need a map (bringing one is highly recommended, however). Travelers simply follow the route markers—gold clamshell designs on blue backgrounds posted on buildings or painted on rocks and trail posts.

Walking is not the only option. Bicycles are common along the Camino and will cut the time needed to complete the pilgrimage in half. Arriving in Santiago on horseback is another option, as is walking with a donkey in tow, carrying the bags.

Every town along the route has an official Camino *albergue*, or hostel, often in an ancient monastery or original pilgrim's hospice. They generally accommodate between 40 and 150 people. You can bunk for free—though a donation is expected—in the company of fellow walkers, but may only stay one night, unless severe Camino injuries prevent you from moving on. Be aware that these places can fill up fast. Walkers get first priority, followed by cyclists and those on horseback, with organized walking groups at the bottom of the pecking order. (Sometimes you need to wait until

THE MODERN PILGRIM

The modern pilgrim has technology at his or her fingertips. The official Xacabeo Web site (🌐 www.camino.xacobeo.es/en) can not only help you plan your trip, with detailed route maps and hostel locations, it also has a Xacoblog where you can share videos, photos, and comments, as well as a forum for asking questions and getting feedback. A cell phone application helps you check routes, hostels, and sites to see while you're walking.

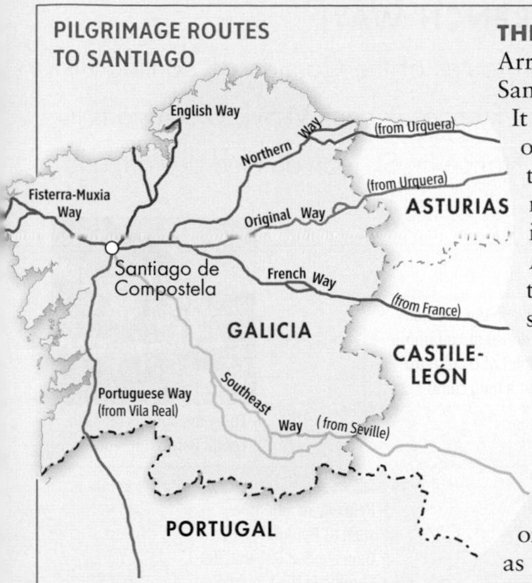

after lunch for them to open.) If there is no room at the official albergues, there are plenty of paid hostels along the route. Wherever you stay, get your Pilgrims' Passport, or *credencial*, stamped, as proof of how far you've walked.

A typical day on the Camino involves walking hard through the morning to the next village in time to get a free bed. The afternoon is for catching up with fellow pilgrims, having a look around town, and doing a bit of washing. The Spanish people you meet along the way and the camaraderie with fellow pilgrims is a highlight of the trip for many.

Some albergues serve a communal evening meal, but there is always a bar in town that offers a lively atmosphere and a cheap (8–10 euros) Pilgrim's set menu (quality and fare varies; it consists of three courses plus bread and beverage). Sore feet are compared, local wine is consumed, and new walking partners are found for the following day's stage. Just make sure you get back to the albergue before curfew, around 10 or 11, or you may find a locked door.

THE END OF THE LINE

Arriving at the end of the Camino de Santiago is an emotional experience. It is common to see small groups of pilgrims, hands clasped tightly together, tearfully approaching the moss- and lichen-covered cathedral in Santiago's Plaza del Obradoiro. After entering the building through the Pilgrim's Door and hugging the statue of St. James, a special mass awaits them at midday, the highlight of which is seeing the *Botafumeiro*, a giant incense-filled censer, swinging from the ceiling.

Those that have covered more than 62 miles (100 kilometers) on foot, or twice that distance on a bicycle—as evidenced by the stamped passport—can then collect their *Compostela* certificate from the Pilgrim's office (near the cathedral, at Rúa do Vilar 1). Each day, the first 10 pilgrims to request it are entitled to free meals for three days at the Hostal de los Reyes Catolicos, once a pilgrims' hospice, and now a five-star parador hotel next to the cathedral. Travelers who want to experience more scenery and gain the achievement of going to the "ends of the Earth" continue on to Finisterre at the western tip of Galicia's Atlantic coast, once thought to be the end of the world.

On the Camino, all roads lead to the cathedral at Santiago de Compostela.

THE CAMINO FRANCÉS (FRENCH WAY)

The most popular of the seven main routes of the Camino de Santiago is the 497-mile (800-kilometer) Camino Francés (French Way), which starts in Spain (in Roncesvalles or Jaca) or in France (in St. Jean de Pied de Port) and

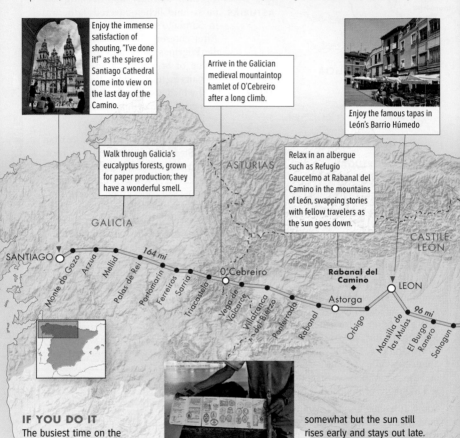

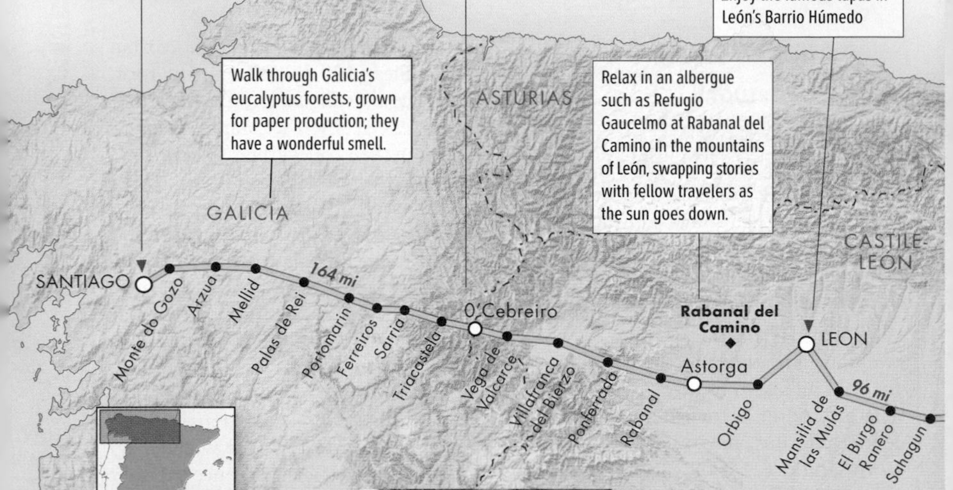
Enjoy the immense satisfaction of shouting, "I've done it!" as the spires of Santiago Cathedral come into view on the last day of the Camino.
Arrive in the Galician medieval mountaintop hamlet of O'Cebreiro after a long climb.
Enjoy the famous tapas in León's Barrio Húmedo
Walk through Galicia's eucalyptus forests, grown for paper production; they have a wonderful smell.
Relax in an albergue such as Refugio Gaucelmo at Rabanal del Camino in the mountains of León, swapping stories with fellow travelers as the sun goes down.
ASTURIAS
GALICIA
CASTILE-LEÓN
SANTIAGO
164 mi
Monte do Gozo
Arzua
Mellid
Palas de Rei
Portomarin
Ferreiros
Sarria
Triacastela
O'Cebreiro
Vega de Valcarce
Villafranca del Bierzo
Ponferrada
Rabanal
Rabanal del Camino
Astorga
Orbigo
LEON
96 mi
Mansilia de las Mulas
El Burgo Ranero
Sahagun

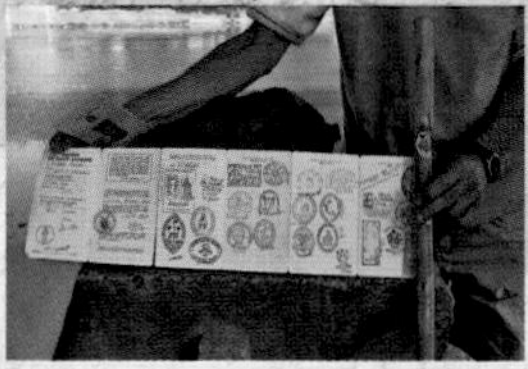

Take home a record of your trip.

IF YOU DO IT

The busiest time on the Camino is in the summer months, from June to September, when many Spaniards make the most of their summer holidays journeying the route. That means crowded paths and problems finding a room at night, particularly if you start the Camino on the first few days of any month. This time of year is also very hot. To avoid the intense heat and crowds, many pilgrims choose to start the Camino in April, May, or September. Making the journey in winter is not advised, as Galicia and central Spain can get very cold at that time of year. September is ideal because the heat has abated somewhat but the sun still rises early and stays out late.

You will need to be fully prepared for tough walking conditions before you set out. The single most important part of your equipment is your hiking boot, which should be as professional as your budget allows and well worn in before you hit the trail. Other essentials include a good-quality—and water-

crosses the high meseta plains into Galicia. The Camino Norte (Northern Way), which runs through the woodlands of Spain's rugged north coast, is also gaining in popularity.

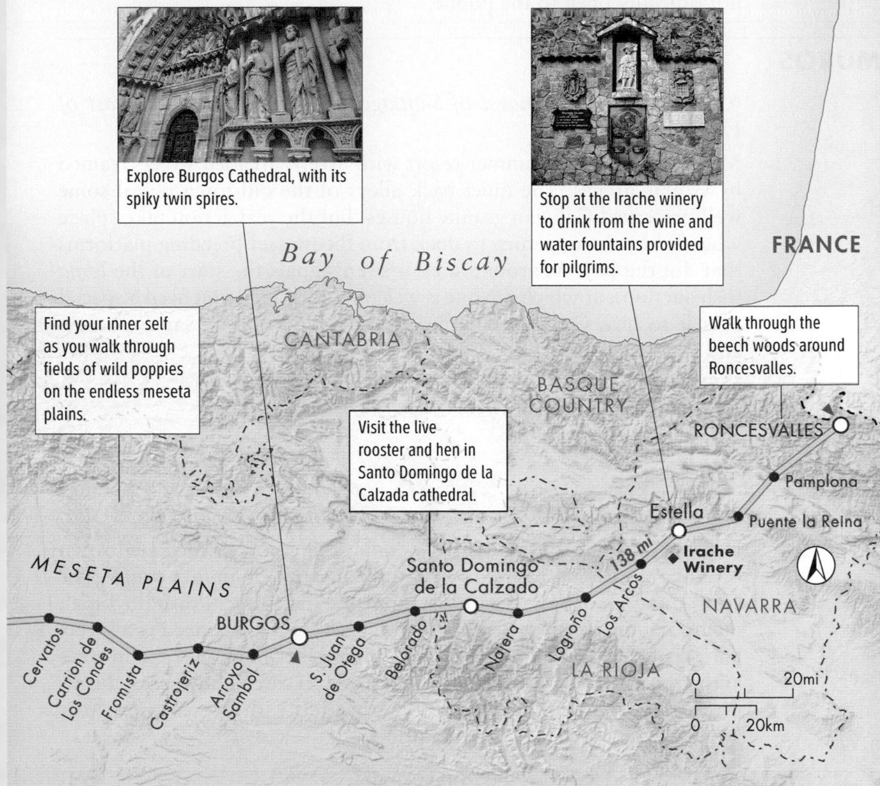
Explore Burgos Cathedral, with its spiky twin spires.
Stop at the Irache winery to drink from the wine and water fountains provided for pilgrims.
Bay of Biscay
FRANCE
Find your inner self as you walk through fields of wild poppies on the endless meseta plains.
CANTABRIA
Walk through the beech woods around Roncesvalles.
BASQUE COUNTRY
Visit the live rooster and hen in Santo Domingo de la Calzada cathedral.
RONCESVALLES
Pamplona
Estella
Puente la Reina
138 mi
Irache Winery
MESETA PLAINS
Santo Domingo de la Calzado
NAVARRA
BURGOS
Cervatos
Carrion de Los Condes
Fromista
Castrojeriz
Arroyo Sambol
S. Juan de Otega
Belorado
Najera
Logroño
Los Arcos
LA RIOJA
0
20mi
0
20km

proof (it rains year-round in Galicia)—backpack, sleeping bag, sunscreen, and a medical kit, including Vaseline and blister remedies for sore feet. Don't forget a set of earplugs as well, to keep out the sound of other pilgrims' snores and dawn departures.

To get hold of your *credencial,* or pilgrim's passport, contact one of the Camino confraternity groups. These are not-for-profit associations formed by previous pilgrims to help those who are thinking about doing the Camino (see *www.csj.org.uk/other-websites.htm* for a list of groups). You can also pick up a passport at many of the common starting points, such as the abbey in Roncesvalles, the cathedral in Le Puy, and local churches and Amigos del Camino de Santiago in villages throughout Spain. In some cases, even police stations and city halls have them.

Many albergues throughout Spain also can provide you with a valid *credencial* for a small fee.

HELPFUL WEB SITES

www.xacobeo.es/en
www.santiago-today.com
www.csj.org.uk
www.caminodesantiago.me.uk
www.albergue.caminodesantiago.me

FISTERRA

50 km (31 mi) west of Santiago, 75 km (48 mi) southwest of A Coruña.

There was a time when this lonely, windswept outcrop over raging waters was thought to be the end of the earth—the *finis terrae*. All that's left is a run-down stone *faro* (lighthouse) perched on a cliff and not officially open to the public.

MUROS

65 km (40 mi) southwest of Santiago, 55 km (34 mi) southeast of Fisterra.

Muros is a popular summer resort with lovely, arcaded streets framed by Gothic arches. The quiet back alleys of the old town reveal some well-preserved Galician granite houses, but the real action takes place when fishing boats return to dock from the mussel-breeding platforms that dot the bay. At around 6 PM a siren signals the start of the *lonja* (fish auction), at which anyone is welcome, although you need a special license to buy. Good nearby beaches include Praia de San Francisco and Praia de Area.

ESSENTIALS

Visitor Information Muros (☎ *981/826050*).

NOIA

30 km (19 mi) east of Muros, 36 km (22 mi) west of Santiago.

Deep within the Ría de Muros y Noia, the compact medieval town of Noia nuzzles up to the foot of the Barbanza mountain range. The Gothic church of **San Martín** rises over the old town's Praza do Tapal, facing resolutely out to sea. In the town center, **La Alameda** is a lovely park that gives way to a tiled pedestrian street lined with palm trees and wrought-iron and stone benches. You can catch glimpses of the *ría* through the trees; in the summer, the street fills with terrace cafés. Near Noia are the beaches of Testal and Boa.

PONTEVEDRA

55 km (34 mi) southeast of Noia, 59 km (37 mi) south of Santiago.

At the head of its *ría,* Pontevedra is approached through prefab suburbs, but the old quarter is well preserved and largely unspoiled. Speckled with bars, it can get very lively on weekends.

ESSENTIALS

Bus Station Pontevedra (✉ *Calvo Sotelo s/n* ☎ *986/852408*).

Visitor Information Pontevedra (✉ *Calle de Xeneral Gutiérrez Mellado 1* ☎ *986/850814* ✉ *La Herreria* ⏲ *July–Sept., outdoor kiosks*).

The 16th-century seafarers' basilica of **Santa María Mayor**, with a 1541 facade, has lovely, sinuous vaulting and, at the back of the nave, a Romanesque portal. There's also an 18th-century Christ by the Galician

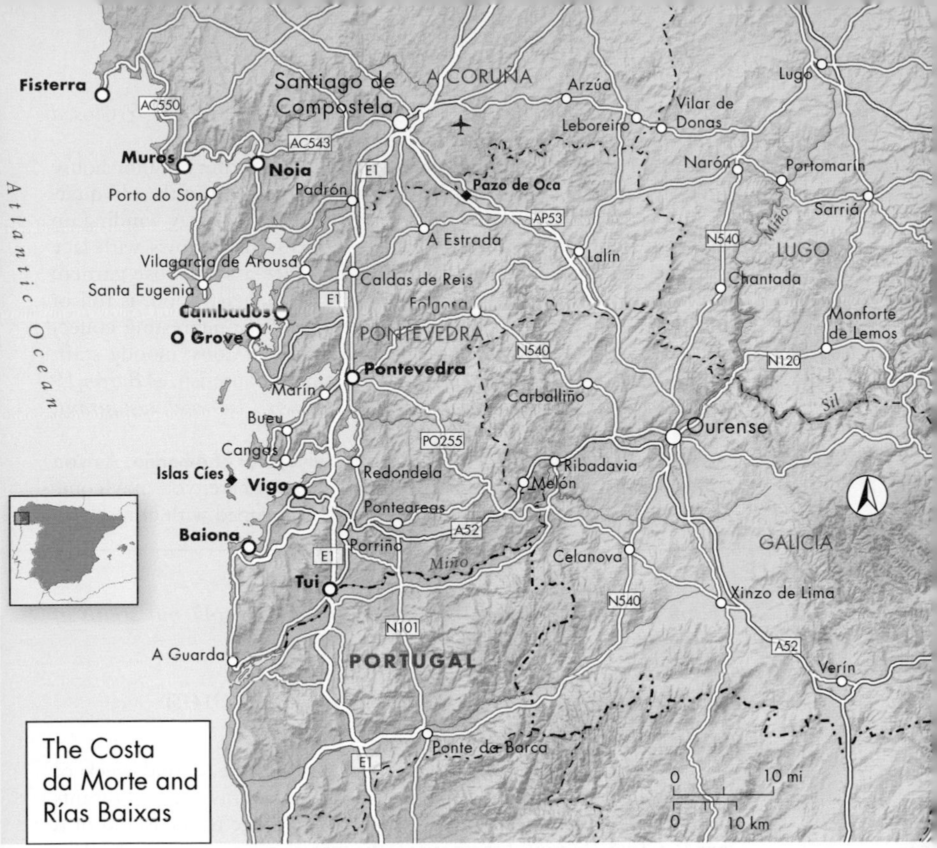

The Costa da Morte and Rías Baixas

sculptor Ferreiro. ✉ *Av. de Santa María s/n* ☎ *986/869902* 🎫 *Free* 🕓 *Daily 11–1 and 6–8.*

★ Pontevedra's **Museo Provincial** is in two 18th-century mansions connected by a stone bridge. Displays include exquisite Celtic jewelry, silver from all over the world, and several large model ships. The original kitchen, with stone fireplace, is intact; nearby, you can descend steep wooden stairs to the reconstructed captain's chamber on the battleship *Numancia,* which limped back to Spain after the Dos de Mayo battle with Peru in 1866. Complete the loop by going upstairs in the first building, where there are Spanish and Italian paintings and some inlay work. ✉ *Praza de Leña* ☎ *986/851455* 🎫 *Free* 🕓 *Tues.–Sat. 10–2 and 4–7, Sun. 11–2.*

WHERE TO EAT AND STAY

$$$–$$$$ SPANISH ★ ✕ **Casa Solla**. Pepe Solla brings Galicia's bounty to his terrace garden restaurant, 2 km (1 mi) outside of town toward O Grove. Try the *menu degustación* (tasting menu) to sample a selection of regional favorites, such as *lomo de caballa* (grilled mackerel), *caldo gallego de chorizo* (Galician chorizo sausage soup), *merluza con acelga* (cod with chard), or *jarrete de cordero* (sliced lamb shank). Finish off with a selection of Galician cheeses and *torrija con flan de coco y mango* (bread pudding with mango and coconut flan). ✉ *Av. Sineiro 7, Ctra. de La Toja, Km*

2, San Salvador de Poio ☎ 986/872884 ▭ AE, DC, MC, V ⏲ Closed Mon. and late Dec.–early Jan. No dinner Thurs. and Sun.

$$$ **Casa del Barón (Parador de Pontevedra).** A 16th-century manor house built on the foundations of a Roman villa in the heart of the old quarter, this rather dark parador has a baronial stone stairway winding up from the front lobby. Guest rooms have recessed windows with lace curtains and large wooden shutters; some face a small rose garden. The restaurant ($$–$$$$), which serves fine Galician food, is full of antique mirrors, candelabras, and portraits. **Pros:** interesting collection of bric-a-brac; tranquil yet central location. **Cons:** moody staff; pokey corridors; gloomy rooms—a bit haunted house-ish. ✉ *Barón 19* ☎ *986/855800* 🌐 *www.parador.es* *47 rooms* *In-hotel: restaurant, bar, Wi-Fi hotspot* ▭ *AE, DC, MC, V.*

EN ROUTE

Driving west on the C550, you'll pass the **vineyards of Albariño.** As you wind your way through the small towns around here, you may come across the occasional donkey hauling wagons heaped with grapes.

O GROVE

31 km (19 mi) northwest of Pontevedra, 75 km (47 mi) south of Santiago.

ESSENTIALS

Visitor Information O Grove (✉ *Pl. de O Corgo 1* ☎ *986/731415*).

EXPLORING

O Grove throws an illustrious shellfish festival the second week of October, but you can enjoy the day's catch in taverns and restaurants year-round. From O Grove, you can cross a bridge to the island of **A Toxa** (La Toja), famous for its spas—the waters are said to have healing properties. Legend has it that a man abandoned an ailing donkey here and found it up on all fours, fully rejuvenated, upon his return. The island's south side has a palm-filled garden anchored on one side by the **Capilla de San Sebastián,** a tiny church covered in cockleshells.

Nearby Reboredo is the home of **Acquarium/Galicia**, one of Spain's finest aquariums, showcasing Galician marine life in an original and interactive manner. ✉ *Punta Moreiras s/n* ☎ *986/731515* 🌐 *www.acquariumgalicia.com* *€9* ⏲ *Daily 11–2 and 4:30–7:30.*

WHERE TO EAT AND STAY

$$–$$$$ SEAFOOD **✕ El Crisol.** Photos of famous diners greet you as you enter this secluded spot, which has been serving lobster, shrimp, spider crabs, scallops, and freshly caught fish from Pontevedra's *ría* for more than 70 years. If you can't make up your mind, the house *sopa de pescados mixtos* (mixed-fish soup) combines most of the above and is an appropriate dish, given the establishment's name, which means "the melting pot." Save room for the *torta de queso,* a rich cheesecake dessert. ✉ *Hospital 10* ☎ *986/730029* ▭ *AE, DC, MC, V* ⏲ *Closed Mon. Sept.–June. No lunch Mon. July and Aug.*

$$$$ **Gran Hotel Hesperia La Toja.** Extravagant and exorbitant (for the region), this classic spa hotel is on the breezy island of La Toja, just across the bridge from O Grove. Surrounded by pine trees and spilling

out onto a delightful golf course, the hotel has simple guest rooms, their charm slightly faded compared with the grandiose formality of the foyers and salons. Try to book a room with a sea view. **Pros:** glittering sea views; golf course; excellent services. **Cons:** expensive; rather noisy rooms. ✉ *Isla de la Toja* ☎ *986/730025* 🌐 *www.hesperia.com* *197 rooms* *In-room: Wi-Fi. In-hotel: restaurant, bar, golf course, tennis court, pool, gym, spa, beachfront* ▭ *AE, DC, MC, V.*

CAMBADOS

34 km (21 mi) north of Pontevedra, 61 km (37 mi) southwest of Santiago.

4

This breezy seaside town has a charming, almost entirely residential old quarter. The impressive main square, **Praza de Fefiñanes,** is bordered by an imposing Albariño bodega.

WHERE TO EAT AND STAY

$$–$$$$ SEAFOOD ★ ✕ **María José.** From its privileged first-floor spot across from the parador, the Ribadomar family produces inventive dishes like scallop salad, mango soup with mascarpone ice cream, or salmon with anchovy mayonnaise. Specialties are *arroz de marisco caldoso* (shellfish, stock, and rice) and *mariscada* (fresh seafood). ✉ *San Gregorio 2* ☎ *986/542281* ▭ *MC, V* ⊗ *Closed last wk in Dec. and 1st wk in Jan. and Mon. Oct.–June. No dinner Sun. Oct.–June.*

$$$ **Parador de Cambados (El Albariño).** The bar of this airy mansion is large and inviting, with natural light and wooden booths. Rooms are warmly furnished with wrought-iron lamps, area rugs, and full-length wood shutters over small-pane windows. The kitchen's ($$–$$$$) *lenguado al vino albariño* (sole in Albariño wine sauce) is divine, as are the empanadas filled with cockles. **Pros:** easily accessible; comfortable rooms; excellent dining. **Cons:** a bit pricey. ✉ *Paseo de Cervantes s/n* ☎ *986/542250* 🌐 *www.parador.es* *58 rooms* *In-hotel: Wi-Fi hotspot, restaurant, tennis court, pool* ▭ *AE, DC, MC, V.*

SHOPPING

Cambados is the hub for Albariño, one of Spain's best white wines—full bodied and fruity, yet fresh. **A Casa do Albariño** (✉ *Rúa Principe 3* ☎ *986/542236*) is a tiny, tasteful emporium of Galician wines and cheeses. Head to **Cucadas** (✉ *Praza de Fefiñanes* ☎ *986/542511*) for a particularly large selection of baskets, copper items, and lace.

VIGO

31 km (19 mi) south of Pontevedra, 90 km (56 mi) south of Santiago.

Vigo's formidable port is choked with trawlers and fishing boats and lined with clanging shipbuilding yards. Its sights (or lack thereof) fall far short of its commercial swagger. The city's casual appeal lies a few blocks inland, where the port commotion gives way to the narrow, dilapidated streets of the old town.

ESSENTIALS

Bus Station Vigo (✉ *Av. de Madrid 57* ☎ *986/373411*).

The coastline of Baiona is one of the first things the crew of Columbus's ship the *Pinta* saw when they returned from their discovery of America.

Visitor Information Vigo (✉ *C. Cánovas del Castillo 22* ☎ *986/430577*).

EXPLORING

From 8:30 to 3:30 daily, on **Rúa Pescadería** in the barrio called La Piedra, Vigo's famed *ostreras*—a group of rubber-gloved fisherwomen who have been peddling fresh oysters to passersby for more than 50 years—shuck the bushels of oysters hauled into port that morning. Healthy rivalry has made them expert hawkers who cheerfully badger all who walk by. When you buy a dozen (for about €6), the women plate them and plunk a lemon on top; you can then take your catch into any nearby restaurant and turn it into a meal. A short stroll southwest of the old town brings you to the fishermen's barrio of **El Berbés** with its pungent and cacophonous *lonja* (fish market), where fishermen sell their morning catch to vendors and restaurants. **Ribera del Berbés,** facing the port, has several seafood restaurants, most with outdoor tables in summer. South of Vigo's old town is the hilltop **Parque del Castro** (✉ *Between Praza de España and Praza do Rei, beside Av. Marqués de Alcedo*), a quiet, stately park with sandy paths, palm trees, mossy embankments, and stone benches. Atop a series of steps are the remains of an old fort and a *mirador* (lookout) with fetching views of Vigo's coastline and the Islas Cíes.

Islas Cies. The Cíes Islands, 35 km (21 mi) west of Vigo, are a nature reserve and one of the last unspoiled refuges on the Spanish coast. From July to September, about eight boats a day leave Vigo's harbor, returning later in the day, for the round-trip fare of €12. The 45-minute ride brings you to white-sand beaches where birds abound, and the only land transportation is your own two feet: it takes about an hour to cross the main island.

WHERE TO EAT

$–$$$ SPANISH **Bar Cocedero La Piedra.** This jovial tapas bar is perfectly located to relieve the Rúa Pescadería fisherwomen of their freshest catch, and it does a roaring lunch trade with Vigo locals. The chefs serve heaping plates of *mariscos* (shellfish) and scallops with roe at market prices. Fresh and fruity Albariño wines are the beverages of choice; the chummy, elbow-to-elbow crowd sits at round tables covered with paper, although on a nice day you might want to grab a seat on the terrace to enjoy your oysters and watch the old town bustle. ✉ *Rúa Pescadería 3* ☎ *986/413204* ▭ *AE, DC, MC, V.*

$$–$$$$ SPANISH **El Mosquito.** Signed photos from the likes of King Juan Carlos and Julio Iglesias cover the walls of this elegant rose- and stone-wall restaurant, open since 1928. The brother-and-sister team of Manolo and Carmiña has been at the helm for the last few decades, and their specialties include *lenguado a la plancha* (grilled sole) and *navajas* (razor clams). The *tocinillos,* a sugary, caramel flan, is also definitely worth trying. The restaurant's name refers to an era when wine arrived in wooden barrels: if mosquitoes gathered at the barrel's mouth, it held good wine. ✉ *Praza da Pedra 4* ☎ *986/433570* ▭ *AE, DC, MC, V* ⊗ *Closed Sun. and Aug.*

$–$$ SPANISH **Tapas Areal.** This ample and lively bar flanked by ancient stone and exposed redbrick walls is a good spot for tapas and beer or Albariños and Ribeiros. ✉ *México 36* ☎ *986/418643* ▭ *MC, V.*

BAIONA

12 km (8 mi) southwest of Vigo.

At the southern end of the AP9 freeway and the Ría de Vigo, Baiona (Bayona in Castilian) is a summer haunt of affluent Gallegos. When Columbus's *Pinta* landed here in 1492, Baiona became the first town to receive the news of the discovery of the New World. Once a castle, **Monte Real** is one of Spain's most popular paradors; walk around the battlements for superb views. Inland from Baiona's waterfront, Paseo Marítima, a jumble of streets, has seafood restaurants and lively cafés and bars. Calle Ventura Misa is one of the main drags. On your way into or out of town, check out Baiona's **Roman bridge.** The best nearby beach is Praia de América, north of town toward Vigo.

WHERE TO STAY

$$$$ Fodor's Choice ★ **Parador de Baiona.** This baronial parador was built inside the walls of a medieval castle on a hilltop. Rooms are plush, and some have balconies with ocean views toward the Islas Cíes. The restaurant serves fine seafood; try a sampler of *entremeses variados* (mixed appetizers) or a *parillada de pescados* (grilled swordfish, salmon, and cod). **Pros:** stupendous medieval architecture; views of the *ría*; luxurious bathrooms. **Cons:** especially pricey for rooms with sea views (almost double the cost of a room with a patio view); occasional problems with plumbing. ✉ *Ctra. de Baiona at Monterreal* ☎ *986/355000* 🌐 *www.parador.*

es 122 *rooms* *In-hotel: restaurant, bar, tennis court, pool, gym, beachfront, Wi-Fi hotspot* AE, DC, MC, V.

TUI

14 km (9 mi) southeast of Baiona, 26 km (16 mi) south of Vigo.

From Vigo, take the scenic coastal route PO552, which goes up the banks of the Miño River along the Portuguese border, or, if time is short, jump on the inland A55; both routes lead to Tui, where steep, narrow streets rich with emblazoned mansions suggest the town's past as one of the seven capitals of the Galician kingdom. Today it's an important border town; the mountains of Portugal are visible from the cathedral. Across the river in Portugal, the old fortress town of Valença contains reasonable shops, bars, restaurants, and a hotel with splendid views of Tui.

Crucial during the medieval wars between Castile and Portugal, Tui has a 13th-century **cathedral** that looks like a fortress. The cathedral's majestic cloisters surround a lush formal garden. *Pl. de San Fernando* *986/600511* €2 *Daily 9:30–1:30 and 4–7.*

WHERE TO EAT AND STAY

$$$ **Parador de Tui.** This stately granite-and-chestnut hotel on the bluffs overlooking the Miño is filled with art by locals. Guest rooms are furnished with antiques and light-color fabrics. Views of the woods surround the dining room ($$–$$$$), where specialties from the river Miño include Atlantic salmon, lamprey eel, sea trout, and river trout. For dessert, try the *pececitos,* almond-flavor pastries made by local convent nuns. **Pros:** enticing gardens; varied services; fine fish cuisine. **Cons:** a bit of a walk from Tui proper; not inexpensive. *Av. del Portugal s/n* *986/600300* *www.parador.es* *32 rooms* *In-hotel: restaurant, bar, tennis court, pool, Wi-Fi hotspot, parking (free)* AE, DC, MC, V.

A CORUÑA AND RÍAS ALTAS

Galicia's gusty and rainy northern coast has inspired poets to wax lyrical about raindrops falling continuously on one's head. The sun does shine between bouts of rain, though, suffusing town and country with a golden glow. North of A Coruña, the Rías Altas (Upper Estuaries) notch the coast as you head east toward the Cantabrian Sea.

A CORUÑA

57 km (35 mi) north of Santiago.

One of Spain's busiest ports, A Coruña (La Coruña in Castilian) prides itself on being the most progressive city in the region. The weather can be fierce, wet, and windy—hence the glass-enclosed, white-pane galleries on the houses lining the harbor.

GETTING HERE AND AROUND

The A9 motorway provides excellent access to and from Santiago de Compostela, Pontevedra, Vigo, and Portugal, while Spain's north coast and France are accessible along the N634.

Buses run every hour from A Coruña to Santiago. Trains also operate on an hourly basis to Santiago and Pontevedra from the city's San Cristóbal rail station; Madrid can be reached in eight hours on the fast track Talgo service.

Outside the old town, the city's local buses shuttle back and forth between the Darsena de la Marina seafront and relatively far-flung attractions such as the Domus science museum and Torre de Hercules lighthouse.

ESSENTIALS

Bus Station A Coruña (✉ *Caballeros 21* ☎ *981/184335*).

Train Station San Cristóbal station (✉ *C. Joaquín Planells*).

Visitor Information A Coruña (✉ *Edificio Sol, Rúa Sol s/n* ☎ *981/184344*).

EXPLORING

To see why sailors once nicknamed A Coruña *la ciudad de cristal* (the glass city), stroll **Dársena de la Marina**, said to be the longest seaside promenade in Europe. Although the congregation of boats is charming, the real sight is across the street: a long, gracefully curved row of houses. Built by fishermen in the 18th century, they face *away* from the sea—at the end of a long day, these men were tired of looking at the water. Nets were hung from the porches to dry, and fish was sold on the street below. When Galicia's first glass factory opened nearby, someone thought to enclose these porches in glass, like the latticed stern galleries of oceangoing galleons, to keep wind and rain at bay. The resulting **glass galleries** ultimately spread across the harbor and eventually throughout Galicia.

Plaza de María Pita is the focal point of the *ciudad vieja* (old town). Its north side is given over to the neoclassical **Palacio Municipal,** or city hall, built 1908–12 with three Italianate domes. The **monument** in the center, built in 1998, depicts the heroine Maior (María) Pita. When England's Sir Francis Drake arrived to sack A Coruña in 1589, the locals were only half finished building the defensive Castillo de San Antón, and a 13-day battle ensued. When María Pita's husband died, she took up his lance, slew the Briton who tried to plant the Union Jack here, and revived the exhausted Coruñesos, inspiring other women to join the battle.

The 12th-century church of **Santiago** (✉ *Pl. de la Constitución s/n*), the oldest church in A Coruña, was the first stop on the *camino inglés* (English route) toward Santiago de Compostela. Originally Romanesque, it's now a hodgepodge of Gothic arches, a baroque altarpiece, and two 18th-century rose windows.

The **Colegiata de Santa María** (✉ *Pl. de Santa María*) is a Romanesque beauty from the mid-13th century, often called Santa María del Campo (St. Mary of the Field) because it was once outside the city walls. The facade depicts the Adoration of the Magi; the celestial figures include St. Peter, holding the keys to heaven. Because of an architectural miscalculation the roof is too heavy for its supports, so the columns inside lean outward and the buttresses outside have been thickened.

At the northeastern tip of the old town is the **Castillo de San Antón** (St. Anthony's Castle), a 16th-century fort. Inside is A Coruña's **Museum of Archaeology,** with remnants of the prehistoric Celtic culture that once thrived in these parts. The collection includes silver artifacts as well as pieces of the Celtic stone forts called *castros.* ☎ *981/205994* 🎫 *€2* ⏲ *Daily 10–2 and 4–7:30.*

Across town, on a hill, is the **Casa de las Ciencias** (Science Museum), a hands-on museum where children can learn the principles of physics and technology. ✉ *Parque de Santa Margarita* ☎ *981/189844* 🌐 *www.casaciencias.org* 🎫 *Museum €2, planetarium €1* ⏲ *Daily 10–7.*

Much of A Coruña sits on a peninsula, on the tip of which is the **Torre de Hercules**—the oldest still-functioning lighthouse in the world. Originally built during the reign of Trajan, the Roman emperor born in Spain in AD 98, the lighthouse was rebuilt in the 18th century and looks strikingly modern; all that remains from Roman times are inscribed foundation stones. Scale the 245 steps for superb views of the city and coastline—if you're here on a summer weekend, the tower opens for views of city lights along the Atlantic. Lining the approach to the lighthouse are sculptures depicting figures from Galician and Celtic legends. ✉ *Ctra. de la Torre s/n* ☎ *981/223730* 🎫 *€2* ⏲ *Sept.–June, daily 10–6; July and Aug., daily 10–8:45.*

Designed in the shape of a ship's sail by Japanese architect Arata Isozaki, the **Domus/Casa del Hombre** (Museum of Mankind) is dedicated to the study of the human being, particularly the human body. Many exhibits are interactive. An IMAX film shows a human birth. ✉ *C. Santa Teresa 1* ☎ *981/189840* 🌐 *www.casaciencias.org* 🎫 *Museum €2, IMAX €1* ⏲ *Daily 10–7.*

WHERE TO EAT AND STAY

$$–$$$$ SPANISH ★ ✕ **Adega o Bebedeiro.** Steps from the ultramodern Domus, this tiny restaurant is beloved by locals for its authentic food and low prices. It feels like an old farmhouse, with stone walls and floors, a fireplace, pine tables and stools, and dusty wine bottles (*adega* means "wine cellar"). Appetizers such as *setas rellenas de marisco y salsa holandesa* (wild mushrooms with seafood and hollandaise sauce) are followed by fresh fish at market prices and an ever-changing array of delicious desserts. ✉ *C. Ángel Rebollo 34* ☎ *981/210609* 💳 *AE, DC, MC, V* ⏲ *Closed Mon., last 2 wks in June, and last 2 wks in Dec. No dinner Sun.*

$$$–$$$$ SPANISH ✕ **Casa Pardo.** Near the port, this chic, double-decker dining room has soft ocher tones, with perfectly matched wood furniture. Try the *zamburiñas rebazadas* (battered mini scallops) and the *rape a la cazuela* (bay leaf–scented monkfish and potatoes sprinkled with paprika, baked in a clay casserole) to find out why this establishment was the first in A Coruña to be awarded a Michelin star. For dessert, there's flaky pastry with banana cream or chocolate soufflé. ✉ *Novoa Santos 15* ☎ *981/287178* 💳 *AE, DC, MC, V* ⏲ *Closed Sun.*

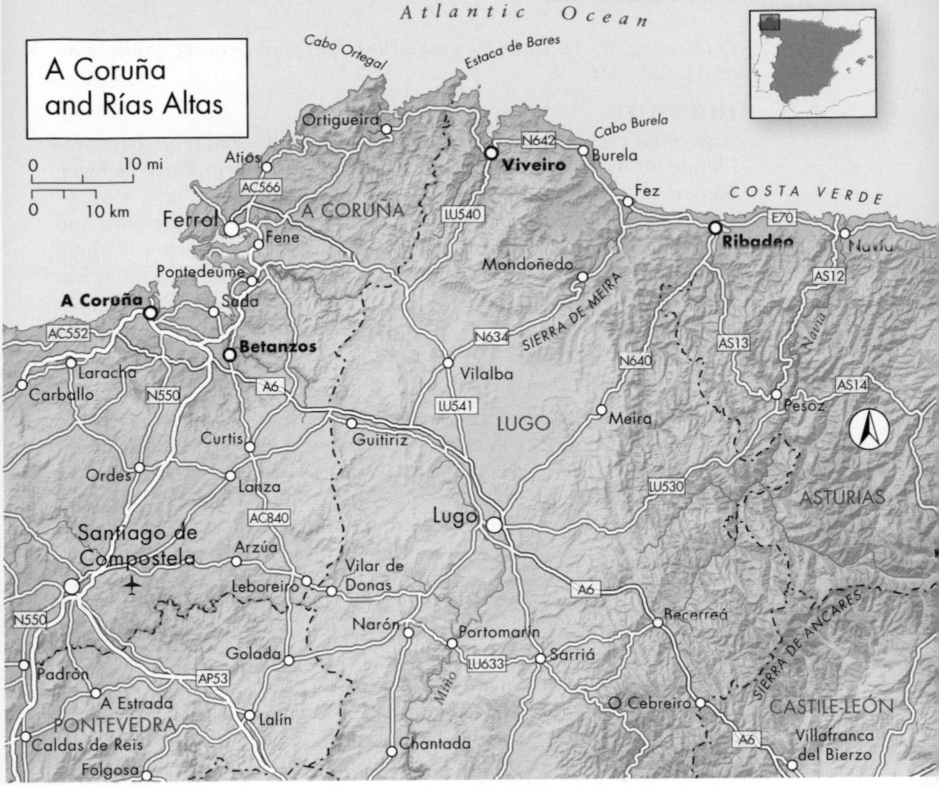

$$–$$$$
SEAFOOD

✕ **El Coral**. The window is an altar of shellfish, with varieties of mollusks and crustaceans you've probably never seen before. Inside, wood-panel walls, crystal chandeliers, and 12 white-clad tables help create an elegant yet casual experience. Specialties include *turbante de mariscos* (a platter—literally, a "turban"—of steamed and boiled shellfish). ✉ *Callejón de la Estacada 9, at Av. Marina* ☎ *981/200569* ✍ *Reservations essential* ▬ *AE, DC, MC, V* ⏲ *Closed Sun.*

$$–$$$
SEAFOOD
★

✕ **La Penela**. The smart, contemporary, bottle-green dining room is the perfect place to feast on fresh fish while sipping Albariño—try at least a few crabs or mussels with béchamel, for which this restaurant is locally famous. If shellfish isn't your speed, the roast veal is also popular. The restaurant occupies a modernist building on a corner of the lively Praza María Pita. Some tables have views of the harbor, or you can eat in a glassed-in terrace on the square. ✉ *Praza María Pita 12* ☎ *981/209200* ▬ *AE, DC, MC, V* ⏲ *Closed Sun. and Jan. 10–25.*

$$$

🏨 **Hesperia Finisterre.** This grande dame, where the old town joins the bay, is the oldest and busiest of A Coruña's top hotels. A favorite with business folk and families, it has large rooms with modern wood furnishings and bright upholstery. Ask for a room overlooking the bay. **Pros:** port and city views; helpful staff; good leisure activities. **Cons:** inconvenient outdoor parking; unimpressive breakfast. ✉ *Paseo del Parrote 2* ☎ *981/205400* 🌐 *www.hesperia-finisterre.com* 🛏 *92 rooms*

In-room: Wi-Fi. In-hotel: restaurant, bar, tennis courts, pools, gym *AE, DC, MC, V.*

NIGHTLIFE

Begin your evening in the **Plaza de María Pita**—cafés and tapas bars proliferate off its western corners and inland. **Calles Franja, Riego de Agua, Barrera,** and **Galera** and the **Plaza del Humor** have many bars, some of which serve Ribeiro wine in bowls. Night owls head for the posh and pricey clubs around **Praia del Orzán** (Orzán Beach), particularly along Calle Juan Canalejo. For lower-key entertainment, the old town has cozy taverns. Try **A Roda 2** (✉ *Capitán Troncoso 8* ☎ *981/228671*) for tapas (such as octopus in its own ink and garlic garbanzo beans) and a lively evening crowd.

SHOPPING

Calle Real has boutiques with contemporary fashions. A stroll down **Calle San Andrés,** two blocks inland from Calle Real, or **Avenida Juan Flórez,** leading into the newer town, may yield some sartorial treasures. Galicia has spawned some of Spain's top designers, notably **Adolfo Dominguez** (✉ *Av. Finisterre 3* ☎ *981/252539*). For hats and Galician folk clothing, stop into **Sastrería Iglesias** (✉ *Rúa Rego do Auga 14* ☎ *981/221634*)—founded in 1864—where artisan José Luis Iglesias Rodrígues sells his textiles. Authentic Galician *zuecos* (hand-painted wooden clogs) are still worn in some villages to navigate mud; the cobbler **José López Rama** (✉ *Rúa do Muiño 7* ☎ *981/701068*) has a workshop 15 minutes south of A Coruña in the village of Carballo.The glazed terra-cotta ceramics from Bunho, 40 km (25 mi) west of A Coruña on C552, are prized by aficionados—to see where they're made, drive out to Bunho itself, where potters work in private studios all over town. Stop in to **Alfarería y Cerámica de Buño** (✉ *C. Barreiros s/n, Bunho* ☎ *981/721658*) to see the results.A wide selection of classic blue-and-white pottery is sold at **Cerámicas del Castro** (✉ *O Castro s/n, Sada* ☎ *981/620200*), north of Coruña in Sada.

BETANZOS

★ *25 km (15 mi) east of A Coruña, 65 km (40 mi) northeast of Santiago.*

The charming, slightly ramshackle medieval town of Betanzos is still surrounded by parts of its old city wall. It was an important Galician port in the 13th century but is now silted up.

ESSENTIALS

Visitor Information Betanzos (✉ *Pr. Irmáns García Naveira s/n* ☎ *981/776666*).

EXPLORING

The 1292 monastery of **San Francisco** was converted into a church in 1387 by the nobleman Fernán Perez de Andrade, whose magnificent sepulchre, to the left of the west door, has him lying on the backs of a stone bear and boar, with hunting dogs at his feet and an angel receiving his soul by his head. The 15th-century church of **Santa María de Azougue, a few steps uphill,** has Renaissance statues that were stolen in 1981

A Coruña is a major port town, but fashionistas might know it as where the first Zara clothing shop opened, back in 1975.

but subsequently recovered. The tailors' guild put up the Gothic-style church of **Santiago**, which includes a Door of Glory inspired by the one in Santiago's cathedral. Above the door is a carving of St. James as the Slayer of the Moors.

VIVEIRO

★

The once-turreted city walls of this popular summer resort are still partially intact. Two festivals are noteworthy here: the **Semana Santa** processions, when penitents follow religious processions on their knees, and the **Rapa das Bestas**, a colorful roundup of wild horses the first Sunday in July (on nearby Monte Buyo).

ESSENTIALS

Visitor Information Viveiro (✉ *Avda. Ramón Canosa s/n* ☎ *982/560879*).

WHERE TO EAT AND STAY

$$$ **Hotel Ego.** The view of the *ría* from this hilltop hotel outside Viveiro is unbeatable, and every room has one. The glassed-in breakfast room also faces the *ría,*as well as a cascade of trees; on a rainy day, you'd much rather be cooped up here than in town. Adjoining the hotel is the elegant Nito restaurant ($$–$$$$), which serves excellent Galician cuisine, such as *percebes* (gooseneck barnacles), spider crab, and lobster. **Pros:** hilltop views; relaxing public areas and spa. **Cons:** lacks distinctive character; airport terminal facade. ✉ *Playa de Area, off N642* ☎ *982/560987* *29 rooms* *In-room: Wi-Fi. In-hotel: restaurant, bar* *AE, MC, V.*

A perfect day at Castro beach in Ribadeo

OFF THE BEATEN PATH

Distinctive blue-and-white-glazed contemporary ceramics are made at **Cerámica de Sargadelos** (✉ *Ctra. Paraño s/n, Cervo* ☎ *982/557841*), 21 km (13 mi) east of Viveiro. Watch artisans work weekdays 8:30–12:30 and 2:30–5:30. Shop hours are 11–2 and 4–7 on weekends and holidays.

RIBADEO

50 km (31 mi) southeast of Viveiro.

Perched on the broad *ría* of the same name, Ribadeo is the last coastal town before Asturias. The views up and across the estuary are marvelous—depending on the wind, the waves appear to roll *across* the ría rather than straight inland. Salmon and trout fishermen congregate upriver.

ESSENTIALS

Visitor Information Ribadeo (✉ *Pl. de España* ☎ *982/128689*).

WHERE TO EAT AND STAY

$$$ **Parador de Ribadeo.** Most rooms have glassed-in sitting areas with views (Room 208 has the best) across the *ría* to Asturias. Parquet floors and harvest-yellow walls are accented by watercolors of the area. In the dining room ($$–$$$$) a cornucopia of shellfish is served, much of it swimming around in a holding tank before you make your selection. Try the *sopa de mariscos (*seafood soup with a pastry top) and the ice cream flavored with Tetilla cheese and drizzled with honey. Fishing, horseback riding, and boating can be arranged. **Pros:** balconies in rooms; *ría* views; tasty seafood. **Cons:** rooms are smallish; restaurant opens at

9 PM. ✉ *Amador Fernández 7* ☎ *982/128825* 🌐 *www.parador.es* ⇨ *46 rooms, 1 suite* ♨ *In-hotel: restaurant, bar* ▭ *AE, DC, MC, V.*

ASTURIAS

As you cross into the Principality of Asturias, the intensely green countryside continues, belying the fact that this is a major mining region once exploited by the Romans for its iron and gold-rich earth. Asturias is bordered to the southeast by the imposing Picos de Europa, which are best accessed via the scenic coastal towns of Llanes or Ribadesella.

LUARCA

4

75 km (47 mi) east of Ribadeo, 92 km (57 mi) northeast of Oviedo.

The village of Luarca is tucked into a cove at the end of a final twist of the Río Negro, with a fishing port and, to the west, a sparkling bay. The town is a maze of cobblestone streets, stone stairways, and whitewashed houses, with a harborside decorated with painted flowerpots.

ESSENTIALS

Visitor Information Luarca (✉ *Calle Caleros 11* ☎ *985/640083*).

WHERE TO EAT AND STAY

$$–$$$$ SPANISH ★ ✕ **Casa Consuelo.** Four miles west of Luarca in Otur, which has a delightful beach, Casa Consuelo is one of the most popular spots on Spain's northern coast. It first opened in 1935 and is famed for *merluza* (hake) served with the northern Spanish delicacy *angulas* (baby eels) and blue cheese (about €55 for two, depending on market prices). This dish and the busy restaurant itself, whose name means "house of comfort," are not to be missed; portions are generous. ✉ *Ctra. N634, Km 511, 6 km (4 mi) west of Luarca, Otur* ☎ *985/641809* 🌐 *www.casaconsuelo.com* ✍ *Reservations essential* ▭ *AE, DC, MC, V* ⊙ *Closed Mon.*

$–$$$ SEAFOOD ✕ **El Barómetro.** In a 19th-century building decorated with an ornate barometer to gauge the famously unpredictable local weather, this small, family-run seafood eatery in the middle of the harborfront has an inexpensive *menú del día* (daily menu) and a good choice of local fresh fish, including *calamares* (squid) and *espárragos rellenos de erizo de mar* (asparagus stuffed with sea urchins). For a bit more money, you can dig into *bogavante,* a large-claw lobster. For dessert, the cheesecake is highly rated. ✉ *Paseo del Muelle 4* ☎ *985/470662* ▭ *MC, V* ⊙ *Closed late Sept.–late Oct. No dinner Wed.*

$$ 🏨 **Hotel Villa La Argentina.** This charming Asturian mansion on the hill above Luarca was built in 1899 by a wealthy Indiano (a Spaniard who made his fortune in South America). On-site are a small antiques museum and an old coach house, surrounded by palm trees and imported shrubs. You can choose between the newly constructed apartments in the garden or the Belle Epoque suites in the main building, one of which has a pleasant glassed-in reading room. **Pros:** friendly staff; lovely gardens; peace and quiet. **Cons:** a short walk from town. ✉ *Villar de Luarca s/n* ☎ *985/640102* 🌐 *www.villalaargentina.com* ⇨ *9*

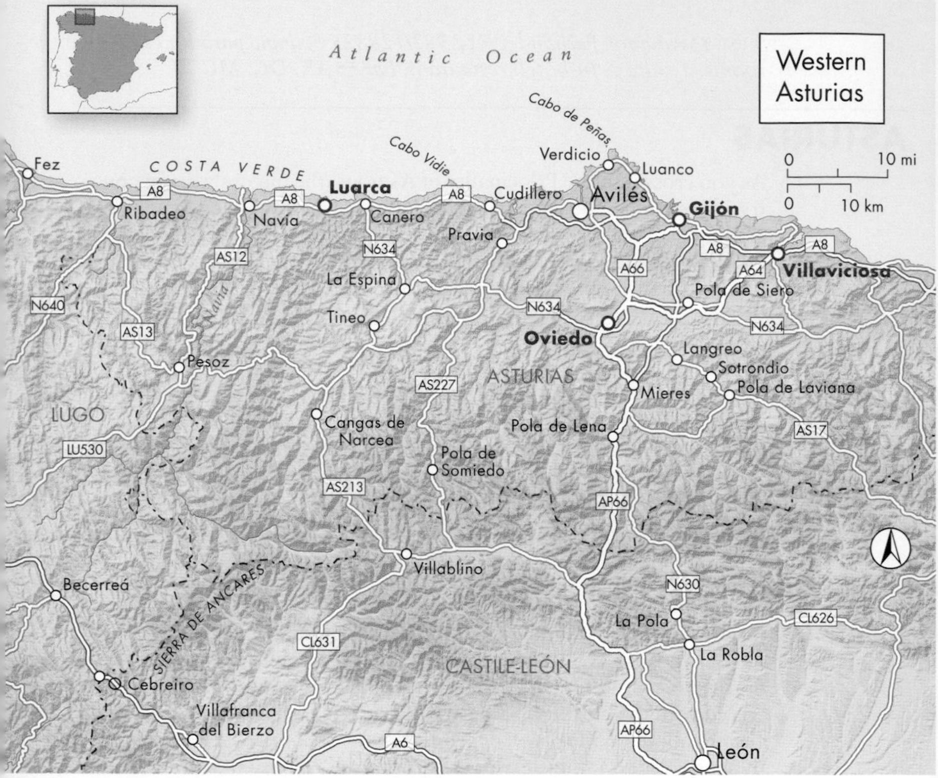

rooms, 3 suites ♿ *In-room: Wi-Fi. In-hotel: restaurant, bar, tennis court, pool* ▭ *DC, MC, V* ⊙ *Closed early Jan.–mid-Mar.*

EN ROUTE

The coastal road leads to the little fishing village of **Cudillero** (35 km [22 mi] east of Luarca), clustered around its tiny port. The emerald green of the surrounding hills, the bright blue of the water, and the white of the houses make this village one of the prettiest in Asturias. Seafood and cider restaurants line the central street that turns into a boat ramp at the bottom of town.

OVIEDO

92 km (57 mi) southeast of Luarca, 50 km (31 mi) southeast of Cudillero, 30 km (19 mi) south of Gijón.

Inland, the Asturian countryside starts to look more prosperous. Wooden, thatch-roof horreos (granaries) strung with golden bundles of drying corn replace the stark granite sheds of Galicia. A drive through the hills and valleys brings you to the capital city, Oviedo. Though primarily industrial, Oviedo has three of the most famous pre-Romanesque churches in Spain and a large university, giving it both ancient charm and youthful zest. Start your explorations with the two exquisite 9th-century chapels outside the city, on the slopes of Monte Naranco.

GETTING HERE AND AROUND

Oviedo is served by the A66 tollway, which links to Gijón and Avilés, where you can get on the A8 west to A Coruña or east toward Santander. Madrid is reached on the N630 south.

There are several buses per day to Gijón (30 minutes) and to Santiago and A Coruña (5 hours). Madrid is 5½ hours away by rail from Oviedo's RENFE station, situated on Calle Uría. The FEVE service operates across the north coast, with Gijón easily reached in half an hour and Bilbao just under eight hours away.

Local buses operate along the main arteries of Oviedo, between the rail station and shopping areas, but skirt around the rim of the historical center, where Oviedo's oldest buildings are clustered in the labyrinth of streets around the Plaza Alfonso. Considering the short distances, walking is the best option, though taxis are inexpensive.

ESSENTIALS

Bus and Train Station (✉ *Cl. Pepe Cosmen s/n* ☎ *901/499949*).

Visitor Information (✉ *Calle Uría*).

EXPLORING

★ The church of **Santa María del Naranco**, with superb views, and its plainer sister, **San Miguel de Lillo** (275 meters uphill), are the jewels of an early architectural style called Asturian pre-Romanesque, a more primitive, hulking, defensive line that preceded Romanesque architecture by nearly three centuries. Commissioned as part of a summer palace by King Ramiro I when Oviedo was the capital of Christian Spain, these masterpieces have survived for more than 1,000 years. The **Reception Center** (☎ *985/114901* ⏲ *Wed.–Mon. 11–1:30 and 4–6*) near the site provides videos that explain the architecture. ✉ *Ctra. de los Monumentos, 2 km (1 mi) north of Oviedo* ☎ *676/032087* 🎫 *€2.20 (includes guided tour), free Mon. (without guided tour)* ⏲ *Apr.–Sept., Tues.–Sat. 9:30–1 and 3:30–7, Sun. and Mon. 9:30–1; Oct.–Mar., Tues.–Sat. 10–12:30 and 3–4:30, Sun. and Mon. 10–12:30.*

Oviedo's Gothic **cathedral** was built between the 14th and the 16th centuries around the city's most cherished monument, the **Cámara Santa** (Holy Chamber). King Ramiro's predecessor, Alfonso the Chaste (792–842), built it to hide the treasures of Christian Spain during the struggle with the Moors. Damaged during the Spanish civil war, it has since been rebuilt. Inside is the gold-leaf **Cross of the Angels,** commissioned by Alfonso in 808 and encrusted with pearls and jewels. On the left is the more elegant **Victory Cross,** actually a jeweled sheath crafted in 908 to cover the oak cross used by Pelayo in the battle of Covadonga. ✉ *Pl. Alfonso II El Casto* ☎ *985/221033* 🎫 *Cathedral free, Cámara Santa and Museum €3.50* ⏲*, July–Sept., weekdays 10:15–7:15, Sat. 10:15–5:15. Oct.–June, weekdays 10–1 and 4–6; Sun. for mass only, at 10* AM *and 11* AM.

Across the Plaza Alfonso is the still-inhabited 15th-century **Palacio de la Rúa**, the oldest palace in town. Behind the cathedral, the **Museo Arqueológico,** housed in the splendid Monastery of San Vicente, contains fragments of pre-Romanesque buildings. ✉ *San Vicente 3* ☎ *985/215405* 🎫 *Free* ⏲ *Tues.–Sat. 10–1:30 and 4–6, Sun. 11–1.*

WHERE TO EAT AND STAY

$$$–$$$$ SPANISH ★ **Casa Fermín**. Skylights, plants, and an air of modernity belie the age of this sophisticated restaurant, which opened in 1924. Founder Luis Gil introduced traditional Asturian cuisine at seminars around the world. Specialties include *pulpo rustido con crema de patata, ajos frecos y aceite de perejil* (roasted octopus with creamed potatoes, fresh garlic, and parsley oil), *caramelos de morcilla con salsa de cerezas* (caramelized black pudding with cherry sauce), and wild game in season. If you're feeling adventurous, wash it all down with a Bloody Mary *con berberechos* (with cockles). *Calle San Francisco 8* *985/216452* *AE, DC, MC, V* *Closed Sun.*

$$ SPANISH ★ **La Máquina**. For the best *fabada* (bean-and-sausage stew) in Asturias, head 6 km (4 mi) outside Oviedo toward Avilés and stop at the farmhouse with the miniature locomotive out front. The creamy fava beans of the signature dish are heaped with delicious hunks of morcilla sausage, chorizo, and Tocino ham. To leave without trying the *arroz con leche* (rice pudding), though, would be imponderable. The simple, whitewashed dining room has attracted diners from across Spain for decades, some of whom think nothing of making a weekend trip just to eat here. *Av. Conde de Santa Bárbara 59, Lugones* *985/263636* *DC, MC, V* *Closed Sun. and mid-June–mid-July. No dinner.*

$$$ **Barceló Oviedo Cervantes**. A playful revamp of this town house in the city center has seen a neo-Moorish–style portico added to the original latticed facade, while public areas have a quirky, informal feel. Delicious seafood from the Bay of Biscay is served in the restaurant. To soak up the luxury, ask for a room with an in-bath home entertainment system. **Pros:** helpful and amiable staff; playful art and design features; central location close to rail station. **Cons:** uninteresting views; confusing light switches. *Cervantes 13* *985/255000* *www.barcelo.com* *72 rooms* *In-hotel: restaurant, bar, Wi-Fi hotspot, parking (paid)* *AE, DC, MC, V.*

$$$$ Fodor's Choice ★ **Hotel de la Reconquista**. An 18th-century hospice emblazoned with a huge stone coat of arms, the ultraluxurious Reconquista costs almost twice as much as any other hotel in Asturias and is by far the most distinguished hotel in Oviedo. The wide lobby, encircled by Doric pillars and an oak balcony, is decked out with velvet upholstery and 18th-century paintings. Guest rooms are large and modern, with comfortable beds and large armchairs. **Pros:** enormous rooms; palatial public areas; historic feel. **Cons:** expensive; poorly lit rooms; ambience can be rather haughty. *Calle Gil de Jaz 16* *985/241100* *www.hoteldelareconquista.com* *132 rooms, 10 suites* *In-room: Wi-Fi. In-hotel: restaurant, bar* *AE, DC, MC, V.*

NIGHTLIFE AND THE ARTS

The old town's main strip of dance clubs is on **Calle Canóniga**. A rather rowdy town after dark, Oviedo has plenty in the way of loud live music. **Calle Carta Puebla** is packed with pubs, many of which are Irish, owing to the region's Celtic heritage.

SHOPPING

Some antiques shops are clustered together for a few blocks on **Calle de Mon**. On Thursday and Sunday mornings a colorful outdoor market, **El Rastrillo**, is held in El Fontan.Shops throughout the city carry **azabache jewelry** made of jet. For handcrafted leather bags and belts, check out **Artesania Escanda** (✉ *Jovellanos 5* ☎ *985/210467*). Vacuum-packed *fabada* is sold at **Casa Veneranda** (✉ *Melquíades Álvarez 23* ☎ *985/212454*).

GIJÓN

30 km (19 mi) north of Oviedo.

Gijón is part fishing port, part summer resort, and part university town. It's packed with cafés.

ESSENTIALS

Visitor Information Gijón (✉ *Calle Rodriguez San Pedro s/n* ☎ *985/341771*).

EXPLORING

The promenade along **Praia San Lorenzo** extends from one end of town to the other. Across the narrow peninsula and the Plaza Mayor is the harbor, where the fishing fleet comes in with the day's catch.The steep peninsula is the old fishermen's quarter, **Cimadevilla**, now the hub of Gijón's nightlife. From the park at the highest point on the headland, beside Basque artist Eduardo Chillida's massive sculpture *Elogio del Horizonte* (In Praise of the Horizon), there's a panoramic view of the coast and city.

Termas Romanas (Roman baths*)*, dating to the time of Augustus, are under the plaza at the end of the beach. ✉ *Campo Valdés* ☎ *985/185151* 🎫 *€2.40* ⏲ *Tues.–Sat. 9:30–2 and 5–7:30, weekends 10–2 and 5–7:30.*

The **Museo de la Gaita** (Bagpipe Museum*)* is across the river on the eastern edge of town, past Parque Isabel la Católica. A collection of bagpipes from all over the world is augmented by workshops where you can see the instruments crafted. ✉ *Paseo del Doctor Fleming 877, La Güelga s/n* ☎ *985/182960* 🎫 *€2.35* ⏲ *Sept.–June, Tues.–Sat. 10–1 and 5–8, Sun. 11–2 and 5–7; July and Aug., Tues.–Sat. 11–1 and 5–7, Sun. 11–2 and 5–8.*

WHERE TO EAT AND STAY

$$$–$$$$ SPANISH ✕ **El Puerto.** This glass-enclosed dining room overlooks the harbor and serves fine, imaginative shellfish, seafood, and meats. Locals claim that the best meals in Gijón are to be had here, and the *merluza con bogavante en salsa verde* (hake and lobster with a parsley sauce) is a house specialty, though if you're really hungry, try the four-plate menu or *parillada de mariscos* (mixed grilled shellfish); El Puerto prides itself on its Cantabrian catch. Game is also served in season, and the wine list is substantial. ✉ *Calle Claudio Alvargonzález* ☎ *985/349096* ✍ *Reservations essential* 💳 *AE, DC, MC, V* ⏲ *No dinner Sun.*

$$$ 🏨 **Parador de Gijón.** In an old water mill in a park not far from the San Lorenzo Beach, this parador is one of the simplest and friendliest in Spain. Rooms in the newer wing are small, with wood floors and pine shutters, but most have wonderful views over the lake or the park. In the restaurant ($–$$$), try the caldereta de marisco (an aromatic seafood stew made with crab, lobster, and shrimp), chopa a la sidra (sea chub cooked in cider), or tigres (spicy stuffed mussels). For dessert, try fresh figs (in season) with pungent Cabrales cheese. **Pros:** park views; friendly staff; great food. **Cons:** austere guest rooms; badly thought-out bathrooms; difficult to find. ✉ *Calle Torcuato Fernández Miranda 15* ☎ *985/370511* 🌐 *www.parador.es* *40 rooms* *In-hotel: restaurant, Wi-Fi hotspot* ▭ *AE, DC, MC, V.*

EN ROUTE

East of Gijón is apple-orchard country, source of the famous hard cider of Asturias. Rolling green hills, grazing cows, and white chalets make a remarkably Alpine landscape.

VILLAVICIOSA

32 km (20 mi) east of Gijón, 45 km (28 mi) northeast of Oviedo.

Cider-capital Villaviciosa has a large dairy and several bottling plants as well as an attractive old quarter. The Hapsburg Emperor Charles V first set foot in Spain just down the road from here. The town's annual five-day Fiesta de la Manzana (Apple Festival) begins the first Friday after September 8.

ESSENTIALS

Visitor Information Villaviciosa (✉ *Parque Vallina* ☎ *985/891759*).

EXPLORING

To taste the regional hard cider, stop into **El Congreso** (✉ *Pl. Generalísimo 25* ☎ *No phone*), a popular *sidrería* (cider house) that also serves tasty tapas and shellfish straight from the tank.

WHERE TO STAY

$ **Carlos I.** Right in the pedestrian heart of the *casco antiguo* (old town), this late-17th-century mansion is loaded with character. From the crests emblazoned on the facade to the wood floors, antique furniture, plants, and oil paintings, not to mention the cozy, tile-floored bar-cafeteria, the Carlos I is a local classic, and relatively cheap as well. Guest rooms are spotless and comparatively large. **Pros:** great location; oozes historical character; clean and tidy. **Cons:** old bath facilities; noisy in morning. ✉ *Pl. Carlos I 4* ☎ *985/890121* 📠 *985/890051* *16 rooms* *In-hotel: bar* ▭ *MC, V.*

RIBADESELLA

67 km (40 mi) east of Gijón, 84 km (50 mi) northeast of Oviedo.

The N632 twists around green hills dappled with eucalyptus groves, allowing glimpses of the sea and sandy beaches below and the snow-capped Picos de Europa looming inland. This fishing village and beach resort is famous for its seafood, its cave, and the canoe races held on the Sella River the first Saturday of August.

ESSENTIALS

Visitor Information Ribadesella (✉ *C. Marqueses de Argüelles s/n* ☎ *985/860038* ⏲ *Closed Mon.*).

DID YOU KNOW?

Gijón is a popular stop for travelers in Asturias: it's a large port city with a bit of everything, including a popular summer beach and lots of cafés.

Villaviciosa, home to the Church of San Salvador de Valdediós, is best known as the cider capital of the region.

EXPLORING

Discovered in 1968 by Señor Bustillo, the **Cueva Tito Bustillo** (Tito Bustillo Cave) has 20,000-year-old paintings on par with those in Lascaux, France, and Altamira. Giant horses and deer prance about the walls. To protect the paintings, no more than 375 visitors are allowed inside each day. The guided tour is in Spanish. There's also a museum of Asturian cave finds open year-round. ☎ *985/861120* 🌐 *www.titobustillo.com* 🎟 *€4* ⏲ *Museum and cave Apr.–Sept., Wed.–Sun. 10–4:30.*

LLANES

40 km (25 mi) east of Ribadesella.

This sprightly beach town is on a pristine stretch of the Costa Verde. The shores in both directions outside town have vistas of cliffs looming over white-sand beaches and isolated caves. Inland, the landscape rises impessively into the mountains of the Sierra de Cuera, which provides a scenic shortcut to Arenas de Cabrales and the Picos de Europa via the N7 road.

ESSENTIALS

Visitor Information Llanes (✉ *Calle La Torre, Alfonso IX s/n* ☎ *985/400164*).

EXPLORING

The peaceful, well-conserved **Plaza Cristo Rey** marks the center of the old town, partially surrounded by the remains of its medieval walls. The 13th-century church of **Santa María** rises over the square. Nearby, off Calle Alfonso IX, a medieval tower houses the tourist office. A long canal, connected to a small harbor, cuts through the heart of Llanes, and along its banks rise colorful houses with glass galleries against a backdrop of the Picos de Europa. At the daily portside fish market, usually held around 1 PM, vendors display heaping mounds of freshly caught seafood. Steps from the old town is **Playa del Sablón**, a little swath of sand that gets crowded on summer weekends. On the eastern edge of town is the larger **Playa de Toró**. Just 1 km (½ mi) east of Llanes is one of the area's most secluded beaches, the immaculate **Playa Ballota**, with private coves for picnicking and one of the few stretches of nudist sand in Asturias. West of Llanes, the most pleasant beaches lie between the towns of Barro and Celorio.

CIDER HOUSE RULES

In order to aerate the cider, cider houses generally insist that either you or your waiter pour it from overhead to a glass held at knee level. This process is called the *escancio* (pouring), a much-valued skill around which entire tournaments are held. Give it a try; spilling is allowed. The region's main cider center is in Villaviciosa.

4

Dotting the Asturian coast east and west of Llanes are *bufones* (blowholes), cave-like cavities that expel water when waves are sucked in. Active blowholes shoot streams of water as high as 100 feet into the air; unfortunately, it's hard to predict when this will happen, as it depends on the tide and the size of the surf. They are clearly marked so you can find them, and there are barriers to protect you when they expel water. There's a blowhole east of Playa Ballota; try to watch it in action from the **Mirador Panorámico La Boriza**, near the entrance to the golf course. If you miss it, the view is still worth a stop—on a clear day you can see the coastline all the way east to Santander.

WHERE TO EAT AND STAY

$–$$ SEAFOOD ✕ **La Casa del Mar.** Llanes has prettier, cleaner, and less noisy places to enjoy seafood, but if you fancy rubbing shoulders with Asturian fishermen and eating their catch cooked just the way they like it, then this spot by the port, guarded by a parrot named Paco, is for you. The glassed-in terrace has a view of the small harbor bobbing with boats, and the menu offers such simple local treats as baby squid in ink, spider crab, seafood meatballs, and razor clams, all with a minimum of fuss but maximum value. ✉ *Plaza Magdalena Muelle s/n, Calle Marinero* ☎ *985/401205.*

$$$ **La Posada de Babel.** This exquisite family-run inn just outside Llanes stands among oak, chestnut, and birch trees on the edge of the Sierra de Cuera. There is some unusual architecture, including a granary converted into a guestroom but expect plenty of personal attention and roaring fires in the public rooms. **Pros:** extremely amiable staff; comfy base for hiking. **Cons:** slippery stairs to certain rooms; closed in winter. ✉ *La Pereda s/n* ☎ *985/402525* 🌐 *www.laposadadebabel.com* *13 rooms* *In-hotel: restaurant, bar, bicycles, Wi-Fi hotspot* *DC, MC, V* *Closed Nov.–Feb.*

THE PICOS DE EUROPA

With craggy peaks soaring up to the 8,688-foot Torre Cerredo, the northern skyline of the Picos de Europa has helped seafarers and fishermen navigate the Bay of Biscay for ages. To the south, pilgrims on their way to Santiago enjoy distant but inspiring views of the snowcapped range from the plains of Castile between Burgos and León. Over the years, regular, very heavy rain and snow have created canyons plunging 3,000 feet, natural arches, caves, and sinkholes (one of which is 5,213 feet deep).

The Picos de Europa National Park, covering 646.6 square km (250 square mi), is perfect for climbers and trekkers: you can explore the main trails, hang glide, ride horses, cycle, or canoe. There are two adventure-sports centers in Cangas de Onís, near the Roman Bridge.

CANGAS DE ONÍS

25 km (16 mi) south of Ribadesella, 70 km (43 mi) east of Oviedo.

The first capital of Christian Spain, Cangas de Onís is also the unofficial capital of the Picos de Europa National Park. Partly in the narrow valley carved by the Sella River, it has the feel of a mountain village.

ESSENTIALS

Visitor Information Cangas de Onís (✉ *Calle Camila Beceña 1* ☎ *985/848005*).

EXPLORING

A high, humpback **medieval bridge** (also known as the Puente Romano, or Roman Bridge, because of its style) spans the Sella River gorge with a reproduction of Pelayo's Victory Cross, or La Cruz de la Victoria, dangling underneath.To help plan your rambles, consult the scale model of the park outside the **Picos de Europa visitor center** (✉ *Casa Dago, Av. Covadonga 43* ☎ *985/848614*). The store opposite (at No. 22), El Llagar, sells maps and guidebooks, a few in English.

WHERE TO EAT AND STAY

$–$$$ SPANISH ✕ **Sidrería Los Arcos.** This busy tavern on one of the town's main squares has lots of polished wood and serves local cider, fine Spanish wines, and sizzling T-bone steaks. The mouth-watering selection of *tapas* includes *revuelto de morcilla* (scrambled eggs with blood sausage), which is served on *torto de maíz* (a corn pastry base), and *pulpo de pedreu sobre crema fina de patata, oricios y germinados ecologicos* (octopus with creamed potato, sea urchins, and bean sprouts). ✉ *Pl. del Ayuntamiento, enter on Av. Covadonga* ☎ *985/849277* ▭ *AE, MC, V* ⊙ *Closed Feb.*

$$ 🏨 **Aultre Naray.** This 19th-century mansion overlooking the Escapa mountain range is a rare find. It's perfectly placed for hiking, camping, canoeing, and swimming (which the staff can help organize). Despite the wooden beams and many original features, it's not rustic—guest rooms have modern furniture, plenty of light, and, in some cases, pleasant sitting rooms. The hotel is 15 km (9 mi) east of town. **Pros:** fine base for outdoor activities; great views. **Cons:** a bit of a hike from

A GOOD TOUR: THE PICOS DE EUROPA

The best-known road trip in the Picos connects **Cangas de Onís** and **Riaño** along the twisting Sella River Gorge. Part of this trip is along the **Ruta de los Beyos** through the Beyo Canyon, on the N625 road. It's a two-hour drive up to the pass at **Puerto del Pontón** (Pontón Pass; 4,232 feet). Just beyond the pass, turn left (northeast) and drive up to the **Puerto de Panderruedas** (4,757 feet) for a panoramic view of the peaks, especially in the early evening sun. From here you can descend northeast to the town of Posada de Valdeón and continue to Caín for a look at the famous Ruta del Cares. Another drive, beginning from Cangas de Onís, takes you up past Covadonga to Lakes Enol and Ercina on the AS262.

For the **Ruta del Cares,** drive east on the AS114 from **Cangas de Onís** toward **Panes,** stopping just before **Arenas de Cabrales** at the *mirador* (lookout) onto the **Naranjo de Bulnes,** a huge tooth of rock way up in the peaks. The mountain was named for its occasional tendency to glow orange (*naranja)* at sunrise and sunset. At **Arenas de Cabrales** turn south onto the AS264 road to reach **Poncebos**, where you can leave the car for the four-hour Ruta de Cares walk to **Caín** through the **Garganta de Cares** gorge. The canyon presents itself fairly soon, so you can turn back without pangs if you don't want to make the full hike. This route is popular, so arrive in Poncebos early in the day to avoid parking problems.

If you have another day, leave **Cangas** and drive via **Panes** and **Potes** to the eastern, Cantabrian portion of the park, where you can stay at the **Parador de Fuente Dé.** South of Panes, turn right at **Urdón**'s hydroelectric power station to **Tresviso** for unforgettable views and a chance to buy some local cheese. South of **La Hermida** on the N621 the **Garganta de La Hermida** cuts through sheer 600-foot limestone cliffs up to **Potes**.

West of **Potes** off the CA185 is the **Monasterio de Santo Toribio de Liébana,** with a 13th-century Gothic church and 17th-century cloisters. The CA185 ends at **Fuente Dé**, where a cable car can whisk you to the top of the Picos. South of **Potes** the N621 continues to Riaño, a two-hour drive. About halfway there, **Puerta de San Glorio** is the jumping-off point for the 2.2-km (1.3-mi) walk up to the Monumento al Oso, where a white stone bear marks another splendid view.

Cangas. ✉ *N634, Km 335, Peruyes* ☎ *985/840808* 🌐 *www.aultrenaray.com* ⇆ *10 rooms* ♨ *In-hotel: restaurant, bar, Wi-Fi hotspot* ▭ *DC, MC, V.*

¢ 🏨 **La Naturaleza**. The name means "nature," and this hotel, poised among ancient chestnuts at the foot of the Ruta del Cares and enjoying views of Arenas de Cabrales and the Sella River, is surrounded by its namesake, in glorious abundance. The location, at one of the main gateways into the Picos de Europa, is ideal, and the six bright, comfy rooms all have large, clean bathrooms. There's a welcoming cozy fireplace in the lounge. **Pros:** nice vistas; pleasant wooden balconies; comfortable and cozy throughout. **Cons:** only six rooms; doesn't accept credit cards. ✉ *Calle La Segada* ☎ *985/846487* 📠 *985/846101* 🛏 *6 rooms* 🖒 *In-room: no a/c. In-hotel: restaurant, bar* 💳 *No credit cards* ⏲ *Closed Dec. and Jan.*

$$$ ★ **Parador de Cangas de Onís**. On the banks of the Sella River just west of Cangas, this friendly parador is part 8th-century Benedictine monastery and part modern wing: the older building has 11 period-style rooms. Excellent local dishes ($$–$$$), such as *merluza del Cantabrica a la sidra* (hake cooked in cider) garnished with asparagus, are served in the dining room. **Pros:** helpful staff; gorgeous riverside location with mountain views; oodles of history. **Cons:** limited menu; chilly corridors. ✉ *Monasterio de San Pedro de Villanueva, Ctra. N624, from N634, take right turn for Villanueva* ☎ *985/849402* 🌐 *www.parador.es* 🛏 *64 rooms* 🖒 *In-hotel: restaurant, bar* 💳 *AE, DC, MC, V.*

COVADONGA

14 km (9 mi) southeast of Cangas de Onís.

To see high alpine meadowland, some rare Spanish lakes, and views over the peaks and out to sea (if the mist ever disperses), take the narrow road up past Covadonga to **Lake Enol,** stopping for the view en route. Starting to the right of the lake, a three-hour walk takes in views from the **Mirador del Rey,** where you can find the grave of pioneering climber Pedro Pidal. Farther up the road from Lake Enol are a summer-only tourist office and **Lake Ercina,** where Pope John Paul II picnicked during his 1989 tour of Asturias and Galicia.

ESSENTIALS

Visitor Information Covadonga (✉ *Av. Covadonga s/n, Pl. del Ayuntamiento* ☎ *985/846035*).

EXPLORING

NEED A BREAK?

Near Lake Enol is the Restaurante el Casín (✉ *Ctra. Santander–Oviedo s/n, Ribadesella* ☎ *985/860231*), with a small terrace bar overlooking the mountains and the lake. The set menu is €9; à la carte options include roasts and restorative *fabada* stews. It's closed January and February.

★ Covadonga's **shrine** is considered the birthplace of Spain. Here, in 718, a handful of sturdy Asturian Christians led by Don Pelayo took refuge in the Cave of St. Mary, about halfway up a cliff, where they prayed to the Virgin Mary to give them strength to turn back the Moors. Pelayo and his followers resisted the superior Moorish forces and set up a Christian kingdom that eventually led to the Reconquest. The cave has an 18th-century statue of the Virgin and Don Pelayo's grave. Covadonga itself has a **basilica,** and the **museum** has the treasures donated to the Virgin of the Cave, including a crown studded with more than a thousand diamonds. ☎ *985/846096* 🎫 *€3* ⏲ *Daily 10:30–2 and 4–7:30.*

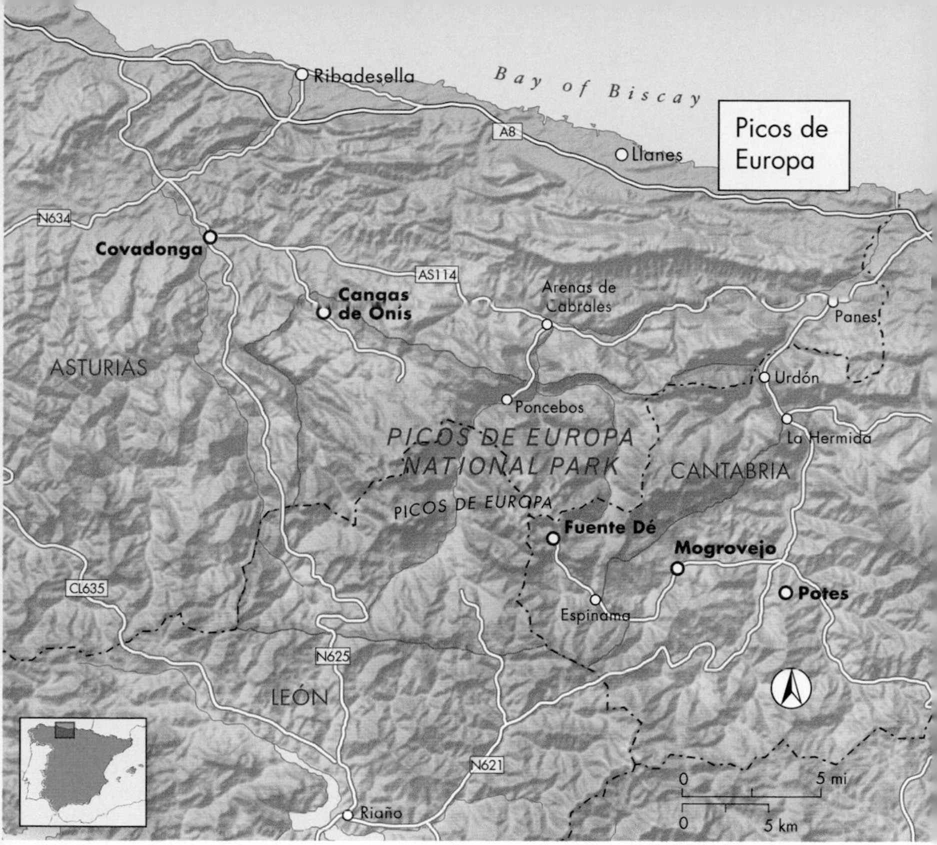

POTES

51 km (31 mi) southwest of San Vicente de la Barquera, 115 km (69 mi) southwest of Santander, 173 km (104 mi) north of Palencia, 81 km (50 mi) southeast of Cangas de Onis.

Known for its fine cheeses made of milk from cows, goats, and sheep, the region of La Liébana is a highland domain well worth exploring. Potes, the area's main city, is named for and sprinkled with ancient bridges and surrounded with the stunning 9th-century **monasteries** of Santo Toribio de Liébana, Lebeña, and Piasca. The gorges of the Desfiladero de la Hermida pass are 3 km (2 mi) north, and the rustic town of Mogrovejo is on the way to the vertiginous cable car at Fuente Dé, 25 km (15 mi) west of Potes.

ESSENTIALS

Visitor Information Potes (✉ *Independencia 30* ☎ *942/730787*).

EXPLORING

As you approach the parador of **Fuente Dé**, at the head of the valley northwest of the hamlet of Espinama you'll see a wall of gray stone rising 6,560 feet straight into the air. Visible at the top is the tiniest of huts: El Mirador del Cable (the cable-car lookout point). Get there via

Hiking in the Picos de Europa

a 2,625-foot funicular (€14 round-trip). At the top, you can hike along the Ávila Mountain pasturelands, rich in wildlife, between the central and eastern massifs of the Picos. There's an official entrance to Picos de Europa National Park here.

WHERE TO EAT AND STAY

$–$$$ SPANISH **El Bodegón**. A simple, friendly, and cozy space awaits behind the ancient stone facade, 200 meters from the main plaza. Part of the house is original, but much has been renovated, providing an attractive combination of traditional mountain design and modern construction. The menu focuses on standard highland comfort food, such as a delicious *cocido montañes* (mountain stew of sausage, garbanzo beans, and vegetables) at a rock-bottom price. The €9 lunch menu is one of the best values for miles around. ✉ *San Roque 4* ☎ *942/730247* 💳 *AE, DC, MC, V* ⏲ *Closed Mon.*

$$$ **Parador de Fuente Dé**. This modern parador is in a valley beside the cable car that ascends a soaring rock face to 2,705 feet in about four minutes. Somewhat spartan, it's a fine no-frills base for serious climbers and walkers and has a good restaurant ($$–$$$) with *cocido lebaniego* (a sturdy local stew) and steaks topped with Cabrales, local blue cheese. The parador is east of the Cantabrian border, 23 km (14 mi) west of Potes. **Pros:** mountainside location; next to cable car; cheap for a parador. **Cons:** simply furnished; limited access in winter snow. ✉ *Fuente Dé* ☎ *942/736651* 🌐 *www.parador.es* *78 rooms* *In-hotel: restaurant, bar, Wi-Fi hotspot* 💳 *AE, DC, MC, V* ⏲ *Closed Dec.–Feb.*

CANTABRIA

Historically part of Old Castile, the province of Cantabria was called Santander until 1984, when it became an autonomous community. The most scenic route from Madrid via Burgos to Santander is the slow but spectacular N62, past the Ebro reservoir. Faster and safer is the N627 from Burgos to Aguilar de Campóo connecting to the A67 freeway down to Santander.

SANTANDER

★ *390 km (242 mi) north of Madrid, 154 km (96 mi) north of Burgos, 116 km (72 mi) west of Bilbao, 194 km (120 miles) northeast of Oviedo.*

One of the great ports on the Bay of Biscay, Santander is surrounded by beaches that are by no means isolated, yet it lacks the package-tour feel of so many Mediterranean resorts. A fire destroyed most of the old town in 1941, so the rebuilt city looks relatively modern, and although it has traditionally been a conservative stronghold loyal to the Spanish state (in contrast to its Basque neighbors), Santander is especially lively in summer, when its summer-university community and music-and-dance festival fill the city with students and performers.

Portus Victoriae, as Santander was then called, was a major port in the 1st-to-4th-century Roman Hispania Ulterior (and even earlier under the aboriginal Cántabros). Commercial life accelerated between the 13th and 16th centuries, but the waning of Spain's naval power and a series of plagues during the reign of Felipe II caused Santander's fortunes to plummet in the late 16th century. Its economy revived after 1778, when Seville's monopoly on trade with the Americas was revoked and Santander entered fully into commerce with the New World. In 1910 the Palacio de la Magdalena was built by popular subscription as a gift to Alfonso XIII and his queen, Victoria Eugenia, lending Santander prestige as one of Spain's royal watering spots.

Santander benefits from promenades and gardens, most of which face the bay. Walk east along the Paseo de Pereda, the main boulevard, to the Puerto Chico, a small yacht harbor. Then follow Avenida Reina Victoria to find the tree-lined park paths above the first of the city's beaches, Playa de la Magdalena. Walk onto the Península de la Magdalena to the Palacio de la Magdalena, today the summer seat of the University of Menéndez y Pelayo. Beyond the Magdalena Peninsula, wealthy locals have built mansions facing the long stretch of shoreline known as El Sardinero, Santander's best beach.

GETTING HERE AND AROUND

Santander itself is easily navigated on foot, but if you're looking to get to El Sardinero beach take the bus from the central urban transport hub at Jardines de Pereda.

ESSENTIALS

Bus Station Santander (✉ *C. Navas de Tolosa s/n* ☎ *942/211995*).

Train Station Santander (✉ *Estación de Santander, C. Rodríguez s/n* ☎ *942/210211*).

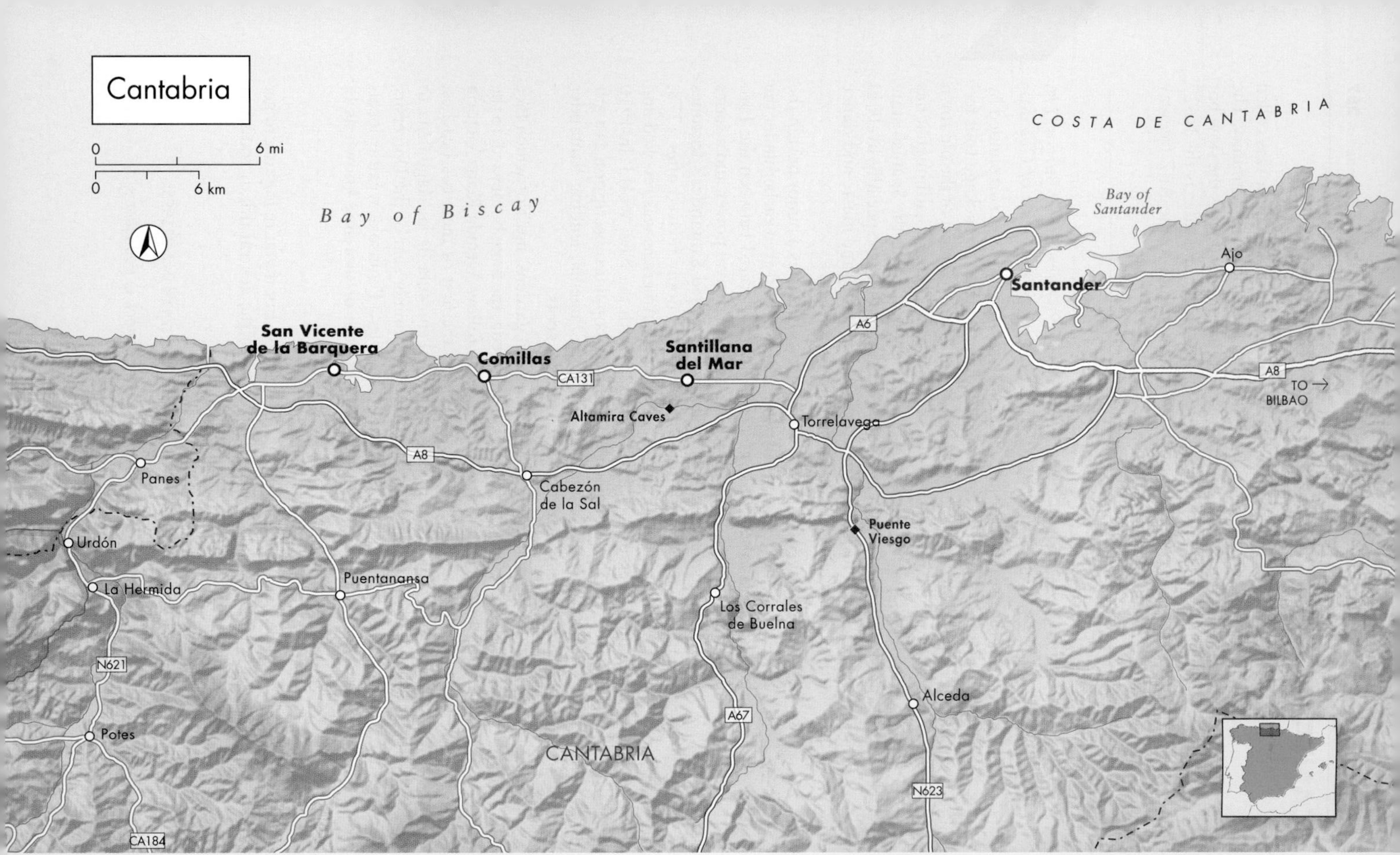
Cantabria
0
6 mi
0
6 km
Bay of Biscay
COSTA DE CANTABRIA
Bay of Santander
Santander
Ajo
A8
TO → BILBAO
A6
San Vicente de la Barquera
Comillas
CA131
Santillana del Mar
Altamira Caves
Torrelavega
A8
Panes
Cabezón de la Sal
Puente Viesgo
Urdón
La Hermida
Puentanansa
Los Corrales de Buelna
N621
Alceda
A67
Potes
CANTABRIA
N623
CA184

Visitor Information Santander (✉ *Jardines de Pereda* ☎ *942/216120* ✉ *Plaza de Velarde 5* ☎ *942/310708*).

EXPLORING

The blockish **Catedral de Santander** marks the transition between Romanesque and Gothic. Though largely rebuilt in the neo-Gothic style after serious damage in the 1941 fire, the cathedral retained its 12th-century crypt. The chief attraction here is the tomb of Marcelino Menéndez y Pelayo (1856 1912), Santander's most famous literary figure. The cathedral is across Avenida de Calvo Sotelo from the Plaza Porticada. ✉ *Somorrostro s/n* ☎ *942/226024* *Free* ⏲ *Weekdays 10–1 and 4–7:30, weekends 8–2 and 4:30–8.*

The **Museo Municipal de Bellas Artes** (Municipal Museum of Fine Arts) has works by Flemish, Italian, and Spanish artists. Goya's portrait of absolutist king Fernando VII is worth seeking out; the smirking face of the lion at the king's feet clues you in to the artist's feelings toward his patron. The same building holds the **Biblioteca Menéndez y Pelayo** (☎ *942/203120*), a library with some 50,000 volumes, and the writer's study, kept as it was in his day. ✉ *C. Rubio s/n* ☎ *942/203123* *Free* ⏲ *Museum Tues.–Fri. 10:15–1 and 5:30–9, Sat. 10–1. Library weekdays 9–2 and 4–9:30, Sat. 9–1:30.*

In the old city, the center of life is the **Plaza Porticada**, officially called the Plaza Velarde. In August this unassuming little square is the seat of Santander's star event, the outdoor International Festival of Music and Dance.

WHERE TO EAT AND STAY

$$–$$$ SPANISH ✕ **Bodega del Riojano**. The paintings on wine-barrel ends that decorate this classic restaurant have given it the nickname Museo Redondo (Round Museum). The building dates back to the 16th century, when it was a wine cellar, which you can see in the heavy wooden beams overhead and the rough and rustic tables. With culinary specialties from La Rioja and fresh seafood from the Bay of Biscay, there is much to choose from. The menu changes daily and seasonally, but the fish of the day is a sure bet. ✉ *Río de la Pila 5* ☎ *942/216750* ▭ *AE, DC, MC, V* ⏲ *Closed Mon. No dinner Sun. Oct.–May.*

$$–$$$$ SPANISH ✕ **Zacarías**. Whether you're looking for a brief tapas interlude or a full dinner, try this popular rustic and refined interior patio ringed with a lovely upstairs balcony. Zacarías is an institution in Santander and justly famous for its seafood and upland dishes of all kinds. Try the *maganos de guadañeta* (calamari and caramelized onion) or the *huevos de arcipreste de hita con langosta* (eggs with lumpfish caviar and lobster). Owner and chef Zacarías Puente Herboso is also a somewhat legendary food writer and an authority on Cantabrian recipes. ✉ *General Mola 41* ☎ *942/212333* ▭ *AE, DC, MC, V.*

$$–$$$$ ★ **Bahía**. Classical decor combined with state-of-the-art technology and contemporary furnishings make this Santander's finest hotel, a grand and comfortable perch overlooking the water. Rooms are spacious and filled with gauzy drapes and noble pieces of oak and mahogany furniture, while the public spaces are ample and elegant, recalling Santander's regal past as a summer watering spot for the Spanish royal family

during the late 19th and early 20th centuries. **Pros:** at the nerve center of town; great for watching maritime traffic. **Cons:** nearby cathedral bells can be noisy if you're not on the sea side of the hotel; not right on the beach. ✉ *Av. Alfonso XIII 6* ☎ *942/205000* 🌐 *www.hotelbahia.com* ⇨ *188 rooms* ♨ *In-room: Wi-Fi. In-hotel: restaurant, bar, Wi-Fi hotspot, parking (paid)* ▭ *AE, DC, MC, V.*

$$–$$$ **Las Brisas.** Jesús García runs this 80-year-old mansion as an upscale, cottage-style hotel by the sea. Each room or apartment is different, from dollhouselike alcoves to an odd but attractive family duplex apartment. The basement bar and breakfast room are especially cozy and full of agreeable kitsch. The hotel is a short walk from the beach, and many of the rooms have fine views out to sea. **Pros:** proximity to the shore; fresh and briny Atlantic air. **Cons:** mildly disorganized; some rooms are a bit cramped. ✉ *C. la Braña 14* ☎ *942/270991 or 942/275011* 🌐 *www.hotellasbrisas.net* ⇨ *13 rooms, 12 apartments* ♨ *In-hotel: bar* ▭ *AE, DC, MC, V.*

SHOPPING

Santander's ceramics emporium **La Muralla** (✉ *Calle Arrabal 17* ☎ *942/229292*) is known as the best in town. For fashions in a designer setting **Del Rosa al Amarillo** (✉ *Calle Hernán Cortés 37* ☎ *942/312800*) carries a full range of hot items. For footwear, **Loocky** (✉ *Santa Clara 2* ☎ *942/390438*) is tops. Fine foods, including the Santanderino specialty *dulces pasiegos* (light and sugary cakes), can be sampled and purchased at **Mantequerías Cántabras** (✉ *Plaza de Italia s/n* ☎ *942/272899*).

SANTILLANA DEL MAR

Fodor's Choice ★ *29 km (18 mi) west of Santander.*

ESSENTIALS

Visitor Information Santillana del Mar (✉ *Jesús Otero 20* ☎ *942/818812*).

EXPLORING

This stunning ensemble of 15th- to 17th-century stone houses is one of Spain's greatest troves of medieval and Renaissance architecture. The town is built around the **Colegiata**, Cantabria's finest Romanesque structure, with a 17th-century altarpiece, the tomb of local martyr Santa Juliana, and sculpted capitals depicting biblical scenes. The adjoining Regina Coeli convent has a **Museo Diocesano** (☎ *942/840317*) with liturgical art. ✉ *Av. Le Dorat 2* ☎ *942/818004* 🌐 *www.santillanamuseodiocesano.com* 🎫 *€3* ⏲ *Daily 10–2 and 4–7; closed Mon. Oct.–May.*

The world-famous **Altamira Caves**, 3 km (2 mi) southwest of Santillana del Mar, have been called the Sistine Chapel of prehistoric art for the beauty of their drawings, believed to be some 20,000 years old. First uncovered in 1875, the caves are a testament to early mankind's admiration of beauty and surprising technical skill in representing it, especially in the use of rock forms to accentuate perspective. The caves are closed to visitors, but the reproduction in the **museum** is open to all. ✉ *Museo de Altamira, Santillana del Mar, Cantabria* ☎ *942/818005* 🌐 *museodealtamira.mcu.es* 🎫 *€3* ⏲ *May–Oct. Tues.–Sat. 9:30-8, Sun. 9:30–3; Nov.–Apr. Tues.–Sat. 9:30–6, Sun. 9:30–3.*

The reproduction cave at the Altamira museum displays paintings of bison.

WHERE TO STAY

$$ **Casa del Organista.** A cozy 18th-century house with comfortable and tastefully appointed whitewashed rooms, this is a handy alternative to the pricier and more famous national paradors nearby. A typical *casona montañesa* (noble mountain town house) with painstakingly crafted stone and wood details, this intimate hideaway offers a countrified but elegant base camp for exploring one of Spain's finest Renaissance towns. **Pros:** personal and friendly service; lovely, warm decor. **Cons:** limited availability and difficult to book in high season; some rooms are very small. ⊠ *Los Hornos 4* ☎ *942/840352* 🌐 *www.casadelorganista.com* *14 rooms* *In-hotel: restaurant, Wi-Fi hotspot* *AE, DC, MC, V* *Closed Dec. 15–Jan. 15.*

$$$ Fodor's Choice ★ **Parador de Santillana Gil Blas.** Built in the 16th century, this lovely stone palace occupies what used to be the summer home of the Barreda-Bracho family. Rooms are baronial, with heavy wood beams overhead and splendid antique furnishings. The spacious dining hall ($$–$$$$) has a medieval feel and specializes in local cuisine as well as roasts and hearty stews and soups in the Castilian tradition. **Pros:** storybook surroundings; elegant and attentive service. **Cons:** a little breezy and chilly in winter. ⊠ *Pl. Ramón Pelayo 11* ☎ *942/028028* 🌐 *www.parador.es* *27 rooms* *In-hotel: restaurant, bar, Wi-Fi hotspot, parking (paid)* *AE, DC, MC, V.*

OFF THE BEATEN PATH

Puente Viesgo. In 1903 this 16th-century hamlet in the Pas Valley excavated four caves under the 1,150-foot peak of Monte del Castillo, two of which—Cueva del Castillo and Cueva de las Monedas—are open to the public. Bison, deer, bulls, and even humanoid stick figures are depicted; the oldest designs are thought to be 35,000 years old. Most

DID YOU KNOW?

Santillana del Mar is sometimes called the Town of Three Lies because it doesn't have a saint (Santo), flat lands (llana), or a sea (Mar), as are implied, but the name acutally derives from the local martyr, Santa Juliana (Santa Illana), whose remains are kept in the Colegiata.

arresting are the paintings of 44 hands (curiously, 35 of them left), reaching out through time. The painters are thought to have blown red pigment around their hands through a hollow bone, leaving the negative image. Reservations are advised. ✉ *N623, Km 28, from Santander* ☎ *942/598425* 🌐 *www.culturadecantabria.es* 🎟 *€4 per cave* ⏲ *May–Sept., daily 10–2 and 4–7; Oct.–Apr., Wed.–Sun. 9:30–4.*

COMILLAS

49 km (30 mi) west of Santander.

This astounding pocket of Catalan Art Nouveau architecture in the green hills of Cantabria will make you rub your eyes in disbelief. The Marqués de Comillas, a Catalan named Antonio López y López (1817–83) whose daughter Isabel married Antoni Gaudí's patron Eusebi Güell, was the wealthiest and most influential shipping magnate of his time and a fervent patron of the arts, and he encouraged the great Moderniste architects to use his native village as a laboratory. Gaudí's 1883–89 green-and-yellow-tile villa, El Capricho (a cousin of his Casa Vicens in Barcelona), is the town's main Moderniste attraction. The town cemetery is filled with Art Nouveau markers and monuments, most notably an immense angel by eminent Catalan sculptor Josep Llimona.

ESSENTIALS

Visitor Information Comillas (✉ *Plaza Joaquin del Pièlago* ☎ *942/722591*).

EXPLORING

Palacio Sobrellano, built in the late 19th century by Catalan architect Joan Martorell for the Marqués de Comillas, is an exuberant neo-Gothic mansion with surprising collections of everything from sculpture and painting to archaeology and ethnographical material. The chapel has benches and kneeling stalls that were designed by Gaudí. ☎ *942/720339* 🌐 *www.culturadecantabria.es* 🎟 *€3 palace, €6 palace and chapel* ⏲ *Sept.–May, Wed.–Sun. 10:30–2 and 4–7:30; June–Sept., daily 10–9.*

WHERE TO EAT

$$$–$$$$ SPANISH ✕ **El Capricho de Gaudí**. Dining in a Gaudí creation is an opportunity not to be taken lightly, especially if the visual rush is accompanied by *vieiras y pulpo al pilpil de rape*(scallops, octopus, and monkfish in a garlic-and-chili sauce), fresh turbot with young garlic, or roast lamb from the verdant hills of Cantabria. This unique spot may be somewhat overpriced, but even for a cup of coffee or a bowl of soup it's an unforgettable and unique chance to break bread in the same space where the great Moderniste took some of his first steps as a young architect. ✉ *Barrio de Sobrellano* ☎ *942/720365* 💳 *AE, DC, MC, V* ⏲ *Closed Jan. 15–Feb. 15 and Mon. Oct.–May. No dinner Sun.*

SAN VICENTE DE LA BARQUERA

64 km (40 mi) west of Santander, 15 km (9 mi) west of Comillas.

Important as a Roman port long before many other larger, modern shipping centers (such as Santander) were, San Vicente de la Barquera is one of the oldest and most beautiful maritime settlements in northern Spain. The 28 arches of the ancient bridge **Puente de la Maza,** which spans the *ría* (fjord), welcome you to town.

ESSENTIALS

Visitor Information San Vicente de la Barquera (✉ *Av. Generalísimo 20* ☎ *942/710797*).

EXPLORING

Thanks to its exceptional Romanesque portals, the 15th-century church of **Nuestra Señora de los Angeles** (Our Lady of the Angels) is among San Vicente's most memorable sights.Make sure you check out the arcaded porticoes of the **Plaza Mayor** and the view over the town from the Unquera road (N634) just inland. San Vicente celebrates **La Folía** in late April (the name translates roughly as "folly," and the exact date depends not only on Easter but on the high tide) with a magnificent maritime procession: the town's colorful fishing fleet accompanies the figure of La Virgen de la Barquera as she is transported in part by boat from her sanctuary outside town to the village church. There she's honored with folk dances and songs before being returned to her hermitage.

Bilbao and the Basque Country

WITH CANTABRIA, NAVARRA, AND LA RIOJA

WORD OF MOUTH

"San Sebastian is stunning, beautiful, classy, quaint, you can walk everywhere, has some of the world's best beaches in town and nearby, the world's best chefs, an amazing jazz festival in Aug. I wish I could spend a month there every year."

—Egbert

WELCOME TO BILBAO AND THE BASQUE COUNTRY

TOP REASONS TO GO

★ **The Basque Coast:** From colorful fishing villages to tawny beaches to Europe's longest surfing wave, the Basque Coast always delights the eye.

★ ***Tapas* in San Sebastián:** Nothing matches San Sebastián's old quarter, with the laughter of tavern hoppers tippling and grazing at counters heaped with colorful morsels.

★ **Bilbao for Art and Architecture:** The titanium Guggenheim and the Museo de Bellas Artes (Fine Arts Museum) shimmer where steel mills and shipyards once stood, while verdant pastures loom above and beyond.

★ **Running with the Bulls in Pamplona:** Running with a pack of wild animals (and people) will certainly get the adrenaline pumping, but you might prefer to be a spectator.

★ **Rioja's Wine Country:** Spain's premier winegrowing region in La Rioja Alta and La Rioja Alavesa is filled with wine-tasting opportunities and fine cuisine.

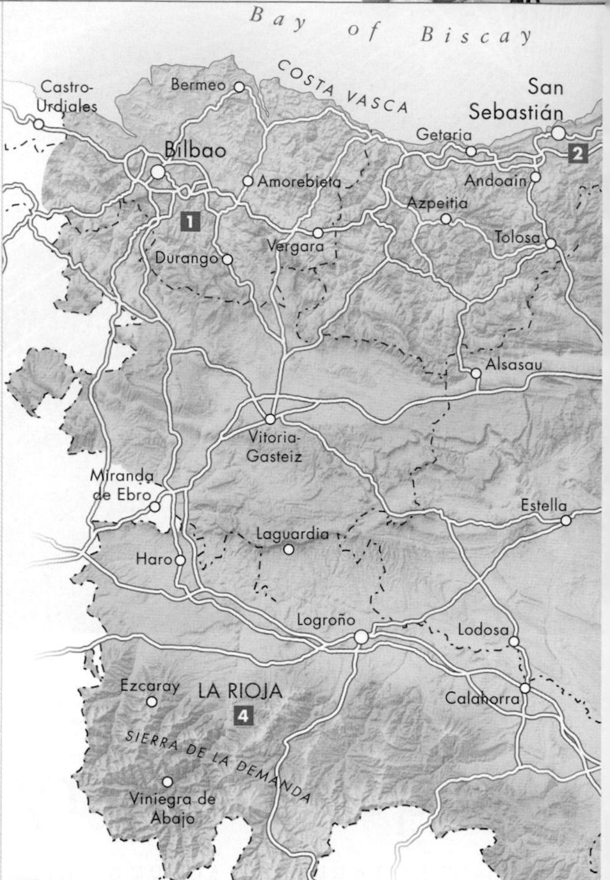

1 Bilbao and the Basque Country. The contrast between Bilbao and the rest of the Basque Country makes each half of the equation better: a city famous for steel and shipbuilding turned into a shimmering art and architecture hub, surrounded by sylvan hillsides, tiny fishing ports, and beautiful beaches.

2 San Sebastián to Hondarribia/Fuenterrabía. San Sebastián lures travelers with its sophistication and wide beach. Nearby Hondarribia is a fishing port on the Bidasoa river estuary border with France.

3 Navarra and Pamplona. This region offers much beyond Pamplona's running-with-the-bulls blowout party. The green Pyrenean hills to the north contrast with the lunar Bárdenas Reales to the southeast, and the wine country south of Pamplona leads to lovely Camino de Santiago way stations like Estella. Medieval Vitoria is the capital of the Alava and the whole Basque Country and is relatively undiscovered by tourists.

4 La Rioja. Spain's wine country is dedicated to tastes of all kinds. The Sierra de la Demanda mountain range offers culinary destinations such as Ezcaray's Echaurren or Viniegra de Abajo's Venta de Goyo, while the towns of Logroño, Haro, and Laguardia are well endowed with superb architecture and gastronomy.

GETTING ORIENTED

Bordering the coastline of the Bay of Biscay, the Basque Country and, farther inland, Navarra and La Rioja are a Spain apart—a land of moist green foothills, lush vineyards, and rolling meadowlands. A fertile slot between the Picos de Europa and the Pyrenees mountain ranges that stretch from the Mediterranean Cap de Creus all the way to Finisterre (Land's End) on the Atlantic in northwestern Galicia, this northern Arcadia is an often rainy but frequently comforting reprieve from the bright, hot Spanish *meseta* (high plain or tableland) to the south.

BILBAO AND THE BASQUE COUNTRY PLANNER

When to Go

Mid-April through June, September, and October are the best times to enjoy the temperate climate and both the coastal and upland landscapes of this wet and grassy corner of Spain—though any time of year except August, when Europeans are on vacation, is nearly as good.

Pamplona in July is bedlam, though for party animals it's heaven.

The Basque Country is rainy in winter, but the wet Atlantic weather is always invigorating and, as if anyone needed it in this culinary paradise, appetite-enhancing. Much of the classically powerful Basque cuisine evolved with the northern maritime climate in mind.

The September film festival in San Sebastián coincides with the spectacular whaleboat regattas, while the beaches are still ideal and largely uncrowded.

When you're looking for a place to stay, note that the largely industrial and well-to-do north is an expensive part of Spain, which is reflected in room rates. San Sebastián is particularly pricey, and Pamplona rates triple during San Fermín in July. Reserve ahead for Bilbao, where the Guggenheim is filling hotels, and nearly everywhere else in summer.

Festivals

Glitterati descend on San Sebastián for its international **film festival** in the second half of September (exact dates vary, check *www.sansebastianfestival.com*). The same goes for the late-July **jazz festival** (*www.heinekenjazzaldia.com*), which draws many of the world's top performers. Saint's day is celebrated here January 19–20 with **La Tamborrada,** when 100-odd platoons of chefs and Napoleonic soldiers parade hilariously through the streets.

Pamplona's feast of **San Fermín** (July 6–14), made famous by Ernest Hemingway in *The Sun Also Rises*, remains best known for its running of the bulls. Bilbao's **Semana Grande** (Grand Week), in early August, is notorious for the largest bulls of the season and a fine series of street concerts.

Near San Sebastián, in the first week of August, the fishing village of **Getaria** celebrates Juan Sebastián Elkano's completion of Ferdinand Magellan's voyage around the world every other year. The fiestas include a solemn procession up from the port of the weather-beaten, starving survivors and a week of feasts, dances, and street parties.

Vitoria's weeklong **Fiesta de la Virgen Blanca** (Festival of the White Virgin) celebrates the city's patron saint with bullfights and more August 4–9.

If You Like Beaches

Between Bilbao and San Sebastián, the smaller beaches at Zumaia, Getaria, and Zarautz are usually quiet. San Sebastián's best beach, La Concha, which curves around the bay along with the city itself, is scenic and clean but packed in summer; Ondarreta, at the western end of La Concha, is often less crowded. Surfers gather at Zurriola on the northern side of the Urumea River. Hondarribia, the last stop before the French border, has a vast expanse of fine sand along the Bidasoa estuary.

Eat, Drink, and Be Merry . . . And Hike Off Those Calories

The concentration of celebrated chefs around San Sebastián is so dazzling that food is a natural rallying point here. There are famous names as well as rising stars in and around the Basque Country. Meanwhile, the excellence of ordinary food prepared with no gourmet pretensions beyond happy dining is everywhere.

Not surprisingly, maintaining an appetite (and some semblance of a waistline) can become a problem on a food safari—and hiking is the answer. Bring good walking shoes and check with local tourist offices for classic hikes such as the full-day walk over the Pyrenees from St-Jean-Pied-de-Port to upper Navarra's Roncesvalles, a unique way to get a never-to-be-forgotten feel for the Pyrenean portal. The network of trails and ancient cobblestone Roman roads up the Basque coast from Zumaia to Getaria, Zarautz, San Sebastián, and all the way to France will offer a look at corners of the Basque Country not seen from the freeways. From San Sebastián, the red-and-white GR (Gran Recorrido) markings at the end of the Zurriola beach will start you on a gorgeous three-hour hike to Pasajes de San Pedro, where a two-minute boat ride will whisk you across the Rentería shipping passage to Pasajes de San Juan (Pasaia Donibane in Euskera) and the town's several first-rate dining opportunities.

WHAT IT COSTS IN BILBAO (IN EUROS)

	¢	$	$$	$$$	$$$$
Restaurants	under €8	€9–€11	€12–€18	€19–€25	over €25
Hotels	under €75	€75–€100	€101–€150	€151–€190	over €190

Prices are per person for a main course at dinner, and for two people in a standard double room in high season, excluding tax.

WHAT IT COSTS IN THE REST OF BASQUE COUNTRY (IN EUROS)

	¢	$	$$	$$$	$$$$
Restaurants	under €8	€8–€12	€13–€17	€18–€22	over €22
Hotels	under €60	€60–€90	€91–€125	€126–€180	over €180

Prices are per person for a main course at dinner, and for two people in a standard double room in high season, excluding tax.

Planning Your Time

A road-trip through Basque Country, Navarra, and La Rioja would require at least a week but a glimpse, however brief, of Bilbao and its Guggenheim, but you can get away with just two days in Bilbao itself. San Sebastián and La Concha Beach, the Baztán Valley, Pamplona, Laguardia, and La Rioja's wine capital at Haro are the top must-see elements in a classic whirlwind tour.

If you doubled the time and spent two days in each of these destinations, the next tier of unmissable spots might include Mundaka and the Vizcayan Coast west of Bilbao, Getaria, Pasajes de San Juan, Hondarribia in and around San Sebastián, and Logroño in La Rioja.

Even better, if you found a few weeks to wander in a relaxed fashion, you could make it up as you went along, counting on off-season space available in most hotels and paradors, while crisscrossing the France–Spain border. La Rioja's Sierra de la Demanda also has some of the finest landscapes in Spain (not to mention culinary pilgrimages to Echaurren in Ezcaray or Venta de Goyo in Viniegra de Abajo).

5

GETTING HERE AND AROUND

By Air

Bilbao's airport serves much of this area, and there are smaller airports at Hondarribia (serving San Sebastián), Vitoria, Logroño, and Pamplona.

By Bus

Daily bus service connects the major cities to Madrid, Zaragoza, and Barcelona (with a layover or transfer to Spain's other destinations). The trip between Barcelona and Bilbao takes 7 to 8 hours. Reserve online at *www.alsa.es.*

Bus service between cities and smaller towns is comprehensive, but few have central bus stations; most have numerous bus lines leaving from various points in town.

By Car

Even the remotest points are an easy one-day drive from Madrid, and northern Spain is superbly covered by freeways.

The drive from Madrid to Bilbao is 397 km (247 mi)—about five hours; follow the A1 past Burgos to Miranda del Ebro, where you pick up the AP68. Car rentals are available in the major cities: Bilbao, Pamplona, San Sebastián, and Vitoria. Cars can also be rented at Hondarribia (Fuenterrabía) and the San Sebastián (Donostia) airport.

By Taxi

Taxis normally can be hailed on the street, though from more remote spots, such as Pedro Subijana's Akelaŕe restaurant on Igueldo above San Sebastián, the maître d' will need to call a taxi for you.

By Train

Direct RENFE trains from Madrid run to Bilbao (at 8 AM and 4:10 PM), San Sebastián (at 8 AM and 4:10 PM), Pamplona (7:35, 10:35, 3:05, and 7:35), Vitoria (8, 8:30, 1:13, 4:10, and 5:30), and Logroño (6:35). A car is the most convenient way to get around here, but if this isn't an option, many cities are connected by RENFE trains, and the regional company FEVE runs a delightful narrow-gauge train that winds through stunning landscapes. From San Sebastián, lines west to Bilbao and east to Hendaye depart from Estación de Amara; most long-distance trains use Estación del Norte. See the Travel Smart chapter for more information about train travel.

DID YOU KNOW?

The French sculptress Louise Bourgeois's (1911-2010) giant spider Maman, stands over 30 feet tall, outside the entrance to the Guggenheim.

EATING AND DRINKING WELL IN THE BASQUE COUNTRY

Basque cuisine, Spain's most prestigious regional gastronomy, derives from the refined French sensibility about cooking combined with a rough and tumble passion for the camaraderie of the table and for perfectly prepared seafood, meat, and vegetables.

Top left: A *nueva cocina* interpretation of the classic *bacalao al pil-pil*. Top right: A colorful bowl of marmtako stew. Bottom left: An expensive plate of *angulas*.

An ancestral passion for food combined with fine raw ingredients from the Atlantic and the verdant pre-Pyrenean hills has made Basque cuisine famous. The so-called *nueva cocina vasca* (new Basque cooking) is now about 30 years old, but it was originally inspired by the Nouvelle Cuisine of neighboring France, and meant the invention of streamlined versions of classic Basque dishes such as *marmitako* (tuna and potato stew).

Though experts have often defined Basque cooking as simply "the art of preparing fish" there is no dearth of lamb, beef, goat, or pork in the Basque diet or on menus. Cooking both beef and fish over coals is a popular favorite as are—new Basque cooking notwithstanding—bracing stews combining legumes such as lentils and garbanzos with sausage.

CIDER

Don't miss a chance to go to a *sidrería*, a cider house where the cider is poured from overhead and quaffed in a single gulp. *Chuletas de buey* (garlicky beefsteak grilled over coals) and *tortilla de bacalao* (cod omelet) provide ballast for hard apple cider al txotx. The cider-cod combination is linked to the Basque whalers who carried longer-lasting cider rather than wine in their galleys.

BESUGO A LA DONOSTIARRA

Besugo (sea bream) cooked San Sebastián style is baked in the oven covered with flakes of garlic that look like scales (but taste better), with a last-minute splash of vinegar and parsley on top. The flesh of the sea bream is flaky and firm and the aroma of the fresh fish and garlic is ambrosial.

BACALAO

Codfish, a Basque favorite since the Stone Age, comes in various guises. *Bacalao al pil-pil* (stewed codfish) is a classic Bilbao specialty boiled—rather than fried—with garlic and olive oil in its own juices. The "pil-pil" refers to the sound of the emulsion of cod and olive oil bubbling up from the bottom of the pan. Served with a red chili pepper, this is a beloved Basque delicacy.

TUNA AND POTATO STEW

Using the dark maroon-color meat of the Thunnas Albacares, marmitako, a stick-to-your-ribs potato, tuna, and red pepper stew is the classic Basque fishermen's concoction made for the restoration of weather-beaten seafarers. Taken from the French name of the cooking pot (marmite), there are marmitako competitions held annually, which combine the Basque passion for sport with their devotion to food.

OX

Oxen in the Basque country have traditionally been work animals and all but

family members, used for farm labors and fed and maintained with great reverence and care. When sacrificed for meat at the age of 12 or 13, their flesh is tender and marbled with streaks of fat rich with grassy aromas and tastes. Many of today's ox steaks (Txuleta de buey) may not be from authentic work oxen, but the quality of the meat, tender and fragrant, cooked over coals with garlic and a few flakes of sea salt, is dark and delicious.

WINE

Basque *txakolí,* a young white wine made from tart green grapes, is refreshing with either seafood or meat. Purists insisting on Basque wine with their Basque cuisine, though, could choose a Rioja Alavesa, from the part of the Rioja winegrowing country north of the Ebro.

BABY EELS

Angulas, known as elvers in English, are a Basque delicacy that has become an expensive treat, with prices reaching 1,000 euros a kilogram (about 2.2 pounds). The 3- to-4-inch-long eels look like spaghetti, but with tiny black eyes, and are typically served in a small earthenware dish sizzling with olive oil, garlic, and a single slice of chili. A special wooden fork is used to eat them, to avoid any metallic taste, and because the wood works better with the slippery eels.

Updated by George Semler and Kati Krause

Northern Spain is a misty land of green hills, low russet rooflines, and colorful fishing villages; it's also home to the formerly industrial city of Bilbao, reborn as a center of art and architecture. The semiautonomous Basque Country, with its steady drizzle (onomatopoetically called the *sirimiri*), damp verdant landscape, and rugged coastline, is a distinct national and cultural entity within the Spanish state.

Navarra is considered Basque in the Pyrenees and merely Navarran in its southern reaches, along the Ebro River. La Rioja, tucked between the Sierra de la Demanda (a small-to-midsize mountain range that separates La Rioja from the central Castilian steppe) and the Ebro River, is Spain's premier wine country.

Called the País Vasco in Castilian Spanish and Euskadi in the linguistically mysterious, non-Indo-European Basque language called Euskera, the Basque region is more a country within a country, or a nation within a state (the semantics are much debated). The Basques are known to love competition—it has been said that they will bet on anything that has numbers on it and moves (horses, dogs, runners, weight lifters). Such traditional rural sports as chopping mammoth tree trunks, lifting boulders, and scything grass reflect the Basques' attachment to the land and to farm life as well as an ingrained enthusiasm for feats of strength and endurance. Even poetry and gastronomy become contests in Euskadi, as *bertsolaris* (amateur poets) improvise duels of sharp-witted verse, and male-only gastronomic societies compete in cooking contests to see who can make the best *sopa de ajo* (garlic soup) or *marmitako* (tuna stew).

The much-reported-on Basque separatist movement is made up of a small but radical sector of the political spectrum. The terrorist organization known as ETA, or Euskadi Ta Askatasuna (Basque Homeland and Liberty), has killed nearly 900 people in more than 35 years of violence. Conflict has waxed and waned over the years, though it has never affected travelers. When ETA declared a permanent cease-fire in April

2006, hope flared for an end to Basque terrorism until a late-December bomb at Madrid's Barajas airport killed two and brought progress to a halt. In early 2009 Basque lehendakari (president) Juan José Ibarretxe and the PNV (Basque Nationalist Party) lost, albeit narrowly, the Basque presidency in favor of Patxi López of the PSOE (Spanish Socialist Party) in coalition with the PP (the right wing Partido Popular), reflecting voter weariness with the nationalist cause.

EXPLORING THE REGIONS

Northern Spain's Bay of Biscay area, at the western end of the Pyrenees along the border with France, is where the Cantabrian Cordillera and the Pyrenees nearly meet. The green foothills of Basque Country gently fill this space between the otherwise unbroken chain of mountains that rises from the Iberian Peninsula's easternmost point at northern Catalonia's Cap de Creus and ends at western Galicia's Fisterra, or Finisterre (Land's End). Navarra—part Basque and part Castilian-speaking Navarrese—lies just southeast and inland of the Basque Country, with the backdrop of the Pyrenees rising up to the north. La Rioja, below Navarra, nestles in the Ebro River valley under the Sierra de la Demanda to the south and stretches east and downriver to Calahorra and the edge of Spain's central *meseta* (plains).

5

BILBAO AND THE BASQUE COAST TO GETARIA (GUETARIA)

Starring Frank Gehry's titanium brainchild—the Museo Guggenheim Bilbao—Bilbao has established itself as one of Spain's 21st-century darlings. The area around the coast of Vizcaya and east into neighboring Guipúzcoa province to Getaria and San Sebastián is a succession of colorful ports, ocher beaches, and green hills.

BILBAO

34 km (21 mi) southeast of Castro-Urdiales, 116 km (72 mi) east of Santander, 397 km (247 mi) north of Madrid.

Fodor's Choice ★

Time in Bilbao (Bilbo, in Euskera) may be recorded as BG or AG (Before Guggenheim, After Guggenheim). Never has a single monument of art and architecture so radically changed a city—or, for that matter, a nation, and in this case two: Spain and Euskadi. Frank Gehry's stunning museum, Norman Foster's sleek subway system, the glass Santiago Calatrava footbridge, and the leafy park and commercial complex in Abandoibarra have all helped foster a cultural revolution in the commercial capital of the Basque Country.

Greater Bilbao encompasses almost 1 million inhabitants, nearly half the total population of the Basque Country. Founded in 1300 by Vizcayan noble Diego López de Haro, Bilbao became an industrial center in the mid-19th century, largely because of the abundance of minerals in the surrounding hills. An affluent industrial class grew up here, as did the working-class suburbs that line the Margen Izquierda (Left Bank) of the Nervión estuary.

Bilbao's new attractions get more press, but the city's old treasures still quietly line the banks of the rust-color Nervión River. The **Casco Viejo** (Old Quarter)—also known as Siete Calles (Seven Streets)—is a charming jumble of shops, bars, and restaurants on the river's Right Bank, near the Puente del Arenal bridge. Throughout the old quarter are ancient mansions emblazoned with family coats of arms, noble wooden doors, and fine ironwork balconies. Carefully restored after devastating floods in August 1983, this upscale shopping district is replete with excellent taverns, restaurants, and nightlife. The most interesting square is the 64-arch Plaza Nueva, where an outdoor market is pitched every Sunday morning.

Walking the banks of the Nervión is a satisfying jaunt. After all, this was how—while out on a morning jog—the Guggenheim's director, Thomas Krens, first discovered the perfect spot for his project, nearly opposite the right bank's Deusto University. From the Palacio de Euskalduna upstream to the colossal Mercado de la Ribera, parks and green zones line either side of the river. An amble here will offer even more when César Pelli's Abandoibarra project fills in the half mile between the Guggenheim and the Euskalduna bridge with a series of parks, the Deusto University library, the Meliá Bilbao Hotel, and a major shopping center.

On the Left Bank, the wide, late-19th-century boulevards of the **Ensanche** neighborhood, such as Gran Vía (the main shopping artery) and Alameda Mazarredo, are the city's more formal face. Bilbao's cultural institutions include, along with the Guggenheim, a major museum of fine arts (the Museo de Bellas Artes) and an opera society (ABAO: Asociación Bilbaína de Amigos de la Ópera) with 7,000 members from all over Spain and parts of southern France. In addition, epicureans have long ranked Bilbao's culinary offerings among the best in Spain. Don't miss a chance to ride the speedy and quiet trolley line, the Euskotram, for a trip along the river from Atxuri Station to Basurto's San Mamés soccer stadium, reverently dubbed "La Catedral del Fútbol" (the Cathedral of Football).

GETTING HERE AND AROUND

Bilbao's Euskotram, running up and down the Ría de Bilbao (aka River Nervión) past the Guggenheim to the Mercado de la Ribera, is an attraction in its own right: silent, swift, and panoramic as it glides up and down its grassy runway. The EuskoTren leaving from Atxuri Station north of the Mercado de la Ribera runs along a spectacular route through Gurenica and the Urdaibai Nature Preserve to Mundaka, probably the best way short of a boat to see this lovely wetlands preserve.

The Creditrans ticket is good for tram, metro, and bus travel and is available in values of €5, €10, and €15, though the €5 ticket should suffice for the few subway hops you might need to get around town. Creditrans can be purchased at newspaper stands, bus stops, metro stations, and from some drivers. Pass your ticket through the machine as you get on and off metros, tramways, or buses and it is charged according to the length of your trip. Transfers cost extra. A single in-town (Zone 1) ride costs about €1 and can be purchased from a driver; with a Creditrans transaction the cost is reduced to about €0.93

Bilbobus provides bus service 6 AM–10:20 PM. Plaza Circular and Plaza Moyúa are the principal hubs for all lines. Once the metro and normal bus routes stop service, take a night bus, known as a *Gautxori* (Night bird). Six lines run radially between Plaza Circular and Plaza Moyúa and the city limits 11:30 PM–2 AM weekdays and until 6 AM on Saturday.

Metro Bilbao is lineal, running down the Nervión estuary from Basauri, above, or east of, the Casco Viejo, all the way to the mouth of the Nervión at Getxo, before continuing to the beach town of Plentzia. There is no main hub, but the Moyúa station is the most central stop and lies in the middle of Bilbao's Ensanche, or modern (post-1860) part. The second subway line runs down the left bank of the Nervión to Santurtzi. The fare is €1.30.

5

TOURS

Bilbao's tourist office, Iniciativas Turísticas, conducts weekend guided tours in English and Spanish. The Casco Viejo tour starts at 10 AM at the tourist office on the ground floor of the Teatro Arriaga. The Ensanche and Abandoibarra tour begins at noon at the tourist office to the left of the Guggenheim entrance. The tours last 90 minutes and cost €4.50.

Bilbao Paso a Paso arranges custom-designed visits and tours of Bilbao throughout the week.

Stop Bilbao leads visits and tours of Bilbao and the province of Vizcaya.

ESSENTIALS

Bus and Subway Informaton Bilbobus (☎ *94/448–4080*). **Euskotram** (✉ *Atxuri 6 Casco Viejo* ☎ *902/543210*). **Metro Bilbao** (✉ *Atxuri 10 Casco Viejo* ☎ *94/425–4000*).

Bus Station Termibus Bilbao (✉ *Gurtubay 1, San Mamés* ☎ *94/439–5077* 🌐 *www.termibus.es* Ⓜ *San Mamés*).

Tour Information Bilbao Paso a Paso (✉ *Calle Mitxel Labegerie 1 [5–1]* ☎ *94/415–3892* 🌐 *www.bilbaopasoapaso.com*). **Iniciativas Turísticas** (✉ *Pl. Ensanche 11* ☎ *94/479–5760* 🌐 *www.bilbao.net*). **Stop Bilbao** (✉ *Gran Vía 80* ☎ *94/442–4689* 🌐 *www.stop.es*).

Train Station Bilbao (✉ *Estación del Abando, Calle Hurtado de Amézaga* ☎ *94/423–8623 or 94/423–8636*). **FEVE** (✉ *Estación de FEVE, next to Estación del Abando* ☎ *94/423–2266* 🌐 *www.feve.es*). **EuskoTren** (✉ *Estación de Atxuri, north of Mercado de la Ribera, Bilbao* ☎ *94/433–8007* 🌐 *www.euskotren.es*).

Visitor Information Bilbao Iniciativas Turísticas (✉ *Pl. Ensanche 11 El Ensanche* ☎ *94/479–5760* 🌐 *www.bilbao.net* ✉ *Aeropuerto de Loiu* ☎ *94/471–0310* ✉ *Av. de Abandoibarra 2* ☎ *94/479–5760* ✉ *Teatro Arriaga office, Pl. Arriaga 1 Casco Viejo* ☎ *No phone*).

The Guggenheim may be the most famous art museum in Bilbao these days, but the Museum of Fine Arts is also a very worthwhile destination.

TOP ATTRACTIONS

8 **AlhóndigaBilbao.** Once an early-20th-century municipal wine storage facility used by Bilbao's Rioja wine barons, this city block–size, Philippe Starck–designed civic center is filled with shops, cafés, restaurants, movie theaters, swimming pools, fitness centers, and nightlife opportunities at the very heart of the city. Conceived as a hub for entertainment, culture, wellness, and civic coexistence, AlhóndigaBilbao's opening in spring 2010 added another star to Bilbao's cosmos of architectural and cultural offerings. ✉ *Alameda Recalde 56 El Ensanche* ☎ *94/470–3458* 🌐 *www.alhondigabilbao.com* Ⓜ *Moyúa.*

18 **Ascensor de Begoña** *(Begoña Elevator)*. This popular Bilbao landmark is an elevator that connects the Casco Viejo with points overlooking the city. La Basilica de la Begoña is the classic pilgrimage and site of weddings and christenings. ✉ *Entrance at Calle Esperanza 6 Casco Viejo* 🎫 *€0.40* Ⓜ *Casco Viejo.*

4 **Museo de Bellas Artes** *(Museum of Fine Arts)*. Considered one of the top five museums in a country that has a staggering number of museums and great paintings, the Museo de Bellas Artes is like a mini-Prado, with representatives from every Spanish school and movement from the 12th through the 20th centuries. The museum's fine collection of Flemish, French, Italian, and Spanish paintings includes works by El Greco, Francisco de Goya y Lucientes, Diego Velázquez, Zurbarán, José Ribera, Paul Gauguin, and Antoni Tàpies. One large and excellent section traces developments in 20th-century Spanish and Basque art alongside works by better-known European contemporaries, such as Fernand Léger and Francis Bacon. Look especially for Zuloaga's famous portrait

Fodor's Choice ★

of La Condesa Mathieu de Moailles and Joaquín Sorolla's portrait of Basque philosopher Miguel de Unamuno. A statue of Zuloaga outside greets visitors to this sparkling collection at the edge of Doña Casilda Park and on the left bank end of the Deusto bridge, five minutes from the Guggenheim. Three hours might be barely enough to appreciate this international and pan-chronological painting course. The museum's excellent Arbolagaña restaurant offers a stellar lunch break to break up the visit. ✉ *Museo Plaza 2D Parque de Doña Casilda de Iturrizar, El Ensanche* ☎ *94/439–6060* 🌐 *www.museobilbao.com* 🎟 *€5.50; Bono Artean combined ticket with Guggenheim (valid 1 yr) €15; free Wed.* ⏲ *Tues.–Sat. 10–1:30 and 4–7:30, Sun. 10–2* Ⓜ *Moyúa.*

5 **Museo Guggenheim Bilbao.** Described by the late Spanish novelist Manuel
Fodor's Choice ★ Vázquez Montalbán as a "meteorite," the Guggenheim, with its eruption of light in the ruins of Bilbao's failed shipyards and steelworks, has dramatically reanimated this onetime industrial city. How Bilbao and the Guggenheim met is in itself a saga: Guggenheim director Thomas Krens was looking for a venue for a major European museum, having found nothing acceptable in Paris, Madrid, or elsewhere, and glumly accepted an invitation to Bilbao. Krens was out for a morning jog when he found it—the empty riverside lot once occupied by the Altos Hornos de Vizcaya steel mills. The site, at the heart of Bilbao's traditional steel and shipping port, was the perfect place for a metaphor for Bilbao's macro-reconversion from steel to titanium, from heavy industry to art, as well as a nexus between the early-14th-century Casco Viejo and the new 19th-century Ensanche and between the wealthy right bank and working-class left bank of the Nervión River.

Frank Gehry's gleaming brainchild, opened in 1997 and hailed as "the greatest building of our time" by architect Philip Johnson and "a miracle" by Herbert Muschamp of the *New York Times,* has sparked an economic renaissance in the Basque Country after more than a half century of troubles. In its first year, the Guggenheim attracted 1.4 million visitors, three times the number expected and more than both Guggenheim museums in New York during the same period.

At once suggestive of a silver-scaled fish and a mechanical heart, Gehry's sculpture in titanium, limestone, and glass is the perfect habitat for the contemporary and postmodern artworks it contains. The smoothly rounded jumble of surfaces and cylindrical shapes recalls Bilbao's shipbuilding and steel-manufacturing past, whereas the transparent and reflective materials create a shimmering, futuristic luminosity. With the final section of the La Salve bridge over the Nervión folded into the structure, the Guggenheim is both a doorway to Bilbao and an urban forum: the atrium looks up into the center of town and across the river to the Old City and the green hillsides of Artxanda where livestock graze tranquilly. Gehry's intent to build something as moving as a Gothic cathedral in which "you can feel your soul rise up," and to make it as poetically playful and perfect as a fish—per the composer Franz Schubert's ichthyological homage in his famous "Trout Quintet"—is patent: "I wanted it to be more than just a dumb building; I wanted it to have a plastic sense of movement!"

Covered with 30,000 sheets of titanium, the Guggenheim became Bilbao's main attraction overnight. Despite unexpected cleaning problems (Bilbao's industrial grime knows no equal), which were solved in 2002 using a customized procedure, the museum's luster endures. The enormous atrium, more than 150 feet high, connects to the 19 galleries by a system of suspended metal walkways and glass elevators. Vertical windows reveal the undulating titanium flukes and contours of this beached whale. The free Audio Guía explains everything you always wanted to know about modern art, contemporary art, and the Guggenheim. Frank Gehry talks of his love of fish and how his creative process works, while the pieces in the collection are presented one by one (an Oskar Kokoschka painting includes a description of Alma Mahler's lethal romance with the painter).

The collection, described by Krens as "a daring history of the art of the 20th century," consists of more than 250 works, most from the New York Guggenheim and the rest acquired by the Basque government. The second and third floors reprise the original Guggenheim collection of Abstract Expressionist, Cubist, Surrealist, and geometrical works. Artists whose names are synonymous with the art of the 20th century (Wassily Kandinsky, Pablo Picasso, Max Ernst, Georges Braque, Joan Miró, Jackson Pollock, Alexander Calder, Kazimir Malevich) and European artists of the 1950s and 1960s (Eduardo Chillida, Tàpies, Jose Maria Iglesias, Francesco Clemente, and Anselm Kiefer) are joined by contemporary figures (Bruce Nauman, Juan Muñoz, Julian Schnabel, Txomin Badiola, Miquel Barceló, Jean-Michel Basquiat). The ground floor is dedicated to large-format and installation work, some of which—like Richard Serra's *Serpent*—was created specifically for the space. Claes Oldenburg's *Knife Ship,* Robert Morris's walk-in *Labyrinth,* and pieces by Joseph Beuys, Christian Boltanski, Richard Long, Jenny Holzer, and others round out the heavyweight division in one of the largest galleries in the world.

On holidays and weekends lines may develop, though between the playful clarinetist making a well-deserved killing on the front steps and the general spell of the place (who can be irked in the shadow of Jeff Koons's flower-covered, 40-foot-high *Puppy*), no one seems too impatient. Advance tickets from Servicaixa ATMs or, in the Basque Country, the BBK bank machines are a way to miss the line. Failing that (sometimes they run out), go around at closing time and buy tickets for the next few days. The museum has no parking of its own, but underground lots throughout the area provide alternatives; check the Web site for information. ✉ *Abandoibarra Etorbidea 2, El Ensanche* ☎ *94/435–9080* 🌐 *www.guggenheim-bilbao.es* 🎫 *€13; Bono Artean combined ticket with Museo de Bellas Artes €15* 🕒 *Tues.–Sun. 11–8* Ⓜ *Moyúa.*

❷ **Museo Marítimo Ría de Bilbao** *(Maritime Museum of Bilbao).* This interesting nautical museum on the left bank of the Ría de Bilbao reconstructs the history of the Bilbao waterfront and shipbuilding industry beginning with medieval times. Temporary exhibits range from visits by extraordinary seacraft such as tall ships or traditional fishing vessels to thematic displays on 17th- and 18th-century clipper ships or

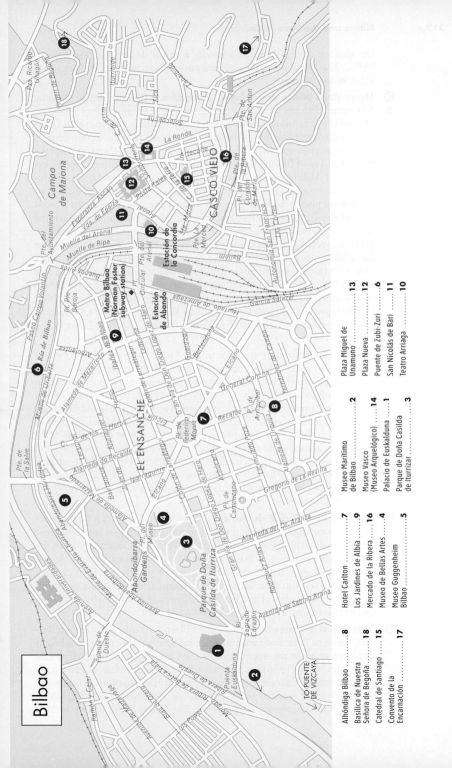

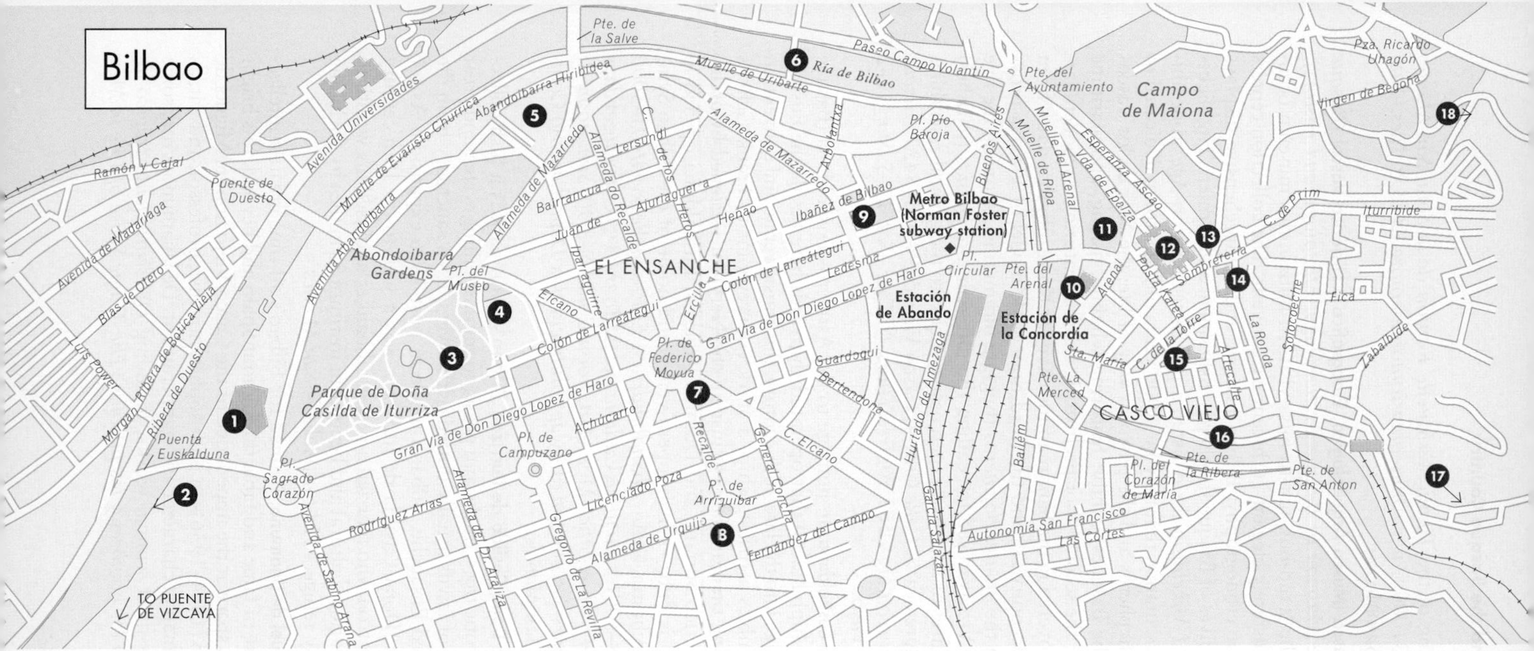

Alhóndiga Bilbao **8**	Hotel Carlton **7**	Museo Marítimo de Bilbao **2**	Plaza Miguel de Unamuno **13**
Basilica de Nuestra Señora de Begoña **18**	Los Jardines de Albia **9**	Museo Vasco (Museo Arqueológico) **14**	Plaza Nueva **12**
Catedral de Santiago **15**	Mercado de la Ribera **16**	Palacio de Euskalduna **1**	Puente de Zubi-Zuri **6**
Convento de la Encarnación **17**	Museo de Bellas Artes **4**	Parque de Doña Casilda de Iturrizar **3**	San Nicolás de Bari **11**
	Museo Guggenheim Bilbao **5**		Teatro Arriaga **10**

the sinking of the *Titanic.* ✉ *Muelle Ramón de la Sota, San Mamés* ☎ *902/131000* 🌐 *www.museomaritimobilbao.org* 🎫 *€5* ⏲ *Tues.–Sun. 10–8* Ⓜ *San Mamés.*

14 ★ **Museo Vasco (Museo Arqueológico, Etnográfico e Histórico Vasco)** *(Basque Museum; Museum of Basque Archaeology, Ethnology, and History).* One of the stand-out, not-to-miss visits in Bilbao, this museum occupies an austerely elegant 16th-century convent. The collection centers on Basque ethnography, Bilbao history, and comprehensive displays from the lives of Basque shepherds, fishermen, and farmers. Highlights include *El Mikeldi* in the cloister, a pre-Christian Iron-Age stone animal representation that may be 4,000 years old; the room dedicated to Basque shepherds and the pastoral way of life; the Mar de los Vascos (Sea of the Basques) exhibit featuring whaling, fishing, and maritime activities; the second-floor prehistoric exhibit featuring a wooden harpoon recovered in the Santimamiñe caves at Kortezubi that dates from the 10th century BC; and the third-floor scale model of Vizcaya province with the *montes bocineros* (bugling mountains), showing the five peaks of Vizcaya used for calling the different *anteiglesias* (parishes) with bonfires or *txalaparta* (percussive sticks) to the general assemblies held in Gurenica. ✉ *Calle Cruz 4, Casco Viejo* ☎ *94/415–5423* 🌐 *www.euskal-museoa.org* 🎫 *€3.50; free Thurs.* ⏲ *Tues.–Sat. 11–5, Sun. 11–2* Ⓜ *Casco Viejo.*

1 **Palacio de Euskalduna.** In homage to the Astilleros Euskalduna (Basque Country shipbuilders) that operated shipyards here beside the Euskalduna bridge into the late 20th century, this music venue and convention hall resembles a rusting ship, a stark counterpoint to Frank Gehry's shimmering titanium fantasy just up the Nervión. Designed by architects Federico Soriano and Dolores Palacios, Euskalduna opened in 1999 and is Bilbao's main opera venue and home of the Bilbao Symphony Orchestra. ✉ *Av. Abandoibarra 4 El Ensanche* ☎ *94/403–5000* 📠 *94/403–5001* 🌐 *www.euskalduna.net* 🎫 *Tour €3* ⏲ *Office weekdays 9–2 and 4–7; box office Mon.–Sat. noon–2 and 5–8:30, Sun. noon–2; guided tours Sat. at noon or by appointment (fax Departamento Comercial)* Ⓜ *San Mamés.*

3 **Parque de Doña Casilda de Iturrizar.** Bilbao's main park is a lush collection of exotic trees, ducks and geese, fountains, falling water, and great expanses of lawns usually dotted with lovers. It's a sanctuary from the hard-edged Ensanche, Bilbao's modern, post-1876 expansion. As for the name, Doña Casilda de Iturrizar was a well-to-do 19th-century Bilbao matron who married a powerful banker and used his wealth to support various cultural and beneficent institutions in the city, including this grassy refuge. ✉ *El Ensanche* Ⓜ *San Mamés.*

13 **Plaza Miguel de Unamuno.** Named for Bilbao's all-time greatest intellectual, figure of fame and fable throughout Spain and beyond, this bright and open space at the upper edge of the Casco Viejo honors Miguel de Unamuno (1864–1936)—a philosopher, novelist, professor, and wit, as well as a man of character and temperament. De Unamuno wrote some of Spain's most seminal works, including *Del sentimiento trágico de la vida en los hombres y los pueblos* (*The Tragic Sense of Life in Men*

The exterior of the Bilbao Guggenheim is immediately recognized by many, but the interior is known for its large spaces, all the better to appreciate the stunning works of art.

and Nations); his *Niebla* (*Mist*) has been generally accepted as the first existentialist novel, published in 1914 when Jean-Paul Sartre was but nine years old. Remembrances to Unamuno in the Casco Viejo include the philosopher's bust here, his birthplace at No. 7 Calle de la Cruz, and the nearby Filatelia Unamuno, a rare stamp emporium that is a favorite of collectors. M *Casco Viejo*.

12 **Plaza Nueva.** This 64-arch neoclassical plaza seems to be typical of every Spanish city from San Sebastián to Salamanca to Seville. With its Sunday-morning market, its December 21 natural-produce Santo Tomás market, and its permanent *tapas* and restaurant offerings, Plaza Nueva is an easy place in which to spend a lot of time. It was finished in 1851 as part of an ambitious housing project designed to ease the pressure on limited mid-19th-century Bilbao space. Note the size of the houses' balconies: it was the measure—the bigger, the better—of the social clout of their inhabitants. The tiny windows near the top of the facades were servants' quarters. The building behind the powerful coat of arms at the head of the square was originally the Diputación, or provincial government office, but is now the **Academia de la Lengua Vasca** (Academy of the Basque Language). The coat of arms shows the tree of Gurenica, symbolic of Basque autonomy, with the two wolves representing Don Diego López de Haro (López derives from *lupus,* meaning wolf). The bars and shops around the arcades include two **Victor Montes** establishments, one for *tapas* at Plaza Nueva 8 and the other for more serious sit-down dining at Plaza Nueva 2. The **Café Bar Bilbao,** at Plaza Nueva 6, also known as Casa Pedro, has photos of early Bilbao, while the **Argoitia,** at No. 15 across the square, has a nice angle on the midday

sun and a coat of arms inside with the *zatzpiakbat* ("seven-one" in Basque), referring to the cultural unity of the three French and four Spanish Basque provinces. Ⓜ *Casco Viejo.*

6 **Puente de Zubi-Zuri.** Santiago Calatrava's signature span (the name means "white bridge" in Euskera) connects Campo Volantín on the right bank with the Ensanche on the left. Just a few minutes east of the Guggenheim, the playful seagull-shape bridge swoops brightly over the dark Nervión. The Plexiglas walkway suggests walking on water, though wear and tear has reduced the surface from transparent to merely translucent. ✉ *El Ensanche* Ⓜ *Moyúa.*

OFF THE BEATEN PATH

Funicular de Artxanda. The panorama from the hillsides of Artxanda is the most comprehensive view of Bilbao, and the various typical *asadors* (roasters) here serve delicious beef or fish cooked over coals. ✉ *Entrance on Pl. de Funicular s/n, Matiko* ☎ *94/445–4956* 🎟 *€0.90* Ⓜ *Casco Viejo.*

11 **San Nicolás de Bari.** Honoring the patron saint of mariners, San Nicolás de Bari, the city's early waterfront church, was built over an earlier eponymous hermitage and opened in 1756. With a powerful facade over the Arenal, originally a sandy beach, San Nicolás was much abused by French and Carlist troops throughout the 19th century. Sculptures by Juan Pascual de Mena adorn the inside of the church. Look for the oval plaque to the left of the door marking the high-water mark of the flood of 1983. ✉ *Pl. de San Nicolás 1, Casco Viejo* ☎ *94/416–3424* Ⓜ *Casco Viejo.*

10 ★ **Teatro Arriaga.** A hundred years ago, this 1,500-seat theater was as exciting a source of Bilbao pride as the Guggenheim is today. Built between 1886 and 1890, when Bilbao's population was a mere 35,000, the Teatro Arriaga represented a gigantic per-capita cultural investment. Always a symbol of Bilbao's industrial might and cultural vibrancy, the original "Nuevo Teatro" (New Theater) de Bilbao was a lavish Belle Époque, neo-baroque spectacular modeled after the Paris Opéra by architect Joaquín Rucoba (1844–1909). The theater was renamed in 1902 for the Bilbao musician thought of as "the Spanish Mozart," Juan Crisóstomo de Arriaga (1806–26).

After a 1914 fire, the new version of the theater opened in 1919. Following years of splendor, the Teatro Arriaga (along with Bilbao's economy) gradually lost vigor; it closed down in 1978 for restoration work that was finally concluded in 1986. Now largely eclipsed by the splendid and more spacious Palacio de Euskalduna, the Arriaga stages opera, theater, concerts, and dance events from September through June. Walk around the building to see the stained glass on its rear facade and the exuberant caryatids holding up the arches facing the river. ✉ *Pl. Arriaga 1, Casco Viejo* ☎ *94/416–3333* 🌐 *www.teatroarriaga.com* Ⓜ *Casco Viejo.*

WORTH NOTING

20 **Basílica de Nuestra Señora de Begoña.** Bilbao's most cherished religious sanctuary, dedicated to the patron saint of Vizcaya, can be reached by the 313 stairs from Plaza de Unamuno or by the gigantic elevator (the Ascensor de Begoña) looming over Calle Esperanza 6 behind the San Nicolás church. The church's Gothic nave was begun in 1519 on the

site of an early hermitage, where the Virgin Mary was alleged to have appeared long before. Finished in 1620, the basilica was completed with the economic support of the shipbuilders and merchants of Bilbao, many of whose businesses are commemorated on the inner walls of the church. The high ground the basilica occupies was strategically important during the Carlist Wars of 1836 and 1873, and as a result La Begoña suffered significant damage that was not restored until the beginning of the 20th century. Comparable in importance (if not in geographical impact) to Barcelona's Virgen de Montserrat, the Basílica de la Begoña is where the Athletic de Bilbao soccer team makes its pilgrimage, some of the players often barefoot, in gratitude for triumphs. ✉ *Calle Virgen de Begoña 38, Begoña* ☎ *94/412–7091* 🌐 *www.basilicadebegona.com* 🎫 *Free* 🕐 *Weekdays 9:30–1:30 and 4:30–8:30* Ⓜ *Casco Viejo.*

5

⓯ **Catedral de Santiago** *(St. James's Cathedral).* Bilbao's earliest church was a pilgrimage stop on the coastal route to Santiago de Compostela. Work on the structure began in 1379, but fire delayed completion until the early 16th century. The florid Gothic style with Isabelline elements features a nave in the form of a Greek cross, with ribbed vaulting resting on cylindrical columns. The notable outdoor arcade, or *pórtico,* was used for public meetings of the early town's governing bodies. ✉ *Pl. de Santiago 1, Casco Viejo* ☎ *94/415–3627* 🎫 *Free* 🕐 *Tues.–Sat. 10–1:30 and 4–7, Sun. 10:30–1:30* Ⓜ *Casco Viejo.*

⓱ **Convento de la Encarnación.** The Basque Gothic architecture of this early-16th-century convent, church, and museum gives way to Renaissance and baroque ornamentation high on the main facade. The **Museo Diocesano de Arte Sacro** (Diocesan Museum of Sacred Art) occupies a carefully restored 16th-century cloister. The inner patio alone, ancient and intimate, more than amortizes the visit. On display are religious silverwork, liturgical garments, sculptures, and paintings dating back to the 12th century. The convent is across from the Atxuri station just upstream from the Puente de San Antón. ✉ *Pl. de la Encarnación 9, Casco Viejo* ☎ *94/432–0125* 🎫 *Free* 🕐 *Tues.–Sat. 10:30–1:30 and 4–7, Sun. 10:30–1* Ⓜ *Casco Viejo.*

❾ **Los Jardines de Albia.** One of the two or three places all *bilbainos* will insist you see is this welcoming green space in the concrete and asphalt surfaces of this part of town. Overlooking the square is the lovely Basque Gothic **Iglesia de San Vicente Mártir,** its Renaissance facade facing its own Plaza San Vicente. The amply robed sculpture of the Virgin on the main facade, as the story goes, had to be sculpted a second time after the original version was deemed too scantily clad. The Jardines de Albia are centered on the bronze effigy of writer Antonio de Trueba by the famous Spanish sculptor Mariano Benlliure (1866–1947), creator of monuments to the greatest national figures of the epoch. ✉ *Calle Colón de Larreátegui s/n, El Ensanche* Ⓜ *Moyúa.*

⓰ **Mercado de la Ribera.** This triple-decker ocean liner with its prow headed down the estuary toward the open sea is one of the best markets of its kind in Europe, as well as one of the biggest, with more than 400 retail stands covering 37,950 square feet. Like the architects of the

The streets of Bilbao's old town offer many welcoming shops, cafés, and restaurants.

Guggenheim and the Palacio de Euskalduna nearly 75 years later, the architect here was not unplayful with this well-anchored ocean-going grocery store in the river. From the stained-glass entryway over Calle de la Ribera to the tiny catwalks over the river or the diminutive restaurant on the second floor, the market is an inviting place. Look for the farmers' market on the top floor, and down on the bottom floor ask how fresh a fish is some morning and you might hear, "Oh, that one's not too fresh: caught last night." ✉ *Calle de la Ribera 20, Casco Viejo* ☎ *94/415–3136* ⏲ *Mon.–Sat. 8* AM*–1* PM Ⓜ *Casco Viejo.*

TAPAS BARS

$$–$$$ TAPAS ✕ **La Gallina Ciega.** With some of Bilbao's finest *pintxos* (morsels impaled on toothpicks) at the bar and a single table serving the chef's daily whim, this modern, clean-lined tavern decorated in eclectic patterns of wood, glass, and marble is one of Bilbao's favorite foodie haunts. The table, as might be expected, is rarely empty and must be reserved well in advance. ✉ *Máximo Aguirre 2, El Ensanche* ☎ *94/442–3943* ▭ *AE, DC, MC, V* Ⓜ *Moyúa.*

$–$$ TAPAS ✕ **La Taberna de los Mundos.** Sandwich-maker Ander Calvo is famous throughout Spain, and his masterpiece is a sandwich on ciabatta of melted goat cheese with garlic, wild mushrooms, organic tomatoes, and sweet red piquillo peppers on a bed of acorn-fed wild Iberian ham. Calvo's two restaurants in Bilbao and one in Vitoria include creative interpretations of the sandwich along with photography, art exhibits, travel lectures, and a global interest reflected in his obsession with early maps and navigational techniques. ✉ *Calle Lutxana 1, El Ensanche*

CLOSE UP

Abandoibarra: Bilbao's New Heart

The Abandoibarra project covers nearly a full square mile along the Nervión estuary. Formerly occupied by docks, warehouses, and shipyards, two thirds of this new urban center are now parks and open spaces. Javier López Chollet's 280,000-square-foot Ribera Park borders the Parque de Doña Casilda between the Guggenheim and Palacio de Euskalduna. This green space joins the quais of La Naja, Ripa, and Uribitarte to connect with the Olabeaga park downriver, creating a riverside promenade more than 3 km (2 mi) long.

The head architect for the project is the Connecticut-based César Pelli, designer of New York's World Financial Center and its Winter Garden fronting the Hudson River. Offices are also part of the project, as well as five apartment blocks and a residential building by Basque architect Luis Peña Ganchegui. Other buildings include the Meliá Bilbao Hotel (formerly the Sheraton Bilbao) by the Mexican architect Ricardo Legorreta; and American Robert Stern's shopping and leisure center, Zubiarte. Flanking the riverside thoroughfare named for Bilbao businessman and benefactor Ramón Rubial are the auditorium of the University of the Basque Country and the Deusto University library. Pedro Arrupe's footbridge, an exercise in rationalism with a simple geometrical form, connects Abandoibarra and Deusto University. The footbridge creates a complete urban promenade joining the Avenue of the Universities, the riverside walk, and the new streets of Abandoibarra, the culminating act of the revitalized, 21st-century Bilbao.

☎ 94/416–8181 🌐 www.delosmundos.com ▭ AE, DC, MC, V ⏲ Closed Mon. mid-Sept.–mid-June Ⓜ Moyúa.

¢–$ TAPAS ✕ **Txiriboga Taberna.** Specialists in *croquetas* (croquettes) made of ham, chicken, or wild mushrooms, this little hole-in-the-wall, a simple no-frills local favorite and semi-secret hideout, also has a back room for sit-down dining. The historic photographs on the walls add to the authenticity, but the croquetas (in Euskera *kroketak*) speak for themselves. *✉ Santa Maria Kalea 13, Casco Viejo ☎ 94/415–7874 ▭ AE, DC, MC, V ⏲ Closed Mon. Ⓜ Casco Viejo.*

$–$$ TAPAS ✕ **Victor Montes.** A hot spot for the daily *tapeo* (tapas tour), this place is always crowded with congenial grazers. The well-stocked counter might offer anything from wild mushrooms to *txistorra* (spicy sausages), Idiazabal (Basque smoked cheese), or, for the adventurous, *huevas de merluza* (hake roe), all taken with splashes of Rioja, *txakolí* (a young, white brew made from tart green grapes), or cider. *✉ Pl. Nueva 8, Casco Viejo ☎ 94/415–7067 🌐 www.victormontesbilbao.com ✍ Reservations essential ▭ AE, DC, MC, V ⏲ Closed Sun. and Aug. 1–15 Ⓜ Casco Viejo.*

¢–$ TAPAS ✕ **Xukela.** Amid bright lighting and a vivid palette of green and crimson morsels of ham and bell peppers lining his bar, chef Santiago Ruíz Bombin creates some of the tastiest and most interesting and varied *pintxos* (miniature cuisine presented on toothpicks) in all of tapasdom. The tavern has the general feel of a small library, lined with

5

books, magazines, paintings, and little reading nooks. Drinks range from beer to the acidic Basque *txakolí* to a handsome selection of red and white wines from all over Spain. ✉ *Calle del Perro 2, Casco Viejo* ☎ *94/415–9772* ▭ *AE, DC, MC, V* Ⓜ *Casco Viejo.*

BILBAO BLUE

The Guggenheim office building near Jeff Koons's *Puppy* is startlingly, deeply, enormously blue. While working on the Guggenheim, Frank Gehry fell in love with this "Bilbao blue," so-called for the vivid blue sky seen on rare days over Bilbao when the Atlantic drizzle–the famous Basque *siri-miri*–permits. Curiously, as a result of either the Guggenheim's reflected light, less industrial smog, or climate change, Bilbao's blue skies have become more frequent but less intense, leaving the Guggenheim offices and the Perro Chico restaurant, Gehry's favorite, among the few surviving outbursts of the city's emblematic color.

WHERE TO EAT

$$$–$$$$ CONTEMPORARY ✕ **Aizian.** Euskera for "in the wind," the hotel restaurant for the Meliá Bilbao, under the direction of chef José Miguel Olazabalaga, has become one of the city's most respected dining establishments. Typical Bilbaino culinary classicism doesn't keep Olazabalaga from creating surprising reductions and contemporary interpretations of traditional dishes such as *vieiras sobre risotto crujiente de hongos* (scallops on a crunchy wild mushroom risotto) or *la marmita de chipirón* (a stew of sautéed cuttlefish with a topping of whipped potatoes covering the sauce of squid ink). The clean-lined contemporary dining room and the streamlined, polished cuisine are a perfect match. ✉ *C. Lehendakari Leizaola 29, El Ensanche* ☎ *94/428–0039* 🌐 *www.restaurante-aizian.com* ▭ *AE, DC, MC, V* ⊗ *Closed Sun. and Aug. 1–15* Ⓜ *San Mamés.*

$$$–$$$$ CONTEMPORARY Fodor's Choice ★ ✕ **Arbolagaña.** On the top floor of the Museo de Bellas Artes, this elegant space has bay windows overlooking the lush Parque de Doña Casilda. Chef Aitor Basabe's modern cuisine offers innovative versions of Basque classics such as codfish on toast, venison with wild mushrooms, or rice with truffles and shallots. The €42 *menú de degustación* (tasting menu) is a superb affordable luxury, while the abbreviated menú de trabajo (work menu) provides a perfect light lunch. ✉ *Alameda Conde Arteche s/n, El Ensanche* ☎ *94/442–4657* ✍ *Reservations essential* ▭ *AE, DC, MC, V* ⊗ *Closed Easter wk, July 15–30, and Mon. No dinner Tues., Wed., and Sun.* Ⓜ *Moyúa.*

$–$$ BASQUE ✕ **Arriaga.** The cider-house experience is a must in the Basque Country. Cider *al txotx* (poured straight out of the barrel), sausage stewed in apple cider, codfish omelets, *txuleton de buey* (beefsteaks), and Idiazabal cheese with quince jelly are the classic fare. Reserving a table is a good idea, especially on weekends. ✉ *Santa Maria 13, Casco Viejo* ☎ *94/416–5670* ▭ *AE, DC, MC, V* ⊗ *No dinner Sun.* Ⓜ *Casco Viejo.*

$$$$ SEAFOOD ✕ **Bermeo.** Named after and decorated in the style of the coastal fishing village to the north, this perennially top Bilbao restaurant in the Hotel Ercilla specializes in fresh market cuisine and traditional Basque interpretations of fish, shellfish, and seafood of all kinds. The *rodaballo* (turbot) in vinaigrette sauce is a good choice. ✉ *Calle Ercilla 37, El*

Ensanche ☎ *94/470–5700* ✍ *Reservations essential* ▭ *AE, DC, MC, V* ⊙ *Closed Aug. 1–15. No lunch Sat. No dinner Sun.* Ⓜ *Moyúa.*

$–$$ CAFÉ Fodor'sChoice ★ **Café Iruña.** The Iruña (it means Pamplona, in Euskera), an essential Bilbao haunt on the Ensanche's most popular garden and square, Los Jardines de Albia, is famous for its decor and its boisterous ambience. The neo-Mudéjar dining room overlooking the square is the place to be (if they try to stuff you in the back dining room, resist or come back another time). The bar has two distinct sections: the elegant side near the dining room, and the older, more bare-bones Spanish side on the Calle Berástegui, with its plain marble counters and *pinchos morunos de carne de cordero* (lamb brochettes) as the house specialty. ✉ *Calle Berástegui 5, El Ensanche* ☎ *94/423–7021* Ⓜ *Moyúa.*

$$$–$$$$ BASQUE Fodor'sChoice ★ ✕ **Casa Rufo.** Charming and cozy, this series of nooks and crannies tucked into a fine food, wine, olive-oil, cheese, and ham emporium has become famous for its *txuleta de buey* (beef chops). Let the affable owners size you up and bring on what you crave. The house wine is an excellent Crianza (two years in oak, one in bottle) from La Rioja, but the wine list offers a good selection from Ribera de Duero, Somantano, and El Priorat as well. ✉ *Calle Hurtado de Amézaga 5 El Ensanche* ☎ *94/443–2172* ✍ *Reservations essential* ▭ *AE, DC, MC, V* ⊙ *Closed Sun.* Ⓜ *Abando.*

$$$–$$$$ SPANISH Fodor'sChoice ★ ✕ **El Perro Chico.** The global glitterati who adopted post-Guggenheim Bilbao favor this spot across the Puente de la Ribera footbridge below the market. Frank Gehry discovered the color "Bilbao blue"—the azure of the skies over (usually rainy) Bilbao—on the walls here and used it for the Guggenheim's office building. Chef Rafael García Rossi and owner Santiago Diez Ponzoa run a happy ship. Noteworthy are the *alcachofas con almejas* (artichokes with clams), the extraordinarily light *bacalao con berenjena* (cod with eggplant), and the dark and fresh *pato a la naranja* (duck à l'orange). ✉ *Calle Aretxaga 2, El Ensanche* ☎ *94/415–0519* ✍ *Reservations essential* ▭ *AE, DC, MC, V* ⊙ *Closed Sun. No lunch Mon.* Ⓜ *Casco Viejo.*

$$$–$$$$ CONTEMPORARY ✕ **Etxanobe.** This luminous corner of the Euskalduna palace overlooks the Nervión River, the hills of Artxanda, and Bilbao. Fernando Canales creates sleek, homegrown contemporary cuisine using traditional ingredients. Standouts are the five codfish recipes, the duckling with Pedro Ximenez sherry, poached eggs with lamb kidneys and foie gras, and the braised scallops with shallot vinaigrette. ✉ *Av. de Abandoibarra 4, El Ensanche* ☎ *94/442–1071* ▭ *AE, DC, MC, V* ⊙ *Closed Sun. and Aug. 1–20* Ⓜ *San Mamés.*

$$$–$$$$ BASQUE ✕ **Guetaria.** A longtime local favorite for fresh fish and meats cooked over coals, this family operation is known for first-rate ingredients lovingly prepared. Named for the famous fishing village just west of San Sebastián long known as la cocina de Guipúzcoa (the kitchen of Guipúzcoa province), Bilbao's Guetaria does its namesake justice. The kitchen, open to the clientele, cooks *lubina* (sea bass), *besugo* (sea bream), *dorada* (gilthead bream), *txuletas de buey* (beef chops), and *chuletas de cordero*(lamb chops) to perfection in a classic *asador* (barbecue) setting. ✉ *Colón de Larreátegui 12, El Ensanche* ☎ *94/424–*

3923 🌐 *www.guetaria.com* ✍ *Reservations essential* 💳 *AE, DC, MC, V* ⏲ *Closed Easter wk* Ⓜ *Moyúa.*

$$$–$$$$ BASQUE ✕ **Guggenheim Bilbao.** Complementing the Guggenheim's visual feast with more sensorial elements, this spot overseen by Martín Berasategui is on everyone's short list of Bilbao restaurants. Try the *lomo de bacalao asado en aceite de ajo con txangurro a la donostiarra i pil-pil* (cod flanks in garlic oil with crab San Sebastián–style and emulsified juices), a postmodern culinary pun on Bilbao's traditional codfish addiction. A lobster salad with lettuce-heart shavings and tomatoes at a table overlooking the Nervión, the University of Deusto, and the heights of Artxanda qualifies as a perfect 21st-century Bilbao moment. ✉ *Av. Abandoibarra 2, El Ensanche* ☎ *94/423–9333* ✍ *Reservations essential* 💳 *AE, DC, MC, V* ⏲ *Closed Mon. and late Dec.–early Jan. No dinner Sun. and Tues.* Ⓜ *Moyúa.*

$$$$ BASQUE Fodor's Choice ★ ✕ **Guria.** Born in the smallest village in Vizcaya, Arakaldo, Guria's founder, the late Genaro Pildain, learned cooking from his mother and focused more on potato soup than truffles and caviar. Don Genaro's influence is still felt here in the restaurant's streamlined traditional Basque cooking that dazzles with simplicity. Every ingredient and preparation is perfect, from *alubias "con sus sacramentos"* (fava beans, chorizo, and blood sausage) to *crema de puerros y patatas* (cream of potato and leek soup) to lobster salad with, in season, *perretxikos de Orduña* (wild mushrooms). ✉ *Gran Vía 66, El Ensanche* ☎ *94/441–5780* ✍ *Reservations essential* 💳 *AE, DC, MC, V* ⏲ *No dinner Sun.* Ⓜ *Indautxu.*

$–$$ CONTEMPORARY Fodor's Choice ★ ✕ **Kiskia.** A modern take on the traditional cider house, this rambling tavern near the San Mamés soccer stadium serves the classical *sidrería* menu of chorizo sausage cooked in cider, codfish omelet, *txuleta de buey* (beef chop), Idiazabal (Basque smoked cheese) with quince jelly and nuts, and as much cider as you can drink, all for €25. Actors, sculptors, writers, soccer stars, and Spain's who's who frequent this boisterous marvel. ✉ *Pérez Galdós 51, San Mamés* ☎ *94/441–3469* 💳 *AE, DC, MC, V* ⏲ *No dinner Sun.–Tues.* Ⓜ *San Mamés.*

$–$$ CONTEMPORARY ✕ **La Deliciosa.** For carefully prepared food at friendly prices, this simply designed, intimate space is one of the best values in the Casco Viejo. The *crema de puerros* (cream of leeks) is as good as any in town, and the *dorada al horno* (roast gilthead bream) is fresh from the nearby La Ribera market. ✉ *Jardines 1, Casco Viejo* ☎ *94/415–0944* 💳 *AE, DC, MC, V* Ⓜ *Casco Viejo.*

$$ BASQUE ✕ **Txakolí de Artxanda.** The funicular from the end of Calle Múgica y Butrón up to the mountain of Artxanda deposits you next to an excellent spot for a roast of one kind or another after a hike around the heights. Whether ordering lamb, beef, or the traditional Basque *besugo* (sea bream), you can't go wrong at this picturesque spot with unbeatable panoramas over Bilbao. ✉ *Monte Artxanda, El Arenal* ☎ *94/445–5015* 💳 *AE, DC, MC, V* ⏲ *Closed Mon. mid-Sept.–mid-June* Ⓜ *Abando.*

WHERE TO STAY

$$$ Fodor's Choice ★ 🏨 **Gran Hotel Domine.** As much modern design celebration as hotel, this Silken chain establishment directly across the street from the Guggenheim showcases the conceptual wit of Javier Mariscal, creator

Continued on page 325

BASQUE SPOKEN HERE

While the Basque Country's future as an independent nation-state has yet to be determined, the quirky, fascinating culture of the Basque people is not restricted by any borders. Experience it for yourself in the food, history, and sport.

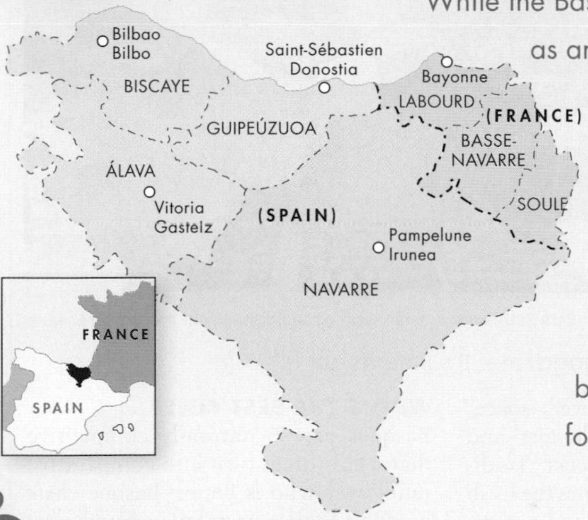

Basque solar cross

The cultural footprints of this tiny corner of Europe, which straddle the Atlantic end of the border between France and Spain, have already touched down all over the globe. The sport of jai-alai has come to America. International magazines give an ecstatic thumbs-up to Basque cooking. Historians are pointing to Basque fishermen as the true discoverers of North America. And bestsellers, not without irony, proclaim *The Basque History of the World*. As in the ancient 4 + 3 = 1 graffiti equation, the three French (Labourd, Basse Navarre, and Soule) and the four Spanish (Guipúzcoa, Vizcaya, Alava, and Navarra) Basque provinces add up to a single people with a shared history. Although nationless, Basques have been Basques since Paleolithic times.

Stretching across the Pyrénées from Bayonne in France to Bilbao in Spain, the New Hampshire-sized Basque region retains a distinct culture, neither expressly French nor Spanish, fiercely guarded by its three million inhabitants. Fables stubbornly connect them with Adam and Eve, Noah's Ark, and the lost city of Atlantis, but a leading genealogical theory points to common bloodlines with the Celts. The most tenable theory is that the Basques are descended from aboriginal Iberian peoples who successfully defended their unique cultural identity from the influences of Roman and Moorish domination.

It was only in 1876 that Sabino Arana—a virulent anti-Spanish fanatic—proposed the ideal of a "pure" Basque independent state. That dream was crushed by Franco's dictatorial reign (1939–75, during which many Spanish Basques emigrated to France) and was immortalized in Pablo Picasso's *Guernica*. This famous painting, which depicts the catastrophic Nazi bombing of the Basque town of Guernika stands not only as a searing indictment of all wars but as a reminder of history's brutal assault upon Basque identity.

"THE BEST FOOD YOU'VE NEVER HEARD OF"

(left) Zurrukutuna, garlic soup with codfish. (right) Preparing canapes.

So says *Food & Wine* magazine. It's time to get filled in.

An old saying has it that every soccer team needs a Basque goaltender and every restaurant a Basque chef. Traditional Basque cuisine combines the fresh fish of the Atlantic and upland vegetables, beef, and lamb with a love of sauces that is rare south of the Pyrénées. Today, the *nueva cocina vasca* (new Basque cooking) movement has made Basque food less rustic and much more nouvelle. And now that pintxos (the Basque equivalent of tapas) have become the rage from Barcelona to New York City, Basque cuisine is being championed by foodies everywhere. Even superchef Michel Guérard up in Eugénie-les-Bains has, though not himself a Basque, influenced and been influenced by the master cookery of the Pays Basque.

WHO'S THE BEST CHEF?

Basques are so naturally competitive that meals often turn into comparative rants over who is better: Basque chefs based in France or in Spain. Some vote for Bayonne's Jean-Claude Tellechea (his L'Auberge du Cheval Blanc is famed for groundbreaking surf-and-turf dishes like hake roasted in onions with essence of poultry) or St-Jean-Pied-de-Port's Firmin Arrambide (based at his elegant Les Pyrénées inn). Others prefer the postmodern lobster salads found over the border in San Sebastián and Bilbao, created by master chefs Juan Mark Arzak, Pedro Subijana, and Martin Berasategui, with wunderkind Andoni Aduriz and the Arbelaitz family nipping at their culinary heels.

SIX GREAT DISHES

Angulas. Baby eels, cooked in olive oil and garlic with a few slices of guindilla pepper.

Bacalao al pil-pil. Cod cooked at a low temperature in an emulsion of olive oil and fish juices, which makes a unique pinging sound as it sizzles.

Besugo. Sea bream, or besugo, is so revered that it is a traditional Christmas dish. Enjoy it with sagardo, the signature Basque apple cider.

Marmitako. This tuna stew with potatoes and pimientos is a satisfying winter favorite.

Ttoro. Typical of Labourd fishing villages such as St-Jean-de-Luz, this peppery Basque bouillabaisse is known as *sopa de pescado* (fish soup) south of the French border.

Txuleta de buey. The signature Basque meat is ox steaks marinated in parsley and garlic and cooked over coals.

BASQUE SPORTS: JAI-ALAI TO OXCART-LIFTING

Sports are core to Basque society, and virtually no one is immune to the Basque passion for competing, betting, and playing.

Over the centuries, the rugged physical environment of the Basque hills and the rough Cantabrian sea traditionally made physical prowess and bravery valued attributes. Since Basque mythology often involved feats of strength, it's easy to see why today's Basques are such rabid sports fans.

PELOTA

A Basque village without a frontón (pelota court) is as unimaginable as an American town without a baseball diamond. "The fastest game in the world," pelota is called *jai-alai* in Basque (and translated officially as "merry festival"). With rubber balls flung from hooked wicker gloves at speeds up to 150 mph—the impact of the ball is like a machine-gun bullet—jai-alai is mesmerizing. It is played on a three-walled court 175 feet long and 56 feet wide with 40-foot side walls.

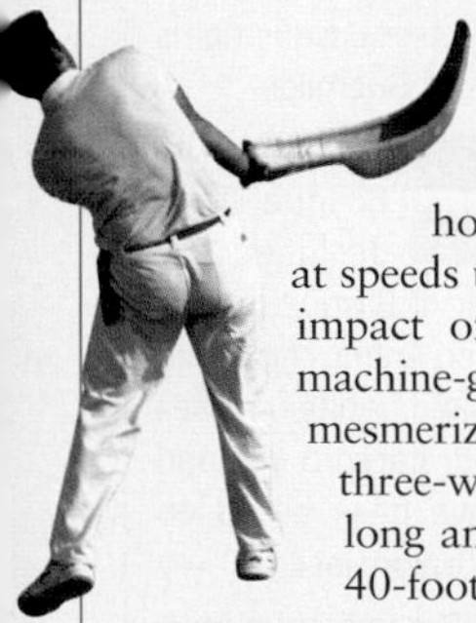

Whether singles or doubles, the object is to angle the ball along or off of the side wall so that it cannot be returned. Betting is very much part of pelota and courtside wagers are brokered by bet makers as play proceeds. While pelota is the word for "ball," it also refers to the game. There was even a recent movie in Spain entitled *La Pelota Vasca*, used metaphorically to refer to the greater "ball game" of life and death.

HERRIKIROLAK

Herrikirolak (rural sports) are based on farming and seafaring. Stone lifters (*harrijasotzaileak* in Euskera) heft weights up to 700 pounds. *Aizkolari* (axe men) chop wood in various contests, *Gizon proba* (man trial) pits three-man teams moving weighted sleds; while *estropadak* are whaleboat rowers who compete in spectacular regattas (culminating in the September competition off La Concha beach in San Sebastián). *Sokatira* is tug of war, and *segalariak* is a scything competition. Other events include oxcart-lifting, milk-can carrying, and ram fights.

SOCCER

When it comes to soccer, Basque goaltenders have developed special fame in Spain, where Bilbao's Athletic Club and San Sebastián's Real Sociedad have won national championships with budgets far inferior to those of Real Madrid or FC Barcelona. Across the border, Bayonne's rugby team is a force in the French national competition; the French Basque capital is also home to the annual French pelota championship.

HABLA EUSKERA?

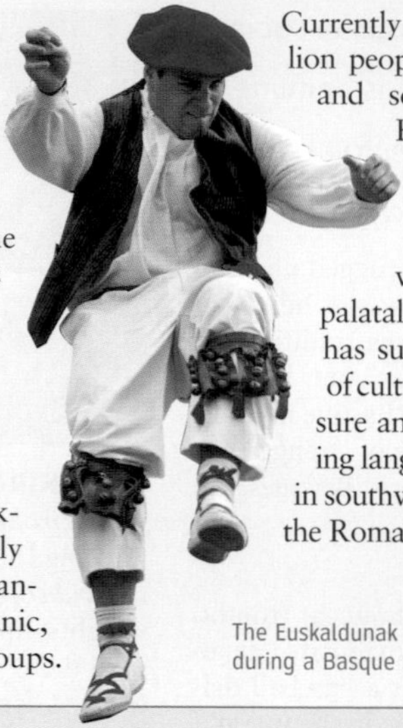

Although the Basque people speak French north of the border and Spanish south of the border, they consider Euskera their first language and identify themselves as the *Euskaldunak* (the "Basque speakers"). Euskera remains one of the great enigmas of linguistic scholarship. Theories connect it with everything from Sanskrit to Japanese to Finnish.

What is certain is where Euskera did not come from, namely the Indo-European family of languages that includes the Germanic, Italic, and Hellenic language groups.

Currently used by about a million people in northern Spain and southwestern France, Euskera sounds like a consonant-ridden version of Spanish, with its five pure vowels, rolled "r," and palatal "n" and "l." Basque has survived two millennia of cultural and political pressure and is the only remaining language of those spoken in southwestern Europe before the Roman conquest.

The Euskaldunak celebrate their heritage during a Basque folk dancing festival.

A BASQUE GLOSSARY

Aurresku: The high-kicking *espata danza* or sword dance typically performed on the day of Corpus Christi in the Spanish Basque Country.

Akelarre: A gathering of witches that provoked witch trials in the Pyrénées. Even today it is believed that *jentilak* (magic elves) inhabit the woods and the Olentzaro (the evil Basque Santa Claus) comes down chimneys to wreak havoc—a fire is kept burning to keep him out.

Boina: The Basque beret or *txapela,* thought to have developed as the perfect protection from the siri-miri, the perennial "Scotch mist" that soaks the moist Basque Country.

Eguzki: The sun worship was at the center of the pagan religion that, in the Basque Country, gave way only slowly to Christianity. The Basque solar cross is typically carved into the east-facing facades of ancient *caserios* or farmhouses.

Espadrilles: Rope-soled canvas Basque shoes, also claimed by the Catalans, developed in the Pyrénées and traditionally attached by laces or ribbons wrapped up the ankle.

Etxekoandre: The woman who commands all matters spiritual, culinary, and practical in a traditional Basque farmhouse. Basque matriarchal inheritance laws remain key.

Fueros: Special Basque rights and laws (including exemption from serving in the army except to defend the Basque Country) originally conceded by the ancient Romans and abolished at the end of the Carlist Wars in 1876 after centuries of Castilian kings had sworn to protect Basque rights at the Tree of Guernika.

Ikurriña: The Basque flag, designed by the founder of Basque nationalism, Sabino Arana, composed of green and white crosses over a red background and said to have been based on the British Union Jack.

Lauburu: Resembling a four-leaf clover, lau (four) buru (head) is the Basque symbol.

Twenty: Basques favor counting in units of twenty (*veinte duros*—20 nickels—is a common way of saying a hundred pesetas, for example).

Txakolí: A slightly fizzy young wine made from grapes grown around the Bay of Biscay, this fresh, acidic brew happily accompanies tapas and fish.

of Barcelona's 1992 Olympic mascot Cobi, and the structural know-how of Bilbao architect Iñaki Aurrekoetxea. With adjustable windowpanes reflecting Gehry's titanium leviathan and every lamp and piece of furniture embodying Mariscal's playful whimsy, this is the brightest star in Bilbao's design firmament. Comprehensively equipped and comfortable, it's the next best thing to moving into the Guggenheim. **Pros:** at the very epicenter and, indeed, part of Bilbao's art and architecture excitement; the place to cross paths with Catherine Zeta-Jones or Antonio Banderas. **Cons:** hard on the wallet and a little full of its own glamour. ✉ *Alameda de Mazarredo 61, El Ensanche* ☎ *94/425–3300* 🖷 *94/425–3301* 🌐 *www.granhoteldominebilbao.com* *139 rooms, 6 suites* *In-room: Wi-Fi. In-hotel: restaurant, bar, gym, parking (paid)* ▭ *AE, DC, MC, V* 🍴 *EP* Ⓜ *Moyúa.*

¢ **Hostal Mendez.** This may be the best value in town, with small but impeccable and well-appointed rooms, some of which (nos. 1 and 2) overlook the facade of the Palacio Yohn (pretty views but noisy at night). A brace of handsome sculpted setters stands vigil at the bottom of lovely, creaky wooden stairs. Fourth-floor rooms are even less expensive in this century-old walk-up building. **Pros:** excellent value and location in the middle of the Casco Viejo. **Cons:** with no air-conditioning, summer on the street side with the windows can be very noisy. ✉ *Santa María Kalea 13, Casco Viejo* ☎ *94/416–0364* 🌐 *www.pensionmendez.com* *12 rooms* *In-room: no a/c* ▭ *AE, DC, MC, V* 🍴 *EP* Ⓜ *Casco Viejo.*

$$$ **Hotel Carlton.** Luminaries who have trod the halls of this elegant white elephant of a hotel include Orson Welles, Ava Gardner, Ernest Hemingway, Lauren Bacall, Federico García Lorca, Albert Einstein, and Alfonso XIII, grandfather of Spain's King Juan Carlos I. During the Spanish civil war it was the seat of the Republican Basque government; later it housed a number of Nationalist generals. The hotel exudes old-world grace and charm along with a sense of history. Squarely in the middle of the Ensanche, the Carlton is equidistant from the Casco Viejo and Abandoibarra area. **Pros:** historic, old-world surroundings that remind you that Bilbao has an illustrious past. **Cons:** also surrounded by plenty of concrete and urban frenzy. ✉ *Pl. Federico Moyúa 2, El Ensanche* ☎ *94/416–2200* 🌐 *www.hotelcarlton.es* *135 rooms, 7 suites* *In-room: Wi-Fi. In-hotel: restaurant, bar, parking (paid)* ▭ *AE, DC, MC, V* 🍴 *EP* Ⓜ *Moyúa.*

¢–$ **Iturrienea Ostatua.** Extraordinarily beautiful, this traditional Basque
Fodor's Choice ★ town house one flight above the street in Bilbao's Old Quarter has charm to spare. With wooden ceiling beams, stone floors, and ethnographical and historical objects including a portable Spanish civil war combat confessional, there is plenty to learn and explore without leaving the hotel. The staff is extraordinarily friendly and helpful. **Pros:** budget friendly; exquisite rustic decor. **Cons:** nocturnal noise on the front side, especially on Friday and Saturday nights in summer, means you should try for a room in the back or bring earplugs. ✉ *Santa María Kalea 14, Casco Viejo* ☎ *94/416–1500* 🌐 *www.iturrieneaostatua.com* *21 rooms* *In-room: no a/c* ▭ *AE, DC, MC, V* 🍴 *EP* Ⓜ *Casco Viejo.*

$$$–$$$$ Fodor's Choice ★ **López de Haro.** This luxury hotel, five minutes from the Guggenheim, is becoming quite a scene now that the city is a bona fide nexus for contemporary art. A converted 19th-century building, López de Haro has an English feel and all the comforts your heart desires. Rooms are classical in design and feel, yet contemporary in equipment and comfort. The excellent restaurant, the Club Náutico, serves modern Basque dishes created by Alberto Vélez—a handy alternative on one of Bilbao's many rainy evenings. **Pros:** state-of-the-art comfort, service, and cuisine in a traditional and aristocratic setting. **Cons:** a less than relaxing, slightly hushed and stuffy scene; not for the shorts and tank top set. ✉ *Obispo Orueta 2, El Ensanche* ☎ *94/423–5500* 🌐 *www.hotellopezdeharo.com* *49 rooms, 4 suites* *In-room: Wi-Fi. In-hotel: restaurant, bar, parking (paid)* *AE, DC, MC, V* *EP* Ⓜ *Moyúa.*

$$–$$$ **Miró Hotel.** Perfectly placed between the Guggenheim and Bilbao's excellent Museo de Bellas Artes, this boutique hotel refurbished by Barcelona fashion designer Toni Miró competes with the reflecting facade of Javier Mariscal's Domine just up the street. Comfortable and daringly innovative, it is one of the city's sleek new fleet of hotels inspired by the world's most talked-about and architecturally revolutionary art museum. Rooms are spacious, lavishly draped in subdued mauves and salmon-hued fabrics, and very-high-tech contemporary. **Pros:** a design refuge that places you in the eye of Bilbao's art and architecture hurricane. **Cons:** not unpretentious; a hint of preciosity pervades these ultrachic halls. ✉ *Alameda de Mazarredo 77, El Ensanche* ☎ *94/661–1880* 🌐 *www.mirohotelbilbao.com* *50 rooms* *In-room: Wi-Fi. In-hotel: restaurant, bar, gym, spa, parking (paid)* *AE, DC, MC, V* *EP* Ⓜ *Moyúa.*

$$ **Petit Palace Arana.** Next to the Teatro Arriaga in the Casco Viejo, this design has a blended style of contemporary and antique: centenary limestone blocks, exposed brickwork, hand-hewn beams, and spiral wooden staircases are juxtaposed with clean new surfaces of glass and steel. The standard rooms and the showers are a tight fit, and the street below can be noisy on weekends, depending on your location. Fifteen executive rooms have exercise bikes and computers, and all rooms have hot tubs with hydromassage and computer hookups. **Pros:** in the heart of traditional Bilbao. **Cons:** the night can be noisy on the Casco Viejo side of the building. ✉ *Bidebarrieta 2, Casco Viejo* ☎ *94/415–6411* 🌐 *www.petitpalacearana.com* *64 rooms* *In-room: Wi-Fi. In-hotel: bar* *AE, DC, MC, V* *EP* Ⓜ *Abando, Casco Viejo.*

$ **Sirimiri.** A small, attentively run hotel near the Atxuri station, this modest spot has modern rooms with views over some of Bilbao's oldest architecture. The buffet-style breakfast is excellent, and the owner and manager offer helpful with advice about Bilbao. **Pros:** handy to the Mercado de la Ribera, Casco Viejo, and the Atxuri train station. **Cons:** tight quarters; noisy on weekends. ✉ *Pl. de la Encarnación, Casco Viejo* ☎ *94/433–0759* 🌐 *www.hotelsirimiri.com* *28 rooms* *In-hotel: restaurant, bar, gym, parking (paid)* *AE, DC, MC, V* *EP* Ⓜ *Casco Viejo.*

SPORTS AND THE OUTDOORS

"Sports" in Bilbao means the Athletic de Bilbao soccer team, traditionally one of Spain's top *fútbol* powers during the city's heyday as an industrial power. While it has been 30 years or so since Bilbao has won a league title, "the lions" are often in the top half of the league standings and seem to take special pleasure in tormenting powerhouses Madrid and Barcelona. The local rivalry with San Sebastián's Real Sociedad is as bitter as baseball's Yankees–Red Sox feud. Athletic de Bilbao's headquarters on Alameda de Mazarredo occupy a lovely mansion, while **San Mamés Stadium** (✉ *Rafael Moreno Pichichi s/n, San Mamés* ☎ *94/441–3954* Ⓜ *San Mamés*) is the place to buy tickets to games and have a look through the Museo del Athletic de Bilbao. The stadium has always been known as *La Catedral* (The Cathedral).

BULLFIGHTS

Bilbao's Semana Grande (Grand Week), in early August, is famous for scheduling Spain's largest bullfights of the season, an example of the Basque Country's tendency to favor contests of strength and character over art. Bullfights take place in the **Plaza de Toros Vista Alegre** (✉ *Pl. Vista Alegre s/n, San Mamés* ☎ *94/444–8698* 🌐 *www.torosbilbao.com* Ⓜ *San Mamés*).

5

SHOPPING

The main stores for clothing are found around Plaza Moyúa in the Ensanche, along streets such as Calle Iparraguirre and Calle Rodríguez Arias. The Casco Viejo has dozens of smaller shops, many of them handsomely restored early houses with gorgeous wooden beams and ancient stones, specializing in an endless variety of products from crafts to antiques. Wool items, foodstuffs, and wood carvings from around the Basque Country can be found throughout Bilbao. *Txapelas* (berets or Basque *boinas*) are famous worldwide and make fine gifts. Best when waterproofed, they'll keep you remarkably warm in rain and mist.

The city is home to international fashion names from Coco Chanel to Zara to Toni Miró, Calvin Klein, and Adolfo Domínguez. The ubiquitous department store Corte Inglés is an easy one-stop shop, if a bit massified and routine. Benetton and Marks & Spencer grace Bilbao's Gran Vía.

EN ROUTE

From Bilbao, drive northwest down the Nervión to Neguri and Getxo and follow the coast road around through Baquio, Bermeo, and Mundaka to Gurenica before proceeding east—this is the scenic route but well worth the extra time. Depending on stops for lunch or sprawling on a breezy beach, this can be a two-to-six-hour drive, all of it spectacularly scenic. The other choice is to pick up the A8 toll road east toward San Sebastián and France, exiting for Gurenica and the BI635 coast road through Vizcaya's hills.

SAN JUAN DE GAZTELUGATXE

37 km (23 mi) northeast of Bilbao.

★ This tiny, gemlike hermitage clinging to its rocky promontory over the Bay of Biscay is 231 steps up along a narrow corridor built into the top of a rocky ledge connecting what would otherwise be an island to the mainland. A favorite pilgrimage for Bilbaínos on holidays, the Romanesque chapel is said to have been used as a fortress by the Templars in the 14th century.

A HEAVENLY STROLL

A walk around San Juan de Gaztelugatxe's chapel bell tower is said to cure nightmares and insomnia, and to make wishes come true.

MUNDAKA

37 km (22 mi) northeast of Bilbao.

Tiny Mundaka, famous with surfers all over the world for its left-breaking roller at the mouth of the Ría de Guernica, has much to offer nonsurfers as well. The town's elegant summer homes and stately houses bearing family coats of arms compete for pride of place with the hermitage on the Santa Catalina peninsula and the parish church's Renaissance doorway.

ESSENTIALS

Visitor Information Mundaka (✉ *Kepa Deuna* ☎ *946/177201*).

WHERE TO EAT AND STAY

$$–$$$ SEAFOOD ✕ **Casino José Mari**. Built in 1818 as a fish auction house for the local fishermen's guild, this building, with wonderful views of Mundaka's beach, is now a fine restaurant and a well-known and respected eating club. The public is welcome, and the Casino is a favorite place for lunches and sunset dinners in summer, when you can sit in the glassed-in, upper-floor porch. Very much a semi-secret local haunt, the club serves excellent fish caught, more often than not, by the members themselves. ✉ *Parque Atalaya, center of town* ☎ *94/687–6005* ▭ *AE, MC, V.*

$–$$$ SEAFOOD ✕ **Portuondo**. Spectacular terraces outside a traditional *caserío* (Basque farmhouse) overlooking the Laida beach, the aromas of beef and fish cooking over coals, and a comfortable country dining room upstairs, and an easy 15-minute walk outside of Mundaka all make this a good stop for lunch or (in summer) dinner. Offerings are balanced between meat and seafood, the wine list covers an interesting selection of wines from all over Spain, and the *tapas* area downstairs crackles with life on weekends and during the summer. ✉ *Portuondo Auzoa 1* ☎ *94/687–6050* ⏲ *Closed Dec. 9–Jan. 15. No dinner Sun.–Thurs. Jan.–June* ▭ *AE, MC, V.*

$$ ★ **Atalaya**. Tastefully converted from a private house, this 1911 landmark 37 km (22 mi) from Bilbao has become a big favorite for quick railroad-getaway overnights from Bilbao and the Guggenheim. (The train ride out is spectacular.) Guest rooms are charming and comfortable; those upstairs have balconies with marvelous views. Room No. 22 is the best in the house. The breakfast room is cheerful and light. **Pros:** intimate retreat from Bilbao's sprawl and bustle; friendly family service. **Cons:** tight quarters in some rooms. ✉ *Paseo de Txorrokopunta 2* ☎ *94/617–7000* 🌐 *www.atalaya-hotel.es* *13 rooms* *In-room: Wi-Fi. In-hotel: restaurant, bar, parking (free)* ▭ *AE, DC, MC, V.*

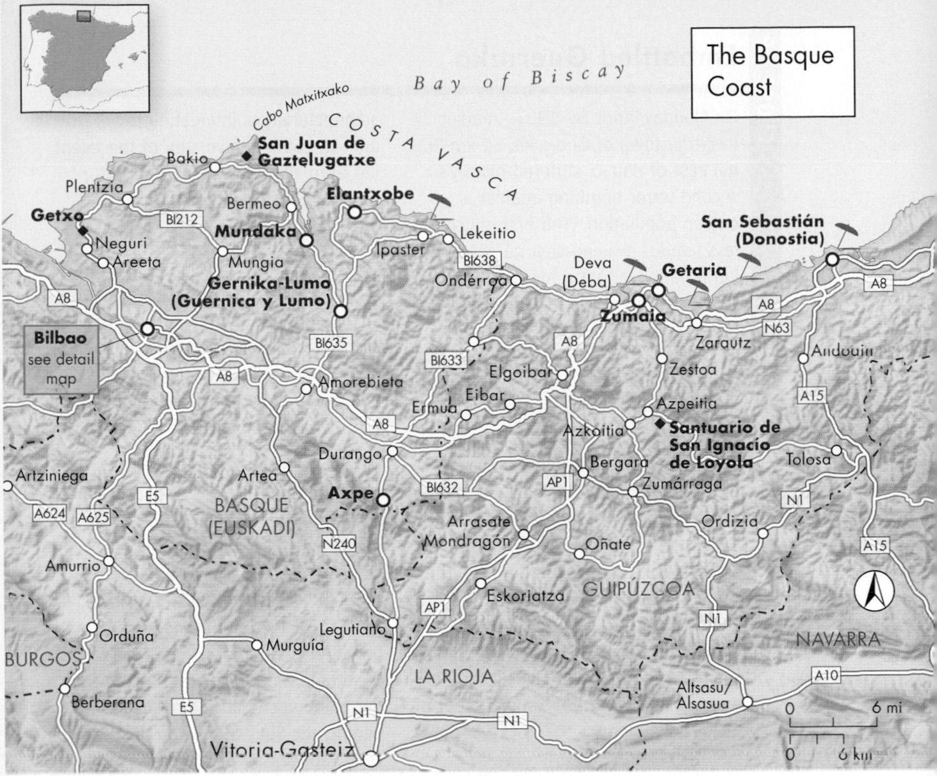

EN ROUTE

From Mundaka, follow signs for Gurenica, stopping at the Mirador de Portuondo—a roadside lookout on the left a kilometer outside of Mundaka (BI635, Km 43)—for an excellent view of the estuary. The restaurant Portuondo (⇨ *see Mundaka)* serves excellent tapas and Basque cooking on a terrace overlooking the Laida beach and the estuary.

AXPE

47 km (28 mi) southeast of Bilbao.

The village of Axpe, in the valley of Atxondo, nestles under the limestone heights of 4,777-foot Amboto—one of the highest peaks in the Basque Country outside of the Pyrenees. Home of the legendary Basque mother of nature, Mari Urrika or Mari Anbotokodama (María, Our Lady of Amboto), Amboto, with its spectral gray rock face, is a sharp contrast to the soft green meadows running up to the very foot of the mountain. According to Basque scholar and ethnologist José María de Barandiarán in his *Mitología Vasca* (*Basque Mythology*), Mari was "a beautiful woman, well constructed in all ways except for one foot, which was like that of a goat."

CLOSE UP

Embattled Guernika

On Monday, April 26, 1937—market day—the town of Guernika, 15 km (9 mi) east of Bilbao, suffered history's second terror bombing against a civilian population. (The first, much less famous, was against neighboring Durango, about a month earlier.) Gurenica, a rural market town, had been one of the keys to the Basque identity since the 14th century: Since the Middle Ages, Spanish sovereigns had sworn under the ancient oak tree of Gurenica to respect Basque *fueros* (special local rights—the kind of local autonomy that was anathema to the *generalísimo*'s Madrid-centered "National Movement," which promoted Spanish unity over local identity). The planes of the Nazi Luftwaffe were sent with the blessings of General Francisco Franco to experiment with saturation bombing of civilian targets and to decimate the traditional seat of Basque autonomy.

When the raid ended, more than 1,000 civilians lay dead or dying in the ruins, and today Gurenica remains a symbol of independence in the heart of every Basque, known to the world through Picasso's famous canvas *Guernica* (now in Madrid's Centro de Arte Reina Sofía). The city was destroyed—though the oak tree miraculously emerged unscathed—and has been rebuilt as a modern, architecturally uninteresting town. Not until the 60th anniversary of the event did Germany officially apologize for the bombing.

When Spain's Second Republic commissioned Picasso to create a work for the Paris 1937 International Exposition, little did he imagine that his grim canvas protesting the bombing of a Basque village would become one of the most famous paintings in history.

Picasso's painting had its own struggle. The Spanish Pavilion in the 1937 International Exposition in Paris nearly substituted a more upbeat work, using *Guernica* as a backdrop. In 1939, Picasso ceded *Guernica* to New York's Museum of Modern Art on behalf of the democratically elected government of Spain—stipulating that the painting should return only to a democratic Spain. Over the next 30 years, as Picasso's fame grew, so did *Guernica*'s—as a work of art and symbol of Spain's captivity.

When Franco died in 1975, two years after Picasso, negotiations with Picasso's heirs for the painting's return to Spain were already under way. Now on display at Madrid's Centro de Arte Reina Sofía, *Guernica* is home for good.

GETTING HERE

To reach Axpe from Bilbao, drive east on the A8/E70 freeway toward San Sebastián. Get off at the Durango exit 40 km (24 mi) from Bilbao and take the BI632 toward Elorrio. At Apatamonasterio turn right onto the BI3313 and continue to Axpe.

WHERE TO EAT AND STAY

$$–$$$$ SPANISH Fodor's Choice ★ **Etxebarri.** Bittor Etxebarri and his development of innovative techniques for cooking over coals have been hot news around the Iberian Peninsula for a decade now, with woods and coals tailored to different ingredients and new equipment such as the pan to char-grill *angulas*

(baby eels) improvised. Everything from clams and fish to meats and even the rice with langoustines is healthy, flavorful, and exciting as prepared and served in this blocky stone house in the center of a tiny mountain town. ✉ *Pl. San Juan 1* ☎ *94/658–3042* 🌐 *www.asadoretxebarri.com* ▭ *AE, DC, MC, V* ⊗ *Closed Mon. Lunch only except Sat.*

$$ Fodor's Choice ★ **Mendi Goikoa.** This handsome group of hillside farmhouses is among the province of Vizcaya's most exquisite hideaways. The lower farmhouse, Mendi Bekoa ("lower mountain" in Euskera), has stunning rooms, an elegant breakfast room, and a glassed-in terrace overlooking the valley. At the restaurant Mendi Goikoa ("upper mountain"; $$–$$$$), heavy beams loom overhead and a fire usually crackles in the far corner. The *pichón de Navaz a la parrilla* (Navaz wood pigeon cooked over coals) and the *txuleta de buey* (beef chop) are memorable. **Pros:** gorgeous setting; smart and attentive service. **Cons:** beds not always entirely comfortable; rooms poorly lit. ✉ *Barrio San Juan 33* ☎ *94/682–0833* 🌐 *www.mendigoikoa.com* *11 rooms* *In-room: Wi-Fi. In-hotel: restaurant* ▭ *AE, DC, MC, V* ⊗ *Closed Dec. 22–Jan. 17. Restaurant closed Mon. No dinner Sun.*

5

ELANTXOBE

27 km (17 mi) from Bermeo.

The tiny fishing village of Elantxobe (Elanchove, in Spanish) is surrounded by huge, steep cliffs, with a small breakwater that protects its fleet from the storms of the Bay of Biscay. The view of the port from the upper village is breathtaking, and the lower fork in the road leads to it.

WHERE TO STAY

¢–$ **Casa Rural Arboliz.** On a bluff overlooking the Bay of Biscay about 2 km (1 mi) outside of Elantxobe on the road to Lekeitio, this rustic inn is removed from the harborside bustle, offering a breath of the country life on the Basque coast. The cheerful, newly renovated rooms have terraces overlooking the sea, and there are two suites that are good for families. **Pros:** bucolic setting. **Cons:** could be too isolated and quiet for some. ✉ *Arboliz 12, Ibarranguelua* ☎ *94/627–6283* 🌐 *www.arboliz.com* *6 rooms* *In-room: Wi-Fi. In-hotel: parking (free)* ▭ *AE, DC, MC, V.*

¢ **Itsasmin Ostatua.** At the foot of Monte Ogoño in the upper part of the charming and colorful fishing and seafaring village of Elantxobe, this cozy place rents simple, cheery rooms and serves home-cooked Basque cuisine in its diminutive dining room ($–$$). Rooms with wood beams overhead look directly down into the deepwater harbor below; fourth-floor rooms have the best views. The hotel is a family enterprise, and the staff is unfailingly cheerful and helpful. **Pros:** part of the hustle and bustle of village life; simple and comfortable. **Cons:** tight quarters in some rooms; rooms facing the square can be noisy on weekends. ✉ *Nagusia 32* ☎ *94/627–6174* 🌐 *www.itsasmin.com* *12 rooms* *In-hotel: restaurant* ▭ *AE, DC, MC, V* ⊗ *Closed Jan. 6–Feb. 6.*

OFF THE BEATEN PATH

The Sanctuary of St. Ignatius of Loyola, in Cestona, about 34 km (21 mi) southwest of San Sebastián, is an exuberant baroque structure erected in honor of Iñigo Lopez de Oñaz y Loyola (1491–1556) after he was canonized as Ignacio de Loyola in 1622 for his defense of the Catholic Church against the tides of Martin Luther's Reformation. Almost two centuries later, Roman architect Carlos Fontana designed the basilica that memorializes the saint. The ornate construction contrasts with the austere ways of St. Ignatius himself, who took vows of poverty and chastity after his conversion. Polychrome marble, flamboyant altar work, and a huge but delicate dome decorate the interior. The fortresslike tower house has the room where Ignatius (Iñigo, in Euskera) experienced conversion while recovering from his wound in an intra-Basque battle.

GETARIA AND ZUMAIA

22 km (14 mi) west of San Sebastián.

Zumaia and Getaria are connected along the coast road and by several good footpaths.

Zumaia, a cozy little port and summer resort with the estuary of the Urola River flowing (back and forth, according to the tide) through town. The **Museo Zuloaga** (☎ *943/862341* 🌐 *www.ignaciozuloaga.com*), on N634 at the eastern edge of town, has an extraordinary collection of paintings by Goya, El Greco, Zurbarán, and others, in addition to works by the Basque impressionist Ignacio Zuloaga. The museum is open Easter–September 15, Wednesday–Sunday 4–8. The rest of the year it's open by prior arrangement only. Admission is €6 (€8 September–April).

Getaria (Guetaria, in Spanish) is known as *la cocina de Guipúzcoa* (the kitchen of Guipúzcoa province) for its many restaurants and taverns. It was also the birthplace of Juan Sebastián Elcano (1460–1526), the first circumnavigator of the globe and Spain's most emblematic naval hero. Elcano took over and completed Magellan's voyage after Magellan was killed in the Philippines in 1521. The town's galleonlike **church** has sloping wooden floors resembling a ship's deck. **Zarautz,** the next town over, has a wide beach and many taverns and cafés.

ESSENTIALS

Visitor Information Getaria (✉ *Parque Aldamar 2* ☎ *943/140957*). **Zumaia** (✉ *Pl. de Itzurun s/n* ☎ *943/143396*).

WHERE TO EAT AND STAY

$–$$ SPANISH ✕ **Bedua.** Zumaia natives like to access this rustic hideaway by boat when the tide is right, though you can also drive. A specialist in *tortilla de patatas con pimientos verdes de la huerta* (potato omelet with homegrown green peppers), Bedua is also known for *tortilla de bacalao* (codfish omelet), *txuleta de buey* (beef chop), and fish of all kinds, especially the classic *besugo* (sea bream) cooked *a la donostiarra* (roasted and covered with a sauce of garlic and vinegar). Txakolí from nearby Getaria is the beverage of choice. ✉ *Cestona, Barrio Bedua, 3 km (2 mi) up Urola from Zumaia* ☎ *943/860551* ▭ *MC, V.*

$$$–$$$$ SPANISH ★ ✕ **Kaia Kaipe.** Suspended over Getaria's colorful and busy fishing port and with panoramas looking up the coast past Zarautz and San Sebastián all the way to Biarritz, this spectacular place puts together exquisite fish soups and serves fresh fish right off the boats—you can

DID YOU KNOW?

The tart green grapes of Getaria's sprawling vineyards are used to make the Basque *txakolí*, a young, slightly effervescent, refreshing white wine.

watch them being unloaded below. The town is the home of Txomin Etxaniz, the premier *txakolí* (tart young Basque white wine), and this is the ideal place to drink it. ✉ *General Arnao 4* ☎ *943/140500* ▭ *AE, DC, MC, V* ⊙ *Closed Mar. 1–17 and Oct. 12–31. No dinner Mon. and Wed.*

¢ **Iribar**. The Iribar family has been grilling fish and beef over coals here for more than half a century. A few years ago they teamed up with an ambitious young chef who has added a modern touch to this family-friendly and traditional restaurant just uphill from Getaria's singular church ($–$$$). The rooms are impeccable, inexpensive, and some of the only berths available in the heart of this schooner-like historic village. **Pros:** historic monument; sweet family; excellent dining opportunity. **Cons:** tiny rooms; hard to get a car close to the hotel. ✉ *Kale Nagusia 34* ☎ *943/140406* 🖷 *943/140953* *4 rooms* *In-hotel: restaurant, bar* ▭ *AE, DC, MC, V* ⊙ *Closed Thurs. and Oct. 1–15 and Apr. 1–15. No dinner Wed.*

$ **Landarte**. For a taste of life in a Basque *caserío* (farmhouse), spend a night or two in this lovely restored 16th-century country manor house an hour's walk from Getaria. The walk down to town will prime you for the pleasures of Basque dining, while the hike back up will prepare you for still more. Stone walls, hand-hewn beams, sea views, and happy and helpful hosts make this a top choice. **Pros:** great location; cheery family. **Cons:** excessively rustic; cramped bathrooms. ✉ *Ctra. de Artadi 1, Zumaia* ☎ *943/865358* 🌐 *www.landarte.net* *6 rooms* *In-room: no a/c, Wi-Fi. In-hotel: parking (free)* ▭ *AE, DC, MC, V.*

$–$$$ **Saiaz Getaria**. For panoramic views over the Bay of Biscay, this 15th-century house on Getaria's uppermost street is a perfect refuge in this little village on a peninsula. The beautifully decorated rooms on the street side have heavy stone walls, but the plainer rooms on the sea side have the spectacular views. The long surfing wave crashing into the beach down below provides perfect water music for sleeping. **Pros:** opportunity to stay in a noble house in a unique fishing village. **Cons:** rooms on the sea side are small and undistinguished except for the views. ✉ *Roke Deuna 25* ☎ *943/140143* 🌐 *www.saiazgetaria.com* *17 rooms* *In-room: Wi-Fi. In-hotel: bar* ▭ *AE, DC, MC, V* ⊙ *Closed Dec. 20–Jan. 6.*

OFF THE BEATEN PATH

For a look at an authentic Basque farmhouse, or *caserío,* where the Urdapilleta family farms pigs, sheep, cattle, goats, chickens, and ducks, take a detour up to the village of Bidegoian (8 km [5 mi] short of Tolosa on the Azpeitia–Tolosa road). **Pello Urdapilleta** (which means "pile of pigs" in Euskera) sells artisanal cheeses and sausages and will show you how upland Basques have traditionally lived and farmed. ✉ *Elola Azpikoa Baserria, Bidegoian* ☎ *943/681006.*

SAN SEBASTIÁN TO HONDARRIBIA

Graceful, chic San Sebastián invites you to slow down: you can stroll the beach here or wander the streets. East of the city is Pasajes, from which the Marquis de Lafayette set off to help the rebelling forces in the American Revolution and where Victor Hugo spent a winter writing.

Just shy of the French border, you'll hit Hondarribia, a brightly painted, flower-festooned port town.

SAN SEBASTIÁN

Fodor's Choice ★ *100 km (62 mi) northeast of Bilbao.*

San Sebastián (Donostia, in Euskera) is a sophisticated city arched around one of the finest urban beaches in the world, **La Concha** (The Shell), so named for its resemblance to the shape of a scallop shell, with Ondarreta and Zurriola beaches at the southwestern and northeastern ends. The promontories of Monte Urgull and Monte Igueldo serve as bookends for La Concha, while Zurriola has Monte Ulía rising over its far end. The best way to see San Sebastián is to walk around: promenades and pathways lead up the hills that surround the city. The first records of San Sebastián date from the 11th century. A backwater for centuries, the city had the good fortune in 1845 to attract Queen Isabella II, who was seeking relief from a skin ailment in the icy Atlantic waters. Isabella was followed by much of the aristocracy of the time, and San Sebastián became a favored summer retreat for Madrid's well-to-do.

San Sebastián is divided by the **Urumea River,** which is crossed by three bridges inspired by late-19th-century French architecture. At the mouth of the Urumea, the incoming surf smashes the rocks with such force that white foam erupts, and the noise is wild and Wagnerian. The city is laid out with wide streets on a grid pattern, thanks mainly to the 12 different times it has been all but destroyed by fire. The last conflagration came after the French were expelled in 1813; English and Portuguese forces occupied the city, abused the population, and torched the place. Today, San Sebastián is a seaside resort on par with Nice and Monte Carlo. It becomes one of Spain's most expensive cities in the summer, when French vacationers descend in droves. It is also, like Bilbao, a center of Basque nationalism.

San Sebastián's neighborhoods include La Parte Vieja, tucked under Monte Urgull north of the mouth of the Urumea River; Gros (so named for a corpulent Napoleonic general) across the Urumea to the north; Centro, the main city nucleus around the cathedral; Amara farther east toward the Anoeta sports complex; La Concha at stage center around the beach; and El Antiguo at the western end of La Concha. Igueldo is the high promontory over the city at the southwestern side of the bay. Alto de Miracruz is the high ground to the northeast toward France; Errenteria is inland east of Pasaia; Oiartzun is a village farther north; Astigarraga is in apple-cider country to the east of Anoeta.

GETTING HERE AND AROUND

San Sebastián is a very walkable city, though local buses (€1.30) are also convenient. Buses for Pasajes, Errenteria, Astigarraga, and Oiartzun originate in Calle Okendo, one block west of the Urumea River behind the Hotel Maria Cristina. Bus A-1 goes to Astigarraga; A-2 is the bus to Pasajes (Pasaia in Euskera).

The EuskoTren, the city train, is popularly known as "El Topo" (The Mole) for the amount of time it spends underground and originates at the Amara Viejo station in Paseo Easo and tunnels its way to Hendaye, France, hourly in 45 minutes. EuskoTren also serves Zarautz (€1.50) in 40 minutes.

For the funicular up to Monte Igueldo (☎ *943/213525* 🌐 *www.monteigueldo.es* 🎟 *€2.50*) the station is just behind Ondarreta beach at the western end of La Concha.

ESSENTIALS

Bus Information Local info (☎ *943/000200* 🌐 *www.dbus.es*). **Bus station** (✉ *C. Sancho el Sabio 33* ☎ *943/463974*).

Car Rental Europcar (✉ *Aeropuerto de San Sebastián (Hondarribia [Fuenterrabía]), San Sebastián* ☎ *943/668530*).

Train Information EuskoTren (☎ *93/013500* 🌐 *www.euskotren.es* 🎟 *€1.50*). **San Sebastián train station** (✉ *Estación de Amara, Pl. Easo 9* ☎ *943/450131 or 943/471852*✉ *Estación del Norte, Av. de Francia* ☎ *943/283089 or 943/283599*).

Visitor Information San Sebastián–Donostia (✉ *Erregina Erregentearen 3* ☎ *943/481166*).

EXPLORING

Every corner of Spain champions its culinary identity, but San Sebastián's refined fare is in a league of its own. Many of the city's restaurants and *tapas* spots are in the **Parte Vieja** (Old Quarter), on the east end of the bay beyond the elegant **Casa Consistorial** (City Hall) and formal **Alderdi Eder** gardens. The building that now houses city hall began as a casino in 1887; after gambling was outlawed early in the 20th century, the town council moved here from the Plaza de la Constitución, the Old Quarter's main square.

The tiny **Isla de Santa Clara**, right in the entrance to the bay, protects the city from Bay of Biscay storms; this makes La Concha one of the calmest beaches on Spain's entire northern coast. A large hill dramatically dominates each side of the entrance to the bay.

A visit to **Monte Igueldo**, on the western side of the bay, is a must. (You can drive up for a toll of €1.70 per person or take the funicular—it runs from 10 AM to 9 PM in summer, 11–6 in winter, with departures every 15 minutes.) From the top, you get the remarkable panorama for which San Sebastián is famous: gardens, parks, wide tree-lined boulevards, Belle Epoque buildings, and, of course, the bay itself.

Designed by the world-renowned Spanish architect Rafael Moneo and situated at the mouth of the Urumea River, the **Kursaal** is San Sebastián's postmodern concert hall, film society, and convention center. The gleaming cubes of glass that make up this bright complex were conceived as a perpetuation of the site's natural geography, an attempt to "underline the harmony between the natural and the artificial" and to create a visual stepping-stone between the heights of Monte Urgull and Monte Ulía. It has two auditoriums, a gargantuan banquet hall, meeting rooms, exhibition space, and a sibling set of terraces overlooking

the estuary. The restaurant **Ni Neu** is an excellent spot for a meal or *tapas*. ✉ *Av. de la Zurriola, Gros* ☎ *943/003000* 🌐 *www.kursaal.org* ⏲ *Guided tours daily at 1:30 (€3). For guided tours in English make arrangements in advance.*

Just in from the harbor, in the shadow of Monte Urgull, is the baroque church of **Santa María**, with a stunning carved facade of an arrow-riddled St. Sebastian. The interior is strikingly restful; note the ship above the saint, high on the altar.

Looking straight south from the front of Santa María, you can see the facade and spires of the **Catedral Buen Pastor** (Cathedral of the Good Shepherd*)* across town.

QUICK BITES

Steps from the facade of Santa María, in the heart of the old quarter, have a *chocolate con nata*—thick, dark hot chocolate with whipped cream—at the tiny café Kantoi (✉ *C. Mayor 10, Parte Vieja*).

The **Museo de San Telmo** is in a 16th-century monastery behind the Parte Vieja, to the right of the church of Santa María, though it's closed for renovations until at least mid-2011, after which admission cost and hours may change. The former chapel, now a lecture hall, was painted by José María Sert (1876–1945), creator of notable works in Barcelona's city hall, London's Tate Gallery, and New York's Waldorf-Astoria hotel. Here, Sert's characteristic tones of gray, gold, violet, and earthy russet enhance the sculptural power of his work, which portrays events from Basque history. The museum displays Basque ethnographic items, such as prehistoric steles once used as grave markers and paintings by Zuloaga, Ribera, and El Greco. ✉ *Pl. de Ignacio Zuloaga s/n, Parte Vieja* ☎ *943/424970* 🎫 *Free* ⏲ *Tues.–Sat. 10:30–1:30 and 4–8, Sun. 10:30–2.*

OFF THE BEATEN PATH

Chillida Leku. In the Jáuregui section of Hernani, 10 minutes south of San Sebastián (close to both Martín Bersategui's restaurant in nearby Lasarte *and* the cider houses of the Astigarraga neighborhood, like Sidrería Petritegui), the Eduardo Chillida Sculpture Garden and Museum, in a 16th-century farmhouse, is a treat for anyone interested in contemporary art. ✉ *Caserío Zabalaga, Barrio Jáuregui 66, Lasarte*

San Sebastián's famed, curving La Concha beach

☎ *943/336006* 🌐 *www.museochillidaleku.com* 🎟 *€9* ⏲ *Closed Tues. (except July and Aug.) and Dec. 25–Jan. 1.*

TAPAS BARS

$–$$ Fodor's Choice ★ **A Fuego Negro.** This fabulous, relatively new tapas bar surprises with dramatic black and red decor, hip-hop music, and a fresh approach to traditional fare, such as small salads, *pintxos* to be eaten with a spoon, deconstructed aperitifs, and "tasting kits." ✉ *C. 31 de Agosto 31, Parte Vieja* ☎ *650/135373* 🌐 *www.afuegonegro.com.*

$$$–$$$$ ★ **Aloña Berri Bar.** Perennial winner of *tapas* championships, this spot across the Urumea River in Gros is well worth the walk. José Ramon Elizondo's miniature creations, from *contraste de pato* (duck à l'orange) to his Moorish-based *bastela de pichón* (pigeon pie), are excellent, if on the expensive side. Make sure to try the excellent crisp asparagus coated with burnt garlic. ✉ *C. Bermingham 24, Gros* ☎ *943/290818.*

¢–$ **Bar Gorriti.** Next to the open-air La Brecha Market, this traditional little *pinchos* bar is a classic, filled with good cheer and delicious *tapas.* ✉ *C. San Juan 3, Parte Vieja* ☎ *943/428353.*

¢–$ **Goiz Argi.** The specialty of this tiny bar—and the reason locals flock here on weekends—is the crisp yet juicy prawn brochette, even tastier as this is one of the city's few nonsmoking establishments. ✉ *Fermín Calbetón 4, Parte Vieja* ☎ *943/425204.*

¢–$ **La Cepa.** This booming and boisterous tavern has been around virtually forever (it opened in 1948). Everything from the ibérico ham to the little olive, pepper, and anchovy combos called "penalties" will whet your appetite. ✉ *C. 31 de Agosto 7, Parte Vieja* ☎ *943/426394.*

$-$$ **La Cuchara de San Telmo.** This bar opposite the San Telmo museum is popular and lively, so be prepared for some good-natured elbowing along with the excellent, freshly prepared pinchos such as ox in grainy mustard or cod in beer tempura. ✉ *C. 31 de Agosto 28, Parte Vieja* ☎ *943/435446.*

$$-$$$ ★ **Zeruko.** It may look like just another tapas bar, but the pinchos served here are among the most advanced and beautiful concoctions you'll find in the region. Don't miss the bacalao al pil pil (cod in a sauce of garlic and oil) that cooks itself on your plate. ✉ *Pescadería 10, Parte Vieja* ☎ *943/423451.*

WHERE TO EAT

$$$$ LA NUEVA COCINA ✕ **Akelarre.** On the far side of Monte Igueldo (and the far side of culinary tradition, as well) presides Chef Pedro Subijana, one of the most respected and creative chefs in the Basque Country. Prepare for tastes of all kinds, from Pop Rocks in blood sausage to mustard ice cream on tangerine peels. At the same time, Subijana's "straight" or classical dishes are monuments to traditional cookery and impeccable: try the venison with apple and smoked chestnuts or the *lubina* (sea bass) with *percebes* (goose barnacles). *EPaseo del Padre Orkolaga 56, Igueldo* ☎ *943/311209* ✍ *Reservations essential* ▭ *AE, DC, MC, V* ⊙ *Closed Feb., Oct. 1–15, Tues. Jan.–June, and Mon. except holidays and evenings preceding holidays. No dinner Sun.*

$$$$ BASQUE Fodor's Choice ★ ✕ **Arzak.** Renowned chef Juan Mari Arzak's little house at the crest of Alto de Miracruz on the eastern outskirts of San Sebastián is internationally famous, so reserve well in advance. Here, traditional Basque products and preparations are enhanced to bring out the best in the natural materials. The ongoing culinary dialogue between Juan Mari and his daughter Elena, who share the kitchen, is one of the most endearing attractions here. They disagree often, but it's all in the family, and the food just gets better and better. The sauces are perfect, and every dish looks beautiful, but the prices (even of appetizers) are astronomical. ✉ *Av. Alcalde Jose Elosegui 273, Alto de Miracruz* ☎ *943/278465* 🖷 *943/272753* ✍ *Reservations essential* ▭ *AE, DC, MC, V* ⊙ *Closed Sun and Mon., last 2 wks in June, and Nov. 1–29. No dinner Sun.*

$$$$ SPANISH Fodor's Choice ★ ✕ **Martín Berasategui.** One of the top four restaurants in San Sebastián (along with Akelaŕe, Arzak, and Mugaritz), the sure bet here is the *lubina asada con jugo de habas, vainas, cebolletas y tallarines de chipirón* (roast sea bass with juice of fava beans, green beans, baby onions, and cuttlefish shavings), but go with whatever Martín suggests, especially if it's woodcock, *pichón de Bresse* (Bresse wood pigeon), or any other kind of game. Lasarte, also the site of San Sebastián's lush green racetrack, is 8 km (5 mi) south of San Sebastián. ✉ *Loidi Kalea 4, Lasarte* ☎ *943/366471* ▭ *AE, DC, MC, V* ⊙ *Closed Mon., Tues., and mid-Dec.–mid-Jan. No lunch Sat. No dinner Sun.*

$$$$ SPANISH Fodor's Choice ★ ✕ **Mugaritz.** This farmhouse in the hills above Errenteria 8 km (5 mi) northeast of San Sebastián is surrounded by spices and herbs tended by boy-genius chef Andoni Luis Aduriz and his crew. In a rustic setting with a modern, open feeling, Aduriz demonstrates his mastery over vegetables, foie, and combining seafood with products of the nearby fields and forest. If you can resist the tasting menu and order carefully

à la carte, Aduriz's inventive, contemporary cuisine is within reach of the non-tycoon budget at about €65 a head. ✉ *Aldura Aldea 20, Otzazulueta Baserria, Errenteria* ☎ *943/518343* ▭ *AE, DC, MC, V* ⊙ *Closed Mon., wk before Easter, and Dec. 15–Jan. 15. No dinner Sun. No lunch Tues.*

$$$–$$$$ SPANISH

✕ **Ni Neu.** In early 2010, Adoni Aduriz's Ni Neu ("Me, Myself" in Euskera, the Basque language) replaced Martín Berasategui's Kursaal in this bright corner of Rafael Moneo's dazzling Kursaal complex at the mouth of the Urumea River. The new formula here has been christened bistronómico, a term coined by French chef Sebastián Demorand to describe a less formal family bistrot environment with more affordable and creative cuisine. Eggs fried at a low temperature with potatoes and codfish broth and pork ribs cooked for 40 hours and accompanied by creamy chicory and vanilla rice are two examples of comfort food with creative touches. In the back of the restaurant a tapas bar offers abbreviated versions of dishes that appear on the menu. ✉ *Zurriola Pasealekua 1, Gros* ☎ *943/003162* ▭ *AE, DC, MC, V* ⊙ *Closed Mon. No dinner Tues., Wed., and Sun.*

$$–$$$ BASQUE

✕ **Sidrería Petritegui.** For hearty dining and a certain amount of carousing and splashing around in hard cider, make this short excursion east of San Sebastián to the town of Astigarraga. Gigantic wooden barrels line the walls, and *sidra al txotx* (cider drawn straight from the barrel) is classically accompanied by cider-house specialties such as *tortilla de bacalao* (codfish omelet), *txuleta de buey* (beef chop), the smoky local sheep's-milk cheese from the town of Idiazabal, and, for dessert, walnuts and *membrillo* (quince jelly). ✉ *Ctra. San Sebastián–Hernani, Km 7, Astigarraga* ☎ *943/457188* ▭ *No credit cards* ⊙ *No lunch weekdays.*

$$$$ SPANISH ★

✕ **Urepel.** Too many cooks may spoil the broth, but not in this family enterprise. Peru Almandoz is the head chef, but the whole family works as a team. The cuisine balances classic and contemporary elements with typical Urepel inventions such as *chicharro al escama dorada* (a skinned, deboned mackerel served under a layer of golden-brown, sliced potatoes) or the unusual foie gras wrapped with veal. The appetizer of finely caramelized scallops with caviar is also excellent. ✉ *Paseo de Salamanca 3, Parte Vieja* ☎ *943/424040* ▭ *AE, DC, MC, V* ⊙ *Closed Sun. and Christmas and Easter wks.*

$$$$ SPANISH Fodor's Choice ★

✕ **Zuberoa.** Working in a 15th-century Basque farmhouse 9½ km (6 mi) northeast of San Sebastián outside the village of Oiartzun, Hilario Arbelaitz has long been one of San Sebastián's most celebrated chefs due to his original yet simple management of prime raw materials such as tiny spring cuttlefish, baby octopi, or woodcock. The *lenguado con verduritas y chipirones* (sole with baby vegetables and cuttlefish) is a tour de force. The atmosphere is unpretentious: just a few friends sitting down to dine simply—but very, very well. ✉ *Pl. Bekosoro 1, Oiartzun* ☎ *943/491228* ▭ *AE, DC, MC, V* ⊙ *Closed Sun., Wed., Jan. 1–15, Apr. 21–May 5, and Oct. 15–30.*

WHERE TO STAY

$$$$ ★ **Hotel María Cristina**. The graceful beauty of the Belle Epoque is embodied here, in San Sebastián's most luxurious hotel, which sits on the elegant west bank of the Urumea River. The grandeur continues in salons filled with Oriental rugs, potted palms, and Carrara marble columns and in bedrooms to match, with gold fixtures and wood wardrobes. Marble bathrooms add still more style. A piano player pounds out an eclectic medley of tunes nightly at the bar. **Pros:** polished service; supreme elegance; *the* place to stay. **Cons:** certain staffers are occasionally stiff; restaurant disappointing. ✉ *Paseo República Argentina 4, Centro* ☎ *943/437600* 🌐 *www.starwoodhotels.com.com* *108 rooms, 28 suites* *In-room: safe, Wi-Fi. In-hotel: restaurant, room service, bar, laundry service, parking (paid)* ▭ *AE, DC, MC, V.*

TESTOSTERONE ASYLUM

The Basque Country's men-only eating societies may seem another example of Spain's stereotypical machismo, but ethnologists and sociologists have long defined Basque society as a powerful matriarchy wherein the authority of the *etxekoandre* (the female house honcho) was so absolute that men became kitchen exiles. Eating societies were initially drinking clubs for men. Food came later, and, with the Basque passion for competition, cooking contests and the pursuit of culinary excellence followed. Today, there are also coed and all-women eating clubs.

$–$$$ **Hotel Parma**. Overlooking the Kursaal concert hall and the Zurriola beach at the mouth of the Urumea River, this small but bright new hotel is also at the edge of the Parte Vieja, San Sebastián's prime grazing area for *tapas* and vinos. Some of the cheerfully decorated rooms (though not all) have views northeast across the Urumea River and out to sea. **Pros:** location; views; the crashing of the waves. **Cons:** rooms are a bit cramped and cluttered; room decor is efficient but drab. ✉ *Paseo de Salamanca 10, Parte Vieja* ☎ *943/428893* 🌐 *www.hotelparma.com* *27 rooms* *In-room: Wi-Fi* ▭ *AE, DC, MC, V.*

$$$–$$$$ **Londres y de Inglaterra**. On the main beachfront promenade overlooking La Concha, this stately hotel has an old-world feel and aesthetic that starts in the bright, formal lobby and continues throughout the hotel. The bar and restaurant face the bay, and the guest rooms with views west out to sea are some of the best in town. **Pros:** sunsets from rooms on the Concha side are stunning; great location over the beach. **Cons:** some rooms in disrepair and in need of updating; street side can be noisy on weekends. ✉ *Zubieta 2, La Concha* ☎ *943/440770* 🌐 *www.hlondres.com* *139 rooms, 9 suites* *In-room: Wi-Fi. In-hotel: restaurant, bar, laundry service, parking (paid)* ▭ *AE, DC, MC, V.*

$ **Pensión Bellas Artes**. This tiny, family-run hotel not far from San Sebastián's cathedral stands out for the personal attention and advice given to guests by owner Leire and her mother. Rooms are simple but of a decent size, and details like fresh flowers every morning add to the feeling that you're staying at someone's home rather than a hotel. **Pros:** friendly service; warm atmosphere. **Cons:** intimate layout means a

5

Continued on page 346

MINIATURE FOOD, MAXIMUM FLAVOR

An Introduction to TAPAS

Virtually every day, coworkers head to a tapas bar after work for a *caña* (a 4- to 6-oz beer) that's almost always paired with a tapa or two. On weeknights, families crowd around tables, drinking and filling up on several tapas or sharing some *raciones*, which are shared among two or three people. In the evenings, people do tapas crawls, the Spanish version of

Defining tapas as merely a snack is, for a Spaniard, like defining air as an occasional breathable treat. If that sounds a little dramatic, consider how this bite-size food influences daily life across all regions and classes throughout Spain.

THE HISTORY OF SHRINKING PORTIONS

The origin of tapas is the stuff of heated tapas-bar debates. Various reports cloud the history of when and how it started. Some credit Alfonso X's diet and his delicate stomach. However, the most commonly accepted explanation is that a flat object (be it a slice of bread or a flat card with some nuts or sunflower seeds) was used to cover the rim of wine glasses to keep dive-bombing fruit flies out. (To cover something up is "tapar" in Spanish.)

a pub crawl, where *croquetas* balance out rich wine. Sometimes the spread for a *pica-pica* (a nibbling marathon), with *tortilla española* (Spanish omelet with potato), *aceitunas* (olives), *chorizo,* and *jamón,* will replace lunch or dinner outright. Eating tapas is such a way of life that a verb had to be created for it: *tapear* (to eat tapas) or *ir a tapeo* (to go eat tapas). The staff of life in Spain isn't bread. It's finger food.

TAPAS ACROSS SPAIN

MADRID

It is often difficult to qualify what is authentically from Madrid and what has been gastronomically cribbed from other regions, thanks to Madrid's melting-pot status for people and customs all over Spain. While *croquetas, tortilla de patata,* and even *paella* can be served as tapas, *patatas bravas* and *calamares* can be found in almost any restaurant in Madrid. The popular *patatas* are a very simple mixture of fried or roasted potatoes with a "Brava" sauce that is slightly spicy—surprising, given a country-wide aversion for dishes with the slightest kick. The *calamares*, fried in olive oil, can be served alone or with alioli sauce, mayonnaise, or—and you're reading correctly—in a sandwich. A slice of lemon usually accompanies your serving.

ANDALUSIA

Known for the warmth of its climate and its people, Andalusian bars tend to be very generous with their tapas—maybe in spite of the fact that they aren't exactly celebrated for their culinary inventiveness. But tapas here are traditional and among the best. Many times ordering a drink will bring you a sandwich large enough to make a meal, or a bowl of gazpacho that you could swim in. Seafood is also extremely popular in Andalusia, and you will find tapas ranging from sizzling prawns to small anchovies soaked in vinegar or olive oil.

Pescado frito (fried fish) and *albóndigas* (meatballs) are two common tapas in the region, and it's worth grazing multiple bars to try the different preparations. The fish usually includes squid, anchovies, and other tiny fish, deep fried and served as is. Since the bones are very small, they are not removed and considered fine for digestion. If this idea bothers you, sip some more wine. The saffron-almond sauce (*salsa de almendras* y *azafrán*) that accompanies the meatballs might very well make your eyes roll with pleasure. And since saffron is not as expensive in Spain as it is in the United States, the meatballs are liberally drenched in it.

Not incidentally, Spain's biggest export, olives, grows in Andalusia, so you can expect many varieties among the tapas served with your drinks.

Tortilla de patata

Calamares

Fried anchovy fish

Albondigas

BASQUE COUNTRY

More than any other community in Spain, the Basque Country is known for its culinary originality. The tapas, like the region itself, tend to be more expensive and inventive. And since the Basques insist on doing things their way, they call their unbelievable bites *pintxos* (or *pinchos* in Spanish) rather than tapas. *Gildas*, probably the most ordered *pintxo* in the Basque Country, is a simple toothpick skewer composed of a special green pepper (called *guindilla vasca*), an anchovy, and a pitted olive. All the ingredients must be of the highest quality, especially the anchovy, which should be marinated in the best olive oil and not be too salty. *Pimientos rellenos de bacalao* (roasted red peppers with cod) is also popular, given the Basque Country's adjacency to the ocean. The festive color of the red peppers and the savoriness of the fish make it a bite-sized Basque delicacy.

Red and green pepper *pintxos*

A spread of tapas selections

GET YOUR TAPAS ON

Madrid

El Bocaíto. Here you'll find the best *pescaito frito* (deep-fried whitebait) and a huge assortment of *tostas* (toast points with different toppings). ✉ *Libertad 6, Chueca* ☎ *91/532–1219.*

Estay. You'll find delicious *tortilla española con atun y lechuga* (Spanish omelet with tuna and lettuce) and excellent *rabas* (fried calamari). ✉ *Hermosilla 46, Salamanca* ☎ *91/578–0470.*

Andalusia

El Churrasco. The meats are delicious, but don't miss the *berenjenas crujientes con salmorejo* (crispy fried eggplant slices with thick gazpacho). ✉ *Romero 16, Judería, Córdoba* ☎ *95/729–0819.*

El Rinconcillo. It's great for the view of the Iglesia de Santa Catalina and a *caldereta de venado* (venison stew). ✉ *C. Gerona 40, Barrio de la Macarena, Seville* ☎ *95/422–3183.*

The Basque Country

Aloña Berri Bar. The repeat winner of tapas championships, its *contraste de pato* (duck à l'orange) and *bastela de pichón* (pigeon pie) makes foodies swoon. ✉ *C. Bermingham 24, Gros, San Sebastián* ☎ *94/329–0818.*

Xukela. Tasty and interersting *pintxos* are served at this atmospheric tavern. ✉ *C. del Perro 2, Bilbao, Casco Viejo* ☎ *94/415–9772.*

Bite-size food and drink

A wine pairing

lack of privacy. ✉ *Urbieta 64, Centro* ☎ *943/474905* 🌐 *www.pensionbellasartes.com* 10 rooms *In-room: Wi-Fi* ▭ *AE, DC, MC, V.*

NIGHTLIFE

Akerbeltz (✉ *Mari Kalea 10, Parte Vieja* ☎ *943/460934*), at the corner over the port to the left of Santa María del Coro and the Gaztelubide eating society, is a cozy late-night refuge for music and drinks. San Sebastián's top disco is **Bataplan** (✉ *Paseo de la Concha s/n, Centro* ☎ *943/460439*), near the western end of La Concha. **Bebop** (✉ *Paseo de Salamanca 3, Parte Vieja* ☎ *943/429869*), a publike bar on the edge of the Urumea River, has regular Latin and jazz concerts. **Friends** (✉ *Blvd. Zumardía 27, Centro* ☎ *943/217678*), near the Parte Vieja, is a hot spot. **Kabutzia** (✉ *Paseo del Muelle s/n, Centro* ☎ *943/429725*), above the Club Nautico seaward from the Casino, is a busy night haunt. **La Rotonda** (✉ *Paseo de la Concha 6, Centro* ☎ *943/429095*), across the street from Bataplan, below Miraconcha, is a top nightspot.

SHOPPING

San Sebastián is nonpareil for stylish home furnishings and clothing. Wander Calle San Martín and the surrounding pedestrian-only streets to see what's in the windows. **Bilintx** (✉ *C. Fermín Calbetón 21, Parte Vieja* ☎ *943/420080*) is one of the city's best bookstores.Stop into **Maitiena** (✉ *Av. Libertad 32, Centro* ☎ *943/424721*) for a fabulous selection of chocolates. **Ponsol** (✉ *C. Narrica 4, Parte Vieja* ☎ *943/420876*) is the best place to buy Basque berets; the Leclerq family has been hatting (and clothing) the locals for three generations.

PASAJES DE SAN JUAN

10 km (6 mi) east of San Sebastián.

★ Generally marked as Pasaia Donibane, in Euskera, there are actually three towns around the commercial port of Rentería: **Pasajes Ancho,** an industrial port; **Pasajes de San Pedro,** a large fishing harbor; and historic **Pasajes de San Juan,** a colorful cluster of 18th- and 19th-century buildings along the channel to the sea. Best reached by driving into Pasajes de San Pedro, on the San Sebastián side of the strait, and catching a launch across the mouth of the harbor (about €0.75, depending on the time of day)—this is too sweet a side trip to pass up.

In 1777, at the age of 20, General Lafayette set out from Pasajes de San Juan to aid the American Revolution. Victor Hugo spent the summer of 1843 here writing his *Voyage aux Pyrénées*. The **Victor Hugo House** is the home of the tourist office and has an exhibit of traditional village dress. **Ontziola,** a research center for traditional wooden boat design, is directed by Xavier Agote, who taught boatbuilding in Rockland, Maine. Pasajes de San Juan can be reached via Pasajes de San Pedro from San Sebastián by cab or bus. Or, if you prefer to go on foot, follow the red-and-white-blazed GR trail that begins at the east end of the Zurriola beach—you're in for a spectacular three-hour hike along the rocky coast. By car, take N1 for France and, after passing Juan Mari Arzak's landmark restaurant, Arzak, at Alto de Miracruz, look for a marked left turn into Pasaia or Pasajes de San Pedro.

WHERE TO EAT

$$–$$$ BASQUE Fodor's Choice ★ **Txulotxo.** Cozy and friendly, this picturesque and unusual restaurant sits like a matchbox on stilts at the edge of the Rentería shipping passage, in the shadow of the occasional freighter passing only a few dozen yards away. The *sopa de pescado* (fish soup), thick and piping hot, is among the best available on the Basque coast, and the fresh grilled sole and monkfish, not to mention the pimiento-wrapped *bacalao* (codfish), are equally superb. Make sure you leave some time to stroll around town. *Donibane 71, Pasajes de San Juan 943/523952 Reservations essential AE, DC, MC, V Closed Tues. and Dec. 23–Jan. 15. No dinner Sun.*

WORD OF MOUTH

"Just back from a weekend at Hondarribia, an underrated town for no reason at all. Every time I go there I find another new reason to love it. Basque mediaeval streets, dozens of cozy corners, a parador in a fortress, great *pintxos* and great food, friendly atmosphere everywhere. A must."
—mikelg

5

HONDARRIBIA

12 km (7 mi) east of Pasajes.

Hondarribia (Fuenterrabía, in Spanish) is the last fishing port before the French border. Lined with fishermen's homes and small fishing boats, the harbor is a beautiful but touristy spot. If you have a taste for history, follow signs up the hill to the medieval bastion and onetime castle of Carlos V, now a parador.

ESSENTIALS

Visitor Information Hondarribia (*Javier Ugarte 6 943/645458*).

WHERE TO EAT AND STAY

$$$$ SEAFOOD **Alameda.** Hot young Hondarribia star chefs Gorka and Kepa Txapartegi opened this restaurant in 1997 after working with, among others, Lasarte's master chef Martín Berasategui. The elegantly restored house in upper Hondarribia is a delight, as are the seasonally rotated combinations of carefully chosen ingredients, from duck to foie gras to vegetables. Both surf and turf selections are well served here, from ibérico ham to fresh tuna just in from the Atlantic. The terrace is the place to be on balmy summer evenings. *Minasoroeta 1 943/642789 AE, DC, MC, V Closed Mon., 2 wks at Christmas and 2 wks in Feb. No dinner Sun.*

$$–$$$ SEAFOOD ★ **La Hermandad de Pescadores.** This central restaurant with wooden tables and a handsome mahogany bar is owned by the local fishermen's guild and serves simple, hearty fare at better than reasonable prices. Try the *sopa de pescado* (fish soup), the *mejillones* (mussels), or the *almejas a la marinera* (clams in a thick, garlicky sauce). If you are careful to come not at peak hours (2–4 and 9–11), you'll be able to find space at the long, communal, and fraternal boards. *C. Zuloaga s/n 943/642738 AE, DC, MC, V Closed Wed., Christmas through Jan., 1 wk in May, and 1 wk in Oct. No dinner Tues.*

¢ **Caserío "Artzu."** This family barn and house, with its classic low, wide roofline, has been here in one form or another for some 800 years. Just west of the hermitage of Nuestra Señora de Guadalupe, 5 km (3 mi) above Hondarribia, Artzu offers modernized accommodations in an ancient *caserío* overlooking the junction of the Bidasoa estuary and the Atlantic. Better hosts than this warm, friendly clan are hard to find. **Pros:** good value; friendly family. **Cons:** beds only moderately comfortable; bathrooms small. ✉ *Barrio Montaña* ☎ *943/640530* 🌐 *www.euskalnet.net/casartzu* 🛏 *6 rooms, 1 with bath* 👍 *In-room: no a/c, no TV, Wi-Fi. In-hotel: restaurant, bar* 💳 *No credit cards.*

$$$–$$$$ **Parador de Hondarribia.** Also known as Parador El Emperador, this medieval bastion dates from the 10th century and housed imperial Spain's founding Emperor Carlos V in the 16th century. Replete with suits of armor and other chivalric bric-a-brac, the place feels like a movie set (and has occasionally been used as one). Many rooms have views of the Bidasoa estuary. Reserve ahead and ask for one of the three "special" rooms, with canopy beds and baronial appointments, well worth the moderate extra expense. **Pros:** great views; impeccably comfortable. **Cons:** slightly chilly (typical parador) service; no restaurant. ✉ *Pl. de Armas 14* ☎ *943/645500* 🌐 *www.parador.es* 🛏 *36 rooms* 👍 *In-room: Wi-Fi. In-hotel: bar, parking (paid)* 💳 *AE, DC, MC, V.*

EN ROUTE

The fastest route from San Sebastián to Pamplona is the A15 Autovía de Navarra, which cuts through the Leizarán Valley and gets you there in about 45 minutes. Somewhat more scenic, if slower (two hours) and more tortuous, is the 134-km (83-mi) drive on C133, which starts near Hondarribia and follows the Bidasoa River (the border with France) up through Vera de Bidasoa. When C133 meets N121, you can turn left up into the lovely Baztán Valley or right to continue through the Velate pass to Pamplona.

NAVARRA AND PAMPLONA

Bordering the French Pyrenees and populated largely by Basques, Navarra grows progressively less Basque toward its southern and eastern edges. Pamplona, the ancient Navarran capital, draws crowds with its annual feast of San Fermín, but medieval Vitoria, in the Basque province of Alava, is largely undiscovered by tourists. Olite, south of Pamplona, has a storybook castle, and the towns of Puente la Reina and Estella are visually indelible stops on the Camino de Santiago.

PAMPLONA

79 km (47 mi) southeast of San Sebastián.

Pamplona (Iruña, in Euskera) is known worldwide for its running of the bulls, made famous by Ernest Hemingway in his 1926 novel *The Sun Also Rises.* The occasion is the festival of San Fermín, July 6–14, when Pamplona's population triples (along with hotel rates), so reserve rooms months in advance. Every morning at 8 sharp a rocket is shot off, and the bulls kept overnight in the corrals at the edge of town are run through a series of closed-off streets leading to the bullring, a 902-yard dash. Running before them are Spaniards and foreigners feeling festive enough to risk goring. The degree of peril in the running (or *encierro*,

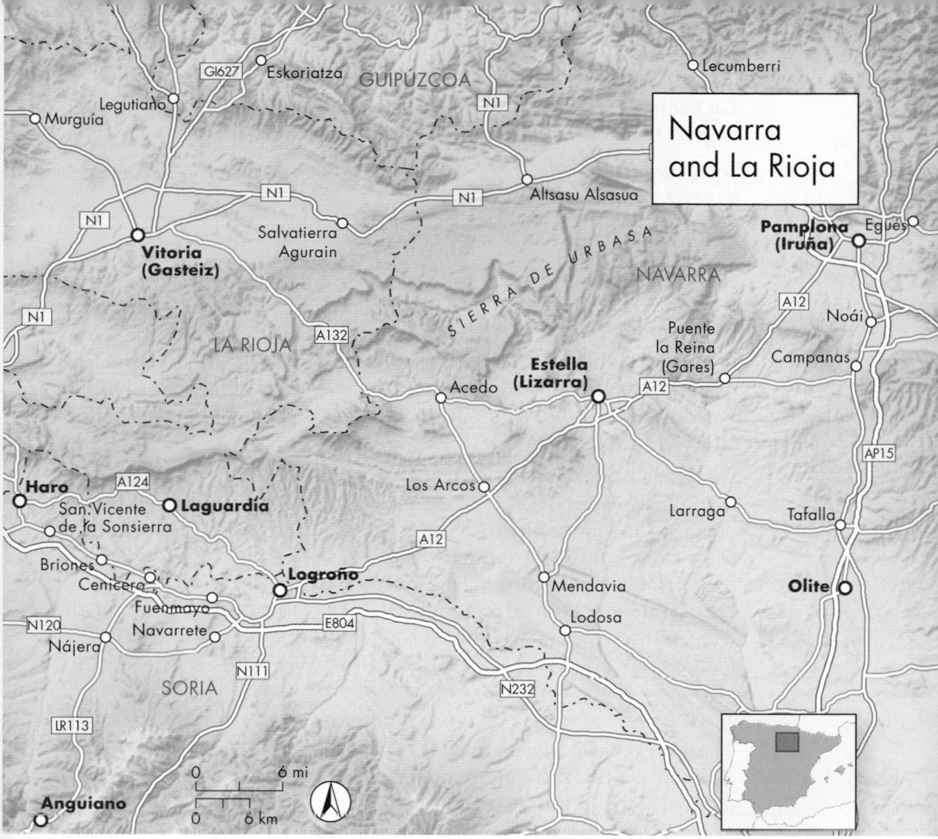

meaning "enclosing) is difficult to gauge. Serious injuries occur nearly every day during the festival; deaths are rare but always a possibility. What's certain is the sense of danger, the mob hysteria, and the exhilaration. Tickets to the bullfights (*corridas*), as opposed to the running, to which access is free, can be difficult to get.

Founded by the Roman emperor Pompey as Pompaelo, or Pampeiopolis, Pamplona was successively taken by the Franks, the Goths, and the Moors. In 750, the Pamplonians put themselves under the protection of Charlemagne and managed to expel the Arabs temporarily. But the foreign commander took advantage of this trust to destroy the city walls; when he was driven out once more by the Moors, the Navarrese took their revenge, ambushing and slaughtering the retreating Frankish army as it fled over the Pyrenees through the mountain pass of Roncesvalles in 778. This is the episode depicted in the 11th-century *Song of Roland*, although the anonymous French cast the aggressors as Moors. For centuries after that, Pamplona remained three argumentative towns until they were forcibly incorporated into one city by Carlos III (the Noble, 1387–1425) of Navarra.

ESSENTIALS

Bus Station Pamplona (✉ Yanguas y Miranda 2 ☎ *948/203566*).

Car Rentals Europcar (✉ *Av. Pio XII 43, Pamplona* ☎ *948/172523* ✉ *Aeropuerto de Pamplona* ☎ *948/312798*).

Train Information Pamplona (✉ *Estación de Pamplona, Ctra. de San Sebastián* ☎ *948/130202*).

Visitor Information Pamplona (✉ *HilarionEslava 1* ☎ *848/420420*).

EXPLORING

Pamplona's most remarkable civil building is the ornate **ayuntamiento** *(town hall)* on the Plaza Consistorial, with its rich ocher facade setting off brightly gilded balconies. The interior is a lavish wood-and-marble display of wealth reminding visitors that Navarra was always a wealthy kingdom of its own. The present building was erected between 1753 and 1759.

Pamplona's **cathedral**, set near the portion of the ancient walls rebuilt in the 17th century, is one of the most important religious buildings in northern Spain, thanks to the fragile grace and gabled Gothic arches of its cloister. Inside are the tombs of Carlos III and his wife, marked by an alabaster sculpture. The **Museo Catedralicio Diocesano** (Diocesan Museum) houses religious art from the Middle Ages and the Renaissance. Call in advance for guided tours in English. ✉ *C. Dormitaleria 3–5* ☎ *948/212594* *€4.50* *Museum July 15–Sept. 15, weekdays 10–7, Sat. 10–2; Sept. 15–July 15, weekdays 10–2 and 4–7, Sat. 10–2.*

The central **Ciudadela**, an ancient fortress, is a parkland of promenades and pools. Walk through in late afternoon, the time of the *paseo* (traditional stroll), for a taste of everyday life here.

Archivo Real y General de Navarra. This Rafael Moneo–designed archive of glass and stone ingeniously contained within a Romanesque palace is Pamplona's architectural treasure. Containing papers and parchments going back to the 9th century, the archive holds 23,000 linear meters of documents and has room for 17,000 meters more. The library and reading rooms are lined with cherry wood and covered with a gilded ceiling. ✉ *Dos de Mayo s/n* ☎ *848/424609* *www.cfnavarra.es*.

On Calle Santo Domingo, in a 16th-century building once used as a hospital for pilgrims on their way to Santiago de Compostela, is the **Museo de Navarra**, with a collection of regional archaeological artifacts and historical costumes. ✉ *C. Santo Domingo 47* ☎ *848/426492* *www.cfnavarra.es* *€2.50* *Tues.–Sat. 9.30–2 and 5–7, Sun. 11–2.*

One of Pamplona's greatest charms is the warren of small streets near the **Plaza del Castillo** (especially Calle San Nicolás), which are filled with restaurants, taverns, and bars. Pamplonicas are hardy, rough-and-tumble sorts, well known for their eagerness and capacity to eat and drink.

QUICK BITES

Pamplona's gentry has been flocking to the ornate, French-style Café Iruña (✉ *Pl. del Castillo 44* ☎ *948/222064* *www.cafeiruna.com*) since 1888, but Ernest Hemingway made it part of world literary lore in *The Sun Also*

***Rises* in 1926. You can still have a drink with a bronze version of the author at his favorite perch at the far end of the bar.**

OFF THE BEATEN PATH

Fundación–Museo Jorge Oteiza. Just 8 km (5 mi) east of Pamplona on the road toward France, this museum dedicated to the father of modern Basque art is a must-visit. Jorge Oteiza (1908–2003), in his seminal treatise, *Quosque Tandem,* called for Basque artists to find an aesthetic of their own instead of attempting to become part of the Spanish canon. Rejecting ornamentation in favor of essential form and a noninvasive use of space, Oteiza created a school of artists of which the sculptor Eduardo Chillida (1924–2002) was the most famous. The building itself, Oteiza's home for more than two decades, is a large cube of earth-color concrete designed by Oteiza's longtime friend, Pamplona architect Francisco Javier Sáenz de Oiza.The sculptor's living quarters, his studio and laboratory, and the workshop used for teaching divde the museum into three sections. ✉ *Alzuza, Ctra. N150, Km 8, from Pamplona* ☎ *948/332074* 🌐 *www.museooteiza.org* €4 ⏲ *Mid-Sept.–mid-June, Tues.–Fri. 10–3, weekends 11–7; mid-June–mid-Sept., Tue.–Sat. 11–7, Sun. 11–3.*

5

WHERE TO EAT AND STAY

$$$$ ✕ **Europa.** Generally considered Pamplona's best restaurant, the Europa, in the hotel of the same name, offers a decidedly epicurean take on traditional Navarran cooking. The small and light first-floor dining room offers the perfect backdrop to dishes like slow-cooked lamb and pork, or the best *bacalao al pil pil* you may try on your trip. A la carte dining is expensive, but there are excellent tasting menus available for €45 and €65. ✉ *C. Espoz y Mina 11* ☎ *948/221800* 🌐 *www.hreuropa.com* ▭ *AE, DC, MC, V C*

¢–$$ SPANISH ✕ **Gaucho.** A legendary address for *tapeo* (*tapas* grazing) and *txikiteo* (wine tippling), this small tavern serves some of the best *tapas* in Pamplona. Just off Plaza del Castillo, in the eye of the hurricane during *San Fermín*, there is a surprising sense of peace and quiet here, even as the fiesta spins out of control outside. *Tapas* range from the classical *chistorra* (spicy sausage) to contemporary creations such as the deconstructed *vieira* (scallop), an apt metaphor for Pamplona's blend of old and new. ✉ *Espoz y Mina 4* ☎ *948/225073* ▭ *AE, DC, MC, V* ⏲ *Closed July 15–30.*

$$$–$$$$ SPANISH ✕ **Josetxo.** This warm, family-run restaurant in a stately mansion with classically elegant decorations is one of Pamplona's finest addresses for refined cuisine. Traditional, international, Navarran, and contemporary culinary techniques and tastes all find a place on the menu. House favorites range from *hojaldre de marisco* (shellfish pastry) to an *ensalada de langosta* (lobster salad) appetizer and *muslo de pichón relleno de trufa y foie* (pigeon drumstick stuffed with truffles and foie gras). ✉ *Pl. Príncipe de Viana 1* ☎ *948/222097* ▭ *AE, DC, MC, V* ⏲ *Closed Sun. except during San Fermín, and Aug.*

$–$$$ **Europa.** A modest, family-run hotel a block and half from the bullring and within shouting distance of party-central Plaza del Castillo, this is a handy alternative to the grand hotels of Pamplona. The bathrooms have cool marble floors. The restaurant, on the ground floor, is one of the

CLOSE UP

Running with the Bulls

In *The Sun Also Rises,* Hemingway describes the Pamplona *encierro* (bull running) in anything but romantic terms. Jake Barnes hears the rocket, steps out on his balcony, and watches the crowd run by: men in white with red sashes and neckerchiefs, those behind running faster than the bulls. "One man fell, rolled to the gutter, and lay quiet." It's a textbook move, and first-rate observation and reporting. An experienced runner who falls remains motionless (bulls respond to movement). In the next *encierro* in the novel, a man is gored and dies. The waiter at the Iruña café mutters, "You hear? Muerto. Dead. He's dead. With a horn through him. All for morning fun."

Despite this, generations of young Americans and other internationals have turned this barnyard bull-management maneuver into one of the Western world's most famous rites of passage. The idea is simple: At daybreak, six fighting bulls are guided through the streets by 8 to 10 *cabestros,* or steers (also known as *mansos,* meaning "tame"), to the holding pens at the bullring, from which they will emerge to fight that afternoon. The course covers 924 yards. The Cuesta de Santo Domingo down to the corrals is the most dangerous part of the run, high in terror and short in distance. The walls are sheer, and the bulls pass quickly. The fear here is of a bull hooking along the wall of the Military Hospital on his way up the hill, forcing runners out in front of the speeding pack in a classic hammer and anvil movement. Mercaderes is next, cutting left for about 100 yards by the town hall, then right up Calle Estafeta. The outside of each turn and the centrifugal force of 10,000 kilos (22,000 pounds) of bulls and steers are to be avoided here. Calle Estafeta is the bread and butter of the run, the longest (about 400 yards), straightest, and least complicated part of the course.

The classic run, a perfect blend of form and function, is to remain ahead of the horns for as long as possible, fading to the side when overtaken. The long gallop up Calle Estafeta is the place to try to do it. The trickiest part of running with the bulls is splitting your vision so that with one eye you keep track of the bulls behind you and with the other you avoid falling over runners ahead of you.

At the end of Estafeta the course descends left through the *callejón,* the narrow tunnel, into the bullring. The bulls move more slowly here, uncertain of their weak forelegs, allowing runners to stay close and even to touch them as they glide down into the tunnel. The only uncertainty is whether there will be a pileup in the tunnel. The most dramatic photographs of the *encierro* have been taken here, as the galloping pack slams through what occasionally turns into a solid wall of humanity. If all goes well—no bulls separated from the pack, no mayhem—the bulls will have arrived in the ring in less than three minutes.

The cardinal crime, punishable by a $1,000 fine, is to attempt to attract a bull, thus removing him from the pack and creating a deadly danger. After 14 years without a fatality, a young man was gored to death in July 2009.

DID YOU KNOW?

The distance from the corral where the bulls are kept to the bullring where they'll fight in the afternoon is about 825 metres (about 1,066 feet); the average person running with the bulls covers it in about 3 minutes.

best in Navarra, and there is generally an offer on whereby hotel guests can enjoy this gourmet haven at much less than the usual prices. **Pros:** central location; good value; excellent cooking. **Cons:** noisy during the fiesta unless you score an interior room; rooms on the small side. ✉ *C. Espoz y Mina 11* ☎ *948/221800* 🌐 *www.heuropa.com* *25 rooms* *In-room: Wi-Fi. In-hotel: restaurant* ▭ *AE, DC, MC, V.*

$$$$ **Gran Hotel La Perla.** La Perla is the oldest hotel in Pamplona and, after several years of refurbishing, has reinvented itself as a luxury lodging option. Rooms have been modernized and redecorated in plush pastels and sleek contemporary lines. Several have retained their early-20th-century decor, among them Hemingway's (No. 201, from which he watched the running of the bulls in 1924). The hotel founder's son, Lalo Moreno, was a bullfighter, and the mounted heads of two of his taurine adversaries preside over the restaurant. Prices triple during San Fermín. **Pros:** read your worn copy of *The Sun Also Rises* in the place where the book was first conceived; impeccable comfort. **Cons:** round-the-clock mayhem during San Fermín. ✉ *Pl. del Castillo 1* ☎ *948/223000* 🌐 *www.granhotellaperla.com* *44 rooms* *In-room: refrigerator, Wi-Fi. In-hotel: restaurant, bar, parking (paid)* ▭ *AE, DC, MC, V.*

$$$$ **Palacio Guendulain.** This 18th-century palace in the center of town has been restored to the original architecture and aristocratic decor, including the wooden ceilings and the grand staircase. Even the collection of carriages of the counts of Guendulain—who continue to live in the building—is on display and many of the sumptuous rooms have original furniture. This one is worth the splurge. **Pros:** opportunity to stay in a historical monument; central location; outstanding service. **Cons:** provides little refuge from the mayhem during San Fermín. ✉ *Zapatería 53* ☎ *948/225532* 🌐 *www.palacioguendulain.com* *23 rooms, 2 suites* *In-room: Wi-Fi. In-hotel: restaurant, bar, laundry service, parking (paid)* ▭ *AE, DC, MC, V.*

NIGHTLIFE

The city has a thumping student life year-round, especially along the length of Calle San Nicolas. For an ultra-up-to-date nightspot, try **Dodo Club** (✉ *San Roque 7* ☎ *948/198989*), where breakfast, lunch, free Wi-Fi, and DJs keep things lively around the clock. **Marengo** (✉ *Av. Bayona 2* ☎ *948/265542* *€10* ⏲ *11* PM–6 AM) is a barnlike rager filled until dawn with young singles and couples. Dress up or you might flunk the bouncer's inspection.

SHOPPING

Botas are the wineskins from which Basques typically drink at bullfights or during fiestas. The art lies in drinking a stream of wine from a *bota* held at arm's length without spilling a drop, if you want to maintain your honor (not to mention your clean shirt). You can buy empty *botas* in any Basque town, but Pamplona's **Anel** (✉ *C. Comedías 7*) sells the best brand, Las Tres Zetas—"The Three Zs," written as ZZZ. **Hijas de C. Lozano** (✉ *C. Zapatería 11*) sells *café y leche* (coffee and milk) toffees that are prized all over Spain. **Salcedo** (✉ *C. Estafeta 37*), open since 1800, invented and still sells almond-based *mantecadas* (powder cakes), as well as *coronillas* (delightful almond-and-cream concoctions).

OFF THE BEATEN PATH

Olite, 41 km (25 mi) south of Pamplona, offers an unforgettable glimpse into the Spain of the Middle Ages, including the 11th-century church of **San Pedro,** revered for its finely worked Romanesque cloisters and portal. It's the town's **castle** (*€3.10* *Daily 10–7*), though, restored by Carlos III in the French style and brimming with ramparts, crenellated battlements, and watchtowers, that captures the imagination most. You can walk the ramparts, and should you get tired or hungry, part of the castle has been converted into a parador, making a fine place to catch a bite or a few z's. *www.parador.com.*

ESTELLA

43 km (27 mi) southwest of Pamplona, 48 km (30 mi) northeast of Logroño.

Once the seat of the Royal Court of Navarra, Estella (Lizarra, in Euskera) is an inspiring stop on the Camino de Santiago.

ESSENTIALS

Visitor Information Estella (*San Nicolás 4* *948/556301*).

The heart of Estella is the arcaded Plaza San Martín and its chief civic monument, the 12th-century **Palacio de los Reyes de Navarra** (Palace of the Kings of Navarra). **San Pedro de la Rúa** (*C. San Nicolás s/n*) has a beautiful cloister and a stunning carved portal.

Across the River Ega from San Pedro, the doorway to the **church of San Miguel** has fantastic relief sculptures of St. Michael the Archangel battling a dragon.The **Iglesia del Santo Sepulcro** (Church of the Holy Sepulchre *C. Curtidores s/n*) has a beautiful fluted portal. **Santa María Jus del Castillo** (*C. Curtidores s/n*), converted from a synagogue in 1145, is the only vestige of Estella's medieval Jewish quarter. The **Monasterio de Irache** (*Ctra. de Logroño, Km 3*) dates from the 10th century but was later converted by Cistercian monks to a pilgrims' hospital; next door is the famous brass faucet that supplies pilgrims with free-flowing holy wine.

VITORIA-GASTEIZ

93 km (56 mi) west of Pamplona, 115 km (71 mi) southwest of San Sebastián, 64 km (40 mi) southeast of Bilbao.

Vitoria's standard of living is currently rated among the highest in Spain, based on such criteria as square meters of green space per inhabitant (14), sports and cultural facilities, and pedestrian-only zones. The capital of the Basque Country, and its second-largest city after Bilbao, Vitoria (Gasteiz, in Euskera) is nevertheless in many ways Euskadi's least Basque city. Neither a maritime city nor a mountain enclave, Vitoria occupies the steppelike *meseta de Alava* (Alava plain) and functions as a modern industrial center with a surprisingly medieval Casco Antiguo (Old Quarter), which serves as a striking example of the successful integration of ancient and modern architecture. Founded by Sancho el Sabio (the Wise) in 1181, the city was built largely of granite rather than sandstone, so Vitoria's oldest streets and squares seem especially dark, weathered, and ancient.

GETTING AROUND

Vitoria is a big city, but the area you'll spend your time in is small, only about 1 km (½ mi) square, and easily walkable.

ESSENTIALS

Bus Station Vitoria (✉ *C. de los Herran 50* ☎ *945/258400*).

Car Rentals Europcar (✉ *Adriano VI 29* ☎ *945/200433*).

Visitor Information Vitoria-Gasteiz (✉ *Pl. General Loma 1* ☎ *945/161598*).

EXPLORING

★ **Artium.** Officially titled Centro-Museo Vasco de Arte Contemporáneo, this former bus station was opened in 2002 by King Juan Carlos I, who called it "the third leg of the Basque art triangle, along with the Bilbao Guggenheim and San Sebastián's Chillida Leku." The museum's permanent collection—including 20th- and 21st-century paintings and sculptures by Jorge Oteiza, Chillida, Agustín Ibarrola, and Nestor Basterretxea, among many others—makes it one of Spain's finest treasuries of contemporary art. ✉ *Calle de Francia 24* ☎ *945/209020* 🌐 *www.artium.org* 🎫 *Free (donations welcome)* ⏲ *Tues.–Sun. 11–8.*

Plaza de la Virgen Blanca, in the southwest corner of old Vitoria, is ringed by noble houses with covered arches and white-trim glass galleries. The monument in the center commemorates the Duke of Wellington's defeat of Napoléon's army here in 1813. For lunch, coffee, or *tapas*, look to the plaza's top left-hand corner for the Cafeteria de la Virgen Blanca, with its giant wooden floorboards.The **Plaza de España**, across Virgen Blanca past the monument and the handsome El Victoria café, is an arcaded neoclassical square with the austere elegance typical of formal 19th-century squares all over Spain.The **Plaza del Machete**, overlooking Plaza de España, is named for the sword used by medieval nobility to swear allegiance to the local *fueros* (special Basque rights and privileges). A jasper niche in the lateral facade of the Gothic church of **San Miguel Arcángel** (✉ *Pl. del Machete*) contains the Virgen Blanca (White Virgin), Vitoria's patron saint.

The 15th-century **Torre de Doña Otxanda** (✉ *Calle Siervas de Jesús24*) houses Vitoria's **Museo de Ciencias Naturales** (Museum of Natural Sciences), which contains interesting botanical, zoological, and geological collections along with the museum's most prized items: pieces of amber from the nearby archeological site at Peñacerrada-Urizaharra.

The **Catedral de Santa María** (✉ *Cuchillería 95*), which dates back to the 14th century, is currently being restored but can still be visited; it's a unique opportunity to study the building's architecture from the foundation up. A prominent and active supporter of the project is the American writer Ken Follett, and a statue of him has been placed on one side of the cathedral.

The **Torre de los Anda** (✉ *C. Fray Zacarías Martinez s/n*) is across from the exquisitely sculpted Gothic doorway on the western facade of the cathedral. Go into the courtyard on the west side of this square; in

The Plaza de la Virgen Blanca is surrounded by magisterial buildings.

the far right corner, you'll find the sculpted head of a fish protruding from the grass in front of an intensely ornate door. Walk through Calle Txikitxoa and up Cantón de Santa María behind the Catedral de Santa María, noting the tiny hanging rooms and alcoves that have been added to the back of the apse over the centuries, clinging across corners and filling odd spaces.

The lovely plateresque facade of the 16th-century **Palacio de Escoriaza-Esquibel** (⊠ *C. Fray Zacarías Martinez 5*) overlooks an open space.Don't miss the austere **Palacio Villasuso** (⊠ *C. Fray Zacarías Martinez*), built in 1538. It's down toward the Plaza del Machete, across from the church of San Miguel. The **Casa del Cordón** (⊠ *C. Cuchillería*), a 15th-century structure with a 13th-century tower, stands at No. 24, identifiable by the Franciscan *cordón* (rope) decorating one of the pointed arches on the facade.

★ The 1525 Palacio de Bendaña and the adjoining bronze-plated building are home to one of Vitoria's main attractions, the **Bibat**, which combines the Museo Fournier de Naipes (Playing-Card Museum) with the **Museo de la Arqueología.** The project, by Navarran architect Patxi Mangado, is a daring combination of old and new architecture, though it was dubbed "the chest" because of its dark facade. The palacio houses the playing-card collection of Don Heraclio Fournier, who, in 1868, founded a playing-card factory, started amassing cards, and eventually found himself with 15,000 sets, the largest and finest such collection in the world. As you survey rooms of hand-painted cards, the distinction between artwork and game piece is quickly scrambled. The oldest sets date from the 12th century, making them older than the building, and the story parallels the history of printing. The most unusual and finely painted sets come from Japan, India (the Indian cards are round), and the international practice of tarot. The Archeology Museum, in the new building, has paleolithic dolmens, Roman art and artifacts, medieval objects, and the famous *stele del jinete* (stele of the horseback rider), an early Basque tombstone. ✉ *C. Cuchillería 54* ☎ *945/203707* *Free* ⏲ *Tues.–Fri. 10–2 and 4–6:30, Sat. 10–2, Sun. 11–2.*

Parque de la Florida (✉ *South of Pl. de la Virgen Blanca*) is a nice respite during a tour of Vitoria.Just south of the park, the **Museo Provincial de Armería** (Provincial Arms Museum) has prehistoric hatchets, 20th-century pistols, and a sand-table reproduction of the 1813 battle between the Duke of Wellington's troops and the French. ✉ *Paseo Fray Francisco de Vitoria 3* ☎ *945/181925* *Free* ⏲ *Tues.–Fri. 10–2 and 4–6:30, Sat. 10–2, Sun. 11–2.*

The **Museo de Bellas Artes** (*Museum of Fine Arts*✉ *Paseo Fray Francisco de Vitoria 8*) has paintings by Ribera, Picasso, and the Basque painter Zuloaga.

WHERE TO EAT AND STAY

$$–$$$$ SPANISH ★ ✕ **El Portalón**. With dark, creaky wood floors and staircases, bare brick walls, and ancient beams, pillars, and coats of arms, this rough and rustic 15th-century inn turns out classical Castilian and Basque specialties that reflect Vitoria's geography and social history. The wine cellar is a gold mine. Try the *lomo de cebón asado en su jugo con puré de manzanas* (filet mignon with apple puree) or any of the *merluza* (hake) preparations. ✉ *C. Correría 147–149* ☎ *945/142755* ▭ *AE, DC, MC, V* ⏲ *Closed last 3 wks in Aug., Easter wk, and Dec. 24–Jan. 4. No dinner Sun.*

$$$ ★ **Parador de Argómaniz**. About 15 minutes east of Vitoria off N104 toward Pamplona, this 17th-century palace has panoramic views over the Alava plains and retains a powerful sense of mystery and romance, with long stone hallways punctuated by imposing antiques. Rooms have polished wood floors, and some have glass-enclosed sitting areas and/or hot tubs. The wood-beam dining room ($$–$$$$) on the third floor makes each meal feel like a baronial feast. **Pros:** contemporary rooms and comforts; gorgeous details and surroundings. **Cons:** isolated. ✉ *N1, Km 363, Argómaniz* ☎ *945/293200* 🌐 *www.parador.es* *53 rooms* *In-room: Wi-Fi. In-hotel: restaurant, bar, parking (free)* ▭ *AE, DC, MC, V.*

LAGUARDIA

66 km (40 mi) south of Vitoria, 17 km (10 mi) northwest of Logroño.

Founded in 908 to stand guard—as its name suggests—over Navarra's southwestern flank, Laguardia is on a promontory overlooking the Ebro River and the vineyards of the Rioja Alavesa–La Rioja wine country north of the Ebro in the Basque province of Alava. Flanked by the Sierra de Cantabria, the town rises shiplike, its prow headed north, over the sea of surrounding vineyards. Ringed with walls, Laguardia's dense cluster of emblazoned noble facades and stunning patios may have no equal in Spain. Stroll by the 50 or so houses with coats of arms and medieval or Renaissance masonry.

ESSENTIALS

Visitor Information Laguardia (✉ *Pl. San Juan 1* ☎ *945/600845*).

EXPLORING

Starting from the 15th-century Puerta de Carnicerías, or Puerta Nueva, the central portal off the parking area on the east side of town, the first landmark is the 16th-century **ayuntamiento** (town hall), with its imperial shield of Carlos V. Farther into the square is the current town hall, built in the 19th century. A right down Calle Santa Engracia takes you past impressive facades—the floor inside the portal at No. 25 is a lovely stone mosaic, and a walk behind the triple-emblazoned 17th-century facade of No. 19 reveals a stagecoach, floor mosaics, wood beams, and an inner porch.The Puerta de Santa Engracia, with an image of the saint in an overhead niche, opens out to the right, and on the left, at the entrance to Calle Víctor Tapia, house No. 17 bears a coat of arms with the Latin phrase LAUS TIBI (Praise Be to Thee). Laguardia's crown architectural jewel is Spain's only Gothic polychrome portal, on the church of **Santa María de los Reyes**. Protected by a posterior Renaissance facade, the door centers on a lovely, lifelike effigy of La Virgen de los Reyes (Virgin of the Kings), sculpted in the 14th century and painted in the 17th by Ribera.

To the north of the ornate castle and hotel El Collado is the monument to the famous Laguardia composer of fables, Felix María Samaniego (1745–1801), heir to the tradition of Aesop and Jean de La Fontaine. Walk around the small, grassy park to the Puerta de Páganos and look right—you can see Laguardia's oldest civil structure, the late-14th-century **Casa de la Primicia**, at Calle Páganos 78 (where fresh fruit was sold). If you walk left of the Casa de la Primicia, past several emblazoned houses to Calle Páganos 13, you can see the *bodega* (wine cellar) at the Posada Mayor de Migueloa, which is usually full and busy. Go through the corridor to the Posada's Calle Mayor entryway and walk up to the **Juanjo San Pedro** gallery at Calle Mayor 1, filled with antiques and artwork.

★ **Herederos de Marqués de Riscal.** The village of Elciego, 6 km (4 mi) southeast of Laguardia is the site of the historic Marqués de Riscal winery. Tours of the vineyards—among the most legendary in La Rioja—as well as the cellars are conducted in various languages, including English. Reservations are required. ✉ *C. Torrea 1, Elciego* ☎ *945/180888* 🌐 *www.marquesderiscal.com* 🎟 *€10* ⏲ *Tours every day but times vary; book ahead.*

WHERE TO EAT AND STAY

$$–$$$ SPANISH ✕ **Marixa.** Aficionados travel great distances to dine in the lovely restaurant, known for its excellent roasts, views, and value, in the Marixa hotel. The heavy, wooden interior is ancient and intimate, and the cuisine is Vasco-Riojano, combining the best of both worlds. House specialties are Navarran vegetable dishes and meat roasted over coals. There are 10 guest rooms ($$), as well, which are modern and cheery though not particularly charming. ✉ *C. Sancho Abarca 8* ☎ *945/600165*

🌐 *www.hotelmarixa.com* ⇆ *10 rooms* ▭ *AE, DC, MC, V* ⊗ *Closed mid-Dec.–mid-Jan.*

$$$$ ★ **Hotel Marqués de Riscal.** Frank Gehry's explosion of genius looks as if a colony from outer space has taken up residence (or crashed) in the middle of La Rioja's oldest vineyards *(see below)*, 6 km (4 mi) outside of Laguardia. The jumble of pink and gold titanium sheets and stainless steel curves around rectilinear sandstone surfaces is something like a pile of gift wrap, and with the winery's visitor center, the historic cellars, and the rolling hills offering activities from horseback riding to golf, visitors here have plenty to do. The spa provides new ways to use grape juice, while La Rioja's star chef Francis Paniego's gourmet restaurant ($$$$) delights the palate. **Pros:** dazzling environment; superb dining. **Cons:** expensive. ✉ *C. Torrea 1, Elciego* ☎ *945/180880* 🌐 *www.luxurycollection.com* ⇆ *43 rooms, 11 suites* ♁ *In-room: Wi-Fi. In-hotel: restaurant, bar, spa, parking (free)* ▭ *AE, DC, MC, V.*

$$ **Posada Mayor de Migueloa.** This 17th-century palace is a beauty, and the property includes a tavern ($$–$$$$) at Calle Páganos 13, where recommendations include starters like *patatas a la riojana* (potatoes with chorizo) and *pochas con chorizo y costilla* (beans with sausage and lamb chop) and mains ranging from beef with foie gras to *venado con miel y pomelo* (venison with a honey-and-grapefruit sauce). Guest rooms have beautiful, original, rough-hewn ceiling beams. **Pros:** beautiful rooms; gorgeous stone entryway floors. **Cons:** in a pedestrianized area a long way from your car; rooms on the front side exposed to boisterous racket on weekends; expensive restaurant sometimes misses. ✉ *C. Mayor de Migueloa 20* ☎ *945/621175* 🌐 *www.mayordemigueloa.com* ⇆ *8 rooms* ♁ *In-room: Wi-Fi. In-hotel: restaurant, bar* ▭ *AE, DC, MC, V* ⊗ *Closed mid-Dec.–mid-Jan.*

LA RIOJA

A natural compendium of highlands, plains, and vineyards drained by the Ebro River, La Rioja (named for the River Oja) has historically produced Spain's finest wines. Most inhabitants live along the Ebro, in the cities of Logroño and Haro, though the mountains and upper river valleys hold many treasures. A mix of Atlantic and Mediterranean climates and cultures with Basque overtones and the *meseta*'s arid influence, La Rioja is composed of the Rioja Alta (Upper Rioja), the moist and mountainous western end, and the Rioja Baja (Lower Rioja), the lower, dryer eastern extremity, more Mediterranean in climate. Logroño, the capital, lies between the two.

LOGROÑO

92 km (55 mi) southwest of Pamplona on NIII.

A busy industrial city of 130,000, Logroño's lovely old quarter is bordered by the Ebro and the medieval walls, with **Breton de los Herreros** and **Muro Francisco de la Mata** the most characteristic streets.

Near Logroño, the Roman bridge and the *mirador* (lookout) at **Viguera** are the main sights in the lower Iregua Valley. According to legend,

Santiago (St. James) helped the Christians defeat the Moors at the **Castillo de Clavijo,** another panoramic spot. The **Leza (Cañon) del Río Leza** is La Rioja's most dramatic canyon.

Logroño's dominant landmarks are the finest sacred structures in Rioja.

ESSENTIALS

Bus Station Logroño (✉ *Av. España 1* ☎ *941/235983*).

Train Station Logroño (✉ *Estación de Logroño, Pl. de Europa* ☎ *941/240202*).

Visitor Information Logroño (✉ *Portales 50* ☎ *941/273353*).

EXPLORING

The 11th-century church of **Santa María del Palacio** (✉ *C. Ruavieja s/n*) is known as La Aguja (The Needle) for its pyramid-shaped, 45-yard Romanesque-Gothic tower.The church of **Santiago el Real** (Royal St. James✉ *Pl. de Santiago s/n*), reconstructed in the 16th century, is noted for its equestrian statue of the saint (also known as Santiago Matamoros: St. James the Moorslayer), which presides over the main door.**San Bartolomé** (✉ *C. San Bartolomé 2*) is a 13th- to 14th-century French Gothic church with an 11th-century Mudejar tower and an elaborate 14th-century Gothic doorway.The **Catedral de Santa María de La Redonda** (✉ *C. Portales 14*) is noted for its twin baroque towers. Many of Logroño's monuments, such as the elegant **Puente de Piedra** (Stone Bridge), were built as part of the Camino de Santiago pilgrimage route.

WHERE TO EAT AND STAY

For *tapas*, **Calle Laurel** or *el sendero de los elefantes* (the path of the elephants)—an allusion to *trompas* (trunks), Spanish for a snootful—offers bars with signature specialties: Bar Soriano for "*champis*" (*champiñones*, or mushrooms), Blanco y Negro for "*matromonio*" (anchovies on cheese), Casa Lucio for *migas de pastor* (sausage with garlic and bread crumbs), and La Travesía for potato omelet. If you're ordering wine, a Crianza brings out the crystal, a young Cosechero comes in small glasses, and Reserva (selected grapes aged three years in oak and bottle) elicits snifters for proper swirling, smelling, and tasting.

$$–$$$$ SPANISH ✕ **Asador Emilio.** The Castilian rustic decor here includes a coffered wood ceiling that merits a long look. Roast lamb cooked over wood coals is the specialty, but *alubias* (kidney beans) and *migas de pastor* (literally, "shepherd's bread crumbs," cooked with garlic and sausage) are hard to resist. The wine list, not surprisingly, is stocked with most of La Rioja's top finds, from Roda I to Barón de Chirel Reserva. ✉ *República Argentina 8* ☎ *941/233141* ▭ *AE, DC, MC, V* ⊙ *Closed Sun. except May. No dinner Sun.*

$–$$$ SPANISH ✕ **El Cachetero.** Local fare based on roast lamb, goat, and vegetables is the rule at this family-run favorite in the middle of Logroño's main food and wine preserve. Coming in from Calle del Laurel is something like stepping through the looking glass: from street pandemonium to the peaceful hush of this culinary sanctuary. Though the dining room is classical and elegant, with antique furnishings and a serious look, the cuisine is homespun, based on seasonally changing raw materials.

The fertile soil and fields of the Ebro River Valley make some of Spain's most colorful landscapes.

Patatas a la riojana (potatoes stewed with chorizo) is a classic dish here. ✉ *C. Laurel 3* ☎ *941/228463* ▭ *AE, DC, MC, V* ⏲ *Closed Sun. and last wk in Aug. No dinner Wed.*

$–$$$$ SPANISH ★ ✕ **La Rueda.** Cándida Calleja's upstairs perch over the intersection of the Calle and Travesía del Laurel *tapas*-grazing scene is close enough to the action below but removed enough to be pleasant. Memorable dishes include *jamón ibérico de bellota* (acorn-fed ham) or *revuelto de gambas y puntas de espárragos trigueros* (eggs scrambled with shrimp and wild asparagus). If trout is on the menu, don't hesitate: Cándida knows how to cook it. The downstairs bar serves excellent *sepia* (cuttlefish) with cool hits of Rojanda, La Rueda's own fresh young white wine. ✉ *Travesía del Laurel 1* ☎ *941/227986* ▭ *AE, DC, MC, V* ⏲ *Closed Sun. and Aug.*

$$ **Herencia Rioja.** This modern hotel near the old quarter has contemporary and comfortable rooms, first-rate facilities, a well-trained staff, a fine restaurant ($$–$$$$) with a good wine list, a grill for cooking over coals, and a healthy, businesslike buzz about it. The halls and corridors are somewhat somber and over-lavishly draped with fabrics, but the efficiency of the place makes up for its aesthetic shortcomings. **Pros:** top comfort; two steps from Calle del Laurel's tapas bonanza. **Cons:** undistinguished modern building; lugubrious interiors. ✉ *Marqués de Murrieta 14* ☎ *941/210222* 🌐 *www.nh-hoteles.es* *81 rooms, 2 suites* *In-room: refrigerator, Wi-Fi. In-hotel: restaurant, bar, gym* ▭ *AE, DC, MC, V.*

$ **Marqués de Vallejo.** Close to—but not overwhelmed by—the food- and wine-tasting frenzy of nearby Calle del Laurel, this small, family-run hotel within view of the cathedral is nearly dead center amid the most important historic sites and best architecture that Logroño has to offer. Rooms are on the small side but cozy. Stash your car in the garage beneath the nearby Plaza del Espolón. **Pros:** central location; traditional Logroño architecture with renovated interior. **Cons:** street-side rooms can be noisy in summer when windows are open. ✉ *Marqués de Vallejo 8* ☎ *941/248333* 🌐 *www.hotelmarquesdevallejo.com* *30 rooms* *In-room: refrigerator, Wi-Fi. In-hotel: restaurant, bar* 💳 *AE, DC, MC, V.*

LA RIOJA ALTA

The Upper Rioja, the most prosperous part of La Rioja's wine country, extends from the Ebro River to the Sierra de la Demanda. La Rioja Alta has the most fertile soil, the best vineyards and agriculture, the most impressive castles and monasteries, a ski resort at Ezcaray, and the historic economic advantage of being on the Camino de Santiago.

5

From Logroño, drive 12 km (7 mi) west on N120 to **Navarrete** to see its noble houses and 16th-century Santa María de la Asunción church.

Nájera, 15 km (9 mi) west of Navarrete, was the court of the kings of Navarra and capital of Navarra and La Rioja until 1076, when La Rioja became part of Castile and the residence of the Castilian royal family. The monastery of **Santa María la Real**, "pantheon of kings," is distinguished by its 16th-century Claustro de los Caballeros (Cavaliers' Cloister), a flamboyant Gothic structure with 24 lacy plateresque Renaissance arches overlooking a grassy patio. The sculpted 12th-century tomb of Doña Blanca de Navarra is the monastery's best-known sarcophagus, while the 67 Gothic choir stalls dating from 1495 are among Spain's best. ✉ *Calle de Monasterio s/n, Nájera* ☎ *941/361083* 🌐 *www.santamarialareal.net* *€3* *Tues.–Sat. 10–1 and 4–7, Sun. 10–12:30 and 4–6.*

Santo Domingo de la Calzada, 20 km (12 mi) west of Nájera on the N120, has always been a key stop on the Camino. Santo Domingo was an 11th-century saint who built roads and bridges for pilgrims and founded the hospital that is now the town's parador. The cathedral is a Romanesque-Gothic pile containing the saint's tomb, choir murals, and a walnut altarpiece carved by Damià Forment in 1541. The live hen and rooster in a plateresque stone chicken coop commemorate a legendary local miracle in which a pair of roasted fowl came back to life to protest the innocence of a pilgrim hanged for theft. Be sure to stroll through the town's beautifully preserved medieval quarter.

Enter the Sierra de la Demanda by heading south 14 km (8½ mi) on LO810. Your first stop is the town of **Ezcaray**, with its aristocratic houses emblazoned with family crests, of which the **Palacio del Conde de Torremúzquiz** (Palace of the Count of Torremúzquiz) is the most distinguished. Good excursions from here are the Valdezcaray winter-sports center; the source of the River Oja at Llano de la Casa; La Rioja's highest point, the 7,494-foot Pico de San Lorenzo; and the Romanesque church of Tres Fuentes, at Valgañón. The town of **San Millán de la Cogolla** is southeast of Santo Domingo de la Calzada. Take LO809 southeast through Berceo to the Monasterio de Yuso, where a 10th-century manuscript on St. Augustine's *Glosas Emilianenses* has notes in what is considered the earliest example of the Spanish language, the vernacular Latin dialect known as Roman Paladino. The nearby Visigothic Monasterio de Suso is where Gonzalo de Berceo, recognized as the first Castilian poet, wrote and recited his 13th-century verse in the Castilian tongue, now the language of more than 300 million people.

HARO'S WINE WAR

June 29, the Fiesta de San Pedro, marks the Batalla del Vino in Haro. Begun around 1710 as a jocular commemoration of a territorial dispute between the towns of Haro and Miranda de Ebro, hundreds of local revelers and visitors throw some 60,000 liters of not very good wine at each other using everything from buckets to vats, hoses, and water pistols. Traditional fiesta attire is white, which quickly becomes a pink-purple. Traditional dances are performed.

WHERE TO STAY

$–$$ Fodor's Choice ★ **Echaurren.** This rambling roadhouse in Ezcaray, 61 km (37 mi) southwest of Logroño, is 7 km (4 mi) below Valdezcaray, La Rioja's best ski resort. Echaurren is famous for fine traditional cuisine ($$–$$$) engineered by Marisa Sanchez and the postmodern creations of her son, Francis Paniego. Marisa's *patatas a la riojana* (potatoes stewed with peppers and chorizo) are a classic, while Francis, a youthful master chef, experiments with wood coals and aromas and also directs the superb Hotel Marqués de Riscal restaurant in Elciego. Rooms are comfortable, and the staff is warm and engaging. **Pros:** traditional building; comfortable beds; family service. **Cons:** the bells from the church across the way. ✉ *Padre José García 19, Ezcaray* ☎ *941/354047* 🌐 *www.echaurren.com* *25 rooms* *In-room: refrigerator, Wi-Fi. In-hotel: restaurant, bar, parking (paid)* *AE, DC, MC, V.*

$$–$$$ ★ **Hospedería del Monasterio de San Millán.** Declared a World Heritage Site by UNESCO, this magnificent inn occupies a wing of the historic Monasterio de Yuso, famous as the birthplace of the Spanish language. Heavy medieval stone walls conceal a surprisingly contemporary and minimalist interior, with an elongated baronial dining room that serves regional dishes from La Rioja. Guest rooms are elegant and may seem austere at first glance, but the converted and restored monastery has all the modern comforts of any first-class hotel. **Pros:** historic site; graceful building. **Cons:** somewhat isolated; monastic decor. ✉ *Monasterio de Yuso, San Millán de la Cogolla* ☎ *941/373277* 🌐 *www.sanmillan.com* *22 rooms, 3 suites* *In-room: refrigerator, Wi-Fi. In-hotel: restaurant, bar* *AE, DC, MC, V.*

HARO

49 km (29 mi) west of Logroño.

ESSENTIALS

Visitor Information Haro (✉ *Pl. Monseñor Florentino Rodríguez* ☎ *941/303366*).

EXPLORING

Haro is the wine capital of La Rioja. Its **Casco Viejo** (Old Quarter) and best taverns are concentrated along the loop known as La Herradura (the Horseshoe), with the Santo Tomás church at the apex of its curve and Calle San Martín and Calle Santo Tomás leading down to the upper left-hand (northeast) corner of Plaza de la Paz. Up the left side of the horseshoe, Bar La Esquina is the first of many fine *tapas* bars. Bar Los Caños, behind a stone archway at San Martín 5, is built into the vaults and arches of the former church of San Martín and serves excellent local Crianzas and Reservas and a memorable *pincho* of quail egg, anchovy, hot pepper, and olive.

Haro's century-old **bodegas** (wineries) have been headquartered in the *barrio de la estación* (train-station district) ever since the railroad opened in 1863. Guided tours and tastings, some in English, can be arranged at the facilities themselves or through the tourist office.

The architectural highlight of Haro is the church of **Santo Tomás**, a single-naved Renaissance and late Gothic church completed in 1564, with an intricately sculpted plateresque portal on the south side and a gilded baroque organ facade towering over the choir loft.

5

WHERE TO STAY

$$ **Los Agustinos.** Haro's best hotel is built into a 14th-century monastery with a cloister (now a beautiful covered patio) that's considered one of the best in La Rioja. Arches, a great hall, and Renaissance tapestries complete the medieval look. The restaurant serves creditable local fare in two comfortable dining rooms, and the glassed-in wine cellar holds Haro's greatest treasures. **Pros:** gorgeous public rooms; cozy hotel bar; close to town center but in a quiet corner. **Cons:** unexciting room decor; staff not very helpful. ✉ *San Agustín 2* ☎ *941/311308* 🌐 *www.hotellosagustinos.com* *60 rooms, 2 suites* *In-room: refrigerator, Wi-Fi. In-hotel: restaurant, bar* 💳 *AE, DC, MC, V.*

THE HIGHLANDS

The rivers forming the seven main valleys of the Ebro basin originate in the Sierra de la Demanda, Sierra de Cameros, and Sierra de Alcarama. **Ezcaray** is La Rioja's skiing capital in the **valley of the Rio Oja,** just below Valdezcaray in the Sierra de la Demanda. The upper **Najerilla Valley** is La Rioja's mountain sanctuary, an excellent hunting and fishing preserve. The Najerilla River, a rich chalk stream, is one of Spain's best trout rivers. Look for the Puente de Hiedra (Ivy Bridge), its heavy curtain of ivy falling to the surface of the Najerilla above Anguiano. The **Monasterio de Valvanera,** off C113 near Anguiano, is the sanctuary of La Rioja's patron saint, the Virgen de Valvanera, a 12th-century Romanesque wood carving of the Virgin and Child. **Anguiano** is renowned for its Danza de los Zancos (Dance of the Stilts), held July 22, when dancers on wooden stilts plummet down through the steep streets of the town into the arms of the crowd at the bottom. At the valley's highest point are the Mansilla reservoir and the Romanesque Ermita de San Cristóbal (Hermitage of St. Christopher).

The upper **Iregua Valley,** off N111, has the prehistoric Gruta de la Paz caves at Ortigosa. The artisans of **Villoslada del Cameros** make the region's famous patchwork quilts, called *almazuelas*. Climb to **Pico Cebollera** for a superb view of the valley. Work back toward the Ebro along the River Leza, through Laguna de Cameros and San Román de Cameros (known for its basket weavers), to complete a tour of the Sierra del Cameros. The upper **Cidacos Valley** leads to the **Parque Jurásico** (Jurassic Park) at Enciso, famous for its dinosaur tracks. The main village in the upper **Alhama Valley** is **Cervera del Rio Alhama,** a center for handmade *alpargatas* (rope-sole shoes).

WHERE TO EAT AND STAY

$–$$$ SPANISH ✕ **La Herradura.** High over the ancient bridge of Anguiano, this is an excellent place to try the local specialty, *caparrones colorados de Anguiano con sus sacramentos* (small, red kidney beans stewed with sausage and fatback) made with the much-prized, extra-tasty hometown bean. Unpretentious and family run, La Herradura ("horseshoe") is a local favorite usually filled with Riojanos and trout fishermen taking a break from the river. The house wine is an acceptable and inexpensive Uruñuela *cosechero* (young wine of the year) from the Najerilla Valley. ✉ *Ctra. de Lerma, Km 14, Anguiano* ☎ *941/377151* ▭ *MC, V.*

¢ **Hospedería Abadía de Valvanera.** A 16th-century monastery atop a 9th-century hermitage, this is an ideal base for hiking, but note that the 12th-century carving of the Virgin of Valvanera receives an overnight harvest pilgrimage from Logroño every October 15, and it's very hard to book then. Patroness of the grape harvest and barren couples, the Virgin is portrayed with a pomegranate (symbolizing fertility) and vines. Her infant is said to have turned away in embarrassment when a hopeful couple performed the procreative act on the altar. Rooms are simple and the restaurant ($–$$) offers local dishes at unbeatable prices. **Pros:** cool air during summer heat; simplicity and silence. **Cons:** spartan accommodations; limited dining choices. ✉ *Monasterio de Valvanera s/n, 5 km (3 mi) west of LR113* ☎ *941/377044* 🌐 *www.abadiavalvanera.com* *28 rooms* *In-room: no a/c, no TV. In-hotel: restaurant* ▭ *AE, DC, MC, V.*

¢ **Venta de Goyo.** A favorite with anglers and hunters in season, this cheery spot across from the mouth of the Urbión River (where it meets the Najerilla) has wood-trim bedrooms with red-check bedspreads and an excellent restaurant ($$–$$$$) specializing in venison, wild boar, partridge, woodcock, and game of all kinds. Juan Carlos Jiménez and his nephew, chef Juan Carlos Esteban, serve some of the best *caparrones* (pygmy red beans from Anguiano) in La Rioja. **Pros:** excellent game and mountain cooking; charming rustic bar; unforgettable homemade jams. **Cons:** next to road; hot in summer. ✉ *Ctra. LR113, Km 24.6, Viniegra de Abajo* ☎ *941/378007* 📠 *941/378048* *22 rooms* *In-hotel: restaurant, bar* ▭ *AE, DC, MC, V.*

6

The Pyrenees

WORD OF MOUTH

"I like the Roncal Valley for its dynamic scenery and great cheese. The Baztan Valley, which leads you to San Sebastian-Donostia, is beautiful. A walk through the Irati Forest is also worth the trip."

—Robert2533

WELCOME TO THE PYRENEES

TOP REASONS TO GO

★ **Pyrenean Gems:** Stop at Taüll and see the exquisite Romanesque churches and mural paintings of the Nogeura de Tor valley.

★ **Spain's Grand Canyon:** Walk through the Parque Nacional de Ordesa y Monte Perdido for stunning scenery, complete with marmots and mountain goats.

★ **Basque Navarra:** Explore the lush and verdant Basque highlands of the Baztán Valley, and then follow the Bidasoa River down to colorful Hondarribia and the sparkling Bay of Biscay.

★ **Skiing at the chic Vall d'Aran resort of Baqueiria-Bequet:** With 57 mi of the most varied pistes in the Pyrenees, this is where King Juan Carlos I skis with his family.

★ **The cogwheel train at Ribes de Freser, near Ripoll:** Ride up a gaping gorge to the sanctuary and ski station at Val de Núria, where there's a stunning hike to the remote highland valley and refuge of Coma de Vaca.

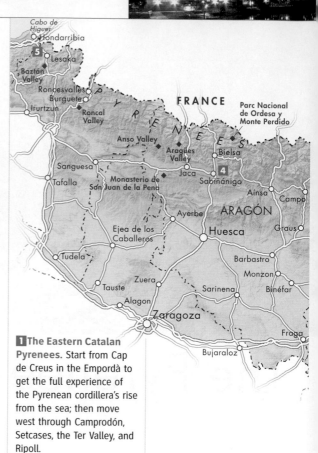

1 The Eastern Catalan Pyrenees. Start from Cap de Creus in the Empordà to get the full experience of the Pyrenean cordillera's rise from the sea; then move west through Camprodón, Setcases, the Ter Valley, and Ripoll.

2 La Cerdanya. The widest and sunniest valley in the Pyrenees, La Cerdanya is an east–west expanse that straddles the French border between two forks of the Pyrenean cordillera. The Segre River flows down the center of the valley, while snowcapped peaks rise to the north and south.

3 Western Catalan Pyrenees. West of La Seu d'Urgell, the western Catalan Pyrenees include the Vall de Aran, the Parc Nacional d'Aigüestortes i Estany de Sant Maurici, and the Noguera de Tor valley with its Romanesque treasures.

4 Aragón and the Central Pyrenees. Benasque is the jumping off point for Aneto, the highest peak in the Pyrenees. San Juan de Plan, Gistaín, and Bielsa are typical mountain enclaves. Parque Nacional de Ordesa y Monte Perdido is an unforgettable daylong or two-day trek. Jaca and the Hecho, Ansó, and Roncal valleys are Upper Aragón at its purest, while Huesca and Zaragoza are good lowland alternatives in case bad weather blows you out of the mountains.

5 The Western and Basque Pyrenees. Beginning in the Roncal Valley, the language you hear may be Euskera, the non–Indo-European tongue of the Basques. The highlands of Navarra, from Roncesvalles and Burguete down through the Baztán Valley to Hondarribia, are a magical realm of rolling hillsides and emerald pastures.

GETTING ORIENTED

The Pyrenean valleys, isolated from each other and the world below for many centuries, retain a rugged mountain character, mixing distinct traditions with a common highland spirit of magic and mystery. Spain's natural border with France was a nexus where medieval people took refuge and exchanged culture and learning. A haven from the 8th-century Moorish invasion, the Pyrenees became an unlikely repository of Romanesque art and architecture as well as a natural preserve of wildlife and terrain.

THE PYRENEES PLANNER

When to Go

If you're a hiker, stick to the summer (June to September, especially July), when the weather is better and there's less chance of a serious snowfall—not to mention blizzards or lightning storms at high altitudes.

October, with comfortable daytime temperatures and chillier evenings, is ideal for enjoying the still-green Pyrenean meadows and valleys and hillside hunts for wild mushrooms.

November brings colorful leaves, the last mushrooms, and the first frosts.

For skiing, come between December and April. The green springtime thaw, from mid-March to mid-April, is spectacular for skiing on the snowcaps and trout fishing or golfing on the verdant valley floors.

August is the only crowded month, when all of Europe is on summer vacation and the cooler highland air is at its best.

About the Hotels

Most hotels in the Pyrenees are informal and outdoorsy, with a large fireplace in one of the public rooms. They are usually built of wood and slate under a steep roof, blending in with the surrounding mountains. Options include friendly family-owned establishments, rooms in Basque *caseríos* (farmhouses), and town houses. Larger chain-type hotels are almost unheard of here.

Four Ways to Say Hello in the Pyrenees

In Spanish: "Buenos días"

In Catalan: "Bon dia"

In Euskera (Basque): "Egun on"

In Fabla Aragonesa: "Buen Diya"

Take a Tour

There are wonderful outdoor activities to be experienced in the Pyrenees and plenty of guides and outfitters to help. Alto Aragon organizes trekking, horseback riding, adventure sport, and ornithology tours.

Well populated with trout, the Pyrenees' cold-water streams provide excellent angling from mid-March to the end of August. Notable places to cast a line are the Segre, Aragón, Gállego, Noguera Pallaresa, Arga, Esera, and Esca rivers. Pyrenean ponds and lakes also tend to be rich in trout. Ramón Cosiallf and his company Danica can take you fly-fishing anywhere in the world by horse or helicopter, but the Pyrenees is their home turf. For about €150 a day (depending on equipment), you'll be whisked to high Pyrenean lakes and ponds, streams and rivers, armed with equipment and expertise.

Contacts Danica (☎ *659/735376 or 974/553493* 🌐 *www.danicaguias.com*). **Alto Aragon** (☎ *974/371281* 🌐 *www.altoaragon.co.uk*).

Hiking the Pyrenees

There are many reasons to visit the Pyrenees: it's gorgeous; it has fabulous skiing, art, and architecture; but hiking affords an ideal view of the scenery and is one of the best ways to drink in the stunning landscape. No matter how spectacular the mountains seem from paved roads, they are exponentially more stunning from upper hiking trails and high *pistas forestales* (forest tracks) that are best traveled in four-wheel-drive vehicles. Day hikes or overnight two-day treks to mountain *refugios* (*refugis in Catalan*), especially in the Ordesa or Aigüestortes national parks, reveal the full natural splendor of the Pyrenees.

Local tourist offices can provide maps and recommend day hikes, while specialized bookshops such as Barcelona's Quera (Carrer Petritxol 2) have complete Pyrenean maps as well as books with detailed hiking instructions for the entire mountain range from the Atlantic to the Mediterranean. Some books to look for include *The Pyrenees* by Kev Reynolds (Cicerone Press), with practical info, maps, and photos by one of the UK's most widely used publishers of guidebooks for the outdoors, and *Trekking in the Pyrenees* (Trailblazer Publications). Also check out 🌐 *www.pyrenees-pirinoes.org* for trails and information.

Hiking in the Pyrenees should always be undertaken carefully: proper footwear, headwear, water supply, and weather-forecast awareness are essential. Even in the middle of summer, a sudden snowstorm can turn a day hike to tragedy. *See the "Hiking in the Pyrenees" box in this chapter for more details.*

WHAT IT COSTS (IN EUROS)

	¢	$	$$	$$$	$$$$
Restaurants	under €8	€8–€12	€13–€17	€18–€22	over €22
Hotels	under €60	€60–€90	€91–€125	€126–€180	over €180

Prices are per person for a main course at dinner, and for two people in a standard double room in high season, excluding tax.

Planning Your Time

You could walk all the way from the Atlantic to the Mediterranean in 43 days, but not many have that kind of vacation time. With 10 to 14 days you can drive from sea to sea: from a wade in the Mediterranean at Cap de Creus to Hondarribia and the Cabo Higuer lighthouse on the Bay of Biscay. A week is best for a single area—La Cerdanya and the Eastern Catalan Pyrenees; the Western Catalan Pyrenees and Vall d'Aran; Jaca and the central Pyrenees; or the Basque Pyrenees north of Pamplona.

A day's drive up through Figueres (in Catalonia) and Olot will bring you to **Camprodón. Sant Joan de les Abadesses** and **Ripoll** are important stops, especially for the famous Sant Maria de Ripoll portal. La Cerdanya's **Puigcerdà, Llívia,** and **Bellver de Cerdanya** are must-visits, too.

To the west is **La Seu d'Urgell** on the way to **Parc Nacional d'Aigüestortes i Estany de Sant Maurici,** the **Vall d'Aran,** and the winter-sports center Baqueira-Beret. Stop at **Taüll** and the **Noguera de Tor** valley's Romanesque churches. Farther west, **Benasque** is the jumping off point for Aneto, the highest peak in the Pyrenees.

Parque Nacional de Ordesa y Monte Perdido is Spain's grandest canyon—sort of a junior version of North America's Grand Canyon—while **Jaca** is the central Pyrenees' most important town.

6

GETTING HERE AND AROUND

By Air

Barcelona's international airport, El Prat de Llobregat (⇨ *Barcelona*), is the largest gateway to the Catalan Pyrenees. Farther west, the airports at Zaragoza, Pamplona, and Hondarribia (Fuenterrabía) serve the Pyrenees of Aragón, Navarra, and the Basque Country.

By Train

There are three small train stations deep in the Pyrenees: Puigcerdà, in the Cerdanya Valley; La Pobla de Segur, in the Noguera Pallaresa Valley; and Canfranc, north of Jaca, below the Candanchú and Astún ski resorts. The larger gateways are Huesca and Lleida. From Madrid, connect through Barcelona for the eastern Pyrenees, Zaragoza and Huesca for the central Pyrenees, and Pamplona or San Sebastián for the western Pyrenees.

By Bus

Bus travel in the Pyrenees is the only way to cross from east to west (or vice versa), other than hiking or driving, and requires some zigzagging up and down. In most cases, four buses daily connect the main pre-Pyrenean cities (Barcelona, Zaragoza, Huesca, and Pamplona) and the main highland distributors (Puigcerdà, La Seu d'Urgell, Vielha, Benasque, and Jaca). The time lost waiting for buses makes this option a last resort.

Bus Lines **Ágreda La Oscense** (✉ *Paseo María Agustín 7, Zaragoza* ☎ *976/229343* ✉ *Estación Intermodal, Ronda de la Estación s/n, Huesca* ☎ *974/210700*). **Alsina Graells** (✉ *Calle Ali Bei 80, Barcelona* ☎ *93/265–6866* ✉ *Av. Garriga i Masó s/n, La Seu d'Urgell* ☎ *972/350020* ✉ *Calle Saracibar s/n, Lleida* ☎ *973/271470*). **La Baztanesa** (✉ *Calle Yanguas y Miranda 2, Pamplona* ☎ *948/222223*). **La Roncalesa** (✉ *Estación de Autobuses, Calle Conde Oliveta 6, Pamplona* ☎ *948/300257*).

By Car

The most practical way to tour the Pyrenees is by car. The Eje Pirenaico (Pyrenean Axis), or N260, is a carefully engineered, safe, cross-Pyrenean route that connects Cap de Creus, the Iberian Peninsula's easternmost point on the Mediterranean Costa Brava east of Girona and Cadaqués, with Cabo de Higuer, the lighthouse west of Hondarribia at the edge of the Atlantic Bay of Biscay.

The Collada de Toses (Tosses Pass) to Puigcerdà is the most difficult route into the Cerdanya Valley, but it's cost-free, has spectacular scenery, and you get to include Camprodón, Olot, and Ripoll in your itinerary. Safer and faster but more expensive (tolls total more than €20 from Barcelona to Bellver de Cerdanya) is the E9 through the Tuñel del Cadí. Once you're there, most of the Cerdanya Valley's two-lane roads are wide and well paved. As you go west, roads can be more difficult to navigate, winding dramatically through mountain passes.

DID YOU KNOW?

Trekking in the Pyrenees can be a very serious endeavor—it's possible to walk the entire way from the Atlantic Coast to the Mediterranean (it'll take about 43 days)—but there are also shorter, just as stunning, one- or two-day hikes.

EATING AND DRINKING WELL IN THE PYRENEES

Top left: Some typical dishes: grilled T-bone steak, chorizo and *longaniza* sausage with grilled peppers. Top right: A sampling of wild mushrooms. Bottom left: Spring duckling with potatoes.

Pyrenean cuisine is hearty mountain fare characterized by thick soups, stews, roasts, and local game. Ingredients are prepared with slightly different techniques and recipes in each different valley, village, and kitchen.

The three main culinary schools across the Pyrenees match the three main cultural identities of the area—from east to west, they are Catalan, Aragonese, and Basque. Within these three main groups there are further subdivisions corresponding to the valleys or regions of La Garrotxa, La Cerdanya, Ribagorça, Vall d'Aran, Benasque, Alto Aragón, Roncal, and Baztán. Game is common throughout. Trout, mountain goat, deer, boar, partridge, rabbit, duck, and quail are roasted over coals or cooked in aromatic stews called *civets* in Catalonia and *estofadas* in Aragón and the Basque Pyrenees. Fish and meat are often seared on slabs of slate (*a la llosa* in Catalan, *a la piedra* in Castilian Spanish). Sheep, goat, and cow cheeses vary from valley to valley, along with types of sausages and charcuterie.

WILD MUSHROOMS

Valued for their aromatic contribution to the taste process (the truffle is a delicious example), wild mushrooms impart the musky scent of the forest floor and go well with meat or egg dishes. Dishes to look for include *rovellones* (saffron milk cap) sautéed with parsley, olive oil, and garlic, to *camagrocs* (yellow foot mushroom, a type of chanterelle) scrambled with eggs.

HIGHLAND SOUPS

As with all mountains soups, *sopa pirenaica* combines restorative animal fat protein with vegetables and the high altitude need for liquids. Always advisable and delicious when hiking in the mountains, the Spanish version of the French *garbure,* the classic mountain soup from the north side of the Pyrenees, mixes legumes, vegetables, potatoes, pork, hen, and sometimes lamb or wild boar into a tasty and restorative meal that will help hikers recover energy and be ready to go again the next morning. *Olha Aranesa* (Aranese soup) is another Pyrenean power soup, with vegetables, legumes, pork, hen, and beef in a long-cooked and slowly simmered unctuous stew. Similar to the ubiquitous Catalan *escudella,* another Pyrenean favorite, the *olha aranesa* combines chickpeas and pasta with a variety of meat and vegetables and is served, like the *cocido madrileño,* in various stages: soup, legumes, vegetables, and meats.

PYRENEAN STEWS

Wild boar stew is known by different names in the various languages of the Pyrenees—*civet de porc senglar* in Catalan, *estofado de jabalí* in Spanish. A dark and gamey treat in cold weather, wild boar is prepared in many ways between Catalonia, Aragón, and the Basque Country but most recipes include onions, carrots, mushrooms, laurel, oranges, leeks, peppers, dry sherry,

brown sugar, and sweet paprika. *Civet d'isard* (mountain goat stew), known as *estofado de ixarso* in the Pyrenees of Aragón, is another favorite, prepared in much the same way but with a more delicate taste.

TRINXAT

The Catalan verb *trinxar* means to chop or shred, and *trinchat* is winter cabbage, previously softened by frost, chopped fine and mixed with mashed potato and fatback or bacon. A quintessential high-altitude comfort food, *trinxat* juxtaposes the acidity of the cabbage with the saltiness of the pork, and the potato acts as the unifying element.

DUCK WITH TURNIPS

The traditional dish, tiró amb naps, goes back, as do nearly all European recipes that make use of turnips, to pre-Columbian times before the discovery of the potato in the New World. The frequent use of duck (*pato* in Spanish, *anec* in Catalan, *tiró* in La Cerdanya) in the half-France, half-Spain, all-Catalan Cerdanya valley two hours north of Barcelona is a taste acquired from the French southwest just over the Pyrenees.

6

Updated by
Paul Cannon

Separating the Iberian Peninsula from the rest of the European continent, the snowcapped Pyrenees have always been a special realm, a source of legend and superstition. To explore the Pyrenees fully—appreciating the flora and fauna, the local gastronomy, the remote glacial lakes and streams, the Romanesque art in a thousand hermitages—could take a lifetime.

Each Pyrenean mountain system is drained by one or more rivers, forming some three dozen valleys between the Mediterranean and the Atlantic; these valleys were all but completely isolated until around the 10th century. Local languages still abound, with Castilian Spanish and Euskera (Basque) in upper Navarra; Grausín, Belsetán, Chistavino, Ansotano, Cheso, and Patués (Benasqués) in Aragón; Aranés, a dialect of Gascon French, in the Vall d'Aran; and Catalan at the eastern end of the chain from Ribagorça to the Mediterranean.

Throughout the centuries, the Pyrenees have remained a strategic barrier and stronghold to be reckoned with. The Romans never completely subdued Los Vascones (as Greek historian Strabo [63–21 BC] called the Basques) in the western Pyrenean highlands. Charlemagne lost Roland and his rear guard at Roncesvalles in 778, and his Frankish heirs lost all of Catalonia in 988. Napoléon Bonaparte never completed his conquest of the peninsula after 1802, largely because of communications and supply problems posed by the Pyrenees, and Adolf Hitler, whether for geographical or political reasons, decided not to use post–civil war Spain to launch his African campaign in 1941. A D-Day option to make a landing on the beaches of northern Spain was scrapped because the Pyrenees looked too easily defendable (you can still see the south-facing German bunkers on the southern flanks of the western Pyrenean foothills). Meanwhile, the mountainous barrier provided a path to freedom for downed pilots, Jewish refugees, and POWs fleeing the Nazis, just as it later meant freedom for political refugees running north from the Franco regime.

EXPLORING THE PYRENEES

As the crow flies, the Pyrenees stretch 435 km (270 mi) along Spain's border with France, though the sinuous borderline exceeds 600 km (370 mi). A drive across the N260 trans-Pyrenean axis connecting the destinations in this region would exceed 800 km (495 mi). The three groupings across the cordillera are the Catalan Pyrenees, from the Mediterranean to the Noguera Ribagorçana River south of Vielha; the central Pyrenees of Aragón, extending west to the Roncal Valley; and the Basque Pyrenees, falling gradually westward through the Basque Country to the Bay of Biscay and the Atlantic Ocean. The highest peaks are in Aragón—Aneto, in the Maladeta massif; Posets; and Monte Perdido, all of which are about 11,000 feet above sea level. Pica d'Estats (10,372 feet) is Catalonia's highest peak, and Pic d'Orhi (6,656 feet) is the highest in the Basque Pyrenees.

EASTERN CATALAN PYRENEES

Catalonia's easternmost Pyrenean valley, the Vall de Camprodón, is still hard enough to reach that, despite pockets of Barcelona summer colonies, it has retained much of its agricultural culture and mountain wildness. It has several exquisite towns and churches and, above all, mountains, such as the Sierra de Catllar. Vallter 2000 and Núria are ski resorts at the eastern and western ends of the Pyrenees heights on the north side of the valley, but the middle reaches and main body of the valley have remained pasture for sheep, cattle, and horses and de facto natural parks.

GETTING HERE AND AROUND

To reach the Vall de Camprodón from Barcelona, you can take the N152 through Vic and Ripoll. From the Costa Brava go by way of either Figueres or Girona, Besalú, and the Capsacosta tunnel. From France, drive southwest through the Col (Pass) d'Ares, which enters the head of the valley at an altitude of 5,280 feet from Prats de Molló.

CAMPRODÓN

127 km (80 mi) northwest of Barcelona.

Camprodón, the capital of its *comarca* (county), lies at the junction of the Ter and Ritort rivers—both excellent trout streams. The rivers flow by, through, and under much of the town, giving it a highland waterfront character (as well as a long history of flooding). The town owes much of its opulence to the summer folks from Barcelona who built mansions along **Passeig Maristany**, the leafy promenade at its northern edge.

ESSENTIALS

Visitor Information Camprodón (✉ *Pl. de Espanya 1* ☎ *972/740–0010*).

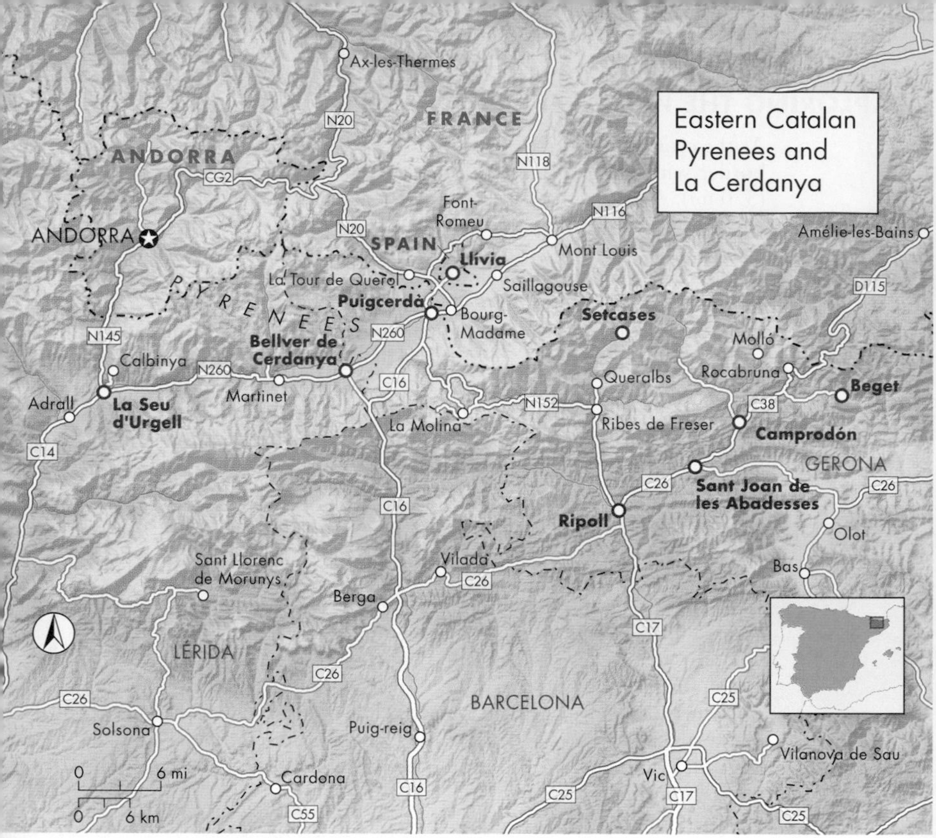

EXPLORING

Museu Isaac Albéniz. Camprodón's most famous son is composer Isaac Albéniz (1860–1909), whose celebrated classical-guitar piece *Asturias* is one of Spain's best-known works. The house and its contents introduce visitors to the life and times of Albéniz, who spent more than 20 years in exile in France, where he became friends with musical luminaries such as Pablo Casals, Claude Debussy, and Gabriel Fauré. ✉ *Carrer Sant Roc 22* ☎ *972/741166* *€3* ⏲ *Wed.–Mon. 11–2 and 4–7.*

Camprodón's best-known symbol is the elegant **12th-century stone bridge** that broadly spans the Ter River in the center of town.

WHERE TO STAY

¢–$ **Fonda Rigà.** A renovated highland inn with comfortable rooms and spectacular views, this mountain perch is 10 km (6 mi) up the Ter Valley from Camprodón, and is an excellent base camp for hikers, wild-mushroom seekers, equestrian enthusiasts, and anyone interested in Pyrenean flora and fauna. Rooms are basic, with bright wood walls and cheerful decor. The restaurant has panoramic views over the valley and specializes in meat cooked over coals. **Pros:** the views and the peace and quiet; newly renovated rooms and facilities. **Cons:** a serious 5 km (3 mi) drive above the valley floor; remote from Camprodón. ✉ *Ctra. de Tregurà de Dalt, Km 4.8* ☎ *972/136000* 🌐 *www.fondariga.*

com ⇨ *16 rooms* ♢ *In-room: no a/c, Wi-Fi. In-hotel: restaurant, bar, Wi-Fi hotspot, parking (paid)* ▭ *AE, DC, MC, V.*

$$–$$$ **L'Hotel de Camprodón.** An elegant Moderniste building with rooms over the river on one side and over the bustling Plaça Dr. Robert on the other, this is a perfect destination for getting a sense of this stylish little mountain hub. Rooms are furnished with tasteful simplicity, and those with terraces look down at the graceful span of Camprodón's emblematic Pont Nou, with mallards splashing alongside brightly speckled (and legally protected) native Pyrenean trout. The Sunday market in the square is an important weekly event with natural-food products and crafts. **Pros:** central location; cozy and intimate public rooms. **Cons:** rooms on the square noisy in summer; no Wi-Fi in rooms. ✉ *Pl. Dr. Robert 3* ☎ *972/740013* ⊕ *www.hotelcamprodon.com* ⇨ *38 rooms* ♢ *In-room: no a/c. In-hotel: restaurant, bar, pool, Wi-Fi hotspot, parking (free)* ▭ *AE, DC, MC, V.*

SHOPPING

Cal Xec (✉ *C. Isaac Albéniz 1* ☎ *972/740084*), the legendary sausage and cheese store at the end of the Camprodón Bridge, also sells the much-prized, vanilla-flavored Birbas cookies.

EN ROUTE

From Camprodón, take C38 north toward Molló and the French border at Col d'Ares. After 3 km (1.8 mi) turn east toward **Rocabruna,** a village of crisp, clean Pyrenean stone houses at the source of the clear Beget River. The village is famous for the excellent Can Po restaurant *(⇨ Beget, below)*, a destination for gastronomical pilgrims on the way to Beget.

BEGET

★ *17 km (11 mi) east of Camprodón.*

The village of Beget, considered Catalonia's *més bufó* (cutest), was completely cut off from motorized vehicles until the mid-1960s, when a *pista forestal* (a jeep track) was laid down; in 1980 Beget was finally fully connected to the rest of the world by an asphalt roadway, which can be hazardous when mist descends, as it often does. Beget's 30 houses are eccentric stone structures with heavy wooden doors and a golden color peculiar to the Camprodón Valley. Graceful stone bridges span the stream where protected trout feast.

EXPLORING

The 11th-century Romanesque church of **Sant Cristófol** has a diminutive bell tower and a rare 6-foot Majestat—a polychrome wood carving of Christ in a head-to-foot tunic, dating from the 12th or 13th century. The church is usually closed, but townsfolk can direct you to the keeper of the key.

WHERE TO EAT

$$–$$$$ SPANISH ★ ✕ **Can Po.** This ancient, ivy-covered, Pyrenean stone-and-mortar farmhouse perched over a deep gully in nearby Rocabruna is famed for carefully prepared local dishes like *vedella amb crema de ceps* (veal in wild mushroom sauce) and the Catalan classic *anec amb peres* (duck stewed with pears). Try the *civet de porc senglar* (stewed wild boar) in

season (winter) or any of the many varieties of wild mushrooms that find their way into the kitchen at this rustic mountain retreat. ✉ *Ctra. de Beget s/n, Rocabruna* ☎ *972/741045* ▬ *AE, DC, MC, V* ⏲ *Closed Mon.–Thurs. mid-Sept.–mid-July, Dec. 26–Jan. 6 and Easter wk.*

SETCASES

11 km (7 mi) northwest of Camprodón, 91 km (56 mi) northwest of Girona.

Although Setcases ("seven houses") is somewhat larger than its name would imply, this tiny village nestled at the head of the valley has a distinct mountain spirit.

ESSENTIALS

Visitor Information Setcases (✉ *Carrer del Rec 5* ☎ *972/136089*).

EXPLORING

On the road back down the valley from Setcases, **Llanars,** just short of Camprodón, has a 12th-century Romanesque church, **San Esteban,** of an exceptionally rich shade of ocher. The wood-and-iron portal depicts the martyrdom of St. Stephen.

WHERE TO EAT AND STAY

$–$$$ SPANISH ✕ **Can Tomàs.** On the immediate left coming into town, this unusual place, covered with lovingly rendered portraits of wild mushrooms, specializes in aromatic upland fungi used in original ways. The *arròs de bolets* (a paella with wild mushrooms) is the house standard, but the *encenalls de foie i tòfona* (shavings of duck liver with black truffles) and the cuttlefish with meatballs and *rossinyols*—chanterelle mushrooms, widely considered to be the most delicious of wild fungi—give an idea of the creative and international flavor of this little gem. ✉ *Carrer de Jesús 10, Setcases* ☎ *972/136004* 🌐 *www.cantomas.com* ▬ *AE, DC, MC, V* ⏲ *Closed Wed.*

$$–$$$$ 🏨 **La Coma.** *Coma* is Catalan Pyrenean dialect for "high and fertile meadow"—nothing to do with the English word for profound unconsciousness. The proprietors are kind country folk who know the mountains and can help plan excursions. Rooms are in the modern stone house and done in bright wood trim. The restaurant ($–$$), with garden seating in summer, specializes in mountain *civets* (stews) and *escudellas* (a typical Catalan thick stew of vegetables, beans, pasta, and pork). **Pros:** cozy sense of being as far into the Pyrenees as you can get; good mountain food in rustic dining room. **Cons:** rooms are austere; location at the entrance to town means it can get a bit too busy at times. ✉ *Setcases* ☎ *972/136074* 🌐 *www.hotellacoma.com* 🛏 *22 rooms* 🖒 *In-room: no a/c. In-hotel: restaurant, pool, gym, Wi-Fi hotspot* ▬ *AE, DC, MC, V.*

SPORTS AND THE OUTDOORS

The **Vallter 2000 ski area** (☎ *972/136057* 🌐 *www.vallter2000.com*) above Setcases—built into a glacial cirque reaching a height of 8,216 feet—has a dozen lifts and, on very clear days at the top, views east all the way to the Bay of Roses on the Costa Brava.

SANT JOAN DE LES ABADESSES

21 km (13 mi) southeast of Setcases, 14 km (9 mi) south of Camprodón.

The site of an important church, Sant Joan de les Abadesses is named for the 9th-century abbess Emma and her successors. Emma was the daughter of Guifré el Pilós (Wilfred the Hairy), hero of the Christian Reconquest of Ripoll and proclaimed founder of the Catalan "nation." The town's arcaded Plaça Major offers a glimpse of the town's medieval past, as does the broad, elegant, 12th-century bridge over the Ter.

ESSENTIALS

Visitor Information Sant Joan de les Abadesses (✉ *Pl. de la Abadía 9* ☎ *972/720599*).

EXPLORING

The altarpiece in the 12th-century Romanesque church of **Sant Joan** (✉ *Pl. de la Abadía s/n* ☎ *972/720013*), a 13th-century polychrome wood sculpture of the Descent from the Cross, is one of the most expressive and human of that epoch.

6

RIPOLL

10 km (6 mi) southwest of Sant Joan de les Abadesses, 105 km (62 mi) north of Barcelona, 65 km (40 mi) southeast of Puigcerdà.

One of the first Christian strongholds of the Reconquest and a center of religious erudition during the Middle Ages, Ripoll is known as the *bressol* (cradle) of Catalonia's liberation from Moorish domination and the spiritual home of Guifré el Pilós, who was the first count of Barcelona and is often claimed, despite threadbare evidence, to have founded the Catalan "nation" in the late 9th century. A dark, mysterious country town built around a **9th-century Benedictine monastery,** Ripoll was a focal point of culture throughout French Catalonia and the Pyrenees, from the monastery's 879 founding until the mid-1800s, when Barcelona began to eclipse it.

ESSENTIALS

Visitor Information Ripoll (✉ *Pl. de l'Abat Oliva* ☎ *972/702351*).

EXPLORING

Decorated with a pageant of biblical figures, the 12th-century doorway to the church of **Santa Maria** is one of Catalonia's great works of Romanesque art, crafted as a triumphal arch by stone masons and sculptors of the Roussillon school, which was centered around French Catalonia and the Pyrenees. You can pick up a guide to the figures on the portal either in the church or at the information kiosk nearby. 🎫 *Cloister and door €4, museum €6.50* ⏲ *Tues.–Sun. 10–2 and 3–7.*

Fourteen kilometers (9 mi) north of Ripoll, the **cogwheel train** (☎ *972/732020*) ride from Ribes de Freser up to Núria provides one of Catalonia's most unusual excursions; in few other places in Spain does a train make such a precipitous ascent. Known as the *cremallera* (zipper), the line was completed in 1931 to connect Ribes with the Santuari de la Mare de Déu de Núria (Mother of God of Núria) and with mountain hiking and skiing. The ride takes 45 minutes and costs €19.50 round-trip. **Núria**, at an altitude of 6,562 feet at the foot of Puigmal, is a ski area. From here there's an often dramatic—occasionally heart-stopping—trail, best done in the summer months, called the Camino dels Enginyers, or "engineers" path, a three hour jaunt partially aided at one point with a cable handrail, to the remote highland valley of Coma de Vaca, where the reward of a cozy refuge (☎ *949/229012*) and hearty replenishment await. Make sure there's space by phoning ahead. The next morning you can descend along the riverside Gorges de Freser trail, another three hour walk, down to Queralbs, where there are connecting trains to Ribes de Freser.

The legend of the **Santuari de la Mare de Déu de Núria**, a Marian religious retreat, is based on the story of Sant Gil of Nîmes, who did penance in the Núria Valley during the 7th century. The saint left behind a wooden statue of the Virgin Mary, a bell he used to summon shepherds to prayer, and a cooking pot; 300 years later, a pilgrim found these treasures in this sanctuary. The bell and the pot came to have special importance to barren women, who, according to local credence, were blessed with as many children as they wished after placing their heads in the pot and ringing the bell. ✉ *Núria* *Free* *Daily except during Mass.*

WHERE TO STAY

¢–$ **Hotel Vall de Núria.** A simple barracks-like hybrid of a mountain refuge and a hotel, this alpine dormitory and the Alberg (100 yards higher up the slope) offer comfortable lodging and dining at an altitude of 2,000 meters above sea level. For a day's outing or as a starting point for a major hike (12 hours) to Ulldeter, above Setcases, or even a weeklong walk to the Mediterranean, this is a handy spot, accessible only by the cogwheel train from Ribes de Freser. **Pros:** perfect location in the heart of the Pyrenees; pristine mountain air; simplicity. **Cons:** a rambling dormitory redolent of boarding school; quasi-monastic austerity. ✉ *Estación de Montaña Vall de Núria, Queralbs* ☎ *972/732000* *www.valldenuria.com* *65 rooms* *In-room: Wi-Fi. In-hotel: restaurant, bar, tennis court, Internet terminal* *AE, MC, V.*

LA CERDANYA

The Pyrenees' widest, sunniest valley is said to be in the shape of the handprint of God. High pastureland bordered north and south by snow-covered peaks, La Cerdanya starts in France, at Col de la Perche (near Mont Louis), and ends in the Spanish province of Lleida, at Martinet. Split between two countries and subdivided into two more provinces on each side, the valley has an identity all its own. Residents on both sides of the border speak Catalan, a Romance language derived from early Provençal French, and regard the valley's political border with undisguised hilarity. Unlike any other valley in the upper Pyrenees, this one runs east–west and thus has a record annual number of sunlight hours.

> **TIP**
>
> If you're planning a long-distance hiking trip, local bus connections will get you to your starting point and retrieve you from the finish line.

$$$–$$$$ **Villa Paulita.** This stately townhouse complex at the edge of Puigcerdà's iconic lake has vaulted to the forefront of the Cerdanya's dining and lodging options since opening in 2008. Along with perfection in peace and comfort, the hotel restaurant, L'Estany Senzone ($$$–$$$$), directed by chef Josep Maria Masó, is one of the two or three best dining establishments in the Pyrenees. **Pros:** near the center of the town's markets, restaurants, and general action but tucked into a scenic and silent northeast corner. **Cons:** so self-sufficient and peaceful it's easy to forget the many pleasures of exploring the Cerdanya Valley. ✉ *Av. Pons i Gasch 15* ☎ *972/884622* 🌐 *www.hospes.com* *38 rooms* *In-room: refrigerator, Wi-Fi. In-hotel: restaurant, bar, golf course, tennis court, pool, Wi-Fi hotspot* 💳 *AE, DC, MC, V.*

NIGHTLIFE

Young Spanish and French night owls fill the town's many clubs until dawn. **Le Clochard** (✉ *Carrer Major 54* ☎ *972/881615*) is a thronged pub in the center of town. **Transit** (✉ *Casino 3* ☎ *972/881606*) is midtown Puigcerdà's rock-until-dawn favorite.

SHOPPING

Puigcerdà is one big shopping mall and long a nexus for contraband clothes, cigarettes, and other items smuggled across the French border. **Carrer Major** is an uninterrupted row of stores selling everything: books, jewelry, fashion, and sports equipment.

The **Sunday market** in Plaça del Cuartel, like those in most Cerdanya towns, is a great place to look for local specialties such as herbs, goat cheese, wild mushrooms, honey, and basketry.

For the best *margaritas* in town (no, not those; these are crunchy-edged madeleines made with almonds), look for the oldest commercial establishment in Catalonia: **Pasteleria Cosp** (✉ *Carrer Major 20* ☎ *972/880103*), founded in 1806.

LLÍVIA

6 km (4 mi) northeast of Puigcerdà.

A Spanish enclave in French territory, Llívia was marooned by the 1659 Peace of the Pyrenees treaty, which ceded 33 villages to France. Incorporated as a *vila* (town) by royal decree of Carlos V—who spent a night here in 1528 and was impressed by the town's beauty and hospitality—Llívia managed to remain semantically Spanish.

ESSENTIALS

Visitor Information Llívia (✉ *Carrer dels Forns 10* ☎ *972/896313*).

EXPLORING

At the upper edge of town, the fortified church **Mare de Déu dels Àngels** (✉ *Carrer dels Forns 13* ☎ *972/896301*) is an acoustic gem; check to see if any choral events are scheduled, especially in August and December, when the Llívia music festival schedules top classical groups.

Across from the church is the ancient pharmacy **Museu de la Farmacia** (✉ *Carrer dels Forns 12* ☎ *972/880103* ⏲ *Daily Tues.–Fri. 10–4:20, weekends 10–1:50*), founded in 1415 and thought to be the oldest in Europe.Look for the **mosaic** in the middle of town commemorating Lampègia, *princesa de la pau i de l'amor* (princess of peace and of love), erected in memory of the red-haired daughter of the duke of Aquitania and lover of Munuza, a Moorish warlord who governed the Cerdanya during the Arab domination.

WHERE TO EAT

$$–$$$$ SPANISH ★ ✕ **Can Ventura.** Inside a flower-festooned 17th-century town house made of ancient stones, Jordi Pous's epicurean oasis is a handsome dining space and one of the Cerdanya's best addresses for both fine cuisine and good value. Beef *a la llosa* (seared on slabs of slate) and duck with pears and *naps* (turnips) are house specialties, and the wide selection of *entretenimientos* (hors d'oeuvres or tapas) is the perfect way to begin. Ask Jordi, an encyclopedic food and wine savant, about wine selections, game, and wild mushrooms in season. ✉ *Pl. Major 1* ☎ *972/896178* *Reservations essential* ▭ *AE, DC, MC, V* ⏲ *Closed Mon., June 20–July 15; Tues. July 16–Oct.*

$$$–$$$$ SPANISH Fodor'sChoice ★ ✕ **La Formatgeria de Llívia.** Conveniently situated on Llívia's eastern edge (en route to Saillagousse, France), this restaurant is in a former cheese factory that still makes fresh Mató cheese while you watch; there are tasting tables in the bar for these cheese-sampling sessions. Juanjo Meya and his wife, master chef Marta Pous, have had great success offering fine local cuisine, panoramic views looking south toward Puigmal and across the valley, and general charm and good cheer. The innovative tasting menu adds a creative dimension to the restaurant. ✉ *Pl. de Rô, Gorguja* ☎ *972/146279* *Reservations essential* ▭ *AE, DC, MC, V* ⏲ *Closed June 20–July 12, Tues. and Wed.*

BELLVER DE CERDANYA

★ *31 km (19 mi) southwest of Llívia, 25 km (16 mi) southwest of Puigcerdà.*

Bellver de Cerdanya has preserved its slate-roof and fieldstone Pyrenean architecture more successfully than many of the Cerdanya's larger towns. Perched on a promontory over the **Río Segre,** which winds around much of the town, Bellver is a mountain version of a fishing village—trout fishing, to be exact. The town's Gothic church of **Sant Jaume** and the arcaded **Plaça Major,** in the upper part of town, are lovely examples of traditional Pyrenean mountain-village design.

ESSENTIALS

Visitor Information Bellver de Cerdanya (✉ *Pl. de Sant Roc 9* ☎ *973/510229*).

WHERE TO EAT AND STAY

$ **Fonda Biayna.** A rustic retreat with woodsy furnishings that seems happily stuck in an early Pyrenean time warp, this hotel has simple and cozy guest rooms. The Catalan fare ($–$$$) includes such dishes as roast rabbit *allioli* (a sauce of garlic and olive oil), *civet de jabalí* (wild boar stew), and *confit d'anec amb monguetes seques* (duck confit with green beans). **Pros:** creaky floors and antiques add to the charm; cozy sense of traditional Pyrenean way of life. **Cons:** rooms are small; can be hot in summer. ✉ *Carrer Sant Roc 11* ☎ *973/510475* 🌐 *www.fondabiayna.com* *16 rooms* *In-room: no phone, no a/c, no TV, Wi-Fi. In-hotel: restaurant, Wi-Fi hotspot* *AE, DC, MC, V.*

LA SEU D'URGELL

Fodor's Choice ★ *20 km (12 mi) south of Andorra la Vella (in Andorra), 50 km (31 mi) west of Puigcerdà.*

La Seu d'Urgell is an ancient town facing the snowy rock wall of the Sierra del Cadí. As the seat (*seu*) of the regional archbishopric since the 6th century, it has a rich legacy of art and architecture. The Pyrenean feel of the streets, with their dark balconies and porticoes, overhanging galleries, and colonnaded porches—particularly **Carrer dels Canonges**—makes Seu mysterious and memorable. Look for the medieval **grain measures** at the corner of Carrer Major and Carrer Capdevila. The tiny food shops on the arcaded Carrer Major are good places to assemble lunch for a hike.

ESSENTIALS

Bus Station La Seu d'Urgell (✉ *Av. Garriga i Masó s/n, La Seu d'Urgell* ☎ *973/350020*).

Visitor Information La Seu d'Urgell (✉ *Av. Valls d'Andorra 33* ☎ *973/351511*).

EXPLORING

★ The 12th-century **Catedral de Santa Maria** is the finest cathedral in the Pyrenees, and the sunlight casting the rich reds and blues of Santa Maria's southeastern rose window into the deep gloom of the transept is a moving sight. The 13th-century cloister is famous for the individually carved, often whimsical capitals on its 50 columns, crafted by the same Roussillon school of masons who carved the doorway on the church of Santa Maria in Ripoll. Don't miss the haunting, 11th-century chapel of **Sant Miquel** or the **Diocesan Museum,** which has a striking collection of medieval murals from various Pyrenean churches and a colorfully illuminated 10th-century Mozarabic manuscript of the monk Beatus de Liébana's commentary on the apocalypse, along with a short film explaining it. ✉ *Pl. dels Oms* ☎ *973/350981* *Cathedral, cloister, and museum €4* ⏲ *Daily 9–1 and 4–8.*

WHERE TO EAT AND STAY

$$–$$$$ SPANISH ✕ **Cal Pacho.** Sample traditional Pyrenean and Mediterranean specialties at very reasonable prices in this dark, rustic spot, built in the typical mountain style with stone and wooden beams. It's a family-run restaurant popular with the locals, and the Río Segre and the Olympic Park, which teems with kayakers, are just a few steps away from this cozy

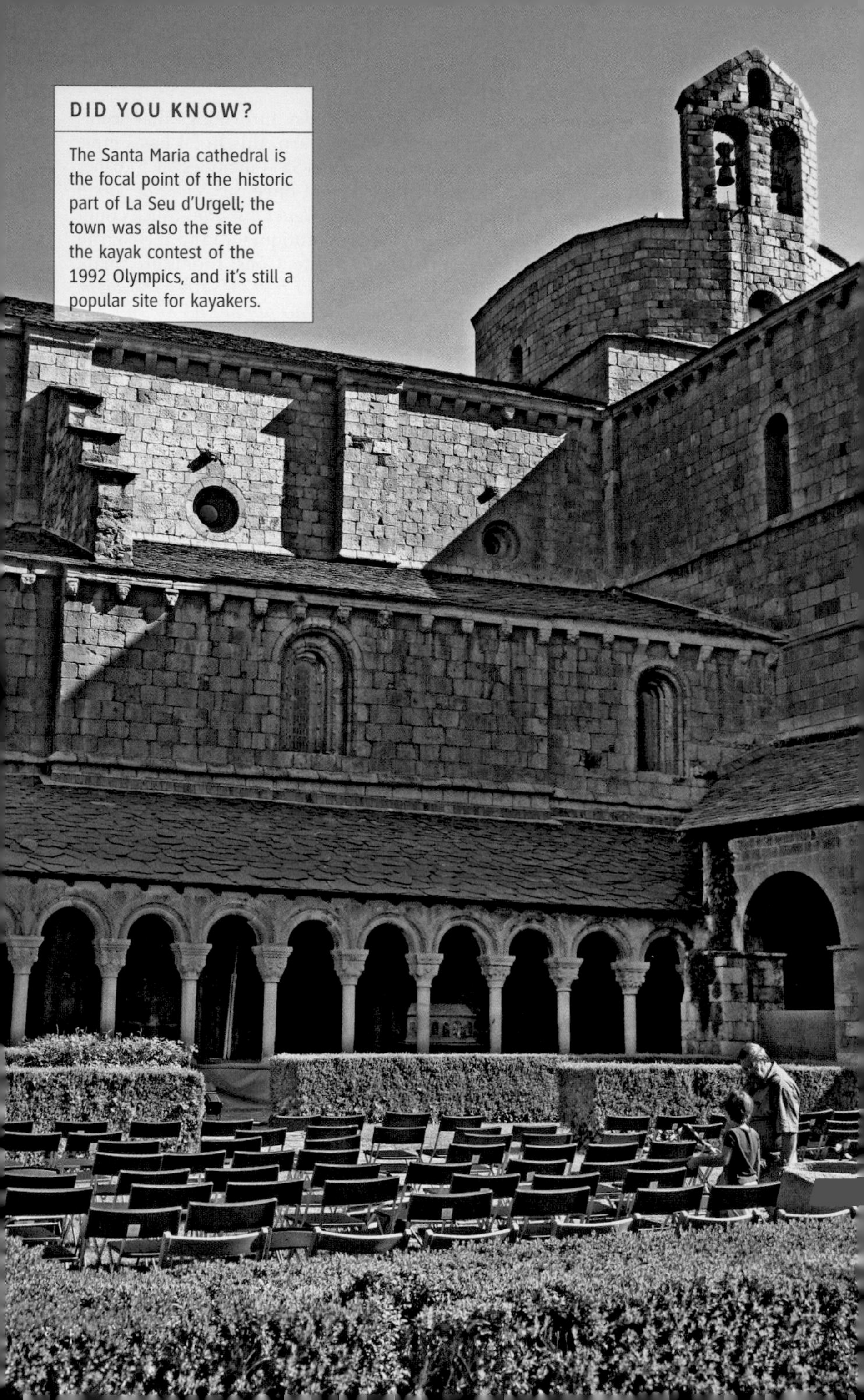

DID YOU KNOW?

The Santa Maria cathedral is the focal point of the historic part of La Seu d'Urgell; the town was also the site of the kayak contest of the 1992 Olympics, and it's still a popular site for kayakers.

nook in the lower part of town. Count on the filling *escudella* (mountain soup of vegetables, pork or veal, and noodles) in winter, and lamb, sausage, or trout cooked over coals or on slate year-round. ✉ *Carrer La Font 11* ☎ *973/352719* ▭ *AE, DC, MC, V.*

¢–$ **Cal Serni.** Ten minutes north of La Seu d'Urgell (off the road to Andorra) in the Pyrenean village of Calbinyà—which has a Museu del Pagès (Farmers' Museum) and a 16th-century farmhouse—is this lovely inn with rustic charm and inexpensive meals. The inn's owners often accompany guests into the woods to help identify mushrooms and berries and will be only too delighted to show you how to make delicious jams and conserves and how to cure meats during *la matanza*, the killing season. **Pros:** mountain authenticity just minutes from La Seu; good value. **Cons:** small rooms; no Internet. ✉ *Ctra. de Calbinyà s/n, Valls de Valira* ☎ *973/352809* 🌐 *www.calserni.com* *6 rooms* *In-hotel: restaurant* ▭ *AE, DC, MC, V.*

$$$$ Fodor's Choice ★ **El Castell de Ciutat.** Just outside La Seu, this wood-and-slate structure beneath La Seu's castle is one of the finest places to stay in the Pyrenees. Rooms on the second floor have balconies overlooking the river; those on the third have slanted ceilings and dormer windows. Suites include a salon. The internationally acclaimed restaurant, Tapies ($$$$), specializes in mountain cuisine, particularly Pyrenean *bolets* (mushrooms) and *caza* (game) from the Cerdanya valley. Reserve in advance during summer or Easter week. **Pros:** best restaurant for many miles; supremely comfortable rooms. **Cons:** right next to a busy highway; misses out on the feel of the town of La Seu. ✉ *Ctra. de Lleida (N260), Km 229* ☎ *973/350000* 🌐 *www.hotelelcastell.com* *32 rooms, 6 suites* *In-room: Wi-Fi. In-hotel: restaurant, pools, gym, Wi-Fi hotspot* ▭ *AE, DC, MC, V.*

$$$ **Parador de la Seu d'Urgell.** These comfortable quarters right in the center of town are built into the 12th-century church and convent of Sant Domènec. The interior patio—the cloister of the former convent—is a tranquil hideaway, lush with vegetation. Rooms are spare and simple but warm, and some have views of the mountains. **Pros:** next to the Santa Maria cathedral; handy for wandering through the town. **Cons:** minimalist lines and contemporary interior design clash with the medieval feel of this mountain refuge. ✉ *Carrer Sant Domènec 6* ☎ *973/352000* 🌐 *www.parador.es* *77 rooms, 1 suite* *In-hotel: restaurant, pool, gym* ▭ *AE, DC, MC, V.*

WESTERN CATALAN PYRENEES

"The farther from Barcelona, the wilder" is the rule of thumb, and this is true of the rugged countryside and fauna in the western part of Catalonia. Three of the greatest destinations in the Pyrenees are here: the Garonne-drained, Atlantic-oriented Vall d'Aran; the Noguera de Tor Valley (aka Vall de Boí), with its matching set of gemlike Romanesque churches; and Parc Nacional d'Aigüestortes i Estany de Sant Maurici, which has a network of pristine lakes and streams. The main geographical units in this section are the valley of the Noguera Pallaresa River,

6

the Vall d'Aran headwaters of the Atlantic-bound Garonne, and the Noguera Ribagorçana River valley, Catalonia's western limit.

SORT

★ *59 km (37 mi) west of La Seu d'Urgell.*

The capital of the Pallars Sobirà (Upper Pallars Valley) is a center for skiing, fishing, and white-water kayaking. Don't be fooled by the town you see from the main road: one block back, Sort is honeycombed with tiny streets and protected corners built to stave off harsh winter weather.

GETTING HERE

To get here from La Seu d'Urgell, take N260 toward Lleida, head west at Adrall and drive 53 km (33 mi) over the Cantó Pass to Sort.

ESSENTIALS

Visitor Information Pallars Sobirà (✉ *Camí de la Cabanera* ☎ *973/621002* 🌐 *www.pallarssobira.info*).

WHERE TO EAT

$$–$$$$ SPANISH ★ ✕ **Fogony**. If you hit Sort at lunchtime, Fogony, one of the finest dining establishments in the Pyrenees, is an excellent reason to stop. Come here for contemporary creations such as suckling pig (*cochinillo*) with tangerine crepes, *colmenillas con salsa de foie de pato macerado con Armagnac y Oporto* (wild mushrooms with sauce of duck liver macerated in Armagnac and port wine), or the *carré de cordero con falsas migas y espuma de patata* (lamb medallion with false bread crumbs and foam of potato). ✉ *Av. Generalitat 45* ☎ *973/621225* ▭ *AE, DC, MC, V* ⊙ *Closed 2 wks in Jan. Closed Mon. except Christmas wk, Easter wk, and Aug. No dinner Sun.*

PARC NACIONAL D'AIGÜESTORTES I ESTANY DE SANT MAURICI

★ *After Escaló, 12 km (7 mi) northwest of Llavorsí, the road to Espot and the park veers west.*

Running water and the abundance of high mountain terrain are the true protagonists in this wild domain in the shadow of the twin peaks of Els Encantats. More than 300 glacial lakes and lagoons drain through flower-filled meadows and woods to the two Noguera River watercourses: the Pallaresa to the east and the Ribagorçana to the west. The water is surrounded by bare rock walls carved out by the glacier that left these jagged peaks and moist pockets. The land ranges from soft lower meadows below 5,000 feet to the highest crags at nearly double that height: the twin Encantats measure more than 9,000 feet, and surrounding peaks Beciberri, Peguera, Montarto, and Amitges hover between 8,700 feet and just under 10,000 feet.

The nine mountain refuges are the stars of the Pyrenees, ranging from the 12-bunk Beciberri, the highest bivouac in the Pyrenees at 9,174 feet, to the 80-bunk, 7,326-foot Ventosa i Calvell at the foot of Punta Alta.

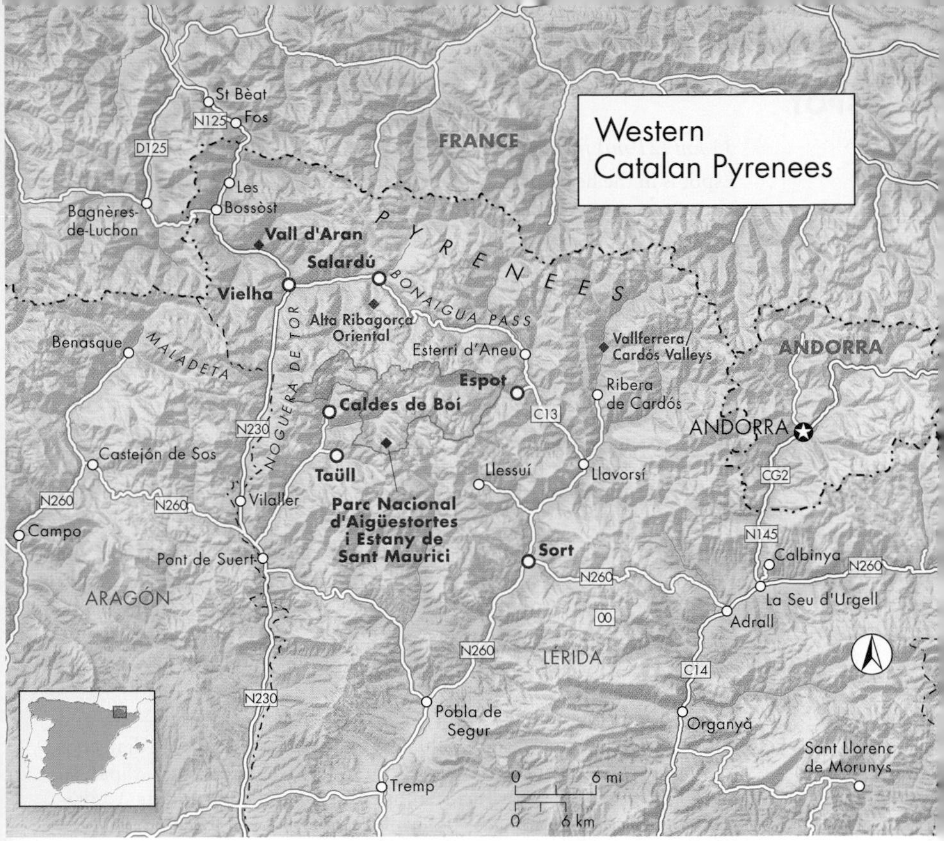

Between June and September these mountain accommodations fill with tired and hungry hikers sharing trail tips and lore.

The park has strict rules: no camping, no fires, no vehicles beyond certain points, no unleashed pets. Entrance is free, and it is accessible from the Noguera Pallares and Ribagorçana valleys and from Espot and Boí. For information and refuge reservations, contact the **park administration offices** (☎ *973/694000 Barruera, 973/696189 Boí, 973/624036 Espot* 🌐 *www.mma.es/parques/lared.com*).

WHERE TO STAY

There are no hotels in the park, but the nine refuges have staff who provide beds and dinner for hikers from June to October and during shorter periods at Christmas and Easter. When they are not open or staffed, shelter is available in parts, and fireplaces can be used for cooking, but food and utensils must be supplied by hikers. The 66-bunk **Refugi d'Amitges** (☎ *973/250109*) is near the Amitges lakes, at 7,920 feet. The 24-bunk **Refugi Ernest Mallafré** (☎ *973/250118*) is at the foot of Els Encantats, near Lake Sant Maurici. **Refugi Josep Maria Blanc** (☎ *973/250108*), at 7,755 feet, offers 40 bunks at the base of a peninsula reaching out into the Tort de Peguera Lake.

ESPOT

33 km (21 mi) from Sort.

Espot is in the heart of the valley, along a clear stream, next to the eastern entrance of Aigüestortes–Sant Maurici National Park.

ESSENTIALS

Visitor Information Espot (✉ *Pl. Major s/n* ☎ *973/624036*).

EXPLORING

Super-Espot is the local ski area. The **Pont de la Capella** *(Chapel Bridge)*, a perfect, mossy arch over the flow, looks as though it might have grown directly out of the Pyrenean slate.

VALL D'ARAN AND ENVIRONS

From Esterri d'Aneu, the valley runs 46 km (27 mi) east to Vielha over the Bonaigua Pass.

The Vall d'Aran is at the western edge of the Catalan Pyrenees and the northwestern corner of Catalonia. North of the main Pyrenean axis, it's the Catalan Pyrenees' only Atlantic valley, opening north into the plains of Aquitania and drained by the Garonne, which flows into the Atlantic Ocean above Bordeaux. The 48-km (30-mi) drive from Bonaigua Pass to the Pont del Rei border with France follows the riverbed.

The valley's Atlantic personality is evidenced by its climate—wet and cold—and its language: the 6,000 inhabitants speak Aranés, a dialect of Gascon French derived from the Occitanian language group. (Spanish and Catalan are also universally spoken.) Originally part of the Aquitanian county of Comminges, the Vall d'Aran maintained feudal ties to the Pyrenees of Spanish Aragón and became part of Catalonia-Aragón in the 12th century. In 1389 the valley was assigned to Catalonia.

Neither as wide as the Cerdanya nor as oppressively narrow and vertical as Andorra, the Vall d'Aran has a sense of well-being and order, an architectural harmony unique in Catalonia. The clusters of iron-gray slate roofs, the lush vegetation, and the dormer windows (a sign of French influence) all make the Vall d'Aran a distinct geographic and cultural pocket that happens to have washed up on the Spanish side of the border.

Hiking and climbing are popular here; guides are available year-round and can be arranged through the **tourist office** (☎ *973/640110*) in Vielha.

VIELHA

79 km (49 mi) northwest of Sort, 297 km northwest of Barcelona, or 160 km north of Lleida.

Vielha (Viella, in Spanish), capital of the Vall d'Aran, is a lively crossroads vitally involved in the Aranese movement to defend and reconstruct the valley's architectural, institutional, and linguistic heritage.

ESSENTIALS

Visitor Information Vielha (✉ *Carrer Sarriulera 10* ☎ *973/640110*).

CLOSE UP

Hiking in the Pyrenees

Walking the Pyrenees, with one foot in France and the other in Spain, is an exhilarating experience within reach of the moderately fit.

In fall and winter the Alberes Mountains between Cap de Creus, the Iberian Peninsula's easternmost point, and the border with France at Le Perthus are a grassy runway between the Côte Vermeille's to the north and the moist green patchwork of the Empordá to the south. The well-marked GR (Gran Recorrido) 11 is a favorite two-day spring or autumn hike, with an overnight stay at the Refugi de la Tanyareda, just below Puig Neulós, the highest point in the Alberes.

The eight-hour walk from Coll de Núria to Ulldeter over the Sierra Catllar, above Setcases, is another grassy corridor in good weather from April to October. The luminous Cerdanya Valley is a hiker's paradise year-round, while the summertime round-Andorra hike is a memorably scenic 360-degree tour of the tiny country.

The Parc Nacional d'Aigüestortes i Estany de Sant Maurici is superb for trekking from spring through fall. The ascent of the hightest peak in teh Pyrenees, the 11,168-foot Aneto peak above Benasque, is a long day's round-trip best approached in summer and only by fit and experienced hikers. Much of the hike is over the Maladeta glacier, from the base camp at the Refugio de La Renclusa, where you can rent crampons and ice axes.

In Parque Nacional de Ordesa y Monte Perdido you can take day trips up to the Cola de Caballo waterfall and back around the southern rim of the canyon or, for true mountain goats, longer hikes via the Refugio de Góriz to La Brèche de Roland and Gavarnie or to Monte Perdido, the parador at La Pineta, and the village of Bielsa. Another prized walk has bed and dinner in the base camp town of Torla or a night up at the Refugio de Goriz at the head of the valley.

The section of the Camino de Santiago walk from Saint-Jean-Pied-de-Port to Roncesvalles is a marvelous 8- to 10-hour trek and manageable any time of year, though weather reports should be checked carefully from October to June.

Local *excursionista* (outing) clubs can help you get started; local tourist offices may also have brochures and rudimentary trail maps. Keep in mind that the higher reaches are safely navigable only in summer.

Contacts Centre Excursionista de Catalunya (✉ *Carrer Paradís 10, Barcelona* ☎ *93/315–2311*). **Cercle d'Aventura** (☎ *972/881017*). **Giroguies** (☎ *636/490830* 🌐 *www.giroguies.com*). **Guies de Meranges** (☎ *616/855535*). **Guies de Muntanya** (☎ *629/591614* 🌐 *www.guiesdemuntanya.com*).

6

EXPLORING

The octagonal, 14th-century bell tower on the Romanesque parish church of **Sant Miquel** is one of the town's trademarks, as is its 15th-century Gothic altar. The partly damaged 12th-century wood carving *Cristo de Mig Aran,* displayed under glass, evokes a sense of mortality and humanity with a power unusual in medieval sculpture.

North of Vielha, the tiny villages over the Garonne River hold intriguing little secrets, such as the sculpted Gallo-Roman heads (funeral stelae, or stone slabs, restored in the 12th century) carved into the village portal at **Gausac**. The bell tower in **Vilac** has an eccentric charm. **Vilamós**'s church, the oldest in the valley, is known for the three curious carved figures, thought to be Gallo-Roman funeral stelae, on its facade. Beautifully carved capitals on the supporting columns adorn the porticoed square in the border village of **Bossòst**. East of Vielha is the village of **Escunhau**, with steep alley stairways. **Arties** makes a good stop, with its famous Casa Irene restaurant and historic parador.

WHERE TO EAT AND STAY

$$–$$$ SPANISH ★ **Era Mola**. Also known as Restaurante Gustavo y María José, this rustic former stable with whitewashed walls serves French-inspired Aranese cuisine. Duck, either stewed with apples or served with *carradetas* (wild mushrooms from the valley), and roast kid or lamb are favorites. The wine list is particularly strong in Rioja, Ribera de Duero, and Somontano reds, as well as full-bodied whites such as Albariños from Rías Baixas and Ruedas from Valladolid. *Carrer Marrec 14* *973/642419* *Reservations essential* *AE, DC, MC, V* *No lunch weekdays Dec.–Apr.*

$$$–$$$$ ★ **Casa Irene**. A rustic haven, this inn 6 km (4 mi) east of Vielha is known for fine mountain cuisine with a French flair. Three tasting menus ($$$–$$$$) and dishes such as poached foie gras in black truffles and roast wood pigeon with cream of artichoke have made Irene a national treasure. The personal style and spacious and elegant rooms make this a highly recommendable address for lodging as well as food. **Pros:** small and personalized; aesthetically impeccable. **Cons:** streetside rooms can be noisy on summer nights. *Carrer Major 3, Arties* *973/644364* *www.hotelcasairene.com* *22 rooms* *In-room: Wi-Fi. In-hotel: restaurant, Wi-Fi hotspot, parking (paid)* *Reservations essential* *AE, DC, MC, V* *Closed Nov. and May.*

$$$ **Parador de Arties**. Built around the Casa de Don Gaspar de Portolà, once home to the founder of the colony of California, this modern parador has sweeping views of the Pyrenees. Just 7 km (4 mi) from the Baqueira ski slopes and 2½ km (1½ mi) south of Vielha, it's big enough to be festive but small enough for intimacy. The restaurant ($$–$$$) specializes in Pyrenean soups and stews such as *civet de jabalí* (wild boar stew). **Pros:** marvelous panoramas; quiet and personal for a parador. **Cons:** neither at the foot of the slopes nor in the thick of the Vielha après-ski vibe; requires driving. *Ctra. Baqueira-Beret s/n, Arties* *973/640801* *www.parador.es* *54 rooms, 3 suites* *In-hotel: restaurant, pools, gym, parking (paid)* *AE, MC, V.*

$$$ **Parador de Vielha**. This modern granite parador has a semicircular salon with huge windows and spectacular views over the Maladeta peaks of the Vall d'Aran. Rooms are furnished with traditional carved-wood furniture and floor-to-ceiling curtains. The light-flooded restaurant ($$–$$$) serves Catalan and Pyrenean cuisine, ranging from *espinacas a la catalana* (spinach sautéed in olive oil with pine nuts, raisins, and garlic) to *civet d'isard* (wild mountain-goat stew). **Pros:** terrific observation post; comfortable and relaxed. **Cons:** somewhat overpopulated when

fully booked; overmodern and functional design. ✉ *Ctra. del Túnel s/n* ☎ *973/640100* 🌐 *www.parador.es* *118 rooms* *In-hotel: restaurant, pool, spa, Wi-Fi hotspot, parking (free)* ▭ *AE, MC, V.*

NIGHTLIFE

Bar Era Crin (✉ *Carrer Sortaus 2, Escunhau* ☎ *973/642061*) has live performances and pop rock to dance to. **Bar la Lluna** (✉ *Carrer Major 10, Arties* ☎ *973/641115*), a local favorite, occupies a typical Aranese house and has live performances on Wednesday. **Eth Clòt** (✉ *Pl. Sant Orenç, Arties* ☎ *973/642060*) is a hot *bar musicale*. **Glass** (✉ *Centro Comercial Elurra, Betrén* ☎ *973/640332*) is in a commercial complex near Vielha that's filled with a dozen music bars, pubs, and discos.

SALARDÚ

9 km (6 mi) east of Vielha.

Salardú is a pivotal point in the Vall d'Aran, convenient to Tredós, the Montarto peak, the lakes and Circ de Colomers, Aigüestortes National Park, and the villages of Unha and Montgarri. The town itself, with just over 700 inhabitants, is known for its steep streets and its octagonal fortified bell tower. The 12th-century **Sant Andreu** church's Romanesque wood sculpture of Christ is said to have miraculously floated up the Garonne River.

The tiny village of **Unha** perches on a promontory 3 km (2 mi) above Salardú, with the elegant Ço de Brastet (Brastet House) at its entrance. Unha's 12th-century church of Santa Eulàlia has a curiously bulging 17th-century bell tower.East of Salardú is the village of **Tredós**, home to the Romanesque church of Santa Maria de Cap d'Aran—symbol of the Aranese independence movement and meeting place of the valley's governing body, the Conselh Generau, until 1827.

OFF THE BEATEN PATH

Santa Maria de Montgarri. Partly in ruins, this 11th-century chapel was once an important way station on the route into the Vall d'Aran from France. The beveled, hexagonal bell tower and the rounded stones, which look as if they came from a brook bottom, give the structure a stippled appearance not unlike that of a Pyrenean trout. The Romería de Nuestra Señora de Montgarri (Feast of Our Lady of Montgarri), on July 2, is a country fair with dancing, game playing, and general carrying-on. The sanctuary is 12 km (7 mi) northeast of the town of Bagergue, which is just north of Salardú.

WHERE TO EAT AND STAY

$$–$$$ SPANISH

✕ **Casa Rufus.** Fresh pine on the walls and underfoot, red-and-white checked curtains, and snowy white tablecloths cozily furnish this restaurant nestled in the tiny, gray-stone village of Gessa, between Vielha and Salardú. Rufus, who also runs the ski school at Baqueira, is especially adept with local country cooking; try the *conejo relleno de ternera* (rabbit stuffed with veal) or one of the *civets* (stews) of mountain goat or venison, which, if on the menu, shouldn't be missed. ✉ *Sant Jaume 8, Gessa* ☎ *973/645246 or 973/645872* ▭ *MC, V* ⏲ *Closed May–mid-July, Nov., and weekdays in Oct. No dinner Sun. No lunch weekdays mid-Sept.–Apr.*

$$$$ ★ **Meliá Royal Tanau.** This luxurious hotel 7 km (4 mi) east of Salardú is next to the lifts and offers everything from hydrotherapy massage to fine cuisine (with prices to match: $$$–$$$$). Considered one of the top skiing hotels in the Pyrenees, the Royal Tanau will pamper you carefully between assaults on the snowy heights. Top-floor rooms can be snug, but duplex apartments have sleeping lofts with skylights opening into the starry Pyrenean firmament. **Pros:** among the top Pyrenean skiing accommodations; intimate and low-key luxe. **Cons:** some rooms are on the small side; occasional design and layout lapses. ✉ *Ctra. Baqueira-Beret, Km 7* ☎ *973/644446* 🌐 *www.meliaroyaltanau.solmelia.com* *30 rooms, 15 apartments* *In-room: no a/c, Wi-Fi. In-hotel: restaurant, pool, Wi-Fi hotspot* *AE, MC, V.*

$$$$ **Val de Ruda.** For rustic surroundings light on luxury but long on comfort and an outdoorsy, alpine feeling, this modern-traditional construction is a good choice. Just a two-minute walk to the lift, the Val de Ruda was one of the first skiing hotels to be built here, in the early 1980s. This glass, wood, and stone refuge has a friendly staff and pine- and oak-beam warmth for après-ski wining and dining. **Pros:** warm and welcoming after a day in the mountains; friendly family service. **Cons:** some of the dormer rooms are cozy but tiny. ✉ *Ctra. Baqueira-Beret Cota 1500* ☎ *973/645258* 🌐 *www.valderuda-bassibe.com* *34 rooms* *In-room: no a/c. In-hotel: restaurant, bar, Wi-Fi hotspot* *AE, DC, MC, V.*

NIGHTLIFE

Pachá (✉ *Baqueira* ☎ *973/646444*) has successfully extended its disco tentacles from Ibiza to Barcelona to Baqueira.

SPORTS AND THE OUTDOORS

Skiing, white-water rafting, hiking, climbing, horseback riding, and fly-fishing are available throughout the Vall d'Aran. Consult the Vielha **tourist office** (☎ *973/640110*) for information.

SKIING The **Baqueira-Beret Estación de Esquí** *(Baqueira-Beret Ski Station)* offers Catalonia's most varied and reliable skiing. The station's 87 km (57 mi) of *pistas* (slopes), spread over 53 runs, range from the gentle Beret slopes to the vertical chutes of Baqueira. The Bonaigua area is a mixture of steep and gently undulating trails with some of the longest, most varied runs in the Pyrenees. The internationally International Ski Federation–classified super-giant slalom run in Beret is the star attraction, although the Hotel Pirene runs carefully guided helicopter outings to the surrounding peaks of Pincela, Areño, Parros, Mall de Boulard, Pedescals, and Bassibe, among others. A dozen restaurants and four children's areas are scattered about the facilities, and the thermal baths at Tredós are 4 km (2½ mi) away. ✉ *Salardú* ☎ *973/639010* 🌐 *www.baqueira.es.*

OFF THE BEATEN PATH

The **Vall de Joeu** (Joeu Valley), above the town of Les Bordes, 9 km (6 mi) northwest of Vielha, was for centuries the unsolved mystery of Vall d'Aran hydraulics. The Joeu River, one of the two main sources of the Garonne, appears to rise at Artiga de Lin, where it then cascades down in the Barrancs Waterfalls. On July 19, 1931, speleologist Norbert Casteret proved, by dumping 132 pounds of colorant into a cavern in neighboring Aragón, that this "spring" was actually glacier

DID YOU KNOW?

The mountain town of Salardu is part of the Naut Aran (literally "upper valley") municipality of Spain's Aran Valley. Not surprisingly, the area is major draw for skiiers.

runoff from the Maladeta massif in the next valley to the southwest. The glacier melt flows into a huge crater, Els Aïgualluts, and reappears 4 km (3 mi) northeast at the Uelhs deth Joeu (Eyes of Jupiter, so named for the Roman deity's association with the heavens, weather, rainfall, and agriculture), in Aranés, where it flows north toward the Garonne, eventually emptying into the Atlantic.

TAÜLL

58 km (36 mi) south of Vielha.

Taüll is a town of narrow streets and tight mountain design—wooden balconies and steep slate roofs. The famous Taüll churches of Sant Climent and Santa Maria are among the best examples of Romanesque architecture in the Pyrenees. Other important churches near Taüll include Sant Feliu, at Barruera; Sant Joan Baptista, at Boí; Santa Maria at Cardet; Santa Maria at Col; Santa Eulàlia, at Erill-la-vall; La Nativitat de la Mare de Deu and Sant Quirze, at Durro; Sant Llorenç, at Sarais; and Sant Nicolau, in the Sant Nicolau Valley, at the entrance to Aigüestortes–Sant Maurici National Park.

ESSENTIALS

Visitor Information Taüll (✉ *Av. Valira s/n* ☎ *973/694000*).

EXPLORING

Taüll has a ski resort, **Bohí Taüll**, at the head of the Sant Nicolau Valley.

★ At the edge of town is the exquisite three-nave Romanesque church of **Sant Climent**, built in 1123. The six-story belfry has exceptionally harmonious proportions, Pyrenean stone that changes hues with the light, and a sense of intimacy that creates notable balance. In 1922 Barcelona's Museu Nacional d'Art de Catalunya became the home of the church's murals, including the famous *Pantocrator*, the work of the "Master of Taüll." The murals presently in the church are reproductions. *€3* *Daily 10–2 and 4–8.*

CALDES DE BOÍ

6 km (4 mi) north of Taüll.

ESSENTIALS

Visitor Information Vall de Boí (✉ *Pg. Sant Feliu 43* ☎ *973/694000*).

EXPLORING

Caldes de Boí. The thermal baths in the town of Caldes de Boí include, between hot and cold sources, 40 springs. The caves inside the bath area are a singular natural phenomenon, with thermal steam seeping through the cracks in the rock. Take advantage of the baths' therapeutic qualities at either Hotel Caldas or Hotel Manantial—services range from a bath, at €8 to €12, to an underwater body massage for €19. People with arthritis are frequent takers. ✉ *Hotel Caldas* ☎ *973/696220* ✉ *Hotel Manantial* ☎ *973/696210* *www.caldesdeboi.com* *Hotels and baths closed Oct.–May.*

WHERE TO EAT AND STAY

¢ SPANISH **Fondevila.** Wooden trim and simple country furnishings warm the interior of this stone structure 3 km (2 mi) north of Taüll. The rooms are generously proportioned, handsomely furnished, and cozy. The country cuisine ($–$$) includes game in season and various Catalan specialties, from hearty stews such as *escudella* and *civet de porc senglar* (wild boar stew) to venison and *anec amb peres* (duck stewed with pears). **Pros:** friendly and intimate service; simple mountain lodging; top value. **Cons:** sparse room decor may seem stark. ✉ *Carrer Única s/n, Boí* ☎ *973/696011* *46 rooms* *In-room: no a/c, Wi-Fi. In-hotel: restaurant* ▭ *AE, DC, MC, V* ⊙ *Closed Nov. 10–Dec. 26 and Jan. 7–Feb. 1.*

ARAGÓN AND CENTRAL PYRENEES

The highest, wildest, and most spectacular range of the Pyrenees is the middle section, farthest from sea level. From Benasque on Aragón's eastern side to Jaca at the western edge are the great heights and most dramatic landscapes of Alto Aragón (Upper Aragón), including the Maladeta (11,165 feet), Posets (11,070 feet), and Monte Perdido (11,004 feet) peaks, the three highest points in the Pyrenean chain.

Communications between the high valleys of the Pyrenees were all but nonexistent until the 19th century: four-fifths of the region had never seen a motor vehicle of any kind until well into the 20th century, and the 150-km (93-mi) border with France between Portalet de Aneu and Vall d'Aran had never had an international crossing. This combination of high peaks, deep defiles, and isolation has produced some of the Iberian Peninsula's best-preserved towns and valleys. Today, numerous ethnological museums bear witness to a way of life that has nearly disappeared since the 1950s. Residents of Upper Aragón speak neither Basque nor Catalan, but local dialects, such as Grausín, Chistavino, Belsetá, and Benasqués (collectively known as *fabla*), which have more in common with each other and with Occitanian or Langue d'Oc (the southwestern French language descended from Provençal) than with modern Spanish and French. Furthermore, each valley has its own variations on everything from the typical Aragonese folk dance, the *jota,* to cuisine and traditional costume.

The often bypassed cities of Huesca and Zaragoza are both useful Pyrenean gateways and historic destinations in themselves. With its ancient *casco viejo* (old city) around the immense basilica of La Pilarica, Zaragoza is much more than just an unavoidable link between Barcelona and Bilbao; and Huesca has a memorable old quarter. Both cities retain an authentic provincial character that is refreshing in today's cosmopolitan Spain.

6

HUESCA

75 km (46 mi) southwest of Aínsa, 72 km (45 mi) northeast of Zaragoza, 123 km (74 mi) northwest of Lleida.

Capital of Aragón until the royal court moved to Zaragoza in 1118, Huesca was founded by the Romans more than a thousand years earlier; the city became an independent state with a senate and an excellent school system organized by the Roman general Sertorius in 77 BC. Much later, after centuries of Moorish rule, Pedro I of Aragón liberated Huesca in 1096. The town's university was founded in 1354 and now specializes in Aragonese studies.

ESSENTIALS

Bus Station Huesca (✉ *Ronda de la Estación s/n, Huesca* ☎ *974/210700*).

Visitor Information Huesca (✉ *Pl. López Allué s/n* ☎ *974/292170*).

EXPLORING

An intricately carved gallery tops the eroded facade of Huesca's 13th-century Gothic **cathedral**. Damián Forment, a disciple of the 15th-century Italian master sculptor Donatello, created the alabaster altarpiece with scenes from the Crucifixion. ✉ *Pl. de la Catedral s/n* ☎ *974/220676* *Free* ⏲ *Mon.–Sat. 8–1 and 4–6:30.*

Twice daily, the Huesca tourist office (in the former market at Plaza Luis Lopez Allué) accompanies visitors into the Renaissance **ayuntamiento** *(*town hall*)* to see the 19th-century painting of the 12th-century beheading of a group of uncooperative nobles ordered by Ramiro II. King Ramiro, having called a meeting for the purported pouring of a giant bell that would be audible throughout Aragón, proceeded to massacre the leading troublemakers, and the expression *como la campana de Huesca* ("like the bell of Huesca") is still sometimes used to describe an event of surprising resonance. ✉ *Pl. de la Catedral 1* ☎ *974/292170* *Free* ⏲ *Mon.–Sat. at noon and 6.*

The **Museo Arqueológico Provincial** is an octagonal patio ringed by eight chambers, including the **Sala de la Campana** (Hall of the Bell), where the beheadings of 12th-century nobles took place. The museum is in parts of what was once the royal palace of the kings of Aragón and holds paintings by Aragonese primitives, including *La Virgen del Rosario* by Miguel Jiménez, and several works by the 16th-century Maestro de Sigena. ✉ *Pl. de la Universidad* ☎ *974/220586* *Free* ⏲ *Tues.–Sat. 10–2 and 5–8, Sun. 10–2.*

The church of **San Pedro el Viejo** has an 11th-century cloister. Ramiro II and his father, Alfonso I—the only Aragonese kings not entombed at San Juan de la Peña—rest in a side chapel. ✉ *Pl. de San Pedro s/n* ☎ *974/222387* *Free* ⏲ *Mon.–Sat. 10–2 and 6–8.*

OFF THE BEATEN PATH

Castillo de Loarre. This massively walled 11th-century monastery, 36 km (22 mi) west of Huesca off Route A132 on A1206, is nearly indistinguishable from the rock outcroppings that surround it. Inside the walls are a church, a tower, a dungeon, and even a medieval toilet with views of the almond and olive orchards in the Ebro basin.

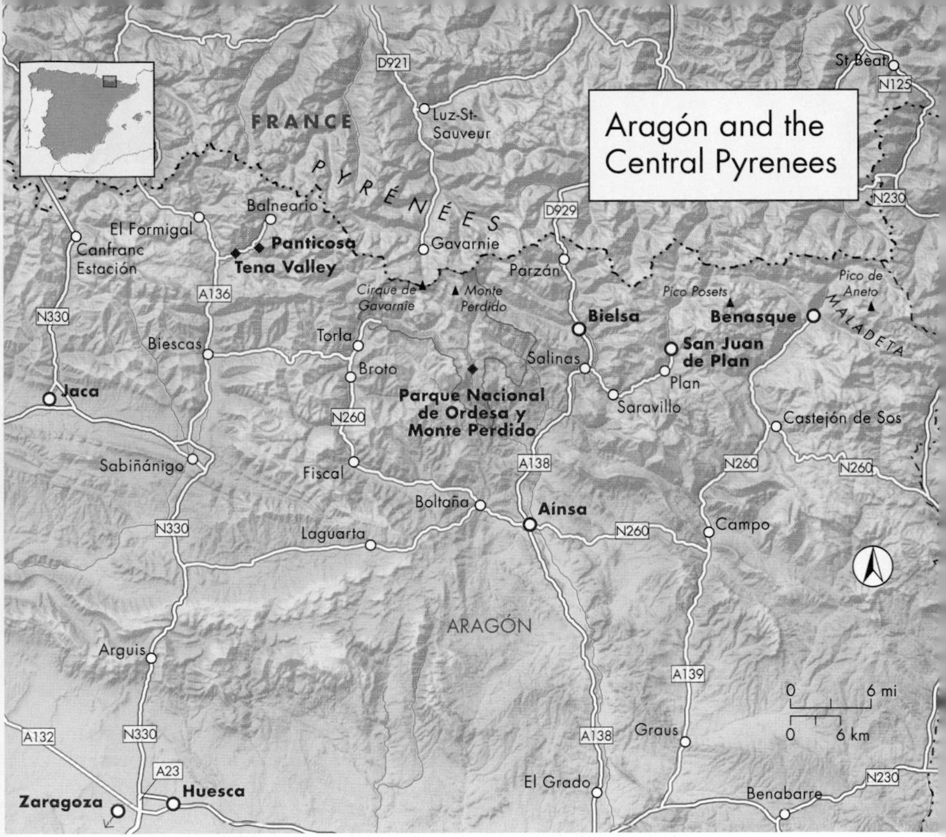

WHERE TO EAT AND STAY

$$–$$$$ SPANISH ✕ **Las Torres.** Huesca's top dining establishment makes inventive use of first-rate local ingredients ranging from wild mushrooms to wild boar, venison, and lamb. The glass-walled kitchen is as original as the cooking that emerges from it, and the wine list is strong in Somontanos, Huesca's own Denomination of Origin. Look for *lomo de ternasco cocinado a baja temperatura con embutidos de Graos* (veal cooked at low temperature with Graos sausage) or *paticas de cordero deshuesados* (boned lamb's trotters) for a taste of pure upper Aragón. ✉ *María Auxiliadora 3* ☎ *974/228213* 🌐 *www.lastorres-restaurante.com* ▭ *AE, DC, MC, V* ⊙ *Closed 2 wks at Easter, Aug. 16–31, and Sun.*

$$–$$$ **Pedro I de Aragón.** This modern structure over the leafy Parque Miguel Servet is lush with mirrors and marble in the lobby and pine pine furniture in the rooms. Comfort is the objective here, and the accommodations and service are the best in Huesca, although the decor is somewhat stuck in a generic 1960s time warp. **Pros:** efficient and modern. **Cons:** exterior rooms noisy on summer weekends; no style but very comfortable. ✉ *Parque 34* ☎ *974/220300* 🌐 *www.gargallo-hotels.com* *125 rooms, 4 suites* *In-room: no a/c. In-hotel: restaurant, bar, pool, Wi-Fi hotspot* ▭ *AE, DC, MC, V.*

¢ **San Marcos.** This elegant building dates from the late 19th century, though the public spaces have been updated for comfort. A family-run

Mountain trekking in the Huesca province

enterprise with a personal touch, it has rooms that are small and simply but recently decorated with fresh pine furniture and impeccable bathroom facilities. Outside the 1st-century Roman walls, the hotel is a five-minute walk from Huesca's cathedral. **Pros:** convenient central location; historic and elegant building; good value. **Cons:** rooms can seem cluttered and somewhat cramped. ✉ *San Orencio 10* ☎ 📠 *974/222931* *29 rooms* *In-room: no a/c, Wi-Fi. In-hotel: restaurant, bar, pool* *AE, DC, MC, V.*

ZARAGOZA

72 km (43 mi) southwest of Huesca, 138 km (86 mi) west of Lleida, 307 km (184 mi) northwest of Barcelona, 164 km (98 mi) southeast of Pamplona, 322 km (193 mi) northeast of Madrid.

In high spirits after the 2008 Universal Exposition (based on the theme of water and its own mighty Ebro River), Zaragoza is now about as exciting as it's ever been. This traditionally provincial city is experiencing its greatest boom since the Romans established a thriving river port here in 25 BC. Rated one of Spain's most desirable places to live because of its air quality, low cost of living, and low population density, Zaragoza seems full of self-contained well-being. Despite its hefty size (pop. 660,895), this sprawling provincial capital midway between Barcelona, Madrid, Bilbao, and Valencia is a detour from the tourist track connected by the AVE, Spain's high-speed railroad, with both Madrid and Barcelona only 90 minutes away.

Straddling Spain's greatest river, the Ebro, 2,000-year-old Zaragoza was originally named Caesaraugusta, for Roman emperor Augustus. Its legacy contains everything from Roman ruins and Jewish baths to Arab, Romanesque, Gothic-Mudejar, Renaissance, baroque, neoclassical, and Art Nouveau architecture. Parts of the **Roman walls** are visible near the city's landmark, Basílica de Nuestra Señora del Pilar. Nearby, the medieval **Puente de Piedra** (Stone Bridge) spans the Ebro. Checking out the **Lonja** (Stock Exchange), the Moorish **Aljafería** (Fortified Palace and Jewel Treasury), the **Mercado de Lanuza** (Produce Market), and the many **churches** in the old town is a good way to navigate Zaragoza's jumble of backstreets.

A PAMPLONA ALTERNATIVE

For an unspoiled Pamplona-like fiesta in another pre-Pyrenean capital, with bullfights, *encierros* (running of the bulls through the streets), and all-night revelry, try Huesca's San Lorenzo celebration August 9–15. Spain's top bullfighters are the main attraction, along with concerts, street dances, and liberal tastings of the excellent Somontano wines of upper Huesca. *Albahaca* (basil) is the official symbol of Huesca, and the ubiquitous green sashes and bandannas will remind you that this is Huesca, not Pamplona (where red is the trimming).

Excursions from Zaragoza include Francisco José de Goya y Lucientes's birthplace at **Fuendetodos,** 44 km (26 mi) to the southeast, and **Belchite,** another 20 km (12 mi) east of Fuendetodos, site of the ruins of a town destroyed in one of the fiercest battles of the Spanish civil war and left untouched since as a reminder of the tragedy of war.

ESSENTIALS

Bus Station Zaragoza (✉ *Paseo María Agustín 7* ☎ *976/229343*).

Visitor Information Zaragoza (central square) (✉ *Pl. de Nuestra Señora del Pilar* ☎ *902/412008*). **Zaragoza** (✉ *Calle Torreon de la Zuda, Glorieta de Pío XII* ☎ *902/412008*). **Zaragoza (train station)** (✉ *Rioja 33, Estación Zaragoza-Delicias* ☎ *902/432343*).

EXPLORING

Hulking on the banks of the Ebro, the **Basílica de Nuestra Señora del Pilar** (Basilica of Our Lady of the Pillar), affectionately known as "La Pilarica," is Zaragoza's symbol and pride. An immense baroque structure with no fewer than 11 tile cupolas, La Pilarica is the home of the Virgen del Pilar, the patron saint not only of peninsular Spain but of the entire Hispanic world. The fiestas honoring this most Spanish of saints, held the week of October 12, are events of extraordinary pride and Spanish fervor, with processions, street concerts, bullfights, and traditional *jota* dancing. The cathedral was built in the 18th century to commemorate the appearance of the Virgin on a pillar (*pilar*), or pedestal, to St. James, Spain's other patron saint, during his legendary incarnation as Santiago Matamoros (St. James the Moorslayer) in the 9th century. La Pilarica herself resides in a side chapel that dates from 1754. The frescoes in the cupolas, some of which are attributed to the young Goya, are among the basilica's treasures. The **Museo Pilarista** holds drawings and some of the Virgin's jewelry. The bombs displayed to the right of the altar of La Pilarica chapel fell through the roof of the church in 1936 and miraculously failed to explode. You can still see one of the holes overhead to the left. Behind La Pilarica's altar is the tiny opening where the devout line up to kiss the rough marble pillar where La Pilarica was allegedly discovered. ✉ *Pl. del Pilar s/n* 🎫 *Basilica free, museum €2* ⏲ *Basilica daily 5:45 AM–9:30 PM, museum daily 9–2 and 4–6.*

The **Iglesia de la Magdalena**, next to the remains of the Roman forum, has an ancient brick Mudejar bell tower and is usually open in the mornings. ✉ *Pl. de la Magdalena s/n* ☎ *976/299598.*

Zaragoza's cathedral, **La Seo** *(Catedral de San Salvador)*, at the eastern end of the Plaza del Pilar, is the city's bishopric, or diocesan *seo* (seat). An amalgam of architectural styles ranging from the Mudejar brick-and-tile exterior to the Gothic altarpiece to exuberant Churrigueresque doorways, the Seo nonetheless has an 18th-century baroque facade that seems to echo those of La Pilarica. The **Museo de Tapices** within contains medieval tapestries. The nearby medieval **Casa y Arco del Deán** form one of the city's favorite corners. ✉ *Pl. del Pilar* 🎫 *Cathedral €2.50, museum €2* ⏲ *Cathedral Mon.–Sat. 10–2 and 4–8, Sun. 5–8; museum Tues.–Sat. 10–2 and 4–6, Sun. 10–2.*

The **Museo Camón Aznar** has a fine collection of Goya's works, particularly engravings. ✉ *Carrer Espoz y Mina 23* ☎ *976/397328* 🎫 *Free* ⏲ *Tues.–Fri. 9–2 and 6–9, Sat. 10–2 and 6–9, Sun. 11–2.*

The **Museo del Centro de Historia** exhibits a wide range of memorabilia from Zaragoza's 2,000-year history, including audiovisual studies of different facets. The section on the Ebro River and the Roman exploitation of the port of Zaragoza are especially interesting. ✉ *Pl. San Agustín 2* ☎ *976/205640* 🎫 *Free* ⏲ *Tues.–Sat. 10–7:15, Sun. 10–1:15.*

The **Museo del Foro** displays remains of the Roman forum and the Roman sewage system, though the presentation is in Spanish only. Two more Roman sites, the **thermal baths** at Calle de San Juan y San Pedro and the **river port** at Plaza San Bruno, are also open to the public. ✉ *Pl. de la Seo s/n* ☎ *976/399752* 🎫 *€2.50* ⏲ *Tues.–Sat. 10–2 and 5–8, Sun. 10–2.*

The **Museo Pablo Gargallo** is one of Zaragoza's most treasured and admired gems, both for the palace in which it is housed and for its collection—Gargallo, born near Zaragoza in 1881, was one of Spain's greatest modern sculptors. ✉ *Pl. de San Felipe 3* ☎ *976/724922* 🎫 *Free* ⏲ *Tues.–Sat. 9–2 and 5–9, Sun. 9–2.*

The **Museo Provincial de Bellas Artes** contains a rich treasury of works by Zaragoza's emblematic painter, Goya, including his portraits of Fernando VII, and his best graphic works: *Desastres de la guerra, Caprichos,* and *La tauromaquia.* ✉ *Pl. de los Sitios 5* ☎ *976/222181* 🎫 *Free* ⏲ *Tues.–Sat. 10–2 and 5–8, Sun. 10–2.*

The **Museo del Teatro Romano** showcases a restored Roman amphitheater as well as the objects recovered during the excavation process, including theatrical masks, platters, and even Roman hairpins. ✉ *Calle San Jorge 12* ☎ *976/205088* 🎫 *€3.50* ⏲ *Tues.–Sat. 10–9, Sun. 10–2.*

Overlooking the Ebro River and Zaragoza's Basilica of Our Lady of the Pillar

The **Palacio de La Aljafería** completes the trio of Spain's great Moorish palaces. If Córdoba's Mezquita shows the energy of the 10th-century Caliphate and Granada's Alhambra is the crowning 14th-century glory of Al-Andalus (the 789-year Moorish empire on the Iberian Peninsula), then the late-11th-century Aljafería can be seen as the intermediate step. Originally a fortress and royal residence, and later a seat of the Spanish Inquisition, the Aljafería is now the home of the Cortes (Parliament) de Aragón. The 9th-century Torre del Trovador (Tower of the Troubadour) appears in Giuseppe Verdi's opera *Il Trovatore.* ✉ *Diputados s/n* ☎ *976/289683* *€3* *Mon.–Wed. and weekends 10–2 and 4–7, Fri. 4–7.*

OFF THE BEATEN PATH

Monasterio de Piedra. An hour's drive south of Zaragoza brings you to the Cistercian Monasterio de Piedra, a lush oasis on the arid Aragonese *meseta* (plain). Founded in 1195 by Alfonso II of Aragón and named for the nearby Río Piedra (Stone River, so-called for the calcified limestone deposits along its banks), the monastery has a 16th-century Renaissance section that is now a moderately priced private hotel (rooms range in price from €115 to €170). The 12th-century cloister, wine museum, and caves, waterfalls, and walkways suspended over the riverbed are spectacular. If you can't stay overnight, you can wander the park for €14. **Pros:** peaceful getaway with top comfort and splendid views; sound of falling water. **Cons:** rooms somewhat monastic and austere; faulty fittings. ✉ *Rte. C202 south of Calatayud, just beyond Nuévalos* ☎ *902/196052* *www.monasteriopiedra.com* *63 rooms* *In-hotel: restaurant, bar, parking* *AE, DC, MC, V.*

WHERE TO EAT AND STAY

$–$$$ SPANISH
Casa Emilio. One of the city's most popular restaurants with artists, journalists, and writers, this relaxed and easygoing haven of straightforward cooking and conversation near the Aljafería and the train station offers excellent value and a friendly environment. Specialties include *revuelto de bacalao al ajoarriero* (cod and scrambled eggs), *ventresca de bonito marinada* (marinated tuna belly), and *ternasco al horno de leña* (young lamb roasted in a wood oven). The house wines, usually from Somontano, are of good value and quality. *Av. Madrid 3–5* *976/435839* *AE, DC, MC, V.*

$$$–$$$$ SPANISH
La Bastilla. In what was once the granary of the 13th-century Santo Sepulcro convent, with heavy stone battlements from the Roman walls showing here and there around the dining room, this is one of Zaragoza's most polished and gastronomically respected dining establishments. In winter, the black-truffle tasting menu offers a succession of truffle-studded dishes from foie gras to onion soup, Morcilla (blood) sausage soaked in cider, or veal with *moixardinas* (wild mushrooms). The wine list has some interesting Somontano, Ribera de Duero, and Rioja selections. *Coso 177* *976/298449* *Reservations essential* *AE, DC, MC, V.*

$–$$ SPANISH ★
Los Victorinos. This rustic tavern heavily adorned with bullfight-related paraphernalia—Victorinos are a much-feared and respected breed of fighting bulls—offers an elaborate and inventive selection of *pinchos* (morsels impaled on toothpicks) and original tapas of all kinds. *Jamón ibérico de bellota* (acorn-fed Iberian ham), Spain's equivalent of caviar, is always a natural choice for nutty aromas and exquisite taste, but also look for quail eggs and the classic *gilda*—olives, green peppers, and anchovies on a toothpick. Tucked in behind the Seo, this local secret opens at 7:30 every evening. *Calle José de la Hera 6* *976/394213* *AE, DC, MC, V* *No lunch.*

$–$$
Las Torres. The rooms are small, but the scenery is hard to beat: you may even be able to admire the domes of La Pilarica from your pillow. If you're a light sleeper, you may need earplugs to muffle the bonging of the bells—they ring every 15 minutes all through the night; interior rooms are much quieter. **Pros:** excellent location on central square of old town; top value in town. **Cons:** rooms on the Pilarica side over the square can be noisy in summer. *Pl. del Pilar 11* *976/394250* *www.hotellastorres.com* *54 rooms* *In-hotel: parking (paid)* *AE, DC, MC, V.*

$$$–$$$$ ★
Palafox. One of Zaragoza's top accommodations, the Palafox combines contemporary design-chic with traditional urban service and elegance. Rooms are equipped with state-of-the-art gadgets, including flat-screen TVs and Jacuzzis. The bathrooms are almost private spas. The restaurant, Aragonia Paradís, holds its own with any place in town, with a selection of more than 2,000 wines and the best Havana cigar collection in Aragón. **Pros:** top comfort and service; bright reception area. **Cons:** modern and somewhat antiseptic. *Marqués Casa Jiménez s/n* *976/237700* *www.palafoxhoteles.com* *160 rooms* *In-room: refrigerator, Wi-Fi. In-hotel: restaurant, bar, pool, gym, parking (paid)* *AE, DC, MC, V.*

SHOPPING

El Tubo (✉ *Cinegio 10* ☎ *976/391177*) is Zaragoza's best store for handmade leather boots from all over Spain.

BENASQUE

Fodor's Choice ★ *79 km (49 mi) southwest of Vielha.*

Benasque, Aragón's easternmost town, has always been an important link between Catalonia and Aragón. This elegant mountain hub with a population of just over 1,500 harbors a number of notable buildings, including the 13th-century Romanesque church of **Santa Maria Mayor** and the ancient, dignified manor houses of the town's old families, such as the **palace of the counts of Ribagorça,** on Calle Mayor, and the **Torre Juste.** Take a walk around and peer into the entryways and patios of these palatial facades, left open just for this purpose.

ESSENTIALS

Visitor Information Benasque (✉ *Pl. Mayor 5* ☎ *974/551289*).

EXPLORING

Anciles, 2 km (1 mi) south of Benasque, is one of Spain's best-preserved and best-restored medieval villages, a collection of farmhouses and *palacetes* (town houses). The summer classical music series is a superb collision of music and architecture, and the village restaurant, Ansils, combines modern and medieval motifs in both cuisine and design.

OFF THE BEATEN PATH

Pico De Aneto. Benasque is the traditional base camp for excursions to Aneto, which, at 11,168 feet, is the highest peak in the Pyrenees. You can rent crampons and a *piolet* (ice ax) for the two- to-three-hour crossing of the Aneto glacier at any sports store in town or at the Refugio de la Renclusa—a way station for mountaineers—an hour's walk above the parking area, which is 17 km (11 mi) north of Benasque, off A139. The trek to the summit and back is not difficult, just long—some 20 km (12 mi) round-trip, with a 1,500-yard vertical ascent. Allow a full 12 hours.

WHERE TO EAT AND STAY

$$–$$$$ SPANISH

✕ **Asador Ixarso.** Roast goat or lamb cooked over a raised fireplace in the corner of the dining room is why this place is a fine refuge in chilly weather. The *revuelto de setas* (eggs scrambled with wild mushrooms) is a classic highland specialty, while the salads are varied and refreshing, especially after a morning or afternoon of skiing, hiking, or climbing. The mixed grill is a house favorite, and the opportunity to try whatever game—venison, wild boar, or partridge—is on the menu should not be missed. ✉ *Calle San Pedro 9* ☎ *974/552057* ▭ *AE, DC, MC, V* ⊙ *Closed weekdays mid-Sept.–1st wk in Dec. and Easter–June.*

$$–$$$$ SPANISH

✕ **Restaurante Ansils.** This rustic spot near Anciles on the Benasque-Anciles road is ingeniously designed in glass, wood, and stone and specializes in local Benasqué and Aragonese dishes, such as *civet de jabalí* (wild boar stew) and *recau* (a thick vegetable broth). *Estofada de perdiz* (partridge stew) is a perennial house favorite. The restaurant is sometimes closed unexpectedly on weekdays and out of season, so check before you go. Memorable and multitudinous holiday meals are

The city of Benasque, nestled in the valley

served on Christmas and Easter; reserve well in advance. ✉ *Calle Gral. Ferraz 13, Anciles* ☎ *974/551150* ▭ *AE, DC, MC, V* ⊙ *Closed weekdays Oct.–June.*

$–$$ **Gran Hotel Benasque.** This spacious, modern hotel within walking distance from Benasque is bracketed by the highest crests in the Pyrenees (Aneto and Posets) and serves as an impeccably comfortable base for exploring them. The wood-paneled guest rooms, contrary to the Iberian norm, are carpeted; the top rooms have skylights. The restaurant's mountain fare ($$–$$$ for set menu only) includes *sopa Benasquesa* (a thick highland stew) and *crepas Aneto* (crepes with ham, wild mushroom, and béchamel sauce). **Pros:** bucolic setting just outside of town; easy access to lovely village of Ansils. **Cons:** modern building with more efficiency than charm; characterless room decor. ✉ *Ctra. de Anciles s/n* ☎ *974/551011* 🌐 *www.hotelesvalero.com* *69 rooms* *In-room: refrigerator, Wi-Fi. In-hotel: restaurant, bar, pools, gym* ▭ *AE, MC, V* ⊙ *Closed Nov.*

$–$$ **Hospital de Benasque.** About 13 km (8 mi) north of Benasque off the A139 road, this mountain retreat constructed and furnished in stone and wood is an ideal base camp for hiking and cross-country skiing. Rooms are simple, with clean lines, and the restaurant ($$–$$$) serves classical Pyrenean fare in a glassed-in dining room flooded with natural light. **Pros:** lovely location in a wide meadow surrounded by peaks; literally a breath of fresh air. **Cons:** rooms are spartan; can get hot on summer days. ✉ *Camino Real de Francia s/n* ☎ *974/552012* 🌐 *www.llanosdelhospital.com* *57 rooms* *In-room: no a/c, Wi-Fi. In-hotel: restaurant, bar, parking (free)* ▭ *AE, DC, MC, V.*

SPORTS AND THE OUTDOORS

The **Cerler ski area** (☏ *974/551012* 🌐 *www.cerler.com*), 6 km (4 mi) east of Benasque on the Cerler road, covers the slopes of the Cogulla peak. Built on a shelf over the valley at an altitude of 5,051 feet, Cerler has 26 ski runs, three lifts, and a guided helicopter service to drop you at the highest peaks. The outfitter **Danica Guías de Pesca** (☏ *974/553493 or 659/735376* 🌐 *www.danicaguias.com*) can show you the top spots and techniques for Pyrenean fly-fishing.

AÍNSA

66 km (41 mi) southwest of Benasque.

Aínsa's arcaded Plaza Mayor and old town are classic examples of medieval village design, with heavy stone archways and tiny windows.

ESSENTIALS

Visitor Information Aínsa (✉ *Av. Pirenaica 1* ☏ *974/500767*).

EXPLORING

The 12th-century Romanesque church of **Santa María** has a quadruple-vaulted door. ✉ *Old Quarter* 🎫 *Free* ⏲ *Daily 9–2 and 4–8.*

6

WHERE TO EAT AND STAY

$$–$$$$ SPANISH ✕ **Bodegas del Sobrarbe.** Lamb and suckling pig or kid roasted in a wood oven are among the specialties at this excellent restaurant built into an 11th-century wine cellar. The setting is medieval, with vaulted ceilings made of heavy wood and stone. After the welcoming bar at the entrance, a succession of small dining rooms under arches gives a sense of privacy. The tables are decorated with hand-crafted ceramic tiles from Teruel, and the ambience is mountain rustic. ✉ *Pl. Mayor 2* ☏ *974/500237* ▭ *AE, DC, MC, V* ⏲ *Closed Jan. and Feb.*

¢–$ 🏨 **Casa Cambra.** A once-abandoned village between Barbastro and Aínsa is home to this little inn, a perfect base for hiking and mountain sports of all kinds. The restored 18th-century town house of stone and timber has rooms for two to four people and is part of a tourist complex that includes a restaurant and a variety of lodging arrangements. **Pros:** rural tourism in a pretty setting; family-run intimate accommodation. **Cons:** close quarters and thin walls in some rooms can be detrimental to privacy. ✉ *Ctra. Barbastro–Aínsa, A138, Km 41.8, Morillo de Tou* ☏ *974/500793* 🌐 *www.morillodetou.com* *17 rooms* *In-room: no a/c, no TV* ▭ *MC, V.*

SAN JUAN DE PLAN AND THE GISTAÍN VALLEY

14 km (8 mi) east of Salinas.

This detour begins with a well-marked road heading east of Salinas, 25 km (15 mi) north of Aínsa. The Cinqueta River drains the Gistaín Valley, flowing by or through the mountain villages of Sin, Señes, Saravillo, Serveta, and Salinas. The town of San Juan de Plan presides at the head of the valley, where an ethnographic museum, a water-powered sawmill, and an early-music and dance ensemble are the pride of the region. The mid-February carnival is among the most distinct and traditional celebrations in the Pyrenees.

ESSENTIALS

Visitor Information Plan (✉ *Calle Capilleta* ☎ *974/506400*).

EXPLORING

The **Museo Etnológico** is a fascinating glimpse into a traditional way of life (dress, kitchen utensils, bedclothes, field tools) that endured largely intact until about 1975. ✉ *Pl. Mayor s/n* ☎ *974/506062* *€3.50* ⏲ *Daily 9–2 and 4–8.*

WHERE TO STAY

¢–$ ★ **Casa la Plaza.** Josefina Loste's pleasant country inn has rustic, cozy rooms with antique furniture and sloping ceilings—each is tucked into and under the eaves in a different way. The restaurant ($–$$$) serves excellent local dishes using fresh mountain products prepared lovingly, using traditional recipes in inventive ways. **Pros:** charming decor and sense of authentic Pyrenean village life; excellent fare at the hotel restaurant. **Cons:** rooms are not very spacious and can feel slightly cluttered. ✉ *Pl. Mayor s/n* ☎ *974/506052* *13 rooms* *In-room: no a/c. In-hotel: restaurant, bar* *AE, DC, MC, V* ⏲ *Closed sporadically Oct.–May; call to confirm.*

BIELSA

34 km (21 mi) northeast of Aínsa.

Bielsa, at the confluence of the Cinca and Barrosa rivers, is a busy summer resort with some lovely mountain architecture and an ancient, porticoed town hall. Northwest of Bielsa the **Monte Perdido glacier** and the icy **Marboré Lake** drain into the **Pineta Valley** and the Pineta Reservoir. You can take three- or four-hour walks from the parador up to Larri, Munia, or Marboré Lake among remote peaks.

ESSENTIALS

Visitor Information Bielsa (✉ *Pl. Mayor s/n* ☎ *974/501127*).

WHERE TO EAT AND STAY

¢–$ ★ **Hotel Valle de Pineta.** This corner castle overlooking the river junction is the most spectacular nest and refuge in town. The restaurant ($$–$$$), offering classic Aragonese and Pyrenean fare, is excellent and the views from the floor-to-ceiling windows are superb. Try for the top corner room, which looks across both the Barrosa and Cinca valleys. **Pros:** central location in the village center; family service. **Cons:** upper rooms are cozy but tiny; it gets hot if the wind dies down during the hottest part of summer. ✉ *Calle Baja s/n* ☎ *974/501010* *www.hotelvalledepineta.com* *26 rooms* *In-room: no a/c. In-hotel: restaurant, bar, pool, Wi-Fi hotspot* *AE, DC, MC, V* ⏲ *Closed Nov., Jan., and Feb.*

$$$ **Parador de Bielsa.** Glass, steel, and stone define this modern structure overlooking the national park, the peak of Monte Perdido, and the source of the Cinca River. Rooms are done in bright wood, but the best part is the proximity to the park and the views. The restaurant ($$–$$$) specializes in Aragonese mountain dishes, such as *pucherete de Parzán* (a stew with beans, sausage, and vegetables). **Pros:** surrounded by nature in complete comfort; views of the highest peaks in the Pyrenees;

country cooking. **Cons:** parador service as usual; a little chilly at 4,455 feet above sea level. ✉ *Ctra. Valle de Pineta s/n* ☎ *974/501011* 🌐 *www.parador.es* *39 rooms* *In-room: no a/c, Wi-Fi. In-hotel: restaurant, bar* *AE, DC, MC, V.*

EN ROUTE

You can explore the **Valle del Cinca** from the river's source at the head of the valley above Bielsa. From Bielsa, drive back down to Aínsa and turn west on N260 (alternately marked C138) for Broto.

PARQUE NACIONAL DE ORDESA Y MONTE PERDIDO

Fodor's Choice ★

108 km (67 mi) west of Bielsa; from Aínsa, turn west on N260 for the 53-km (33-mi) drive to Torla (park entrance).

ESSENTIALS

Visitor Information Torla (✉ *C. Fatás s/n* ☎ *974/486378*).

EXPLORING

The **Ordesa and Monte Perdido National Park** is one of Spain's great but often overlooked wonders; some consider it a junior version of North America's Grand Canyon. The entrance lies under the vertical walls of Monte Mondarruego, source of the Ara River and its tributary, the Arazas, which forms the famous Ordesa Valley. The park was founded by royal decree in 1918 to protect the natural integrity of the central Pyrenees, and it has expanded from 4,940 to 56,810 acres as provincial and national authorities have added the Monte Perdido massif, the head of the Pineta Valley, and the Escuain and Añisclo canyons. Defined by the Ara and Arazas rivers, the Ordesa Valley is endowed with pine, fir, larch, beech, and poplar forests; lakes, waterfalls, and high mountain meadows; and protected wildlife, including trout, boar, chamois, and the *Capra pyrenaica* mountain goat.

Well-marked and well-maintained mountain trails lead to waterfalls, caves, and spectacular observation points. The standard tour, a full day's hike (eight hours), runs from the parking area in the Pradera de Ordesa, 8 km (5 mi) northeast of Torla, up the Arazas River, past the *gradas de Soaso* (Soaso risers, a natural stairway of waterfalls) to the *cola de caballo* (horse's tail), a lovely fan of falling water at the head of the Cirque de Cotatuero, a sort of natural amphitheater. A return walk on the south side of the valley, past the Refugio de los Cazadores (hunters' hut), offers a breathtaking view followed by a two-hour descent back to the parking area. A few spots, although not technically difficult, may seem precarious. Information and guidebooks are available at the booth on your way into the park at Pradera de Ordesa. The best time to come is May to mid-November but check conditions with regional tourist offices before driving into a blizzard in May or missing out on *el veranillo de San Martín* ("Indian summer") in fall. ☎ *974/243361 Pradera de Ordesa information office* 🌐 *www.ordesa.net* *Free.*

EN ROUTE

Broto is a prototypical Aragonese mountain town with an excellent 16th-century Gothic church. Nearby villages, such as **Oto,** have stately manor houses with classic local features: baronial entryways, conical chimneys, and wooden galleries. **Torla** is the park's entry point and a popular base camp for hikers.

DID YOU KNOW?

The Ordesa and Monte Perdido National Park is sometimes called a junior version of the Grand Canyon. One of the reasons this region was designated as a national park was to protect the Pyrenean Ibex, which nevertheless became extinct in 2000.

WHERE TO EAT AND STAY

$–$$ SPANISH ✕ **El Rebeco.** In this graceful, rustic building in the upper part of town, the dining rooms are lined with historic photographs of Torla during the 19th and 20th centuries. The black marble-and-stone floor and the *cadiera*—a traditional open fireplace room with an overhead smoke vent—are extraordinary original elements of Pyrenean architecture. In late fall and winter, *civets* (stews) of deer, boar, and mountain goat are the order of the day. In summer, lighter fare and hearty mountain soups restore hikers between treks. ✉ *Calle Lafuente 55, Torla* ☎ *974/486066* ▭ *AE, DC, MC, V* ⊙ *Closed Dec.–Easter.*

$ 🏨 **Villa de Torla.** This classic mountain refuge has rooms of various shapes and sizes, all with typical Pyrenean details dominated by stone floors and fresh wood paneling and trim. Sun decks, terraces, and a private dining room make it easy to forget that "Spain's Grand Canyon" is just a few minutes up the valley. **Pros:** in the middle of a postcard-perfect Pyrenean village; helpful staff. **Cons:** rooms on the street side can be noisy on weekends and summer nights. ✉ *Pl. Aragón 1* ☎ *974/486156* 🌐 *www.hotelvilladetorla.com* *38 rooms* *In-hotel: restaurant, bar, pool, parkingWi-Fi hotspot* ▭ *AE, DC, MC, V.*

EN ROUTE

Follow N260 (sometimes marked C140) west over the Cotefablo Pass from Torla to Biescas. This route winds interminably through the pine forest leading up to and down from the pass; expect it to take five times longer than it looks like it should on a map.

PANTICOSA AND THE TENA VALLEY

40 km (25 mi) northwest of Ordesa.

The Valle de Tena, a north–south hexagon of 400 square km (154 square mi), is formed by the Gállego River and its tributaries, principally the Aguaslimpias and the Caldares. A glacial valley surrounded by peaks rising to more than 10,000 feet (such as the 10,900-foot Vignemale), Tena is a busy hiking and winter-sports center.

ESSENTIALS

Visitor Information Panticosa (✉ *C. San Miguel 37* ☎ *974/487318*).

EXPLORING

Sallent de Gállego, at the head of the valley, has long been a jumping-off point for excursions to **Aguaslimpias, Piedrafita,** and the meadows of the Gállego headwaters at **El Formigal** (a major ski area) and **Portalet.** The lovely Pyrenean *ibon* (glacial lake) of **Respumoso** is accessible by a 2½-hour walk above the old road from Sallent to Formigal. The villages lining the valley are each unique, with Tramacastilla, Escarrilla, and Piedrafita especially representative of ancient Pyrenean village architecture. **Lanuza**, a ghost town since the reservoir built in 1975 flooded half the village, comes alive every July when a floating stage hosts performers in the Pirineos Sur music festival.

WHERE TO EAT AND STAY

$–$$ SPANISH ✕ **Mesón Sampietro.** This cozy tavern and restaurant, a family spot not far from Panticosa's quirky and lovely church, bustles and booms after the skiing or hiking day comes to a close. The house specialty, potatoes in olive oil, garlic, parsley, and vinegar, is an Aragonese favorite not to be missed. Take a seat at one of the traditional *susulia* benches—they have little fold-down tables between the two seats, making them perfect for warm winter dinners in front of a roaring fire. ✉ *C. La Parra 5, Panticosa* ☎ *974/487244* ▭ *AE, DC, MC, V.*

$$$$ **Gran Hotel**. The most complete comfort available in Panticosa, this modern hotel with a palatial facade in the former thermal spa zone above town is a perfect base camp for hiking and skiing. Oak floors, along with marble paving in the bathrooms, set the tone for this lovingly restored mountain resort complex that ranks as one of the best in the Pyrenees. **Pros:** impeccable service and infrastructure; spectacular views into the mountains. **Cons:** not really part of the Panticosa ski scene; far from restaurants and town nightlife. ✉ *Balneario de Panticosa, Panticosa* ☎ *974/487616* 🌐 *www.panticosa.com* *38 rooms, 4 suites* *In-room: Wi-Fi. In-hotel: restaurant, spa* ▭ *AE, DC, MC, V* ⏲ *Closed Oct.–Dec.*

JACA

24 km (15 mi) southwest of Biescas.

Jaca, the most important municipal center in Alto Aragón (with a population of more than 12,000), is anything but sleepy. Bursting with ambition and blessed with the natural resources and first-rate facilities to express their relentless drive, Jacetanos are determined to make their city the site of a Winter Olympics someday. Founded in 1035 as the kingdom of Jacetania, Jaca was an important stronghold during the Christian Reconquest of the Iberian Peninsula and proudly claims never to have bowed to the Moorish invaders. Indeed, on the first Friday of May the town still commemorates the decisive battle in which the appearance of a battalion of women, their hair and jewelry flashing in the sun, so intimidated the Moorish cavalry that they beat a headlong retreat.

GETTING HERE

Drive down the Tena Valley through Biescas; a westward turn at Sabiñánigo onto N330 leaves a 14-km (9-mi) drive to Jaca.

ESSENTIALS

Visitor Information Jaca (✉ *Pl. San Pedro 11–13* ☎ *974/360098*).

EXPLORING

An important stop on the pilgrimage to Santiago de Compostela, Jaca has the 11th-century **Catedral de Santa María**, one of the oldest in Spain. **The Museo Diocesano,** near the cloisters, is filled with excellent Romanesque and Gothic murals and artifacts. ☎ *974/356378 Museo* *€5* ⏲ *June–Sept., Tues.–Sun. 10–2 and 4–8; Oct.–May, Tues.–Sun. 10–2 and 4–7.*

The door to Jaca's **ayuntamiento** (*Town hall* ✉ *Calle Mayor 24* ☎ *974/355758*) has a notable Renaissance design.The massive **Ciudadella** (Citadel) is a good example of 17th-century military architecture. It has a display of thousands of military miniatures. ✉ *Av. Primer Viernes de Mayo s/n* ☎ *974/363746* *€5* ⏲ *Daily 11–noon and 4–6.*

QUICK BITES

One of Jaca's most emblematic restaurants is La Campanilla (✉ *Escuelas Pías 8*), behind the *ayuntamiento*. The baked potatoes with garlic and olive oil are an institution.

In summer a free guided tour departs from the local RENFE station, covering the valley and the mammoth belle epoque railroad station at **Canfranc**, surely the largest and most ornate building in the Pyrenees, soon to open as a new luxury hotel. The train ticket costs €3.50; ask the tourist office for schedules.

WHERE TO EAT AND STAY

¢–$$ SPANISH ★ ✕ **El Fau.** Tucked in next to the cathedral, El Fau overlooks Jaca's finest carved capitals and serves excellent *cazuelitas*, small earthenware casseroles containing anything from piping-hot garlic shrimp to wild mushrooms to small portions of *civet de jabalí* (wild boar stew). In summer the cold beer really hits the spot, and the terrace fills with locals and travelers replenishing their energy after hiking and climbing excursions. A predinner, prenightlife stop ideal for connecting with old friends or making new ones, this is the town clearinghouse for party recruitment. ✉ *Pl. de la Catedral* ☎ *974/361594* ▭ *AE, DC, MC, V* ⊙ *Closed Mon.*

$$–$$$$ SPANISH ✕ **La Cocina Aragonesa.** This Jaca mainstay in the Hotel Conde Aznar is an elegant, rustic space decorated with local farming and mountaineering objects and centered on a mammoth fireplace. Its Aragonese/Basque cuisine is justly famous around town and beyond for constantly changing, fresh and innovative creations, especially game in season: venison, wild boar, partridge, and duck. Try the *perdiz roja estofada con foie* (redleg partridge stuffed with foie gras) or the *cebollitas glaseadas y trufa negra* (glazed baby onions with black truffles). ✉ *Cervantes 5* ☎ *974/361050* ▭ *AE, DC, MC, V* ⊙ *Closed Nov. 15–30 and Wed. June–Sept.*

$–$$$ SPANISH ✕ **La Tasca de Ana.** Ana's *tasca* (tavern) is one of Jaca's simplest and best for lamb or beef cooked over coals and a hefty repertoire of satisfying highland cuisine. Nearly anyone in town will send you here for superb tapas of every kind. Invent your own meal by starting with a round of olives and working through, say, cured *jamón ibérico de bellota* (acorn-fed Iberian ham), *sepia* (cuttlefish), *albóndigas* (meatballs), and *civet de jabalí* (wild boar stew), concluding with the famous sheep cheese from the neighboring Roncal Valley. ✉ *Pl. Ramiro I 3* ☎ *974/363621* ▭ *AE, DC, MC, V* ⊙ *Closed Mon.*

$–$$ **Gran Hotel.** This rambling hotel, Jaca's traditional official clubhouse, is central to life, sports, and tourism in this Pyrenean hub. A mid-20th-century structure made of wood, stone, and glass, the complex includes a garden and a separate dining wing with a restaurant serving creditable Aragonese cuisine. The streamlined and comfortable rooms have rich colors and practical wood furniture. **Pros:** quiet location just west of the town center; professional and polished service. **Cons:** modern and functional construction with no special charm or Pyrenean ambience; neo-motel-room decor. ✉ *Paseo de la Constitución 1* ☎ *974/360900* 🌐 *www.inturmark.es* *165 rooms* *In-hotel: restaurant, pool, Wi-Fi hotspot* ▭ *AE, DC, MC, V.*

$–$$ **Hotel Mur.** A simple but sound lodging option in the middle of Jaca, this hotel offers traditional highland decor, helpful staff, and a central location from which to cruise the après-ski scene. The restaurant serves Pyrenean and Aragonese cooking at excellent prices, especially on weekdays when the €12 *menu del peregrino* (pilgrims' menu) offers *boliches de Embún* (particularly prized white beans from the mountain town of Embún) stewed with sausage or the classic Aragonese *migas de pastor* (shepherd's bread crumbs). **Pros:** great location; friendly family management. **Cons:** tight quarters in some of the smaller rooms; street noise in exterior rooms on weekends. ✉ *Santa Orosia 1* ☎ *974/360100* 🌐 *www.hotelmur.com* *72 rooms* *In-room: no a/c. In-hotel: restaurant, Wi-Fi hotspot* *AE, DC, MC, V.*

NIGHTLIFE

Discos such as Santa Locura and La Trampa throng with skiers and hockey players in season (October–April), but the main nocturnal attractions are Jaca's so-called *bares musicales* (music bars), usually less loud and smoky than the discos. Most of these are in the old town, in Calle Ramiro I and along Calle Gil Bergés and Calle Bellido.

SPORTS AND THE OUTDOORS

The **ski areas** of Candanchú and Astún are 32 km (20 mi) north of Jaca, on the road to Somport and the French border.

THE WESTERN AND BASQUE PYRENEES

The Aragüés, Hecho, and Ansó valleys, drained by the Estarrún, Osia, Veral, and Aragón Subordán rivers, are the westernmost valleys in Aragón and rank among the most pristine parts of the Pyrenees. Today these sleepy hollows are struggling to generate an economy that will save this endangered species of Pyrenean life. With only cross-country (Nordic) skiing available, this is a region less frequented by tourists. As you move west into the Roncal Valley and the Basque Country, you will note smoother hills and softer meadows as the rocky central Pyrenees of Aragón begin to descend toward the Bay of Biscay. These wet and fertile uplands and verdant beech forests seem reflected in the wide lines and flat profiles of the Basque *caseríos* (farmhouses) hulking firmly into the landscape. The Basque highlands of Navarra from Roncal through the Irati Forest to Roncesvalles and along the Bidasoa River leading down to the Bay of Biscay seem like an Arcadian paradise as the jagged Pyrenean peaks give way to sheep-filled pasturelands.

GETTING HERE

To get to the westernmost Pyrenean valleys in Aragón from Jaca, head west on N240 for 20 km (12 mi), take a hard right at Puente de la Reina (after turning right to cross the bridge), and continue north along the Aragón Subordán River. The first right after 15 km (9 mi) leads into the Aragüés Valley along the Osia River to Aisa and then Jasa.

MONASTERIO DE SAN JUAN DE LA PEÑA

★ 22 km (14 mi) southwest of Jaca.

South of the Aragonese valleys of Hecho and Ansó is the Monastery of San Juan de la Peña, a site connected to the legend of the Holy Grail and another "cradle" of Christian resistance during the 700-year Moorish occupation of Spain. Its origins can be traced to the 9th century, when a hermit monk named Juan settled here on the *peña* (cliff). A monastery was founded on the spot in 920, and in 1071 Sancho Ramirez, son of King Ramiro I, made use of this structure, which was built into the mountain's rock wall, to found the Benedictine Monasterio de San Juan de la Peña. The **cloister,** tucked under the cliff, dates from the 12th century and contains intricately carved capitals depicting biblical scenes. From Jaca, drive 11 km (7 mi) west on N240 toward Pamplona to a left turn clearly signposted for San Juan de la Peña. From there it's another 11 km (7 mi) to the monastery. ✉ *Off N240* ☎ *974/355119* 🌐 *www.monasteriosanjuan.com* 🎫 *€12* 🕐 *Oct.– Mar., Tues.–Sun. 10–3:30; Mar.–June, Tues.–Sun. 10–2 and 3–8; July–Sept., daily 10–2 and 3:30–7.*

6

ARAGÜÉS VALLEY

Aragüés del Puerto is 2 km (1 mi) northwest of Jaca.

ESSENTIALS

Visitor Information Ayuntamiento: Aragüés del Puerto (✉ *Pl. Mayor 1* ☎ *974/371447*).

EXPLORING

Aragüés del Puerto is a tidy mountain village with stone houses and lovely little corners, doorways, and porticoes. The distinctive folk dance in Aragüés is the *palotiau,* a variation of the *jota* performed only in this village.The **Museo Etnográfico** (Ethnographic Museum*)*, in an ancient chapel in Aragüés del Puerto (ask for the caretaker at the town hall), offers a look into the past, from the document witnessing the 878 election of Iñigo Arista as king of Pamplona to the quirky manual wheat grinder.At the source of the River Osia, the Lizara **cross-country ski area** is in a flat expanse between the Aragüés and Jasa valleys. Look for 3,000-year-old megalithic dolmens sprinkled across the flat.

HECHO AND ANSÓ VALLEYS

Hecho Valley is 49 km (30 mi) northwest of Jaca, Ansó Valley is 25 km (15 mi) west of Hecho.

GETTING HERE AND AROUND

You can reach the Valle de Hecho from the Aragüés Valley by returning to the valley of the Aragón-Subordan and turning north again on the A176.

ESSENTIALS

Visitor Information Hecho (✉ *Pallar d'Agustín* ☎ *974/375505*).

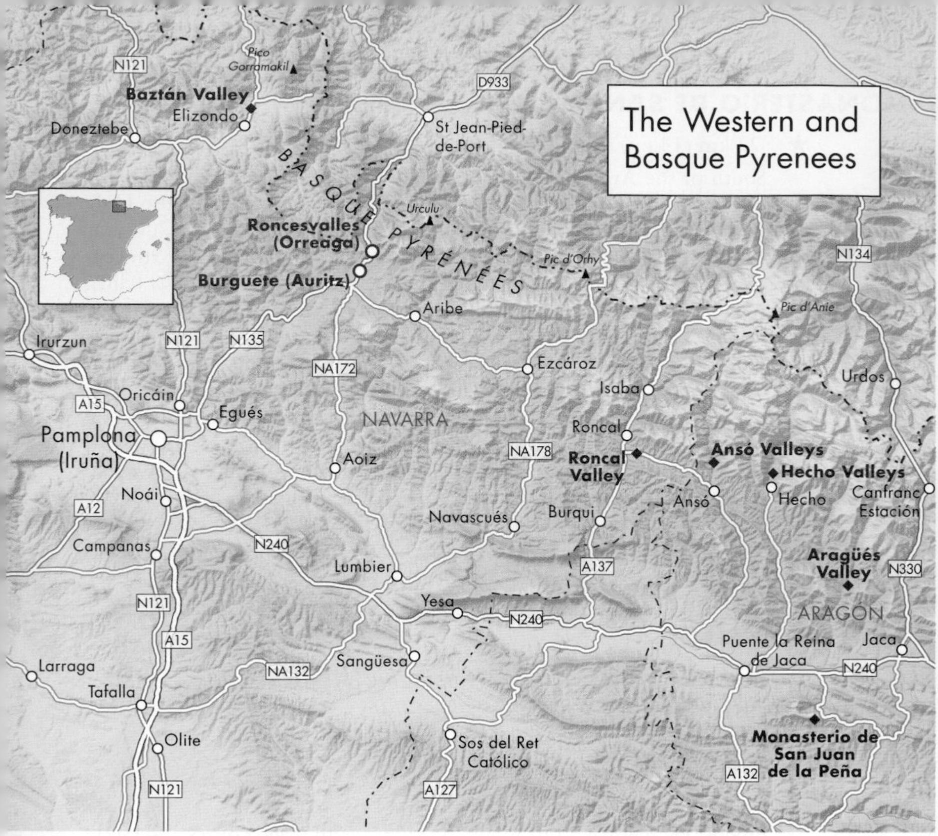

EXPLORING

The **Monasterio de San Pedro de Siresa**, above the town of Hecho, is the area's most important monument, a 9th-century retreat of which only the 11th-century church remains. Cheso, a medieval Aragonese dialect descended from the Latin spoken by the Siresa monks, is thought to be the closest to Latin of all Romance languages and dialects. It has been kept alive in the Hecho Valley, especially in the works of the poet Veremundo Méndez Coarasa. ✉ *Calle San Pedro, Siresa* 🎫 *Free* ⏲ *July and Aug., daily 11–1 and 5–8; other months, call Ayuntamiento de Siresa (974/375002) for key.*

The **Selva de Oza** *(Oza Forest)*, at the head of the Hecho Valley, is above the **Boca del Infierno** (Mouth of Hell), a tight draw where road and river barely squeeze through. Beyond the Oza Forest is a **Roman road** used before the 4th century to reach France through the Puerto del Palo—one of the oldest routes across the border on the pilgrimage to Santiago de Compostela.

The **Valle de Ansó** is Aragón's western limit. Rich in fauna (mountain goats, wild boar, and even a bear or two), the Ansó Valley follows the Veral River up to Zuriza.The three **cross-country ski areas** above Zuriza are known as the Pistas de Linza.Near Fago is the sanctuary of the **Virgen de Puyeta**, patron saint of the valley. Towering over the head of the valley is Navarra's highest point, the 7,989-foot **Mesa de los Tres Reyes** *(*Plateau of the Three Kings*)*, named not for the Magi but for the kings of Aragón, Navarra, and Castile, whose 11th-century kingdoms bordered here, allowing them to meet without leaving their respective realms.Try to be in the town of **Ansó** on the last Sunday in August, when residents dress in their traditional medieval costumes and perform ancestral dances of great grace and dignity.

WHERE TO EAT AND STAY

¢ **Gaby-Casa Blasquico.** This cozy inn, famed as Hecho's top restaurant ($$–$$$), is known for its Aragonese mountain cuisine. Especially strong on game recipes, the menu also has superb Pyrenean lamb and vegetable dishes and innovative creations such as foie gras with Coca-Cola sorbet. Call ahead for reservations, as Gaby often opens for anyone who reserves in advance, even if the place is theoretically closed. **Pros:** cozy mountain chalet with flowered balconies; two cute dormered rooms; fine mountain cuisine. **Cons:** rooms lack space; public rooms cluttered with memorabilia. ✉ *Pl. Palacio 1, Hecho* ☎ *974/375007* 🌐 *www.casablasquico.com* *Reservations essential* *6 rooms* *In-room: no a/c, Wi-Fi. In-hotel: restaurant, Internet terminal* *MC, V* ⏲ *Closed 1st 2 wks in Sept.; restaurant closed weekdays Sept.–Easter wk.*

$ **Usón.** For a base camp for exploring the upper Hecho Valley or the Oza Forest, look no further. The staff at this friendly little Pyrenean inn will tell you where to rent a bike, get you a trout-fishing permit, or send you off in the right direction for a climb or hike. Rooms are simple and airy and decorated with colorful fabrics and quilts. The hotel, equipped with solar panels, generates its own energy. **Pros:** friendly service; great value; stunning views into the mountains. **Cons:** no elevator; remote setting. ✉ *Ctra. Selva de Oza, HU2131, Km 7, Usón* ☎ *974/375358* 🌐 *www.hoteluson.com* *8 rooms, 4 apartments* *In-room: no a/c. In-hotel: restaurant, Internet terminal* *MC, V* ⏲ *Closed Nov. 2–Mar. 15.*

EN ROUTE

From Ansó, head west to Roncal on the narrow and winding but panoramic 17-km (11-mi) road through the Sierra de San Miguel. To enjoy this route fully, count on taking a good 45 minutes to reach the Esca River and the Valle de Roncal.

RONCAL VALLEY

17 km (11 mi) west of Ansó Valley.

The Roncal Valley, the eastern edge of the Basque Pyrenees, is famous for its eponymous sheep's-milk cheese and as the birthplace of Julián Gayarre (1844–90), the leading tenor of his time. The 34-km (21-mi) drive through the towns of **Burgui** and **Roncal** to **Isaba** winds through green hillsides and *caseríos*, classical Basque farmhouses covered by long, sloping roofs designed to house animals on the ground floor and the family up above to take advantage of the body heat of the livestock. Burgui's red-tile roofs backed by rolling pastures contrast with the vertical rock and steep slate roofs of the Aragonese and Catalan Pyrenees; Isaba's wide-arched bridge across the Esca is a graceful reminder of Roman aesthetics and engineering techniques.

6

GETTING HERE

To get to the valley from Jaca, take N240 west along the Aragón River; a right turn north on NA137 follows the Esca River from the head of the Yesa Reservoir up the Roncal Valley.

ESSENTIALS

Visitor Information Roncal (✉ *C. Iriartea s/n* ☎ *948/475256*).

EXPLORING

Try to be in the Roncal Valley for **El Tributo de las Tres Vacas** (the Tribute of the Three Cows), which has been celebrated every July 13 since 1375. The mayors of the valley's villages, dressed in traditional gowns, gather near the summit of San Martín to receive the symbolic payment of three cows from their French counterparts, in memory of the settlement of ancient border disputes. Feasting and celebrating follow.

The road west (NA140) to **Ochagavia** through the Puerto de Lazar (Lazar Pass) has views of the Anie and Orhi peaks, towering over the French border.Two kilometers (1 mi) south of Ochagavia, at Escároz, a small secondary roadway winds 22 km (14 mi) over the Abaurrea heights to **Aribe**, known for its triple-arched medieval bridge and ancient *horreo* (granary). A 15-km (9-mi) detour north through the town of Orbaiceta up to the headwaters of the Irati River, at the Irabia Reservoir, gets you a good look at the **Selva de Irati** *(*Irati Forest*)*, one of Europe's major beech forests and the source of much of the timber for the fleet Spain commanded during its 15th-century golden age.

RONCESVALLES (ORREAGA)

★ *64 km (40 mi) northwest of Isaba in the Roncal Valley, 2½ km (1½ mi) north of Burguete, 48 km (30 mi) north of Pamplona.*

Roncesvalles (often listed as Orreaga, in Euskera) is the site of the Colegiata, cloister, hospital, and 12th-century **chapel of Santiago,** the first Navarran church on the Santiago pilgrimage route.

ESSENTIALS

Visitor Information Orreaga-Roncesvalles (✉ *C. Única s/n* ☎ *948/760301*).

EXPLORING

The **Colegiata** (*Collegiate Church* ✉ *Ctra. Pamplona–Francia [N135], Km 48* 🌐 *www.roncesvalles.es*), built at the orders of King Sancho VII el Fuerte (the Strong), houses the king's tomb, which measures more than 7 feet long. The 3,468-foot **Ibañeta Pass**, above Roncesvalles, is a gorgeous route into France. A *menhir* (monolith) marks the traditional site of the legendary battle in *The Song of Roland* in which Roland fell after calling for help on his ivory battle horn. The well-marked eight-hour walk to or from St-Jean-Pied-de-Port (which does *not* follow the road) is one of the most beautiful and dramatic sections of the pilgrimage.

The San Juna de la Pena monastery at Jaca

BURGUETE (AURITZ)

2 km (1 mi) south of Roncesvalles, 120 km (75 mi) northwest of Jaca.

Burguete (Auritz in Euskera) lies between two mountain streams forming the headwaters of the Urobi River. The town was immortalized in Ernest Hemingway's *The Sun Also Rises,* with its evocative description of trout fishing in an ice-cold stream above a Navarran village.

ESSENTIALS

Visitor Information Ochagavia (✉ *C. Labaria 25* ☎ *948/890641*).

WHERE TO EAT AND STAY

¢ **Hostal Burguete.** In his 1926 novel *The Sun Also Rises*, Hemingway's character Jake Barnes spends time here clearing his head before plunging back into the psychodrama of the San Fermín Festival and his impossible passion for Lady Brett Ashley. The inn still works for this sort of thing, though there aren't as many trout around these days. Good value and simple Navarran cooking ($–$$$) make this stalwart Basque town house a good stop. You might even be able to sleep in Hemingway's bed; his room is kept exactly as it was when the novelist bunked here in 1924. **Pros:** special for Hemingway fans; good value. **Cons:** room decor is stark; beds may actually be from the 1920s. ✉ *Calle Única 51* ☎ *948/760005* 🖷 *948/790488* *22 rooms* *In-room: no a/c. In-hotel: restaurant, Wi-Fi hotspot* 💳 *AE, DC, MC, V* ⏲ *Closed Feb. and Mar.*

EN ROUTE

To skip Pamplona and stay on the trans-Pyrenean route, continue 21 km (13 mi) southwest of Burguete on NA135 until you reach NA138, just before Zubiri. A right turn takes you to Urtasun, where the small NA252 leads left to the town of Iragui and over the pass at Col d'Egozkue (from which there are superb views over the Arga and Ultzana River valleys) to Olagüe, where it connects with NA121 some 20 km (12 mi) north of Pamplona. Turn right onto N121A and climb over the Puerto de Velate (Velate Pass)—or, in bad weather or a hurry, through the tunnel—to the turn for Elizondo and the Baztán Valley, N121B. (Take a good map if you're setting off into the hills.)

BAZTÁN VALLEY

80 km (50 mi) north of Pamplona.

Tucked neatly over the headwaters of the Bidasoa River, under the peak of the 3,545-foot Garramendi Mountain, which looms over the border with France, the rounded green hills of the Valle de Baztán make an ideal halfway stop between the central Pyrenees and the Atlantic. Each village in this enchanted Navarran valley seems smaller and simpler than the next: tiny clusters of whitewashed, stone-and-mortar houses with red-tile roofs group around a central *frontón* (handball court).

ESSENTIALS

Visitor Information Elizondo (✉ *Palacio de Arizkunenea* ☎ *948/581279*).

WHERE TO EAT AND STAY

$–$$ BASQUE ★ ✕ **Galarza.** The kitchen in this small but stalwart stone town house overlooking the trout-infested Baztán River turns out excellent Basque fare, with a Navarran emphasis on vegetables. Try the *txuritabel* (roast lamb with a special stuffing of egg and vegetables), which is best in the spring (though available year-round), or *txuleta de ternera* (grass-fed veal raised in the valley), good any time of year. *Rape con hongos* (monkfish with wild mushrooms) is another favorite here; the desserts feature delicious homemade *cuajada* (custard). ✉ *Calle Santiago 1, Elizondo* ☎ *948/580101* ▭ *MC, V* ⌚ *Closed late Sept.–early Oct.*

¢ ★ **Fonda Etxeberria.** In an old farmhouse with creaky floorboards and ancient oak doors, this tiny *caserío* (Basque farmhouse) inn has small, handsome rooms. The palatial bathrooms are shared by guests (usually one bathroom per two to three rooms). The restaurant ($–$$) prepares simple country dishes such as *alubias de Navarra estofadas* (Navarran white beans stewed with chorizo), *trucha a la Navarra* (trout sautéed and stuffed with ham), and roast lamb. **Pros:** an authentic Basque farmhouse in a remote Pyrenean village; friendly family service. **Cons:** rooms have squeaky beds and floorboards; shared baths. ✉ *Kalea Antxitonea Trinketea (next to frontón court) s/n Arizkun* ☎ *948/453013* ⎙ *948/453433* *16 rooms without bath* *In-room: no a/c, no TV. In-hotel: restaurant* ▭ *MC, V.*

Barcelona

WORD OF MOUTH

"I think I fell in love with Barcelona at first sight. It's cosmopolitan, urban, quaint, vibrant . . . the architectural mix of modern, Modernisme, and old. And the Mediterranean feeling . . . the beaches, ferries pulling in and out of the port . . . It's simply one of the most beautiful and exciting cities of this planet."

—Cowboy1968

WELCOME TO BARCELONA

TOP REASONS TO GO

★ **La Boqueria:** Barcelona's produce market is the most exciting midcity cornucopia in the world.

★ **Santa Maria del Mar:** The church is peerless in its Mediterranean Gothic style; hearing Renaissance choral music here is one of the ultimate sensory experiences.

★ **La Sagrada Família:** Gaudí's stalagmites, stalactites, and cylindrical towers add up to the city's most surprising architectural marvel.

★ **El Palau de la Música Catalana:** Cavalry erupts from the wings and a stained-glass chandelier plummets from above; this Art Nouveau tour de force is alive with music before the first note sounds.

★ **Fashion and Design:** How could a city famous for its architecture fail to offer a fleet of innovative clothing designers and chic shops?

★ **Castellers and Sardanas:** Human castles and Catalonia's national dance are two of the beloved symbols of this nation-within-a-nation.

1 La Rambla and El Raval. Ciutat Vella (the Old City) is bisected by the Rambla, home of the Boqueria market. The Raval is a multicultural sprawl, spread out around the MACBA contemporary art museum and the medieval Hospital de la Santa Creu.

2 Barri Gòtic and Born-Ribera. Northeast of the Rambla, the Gothic Quarter is a jumble of ancient (mostly pedestrianized) streets filled with shops, cafés, and 14th-century architecture. Born-Ribera is around Santa Maria del Mar.

3 Barceloneta, Ciutadella, and Port Olímpic. Barceloneta is a charming fisherman's village, with seafood restaurants and sandy beaches. Port Olímpic is a

GETTING ORIENTED

The baseball diamond–shape area at the bottom of Barcelona is Ciutat Vella (Old City): it's the heart of the city and a sensory feast, from the Rambla's human parade and the Boqueria's fish, fruit, and vegetables to the steamy corners of the Born. The checkerboard grid expanse north of Ciutat Vella is the post-1860 Eixample (Expansion), rich in Moderniste architecture. Gaudí will take you into the outlying villages of Gràcia and Sarrià, paintings will lead you to the Montjuïc promontory, and music will bring you into the city's finest architecture. In Barcelona, a city addicted to the avant-garde, uncommon originality is a common virtue.

massive succession of restaurants and discos. Ciutadella, originally a fortress, is now a park with the city zoo.

4 The Eixample. The post-1860 Eixample spreads out above Plaça de Catalunya and contains most of the city's Art Nouveau architecture, including Gaudí's Sagrada Família, along with hundreds of shops and places to eat.

5 Upper Barcelona. The village of Gràcia nestles above the Diagonal, with Gaudí's Park Güell at its upper edge. The Pedralbes monastery and cloister, and a rustic village trapped by urban encroachment.

6 Montjuïc. The promontory over the south side of the city lacks a real street vibe but the artistic treasure massed here is not to be missed: Miró, the MNAC, Mies van der Rohe, and CaixaForum.

7 Side Trips. The Benedictine monastery of Montserrat is a popular pilgrimage and an easy trip out of town. Sitges has a lovely beach, while Santes Creus and Poblet are interesting Cistercian monasteries.

BARCELONA PLANNER

Festivals and When to Go

Summer can be very hot in Barcelona, and many of the best restaurants and musical venues are closed in August. On the other hand, **El Grec** (🌐 *www.barcelonafestival.com*), the summer music festival in June and July, is a delight, and the August **Gràcia Festa Major** is a major block party.

October through June is the time to come to Barcelona, with mid-November–early April pleasantly cool and the rest of the time ideally warm. The **International Music Festival** is in September, and there's an **international jazz festival** in November. Late February's **Carnaval** and *calçot* (long-stemmed onion) season are spectacular and delicious. April and May are best of all: the **Sant Jordi** lovers' day on April 23 and the **Sant Ponç** celebration of natural produce on May 11 are among the most magical moments of the year.

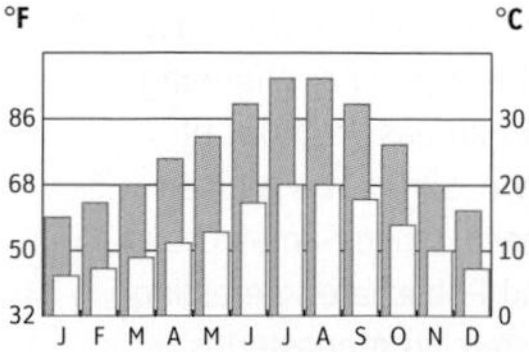

Tours

Bike Tours: Fat Tire Bike Tours and Un Cotxe Menys—"One Car Less," in Catalan—both organize popular guided outings in English.

Boat Tours: Golondrina harbor boats make trips around the harbor from the Portal de la Pau, near the Columbus Monument. The fare is €7.50 for a 40-minute tour. They also have 90-minute (€14) rides in glass-bottom catamarans that parallel the coast up past Barcelona's Olympic Port to the Fòrum complex at the northeastern end of the Diagonal.

Bus Tours: From mid-June to mid-October, the Bus Turistic (9:30–7:30 every 30 minutes) runs a circuit past all the important sights. A day's ticket, which you buy on the bus, costs €9 (€6 half day) and covers the fare for the Tramvía Blau, funicular, and Montjuïc cable car, too. The ride starts at the Plaça de Catalunya. Julià Tours and Pullmantur also run day and half-day excursions outside the city. Popular trips are those to Montserrat and the Costa Brava resorts, the latter including a cruise to the Medes Isles.

Walking Tours: The **Barcelona Tourist Office (Turisme de Barcelona)** has daily English-language walking tours of the Gothic Quarter at 10 AM for €12. **Ruta Picasso** tours Barcelona's Picasso sites in English Tuesday, Thursday, and Saturday at 4 PM for €18, including tickets to the Picasso Museum. The **Ruta Moderniste** tours cover the city's best Art Nouveau architecture in English on Friday at 4 PM (6 PM June–Sept.). **Ruta Gourmet** tours take walkers through emblematic points of the city's gastronomic life, with tastings, for €18. **Urbancultours** has English-language walking tours covering the medieval Jewish quarter and other sights.

Contacts Bus Turistic (☎ *93/285–3834* 🌐 *www.tmb.net*). **Fat Tire** (☎ *93/342–9275* 🌐 *www.fattirebiketours.com/barcelona.com*). **Golondrina** (☎ *93/442–3106* 🌐 *www.lasgolondrinas.com*). **Julià Tours** (☎ *93/317–6454*). **Pullmantur** (☎ *93/318–5195*). **Ruta Gourmet** (☎ *93/285–3832* 🌐 *www.atrapalo.com*). **Turisme de Barcelona** (☎ *93/285–3832* 🌐 *www.barcelonaturisme.com*). **Un Cotxe Menys** (☎ *93/268–2105* 🌐 *www.bicicletabarcelona.com*).

Epicurean Barcelona

"Barcelona, as nowhere else, has always understood that culture was not the butter on the bread of life . . . but the bread itself!" —Robert Hughes

For music lovers: Musical events in Barcelona are worth advance planning. Check schedules for the Liceu opera house, the Palau de la Música Catalana, the Auditori, or the many churches (especially Santa Maria del Mar) that hold concerts. Performances of Handel's *Messiah* at Christmas and Mozart's *Requiem* at Easter are annual highlights. The **Festival de Música Antiga** (Early Music Festival) in late April to early May brings classical music into some of the Gothic Quarter's prettiest squares and patios.

For foodies: Reserve well in advance for Barcelona's top gourmet restaurants, including Comerç 24, Drolma, Alkimia, and, especially, Santi Santamariá's El Racó de Can Fabes outside of town in Sant Celoni and Carme Ruscalleda's Sant Pau in Sant Pol de Mar. Ferran Adrià's world-famous El Bulli, at Cala Montjoi near Roses, is almost impossible to book, open only from mid-June to mid-December, and said to be closing for at least two years as of 2012.

Event Listings

El Pais and *La Vanguardia* have daily listings for art openings and concerts (including many free ones), under their Agenda headings. Keeping an eye on these listings can guide you to some of Barcelona's best events, often with *tapas* and *cava* included. Performances of Castellers, the human tower squads unique to Catalonia, are announced in the weekend agenda section. *La Guia del Ocio* comes out every Thursday and lists the top musical and cultural events for the week; many hotels hand out this guide gratis.

WHAT IT COSTS (IN EUROS)

	¢	$	$$	$$$	$$$$
Restaurants	under €10	€10–€15	€16–€22	€23–€29	over €29
Hotels	under €75	€75–€124	€125–€174	€175–€225	over €225

Prices are per person for a main course at dinner, and for two people in a standard double room in high season, excluding tax.

Planning Your Time

The Rambla is the icebreaker for most trips to Barcelona, starting in Plaça de Catalunya and moving down toward the port past the Boqueria market with all its colors and aromas. Other must-sees on the Rambla are the Liceu opera house, Plaça Reial, and Gaudí's Palau Güell. Main Gaudí masterworks around town include the Sagrada Família church, Park Güell, Casa Batlló, Casa Milà (La Pedrera), and Casa Vicens.

The Gothic Quarter is a warren of Roman and medieval alleys. Once the Roman Forum, Plaça Sant Jaume opens up between the municipal and Catalonian government palaces. Across Via Laietana, the Born-Ribera neighborhood centers on the exquisite Mediterranean Gothic Santa Maria del Mar basllIca, a step away from the Picasso Museum. A 15-minute walk east from Santa Maria del Mar is Barceloneta, the traditional fishermen's quarter, with popular beaches and a dozen good seafood restaurants.

El Raval, home of the medieval hospital, one of the city's finest Gothic spaces, is a good morning's hike. Gràcia and Sarrià are both interesting half-day explorations, while Montjuïc has the Museu Nacional d'Art de Catalunya, the Miró Fundació, and the Mies van der Rohe Pavilion.

7

GETTING HERE AND AROUND

By Air

Barcelona's main airport is El Prat de Llobregat, 14 km (9 mi) south of Barcelona. A few international and domestic flights (Madrid, Majorca, etc.) land in Girona, an hour north of the city.

The Aerobus leaves El Prat for Plaça de Catalunya every 15 minutes (6 AM–11 PM) on weekdays and every 30 minutes (6:30 AM–10:30 PM) on weekends. From Plaça de Catalunya, it leaves for the airport every 15 minutes (5:30 AM–10 PM) on weekdays and every 30 minutes (6:30 AM–10:30 PM) on weekends. The fare is €5 (round-trip €9).

Cab fare from the airport into town is about €30.

The RENFE airport train is inexpensive and efficient, but runs only every 20 to 30 minutes. From the airport, the RENFE station is a 10- to 15-minute walk (with moving walkway) from the gates. Trains run between 6 AM and midnight, stopping at the Estació de Sants, then Passeig de Gràcia, and end at Estació de França. Trains to the airport leave Estació de Sants every 20 minutes from 5:25 AM to midnight. The one-way fare is €2.90. The 10-ride T-10 metro ticket (see By Bus) includes service to the airport station for the price of a single ride.

By Bus

Barcelona's main bus station is Estació del Nord, east of the Arc de Triomf. Buses also depart from the Estació de Sants and from the depots of Barcelona's various private bus companies. You're best off reserving online or through a travel agent, who can quickly book you the best bus passage to your destination (see the Travel Smart chapter for contacts).

By Train

Almost all long-distance trains arrive and depart from Estació de Sants. En route to or from Sants, some trains stop at another station on Passeig de Gràcia at Carrer Aragó, which can be a good way to avoid the long lines that form at Sants during holidays, though it is even better to deal directly with 🌐 *www.renfe.es*. The Estació de França, near the port, now handles only a few long-distance trains within Spain. The air shuttle (or a scheduled flight) between Madrid and Barcelona can, if all goes well, get you door to door in less than three hours for only about €40 more than the cost of a train. The AVE, the high-speed RENFE train, now connects Barcelona and Madrid in 2 hours, 38 minutes, for €120.40. Booking two weeks in advance can cut the ticket cost to €48.

The FCG (Ferrocarril de la Generalitat) train from Plaça de Catalunya through the center of town to Sarrià and outlying cities is a commuter train that gets you to within walking distance of nearly everything in Barcelona. Transfers to the regular city metro are free.

By Foot

Modern Barcelona, above the Plaça de Catalunya, is built on a grid system, but the old town, from the Plaça de Catalunya to the port, is a labyrinth of narrow streets, so you'll need a good street map. Most sightseeing can be done on foot—you won't have any choice in the Barri Gòtic—but you'll have to use the metro, buses, or taxis to link sightseeing areas.

By Bus, Subway, and Tram

City buses run daily 5:30 AM–11:30 PM. Route maps are displayed at bus stops. Schedules are available at bus and metro stations or at ⊕ *www.bcn.es/guia/welcomea.htm.*

Barcelona's new tramway system is divided into two subsectors: Trambaix serves the western end of the Diagonal, and Trambesòs serves the eastern end.

The subway is the fastest, cheapest, and easiest way to get around Barcelona. Metro lines are color coded, and the FGC trains (Ferrocarriles de la Generalitat de Catalunya, part of the city underground system) are marked with a reclining S-like blue-and-white icon. Lines 2, 3, and 5 run weekdays 5 AM–midnight. Lines 1 and 4 close at 1 AM. On Friday, Saturday, and holiday evenings all trains run until 2 AM. The FGC Generalitat trains run until 12:30 AM on weekdays and Sunday and until 2:15 AM on weekends and eves of holidays. *See the inside back cover for a map of the Barcelona metro.*

The Montjuïc Funicular runs from the junction of Avinguda del Paral.lel and Nou de la Rambla to the Miramar station on Montjuïc (Paral.lel). It operates daily 11 AM–9:30 PM in summer and on weekends and holidays, and 11 AM–8 PM in winter; the fare is €1.40.

Bus, subway, and tram fares are a flat fee of €1.40 no matter how far you travel (with free transfers for up to 75 minutes), but it's more economical to buy a Targeta T-10 (valid for bus or metro FGC Generalitat trains, the Tramvía Blau blue tram, and the Montjuïc Funicular; 10 rides for €7.70). The Dia T-1 pass is valid for one day of unlimited travel on all subway, bus, and FGClines, but the Targeta T-10 is generally a better value than the Día T-1 if you'll be in town more than a day.

Contacts Tram BCN (☎ *902/193275* ⊕ *www.trambcn.com*). **Transports Metropolitans de Barcelona (TMB)** (☎ *93/298–7000* ⊕ *www.tmb.net*).

Visitor Information

Turisme de Barcelona (☎ *93/368–9700* ⊕ *www.barcelonaturisme.com*).

Discounts and Deals

The moderately worthwhile **Barcelona Card** comes in two-, three-, four-, and five-day versions: for €27, €33, €37.50, and €44 (2010 prices). You get unlimited travel on public transport and discounts at 27 museums, 10 restaurants, 14 leisure sights, and 20 stores. Caveat: the restaurants and shops covered are generally mediocre, and the only important museum savings is 20% at the expensive Casa Batlló. You can get the card in Turisme de Barcelona offices in Plaça de Catalunya and Plaça Sant Jaume and in the Sants train station, the El Prat airport, the El Corte Inglés department store, and the Barcelona Aquarium, among other sites.

By Taxi

Taxis are black and yellow and show a green rooftop light when available for hire. The meter starts at €1.80 (€1.90 at night and on weekends and holidays). There are supplements for luggage, night travel, Sundays and holidays, rides from a station or to the airport, and for trips to or from the bullring or a soccer (*fútbol*) match. On Friday and Saturday nights between midnight and 6 AM there is an automatic supplement of €4. There are cab stands all over town, and you can also hail cabs on the street.

EATING AND DRINKING WELL IN BARCELONA

Barcelona cuisine draws from Catalonia's rustic country cooking and uses ingredients from the Mediterranean, the Pyrenees, and inland farmlands. Historically linked to France and Italy, cosmopolitan influences and experimental contemporary innovation have combined to make Barcelona an important food destination.

Top left: A stew of broad beans and sausages. Top right: Esqueixada, the Catalan cod salad. Bottom left: A dessert of honey with fresh cheese.

CAVA

Order champagne in Barcelona and you might get anything from French bubbly to dirty looks. Ask, instead, for *cava*, the local sparkling wine from the Penedès wine-growing region 40 km southwest of the city. Catalan winemaker Josep Raventós created cava after phylloxera wiped out nearly all of Europe's vineyards. It has an earthier, darker taste than champagne, with larger and zestier bubbles.

The Mediterranean diet of seafood, vegetables, olive oil, and red wine comes naturally to Barcelona. A dish you'll see on many menus is *pa amb tomaquet*: bread rubbed with garlic and ripe tomato, then drizzled with olive oil. Fish of all kinds, shrimp, shellfish, and rice dishes combining them are common, as are salads of seafood and Mediterranean vegetables. Vegetable and legume combinations are common. Seafood and upland combinations, the classic *mar i muntanya* (surf and turf) recipes, join rabbit and prawns or cuttlefish and meatballs, while salty and sweet tastes—a Moorish legacy—are found in duck with pears or goose with figs.

SALADS

Esqueixada is a cold salad consisting of strips of raw, shredded, salt-cured cod marinated in oil and vinegar with onions, tomatoes, olives, and red and green bell peppers. Chunks of dried tuna can also be included and chickpeas, roast onions, and potatoes can be added, too. *Escalibada* is another classic Catalan salad of red and green bell peppers and eggplant that have been roasted over coals, cut into strips, and served with onions, garlic and olive oil.

LEGUMES

Botifarra amb mongetes (sausage with white beans) is the classic Catalan sausage made of pork and seasoned with salt and pepper, grilled and served with stewed white beans and *allioli* (an olive oil and garlic emulsion); *botifarra* can also be made with truffles, apples, egg, wild mushrooms, and even chocolate. *Mongetes de Santa Pau amb calamarsets* (tiny white beans from Santa Pau with baby squid) is a favorite *mar i muntanya.*

VEGETABLES

Espinaques a la catalana (spinach with pine nuts, raisins, and garlic) owes a debt to the Moorish sweet-salt counterpoint and to the rich vegetable-growing littoral along the Mediterranean coast north and south of Barcelona. Bits of bacon, fatback, or *ibérico* ham may be added and some recipes use fine flakes of

almonds as well. *Albergínies* (eggplant or aubergine) is a favorite throughout Catalunya, whether roasted, stuffed, or stewed, while *carxofes* (artichokes) fried to a crisp or stewed with rabbit is another staple.

FISH

Llobarro a la sal (sea bass cooked in salt) is baked in a shell of rock salt that hardens and requires a tap from a hammer or heavy knife to break and serve. The salt shell keeps the juices inside the fish and the flesh flakes off in firm chunks, while the skin of the fish prevents excessive saltiness from permeating the meat. *Suquet* is another favorite fish stew, with scorpion fish, monkfish, sea bass, or any combination thereof stewed with potatoes, onions, and tomatoes.

DESSERTS

Crema Catalana (Catalan cream) is the most popular dessert in Catalonia, a version of the French *crème brûlée,* custard dusted with cinnamon and confectioner's sugar and burned with a blowtorch (traditionally, a branding iron was used) before serving. The branding results in a hardened skim of caramelized sugar on the surface. The less sweet and palate-cleansing *mel i mató* (honey and fresh cheese) is a close second in popularity.

BARCELONA'S BEST BEACHES

It's an unusual combination in Europe: a major metropolis fully integrated with the sea. Barcelona's 4.2 km (2.5 mi.) of beaches allow for its yin/yang of urban energy and laid-back beach vibe. When you're ready for a slower pace, seek out a sandy refuge.

Top left: Barcelona's Bogatell beach was created for the Barcelona Olympic Games. Top right: Palm trees at the beach in Barcelona. Bottom left: Modern art at La Barceloneta.

Over the last decade, Barcelona's *platjas* (beaches) have improved and multiplied in number. Barceloneta's southwestern end is the Platja de Sant Sebastià, followed northward by the platjas de Sant Miquel, Barceloneta, Passeig Marítim, Port Olímpic, Nova Icària, Bogatell, Mar Bella (the last football-field length of which is a nudist enclave), La Nova Mar Bella, and Llevant. The Barceloneta beach is the most popular stretch, easily accessible by several bus lines, notably the No. 64 bus and by the L4 metro stop at Barceloneta or at Ciutadella–Vil.la Olímpica. The best surfing stretch is at the northeastern end of the Barceloneta beach, while the boardwalk itself offers miles of runway for walkers, bicyclers, and joggers. Topless bathing is common on all beaches in and around Barcelona.

WORD OF MOUTH

"Any beach recommendations in Barcelona?"
—robinlb

"The beaches between Port Olimpic and Barceloneta... near Barceloneta [it's] a bit more popular because you have small supermarkets a stone's throw away from the beach... try to avoid Sundays because it gets really busy, and the beach bars (almost) double their prices." —Cowboy 1968

PLATJA DE LA BARCELONETA

Just to the left at the end of Passeig Joan de Borbó, this is the easiest beach to get to, hence the most crowded and the most fun from a people-watching standpoint. Along with swimming, there are windsurfing and kite surfing rentals to be found just up behind the beach at the edge of La Barceloneta. Rebecca Horn's sculpture L'Estel Ferit, a rusting stack of cubes, expresses nostalgia for the beach shack restaurants that lined the beach here until 1992. Surfers trying to catch a wave wait just off the breakwater in front of the excellent beachfront Agua restaurant.

PLATJA DE LA MAR BELLA

Closest to the Poblenou metro stop near the eastern end of the beaches, this is a thriving gay enclave and the unofficial nudist beach of Barcelona (but clothed bathers are welcome, too). The water sports center Base Nàutica de la Mar Bella rents equipment for sailing, surfing, and windsurfing. Outfitted with showers, safe drinking fountains, and a children's play area, La Mar Bella also has lifeguards who warn against swimming near the breakwater. The excellent Els Pescadors restaurant is just inland on Plaça Prim.

PLATJA DE LA NOVA ICÀRIA

One of Barcelona's most popular beaches, this strand is just east of the Olympic Port with the full range of

entertainment, restaurant, and refreshment venues close at hand. (Mango and El Chiringuito de Moncho are two of the most popular restaurants.) The beach is directly across from the neighborhood built as the residential Olympic Village for Barcelona's 1992 Olympic Games, an interesting housing project that has now become a popular residential neighborhood.

PLATJA DE SANT SEBASTIÀ

Barceloneta's most southwestern beach (to the right at the end of Passeig Joan de Borbó) now stretches out in the shadow of the W Hotel, somewhat compromising its role as the oldest and most historic of the city beaches. But it was here 19th-century barcelonins cavorted in bloomers and bathing costumes. The right end of the beach is the home of the Club Natació de Barcelona and there is a semi-private feel that the beaches farther east seem to lack.

PLATJA DE GAVÀ-CASTELLDEFELS

A 15-minute train ride south of Barcelona near the Gavà stop is a wider and wilder beach, with better water quality and a windswept strand that feels light years removed from the urban sprawl and somewhat dusty beaches of Barcelona. Alighting at Gavà and returning from Castelldefels allows a hike down the beach to Can Patricio or any of the other beach restaurants dishing out delicacies like calçots or paella.

Updated by George Semler

Capital of Catalonia, 2,000-year-old Barcelona commanded a vast Mediterranean empire when Madrid was still a dusty Moorish outpost on the Spanish steppe. Relegated to second-city status only after Madrid became the seat of the royal court in 1561, Barcelona, one of Europe's most visually stunning cities, has long rivaled and often surpassed Madrid's economic and political might.

Barcelona balances the medieval intimacy of its Gothic Quarter with the grace and distinction of the wide boulevards in the Moderniste Eixample—just as the Mediterranean Gothic elegance of the church of Santa Maria del Mar provides a perfect counterpoint to Gaudí's riotous Sagrada Família. Ludwig Mies van der Rohe's pavilion seems even more minimalist after a look at the Art Nouveau Palau de la Música Catalana, while such exciting contemporary creations as Ricardo Bofill's neoclassical Parthenon-under-glass Teatre Nacional de Catalunya, Frank Gehry's waterfront goldfish, Norman Foster's Torre de Collserola, and Jean Nouvel's Torre Agbar all add spice to Barcelona's visual soup. Meanwhile, Barcelona's fashion industry is pulling even with those of Paris and Milan, and FC (Futbol Club) is Barcelona's perennial contender for European Championships and the world's most glamorous soccer club.

Barcelona has long had a frenetically active cultural life. It was the home of architect Antoni Gaudí, whose buildings are the most startling statements of Modernisme. Other leading Moderniste architects of the city include Lluís Domènech i Montaner and Josep Puig i Cadafalch, and the painters Joan Miró, Salvador Dalí, and Antoni Tàpies are also strongly identified with Catalonia. Pablo Picasso spent his formative years in Barcelona, and one of the city's treasures is a museum devoted to his works. Barcelona's opera house, the Liceu, is the finest in Spain, and the city claims such native Catalan musicians as cellist Pablo (Pau, in Catalan) Casals, opera singers Montserrat Caballé and José (Josep) Carreras, and early music viola da gamba master Jordi Savall.

In 133 BC the Roman Empire annexed Barcino; Visigoths roared down from the north in the 5th century; the Moors invaded in the 8th; and in the 9th, the Franks, under Charlemagne, captured Catalonia and made it their buffer zone at the edge of the Moors' Iberian empire. By 988, the autonomous Catalonian counties had gained independence from the Franks, but in 1137 Catalonia was, through marriage, united with the House of Aragón. Another marriage, that of Ferdinand II of Aragón and Isabella of Castile (and queen of León) in 1474, brought Aragón and Catalonia into a united Spain. As the economic capital of Aragón's Mediterranean empire, Barcelona grew powerful between the 12th and 14th centuries and began to falter only when maritime emphasis shifted to the Atlantic after 1492. Despite Madrid's power as the seat of Spain's Royal Court, Catalonia enjoyed autonomous rights and privileges until 1714, when, in reprisal for having backed the Austrian Hapsburg pretender to the Spanish throne, all institutions and expressions of Catalan identity were suppressed by Felipe V of the French Bourbon dynasty. Not until the mid-19th century would Barcelona's industrial growth bring about a renaissance of nationalism and a cultural flowering that recalled Catalonia's former opulence.

Catalan nationalism continued to strengthen in the 20th century. After the abdication of Alfonso XIII and the establishment of the Second Spanish Republic in 1931, Catalonia enjoyed renewed autonomy and cultural freedom. Once again backing a losing cause, Barcelona was a Republican stronghold and hotbed of anti-fascist sentiment during the 1936–39 civil war, with the result that Catalan language and identity were suppressed under the regime of Francisco Franco (1939–75) by such means as book burning, the renaming of streets and towns, and the banning of the Catalan language in schools and the media. This repression had little lasting effect; Catalans jealously guard their language and culture and generally think of themselves as Catalans first, Spaniards second.

Catalonian home rule was granted after Franco's death in 1975, and Catalonia's governing body, the ancient Generalitat, was reinstated in 1980. Catalan is now Barcelona's co-official language, along with Castilian Spanish, and is eagerly promoted through free classes funded by the Generalitat. Street names are signposted in Catalan, and newspapers, radio stations, and a TV channel publish and broadcast in Catalan.

EXPLORING BARCELONA

Barcelona has several main areas to explore. Between Plaça de Catalunya and the port lies the Old City, or Ciutat Vella, including El Barri Gòtic (the Gothic Quarter); the shop-, bar-, and *tapas*-rich La Ribera (the waterfront, also known as Born-Ribera); the populous central promenade of the Rambla; and El Raval, the former slums or outskirts southwest of the Rambla. Above Plaça de Catalunya is the grid-pattern expansion known as the Eixample (literally, the "Expansion") built after the city's third series of defensive walls were torn down in 1860; this area contains most of Barcelona's Moderniste architecture. Farther north and west, Upper Barcelona includes the former outlying towns of

Gràcia and Sarrià, Pedralbes, and, rising up behind the city, Tibidabo and the green hills of the Collserola nature preserve.

Though built in the mid-18th century, Barceloneta is generally considered part of Ciutat Vella. The Port Olímpic, a series of vast terrace restaurants and discos, is just beyond the Frank Gehry goldfish and the Hotel Arts. The Ciutadella park, once a fortress built not to protect but to dominate Barcelona, is just inland.

A final area, less important from a visitor's standpoint, is Diagonal Mar, from Torre Agbar and Plaça de les Glòries, east to the mouth of the River Besòs. This is the new Barcelona built for the 2004 Fòrum de les Cultures.

Numbers in the text correspond to numbers in the margins and on chapter maps.

CIUTAT VELLA: THE RAMBLA AND EL RAVAL

Barcelona's best-known promenade is a constant and colorful flood of humanity that flows past flower stalls, bird vendors, mimes, musicians, newspaper kiosks, and outdoor cafés; traffic plays second fiddle to the endless *paseo* (stroll) of locals and travelers alike. The poet Federico García Lorca called this street the only one in the world that he wished would never end. The whole avenue is referred to as Las Ramblas (Les Rambles, in Catalan) or La Rambla, but each section has its own name: Rambla Santa Monica is at the southeastern, or port, end; Rambla de les Flors in the middle; and Rambla dels Estudis at the top, near Plaça de Catalunya. El Raval is the area to the west of the Rambla, originally a slum outside Barcelona's second set of walls. Alas, Rambla-happy tourists are tempting prey for thieves and scam artists. Do *not* play the shell game (Barcelona's local three-card monte), keep maps and guidebooks hidden so you are not obviously a tourist, conceal cameras, and leave wallets and passports in your hotel safe.

A GOOD WALK

Start on the Rambla opposite the Plaça Reial, near the Drassanes metro stop, and wander down toward the sea to the **Columbus Monument** ❶ and the Rambla de Mar boardwalk, perhaps stopping to investigate the **Museu Marítim** ❷ and its medieval Drassanes Reials shipyards. Gaudí's **Palau Güell** ❸, on Carrer Nou de la Rambla, is the next stop before the **Gran Teatre del Liceu** ❹. For a little detour, head over to **Sant Pau del Camp** ❺, which will take you through Barcelona's fairly tame red-light district, the Barri Xinès, on the way. Back on the Rambla, you can take in the facade and perhaps some savories at **Antigua Casa Figueres** ❻, stroll through the **Boqueria** ❼ food market, and then cut around to the courtyards of the medieval **Antic Hospital de la Santa Creu** ❽. The **Museu d'Art Contemporani de Barcelona** (MACBA) ❾, a short detour away, is an excellent place to spend an hour or two.

TIMING This walk covers 3 km (2 mi). With brief stops, allow three hours; add another hour or two for the MACBA.

Antic Hospital de la Santa Creu **8**
Antigua Casa Figueres **6**
Boqueria **7**
Gran Teatre del Liceu **4**
Monument a Colom **1**
Museu d'Art Contemporani de Barcelona (MACBA) **9**
Museu Marítim **2**
Palau Güell **3**
Port **10**
Sant Pau del Camp **5**

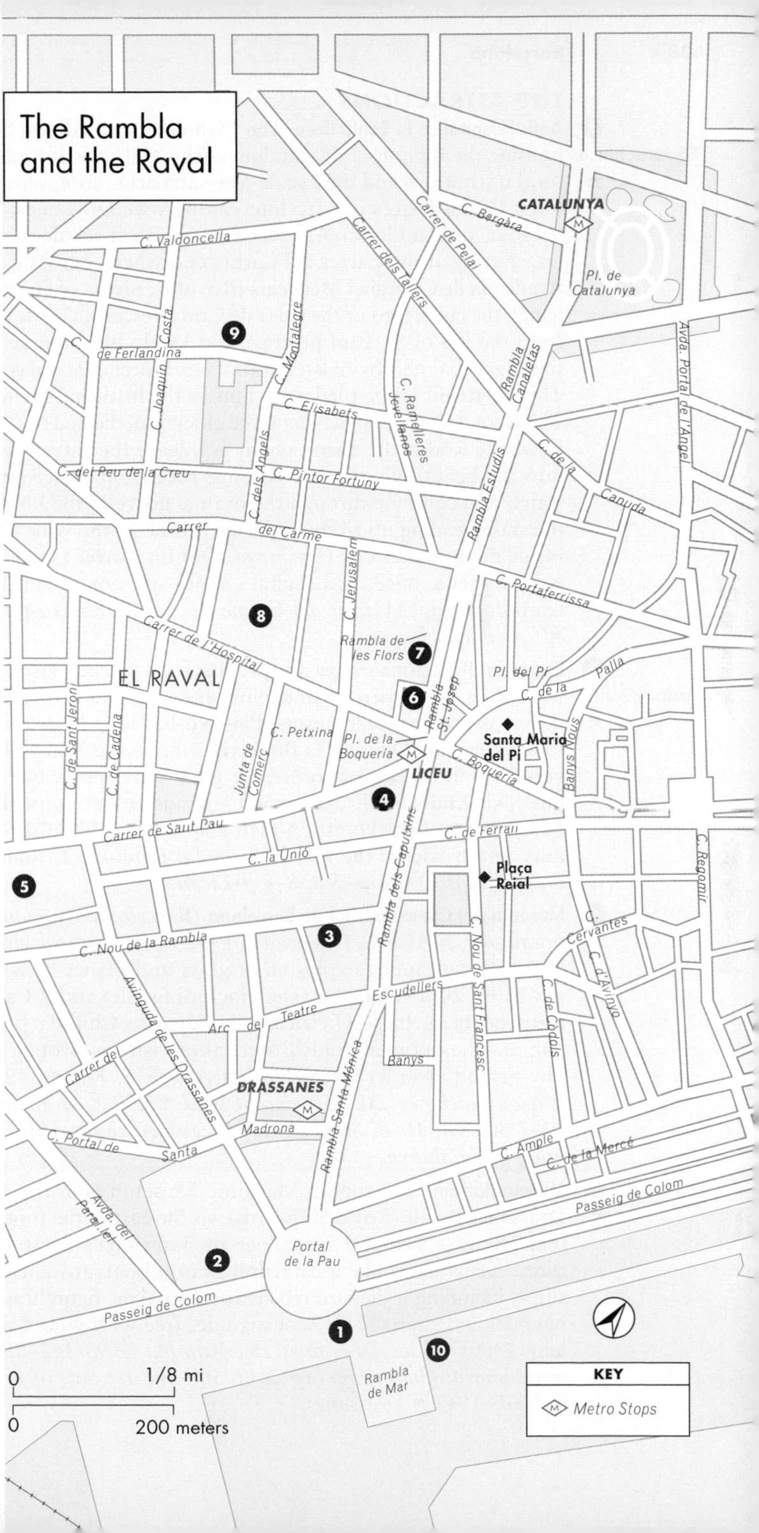

TOP ATTRACTIONS

8 Fodor's Choice ★ **Antic Hospital de la Santa Creu.** The 15th-century medieval hospital, now housing the Biblioteca de Catalunya (the "Library of Catalunya") cultural institutions and the Escola Massana art school, is one of the four finest Gothic spaces in Barcelona (along with Drassanes, Santa Maria del Mar, and La Llotja). Approach it from the back door of the Boqueria, starting at the Carrer del Carme end where, across from the **Reial Acadèmia de Cirurgia i Medecina (Royal Academy of Surgery and Medicine)**, the courtyard of the Casa de Convalescència leads in past scenes from the life of St. Paul portrayed in lovely blue-and-yellow ceramic tiles hand-painted by master craftsman Llorenç Passolas in 1680–81. The green-and-white-tiled patio houses the **Institut d'Estudis Catalans**. The second-floor garden behind the clock is dedicated to Catalan novelist Mercé Rodoreda. Turn right as you leave the entryway, take a look into the beautifully vaulted reading rooms on either side down the stairs, and continue through the orange grove in the hospital patio to the stairs leading up to the right for a look at the wide Gothic arches inside the Biblioteca de Catalunya. Out on Carrer Hospital to the left is **La Capella,** once the hospital chapel and now a gallery with contemporary art. ✉ *Carrer del Carme 45, or Carrer Hospital 56, Raval* Ⓜ *Catalunya, Liceu.*

7 Fodor's Choice ★ **Boqueria.** Barcelona's most spectacular food market, also known as the Mercat de Sant Josep, is an explosion of life and color sprinkled with delicious little bar-restaurants. **Pinotxo** has long been a sanctuary for food lovers and **Quim de la Boqueria** is hot on its heels. **El Kiosco Universal,** on the northeast corner, has great atmosphere but only average fare. Don't miss mushroom expert and author Petràs and his Fruits del Bosc (Fruits of the Forest), a mad display of wild mushrooms, herbs, nuts, and berries at the very back. ✉ *La Rambla 91, Rambla* 🌐 *www.boqueria.info* ⏲ *Mon.–Sat. 8–8* Ⓜ *Liceu.*

9 **Museu d'Art Contemporani de Barcelona** *(Barcelona Museum of Contemporary Art, MACBA).* Designed in 1992 by American architect Richard Meier, this gleaming explosion of glass and planes of white contains works by 20th-century masters including Alexander Calder, Robert Rauschenberg, Jorge Oteiza Enbil, Eduardo Chillida Juantegui, and Tàpies. The optional guided tour takes visitors through the philosophy behind abstract art. ✉ *Pl. dels Àngels 1, Raval* ☎ *93/412–0810* 🌐 *www.macba.es* 🎫 *€7.50, except Wed. €3.50* ⏲ *Mon. and Wed.–Fri. 11–7:30, Sat. 10–8, Sun. 10–3; free guided tours daily at 6, Sun. at noon* Ⓜ *Catalunya.*

2 ★ **Museu Marítim.** The superb Maritime Museum is in the 13th-century **Drassanes Reials** (Royal Shipyards), to the east at the foot of the Rambla. The vast medieval space, one of Barcelona's finest Gothic structures, seems more like a cathedral than a boatyard and is filled with ships, including a life-size reconstructed galley, figureheads, and early navigational charts. The Acoustiguide, free with your ticket, is excellent. ✉ *Av. de les Drassanes s/n, Rambla* ☎ *93/342–9920* 🌐 *www.museumaritimbarcelona.org* 🎫 *€6.50; free 1st Sat. of month after 3* ⏲ *Daily 10–7* Ⓜ *Drassanes.*

One of the earliest medical complexes in Europe is the Antic Hospital de la Santa Creu i Sant Pau.

3 ★ **Palau Güell.** Antoni Gaudí built this mansion during the years 1886–89 for his patron, textile baron Count Eusebi de Güell, and soon found himself in the international limelight. The dark facade is a dramatic foil for the treasure house inside, where spear-shape Art Nouveau columns frame the windows and prop up a series of intricately coffered wood ceilings. Gaudí is most himself on the roof, where his playful, polychrome ceramic chimneys fit right in with his later works like Park Güell and La Pedrera. The palace is only partially open (and has free entry) during restorations, which will extend at least through 2009. Check the Web site for updates. ✉ *Carrer Nou de la Rambla 3–5, Rambla* ☎ *93/317–3974* 🌐 *www.palauguell.cat* ⏲ *Tues.–Sat. 10–2:30* Ⓜ *Drassanes, Liceu.*

5 Fodor's Choice ★ **Sant Pau del Camp.** Barcelona's oldest church was originally outside the city walls (*del camp* means "in the fields") and was a Roman cemetery as far back as the 2nd century AD, according to archaeological evidence. What you see now was built in 1127 and is the earliest Romanesque structure in Barcelona, redolent of the pre-Romanesque Asturian churches or the pre-Romanesque Sant Michel de Cuxà in Prades, Catalunya Nord (Catalonia North, aka southern France). Elements of the church (the classical marble capitals atop the columns in the main entry) are thought to be from the 6th and 7th centuries. The hulking mastodonic shape of the church is a reflection of the defensive mentality of Barcelona's early Christians, for whom the bulwark of the church served as a spiritual, if not physical, refuge during an era of Moorish sackings and invasions. Check for musical performances here because the church is an acoustical gem. Note the stained-glass window

high on the facade facing Carrer Sant Pau: if Santa Maria del Pi's rose window is Europe's largest, this is quite probably the smallest. The tiny cloister, the only way in during afternoon opening hours, is Sant Pau del Camp's best feature, one of Barcelona's semisecret treasures. From inside the church, the right side of the altar leads out into this patio surrounded by porches or arcades. Sculpted Corinthian capitals portraying biblical scenes support triple Mudejar arches. ✉ *Sant Pau 101, Raval* ☎ *93/441–0001* ⏲ *Cloister weekdays 4:30–7:30. Sun. mass at 10:30, 12:30, and 8* PM Ⓜ *Catalunya, Liceu, Paral.lel.*

WATCH YOUR STUFF

While muggings are practically unheard of in Barcelona, petty thievery is common. Handbags, backpacks, camera cases, and wallets are favorite targets, so tuck those away. Handbags hooked over chairs, on the floor or sidewalk under your feet, or dangling from hooks under bars are easy prey. Even a loosely carried bag is tempting. Should you carry a purse, use one with a short strap that tucks tightly under your arm without room for fleet hands to unzip it.

WORTH NOTING

6 **Antigua Casa Figueres.** This Moderniste café, grocery, and pastry store on the corner of Carrer Petxina has a splendid mosaic facade and exquisite Art Nouveau fittings. The best way to get a close look at them is to sit down for a hot chocolate, tea, or coffee. The fluffy (and very sweet) *ensaimadas,* spiraling Mallorcan pastries sprinkled with confectioner's sugar, are hard to resist. ✉ *La Rambla 83, Rambla* ☎ *93/301–6027* 🌐 *www.escriba.es* ⏲ *Daily 8:30* AM*–9* PM Ⓜ *Catalunya, Liceu.*

4 **Gran Teatre del Liceu.** Along with Milan's La Scala, Barcelona's opera house has long been considered one of the most beautiful in Europe. First built in 1848, it burned down in 1861, was bombed in 1893, and was again gutted by a blaze of mysterious origins in early 1994. In 1999, a restored and renewed Liceu, equipped for modern productions, opened anew. Even if you don't see an opera, don't miss the tour: regular tours are 70 minutes; express tours are 20. Under the opera house, with entrances on Carrer Sant Pau and the Rambla, Espai Liceu has a cafeteria; a shop specializing in opera-related gifts, books, and recordings; an intimate 50-person-capacity circular concert hall; and a Mediateca with recordings and films of past opera productions. ✉ *La Rambla 51–59, Rambla* ☎ *93/485–9900* 🌐 *www.liceubarcelona.com* 🎫 *Guided tours €8.50, 20-min self-guided express tour €4* ⏲ *Tours daily at 10* AM *in Spanish and English, self-guided express tours daily at 11:30, noon, 12:30, and 1. The backstage tour at 9:30* AM *(€10) must be arranged by reservation:* ☎ *93/485–9900* ✉ *visites£liceubarcelona.com* Ⓜ *Liceu.*

1 **Monument a Colom** *(Columbus Monument).* This 60-meter-tall (200-foot-tall) monument at the foot of the Rambla marks the spot where Christopher Columbus stepped back onto Spanish soil in 1493 after discovering America. A viewing platform at the top (reached by elevator; entrance is on the harbor side) gives a bird's-eye view of the city. ✉ *Portal de la Pau s/n, Rambla* ☎ *93/302–5224* 🎫 *€3* ⏲ *Daily 9–8:30* Ⓜ *Drassanes.*

10 **Port.** Beyond the Monument a Colom—behind the Duana, or former customs building (now site of the Barcelona Port Authority)—is the **Rambla de Mar,** a boardwalk with a drawbridge. The Rambla de Mar extends out to the **Moll d'Espanya,** with its Maremagnum shopping center, IMAX theater, and aquarium. Next to the Duana, you can board a Golondrina boat for a tour of the port, to go up the coast to the Olympic Port, or to go to the Fòrum complex at Diagonal Mar. From the Moll de Barcelona's Torre de Jaume I, just to the southeast, you can catch a cable car to Montjuïc or Barceloneta.

CIUTAT VELLA: EL BARRI GÒTIC AND BORN-RIBERA

The Gothic Quarter winds through the church and Plaça of the church of Santa Maria del Pi, the Roman Barcelona around the cathedral, the Plaçà del Rei, past the city's administrative centers at Plaça Sant Jaume with the Jewish Quarter tucked in beside it, and through the Sant Just neighborhood northeast of Plaça Sant Jaume. Across Via Laietana is the Barri de la Ribera, or Born-Ribera, once the waterfront district around the basilica of Santa Maria del Mar. Born-Ribera includes the Museu Picasso and Carrer Montcada, Barcelona's most aristocratic street in the 14th and 15th centuries. Much of the Barri de la Ribera was torn down in 1714 by the victorious Spanish and French army of Felipe V to create a *glacis,* an open no-man's land outside the walls of the occupying stronghold, La Ciutadella fortress.

On the northeastern edge of this area, Barcelona's old textile neighborhood, around the church of Sant Pere de les Puelles, includes the flagship of the city's Moderniste architecture: the Palau de la Música Catalana, as well as the Mercat de Santa Caterina, a produce market with several dining options.

TOP ATTRACTIONS

2 **Centre d'Interpretació del Call** *(Center for the Interpretation of the Jewish Quarter).* This 14th-century building in the heart of the *call* is one of the few buildings in the area with its original stones and features still intact. On display are 13th- and 14th-century objects found in the *call* during archaeological excavations, including dishes with Hebrew letters and a facsimile of an illustrated manuscript (the Sarajevo Haggadah), depicting 15th-century scenes. There are also two tombstones with Hebrew inscriptions. The center runs walking tours and discussions about medieval Barcelona and its Jewish community, lectures by experts on Hebrew history and culture, tastings of Catalan-Jewish cuisine, Jewish storytelling sessions, and summer-school activities. ✉ *Placeta de Manuel Ribé, Barri Gòtic* ☎ *93/256–2122* 🌐 *www.calldebarcelona.org* ⏲ *Wed.–Fri. 10–2, Sat. 11–6, Sun. 11–3* Ⓜ *Jaume I.*

11 **El Born.** Once the site of medieval jousts, the Passeig del Born is at the end of Carrer Montcada behind the church of Santa Maria del Mar. The numbered cannonballs under the benches are in memory of the 1714 siege of Barcelona that concluded the 14-year War of the Spanish Succession. The Bourbon forces obliged residents to tear down more than 900 of their own houses, about a fifth of the city at that time, to create an open no-man's land for the fortress built for the occupying army of

Catedral de la Seu 4
Centre d'Interpretació del Call 2
El Born 11
Museu d'Història de la Ciutat 7
Museu Frederic Marès 5
Museu Picasso 9
Palau de la Música Catalana 8
Plaça del Rei 6
Plaça Reial 1
Plaça Sant Jaume 3
Santa Maria del Mar 10

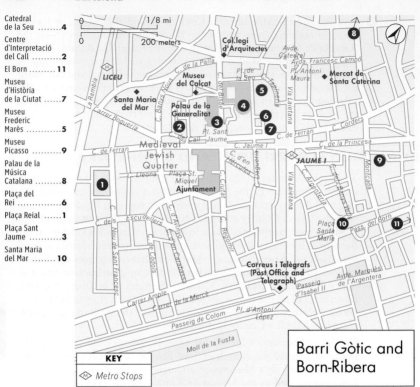

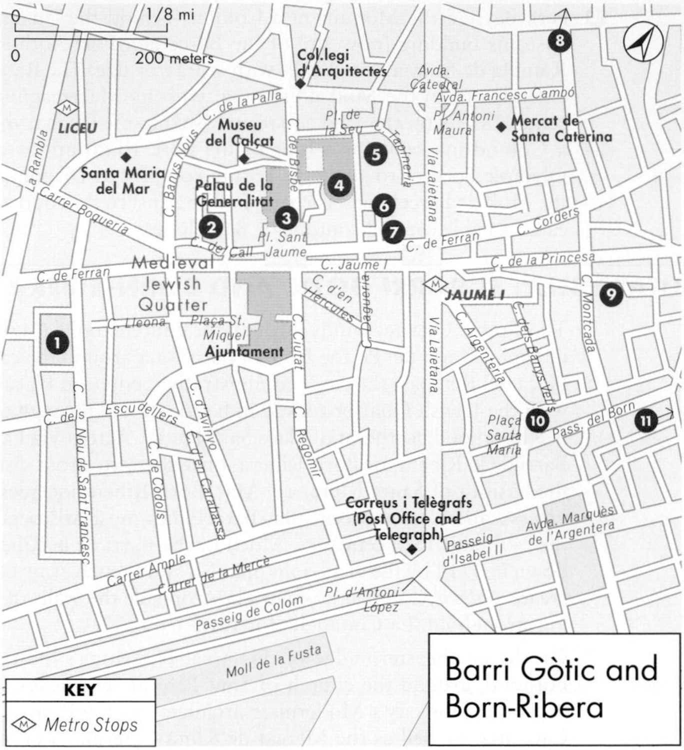

the great villain of Barcelona history: Felipe V, grandson of Louis XIV. Walk down to the Born itself—a great iron hangar designed by Josep Fontseré in 1876. It was modeled after Les Halles, which used to be Paris's beloved midcity produce market. Renovations of El Born uncovered the perfectly preserved lost city of 1714, complete with blackened fireplaces, taverns, wells, and the canal that brought water into the city. Sand dunes visible in the cellars attest to La Ribera's early position on the Barcelona waterfront before landfill created Barceloneta and the present harbor. Pending development of a history walk through the streets and houses, the Museu d'Història de la Ciutat (see below) offers free visits overlooking the ruins of the 14th-to-18th-century Barri de la Ribera, weekends 10–3. ✉ *Born-Ribera* ☎ *93/315–1111 Museu de Història de la Ciutat* Ⓜ *Jaume I.*

❼ **Museu d'Història de la Ciutat** *(City History Museum)*. This fascinating museum traces the evolution of Barcelona from its first Iberian settlement to its alleged founding by the Carthaginian Hamilcar Barca in about 230 BC, to Roman and Visigothic times and beyond. Antiquity is the focus here: Romans took the city during the Punic Wars, and the striking underground remains of their Colonia Favencia Julia Augusta Paterna Barcino, through which you can roam on metal walkways, are the museum's main treasure. Archaeological finds include parts of

CLOSE UP

Picasso's Barcelona

Barcelona's claim to Pablo Picasso (1881–1973) has been contested by Málaga, the painter's birthplace; by Madrid, where his painting *Guernica* hangs; and even by the town of Gernika itself, victim of the 1937 Luftwaffe saturation bombing that inspired the famous canvas. Picasso, a staunch Franco opponent after the war, refused to return to Spain (he had been dividing his time between Paris and Barcelona). In turn, the Franco regime allowed no public display of Picasso's work until 1961, when the artist's *Sardana* frieze at Barcelona's Architects' Guild was unveiled. Picasso did not set foot on Spanish soil for the last 39 years of his life.

The artist spent a sporadic but formative period of his youth in Barcelona (between 1895 and 1904), after which he moved to Paris to join its fertile art scene. Picasso's father had been appointed art professor at the Reial Acadèmia de les Belles Arts in La Llotja, and Picasso, a precocious draftsman, began advanced classes in the academy at the age of 15. A few years later, working in different studios between academic stints in Madrid, the young artist first exhibited at Els Quatre Gats, a tavern still thriving on Carrer Montsió. Much intrigued with the Bohemian life of Barcelona's popular neighborhoods, Picasso was inspired to make his early Cubist painting *Les Demoiselles d'Avignon* not by the French town but by the Barcelona street Carrer d'Avinyó, then known for its brothel. After his move to Paris, Picasso returned occasionally to Barcelona until his last visit in the summer of 1934.

Considering Picasso's off-and-on tenure in Barcelona, followed by his self-imposed exile, it's remarkable that the city and the artist should be so intertwined in the world's perception. The Picasso Museum, although an excellent visit, is only the fourth-most important art venue on any art connoisseur's list of Barcelona galleries. The museum was the brainchild of the artist's longtime friend Jaume Sabartés, who believed that his vast private collection of Picasso works should be made public. After much wrangling with the Franco regime, loath to recognize publicly such a prominent anti-Franco figure and the author of a work titled *The Dream and the Lie of Franco* (1937), the Picasso Museum finally opened in 1963. **Iconoserveis Culturals** (✉ *C. Muntaner 185, Eixample* ☎ *93/410–1405* 🌐 *www.iconoserveis.com*) gives walking tours through the key spots in Picasso's Barcelona life, covering studios, galleries, taverns, the Picasso family apartments, and the painter's favorite haunts and hangouts.

walls, fluted columns, and recovered busts and vases. Above ground, off the Plaça del Rei, the **Palau Reial Major,** the splendid **Saló del Tinell,** the chapel of **Santa Àgata,** and the **Torre del Rei Martí,** a lookout tower with views over the Barri Gòtic, complete the self-guided tour. ✉ *Plaça del Rei s/n, Barri Gòtic* ☎ *93/256–2100* 🌐 *www.museuhistoria.bcn.cat* 🎟 *€5.50 (includes admission to Monestir de Pedralbes, Centre d'Interpretació del Park Güell, Centre d'Interpretació del Call, Centre d'Interpretació Històrica, Refugi 307, and Museu-Casa Ver-*

DID YOU KNOW?

The Palau de la Música Catalana was created to encourage musical knowledge at a popular level, as opposed to the Liceu Opera House, which was identified with the Catalan aristocracy.

daguer) ⏲ *Oct.–May, Tues.–Sat. 10–2 and 4–7, Sun. 10–3; June–Sept., Tues.–Sat. 10–7, Sun. 10–3* Ⓜ *Catalunya, Liceu, Jaume I.*

9 **Museu Picasso.** Picasso spent key formative years (1895–1904) in Barcelona, when he was a young bohemian, and never forgot these good times. A collection of his work can be found in Carrer Montcada, known for Barcelona's most elegant medieval and Renaissance palaces, five of which are occupied by the Picasso Museum. Picasso's longtime crony and personal secretary, Jaume Sabartés, donated his private collection to this museum in 1960, and Picasso himself donated another 1,700 works in 1970. Though the 3,600-work permanent collection is strong on his early production, don't expect to find many of the artist's most famous works. Displays include childhood and adolescent sketches, works from Picasso's Blue and Rose periods, and the famous 44 Cubist studies based on Diego Velázquez's painting *Las Meninas*. The sketches, oils, schoolboy caricatures, and drawings from Picasso's early years in La Coruña and later in Barcelona are perhaps the most fascinating part of the museum, showing the facility the artist possessed from an early age. His *La Primera Communión* (First Communion), painted at the age of 15, for which he was given a short review in the local press, was an important achievement for the young Picasso, and the *Las Meninas* studies and the bright *Pichones (Pigeons)* series provide a final explosion of color and light. *Suite 156,* a series of erotic and playful drawings on display when temporary exhibits allow space, may be the best of all. ✉ *Carrer Montcada 15–23, Born-Ribera* ☎ *93/319–6310* 🌐 *www.museupicasso.bcn.cat* 🎫 *€9.50; free 1st Sun. of month* ⏲ *Tues.–Sun. 10–8* Ⓜ *Catalunya, Liceu, Jaume I.*

Fodor's Choice ★

QUICK BITES

Mercat de Santa Caterina. This marketplace, a splendid carnival of colors and roller-coaster rooftops, was restored by the late Enric Miralles (though the project was finished in 2005 by his widow, architect Benedetta Tagliabue). Inside, undulating wood and colored ceramic mosaics recall both Gaudí and Miró, and there is an archaeological display explaining more than 2,000 years of the site's history. The spacious Cuines Santa Caterina restaurant has a unique crossword-style menu, listing food products across the top and world cuisines such as Asian, Mediterranean, and vegetarian down the left margin. ✉ *Av. Francesc Cambo 16, Born-Ribera* ☎ *93/268–9918* 🌐 *www.mercatsbcn.com* Ⓜ *Jaume I, Catalunya.*

8 **Palau de la Música Catalana.** A riot of color and form, Barcelona's Music Palace is the flagship of the city's Moderniste architecture. Designed by Lluís Domènech i Montaner in 1908, it was originally conceived by the Orfeó Català musical society as a vindication of the importance of music at a popular level—as opposed to the Liceu opera house's identification with the Catalan (often Castilian-speaking monarchist) aristocracy. The Palau's exterior is remarkable in itself, albeit hard to see because there's no room to back up and behold it. Above the main entrance are busts of the composers Giovanni Pierluigi da Palestrina, Johann Sebastian Bach, Ludwig van Beethoven, and (around the corner on Carrer Amadeu Vives) Richard Wagner. Look for the colorful mosaic

Fodor's Choice ★

pillars on the upper level, a preview of what's inside. The Miquel Blay sculptural group at the corner of Sant Pere Més Alt and Amadeu Vives depicts everyone from St. George the dragon slayer (at the top) to fishermen with oars over their shoulders.

The interior is an uproar. Wagnerian cavalry erupts from the right side of the stage over a heavy-browed bust of Beethoven, and Catalonia's popular music is represented by the flowing maidens of Lluís Millet's song "Flors de Maig" ("Flowers of May") on the left. Overhead, an inverted stained-glass cupola seems to offer the divine manna of music, and painted rosettes and giant peacock feathers explode from the tops of the walls. Even the stage is populated with muselike Art Nouveau musicians, each half bust and half mosaic. The visuals alone make music sound different in here, and at any important concert the excitement is palpably thick; if you can't attend one, take a tour of the hall. *Ticket office✉ Carrer Palau de la Música 4–6, just off Via Laietana, around corner from hall, Sant Pere ☎ 902/442882 🌐 www.palaumusica.org 🎫 Tour €10 ⏲ Sept.–June, tours daily 10–3:30; July and Aug., tours daily 10–7* Ⓜ *Catalunya.*

❻ **Plaça del Rei.** Chronicled in legend, song, and painting, this austere medieval square has long been believed to be the scene of Christopher Columbus's triumphal return from his first voyage to the New World, with Ferdinand and Isabella receiving "the discoverer" on the stairs—though it turns out the king and queen were actually at a summer palace outside of town. Also around the square, as you face the stairway, are the dark 15th-century **Torre Mirador del Rei Martí** (King Martin's Watchtower); to the left is the 16th-century **Palau del Lloctinent** (Lieutenant's Palace) and archive of the Corona d'Aragó with its gorgeous patio, a coffered ceiling in the shape of an inverted boat over the stairway, a Josep Maria Subirachs sculpted bronze door, and a display on the life of Jaume I, founder of the Catalan nation. The 14th-century **Capilla Reial de Santa Àgueda** (Royal Chapel of Saint Agatha) is to the right of the stairway, and, on Carrer Veguer, the **Palau Clariana-Padellàs** (Clariana-Padellàs Palace), moved here stone by stone from Carrer Mercaders in the early 20th century, is at the entrance to the Museu d'Història de la Ciutat. Ⓜ *Catalunya, Liceu, Jaume I.*

❼ **Plaça Reial.** Seedy around the edges but elegant and neoclassical in design, this symmetrical mid-19th-century arcaded square is bordered by ocher facades with balconies overlooking the **Fountain of the Three Graces** and lampposts designed by Gaudí. Restaurants and cafés, sadly identifiable as tourist traps by the photo-menus (the only good one is Taxidermista; see the listing below), line the square. On Sunday morning, crowds gather to sell and trade stamps and coins. Ⓜ *Catalunya, Liceu.*

❽ **Plaça Sant Jaume.** Two thousand years ago, this formal square was the center of the Roman forum, which seems fitting for the modern-day site of both Catalonia's and Barcelona's government seats. The **Palau de la Generalitat,** seat of the Catalan government, is a majestic 15th-century palace—through the front windows you can see the gilded ceiling of the Saló de Sant Jordi (Hall of St. George), named for Catalonia's dragon-

DID YOU KNOW?

The imposing Gothic church of Santa Maria del Mar stands out in Barcelona as a dramatic counterpart to the city's exuberant Moderniste architecture.

slaying patron saint. ✉ *Pl. Sant Jaume 1, Barri Gòtic* ☎ *93/402–7000* 🌐 *www.bcn.es* ⏲ *Sun. 10–1* Ⓜ *Catalunya, Liceu, Jaume I.*

10 Fodor's Choice ★ **Santa Maria del Mar.** The most breathtakingly symmetrical and graceful of all Barcelona's churches is on the Carrer Montcada end of Passeig del Born. It's an early Gothic basilica with Romanesque echoes and overtones; simple and spacious, this pure, classical space enclosed by soaring columns is something of an oddity in ornate and complex Moderniste Barcelona. Santa Maria del Mar (Saint Mary of the Sea) was built from 1329 to 1383, an extraordinarily prompt construction time in that era, in fulfillment of a vow made a century earlier by Jaume I to build a church to watch over all Catalan seafarers. The architect in charge of the construction, a mere stonemason named Montagut de Berenguer, designed a bare-bones basilica (an oblong Roman royal hall used for public meetings and later adapted for early Christian or medieval churches) that's now considered the finest existing example of Catalan (or Mediterranean) Gothic architecture. The number eight (or multiples thereof)—the medieval numerological symbol for the Virgin Mary—runs through every element of the basilica's construction: 16 octagonal pillars rise 16 meters before arching out another 16 meters to the painted keystones at the apex of the arches 32 meters overhead. The sum of the lateral aisles, 8 meters each, equals the width of the center aisle, and the difference in height between the central and lateral naves, 8 meters, equals their width. The result of all this proportional balance is a tonic sense of peace and enlightenment, an almost mystical poise enhanced by a lovely rose window whose circular mass in blues and crimsons perfectly offsets the golden sandstone verticality of the columns. Any excuse to spend time in Santa Maria del Mar, from eavesdropping on a wedding to hearing a concert to using it as a shortcut through to the Passeig de Born, is valid. ✉ *Pl. de Santa Maria, Born-Ribera* ☎ *93/310–2390* ⏲ *Daily 9–1:30 and 4:30–8* Ⓜ *Catalunya, Jaume I.*

The cemetery on the eastern side of the church of Santa Maria del Mar, known as the Cemetery of the Mulberry trees, has been turned into a public plaza where there is a low marble monument inscribed EN EL FOSSAR DE LES MORERES NO S'HI ENTERRA CAP TRAIDOR, or "In the cemetery of the mulberry trees no traitor lies." It refers to the story of the graveyard keeper who refused to bury those who had fought on the invading side during the War of the Spanish Succession, in 1714, even when one of them turned out to be his son. The torch-sculpture over the monument, often referred to as a *pebetero* (Bunsen burner), was erected in 2002. ✉ *Fossar de les Moreres, La Ribera* Ⓜ *Jaume I.*

WORTH NOTING

4 **Catedral de la Seu.** On Saturday afternoons, Sunday mornings, and occasional evenings, Barcelona folk gather in the Plaça de la Seu to dance the *sardana,* a somewhat demure circle dance and a great symbol of Catalan identity. The Gothic cathedral was built between 1298 and 1450, with the spire and neo-Gothic facade added in 1892. Architects of Catalan Gothic churches strove to make the high altar visible to the entire congregation, hence the unusually wide central nave and slender side columns. The first thing you see upon entering the Catedral de la

Seu are the high-relief sculptures on the choir stalls, telling the story of **Santa Eulàlia** (Barcelona's co-patron along with La Mercé, Our Lady of Mercy). The first scene, on the left, shows St. Eulàlia in front of the Roman Consul Decius with her left hand on her heart and her right hand pointing at a cross in the distance. In the next scene, Eulàlia is tied to a column and whipped by Decius's thugs. To the right of the choir entrance, the senseless Eulàlia is hauled away, and in the final scene she is lashed to the X-shape cross upon which she was crucified in the year 303.To the right is a sculpture of St. Eulàlia with her cross, resurrected as a living saint. Other highlights are the beautifully carved choir stalls, St. Eulàlia's tomb in the crypt, and the battle-scarred crucifix in the Lepanto Chapel to the right of the main entrance. The tall cloisters surround a tropical garden, and outside, at the building's front right corner, is the intimate Santa Llúcia chapel. The cathedral is floodlit in striking yellows at night, and the stained-glass windows are backlit. During the so-called Special Visits, from 1 to 5, visitors can see the entire cathedral, museum, bell tower, and rooftop. ✉ *Pl. de la Seu, Barri Gòtic* ☎ *93/342–8260* 🌐 *www.catedralbcn.org* 🎫 *1–5* PM *Special Visit: €5.50; the rest of the time free* 🕓 *Daily 7:45* AM*–7:45* PM Ⓜ *Catalunya, Liceu, Jaume I.*

5 **Museu Frederic Marès** *(Frederic Marès Museum)*. You can browse for hours amid the miscellany assembled by the early-20th-century sculptor-collector Frederic Marès in this trove of art and odds and ends. Everything from paintings and polychrome wood carvings, such as Juan de Juní's 1537 masterpiece *Pietà* and the Master of Cabestany's late-12th-century sculpture *Apparition of Christ to His Disciples at Sea,* to Marès's collection of pipes and walking sticks is stuffed into this rich potpourri. ✉ *Pl. Sant Iu 5, Barri Gòtic* ☎ *93/310–5800* 🌐 *www.museumares.bcn.es* 🎫 *€4.50; free 1st Sun. of month and Wed. afternoon* 🕓 *Tues.–Sat. 10–7, Sun. 10–3* Ⓜ *Catalunya, Liceu, Jaume I.*

BARCELONETA, LA CIUTADELLA, AND PORT OLÍMPIC

Barceloneta, once the open sea, was silted in and became a salt marsh until 1753, when French military engineer Prosper de Verboom designed a housing project for families who had lost their homes in La Ribera. The beach here is popular and clean Today, Port Olímpic, along the sport marina northeast of the Hotel Arts, is mainly taken up with tourist-filled terrace restaurants and high-decibel discos—it's probably best avoided if this isn't your taste. The Ciutadella, once the fortress that kept watch over Barcelona, is now a leafy park with the city zoo, the Catalan parliament, and pools and waterfalls.

TOP ATTRACTIONS

6 **Barceloneta.** Once Barcelona's pungent fishing port, Barceloneta retains much of its salty maritime flavor. It's an exciting and colorful place to walk through, with narrow streets and lines of laundry snapping in the breeze. Stop in Plaça de la Barceloneta to see the baroque church of **Sant Miquel del Port,** with its oversize sculpture of the winged archangel. Look for the splendidly remodeled Barceloneta market and its upstairs and downstairs restaurants, Lluçanès and Els Fogons de la Barceloneta.

The original two-story houses and the restaurant Can Solé on Carrer Sant Carles are historic landmarks. Barceloneta's surprisingly clean and sandy **beach**, though overcrowded in midsummer, offers swimming, surfing, and a lively social scene from late May through September.

QUICK BITES

Friendly Can Manel la Puda (✉ *Passeig de Joan de Borbó 60–61* ☎ *93/221–5013*), in Barceloneta, is always good for an inexpensive feast. Serving lunch until 4 and starting dinner at 7, it's a popular place for *suquets* (fish stew), paella, and *arròs a banda* (rice with shelled seafood). It's closed Monday.

WORTH NOTING

❶ **Arc del Triomf.** This imposing, exposed-redbrick arch on Passeig de Sant Joan was built by Josep Vilaseca as the grand entrance for the Universal Exposition of 1888. Similar in size and sense to the triumphal arches of ancient Rome, this one refers to Jaume I El Conqueridor's 1229 conquest of the Moors in Mallorca—the bats, on either side of the arch, are always part of Jaume I's coat of arms.

❷ **Castell dels Tres Dragons** *(Castle of the Three Dragons)*. Built by Domènech i Montaner as a restaurant for the Universal Exposition of 1888, this arresting structure was named in honor of a popular mid-19th-century comedy by the father of the Catalan theater, Serafí Pitarra. Greeting you on the right as you enter the Ciutadella from Passeig Lluí Companys, the building has exposed brickwork and visible iron supports, both radical innovations of their time. Moderniste architects later met here to exchange ideas and experiment with traditional crafts. The castle now holds Barcelona's **Museum of Zoology**. ✉ *Passeig Picasso 5, La Ciutadella* ☎ *93/319–6912* 🌐 *www.bcn.es/medciencies* 🎫 *€4.50* ⏱ *Tues., Wed., and Fri.–Sun. 10–2:30, Thurs. 10–6:30* Ⓜ *Arc de Triomf.*

❼ **El Transbordador Aeri del Port** *(cable car)*. The creaky-looking but recently refurbished (2006) cable car leaving from the tower at the end of Passeig Joan de Borbó connects the Torre de San Sebastián on the Moll de Barceloneta, the tower of Jaume I in the boat terminal, and the Torre de Miramar on Montjuïc. The Torre de Altamar restaurant in the tower at the Barceloneta end serves excellent food and wine and has nonpareil views. ✉ *Passeig Joan de Borbó s/n, Barceloneta* ☎ *93/225–2718* 🎫 *€12.50 round-trip, €9 one-way* ⏱ *Daily 10:45–7* Ⓜ *Barceloneta.*

❸ **La Cascada.** Take a break by the Ciutadella's lake; behind it, you'll find the monumental *Cascada* (Falls) fountain, by Josep Fontseré, designed for the Universal Exposition of 1888. The waterfall's rocks were the work of a young architecture student named Antoni Gaudí—his first public work, appropriately natural and organic, a hint of things to come. ✉ *La Ciutadella* Ⓜ *Arc de Triomf, Ciutadella.*

❺ **Museu d'Història de Catalunya.** Built into what used to be a port warehouse, this state-of-the-art museum is interactive (visitors can try on armor, ride a mechanical horse, or activate computerized displays), making you part of Catalonian history. Beginning with prehistoric times, the emergence of the language and identity of Catalonia is traced through more than 3,000 years into the contemporary democratic era. Explanations of the exhibits appear in Catalan, Castilian, and English.

Arc de Triomf 1
Barceloneta 6
Castell dels Tres Dragons.....2
La Cascada 3
Museu d'Història de Catalunya 5
Parc de la Ciutadella 4
El Transbordador Aeri del Port 7

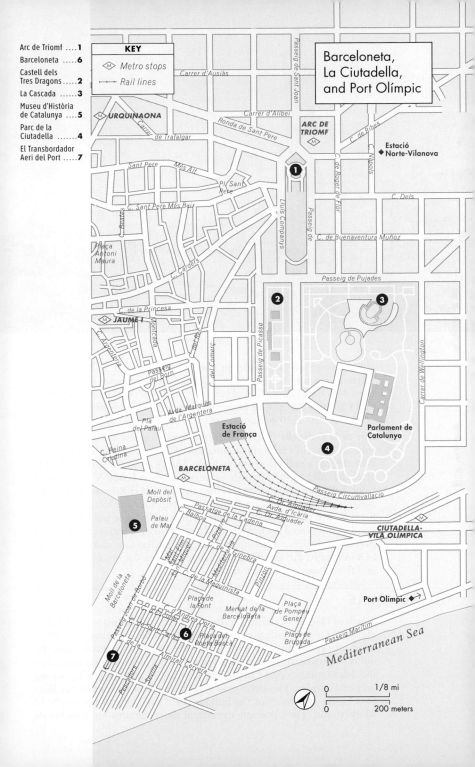

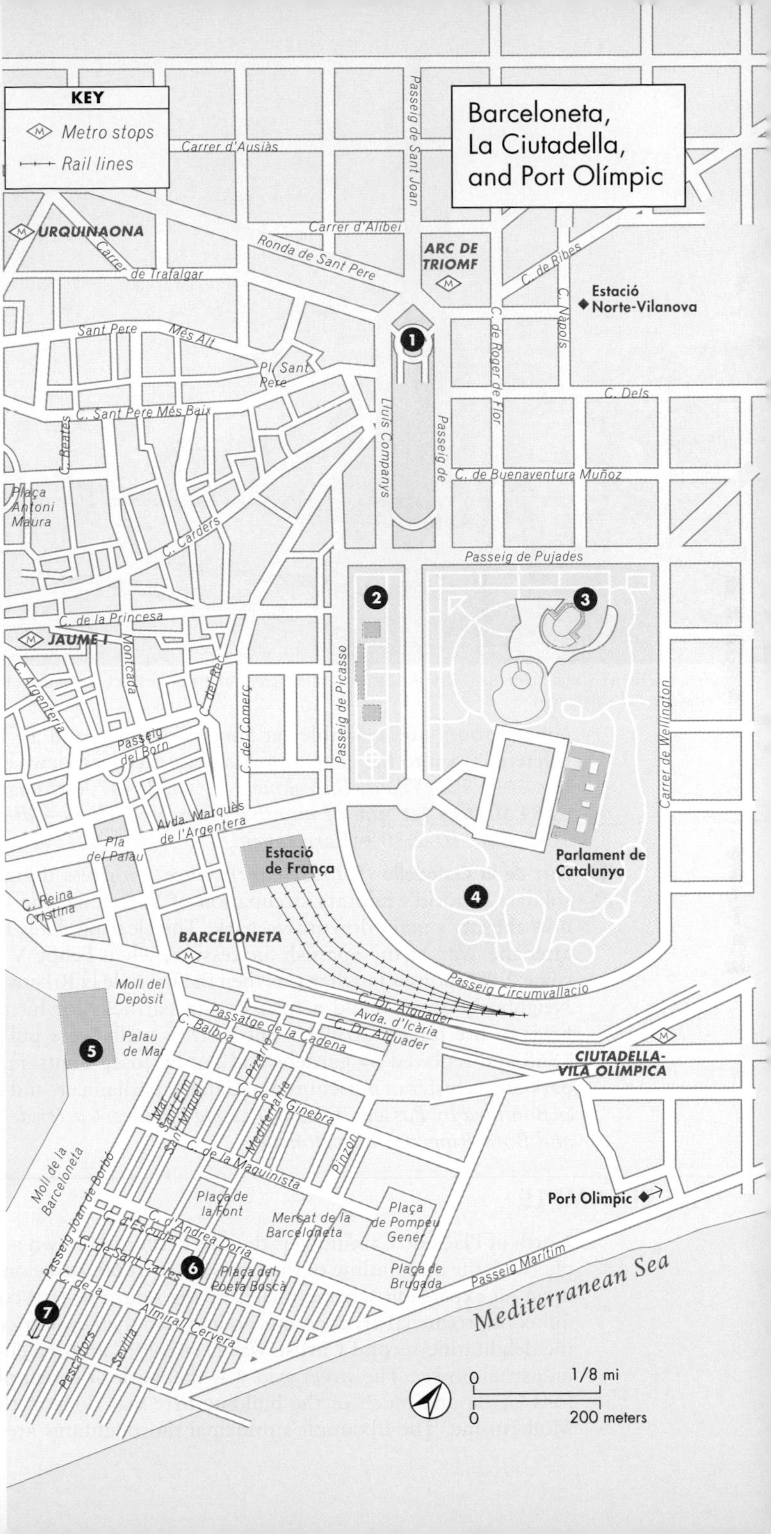

Rebecca Horn's sculpture on Barceloneta's beach is reminiscent of the little shack restaurants that once crowded this sandy spot.

Guided tours are available on Sunday at noon and 1. The rooftop cafeteria, open to the general public, has excellent views over the harbor. ✉ *Pl. Pau Vila 3, Barceloneta* ☎ *93/225–4700* 🌐 *www.mhcat.net* 🎟 *€4.50; free 1st Sun. of month* ⏲ *Tues. and Thurs.–Sat. 10–7, Wed. 10–8, Sun. 10–2:30* Ⓜ *Barceloneta.*

4 **Parc de la Ciutadella** *(Citadel Park).* Once a fortress designed to consolidate Madrid's military occupation of Barcelona, the Ciutadella is now the city's main downtown park. The clearing dates from shortly after the War of the Spanish Succession, when Felipe V demolished some 2,000 houses in what was then the Barri de la Ribera (Waterfront Neighborhood) to build a fortress and barracks for his soldiers and fields of fire for his artillery. The fortress walls were pulled down in 1868 and replaced by gardens laid out by Josep Fontserè. Within the park are a cluster of museums, the Catalan parliament, and the city **zoo.** ✉ *Bounded by Passeig Picasso, Passeig Pujades, Carrer de Wellington, and Born-Ribera* Ⓜ *Barceloneta.*

THE EIXAMPLE

North of Plaça de Catalunya is the checkerboard known as the Eixample. With the dismantling of the city walls in 1860, Barcelona embarked upon an expansion scheme fueled by the return of rich colonials, the influx of provincial aristocrats who had sold their country estates after the debilitating second Carlist War (1847–49), and the city's growing industrial power. The street grid was the work of urban planner Ildefons Cerdà and much of the building here was done at the height of Modernisme. The Eixample's principal thoroughfares are Rambla de

Catalunya and Passeig de Gràcia, where the city's most elegant shops vie for space among its best Art Nouveau buildings.

A GOOD TOUR

Starting in the Plaça de Catalunya, walk up Passeig de Gràcia until you reach the corner of Consell de Cent, where you'll enter the vortex of Moderniste architecture, the **Manzana de la Discòrdia** ❶. The **Casa Montaner i Simó–Fundació Tàpies** ❷ is around the corner on Carrer Aragó. Gaudí's **Casa Milà** ❸, known as La Pedrera, is three blocks farther up Passeig de Gràcia; after touring the interior and rooftop, walk up Passeig de Gràcia to the **Vinçon**, one of Barcelona's top design stores, with views into the back of Casa Milà. Just around the corner, at Diagonal 373, is Puig i Cadafalch's intricately sculpted **Palau Baró de Quadras**, now housing the Casa Asia cultural center. Two minutes farther east is his Nordic castlelike **Casa de les Punxes** ❹ at No. 416–420. From here it's a 10-minute walk to yet another Puig i Cadafalch masterpiece, **Casa Macaia**. Finally, walk another 15 minutes along Carrer Provença to Gaudí's emblematic **Temple Expiatori de la Sagrada Família** ❺. If you've still got energy and curiosity to burn, stroll over to Domènech i Montaner's **Hospital de Sant Pau** ❻.

TIMING Depending on how many taxis you take, this is a four- to five-hour tour, so plan your exploring around a good lunch. Add an hour to two hours each to visit Casa Battló, Casa Milà, and the Sagrada Família, or plan to return later.

TOP ATTRACTIONS

❸ ★ **Casa Milà.** Gaudí's Casa Milà, usually referred to as **La Pedrera** (The Stone Quarry), has a curving stone facade that bobs around the corner of the block. When the building was unveiled, in 1910, residents weren't enthusiastic about the cavelike balconies on their most fashionable street. Don't miss Gaudí's rooftop chimney park, especially in late afternoon, when the sunlight slants over the city into the Mediterranean. The handsome **Espai Gaudí** (Gaudí Space) in the attic has excellent critical displays of Gaudí's works, theories, and techniques, including an upside-down model of the Sagrada Família made of hanging beads. The **Pis de la Pedrera,** a restored apartment, gives an interesting glimpse into the life of its resident family in the early 20th century. Guided tours are offered weekdays at 6 PM and weekends at 11 AM. ✉ *Carrer Provença 261–265, Eixample* ☎ *902/400973* 🎟 *€8.50* ⏲ *Daily 9–6:30; guided tours weekdays at 6* PM, *weekends*

CATALAN FOR BEGINNERS

Catalan is derived from Latin and Provençal French, whereas Spanish is heavy on Arabic vocabulary and phonetics. For language exchange *(intercambios)*, check the bulletin board at the central university Philosophy and Letters Faculty on Gran Via or any English bookstore for free half-hour exchanges of English for Catalan (or Spanish), a great way to get free private lessons and meet locals. Who knows? With the right chemistry, intercambios can lead to cross-cultural friendships and even romance. Who said the language of love is French?

at 11 AM. *Espai Gaudí roof terrace open for drinks evenings June–Sept.* Ⓜ *Diagonal, Provença.*

❶ **Manzana de la Discòrdia.** A pun on the Spanish word *manzana,* meaning both city block and apple, the reference is to the classical myth of the Apple of Discord, in which Eris, goddess of strife, drops a golden apple with the inscription "to the fairest." The goddesses Hera, Athena, and Aphrodite all claim the apple; Paris is chosen to settle the dispute and awards the apple to Aphrodite, who promises him Helen, the most beautiful of women, triggering the Trojan War. On this city block you can find the architectural counterpoint, where the three main Moderniste architects go hand to hand, drawing steady crowds of architecture buffs. Of the three, Casa Batlló is clearly the star.

Fodor's Choice ★

Casa Lleó Morera (No. 35) was extensively rebuilt (1902–06) by Domènech i Montaner and is a treasure chest of Modernisme. The facade is covered with ornamentation and sculptures of female figures using the modern inventions of the age: the telephone, the telegraph, the camera, and the Victrola. The inside is closed to the public, but a quick glimpse into the entryway on the corner gives an idea of what's upstairs.

The pseudo-Flemish **Casa Amatller** (No. 41) was built by Puig i Cadafalch in 1900 as a residence for the chocolatier Antoni Amattler. Puig i Cadafalch's architectural historicism sought to recover Catalonia's proud past, in combination with eclectic elements from Flemish and Netherlandish architectural motifs. The sculptures by Eusebi Arnau range from St. George and the dragon to a handless drummer with his dancing bear. The flowing-haired "Princesa" is thought to be Amatller's daughter, and the animals up above pour chocolate, a reference to the source of the Amatller family fortune. Casa Amatller is closed to the public (call or ask about any change in this), but an office on-site dispenses tickets for the Ruta del Modernisme tour (⇨ *see the Moderniste Barcelona box for details).*

At No. 43, the colorful and bizarre **Casa Batlló**—Gaudí at his most spectacular—with its mottled facade resembling anything from an abstract pointillist painting to rainbow sprinkles on an ice-cream cone, is usually easily identifiable by the crowd of tourists snapping photographs on the sidewalk. Nationalist symbolism is hard at work here: the scaly roofline represents the Dragon of Evil impaled on St. George's cross, and the skulls and bones on the balconies are the dragon's victims. These motifs allude to Catalonia's Middle Ages, with its codes of chivalry and religious fervor. The interior design follows a gently swirling maritime motif in stark contrast to the terrestrial strife represented on the facade. ✉ *Passeig de Gràcia 43, between Carrer Consell de Cent and Carrer Aragó, Eixample* ☎ *93/216–0306* 🌐 *www.casabatllo.es* 🎫 *€17* 🕘 *Daily 9–8* Ⓜ *Passeig de Gràcia.*

❺ **Temple Expiatori de la Sagrada Família.** Looming over Barcelona like a magical midcity massif of needles and peaks left by eons of wind erosion and fungal exuberance, Barcelona's most unforgettable landmark, Antoni Gaudí's Sagrada Família, was conceived as nothing short of a Bible in stone. This landmark is one of the most important architec-

Fodor's Choice ★

Casa Milà 3	Manzana de la Discòrdia (Casa Lleó Morera, Casa Amatller, Casa Batlló) 1
Casa Montaner i Simó—Fundació Tàpies 2	Temple Expiatori de la Sagrada Família 5
Casa de les Punxes 4	
Hospital de Sant Pau 6	

CLOSE UP

Moderniste Barcelona

Characterized by intense ornamentation and natural or organic lines and forms, Modernisme (Art Nouveau) swept Europe between 1880 and 1914, proliferating wildly in Barcelona. Beginning with the city's Universal Exposition of 1888, the playful Catalan artistic impulse (evidenced in the works of Gaudí, Miró, and Dalí) and Barcelona's late-19th-century industrial prosperity teamed up with a surge in Catalonian nationalism to run rampant in the Eixample neighborhood, where bourgeois families competed with each other by decorating their opulent mansions.

A cultural movement that went beyond architecture, Modernisme affected everything from clothes to hairstyles to tombstones. The curved line replaced the straight, natural elements such as flowers and fruit were sculpted into facades, and the classical and pragmatic gave way to decorative ebullience.

Barcelona's Palau de la Música Catalana by Domènech i Montaner is a stunning compendium of Art Nouveau techniques, including acid-engraved and stained glass, polychrome ceramics, carved wooden arches, and sculpture. Josep Puig i Cadafalch's Casa Amatller and his Casa de les Punxes are examples of Modernisme's eclectic, historical tendency. Josep Graner i Prat's Casa de la Papallona, Joan Rubió Bellver's Casa Golferichs, Antoni Gaudí's Casa Batlló, and Salvador Valeri i Pupurull's Casa Comalat converted Barcelona's Eixample into a living Moderniste museum.

The **Ruta del Modernisme** is an itinerary through the Barcelona of Gaudì, Domènech i Montaner, and Puig i Cadafalch, just some of the architects who made Barcelona the world capital of Modernisme in the late 19th and early 20th centuries. Palaces, private houses, the temple that has become a symbol of the city, and a huge hospital join pharmacies, lampposts, and benches—115 works in all—tracing Art Nouveau's explosion in Barcelona.

There are three Modernisme Centers—Centre d'Informació de Turisme de Barcelona (Plaça de Catalunya 17, Soterrani), Hospital de la Santa Creu i Sant Pau (Pavelló de Santa Apol. lònia, Carrer Sant Antoni Claret 167), and Pavellons Güell (Av. de Pedralbes 7)—that sell items related to the route, including a **guide book**, which has discount vouchers good for up to 50% off admission fees to all Moderniste monuments in the city and in another 13 towns. For more details call ☎ *902/076621* or check out 🌐 *www.rutadelmodernisme.com.*

tural creations since the 19th century, though its construction, begun in 1882, is still underway.

Start at the **Nativity facade,** where Gaudí addresses the fundamental mystery of Christianity: why does God the Creator become, through Jesus Christ, a creature? Gaudí's answer-in-stone is that God wanted to free man from the slavery of selfishness, symbolized here by the iron fence around the serpent at the base of the central column. The column depicts the genealogy of Christ. Overhead are the constellations in the Christmas sky at Bethlehem. Higher up is the Crowning of the Virgin

RECOMMENDED MODERNISTE MONUMENTS

- Casa Amatller
- Casa Batlló
- Casa Calvet
- Casa Comalat
- Casa de les Punxes (Casa Terrades)
- Casa Fuster
- Casa Lleó Morera
- Casa Macaya
- Casa Milà (La Pedrera)
- Casa Planells
- Casa Thomas
- Casa Vicens
- Conservatori Municipal de Música
- CosmoCaixa, Museu de la Ciència
- Hidroelèctrica
- Hospital de la Santa Creu i Sant Pau
- Museu Nacional d'Art de Catalunya (MNAC)
- Museu de Zoologia
- Observatori Fabra
- Palau de la Música Catalana
- Palau del Baró de Quuadras
- Palau Montaner
- Pavellons Güell
- Temple Expiatori de la Sagrada Família
- Torre Bellesguard

under an overhang, atop which is a pelican feeding its young with its blood, a symbol of the eucharistic sacrifice. Below, two angels adore the initials of Christ (JHS) under the symbols of the cross, the Alpha and Omega. The cypress at the top is the evergreen symbol of eternity pointing to heaven; the white doves, souls seeking eternity.

To the right, the Portal of Faith, above Palestinian flora and fauna, shows scenes from the youth of Jesus, including his preaching at the age of 13. Higher up are grapes and wheat, symbols of the eucharist, and a sculpture of a hand and eye, symbols of divine providence. The left-hand Portal of Hope begins at the bottom with flora and fauna from the Nile; the Slaughter of the Innocents; the flight of the Holy Family into Egypt; Joseph, surrounded by his carpenter's tools, contemplating his son; and the marriage of Joseph and Mary. Above this is a sculpted boat with anchor (representing the church), piloted by St. Joseph assisted by the Holy Spirit. Overhead is a typical spire from the Montserrat massif. Gaudí intended these towers to house a system of bells capable of playing more complex music than standard bell systems. The towers' peaks represent the apostles' successors in the form of miters, the official headdress of bishops of the Western church.

The **Passion facade** on the southwestern side, at the entrance to the grounds, is a dramatic contrast to the Nativity facade. Josep Maria Subirachs, the sculptor chosen in 1986 to execute Gaudí's plans—initially an atheist, and author of statements such as "God is one of man's greatest creations"—now confesses to a respectful agnosticism. Known for his distinctly angular, geometrical interpretations of the human form, Subirachs boasted that his work "has nothing to do with

Continued on page 464

GAUDÍ

ARCHITECTURE THROUGH THE LOOKING GLASS

(left) The undulating rooftop of Casa Batlló. (top) Construction continues on la Sagrada Família.

Before his 75th birthday in 1926, Antonio Gaudí was hit by a trolley car while on his way to Mass. The great architect—initially unidentified—was taken to the medieval Hospital de la Santa Creu in Barcelona's Raval and left in a pauper's ward, where he died two days later without regaining consciousness. It was a dramatic and tragic end for a man whose entire life seemed to court the extraordinary and the exceptional.

Gaudí's singularity made him hard to define. Indeed, eulogists at the time, and decades later, wondered how history would treat him. Was he a religious mystic, a rebel, a bohemian artist, a Moderniste genius? Was he, perhaps, all of these? He certainly had a rebellious streak, as his architecture stridently broke with tradition. Yet the same sensibility that created the avant-garde benchmarks Park Güell and La Pedrera also created one of Spain's greatest shrines to Catholicism, the *Temple Expiatori de la Sagrada Família* (Expiatory Temple of the Holy Family), which architects agree is one of the world's most enigmatic structures; work on the cathedral continues to this day. And while Gaudí's works suggest a futurist aesthetic, he also reveled in the use of ornamentation, which 20th century architecture largely eschewed.

What is no longer in doubt is Gaudí's place among the great architects in history. Eyed with suspicion by traditionalists in the 1920s and 30s, vilified during the Franco regime, and ultimately redeemed as a Barcelona icon after Spain's democratic transition in the late 70s, Gaudí has finally gained universal admiration.

THE MAKING OF A GENIUS

Gaudí was born in 1852 the son of a boilermaker and coppersmith in Reus, an hour south of Barcelona. As a child, he helped his father forge boilers and cauldrons in the family foundry, which is where Gaudí's fascination with three-dimensional and organic forms began. Afflicted from an early age with reoccuring rheumatic fever, the young architect devoted his energies to studying and drawing flora and fauna in the natural world. In school Gaudí was erratic: brilliant in the subjects that interested him, absent and disinterested in the others. As a seventeen-year-old architecture student in Barcelona, his academic results were mediocre. Still, his mentors agreed that he was brilliant.

Unfortunately being brilliant didn't mean instant success. By the late 1870s, when Gaudí was well into his twenties, he'd only completed a handful of projects, including the Plaça Reial lampposts, a flower stall, and the factory and part of a planned workers' community in Mataró. Gaudí's career got the boost it needed when, in 1878, he met Eusebi Güell, heir to a textiles fortune and a man who, like Gaudí, had a refined sensibility. (The two bonded over a mutual admiration for the visionary Catalan poet Jacint Verdaguer.) In 1883 Gaudí became Güell's architect and for the next three decades, until Güell's death in 1918, the two collaborated on Gaudí's most important architectural achievements, from high-profile endeavors like Palau Güell, Park Güell, and Pabellones Güell to smaller projects for the Güell family.

(top) Interior of Casa Batlló. (bottom) Chimneys on rooftop of Casa Milà recall helmeted warriors or veiled women.

GAUDÍ TIMELINE

1883–1884

Gaudí builds a summer palace, *El Capricho* in Comillas, Santander for the brother-in-law of his benefactor, Eusebi Güell. Another gig comes his way during this same period when Barcelona ceramics tile mogul Manuel Vicens hires him to build his town house, *Casa Vicens*, in the Gràcia neighborhood.

El Capricho

1884–1900

Gaudí whips up the Pabellones Güell, Palau Güell, the Palacio Episcopal of Astorga, Barcelona's Teresianas school, the Casa de los Botines in León, Casa Calvet, and Bellesguard. These have his classic look of this time, featuring interpretation of Mudéjar (Moorish motifs), Gothic, and Baroque styles.

Palacio Episcopal

BREAKING OUT OF THE T-SQUARE PRISON

If Eusebi Güell had not believed in Gaudí's unusual approach to Modernisme, his creations might not have seen the light of day. Güell recognized that Gaudí was imbued with a vision that separated him from the crowd. That vision was his fascination with the organic. Gaudí had observed early in his career that buildings were being composed of shapes that could only be drawn by the compass and the T-square: circles, triangles, squares, and rectangles—shapes that in three dimensions became prisms, pyramids, cylinders and spheres. He saw that in nature these shapes are unknown. Admiring the structural efficiency of trees, mammals, and the human form, Gaudí noted ". . . neither are trees prismatic, nor bones cylindrical, nor leaves triangular." The study of natural forms revealed that bones, branches, muscles, and tendons are all supported by internal fibers. Thus, though a surface curves, it is supported from within by a fibrous network that Gaudí translated into what he called "ruled geometry," a system of inner reinforcement he used to make hyperboloids, conoids, helicoids, or parabolic hyperboloids.

These tongue-tying words are simple forms and familiar shapes: the femur is hyperboloid; the way shoots grow off a branch is helicoidal; the web between your fingers is a hyperbolic paraboloid. To varying degrees, these ideas find expression in all of Gaudí's work, but nowhere are they more clearly stated than in the two masterpieces La Pedrera and Park Güell.

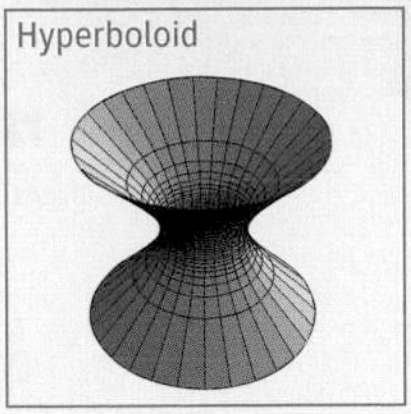

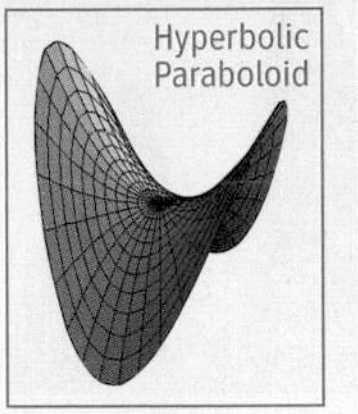

The top of the gatehouse in Park Güell at the main entrance; note the mushroom-like form.

1900–1917

Gaudí's Golden Years—his most creative, personal, and innovative period. Topping each success with another, he tackles Park Güell, the reform of Casa Batlló, the Güell Colony church, Casa Milà (La Pedrera), and the Sagrada Família school.

Casa Batlló's complex chimneys

1918–1926

A crushing blow: Gaudí suffers the death of his assistant, Francesc Berenguer. Grieving and rudderless, he devotes himself fully to his great unfinished opus, la Sagrada Família—to the point of obsession. On June 10th, 1926, he's hit by a trolley car. He dies two days later.

La Sagrada Família

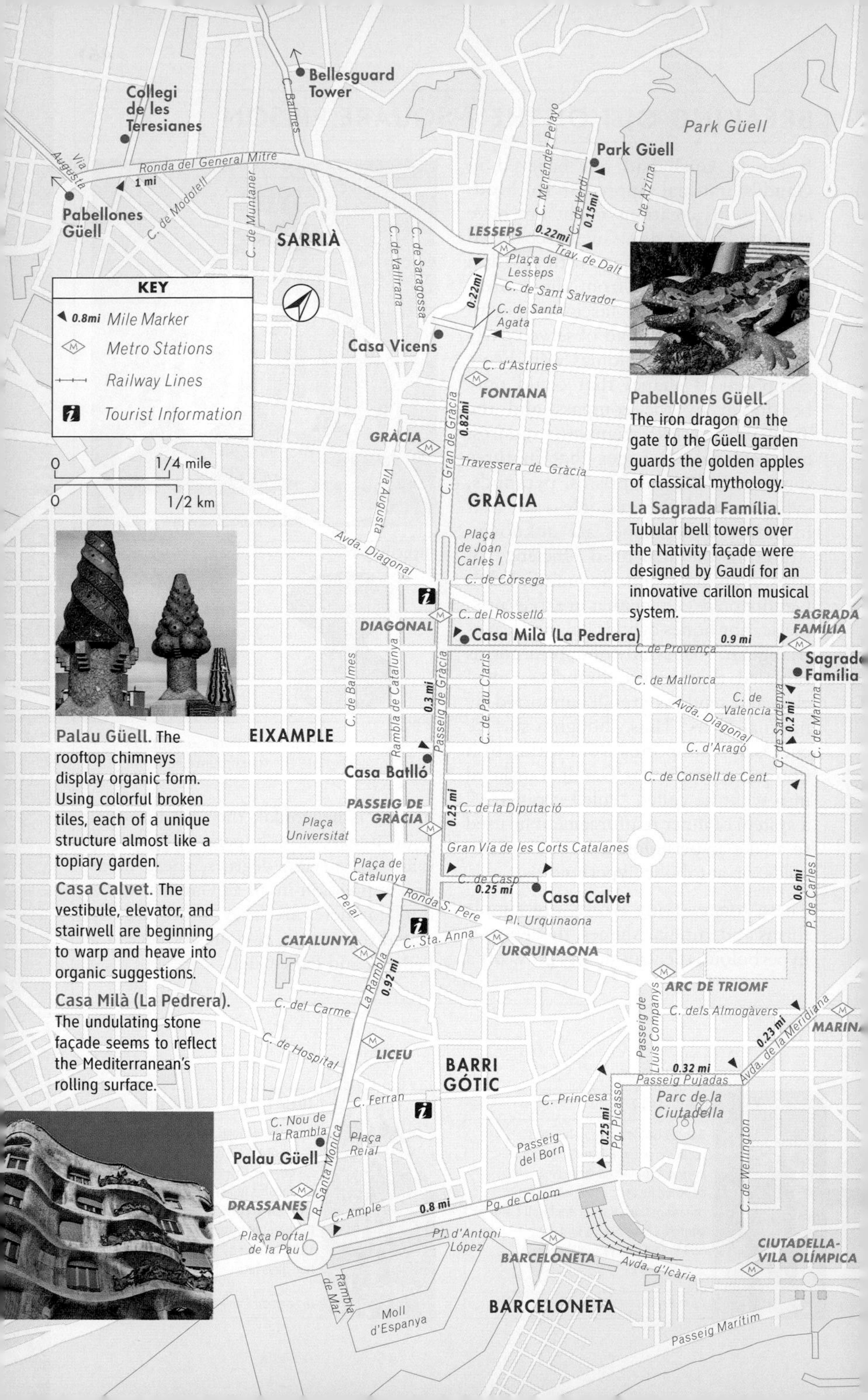

Pabellones Güell. The iron dragon on the gate to the Güell garden guards the golden apples of classical mythology.

La Sagrada Família. Tubular bell towers over the Nativity façade were designed by Gaudí for an innovative carillon musical system.

Palau Güell. The rooftop chimneys display organic form. Using colorful broken tiles, each of a unique structure almost like a topiary garden.

Casa Calvet. The vestibule, elevator, and stairwell are beginning to warp and heave into organic suggestions.

Casa Milà (La Pedrera). The undulating stone façade seems to reflect the Mediterranean's rolling surface.

HOW TO SEE GAUDÍ IN BARCELONA

Few architects have left their stamp on a major city as thoroughly as Gaudí did in Barcelona. Paris may have the Eiffel Tower, but Barcelona has Gaudí's still unfinished masterpiece, the **Temple Expiatori de la Sagrada Família,** the city's most emblematic structure. Dozens of other buildings, parks, gateways and even paving stones around town bear Gaudí's personal Art Nouveau signature, but the continuing progress on his last and most ambitious project makes his creative energy an ongoing part of everyday Barcelona life in a unique and almost spectral fashion.

(top) The serpentine ceramic bench at Park Güell, designed by Gaudí collaborator Josep Maria Jujol, curves sinuously around the edge of the open square. (bottom) Sculptures by Josep María Subirachs grace the temple of the Sagrada Família.

In Barcelona, nearly all of Gaudí's work can be visited on foot or, at most, with a couple of metro or taxi rides. A walk from **Palau Güell** near the Mediterranean end of the Rambla, up past **Casa Calvet** just above Plaça Catalunya, and on to **Casa Batlló** and **Casa Milà** is an hour's stroll, which, of course, could take a full day with thorough visits to the sites. **Casa Vicens** is a half hour's walk up into Gràcia from **Casa Milà. Park Güell** is another thirty- to forty-minute walk up from that. **La Sagrada Família,** on the other hand, is a good hour's hike from the next nearest Gaudí point and is best reached by taxi or metro. The **Teresianas** school, the **Bellesguard Tower,** and **Pabellones Güell** are within an hour's walk of each other, but to get out to Sarrià you will need to take the comfortable Generalitat (FGC) train.

Gaudí." When in 1990 artists, architects, and religious leaders called for his resignation after he sculpted an anatomically complete naked Christ on the cross, Subirachs defended the piece as part of the realism of the scene. Despite his staunch ideological and esthetic independence from the master, Subirachs pays double homage to Gaudí in the Passion facade: over the left side of the main entry is the blocky figure of Gaudí making notes or drawings, and the Roman soldiers are modeled on Gaudí's helmeted chimneys on the roof of La Pedrera.

Framed by leaning tibialike columns representing the bones of the dead, the scenes begin at the left of the facade with the Last Supper. The faces of the disciples are contorted in confusion and dismay, especially that of Judas, who clutches a bag of money behind his back over the figure of a reclining hound (a symbol of fidelity contrasting with his treachery). The next sculptural group represents the prayer in the Garden of Gethsemane and Peter awakening, followed by the kiss of Judas.

In the center, Jesus is lashed to a pillar during his flagellation, a tear track carved into his expressive countenance. The column's top stone is off-kilter, a reminder of the stone to be removed from Christ's sepulchre. The knot and broken reed at the base of the pillar symbolize Jesus's physical and psychological suffering. To the right of the door is a rooster, with Peter lamenting his third denial of Christ "before the cock crows." Farther to the right are Pilate and Jesus with a crown of thorns, and just above, back on the left, is Simon of Cyrene helping Jesus with the cross after his first fall. Over the center, where Jesus consoles the women of Jerusalem ("Don't cry for me; cry for your children"), is a faceless Veronica—faceless because her story is considered apocryphal—holding the veil with which she wiped Christ's face, only to find his likeness miraculously imprinted upon it. To the left is a sculpture of Gaudí making notes, John the Evangelist in stone, and, farther left, the equestrian figure of a centurion piercing the side of the church, which represents the body of Christ, with his spear. Above are the soldiers rolling dice for Christ's clothing and the naked, crucified Christ. The moon to the right of the cross refers to the darkness at the moment of Christ's death and to the full moon of Easter; to the right are Peter and Mary at the sepulchre, the egg above Mary symbolizing the Resurrection. At Christ's feet is a figure with a furrowed brow, perhaps suggesting the agnostic's anguished search for certainty, thought to be a self-portrait of Subirachs characterized by the sculptor's giant hand and an "S" on his right arm. High above is a gold figure of the resurrected Christ.

Future of the project. The 125th anniversary of the laying of the first stone was celebrated on March 19, 2007. Plans for the building have been scaled back since it was first conceived by Gaudi, but intentions for its completion are still impressive. Towers to be completed over the apse include those dedicated to the four evangelists (Matthew, Mark, Luke, and John), the Virgin Mary, and the highest of all, dedicated to Christ. The main facade will face east across Carrer Mallorca and a wide esplanade that will be created by the demolition of an entire city block of apartment houses built during the 1960s. The apse is expected to be covered by November 7, 2010, when Pope Benedict XVI is scheduled to consecrate the church and offer a prayer in the crypt at Gaudí's tomb. Predictions on the completion of the Glory Facade range from 2017 to 2026, the 100th anniversary of Gaudí's death. ✉ *Mallorca 401, Eixample* ☎ *93/207–3031* 🌐 *www.sagradafamilia.org* 🎟 *€11, bell-tower elevator €2.50* ⏲ *Oct.–Mar., daily 9–6; Apr.–Sept., daily 9–8* Ⓜ *Sagrada Família.*

WORTH NOTING

4 **Casa de les Punxes** *(House of the Spikes).* Also known as Casa Terrades, for the family that commissioned it, this cluster of six conical towers ending in impossibly sharp needles is one of several Puig i Cadafalch inspirations rooted in the Gothic architecture of northern Europe, an ur-Bavarian or Danish castle in downtown Barcelona. It's one of the few freestanding Eixample buildings visible from 360 degrees. Nearby is the **Casa Àsia–Palau Baró de Quadras** (Av. Diagonal 373), a neo-Gothic and plateresque (intricately carved in silversmithlike detail) house built by Puig i Cadafalch in 1904 for Baron Quadras. Its facade has some of the most spectacular Eusebi Arnau sculptures in town. Look for St. George slaying the dragon, and don't miss the alpine chaletlike windows across the top floor. The architect's **Casa Macaia** (Passeig de Sant Joan 108) is also worth walking past. ✉ *Av. Diagonal 416–420, Eixample* Ⓜ *Diagonal.*

2 **Casa Montaner i Simó–Fundació Tàpies.** This modern, airy building showcases the work of contemporary Catalan painter Antoni Tàpies, as well as temporary exhibits. ✉ *Carrer Aragó 255, Eixample* ☎ *93/487–0315* 🎟 *€5* ⏲ *Tues.–Sun. 10–8.*

6 **Hospital de Sant Pau.** Certainly one of the most beautiful hospital complexes in the world, a 10-minute walk down Avinguda Gaudí from the Sagrada Família, the Hospital de Sant Pau is notable for its Mudejar motifs and sylvan plantings. The hospital wards are set among gardens under exposed brick facades intensely decorated with mosaics and polychrome ceramic tile. Begun in 1900, this monumental production won Lluís Domènech i Montaner his third Barcelona "Best Building" award, in 1912. (His previous two prizes were for the Palau de la Música Catalana and Casa Lleó Morera.) The Moderniste enthusiasm for nature is apparent here; the architect believed patients are more apt to recover if they are surrounded by trees and flowers rather than ensconced in sterile hospital wards. Domènech i Montaner also believed in the therapeutic properties of form and color and decorated the hospital with Pau Gargallo sculptures and colorful mosaics. ✉ *Carrer Sant Antoni Maria Claret 167, Eixample* ☎ *93/291–9000* 🌐 *www.santpau.es* 🎟 *Free; tour €5* ⏲ *Daily 9–8; tours weekends 10–2, weekdays by advance arrangement* Ⓜ *Hospital de Sant Pau.*

UPPER BARCELONA, WITH PARK GÜELL

Barcelona's upper reaches begin with Pedralbes, a neighborhood of graceful mansions grouped around a stunning Gothic monastery. Park Güell is Gaudí's Art Nouveau urban garden. Gràcia and Sarrià were outlying villages swallowed up by the expanding metropolis. Note that the Monestir de Pedralbes closes at 2, so it's a good place to start the day.

TOP ATTRACTIONS

2 **Casa Vicens.** Gaudí's first important commission as a young architect was built between 1883 and 1885, at which time he had not yet thrown away his architect's tools, particularly the T-square. The historical eclecticism of the early Art Nouveau movement is evident in the Orientalist themes and Mudejar details lavished on the facade. The house was commissioned by a ceramics merchant, which may explain the eye-catching colored ceramic tiles that render most of the facade a striking checkerboard—Barcelona's first example of this now-omnipresent technique. The palm leaves on the gate and surrounding fence have been attributed to Gaudí's assistant Francesc Berenguer, and the comic iron lizards and bats oozing off the facade are Gaudí's playful nod to the Gothic gargoyle. ✉ *Carrer de les Carolines 24–26, Gràcia* Ⓜ *Gràcia, Fontana.*

3 **Gràcia.** Gràcia isn't just a neighborhood; it's a state of mind, a virtual village republic that has periodically risen in rebellion against city, state, and country. The street names (Llibertat, Fraternitat, Progrès, Venus) reveal the ideological history of this nucleus of working-class sentiment. Barcelona's first collectivized manufacturing operations (i.e., factories) were clustered here—a dangerous precedent, as workers organized into radical groups ranging from anarchists to feminists to Esperantists. Once an outlying town, Gràcia joined Barcelona only under duress and attempted to secede from the Spanish state in 1856, 1870, 1873, and 1909. Lying above the Diagonal from Carrer de Córsega up to Park Güell, this jumble of streets is filled with appealing bars and restaurants, movie theaters, and outdoor cafés, usually thronged with hip couples. The August Festa Major fills the streets with the rank-and-file residents of this lively yet intimate little pocket of resistance to Organized Life.

1 **Monestir de Pedralbes.** One of Barcelona's hidden treasures, this convent was founded by Reina Elisenda, widow of Catalonia's Sovereign Count Jaume II, for Clarist nuns in 1326. The Gothic cloister is the finest in Barcelona. The abess's day cell, the Capella de Sant Miquel, has murals painted in 1346 by Ferrer Bassa, a Catalan master much influenced by the Italian Renaissance. Scratched into the painting, on the right side between Sts. Francis and Clare, you can make out what is widely considered Barcelona's earliest graffito: *Joan no m'oblides* (John, don't forget me), proof that not all of the novitiates were there by choice. You can also visit the medieval living quarters and kitchen. Look for the ruts broken into the arcaded walkways by Napoleonic cannon during the 1809 French occupation. The museum shows religious paintings and artifacts collected over the centuries. ✉ *Baixada Monestir 9, Pedralbes* ☎ *93/203–9282* 🌐 *www.museuhistoria.bcn.es* 🎫 *€5.50; free 1st Sun. of month. Ticket also includes admission to Museu Històrica de la Ciutat, Centre d'Interpretació del Park Güell, Centre d'Interpretació del Call, Centre d'Interpretació Històrica, Refugi 307, and Museu-Casa Verdaguer* ⏲ *Oct.–May, Tues.–Sun. 10–2; June–Sept., Tues.–Sun. 10–5* Ⓜ *Reina Elisenda.*

Fodor's Choice ★

4 **Park Güell.** Güell Park is one of Gaudí's, and Barcelona's, most pleasant and visually stimulating places to spend a few hours; it's light and playful, alternately shady, green, floral, and sunny. Named for and

Fodor's Choice ★

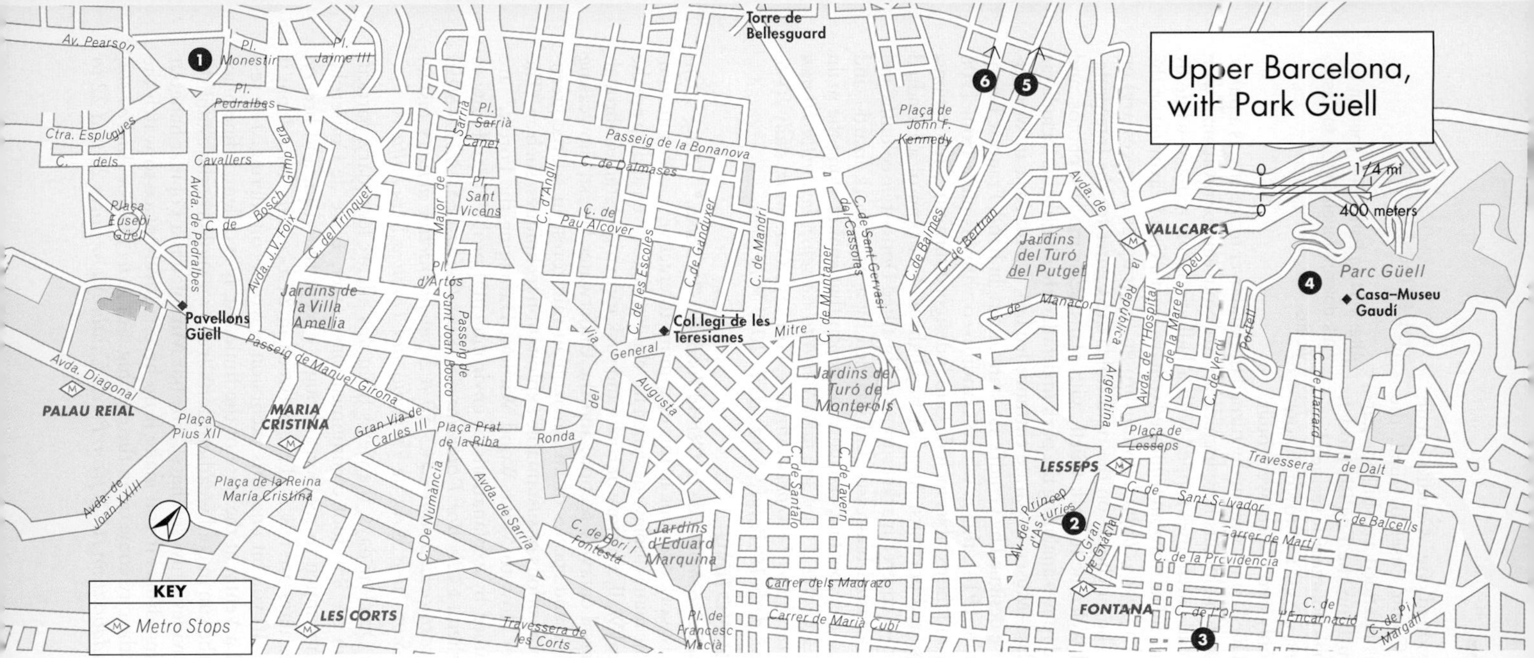

Casa Vicens 2
Gràcia 3
Monestir de Pedralbes 1
Park Güell 4
Tibidabo 6
Torre de Collserola 5

commissioned by Gaudí's main patron, Count Eusebio Güell, the park was intended as a hillside garden suburb on the English model. Barcelona's bourgeoisie seemed happier living closer to "town," however, so only two houses were built, and the Güell family eventually turned the land over to the city as a public park. Gaudí highlights here include an Art Nouveau extravaganza with gingerbread gatehouses topped with a hallucinogenic red-and-white fly Amanita wild mushroom (rumored to have been a Gaudí favorite) on the right and a *phallus impudicus* mushroom (no translation necessary) on the left. The gatehouse on the right holds the **Center for the Interpretation and Welcome to Park Güell,** with plans, scale models, photos, and suggested routes analyzing the park in detail. Other highlights include the **Gaudí Casa–Museu** (separate entrance fee €4), a pink Alice in Wonderland house designed by Gaudí's assistant and right hand, Francesc Berenguer (1866–1914); this is where Gaudí lived with his niece from 1906 to 1926, and the exhibits include Gaudí-designed furniture, decorations, drawings, and portraits. Another highlight is the Room of a Hundred Columns—a covered market supported by tilted Doric-style columns and mosaic-encrusted buttresses and guarded by a patchwork lizard—and the fabulous serpentine, polychrome bench that snakes along the main square. ✉ *Carrer d'Olot s/n; take Metro to Lesseps; then walk 10 min uphill or catch Bus 24 to park entrance, Gràcia* ⏲ *Oct.–Mar., daily 10–6; Apr.–June, daily 10–7; July–Sept., daily 10–9* Ⓜ *Lesseps.*

> **TOURING TIP**
>
> After visiting Park Güell, you can walk down through Gràcia to Casa Vicens.

WORTH NOTING

OFF THE BEATEN PATH

CosmoCaixa–Museu de la Ciència Fundació "La Caixa." Young scientific minds work overtime in this ever-more-interactive science museum. Among the many displays designed for children ages seven and up are the Geological Wall, a history of rocks and rock formations studied through a transversal cutaway section, and the Underwater Forest, showcasing the climate and species of an Amazonian rain forest in a large greenhouse. Expositions of sustainable exploitation techniques, such as "The Red Line: How to Make Wood Without Damaging the Forest," are accompanied by explanations of environmental problems and how to correct them. ✉ *Teodor Roviralta 55, Sant Gervasi* ☎ *93/212–6050* 🌐 *www.cosmocaixa.com* 🎟 *€3.50 (€2 per interactive activity inside)* ⏲ *Tues.–Sun. 10–8* Ⓜ *Av. de Tibidabo and Tramvía Blau halfway.*

6 **Tibidabo.** On clear days, the views from this hill are legendary, particularly from the 850-foot communications tower, Torre de Collserola. There's not much to see here, though, except the vista, and breezy, smog-free days are few and far between in 21st-century Barcelona; if (and only if) you hit one, this excursion is worth considering. The restaurant **La Venta,** at the base of the funicular, is excellent, a fine place to sit in the sun in cool weather (don't fret over sunburn; the establishment provides straw sun hats). The bar **Mirablau** is a popular hangout for evening drinks if you make it up here, a lovely place to watch the lights of the city come on in the evening. ✉ *Pl. del Doctor Andreu s/n; take Tibidabo train (U-7) from Pl. de Catalunya or buses 24 and 22 to*

DID YOU KNOW?

Park Güell was originally built to be a private garden community. One of the houses built here became Gaudí's residence from 1906 to 1926.

Pl. Kennedy. At Av. Tibidabo, catch Tramvía Blau (Blue Trolley), which connects with funicular to summit Ⓜ *Tibidabo.*

5 **Torre de Collserola.** Created by Norman Foster, the Collserola Tower was erected for the 1992 Olympics amid controversy over defacement of the traditional mountain skyline. An immense communications mast with a cylindrical midsection housing an observation deck, it's now considered the best piece of contemporary architecture in the city's upper reaches. ✉ *Av. de Vallvidrera, Tibidabo* ✥ *Take funicular up to Tibidabo; from Pl. Tibidabo there is free transport to tower* ☎ *93/211–7942* 🌐 *www.torredecollserola.com* 🎫 *€5.50* ⏲ *Wed.–Fri. 11–2:30 and 3:30–6, weekends 11–6* Ⓜ *Tibidabo.*

MONTJUÏC

This far-flung, leafy park on a hill to the south of town requires some hiking between sights and lacks the intensity and color of Barcelona street life, but the art is world class. Named for the Roman god Jove, or Jupiter, Montjuïc is best reached by taxi, by Bus 61, on foot from Plaça Espanya, or by the funicular that operates from the Paral.lel. The cross-harbor cable car from Barceloneta or from the Jaume I midstation in the port is another, spectacular, approach (acrophobes, be warned).

Walking from sight to sight on Montjuïc is possible but not recommended. You'll want fresh feet to see the sights here, especially the vast art displays in the Palau Nacional and the Miró Foundation. Ⓜ *Paral.lel.*

TOP ATTRACTIONS

6 **Fundació Miró.** The Miró Foundation was a gift from the artist Joan Miró to his native city and is one of Barcelona's most exciting showcases of contemporary art. The airy white building was designed by Josep Lluís Sert and opened in 1975; an extension was added by Sert's pupil Jaume Freixa in 1988. Miró's unmistakably playful and colorful style, filled with Mediterranean light and humor, seems a perfect contrast with its minimalist surroundings. Exhibits and retrospectives here tend to be progressive and provocative. Look for Alexander Calder's mercury fountain. Miró himself rests in the cemetery on Montjuïc's southern slopes. During the Franco regime, which he strongly opposed, Miró first lived in self-imposed exile in Paris then moved to Majorca in 1956. When he died in 1983, the Catalans gave him a send-off amounting to a state funeral. ✉ *Av. Miramar 71, Montjuïc* ☎ *93/443–9470* 🌐 *www.bcn.fjmiro.es* 🎫 *€8.50* ⏲ *Tues., Wed., Fri., and Sat. 10–7, Thurs. 10–9:30, Sun. 10–2:30.*

Fodor's Choice ★

3 **Mies van der Rohe Pavilion.** The reconstructed Mies van der Rohe Pavilion (the German contribution to the International Exposition of 1929) is a "less is more" study in interlocking planes of white marble, green onyx, and glass, the aesthetic opposite of the Moderniste Palau de la Música. ✉ *Av. Marquès de Comillas s/n, Montjuïc* ☎ *93/423–4016* 🌐 *www.miesbcn.com* 🎫 *€4.50* ⏲ *Daily 10–8.*

4 **Museu Nacional d'Art de Catalunya** *(MNAC, Catalonian National Museum of Art)*. Housed in the imposingly domed, towered, frescoed, and columned **Palau Nacional,** built in 1929 as the centerpiece of the World's

Fodor's Choice ★

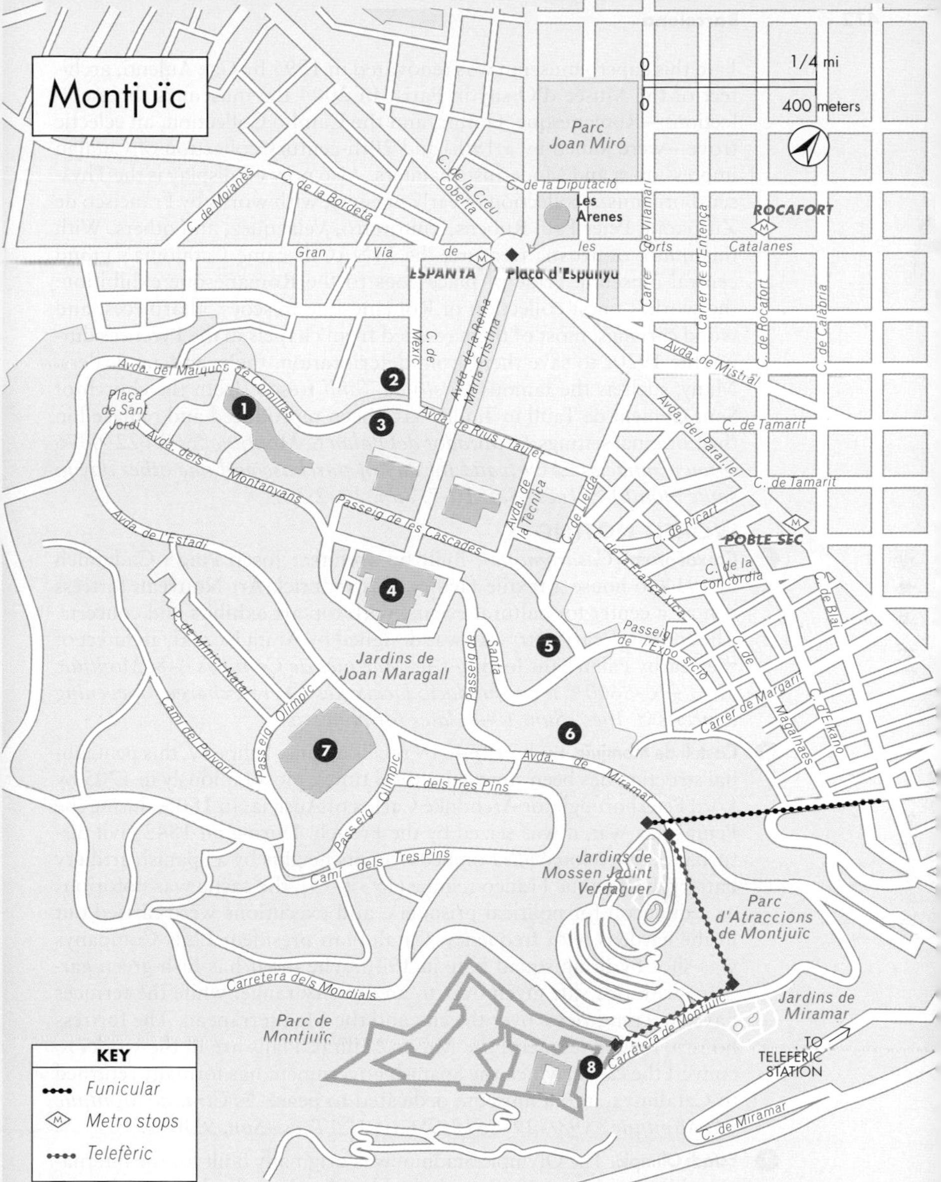

CaixaForum (Casaramona) **2**

Castell de Montjuïc **8**

Estadi Olímpic **7**

Fundació Miró **6**

Mies van der Rohe Pavilion **3**

Museu d'Arqueologia de Catalunya **5**

Museu Nacional d'Art de Catalunya **4**

Poble Espanyol **1**

Fair, this superb museum was renovated in 1995 by Gae Aulenti, architect of the Musée d'Orsay in Paris. In 2004 the museum's three collections—Romanesque, Gothic, and the Cambó Collection, an eclectic trove—were joined by a 19th- and 20th-century collection of Catalan impressionist and Moderniste painters. Also now on display is the Thyssen-Bornemisza collection of early masters, with works by Francisco de Zurbarán, Peter Paul Rubens, Tintoretto, Velázquez, and others. With this influx of artistic treasure, the MNAC became Catalonia's grand central museum. Pride of place goes to the Romanesque exhibition: the world's finest collection of Romanesque frescoes, altarpieces, and wood carvings, most of them rescued from chapels in the Pyrenees during the 1920s to save them from deterioration, theft, and art dealers. Many, such as the famous *Cristo de Taüll* fresco (from the church of Sant Climent de Taüll in Taüll), have been reproduced and replaced in their original settings. ✉ *Mirador del Palau 6, Montjuïc* ☎ *93/622–0376* 🌐 *www.mnac.es* 🎫 *€9 (valid for day of purchase and one other day in same month)* ⏲ *Tues.–Sat. 10–7, Sun. 10–2:30.*

WORTH NOTING

2 **CaixaForum** *(Casaramona)*. Built by architect Josep Puig i Cadafalch in 1911 to house a textile factory, this redbrick Art Nouveau fortress is now a center for cultural events, with top art exhibits and concerts. The contemporary entryway was designed by Arata Isozaki, architect of the nearby Palau Sant Jordi. ✉ *Av. Marquès de Comillas 6–8, Montjuïc* ☎ *93/476–8600* 🌐 *www.fundacio.lacaixa.es* 🎫 *Free; charge for evening concerts* ⏲ *Tues.–Sun. 10–8; later for concerts.*

8 **Castell de Montjuïc.** Built in 1640 by rebels against Felipe IV, this pentagonal structure has been stormed several times, most famously in 1705 by Lord Peterborough for Archduke Carlos of Austria. In 1808, during the Peninsular War, it was seized by the French. During an 1842 civil disturbance, Barcelona was bombed from its heights by a Spanish artillery battery. During the Franco regime (1939–75), the castle was notorious as a dungeon for political prisoners, and executions were carried out in the gardens with frequency. Catalonian president Lluís Companys was shot by firing squad here in 1940. The moat has lush green gardens, with one side given over to an archery range, while the terraces have sweeping views over the city and the Mediterranean. The fortress houses, for the moment, the Museu Militar. Plans are in the works to convert the castle, which the Spanish government has formally returned to Catalunya, into a museum dedicated to peace. ✉ *Ctra. de Montjuïc 66, Montjuïc* ☎ *93/329–8613* 🎫 *€3.50* ⏲ *Tues.–Sun. 9:30–8.*

7 **Estadi Olímpic.** The Olympic Stadium was originally built for the International Exposition of 1929, with the idea that Barcelona would then be the site of the 1936 Olympics (ultimately staged in Hitler's Berlin). After failing twice, Barcelona celebrated the attainment of its long-cherished goal by renovating the semiderelict stadium in time for 1992, providing seating for 70,000. The **Galeria Olímpica,** a museum about the Olympic movement in Barcelona, displays objects and shows replays from the 1992 games. An information center traces the history of the modern Olympics from Athens in 1896 to the present. ✉ *Passeig Olímpic*

Architect Arata Isozaki designed the futuristic Palau Sant Jordi Sports Palace.

17–19, Montjuïc ☎ 93/426–0660 🌐 www.fundaciobarcelonaolimpica.es 🎫 Gallery €4.50 ⏲ Tues.–Sat. 10–2 and 4–7.*

❺ **Museu d'Arqueologia de Catalunya.** Just downhill to the right of the Palau Nacional, the Museum of Archaeology holds important finds from the Greek ruins at Empúries, on the Costa Brava shown alongside fascinating objects from and explanations of Megalithic Spain. ✉ *Passeig Santa Madrona 39–41, Montjuïc* ☎ *93/424–6577* 🌐 *www.mac.es* 🎫 *€3.50* ⏲ *Tues.–Sat. 9:30–7, Sun. 10–2:30.*

❶ **Poble Espanyol.** The Spanish Village was created for the International Exposition of 1929. A sort of artificial Spain-in-a-bottle, with reproductions of the country's architectural styles, it takes you from the walls of Ávila to the wine cellars of Jerez de la Frontera with shops, houses, and crafts workshops en route. The liveliest time to come is at night, and a reservation at one of the half dozen restaurants gets you in free, as does the purchase of a ticket for either of the two discos or the Tablao del Carmen flamenco club. ✉ *Av. Marquès de Comillas s/n* ☎ *93/508–6300* 🌐 *www.poble-espanyol.com* 🎫 *€8* ⏲ *Mon. 9 AM–8 PM, Tues.–Thurs. 9 AM–2 AM, Fri. 9 AM–4 AM, Sat. 9 AM–5 AM, Sun. 9 AM–midnight.*

BARS AND CAFÉS

Use the coordinate (⊕ B2) at the end of each listing to locate a site on the corresponding map.

Barcelona may have more bars and cafés per capita than any other place in the world, from colorful *tapas* spots to sunny outdoor cafés, tearooms, chocolaterias, *cocteleríás* (cocktail bars), *whiskerias* (often singles bars filled with professional escorts), *xampanyerias* (serving champagne and cava), and beer halls. Most cafés are open long hours, roughly 9 AM to 2 AM; bars from about noon to 2 AM.

CAFÉS

BARRI GÒTIC

¢–$ CAFÉ **Els Quatre Gats.** Picasso staged his first exhibition here, in 1899, and Gaudí and the Catalan impressionist painters Ramón Casas and Santiago Russinyol held meetings of their Centre Artistic de Sant Lluc here in the early 20th century. The restaurant is undistinguished, but the café is a good place to read and people-watch. ✉ *Montsió 3, Barri Gòtic* ☎ *93/302–4140* ⏲ *Daily 8 AM–1 AM* Ⓜ *Catalunya* ✣ *D4.*

¢–$ CAFÉ **Schilling.** Near Plaça Reial, the hip Schilling is always packed. Have coffee by day, drinks and tapas by night. ✉ *Ferran 23, Barri Gòtic* ☎ *93/317–6787* ⏲ *Daily 10 AM–2 AM* Ⓜ *Liceu* ✣ *D5.*

BORN-RIBERA

¢–$ CAFÉ **Café de la Princesa.** Behind Carrer Montcada and the Picasso Museum, this little boutique, restaurant, and café is a unique space dedicated to design, crafts, books, and wine and food tastings. ✉ *Flassaders 21, Born-Ribera* ☎ *93/268–2181* ⏲ *Daily 9 AM–2 PM and 4:30 PM–8 PM* Ⓜ *Jaume I* ✣ *E5.*

EIXAMPLE

¢–$ CAFÉ **Café Paris.** This is a lively place where everyone from Prince Felipe, heir to the Spanish throne, to poet/pundit James Townsend Pi Sunyer has been spotted. The tapas are excellent, and the beer is cold. ✉ *Carrer Aribau 184, at Carrer Paris, Eixample* ☎ *93/209–8530* ⏲ *Daily 6 AM–2 AM* Ⓜ *Provença* ✣ *C1.*

¢–$ CAFÉ **La Bodegueta.** If you can locate this dive (it's two steps below sidewalk level), you'll find a dozen small tables, a few spots at the marble counter, and happy people drinking coffee or beer, usually accompanied by the establishment's excellent *pa amb tomàquet* (toasted bread with squeezed tomato, olive oil, and either Manchego cheese or Iberian cured ham). ✉ *Rambla de Catalunya 100, Eixample* ☎ *93/215–4894* ⏲ *Daily 8 AM–2 AM* Ⓜ *Provença* ✣ *D2.*

RAMBLA

¢–$ CAFÉ **Café de l'Opera.** Opposite the opera house, this high-ceilinged Art Nouveau space has welcomed operagoers and performers for more than 100 years. ✉ *Rambla 74, Rambla* ☎ *93/317–7585* ⏲ *Daily 9:30 AM–2:15 AM* Ⓜ *Liceu* ✣ *D5.*

¢–$ CAFÉ **Café Viena.** This little classic is always packed with locals and international travelers enjoying what Mark Bittman of *the New York Times* has consecrated as "the best sandwich in the world." The *flautas de jamón ibérico* (thin bread "flutes" of Ibérico ham anointed with tomato) may not be made with the absolute top level of acorn-fed ham, but they're close enough for a high pass and, at less than €7, a great value accompanied by an icy *caña* (draft beer). ✉ *Rambla dels Estudis 115, Rambla* ☎ *93/317–1492* ⏲ *Daily 9 AM–2 AM* Ⓜ *Catalunya* ✣ *D4.*

¢–$ CAFÉ **Café Zurich.** This classic spot at the top of the Rambla is the city's prime meeting point. The outdoor tables offer peerless people-watching, and the interior is high-ceilinged and elegant. ✉ *Pl. Catalunya 1, Rambla* ☎ *93/317–9153* ⏲ *Daily 9* AM*–2* AM Ⓜ *Catalunya* ✥ *D4.*

TAPAS BARS

Because of Catalonia's distinct social mores, *tapas* were not, historically, an important part of Barcelona life. Today, however, astute Catalan and Basque chefs are busy transforming the city into an emerging *tapas* capital (until now, San Sebastian, Sevilla, Cadiz, or perhaps Madrid led the *tapas* charge). Especially around Santa Maria del Mar and the Passeig del Born area, nomadic wine tippling and *tapas* tasting are proliferating. For the most part, beware of *tapas* bars along Passeig de Gràcia, where the offerings are usually microwaved and far from Barcelona's best. Many *tapas* bars are open from early in the morning until late at night.

BARCELONETA

¢–$$ TAPAS ✗ **El Vaso de Oro.** A favorite with food lovers from Barcelona and beyond, this often overcrowded little counter serves some of the best beer and tapas in town. Avoid peak local lunch and dinner hours (2–4 PM and 9–11 PM) for better luck finding space at the bar. ✉ *Balboa 6, Barceloneta* ☎ *93/319–3098* ⏲ *Daily 9* AM*–midnight* Ⓜ *Barceloneta* ✥ *E6.*

BARRI GÒTIC

¢–$ TAPAS ✗ **El Irati.** The only drawback to this lively Basque bar is that it's harder to squeeze into than the Barcelona metro at rush hour, so come early-ish, at 1 PM or 7:30 PM. Skip the tapas on the bar and opt for the plates brought out piping hot from the kitchen; accompany them with cold, refreshing *txakolí*, a Basque white wine. The restaurant in back is excellent. ✉ *Cardenal Casañas 17, Barri Gòtic* ☎ *93/302–3084* ⏲ *Tues.–Sat. noon–midnight, Sun. noon–4* Ⓜ *Liceu* ✥ *D4.*

BORN-RIBERA

¢–$ TAPAS Fodor's Choice ★ ✗ **Cal Pep.** A two-minute walk east from Santa Maria del Mar toward the Estació de França, Pep has some of Barcelona's best and freshest selections of tapas, cooked and served piping hot in a boisterous space. The house wines are good, but the Torre la Moreira Albariño white perfectly complements Pep's offerings. ✉ *Pl. de les Olles 8, Born-Ribera* ☎ *93/319–6183* ⏲ *Tues.–Sat. 1–4 and 8–11, Mon. 8–11* Ⓜ *Jaume I* ✥ *E5.*

¢–$ TAPAS ✗ **El Xampanyet.** Hanging *botas* (leather wineskins) mark this lively *xampanyeria* (champagne bar), just down the street from the Picasso Museum. Avoid the oversweet house sparkling wine (it's not cava), and pick draft beer or wine. Indulge in *pa amb tomàquet* (toasted bread with squeezed tomato and olive oil) served on marble-top tables near walls decorated with azulejos (glazed tiles). ✉ *Montcada 22, Born-Ribera* ☎ *93/319–7003* ⏲ *Tues.–Sat. noon–4 and 6:30–midnight, Sun. noon–4* Ⓜ *Jaume I* ✥ *E5.*

¢–$ TAPAS ✗ **Sagardi.** This attractive wood-and-stone cider-house replica comes close to re-creating its Basque prototype with its ersatz cider barrel shooting frothy blasts into wide-mouthed glasses. The hot tapas from the kitchen are much better than the overly breaded morsels on display. The restaurant in the back cooks first-rate *txuletas de buey* (beefsteaks)

7

Café Zurich has been a popular meeting spot for locals since the 1920s.

over coals. ✉ *Carrer Argenteria 62, Born-Ribera* ☎ *93/319–9993* ⏲ *Daily 1:30–3:30 and 8–midnight* Ⓜ *Jaume I* ✥ *E5.*

EIXAMPLE

$–$$$ TAPAS ✕ **Casa Lucio.** This small but expensive dazzler just two blocks south of the Mercat de Sant Antoni is worth tracking down for its original and delicious tapas. ✉ *Viladomat 59, Eixample* ☎ *93/424–4401* ⏲ *Mon.–Sat. 1–4 and 8–11* Ⓜ *Sant Antoni* ✥ *B4.*

¢–$$ TAPAS ✕ **Ciudad Condal.** At the bottom of Ramba Catalunya, this place with a long wooden bar covered with *tapas* is always filled with a throng of hungry, mostly international, clients. A good late-night or postconcert solution, there's usually room to squeeze in at the bar, though reservations à table provide more seclusion and space. ✉ *Rambla de Catalunya 18, Eixample* ☎ *93/318–1997* ⏲ *Daily 7:30 AM–1:30 AM* Ⓜ *Passeig de Gràcia* ✥ *D3.*

¢–$$ TAPAS ★ ✕ **Inòpia Clàssic Bar.** Albert Adrià, younger brother of famous chef Ferran Adrià, opened this tapas bar near the Mercat de Sant Antoni, which has uniformly excellent products and preparations. ✉ *Tamarit 104, Eixample* ☎ *93/424–5231* ⏲ *Tues.–Sat. 7:30–11, Sun. 1–4* Ⓜ *Rocafort, Poble Sec* ✥ *A4.*

¢–$$ TAPAS ✕ **Mantequeria Can Ravell.** Lovers of exquisite wine, ham, cheese, cigars, caviar, and any other delicacy you can think of, this is your spot. The backroom table is first-come, first-served, where strangers share tales, tastes, and textures. The upstairs dining room, through the kitchen and up a spiral staircase, serves lunch (and dinner Thursday and Friday) and has a *Through the Looking-Glass* vibe. ✉ *Carrer Aragó 313, Eixample* ☎ *93/457–5114* ⏲ *Mon. 10–7, Tues. and Wed. 10–9, Thurs. and Fri. 10–10, Sat. 10–6* Ⓜ *Passeig de Gràcia* ✥ *E2.*

WORD OF MOUTH

"The food in Barcelona is great, the culture is quite offbeat, and there is a general air of revelry and youth all over town." —nessundorma

¢–$$ TAPAS **Paco Meralgo.** The name, a pun on *para comer algo* (to eat something), may be only marginally amusing, but the tapas here are no joke, and whether à table, at the counter, or in the private dining room upstairs, this glittery space always rocks. ✉ *Carrer Muntaner 171, Eixample* ☎ *93/430–9027* ⏲ *Mon.–Sat. 1–4 and 8–midnight* Ⓜ *Provença* ✣ *C1.*

¢–$$ TAPAS **Tapaç 24.** Carles Abellán has done it again. His irrepressibly creative Comerç 24 has been a hit since the day it opened, and his new *tapas* emporium is headed in the same direction. Abellán shows us how much he admires traditional Catalan and Spanish bar food, from *patatas bravas* (potatoes in hot sauce) to *croquetas de jamón ibérico* (croquettes made of Iberian ham). ✉ *Carrer Diputació 269, Eixample* ☎ *93/488–0977* ⏲ *Mon.–Sat. 8 AM–midnight* Ⓜ *Passeig de Gràcia* ✣ *D3.*

POBLE SEC

¢–$$ TAPAS **Quimet-Quimet.** This tiny foodie haunt lined with wine and whiskey bottles is stuffed with products and people. Come before 1:30 PM or 7:30 PM and you'll generally find a stand-up table. ✉ *Poeta Cabanyés 25, Poble Sec* ☎ *93/442–3142* ⏲ *Weekdays noon–4 and 7–10:30, Sat. noon–4* Ⓜ *Paral.lel* ✣ *B5.*

7

WHERE TO EAT

Barcelona's restaurant scene is an ongoing surprise. Between the cutting-edge of avant-garde culinary experimentation and the cosmopolitan and rustic dishes of traditional Catalan fare, there's a fleet of inventive chefs producing some of Europe's finest Mediterranean cuisine.

MEALTIMES AND RESERVATIONS

Barcelona dines late. Lunch is served 2–4 and dinner 9–11. If you arrive a half hour early, you may score a table but miss the life and fun of the place. Restaurants serving continuously 1 PM–1 AM are rarely the best ones (Botafumeiro is an exception). Hunger attacks between meals are easily resolved in the city's numerous cafés and *tapas* bars.

RESERVATIONS

Nearly all of Barcelona's best restaurants require reservations. As the city has grown in popularity, more and more receptionists are perfectly able to take your reservations in English. Your hotel concierge will also be happy to call and reserve you a table.

DEALS AND DISCOUNTS

Menús del día (menus of the day), served only at lunchtime, are good values. In general, beware the advice of hotel concierges and taxi drivers, who have been known to warn that the place you are going is either closed or no good anymore and to recommend places where they get kickbacks.

BEST BETS FOR BARCELONA DINING

Need a cheat sheet for Barcelona's thousands of restaurants? Fodor's writers have selected some of their favorites by price, cuisine, and experience. You can also search by neighborhood, and find specific details about a restaurant in our full reviews. *¡Bon profit!* (That's Catalan for "good eating!")

Fodor's Choice ★

Botafumeiro, $$$$, p. 489
Ca l'Isidre, $$$, p. 483
*Cal Pep, ¢, p. 475
Can Fabes, $$$, p. 491
Casa Leopoldo, $$$, p. 483
Cinc Sentits, $$, p. 486
Comerç 24, $$$, p. 482
Drolma, $$$$, p. 486
Manairó, $$$, p. 488
Silvestre, $, p. 490
Tram-Tram, $$$, p. 491

By Price

¢

*Cal Pep, p. 475

$

Can Manel la Puda, p. 484
Folquer, p. 489
Silvestre, p. 490

$$

Café de l'Acadèmia, p. 479
Can Majó, p. 484
Cinc Sentits, p. 486
Cometacinc, p. 479
La Taxidermista, p. 482
Suquet de l'Almirall, p. 484
Vivanda, p. 491

$$$

Ca l'Isidre, p. 483
Can Fabes, p. 491
Comerç 24, p. 482
Manairó, p. 488
Tram-Tram, p. 491

$$$$

Botafumeiro, p. 489
Can Gaig, p. 485
Drolma, p. 486

By Cuisine

BASQUE

Ipar-Txoko, p. 489

CONTEMPORARY CATALAN

L'Olivé, p. 487

LA NUEVA COCINA/ EXPERIMENTAL CUISINE

Alkimia, p. 485
Cinc Sentits, p. 486
Comerç 24, p. 482
Manairó, p. 488

MEDITERRANEAN

Ca l'Isidre, p. 483
Can Gaig, p. 485
Cinc Sentits, p. 486

PAELLA

Barceloneta, p. 483
Can Majó, p. 484
Suquet de l'Almirall, p. 484

SEAFOOD

Antiga Casa Solé, p. 483
Botafumeiro, p. 489
El Lobito, p. 484

TAPAS

*Cal Pep, p. 475
*Casa Lucio, p. 476
*El Vaso de Oro, p. 475
*Inòpia Clàssic Bar, p. 476
*Mantequeria Can Ravell, p. 476
*Sagardi, p. 475
*Tapaç 24, p. 477

TRADITIONAL CATALAN

Antiga Casa Solé, p. 483
Ca l'Isidre, p. 483
Can Gaig, p. 485
Casa Leopoldo, p. 483
Drolma, p. 486
Tram-Tram, p. 491

By Experience

BEST BANG FOR YOUR BUCK

Barceloneta, p. 483
*Cal Pep, p. 475
Silvestre, p. 490
Vivanda, p. 491

GREAT VIEW

Dos Cielos, p. 486
Torre d'Altamar, p. 485

YOUNG AND HAPPENING

Cinc Sentits, p. 486
Comerç 24, p. 482
Manairó, p. 488
Nonell, p. 479

Tapas bars and cafés are marked with *, see previous section of chapter.

RESTAURANT REVIEWS

Listed alphabetically within neighborhoods.

Use the coordinate (⊕ B2) at the end of each listing to locate a site on the corresponding map.

CIUTAT VELLA (OLD CITY): BARRI GÒTIC, BORN-RIBERA, RAMBLA, AND RAVAL

Chic new restaurants and cafés seem to open daily in the old city.

BARRI GÒTIC

$$ CATALAN

✕ **Café de l'Acadèmia.** With wicker chairs, stone walls, and background classical music, this place is sophisticated-rustic, and the excellent contemporary Mediterranean cuisine specialties such as *timbal d'escalibada amb formatge de cabra* (roast vegetable salad with goat cheese) and *crema de pastanaga amb gambes i virutes de parmesá* (cream of carrot soup with shrimp and Parmesan cheese shavings) make it more than a mere café. Politicians and functionaries from the nearby Generalitat frequent this dining room, which is always lively. Be sure to reserve at lunchtime. ✉ *Lledó 1, Barri Gòtic* ☎ *93/319–8253* ▭ *AE, DC, MC, V* Ⓜ *Jaume I* ⊕ *D5.*

$$ CATALAN

✕ **Cometacinc.** This stylish place in the Barri Gòtic, an increasingly chic neighborhood of artisans and antiquers, is a fine example of Barcelona's new-over-old architecture and interior design panache. The 30-foot floor-to-ceiling wooden shutters are a visual feast, and the carefully prepared interpretations of old standards such as the *carpaccio de toro de lidia* (bull carpaccio) with basil sauce and pine nuts awaken the palate brilliantly. The separate dining room, for anywhere from a dozen to two dozen diners, is a perfect place for a private party. ✉ *Carrer Cometa 5, Barri Gòtic* ☎ *93/310–1558* ▭ *AE, DC, MC, V* ⊗ *Closed Tues.* Ⓜ *Jaume I* ⊕ *D5.*

$$–$$$ ECLECTIC

✕ **Cuines Santa Caterina.** A lovingly restored market designed by the late Enric Miralles and completed by his widow Benedetta Tagliabue provides a spectacular setting for one of the city's most original dining operations. Under the undulating wooden superstructure of the market, the breakfast and tapas bar, open from dawn to midnight, offers a variety of culinary specialties cross-referenced by culture (Mediterranean, Asian) and product (pasta, rice, fish, meat), all served on sleek counters and long wooden tables. ✉ *Av. Francesc Cambó, Barri Gòtic* ☎ *93/268–9918* ▭ *AE, DC, MC, V* Ⓜ *Catalunya, Liceu, Jaume I* ⊕ *E4.*

$$–$$$ ECLECTIC

✕ **Nonell.** With cosmopolitan cuisine and the polished and polyglot service to go with it, this relatively recent addition to the city's gastronomic scene is succeeding well. Dishes range from classic Mediterranean to Castilian roast suckling pig to Middle Eastern creams and sauces. The wine list is largely original, featuring labels you may never have heard of but will be glad to get to know; service is impeccable and often delivered in perfect English. ✉ *Pl. Isidre Nonell, Barri Gòtic* ☎ *93/301–1378* ▭ *AE, DC, MC, V* Ⓜ *Catalunya, Liceu* ⊕ *D4.*

$$ JAPANESE

✕ **Shunka.** Widely regarded as Barcelona's finest Japanese restaurant, this cozy hideaway behind the Hotel Colón serves straight across the

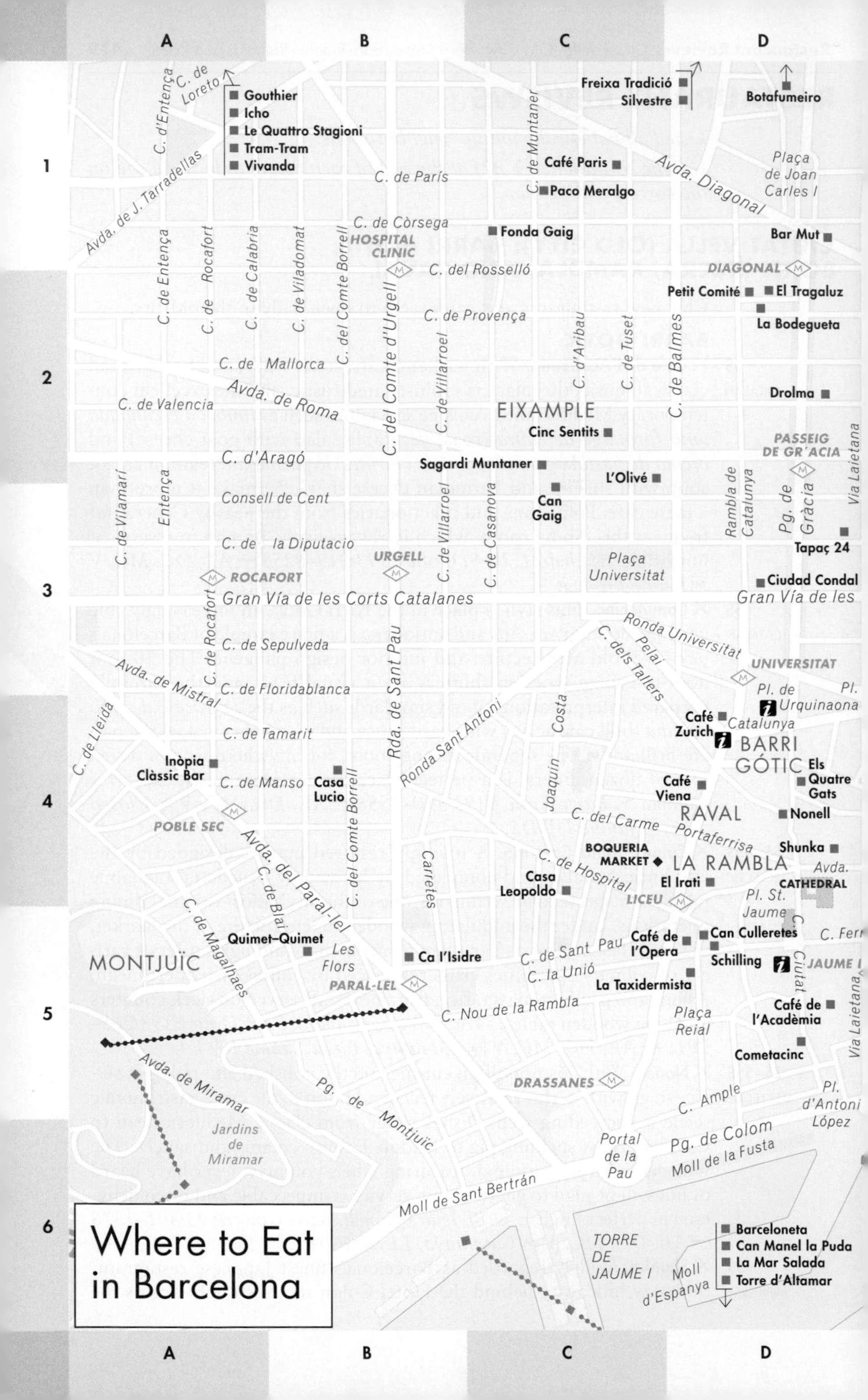

Where to Eat in Barcelona

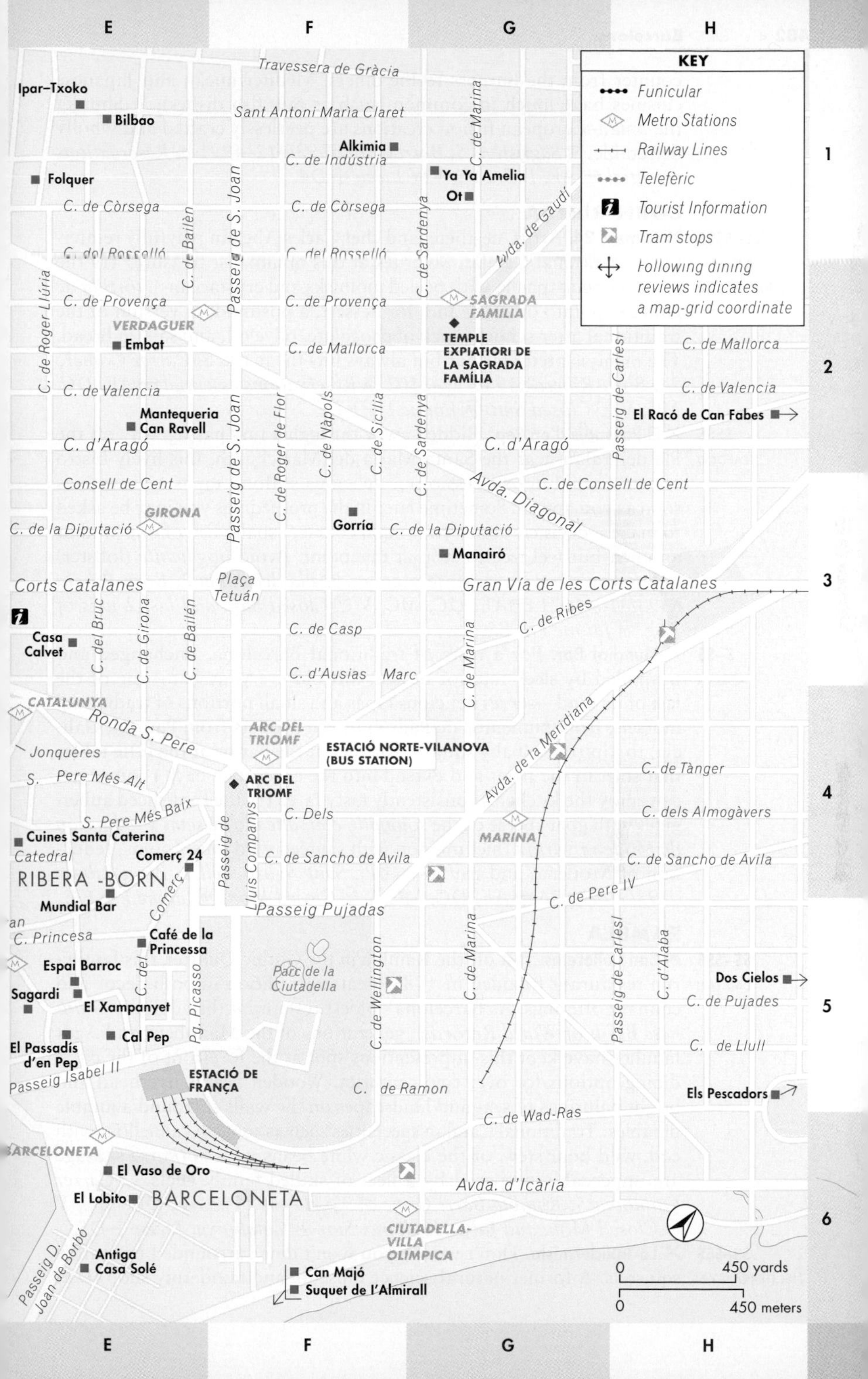
E
F
G
H
1
2
3
4
5
6
KEY
Funicular
Metro Stations
Railway Lines
Teleféric
Tourist Information
Tram stops
Following dining reviews indicates a map-grid coordinate
Travessera de Gràcia
Sant Antoni Maria Claret
C. de Indústria
C. de Còrsega
C. del Rosselló
C. de Provença
C. de Mallorca
C. de Valencia
C. d'Aragó
Consell de Cent
C. de Consell de Cent
C. de la Diputació
Corts Catalanes
Gran Vía de les Corts Catalanes
Avda. Diagonal
Avda. de Gaudí
C. de Roger Llúria
C. de Bailèn
Passeig de S. Joan
C. de Roger de Flor
C. de Nàpols
C. de Sicília
C. de Sardenya
C. de Marina
Passeig de Carlesl
Ipar–Txoko
Bilbao
Folquer
Alkimia
Ya Ya Amelia
Ot
VERDAGUER
Embat
SAGRADA FAMILIA
TEMPLE EXPIATIORI DE LA SAGRADA FAMÍLIA
Mantequeria Can Ravell
El Racó de Can Fabes
GIRONA
Gorría
Manairó
Plaça Tetuán
C. de Ribes
C. de Casp
C. d'Ausias Marc
C. del Bruc
C. de Girona
Casa Calvet
CATALUNYA
Ronda S. Pere
Jonqueres
S. Pere Més Alt
S. Pere Més Baix
ARC DEL TRIOMF
ESTACIÓ NORTE-VILANOVA (BUS STATION)
Avda. de la Meridiana
C. de Tànger
C. dels Almogàvers
C. Dels
MARINA
C. de Sancho de Avila
C. de Pere IV
Cuines Santa Caterina
Catedral
Comerç 24
RIBERA -BORN
Passeig de Lluís Companys
Mundial Bar
Passeig Pujadas
C. Princesa
Café de la Princessa
Espai Barroc
Sagardi
El Xampanyet
C. del Comerç
Pg. Picasso
Parc de la Ciutadella
C. de Wellington
C. d'Alaba
Dos Cielos
C. de Pujades
C. de Llull
El Passadís d'en Pep
Cal Pep
Passeig Isabel II
ESTACIÓ DE FRANÇA
C. de Ramon
C. de Wad-Ras
Els Pescadors
BARCELONETA
El Vaso de Oro
El Lobito
Avda. d'Icària
CIUTADELLA-VILLA OLIMPICA
Antiga Casa Solé
Passeig D. Joan de Borbó
Can Majó
Suquet de l'Almirall
0
450 yards
0
450 meters

counter from the burners to the diners. Mediterranean and Japanese cuisines have much in common (such as raw fish dishes); at Shunka the Asian–European fusion creations are peerlessly crafted and wholly delectable. ✉ *Sagristans 5, Barri Gòtic* ☎ *93/412–4991* ✍ *Reservations essential* ▭ *AE, DC, MC, V* Ⓜ *Liceu* ✣ *D4.*

BORN-RIBERA

$$$–$$$$ CATALAN Fodor's Choice ★ ✕ **Comerç 24.** Artist, aesthete, and chef Carles Abellán playfully reinterprets traditional Catalan favorites at this minimalist treasure. Try the *arròs a banda* (paella with peeled mollusks and crustaceans), *tortilla de patatas* (potato omelet), and, for dessert, a postmodern version of the traditional after-school snack of chocolate, olive oil, and salt on bread. The menu is pretty far out but always hits the mark. ✉ *Carrer Comerç 24, Born-Ribera* ☎ *93/319–2102* ✍ *Reservations essential* ▭ *AE, DC, MC, V* ⊙ *Closed Sun.* Ⓜ *Jaume I* ✣ *E4.*

$$$$ SEAFOOD ✕ **El Passadís d'en Pep.** Hidden away through a tiny passageway off the Pla del Palau near the Santa Maria del Mar church, this lively bistro serves a rapid-fire succession of delicious seafood tapas and wine as soon as you appear. Sometime later in the proceedings you may be asked to make a decision about your main course, usually fish of one kind or another, but feel free to stop at this point. Avoid *bogavante* (lobster) unless you're on an expense account. ✉ *Pla del Palau 2, Born-Ribera* ☎ *93/310–1021* ▭ *AE, DC, MC, V* ⊙ *Closed Sun. and last 2 wks of Aug.* Ⓜ *Jaume I* ✣ *E5.*

$–$$ CATALAN ✕ **Mundial Bar.** For a taste of traditional Barcelona, unchanged and unspoiled by sleek interior design, this old everyday bar—one of the last of its kind—serves delicious tapas and small portions of traditional morsels, from pimientos de Padrón (green peppers from Padrón, Galicia) to xipirones (baby squid). Whether at the bar or at the little tables that start in the front and extend into the cavernous back rooms, you can enjoy the kitchen's consistently tasty fare. Try the thin-sliced aubergines with goat cheese or the *solomillo con salteado de setas y reducción de Módena y trufa* (filet mignon with sautéed wild mushrooms, reduction of Módena, and truffles). ✉ *Pl. Sant Agustí Vell 1, Born-Ribera* ☎ *93/319–9056* ▭ *AE, DC, MC, V* ⊙ *Closed Mon.* Ⓜ *Jaume I* ✣ *E4.*

RAMBLA

$$–$$$ CATALAN ✕ **Can Culleretes.** Just off the Rambla in the Gothic Quarter, this family-run restaurant founded in 1786 breathes tradition in both decor and culinary offerings. As Barcelona's oldest restaurant (listed in the *Guinness Book of World Records*), generations of the Manubens and Agut families have kept this unpretentious spot at the forefront of the city's dining options for over two centuries. Wooden beams overhead and bright paintings of sea- and landscapes on the walls surround a jumble of tables. Traditional Catalan specialties such as spinach cannelloni with cod, wild boar stew, or the classic white beans with *botifarra* sausage are impeccably prepared by a fleet of skilled family chefs. ✉ *Carrer Quintana 5, Rambla/Barri Gòtic* ☎ *93/317–6485* ▭ *AE, DC, MC, V* ⊙ *Closed Mon. and July. No dinner Sun.* Ⓜ *Catalunya, Liceu* ✣ *D5.*

$$–$$$ MEDITERRANEAN ✕ **La Taxidermista.** Don't worry: you won't dine surrounded by stuffed squirrels. A former natural-science museum and taxidermy shop (Dalí

once purchased 200,000 ants and a stuffed rhinoceros here), this is the only recommendable restaurant in the sunny Plaça Reial. Decorator Beth Gali designed the interior around original beams and steel columns. Delicacies such as *bonito con escalibada y queso de cabra* (white tuna with braised aubergines, peppers, and goat cheese) are served at outside tables best enjoyed in the winter sun. ✉ *Pl. Reial 8, Rambla* ☎ *93/412–4536* ▭ *AE, DC, MC, V* ⊙ *Closed Mon.* Ⓜ *Liceu* ⊕ *D5.*

RAVAL

$$$–$$$$ CATALAN Fodor's Choice ★ **✕ Ca l'Isidre.** A favorite with Barcelona's art mob, this place is shellacked with pictures and engravings, some original, by Dalí and other art stars. Just inside the Raval from Avinguda del Paral.lel, the restaurant relies on fresh produce from the nearby Boqueria for its traditional Catalan cooking. The restaurant's wines are invariably novelties from all over the Iberian Peninsula; ask owner Isidre Gironés's advice and you will get a great wine as well as an enology, geography, and history course delivered with charm, brevity, and wit. The slight French accent in the cuisine is evident in the superb homemade foie gras. Come and go by cab at night; it's not easy to find, and the streets here can be sketchy. ✉ *Les Flors 12, Raval* ☎ *93/441–1139* ✍ *Reservations essential* ▭ *AE, MC, V* ⊙ *Closed Sun., Easter wk., and mid-July–mid-Aug.* Ⓜ *Paral. lel* ⊕ *B5.*

$$$–$$$$ CATALAN Fodor's Choice ★ **✕ Casa Leopoldo.** Hidden in a dark Raval pocket west of the Rambla, this restaurant owned by the Gil family serves fine seafood and Catalan fare. To get here, approach along Carrer Hospital, take a left through the Passatge Bernardí Martorell, and go 50 feet right on Sant Rafael to the Gil front door. Try the *revuelto de ajos tiernos y gambas* (eggs scrambled with young garlic and shrimp) or the famous *cap-i-pota* (stewed head and hoof of pork). Albariños and Priorats are among Rosa Gil's favorite wines. ✉ *Sant Rafael 24, Raval* ☎ *93/441–3014* ▭ *AE, DC, MC, V* ⊙ *Closed Mon. No dinner Sun.* Ⓜ *Liceu* ⊕ *C4.*

BARCELONETA AND THE PORT OLÍMPIC

Barceloneta and the Port Olímpic (Olympic Port) have little in common beyond their seaside location: the former is a traditional fishermen's quarter; the latter is a crazed disco strip with thousand-seat restaurants.

$$$–$$$$ SEAFOOD **✕ Antiga Casa Solé.** Just two blocks from Barceloneta's prettiest square, the charming Plaça de ~~Sant~~ Miquel, this traditional midday Sunday pilgrimage site occupies a typical waterfront house and serves fresh, well-prepared seafood. Whether it's *llenguado a la plancha* (grilled sole) or the exquisite *arròs negre amb sepia en su tinta* (black rice with squid in its own ink), everything here comes loaded with taste. In winter try to get close to the open kitchen for the aromas, sights, sounds, and warmth. ✉ *Sant Carles 4, Barceloneta* ☎ *93/221–5012* ▭ *AE, DC, MC, V* ⊙ *Closed Mon. and last 2 wks of Aug. No dinner Sun.* Ⓜ *Barceloneta* ⊕ *E6.*

$$–$$$ SEAFOOD **✕ Barceloneta.** This enormous riverboat-like building at the end of the yacht marina in Barceloneta is hardly an intimate space where the chef greets every patron. On the other hand, the food is delicious, the service

7

impeccable, and the hundreds of fellow diners make the place feel like a cheerful New Year's Eve celebration. Rice and fish dishes are the house specialty, and the salads are excellent. ✉ *L'Escar 22, Barceloneta* ☎ *93/221–2111* ▭ *AE, MC, V* Ⓜ *Barceloneta* ✢ *D6.*

$$–$$$ SEAFOOD Fodor's Choice ★ ✕ **Can Majó.** At the edge of the beach in Barceloneta, this is one of Barcelona's premier seafood restaurants. House specialties are *caldero de bogavante* (a cross between paella and lobster bouillabaisse) and *suquet* (fish stewed in its own juices), but whatever you choose will be excellent. In summer the terrace overlooking the Mediterranean is the closest you can now come to the Barceloneta *chiringuitos* (shanty restaurants) that used to line the beach here. ✉ *Almirall Aixada 23, Barceloneta* ☎ *93/221–5455* ▭ *AE, DC, MC, V* ⏲ *Closed Mon. No dinner Sun.* Ⓜ *Barceloneta* ✢ *F6.*

$–$$ MEDITERRANEAN ✕ **Can Manel la Puda.** The first choice for paella in the sun, year-round, Can Manel is near the end of the main road out to the Barceloneta beach and closes between 4 and 7. *Arròs a banda* (rice with peeled shellfish) and paella *marinera* (with seafood) or *fideuá* (with noodles) are delicious. The paella, prepared for a minimum of two diners, will easily feed three, or even four if you're planning to dine a few more times that day. ✉ *Passeig Joan de Borbó 60, Barceloneta* ☎ *93/221–5013* ▭ *AE, DC, MC, V* ⏲ *Closed Mon.* Ⓜ *Barceloneta* ✢ *D6.*

$$–$$$ SEAFOOD ✕ **El Lobito.** Although it can get filled to the gills with diners in full feeding frenzy spilling out onto the terrace in summer, the only thing really wrong with this place is that the portions are too big. Fish and seafood flow out of the kitchen, and the uproar tells you everyone's here to have fun. The wine list meets the standards of the pure, excellent seafood. ✉ *Ginebra 9, Barceloneta* ☎ *93/319–9164* ▭ *AE, DC, MC, V* ⏲ *Closed Mon.* Ⓜ *Barceloneta* ✢ *E6.*

$$–$$$ SEAFOOD ✕ **Els Pescadors.** A kilometer northeast of the Olympic Port in the interesting Sant Martí neighborhood, this handsome late-19th-century bistro-style dining room has a lovely terrace on a little square shaded by immense ficus trees. Kids can range freely in the traffic-free square while their parents concentrate on well-prepared seafood specialties such as paella, fresh fish, or *fideuá* (paella made with noodles). ✉ *Pl. de Prim 1, Sant Martí* ☎ *93/225–2018* ▭ *AE, MC, V* ⏲ *Closed Mon.* Ⓜ *Poblenou* ✢ *H5.*

$–$$ SEAFOOD ✕ **La Mar Salada.** A handy alternative next door to the sometimes crowded Can Manel la Puda, this sunny little seafood-and-rice restaurant whips up excellent paella, black rice, *fideuá* (paella made with vermicelli noodles), bouillabaisse, and fresh fish. Order an Albariño white wine from Galicia's Rias Baixas and a mixed salad—you can't do much better for value and quality in Barceloneta. ✉ *Passeig Joan de Borbó 58, Barceloneta* ☎ *93/221–2127* ▭ *AE, MC, V* ⏲ *Closed Tues.* Ⓜ *Barceloneta* ✢ *D6.*

$$–$$$ SEAFOOD ✕ **Suquet de l'Almirall.** With a handy terrace for alfresco dining in summer, "The Admiral's Fish Stew" indeed serves fare fit for the admiralty. Specializing in rice dishes and *caldoso de bogavante,* an abundantly brothy rice dish with lobster, this is one of Barceloneta's best. ✉ *Passeig Joan de Borbó 65, Barceloneta* ☎ *93/221–6233* ▭ *AE, DC, MC, V* ⏲ *Closed Mon. No dinner Sun.* Ⓜ *Barceloneta* ✢ *F6.*

$$$–$$$$ MEDITERRANEAN ✕ **Torre d'Altamar.** Seafood of every stripe, spot, fin, and carapace emanates from the kitchen here, but the filet mignon under a colossal slab of foie is a tour de force. Housed inside the cable-car tower over the far side of the port, this restaurant has spectacular views of Barcelona as well as far out into the Mediterranean. ✉ *Passeig Joan de Borbó 88–Torre de San Sebastián, Barceloneta* ☎ *93/221–0007* ▭ *AE, DC, MC, V* ⊙ *Closed Sun. No lunch Mon.* Ⓜ *Barceloneta* ✥ *D6.*

EIXAMPLE

Eixample dining, invariably upscale and elegant, ranges from traditional cuisine to designer fare in sleek minimalist spaces.

$$$–$$$$ CATALAN ✕ **Alkimia.** Chef Jordi Vilà is making news here with his inventive creations and tasting menus at €44 and €58 that pass for a bargain at the top end of Barcelona culinary culture. It's usually packed, but the alcoves are intimate and the stark decor is parceled out among them. Vilà's deconstructed *pa amb tomàquet* (in classical usage, toasted bread with olive oil and squeezed tomato) in a shot glass gives a witty culinary wink before things get serious with fish options like red mullet with yogurt and pickled cauliflower, or john dory with candied tomato and black olives. A dark-meat course, venison or beef, brings the taste progression to a close before dessert provides more comic relief. Alkimia, as its name suggests, is pure magic. ✉ *Indústria 79, Eixample* ☎ *93/207–6115* ▭ *AE, DC, MC, V* ⊙ *Closed Sat. lunch, Sun., Easter wk, and Aug. 1–21* Ⓜ *Sagrada Família* ✥ *F1.*

$$–$$$ CATALAN ✕ **Bar Mut.** This elegant retro space just above the Diagonal serves first-rate products ranging from wild sea bass to the best Ibérico hams. Crowded, expensive, noisy, chaotic, and delicious, it's everything a great tapas bar or restaurant should be. The name is a play on the word vermut (vermouth), which, not so long ago, was about as close to tapas as Barcelona was apt to get. The wine selections and range of dishes proposed on the chalkboard behind the bar are creative and traditional. Don't let the friendly and casual feel of the place lull you into thinking that la cuenta (the check) will be anything but deadly serious. ✉ *Pau Claris 192, Eixample* ☎ *93/217–4338* ▭ *AE, DC, MC, V* ⊙ *Provença, Diagonal* ✥ *D1.*

$$$$ CATALAN ✕ **Can Gaig.** This Barcelona favorite is justly famous for combining superb interior design with carefully prepared cuisine. Market-fresh ingredients and original combinations are solidly rooted in traditional recipes from Catalan home cooking, while the menu balances seafood and upland specialties, game, and domestic raw materials. Try the *perdiz asada con jamón ibérico* (roast partridge with Iberian ham) or, if it's available, *becada* (woodcock), of which chef Carles Gaig is a recognized master. ✉ *Carrer d'Aragó 214, Eixample* ☎ *93/429–1017* ✍ *Reservations essential* ▭ *AE, DC, MC, V* ⊙ *Closed Mon., Easter wk, and Aug.* Ⓜ *Passeig de Gràcia* ✥ *C3.*

$$$–$$$$ MEDITERRANEAN ✕ **Casa Calvet.** It's hard to pass up the opportunity to break bread in one of the great Moderniste's creations. Designed by Antoni Gaudí from 1898 to 1900, the Art Nouveau Casa Calvet includes this graceful dining room ornamented with looping parabolic door handles, polychrome

stained glass, etched glass, and wood carved in floral and organic motifs. The Catalan and Mediterranean fare is light and contemporary, though refreshingly innocent of *nueva cocina* influence. ✉ *Casp 48, Eixample* ☎ *93/412–4012* ▬ *AE, DC, MC, V* ⏲ *Closed Sun. and last 2 wks of Aug.* Ⓜ *Urquinaona* ✣ *E3.*

$$–$$$ CATALAN Fodor's Choice ★ ✕ **Cinc Sentits.** The engaging Artal family—maître d' and owner Rosa, server and eloquent food narrator Amy, and chef Jordi—a Catalan family with a couple of decades in Canada and the United States, offers a unique Barcelona experience: cutting-edge contemporary *cuina d'autor* in a minimalist setting explained in detail in native English. Two fixed menus—one for "Essences" and the other for "Sensations"—provide a wide range of tastes and textures. At the end of the meal a printout reprises the mini-courses and wines that have just crossed your palate. This is foodie nirvana. ✉ *Aribau 58, Eixample* ☎ *93/323–9490* ▬ *AE, DC, MC, V* ⏲ *Closed Sun. No dinner Mon.* Ⓜ *Provença* ✣ *C2.*

$$$–$$$$ MEDITERRANEAN ✕ **Dos Cielos.** Twins Javier and Sergio Torres have leapt to the top of Barcelona's culinary charts as well as to the top tower of the Hotel ME. The restaurant combines Brazilian, French, and Valencian touches reflecting the twins' accumulated culinary experiences around the world, and it only seems fitting that the Torres brothers should be working in a tower and that their restaurant be named Dos Cielos (*cielo* being Spanish for sweetheart; the boys *are* cute). Contemporary innovation wed to profound respect for traditional palates produces an interesting cuisine based on fresh local produce, some of it grown in the hotel's own roof garden. The views over the Mediterranean are spectacular. ✉ *Pere IV 272–286, Eixample* ☎ *93/367–2070* ▬ *AE, DC, MC, V* ⏲ *Closed Sun. and Mon.* Ⓜ *Poble Nou* ✣ *H5.*

$$$$ MEDITERRANEAN Fodor's Choice ★ ✕ **Drolma.** Named (in Sanskrit) for Buddha's feminine side, chef Fermin Puig's intimate perch in the Hotel Majestic was an instant success. The *menú de degustació* (tasting menu) might have pheasant cannelloni in foie-gras sauce with fresh black truffles or giant prawn tails with *trompettes de la mort* (black wild mushrooms) and *sôt-l'y-laisse* (free-range chicken nuggets). Fermin's foie gras *a la ceniza amb ceps* (cooked over wood coals with wild mushrooms)—a recipe rescued from his boyhood farmhouse feasts—is typical of Drolma's signature blend of tradition and inspiration. ✉ *Passeig de Gràcia 70, Eixample* ☎ *93/496–7710* ✍ *Reservations essential* ▬ *AE, DC, MC, V* ⏲ *Closed Sun. and Aug.* Ⓜ *Provença, Passeig de Gràcia* ✣ *D2.*

$$ CATALAN ✕ **Embat.** An embat is a puff of wind or a crashing wave in Catalan, and this relatively new (November 2008) restaurant is indeed a breath of fresh air in the swashbuckling and hyper-commercial Eixample. The market cuisine by partner chefs Santi Rebés and Fidel Puig is always impeccably fresh and freshly conceived, starring thoughtful combinations such as the *cazuelita de alcachofas con huevo poché y papada* (casserole of artichokes and poached egg with pork dewlap) or the *pichón con bizcocho de cacao y cebolla confitada* (wood pigeon with cacao biscuit and onion confit). ✉ *Mallorca 304, Eixample* ☎ *93/458–0885* ▬ *AE, DC, MC, V* ⏲ *Closed Sun. and Mon. No dinner Tues. and Wed.* Ⓜ *Diagonal* ✣ *E2.*

Casa Calvet restaurant offers the chance to dine inside a Moderniste masterpiece.

$–$$ CATALAN **✕ Fonda Gaig.** A rustic interpretation of the traditional cuisine that has made the Gaig family synonymous with top Barcelona dining since 1869, this new enterprise is making a place for itself in Barcelona's relentlessly evolving culinary world. With some of the steam leaking out of the radically innovative and experimental cookery movement led by Ferran Adrià and his restaurant, El Bulli, Carles Gaig and a growing number of top chefs are going back to simpler and more affordable food. Look for standards such as *botifarra amb mongetes de ganxet* (sausage with white beans), *canelons de l'Avia* (grandmother's cannelloni), or *pollastre de gratapallers a la casssola* (stewed free-range chicken). The ample dining room is, in contrast to the cuisine, stylishly contemporary, with comfortable armchairs à table. ✉ *Còrsega 200, Eixample* ☎ *93/453–2020* ▭ *AE, DC, MC, V* ⏲ *Closed Sun. and Mon. No dinner Sun.* Ⓜ *Hospital Clínic, Provença* ✣ *C1.*

$$$–$$$$ BASQUE **✕ Gorría.** Named for founder Fermín Gorría, this is quite simply the best straightforward Basque-Navarran cooking in Barcelona. Everything from the stewed *pochas* (white beans) to the heroic *chuletón* (steak) is as clean, clear, and pure as the Navarran Pyrenees. The Castillo de Sajazarra reserva '95, a semisecret brick-red Rioja, provides the perfect accompaniment at this delicious pocket of Navarra in the Catalan capital. ✉ *Diputació 421, Eixample* ☎ *93/245–1164* ▭ *AE, DC, MC, V* ⏲ *Closed Sun.* Ⓜ *Monumental* ✣ *F3.*

$$$–$$$$ CATALAN **✕ L'Olivé.** Comforting Catalan home cooking means this busy and attractive spot is always packed with trendy diners having a great time. Excellent hearty food, smart service, and some of the best *pa amb tomàquet* (toasted bread with olive oil and tomato) in town leaves you wanting to squeeze in, too. ✉ *Balmes 47, Eixample* ☎ *93/452–1990* ▭ *AE, DC, MC, V* ⏲ *No dinner Sun.* Ⓜ *Provença* ✣ *C2.*

$$$–$$$$ CATALAN **Fodor's Choice** ★ ✗ **Manairó.** A *manairó* is a mysterious Pyrenean elf who helps make things happen, and Jordi Herrera may be a culinary one. A demon with everything from blowtorch-fried eggs to meat cooked *al clavo ardiente* (à la burning nail)—fillets warmed from within by red-hot spikes producing meat both rare and warm and never undercooked—Jordi also cooks cod under a lightbulb at 220°F (*bacalao iluminado*, or illuminated codfish) and serves a palate-cleansing gin and tonic with liquid nitrogen, gin, and lime. The intimate though postmodern, edgy design of the dining room reflects the cuisine perfectly. ✉ *Diputació 424, Eixample* ☎ *93/231–0057* ✍ *Reservations essential* ▭ *AE, DC, MC, V* ⏲ *Closed Sun., Mon., and last 3 wks of Aug.* Ⓜ *Monumental* ✣ *G3.*

$$–$$$ CATALAN ✗ **Ot.** Streamlined and original contemporary recipes make Ot (Otto, in Catalan), just two blocks up from Gaudí's Sagrada Família, a good choice for hungry and foot-weary diners. An eight-course tasting menu (€58 at this writing) composed of two appetizers, two starters, fish, meat, and two desserts is the standard formula. The abbreviated tasting menu (€45) isn't much less expensive, but you get a lot less to eat (one of everything and a choice of fish or meat). The menu changes frequently and includes zingers such as cauliflower soup with herring eggs. ✉ *Carrer Còrsega 537, Eixample* ☎ *93/435–8048* ▭ *AE, DC, MC, V* ⏲ *No lunch Mon.* Ⓜ *Sagrada Família* ✣ *G1.*

$$–$$$ CATALAN ✗ **Petit Comité.** Fermin Puig, of the famous Drolma at the Hotel Majestic, created Petit Comité as a more rustic country cousin of his sleek high-end dining room across the street. Traditional Catalan cooking is the theme in this contemporary space with a square counter in the middle for bar fare. Service around the clock from midday to midnight (1 PM–1 AM) makes reservations essential only at peak hours. Traditional favorites include *trinxat* (chopped cabbage with potato and bacon) or *caneloni amb béchamel de tòfona* (cannelloni with truffled béchamel) and the traditional dessert of *mel i mató* (fresh cheese and honey). ✉ *Passatge de la Concepció 13, Eixample* ☎ *93/550–0620* ✍ *Reservations essential* ▭ *AE, DC, MC, V* ⏲ *Open daily 1 PM–1 AM* Ⓜ *Diagonal* ✣ *D2.*

$$–$$$ BASQUE ✗ **Sagardi Muntaner.** Basque favorites from *alubias de Tolosa* (diminutive but potent black beans from Tolosa) to *pimientos de piquillo* (sweet red bell peppers) to *txuletón de buey* (ox steak) are on the menu at this mid-Eixample address open from noon to midnight every day. The bar displays the full range of typical Basque tapas and serves freezing *txakolí* (a young white wine from the Basque Country) for openers. ✉ *Muntaner 70–72, Eixample* ☎ *93/902–520–522* ▭ *AE, DC, MC, V* Ⓜ *Universitat, Provença* ✣ *C2.*

$$ ECLECTIC ✗ **Ya Ya Amelia.** Just two blocks uphill from Gaudí's Sagrada Família church, this kitchen serves lovingly prepared and clued-in dishes ranging from warm goat-cheese salad to foie (duck or goose liver) to *chuleton de buey a la sal* (beef cooked in salt). The "Ya Ya" (an affectionate term for grandmother in Spanish) was apparently of Basque origin, as the cuisine here is a pleasantly schizoid medley of Basque and Catalan. Serving from noon to 5 and 8 to midnight, the Ya Ya is a welcome relief for the

ravenous and weary fresh from touring the nearby church. ✉ *Sardenya 364, Eixample* ☎ *93/456–4573* ▭ *AE, DC, MC, V* ⊙ *Closed Mon.* Ⓜ *Sagrada Família* ✢ *G1.*

GRÀCIA

This exciting yet intimate neighborhood has everything from the most sophisticated cuisine in town to lively Basque taverns.

¢–$ MEDITERRANEAN ✕ **Bilbao.** A cheery bistro near the bottom of Gràcia, this place is always packed with hungry epicureans having a festive time. Unpretentious, straightforward Mediterranean market cuisine is well prepared and sold at reasonable prices here, but the best feature is the generally gleeful din—a good sign. Try the fried egg with black truffles and look for the Montsant red wines, always great values. ✉ *Perill 33, Gràcia* ☎ *93/458–9624* ▭ *AE, DC, MC, V* ⊙ *Closed Sun.* Ⓜ *Diagonal, Joanic* ✢ *E1.*

$$$$ SPANISH Fodor's Choice ★ ✕ **Botafumeiro.** On Gràcia's main thoroughfare, Barcelona's finest Galician restaurant has maritime motifs, snowy tablecloths, wood paneling, and fleets of waiters in spotless white outfits all moving at the speed of light. The bank-breaking *mariscada Botafumeiro* is a seafood medley of shellfish, fin fish, cuttlefish, and caviar. An assortment of *media ración* (half-ration) selections is available at the bar, where *pulpo a feira* (squid on slices of potato), *jamón ibérico de bellota* (acorn-fed Iberian ham), and *pan con tomate* (toasted bread topped with olive oil and tomato) make peerless late-night snacks. ✉ *Gran de Gràcia 81, Gràcia* ☎ *93/218–4230* ▭ *AE, DC, MC, V* Ⓜ *Gràcia* ✢ *D1.*

$–$$ CATALAN ✕ **Folquer.** This artsy little hideaway at the bottom of Gràcia serves creatively prepared traditional Catalan specialties. Chef Juanjo Carrillo, who has worked with Andoni Aduriz at the famous Mugaritz near San Sebastián, produces surprising combinations such as *tartin de poma amb escalope de foie y salsa lima* (apple tart with breaded duck liver in a lime sauce) or *bacallà amb mongetas vermellas i pil-pil de pernil* (codfish cooked at low temperature with red beans and Ibérico ham gelatin). The two tasting-menu options (€13 and €17) are among Barcelona's top values. ✉ *Torrent de l'Olla 3, Gràcia* ☎ *93/217–4395* ▭ *AE, DC, MC, V* ⊙ *Closed Sun. and last 2 wks of Aug. No lunch Sat.* Ⓜ *Diagonal* ✢ *E1.*

$$–$$$ BASQUE ✕ **Ipar-Txoko.** This excellent little Basque enclave has managed to stay largely under the radar, and for that reason, among others, the cuisine is authentic, the prices are fair, and the service is personal and warm. A balanced menu offers San Sebastián specialties such as *txuleta de buey* (beef steak) or *besugo* (sea bream), flawlessly prepared, while the wine list includes classic Riojas and freezing txakolí from Txomin Etxaniz. ✉ *Carrer Mozart 22, Gràcia* ☎ *93/218–1954* ✍ *Reservations essential* ▭ *AE, DC, MC, V* ⊙ *Closed Sun., Mon., and last 3 wks of Aug.* Ⓜ *Gràcia, Diagonal* ✢ *E1.*

SARRIÀ, PEDRALBES, AND SANT GERVASI

An excursion to the upper reaches of town offers an excellent selection of restaurants, little-known Gaudí sites, shops, cool evening breezes, and a sense of village life in Sarrià.

7

$$$–$$$$ CATALAN

✕ **Freixa Tradició.** When wunderkind molecular gastronomist Ramón Freixa turned the family restaurant back over to his father, Josep Maria Freixa, there was some speculation about the menu's headlong rush into the past. Now that the results are in, Barcelona food cognoscenti are coming in droves for the authentic Catalan fare that dominated the land before experimental cuisine took over the culinary landscape. Creamy rice with cuttlefish, monkfish with fried garlic, pig trotters with prunes and pine nuts, and a robust selection of local specialties are making the new-old Freixa better than ever. ✉ *San Elies 22, Sant Gervasi* ☎ *93/209–7559* ▭ *AE, MC, V* ⊙ *Closed Sun. Easter wk, and Aug.* Ⓜ *Sant Gervasi-Muntaner* ✣ *D1.*

$–$$ FRENCH

✕ **Gouthier.** Thierry Airaud's attractive, minimalist dining space at the bottom of Plaça Sant Vicenç de Sarrià specializes in oysters, caviars, foies (duck and goose livers), and cavas and champagnes to go with these exquisite products. Fortunately, the tasting portions allow you to indulge your wildest food fantasies without sustaining massive financial damage. Ask for advice on oysters and compare different tastes and textures. ✉ *Carrer Mañé i Flaquer 8, Sarrià* ☎ *93/205–9969* ▭ *AE, DC, MC, V* ⊙ *Closed Sun. and Mon.* Ⓜ *Sarrià* ✣ *A1.*

$$$–$$$$ JAPANESE

✕ **Icho.** Asian cuisine expert Ana Saura's much respected restaurant just behind L'Illa Diagonal shopping emporium is widely regarded as offering the best Japanese food in Barcelona. Chef Maestro Tan prepares sushi and sashimi of impeccable quality and purity, often working only three feet away from diners at the polished oak bar, with the best views into the glass-walled kitchen. Cockles steamed in sake, miso soup, prawns in tempura, or sauteed yakisoba noodles with vegetables are excellent starters. Steak tartare made with Wagyu Kobe beef is a specialty of the house, as are the tuna tartare with cream of tofu and wasabi and the scallop tartare. ✉ *Déu i Mata 69, Les Corts* ☎ *93/444–3370* ▭ *AE, DC, MC, V* ⊙ *Closed Sun.* Ⓜ *Les Corts* ✣ *A1.*

$$$–$$$$ ITALIAN

✕ **Le Quattro Stagioni.** For excellent, streamlined Italian fare far from your stereotypical red-sauce joint (think urban postmodern cuisine), this chic spot just down the street from the Tres Torres metro stop is a winner. It's always filled with intriguing-looking bon vivants evenly balanced between hip locals and clued-in tourists, and the garden is cool and fragrant on summer nights. ✉ *Dr. Roux 37, Sant Gervasi* ☎ *93/205–2279* ▭ *AE, DC, MC, V* Ⓜ *Tres Torres* ✣ *A1.*

$–$$ MEDITERRANEAN

Fodor's Choice ★

✕ **Silvestre.** This graceful and easygoing young constellation in Barcelona's culinary galaxy serves modern cuisine to some of the city's most discerning and distinguished diners. Just below Via Augusta, a series of intimate dining rooms and cozy corners are carefully tended by chef Guillermo (Willy) Casañé and his charming wife Marta Cabot, a fluent English–speaking maître d' and partner. Look for fresh market produce lovingly prepared in dishes such as tuna tartare, noodles and shrimp, or wood pigeon with duck liver. Willy's semi-secret list of house wines is always surprising for its quality and value. ✉ *Santaló 101, Sant Gervasi* ☎ *93/241–4031* ▭ *AE, DC, MC, V* ⊙ *Closed Sun., middle 2 wks of Aug., and Easter wk. No lunch Sat.* Ⓜ *Muntaner* ✣ *D1.*

$$$–$$$$ CATALAN Fodor's Choice ★ **Tram-Tram.** At the end of the old tram line above the village of Sarrià, Isidre Soler and his wife, Reyes, have put together one of Barcelona's finest culinary offerings. Try the *menú de degustació* and you might be lucky enough to get marinated tuna salad, cod medallions, and venison filet mignon, among other tasty creations. Perfectly sized portions and a streamlined reinterpretation of space within this traditional Sarrià house—especially in the garden out back—make this a memorable dining experience. ✉ *Major de Sarrià 121, Sarrià* ☎ *93/204–8518* 💳 *AE, DC, MC, V* ⏲ *Closed Sun. and late Dec.–early Jan. No lunch Sat.* Ⓜ *Reina Elisenda* ✣ *A1.*

$$–$$$ MEDITERRANEAN **Vivanda.** Just above Plaça de Sarrià, this leafy garden is especially wonderful between May and mid-October, when outside dining is a delight. The new menu designed by Alkimia's Jordi Vilà has traditional Catalan miniatures *"para picar"* (small morsels), *platillos* (little dishes), and half-rations of meat and fish listed as *platillos de pescado* and *platillos de carne*. The *coca de pa de vidre con tomate* (a delicate shell of bread with tomato and olive oil) and the venisonlike *presa de Ibérico* (fillet of Ibérico pig) are both exquisite. ✉ *Major de Sarrià 134, Sarrià* ☎ *93/203–1918* 💳 *AE, DC, MC, V* ⏲ *Closed Sun.* Ⓜ *Reina Elisenda* ✣ *A1.*

OUTSKIRTS OF BARCELONA

With the many fine in-town dining options available in Barcelona, any out-of-town recommendations must logically rank somewhere in the uppermost stratosphere of gastronomic excellence. Ferran Adrià's El Bulli, in Roses, has an international reputation, is next to impossible to get a reservation at, and is said to be closing for at least two years, from 2012 through 2013.

$$$–$$$$ CATALAN Fodor's Choice ★ **El Rac Can Fabes.** Santi Santamaria's master class in Mediterranean cuisine merits the 45-minute train ride (or 30-minute drive) north of Barcelona to Sant Celoni. One of the six top-rated restaurants in Spain, this is a must for anyone interested in fine dining. Every detail, from the six flavors of freshly baked bread to the cheese selection, is superb. The tasting menu is the wisest solution. The RENFE stations are at Passeig de Gràcia or Sants, but the last train back is at 10:24 PM, so this is a lunchtime-only transport solution if you hope to take only a day; fortunately, five guest rooms are available just a few steps from your last glass of wine. ✉ *Carrer Sant Joan 6, Sant Celoni* ☎ *93/867–2851* 💳 *AE, DC, MC, V* ⏲ *Closed Mon., 1st 2 wks of Feb., and late June–early July. No dinner Sun.* ✣ *M5.*

WHERE TO STAY

Use the coordinate (✣ B2) at the end of each listing to locate a site on the corresponding map.

Barcelona's hotels offer clear distinctions. Hotels in the Ciutat Vella (Old City)—the Gothic Quarter and along the Rambla—are charming and convenient for sightseeing, though sometimes short on peace and quiet. Relative newcomers to the Barcelona hotel fleet, such as the Neri, the Duquesa de Cardona, and the Casa Camper Barcelona, are contemporary design standouts inhabiting medieval architecture, a combination at which Barcelona architects and decorators are peerless. Eixample hotels (including most of the city's best) are late-19th- or early-20th-century town houses restored and converted into exciting modern environments.

Mid-Eixample hotels, including the Hotel Palace (former Ritz), the Claris, the Majestic, the Condes de Barcelona, and the Hotel Omm, combine style and luxury with a sense of place; the peripheral palaces (like the Hotel Arts) are less about Barcelona and more about generic comfort and luxury. Sarrià and Sant Gervasi upper-city hotels get you up out of the urban crush, and Olympic Port and Diagonal Mar hotels are in high-rise towers (requiring transport to and from the real Barcelona). Smaller budget hotels are less than half as expensive as some of the luxury addresses and more a part of city life.

CIUTAT VELLA (OLD CITY)

The Ciutat Vella includes the Rambla, Barri Gòtic, Born-Ribera, and Raval districts between Plaça de Catalunya and the port.

BARRI GÒTIC

$$–$$$ Fodor's Choice ★ **Colón.** There's something clubby about this elegant Barcelona standby, surprisingly intimate and charming for such a sizable operation. The location is ideal—directly across the plaza from the cathedral, overlooking weekend *sardana* dancing, Thursday antiques markets, and, of course, the floodlit cathedral by night. Rooms are comfortable and furnished with traditional pieces, some of them antiques; try to get one with a view of the cathedral. The Colón was a favorite of the artist Joan Miró. **Pros:** walking distance from all of central Barcelona; views of cathedral; friendly staff. **Cons:** slightly old-fashioned; undistinguished dining. ✉ *Av. Catedral 7, Barri Gòtic* ☎ *93/301–1404* 🌐 *www.hotelcolon.es* *140 rooms, 5 suites* *In-room: a/c, safe, refrigerator, Wi-Fi. In-hotel: restaurant, bar* *AE, DC, MC, V* *EP* Ⓜ *Catalunya* ✣ *D4.*

$$$$ **Grand Hotel Central.** At the edge of the Gothic Quarter, very near the Barcelona cathedral, this fashionable midtown hideaway is becoming a magnet for the hip and hot-to-trot. Rooms are flawlessly furnished with stark furniture and equipped with high-tech design features, from flat-screen TVs to DSL hookups. The restaurant, supervised by internationally acclaimed chef Ramón Freixa, is bound for glory, and the roof terrace and top-floor pool offer a unique perch over the city's 2,000-year-old Roman and Gothic central nucleus. The higher the better, as street level can be noisy, soundproofing or not. **Pros:** excellent location between the Gothic Quarter and the Born; attentive service; full gamut of high-tech amenities. **Cons:** the street outside is noisy and fast. ✉ *Via Laietana 30, Barri Gòtic* ☎ *93/295–7900* 🌐 *www.grandhotelcentral.com* *141 rooms, 6 suites* *In-room: Wi-Fi. In-hotel: restaurant, bar, pool, gym, Internet terminal, Wi-Fi hotspot, parking (paid)* *AE, DC, MC, V* *EP* Ⓜ *Catalunya, Jaume I* ✣ *E5.*

BEST BETS FOR BARCELONA LODGING

Having trouble deciding where to stay in Barcelona? Fodor's offers a selective listing of high-quality lodging experiences at every price range, from the city's best budget options to its most sophisticated. Here we've compiled our top recommendations by price and experience; full details are in the reviews that follow. The very best properties—those that provide a particularly remarkable experience—are designated with a Fodor's Choice symbol. Sleep tight!

Fodor's Choice ★

Casa Fuster, $$$, p. 507
Claris, $$$, p. 503
Colón, $$, p. 492
Condes de Barcelona, $$$, p. 503
Duquesa de Cardona, $$$, p. 499
Hostal Gat Raval, $, p. 498
Hotel Granados 83, $$$, p. 504
Hotel Neri, $$$$, p. 496
Hotel Omm, $$$$, p. 504
Majestic, $$$, p. 505
Sant Agustí, $$, p. 499
Turó de Vilana, $$$, p. 507
W Hotel Barcelona, $$$$, p. 502

By Price

$

Hostal Gat Raval, p. 498
Hotel Chic & Basic Born, p. 496

$$

Colón, p. 492
Sant Agustí, p. 499

$$$

Casa Fuster, p. 507
Claris, p. 503
Condes de Barcelona, p. 503
Duquesa de Cardona, p. 499
Hotel Granados 83, p. 504
Majestic, p. 505
Turó de Vilana, p. 507

$$$$

Hotel Arts, p. 502
Hotel Neri, p. 496
Hotel Palace, p. 505
Hotel Omm, p. 504
W Hotel Barcelona, p. 502

By Experience

BEST CONCIERGE

Majestic, p. 505

BEST HIPSTER HOTELS

Hotel Chic & Basic Born, p. 496
Hotel Granados 83, p. 504

BEST FOR HISTORY BUFFS

Colón, p. 492

BEST LOBBY

Claris, p. 503
Hotel Arts, p. 502
W Hotel Barcelona, p. 502

BEST VIEWS

Hotel Arts, p. 502
W Hotel Barcelona, p. 502

CHILD-FRIENDLY

Casa Camper Barcelona, p. 496
Villa Emilia, p. 506

GOOD FOR GROUPS

ME Barcelona, p. 506

MOST ROMANTIC

Hotel Neri, p. 496

Where to Stay in Barcelona

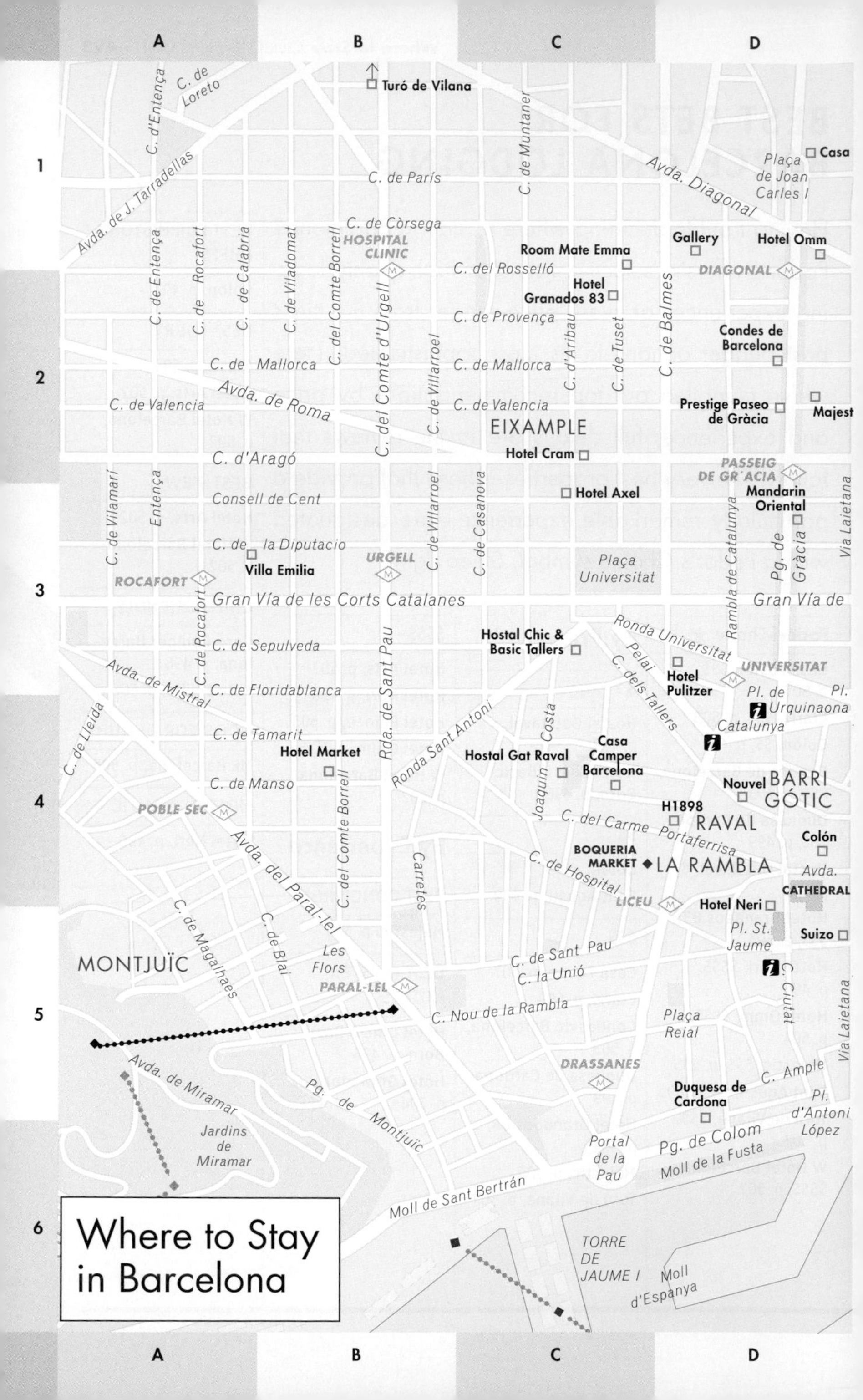

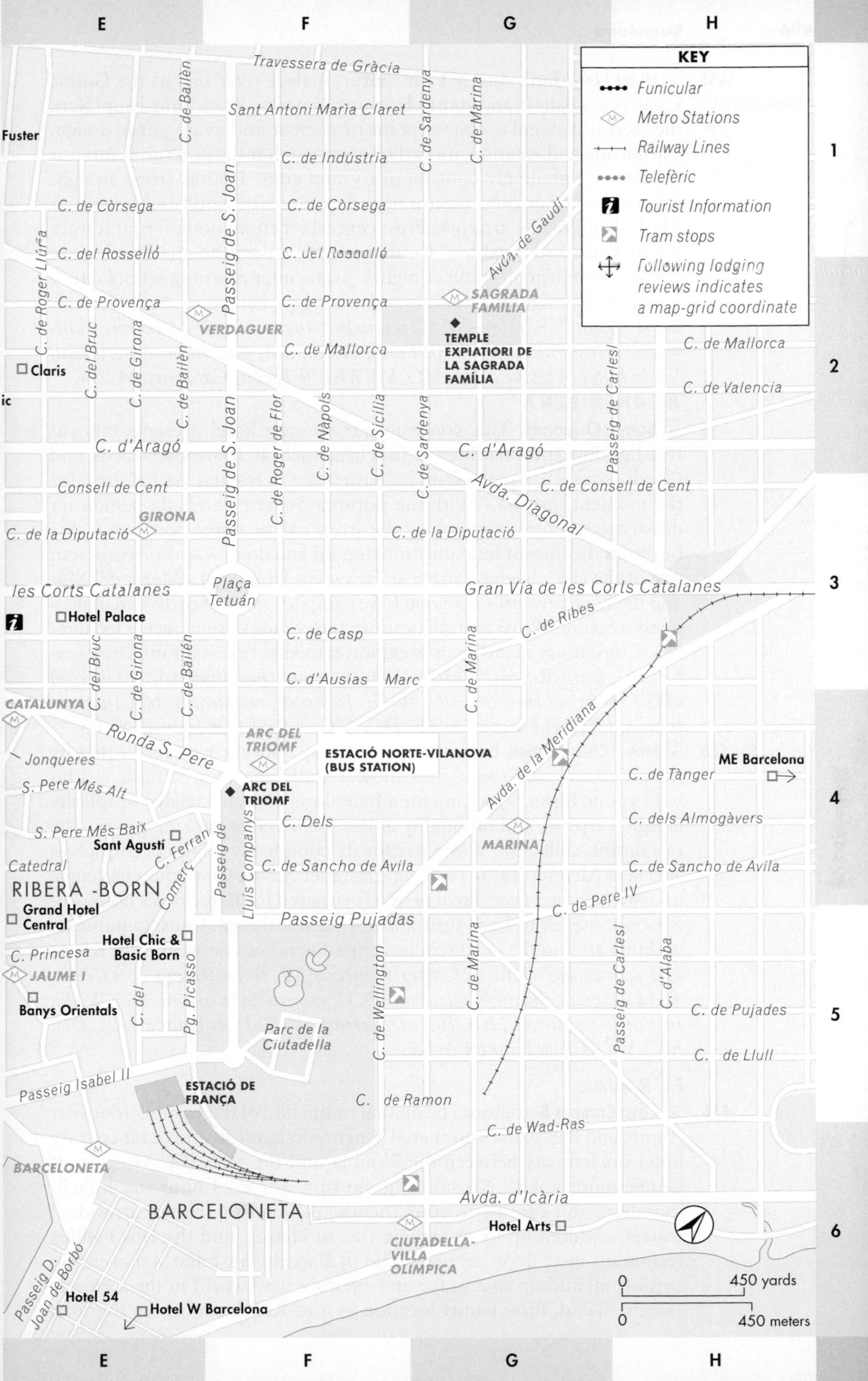

E
F
G
H
KEY
Funicular
Metro Stations
Railway Lines
Telefèric
Tourist Information
Tram stops
Following lodging reviews indicates a map-grid coordinate
1
2
3
4
5
6
Travessera de Gràcia
Sant Antoni Marìa Claret
C. de Bailèn
C. de Sardenya
C. de Marina
Fuster
C. de Indústria
C. de Còrsega
C. de Còrsega
Passeig de S. Joan
Avda. de Gaudí
C. de Roger Llúria
C. del Rosselló
C. del Rosselló
C. de Provença
C. de Provença
SAGRADA FAMILIA
VERDAGUER
TEMPLE EXPIATIORI DE LA SAGRADA FAMÍLIA
C. de Mallorca
C. de Mallorca
Claris
C. del Bruc
C. de Girona
C. de Bailèn
C. de Valencia
Passeig de Carlesi
ic
Passeig de S. Joan
C. de Roger de Flor
C. de Nàpols
C. de Sicilia
C. de Sardenya
C. d'Aragó
C. d'Aragó
Consell de Cent
C. de Consell de Cent
Avda. Diagonal
GIRONA
C. de la Diputació
C. de la Diputació
Plaça Tetuán
les Corts Catalanes
Gran Vía de les Corts Catalanes
Hotel Palace
C. de Ribes
C. de Casp
C. del Bruc
C. de Girona
C. de Bailèn
C. d'Ausias Marc
C. de Marina
CATALUNYA
Avda. de la Meridiana
ARC DEL TRIOMF
Ronda S. Pere
ESTACIÓ NORTE-VILANOVA (BUS STATION)
ME Barcelona
Jonqueres
S. Pere Més Alt
ARC DEL TRIOMF
C. de Tànger
C. Dels
C. dels Almogàvers
S. Pere Més Baix
Sant Agustí
C. Ferran
MARINA
Catedral
Passeig de Lluís Companys
C. de Sancho de Avila
C. de Sancho de Avila
RIBERA -BORN
Comerç
C. de Pere IV
Grand Hotel Central
Passeig Pujadas
Hotel Chic & Basic Born
C. Princesa
C. de Wellington
C. de Marina
Passeig de Carlesi
C. d'Alaba
JAUME I
Pg. Picasso
C. del
C. de Pujades
Banys Orientals
Parc de la Ciutadella
C. de Llull
Passeig Isabel II
ESTACIÓ DE FRANÇA
C. de Ramon
C. de Wad-Ras
BARCELONETA
Avda. d'Icària
BARCELONETA
Hotel Arts
CIUTADELLA-VILLA OLIMPICA
Passeig D. Joan de Borbó
0
450 yards
0
450 meters
Hotel 54
Hotel W Barcelona
E
F
G
H

$$$$ Fodor's Choice ★ **Hotel Neri.** Built into a 17th-century palace over one of the Gothic Quarter's smallest and most charming squares, Plaça Sant Felip Neri, the Neri is a singular counterpoint of ancient and avant-garde design. The facade and location are early Barcelona, but the cavernous interior spaces are unfailingly contemporary and edgy. Rooms stress straight lines, sheer and angular precision, and expanses of wood and stone with Mark Rothko–like artwork. **Pros:** central location; design; roof terrace for cocktails and breakfast. **Cons:** noise from the echo-chamber square can be a problem on summer nights (and winter morning school days); impractical design details such as the hanging bed lights. ✉ *St. Sever 5, Barri Gòtic* ☎ *93/304–0655* 🌐 *www.hotelneri.com* *22 rooms* *In-room: refrigerator, Wi-Fi. In-hotel: restaurant, bar, Internet terminal, Wi-Fi hotspot* *AE, DC, MC, V* *EP* Ⓜ *Liceu, Catalunya* ✣ *D4.*

BORN-RIBERA

$ **Banys Orientals.** This contemporary-design hotel presents innovative lighting and imaginative touches, such as four-poster beds and Gaudí-esque chairs. (Despite its name, the "Oriental Baths" has, for the moment, no spa.) With the popular Senyor Parellada restaurant downstairs, rooms overlooking the street can be noisy, not from traffic but from the flow of humanity moving up and down Carrer Argenteria, one of the city's liveliest arteries. Two steps from Santa Maria del Mar and the Born area, this is a good base camp for most of early Barcelona's finest treasures. **Pros:** central location; interesting design; recent technology. **Cons:** noisy nightlife thoroughfare; mediocre restaurant. ✉ *Argenteria 37, Born-Ribera* ☎ *93/268–8460* 🌐 *www.hotelbanysorientals.com* *56 rooms* *In-room: a/c, Wi-Fi. In-hotel: restaurant, bar, Internet terminal, Wi-Fi hotspot* *AE, DC, MC, V* *EP* Ⓜ *Jaume I* ✣ *E5.*

$$–$$$ **Hotel Chic & Basic Born.** A revolutionary concept best illustrated by the middle-of-your-room glass shower stalls, the Chic & Basic is a hit with young hipsters looking for a Barcelona combo package of splashy design, surprise, and originality at less-than-wallet-rocking prices. The restaurant, called the White Bar for its completely albino decor, serves excellent Mediterranean cooking. Designer Xavier Claramunt has come up with a winner here. **Pros:** perfectly situated for Barcelona's hot Born-Ribera scene; clean-lined sleek and impeccable design. **Cons:** tumultuous nightlife around the hotel requires closed windows on weekends; rooms and spaces are small. ✉ *Carrer Princesa 50, Born-Ribera* ☎ *93/295–4652* 🌐 *www.chicandbasic.com* *31 rooms* *In-room: a/c, Wi-Fi. In-hotel: restaurant, bar, Internet terminal, Wi-Fi hotspot* *AE, DC, MC, V* *EP* Ⓜ *Jaume I* ✣ *E5.*

EL RAVAL

$$$ **Casa Camper Barcelona.** The mutual brainchild of the Camper footwear empire and Barcelona's nonpareil Vinçon design store, this 21st-century hotel sits halfway between the Rambla and the MACBA (Museum of Contemporary Art). No smoking, no tips, a free 24-hour snack facility where you can invite your friends, ecologically recycled residual waters, children up to 12 staying free of charge, and the Dos Palillos restaurant next door, serving some of Barcelona's finest Asian-fusion cuisine, all add up to a brave and exciting new world in the formerly sketchy Raval. **Pros:** handy location in mid-Raval just off the Rambla;

WHERE TO STAY?

	Neighborhood Vibe	Pros	Cons
Ciutat Vella	Busy. The Rambla never sleeps, the Raval is exciting and exotic, the Gothic Quarter is quiet and medieval, and Born-Ribera hums with restaurants and taverns.	The pulse of the metropolis beats strongest here; the Boqueria, Santa Caterina, and Barceloneta markets rage, while must-see sites are only steps away.	The incessant crush of humanity along the Rambla can be overwhelming, though the Gothic Quarter and Born-Ribera are quieter. The Raval is rough and seedy.
Eixample	Some of Gaudí's best buildings line the sidewalks, and many of the city's finest hotels and restaurants are right around the corner. And then there's the shopping...	Eixample remains the world's only Art Nouveau neighborhood, constantly rewarding to the eye. Gaudí's unfinished masterpiece La Sagrada Família is within walking distance.	A bewildering grid without numbers or alphabetization, the Eixample can seem hard-edged compared to the older, quirkier, parts of Barcelona.
Barceloneta and Port Olímpic	The onetime fisherman's quarter, Barceloneta retains its informal and working-class ambience, with laundry flapping over the streets and sidewalk restaurants lining Passeig Joan de Borbó.	Near the beach, this part of town has a laid-back feel. The Port Olímpic is a world apart, but Barceloneta is brimming with the best seafood dining spots in town.	Barceloneta offers few hotel opportunities, while the Port Olímpic's principal offering, the monolithic Hotel Arts, can feel like a tourist colony away from the rest of town.
Pedralbes, Sarrià and Upper Barcelona	Upper Barcelona is leafy and residential, and the air is always a few degrees cooler. Pedralbes holds Barcelona's finest mansions; Sarrià is a rustic village suspended in the urban sprawl.	Getting above the fray and into better air has distinct advantages, and the upper reaches of Barcelona offers them. A 15-minute train ride connects Sarrià with the Rambla.	The only drawback to staying in Upper Barcelona is the 15-minute commute to the most important monuments and attractions. After midnight on weeknights this will require a taxi.

ultramodern technology and concept; handy to MACBA and a handful of trendy shops. **Cons:** snacking redundant, as you're two steps from the Boqueria; no way to get a car close to the hotel door. ⊠ *C. Elisabets 11, Raval* ☎ *93/342–6280* 🌐 *www.casacamper.com* *20 rooms, 5 suites* *In-room: safe, Wi-Fi. In-hotel: restaurant, bicycles, laundry service* ▭ *AE, DC, MC, V* 🍽 *BP* Ⓜ *Catalunya* ⊕ *C4.*

$ **Hostal Chic & Basic Tallers.** Another sleek budget choice in the upper Raval, this even-more-economical version of the Hotel Chic & Basic over in the Born offers three sizes of rooms from medium to extra large, and has a living room called Chill & Basic with Wi-Fi access and free snacks. Other surprising assets include in-room music speakers that allow you to listen to the mix created by the hotel's music director or plug in your own iPod. **Pros:** perfectly designed and situated for an exciting, low-cost Barcelona experience; young and friendly staff. **Cons:** the streets in the Raval can reverberate noisily at night; space is tight in rooms. ⊠ *Carrer Tallers 82, Raval* ☎ *93/302–5183* 🌐 *www.chicandbasic.com* *14 rooms* *In-room: Wi-Fi. In-hotel: Internet*

7

CLOSE UP

Lodging Alternatives

APARTMENT RENTALS

If you want a home base that's roomy enough for a family and comes with cooking facilities, consider a furnished rental. These can save you money, especially if you're traveling with a group. Apartment rentals are increasingly popular in Barcelona these days. Aparthotels rent apartments in residences subdivided into small living spaces at prices generally more economical than hotel rates. Rentals by the day or week can be arranged, though prices may rise for short stays. Prices range from €100 to €300 per day depending on the quality of the accommodations, but perfectly acceptable lodging for four can be found for around €150 per night. Apartment accommodations can be arranged through any of the agencies listed below.

LOCAL APARTMENT AGENCIES

Aparthotel Bertran (☎ *93/212–7550* 🌐 *www.hotelbertran.com*). **Aparthotel Bonanova** (☎ *93/253–1563* 🌐 *www.aparthotelbonanova.com*). **Aparthotel Nàpols** (☎ *93/246–4573* 🌐 *www.napols.net*). **Apartment Barcelona** (☎ *93/215–7934* 🌐 *www.apartmentbarcelona.com*). **Apartments Ramblas** (☎ *93/301–7678* 🌐 *www.apartmentsramblas.com*). **BarcelonaForrent** (☎ *93/457–9329* 🌐 *www.barcelonaforrent.com*). **Barcelona Rentals/Atlanta-Ads** (☎ *404/849–5827* 🌐 *www.atlanta-ads.com*). **Barceloneta Suites** (☎ *93/221–4225* 🌐 *www.barcelonetasuites.com*). **Feel Barcelona** (☎ *93/301–9341* 🌐 *www.feelbarcelona.com*). **Flats By Days** (☎ *93/342–6481* 🌐 *www.flatsbydays.com*). **Friendly Rentals** (☎ *93/268–8051* 🌐 *www.friendlyrentals.com*). **Goben Apartments** (☎ *93/278–1156* 🌐 *www.gobcn.com*). **Lofts & Apartments** (☎ *93/366–8800* 🌐 *www.lofts-apartments.com*). **Oh-Barcelona** (☎ *93/467–3782* 🌐 *www.oh-barcelona.com*). **Rent a Flat in Barcelona** (☎ *93/342–7300* 🌐 *www.rentaflatinbarcelona.com*)

terminal, Wi-Fi hotspot ▭ *AE, DC, MC, V* 🍽 *EP* Ⓜ *Catalunya, Universitat* ✥ *C3.*

¢–$ **Hostal Gat Raval.** This hip little hole-in-the-wall opens into a surprisingly bright and sleekly designed modern space with rooms that come in different shapes, styles, and numbers of beds, all cheerily appointed and impeccably maintained. Just around the corner from the MACBA, the Gat Raval seems to have been influenced by Richard Meier's shining contemporary structure, though you'd never guess it from the street. **Pros:** central location in the deepest Raval; contemporary design; recent technology. **Cons:** noisy street at threshold; somewhat cramped rooms and public spaces; few amenities. ✉ *Joaquin Costa 44, Raval* ☎ *93/481–6670* 🌐 *www.gataccommodation.com* ⇨ *22 rooms* ♁ *In-room: a/c, Wi-Fi. In-hotel: Internet terminal, Wi-Fi hotspot* ▭ *AE, DC, MC, V* 🍽 *BP* Ⓜ *Universitat* ✥ *C4.*

Fodor's Choice ★

$–$$ **Hotel Market.** A wallet-friendly boutique hotel and yet another Barcelona design triumph, the Hotel Market is so named for the Mercat de Sant Antoni. On a little alleyway a block from the market and walking distance from all of the Raval and Gothic Quarter sites and attractions, this ultramodern, high-tech, designer lodging opportunity is one of Barcelona's best bargains. Rooms are simply but solidly furnished with dark-wood trim and beams setting off bright white bedspreads and lacquered surfaces. The hotel restaurant offers superlative fare and excellent value. **Pros:** well equipped, designed, and positioned for a low-cost Barcelona visit; young and friendly staff. **Cons:** rooms are a little cramped. ✉ *Carrer Comte Borrell 68 (entrance at Passatge Sant Antoni Abat 10), Raval* ☎ *93/325–1205* 🌐 *www.markethotel.com.es* *37 rooms* *In-room: a/c, safe, refrigerator, Wi-Fi. In-hotel: restaurant, bar, Internet terminal, Wi-Fi hotspot* ▭ *AE, DC, MC, V* *EP* Ⓜ *Sant Antoni* ✣ *B4.*

$$ Fodor's Choice ★ **Sant Agustí.** In a leafy square just off the Rambla, the Sant Agustí has long been popular with musicians performing at the Liceu opera house. Rooms are small but graceful and attractively designed, with plenty of bright wood trim and clean lines. **Pros:** central location near the Boqueria market, the Rambla, and the opera house; cozy, wood-beamed, traditional design. **Cons:** noisy square usually requiring closed windows; short on amenities and room service. ✉ *Pl. Sant Agustí 3, Raval* ☎ *93/318–1658* 🌐 *www.hotelsa.com* *77 rooms* *In-room: a/c, safe, Wi-Fi. In-hotel: bar, Wi-Fi hotspot* ▭ *AE, DC, MC, V* *EP* Ⓜ *Liceu* ✣ *E4.*

THE RAMBLA

$$$–$$$$ Fodor's Choice ★ **Duquesa de Cardona.** This refurbished 16th-century town house overlooking the port has ultracontemporary facilities with designer touches, all housed in an early-Renaissance structure. The exterior rooms have views of the harbor, the World Trade Center, and the passenger-boat terminals. The hotel is a 10-minute walk from everything in the Gothic Quarter or Barceloneta and no more than a 30-minute walk from the main Eixample attractions. The miniature rooftop pool, more for a dip than a swim, is cooling in summer. **Pros:** contemporary technology in a traditional palace at a key spot over the port; roof terrace with live music in summer. **Cons:** rooms on the small side; roof terrace tiny; sea views restricted by Maremagnum complex. ✉ *Passeig de Colom 12, Rambla* ☎ *93/268–9090* 🌐 *www.hduquesadecardona.com* *44 rooms* *In-room: Wi-Fi. In-hotel: restaurant, pool* ▭ *AE, DC, MC, V* *EP* Ⓜ *Drassanes* ✣ *D5.*

$$$–$$$$ **H1898.** This elegant hotel overlooking the Rambla occupies a building with an illustrious history as the headquarters of the Compañia de Tabacos de Filipinas. Named for the fateful year when Spain was stripped of its final colonial possessions, the Philippines among them, the hotel's elegance pays homage to bygone imperial days and provides a symbol of the city's present opulence. Rooms are superbly equipped with state-of-the-art appliances and decorated in a maritime, South Seas idiom. The upper rooms, with terraces on the side away from the Rambla, have lovely views of Montjuïc, the Mediterranean, and the Collserola hills behind the city. **Pros:** central location on the Rambla; top-level design and technology. **Cons:** subway rumble discernible in lower rooms on Rambla side. ✉ *La Rambla 109, Rambla* ☎ *93/552–9552* 🌐 *www.hotel1898.com* *166 rooms, 3 suites* *In-room: Wi-Fi.*

Fodor's Choice ★

Duquesa de Cardona

Claris

Condes de Barcelona

Sant Agusti

W Hotel Barcelona

Fodor's Choice ★

Casa Fuster

Hotel Omm

Majestic

In-hotel: restaurant, bar, pool, gym, parking (paid) ▭ *AE, DC, MC, V* *EP* Ⓜ *Catalunya* ✥ *D4.*

$$ **Nouvel.** White marble, etched glass, elaborate plasterwork, and carved, dark woodwork blend into this hotel's handsome Art Nouveau interior. Rooms have marble floors, firm beds, and chic bathrooms. The narrow street, just below Plaça de Catalunya, is pedestrian-only and blissfully quiet. **Pros:** centrally positioned; charming Moderniste details; quiet pedestrian street. **Cons:** rooms on the small side; not especially high-tech. ✉ *Santa Anna 18–20, Rambla* ☎ *93/301–8274* 🌐 *www.hotelnouvel.com* *71 rooms* *In-room: a/c, safe, Wi-Fi. In-hotel: restaurant, bar* ▭ *AE, DC, MC, V* *EP* Ⓜ *Catalunya* ✥ *D4.*

BARCELONETA, PORT OLÍMPIC, AND FÒRUM

$$$$ **Hotel Arts.** This luxurious Ritz-Carlton-owned skyscraper overlooks Barcelona from the Olympic Port, providing stunning views of the Mediterranean, the city, and the mountains behind. The hotel's main drawback is that it's somewhat in a world of its own, a short taxi ride (or a good 20-minute walk) from the center of the city. That said, it's an exciting world to be in. True to the name, fine art—from Eduardo Chillida drawings to Susana Solano sculptures—hangs everywhere. Rooms are decorated in contrasting beige and dark-wood accents and stocked with Acqua di Parma toiletries. Sergi Arola's eponymous restaurant is a chic, postmodern culinary playground. **Pros:** excellent views over Barcelona; first-rate, original art all over the halls and rooms; fine restaurants; general comfort and technology. **Cons:** a 20-minute hike from the Born, the nearest point of Barcelona; hotel feels like a colony of (mostly American) tourists set apart from local life. ✉ *Calle de la Marina 19, Port Olímpic* ☎ *93/221–1000* 🌐 *www.hotelartsbarcelona.com* *397 rooms, 59 suites, 27 apartments* *In-room: a/c, safe, refrigerator, Wi-Fi. In-hotel: 3 restaurants, room service, bar, pool, beachfront, laundry service, parking (paid)* ▭ *AE, DC, MC, V* *EP* Ⓜ *Ciutadella–Vil.la Olímpica* ✥ *G6.*

$$$$ Fodor's Choice ★ **W Hotel Barcelona.** Architect Ricardo Bofill's W Barcelona, locally known as Hotel Vela ("Hotel Sail"), opened in late 2009, when the towering sail-shaped monolith's golden glow joined the Hotel Arts as one of the most iconic shapes on the Barcelona waterfront. With top in-room and in-hotel technology joining features such as the WET pool, the Bliss spa, the Living Room/Lobby, and the Whatever/Whenever Service, the W has set its sights on uncontested leadership of the city's hotel scene, with master chef Carles Abellán at the helm of his own eponymous restaurant. **Pros:** unrivaled views and general design excitement and glamour; excellent restaurants; rooms are bright, clean-lined, and have nonpareil views in all directions. **Cons:** the high-rise icon could seem garish to some; a good hike from the Gothic Quarter. ✉ *Pl. Rosa dels Vents 1, Barceloneta* ☎ *93/295–2800* 🌐 *www.starwoodhotels.com* *473 rooms, 67 suites* *In-room: safe, refrigerator, Wi-Fi. In-hotel: 3 restaurants, bar, pool, gym, parking (paid)* ▭ *AE, DC, MC, V* Ⓜ *Barceloneta* *EP* ✥ *E6.*

EIXAMPLE

$$$–$$$$ Fodor's Choice ★ **Claris.** Universally acclaimed as one of Barcelona's best hotels, the Claris is a fascinating mélange of design and tradition. From the street, a late-20th-century glass and steel upper annex seems to have sprouted from the stone and concrete 19th-century town house below. Rooms come in 60 different modern layouts, some with restored 18th-century English furniture and some with contemporary furnishings from Barcelona's playful legion of designers. Lavishly endowed with wood and marble, the hotel also has a Japanese water garden, a rooftop cocktail terrace and pool, and two first-rate restaurants, including East 47, which has become one of the most admired dining spots in Barcelona. **Pros:** elegant service and furnishings; central location for shopping and Moderniste architecture; facilities and technology perfect. **Cons:** noisy corner; bathrooms are designer chic but impractical. ✉ *Carrer Pau Claris 150, Eixample* ☎ *93/487–6262* 🌐 *www.derbyhotels.es* *80 rooms, 40 suites* *In-room: a/c, Wi-Fi. In-hotel: 2 restaurants, bar, pool, gym, laundry service, parking (paid)* *AE, DC, MC, V* *EP* Ⓜ *Passeig de Gràcia* ✣ *E2.*

$$–$$$$ Fodor's Choice ★ **Condes de Barcelona.** One of Barcelona's most popular hotels, the Condes de Barcelona retains a grand charm with a marble-floored pentagonal lobby and the original columns and courtyard dating from the 1891 building. Rooms are decorated in contemporary neutrals. The newest rooms have hot tubs and terraces overlooking interior gardens. An affiliated fitness club around the corner offers golf, squash, and swimming. Chef Martín Berasategui's two restaurants, Lasarte and Loidi, are among Barcelona's most sought-after dining spots. Reserve rooms well in advance—demand is high, and early reservations score bargain rates. **Pros:** elegant Moderniste building with chic contemporary furnishings; prime spot in the middle of the Eixample. **Cons:** too large for much of a personal touch; staff somewhat overextended; restaurant Lasarte difficult to book. ✉ *Passeig de Gràcia 75, Eixample* ☎ *93/467–4780* 🌐 *www.condesdebarcelona.com* *181 rooms, 2 suites* *In-room: a/c, safe, Wi-Fi. In-hotel: 2 restaurants, bar, pools, gym, parking (paid)* *AE, DC, MC, V* *EP* Ⓜ *Passeig de Gràcia* ✣ *D2.*

$$–$$$ **Hotel Axel.** This hotel catering primarily (but by no means exclusively) to gays has spacious and spotless rooms with every possible comfort, a mid-Eixample location in what has come to be known as the "Gayxample." Rooms are soundproof and luminous, decked out in white-on-white decor punctuated by primary colors. Free bottled water is available in every corridor. The hotel restaurant is excellent, and the rooftop Skybar has wonderful views over the city. **Pros:** exciting minimalist contemporary design; graceful public spaces and lighting; friendly service. **Cons:** erotic in-room art could be outside some guests' comfort zone. ✉ *Aribau 33, Eixample* ☎ *93/323–9393* 🌐 *www.hotelaxel.com* *66 rooms* *In-room: a/c, Wi-Fi. In-hotel: restaurant, bar, pool, gym, spa, Internet terminal, Wi-Fi hotspot, parking (paid)* *AE, DC, MC, V* *EP* Ⓜ *Universitat* ✣ *C3.*

$$–$$$$ **Hotel Cram.** A sparkling cast of famous interior decorators had a hand in assembling this Eixample design hotel. The result is a warm avant-garde aesthetic with luxurious details such as high-pressure

showerheads. Just a block behind the leafy, orange tree–filled patio of the University of Barcelona's philology and letters school, a short walk from the central Eixample and the Rambla, home of Carles Gaig's famous restaurant (Can Gaig), the Cram is good place to keep in mind for impeccable accommodations in midtown Barcelona. **Pros:** dazzlingly designed; well positioned for the Eixample and Rambla; smart and friendly staff. **Cons:** Aribau is a major uptown artery, and traffic careens through at all hours; rooms are not spacious. ✉ *Carrer Aribau 54, Eixample* ☎ *93/216–7700* 🌐 *www.hotelcram.com* *67 rooms* *In-room:a/c, refrigerator, Wi-Fi. In-hotel: restaurant, bar, Internet terminal, Wi-Fi hotspot* *AE, DC, MC, V* *EP* Ⓜ *Universitat* ✣ *G9.*

> **WORD OF MOUTH**
>
> "[Hotel Granados 83] has a 4 star superior rating and while the rooms themselves are small, they are so well organized and so attractive that you don't even notice... The staff is very helpful—and hip... I would stay there again and again, especially when the great low season prices are in effect." —JulieVikmanis

$$$–$$$$ Fodor's Choice ★ **Hotel Granados 83.** Constructed with an exposed brick, steel, and glass factory motif with Buddhist and Hindu art giving the hotel a Zen tranquillity, this relative newcomer to the local hotel panorama has established itself as one of Barcelona's best design hotels. A few steps below the Diagonal and well situated for exploring the Eixample and the rest of the city, the hotel, named for Barcelona's famous composer and pianist Enric Granados, is an interesting compendium of materials and taste. Rooms have a certain masculine aesthetic, with leather, chrome, and dark bedding. The first-rate Mediterranean restaurant and the rooftop pool and solarium provide the cherry on top of this sundae. **Pros:** quiet semi-pedestrianized street; elegant building with chic design in wood, marble, and glass; polished service. **Cons:** room prices vary wildly according to availability and season. ✉ *Carrer Enric Granados 83, Eixample* ☎ *93/492–9670* 🌐 *www.derbyhotels.es* *70 rooms, 7 suites* *In-room: a/c, safe, refrigerator, Wi-Fi. In-hotel: restaurant, bar, pools, spa, gym, parking (paid)* *AE, DC, MC, V* *EP* Ⓜ *Provença* ✣ *C2.*

$$$$ Fodor's Choice ★ **Hotel Omm.** Another on Barcelona's lengthening list of design hotels, this postmodern architectural tour de force was conceived by a team of designers who sought to create, in a playful way, a mystic sense of peace mirroring its mantra. Minimalist rooms, a soothing reception area, and even the pool all contribute to this aura. The upper rooms overlook the roof terrace of Gaudí's Casa Milá. The restaurant, Moo, serves modern cuisine orchestrated by the Roca brothers—Joan, Josep, and Jordi—who achieved international prestige with their Celler de Can Roca near Girona. **Pros:** a perfect location for the upper Eixample; a design triumph; a sense of being at the epicenter of style; great nightlife scene around the bar on weekends. **Cons:** slightly pretentious staff; the restaurant is pricey and a little precious. ✉ *Roselló 265, Eixample* ☎ *93/445–4000* 🌐 *www.hotelomm.es* *87 rooms, 4 suites* *In-room: Wi-Fi. In-hotel: restaurant, bar, pool, parking (paid)* *AE, DC, MC, V* *EP* Ⓜ *Diagonal, Provença* ✣ *D2.*

$$$$ **Hotel Palace.** Founded in 1919 by Caesar Ritz, this is the original Ritz, the grande dame of Barcelona hotels, renamed in 2005. The imperial lobby is at once loose and elegant; guest rooms contain Regency furniture, and some have Roman-style mosaics in the baths. You can dine on first-rate French cuisine in the restaurant, Caelis. **Pros:** equidistant from Gothic Quarter and central Eixample; elegant and excellent service; consummate old-world luxury in rooms. **Cons:** a little stuffy; painfully pricey. ✉ *Gran Via 668, Eixample* ☎ *93/318–5200* 🌐 *www.hotelpalacebarcelona.com* *122 rooms* *In-room: a/c, Wi-Fi. In-hotel: restaurant, bar, gym* *AE, DC, MC, V* *EP* Ⓜ *Passeig de Gràcia* ✣ *E3.*

$$–$$$ **Hotel Pulitzer.** Built squarely over the metro's central hub and within walking distance of everything in town, this elegant new hotel could not be better situated to take advantage of Barcelona's many attractions. With ultramodern, high-tech equipment of every stripe—from DSL Internet and Wi-Fi to hot tubs—the Pulitzer combines smart service with chic decor at moderate prices. **Pros:** surprisingly quiet and collected sanctuary considering the central location; well-equipped bar and public Internet rooms; breakfast room bright and cheery. **Cons:** too large and busy for intimacy or much personal attention from staff. ✉ *Vergara 8, Eixample* ☎ *93/481–6767* 🌐 *www.hotelpulitzer.es* *91 rooms* *In-room: safe, Wi-Fi. In-hotel: restaurant, bar, Internet terminal, Wi-Fi hotspot* *AE, DC, MC, V* *EP* Ⓜ *Catalunya* ✣ *D3.*

$$$–$$$$ **Fodor's Choice** ★ **Majestic.** With an unbeatable location on Barcelona's most stylish boulevard, surrounded by fashion emporiums of every denomination, the Majestic is a near-perfect place to stay. The building is part Eixample town house and part modern extension, but pastels and Mediterranean hues warm each room. The superb restaurant, Drolma, is a destination in itself. **Pros:** perfectly placed in the center of the Eixample; good balance between technology and charm; one of Barcelona's best restaurants. **Cons:** facing one of the city's widest, brightest, noisiest, most commercial thoroughfares. ✉ *Passeig de Gràcia 68, Eixample* ☎ *93/488–1717* 🌐 *www.hotelmajestic.es* *271 rooms, 32 suites* *In-room: Wi-Fi. In-hotel: 2 restaurants, bar, pool, gym, parking (paid)* *AE, DC, MC, V* *EP* Ⓜ *Passeig de Gràcia* ✣ *D2.*

$$$–$$$$ **Mandarin Oriental Barcelona.** Since opening with a rush of excitement in November of 2009, this ultracontemporary art-deco palace by Oviedo-born designer Patricia Urquiola has quickly become a Barcelona mainstay at the very hub of the city's elegant Eixample. With views of Gaudí's Casa Batlló, this sleek new lodging option offers rooms overlooking a lush interior landscaped garden or over Passeig de Gràcia just a few blocks down from La Pedrera. Built into a renovated mid-20th-century town house, rooms are light and airy in off-white tones with a hint of Eastern-influenced minimalism. The hotel's gourmet restaurant Moments is managed by one of Catalonia's top chefs, Carme Ruscalleda, with her son Raúl Balam at the burners, while four other restaurants offer different dining environments. **Pros:** gorgeous high-tech equipment and design; central position for shopping and sightseeing. **Cons:** on a busy thoroughfare; slightly overmodern and antiseptic. ✉ *Passeig de Gràcia 38–40, Eixample* ☎ *93/151–8888* 🌐 *www.mandarinoriental.*

7

com 🖅 *98 rooms* ⟐ *In-room:safe, refrigerator, Wi-Fi. In-hotel: 5 res-taurants, bar, pool, spa, Wi-Fi hotspot, parking (paid)* ▤ *AE, DC, MC, V* ⦅◯⦆ *EP* Ⓜ *Passeig de Gràcia, Diagonal, Provença* ✛ *D3.*

$$$$ ⌸ **ME Barcelona.** With the new ME hotel east of Plaça de les Glòries, the Meliá hotel group has taken a serious run at the heights of Barcelona's hotel scene. Everything from the Dos Cielos restaurant with star chefs the Torres twins at the burners to the Angels & Kings pool and restau-rant flamboyantly parades the hippest design. Showers with natural rain showerheads, thread counts in the gazillions, feather pillows provided by Elysian geese, an organic herb garden for the restaurant—the ME has haute details to spare. **Pros:** well placed for a look at the Barcelona of the 21st century; handy to the Sagrada Família, the beach, and the torrid Poble Nou nightlife scene. **Cons:** a long taxi or subway ride from the Gothic Quarter; surrounded by new, high-rise architecture. ✉ *Pere IV 272–286, Eixample* ☏ *93/488–1717* ⊕ *www.me-barcelona.com* 🖅 *259 rooms* ⟐ *In-room: Wi-Fi. In-hotel: 2 restaurants, bar, pool, gym, park-ing (paid)* ▤ *AE, DC, MC, V* ⦅◯⦆ *EP* Ⓜ *Poble Nou* ✛ *H4.*

$$–$$$ ⌸ **Prestige Paseo de Gràcia.** A triumph of design built around a (mostly original) 1930s staircase, this hotel offers purity of line and sleek mini-malism as the reigning aesthetic principles, especially inside the rooms, with their stark monochromatic palette. The roof terrace is a tour de force, the different sections divided by contrasting colors and textures. **Pros:** ideally positioned in the middle of the Eixample; superbly bal-anced minimalist design; elegant service. **Cons:** opens onto a wide, bus-tling, bright, loud boulevard; understaffed, thus poor service; small rooms. ✉ *Passeig de Gràcia 62, Eixample* ☏ *93/272–4180* ⊕ *www. prestige-paseo-de-gracia.com* 🖅 *45 rooms* ⟐ *In-room: a/c, Wi-Fi. In-hotel: 2 restaurants, bar, pool, gym, Internet terminal, Wi-Fi hotspot, parking (paid)* ▤ *AE, DC, MC, V* ⦅◯⦆ *EP* Ⓜ *Passeig de Gràcia* ✛ *D2.*

$–$$ ⌸ **Room Mate Emma.** This 2009 addition to Barcelona's hotel fleet oper-ates under the motto "daring, cheerful, creative" and seems to fill the bill consistently. Along with minimalist lines and design details, Emma's pivotal location allows easy walking to everything in Barcelona (with the exception of Montjuïc and its art treasures). Following the less-is-more leads of architects Mies van der Rohe and, more recently, Rafael Moneo, the contemporary Barcelona aesthetic is sharp and simple, a welcome respite from Modernisme's opulence. The rooms have a certain space-age look, with white-on-white details and a few contrasting doses of purple, while the lobby and public rooms are futuristic and functional in patterned etched glass. **Pros:** perfectly positioned in the center of the Eixample; quintessential minimalist chic; smart, hip staff. **Cons:** on a busy street; lower rooms can be noisy. ✉ *Carrer Rosselló 205, Eix-ample* ☏ *93/238–5606* ⊕ *www.room-matehotels.com* 🖅 *56 rooms* ⟐ *In-room: safe, refrigerator, Wi-Fi. In-hotel: restaurant, bar, Internet ter-minal, Wi-Fi hotspot* ▤ *AE, DC, MC, V* ⦅◯⦆ *EP* Ⓜ *Diagonal* ✛ *C1.*

$$–$$$$ ⌸ **Villa Emilia.** This sleek design hotel offers fine lodging halfway between Sants station and the convention center at prices that are gen-erally affordable, except at moments of peak demand. Rooms on the sixth floor have more light and less noise, while rooms ending in 2 or 8 (68, 62, 58, 52, etc.) are larger and have superior views. If you pick

a room over the street, you'll have views of Montjuïc paired with quiet interiors. All rooms are fully equipped with of-the-moment technology, from Wi-Fi connections to plasma TVs. The seventh-floor roof terrace is a popular spot for breakfast and drinks. **Pros:** popular terrace for drinks and socializing; top technology and gadgetry; easy on the budget. **Cons:** not the most picturesque part of the Eixample; noisy streets. ✉ *Calàbria 115–117, Eixample* ☎ *93/252–5285* 🌐 *www.hotelvillaemilia.com* 53 *rooms* *In-room: cafe, Wi-Fi. In-hotel: bar, Internet terminal, Wi-Fi hotspot* *AE, DC, MC, V* *EP* Ⓜ *Rocafort* ✢ *A3.*

GRÀCIA

$$$–$$$$ **Fodor's Choice** ★

Casa Fuster. Casa Fuster is your only chance to stay in an Art Nouveau building designed by Lluís Domènech i Montaner, architect of the retina-rattling Palau de la Música Catalana. His last project, built in 1911, this elegant hotel at the bottom of the village of Gràcia shows a tendency toward the more classical Noucentisme that followed the decorative delirium of the Moderniste movement. The rooms and public spaces reinforce the Moderniste theme with Gaudí-designed chairs, *trencadis* (broken tile) floors and door handles, and Art Nouveau–inspired lamps and fixtures. The hotel restaurantserves fine Mediterranean cuisine, while the sumptuously decorated Café Vienés was a historic meeting place for Barcelona's movers and shakers of the early 20th century. **Pros:** well placed for exploring Gràcia as well as the Eixample; equidistant from the port and Upper Barcelona's Tibidabo. **Cons:** the design can feel a little heavy and mournful; some in-room facilities look better than they work (such as the showers that require you to spray cold water on yourself to turn them on) ✉ *Passeig de Gràcia 132, Gràcia* ☎ *93/255–300093/255–3002* 🌐 *www.hotelcasafuster.com* *66 rooms, 39 suites* *In-room: a/c. In-hotel: restaurant, room service, bar, pool, gym, laundry service, Wi-Fi hotspot, parking (paid)* *AE, DC, MC, V* *EP* Ⓜ *Diagonal* ✢ *D1.*

SARRIÀ, SANT GERVASI, PUTXET, AND PEDRALBES

$$–$$$$ **Fodor's Choice** ★

Turó de Vilana. Surrounded by bougainvillea-festooned villas above Barcelona's Passeig de la Bonanova, this shiny place has a hot tub in every room, gleaming halls, and public areas of stone, steel, and glass run by a pleasant staff. Rooms are polished with state-of-the-art equipment and contemporary designer furnishings. In summer, Upper Barcelona is noticeably cooler, not to mention quieter at night. The Turó de Vilana is a 10-minute walk from the Sarrià train that connects you with the city center in a quarter of an hour. **Pros:** new furnishings and latest technology in rooms; bright and cheery service and design; verdant and refreshing surroundings. **Cons:** in upper Sarrià and a long way from the center of town. ✉ *Vilana 7, Sant Gervasi* ☎ *93/434–0363* 🌐 *www.turodevilana.com* *20 rooms* *In-room: a/c, Wi-Fi. In-hotel: restaurant, room service, Wi-Fi hotspot, parking (paid)* *AE, DC, MC, V* *EP* Ⓜ *Sarrià* ✢ *D1.*

7

NIGHTLIFE AND THE ARTS

Barcelona's art and nightlife scenes start early and never quite stop. To find out what's on, look in newspapers or the weekly *Guía Del Ocio,* which has a section in English and is available at newsstands all over town. *Activitats,* available at the Palau de la Virreina (*La Rambla 99*) or the Centre Santa Monica (*La Rambla 7*), lists cultural events.

THE ARTS

CASTELLERS AND SARDANAS

The Sunday-morning papers carry announcements for local neighborhood celebrations, flea markets and produce fairs, puppet shows, storytelling sessions for children, sardana dancing, bell-ringing concerts, and, best of all, *castellers* (🌐 *www.bcn.es*) has listings in English. The castellers, complex human pyramids sometimes reaching as high as 10 stories, are a quintessentially Catalan phenomenon that originated in the 17th century, in the Penedés region west of Barcelona. Castellers perform regularly at neighborhood fiestas and key holidays. Sardanas usually begin at 1 PM, Castellers start between 11 AM and noon. Most Sunday-morning events are over by 2, when lunchtime officially reigns supreme.

Sardanas are performed in front of the cathedral at 1 PM every Saturday and Sunday and at different points such as Plaça Sant Jaume during the Festes de la Mercé and other festes.

CLASSICAL MUSIC

The basilica of Santa Maria del Mar, the church of Santa Maria del Pi, the Monestir de Pedralbes, Drassanes Reials, and the Saló del Tinell, among other ancient and intimate spaces, hold concerts.

Barcelona's most famous concert hall is the Moderniste **Palau de la Música Catalana** (✉ *Carrer Palau de la Música 4–6, Sant Pere* ☎ *93/295–7200*), with performances September–June. Tickets range from €6 to €100 and are best purchased well in advance, though a last-minute *palco sin vistas* (box seat with no sight of the stage) is a good way to get into the building for a concert. The contemporary **Auditori de Barcelona** (✉ *Carrer Lepant 150, near Pl. de les Glòries, Eixample* ☎ *93/247–9300*) has classical music, with occasional jazz and pop thrown in. Barcelona's **Gran Teatre del Liceu** (✉ *La Rambla 51–59 [box office: La Rambla de Capuchinos 63], Rambla* ☎ *93/485–9900 box office*) stages operas and recitals.

DANCE

L'Espai de Dansa i Música de la Generalitat de Catalunya (✉ *Travessera de Gràcia 63, Eixample* ☎ *93/414–3133*)—generally listed as L'Espai, or "The Space"—is the prime venue for ballet and modern dance, as well as some musical offerings. **El Mercat de les Flors** (✉ *Carrer Lleida 59, Eixample* ☎ *93/426–1875*), near Plaça d'Espanya, is a traditional venue for modern dance and theater.

FILM

Though many foreign films are dubbed, Barcelona has a full complement of original-language cinema; look for listings marked "v.o." (*versión original*).

Verdi (✉ *Carrer Verdi 32, Gràcia*) screens current releases with original-version soundtracks in a fun neighborhood for pre- and postmovie eating and drinking. The **Icaria Yelmo** (✉ *Salvador Espriu 61, Port Olímpic*) complex in the Olympic Port has the city's largest selection of English-language films. **Renoir Les Corts** (✉ *Eugeni d'Ors 12, behind Diagonal's El Corte Inglés, Diagonal*) is a good choice for recently released English-language features of all kinds. **Casablanca** (✉ *Passeig de Gràcia 115, Eixample*) plays original-language movies, generally art flicks.

FLAMENCO

In Catalunya, flamenco, like bullfighting, is regarded as an import from Andalusia. However, unlike bullfighting, there is a strong interest in and market for flamenco in Barcelona. Tour groups in search of flamenco gravitate to **El Cordobés** (✉ *La Rambla 35, Rambla* ☎ *93/317–6653*). **El Patio Andaluz** (✉ *Aribau 242, Eixample* ☎ *93/209–3378*) has rather touristy flamenco shows twice nightly (10 and midnight) and a karaoke section upstairs. **El Tablao de Carmen** (✉ *Poble Espanyol, Av. Marquès de Comillas s/n Montjuïc* ☎ *93/325–6895*) hosts touring flamenco troupes up on Montjuïc. On the Plaça Reial, **Los Tarantos** (✉ *Pl. Reial 17, Barri Gòtic* ☎ *93/318–3067*) spotlights Andalusia's best flamenco. **Palacio del Flamenco** (✉ *Balmes 139, Eixample* ☎ *93/218–7237* 🌐 *www.palaciodelflamenco.com*) showcases some of Barcelona's best flamenco. Prices start at €*30* for a drink and the show and go up to €40–€60 for dinner and a show.

7

NIGHTLIFE

CABARET

Bcn Seven Dreams (✉ *Pl. Mayor 9, Poble Espanyol, Avda. Marquès de Comillas s/n, Montjuïc* ☎ *93/325–4604*) in Montjuïc's Poble Espanyol, is Barcelona's last true cabaret show, featuring a chorus line, song and dance, and light erotic innuendo. Near the bottom of the Rambla, the minuscule **Bar Pastis** (✉ *Carrer Santa Mònica 4, Rambla* ☎ *93/318–7980*) has live performances and LPs of every song Edith Piaf recorded. **Star Class** (✉ *Av. Sarrià 44, Eixample* ☎ *93/430–9156*) has a combination cabaret and disco program. **Joy's** (✉ *Carrer Rocafort 231, Eixample* ☎ *93/430–9156*) hosts a floor show, cabaret, and dancing.

CASINO

The **Gran Casino de Barcelona** (✉ *Carrer de la Marina, Port Olímpic* ☎ *93/225–7878*), under the Hotel Arts, is open daily 1 PM–5 AM.

JAZZ, BLUES, AND LIVE MUSIC VENUES

BARRI GÒTIC The Gothic Quarter's **Harlem Jazz Club** (✉ *Carrer Comtessa Sobradiel 8, Barri Gòtic* ☎ *93/310–0755*) is small but atmospheric, with good jazz and country bands.

BORN-RIBERA **Nao Colón/Club Bamboo** (✉ *Av. Marques de l'Argentera 19, Born-Ribera* ☎ *93/268–7633*) combines the sounds and the cuisine of the

Barcelona is a happening music destination.

Mediterranean followed by jazz, blues, flamenco, fusion, hard rock, and house after midnight.

EIXAMPLE **Luz de Gas** (✉ *Carrer Muntaner 246, Eixample* ☎ *93/209–7711*) hosts every genre from Irish fusion to Cuban sounds. The bustling **Zacarías** (✉ *Av. Diagonal 477, Eixample* ☎ *93/207–5643*) stages live music from a variety of musical genres, including jazz, rock, folk, and blues.

PORT OLÍMPIC **Luna Mora** (✉ *Port Olímpic, next to Hotel Arts, Port Olímpic* ☎ *93/221–6161*) stages the gamut, from country blues to salsa and soul.

RAMBLA **Jamboree-Jazz and Dance-Club** (✉ *Pl. Reial 17, Rambla* ☎ *93/301–7564*) is a center for jazz, rock, and flamenco.

LATE-NIGHT BARS

Bar musical is Spanish for any bar with music loud enough to drown out conversation. **Port Olímpic** and the Port Vell's **Maremagnum** are wildly active but, compared to other options, better to avoid. Especially in summer and on weekends, these are far from Barcelona's best nightlife options.

EIXAMPLE Two blocks from Velodrom is the intriguing *barmuseo* (bar-cum-museum) **La Fira** (✉ *Carrer Provença 171, Eixample* ☎ *93/323–7271*). **George and Dragon** (✉ *Carrer Diputació 269, Eixample* ☎ *93/488–1765*), named for Barcelona's ubiquitous symbols of good and evil, is a rollicking English pub just off Passeig de Gràcia.

Over by the Sagrada Família, the **Michael Collins Irish Pub** (✉ *Pl. Sagrada Família 4, Eixample* ☎ *93/459–1964*) has a strong Anglo following. **Nick Havanna** (✉ *Carrer Rosselló 208, Eixample* ☎ *93/215–6591*) has, along with a consistently hot program of live music, Barcelona's most entertaining urinals. Café-restaurant-bar **Salero** (✉ *Carrer del Rec 60, Eixample* ☎ *93/488–1765*) is always packed with young miscreants. Above Via Augusta in Upper Barcelona, the **Sherlock Holmes** (✉ *Carrer Copernic 42–44, Eixample* ☎ *93/414–2184*) is an ongoing Brit-fest with live musical performances and dark intimate corners. **Universal** (✉ *Carrer Marià Cubí 182–184, Eixample* ☎ *93/200–7470*) has been the hottest bar in town for 30 years and is still going strong. For a more laid-back scene, with high ceilings, billiards, and *tapas*, visit the new Carles Abellan–catered **Velodrom** (✉ *Carrer Muntaner 211–213, Eixample* ☎ *93/230–6022*), below the Diagonal.

RAMBLA **Glaciar** (✉ *Pl. Reial 13, Rambla* ☎ *93/302–1163*) is *the* spot for young out-of-towners.

RAVAL **Bar Almirall** (✉ *Carrer Joaquin Costa 33, Raval* ☎ *93/412–1535*) has an Art Nouveau chicness. **Bar Muy Buenas** (✉ *Carrer del Carme 63, Raval* ☎ *93/442–5053*) is an Art Nouveau gem.

Downtown, deep in the Barrio Chino, try the **London Bar** (✉ *Carrer Nou de la Rambla 34, Raval* ☎ *93/302–3102*), an Art Nouveau circus haunt with a trapeze suspended above the bar. **L'Ovella Negra** (✉ *Carrer de les Sitges 5, Raval* ☎ *93/317–1087*) is the top student tavern.

UPPER BARCELONA Above Via Augusta, **Opiniao** (✉ *Carrer Ciutat de Balaguer 67, below Bonanova, La Bonanova* ☎ *93/418–3399*) is another Upper-Barcelona dive, aka a hot local club.

NIGHTCLUBS AND DISCOS

Most clubs have a discretionary cover charge and like to inflict it on foreigners, so dress up and be prepared to talk your way past the bouncer. Any story can work; for example, you own a chain of nightclubs and are on a world tour. Don't expect much to happen until 1:30 or 2.

BORN-RIBERA **Luz de Luna** (✉ *Carrer Comerç 21, La Ribera* ☎ *93/310–7542*) lays down wall-to-wall salsa.

EIXAMPLE **Agua de Luna** (✉ *Carrer Viladomat 211, Eixample* ☎ *93/410–0440*) is a torrid salsa scene in the western Eixample. Salsa sizzles at the exuberantly Caribbean **Antilla BCN Latin Club** (✉ *Carrer Aragó 141, Eixample* ☎ *93/451–4564*). A line forms at **Bikini** (✉ *Carrer Deu i Mata 105, at Entença, Eixample* ☎ *93/322–0005*) on festive Saturday nights. **Búcaro** (✉ *Carrer Aribau 195, Eixample* ☎ *93/209–6562*) rocks until dawn, albeit largely for the extremely young. **Buda Barcelona** (✉ *Carrer Pau Claris 92, Eixample* ☎ *93/318–4252*) is the hottest nightspot in the Eixample, with celebrities and glamour galore. **Costa Breve** (✉ *Carrer Aribau 230, Eixample* ☎ *93/200–7346*) accepts postgraduates with open arms. **El Otro** (✉ *Carrer Valencia 166, Eixample* ☎ *93/323–6759*) is kind to aging (over-thirty) miscreants. Still popular, though as much as it once was, is the prisonesque nightclub **Otto Zutz** (✉ *Carrer Lincoln 15, Eixample* ☎ *93/238–0722*), off Via Augusta. **Row Club** (✉ *Carrer Rosselló 208, Eixample* ☎ *93/237–5405*) is big on techno. **Sala Cibeles** (✉ *Carrer de Córsega 363, Eixample* ☎ *93/272–0910*) has a large sound system and singing DJs. The nearly classic **Up and Down** (✉ *Carrer Numancia 179, Eixample* ☎ *93/280–2922*), pronounced "Pen-*dow,*" is a good choice for elegant carousers.

MONTJUÏC **Torres de Avila** (✉ *Av. Marquès de Comillas 25, Montjuïc* ☎ *93/424–9309*), in Pueblo Espanyol, is wild and woolly until broad daylight on weekends.

PEDRALBES **Pachá** (✉ *Carrer Dr. Marañon 17, Pedralbes-Les Corts* ☎ *93/204–0412*) offers two raging discos and a restaurant.

POBLE NOU (EAST BARCELONA) The **Loft** (✉ *Carrer Pamplona 88, Poble Nou* ☎ *93/272–0910*), an offshoot of Sala Razzmatazz, is dedicated to electronic music.

Sala Razzmatazz (✉ *Carrer Almogavers 122, Poble Nou* ☎ *93/320–8200*) offers Friday and Saturday disco madness until dawn. Weeknight concerts have international stars like Ani DiFranco and Enya.

PORT OLÍMPIC The beachfront **CDLC** (✉ *Passeig Maritim 32, Port Olímpic* ☎ *93/224–0470*) has compartmentalized *sofa-camas* (sofa beds of a sort) for prime canoodling. **Shôko** (✉ *Passeig Marítim 36, Port Olímpic* ☎ *93/225–9200*) is an excellent Asian-fusion restaurant until midnight, when it morphs into the beachfront's wildest dance and lounge club.

RAVAL **DosTrece** (✉ *Carrer del Carme 40, Raval* ☎ *93/443–0341*) packs in young internationals for dancing and carousing. **It Café** (✉ *Carrer Joaquin Costa 4, Raval* ☎ *93/443–0341*) is a design oasis not far from the MACBA in the Raval. For big-band tango in an old-fashioned *sala de baile* (dance hall), head to **La Paloma** (✉ *Carrer Tigre 27, Raval* ☎ *93/301–6897*), which has kitschy 1950s furnishings.

TIBIDABO **Danzatoria** (✉ *Av. Tibidabo 61, Tibidabo* ☎ *93/211–6261*), a fusion of Salsitas and Partycular (two former clubs), is a "multispace" with five venues (disco, hall, dance, chill-out, garden) and fills with models and hopeful guys.

SPORTS AND THE OUTDOORS

HIKING

The **Collserola** hills behind the city offer well-marked trails, fresh air, and lovely views. Take the San Cugat, Sabadell, or Terrassa FFCC train from Plaça de Catalunya and get off at Baixador de Vallvidrera; the information center, 10 minutes uphill next to **Vil.la Joana** (now the Jacint Verdaguer Museum), has maps of this mountain woodland 20 minutes from downtown. The walk back into town can take from two to five hours, depending on your speed and the trails you pick. **Club Excursionista de Catalunya** (✉ *Carrer Paradís 10, Barri Gòtic* ☎ *93/315–2311*) has information on hiking in Barcelona and throughout Catalunya.

SOCCER

If you're in Barcelona between September and June, go see the celebrated FC Barcelona play soccer (preferably against Real Madrid, if you can score a ticket) at Barcelona's gigantic stadium, **Camp Nou** (✉ *Carrer Arístides Maillol, Les Corts* ☎ *93/496–3608* 🌐 *www.fcbarcelona.com* 🎫 *Museum €6, combined ticket including tour of museum, field, and sports complex €10* ⏲ *Museum Mon.–Sat. 10–6:30, Sun. 10–2* Ⓜ *Collblanc, Palau Reial*). A worthwhile alternative to seeing a game is the guided tour of the FC Barcelona museum and facilities. The museum has five video screens showing the club's most memorable goals, along with player biographies and displays chronicling the history of one of Europe's most colorful soccer clubs.

SHOPPING

Between the surging fashion scene, a host of young clothing designers, clever home furnishings, rare and delicious foodstuffs, and art and antiques, Barcelona might just be the best place in Spain to unload extra ballast from your wallet. It's true, bargains are few, outside saffron and rope-sole shoes, but quality and selection are excellent. Most stores are open Monday–Saturday 9–1:30 and 5–8. Virtually all are closed on Sunday.

SHOPPING DISTRICTS

Barcelona's prime shopping districts are the Passeig de Gràcia, Rambla de Catalunya, Plaça de Catalunya, Porta de l'Àngel, and Avinguda Diagonal up to Carrer Ganduxer.

For high fashion, browse along **Passeig de Gràcia** and the **Diagonal** between Plaça Joan Carles I and Plaça Francesc Macià. There are two dozen antiques shops in the Gothic Quarter, many off the Passeig de Gràcia on Bulevard dels Antiquaris, and still more in Gràcia and Sarrià. **Bulevard Rosa** is a fashion and shopping mall off Passeig de Gràcia. For old-fashioned Spanish shops, prowl the Gothic Quarter, especially **Carrer Ferran.** The area surrounding **Plaça del Pi,** from the Boqueria to Carrer Portaferrissa and Carrer de la Canuda, is thick with boutiques, jewelry, and design shops. The **Barri de la Ribera,** around Santa Maria del Mar, especially the Born area, has a cluster of design, fashion, and food shops. Design, jewelry, and knickknack shops cluster on Carrer Banys Vells and Carrer Flassaders, near Carrer Montcada. The shopping colossus **L'Illa,** on the Diagonal beyond Carrer Ganduxer, includes the department store FNAC, Custo, and myriad temptations. **Carrer Tuset,** north of the Diagonal, has lots of small boutiques. The **Maremagnum** mall, in Port Vell, is convenient to downtown. **Diagonal Mar,** at the eastern end of the diagonal, and the **Fòrum** complex offer many shopping options in a mega-shopping-mall environment.

SPECIALTY STORES

ANTIQUES

The headquarters of antiques shopping is the Gothic Quarter, where **Carrer de la Palla** and **Carrer Banys Nous** are lined with shops full of prints, maps, books, paintings, and furniture. An antiques market is held in front of the Catedral de la Seu every Thursday from 10 to 8. There are also about 70 shops off Passeig de Gràcia on Bulevard dels Antiquaris. In Upper Barcelona, the entire village of **Sarrià** is becoming an antiquer's destination, with shops along Cornet i Mas, Pedró de la Creu, and Major de Sarrià.

EIXAMPLE **Alcanto** (✉ *Passeig de Gràcia 55–57, Eixample*) is a clearinghouse for buying and selling. **Antiguedades J. Pla** (✉ *Carrer Aragó 517, Eixample*) buys and sells antiques.

The Eixample's **Centre d'Antiquaris** (✉ *Passeig de Gràcia 55, Eixample*) contains 75 antiques stores. Moderniste aficionados should check out **Gothsland** (✉ *Carrer Consell de Cent 331, Eixample*). **Novecento** (✉ *Passeig de Gràcia 75, Eixample*) has antique art and jewelry.

ART

There's a cluster of art galleries on Carrer Consell de Cent between Passeig de Gràcia and Carrer Balmes and around the corner on Rambla de Catalunya. The Born–Santa Maria del Mar quarter is another art destination, along Carrer Montcada and the parallel Carrer Banys Vells.

BARRI GÒTIC Carrer Petritxol, which leads down into Plaça del Pi, is lined with galleries, notably **Sala Parès** (✉ *Carrer Petritxol 5, Barri Gòtic*).

BORN-RIBERA The always ticking **Metrònom** (✉ *Carrer Fussina 4, La Ribera*) at the north end of the Born has a weakness for performance art and edgy erotic installations and photography.

EIXAMPLE **Eude** (✉ *Carrer Consell de Cent 278, Eixample*) showcases young artists. **Fundació La Caixa**✉ *Passeig de Gràcia, Eixample*) has regular exhibits at its Casa Milà gallery on Passeig de Gràcia. **Galeria Joan Prats** (✉ *La Rambla de Catalunya 54, Eixample*) is a veteran, known for the quality of its artists' works. The **Joan Gaspar** (✉ *Pl. Letamendi 1, Eixample*) started with Picasso and Miró. **Sala Dalmau** (✉ *Carrer Consell de Cent 347, Eixample*) is an established art outlet. **Sala Rovira** (✉ *La Rambla de Catalunya 62, Eixample*) has shown top artists Tom Carr and Blanca Vernis.

RAMBLA The **Espai Xavier Miserachs** (✉ *La Rambla 99, Rambla*) in the Palau de la Virreina has eclectic temporary exhibits of painting, photography, design, and illustration.

RAVAL **La Capella de l'Antic Hospital de la Santa Creu** (✉ *Carrer Hospital 56, Raval*) exhibits installations and new art.

BOOKS

BARRI GÒTIC **El Corte Inglés** (✉ *Porta de l'Àngel 19–21, Barri Gòtic*), especially the branch in Porta del Àngel, sells English guidebooks and novels.

EIXAMPLE **Altair** (✉ *Gran Via de les Corts Catalanes 616, Eixample*) is Barcelona's premier travel and adventure bookstore, with many titles in English. **BCN Books** (✉ *Carrer Roger de Llúria 118, Eixample*) is a top store for books in English. **Casa del Llibre** (✉ *Passeig de Gràcia 62, Eixample*) is a book feast, with English titles.

SHOPPING BEST BETS

Best Antiques shopping street: Carrer de la Palla

Best Bling: Majoral

Best Bookstore: La Central

Best Boutique: Custo Barcelona

Best Ceramics Studio: Art Escudellers

Best Cobbler: La Manual Alpargatera

Best Gourmet Food Market: Mantequeria Can Ravell

Best Music Store: Discos Castelló

Best Spice Shop: Casa Gispert

Best Stationery Boutique: Papirum

> **BOOKS AND ROSES**
>
> Barcelona's April 23 Sant Jordi (Saint George) celebration is a Valentine's Day, Catalan-style, when ladies are given roses and men receive books. On that day, Barcelona becomes one huge rose-scented bookstore, with kiosks full of books next to flower sellers lining the Rambla. The rose tradition began with Barcelona's medieval rose festival, and international book day was appended later, to celebrate the April 23, 1616, deaths of both Miguel de Cervantes and William Shakespeare.

Fodor's Choice ★ **La Central** (✉ *Carrer Mallorca 237, Eixample*) is Barcelona's best bookstore. **La Central del Raval** (✉ *Carrer Elisabets 6, Eixample*), in the former chapel of the Casa de la Misericòrdia, sells books on architecture. **Laie** (✉ *Carrer Pau Claris 85, Eixample*) is a book lover's sanctuary, with cultural events as well as stacks.

RAMBLA The bookstore in the **Palau de la Virreina** (✉ *La Rambla 99, Rambla*) has books on art, design, and Barcelona in general.

CLOTHING BOUTIQUES AND JEWELRY

BARRI GÒTIC **El Ingenio** (✉ *Carrer Rauric 6, Barri Gòtic*) has one of the prettiest antique storefronts in town; inside are costumes, puppets, carnival masks, and gadgets for all ages. **May Day** (✉ *C. Portaferrissa 16, Barri Gòtic*) carries cutting-edge clothing, footwear, and accessories.

BORN-RIBERA **Custo Barcelona** (✉ *Pl. de les Olles 7, Born-Ribera*) is becoming a city icon and *the* place for colorful, whimsical, tops that you can immediately wear out at the feeding frenzy going on next door at the Cal Pep *tapas* bar. **Majoral** (✉ *Carrer Argenteria 66, Born-Ribera*) makes and sells organic, almost edible-looking rings, earrings, brooches, pins, and assorted bling. **Otman** (✉ *Carrer Cirera 4, La Ribera*) has light and racy frocks, belts, blouses, and skirts.

EIXAMPLE **Adolfo Domínguez** (✉ *Passeig de Gràcia 35, Av. Diagonal 570, Eixample*) is one of Spain's leading designers. **David Valls** (✉ *C. Valencia 235, Eixample*) represents new, young Barcelona fashion design. **El Bulevard Rosa** (✉ *Passeig de Gràcia 53–55, Eixample*) is a collection of boutiques with the latest outfits.

The two locations of Toni Miró's **Groc** (✉ *C. Muntaner 382, Eixample* ✉ *La Rambla de Catalunya 100, Eixample*) have the latest looks for men, women, and children. **Janina** (✉ *Rambla Catalunya 94, Eixample*) sells trendy and stylish lingerie by La Perla, Eres, Dolce and Gabbana, and others. **Joaquim Berao** (✉ *C. Rosselló 277, Eixample*) is a top jewelry designer. **No Té Nom** (✉ *Carrer Pau Claris 159, Eixample*) means "it has no name" in Catalan; it sells new fabrics and design accessories. **On Land** (✉ *Valencia 273, Eixample*) is all street fashion by the hottest young designers in town.

Galeria Meko (✉ *Sant Pere Més Baix 11, Sant Pere* ☎ *93/268–0222*) is a gorgeously restored 17th-century space showcasing Carmen Pintor's *joieria d'autor* (original jewelry).

CERAMICS

Although perusing smaller establishments is always worthwhile, one of Barcelona's big department stores, **El Corte Inglés,** at Plaça de Catalunya or Avinguda Diagonal (for addresses, look under "Department Stores"), is also a good bet for ceramics.

BARRI GÒTIC **Art Escudellers** (✉ *Carrer Escudellers 23–25, Barri Gòtic*) displays ceramics from more than 200 artisans from all over Spain; Catalonia's famous La Bisbal, Agentona, and La Galera ceramics are well represented with their characteristic cobalt, mustard, and deep green glazed, unglazed, and partially glazed works. **Ítaca** (✉ *Carrer Ferrán 26, Barri Gòtic*) has ceramic plates, bowls, and pottery from Talavera de la Reina and La Bisbal. For Lladró, try **Pla de l'Os** (✉ *Carrer de la Boqueria 3, Barri Gòtic*), off the Rambla.

DEPARTMENT STORES

Spain's ubiquitous **El Corte Inglés** (✉ *Pl. de Catalunya 14, Eixample* ✉ *Porta de l'Angel 19–21, Barri Gòtic* ✉ *Pl. Francesc Macià 58, Sant Gervasi* ✉ *Av. Diagonal 617, Les Corts*) has four locations in Barcelona. On Plaça de Catalunya you can also find the international book and music store **FNAC** and the furniture and household design goods store **Habitat,** also on Carrer Tuset at the Diagonal.

INTERIOR DESIGN AND HOME FURNISHINGS

The area around the church of Santa Maria del Mar, an artisans' quarter since medieval times, is full of cheerful design stores and art galleries.

BARRI GÒTIC Cutlery flourishes at the stately **Ganiveteria Roca** (✉ *Pl. del Pi 3, Barri Gòtic*), opposite the giant rose window of the Santa Maria del Pi church. **Gotham** (✉ *Cervantes 7, Barri Gòtic*), behind Town Hall, restores furniture from the 1950s and 1960s. It's a perennial set for Pedro Almodóvar movies. Amid mouthwatering interior design, **La Comercial** (✉ *Carrer del Rec 52 and 73, La Ribera*), off Passeig del Born, has clothes by international designers. **Sita Murt** (✉ *Carrer d'Avinyó 18, Barri Gòtic*) is a stunning subterranean space with a clever play of mirrors and international collections that include Esteve Sita Murt.

BORN-RIBERA **Estudi Pam2** (✉ *Sabateret 1–3, La Ribera*), behind Carrer Montcada, sells ingenious design items. **Papers Coma** (✉ *Carrer Montcada 20, La Ribera*) has inventive knickknacks. **Suspect** (✉ *Carrer Comerç 29, La Ribera*), north of the Born, specializes in clothes and furniture made by Spastor, a group of Barcelona designers. **Vientos del Sur** (✉ *Carrer Argenteria 78, La Ribera*), part of the Natura chain, has a good selection of textile and wood-carved crafts, as well as clothing and gift items.

EIXAMPLE **bd** (short for *Barcelona Design*✉ *Carrer Mallorca 291–293, Eixample*) is a spare, cutting-edge home-furnishing store in a Moderniste gem, Domènech i Montaner's Casa Thomas. Upscale **Gimeno** (✉ *Passeig de Gràcia 102, Eixample*) has everything from clever suitcases to the latest in furniture design. **Vinçon** (✉ *Passeig de Gràcia 96, Eixample*) occupies a rambling Moderniste house and carries everything from Filofaxes to handsome kitchenware.

FINE FOODS

BARRI GÒTIC **Caelum** (✉ *C. de la Palla 8, Barri Gòtic*) sells crafts and such foods as honey and preserves made in convents and monasteries all over Spain. **La Casa del Bacalao** (✉ *Comtall 8, off Portal del Angel, Barri Gòtic*) specializes in salt cod and books of codfish recipes. **OroLíquido** (✉ *C. de la Palla 8, Barri Gòtic*) sells the finest olive oils from Spain and the world at large.

BORN-RIBERA Behind the Picasso Museum, **Born Cooking** (✉ *Corretger 9, La Ribera*) is a work of art in itself, serving delicious cakes, quiches, and all manner of sweets and savories.**Casa Gispert** (✉ *Carrer Sombrerers 23, La Ribera*), on the inland side of Santa Maria del Mar, is one of the most aromatic and aesthetically perfect shops in Barcelona, bursting with spices, saffron, chocolates, and nuts. **El Magnífico** (✉ *Carrer Argenteria 64, La Ribera*) is famous for its coffees. **Jobal** (✉ *C. Princesa 38, La Ribera*) is a charming and fragrant saffron and spice shop. **La Barcelonesa** (✉ *Carrer Comerç 27, La Ribera*) specializes in dry goods, spices, tea, and saffron. **La Botifarreria de Santa Maria** (✉ *Carrer Santa Maria 4, La Ribera*), next to the church of Santa Maria, has excellent cheeses, hams, pâtés, and homemade *sobrassadas* (pork pâté with paprika). **Tot Formatge** (✉ *Passeig del Born 13, La Ribera*) has cheeses from all over Spain and the world. **Vila Viniteca** (✉ *C. Agullers 7, La Ribera*), near Santa Maria del Mar, is one of the best wine shops in Barcelona; the produce store across the way sells some of the best cheeses around.

EIXAMPLE **La Palmera** (✉ *C. Enric Granados 57, Eixample*) has a superb collection of wines, hams, cheeses, and olive oils.

★ **Mantequeria Can Ravell** (✉ *Carrer Aragó 313, Eixample*), a restaurant and delicatessen, is Barcelona's number-one all-around wine, cheese, ham, and fine foods specialist.

SANT GERVASI **Vilaplana** (✉ *C. Francesc Perez-Cabrero, Sant Gervasi*) is famous for its pastries, cheeses, hams, pâtés, caviars, and fine deli items. **Tutusaus** (✉ *C. Francesc Perez-Cabrero 5, Sant Gervasi*) specializes in fine ibérico hams and superb cheeses from all over Europe.

SARRIÀ **La Cave** (✉ *Av. J. V. Foix 80, Sarrià*) is a wine cellar with flair; bottles are arranged by varietal, price, and taste.

FOOD AND FLEA MARKETS

Barcelona's spectacular food markets include the Mercat de la Llibertat, near Plaça Gal.la Placidia, and Mercat de la Revolució, on Travessera de Gràcia, both in Gràcia. On Thursday, a natural-produce market (honey, cheese) fills Plaça del Pi with interesting tastes and aromas. On Sunday morning, Plaça Reial hosts a stamp and coin market, Plaça Sant Josep Oriol holds a painter's market, and there is a general crafts and flea market near the Columbus Monument at the port end of the Rambla.

BARRI GÒTIC The **Mercat Gòtic** (✉ *Pl. de la Seu, Barri Gòtic*) fills the area in front of the Catedral de la Seu on Thursday.

RAMBLA Fodor's Choice ★ The **Boqueria** (✉ *La Rambla 91, Rambla*) is Barcelona's most colorful food market and the oldest of its kind in Europe. Open Monday to Saturday, 8 to 8, it's most active before 3 PM.

7

EIXAMPLE Barcelona's largest flea market, **Els Encants** (✉ *Dos de Maig, on Pl. de les Glòries, Eixample* Ⓜ *Glòries*) is held Monday, Wednesday, Friday, and Saturday, from 8 to 7.

The **Mercat de Sant Antoni** (✉ *Ronda Sant Antoni, Eixample*) is an old-fashioned food, clothing, and used-book (many in English) market that's best on Sunday. It's currently closed for restoration until 2011.

GIFTS AND MISCELLANY

BARRI GÒTIC **La Manual Alpargatera** (✉ *Carrer d'Avinyó 7, Barri Gòtic*), off Carrer Ferran, specializes in handmade rope-sole sandals and espadrilles. **La Lionesa** (✉ *C. Ample 21, Barri Gòtic*) is an old-timey grocery store. Stationery lovers will want to linger in the Gothic Quarter's **Papirum** (✉ *Baixada de la Llibreteria 2, Barri Gòtic*), a tiny, medievalesque shop with exquisite hand-printed papers and writing implements. **Solé** (✉ *C. Ample 7, Barri Gòtic*) makes shoes by hand and sells others from all over the world.

RAVAL **Baclava** (✉ *C. Notariat 10, Raval*) sells artisanal textile products. Barcelona's best music store is **Discos Castelló** (✉ *Carrer Tallers 3, Raval*). For textiles, try **Teranyina** (✉ *C. Notariat 10, Raval*), which shares an address with Baclava.

SANT PERE **Les Muses del Palau** (✉ *Sant Pere Més Alt 1, Sant Pere*), next to the Palau de la Música Catalana, shows and sells Palau de la Música–themed gifts from neckties to pencils, posters, models, jigsaw puzzles, and teacups.

SIDE TRIPS FROM BARCELONA

MONTSERRAT

50 km (30 mi) west of Barcelona.

GETTING HERE AND AROUND

If you're driving, follow the A2/A7 *autopista* on the upper ring road (Ronda de Dalt), or from the western end of the Diagonal as far as Salida (Exit) 25 to Martorell. Bypass this industrial center and follow signs to Montserrat. Alternatively, you can take a train from the Plaça d'Espanya metro station (hourly 8:36–6:36, connecting with the funicular leaving every 15 minutes) or go on a guided tour with Pullmantur or Julià (⇨ Tour Options *in* Barcelona Planner).

EXPLORING

A favorite side trip from Barcelona is a visit to the shrine of La Moreneta (the Black Virgin of Montserrat), Catalonia's patron saint, in a Benedictine monastery high in the Serra de Montserrat, west of town. These dramatic, sawtooth peaks have given rise to countless legends: here St. Peter left a statue of the Virgin Mary, carved by St. Luke; Parsifal found the Holy Grail; and Wagner sought musical inspiration. Montserrat is as memorable for its strange, pink hills as it is for its religious treasures, so be sure to explore the area. The monastic complex is dwarfed by the grandeur of the jagged peaks, and the crests above bristle with chapels and hermitages. The hermitage of **Sant Joan** can be reached by funicular. The views over the mountains to the Mediterranean and, on a clear day,

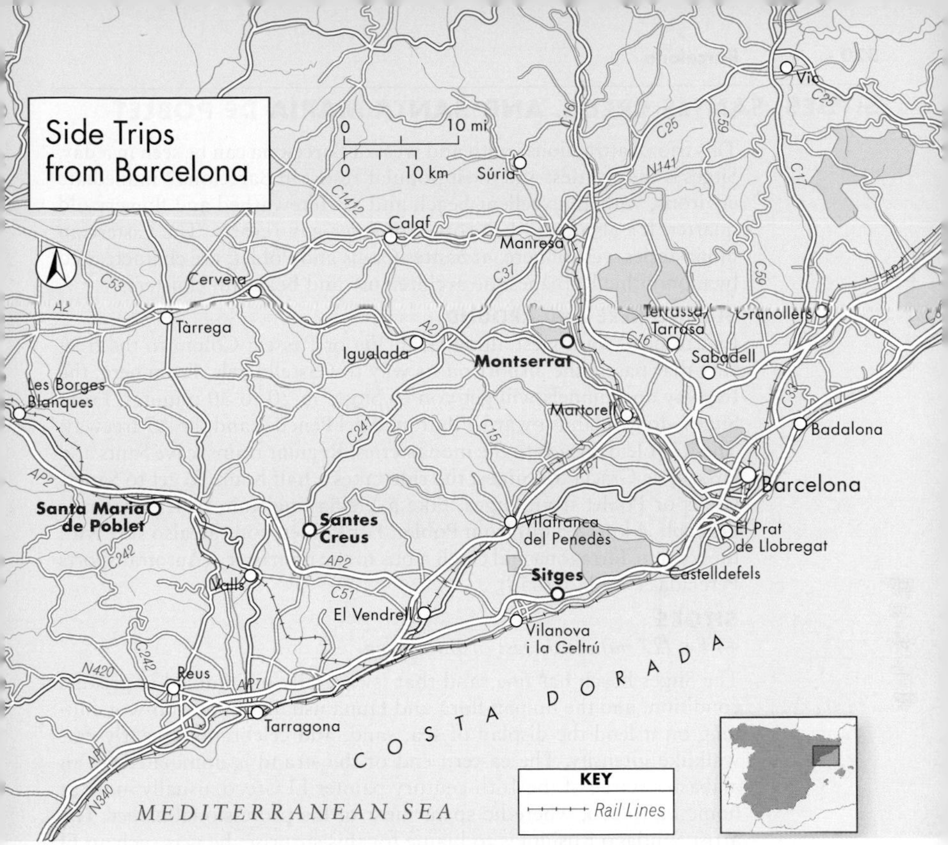

to the Pyrenees are breathtaking; the rugged, boulder-strewn terrain makes for dramatic walks and hikes.

Although a monastery has stood on the same site in Montserrat since the early Middle Ages, the present 19th-century building replaced the rubble left by Napoléon's troops in 1812. The shrine is world-famous and one of Catalonia's spiritual sanctuaries—honeymooning couples flock here by the thousands seeking La Moreneta's blessing on their marriages, and twice a year, on April 27 and September 8, the diminutive statue of Montserrat's Black Virgin becomes the object of one of Spain's greatest pilgrimages.

Only the basilica and museum are regularly open to the public. The **basilica** is dark and ornate, its blackness pierced by the glow of hundreds of votive lamps. Above the high altar stands the famous polychrome statue of the Virgin and Child, to which the faithful can pay their respects by way of a separate door. ☎ *93/877–7777* ⏲ *Daily 6* AM*–10:30* AM *and noon–6:30* PM.

The monastery's **museum** has two sections: the Secció Antiga has old masters, among them works by El Greco, Correggio, and Caravaggio, and the amassed gifts to the Virgin; the Secció Moderna concentrates on recent Catalan painters. ☎ *93/877–7766 abbey and museum* ⏲ *Secció Antiga Tues.–Sat. 10:30–2, Secció Moderna Tues.–Sat. 3–6.*

SITGES, SANTES CREUS, AND SANTA MARIA DE POBLET

This trio of attractions south and west of Barcelona can be seen in a day. Sitges is the prettiest and most popular resort in Barcelona's immediate environs, with an excellent beach and a whitewashed and flowery old quarter. It's also one of Europe's premier gay resorts. The Cistercian monasteries west of here, at Santes Creus and Poblet, are characterized by monolithic Romanesque architecture and beautiful cloisters.

GETTING HERE AND AROUND

By car, head southwest along Gran Via or Passeig Colom to the freeway that passes the airport on its way to Castelldefels. From here, the freeway and tunnels will get you to Sitges in 20 to 30 minutes. From Sitges, drive inland toward Vilafranca del Penedès and the A7 freeway. The A2 (Lleida) leads to the monasteries. Regular trains leave Sants and Passeig de Gràcia for Sitges; the ride takes a half hour. To get to Santes Creus or Poblet from Sitges, take a Lleida-line train to L'Espluga de Francolí, 4 km (2½ mi) from Poblet. For Poblet, you can also stay with the train to Tarragona and catch a bus to the monastery (Autotransports Perelada ☎ *973/202058*).

SITGES

43 km (27 mi) southwest of Barcelona.

The Sitges beach has fine sand that is carefully maintained in pristine condition, and the human flora and fauna usually found sun-worshipping on it lend the display of sea, sand, and celebrants a nearly catwalklike intensity. The eastern end of the strand is dominated by an alabaster statue of the 16th-century painter El Greco, usually more at home in Toledo, where he spent most of his professional career. The artist Santiago Rusiñol is to blame for this surprise; he was such an El Greco fan that he not only installed two El Greco paintings in his Museu Cau Ferrat but also had this sculpture planted on the beach.

The most interesting museum here is the **Cau Ferrat,** founded by Santiago Rusiñol (1861–1931) and containing some of his own paintings together with two El Grecos. Connoisseurs of wrought iron will love the beautiful collection of *cruces terminales,* crosses that once marked town boundaries. Next door is the **Museu Maricel de Mar,** with more artistic treasures; **Casa Llopis,** a romantic villa offering a tour of the house and tasting of local wine, is a short walk across town. ✉ *Fonollar s/n* ☎ *93/894–0364* 🌐 *www.diba.es* 💳 *€3.50 (€6.50 ticket valid for all 3 museums), free 1st Wed. of month* ⏲ *June 14–Sept. 30, Tues.–Sat. 9:30–2 and 4–7, Sun. 10–2; Oct. 1–June 13, Tues.–Sat. 9:30–2 and 3:30–6:30, Sun. 10–2.*

QUICK BITES

Linger over excellent Mediterranean products and cooking with a nonpareil sea view at Vivero (✉ *Passeig Balmins* ☎ *93/894–2149*). The restaurant is closed Monday and serves no dinner from January 1 to May 31.

EN ROUTE

After leaving Sitges, make straight for the A2 *autopista* by way of Vilafranca del Penedès. Wine buffs may want to stop here to taste some excellent Penedès wines; you can tour and sip at the **Bodega Miguel Torres** (✉ *Carrer Comerç 22* ☎ *93/890–0100*). There's an interesting wine

Whitewashed buildings dominate the landscape in Sitges.

museum, **Vinseum** (Museu de les Cultures del Vi de Catalunya) (✉ *Pl. Jaume I 1* ☎ *93/890–0582*), in the Royal Palace, with descriptions of wine-making history. Admission is €5, and it's open Tuesday–Sunday, 10–2 and 4–7.

SANTES CREUS

95 km (59 mi) west of Barcelona.

Founded in 1157, Santes Creus is the first of the monasteries you'll come upon as A2 branches west toward Lleida. Three austere aisles and an unusual 14th-century apse combine with the newly restored cloisters and the courtyard of the royal palace. ✉ *Off A2* ☎ *977/638329* 🎫 *€4* ⊙ *Mid-Mar.–mid-Sept., Tues.–Sun. 10–1:30 and 3–7; mid-Sept.–mid-Jan., Tues.–Sun. 10–1:30 and 3–5:30; mid-Jan.–mid-Mar., Tues.–Sun. 10–1:30 and 3–6.*

Montblanc is off A2 at Salida (Exit) 9, its ancient gates too narrow for cars. A walk through its tiny streets reveals Gothic churches with stained-glass windows, a 16th-century hospital, and medieval mansions.

SANTA MARIA DE POBLET

8 km (5 mi) west of Santes Creus.

Fodor's Choice ★

This splendid Cistercian foundation at the foot of the Prades Mountains is one of the great masterpieces of Spanish monastic architecture. The cloister is a stunning combination of lightness and size, and on sunny days the shadows on the yellow sandstone are extraordinary. Founded in 1150 by Ramón Berenguer IV in gratitude for the Christian Reconquest, the monastery first housed a dozen Cistercians from Narbonne. Later, the Crown of Aragón used Santa Maria de Poblet for religious retreats and burials. The building was damaged in an 1836 anticlerical revolt, and monks of the reformed Cistercian Order have managed the difficult task of restoration since 1940. Today, monks and novices again pray before the splendid retable over the tombs of Aragonese rulers, restored to their former glory by sculptor Frederic Marès; they also sleep in the cold, barren dormitory and eat frugal meals in the stark refectory. ✉ *Off A2* ☎ *977/870254* 🌐 *www.poblet.cat* 🎟 €6 ⏱ *Guided tours by reservation Apr.–Sept., daily 10–12:30 and 3–6; Oct.–Mar., daily 10–12:30 and 3–5:30.*

OFF THE BEATEN PATH

Valls. The town of Valls, famous for its early spring *calçotada* (long-stem onion roast) held on the last Sunday of January, is 10 km (6 mi) from Santes Creus and 15 km (9 mi) from Poblet. Even if you miss the big day, *calçots* are served from November to April at rustic and rambling farmhouses such as **Cal Ganxo** (☎ *977/605960*) in nearby Masmolets, and the Xiquets de Valls, Catalonia's most famous *castellers* (human castlers), might be putting up a human skyscraper.

8

Catalonia, Valencia, and the Costa Blanca

WORD OF MOUTH

"Cadaques is wonderful for walking through narrow streets, with sights around every corner. The beach, though pebbly, is romantic, with colorful fishing boats, and old seamen mending their nets . . . Cadaques' main attraction is Salvador Dalí's private house in Port Lligat, a small village, a few kilometres from Cadaques."

—traveller1959

Join, Ask, Share. www.fodors.com/community/

WELCOME TO CATALONIA, VALENCIA, AND THE COSTA BLANCA

TOP REASONS TO GO

★ **Vist the place where we all got along:** In the old city of Girona, monuments of Christian, Jewish, and Islamic culture are only steps apart.

★ **Valencia:** The past 20 years has seen a transformation of the River Turia into a treasure-trove of museums and concert halls, lovely parks, and architectural wonders.

★ **Catalan Nouveau:** Serious foodies argue that the fountainhead of creative gastronomy has moved from France to Spain—and in particular to the great restaurants of the Ampurdà and Costa Brava.

★ **Hello Dalí:** Surreal doesn't begin to describe the Dalí Museum in Figueres or the wild coast of the artist's home at Cap de Creus.

★ **Burning passions:** Valencia's Las Fallas, in mid-March, a week of fireworks and solemn processions and a finale of spectacular bonfires, is the odds-on favorite for the best festival in Europe.

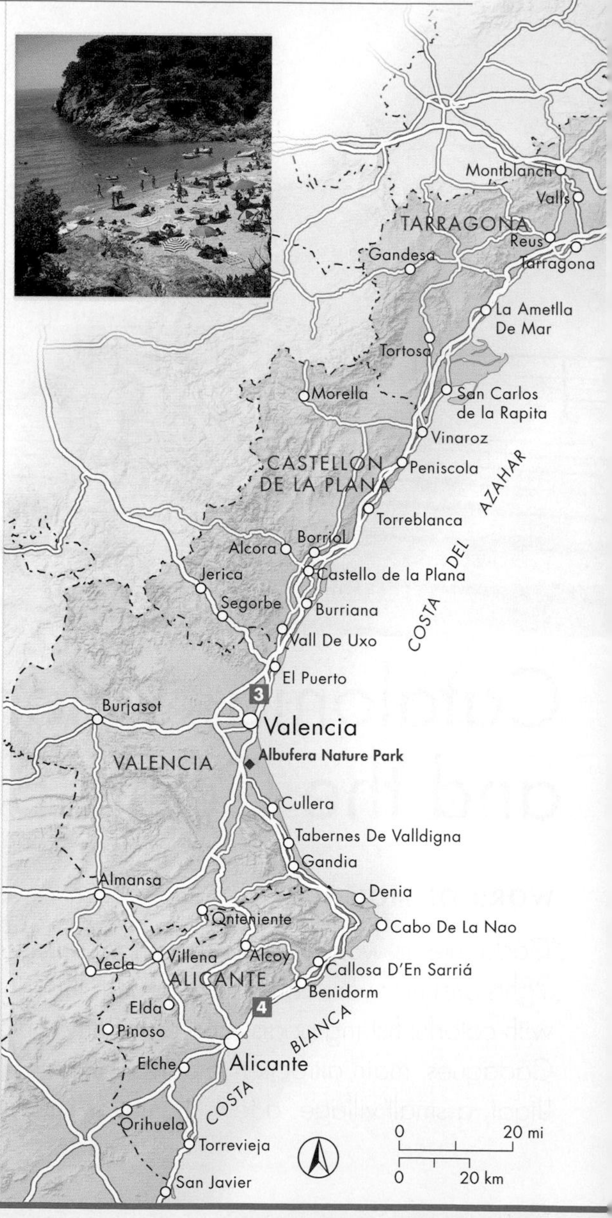

1 Northern Catalonia. Inland and westward from the towns of Girona and Figueres is perhaps the most dramatic and beautiful part of old Catalonia; it's a land of medieval villages and hilltop monasteries, volcanic landscapes, and lush green valleys. The ancient city of Girona, often ignored by people bound for the Costa Brava, is an easy and interesting day trip from Barcelona. The upland towns of Besalú and Olot are Catalonia at its most authentic.

2 Costa Brava. Native son Salvador Dalí put his mark on the northeasternmost corner of Catalonia, where the Costa Brava (literally "rugged coast") begins, especially in the fishing village of Cadaqués and the coast of Cap De Creus. From here, south and west toward Barcelona, lie the beaches, historical settlements, and picturesque towns like Sant Feliu de Guixols that draw millions of summer visitors to the region.

3 Valencia and Environs. Spain's third-largest city, with a rich history and tradition, is now a cultural magnet for its modern art museum and its space-age City of Arts and Sciences complex. The Albufera Nature Park, just to the south, is an important wetland and wildlife sanctuary.

4 Costa Blanca. Culturally and geographically diverse, the Costa Blanca's most populated coastal resorts stretch north from the provincial capital of Alicante. Alicante's historic center and vibrant night-owl scene occupy the hub of a rich agricultural area punctuated by towns like Elche, a UNESCO World Heritage Site. Benidorm has the unenviable reputation of being the largest resort in the world, yet has magnificent sweeping beaches and a something-for-everyone nightlife scene.

GETTING ORIENTED

Year-round, Catalonia is the most visited of Spain's autonomous communities. The Pyrenees that separate it from France provide some of the country's best skiing, while the rugged Costa Brava in the north and the Costa Dorada to the south are havens for sun worshippers. The interior is full of surprises, too: an expanding rural tourism industry and the region's growing international reputation for food and wine give Catalonia a broad-based appeal. Excellent rail, air, and highway connections link Catalonia to the beach resorts and vibrant cities of Valencia, its neighbor to the south.

8

CATALONIA, VALENCIA, AND THE COSTA BLANCA PLANNER

When to Go

Come for the beaches in the hot summer months, but expect crowds and oppressive heat—up to 40°C (104°F). The Mediterranean coast is more comfortable in May and September.

February and March are the peak months for skiing in the Pyrenees. Winter traveling in the region has other advantages: Valencia still has plenty of sunshine, and if you're visiting villages and wineries in the countryside you might find you've got the run of the place! A word of warning: many restaurants outside the major towns may close on weekdays in winter, so call ahead. Museums and centers of interest tend to have shorter winter hours, many closing at 6 PM.

The Costa Blanca beach area gets hot and crowded in summer, and accommodations are at a premium. In contrast, spring is mild and an excellent time to tour the region, particularly the rural areas, where blossoms infuse the air with pleasant fragrances and wildflowers dazzle the landscape.

Dalí and the Costa Brava

Artist Salvador Dalí is entombed beneath the Teatre-Museu Dalí, in Figueres. His former home, a castle in Púbol, is where his wife, Gala, is buried. His summer home in Port Lligat Bay, north of Cadaqués, is now a museum focused on the surrealist's life and work.

Planning Your Time

Not far from Barcelona, the beautiful towns of Vic, Ripoll, Girona, and Cadaqués are easily reachable from the city by bus or train in a couple of hours. Figueres is a must if you want to see the Dalí museum. Girona makes an excellent base from which to explore La Garrotxa; for that, you'll need to rent a car. Tarragona and its environs are definitely worth a few days; it's easily reached from Barcelona via RENFE, or allow an hour and a half to drive, especially on weekends and in summer. If you're driving, a visit to the wineries in the Penedes region en route is well worth the detour. Most of Spain's cava comes from here. The city's Romanic wonders are best seen on foot at a leisurely pace, broken up with a meal at any of its fine seafood restaurants in the Serallo fishing quarter

Valencia is an easy ride from Barcelona on the fast train. If you're taking your time, you might think about stopping in Tarragona on your way (see Side Trips in the Barcelona chapter). From Tarragona it's a comfortable one-hour train ride or drive to Valencia. Valencia and its old town, great markets, the Santiago Calatrava–designed City of Arts and Sciences, and historic buildings can be covered in a few days, but to sample the city's food and get a sense of local life you might want to spend more time in the Barrio del Carmen.

A day trip to the nature reserve at Delta de l'Ebre, outside of Valencia, is also highly recommended.

On the Costa Blanca, Alicante's town hall and travel agencies arrange tours of the city and bus and train tours to Guadalest, the Algar waterfalls, Benidorm, the Peñón de Ifach (Calpe), and Elche.

Festivals and Fiestas

In Valencia, the **Las Fallas** fiestas begin March 1 and reach a climax between March 15 and March 19, El Día de San José (St. Joseph's Day), Father's Day in Spain. Las Fallas originated from St. Joseph's role as patron saint of carpenters; in medieval times, carpenters' guilds celebrated the arrival of spring by cleaning out their shops and making bonfires with scraps of wood. These days it's a 19-day celebration ending with fireworks, floats, carnival processions, and bullfights. On March 19, huge sculptures known as Fallas, effigies of political figures and other personalities, the result of a year's work, are torched to end the fiestas.

Farmhouse Stays in Catalonia

Dotted throughout Catalonia are farmhouses (*casas rurales* in Spanish, and *cases de pagès* or *masies* in Catalan), where you can spend a weekend or longer. Accommodations vary from small, rustic homes to spacious, luxurious farmhouses with fireplaces and pools. Sometimes you stay in a guest room, as at a bed-and-breakfast; in other places you rent the entire house and do your own cooking. Most tourist offices, including the main Catalonia Tourist Office in Barcelona, have info and listings for the *cases de pagès* of the region. You can peruse listings of farmhouses on 🌐 *www.gencat.net*. Several organizations in Spain also have detailed listings and descriptions of Catalonia's farmhouses, and it's best to book through one of these.

Contacts Federació d'Agroturisme i Turisme Rural Comarques de Tarragona (☎ *977/821082* 🌐 *www.agroturisme.org*). **Tural** (☎ *93/539–4678* 🌐 *www.tural.org*).

WHAT IT COSTS (IN EUROS)					
	¢	$	$$	$$$	$$$$
Restaurants	under €8	€8–€12	€13–€17	€18–€22	over €22
Hotels	under €60	€60–€90	€91–€125	€126–€180	over €180

Prices are per person for a main course at dinner, and for two people in a standard double room in high season, excluding tax.

If You Like Beaches

The beaches on the Costa Brava range from stretches of fine white sand to rocky coves and inlets; summer vacationers flock to San Pol, Roses, and Palafrugell; in all but the busiest weeks of July and August, the tucked-away coves of Cap de Creus national park are oases of peace and privacy. Valencia has a long beach that's wonderful for sunning and a promenade lined with paella restaurants; for quieter surroundings, head farther south to El Saler.

The southeastern coastline of the Costa Blanca varies from the long stretches of sand dunes north of Dénia and south of Alicante to the coves and crescents of the Costa Blanca. The benign climate permits lounging on the beach almost year-round. Altea, popular with families, is busy and pebbly, but the old town has retained a traditional pueblo feel with narrow cobbled streets and attractive squares. Benidorm's two white, crescent-shape beaches, packed in summer, extend for more than 5 km (3 mi) and are considered among the best in Spain. Calpe's beaches have the scenic advantage of the sheer outcrop Peñón de Ifach (Cliff of Ifach), which stands guard over stretches of sand to either side. Dénia and Jávea both have family beaches where children paddle in relatively safe waters.

South of Tarragona, Salou has the best beaches, with a lively, palm-lined promenade.

GETTING HERE AND AROUND

By Air

El Prat de Llobregat in Barcelona is the main international airport for the Costa Brava; otherwise, Girona is the closest airport to the region. Valencia has an international airport with direct flights to London, Paris, Brussels, Lisbon, Zurich, and Milan as well as regional flights from Barcelona, Madrid, Málaga, and other cities in Spain. There is a regional airport in Alicante.

There is bus transportation between Girona airport and both Girona and Barcelona.

By Car

A car is extremely useful if you want to explore inland, where much of the driving is smooth, uncrowded, and scenic. Catalonia and Valencia have excellent roads: if you're in the driver's seat the only drawback is the high toll fees on the *autopistas* (highways), but the coastal N340 can get clogged, so you're often better off paying.

By Bus

Bus travel is generally inexpensive and comfortable. Private companies run buses down the coast and from Madrid to Valencia, Benidorm, and Alicante. Alsa is the main bus line in this region; local tourist offices can help with timetables. Sarfa operates buses from Barcelona to Blanes, Lloret, Sant Feliu de Guixols, Platja d'Aro, Palamos, Begur, Roses, and Cadaqués.

Alsa (☎ *902/422242* 🌐 *www.alsa.es*). **Barna Bus** (☎ *93/232–0459*). **Sagales** (☎ *902/130014*, 🌐 *www.sagales.com*). **Sarfa** (✉ *Estació del Nord, Alí Bei 80 Eixample, Barcelona* ☎ *93/265–1158 or 902/302025* Ⓜ *Arc de Triomf*).

By Boat and Ferry

Many short-cruise lines along the coast give you a chance to get a view of the Costa Brava from the sea. Visit the port areas in the main towns listed below and you will quickly spot several tourist cruise lines. Plan on spending around €15–€25, depending on the length of the cruise. The glass-keeled Nautilus boats for observation of the Islas Medes underwater park cost €15 and run on weekends only between October and March.

The shortest ferry connections to the Balearic Islands (100 km to Ibiza) originate in Dénia. Balearia sails to Ibiza, Formentera, and Mallorca; Iscomar sails to Ibiza and then to Palma de Mallorca.

Boat and Ferry Information **Balearia** (☎ *902/160180* 🌐 *www.balearia.com*).**Creuers Badia de Roses** (✉ *Passeig Marítim s/n, Roses* ☎ *972/255499*). **Iscomar** (☎ *902/119128* 🌐 *www.iscomar.com*). **Marina Princess** (✉ *Passeig Marítim 34 L'Estartit* ☎ *972/750643* 🌐 *www.marinaprincess.com*). **Nautilus** (✉ *Passeig Marítim 23 L'Estartit* ☎ *972/751489* 🌐 *www.nautilus.es*). **Roses Serveis Marítims** (✉ *Passeig Marítim s/n, Roses* ☎ *972/152426*). **Viajes Marítimos** (✉ *Passeig Sant Pere 5 Lloret de Mar* ☎ *972/369095* 🌐 *www.viajesmaritimos.com*). **Viatges Marítims Costa Brava** (✉ *Aquarium, L'Estartit* ☎ *972/750880*).

Tours and Outdoor Excursions

Bus and boat tours from Barcelona to Girona and Figueres are run by Julià Travel. Buses leave Barcelona at 9 and return at 6. The price for Girona and Figueres is €66 per person. Pullmantur runs tours to several points on the Costa Brava.

Hiking and walking tours around Valencia and the Costa Blanca are an alternative to relaxing at the beach. The Sierra Mariola and Sierra Aitana regions are both easily accessible from the Costa Blanca resorts, and many companies, including Abdet, Fellwalker, and Mountain Walks, most based in the United Kingdom, offer "walking vacations."

There are also several riding schools, which provide classes as well as trekking opportunities. Pick up brochures at the local tourist offices.

Water sports are widely available, and you can learn to sail in most of the major resorts. Benidorm has a multilingual cable-ski and water-sports center; check 🌐 *www.surf.to/cableski* for more details. Kite-surfing is becoming increasingly popular; the necessary gear is available for rent direct from several beaches, including Santa Pola and Benidorm, and the same applies to windsurfing. Scuba diving is also a favorite and in the smaller coastal towns it's possible to go into reserve waters if you book ahead.

If pedal power is more your thing, several companies offer a range of cycling holidays: Ciclo Costa Blanca is a good place to start.

Contacts Abdet (🌐 *www.abdet.com*). **Ciclo Costa Blanca** (🌐 *www.ciclocostablanca.com*). **Fellwalker** (🌐 *www.fellwalker.co.uk/costablanca.htm*). **Julià Tours** (☎ *93/317–6454* 🌐 *www.juliatravel.com*). **Mountain Walks** (🌐 *www.tk.com*). **Pullmantur** (☎ *93/317–1297* 🌐 *www.pullmanturspain.com*).

By Train

Most of the Costa Brava is *not* served directly by railroad. A local line heads up the coast from Barcelona but takes you only to Blanes; from there it turns inland and connects at Maçanet-Massanes with the main line up to France. Direct trains only stop at major towns, such as Girona, Flaçà, and Figueres. If you want to get off at a small town, be sure to take a local train; or you can take a fast direct train to Girona, for instance, then get off and wait for a local to come by (the words for local, express, and direct are basically the same in Spanish as in English). The stop on the main line for the middle section of the Costa Brava is Flaçà, where you can take a bus or taxi to your final destination. Girona and Figueres are two other towns with major bus stations that feed out to the towns of the Costa Brava. The train serves the last three towns on the north end of the Costa Brava: Llançà, Colera, and Portbou.

Trains reach Valencia from all over Spain, and Estación del Norte is close to the center of town. From Barcelona there are 14 trains a day, including the fast train TALGO, which takes 3½ hours. There are 11 daily trains to Valencia from Madrid; the high-speed train also takes about 3½ hours.

For the Costa Blanca, trains arrive in Alicante. In the southern direction Tarragona is served directly by train.

EATING AND DRINKING WELL IN CATALONIA, VALENCIA, AND THE COSTA BLANCA

Catalonia and Valencia share the classic Mediterranean diet, and Catalans feel right at home with *paella valenciana*. Fish preparations are similar along the coast, though inland favorites vary from place to place.

Top left: *Paella valenciana* in a classic paella pan. Top right: Fresh *calçots*. Bottom left: *Suquet* stew of fish, potatoes, onions, and tomatoes.

Catalonia's northern Alt Empordà region includes grassy inland meadows producing quality beef and the Costa Brava with its fine seafood, such as anchovies from L'Estartit and *gambas* (jumbo shrimp) from Palamós, both deservedly famous. *Romescu*, a blend of almonds, peppers, garlic, and olive oil, is used as a fish and seafood sauce in Tarragona, especially during the *calçotada* (spring onion) feasts in February. The Ebro Delta is renowned for fresh fish and eels, as well as *rossejat* (fried rice in a fish broth with allioli [garlic mayonnaise]). Valencia and the Mediterranean coast are the homeland of *paella valenciana*—a rice dish flavored with saffron that contains seafood, poultry, meat, peas, and peppers. *Arròs a banda* is a variant in which the fish and rice are cooked separately and peeled.

CALÇOTS

One of Catalonia's most beloved feasts is the winter *calçotada* (calçot feast). The *calçot* is a sweet, long-stemmed spring onion discovered by a 19th-century farmer named Xat Benaiges, who extended the scallion's edible portion by packing soil around the base and giving them stockings or shoes (*calçat*). On the last weekend of January, Valls holds a public calçotada where 30,000 gather for calçots, sausage, lamb chops, and young red wine.

RICE

Paella valenciana (Valencian paella) is Spain's most famous contribution to world gastronomy. A simple country concoction dating from the early 18th century, "paella" refers to the pan used to cook the rice, a wide frying pan with short, sturdy handles. Anything available in the fields on any given day, along with rice and olive oil, traditionally went into the paella. *Paella valenciana,* however, has very particular ingredients: it's made with short-grained rice (arroz bomba), chicken, rabbit, *garrofó* (a local legume), tomatoes, green beans, sweet peppers, olive oil, and saffron. Artichokes and peas are also included in season. *Paella marinera* (seafood paella) is a different story: rice, cuttlefish, squid, mussels, shrimp, prawns, lobster, clams, garlic, olive oil, sweet paprika, and saffron, all stewed in fish broth. Many other paella variations are possible, including *paella negra,* a black rice dish made with squid ink, *arròs a banda* made with peeled seafood, and *fideuá,* paella made with vermicelli pasta noodles.

SEAFOOD STEWS

Sepia amb pèsols is a vegetable and seafood *mar i muntanya* (surf 'n turf) beloved on the Costa Brava: cuttlefish and peas are stewed with potatoes, garlic, onions, tomatoes, and a splash of wine. The *picadillo,* or finishing sprinkling of flavors and textures, includes parsley, black pepper, fried bread, pine nuts, olive oil, and salt. *Es niu* ("the nest") of game fowl, cod tripe, cuttlefish, pork, and rabbit is another Costa Brava favorite. Stewed for a good five hours until the darkness of the onions and the ink of the cuttlefish have combined to impart a rich chocolate color to the stew, this is a much-celebrated wintertime classic. You'll also find *suquet de peix,* the Catalan fish stew, made with white fish, at restaurants along the Costa Brava.

FRUIT AND VEGETABLES

Valencia and the eastern Levante region have long been famous as Spain's *huerta* or garden. The alluvial soil of the littoral produces an abundance everything from tomatoes to asparagus, peppers, chard, spinach, onions, artichokes, cucumbers, and the whole range of Mediterranean bounty. Catalonia's Maresme and Empordà regions are also fruit and vegetable bowls making this coastline a rich repository for fresh garden products.

WINES

The Penedès winegrowing region west of Barcelona has been joined by new wine Denominations of Origin from all over Catalonia. Alt Camp, Tarragona, Priorat, Montsant, Costers del Segre, Pla de Bages, Alella, and the Empordà are all producing excellent reds and whites to join Catalonia's sparkling *cava* on local wine lists filled with local surprises.

Updated by George Semler and Kati Krause

The long curve of the Mediterranean from the French border to Costa de Valencia River encompasses the two autonomous communities of Catalonia and Valencia, with the country's second- and third-largest cities (Barcelona and Valencia, respectively). Rivals in many respects, the two communities share a language, history, and culture that set them clearly apart from the rest of Spain.

Girona is the gateway to Northern Catalonia and its attractions—the Pyrenees, the volcanic region of La Garrotxa, and the pristine beaches of the upper Costa Brava. Northern Catalonia is memorable for the soft, green hills of the Ampurdà farm country, the Alberes mountain range at the eastern end of the Pyrenees, and the rugged Costa Brava. Sprinkled across the landscape are *masías* (farmhouses) with austere, staggered-stone roofs and square towers that make them look like fortresses. Even the tiniest village has its church, arcaded square, and *rambla,* where villagers take their evening *paseo*.

The province of Valencia was incorporated into the Kingdom of Aragón, Catalonia's medieval Mediterranean empire, when it was conquered by Jaume I in the 13th century. Along with Catalonia, Valencia became part of the united Spanish state in the 15th century, but defenders of its separate cultural and linguistic identity still resent the centuries of Catalan domination. The Catalan language prevails in Tarragona, a city and province of Catalonia, but Valenciano—a dialect of Catalan—is spoken and used on street signs in the Valencian provinces.

The *huerta* (a fertile, irrigated coastal plain) is devoted mainly to citrus and vegetable farming, which lends color to the landscape and fragrance to the air. Arid mountains form a stark backdrop to the lush coast. Over the years these shores have entertained Phoenician, Greek, Carthaginian, and Roman visitors—the Romans stayed several centuries and left archaeological reminders all the way down the coast, particularly in Tarragona, the capital of Rome's Spanish empire by 218 BC. Rome's dominion did not go uncontested, however; the most serious challenge came from the Carthaginians of North Africa. The three Punic Wars, fought over this territory between 264 and 146 BC, established the reputation of the Carthaginian general Hannibal.

The coastal farmland and beaches that attracted the ancients now call to modern-day tourists, though a chain of ugly developments has marred much of the shore. Inland, however, local culture has survived intact. The rugged and beautiful territory is dotted with small fortified towns, several of which bear the name of Spain's 11th-century national hero, El Cid, as proof of the battles he fought here against the Moors 900 years ago.

EXPLORING THE COSTA BRAVA TO VALENCIA

Named for its wild and rugged coastline, the Costa Brava is where Salvador Dalí got his inspiration. His birthplace, Figueres, is home to his wacky museum, and the whitewashed fishing village of Cadaqués is where he built his even wackier residence.

Visitors are drawn to the Tarragona region for its extensive Roman remains, including its amphitheater and aqueduct. Southwest of Tarragona are the wetlands of the Ebro Delta, rich in birdlife. Inland lie the rugged Sierra de Beceite mountains and the walled town of Morella. The Ebro River snakes its way through the interior, passing through the historical town of Tortosa. The interior is best explored by car, as bus routes are limited. South of Tortosa, lively resort towns—including Benicarló, Peñíscola, and Benicàssim—dot the Costa del Azahar. The region's crown jewel is artistic Valencia.

NORTHERN CATALONIA

Northern Catalonia is for many *the* reason to visit Spain—particularly now that its principal city, Girona, serves as a point of entry to the region for many travelers arriving from the United Kingdom on cheap flights. Girona is a labyrinth of climbing cobblestone streets and staircases, with remarkable Gothic and Romanesque buildings at every turn; the Call—the Jewish Quarter here—is one of the best preserved in Europe. Streets in the modern part of the city are lined with smart shops and boutiques, and the overall quality of life in Girona is considered among the best in Spain.

The nearby towns of Besalu and Figueres couldn't be more different from each other. Figueres is an unexceptional town made exceptional by the Dalí Museum. Besalu is a picture-perfect Romanic village perched on a bluff overlooking the River Fluvia, with several of the most prestigious restaurants in Catalonia. You'll eat well, if not cheaply. Less well known are the medieval towns in and around La Garrotxa: Ripoll, Rupit, and Olot all hold wonderful surprises and probably boast the best produce in the region.

GIRONA

97 km (60 mi) northeast of Barcelona.

Girona (Gerona in Castilian), a city of more than 70,000 inhabitants, keeps intact the magic of its historic past. In fact, with its brooding hilltop castle, soaring cathedral, and dreamy riverside setting it resembles a vision from the Middle Ages. Once called a "Spanish Venice"—although there are no real canals here, just the confluence of four rivers—this city is almost as evocative as that one. With El Call, one of Europe's best-preserved Jewish communities dating from the Middle Ages, and the Arab Baths, lovely Girona is a reminder that Spain's Jewish and Islamic communities both thrived here for centuries. Today, as a university center, it combines past and vibrant present—art galleries, chic cafés, and trendy boutiques have set up shop in many of the restored buildings of the Old Quarter.

The Old Quarter of Girona, called the Força Vella (Old Force, or Fortress), is built on the side of the mountain and is a tightly packed labyrinth of fine buildings, monuments, and steep, narrow cobblestone streets linked with frequent stairways. You can still see vestiges of the Iberian and Roman walls in the cathedral square and in the patio of the old university. Head over from modern Girona (on the west side of the Onyar) to the Old Quarter on the east side. The main street of the Old Quarter is Carrer de la Força, which follows the old Via Augusta, the Roman road that connected Rome with its provinces.

The best way to get to know Girona is by walking along its streets. As you wander through the Força Vella you will be repeatedly surprised by new discoveries. One of Girona's treasures is its setting, as it rises high above the Riu Onyar, where that river merges with the Ter, which flows from a mountain waterfall that can be glimpsed in a gorge above the town. Regardless of your approach to the town, walk first along the west-side banks of the Onyar, between the train trestle and the Plaça de la Independència, to admire the classic view of the Old Town, with its pastel yellow, pink, and orange waterfront facades. Windows and balconies are always draped with colorful drying laundry reflected in the shimmering river and often adorned with fretwork grilles of embossed wood or delicate iron tracery. Cross the Pont de Sant Agustí over to the Old City from under the arcades in the corner of the Plaça de la Independència and find your way to the tourist office, to the right at Rambla Llibertat 1. Then work your way up through the labyrinth of steep streets, using the cathedral's huge baroque facade as a guide.

A special Girona visitor's card allowing free admission to some museums and monuments and discounts at others can be purchased at the tourist-office welcome station. Look for the **Punt de Benvinguda** (✉ *Carrer Berenguer Carnicer 3* ☎ *972/211678* 🌐 *www.girona-net.com*), at the entrance to Girona from the town's main parking area on the right bank of the Onyar River.

GETTING HERE AND AROUND

There are more than 20 daily trains from Barcelona to Girona (continuing on to the French border). Barcelonabus buses take an average of 75 minutes and cost €12 one-way, €21 round-trip. Girona airport is also a

destination for flights from London via the no-frills Ryan Air. Getting around the city is easiest on foot or by taxi; several bridges connect the historic old quarter with the more modern town across the river.

ESSENTIALS

Bus Information Barcelonabus (✉ *Passeig de Sant Joan 52 Girona* ☎ *902/130014*).

Visitor Information Girona (✉ *Rambla de la Libertat 1* ☎ *972/226575* 🌐 *www.ajuntament.gi*).

EXPLORING

Banys Arabs *(Arab Baths)*. A misnomer, the Banys Arabs were actually built by Morisco (workers of Moorish descent who remained in Spain even after the 1492 Expulsion Decree) craftsmen in the late 12th century, long after Girona's Islamic occupation (795–1015) had ended. Following the old Roman model that had disappeared in the West, the custom of bathing publicly may have been brought back from the Holy Land with the Crusaders. These baths are sectioned off into three rooms in descending order; a *frigidarium,* or cold bath, a square room with a central octagonal pool and a skylight with cupola held up by two stories of eight fine columns; a *tepidarium,* or warm bath; and a *caldarium,* or steam room, beneath which is a chamber where a fire was kept burning.

There's more to Girona's cathedral than the 90 steps to get to it; there's much to see inside, including the treasury.

Here the inhabitants of the old Girona came to relax, exchange gossip, or do business. It is known from another public bathhouse in Tortosa, Tarragona, that the various social classes came to bathe by sex and religion on fixed days of the week: Christian men on one day, Christian women on another, Jewish men on still another, Jewish women (and prostitutes) on a fourth, Muslims on others. ✉ *Carrer Ferran el Catòlic s/n* ☎ *972/213262* 🌐 *www.banysarabs.org* 🎫 *€2.50* ⏲ *Apr.–Sept., Mon.–Sat. 10–7, Sun. 10–2; Oct.–Mar., Mon.–Sat. 10–2.*

Fodor's Choice ★ **Cathedral.** At the heart of the Old City, the cathedral looms above 90 steps and is famous for its nave—at 75 feet, the widest in the world and the epitome of the spatial ideal of Catalan Gothic architects. Since Charlemagne founded the original church in the 8th century, it has been through many fires, changes, and renovations, so you are greeted by a rococo-era facade—"eloquent as organ music" and impressively set off by a spectacular flight of 17th-century stairs, which rises from its own plaça. Inside, three smaller naves were compressed into one gigantic hall by the famed architect Guillermo Bofill in 1416. The change was typical of Catalan Gothic "hall" churches, and it was done to facilitate preaching to crowds. Note the famous silver canopy, or *baldaquí* (baldachin). The oldest part of the cathedral is the 11th-century Romanesque **Torre de Carlemany** (Charlemagne Tower).

The cathedral's exquisite 12th-century cloister has an obvious affinity with the cloisters in the Roussillon area of France. Inside the Treasury are a variety of precious objects. They include a 10th-century copy of Beatus's manuscript *Commentary on the Apocalypse* (illuminated in the dramatically primitive Mozarabic style), the Bible of Emperor Charles

V, and the celebrated *Tapís de la Creació* (Tapestry of the Creation), considered by most experts to be the finest tapestry surviving from the Romanesque era (and, in fact, thought to be the needlework of Saxons working in England). It depicts the seven days of Creation as told in Genesis in the primitive but powerful fashion of early Romanesque art and looks not unlike an Asian mandala. Made of wool, with predominant colors of green, brown, and ocher, the tapestry once hung behind the main altar as a pictorial Bible lesson. The four seasons, stars, winds, months of the year and days of the week, plants, animals, and elements of nature circle around a central figure, likening paradise to the eternal cosmos presided over by Christ. In addition to its intrinsic beauty, the bottom band (which appears to have been added at a later date) contains two *iudeis,* or Jews, dressed in the round cloaks they were compelled to wear to set them apart from Christians. This scene is thought to be the earliest portrayal of a Jew (other than biblical figures) in Christian art. ✉ *Pl. de la Catedral* ☎ *972/214426* 🌐 *www.catedraldegirona.org* 🎫 *€5; free Sun.* 🕒 *Nov.–Mar., weekdays 10–7, Sat. 4:30–7, Sun. 10–2, 4:30–7; Apr.–Oct., weekdays 10–8 and 4:30–8, Sat. 4:30–8, Sun. 2–8.*

Centre Bonastruc ça Porta. Housed in a former synagogue and dedicated to the preservation of Girona's Jewish heritage, this center organizes conferences, exhibitions, and seminars. The **Museu de Història dels Jueus** (Museum of Jewish History) contains 21 stone tablets, one of the finest collections in the world of medieval Jewish funerary slabs. These came from the old Jewish cemetery of Montjuïc, revealed when the railroad between Barcelona and France was laid out in the 19th century. Its exact location, about 1½ km (1 mi) north of Girona on the road to La Bisbal and known as La Tribana, is being excavated. The center also holds the **Institut d'Estudis Nahmànides,** with an extensive library of Judaica. ✉ *Carrer de la Força 8* ☎ *972/216761* 🌐 *www.ajgirona.org/call* 🎫 *€3* 🕒 *Mon.–Sat. 10–6, Sun. 10–3.*

El Call. Girona is especially noted for its 13th-century Jewish Quarter, El Call, which can be found branching off Carrer de la Força, south of the Plaça Catedral. The word *call* (pronounced "kyle" in Catalan) may come from an old Catalan word meaning "narrow way" or "passage," derived from the Latin word *callum* or *callis.* Others suggest that it comes from the Hebrew word *Qahal,* meaning "assembly" or "meeting of the community." Owing allegiance to the Spanish king (who exacted tribute for this distinction) and not to the city government, this once prosperous Jewish community—one of the most flourishing in Europe during the Middle Ages—was, at its height, a leading center of learning. An important school of the Kabala was centered here. The most famous teacher of the Kabala from Girona was Rabbi Mossé ben Nahman (also known as Nahmànides, and by the acronym RMBN—or Ramban—taken from the first letters of his title and name), who is popularly believed to be one and the same as Bonastruc ça Porta. Nahmànides wrote an important religious work based on meditation and the reinterpretation of the Bible and the Talmud.

The earliest presence of Jews in Girona is uncertain, but the first historical mention dates from 982, when a group of 25 Jewish families moved

8

to Girona from nearby Juïgues. Jews may have been already present in the region for several hundred years. Today the layout of El Call bears no resemblance to what this area looked like in the 15th century, when Jews last lived here. Space was at a premium inside the city walls in Girona, and houses were destroyed and built higgledy-piggledy one atop the other. The narrow streets, barely wide enough for a single person to pass (they have now been widened slightly), crisscrossed one above the other.

Museu d'Art. The Episcopal Palace near the cathedral contains the wide-ranging collections of Girona's main art museum. You'll see everything from superb Romanesque *majestats* (carved wood figures of Christ) to reliquaries from Sant Pere de Rodes, illuminated 12th-century manuscripts, and works of the 20th-century Olot school of landscape painting. ✉ *Pujada de la Catedral 12* ☎ *972/203834* 🌐 *www.museuart.com* 🎫 *€3.50* ⏲ *Tues.–Sat. 10–7, Sun. 10–2.*

QUICK BITES

Fortify yourself for sightseeing with some superb tea and plump pastries at La Vienesa (✉ *Carrer La Pujada del Pont de Pedra 1* ☎ *972/486046*). One of the town's best-loved gathering points for conversation, this cozy spot is good place to regroup and re-navigate.

Museu del Cinema. An interactive cinema museum, this spot has artifacts and movie-related paraphernalia starting from Chinese shadows, the first rudimentary moving pictures, to Lyon's Lumière brothers. The Cine Nic toy filmmaking machines, originally developed in 1931 by the Nicolau brothers of Barcelona and now being relaunched commercially, allow even novices to put together their own movies. ✉ *Carrer Sèquia 1* ☎ *972/412777* 🌐 *www.museudelcinema.org* 🎫 *€4* ⏲ *May–Sept., Mon.–Sat. 10–8, Sun. 10–3; Oct.–Apr., Mon.–Sat. 10–6, Sun. 10–3.*

Museu d'Història de la Ciutat. On Carrer de la Força, this fascinating museum is filled with artifacts from Girona's long and embattled past. From pre-Roman objects to paintings and drawings from the notorious siege at the hands of Napoleonic troops to the early municipal lighting system and the medieval printing press, there is plenty to see here. You will definitely come away with a clearer idea of Girona's past. ✉ *Carrer de la Força 27* ☎ *972/222229* 🌐 *www.ajuntament.gi/museu_ciutat* 🎫 *€3* ⏲ *May–Sept., Tues.–Sat. 10–2 and 5–7, Sun. 10–3.*

Passeig Arqueològic. The landscaped gardens of this stepped archaeological walk are below the restored walls of the Old Quarter (which you can walk, in parts) and have good views from belvederes and watchtowers. From there, climb through the Jardins de la Francesa to the highest ramparts for a view of the cathedral's 11th-century Charlemagne Tower.

Placeta del Institut Vell. In this small square on Carrer de la Força you can study a tar-blackened 3-inch-long, half-inch-deep groove carved shoulder-high into the stone of the right-hand door post as you enter the square. It indicates the location of a mezuzah, a small case or tube of metal or wood containing a piece of parchment with verses from the Torah (declaring the essence of Jewish belief in one God). Anyone passing through the doorway touched the mezuzah as a sign of devotion. Evidence of the labyrinthine layout of a few street ruts in the

Old Quarter may still be seen inside the antiques store Antiguitats la Canonja Vella at Carrer de la Força 33.

Sant Feliu. The vast bulk of this structure is landmarked by one of Girona's most distinctive belfries, topped by eight pinnacles. One of Girona's most beloved churches, it was repeatedly rebuilt and altered over four centuries and stands today as an amalgam of Romanesque columns, Gothic nave, and baroque facade. It was founded over the tomb of St. Felix of Africa, a martyr under the Roman emperor Diocletian. ✉ *Pujada de Sant Feliu* ☎ *972/201407* ⏲ *Daily 9–10:30, 11:30–1, and 4–6:30.*

Sant Pere. The church of *St. Peter*, across the Galligants River, was finished in 1131, and is notable for its octagonal Romanesque belfry and the finely detailed capitals atop the columns in the cloister. It now houses the **Museu Arqueològic** (Museum of Archaeology), which documents the region's history since Paleolithic times and includes some artifacts from Roman times. ✉ *Carrer Santa Llúcia s/n* ☎ *972/202632* 🎫 *€3* ⏲ *Church and museum daily 10–1 and 4:30–7.*

Torre de Gironella. A five-minute walk uphill behind the cathedral leads to a park and this four-story tower (no entry permitted) dating from the year 1190 that marks the highest point in the Jewish Quarter. Girona's Jewish community took refuge here in early August of 1391, emerging 17 weeks later to find their houses in ruins. Even though Spain's official expulsion decree did not go into effect until 1492, this attack effectively ended the Girona Jewish community. Destroyed in 1404, reconstructed in 1411, and destroyed anew by retreating Napoleonic troops in 1814, the Torre de Gironella was the site of the celebration of the first Hanukkah ceremony in Girona in 607 years, held on December 20, 1998, with Jerusalem's chief Sephardic rabbi Rishon Letzion presiding. ✉ *Ctra. Sant Gregori 91.*

WHERE TO EAT AND STAY

$$–$$$ CATALAN ✕ **Albereda.** Excellent Catalan cuisine with exotic touches is served here in an elegant setting under exposed brick arches. Try the *galeta amb llagostins glaçada* (zucchini bisque with prawns) or the *amanida tèbia d'espàrrecs naturals amb bacallà i cansalada ibérica* (warm asparagus salad with cod and ibérico ham) for a *mar i muntanya* (surf and turf) with the garden thrown in as well. Wild mushrooms, truffles, foie gras, and fresh fish vie for space on this rich menu. ✉ *Carrer Albereda 7 bis* ☎ *972/226002* 🌐 *www.restaurantalbereda.com* 💳 *AE, DC, MC, V* ⏲ *Closed Sun.*

$–$$ CATALAN ★ ✕ **Cal Ros.** Tucked under the arcades just behind the north end of Plaça de la Llibertat, this restaurant combines ancient stone arches with crisp, contemporary furnishings and cheerful lighting. The cuisine is flavorful: hot goat-cheese salad with pine nuts and *garum* (black-olive and anchovy paste, a delicacy dating back to Roman times), *oca amb naps* (goose with turnips), and a blackberry sorbet should not to be missed. ✉ *Carrer Cort Reial 9* ☎ *972/219176* 🌐 *www.calros-restaurant.com* 💳 *AE, DC, MC, V* ⏲ *Closed Mon. No dinner Sun.*

$$$–$$$$ LA NUEVA COCINA Fodor's Choice ★ **Celler de Can Roca.** Despite the almost literal dust-up over Joan Roca's eau de dirt (he made a batter of water and dirt—aka mud—and put it on an oyster), this is universally acclaimed as one of the dozen top restaurants below the Pyrenees. A mile and a half northwest of town on the Taialà road, this is a must-stop for any self-respecting foodie. You can survey the kitchen from the dining room and watch the Roca brothers, Joan and Jordi, in the act of creating their masterful *arròs amb garotes i botifarra negre* (rice with sea urchins and black sausage) and *cua de bou farcida amb foie gras* (oxtail with foie gras). For dessert, try the *pastel calent de xocolata i gingebre* (hot-chocolate ginger cake) or jasmine-tea ice cream. Don't be embarrassed to ask the sommelier for guidance through the encyclopedic wine list. ✉ *Can Sunyer 48* ☎ *972/222157* 🌐 *www.cellercanroca.com* *Reservations essential* ▭ *AE, DC, MC, V* ⊗ *Closed Sun., Mon., and Aug. 24–31.*

$ LA NUEVA COCINA **Mimolet.** Contemporary architecture and cuisine in the old part of Girona make for interesting dining at this sleek and streamlined restaurant just below the Colegiata de Sant Feliu and the Monastery of Sant Pere de Galligants. *Croquetes casolanes* (homemade croquettes) of onion, shrimp, and black sausage or *carpaccio de vedella amb poma, nous i cingles de bertí* (beef carpaccio with apple, walnuts, and a local blue cheese) are typical starters on this rapidly changing seasonal menu. Entrées star grass-fed beef from Girona, lamb, duck, and an anthology of Mediterranean fish and seafood. ✉ *Pou Rodó 12* ☎ *972/202124* 🌐 *www.mimolet.net* ▭ *AE, DC, MC* ⊗ *Closed Sun., Mon., Dec. 23–Jan. 7.*

¢–$ **Bellmirall.** This pretty little hostel across the Onyar in the Jewish Quarter, despite its scarcity of amenities, offers top value in the heart of Girona's most historic section. **Pros:** a budget choice, this hostel provides the basics with perfect aesthetic taste as well. **Cons:** rooms are small, and—without the Internet, TV, and telephone—can feel isolating. ✉ *Carrer Bellmirall 3* ☎ *972/204009* 🌐 *www.grn.es/bellmirall* *7 rooms* *In-room: no a/c, no phone, no TV. In-hotel: Wi-Fi hotspot* ▭ *No credit cards* ⊗ *Closed Jan. and Feb.*

$–$$ ★ **Hotel Històric y Apartaments Històric Girona.** This boutique hotel has one room (the suite) with views of the cathedral and Gothic vaulting overhead. The apartment accommodations are in a 9th-century house, with remnants of a 3rd-century Roman wall and a Roman aqueduct on the ground floor and in one of the apartments. One dining room even contains a wall made in the pre-Roman *opus spicatum* herringbone pattern. Wooden furniture fills the simply but pleasantly furnished rooms. Casilda Cruz rents these good-value apartments in the Old Quarter for as many days as you'd like, from one day to one month. **Pros:** ideal environment for a visit to Europe's best-preserved medieval Jewish Quarter; top technology and comforts. **Cons:** rooms and apartments are a little cramped. ✉ *Carrer Bellmirall 4A* ☎ *972/223583* 🌐 *www.hotelhistoric.com* *8 rooms, 7 apartments, 1 junior suite, 1 suite* *In-room: kitchen, Wi-Fi* ▭ *AE, DC, MC, V*

¢ ★ **Hotel Peninsular.** In a handsomely restored early-20th-century building across the Onyar River with views into Girona's historic Old Quarter, this modest but useful hotel occupies a strategic spot at the end of the

With its picturesque rivers, Girona is often called the Spanish Venice.

Pont de Pedra (Stone Bridge), a Girona landmark in the center of the shopping district. **Pros:** a good location over the Onyar at the hub of Girona life; near the stop for the bus from Girona airport. **Cons:** smallish rooms; sometimes noisy on Friday and Saturday nights. ✉ *Av. Sant Francesc 6* ☎ *902/734541* 🌐 *www.novarahotels.com* *68 rooms* *In-room: a/c, safe, Wi-Fi. In-hotel: bar, Internet terminal* 💳 *AE, DC, MC, V.*

8

NIGHTLIFE AND THE ARTS

Girona is a university town, so the night scene is especially lively during the school year. Trendy young people flock to **Accés 21** (✉ *Carrer Carreras Peralta 7* ☎ *972/213708*). **Babel** (✉ *Carrer Nord 14* ☎ *972/213179*) provides another hot nocturnal address. The older crowd goes to **Cadillac Café** (✉ *Barcelona 130* ☎ *972/228452*), on the road to Palamós. A popular nightspot for the young, hip set is **Platea** (✉ *Carrer Real de Fontclara 4* ☎ *972/227288*).

In summer, nighttime action centers on **Les Carpes de la Devesa** (✉ *Passeig de la Devesa*), a park on the west side of the Onyar River in the modern city. From June to September 15, three awnings, or *carpes*, are set up here so that people can sit outside in the warm weather until the wee hours, enjoying drinks and listening to music.

SHOPPING

If it's jewelry you're looking for, head to **Anna Casals** (✉ *Carrer Ballesteries 33* ☎ *972/410227*). For interior decoration, plastic arts, religious paintings, and sculptures, stop at **Dolors Turró** (✉ *Ballesteries 19* ☎ *972/410193*). **Gluki** (✉ *Carrer Argenteria 26* ☎ *972/201989*) has made chocolate since 1880. Candles are the specialty at **Karla** (✉ *Carrer*

Ballesteries 22 ☎ *972/227210*). All manner of masks, dolls, pottery, and crafts are available at **La Carpa** (✉ *Carrer Ballesteries 37* ☎ *972/212002*). **Torrons Victoria Candela** (✉ *Carrer Anselm Clavé 3* ☎ *972/211103*) specializes in tasty nougat.

Codina (✉ *Carrer Nord 20* ☎ *972/219880*) sells jazzy women's clothes. Young people stock up on threads at **Desideratum** (✉ *Carrer Migdia 30* ☎ *972/221448*). Men will find fine plumage at **Falcó** (✉ *Carrer Josep Maluquer Salvador 16* ☎ *972/207156*). For shoes, go to one of the three locations of **Peacock** (✉ *Carrer Nou 15* ☎ *972/226848* ✉ *Carrer de Santa Clare 31* ☎ *972/201420* ✉ *Carrer Migdia 18* ☎ *972/216115* 🌐 *www.peacock.cat*).

Girona's best bookstore, with a large travel-guide section and a small selection of English fiction, is **Llibreria 22** (✉ *Carrer Hortes 22* ☎ *972/212395* 🌐 *www.llibreria22.net*). For travel books and other editions in English, try **Ulysus** (✉ *Carrer Ballesteries 29* ☎ *972/221773*).

FIGUERES

37 km (23 mi) north of Girona on the A7.

Figueres is the capital of the *comarca* (county) of the Alt Empordà, the bustling county seat of this predominantly agricultural region. Local people come from the surrounding area to shop at its many stores and stock up on farm equipment and supplies. Thursday is market day, and farmers gather at the top of the Rambla to do business and gossip, taking refreshments at cafés and discreetly pulling out and pocketing large rolls of bills, the result of their morning transactions. But among the tractors and mule carts is the main reason tourists come to Figueres: the jaw-dropping Dalí Museum, one of the most visited museums in Spain.

Painter Salvador Dalí is Figueres's most famous son. With a painter's technique that rivaled that of Jan van Eyck, a flair for publicity so aggressive it would have put P. T. Barnum in the shade, and a penchant for shocking (he loved telling people Barcelona's historic Gothic Quarter should be knocked down), Dalí scaled the ramparts of art history as one of the foremost proponents of Surrealism, the art movement launched in the 1920s by André Breton. His most lasting image may be the melting watches in his iconic 1931 painting *The Persistence of Memory.* The artist, who was born and died in Figueres (1904–1989), decided to create a museum-monument to himself during the last two decades of his life. Dalí often frequented the Cafeteria Astòria at the top of the Rambla (still the center of social life in Figueres), signing autographs for tourists or just being Dalí: he once walked down the street with a French omelet in his breast pocket instead of a handkerchief.

GETTING HERE AND AROUND

Figueres is one of the stops on the regular train service from Barcelona to the French border. Local buses are also frequent, especially from nearby Cadaqués, with more than eight services daily. The town is sufficiently small to explore on foot.

CLOSE UP

Catalonia's National Dance

The *sardana,* Catalonia's national dance, is often perceived as a solemn and dainty affair usually danced by senior citizens in front of the Barcelona Cathedral at midday on weekends. Look for an athletic young *colla* (troupe), though, and you'll see the grace and fluidity the *sardana* can create. The mathematical precision of the dance, consisting of 76 steps in sets of four, each dancer needing to know exactly where he or she is at all times, demands intense concentration. Said to be a representation of the passing of time, a choreography of the orbits and revolutions of the moon and stars, the circular *sardana* is recorded in Greek chronicles dating back 2,000 years. Performed in circles of all sizes and by dancers of all ages, the *sardana* is accompanied by the *cobla* (*sardana* combo), five wind instruments, five brass, and the director, who plays a three-holed flute called the *flabiol* and a small drum, the *tabal,* which he wears attached to his flute arm, normally the right.

ESSENTIALS

Visitor Information Figueres (✉ *Pl. del Sol* ☎ *972/503155*).

EXPLORING

Castell de Sant Ferran. An imposing 18th-century fortified castle that is one of the largest in Europe, this structure stands 1 km (½ mi) northwest of town. Only when you start exploring the castle grounds (and walking around its perimeter of roughly 4 km [2½ mi]) can you appreciate how immense it is. The parade grounds extend for acres, and the arcaded stables can hold more than 500 horses. This castle was the site of the last official meeting of the Republican parliament (on February 1, 1939) before it surrendered to Franco's forces. Ironically, it was here that Lieutenant Colonel Antonio Tejero was imprisoned after his failed 1981 coup d'état in Madrid. ✉ *Pujada al Castell s/n* ☎ *972/506094* 🌐 *www.castillosanfernando.org* 🎫 *€3* 🕐 *Mar.–June and mid-Sept.–Oct., daily 10:30–2 and 4–6; July–mid-Sept., daily 10:30–8; Nov.–Feb., daily 10:30–2. Last admission 1 hr before closing.*

Museu del Joguet de Catalunya. Displaying childhood playthings pre–Toys "R" Us, this is Spain's only toy museum. Hundreds of antique dolls are on display. The museum has collections of toys owned by, among others, Salvador Dalí, Federico García Lorca, and Joan Miró. It also hosts Catalonia's only *caganer* exhibit, from mid-December to mid-January in odd-numbered years. These playful little figures of guys (and gals) answering nature's call have long had a special spot in the Catalan *pessebre* (Nativity scene). Farmers are the most traditional figures, squatting discreetly behind the animals, but these days you'll find Barça soccer players and politicians, too. Check with the museum for exact dates. ✉ *Hotel de Figueres, Carrer de Sant Pere 1* ☎ *972/504508* 🌐 *www.mjc.cat* 🎫 *€5* 🕐 *June–Sept., daily 10–1 and 4–7; Oct.–May, Tues.–Sat. 10–6, Sun. 11–2.*

Fodor's Choice ★ **Teatre-Museu Dalí.** "Museum" was not a big enough word for Dalí, so he christened his monument a "Theater." It was, indeed, once the Old

The Dalí Museum in Figueres is itself a work of art. Note the eggs on the exterior: they're a common image. Dalí is buried in the building's crypt.

Town theater, reduced to a ruin in the Spanish civil war. Now topped with a glass geodesic dome and studded with Dalí's iconic egg shapes, the multilevel museum pays homage to his fertile imagination and artistic creativity. It includes gardens, ramps, and a spectacular drop cloth Dalí painted for Les Ballets de Monte Carlo. Don't look for his greatest paintings here, although there are some memorable images, including *Gala at the Mediterranean,* which takes the body of Gala (Dalí's wife) and morphs it into the image of Abraham Lincoln once you look through coin-operated viewfinders. The sideshow theme continues with other coin-operated pieces, including *Taxi Plujós* (Rainy Taxi), in which water gushes over the snail-covered occupants sitting in a Cadillac once owned by Al Capone, or *Sala de Mae West,* a trompe-l'oeil vision in which a pink sofa, two fireplaces, and two paintings morph into the face of Hollywood sex symbol Mae West. Fittingly, another "exhibit" on view is Dalí's own crypt. When his friends considered what flag to lay over his coffin, they decided to cover it with an embroidered heirloom tablecloth instead. Dalí would have liked this unconventional touch, if not the actual site: he wanted to be buried at his castle of Púbol next to his wife, but the then mayor of Figueres took matters into his own hands. All in all, the museum is a piece of Dalí dynamite. The summer night session is a perfect time for a postprandial browse through the world's largest Surrealist museum. ✉ *Pl. Gala-Salvador Dalí 5* ☎ *972/677500* 🌐 *www.salvador-dali.org* 🎟 *€12* ⏲ *Oct.–June, Tues.–Sun. 10:30–5:15; July–Sept., daily 9–7:15; special summer night-time visits July 28–Sept. 2, 10* PM*–1* AM*.*

OFF THE BEATEN PATH

Casa-Museu Gala Dalí. The third point of the Dalí triangle is the medieval castle of Púbol, where the artist's wife, Gala, is buried in the crypt. During the 1970s this was Gala's residence, though Dalí also lived here in the early 1980s. It contains paintings and drawings, Gala's haute-couture dresses, elephant sculptures in the garden, furniture, and other objects chosen by the couple. Púbol, roughly between Girona and Figueres, is near the C255, and is not easy to find. If you are traveling by train, get off at the Flaçà station on the Barcelona–Portbou line of RENFE railways; walk or take a taxi 4 km (2½ mi) to Púbol. By bus, the Sarfa bus company has a stop in Flaçà and on the C255 road, some 2 km (1 mi) from Púbol. ✉ *Púbol* ☎ *972/677500* 🌐 *www.salvador-dali.org* 🎫 *€7* ⏲ *Mid-Mar.–mid-June and mid-Sept.–Oct., Tues.–Sun. 10:30–6; mid-June–mid-Sept., daily 10:30–8. Last admission 45 mins before closing.*

WHERE TO EAT AND STAY

$–$$ SPANISH

Hotel Duràn. Once a stagecoach relay station, the Duràn is now a restaurant and hotel. Dalí had his own private dining room here, and you can take a meal amid pictures of the great Surrealist. Try the *mandonguilles amb sepia al estil Anna* (meatballs and cuttlefish), a *mar i muntanya* (surf and turf) specialty of the house. Rooms ($$) are pretty standard. Pros: good central location; helpful staff; family-friendly. Cons: room decor lacks character; pricey breakfast. ✉ *C. Lasauca 5* ☎ *972/501250* 🌐 *www.hotelduran.com* *65 rooms* *In-room: safe, Internet, Wi-Fi. In-hotel: restaurant, room service, bar, laundry service, Internet terminal, Wi-Fi hotspot, parking (paid)* 💳 *AE, DC, MC, V.*

$–$$ Fodor's Choice ★

Hotel Empordà. Just a mile north of town, this hotel and elegant restaurant ($$–$$$) run by Jaume Subirós is hailed as the birthplace of modern Catalan cuisine and has become a beacon for gourmands seeking superb Catalan cooking. Try the *terrina calenta de lluerna a l'oli de cacauet* (hot pot of gurnard fish in peanut oil) or, if it's winter, *llebre a la Royal* (boned hare cooked in red wine). Guest rooms have parquet floors and sparkling bathrooms, and you can sit in the sun and have a drink on the terrace. The hotel is 1½ km (1 mi) north of town. **Pros:** historic culinary destination; great cuisine. **Cons:** the hotel occupies an unprepossessing roadside lot beside the busy NII highway. ✉ *Ctra. NII, Km 1.5* ☎ *972/500562* 🌐 *www.hotelemporda.com* *42 rooms* *In-room: a/c, Wi-Fi. In-hotel: restaurant, bar, some pets allowed* 💳 *AE, DC, MC, V* *BP.*

BESALÚ

34 km (21 mi) north of Girona, 25 km (15 mi) west of Figueres.

Besalú, the capital of a feudal county until power was transferred to Barcelona at the beginning of the 12th century, remains one of the best-preserved and most evocative medieval towns in Catalonia. Among its main sights are two churches, Sant Vicenç (set on an attractive, café-lined plaza) and Sant Pere, and the ruins of the convent of Santa Maria on the hill above town.

GETTING HERE AND AROUND

With a population of just over 2,000, the village is certainly small enough to stroll, with all the restaurants and sights within easy distance of each other. There is bus service to Besalú from Figueres and the surrounding Costa Brava resorts.

ESSENTIALS

Visitor Information Besalú (✉ *Pl. de la Libertat 1* ☎ *972/591240*).

Guided tours organized by the tourist office visit the *mikvah* (Jewish ritual baths) and the churches (usually closed otherwise). During the Jewish Festival (first week of March) and the Medieval Festival (first weekend in September) residents and costumed actors lead special visits to the historic quarter. The 11th century seems little more than a heartbeat away as a rabbi (an actor) from the old Jewish community shows the mikvah. A walk through the *Call*, or Jewish Quarter, follows. At the church of Sant Pere, with its 13th-century ambulatory, you may hear Gregorian chant. Book at the **tourist office.** ✉ *Pl. de la Llibertat* ☎ *972/591240* 🎫 *€3* ⏲ *Tours July and Aug., Wed. at 11.*

EXPLORING

Convent de Santa Maria. The ruins of the Santa Maria Convent on a hill just outside of town make a good walk and offer a panoramic view over Besalú.

Església de Sant Pere. The 12th-century Romanesque Sant Pere church, part of a 10th-century monastery, is a cavernous yet intimate medieval wonder. ✉ *Pl. de Sant Pere s/n.*

Església de Sant Vicenç. Founded in 977, this pre-Romanesque gem contains the relics of St. Vincent as well as the tomb of its benefactor, Pere de Rovira. La Capella de la Veracreu (Chapel of the True Cross) displays a reproduction of an alleged fragment of the True Cross brought from Rome by Bernat Tallafer in 977 and stolen in 1899. ✉ *Carrer de Sant Vicens s/n*

Pont Fortificat. The town's most emblematic feature is this Romanesque 11th-century fortified bridge with crenellated battlements spanning the Fluvià River.

WHERE TO EAT

$$–$$$ CATALAN ★ ✕ **Els Fogons de Can Llaudes.** A faithfully restored 11th-century Romanesque chapel holds proprietor Jaume Soler's outstanding restaurant, one of Catalonia's best. A typical main dish is *confitat de bou amb patates al morter i raïm glacejat* (beef confit with glacé grapes, served with mashed potatoes). The *menú de degustació* (tasting menu) is recommended; call at least one day in advance to reserve it. ✉ *Prat de Sant Pere 6* ☎ *972/590858* ✍ *Reservations essential* 💳 *AE, MC, V* ⏲ *Closed Tues. and last 2 wks of Nov.*

OLOT

21 km (13 mi) west of Besalú, 55 km (34 mi) northwest of Girona.

Capital of the Garrotxa area, Olot is famous for its 19th-century school of landscape painters and has several excellent Art Nouveau buildings,

Besalú contains astonishingly well-preserved medieval buildings.

including the Casa Solà-Morales, which has a facade by Palau de la Música Catalana architect Lluís Domènech i Montaner. The Sant Esteve church at the southeastern end of Passeig d'en Blay is famous for its El Greco painting *Christ Carrying the Cross* (1605).

EXPLORING

Museu Comarcal de la Garrotxa. *The County Museum of La Garrotxa* contains works of Catalan Modernisme (Art Nouveau) as well as sculptures by Miquel Blay, creator of the long-tressed maidens who support the balconies along Olot's main boulevard, Passeig d'en Blay. ✉ *Carrer Hospici 8* ☎ *972/279130* 🎫 *€3.50* 🕓 *Mon. and Wed.–Sat. 10–1 and 4–7, Sun. 10–1:30.*

WHERE TO EAT AND STAY

$$–$$$ CATALAN ✕ **Ca l'Enric.** Chefs Jordi and Isabel Juncà have become legends in the town of La Vall de Bianya just north of Olot, where symposia on culinary matters such as woodcock preparation have inspired prize-winning books. Cuisine firmly rooted in local products, starring game of all sorts, is taken to another level here. Woodcock in four servings (soup, risotto with wings, drumstick, breast) is the house specialty, but wild boar and local mini-vegetables roasted over coals are also exquisitely prepared. ✉ *Ctra. C 26* ☎ *972/290015* 🌐 *www.calenric.net* ✍ *Reservations essential* 💳 *AE, DC, MC, V* 🕓 *Closed Mon. No dinner Sun., Tues., or Wed. Closed Dec. 24–Jan. 18 and July 1–14.*

$$–$$$ CATALAN ✕ **Les Cols.** Off the road east to Figueres, Fina Puigdevall has made this ancient masia (Catalan farmhouse), with five rooms for overnight stays, a design triumph. The sprawling 18th-century rustic structure is filled with glassed-in halls, intimate gardens, and wrought-iron and

steel details. The cuisine is seasonal and based on locally grown products, from wild mushrooms to the extraordinarily flavorful legumes and vegetables produced by the rich, volcanic soil of La Garrotxa. ✉ *Mas les Cols, Ctra. de la Canya* ☎ *972/261001* 🌐 *www.lescols.com* *Reservations essential* 💳 *AE, DC, MC, V* ⏲ *Closed Jan. 2–22 and July 28–Aug. 14.*

¢ **La Perla d'Olot.** Known for its friendly family ambience, this hotel is always the first in Olot to fill up. On the edge of town toward the Vic road, it's within walking distance of two parks. Rooms are classic and unsurprising, though well equipped and comfortable. **Pros:** relaxed and unpretentious; an easy stop with comfortable rooms and personalized service. **Cons:** a little far from the center of Olot where the locals live. ✉ *Ctra. La Deu 9* ☎ *972/262326* 🌐 *www.laperlahotels.com* *32 rooms, 30 apartments* *In-room: Wi-Fi. In-hotel: restaurant, bar, Internet terminal, some pets allowed* 💳 *AE, DC, MC, V.*

RUPIT

33 km (20 mi) south of Olot, 97 km (60 mi) north of Barcelona.

Rupit is a spectacular stop for its medieval houses and its food, the highlight of which is beef-stuffed potatoes. Built into a rocky promontory over a stream in the rugged Collsacabra region (about halfway from Olot to Vic), the town has some of the most aesthetically perfect **stone houses** in Catalonia, some of which were reproduced for Barcelona's architectural theme park, Poble Espanyol, for the 1929 International Exposition.

GETTING HERE AND AROUND

There is one daily bus from Barcelona (leaving at 6 PM), and the journey takes about two hours. Rupit is delightful to explore on foot and makes a good base for hiking in the surrounding mountainous countryside.

WHERE TO EAT

$$$ SPANISH ★ ✕ **El Repòs.** Hanging over the river that runs through Rupit, this restaurant ($–$$$) serves the best meat-stuffed potatoes around. Ordering a meal is easy: just learn the word *patata*. Other specialties include duck and lamb. The 11 rooms (¢) are rustic but cozy. ✉ *C. Barbacana 1* ☎ *93/852–2100* 💳 *DC, MC, V* ⏲ *Closed weekdays Oct.–Easter but will open by arrangement.*

THE COSTA BRAVA

The Costa Brava (Wild Coast) is a nearly unbroken series of sheer rock cliffs dropping down to crystalline waters, capriciously punctuated with innumerable coves and tiny beaches on narrow inlets, each of which is called a *cala*. It basically begins at Blanes and continues north through 135 km (84 mi) to the French border at Port Bou. Although the area does have spots of real-estate excess, the rocky terrain of many pockets (Tossa, Cap de Begur, and Cadaqués) has discouraged overbuilding. On a good day here, the luminous blue of the sea contrasts with red-brown headlands and cliffs, and the distant lights of fishing boats reflect on wine-color waters at dusk. Umbrella pines escort you to the fringes of secluded coves and sandy white beaches.

GETTING HERE AND AROUND

From Barcelona, the fastest way to the Costa Brava is to start up the inland AP7 *autopista* tollway toward Girona, then take Sortida (Exit) 10 for Blanes, Lloret de Mar, Tossa de Mar, Sant Feliu de Guíxols, S'Agaró, Platja d'Aro, Palamós, Calella de Palafrugell, and Palafrugell. From Palafrugell, you can head inland for La Bisbal and from there on to the city of Girona. From Girona you can easily travel to the inland towns of Banyoles, Besalú, and Olot. To head to the middle section of the Costa Brava, get off at Sortida 6, the first exit after Girona; this will point you directly to the Iberian ruins of Ullastret. To reach the northern part of the Costa Brava, get off the AP7 before Figueres at Sortida 4 for L'Estartit, L'Escala, Empúries, Castelló d'Empúries, Aïguamolls de l'Empordà, Roses, Cadaqués, Sant Pere de Rodes, and Portbou. Sortida 4 will also take you directly to Figueres, Peralada, and the Alberes range. The old national route, NII, is slow, heavily traveled, and more dangerous, especially in summer.

COSTA BRAVA BEACHES AND SITES

BLANES

★ The beaches closest to Barcelona are at **Blanes** (60 km [37 mi] northeast of Barcelona; 45 km [28 mi] south of Girona). The Costa Brava begins here with five different beaches, running from Punta Santa Anna on the far side of the port—a tiny cove with a pebbly beach at the bottom of a chasm encircled by towering cliffs, fragrant pines, and deep blue-green waters—to the 2½-km-long (1½-mi-long) S'Abanell beach, which draws the crowds. Small boats can take you from the harbor to Cala de Sant Francesc or the double beach at Santa Cristina between May and September.

The town's castle of Sant Joan, on a mountain overlooking the town, goes back to the 11th century. The watchtower along the coastline was built in the 16th century to protect against Barbary pirates. Most travelers skip the working port of Blanes.

The summer event in Blanes that everyone waits for is the **fireworks competition,** held every night at 10:30 July 21–27, which coincides with the town's yearly festival. The fireworks are launched over the water from a rocky outcropping in the middle of the seaside promenade known as Sa Palomera while people watch from the beach and surrounding area as more gunpowder is burned in half an hour than at the battle of Trafalgar.

TOSSA DE MAR

The next stop north from Blanes on the coast road is **Tossa de Mar** (80 km [50 mi] northeast of Barcelona, 41 km [25 mi] south of Girona), christened "Blue Paradise" by painter Marc Chagall, who summered here for four decades. The only Chagall painting in Spain, *Celestial Violinist,* is in the **Museu Municipal** (✉ *Pl. Roig i Soler 1* ☎ *972/340709* 🎫 *€3* ⏲ *Oct.–May, Tues.–Sat. 10–2 and 4–8, Sun. 10–2; June–Sept., Tues.–Sat. 10–8, Sun. and Mon. 10–2 and 4–8*). Tossa's walled **medieval town** and pristine beaches are among Catalonia's best.

DID YOU KNOW?

The artist Marc Chagall loved to vacation in Tossa de Mar and felt inspired by its vivid blue ocean landscape.

Set around a blue buckle of a bay, Tossa de Mar is a symphony in two parts: the Vila Vella, or Old Town—a knotted warren of steep, narrow, cobblestone streets with many restored buildings (some dating back to the 14th century)—and the Vila Nova, or New Town. The former is encased in medieval walls and towers, but the New Town is open to the sea and is itself a lovely district threaded by 18th-century lanes. Girdling the Old Town, on the Cap de Tossa promontory that juts out into the sea, the 12th-century walls and towers at water's edge are a local pride and joy, the only example of a fortified medieval town on the entire Catalan coast.

Ava Gardner filmed the 1951 Hollywood extravaganza *Pandora and the Flying Dutchman* here (a statue dedicated to her stands on a terrace on the medieval walls); today the film is compelling for its scenes of an untouched Costa Brava. Things may have changed since those days, but this beautiful village retains much of the magic of the unspoiled Costa Brava. The primary beach at Tossa de Mar is the Platja Gran (Big Beach) in front of the town beneath the walls, and just next to it is Mar Menuda (Little Sea). Small, fat, colorfully painted fishing boats—maybe the same ones that caught your dinner—pull up onto the beach, heightening the charm.

The main bus station (the local tourist office is here) is on Plaça de les Nacions Sense Estat. Take Avinguda Ferran and Avinguda Costa Brava to head down the slope to the waterfront and the Old Town, which is entered by the Torre de les Hores, and head to the Vila Vella's heart, the Gothic church of Sant Vicenç, to saunter around and take a dip in the Middle Ages.

8

WHERE TO EAT AND STAY

$$–$$$ CATALAN **La Cuina de Can Simon.** Elegantly rustic, this restaurant right beside Tossa del Mar's medieval walls serves a combination of classical cuisine with very up-to-date touches. The *caldereta de gambas con verduras y rebanadas de pan con ajo* (shrimp bouillabaisse with vegetables and garlic bread) is a great winter dish. The service is top-shelf, from the welcoming tapa with a glass of *cava* (sparkling wine) to the little pastries accompanying coffee. ✉ *Portal 24, Tossa de Mar* ☎ *972/341269* 🌐 *www.lacuinadecansimo.es* ▭ *AE, DC, MC, V* ⏲ *Closed last 2 wks of Nov.; last 2 wks of Jan.; and Mon. and Tues. Oct.–May. No dinner Sun.*

$–$$ CATALAN **Las Tapas de Can Sisó.** Tucked in under Tossa's defensive walls, this usually booming place has a good-sized terrace and a cozy countrified dining room where tapas, *raciones* (small portions), and full meals are served with elegance and style. Try the *croquetas de espinacas* (spinach croquettes), the *brandada* (purée of cod), or the *cim i tomba* (a Catalan fish and potato stew). ✉ *Pl. de las Armas 1, Tossa de Mar* ☎ *972/340708* ▭ *AE, DC, MC, V* ⏲ *Closed Nov. 10–Dec. 10 and Mon. Oct.–May.*

¢–$ **Hotel Capri.** Maria Eugènia Serrat, a native Tossan, displays local hospitality at her small family hotel. Set on the beach with the medieval walls looming behind it, the hotel has a super location. Rooms are individually decorated in different styles and colors. **Pros:** very warm and personal hostessing; good combination of medieval surroundings and modern technology. **Cons:** tight quarters in general; rooms a little small. ✉ *Passeig del Mar 17, Tossa de Mar* ☎ *972/340358* 🌐 *www.*

hotelcapritossa.com ⇆ *22 rooms* ♨ *In-room: a/c, Wi-Fi. In-hotel: Wi-Fi hotspot, some pets allowed* ▭ *MC, V* ⊙ *Closed Nov.–Mar.* ⊞ *BP.*

$–$$ **Hotel Diana.** Built by the Moderniste architect Antoni Falguera, this Art Nouveau gem is one of the finest places on the Costa Brava to cozy up with a glass of sherry and while away the early evening. Overlooking a beach, the Diana also contains an enticing inner courtyard—a lush garden with palm trees, flowers, and fountains, and inside, a stunning Art Nouveau fireplace that incorporates a bust by Frederic Marés of Falguera's wife. Guest rooms have contemporary furnishings. **Pros:** first-rate art and architecture; verdant surroundings. **Cons:** somewhat lacking in amenities; no Internet terminal. ✉ *Pl. de Espanya 6,Tossa de Mar* ☎ *972/341886* ⊕ *www.diana-hotel.com* ⇆ *20 rooms, 1 suite* ♨ *In-room: a/c, Wi-Fi. In-hotel: bar, Wi-Fi hotspot, some pets allowed* ▭ *AE, DC, MC, V* ⊙ *Closed Nov.–Easter* ⊞ *BP.*

¢ **Hotel Sant March.** This family hotel in the center of Tossa del Mar is two minutes from the beach. The owner's wife and mother-in-law care for an interior garden that is the envy of many and that all rooms open onto, making for much-appreciated tranquility in a sometimes hectic town. **Pros:** intimate, family-run hotel with a warm personal touch. **Cons:** though the rooms are largely shielded from the midtown din, the location is at the very eye of the storm. ✉ *Av. del Pelegrí 2,Tossa de Mar* ☎ *972/340078* ⊕ *www.hotelsantmarch.en.eresmas.com* ⇆ *29 rooms* ♨ *In-hotel: Wi-Fi hotspot, bar* ▭ *AE, DC, MC, V* ⊙ *Closed Oct.–Mar.* ⊞ *BP.*

SANT FELIU DE GUIXOLS

The fishing and shipping town of **Sant Feliu de Guixols** is 23 km (15 mi) north of Tossa de Mar, around hairpin curves, by hidden inlets. Tiny turnouts or parking spots on this route nearly always lead to intimate coves with stone stairways winding down from the road.

The town itself is set in a small bay, and handsome Moderniste mansions line the seafront promenade, recalling former wealth from the cork industry. In front of them, an arching beach of fine white sand leads around to the fishing harbor at its north end. Behind the promenade, a well-preserved old quarter of narrow streets and squares leads to a 10th-century gateway with horseshoe arches (all that remains of a pre-Romanesque monastery); nearby, a church still stands that combines Romanesque, Gothic, and baroque styles.

The Romanesque Benedictine monastery houses the City Museum, **Museu d'Història de la Ciutat,** which contains interesting exhibits about the town's cork and fishing trades and displays local archaeological finds. ✉ *Carrer Abadia s/n* ☎ *972/821575* ▤ *Free* ⊙ *July–Sept., Tues.–Sat. 11–2 and 5–8, Sun. 11–2; Oct.–June, Tues.–Sat. 11–2 and 4–7, Sun. 11–2.*

WHERE TO EAT AND STAY

$–$$ CATALAN ★ ✕ **Can Segura.** Half a block in from the beach at Sant Feliu de Guixols, Can Segura serves home-cooked seafood and upland specialties. The dining room is always full, with customers waiting their turn in the street, but the staff is good at finding spots at the jovially long communal tables. There are very basic rooms (¢) available for overnight sojourns. ✉ *Carrer de Sant Pere 11,Sant Feliu de Guixols 17220* ☎ *972/321009* ▭ *AE, DC, MC, V* ⏲ *Closed Nov.–Easter (except New Year's Eve weekend)* 🍽 *EP.*

$$ CATALAN ★ ✕ **Eldorado.** Lluis Cruanya, who once owned Barcelona's top restaurant and another in Manhattan, has done it again in Sant Feliu de Guixols. With his daughter Suita running the dining room and Iván Álvarez as chef, this smartly designed restaurant with contemporary lines a block back from the beach serves tasty morsels from *llom de tonyina a la plancha amb tomàquets agridolços, ceba i chíps d'escarchofa* (grilled tuna with pickled tomato, baby onions, and artichoke chips) to *llobarro rostít amb emulsió de cítrics i espàrrecs trigueros* (roast sea bass with a citric emulsion and wild asparagus), all cooked to perfection. Try the *patates braves* (new potatoes in *allioli* [garlic mayonnaise] and hot sauce), as good as any in Catalonia. ✉ *Rambla Vidal 19,Sant Feliu de Guixols* ☎ *972/821414* ▭ *AE, DC, MC, V* ⏲ *Closed Tues. Oct.–Easter.*

$$–$$$ CATALAN ★ ✕ **El Dorado Mar.** Around the southern end of the beach at Sant Feliu de Guixols, perched over the entrance to the harbor, this superb family restaurant offers fine fare at unbeatable prices. Whether straight seafood such as *lubina* (sea bass) or *dorada* (gilt-head bream) or *revuelto de setas* (eggs scrambled with wild mushrooms), everything served here is fresh and flavorful. ✉ *Passeig Irla 15,Sant Feliu de Guixols* ☎ *972/326286* ▭ *AE, DC, MC, V* ⏲ *No dinner mid-Oct.–Easter.*

S'AGAR

One of the Costa Brava's best clusters of seaside mansions, **S'Agaró** is 3 km (2 mi) north of Sant Feliu. The 30-minute walk along the **sea wall** from Hostal de La Gavina to Sa Conca Beach is a delight. Likewise, the one-hour hike from Sant Pol Beach over to Sant Feliu de Guixols for lunch and back is a superb look at the Costa Brava at its best.

WHERE TO EAT AND STAY

$$–$$$ CATALAN ★ ✕ **Villa Mas.** For excellent dining at nonstratospheric costs in S'Agaró, this Moderniste villa with a lovely turn-of-the-20th-century zinc bar inside works with fresh products recently retrieved from the Mediterranean. The terrace is a popular and shady spot just across the road from the beach, and the clientele is predominantly young and savvy. ✉ *Platja de Sant Pol 95,S'Agaró* ☎ *972/822526* ▭ *AE, DC, MC, V* ⏲ *Closed Dec. 12–Jan. 12 and Mon. Oct.–Mar. No dinner weekdays Oct.–Mar.*

$$$$ Fodor's Choice ★ 🏨 **L'Hostal de la Gavina.** This is the place for the last remnants of Costa Brava chic. Big wheels such as Cole Porter followed upper-class couples from Barcelona who began honeymooning here in the 1930s. In S'Agaró Vell, on the eastern corner of Sant Pol beach, the hotel is an outstanding display of design and cuisine (don't miss the fresh fish and seafood), opened in 1932 by Josep Ensesa. Guest rooms have fine wood furniture and Oriental rugs. Tennis, golf, and riding are nearby, and on a summer evening the loggia overlooking the sea is sublime. **Pros:** superbly decorated and appointed; wonderful traditional European environment. **Cons:** hard on the budget *and* habit-forming. ✉ *Pl. de la Rosaleda s/n, S'Agaró* ☎ *972/321100* 🌐 *www.lagavina.com* 🛏 *58 rooms, 16 suites* 👍 *In-room: a/c, safe, Wi-Fi. In-hotel: restaurant, pool, tennis court, gym, some pets allowed* ▭ *AE, DC, MC, V* ⏲ *Closed Nov.–Easter (except New Year's weekend).*

CALELLA DE PALAFRUGELL AND AROUND

Up the coast from S'Agaró, a road leads east to **Llafranc,** a small port with quiet waterfront hotels and restaurants, and forks right to **Calella de Palafrugell,** (44 km [27 mi] east of Girona), a pretty fishing village known for its July habaneras festival. (*Habaneras* are Catalan-Cuban sea chants inspired by the Spanish-American War.) Just south is the panoramic promontory **Cap Roig,** with views of the barren Formigues (Ants) Isles and a botanical garden that you can tour with a guide daily (April–September 9–8 and October–December 9–6; weekends only January–February, 9–6) for €4. The left fork drops to **Tamariu,** one of the Costa's prettiest inlet towns. A climb over the bluff leads down to the blindingly white parador at **Aiguablava,** overlooking magnificent cliffs and crags.

WHERE TO EAT AND STAY

$–$$ CATALAN **Pa i Raïm.** "Bread and grapes" in Catalan, this excellent restaurant in Josep Pla's ancestral family home in Palafrugell has one rustic dining room as well as another glassed-in, winter garden space. In summer the leafy terrace is the place to be. The menu ranges from traditional country cuisine to more streamlined contemporary fare such as strawberry gazpacho. The *canelón crujiente de verduritas y setas con romescu* (crisped cannelloni with young vegetables and wild mushrooms with romesco [almonds, peppers, and olive oil] sauce) and the *vieiras y verduritas salteadas con aceite de sésamo* (scallops and baby vegetables sautéed with sesame-seed oil) are two standouts. *Torres i Jonama 56,Palafrugell 972/304572 www.pairaim.com AE, DC, MC, V Closed Dec. 22–Jan. 7, May 11–May 26, and Mon. and Tues. No dinner Sun.*

$$$$ ★ **El Far de Sant Sebastiá.** A 17th-century hermitage attached to a 15th-century watchtower, this jumble of elegant stairways and terraces overlooking the Mediterranean lavishes visitors with a full complement of sensorial rewards and pleasures. Overlooking the Bay of Llafranc from a rocky aerie leading down to a sandy beach, El Far (lighthouse or watchtower) is an hour and a half from Barcelona at the heart of the Costa Brava. Rooms are high-ceilinged and breezy with sea views, and the restaurant ($–$$$) specializes in local Empordà and Mediterranean cuisine. **Pros:** one of the best combinations of graceful architecture and spectacular views on the Costa Brava. **Cons:** somewhat isolated from Costa Brava village life. *Platja de Llafranc, Llafranc–Palafrugell 972/301639 www.elfar.net 9 rooms In-room: a/c, Wi-Fi. In-hotel: restaurant, Wi-Fi hotspot AE, DC, MC, V BP.*

BEGUR AND AROUND

From **Begur**, north of Aiguablava, you can go east through the *calas* or take the inland route past the rose-color stone houses and ramparts of the restored medieval town of **Pals.** Nearby **Peratallada** is another medieval town with fortress, castle, tower, palace, and well-preserved walls. North of Pals there are signs for **Ullastret,** an Iberian village dating from the 5th century BC.

L'Estartit is the jumping-off point for the spectacular **Parc Natural Submarí** (Underwater Natural Park) by the Medes Isles, famous for diving and underwater photography.

The Greco-Roman ruins at **Empúries** are Catalonia's most important archaeological site. This port is one of the most monumental ancient engineering feats on the Iberian Peninsula. As the Greeks' original point of arrival in Spain, Empúries was also where the Olympic Flame entered Spain for Barcelona's 1992 Olympic Games.

WHERE TO EAT AND STAY

$-$$ CATALAN ✕ **Restaurant Ibèric.** This excellent pocket of authentic Costa Brava tastes and aromas serves everything from snails to woodcock in season. Wild mushrooms scrambled with eggs or stewed with hare are specialties here, as are the complex and earthy red wines made by enologist Jordi Oliver of the Oliver Conti vineyard in the Upper Empordà's village of Capmany. ✉ *Carrer Valls 6,Ullastret* ☎ *972/757108* ▭ *AE, DC, MC, V* ⊗ *Closed Mon. No dinner Sun. Nov.–Mar.*

$$$–$$$$ ★ **Hotel Aigua Blava.** What began as a small *hostal* in the mid-1920s is now a full-fledged luxury hotel, run by the fourth generation of the same family. Traditional touches—rocking chairs and wooden furniture in the sitting rooms, black-and-white photos tracing the evolution of the hotel—blend pleasantly with the breezy pastel decoration of the rooms and the luscious sea views. The bright, sun-filled restaurant ($–$$) overlooks the water and serves traditional Mediterranean fish dishes, including *bacalao* (cod) and *merluza* (hake). The hotel is about 9 km (6 mi) north of Calella de Palafrugell. **Pros:** personalized, family-run environment; comfortable and traditional design; surrounded by gardens and greenery. **Cons:** equipment and furnishings are somewhat antique; not a state-of-the-art Jacuzzi-and-spa kind of operation. ✉ *Platja de Fornells, Begur* ☎ *972/624562* 🌐 *www.aiguablava.com* *85 rooms* *In room: a/c, Wi-Fi. In-hotel: restaurant, bar, tennis court, pool, Wi-Fi hotspot* ▭ *AE, DC, MC, V* *BP.*

$$–$$$ ★ **Parador de Aiguablava.** The vista from this modern, blindingly white parador, 9 km (6 mi) north of Calella de Palafrugell, is the classic postcard Costa Brava: the rounded Cala d'Aiguablava wraps around the shimmering blue Mediterranean. On the terrace you can bask in the sun while waves break at the rocky shore and dissolve into white froth below. The parador maximizes its cliff-top perch with large windows everywhere—in the cool-tone rooms, the bright and airy restaurant ($–$$$), and the many comfortable sitting rooms. The restaurant serves fine Costa Brava favorites, including the much-heralded *anchoas* (anchovies) from nearby L'Escala. **Pros:** magnificent surrounding views. **Cons:** the barracks-like alabaster structure atop the cliffs is something of an eyesore. ✉ *Platja d'Aiguablava, Begur* ☎ *972/622162* 🌐 *www.parador.es* *78 rooms* *In-room: a/c. In-hotel: restaurant, pool, gym, Internet terminal* ▭ *AE, DC, MC, V.*

CADAQUÈS AND AROUND

Spain's easternmost town, **Cadaqués**, still has the whitewashed charm that made this fishing village into an international artists' haunt in the early 20th century. The Marítim bar is the central hangout both day and night; after dark, you might also enjoy the Jardí, across the square. Salvador Dalí's house, now a museum, still stands at Port Lligat, a 30-minute walk north of town.

The **Casa Museu Salvador Dalí** was Dalí's summerhouse and a site long associated with the artist's notorious frolics with everyone from poets such as Federico García Lorca and Paul Eluard to filmmaker Luis Buñuel. Filled with bits of the Surrealist's daily life, it's an important point in the "Dalí triangle," completed by the castle at Púbol and the Museu Dalí in Figueres. ✉ *3-km (2-mi) walk north from Cadaqués town center, along beach, Port Lligat* ☎ *972/251015* 🌐 *www.salvador-dali.org* 🎫 *€10* ⏲ *Mar. 15–June 14 and Sept. 16–Jan. 6, Tues.–Sun. 10:30–6; June 15–Sept. 15, daily 9:30–9.*

DALÍ DALLIANCES

Salvador Dalí was as notorious for his bizarre life as for his paintings. In his twenties he was sentimentally involved with Federico García Lorca, though their passion remained unconsummated. Luis Buñuel, author of the surrealist film *Un Chien Andalou* (*An Andalusian Dog*), was another fizzled Dalí romance. When Surrealist poet Paul Éluard visited Port Lligat in 1929, Dalí fell for Éluard's wife, Gala, his muse and lover for life. According to Dalí biographer Ian Gibson the artist's sense of shame, a "pathological shyness," both drove his art and blocked his love life.

The **Castillo Púbol**, Dalí's former castle-home, is now the resting place of Gala, his perennial model and mate. It's a chance to wander through yet more Dalíesque landscape: lush gardens, fountains decorated with masks of Richard Wagner (the couple's favorite composer), and distinctive elephants with giraffe's legs and claw feet. Two lions and a giraffe stand guard near Gala's tomb. ✉ *Pl. Gala Dalí s/n, Púbol-la Pera (Rte. 255 toward La Bisbal, 15 km [9 mi] east of A7)* ☎ *972/488655* 🎫 *€7* ⏲ *Mar. 14–June 14 and Sept. 16–Nov. 2, Tues.–Sun. 10–6; June 15–Sept. 15, daily 10–8; Nov.–Dec., daily 10–5.*

Cap de Creus, north of Cadaqués, Spain's easternmost point, is a fundamental pilgrimage, if only for the symbolic geographical rush. The hike out to the lighthouse—through rosemary, thyme, and the salt air of the Mediterranean—is unforgettable. The Pyrenees officially end (or rise) here. New Year's Day finds mobs of revelers awaiting the first emergence of the "new" sun from the Mediterranean. Gaze down at heart-knocking views of the craggy coast and crashing waves with a warm mug of coffee in hand or fine fare on the table at **Bar Restaurant Cap de Creus**, which sits on a rocky crag above the Cap de Creus.

Fodor's Choice ★ The monastery of **Sant Pere de Rodes,** 7 km (4½ mi) by car (plus a 20-minute walk) above the pretty fishing village El Port de la Selva, is one of the most spectacular sites on the Costa Brava. Built in the 10th and early 11th centuries by Benedictine monks—and sacked and plundered repeatedly since—this Romanesque monolith, now being restored, commands a breathtaking panorama of the Pyrenees, the Empordà plain, the sweeping curve of the Bay of Roses, and Cap de Creus. (Topping off the grand trek across the Pyrenees, Cap de Creus is a spectacular six-hour walk from here on the well-marked GR-11 trail.)

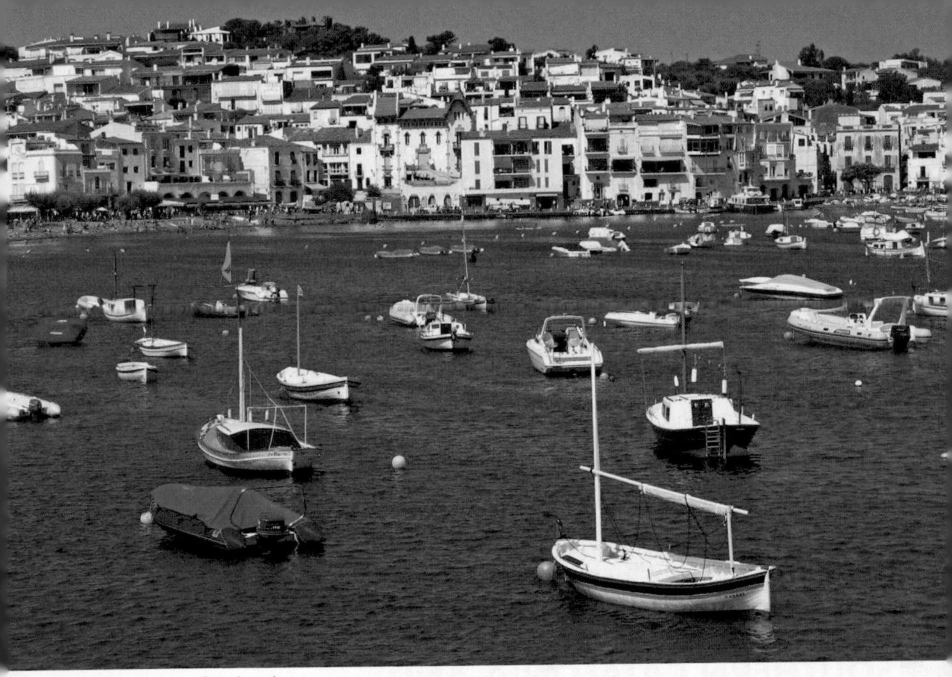

The popular harbor of Cadaqués

WHERE TO EAT AND STAY

$–$$ SEAFOOD **Can Pelayo.** This small family-run spot, hidden behind Plaça Port Alguer a five-minute walk south of Cadaqués town, serves excellent seafood. Straight-up fresh fish is the best bet here: *llobarro* (sea bass), *dorada* (gilt-head bream), or *llenguado* (sole) cooked over coals and accompanied by a green salad and a freezing bottle of a local white wine such as the prize-winning Oliver-Conti Gewürztraminer–sauvignon blanc from nearby Capmany make for an excellent meal. *Carrer Nou 11, Cadaqués* 972/258356 *AE, DC, MC, V* *Closed weekdays Oct.–May.*

¢–$ SPANISH Fodor's Choice ★ **Casa Anita.** Simple, fresh, and generous cuisine is the draw at this tiny place in Cadaqués on the street that leads to Port Lligat and Dalí's house. The crowd's *couleur locale* includes hippies, drifters, beachcombers, and other loafers on a budget. Try the salads and the sardine, mussel, and sea bass dishes, and get here early. *Carrer Miquel Rosset 16, Cadaqués* 972/258471 *AE, DC, MC, V* *Closed last 2 wks of Nov.; mid-Jan.–mid-Feb.; and Mon. Sept.–May*

$$ SEAFOOD ★ **Es Trull.** Some people consider this cedar-shingled cafeteria on the harbor side street in the center Cadaqués to be the best kitchen in town. An ancient olive press in the interior gave Es Trull its name. It specializes in fish dishes such as *escórpora* (scorpion fish) and rice dishes, such as the star player, *arròs de calamar i gambes* (rice with squid and shrimp), or *arròs negre amb calamar i sèpia* (rice in ink of squid and cuttlefish). *Port Ditxós s/n, Cadaqués* 972/258196 *AE, MC, V* *Closed Nov.–Easter.*

$–$$ **Llané Petit.** An intimate, typically Mediterranean bayside hotel, Llané Petit caters to people who want to make the most of their stay in the village and don't want to spend too much time in their hotel rooms. Rooms are simple and serene, and so is the restaurant's cuisine, which uses lots of grilled meats and fish. **Pros:** the semi-private beach next to the hotel is less crowded than the main Cadaqués beach. **Cons:** rooms on the small side; somewhat lightweight beds and furnishings. ✉ *Carrer Dr. Bartomeus 37, Cadaqués* ☎ *972/251020* 🌐 *www.llanepetit.com* *37 rooms* *In-room: a/c, Wi-Fi. In-hotel: restaurant, Internet terminal, Wi-Fi hotspot* ▭ *AE, MC, V* ⏲ *Closed 2 wks in Dec.*

$$–$$$ **Playa Sol.** Open for more than 40 years, this hotel has the experience that comes with age. The rooms are done tastefully in red and ocher; some overlook the sea. The Playa Sol is in the cove of Es Pianc on the left side of the bay of Cadaqués as you face the sea, a five-minute walk from the village center. Boaters will love this place—all types of craft tie up here, as master Costa Brava chronicler Josep Pla spread its fame as the best place to drop anchor in Cadaqués. **Pros:** powerful historic vibrations; a cozy, refuge-in-the-eye-of-the-maelstrom feel. **Cons:** rooms on the small side; public spaces constricted. ✉ *Platja Es Pianc 3 Cadaqués* ☎ *972/258100* 🌐 *www.playasol.com* *49 rooms* *In-room: a/c, Wi-Fi. In-hotel: restaurant, bar, pool, Wi-Fi hotspot* ▭ *AE, DC, MC, V* ⏲ *Closed mid-Nov.–mid-Feb.*

SOUTHERN CATALONIA AND AROUND VALENCIA

South of the Costa Brava, the time machine zooms back to the days of ancient Rome when you arrive in Tarragona, in Roman times regarded as one of the empire's finest creations. Its wine was already famous and its population was the first *gens togata* (literally, the toga-clad race) in Spain, which conferred on them equality with the citizens of Rome. Roman relics, with the Circus Maximus heading the list, are still the evidence of Tarragona's grandeur, and to this the Middle Ages added wonderful city walls and citadels.

Spain's third-largest city and the capital of its region and province, Valencia is equidistant from Barcelona and Madrid. If you have time for a day trip (or you decide to stay in the beach town of El Saler), make your way to the Albufera, a scenic coastal wetland teeming with native wildlife, especially migratory birds.

TARRAGONA

98 km (61 mi) southwest of Barcelona, 251 km (155 mi) northeast of Valencia.

With its vast Roman remains, walls, and fortifications and its medieval Christian monuments, Tarragona was selected by UNESCO in 2000 as a World Heritage Site. The city today is a vibrant center of culture and arts, a busy fishing and shipping port, and a natural jumping-off point for the towns and pristine beaches of the Costa Daurada, 216 km (134 mi) of coastline north of the Costa del Azahar around Tarragona.

Continued on page 564

El Bulli's small pies of crystal almonds with cherries

Icy carrot and passion fruit truffles at El Bulli

Arzak's seabass with vegetable confetti

SPAIN'S FOOD REVOLUTION

Every night is a performance in Spain's houses of haute cuisine, with chefs releasing new "collections" of dishes that thrill more than a diner's tastebuds. One rollercoaster meal may span six hours and more than 30 courses of a few bites apiece. You may not recognize what's on your plate, but that's part of the fun. *by Erica Duecy*

Spain is home to the world's most cutting-edge culinary scene. Chefs of *la nueva cocina*—as the avant-garde movement is called—relentlessly explore new techniques, resulting in dishes that defy convention. By playing with the properties of food, they can turn liquid into solids, and solids into powders. Olive oil "caviar," hot ice cream, and Parmesan "glass" are just a few of the alchemic presentations that have emerged.

Early on, the movement seemed to some critics like experimentation for experimentation's sake. Now it has become more refined, showcasing dishes that pleasure the palate as much as the mind. You're still likely to find yourself sipping rum "snow," eating flavored "air," and handling tweezers as eating utensils. If you decide to pull up a chair at the table of *la nueva cocina*, get ready for an unforgettable eating adventure.

FERRAN ADRIÀ—*LA NUEVA COCINA'S* VISIONARY

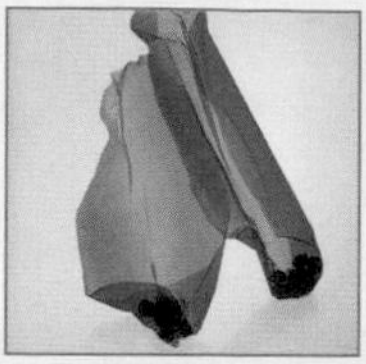

(clockwise from top left): black sesame sponge cake with miso; sea vegetable salad; hibiscus paper with blackcurrant; caviar of snail consomme; the El Bulli kitchen; the staff prepping tomatoes

Adrià has often been called the world's top chef, but his rise to fame didn't happen overnight. Adrià was an emerging talent in 1987 when he attended a cooking demonstration by French chef Jacques Maximin who spoke about his belief that "creativity means not copying." By Adrià's account, that statement transformed his approach to cooking.

The changeover to conceptual cuisine—where techniques and concepts became the driving force for his creativity—occurred in 1994, when Adrià developed a technique for producing dense foam from various liquids. A handful of new techniques emerged in those early years, but "nowadays, that process is accelerated," he says. "Within one year, I am working with several types of techniques."

Some of Adrià's most famous dishes include spherical olives (olive puree and herbs made to look like intact olives), deconstructed Caprese salad, black sesame sponge cake with miso, suckling pig tails with melon consomme, and "co-co," a giant egg made from coconut milk. These creative concoctions are served at El Bulli in meals of 26 to 35 courses, with each course just one or two bites. A meal for one costs about €250, without wine.

EL BULLI'S FUTURE

At the time of this writing, El Bulli's future remains uncertain. Adrià plans to close the restaurant at the end of 2011, and it's still to be determined if that close will be permanent. But don't fret—the El Bulli name lives on, and Adrià has already mentioned a possible culinary institute in its place. Whatever he decides, it's certain that his fans will follow.

TRICKS OF THE TRADE

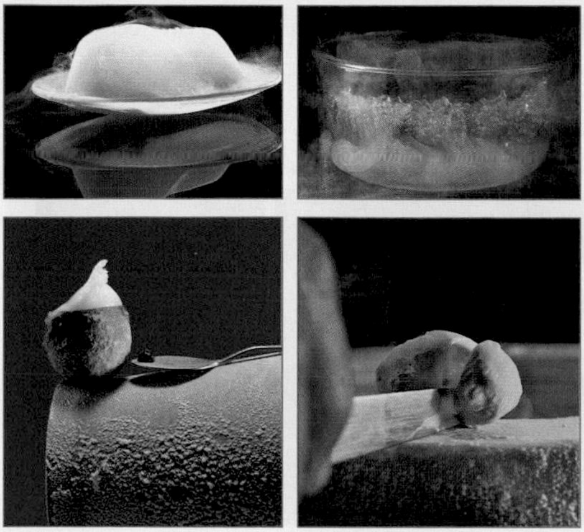

(clockwise from top left): dry ice changes from a solid directly to a gas without becoming liquid; liquid nitrogen boils in a glass container at room temperature; a nitro-cooled pistachio truffle; a nitro-cooled caipirinha with tarragon essence

Many techniques of *la nueva cocina* are borrowed from the food processing industry, including the use of liquid nitrogen, freeze-drying, and gellifying agents. This technological approach to cooking may seem like a departure from Spain's ingredient-driven cuisine, but avant-garde chefs say their creations are no less rooted in Spanish culture than traditional fare.

One leading chef, Juan Mari Arzak, describes his approach as "Basque evolutionary, investigative cuisine." He says, "We are doing things that haven't been done before." Using the freeze-drying technique *lyophilization*, or *LYO*, Arzak makes powders from items like tomatoes and peanuts. "You use the powder to add flavor to things," he says. "If you dust tuna with peanut powder and salt, it concentrates the underlying flavors to make the tuna taste like a more intense version of tuna."

Additionally, an unprecedented spirit of collaboration has defined the movement. "It is true that in other culinary movements chefs have been reluctant to share their knowledge," Adrià says. "Some people ask us, why do you share everything? Why do you share your secrets? The answer is that that's the way we understand cooking—that it's meant to be shared."

HOW DO THEY DO IT?

Daniel Garcia at El Calima using liquid nitrogen

Quick-freezing: Liquid nitrogen can be used to make instant ice cream from any liquid, even olive oil. Just pour olive oil into a bowl of liquid nitrogen, then scoop out the solid that forms.

Spherification: To create a liquidy ball that looks like a raw egg yolk, first mix a puree, say mango puree, with sodium alginate; then ladle it by the spoonful into a bath containing calcium salts. The result is a mango sphere with a liquid center.

Gellification: Liquids like soy sauce can be used to make noodles with this technique. When soy sauce is mixed with methylcellulose, it solidifies and can be extruded through a tube to form soy sauce "noodles."

Freeze-drying: The technique behind instant soup is used to create concentrated powders from items like ham and strawberries. First, the berry is frozen. Then, the pressure is lowered while applying heat so the frozen water in the berry becomes a gas. What remains is a brittle berry that can be crumbled into a powder.

THE SPANISH ARMADA

Among the most recognized contributors to *la nueva cocina* are Juan Mari Arzak, Martín Berasategui, Alberto Chicote, Daniel García, Joan Roca, and Paco Roncero. Here's where to find them:

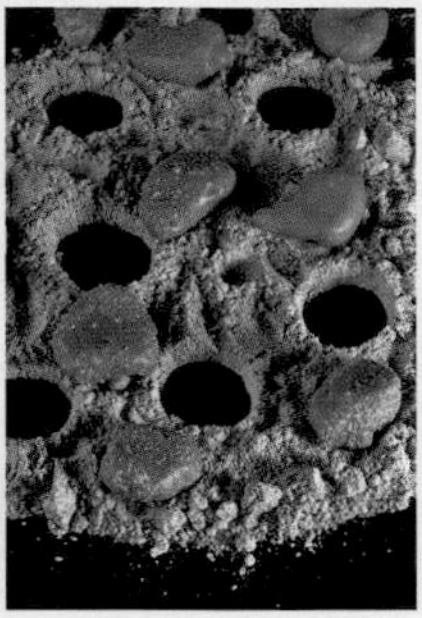

(top left) lobster in crunchy potato shell; (top right) "Lunar Rocks" of frozen cocoa "rocks" and orange-passionfruit syrup pools; (left) Chef Juan Mari Arzak and his daughter Elena

Juan Mari Arzak is recognized for modernizing and reinvigorating Basque cuisine at Restaurante Arzak in San Sebastián. He now operates it with his daughter Elena, who represents the fourth generation of Arzak restaurateurs. Despite his deep culinary roots and decades-long career, Arzak says he works to maintain a fresh perspective. "It's important to look at the world through a cook's eyes, but to think like a little kid," he says. "Because when you are a boy, you have the capacity to be amazed and surprised." **Restaurante Arzak** ✉ Avda. Alcalde Jose Elosegui, 273 / San Sebastián ☎ 943/278465 🌐 www.arzak.info

At his eponymous fine-dining restaurant in Lasarte, **Martín Berasategui** is known for his dedication to local products and fresh flavors. Notable dishes have included foie gras, smoked eel, apple terrine, and *percebes* (barnacles) served with fresh peas in vegetable broth. **Restaurante Martín Berasategui** ✉ Calle Loidi, 1 / Lasarte-Oria ☎ 943/366471 🌐 www.martinberasategui.com

The cuisine at **Alberto Chicote's** Nodo fuses Spanish and Japanese ingredients and techniques. His version of tuna tataki, for example, features seared tuna macerated in soy sauce and rice vinegar, then chopped and served with chilled garlic cream, and garnished with drops of olive oil and black olive powder. **Nodo** ✉ Calle Velázquez, 150 / Madrid ☎ 915/644044 🌐 www.restaurantenodo.es

In his mid-thirties, **Daniel García** is one of the younger practitioners of *la nueva*

cocina, as well as head chef at El Calima, the restaurant in the Hotel Don Pepe in Marbella. "My cultural inspiration comes from the area where I work, in Andalusia, the south of Spain," he says. Acclaimed dishes include gazpacho with anchovies and *queso fresco* snow, and a passionfruit flan with herb broth and eucalyptus-thyme essence. **Restaurante El Calima** ✉ Ave. José Meliá / Marbella ☎ 952/764252 🌐 www.restaurantecalima.com

Joan Roca is chef at El Celler de Can Roca in Girona, which he runs with his two brothers, Josep and Jordi. Roca is known for his work exploring the intersection between aroma and flavor, with dishes such as his "Adaptation of the Perfume *Angel* by Thierry Mugler," featuring cream of toffee, chocolate, gelée of violet and bergamot, and red-fruits ice cream with vanilla. Savories include smoked lemon prawn with green peas and licorice, and white and green asparagus with cardamom oil and truffles. **El Celler de Can Roca** ✉ Carretera de Taialá, 40 / Girona ☎ 972/222157 🌐 www.cellercanroca.com

Chefs in action, demonstrating their creativity in the kitchen: (top) Alberto Chicote with his assistants; (bottom) Martín Berasategui

Paco Roncero is chef at Restaurante La Terraza in Madrid. He is considered one of Ferran Adrià's most outstanding students. "When I started working with Ferran [in 1998], my whole concept of cuisine changed," he says. "I started researching and trying to do new things. Now my cuisine is modern, *vanguardia*, without losing sight of tradition." **Restaurante La Terraza** ✉ Alacalá 15 / Madrid ☎ 915/218700 🌐 www.casinodemadrid.es

Set on a rocky hill overlooking the sea, the ancient Roman stronghold of Tarragona is a bracing architectural mix of past and present. Roman pillars rise amid modern apartment buildings, and a Roman amphitheater shares the city coastline with trawlers and tugboats. Though the modern city is very much an industrial town, with a large port and thriving fishing industry, it has preserved its heritage superbly. Stroll along the town's cliff-side perimeter and you'll see why the Romans set up shop here: Tarragona is strategically positioned at land's edge, its lookout points commanding unobstructed sea views. As capital of the Roman province of Tarraconensis (from 218 BC), Tarraco, as it was then called, formed the empire's principal stronghold in Spain, and by the 1st century BC the city was regarded as one of the empire's finest urban creations. Its wine was already famous, and its people were the first in Spain to become Roman citizens. St. Paul preached here in AD 58, and Tarragona became the seat of the Christian church in Spain until it was superseded by Toledo in the 11th century.

Entering the city from Barcelona, you'll pass the **Triumphal Arch of Berà,** dating from the 3rd century BC, 19 km (12 mi) north of Tarragona; and from the Lleida (Lérida) road, or *autopista,* you can see the 1st-century **Roman aqueduct** that helped carry fresh water 32 km (19 mi) from the Gaià River. Tarragona is divided clearly into old and new by the Rambla Vella; the Old Town and most of the Roman remains are to the north, while modern Tarragona spreads out to the south. You could start your visit at the acacia-lined Rambla Nova, at the end of which is a balcony overlooking the sea, the **Balcó del Mediterràni.** Then walk uphill along the Passeig de les Palmeres; below it is the ancient amphitheater, the curve of which artfully echoes in the modern, semicircular Imperial Tarraco hotel on the passeig.

GETTING HERE AND AROUND

Tarragona is well connected by train: there are hourly trains from Barcelona and regular train service from other major cities, including Madrid.

The bus trip from Barcelona to Tarragona is easy; eight to 10 buses leave Barcelona's Estación Vilanova-Norte every day. Connections between Tarragona and Valencia are frequent. There arealso bus connections with the main Andalusian cities, plus Alicante, Madrid, and Valencia.

The €14 Tarragona Card, valid for 24 hours (€19 for 48 hours), gives free entry to all the city's museums and historical sites, free rides on municipal buses, and discounts at more than 100 shops, restaurants, and bars. It's sold at the main tourist office and at most hotels.

Tours of the cathedral and archaeological sites are conducted by the tourist office.

ESSENTIALS

Visitor Information Tarragona (✉ *Carrer Major 39 [just below cathedral]* ☎ *977/245203*).

EXPLORING

★ **Amphitheater.** The remains of Tarragona's Roman amphitheater, built in the 2nd century AD, have a spectacular view of the sea. This arena with tiered seats was the site of gladiatorial and other contests. You're free to wander through the access tunnels and along the seating rows. Sitting with your back to the sea, you might understand why the emperor Augustus favored Tarragona as a winter resort. In the center of the theater are the remains of two superimposed churches, the earlier of which was a Visigothic basilica built to mark the bloody martyrdom of St. Fructuós and his deacons in AD 259. **■ TIP→ €10 buys a combination ticket card valid for all Tarragona museums and sites.** ✉ *Passeig de les Palmeres* 🎫 *€3, €10 combination ticket valid for all Tarragona museums and sites* ⏲ *June–Sept., Tues.–Sat. 9–9, Sun. 9–3; Oct.–May, Tues.–Sat. 9–5, Sun. 10–3.*

Casa Castellarnau. Now a museum, this Gothic *palauet (*town house) built by Tarragona nobility in the 18th century, includes stunning furnishings from the 18th and 19th centuries. The last member of the Castellarnau family vacated the house in 1954. ✉ *Carrer Cavallers* ☎ *977/242220* 🎫 *€3, €10 combination ticket* ⏲ *June–Sept., Tues.–Sat. 9–9, Sun. 9–3; Oct.–May, Tues.–Sat. 9–7, Sun. 10–3.*

Catedral. Built between the 12th and 14th centuries on the site of a Roman temple and a mosque, this cathedral shows the changes from the Romanesque to Gothic style. The initial rounded placidity of the Romanesque apse, begun in the 12th century, later gave way to the spiky restlessness of the Gothic; the result is somewhat confused. If no mass is in progress, enter the cathedral through the cloister. The main attraction here is the 15th-century Gothic alabaster altarpiece of St. Tecla by Pere Joan, a richly detailed depiction of the life of Tarragona's patron saint. Converted by St. Paul and subsequently persecuted by local pagans, St. Tecla was repeatedly saved from demise through divine intervention. ✉ *Pl. de la Seu* ☎ *977/221736* 🎫 *€3.50* ⏲ *July–mid-Sept., Mon.–Sat. 10–7; mid-Sept.–mid-Nov., Mon.–Sat. 10–5; mid-Nov.–mid-Mar., Mon.–Sat. 10–2; mid-Mar.–June, Mon.–Sat. 10–1 and 4–7; Sun. open for services only.*

Circus Maximus. Students have excavated the vaults of the 1st-century AD Roman arena, near the amphitheater. The plans just inside the gate show that the vaults now visible formed only a small corner of a vast space (350 yards long), where 23,000 spectators gathered to watch chariot races. As medieval Tarragona grew, the city gradually swamped the circus. ✉ *Pl. del Rei* 🎫 *€3, €10 combination ticket* ⏲ *June–Sept., Tues.–Sat. 9–9, Sun. 9–3; Oct.–May, Tues.–Sat. 9–5, Sun. 10–3.*

El Serrallo. The always entertaining fishing quarter and harbor are below the city near the bus station and the mouth of the Francolí River. Attending the afternoon fish auction is a golden opportunity to see how choice seafood starts its journey toward your table in Barcelona or Tarragona. For seafood closer to its source, restaurants in the port such as **Estació Marítima** (✉ *Moll de Costa, Tinglado 4* ☎ *977/232100*) and **Manolo** (✉ *Carrer Gravina 61* ☎ *977/223484*) are excellent choices for no-frills fresh fish in a rollicking environment.

Tarragona's cathedral is a mix of Romanesque and Gothic styles.

★ **Museu Nacional Arqueològic de Tarragona.** A 1960s neoclassical building contains this museum housing the most significant collection of Roman artifacts in Catalonia. Among the items are Roman statuary and domestic fittings such as keys, bells, and belt buckles. The beautiful mosaics include a head of Medusa, famous for its piercing stare. Don't miss the video on Tarragona's history. ✉ *Pl. del Rei 5* ☎ *977/236209* 🎫 *€3.50; free Tues.* ⏲ *June–Sept., Tues.–Sat. 10–8, Sun. 10–2; Oct.–May, Tues.–Sat. 10–1:30 and 4–7, Sun. 10–2.*

Necrópolis i Museu Paleocristià. Just uphill from the fish market is the fascinating early Christian necropolis and museum. ✉ *Av. Ramon y Cajal 80* ☎ *977/211175* 🎫 *€3, €10 combination ticket; free Tues.* ⏲ *June–Sept., Tues.–Sat. 10–1 and 4:30–8, Sun. 10–2; Oct.–May, Tues.–Sat. 10–1:30 and 3–5:30, Sun. 10–2.*

Passeig Arqueològic. A 1½-km (1-mi) circular path skirting the surviving section of the 3rd-century BC Ibero-Roman ramparts, this walkway was built on even earlier walls of giant rocks. On the other side of the path is a glacis, a fortification added by English military engineers in 1707 during the War of the Spanish Succession. Look for the rusted bronze of Romulus and Remus. ✉ *Access from Via de l'Imperi Romà.*

Praetorium. This towering building was Augustus's town house, and is reputed to be the birthplace of Pontius Pilate. Its Gothic appearance is the result of extensive alterations in the Middle Ages, when it housed the kings of Catalonia and Aragón during their visits to Tarragona. The Praetorium is now the city's **Museu d'Història** (History Museum), with plans showing the evolution of the city. The museum's highlight is the **Hippolytus Sarcophagus,** which bears a bas-relief depicting the

CLOSE UP

Reus: Birthplace of Modernisme

No city matches Barcelona, of course, for the sheer density of its Modernisme, but it all began here in **Reus** (13 km [8 mi] northwest of Tarragona), where Antoni Gaudí was born and where his contemporary, Lluís Domènech i Montaner—lesser known but in some ways the more important architect—lived and worked for much of his earlier career. The oldest part of the city, defined by a ring of streets called Ravals where the medieval walls once stood, has narrow streets and promenades with many of Reus's smartest shops, boutiques, and coffeehouses. Inside the ring, and along the nearby Carrer de Sant Joan, are some 20 of the stately homes by Domènech, Pere Caselles, and Joan Rubió that make Reus a must for fans of the Moderniste movement.

The **Gaudí Centre**, a small museum that opened in 2007, showcases the life and work of the city's most illustrious son. There are copies of the models Gaudí made for his major works, a replica of his studio, and his original notebook filled with his thoughts on structure and ornamentation, complaints about clients, and calculations of cost-and-return on his projects—with English translations. A pleasant café on the third floor overlooks the main square of the old city and the bell tower of the Church of Sant Pere. The Centre also houses the **Tourist Office**; come early and book a guided tour that includes the museum (11 AM) and two of Domènech's most important buildings: the Casa Navàs (1 PM) and the Institut Pere Mata (4:30 PM)—neither of which you can visit without the tour. The guided visits to Domènech's works are given October–June only, two Saturdays a month, depending on demand, and only in Catalan; July–September the tours are offered daily (except Sunday) and available in English. ✉ *Pl. del Mercadal 3* ☎ *977/010670* 🌐 *www.gaudicentrereus.com* 🎫 *Museum €6; combination ticket for tour and admission to other city museums €14* ⏲ *Oct.–June, Mon.–Sat. 10–2 and 4–8, Sun. 10–2; July–Sept., Mon.–Sat. 10–8, Sun. 10–2.*

Getting Here: An express bus service operates 23 daily buses between Tarragona (main bus station) and Reus (Plaça de les Oques); the trip takes less than 25 minutes (each way). There are four daily buses between Barcelona and Reus and regular train service connects Reus with Tarragona and main Catalonian and Andalusian cities and destinations.

legend of Hippolytus and Fraeda. You can also access the remains of the Circus Maximus from the Praetorium. ✉ *Pl. del Rei* ☎ *977/241952* 🎫 *€3, €10 combination ticket* ⏲ *June–Sept., Tues.–Sat. 9–9, Sun. 9–3; Oct.–May, Tues.–Sat. 9–7, Sun. 10–3.*

WHERE TO EAT AND STAY

$$$–$$$$ CATALAN ★ ✕ **Joan Gatell.** A short 15-minute hop down the coast to Cambrils will give you a memorable chance to try one of the most famous restaurants in southern Catalonia. The Gatell sisters used to run two restaurants side by side; Fanny now carries on the tradition of exquisite local meals by herself in this one, named after their father, Joan. Try the *fideus negres amb sepionets* (noodle paella with baby squid cooked in squid ink) or *lubina al horno con cebolla y patata* (roast sea bass with onion

and potato). Cambrils is 18 km (11 mi) southwest of Tarragona. ✉ *Passeig Miramar 26, Cambrils* ☎ *977/360057* ▭ *AE, DC, MC, V* ⊙ *Closed Mon., Oct., and late Dec.–Jan. No dinner Sun.*

$–$$ MEDITERRANEAN ✕ **Les Coques.** If you have time for only one meal in the city, take it at this elegant little restaurant in the heart of historic Tarragona. The menu is bursting with both mountain and Mediterranean fare. Meat lovers should try the *costelles de xai* (lamb chops in a dark burgundy sauce); seafood fans should ask for *calamarsets amb favetes* (baby calamari sautéed in olive oil and garlic and served with legumes). ✉ *Baixada Nova del Patriarca 2 bis* ☎ *977/228300* ▭ *AE, DC, MC, V* ⊙ *Closed Sun., 10 days in Feb., and mid-July–mid-Aug.*

$–$$ SPANISH ★ ✕ **Les Voltes.** Built into the vaults of the Roman Circus Maximus, this out-of-the-way spot serves a hearty cuisine. You'll find Tarragona specialties, mainly fish dishes, as well as international recipes, with *calçotada* (spring onions) in winter. (If you want to try calçotadas, you must call to order them a day in advance.) ✉ *Carrer Trinquet Vell 12* ☎ *977/230651* ▭ *MC, V* ⊙ *Closed July and Aug. No dinner Sun., no lunch Mon.*

$–$$ **Imperial Tarraco.** Large and white, this half-moon-shape hotel has a superb position overlooking the Mediterranean. The large public rooms have cool marble floors, black-leather furniture, marble-top tables, and Oriental rugs. Guest rooms are plain but comfortable, and each has a private balcony. Insist on a sea view. **Pros:** facing the Mediterrranean, looking over the fishing port and the Roman amphitheater, a privileged spot. **Cons:** occupies a very busy Tarragona intersection with heavy traffic. ✉ *Passeig Palmeres* ☎ *977/233040* ⊕ *www.husa.es* *170 rooms* *In-room: a/c, Wi-Fi. In-hotel: restaurant, bar, tennis court, pool, Internet terminal* ▭ *AE, DC, MC, V.*

¢ **Plaça de la Font.** The central location and the cute rooms at this budget choice just off the Rambla Vella in the leafy Plaça de la Font make for a comfortable home base in downtown Tarragona. A public parking lot under the square is a boon for those with rental cars, and the rooms with balconies afford a sense of being part of the street life. **Pros:** easy on the budget and comfortable, with charming rooms. **Cons:** rooms are on the small side; best rooms over the square with balconies can be noisy on weekends. ✉ *Pl. de la Font 26* ☎ *977/246134* ⊕ *www.hotelpdelafont.com* *20 rooms* *In room: a/c, Wi-Fi. In-hotel: restaurant, bar, pool, Internet terminal* ▭ *AE, DC, MC, V.*

NIGHTLIFE AND THE ARTS

Nightlife in Tarragona takes two forms: older and quieter in the upper city, younger and more raucous down below. There are some lovely rustic bars in the Casc Antic, the upper section of Old Tarragona. Port Esportiu, a pleasure-boat harbor separate from the working port, has another row of dining and dancing establishments; young people flock here on weekends and summer nights. For a dose of culture with your cocktail, try **Antiquari** (✉ *Santa Anna 3* ☎ *977/241843*), a laid-back bar that hosts readings, art exhibits, and occasional screenings of classic or contemporary films. At **Museum** (✉ *Carrer Sant Llorenç s/n* ☎ *977/240612*) you can relax and have a peaceful drink.

The **Teatre Metropol** (✉ *Rambla Nova 46* ☎ *977/244795*) is Tarragona's center for music, dance, theater, and cultural events ranging from *castellers* (human-castle formations), usually performed in August and September, to folk dances.

SHOPPING

Antigüedades Ciria (✉ *Pla de la Seu 2* ☎ *977/248541*), like other shops in front of the cathedral and in the Plaça Pla de la Seu, has an interesting selection of antiques. You have to haggle for bargains, but **Carrer Major** has some exciting antiques stores. They're worth a thorough rummage, as the gems tend to be hidden.

VALENCIA

357 km (214 mi) southwest of Barcelona, 357 km (214 mi) southeast of Madrid.

Valencia is a proud city. It was the last holdout in Spain to stand with the Republican Loyalists against General Franco before the country fell to 40 years of dictatorship. Today it represents the essence of contemporary Spain—daring design and architecture along with experimental cuisine—but remains deeply conservative and proud of its traditions. Despite its proximity to the Mediterranean, Valencia's history and geography have been defined most significantly by the River Turia and the fertile floodplain (*huerta*) that surrounds it.

The city has been fiercely contested ever since it was founded by the Greeks. El Cid captured Valencia from the Moors in 1094 and won his strangest victory here in 1099: he died in the battle, but his corpse was strapped to his saddle and so frightened the waiting Moors that it caused their complete defeat. In 1102, his widow, Jimena, was forced to return the city to Moorish rule; Jaume I finally drove them out in 1238. Modern Valencia was best known for its flooding disasters until the River Turia was diverted to the south in the late 1950s. Since then the city has been on a steady course of urban beautification. The lovely bridges that once spanned the Turia look equally graceful spanning a wandering municipal park, and the spectacularly futuristic Ciutat de les Arts i les Ciències (City of Arts and Sciences), designed by Valencia-born architect Santiago Calatrava, has at last created an exciting architectural link between this river town and the Mediterranean. If you're in Valencia, an excursion to Albufera Nature Park is a worthwhile day trip.

GETTING HERE AND AROUND

Valencia is well connected by bus and train, with regular service to/from cities throughout the country, including 10 daily express trains to Madrid and around the same number to Barcelona. Valencia's bus station is across the river from the old town; take Bus 8 from the Plaza del Ayuntamiento. Frequent buses make the four-hour trip to/from Madrid and the five-hour trip to/from Barcelona.

Once you're here, the city has an efficient network of buses, trams, and metro. For timetables and more information, stop by the local tourist office.

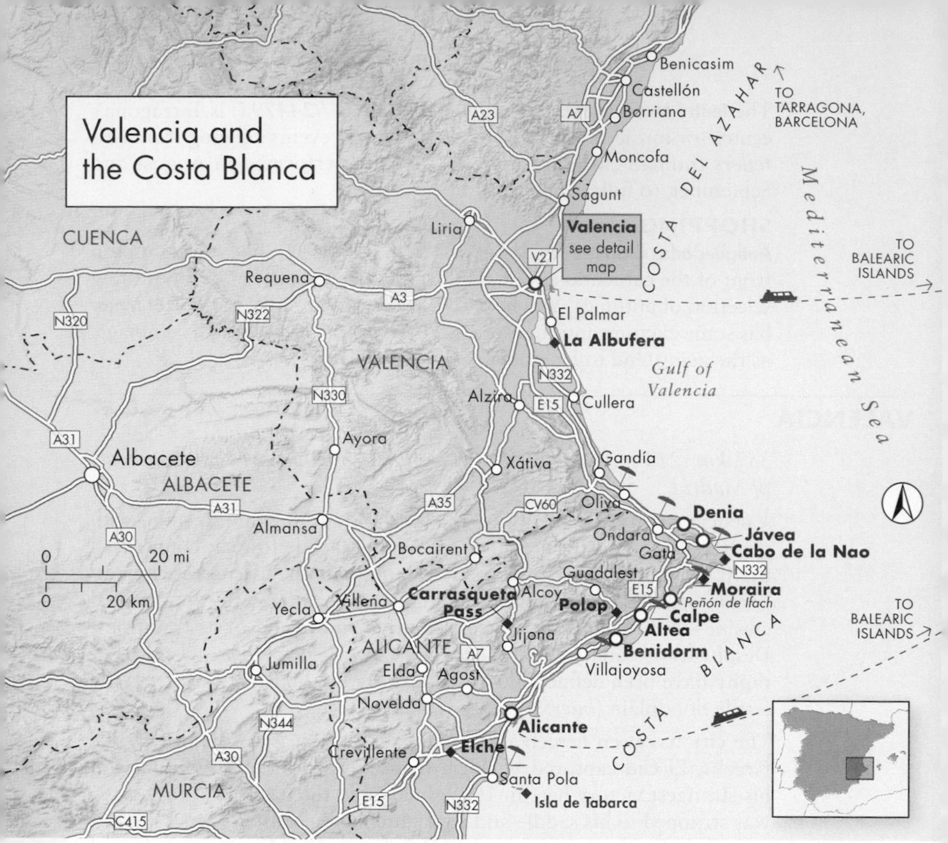

The double-decker Valencia Bus Turístic (daily 10:30–7:30, until 9 in summer; departing every hour) travels through the city passing the main sights: a 24-hour ticket (€14) lets you get on and off at four main boarding points: Plaza de la Reina, Institut Valencià d'Art Modern (IVAM), Museo de Bellas Artes, and Ciutat de les Arts i les Ciències. The same company also offers a two-hour guided trip (€14) to and around Albufera Nature Park, departing from the Plaza de la Reina. In summer (and during the rest of the year, depending on demand) Valencia's regional tourist office also organizes tours of Albufera: you tour the port area before continuing south to the lagoon itself, where you can visit a traditional *barraca* (thatch farmhouse) and end up in the Devesa Gardens (🌐 *www.devesagardens.com*), a nature park around the lake, where you can hire a boat to explore the rice paddies.

ESSENTIALS

Bus Station Valencia (✉ *Av. Menendez Pidal 13* ☎ *963/497222*).

Tour Information Valencia Bus Turístic (☎ *96/341–4400* 🌐 *www.valenciabusturistic.com*).

Train Station Valencia–Estación del Norte (✉ *Pl. de Toros, Valencia* ☎ *902/240202*).

Visitor Information Valencia (✉ *Pl. de la Reina 19* ☎ *963/153931* 🌐 *www.turisvalencia.es*).

EXPLORING

2 **Casa Museo José Benlliure.** The modern Valencian painter-sculptor José Benlliure is known for his portraits and large-scale historical and religious paintings, many of which hang in Valencia's Museo de Bellas Artes (Museum of Fine Arts). Here in his elegant house and studio are 50 of his works, including paintings, ceramics, sculptures, and drawings. On display are also works by his son, Pepino, who painted in the small, flower-filled garden in the back of the house, and iconographic sculptures by Benlliure's brother, the well-known sculptor Mariano Benlliure. To get here, cross the Puente de Serranos, turn right down Calle Blanquerías, and stop at No. 23. ☎ *963/919103* *€2; free weekends and holidays* ⏲ *Tues.–Sat. 10–2 and 4:30–8:30, Sun. 10–3.*

6 **Cathedral.** Valencia's 13th- to 15th-century cathedral is the heart of the city. The building has three portals—Romanesque, Gothic, and rococo. Inside, Renaissance and baroque marble were removed in a successful restoration of the original Gothic style, as is now the trend in Spanish churches. The Capilla del Santo Cáliz (Chapel of the Holy Chalice) displays a purple agate vessel once said to be the Holy Grail (Christ's cup at the Last Supper) and thought to have been brought to Spain in the 4th century. Behind the altar you can see the left arm of **St. Vincent,** who was martyred in Valencia in 304. Stars of the cathedral **museum** are Goya's two famous paintings of St. Francis de Borja, duke of Gandia. To the left of the cathedral entrance is the octagonal tower **El Miguelete,** which you can climb: the roofs of the old town create a kaleidoscope of orange and brown terra-cotta, and the sea appears in the background. It's said that you can see 300 belfries from here, including bright-blue cupolas made of ceramic tiles from nearby Manises. The tower was built in 1381 and the final spire added in 1736. ✉ *Pl. de la Reina* ☎ *963/918127* 🌐 *www.catedraldevalencia.es* *Cathedral and museum €4.50, tower €2* ⏲ *Nov. 1–Mar. 19, Mon.–Sat. 10–5:30; Mar. 20–Oct. 31, Mon.–Sat. 10–6:30, Sun. 2–6:30*

14 **Ciutat de les Arts i les Ciències.** Designed by native son Santiago Calatrava, this sprawling futuristic complex is the home of Valencia's **Museu de les Ciències Príncipe Felipe** (Prince Philip Science Museum), **L'Hemisfèric** (Hemispheric Planetarium), **L'Oceanogràfic** (Oceanographic Park), and **Palau de les Arts** (Palace of the Arts). With resplendent buildings resembling combs and crustaceans, the Ciutat is a favorite of architecture buffs and curious kids. The Science Museum has soaring platforms filled with lasers, holograms, simulators, and hands-on lab experiments. The eye-shaped planetarium projects 3-D virtual voyages on its huge IMAX screen. At the Oceanographic Park you can take a submarine ride through a coastal marine habitat. New additions include an amphitheater, an indoor theater, and a chamber-music hall. ✉ *Av. Autovía del Saler 7* ☎ *902/100031* 🌐 *www.cac.es* *Museu de les Ciències €7.50, L'Hemisfèric €7.50, both €11.20, L'Oceanogràfic €23.90* ⏲ *Museum mid-Sept.–June, Sun.–Fri. 10–8, Sat. 10–9; July–mid-Sept., daily 10–9. L'Oceanogràfic mid-Sept.–June, Sun.–Fri. 10–6, Sat. 10–8; July–mid-*

Fodor's Choice ★

8

CLOSE UP

A Good Walk

A good place to begin your stroll through Valencia's historic center is at the **cathedral** ❻ in the Plaza de la Reina (climb the Miguelete Tower for good city views). Cross the Plaza de la Virgen and before you to the left stands the Gothic **Palau de la Generalitat** ❹. Continuing down Calle Caballeros, you pass Valencia's oldest church, **San Nicolás** ❺. After spending time inside, walk to the Plaza del Mercado and the 15th-century **Lonja de la Seda** ❼. Opposite are the Iglesia de los Santos Juanes, the interior of which was destroyed during the civil war, and the spectacular produce market Mercado Central. Walk down Avenida María Cristina to the **Plaza del Ayuntamiento** ❿, one of the city's liveliest areas. A five-minute walk down Avenida Marqués de Sotelo takes you to the Moderniste **Estación del Norte (North Train Station)** ⓫, next to which is the **Plaza de Toros** ⓬. Head back to the city center via the bustling Plaza del Ayuntamiento and then walk along Calle Poeta Querol to the wedding-cake facade of the **Palacio del Marqués de Dos Aguas** ❾. Cross the Calle Poeta Querol to Plaza Patriarca and enter the **Real Colegio del Patriarca** ❽. Wander old town's streets on your way north toward the Turia River—cross by Puente de la Trinidad to see the **Museo de Bellas Artes** ❸, adjoined by the Jardines del Real (Royal Gardens). Walk up Calle San Pio V to the Puente de Serranos and cross back to the 14th-century twin Torres de Serranos, which once guarded the city's entrance. Turn right for the **Casa Museo José Benlliure** ❷, and continue west another 200 meters to the **Institut València d'Art Modern (IVAM)** ❶. On a separate outing, cross the Turia and stroll south to the **Palau de la Música** ⓭ and **Ciutat de les Arts i les Ciències** ⓮.

TIMING

Allow a day to tour the old quarter, the Museo de Bellas Artes, and the IVAM. Tack on a few hours the next day for the Palau de la Música and Ciutat de les Arts i les Ciències.

Sept. 10–midnight. L'Hemisfèric daily shows generally every hr on hr 11–8; Fri. and Sat., additional show at 9.

⓫ **Estación del Norte.** Designed by Demetrio Ribes Mano in 1917, the train station is a splendid Moderniste structure replete with citrus motifs. ✉ *C. Játiva s/n* ☎ *963/106253.*

❶ **Institut València d'Art Modern (IVAM).** Dedicated to modern and contemporary pieces, the art institute has a permanent collection of 20th-century avant-garde works, European Informalism (including the Spanish artists Antonio Saura, Antoni Tàpies, and Eduardo Chillida), pop art, and photography. The museum is out near the Turia riverbed's elbow. ✉ *Guillem de Castro 118* ☎ *963/863000* 🌐 *www.ivam.es* *€2, free Sun.* ⏲ *July and Aug., Tues.–Sun. 10–10; Sept.–June, Tues.–Sun. 10–8.*

❼ **Lonja de la Seda** *(Silk Exchange).* Downhill from San Nicolás, on the Plaza del Mercado, is the 15th-century Lonja, a product of Valencia's golden age, when the city's prosperity as one of the capitals of the Corona de Aragón made it a leading European commercial and artistic center. The Lonja was constructed as an expression of this splendor.

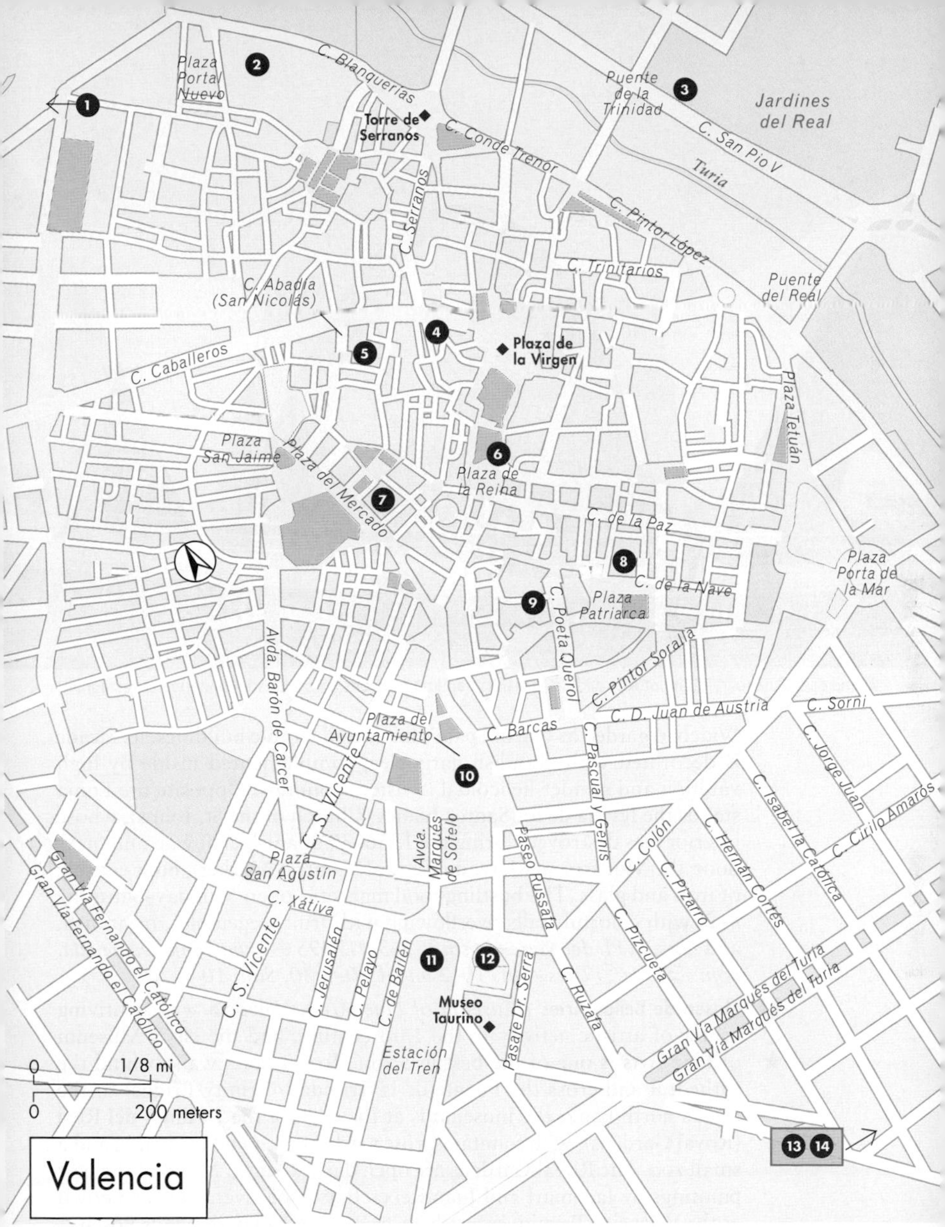

Casa Museo José Benlliure **2**
Cathedral **6**
Ciutat de les Arts i les Ciències **14**
Estación del Tren **11**
Institut Valencià d'Art Modern (IVAM) 1
Lonja de la Seda **7**
Museo de Bellas Artes **3**
Palacio del Marqués de Dos Aguas (Ceramics Museum) **9**
Palau de la Generalitat **4**
Palau de la Música 13
Plaza del Ayuntamiento **10**
Plaza de Toros **12**
Real Colegio del Patriarca **8**
San Nicolás **5**

Valencia's L'Oceanografi (City of Arts and Sciences) has amazing exhibits, as well as an underwater restaurant!

Widely regarded as one of Spain's finest civil Gothic buildings, its facade is decorated with ghoulish gargoyles, complemented inside by high vaulting and slender helicoidal (twisted) columns. Opposite the Lonja stands the **Iglesia de los Santos Juanes** (Church of the St. Johns), whose interior was destroyed during the 1936–39 Spanish civil war, and, next door, the Moderniste **Mercado Central** (Central Market), built entirely of iron and glass. The bustling food market is open Monday–Saturday 8–2, with colorful stalls overflowing with fruit, vegetables, meat, fish, and nuts. ✉ *Pl. del Mercado s/n* ☎ *963/917395* 🌐 *www.lonjadevalencia.com* 🎟 *Free* ⏲ *Tues.–Sat. 10–2 and 4:30–8:30, Sun. 10–3.*

3 ★ **Museo de Bellas Artes** *(Museum of Fine Arts).* Valencia was a thriving center of artistic activity in the 15th century, and the city's Museum of Fine Arts is one of the best in Spain. To get here, walk behind the cathedral and cross the Puente de la Trinidad (Trinity Bridge) to the river's north bank; the museum is at the edge of the **Jardines del Real** (Royal Gardens), with fountains, rose gardens, tree-lined avenues, and a small zoo. The Royal Gardens are open daily 8–dusk. Many of the best paintings by Jacomart and Juan Reixach, two of several artists known as the Valencian Primitives, are here, as is work by Hieronymus Bosch—or El Bosco, as they call him here. The ground floor has the murky, 17th-century Tenebrist masterpieces of Francisco Ribalta and his pupil José Ribera, together with a Diego Velázquez self-portrait and a room devoted to Goya. Upstairs, look for Joaquín Sorolla (Gallery 66), the luminous Valencian painter of everyday Spanish life in the 19th century. ✉ *C. San Pío V 9* ☎ *963/870300* 🌐 *www.museobellasartesvalencia.gva.es* 🎟 *Free* ⏲ *Tues.–Sun. 10–8.*

9 ★ **Palacio del Marqués de Dos Aguas** *(Ceramics Museum).* This building, near the Plaza Patriarca and across Calle Poeta Querol, has a fascinating baroque alabaster facade. Embellished with fruits and vegetables, it centers on the two voluptuous male figures representing the Dos Aguas (Two Waters), in reference to Valencia's two main rivers, the Turia and the Júcar, origin of the noble title of the Marqués de Dos Aguas. The rococo facade was carved in 1740 by Ignacio Vergara. The palace contains the recently reopened **Museo Nacional de Cerámica,** with a magnificent collection of mostly local ceramics. Look for the Valencian kitchen on the second floor. ✉ *C. Poeta Querol 2* ☎ *963/516392* 🎫 *Palace and museum €3, free Sat. afternoon and Sun. morning* ⏲ *Tues.–Sat. 10–2 and 4–8, Sun. 10–2.*

4 **Palau de la Generalitat.** On the left side of the Plaza de la Virgen, fronted by orange trees and box hedges, is the elegant eastern facade of what was once the Gothic home of the Cortes Valencianas (Valencian Parliament), until it was suppressed by Felipe V for supporting the losing side during the 1700–14 War of the Spanish Succession. The two salones (reception rooms) in the older of the two towers have superb woodwork on the ceilings. Don't miss the Salon de los Reyes, a long corridor lined with portraits of Valencia's kings through the ages. Call in advance for permission to enter. ✉ *C. Caballeros 2* ☎ *963/863461* ⏲ *Weekdays 9–2.*

13 **Palau de la Música** *(Music Palace).* On one of the nicest stretches of the Turia riverbed is this huge glass vault, Valencia's main concert venue. Supported by 10 arcaded pillars, the dome gives the illusion of a greenhouse, both from the street and from within its sun-filled, tree-landscaped interior. Home of the Orquesta de Valencia, the main hall also hosts performers on tour from around the world, including chamber and youth orchestras, opera, and an excellent concert series featuring early, baroque, and classical music. For concert schedules, pick up a Turia guide or one of the local newspapers at any newsstand. To see the building without concert tickets, pop into the **art gallery,** which hosts free changing exhibits. ✉ *Paseo de la Alameda 30* ☎ *963/375020* ⏲ *Gallery daily 10:30–1:30 and 5:30–9.*

10 **Plaza del Ayuntamiento.** Down Avenida María Cristina from the market, this plaza is the hub of city life, with the massive baroque facades of the ayuntamiento (city hall) and the central post office facing each other across the park. City Hall itself houses the municipal tourist office and a museum of paleontology. ✉ *Ayuntamiento weekdays 8:30–2:30.*

12 **Plaza de Toros.** Adjacent to the train station is the bullring, one of the oldest in Spain. The best bullfighters are featured during Las Fallas in March, particularly March 18 and 19. Just beyond, down Pasaje Doctor Serra, the **Museo Taurino** (Bullfighting Museum) has bullfighting memorabilia, including bulls' heads and matadors' swords. ✉ *Pasaje Doctor Serra 10* ☎ *963/883738* 🎫 *Free* ⏲ *Bullring and museum Mon. 10–2, Tues.–Sun. 10–8.*

8 **Real Colegio del Patriarca** *(Royal Seminary of the Patriarch).* This seminary, with its church, cloister, and library, is the crown jewel of Valencia's Renaissance architecture and one of the city's finest sites.

Founded by San Juan de Ribera in the 16th century, it has a lovely Renaissance patio and an ornate church, and its museum holds works by Juan de Juanes, Francisco Ribalta, and El Greco. ✉ *C. de la Nave 1* ☎ *963/514176* 🎟 *€1.20* ⏲ *Daily 11–1:30.*

❺ **San Nicolás.** A small plaza contains Valencia's oldest church, once the parish of the Borgia Pope Calixtus III. The first portal you come to, with a tacked-on, rococo bas-relief of the Virgin Mary with cherubs, hints at what's inside: every inch of the originally Gothic church is covered with exuberant early baroque ornamentation. ✉ *C. Caballeros 35* ☎ *963/913317* 🎟 *Free* ⏲ *Open for mass daily 8–9* AM *and 7–8* PM*; Sat. 6:30–8:30* PM*; Sun. various masses 8–1:15.*

WHERE TO EAT

$$$ SPANISH ✕ **Ca'Sento.** Legendary throughout Spain, Ca'Sento has been drawing food lovers on day trips from as far away as Madrid and Barcelona for years. Traditional seafood and rice dishes with contemporary flourishes are Raúl Aleixandre's trademarks in this modern setting backed by generations of family tradition. Be prepared for flan de foie con gelatina de manzana (duck liver flan with apple aspic), cornetes de yuca y txangurro (crab and yuca ice cream cones), gazpacho manchego de lubina (hot sea bass stew), and a complete anthology of original and traditional rice specialties. ✉ *Méndez Núñez 17* ☎ *963/301775* 💳 *AE, DC, MC, V* ⏲ *Closed last 2 wks of Mar., Sun., and Mon.*

$$$ SEAFOOD ✕ **El Timonel.** Decorated like the inside of a yacht, this central restaurant (two blocks east of the bullring) serves outstanding shellfish. The cooking is simple but makes use of the freshest ingredients; try the grilled lenguado (sole) or lubina (sea bass). Also top notch are the eight different kinds of rice dishes, including paella with lobster and arroz a banda, with peeled shrimp, prawns, mussels, and clams. For a sweet finale, try the house special naranjas a la reina, oranges spiced with rum and topped with salsa de fresa (strawberry sauce). Lunch attracts businesspeople, and dinner brings in a crowd of locals and foreigners. ✉ *Félix Pizcueta 13* ☎ *963/526300* 💳 *AE, DC, MC, V* ⏲ *Closed Mon.*

$$$ SPANISH ✕ **La Pepica.** Locals regard this bustling informal restaurant, on the promenade at the El Cabanyal beach, as the best in town for seafood paella. Founded in 1898, the walls of the establishment are covered with signed pictures of appreciative visitors, from Hemingway and Manolete (Valencia is, after all, a bullfight city) to King Juan Carlos and the royal family. Try the *arroz marinero* (seafood paella) topped with shrimp and mussels or hearty platters of *calamares* (squid) and *langostinos* (prawns). Save room for the delectable tarts made with fruit in season. ✉ *Paseo Neptuno 6* ☎ *963/710366* 💳 *AE, DC, MC, V* ⏲ *Closed last 2 wks of Nov. No dinner Mon.–Thurs. Sept.–May.*

$$$ SPANISH ✕ **La Riuà.** A favorite with Valencia's well connected and well-to-do since 1982, this family-run restaurant a few steps from the Plaza de la Reina specializes in seafood dishes like *anguilas* (eels) prepared with *all i pebre* (garlic and pepper), *pulpitos guisados* (stewed baby octopus), and traditional paellas. Lunch begins at 2 and not a moment before. The walls are covered with decorative ceramics and the gastronomic awards the restaurant has won over the years. ✉ *C. del Mar 27* ☎ *963/914571*

Reservations essential ▭ *AE, DC, MC, V* ⊙ *Closed Sun., Easter wk, and Aug. No dinner Mon.*

$ MEDITERRANEAN ✕ **La Sucursal.** La Sucursal is solid proof that Valencia can match the contemporary cuisine of its big brother Barcelona. This thoroughly modern but cozy spot within the IVAM (Institut Valencià d'Art Modern) is simply a taste sensation. You won't leave with a full wallet, but it's unlikely you'll sample venison carpaccio anywhere else or partake of an *arroz caldoso de bogavante* (soupy rice with lobster) any better. The arroz meloso de pulpitos y navajas (creamy rice with baby octopus and razor clams) is yet another creative riff on Valencia's quintessential dish, the paella. Don't hesitate to let the attentive staff make suggestions. ✉ *Guillem de Castro 188* ☎ *963/746665* *Reservations essential* ▭ *AE, DC, MC, V* ⊙ *Closed Sun. No lunch Sat.*

WHERE TO STAY

$$$ ★ **Ad Hoc.** This 19th-century town house, restored in 1994, is on a quiet street at the edge of the old city, a minute's walk from the Plaza Almoina and the Cathedral in one direction, and steps from the Turia gardens in the other. Owner Luis García Alarcón is an antiquarian, and the hotel reflects his eye for classic design and architectural elegance: original decorative brickwork, geometric tile floors, and curved ceiling beams. A buffet breakfast is included. The restaurant ($$$–$$$$) is excellent, too; try the unusual paella with quail and seasonal mushrooms, or the suckling lamb, and top it off with a divine passion-fruit sorbet. **Pros:** ideal location—close to sights but quiet; a courteous, helpful staff; great value. **Cons:** navigating by car and parking can be a nightmare. ✉ *Boix 4* ☎ *963/919140* ⊕ *www.adhochoteles.com* *28 rooms* *In-room: safe, Internet, Wi-Fi. In-hotel: restaurant, room service, laundry service, Internet terminal, Wi-Fi, no-smoking rooms, some pets allowed* ▭ *AE, DC, MC, V.*

$ **Catalonia Excelsior.** For its price category, this hotel in a 1930s building offers the best value. From the Art Deco restaurant-cum-bar, a spiral marble staircase leads to a dark wood-panel salon with a terrace. Rooms have parquet wood floors, modern furnishings, and soothing pastel-colored walls. The general vibe is very friendly, and the hotel is central, just steps from the Plaza del Ayuntamiento. **Pros:** good location, good value. **Cons:** nothing special but fine for a short stay. ✉ *Barcelonina 5* ☎ *963/514612* ⊕ *www.hoteles-catalonia.es* *81 rooms* *In-room: safe, Internet, Wi-Fi. In-hotel: restaurant, bar, Wi-Fi hotspot* ▭ *AE, DC, MC, V.*

$$$ **Neptuno.** This beachfront hotel is a slick modern newcomer to the city's accommodation options. Giant colorful abstracts decorate the public spaces, and the rooms are stylish and minimalist with excellent facilities, including hydromassage tubs, that appeal to business travelers and families. A spacious sun terrace overlooks the tempting swath of beach, while the gourmet restaurant has fast made its mark on the local culinary scene. **Pros:** superb restaurant; great location for families. **Cons:** a 15-minute walk to the historic center; gets booked up early in the summer. ✉ *Paseo de Neptuno 2* ☎ *963/567777* ⊕ *www.hotelneptunovalencia.com* *48 rooms* *In-room: Wi-Fi. In-hotel: restaurant, pool, gym, spa, Wi-Fi hotspot* ▭ *AE, MC, V* *EP.*

8

$$$ **Palau de la Mar**. In a restored 19th-century palace, this self-proclaimed boutique hotel looks out at the Porta de La Mar, which marked the entry to the old walled quarter of Valencia. White marble and frosted glass provide a sense of light and quiet elegance, and the spa is truly luxurious. Ask for a room facing the interior courtyard. The Senzone ($$$$) restaurant serves creative Mediterranean cuisine starring original and suprising rice dishes such as the mar y montaña (surf 'n turf) combining octopus and bacon. **Pros:** big bathrooms with double sinks; great location. **Cons:** rooms on the top floor have low, slanted ceilings. ✉ *Av. Navarro Reverter r 14* ☎ *963/162884* 🌐 *www.hospes.es* *65 rooms* *In-room: safe, DVD (some), Internet, Wi-Fi. In-hotel: restaurant, room service, pool, gym, spa, laundry service, Internet terminal, Wi-Fi hotspot, parking (paid), some pets allowed* 💳 *AE, DC, MC, V.*

$ ★ **Reina Victoria**. Valencia's grande dame is an excellent choice if you want traditional charm and a good location next to the Plaza del Ayuntamiento. The spacious reception rooms have cool marble floors (with rugs to take the chill off), as does the smart, classy restaurant. The smallish guest rooms are clothed in green or burgundy chintz and deep-pile carpets. A buffet breakfast is included in the rate. **Pros:** ideal location; walking distance to both central railway station and major sights of the old city. **Cons:** room soundproofing not up to par; service can be perfunctory. ✉ *Barcas 4* ☎ *963/520487* 🌐 *www.husa.es* *95 rooms* *In-room: safe, refrigerator, Wi-Fi. In-hotel: restaurant, room service, bar, laundry service, Wi-Fi hotspot,* 💳 *AE, DC, MC, V.*

$ **Sidi Saler**. The stretch of coastline just south of Valencia suffers from ongoing construction, but this hotel, surrounded by the El Saler Nature Park, is an oasis of luxury. All the brightly furnished guest rooms have balconies with views of the sea or gardens, and breakfast is included in the price—fill up on a buffet of *revueltos* (scrambled eggs), breads, and fresh fruit. **Pros:** family-friendly; free shuttle bus to/from Valencia; good golfing nearby. **Cons:** rooms a bit overfurnished. ✉ *Gola del Puchol s/n, Playa El Saler* ☎ *961/610411* 🌐 *www.hotelessidi.es* *276 rooms* *In-room: safe, Internet, Wi-Fi. In-hotel: restaurant, room service, bars, tennis court, pools, gym, spa, beachfront, bicycles, laundry service, Internet terminal, Wi-Fi hotspot, parking (free), some pets allowed (fee)* 💳 *AE, DC, MC, V* *BP.*

NIGHTLIFE AND THE ARTS

Sleep is usually anathema here, and you can experience Valencia's nocturnal way of life at any time except summer, when locals disappear on vacation and the international set moves to the beach. Nightlife in the old town centers around Barrio del Carmen, a lively web of streets that unfolds north of Plaza del Mercado. A string of very popular bars and pubs dots Calle Caballeros, leading off Plaza de la Virgen; the Plaza del Tossal also has some popular cafés, as does Calle Alta, off Plaza San Jaime. Some of the funkier, newer places are to be found in and around Plaza del Carmen. Across the river in the new town, look for appealing hangouts along Avenida Blasco Ibáñez and on Plaza de Cánovas del Castillo. Out by the sea, Paseo Neptuno and Calle de Eugenia Viñes are lined with loud clubs and bars most active during the summer. The nightlife and culture review *Turia* is on sale at newsstands, while Hello

DID YOU KNOW?

Valencia's Las Fallas festival in March is a fabulous 19-day celebration. *Fallas* means "bonfires," and a highlight of the party is when effigies of political figures are torched to end the festival.

Valencia, Agenda Urbana, Valencia City, and La Guía Go are available free at tourist offices.

Fodor's Choice ★ If you want nonstop nightlife at its frenzied best, come during the climactic days of **Las Fallas** (🌐 *www.fallas.com*) from March 15 to 19, when revelers throng the streets and last call at many of the bars and clubs isn't until the wee hours, if at all. The **Feria de Julio** (🌐 *www.feriadejulio.com*) is July's monthlong festival of theater, film, dance, and music.

BENICÀSSIM MUSIC FESTIVAL

The coastal town of Benicàssim is backed by the dramatic mountains, and the Mediterranean laps long, sandy swimming beaches. Since the mid-1990s, it's made a name for itself on the indie-music circuit, and thousands descend for the annual **Festival Internacional de Benicàssim** (🌐 *www.fiberfib.com*) in August. Past headlining artists include Nick Cave and Björk.

If you're thinking of overnighting, the 58-room Voramar (*www.voramar.net*), on the beach at the north end of town, is quite pleasant, and the lovely glassed-in restaurant is worth a trip in itself.

The airy, perennially popular, bar–club–performance space **Radio City** (✉ *Santa Teresa 19* ☎ *963/914151*) offers an eclectic nightly showcase from flamenco (on Tuesday at 11 PM) and Afro-jazz fusion to theater. For quiet after-dinner drinks, try the jazzy, lighthearted bar **Café de la Seu** (✉ *Santo Cáliz 7* ☎ *963/915715*), with contemporary art and animal-print chairs. For a taste of *el ambiente andaluz* (Andalusian atmosphere) tuck into tapas and cocktails at **El Albero** (✉ *Ciscar 12* ☎ *963/356273*), which has Andalusian singing at 11 PM Thursday through Saturday. Locals out for a cocktail before hitting the clubs start their evening at **Xuquer Palace** (✉ *Pl. Xuquer 8* ☎ *963/615811*), with Barcelona-style Moderniste furnishings. **Casablanca** (✉ *Eugenia Viñes 152* ☎ *963/713366*) has an elegant postwar look; it's open Thursday through Sunday and has everything from waltz to swing music.**Las Ánimas** (✉ *Pizarro 31* ☎ *963/528842*) is the center city location for the Las Ánimas discos scattered around Valencia, such as **Las Ánimas Puerto** (✉ *Pl. de Las Arenas, Paseo Neptuno, Ediciio Docks s/n* ☎ *963/521342*).**30 y Tantos** (✉ *Eduardo Bosca 29* ☎ *963/521342*) is for over-thirties with music from yesterday and today. Valencia has a lively gay nightlife, with a string of bars and clubs on Calle Quart and around the Plaza del Mercado. Follow the trendsters to the hopping **Venial** (✉ *Quart 26* ☎ *963/917356*), where you can enjoy a tipple or two, groove on the packed dance floor, or just take in the sequined and/or muscled performers strutting their stuff on stage.

SHOPPING

A flea market is held every Sunday morning by the cathedral. Another crafts and flea market takes place on Sunday morning in Plaza Luis Casanova, near Mestalla, Valencia's soccer stadium. If it's great local designer wear you're after, then head straight to the Barrio Carmen.

ALBUFERA NATURE PARK

11 km (7 mi) south of Valencia.

This beautiful freshwater lagoon was named by Moorish poets—*albufera* means "the sun's mirror." Dappled with rice paddies, the Parque Natural de la Albufera is a nesting site for more than 250 bird species, including herons, terns, egrets, ducks, and gulls. Admission is free, and there are miles of lovely walking and cycling trails. Bird-watching companies offer boat rides all along the Albufera.

✉ *Centre d'Informació Raco del'Olla, El Palmar* ☎ *96/162–7345* 🌐 *www.albufera.com* ⏲ *Mon., Wed., and Fri. 9–2, Tues., Thurs., and weekends 9–2 and 3:30–5:30.*

From Valencia, buses depart from the corner of Sueca and Gran Vía de Germanías on the hour (every half hour in summer) daily 7 AM to 9 PM. ☎ *961/627345.*

El Palmar, the major village in the area, has numerous restaurants specializing in paella Valenciana: the most traditional kind is made with rabbit or game birds, though seafood is also popular in this region because it's so fresh.

WHERE TO EAT

$$$ SPANISH ★ ✕ **La Matandeta.** With its white garden walls and rustic interior, this restaurant is a culinary island in the rice paddies for Valencian families who come to the Albufera on Sunday, when many of the city's restaurants are closed. Host-owners Maria Dolores Baixauli and Rafael Gálvez preside over evening meals on the terrace, even as the next generation (Rubén Ruiz Vilanova in the kitchen and Helena Gálvez Baixauli as maitre d') begins to contribute new energy. Fish fresh off the boats are grilled over an open fire, and the traditional main dish is the *paella de pato, pollo, y conejo* (rice with duck, chicken, and rabbit). Choose from 50 types of olive oil on the sideboard for your bread or salad. ✉ *Ctra. CV-1045 (Alfafar/El Saler), Km 4* ☎ *962/112184* 🌐 *www.lamatandeta.com* 💳 *MC, V* ⏲ *Closed Mon.*

THE COSTA BLANCA

The stretch of coastline known as the Costa Blanca (White Coast) begins south of Valencia, near Murcia, and stretches down to Dénia. It's best known for its magic vacation combo of sand, sea, and sun, and there are some excellent, albeit crowded, beaches here, as well as more secluded coves and stretches of sand. Alicante is the largest city and still largely overlooked by visitors, who typically head for the better-known coastal resorts such as Benidorm.

DÉNIA

Fodor's Choice ★ *100 km (62 mi) south of Valencia, 8 km (5 mi) north of Jávea and east of Ondara.*

Widely known as the gastronomic capital of the Costa Blanca, Dénia is a good place to sample Mediterranean seafood—try *picaetes* (tapas in

8

the Valencian dialect) like *sépia y calamar* (squid and cuttlefish), *suquet de rape* (stewed monkfish), or *gambas rojas de Dénia*—a special breed of shrimp found in the waters around Dénia that are served simply boiled or grilled and are nearly as coveted as truffles.

The northernmost beach resort on the Costa Blanca, Dénia is also a busy tourist town known for its fishing boats and fiestas, which culminate in the midsummer Hogueras de San Juan (June 23, St. John's Day eve bonfires). Backed by the Montgó massif, rising to more than 2,100 feet to the west, Dénia's beaches to the north—Les Marines, Les Bovetes, and Les Deveses—are smooth and sandy, whereas the coast to the south is rocky, forming *calas* (tiny secluded inlets that recall the Costa Brava, north of Barcelona).

ESSENTIALS

Visitor Information Dénia (✉ *Pl. Oculista Buigues 9* ☎ *96/642–2367* 🌐 *www.denia.net*).

EXPLORING

Dénia's most interesting architectural attraction is the **Palau del Governador**, the Governor's Palace, within a Moorish-era castle. Overlooking the town, the castle has an interesting archaeological museum as well as a Renaissance bastion and a Moorish portal with a lovely horseshoe arch. ✉ *C. San Francisco s/n* ☎ *96/642–0656* 🎫 *€3* ⏲ *Daily 10–1:30; also Jan.–Mar., Nov., and Dec. 3–6; Apr. and May 4:30–7; June 4–7:30; July and Aug. 5–8:30; Sept. 4–8, and Oct. 3–6:30.*

★ Inland from Dénia, the **Cueva de las Calaveras** (*Cave of the Skulls* ✉ *Ctra. Benidoleig-Pedreguera, Km 1.5, Benidoleig* ☎ *96/640–4235* 🌐 *www.cuevasturisticas.com* 🎫 *€3.50* ⏲ *June–Sept., daily 10–8:30; Oct.–May, daily 10–6*), named for the 12 Moorish skulls found there when the cave was discovered in 1768, was inhabited by Paleolithic humans some 50,000 years ago. More than 400 yards long, the cave of stalactites and stalagmites has a dome rising to more than 60 feet and leads to an underground lake.

WHERE TO EAT AND STAY

$ SEAFOOD ✕ **El Poblet.** Quique Dacosta's exquisite cooking has been making headlines up and down the Costa Blanca and beyond for more than a decade. Patrons get to choose among contemporary rustic dining rooms with views into the kitchen, alfresco tables on the terrace, and the glassed-in pavilion. The cuisine is based on first-rate local produce from the sea and the garden, with an emphasis on avant-garde techniques. Dacosta's repertoire is in constant flux, so the tasting menu is the surest way to experience his latest burst of creativity. The eatery is off Careterra Las Marinas, 3 km northwest of downtown Dénia. ✉ *Calle Rascassa 1* ☎ *96/578–4179* 🌐 *www.elpoblet.com* 💳 *MC, V* ⏲ *Closed Mon. No dinner Sun.*

$$$ SEAFOOD ✕ **El Port.** In the old fishermen's quarter just across from the port, this classic dining spot features all kinds of fish fresh off the boats. There are also shellfish dishes and a full range of rice specialties, from *arros negre* (black rice) to a classic *paella marinera* (seafood and rice). In addition, the tapas here are ample and excellent, while a creditable selection of mouthwatering desserts awaits anyone still hungry enough to consider

trying them. ✉ *Esplanada Bellavista 12* ☎ *96/578–4973* ▭ *AE, MC, V* ⊙ *Closed Mon.*

$$$ SEAFOOD ✕ **El Raset.** Across the harbor, this Valencian favorite has been serving traditional cuisine with a modern twist for 25 years. From a terrace with views of the harbor you can choose from an array of excellent seafood dishes. House specialties include *arroz en caldero* (rice with monkfish, lobster, or prawns) and *gambas rojas* (local red prawns). A la carte dining can be expensive, but set menus are easier on your wallet. The same owners run a very comfortable and modern hotel three houses down on the same street. ✉ *Calle Bellavista 7* ☎ *96/578–5040* 🌐 *www.grupoelraset.com* ▭ *AE, MC, V* ⊙ *Closed Tues. Oct.–May.*

$$$ SEAFOOD ✕ **La Seu.** Under Enrique Martínez, who has studied with some of the country's best chefs, this distinguished restaurant in the center of town continues to reinvent and deconstruct traditional Valencian cuisine. The focus may be on tapas, but what makes La Seu worth a visit is its constantly changing rice dishes made with cod, crayfish, or octopus. You can choose between a bustling, modern tapas area and tables in a warmly lit stone cave. The tasting menu includes tapas and one rice dish, giving you a good impression of the chef's repertoire at an unbeatable price. ✉ *C. Loreto 59* ☎ *96/642–4478* 🌐 *www.laseu.es* ▭ *AE, MC, V* ⊙ *Closed Mon. No dinner Sun.*

$ **Dénia Marriott La Sella Golf Resort and Spa.** This large hotel, about 15 minutes west of Dénia and 1½ km (1 mi) past the small town of La Xara, is ideal if you want to combine sporting facilities and a fine spa with sightseeing and the beaches of the coast. Rooms are larger than what you usually find in the area, and the hotel is child-friendly, with on-site babysitting and a seasonal Kids' Club. **Pros:** many amenities and activities; good for families. **Cons:** large hotel; chain atmosphere. ✉ *Alqueria Ferrando s/n, Jesus Pobre* ☎ *96/645–4054* 🌐 *www.marriott.com* *178 rooms, 8 suites* *In-room: Internet. In-hotel: 2 restaurants, bar, golf course, tennis court, pool, gym, children's programs (ages 4–12), laundry facilities, laundry service, Wi-Fi hotspot, parking (free)* ▭ *AE, DC, MC, V.*

$ **Hotel Chamarel.** Named after a region in Mauritania where seven different cultures are found, this hotel aims to show that different styles can coexist in harmony. Art Deco furniture, bold mix-and-match color schemes, high-tech facilities, and a tranquil patio surrounded by lush greenery all work in harmony to create an oasis. There are two standards of rooms, and the superior ones have four-poster beds, beamed ceilings, spacious bathrooms, and original tiles. A suite in back is perfect for a family. The staff arranges museum visits and water activities at the port. **Pros:** friendly staff; individual attention. **Cons:** no pool; not on the beach. ✉ *Calle Cavallers 13* ☎ *96/643–5007* 🌐 *www.hotelchamarel.com* *13 rooms, 5 suites* *In-room: Wi-Fi. In-hotel: bar, parking (paid), some pets allowed* ▭ *AE, DC, MC, V.*

$ **La Posada del Mar.** Directly under Dénia castle, and a few steps across from the harbor, this hotel is in the 13th-century customs post and has been renovated with a subtle nautical theme, most evident in the portal windows and sailor's-knot ironwork along the staircase. The original Tuscan stone arch has been preserved in the lobby, along with antique vases, giving an ancient but clean Mediterranean feel. Most rooms have generous balconies, and all have views of the harbor and sea. La Posada's rooftop terrace is particularly inviting. **Pros:** serene environment; across from harbor; close to center of town. **Cons:** no pool. ☒ *Pl. de les Drassanes 2* ☎ *96/643–2966* 🌐 *www.laposadadelmar.com* ⇨ *16 rooms, 9 suites* ♁ *In-room: safe, Internet. In-hotel: bar, gym, laundry facilities, Internet terminal, Wi-Fi hotspot, parking (free)* ▭ *AE, DC, MC, V.*

EN ROUTE The Playa del Arenal, a tiny bay cut into the larger one, is worth a visit in the summer. You can reach it via the coastal road, CV736, between Dénia and Jávea.

JÁVEA (XÀBIA)

108 km (67 mi) southeast of Valencia, 92 km (57 mi) northeast of Alicante, 8 km (5 mi) south of Dénia.

On more than 25 km of coast, Jávea is a labyrinth of tiny streets and houses with arched portals and Gothic windows, with an antique aspect contrasted only (and ironically) by its modern church, **Santa María de Loreto.** The church-fortress of **San Bartolomé** is the town's architectural gem with gothic vaulted ceilings inside. Restaurants around the port's **Aduanas del Mar** area serve an excellent variety of versions of the local classic, *arroz a la marinera* (seafood paella).

ESSENTIALS

Visitor Information Jávea (☒ *Pl. Almirante Bastarreche 11* ☎ *96/579–0736* 🌐 *www.xabia.org*).

EXPLORING

The newly renovated **Soler Blasco**, an ethnological and archaeological museum, has a superb set of Iberian gold jewelry discovered in 1904 during building excavation works. ☒ *Pl. dels Germans Segarra 1* ☎ *96/579–1098* ▭ *Free* ⊙ *Mar.–Oct., Tues.–Fri. 10–1 and 6–8, weekends 10–1; Nov.–Feb., Tues.–Sun. 10–1.*

Following the bay south from the town, the beach transforms itself into strange, small rock formations with numerous rock pools. After a mile or so, you reach the small, sandy bay-within-a-bay, the **Playa del Arenal.** This is a nice little resort in its own right, with numerous bars, restaurants, lounges, and shops around the beach.

About 10 km (6 mi) southeast of Jávea, **Cabo de la Nao** (Cape Nao) is a great spur of land jutting into the Mediterranean. As you round the point, you turn from a coast that looks toward Italy to one that faces Africa. The main strip of beach is white pebbles and quite lively. Make your way to Cala de la Granadella beach if you're looking to get away from the mass tourism resort world.

WHERE TO EAT AND STAY

$$$ SPANISH ✕ **Bar El Clavo.** Traditional tapas in this no-frills bar in the port, across the street from the beach, attract a savvy local crowd. The *patatas bravas* (potatoes with hot sauce) are legendary and ideally accompanied by a cold *caña* (draft beer). Try the artichokes and fried fish or the *pulpo gallego* (slices of octopus served with paprika on potato wafers). Reserve in

Dénia's massive fort overlooks the harbor and provides a dramatic element to the skyline, with the Montgó mountains in the background.

advance if you want to ensure a table or take your chances on bar space. ✉ *Almirante Bastarreche 15* ☎ *96/579–1014* ▭ *AE, MC, V.*

$$$ ★ ✕ **La Cocina.** Run by an English couple, La Cocina is a favorite with locals and foreigners alike. Hidden away in a quiet part of the port, this small but comfortable restaurant offers a fresh and modern alternative to most in the area, with a focus on top-notch ingredients and personal service. Favorite dishes include the homemade foie gras and the sirloin steak. The set menus offer an astonishing value for the price, and there are more than 20 wines available by the glass. ✉ *Av. Lepanto 2* ☎ *96/579–5140* ▭ *AE, DC, MC, V.*

$–$$ **El Rodat.** This chic hotel is a comfortable option with lots of extras, including an extensive health and beauty center. The terraced, red stucco buildings have plush, if conservative interiors, with a gold, gray, and cream color scheme. The grounds are home to lofty palms, pine trees, and brilliantly colored mimosa and bougainvillea. Of the two restaurants, El Rodat has more adventurous food than Rodat Terraza. For more privacy, consider renting your own villa with private garden. **Pros:** community feel; many amenities. **Cons:** removed from town and beaches. ✉ *Calle de la Murciana 9, Ctra. al Cabo de la Nao s/n* ☎ *96/647–0710* ⊕ *www.elrodat.com* *34 suites, 8 rooms, 12 villas* *In-room: Wi-Fi. In-hotel: 2 restaurants, bar, tennis court, pool, spa, Internet terminal, parking (free)* ▭ *AE, DC, MC, V.*

$ **Hotel Miramar.** This unpretentious hotel may lack luxuries, but it more than makes up for it with its cheerful service, impeccable rooms, and a location right on the bay-front promenade in the center of town. Rooms with sea views—albeit out of diminutive windows—cost slightly more than interior rooms. **Pros:** fabulous location; good value; friendly staff.

Cons: not much in the way of decor; a bit musty; no pool or terraces. ✉ *Pl. Almirante Bastareche 12* ☎ *96/579–0100* *26 rooms* *In-hotel: restaurant, bar* *MC, V.*

$ **Parador de Jávea.** Ensconced in a lush palm grove with terrific views of the bay, this four-story parador is far more tasteful than many of the high-rise hotels elsewhere on the Costa Blanca. The oak-trim, ceramic-tile guest rooms are airy and pleasant, with wicker furniture. The restaurant is known for its carefully prepared local specialties, most of them from the Mediterranean. **Pros:** beautiful views; cozy room; many activities. **Cons:** modern building lacks charm. ✉ *Av. del Mediterráneo 7* ☎ *96/579–0200* 🌐 *www.parador.es* *70 rooms* *In-room: a/c, Wi-Fi. In-hotel: restaurant, bar, pool, gym* *AE, DC, MC, V.*

CALPE (CALP)

★ *15 km (9 mi) southwest of Jávea, 8 km (5 mi) north of Altea.*

The road from Cabo de la Nao to Calpe is very scenic, winding through the cliffs and hills covered in villas and passing small, rocky, and pebbly bays. Calpe has an ancient history, and its strategic location has attracted Phoenicians, Greeks, Romans, and Moors dedicated to trading, agriculture, and fishing. After the Reconquest by Jaume I in 1240, Christians and Moors lived together peacefully, but between the 14th and 17th centuries they were under almost constant threat from the Barbary Pirates. This led to the construction of numerous fortifications such as the Torreó de la Peça (Tower of the Piece), a defense tower named after an artillery piece used to defend the city. (Two of these cannons can be seen next to the Torreó.) Today the Old Town, full of striking small streets and squares, is a delightful place to wander.

ESSENTIALS

Visitor Information Calpe (✉ *Av. Ejércitos Españoles 30* ☎ *96/583–6920* 🌐 *www.calpe.es*).

EXPLORING

Calpe has always been dominated by the **Peñón d'Ifach**, a huge calcareous rock more than 1,100 yards long, 1,090 feet high, and joined to the mainland by a narrow isthmus. The area is rich in flora and fauna, with more than 300 species of plant life and 80 species of land and marine birds. A visit to the top is not for the fainthearted; wear shoes with traction for the hike, which includes a trip through a tunnel to the summit. The views are spectacular, reaching to the island of Ibiza on a clear day.

★ The fishing industry is still very important in Calpe, and every evening the fishing boats return to port with their catch. The subsequent auction at the **Fish Market** can be watched from the walkway of La Lonja de Calpe. ✉ *Port* ⏲ *Weekdays 4:30–8.*

The **Mundo Marino** company offers a complete range of sailing trips, including cruises between the towns up and down the coast. Some of the vessels have glass bottoms, so you can keep an eye on the abundant marine life. ✉ *Port* 🌐 *www.mundomarino.es.*

WHERE TO EAT AND STAY

$$$ SEAFOOD ✕ **Playa**. Quite simply, this ample and bustling eatery is a seafood and shellfish lovers' paradise, offering a wide selection of fish, rice, and marine dishes at competitive prices. Just opposite the fishing port, the terrace and rambling series of dining rooms can provide everything from a few oysters for a handful of euros up to family-style combination plates for as much as a €100 a throw. The "menu" consists of tables covered with examples of each dish currently available, so diners know exactly what they're getting. ✉ *Explanada del Puerto* ☎ *96/583–0032* ▭ *MC, V.*

CASTLES GALORE

There are close to 100 castles in the Costa Blanca region; most originate from the days of the Moors and were built between the 8th and 13th centuries as a defense against such predictable threats as pirates and other outside invaders. They also protected the city against tax collectors.

$ **Pensión el Hidalgo**. This pleasant family-run *pensión* near the beach has small but cozy rooms that are decorated with a friendly, easygoing feel. Several have private balconies overlooking the Mediterranean. A major perk is the intimate breakfast terrace with a sea view for which you would normally have to pay a premium. **Pros:** beachfront location; reasonable prices. **Cons:** simple decor; you must book far ahead in summer, especially in August. ✉ *Av. Rosa de los Vientos 19, Edificio Santa Marta* ☎ *96/583–9317* 🌐 *www.pensionelhidalgo.com* *9 rooms* *In-hotel: bar* ▭ *MC, V* *BP.*

ALTEA

8

10 km (6 mi) south of Calpe, 11 km (7 mi) north of Benidorm.

Altea is an old fishing village with white houses and a striking church with a blue ceramic-tile dome. One of the best-preserved towns on the Costa Blanca, it serves as a foil to the skyscrapers of Benidorm. The beach is pebbly. North of town, the Altea Hills area is more built up, with pretty villas lining the hills and cliffs.

ESSENTIALS

Visitor Information Altea (✉ *San Pedro 9* ☎ *96/584–4114* 🌐 *www.altea.es*).

WHERE TO EAT AND STAY

$$$ FRENCH ✕ **La Costera**. This popular restaurant and bistro has been taken over by the original owner's daughter and her husband, who scrapped the music shows, removed half the tables, and restored the place to its goat corral origins, although with a feng shui touch. The focus is now on fine French dining, with such specialties as house-made foie gras, roasted *lubina* (sea bass), and *suquet de cola de rape* (stewed monkfish). There's also a variety of game in season, including venison and partridge. Book a table on the small and leafy terrace for a particularly romantic dinner. ✉ *Costera del Mestre la Música 8* ☎ *96/584–0230* 🌐 *www.lacosteradealtea.com* ▭ *MC, V* *Closed Mon.; Sept.-May no lunch Tues.–Fri.; June-Aug. Closed Mon., no lunch.*

$$$ SWISS ✕ **Oustau de Altea**. In one of the prettiest corners of the old part of Altea, this sleek and rustic 200-year-old space, formerly a cloister and

DID YOU KNOW?

The lovely town of Altea (from the Moorish name Althaya, which means "health to all") has a popular seafront promenade; the church is easily recognized by its blue-tile domes.

a school, combines contemporary design details gracefully juxtaposed over a rustic background. Named for the Provençal word for inn or hostelry, Oustau serves polished international cuisine with a French flair, inside and on a terrace. Dishes are named for classic films, such as Love Story (beef and strawberry coulis). Contemporary artists display work here, so the art changes regularly. ✉ *Mayor 5* ☎ *96/584–2078* 🌐 *www.oustau.com* ☞ *Reservations essential* ▭ *MC, V* ⏲ *Closed Feb. and Mon. Oct–June. No lunch.*

$ **Hostal Fornet** Rooms at this pleasant hotel at the highest point of Altea's historic center are modest but squeaky clean, with white walls and pine furnishings. The friendly owners are multilingual, but the real pièce de résistance is the roof terrace with its stunning view of the church's distinctive blue-tiled cupola and surrounding tangle of streets with a Mediterranean backdrop. **Pros:** the views, the staff, and the location; top value. **Cons:** no pool or beach; small rooms; not easy to reach by car. ✉ *C. Beniardá 1* ☎ *96/584–3005* 🌐 *www.albir21-hostalfornet.com* *35 rooms* *In-hotel: restaurant, bar* ▭ *MC, V* ⏲ *Closed Jan.*

BENIDORM

11 km (7 mi) south of Altea, 42 km (26 mi) northeast of Alicante.

Spain's first resort town, Benidorm is an overdeveloped vacationland with a seemingly bottomless capacity for tourists. Hundreds of thousands flock to the twin, white crescent-shape beaches annually. The resulting glut of karaoke clubs and British-run pubs offering all-day breakfasts and satellite soccer games give Benidorm a decidedly un-Spanish feel. Those with children may appreciate the nearby famous Terra Mítica theme park, the animal and water parks, and the available boat trips. For a fantastic view, follow signs to Club Sierra Dorada at the eastern edge of town and climb up to the **Rincón de Loix** (Loix Corner).

8

ESSENTIALS

Visitor Information Benidorm (✉ *Av. Martínez Alejos 16* ☎ *96/585–1311* 🌐 *www.benidorm.org*).

EXPLORING

★ **Excursiones Marítimas Benidorm.** Of the many boat trips offered by this company, the excursion to the Isla de Benidorm, where you can swim and look at the local birdlife, is one of the best. Boats depart every hour, 10–5; the fare is €12.50 for adults. If you want to see more of the beautiful coastline, opt for the one-hour cruise up to Calpe for €20 after which you can do some sightseeing before returning; these trips depart Monday–Saturday at 11:30, with a return sail to Calpe at 5. ☎ *96/585–0052* 🌐 *www.excursionesmaritimasbenidorm.com.*

★ **Terra Mítica.** Owned by Paramount, this is one of Europe's largest theme parks. In addition to many rides, there are shows that include pirate battles, chariot races, and fighting gladiators. ✉ *Just outside Benidorm, Carretera de Benidorm a Finestrat, da de Moralet s/n* ☎ *902/020220* 🌐 *www.terramiticapark.com* *€35* ⏲ *Daily 11–8, some nights/weekends longer hours (call to confirm).*

WHERE TO EAT AND STAY

$$$ ✕ **Casa Toni**. This down-to-earth restaurant offers a welcome escape from the mayhem along the beaches. It's a simple establishment reminiscent of an Andalusian *mesón*, where high-quality products are valued over elaborate dishes. The *ventresca de atún* (marinated tuna belly), the grilled kid ribs, or the Valencian rice dishes will not disappoint you. The bar is a good spot for a quick tapas break. ✉ *Av. De Cuenca s/n* ☎ *96/680–1232* ▭ *AE, DC, MC, V* ⊙ *Closed Mon. No dinner Sun.*

$$$ **Hotel Colón**. Positioned on the front line of the Platja de Ponent (Benidorm's westernmost beach), this family hotel at the edge of the old town has lots to offer. Rooms are decorated in classic Mediterranean blue with sparkling white-tiled bathrooms and go for very reasonable rates. **Pros:** ample sea views; impeccably clean; friendly service. **Cons:** no pool; unsophisticated decor; closed each year for five months. ✉ *Paseo Colón 3* ☎ *96/585–0412* ⊕ *www.hotelcolon.net* *37 rooms* *In-hotel: restaurant, bar, beachfront, Wi-Fi hotspot, some pets allowed* ▭ *MC, V* ⊙ *Closed Nov.–Mar.* *BP.*

NIGHTLIFE

Countless bars and discos with names such as Jockey's and Harrods (reflecting Benidorm's popularity with Brits and Germans) line Avenida de Europa and the Ensanche de la Playa de Levante. The **Benidorm Palace** (✉ *Av. Severo Ochoa* ☎ *96/585–1661* ⊕ *www.benidorm-palace.com*) offers a cabaret Tuesday–Saturday, with Spanish dance, international musical shows, and sometimes even operas. Dinner starts at 8:30; the show at 10. Since its opening in 1977, the Palace, with capacity for 1,500, has been one of the major tourist attractions for the region. Admission for dinner and show is €44; for the show only, it's €27.

ALICANTE (ALACANT)

82 km (51 mi) northeast of Murcia, 183 km (113 mi) south of Valencia by coast road, 42 km (26 mi) south of Benidorm, 55 km (34 mi) south of Alcoy.

The Greeks called it Akra Leuka (White Summit), and the Romans named it Lucentum (City of Light); as a crossroads for inland and coastal routes, Alicante has always been known for its luminous skies. The city is dominated by the Castillo de Santa Bárbara but also memorable is its grand **Esplanada,** lined with date palms. Directly under the castle is the city beach, the Playa del Postiguet, but the city's pride is the long, curved Playa de San Juan, which runs north from the Cap de l'Horta to El Campello.

GETTING HERE AND AROUND

Alicante has two train stations: the main Estación de Madrid and the local Estación de la Marina, from which the local FGV line (not affiliated with RENFE) runs along the Costa Blanca from Alicante to Dénia. The Estación de la Marina is at the far end of Playa Postiguet and can be reached by buses C1 and C2 from downtown.

The small TRAM train goes from the city center on the beach to El Campello. From the same open-air station in Alicante the FGV train departs to Dénia, with stops in El Campello, Benidorm, Altea, Calpe, and elsewhere.

ESSENTIALS

Tram Contact TRAM (*www.tram-alicante.com*).

Visitor Information Alicante (*Rambla Mendez Nuñez 23* *96/520–0000* *www.alicanteturismo.com*).

OLD TOWN

Ayuntamiento. Constructed between 1696 and 1780, the town hall is a beautiful example of baroque civic architecture. Inside, a gold sculpture by Salvador Dalí of San Juan Bautista holding the famous cross and shell rises to the second floor in the stairwell. Ask gate officials for permission to explore the ornate halls and rococo chapel on the first floor. *Pl. de Ayuntamiento* *96/514–9100.*

Basílica de Santa María. Constructed in a Gothic style over the city's main mosque between the 14th and 16th centuries, this is Alicante's oldest house of worship. The main door is flanked by beautiful baroque stonework by Juan Bautista Borja, and the interior highlights are the golden rococo high altar, a Gothic image in stone of St. Mary, and a sculpture of Sts. Juanes by Rodrigo de Osona. The church is across from the Museo de la Asegurada, inside an old granary that is Alicante's oldest public building. *Pl. de Santa María* *96/521–6026* *Tues.–Sun. 4–8:30.*

Concatedral of San Nicolás de Bari. Built between 1616 and 1662 on the site of a former mosque, this church (denominated *con*catedral because it shares the seat of the regional bishopric with the Concatedral de Orihuela) has an austere facade that was designed by Agustín Bernardino, a disciple of the great Spanish architect Juan de Herrera (1530–97), architect of El Escorial. Inside, it's dominated by a dome nearly 150 feet high, a pretty cloister, and a lavish baroque side chapel. Its name comes from the day that Alicante was reconquered, December 6, 1248—the feast day of St. Nicolás. *Pl. Abad Penalva 1* *96/521–2662* *Daily 7:30–12:30 and 5:30–8:30.*

Museo de Bellas Artes Gravina. Inside the beautiful 18th-century Palacio del Conde de Lumiares, MUBAG, as it's best known, has some 500 works of art ranging from the 16th to the early 20th century. *Gravina 13–15* *96/514–6780* *www.mubag.org* *Free* *May–Oct., Tues.–Sat. 10–2 and 5–9; Nov.–Apr., Tues.–Sat. 10–2 and 4–8.*

OUTSIDE OLD TOWN

Capa Collection. Professor Eduardo Capa, of Madrid's Academía Real de Bellas Artes de San Fernando, donated this collection of contemporary Spanish sculpture, the largest in the world. Some 250 of the total of 700 works are permanently displayed here, including pieces by Mariano Benlliure, Dalí, Enrique Pérez Comendador, and Alberto Sánchez. *Castillo de Santa Bárbara* *96/515–2969* *Free* *Tues.–Sat. 10–2 and 4–7, Sun. and holidays 10–2.*

Fodor's Choice ★ **Castillo de Santa Bárbara** *(Saint Barbara's Castle)*. Mount Benacantil, rising to a height of 545 feet, forms a strategic position overlooking not just the city but the sea and the whole Alicante plain for many miles. Remains from civilizations dating from the Bronze Age onward have

8

Alicante's Esplanada de España, lined with date palms, is the perfect place for a stroll.

been found here; the oldest parts, at the highest level, are from the 9th to 13th centuries. This is one of the largest existing medieval fortresses in Europe. It is most easily reached by first walking through a 200-yard tunnel entered from Avenida Jovellanos 1 along Postiguet Beach by the pedestrian bridge, then taking the elevator up 472 feet to the entrance. ✉ *Near Postiguet Beach* ☎ *96/516–2128* 🎫 *Free, elevator €2.40* 🕒 *Elevator and castle daily 10–8 (10 PM June–Aug.); last elevator up at 7 (7:30 PM June–Aug.).*

Museo Arqueológico Provincial. Inside the old hospital of San Juan de Dios, this museum has a collection of artifacts from the Alicante region dating from the Paleolithic era to modern times, with a particular emphasis on Iberian art. The MARQ, as it is known, has won recognition as the European Museum Forum's European Museum of the Year. ✉ *Pl. Dr. Gómez Ulla s/n* ☎ *96/514–9000* 🌐 *www.marqalicante.com* 🎫 *€3* 🕒 *Tues.–Sat. 10–7, Sun. and holidays 10–2.*

Museo de Fogueres. Bonfire festivities are popular in this part of Spain, and the effigies can be elaborate and funny, including satirized political figures and entertainment stars. Every year the best *ninots* (effigies) are saved from the flames and placed in this museum, which also has an audiovisual presentation of the festivities, scale models, photos, and costumes. ✉ *Av. Rambla de Méndez Núñez 29* ☎ *96/514–6828* 🎫 *Free* 🕒 *May–Oct., Tues.–Sun. 10–2 and 5–8; June–Sept., Tues.–Sun. 10–2 and 6–9, Sun. and holidays 10–2.*

Museo Taurino. In the Plaza de Toros, the Bullfighting Museum is a must for taurine aficionados, with fine examples of costumes (the "suits of lights"), bulls' heads, posters, capes, and sculptures. ✉ *Pl. de España*

CLOSE UP

The Oasis of Elche

If Alicante is torrid in summer, Elche (24 km [15 mi] southwest, is even hotter but surrounded by the largest palm forest in Europe, granting some escape from the worst of the heat. The Moors first planted the palms for dates, Europe's most reliable crop, and the trees still produce these. Elche's Palm Grove is the big draw today. The Moors originally irrigated the land and started planting palm trees here, and today there are more than 200,000 palm trees growing within the city. Many of the plantations have been turned into public parks, and efforts are being made to bring back traditional crafts. The blanched palm leaves are used in Elche's two most important cultural events—the Palm Sunday procession and the Mystery Play of Elche. The latter, dating from the Middle Ages and performed every year in mid-August, represents the last days of Mary's life, her death, assumption, and coronation.

You can overnight in this oasis at the Huerto del Cura hotel in the Priest's Grove ($$$) or just stop for lunch at the hotel's Els Capellans ($$$), a culinary sanctuary, where creative cooking is combined with polished service. Expect Mediterranean specialties from *gazpacho de melón y bogavante* (melon and lobster gazpacho) to *arroz con costar* (paella caramelized around the edges). ☎ *96/545–1936* 🌐 *www.huertodelcura.com.*

---

s/n ☎ *96/521–9930* 🎟 *Free* ⏲ *Tues.–Fri. 10:30–1:30 and 5–8, Sat. 10:30–1:30.*

8

WHERE TO EAT AND STAY

$$$ SPANISH ✕ **Cervecería Sento.** The bar and the grill behind it are the center of attention at this historic tapas place just off the Rambla. Fresh squid, calf's liver, and a wide range of vegetables pass incessantly over the sizzling hot plate, creating what many claim are the town's best tapas and *montaditos* (bite-size sandwiches). Try the melt-in-the-mouth *solomillo con foie* (sirloin with foie gras) or the sandwich made with marinated pork, mushrooms, and red peppers accompanied by a glass of red from the excellent wine cellar. ✉ *Calle Teniente Coronel Chapuli s/n* ▭ *MC, V.*

$ ✕ <**Amérigo.** This former Dominican convent is right in the historic center of Alicante. The building blends historic touches with the best of modern design, making it one of the best luxury hotels in the city center. It also incorporates a fashionable tapas bar, a rooftop terrace and pool, and on-site private parking—a real luxury in Alicante. It's a short walk from here to nearby places of interest, including Postiguet Beach. **Pros:** near all museums, the port, and the beach. **Cons:** city center can be hot and busy in summer. ✉ *Rafael Altamira 7* ☎ *96/514–6570* 🌐 *www.hospes.es* *81 rooms* *In-hotel: restaurant, bars, pool, gym, spa, Wi-Fi hotspot, parking (paid)* ▭ *MC, V.*

$ ★ **Les Monges Palace.** In a restored 1912 building, this family-run hostal is in Alicante's central old quarter. Exposed stone walls and ceramic tile floors were lovingly preserved during the restoration. Rooms are furnished with eccentric artwork and quirky charm. The Japanese Suite is equipped with furniture from Japan, a hot tub, and a sauna.

Pros: personalized service; ideal location; plenty of character. **Cons:** all services cost extra; must book well in advance. ✉ *C. San Agustín 4* ☎ *96/521–5046* 🌐 *www.lesmonges.net* *22 rooms, 2 suites* *In-room: a/c, Internet. In-hotel: Internet terminal, Wi-Fi hotspot, parking (paid)* ▭ *MC, V.*

NIGHTLIFE

El Barrio, the old quarter west of Rambla de Méndez Núñez, is the prime nightlife area of Alicante, with music bars and discotheques every couple of steps. In summer, or after 3 AM, the liveliest places are along the water, on the Ruta del Puerto and Ruta de la Madera. It's an Alicante tradition to start the night with overflowing mojitos at **El Coscorrón** (✉ *C. Tarifa 3*). **Astrónomo** (✉ *C. Virgen de Belén 22* ☎ *647/654298*) has a great patio with tiki torches and traditional dancing.

Among the slicker pubs and discos is **Z-Club** (✉ *Calle San Fernando s/n* ☎ *96/521–0646*), where Alicante twentysomethings groove to house and techno. Thirtysomething couples gather at **Byblos Disco** (✉ *C. San Francisco s/n* ☎ *647/654298*).

SHOPPING

Local **crafts** include basketwork, embroidery, leatherwork, and weaving, each specific to a single town or village. The most satisfying places to shop are often neighborhood markets, so inquire about market days. For **ceramics**, travel to the town of Agost, 20 km (12 mi) inland from Alicante. Potters here make jugs and pitchers from the local white clay, with porosity that is ideal for keeping liquids cool.

9

The Balearic Islands

WORD OF MOUTH

"The old train from Palma to Soller is one of life's great small trips . . . Palma is one of Spains great cities, mostly overlooked by tourists. I can't imagine my life as having been complete without a trip to Bar Abaco. In an old manor house with huge vaulted ceilings, the bar is literally full of fresh fruit and flowers."

—markrosy

WELCOME TO THE BALEARIC ISLANDS

TOP REASONS TO GO

★ **Pamper Yourself:** Luxurious boutique hotels on restored and redesigned rural estates are *the* hip accommodations in the Balearics. Many have their own holistic spas: restore and redesign yourself at one of them.

★ **Seafood Delicacies:** Seafood specialties come straight from the boat to portside restaurants all over the islands.

★ **Party Hard:** Ibiza's summer club scene is the biggest, wildest, glitziest in the world.

★ **The Gorgeous Views:** The *miradores* (lookouts) of Majorca's Tramuntana, along the road from Valldemossa to Sóller, highlight the most spectacular seacoast in the Mediterranean.

★ **Palma:** Capital of the Balearics, Palma is one of the unsung great cities of the Mediterranean—a showcase of medieval and modern architecture, a venue for art and music, a mecca for sailors, and a killer place to shop for shoes.

1 Majorca. Palma, the island's capital, is a trove of art and architectural gems. The Tramuntana, in the northwest, is a region of forested peaks and steep sea cliffs that few landscapes in the world can match.

2 Minorca. Mahón, the capital city, commands the largest and deepest harbor in the Mediterranean. Many of the houses above the port date to the 18th-century occupation by the Imperial British Navy.

3 Ibiza (Eivissa). Sleepy from November to May, the island is Party Central in midsummer for retro hippies and nonstop clubbers. Dalt Vila, the medieval quarter of Eivissa, on the hill overlooking the town, is a UNESCO World Heritage site.

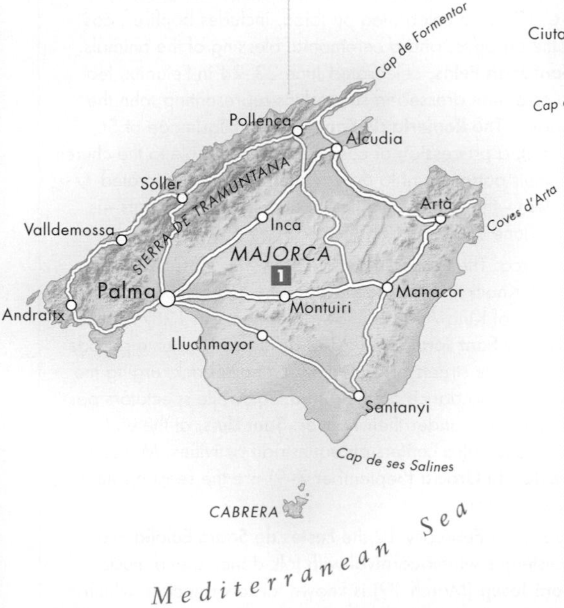

GETTING ORIENTED

The Balearic islands lie 50 to 190 mi off the Spanish mainland, roughly between Valencia and Barcelona. In the center, Majorca, with its rolling eastern plains and mountainous northwest, is the largest of the group. Minorca, its closest neighbor, is virtually flat—but like Ibiza and tiny Formentera to the west, it's blessed with a rugged coastline of small inlets and sandy beaches.

4 Formentera. Partygoers from Ibiza make day trips to chill out at this (comparatively) quiet little island with long stretches of protected beach.

9

THE BALEARIC ISLANDS PLANNER

When to Go

July and August are peak season in the Balearics; it's hot, and even the most secluded beaches are crowded. Weatherwise, May and October are ideal, with June and September just behind. Winter is quiet; it's too cold for the beach but fine for hiking, golfing, and exploring. The clubbing season on Ibiza begins in June.

Note: Between November and February many hotels and restaurants are closed for their own holidays or seasonal repairs.

Local Fiestas

In addition to the major public holidays, towns and villages on each of the islands celebrate a panoply of patron saints' days, fairs, and festivals all their own. Highlights include the following.

Majorca: The **Festival of Sant Antoni d'Abat** (January 16–17), also celebrated on Ibiza, includes bonfires, costume parades, and a ceremonial blessing of the animals. **Sant Joan Pelós**, celebrated June 23–24 in Felanitx, features a man dressed in sheepskins representing John the Baptist. The **Romería de Sant Marçal** (Pilgrimage of St. Mark), a procession of costumed townspeople to the church of their patron saint to draw water from a consecrated cistern—thought to give health and strength of heart—is held June 30 in Sa Cabaneta.

Minorca: The **Processo dels Tres Tocs** (Procession of the Three Knocks) in Ciutadella (January 17) celebrates the victory of King Alfonso III over the Moors in 1287. At the **Feast of Sant Joan** (June 23–24) riders in costume parade through the streets of Ciutadella on horseback, urging the horses up to dance on their hind legs while spectators pass dangerously under their hooves. **Sant Lluís,** at the end of August, also centers on equestrian activities. Mahón's **Fiestas de Gràcia** (September 7–9) are the season's final celebrations.

Ibiza: On February 12 the **Festes de Santa Eulalia** is a boisterous winter carnival with folk dancing and music. **Sant Josep** (March 19) is known for folk dancing, which you can also see in Sant Joan every Thursday evening. On June 23 and 24, is the islandwide **Festa Major de Sant Joan** (Feast of St. John the Baptist). The **Festa del Mar,** honoring Our Lady of Carmen, is held July 16 in Eivissa, Santa Eulalia, Sant Antoni, and Sant Josep, and on Formentera. The festival of **Sant Ciriac** (August 8) celebrates the reconquest of the island from the Moors, and is capped with a watermelon fight beneath the walls of the Old City and a fireworks display.

Formentera: On July 15–16 islanders honor the **Virgen del Carmen,** patron saint of sailors, a blessing of the boats in the harbor.

About the Hotels

Majorca: Majorca's large-scale resorts—more than 1,500 of them—are concentrated mainly on the southern coast and primarily serve the package-tour industry. Perhaps the best accommodations on the island are the number of grand old country estates and town houses that have been converted into boutique hotels, ranging from simple and relatively inexpensive *agroturismos* to stunning outposts of luxury.

Minorca: Apart from a few hotels and hostels in Mahón and Ciutadella, almost all of Minorca's tourist lodgings are in beach resorts. As on the other islands, many of these are fully reserved by travel operators in the high season and often require a week's minimum stay, so it's generally most economical to book a package that combines airfare and accommodations. Alternatively, inquire at the tourist office about boutique and country hotels, especially in and around Sant Lluis.

Ibiza: Ibiza's hotels are mainly in coastal Sant Antoni and Playa d'en Bossa. Many are excellent, but unless you're eager to be part of a mob, Sant Antoni has little to recommend it. Playa d'en Bossa, close to Eivissa, is prettier but lies under a flight path. To get off the beaten track and into the island's largely pristine interior, look for *agroturismo* lodgings in Els Amunts (The Uplands) and in villages such as Santa Gertrudis or Sant Miquel de Balanzat.

Formentera: If July and August are the only months you can visit, reserve well in advance. To get the true feel of Formentera, look for the most out-of-the-way *calas* and fishing villages, especially on the south Platja de Mitjorn coast.

Many hotels on the islands include a Continental or full buffet breakfast in the room rate.

WHAT IT COSTS (IN EUROS)

	¢	$	$$	$$$	$$$$
Restaurants	under €8	€8–€12	€13–€17	€18–€22	over €22
Hotels	under €60	€60–€90	€91–€125	€126–€180	over €180

Prices are per person for a main course at dinner, and for two people in a standard double room in high season, excluding tax.

Planning Your Time

Most European visitors to the Balearics pick an island and stick with it, but you could see all three. Start in Majorca with **Palma.** Begin early at the Cathedral and explore the Llotja, the Almudaina Palace, and the Plaça Major. The churches of Santa Eulalia and Sant Francesc, and the Arab Baths are a must. Staying overnight in Palma means you can sample the nightlife and have time to visit the museums.

Take the old train to **Sóller** and rent a car for a trip over the Sierra de Tramuntana to **Deià, Son Marroig,** and **Valldemossa.** The roads are twisty so give yourself a full day. Spend the night in Sóller and you can drive from there in less than an hour via **Lluc** and **Pollença** to the Roman and Arab remains at **Alcúdia.**

By fast ferry it's just over three hours from Port d'Alcúdia to **Ciutadella,** on Minorca; the port, the **cathedral,** and the narrow streets of the old city can be explored in half a day. Make your way across the island to **Mahón,** and devote an afternoon to the highlights there. From Mahón, you can take a 30-minute interisland flight to **Eivissa.** On Ibiza, plan a full day for the World Heritage site of **Dalt Vila** and the shops of **Sa Penya,** and the better part of another for **Santa Gertrudis** and the north coast. If you've come to Ibiza to party, of course, time has no meaning.

GETTING HERE AND AROUND

By Air

Each of the islands is served by an international airport, all of them within 15 or 20 minutes by car or bus from the capital city. There are daily domestic connections to each from Barcelona (40 min), Madrid, and Valencia: no-frills and charter operators fly to Palma, Mahón, and Eivissa from many European cities, especially during the summer. There are also interisland flights. In high season, book early.

By Bike

The Balearic Islands—especially Formentera and Ibiza—are ideal for exploration by bicycle. Parts of Majorca are quite mountainous, with challenging climbs through spectacular scenery; along some country roads, there are designated bike lanes. Bicycles are easy to rent, and tourist offices have details on recommended routes. Minorca is relatively flat, with lots of roads that wander through pastureland and olive groves to small coves and inlets. Ibiza, too, is relatively flat and easy to negotiate, though side roads can be in poor repair. Formentera is level, with bicycle lanes on all connecting roads.

By Boat and Ferry

From Barcelona: The most romantic way to get to the Balearic Islands is by overnight ferry from Barcelona. Depending on the line and the season, the Trasmediterránea, Balearia, and Iscomar car ferries to Palma, Majorca, sail between 11 and 11:30 PM; you can watch the lights of Barcelona sinking into the horizon for hours—and when you arrive in Palma, around 6 AM, see the spires of the cathedral bathed in the morning sun. All three lines serve Minorca and Ibiza as well. Overnight ferries have lounges and private cabins. Round-trip fares vary with the line, the season, and points of departure and destination but are around €120 for lounges or €280–€360 for a double cabin.

Fast ferries and catamarans, also operated by Trasmediterránea and Balearia, with passenger lounges only, speed from Barcelona to Palma and Alcúdia (Majorca), to Ciutadella (Minorca), and to Eivissa (Ibiza). Depending on the destination, the trip takes between three and five hours.

From Valencia: Trasmediterránea ferries leave Valencia in midmorning for Palma, arriving early evening. There are also ferries from Valencia to Ibiza and Minorca. Departure days and times vary with the season; service is more frequent in summer.

From Denia: Balearia runs a daily two-hour Super Fast Ferry service for passengers and cars between Denia and Eivissa, and a similar three-hour service between Denia and Palma on weekends. Iscomar runs a slower car-and-truck ferry service between Denia and Sant Antoni, Ibiza.

Interisland: Daily ferries connect Alcúdia (Majorca) and Ciutadella (Minorca) in three to four hours, depending on the weather; a hydrofoil makes the journey in about an hour. From May to October, daily hydrofoil service connects Palma and Ibiza; fares range from €15 to €40 one-way. There are frequent car and fast ferry services between Ibiza and Formentera.

Boat and Ferry Information Balearia (*www.balearia.com*). **Formentera port information** (*971/323082*). **Iscomar** (*www.iscomar.com*). **Mediterránea Pitiusa** (*971/322443*). **Trasmapi** (*www.trasmapi.com*). **Trasmediterránea** (*www.trasmediterranea.es*).

Tour Options

Most Majorca hotels and resorts offer guided tours. Typical itineraries are the Caves of Artà or Drac, on the east coast, including the nearby Auto Safari Park and an artificial-pearl factory in Manacor; the Chopin museum in the old monastery at Valldemossa, returning through the writers' and artists' village of Deià; the port of Sóller and the Arab gardens at Alfàbia; the Thursday market and leather factories in Inca; Port de Pollença; Cape Formentor; and northern beaches.

The resorts also run excursions to neighboring beaches and coves—many inaccessible by road—and to the islands of Cabrera and Dragonera. Visitors to Cabrera can take a self-guided tour of the island's underwater ecosystem—using a mask and snorkel with a sound system incorporated; the recording explains the main points of interest as you swim. Contact Excursions a Cabrera or the National Park Office in Palma.

On Minorca, sightseeing trips leave Mahón's harbor from the quayside near the Xoriguer gin factory; several boats have glass bottoms. Fares average around €10. Departure times vary; check with the Tourist Information office on the Moll de Ponent, at the foot of the winding stairs from the old city to the harbor.

Ibiza resorts run trips to neighboring beaches and to smaller islands. Trips from Ibiza to Formentera include an escorted bus tour. In Sant Antoni, which has little to offer in the way of beaches, there are a flotilla of tour organizers to choose from.

Contacts Mahón (✉ *Moll de Llevant 2* ☎ *971/355952*). **Excursions a Cabrera** (☎ *971/649034*). **National Park Office** (✉ *Pl. de España 8* ☎ *971/725010*).

By Taxi

Taxis in Palma are metered. For trips beyond the city, charges are posted at the taxi stands. On Minorca, you can pick up a taxi at the airport or in Mahón or Ciutadella; on Ibiza, taxis are available at the airport and in Eivissa, Figueretas, Santa Eulalia, and Sant Antoni. On Formentera, there are taxis in La Sabina and Es Pujols. Most taxis in Minorca, Ibiza, and Formentera are not metered.

By Train

The public *Ferrocarriles de Mallorca* railway line connects Palma and Inca, with stops at about half a dozen villages en route.

A journey on the privately owned Palma–Sóller railway is a must: completed in 1912, it still uses the carriages of that era. The line trundles across the plain to Bunyola, then winds through tremendous mountain scenery to emerge high above Sóller. An ancient tram connects the Sóller terminus to Port de Sóller, leaving every hour on the hour, 9 to 6; the Palma terminal is near the corner of the Plaça d'Espanya, on Calle Eusebio Estada next to the Inca rail station.

By Car

A car is essential if you want to beach-hop on Majorca or Minorca. Ibiza is best explored by car or motor scooter: many of the beaches lie at the end of rough, unpaved roads. Tiny Formentera can almost be covered on foot, but renting a car at La Sabina is a time-saver.

By Bus

There is bus service on all of the islands, though it's not extensive, especially on Formentera. Check each island's Getting Here and Around information for details.

9

EATING AND DRINKING WELL IN THE BALEARIC ISLANDS

Mediterranean islands should guarantee great seafood—and the Balearics deliver with superb products from the crystalline waters surrounding the archipelago. Inland farms offer free-range beef, lamb, goat, and cheese.

Top left: *Tumbet* is a traditional vegetable dish, served in a clay pot. Top right: Clams are just one of the many seafood options you'll find in the Balearics. Bottom left: Local cheese from Minorca is a delicacy.

Majorcans love their *sopas de peix* (fish soup) and their *panades de peix* (pastries), while Minorca's harbor restaurants are famous for *llagosta* (spiny lobster), grilled or served in a *caldereta*—a soupy stew. Ibiza's fishermen head out into the tiny inlets for sea bass and bream, which are served in beach shacks celebrated for *bullit* (fish casserole), *guisat de marisc* (shellfish stew), and *burrida de ratjada* (ray with almonds). In addition to great seafood, traditional farm dishes range from *sofrit pagès* (sausage with potatoes and red peppers) to *rostit* (oven-roasted pork). Interestingly, mayonnaise is widely thought to have been invented by the French in Mahón, Minorca, after they took the port from the British in 1756.

BALEARIC ALMONDS

Almonds are omnipresent in the Baleares, used in sweets as well as seafood recipes. Typically used in the *picada,* the ground nuts, spices, and herbs on the surface of a dish, almonds are essential to the Balearic economy. After the 19th-century phylloxera plague decimated Balearic vineyards, vines were replaced by almond trees and the almond crop became a staple.

VEGETABLES

The *tumbet mallorquin* is a classic Balearic dish made *of* layers of fried zucchini, bell peppers, potatoes, and eggplant with tomato sauce between each layer. It's served piping hot in individual earthenware casseroles.

SEAFOOD

There are several seafood dishes to look out for in the Balearics. *Burrida de Ratjada* (ray with almonds) is boiled ray fish baked between layers of potato. The *picada* covering the ray during the baking includes almonds, garlic, egg, a slice of fried bread, parsely, salt, pepper, and olive oil. *Caldereta de llagosta* (spiny lobster soup) is a quintessential Minorcan staple sometimes said to be authentic only if the Minorcan spiny lobster is used. A *caldereta* (a soupy stew based on a sofregit of peppers, tomatoes, onions, garlic, and parsely) can be made using a variety of materials from *escupinyes* (tiny clams) to *dàtils* (sea dates), but the spiny lobster version is legendary—especially in the pretty fishing village of Fornells. *Guisat de Marisc* (shellfish stew) is an Ibiza stew of fish and shellfish cooked with a base of onions, potatoes, peppers, and olive oil. Nearly anything that comes out of the waters around Ibiza may well end up in this universal staple.

PORK

Rostit (roast pork) is baked in the oven with liver, eggs, bread, apples, and plums—it's a surprisingly cosmopolitan combination for a country kitchen. *Sobrasada* (pork and paprika paste) is one Majorca's two most iconic food products (the other is the *ensaimada,* a sweet spiral pastry based on *saim,* pork fat). Sobrasada, fine-ground pork seasoned with salt and sweet red paprika, then packed like a sausage, originated in Italy but became popular in Majorca during the 16th century.

MINORCAN CHEESE

Mahón cheese is a Balearic trademark, and Minorca boasts a *Denominación de Origen,* one of the 12 officially designated cheese-producing regions in Spain. The *curado* (fully cured) cheese is the best.

WINE

With just 2,500 acres of vineyards (down from 75,000 in 1891), Majorca's two DO (Denomination of Origin) wine-growing regions—Binissalem, near Palma, and Pla i Llevant on the eastern side of the island—will likely remain under the radar to the rest of the world. While you're here, though, treat yourself to a Torre des Canonge white, a fresh, full, fruity wine, or a red Ribas de Cabrera from the oldest vineyard on the island, Hereus de Ribas in Binissalem, founded in 1711.

BEST BEACHES OF THE BALEARICS

When it comes to oceanfront property, the Balearic Islands have vast and varied resources: everything from long sweeps of beach on sheltered bays to tiny crescents of sand in rocky inlets and coves called *calas*—some so isolated you can reach them only by boat.

Top left: Ibiza is known as party island and the beaches can get crowded. Top right: The upside of the popular beaches are the amenities, like comfy chaises. Bottom left: For peace and quiet, head to Macarella, on Majorca.

Not a few of the Balearic beaches, like their counterparts on the mainland coasts, have become destinations for communities of holiday chalets and retirement homes, with waterfronts lined with shopping centers and the inevitable pizza joints—skip these and head to the simpler and smaller beaches that are in, or abutting the Balearics' admirable number of nature reserves. Granted you'll find few or no services, and be warned that smaller beaches mean crowds in July and August, but these are the Balearics' best beaches. The local authorities protect these areas more rigorously, as a rule, than they do on the mainland, and the beaches are gems. Some of our favorites are on the following page.

BEACH AMENITIES

Be prepared: services at most Balearic beaches are minimal or nonexistent. If you want a deck chair, or something to eat or drink, bring it with you, or make sure to ask around to see if your chosen secluded inlet has at least a chiringuito: a waterfront shack wher the food is likely to feature what the fisherman pulled in that morning.

ES TRENC, MAJORCA

One of the few long beaches on the island that's been spared the development of resort hotels, this pristine 2-mi stretch of soft, white sand southeast of Palma, near Colònia de Sant Jordi, is a favorite with nude bathers—who stay mainly at the west end—and day-trippers who arrive by boat. The water is crystal-clear blue, and shallow for some distance out. There are a few bars and restaurants, and umbrellas and divans for rent. The 10-km (6-mi) walk along the beach from Colònia de Sant Jordi to the Cap Salines lighthouse is one of Majorca's treasures.

PLAYA MAGALUF, MAJORCA

At the western end of the Bay of Palma, about 16 km (10 mi) from the city, this long sandy beach with a promenade makes Magaluf Majorca's liveliest resort destination in July and August. The town is chock-a-block with hotels, holiday apartments, cafés, and clubs, and there are also two water parks in Magaluf—Aqualand and the Western Waterpark—in case the kids tire of windsurfing or kite-surfing.

CALA MACARELLA/CALA MACARETTA, MINORCA

This pair of beautiful secluded coves, edged with pines, is about a 20-minute walk through the woods from the more developed beach at Santa Galdana, on Minorca's south coast. Macarella is the

larger—and busier—of the two; Macaretta, a few minutes farther west along the path, is popular with nude bathers and boating parties. Cala Pregonda, on the north coast of Minorca is a splendid and secluded beach with walk-in access only: it's a lovely crescent cove with pine and tamarisk trees behind and dramatic rock formations at both ends, though it's more difficult to get to.

SES SALINES, IBIZA

Easy to reach from Eivissa, Ibiza's capital, this is one of the most popular beaches on the island, but the setting—in a protected natural park area—has been spared over-development. The beach is relatively narrow, but the fine golden sand stretches nearly a mile along the curve of Ibiza's southernmost bay. Another great choice, on the east coast, is Cala Mastella: a tiny cove tucked away in a pine woods—where a stall on the fisherman's wharf serves the fresh catch of the day.

SES ILLETES, FORMENTERA

The closest beach to the port at La Savina, where the ferries come in from Ibiza, Ses Illetes is Formentera's preeminent party scene: some 2 mi of fine white sand with beach bars and snack shacks, and Jet Skis and windsurfing gear for rent.

9

Updated by Jared Lubarsky

Could anything go wrong in a destination that gets, on average, 300 days of sunshine a year? True, the water is only warm enough for a dip from May through October—but the climate does seem to give the residents of the Balearics a year-round sunny disposition. They are a remarkably hospitable people, not merely because tourism accounts for such a large chunk of their economy, but because history and geography have combined to put them in the crossroads of so much Mediterranean trade and traffic.

The Balearic Islands were outposts, successively, of the Phoenician, Carthaginian, and Roman empires before the Moors invaded in 902 and took possession for some 300 years. In 1235, the Moors were ousted by Jaume I of Aragón, and the islands became part of the independent kingdom of Majorca until 1343, when they returned to the Crown of Aragón under Pedro IV. Upon the marriage of Isabella of Castile to Ferdinand of Aragón in 1469, the Balearics were joined to a united Spain. Great Britain occupied Minorca in 1704, during the War of the Spanish Succession, to secure the superb natural harbor of Mahón as a naval base, but returned it to Spain in 1802 under the Treaty of Amiens.

During the Spanish civil war, Minorca remained loyal to Spain's democratically elected Republican government, while Majorca and Ibiza sided with Franco's insurgents. Majorca became a home base for the Italian fleet supporting the fascist cause. This topic is still broached delicately on the islands; they remain fiercely independent of one another in many ways. Even Mahón and Ciutadella, at opposite ends of Minorca—all of 44 km (27 mi) apart—remain estranged over differences dating from the war.

The tourist boom, which began during Francisco Franco's regime (1939–75), turned great stretches of Majorca's and Ibiza's coastlines into strips of high-rise hotels, fast-food restaurants, and discos.

EXPLORING THE BALEARIC ISLANDS

Majorca and Ibiza are the most heavily developed of the islands, in terms of resorts and tourist infrastructure, and draw most of the foreign visitors, especially from Germany and Great Britain. The north coasts of both have spectacular rocky coastlines, undeveloped areas, and clear waters. Minorca is the preferred destination of Spanish and Catalan families on holiday, and much of it is still farms and pastures, separated with low stone walls, and nature reserves. Formentera has virtually no tourism outside the summer months.

MAJORCA

Saddle-shape Majorca is more than five times the size of either Minorca or Ibiza. The Sierra de Tramuntana, a dramatic mountain range soaring to nearly 5,000 feet, runs the length of its northwest coast, and a ridge of hills borders the southeast shores; between the two lies a flat plain that in early spring becomes a sea of almond blossoms, "the snow of Majorca." The island draws more than 10 million visitors a year, many of them bound for summer vacation packages in the coastal resorts. The beaches are beautiful, but save time for the charms of the northwest and the interior: caves, bird sanctuaries, monasteries and medieval towns, local museums, outdoor cafés, and village markets.

GETTING HERE AND AROUND

From Barcelona, Palma de Majorca is a 50-minute flight, an eight-hour overnight ferry, or a 4½-hour catamaran journey.

If you're traveling by car, Majorca's main roads are well surfaced, and a four-lane, 25-km (15-mi) motorway penetrates deep into the island between Palma and Inca. Palma is ringed by an efficient beltway, the Vía Cintura. For destinations in the north and west, follow the ANDRATX and OESTE signs on the beltway; for the south and east, follow the ESTE signs. Driving in the mountains that parallel the northwest coast and descend to a cliff-side corniche is a different matter; you'll be slowed not only by winding roads but by tremendous views and tourist traffic.

ESSENTIALS

Visitor Information **Oficina de Turismo de Majorca** (✉ *Aeropuerto de Palma* ☎ *971/789556*).

PALMA DE MAJORCA

If you look north of the cathedral (La Seu, or the seat of the bishopric, to Majorcans) on a map of the city of Palma, you can see around the Plaça Santa Eulalia a jumble of tiny streets that made up the earliest settlement. Farther out, a ring of wide boulevards traces the fortifications built by the Moors to defend the larger city that emerged by the 12th century. The zigzags mark the bastions that jutted out at regular intervals. By the end of the 19th century most of the walls had been demolished; the only place where you can still see the massive defenses is at Ses Voltes, along the seafront west of the cathedral.

9

A streambed (*torrent*) used to run through the middle of the old city, dry for most of the year but often a raging flood in the rainy season. In the 17th century it was diverted to the east, along the moat that ran outside the city walls. The stream's natural course is now followed by La Rambla and the Passeig d'es Born, two of Palma's main arteries. The traditional evening *paseo* (promenade) takes place on the Born.

If you come to Palma by car, park in the garage beneath the Parc de la Mar (the ramp is just off the highway from the airport, as you reach the cathedral) and stroll along the park. Beside it run the huge bastions guarding the Almudaina Palace; the cathedral, golden and massive, rises beyond. Where you exit the garage, there's a **ceramic mural** by the late Catalan artist and Majorca resident Joan Miró, facing the cathedral across the pool that runs the length of the park.

If you begin early enough, a walk along the ramparts at Ses Voltes from the *mirador* beside the cathedral is spectacular. The first rays of the sun turn the upper pinnacles of La Seu bright gold and begin to work their way down the sandstone walls. From the Parc de la Mar, follow Avinguda Antoni Maura past the steps to the palace. Just below the Plaça de la Reina, where the **Passeig d'es Born** begins, turn left on Carrer de la Boteria into the Plaça de la Llotja (don't miss a chance to visit the Llotja itself, the Mediterranean's finest civic Gothic building, if it's open), and stroll from there through the Plaça Drassana to the **Museu d'Es Baluard,** at the end of Carrer Sant Pere. Retrace your steps to Avinguda Antoni Maura. Walk up the Passeig d'es Born to Plaça Joan Carles I, then left on Avenida de La Unió and up Carrer de Sant Joan.

GETTING HERE AND AROUND

Palma's Empresa Municipal de Transportes runs 34 bus lines and a tourist train in and around the Majorcan capital. Most buses leave from the city station, next to the Inca railway terminus on the Plaça d'Espanya; a few terminate at other points in Palma. The tourist office on the Plaça d'Espanya has schedules. Bus No. 1 connects the airport with the city center and the port. The No. 21 line connects S'Arenal with the airport. Bus No. 2 circumnavigates the historic city center. Bus No. 20 connects the city center with Porto Pi and the Fundació Pilar i Joan Miró. Fare for a single ride is €1.25.

For sightseeing in Palma, take the open-top City Sightseeing bus that departs from stops throughout the town, including Plaça de la Reina, and travels along the Passeig Marítim and up to the Castell de Bellver. Tickets (€13) are valid for 24 hours, and you can get on and off as many times as you wish. All Palma tourist offices have information and details. Also in Palma, you can hire a horse-drawn carriage with driver at the bottom of the Born, on Avinguda Antonio Maura, in the nearby cathedral square, and on the Plaça d'Espanya, at the side farthest from the railway station. A tour of the city costs €30 for a half hour, €50 for an hour.

Boats from Palma to neighboring beach resorts leave from the jetty opposite the Auditorium, on the Passeig Marítim. The tourist office has a schedule.

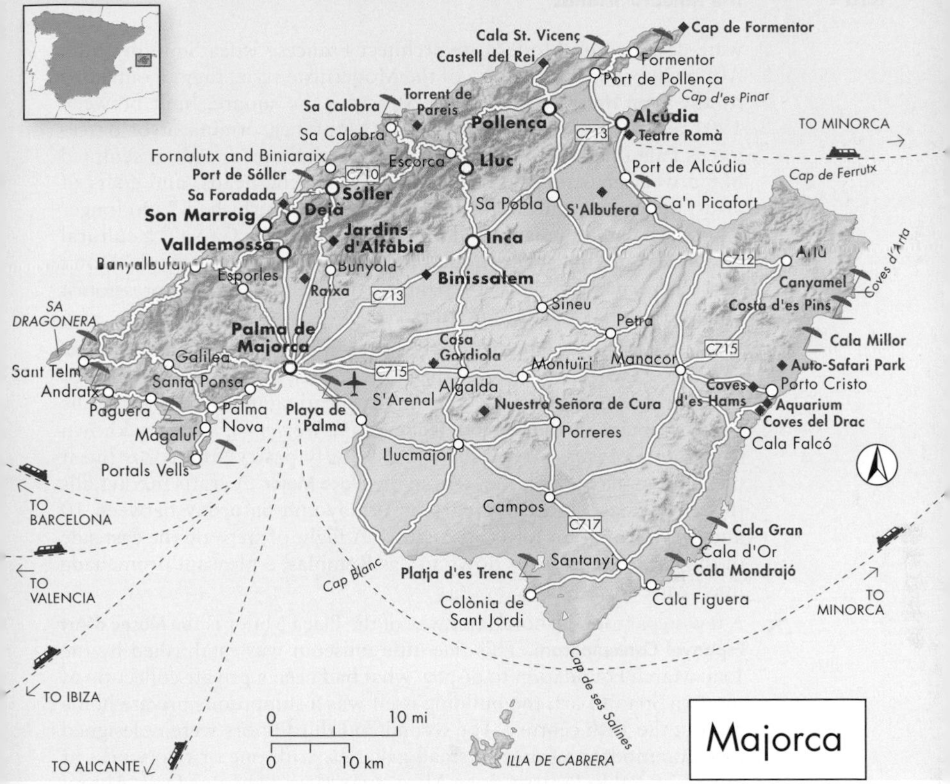

ESSENTIALS

Bike Rentals Bimont (✉ *Camí de Jesús 62, Palma* ☎ *971/731866*). **Embat Ciclos** (✉ *Bartolomé Riutort 27, Palma* ☎ *971/429358*).

Bus Information Empresa Municipal de Transports (🌐 *www.emtpalma.es*).

Bus Station Palma de Majorca (✉ *Estación Central* ☎ *971/752224*).

Taxi Information Associación Fono-Taxi (✉ *Sta. Cnta. Sena 2,Palma* ☎ *971/728081*). **Radio-Taxi** (✉ *Francesc Sancho 7,Palma* ☎ *971/755440*).

Tour Bus Information City Sightseeing (☎ *902/101081*).

Train Station Palma Train Station (✉ *Ferrocarriles de Mallorca, Pl. d'Espanya, Palma* ☎ *971/752245*)

Visitor Information Palma (✉ *Pl. de la Reina 2* ☎ *971/173990* ✉ *Passeig d'es Born 27* ☎ *902/102365* ✉ *Parc de Ses Estacions, across from train station and near Pl. España* ☎ *902/102365*).

EXPLORING

About 110 yards west of the Plaça Joan Carles I, on the Plaça del Mercat, is **San Nicolau** (✉ *Carrer Orfila 1*), a 14th-century church with a hexagonal bell tower. The ornate facades of the **Casas Casasayas** (✉ *Pl. del Mercat 13–14*), on opposite corners of Carrer Santa Cilia, were designed by Moderniste architect Francesc Roca Simó in 1908. Although brilliant examples of the Moderniste style, they're outshone by the **Gran Hotel** (✉ *Pl. Weyler 3*) across the square, built between 1901 and 1903 by Luis Domènech i Montaner, originator of Barcelona's Palau de la Música Catalana. The alabaster facade is sculpted like a wedding cake, with floral motifs, angelic heads, and coats of arms; the original interiors, alas, have been "refurbished." No longer a hotel, the building is owned by the Fundació "La Caixa," a cultural and social organization funded by the region's largest bank. Don't miss the permanent exhibit of paintings by the Majorcan Impressionist Hermenegildo Anglada Camarassa.

Take time to appreciate the neoclassical symmetry of the **Teatre Principal** (☎ *971/725548*), at the top of the Plaça Weyler, Palma's chief venue for opera and classical music. Near the steps leading up to the right of the Teatre Principal is the **Forn des Teatre** (✉ *Pl. Weyler 9*), a bakery known for its *ensaimadas* (a typically Spanish fluffy pastry) and *cocas* (meat pies). From here, climb the steps to the **Plaça Major**. A crafts market fills this elegant neoclassical square on Friday and Saturday between 10 and 2 (Mon.–Sat. in July and August). A flight of steps on the east side of the Plaça Major leads down to **Las Ramblas,** a pleasant promenade lined with flower stalls.

★ A few steps from the north archway of the Plaça Major is the **Museu d'Art Espanyol Contemporani**. This fine little museum was established by the Joan March Foundation to display what had been a private collection of modern Spanish art; the building itself was a sumptuous private home built in the 18th century. The second and third floors were redesigned to accommodate a series of small galleries, with one or two works at most—by Pablo Picasso, Joan Miró, Juan Gris, Salvador Dalí, Antoni Tàpies, and Miquel Barceló, among others—on each wall. ✉ *Carrer Sant Miguel 11* ☎ *971/713515* 🌐 *www.march.es/museupalma* 💵 *Free* 🕒 *Weekdays 10–6:30, Sat. 10:30–2.*

South of the Plaça Major on Carrer Colom, above the Cacao Sampaka chocolate shop in the next small square, is the **Can Forteza Rei** (✉ *Pl. Marqués Palmer 1*), an Art Nouveau delight designed by the original owner, Luis Forteza Rei, in 1909. The building has twisted wrought-iron railings and surfaces inlaid with bits of polychrome tile, signature touches of Antoni Gaudí and his contemporaries. A wonderful carved stone face in a painful grimace flanked by dragons ironically frames the stained-glass windows of a third-floor dental clinic.

Along Carrer Colom is the 17th-century **Ajuntament** (*Town Hall* ✉ *Pl. Cort 1*) ; stop in to see the collection of *gigantes*—the huge painted and costumed mannequins paraded through the streets at festivals—on display in the lobby. The olive tree on the right side of the square is one of Majorca's so-called *olivos milenarios*—purported to be 1,000 years old—and may be even older.

Turn right at the olive tree for a brief detour to the end of the Plaça Cort. On the left at the corner of Carrer de Jaume II is yet another gem of Palma's early Moderniste architecture: the **Can Corbella** (✉ *Pl. Cort 3*), designed in the 1890s by Nicolás Lliteras.

Cathedral of Palma de Majorca

A few steps along the Carrer de la Cadena bring you to the imposing Gothic church of **Santa Eulalia**. In 1435, 200 Jews were converted to Christianity in this church after their rabbis were threatened with being burned at the stake. ✉ *Pl. Santa Eulalia 7, Barrio Antiguo.*

From the Plaça de Sant Eulalia, take the Carrer del Convent de Sant Francesc to the beautiful 13th-century monastery church of **Sant Francesc**, established by Jaume II when his eldest son took monastic orders and gave up rights to the throne. Fra Junípero Serra, the missionary who founded San Francisco, California, was later educated here; his statue stands to the left of the main entrance. The basilica houses the tomb of the eminent 13th-century scholar Ramón Llull. ✉ *Pl. Sant Francesc 7, Barrio Antiguo* 🎫 *€1* 🕒 *Mon.–Sat. 9:30–1 and 3–6, Sun. 9:30–1.*

9

QUICK BITES

The café Ca'n Joan de S'aigo (✉ *C. de Ca'n Sanç 10, Barrio Antiguo* ☎ *971/710759* 🕒 *Mon. and Wed.–Sat. 8 AM–9 PM*), on a side street behind the church of Sant Francesc, is one of Palma's venerable institutions, in business since 1700. Drop in for coffee or hot chocolate with an *ensaimada crema*—a spiral-shape Majorcan pastry with a sinfully rich cream-cheese filling. With its green-glass chandeliers, cane-back chairs, and marble tabletops, the setting is a treat in itself.

From the Plaça Sant Francesc, take Carrer Pere Nadal south toward the bay; the street changes names as it descends, crossing Carrer del Call (in many Spanish cities and towns, the term *call* indicates the site of the medieval Jewish quarter) to become Carrer Santa Clara, then Carrer de Can Pont i Vic. On the left as it turns to Carrer de la Portella is the **Museu de Mallorca**. Housed in the 18th-century ducal palace of the Condes de Ayamans, the museum exhibits the findings of all the major archaeological research on Majorca, from prehistory to the Roman, Vandal, and Moorish occupations. ✉ *Carrer de la Portella 5, Barrio Antiguo* ☎ *971/717540* 🎫 *€2.40* ⏲ *Tues.–Sat. 10–7, Sun. 10–2.*

From the Museu de Majorca, walk down Carrer de la Portella and turn left before the archway at the bottom of the street; follow the signs to one of Palma's oldest monuments, the 10th-century **Banys Arabs** *(Arab Baths)*, in a wonderful walled garden of palms and lemon trees. In its day, it was not merely a public bathhouse but a social institution where you could soak, relax, and gossip with your neighbors. ✉ *Serra 7, Barrio Antiguo* ☎ *971/721549* 🎫 *€2* ⏲ *Dec.–Mar., daily 9–7; Apr.–Nov., daily 9–7:30.*

Fodor's Choice ★ Palma's **cathedral** is an architectural wonder that took almost 400 years to build (1230–1601). The wide expanse of the nave is supported by 14 slender 70-foot-tall columns, which fan out at the top like palm trees. The nave is dominated by an immense rose window, 40 feet in diameter, from 1370. Over the main altar (consecrated in 1346) is the surrealistic **baldoquí** by Antoni Gaudí, completed in 1912: an enormous canopy, with lamps suspended from it like elements of a mobile, rising to a Crucifixion scene at the top. To the right of it, in the Chapel of the Santísimo, is an equally remarkable work by the modern sculptor Miquel Barceló: a painted ceramic tableau that covers the walls of the chapel like a skin. Unveiled in 2007, the tableau is based on the New Testament account of the miracle of the loaves and fishes; Barceló renders this story in a bizarre composition of rolling waves, gaping cracks, protruding fish heads, and human skulls. The **bell tower** above the cathedral's Plaça Almoina door holds nine bells, the largest of which is known as N'Eloi, meaning "Praise." N'Eloi was cast in 1389, weighs 5½ tons, needs six men to ring it, and has shattered stained-glass windows with its sound. ✉ *Pl. Almoina s/n, Barrio Antiguo* ☎ *971/723130* 🌐 *www.catedraldemallorca.org* 🎫 *€4* ⏲ *Apr. and May, weekdays 10–5:15; June–Sept., weekdays 10–6:15; Oct.–Mar., weekdays 10–3:15; year-round, Sat. 10–2:15, Sun. for worship only, 8:30–1:45, 6:30–7:45.*

Opposite Palma's cathedral is the **Palau de l'Almudaina** (Almudaina Palace), residence of the ruling house during the Middle Ages and originally an Arab citadel. It's now a military headquarters and the king's official residence when he is in Majorca. Guided tours generally depart hourly during open hours. ✉ *Carrer Palau Reial s/n, Barrio Antiguo* ☎ *971/214134* 🎫 *€3.20; €4 with a guided tour; audio guide €2* ⏲ *Oct.–Mar., weekdays 10–1:15 and 4–5:15, Sat. 10–1:15; Apr.–Sept., weekdays 10–5:45, Sat. 10–1:15.*

The **Llotja** (Exchange), on the seafront west of the Plaça de la Reina, was built in the 15th century and connects via an interior courtyard to the **Consolat de Mar** (Maritime Consulate). With its decorative turrets, battlements, fluted pillars, and Gothic stained-glass windows—part fortress, part church—it attests to the wealth Majorca achieved in its heyday as a Mediterranean trading power. The interior can be visited

CLOSE UP

A Wine Detour

Binissalem, about a half-hour drive (25 km [15 mi]) from Palma, is the center of one of the island's two D.O. (Denominación de Orígen) registered wine regions and has a riotous harvest festival in mid-September, when surplus grapes are dumped by the truckload for participants to fling at each other. Some of Marjorca's best wineries are here, many of them open for tastings and tours.

One of the largest of Majorca's wineries is **Bodegas José Ferrer** (✉ *Conquistador 103* ☎ *971/511050*). A hard winery to find, but worth a detour as it exports none of its production, is **Bodega Antonio Nadal Ros** (✉ *Camino de Son Roig s/n* ☎ *639/660945*).

only when there are special exhibitions in the Merchants Chamber. ✉ *Pl. de la Llotja 5* ☎ *971/711705* ⏲ *During exhibits, Tues.–Sat. 11–2 and 5–9, Sun. 11–2.*

★ Inaugurated in January 2004, the **Museu d'Es Baluard** *(Museum of Modern and Contemporary Art of Palma)* rises on a long-neglected archaeological site at the western end of the city, parts of which date back to the 12th century. The building itself is an outstanding convergence of old and new: the exhibition space uses and merges into the surviving 16th-century perimeter walls of the fortified city, with a stone courtyard facing the sea and a promenade along the ramparts. There are three floors of galleries, and the collection includes work by Miró, Picasso, Henri Magritte, Tapiès, Alexander Calder, and other major artists. The café-terrace Restaurant del Museu (Tuesday–Sunday 1–4 and 8–11), in the courtyard, affords a fine view of the marina. ✉ *Pl. Porta de Santa Catalina 10, Puig Sant Pere* ☎ *971/908200* 🌐 *www.esbaluard.org* 🎫 *€6 (voluntary donations on Thurs., free on national and regional holidays)* ⏲ *Oct.–June 15, Tues.–Sun. 10–8; June 16–Sept., Tues.–Sun. 10–10.*

The **Castell de Bellver** *(Bellver Castle)* overlooks the city and the bay from a hillside. It was built at the beginning of the 14th century, in Gothic style but with a circular design—the only one of its kind in Spain. An archaeological **museum** of the history of Majorca and a small collection of classical sculpture sit inside. ✉ *Camilo José Cela s/n* ☎ *971/730657* 🎫 *€2.50, free Sun.* ⏲ *Castle and museum Oct.–Mar., Mon.–Sat. 8:30–6:45; Apr.–Sept., Mon.–Sat. 8:30–8:30. Castle only Sun. 10–4:30.*

The permanent collection in the **Museu Fundació Pilar y Joan Miró** (Pilar and Joan Miró Foundation Museum) includes a great many drawings and studies by the Catalan artist, who spent his last years on Majorca, but shows far fewer finished paintings and sculptures than the Fundació Miró in Barcelona. Don't miss the adjacent studio, built for Miró by his friend the architect Josep Lluis Sert. The artist did most of his work here from 1957 on. ✉ *Carrer Joan de Saridakis 29, Cala Major, Marivent* ☎ *971/701420* 🌐 *miro.palmademallorca.es/english/index.htm*

DID YOU KNOW?

The Balearic Islands are filled with secluded coves, or *calas*. Cala Pi, pictured here, is named for the surrounding pine trees: it would be Pine Cove in English.

€6 ⏲ *Sept. 16–May 15, Tues.–Sat. 10–6, Sun. 10–3; May 16–Sept. 15, Tues.–Sat. 10–7, Sun. 10–3.*

WORD OF MOUTH

"Palma and the little towns in the north have lots of foreign residents, but they're still very Spanish. The weather is great, and the people are very friendly." —Fiona

OFF THE BEATEN PATH

Illa de Cabrera. Off the south coast of Majorca lies one of the last unspoiled verdant slivers in the Mediterranean—the Illa de Cabrera, largest of the 19 islands and islets that make up the Cabrera archipelago. Determined to protect its dramatic landscape, wildlife, and lush vegetation, local environmental activists succeeded in 1991 in having it declared a national park. Throughout its history, Cabrera has had its share of visitors, from the Romans to the Arabs. Today, the only intact historical remains are those of a 14th-century castle overlooking the harbor. Tour boats called *golondrinas* make day trips to the island (mainly April–October); contact **Excursiones a Cabrera** (☎ *971/649034* 🌐 *www.excursionsacabrera.com*). Boats generally depart from Colònia de Sant Jordi, 47 km (29 mi) southeast of Palma, around 9:30 AM, returning at 6 PM; tickets are €29, with lunch provided for an additional cost. The trip takes about 30 minutes. Departure times vary, so inquire at any of the Palma tourist offices for current information.

WHERE TO EAT AND STAY

$–$$ SPANISH ✕ **Café la Lonja.** A great spot for hot chocolate or a unique tea or coffee, this classic establishment in the old fishermen's neighborhood has a young vibe that goes well with the decor. Both the sunny terrace in front of the Llotja—a privileged dining spot—and the restaurant inside are excellent places for drinks, *tapas*, baguettes, sandwiches, and salads. The seasonal menu might include a salad of tomato, avocado, and Manchego cheese; fluffy quiche; and *tapas* of squid or mushrooms. It's a good rendezvous point and watering hole. ✉ *Carrer Llotja del Mar 2, La Llotja* ☎ *971/722799* 💳 *AE, MC, V* ⏲ *Closed Sun.*

$$ SPANISH ✕ **La Bóveda.** Within hailing distance of the Llotja, this popular restaurant serves *tapas* and inexpensive platters such as chicken or ham croquettes, grilled cod, garlic shrimp, and *revueltos con setas y jamón* (scrambled eggs with mushrooms and ham). The tables in the back are always at a premium (they're nice and cool on summer days, if you don't mind the smoking), but there's additional seating at the counter or on stools around upended wine barrels. The ample portions of traditional *tapas* are nothing fancy but very good. ✉ *Carrer de la Botería 3, La Llotja* ☎ *971/714863* 💳 *AE, MC, V* ⏲ *Closed Sun.*

$$ 🏨 **Born.** Romanesque arches and a giant palm tree spectacularly cover the central courtyard and reception area of this hotel, which occupies the former mansion of a noble Majorcan family. Guest rooms are modest, though some have the original coffered and painted ceilings, and the rates are more than reasonable. A buffet breakfast is included in the price. **Pros:** convenient for sightseeing; romantic courtyard floodlit at night; fine value for price. **Cons:** small rooms on the street side; poor soundproofing; no elevator. ✉ *Carrer Sant Jaume 3, Centro* ☎ *971/712942* 🌐 *www.hotelborn.com* *31 rooms* *In-hotel: bar, laundry service, Wi-Fi hotspot* 💳 *AE, DC, MC, V* 🍽 *BP.*

$$$ **Dalt Murada.** Dating back to the 15th century, this town house in the old part of Palma was the Sancha Moragues home until 2001, when the family opened it as a hotel. Most of the furniture, paintings, and decor were their own, handed down for generations, but with modernization came enormous Jacuzzi tubs in the tile bathrooms. Weather permitting, a basic breakfast is served in the lovely interior garden, overgrown with bougainvillea and orange and lemon trees. The location, a minute's walk to the cathedral, is ideal. **Pros:** location; helpful service; homey feel. **Cons:** thin walls; a bit pricey for what you get. ✉ *Carrer Almudaina 6A, Barrio Antiguo* ☎ *971/425300* 🌐 *www.daltmurada.com* *16 rooms* *In-room: safe, refrigerator, Wi-Fi. In-hotel: restaurant, bar, laundry service, Internet terminal, Wi-Fi hotspot* 💳 *AE, MC, V* 🍽 *BP.*

$ **Hostal Apuntadores.** It's easy to see why this is Palma's hostelry of choice among budget travelers. It's cheap, the rooftop terrace has arguably the city's best view—overlooking the cathedral and the sea—and it's in the heart of the old town, within strolling distance of the bustling Passeig d'es Born. Rooms are basic, clean, and sizable for the price; ask for one with a balcony. The hotel was last done over in 2007, with double-glazed windows installed on the lower floors. **Pros:** good value for price; good place to meet people. **Cons:** can be noisy; cheapest rooms share bathrooms. ✉ *Carrer Apuntadores 8, Barrio Antiguo* ☎ *971/713491* 🌐 *www.palma-hostales.com* *29 rooms, 18 with bath* *In-room: no phone, refrigerator (some), no TV, Wi-Fi. In-hotel: laundry service, Wi-Fi hotspot* 💳 *MC, V.*

$$$–$$$$ ★ **Palau Sa Font.** Warm Mediterranean tones and crisp, clean lines give this boutique hotel in the center of Palma's shopping district an atmosphere very different from anything else in the city. A 16th-century Episcopal palace, restored as a hotel in 2000, it has ample rooms with linen curtains and plump comforters. From the terrace in the tower, you have 360-degree views of Palma's old quarter. **Pros:** buffet breakfast until 11; helpful English-speaking staff; chic design. **Cons:** pool is small; surroundings can be a bit noisy in midsummer. ✉ *Carrer Apuntadores 38, Barrio Antiguo* ☎ *971/712277* 🌐 *www.palausafont.com* *19 rooms* *In-room: refrigerator, Internet. In-hotel: restaurant, bar, pool, Internet terminal, Wi-Fi hotspot, some pets allowed* 💳 *AE, MC, V* 🍽 *BP.*

$$$$ Fodor's Choice ★ **Reads Hotel and Spa.** A 15-minute drive from Palma, this peaceful retreat centers on a restored 18th-century estate house with its own vineyard. Detached suites have private gardens. Each room is furnished in a different, fanciful style, from Moorish-exotic to traditional Mallorcan and minimalist modern; lobby and lounge areas are filled with antiques from the owner's collection. The spa has an indoor pool and rooms for aesthetic and deep-relaxation treatments. Chef Felix Eschrich presides over the superb Bacchus restaurant ($$$$); serious eaters will book the "chef's table" in the evening—an alcove in the kitchen itself, with seating for six. **Pros:** huge estate good for long walks; indoor/outdoor pools; hands-on programs in the kitchen for serious foodies. **Cons:** no minibars; not really family-friendly. ✉ *Ctra. Santa María–Alaró s/n* ☎ *971/140261* 🌐 *www.readshotel.com* *8 rooms, 15 suites* *In-room: safe, DVD (some). In-hotel: 2 restaurants, room service,*

bar, tennis court, pools, gym, spa, bicycles, no elevator, laundry service, Wi-Fi hotspot, parking (free), some pets allowed, no kids under 12 ☰ *AE, DC, MC, V* 🍽 *BP.*

NIGHTLIFE

Majorca's nightlife is never hard to find. Many of the hot spots are concentrated 6 km (4 mi) west of Palma at **Punta Portals,** in Portals Nous, where King Juan Carlos I often moors his yacht when he's in Majorca in early August for the Copa del Rey international regatta. In Palma, the section of the Passeig Marítim known as **Avinguda Gabriel Roca** is a nucleus of taverns, pubs, and clubs. **Abraxas** (✉ *Paseo Maritimo 42* ☎ *971/455908*) thumps to house music until the wee hours. Once a week (usually Sunday) it hosts a gay night with an infectious anything-goes vibe; the cover charge can be pricey (€10–€20). Outdoor elevators transport you from Avinguda Gabriel Roca to the dance floor at the sleek and futuristic **Tito's** (☎ *971/730017*).

★ The **Plaça de la Llotja** and surrounding streets are where to go for *copas* (drinking, *tapas* sampling, and general carousing). Elegant **Bar Abaco** (✉ *Carrer de Sant Joan 1, La Llotja* ☎ *971/714939*) offers baroque music amid fragrant flowers and fruit.

Carrer Apuntadores, a street on the Born's west side in the old town, is lined with casual bars that appeal especially to night owls in their 20s and 30s. On the weekends, you can often come across impromptu live rock and pop acts performed on small back stages. Some of Palma's best jazz acts play the small, smoky jazz club **Barcelona** (✉ *Carrer Apuntadores 5, La Llotja* ☎ *971/713557*) on weekends.

Join the after-work crowd basking in the Palma of yesteryear at **Cappuccino Grand Café** (✉ *Carrer Sant Miquel 53, La Llotja* ☎ *971/719764*), a fun evening venue (not to be confused with the restaurant and coffeeshop of the same name in the Barrio Antiguo commercial area. **Bluesville** (✉ *Carrer Mas del Morro 3, Barrio Antiguo* ☎ *No phone*) is a laid-back bar popular with both locals and foreigners where you can listen to rock and blues on Saturday nights. In summer (June–September), head to the nearby suburb of Magalluf and dance the night away at the gargantuan disco **BCM Planet Dance** (✉ *Av. S'Olivera s/n, Magalluf* ☎ *971/132715*).

Palma's **Gran Casino de Majorca** is a short distance from the harbor. There's an admission charge of €4, and you'll need your passport to enter; dress is informal, but T-shirts, shorts, and sandals are considered inappropriate. ✉ *Urb. Sol de Majorca s/n, Calvià* ☎ *971/130000* ⏲ *Daily 4* PM*–5* AM.

SPORTS AND THE OUTDOORS

BALLOONING For spectacular views of the island, float up with **Majorca Balloons** (✉ *Palma-Manacor Hwy. Ma-15, Exit 44, Manacor* ☎ *971/818182, mobile 630/076543* 🌐 *www.mallorcaballoons.com*). One-hour flights leave daily, mornings, and afternoons from March to October, weather permitting.

BICYCLING With long flat stretches and heart-pounding climbs, Majorca's 675 km (400 mi) of rural roads adapted for cycling make it the most popular sport on the island; many European professional teams do preseason training here. Tourist board offices have excellent leaflets on bike routes with maps, details about the terrain, sights, and distances.

BIRD-WATCHING Majorca has two notable nature reserves, ideal for bird-watchers. **S'Albufera de Majorca** (✉ *Ctra. Port d'Alcúdia–Ca'n Picafort* ☎ *971/892250* 🌐 *www.mallorcaweb.net/salbufera* ⏲ *Apr.–Sept., daily 9–7; Oct.–Mar., daily 9–5*) is the largest wetlands zone in Majorca. **Sa Dragonera** (☎ *971/180632* ⏲ *Apr.–Sept., daily 9–5; Oct.–Mar., daily 9–4*) has a large colony of sea falcons and is accessible by boat from Sant Elm, the western tip of Majorca. **Cruceros Margarita** (☎ *639/617545*) excursion boats to Sa Dragonera leave from the port of Sant Elm, at the western tip of the island, and from Port d'Andratx, Monday–Saturday (except December and January) at 10:15, 11:15, 12:15, and 1:15. The fare is €10.

GOLF Majorca has more than a score of 18-hole golf courses, among them PGA championship venues of fiendish difficulty. For more information, contact the **Federación Balear de Golf** (*Balearic Golf Federation* ✉ *Av. Jaime III 17, Palma* ☎ *971/722753*).

HANG GLIDING For memorable views of the island, glide above it on an ultralight hang glider. Arrange a trip at **Escuela de Ultraligeros "El Cruce"** (✉ *Ctra. Palma–Manacor, Km 42, Vilafranca de Bonany* ☎ *629/392776*). For hang gliding, contact **Escuela de Parapente Alfàbia** (☎ *687/626536*). **Club Vol Lliure Majorca** (☎ *655/766443* 🌐 *www.cvlmallorca.com*) conducts weekend and intensive hang-gliding courses.

HIKING Majorca is excellent for hiking. In the Sierra de Tramuntana, you can easily arrange to trek one-way and take a boat, bus, or train back. Ask the tourist office for the free booklet *20 Hiking Excursions on the Island of Majorca,* with detailed maps and itineraries. For more hiking information, contact the **Grup Excursionista de Majorca** (*Majorcan Hiking Association* ✉ *Carrer del Horts 1 baixos, Palma* ☎ *971/718823* 🌐 *www.gemweb.org*). A useful travel agency that organizes trekking is **Explorador** (☎ *600/557770* 🌐 *www.islavision.com*).

SAILING For information on sailing, call the **Federación Balear de Vela** (*Balearic Sailing Federation* ✉ *Carrer Joan Miró s/n [San Agustin], Palma* ☎ *971/402412* 🌐 *www.federacionbalearvela.org*). The **Escuela Nacional de Vela de Calanova** (*National Sailing School* ✉ *Av. Joan Miró 327, San Agustí* ☎ *971/402512*) can clue you in about sailing in the Balearics. The **Club de Mar** (✉ *Muelle de Pelaires, south end of Passeig Marítim, Palma* ☎ *971/403611* 🌐 *www.clubdemar-mallorca.com*) is famous among yachties. It has its own hotel, bar, disco, and restaurant. Charter a yacht at **Cruesa Majorca Yacht Charter** (✉ *Carrer Contramuelle Mollet 12, Palma* ☎ *971/282821* 🌐 *www.cruesa.com*).

SCUBA DIVING Ask about scuba diving at **Escuba Palma** (✉ *Av. Rey Jaume I 84, Santa Ponsa* ☎ *971/694968*). **Big Blue** (🌐 *www.bigbluediving.net* ☎ *971/681686*) is a source for all things scuba related.

TENNIS Tennis is very popular here; there are courts at many hotels and private clubs, and tennis schools as well. For information about playing in the area, call the **Federació de Tennis de les Illes Balears** (*Balearic Tennis Federation* ✉ *Av. Alemania 11Palma* ☎ *971/720956*).

Majorca is a popular place for cyclists, and many European professionals train here.

WATER SPORTS You can rent windsurfers and dinghies at most beach resorts, both skin- and scuba diving are excellent, and the island has some 30 yacht marinas. On the northwest coast at Port de Sóller, canoes, windsurfers, dinghies, motor launches, and waterskiing gear are available for rent from Easter to October at **Escola d'Esports Nàutics** (✉ *Calle Marina s/n, Port de Sóller* ☎ *609/354132* 🌐 *www.nauticsoller.com*).

SHOPPING

Majorca's specialties are shoes and leather clothing, porcelain, utensils carved from olive wood, handblown glass, and artificial pearls. Look for designer fashions on the **Passeig des Born** and for antiques on **Costa de la Pols,** a narrow little street near the Plaça Riera. The **Plaça Major** has a modest crafts market Friday and Saturday 10–2 (in summer the market is open Mon.–Sat.; January and February, it's open weekends only). Another crafts market is held May 15–October 15, 8 PM–midnight in **Plaça de les Meravelles.**

Many of Palma's best shoe shops are on Avenida Rei Jaime III, between the Plaça Juan Carles I and the Passeig Mallorca. **Barrats** (✉ *Av. Rei Jaime III 5, Centro* ☎ *971/213024*) specializes in leather coats and shoes for women. **Camper** (✉ *Av. Rei Jaime III 16, Centro* ☎ *971/714635*) has an internationally popular line of sport shoes. **Carmina** (✉ *Avda. de la Unió 4, Centro* ☎ *971/229047*) is the place for top-quality handcrafted men's dress shoes. **Farrutx** (✉ *Passeig des Born 16, Centro* ☎ *971/715308*) gets high prices for its elegant line of women's shoes and bags. **Jaime Mascaró** (✉ *Av. Rei Jaime III 10, Centro* ☎ *971/729842*) is known for its original high-fashion designer shoes for women. Majorca's most popular footwear is the simple, comfortable slip-on espadrille (usually with a leather front over the first half of the foot and a strap across the back of the ankle). Look for a pair at **Alpargatería La Concepción** (✉ *Concepción 17, Barrio Antiguo* ☎ *971/710709*).

Mediterráneo (✉ *Av. Rei Jaume III 11, Centro* ☎ *971/712159*) sells high-quality artificial pearls in its elegant sit-down showroom. **Las Columnas** (✉ *C. Sant Domingo 8, Barrio Antiguo* ☎ *971/712221*) has ceramics from all over the Balearic Islands. Visit **Gordiola** (✉ *Carrer Jaume II 14, Barrio Antiguo* ☎ *971/715518*), glassmakers since 1719, for a variety of original bowls, bottles, plates, and decorative objects. The company's factory is in Alguida, on the Palma–Manacor road, where you can watch the glass being blown and even try your hand at making a piece. Just down the street is **Lafiore** (✉ *Carrer Jaume II 6, Barrio Antiguo* ☎ *971/716517*), the island's other venerable glassmaker, which has its factory showroom in S'Esgleieta, on the road from Palma to Valldemossa. The **Colmado Santo Domingo** (✉ *Carrer Santo Domingo 1* ☎ *971/714887* 🌐 *www.colmadosantodomingo.com* ⏲ *Mon.–Sat. 10–8*) is a wonderful little shop for the artisanal food specialties of Majorca: *sobresada* (soft salami) of black pork, sausages of all sorts, cheeses, jams, and honeys and preserves.

JARDINS D'ALFÀBIA

17 km (10½ mi) north of Palma.

Here's a sound you don't often hear in the Majorcan interior: the sound of falling water. The Moorish viceroy of the island developed the springs and hidden irrigation systems here sometime in the 12th century to create this remarkable oasis on the road to Sóller, with its 40-odd varieties of trees, climbers, and flowering shrubs. The 17th-century manor house, furnished with antiques and painted panels, has a collection of original documents that chronicle the history of the estate. ✉ *Ctra. Palma–Sóller, Km 17* ☎ *971/613123* 🎫 *€4.50* ⏲ *Nov.–Mar., weekdays 9–5:30, Sat. 9–1; Apr.–Oct., Mon.–Sat. 9–6:30.*

SÓLLER

★ *13 km (8½ mi) north of Jardins d'Alfàbia, 30 km (19 mi) north of Palma.*

All but the briefest visits to Majorca should include at least an overnight stay in Sóller, one of the most beautiful towns on the island, notable for the palatial homes built in the 19th and early 20th centuries by the landowners and merchants who thrived on the export of the region's oranges, lemons, and almonds. Many of the buildings here, like the **Church of Sant Bartomeu** and the **Bank of Sóller,** on the Plaça Constitució, and the nearby **Can Prunera,** are gems of the Moderniste style, designed by contemporaries of Antoni Gaudí. The tourist information office in the **Town Hall,** next to Sant Bartomeu, has a walking tour map of the important sites.

GETTING HERE AND AROUND

■TIP→ If you're driving to Sóller from Palma, take the tunnel (€4.45) at Alfàbia, rather than the road over the mountains. The latter is spectacular—lemon and olive trees on stone-walled terraces, farmhouses perched on the edges of forested cliffs—but demanding. Save your strength for even better mountain roads ahead. You can travel in retro style to Sóller from Palma on one of the seven daily trains (round-trip €17) from Plaça d'Espanya—a string of wooden coaches with leather-covered seats dating from 1912.

In Sóller, a charming old trolley car (€4) threads its way from the train station down through town to Port de Sóller.

ESSENTIALS

Trolley Contacts Sóller trolley (✉ *Eusebi Estada 1, Palma de Mallorca* ☎ *902/364711*). Sóller (✉ *Pl. d'Espanya 6* ☎ *902/364711* 🌐 *www.trendesoller.com*).

Visitor Information Port de Sóller (✉ *Canonge Oliver 10* ☎ *971/633042*) Sóller (✉ *Pl. d'Espanya 1* ☎ *971/638008*).

EXPLORING

Sóller's **Station Building Galleries** (✉ *Pl. Espanya 6* ☎ *971/630301* 🎫 *Free* ⏲ *Daily 10:30–6:30*), maintained by the Fundació Tren de l'Art, have two small but remarkable collections, one of engravings by Miró, the other of ceramics by Picasso.

WHERE TO STAY

$$ **El Guía.** Built in 1880, El Guía (The Guide) is furnished in a comfortable mix of rustic and Moderniste styles, with nothing fancy in the way of services or amenities. A few steps from the railroad station, it has a pretty courtyard with wrought-iron gates, rooms with a view of the mountains, and a restaurant ($$–$$$) popular for Majorcan specialties. **Pros:** good value for price; friendly family service; location. **Cons:** just the basics. ✉ *Carrer Castanyer 2* ☎ *971/638686* 🌐 *www.sollernet.com/elguia* *17 rooms* *In-room: a/c (some), no phone, no TV. In-hotel: restaurant, bar, room service, no elevator* ▭ *MC, V* ⏲ *Closed Nov.–Mar.* *BP.*

$$$$ **Gran Hotel Sóller.** Sóller's biggest hotel—a former private estate with an imposing Moderniste façade, converted in 2004—has conference and banquet facilities, and a fitness club with memberships for the local community. The rooms, most with twin beds, are spacious and subdued, with beige upholstery and matching drapes, blue carpeting, and big wardrobes with mirror doors. **Pros:** breakfast on the roof terrace, friendly and efficient service in at least five languages, a minute's walk from the town center. **Cons:** a bit pricier than it should be. ✉ *Carrer Romaguera 18* ☎ *971/630227* 🌐 *www.granhotelsoller.com* *28 rooms, 10 suites* *In-room: safe, refrigerator, DVD (some), Wi-Fi. In-hotel: 2 restaurants, room service, bar, 2 pools, gym, spa, laundry service, Wi-Fi, parking (free), some pets allowed* ▭ *MC, V* *BP.*

$$ **La Vila.** Owner Toni Oliver opened this lovingly restored town house on Sóller's central square in 2006. Rooms (four on the square, four facing the interior garden) are plainly furnished, but the public spaces keep much of the original lush Moderniste detail: coffered ceilings, alabaster walls cut in floral patterns, arches in carved and painted plaster,

a three-story central staircase with a cupola. Book well in advance, on the hotel's Web site. **Pros:** friendly service; good location; palm-shaded garden terrace restaurant. **Cons:** rooms on the square can be noisy; no elevator. ✉ *Pl. Constitució 14* ☎ *971/634641* 🌐 *www.lavilahotel.com* *8 rooms* *In-room: safe, refrigerator, Wi-Fi. In-hotel: restaurant, room service, bar, laundry service, Wi-Fi hotspot* 💳 *MC, V.*

DEIÀ

★ *9 km (5½ mi) southwest of Sóller.*

Deià is perhaps best known as the adopted home of the English poet and writer Robert Graves, who lived here off and on from 1929 until his death in 1985. The village is still a favorite haunt of writers and artists, including Graves's son Tomás, author of *Pa amb Oli (Bread and Olive Oil)*, a guide to Majorcan cooking, and British painter David Templeton. Ava Gardner lived here for a time; so, briefly, did Picasso. The setting is unbeatable; all around Deià rise the steep cliffs of the Sierra de Tramuntana. There's live jazz on summer evenings, and on warm afternoons literati gather at the beach bar in the rocky cove at Cala de Deià, 2 km (1 mi) downhill from the village. Walk up the narrow street to the village church; the small **cemetery** behind it affords views of mountains terraced with olive trees and of the coves below. It's a fitting spot for Graves's final resting place, in a quiet corner.

GETTING HERE AND AROUND

The Palma–Port de Sóller bus passes through Deià five times daily in each direction.

EXPLORING

In 2007, the Fundació Robert Graves opened a museum dedicated to Deià's most famous resident, in **Ca N'Alluny**, the house he built in 1932, overlooking the sea. It's something of a shrine: Graves's furniture and books, personal effects, and the press he used to print many of his works are all preserved. ✉ *Ctra. Deià-Sóller s/n* ☎ *971/636185* 🌐 *www.fundaciorobertgraves.org* *€5* ⏲ *Apr.–Oct., weekdays 10–5, Sat. 10–3; Nov., Feb., and Mar., weekdays 9–4. Sat. 9–2; Dec. and Jan., weekdays 10–3.*

WHERE TO STAY

$$$$ ★ **Es Molí.** A converted 17th-century manor house in the hills above the valley of Deià, the Es Molí is a haven of peace and relaxation, representative of an older sort of luxury (as a hotel it dates to 1965) without the over-the-top pretensions. There are acres of gardens and secluded corners, with deck chairs under the orange trees, as well as bamboo groves and ancient olive trees, and everywhere the sound of water tumbling from a mountain spring. Rooms are spacious and classically furnished; most have private balconies with stone balustrades and stunning views. A shuttle bus runs frequently to the hotel's private cove at Sa Muleta, with a cliff-side solarium and lounge deck. Book early: about half the clientele come back year after year. **Pros:** attentive service; open-air chamber music concerts twice a week at dinner; great value for price. **Cons:** steep climb to rooms in the annex; short season. ✉ *Ctra.*

Valldemossa–Deià s/n ☎ 971/639000 🌐 www.esmoli.com ⇨ 84 rooms, 3 suites ☝ In-room: safe, refrigerator, DVD, Wi-Fi. In-hotel: restaurant, room service, 2 bars, tennis court, pool, gym, laundry service, Wi-Fi hotspot, parking (free) ▭ AE, DC, MC, V ⊙ Closed Nov.–Mar.

$$$$ Fodor's Choice ★ **La Residencia.** Two 16th- to 17th-century manor houses have been artfully combined to make this exceptional hotel on a hill facing the village of Deià. It is superbly furnished with Majorcan antiques, modern canvases, and canopied four-poster beds. Herbs, olives, fruit, and flowers come straight to the kitchen and guest rooms from the hotel's lush landscaped gardens. The annex (built in 2008) has eight rooms on two levels, four with private heated plunge pools. El Olivo, the restaurant ($$$$), offers an inventive Continental menu that includes eclectic but delicious zingers such as lobster with ibérico ham. The hotel has its own shuttle to the sea at Lluc Alcari. **Pros:** impeccable service; view from the terrace. **Cons:** only gnomes can negotiate the stairs to the Tower Suite. ✉ *Son Canals s/n ☎ 971/639011 🌐 www.hotellaresidencia.com ⇨ 36 rooms, 31 suites ☝ In-room: safe, refrigerator, DVD, Internet (some), Wi-Fi. In-hotel: 3 restaurants, room service, bar, tennis courts, pools, gym, spa, bicycles, laundry service, Internet terminal, Wi-Fi hotspot, parking (free), no kids under 10 ▭ AE, DC, MC, V 🍴 BP.*

$$$ **s'Hotel D'Es Puig.** This family-run "hotel on the hill" has a back terrace with a lemon-tree garden and a wonderful view of the mountains; the simply furnished balcony doubles, with exposed beams, share the view. D'Es Puig gets a lot of repeat business from British visitors, so book early. **Pros:** peaceful setting; friendly service. **Cons:** pool is small; beds could be more comfortable; parking difficult. ✉ *Es Puig 4 ☎ 971/639409 or 637/820805 🌐 www.hoteldespuig.com ⇨ 8 rooms ☝ In-room: safe, refrigerator, Wi-Fi. In-hotel: bar, pool, bicycles, laundry service, Wi-Fi hotspot, parking (free) ▭ AE, DC, MC, V ⊙ Closed Dec. and Jan. 🍴 BP.*

SON MARROIG

4 km (2½ mi) west of Deià.

West of Deià is Son Marroig, one of the estates of Austrian archduke Luis Salvador (1847–1915), who arrived in Majorca as a young man and fell in love with the place. The archduke acquired huge tracts of land along the northwest coast, where he built *miradors* at the most spectacular points but otherwise left the pristine beauty of the land intact. Below the *mirador* at Son Marroig you can see **Sa Foradada,** a rock peninsula pierced by a huge archway, where the archduke moored his yacht. Now a museum, the estate house contains the archduke's collections of Mediterranean pottery and ceramics, old Majorcan furniture, and paintings. From April through early October, the Deià International Festival holds classical concerts here. ✉ *Ctra. Deià–Valldemossa s/n ☎ 971/639158 🌐 www.sonmarroig.com 🎫 €3 ⊙ Apr.–Sept., Mon.–Sat. 9:30–7:30; Oct.–Mar., Mon.–Sat. 9:30–5:30.*

On the road south from Deià to Valldemossa is the **Monestir de Miramar,** founded in 1276 by Ramón Llull, who established a school of Asian languages here. It was bought in 1872 by the Archduke Luis Salvador

Majorca's Tramuntana mountains provide excellent views for hikers.

and restored as a *mirador*. Explore the garden and the tiny cloister, then walk below through the olive groves to a spectacular lookout. ✉ *Ctra. Deià–Valldemossa s/n* ☎ *971/616073* 🎫 *€3* 🕐 *Apr.–Oct., Mon.–Sat. 10–7; Nov.–Mar., Mon.–Sat. 9:30–7.*

VALLDEMOSSA

18 km (11 mi) north of Palma.

Visitor Information Valldemossa (✉ *Av. de Palma 7* ☎ *971/612019*).

EXPLORING

The **Reial Cartuja** *(Royal Carthusian Monastery)* was founded in 1339, but when the monks were expelled in 1835, it was privatized, and the cells became apartments for travelers. The most famous lodgers were Frédéric Chopin and his lover, the Baroness Amandine Dupin—a French novelist who used the pseudonym George Sand. The two spent three difficult months here in the cold, damp winter of 1838–39. The tourist office, in the plaza next to the church, sells a ticket good for all of the monastery's attractions.

In the **church,** note the frescoes above the nave—the monk who painted them was Goya's brother-in-law. The **pharmacy,** in the cloisters, was made by the monks in 1723 and is almost completely preserved; from here, a long corridor leads to the apartments occupied by Chopin and Sand, furnished in period style. The piano is original. Nearby, another set of apartments houses the local **museum,** with mementos of Archduke Luis Salvador and a collection of old printing blocks. From here you return to the ornately furnished **King Sancho's palace,** a group of rooms originally built by King Jaume II for his son Sancho. ✉ *Pl. de la Cartuja 11* ☎ *971/612106* 🌐 *www.valldemossa.com* €8 ⏲ *Dec. and Jan., Mon.–Sat. 9:30–5; Feb. and Nov., Mon.–Sat. 9:30–5, Sun. 10–1; Mar.–Oct., Mon.–Sat. 9:30–5:30, Sun. 10–1.*

WHERE TO EAT AND STAY

$$$$ **Gran Hotel Son Net.** About equidistant from Palma and Valldemoss, this restored estate house—parts of which date back to 1672—is one of Majorca's most luxurious hotels. Poplars and palms shade the terrace above the 30-meter pool, with the village of Puigpunyent and the countryside below. Room decor in the main building can be a bit over the top—a lot of red and rose pink—but the bathrooms are truly palatial. A complex of detached suites built in 2008 have private pools, Jaccuzzis on the terrace, fireplaces, and classic-modern furnishing in muted tones of beige and brown. The hotel's showcase restaurant, Oleum, set in an ancient olive press, is an ideal showcase for the creations of chef Sebastian Campins, specializing in Continental cuisine with a Mallorcan accent. **Pros:** attentive staff; family-friendly; convenient to Palma. **Cons:** short season; a bit far from the beaches. ✉ *Carrer Castillo de Son Net, Puigpunyent* ☎ *971/147000* 🌐 *www.sonnet.es* *25 rooms, 6 suites* *In-room: safe, refrigerator, DVD, Wi-Fi. In-hotel: 2 restaurants, room service, bars, pools, gym, spa, bicycles, laundry service, Internet terminal, parking (free)* *AE, DC, MC, V* ⏲ *Closed Nov.–Feb.*

$$$$ ★ **Valldemossa Hotel.** The breathtaking vistas alone are worth a stay. Once part of the Valldemossa Carthusian monastery, this beautifully restored Majorcan stone house–turned–luxury hotel sits on a hill amid acres of olive trees and has sweeping views of the Tramuntana mountains, the town, and the monastery. Modern rooms have snowy white curtains and comforters and antique bedsteads. You can relax on rattan chairs shaded by palms in the sunny patio and then ease into the evening at the elegant restaurant ($$$$), which serves Mediterranean and international dishes. **Pros:** private, with peaceful surroundings. **Cons:** restaurant needs more variety; not especially child-friendly. ✉ *Ctra. Valldemossa s/n* ☎ *971/612626* 🌐 *www.valldemossahotel.com* *4 double rooms, 8 junior suites* *In-room: safe, refrigerator, DVD, Internet, Wi-Fi. In-hotel: restaurant, room service, bar, pools, spa, bicycles, laundry service, Internet terminal, Wi-Fi hotspot, parking (free)* *AE, MC, V* *BP.*

INCA

29 km (17 mi) northeast of Palma.

Inca and environs is shoe heaven: major firms like **Camper** (✉ *Poligon Industrial s/n* ☎ *902/364598*), **Barrats** (✉ *Avda. General Luque 480* ☎ *971/213024*), and **Munper** (✉ *Carrer Jocs 170* ☎ *971/881000*) have their factory showrooms here, and there are dozens of smaller craft ateliers all over town specializing in different kinds of footwear and leather apparel. The Thursday market is the largest on Majorca.

9

WHERE TO EAT

$$ SPANISH — **Celler C'an Amer.** A *celler* is a uniquely Majorcan combination of wine cellar and restaurant, and Inca has no fewer than six. C'an Amer is the best, with heavy oak beams and huge wine vats lining the walls behind the tables and banquettes. Antonia, the dynamic chef-owner, serves some of the best *lechona* (suckling pig) and *tumbet* (vegetables baked in layers) on the island in heroic portions. Winter specialties include a superb oxtail soup prepared with red wine and seasonal mushrooms. After lunch, take your coffee around the corner in the pleasant little church square of Plaça de Santa Maria la Major. ✉ *Carrer Pau 39* ☎ *971/501261* ▭ *AE, MC, V* ⊙ *Closed Sun., May–Oct. (open only for lunch Sat.). Open daily Nov.–Apr.*

ALCÚDIA

54 km (34 mi) northeast of Palma.

The first city on the site of Alcúdia was a Roman settlement, in 123 BC. The Moors reestablished a town here, and after the Reconquest it became a feudal possession of the Knights Templars; the first ring of city walls dates to the early 14th century. Begin your visit at the **Church of Sant Jaume** and walk through the maze of narrow streets inside to the **Porta de Xara,** with its twin crenellated towers.

ESSENTIALS

Visitor Information Alcúdia (✉ *Passeig Marítim s/n* ☎ *971/847241*).

EXPLORING

The **Museu Monogràfic de Pollentia** has a good collection of Roman items. ✉ *Carrer Sant Jaume 30* ☎ *971/547004* 🎫 *€3* ⊙ *Tues.–Fri. 10–3:30, weekends 10–1:30.*

POLLENÇA

5 km (3 mi) inland of the port.

The history of this pretty little town goes back at least as far as the Roman occupation of the island; the only trace of that period is a small **stone bridge** at the edge of town. In the 13th century Pollença and much of the land around it was owned by the Knights Templars—who built the imposing **Church of Nuestra Senyora de Los Ángeles,** on the west side of the present-day Plaça Major. The church looks east to the 330-meter peak of the Puig de Maria, with the 15th-century **sanctuary** at the top. The **Calvari** of Pollença is a flight of 365 stone steps to a tiny **chapel,** and a panoramic view as far as Cap de Formentor. There's a colorful weekly **market** here on Sunday mornings.

ESSENTIALS

Visitor Information Pollença (✉ *Carrer Sant Domingo 2* ☎ *971/535077*).

EXPLORING

OFF THE BEATEN PATH

Cap de Formentor. The winding road north from Port de Pollença to the tip of the island is spectacular. Stop at the **Mirador de la Cruete,** where the rocks form deep narrow inlets of multishaded blue; off to the right,

DID YOU KNOW?

The town of Pollença was built 6 km from the coast and the city's port to avoid pirate attacks.

a winding road leads to a stone tower called the **Talaia d'Albercuix**, at the highest point on the peninsula.

WHERE TO STAY

$$$$ **Barceló Formentor.** Centered in some 3,000 acres of pine forest on the west coast of the Bay of Pollença, this elegant hotel has been in operation since 1929. The elegant white facade and the terrace gardens descending to the beach are glorious with bougainvillea and hibiscus almost year-round. Room furnishings are modern, in soothing pale yellow and green, with figured drapes and exposed ceiling beams. Former guests include the Duke of Windsor, Winston Churchill, Charlie Chaplin, Aristotle Onassis, and the Spanish royal family. **Pros:** long curve of white-sand beach; luxurious public areas; lots of activities for kids. **Cons:** rooms small for the price, especially on the non-seaview side; no nearby choices for dinner out. ✉ *Playa de Formentor s/n, Port de Pollença* ☎ *971/899100* 🌐 *www.barcelo.com* *103 rooms, 21 suites* *In-room: safe, refrigerator, Internet, Wi-Fi. In-hotel: 3 restaurants, bar, tennis courts, pools, gym, beachfront, water sports, laundry service, Internet terminal, Wi-Fi hotspot, parking (free)* *AE, DC, MC, V* *Closed Nov.–Mar.* *BP.*

$$$ **Hotel Juma.** This little hotel on Pollença's main square marked its 100th birthday in 2007. Rooms are small and simply but comfortably furnished with traditional Majorcan pieces and hand-embroidered drapes. It's a good choice for a weekend stay because of the Sunday market in the square. The owners have another seven-room property, L'Hostal, around the corner (✉ *Carrer Mercat 18* ☎ *971/535282* 🌐 *www.hostalpollensa.com)* in an old stable that's been converted to a modern boutique hotel. **Pros:** great location; good breakfast in the bar downstairs; good value for price. **Cons:** parking can be a problem. ✉ *Pl. Major 9 (L'Hostal)* ☎ *971/535002* 🌐 *www.hoteljuma.com* *7 rooms* *In-room: safe, Internet, Wi-Fi (some). In-hotel: bar, laundry service, Wi-Fi hotspot* *AE, MC, V* *BP.*

THE ARTS

★ Pollença hosts an acclaimed international **music festival** in July and August. Founded in 1961, it has brought in such performers as Mstislav Rostropovic, Jessye Norman, the St. Petersburg Philharmonic, the Camerata Köln and the Alban Berg Quartet. Concerts are held in the cloister of the **Convent of Sant Domingo.** Contact the **Festival ticket office** (☎ *971/535077 or 971/534012* 🌐 *www.festivalpollenca.org*).

LLUC

20 km (12 mi) southwest of Pollença.

The **Santuari** in the remote mountain village of Lluc is widely considered Majorca's spiritual heart. La Moreneta, also known as La Virgen Negra de Lluc (the Black Virgin of Lluc), is here in the 17th-century **church.** The **museum** has an eclectic collection of ceramics, paintings, clothing, folk costumes, and religious items. A boys' choir sings psalms in the chapel August–May, weekdays at 11:15 AM and around 4:45 PM, and 11 AM for Sunday mass; hours change during holidays and the summer. The Christmas Eve performance of Cant de la Sibila (Song of the Sybil) is an annual choral highlight. ☎ *971/871525* *Museum €3; monastery free* *Daily 8–8.*

WHERE TO STAY

¢ **Santuari de Lluc.** The Lluc monastery offers simple, clean, and cheap accommodation, mostly in cells once occupied by priests. All have bathrooms and sleep between two and six people. Although the vast building has one bar and three Majorcan restaurants ($–$$), nightlife is restricted, and guests are asked to be silent after 11 PM. ✉ *Santuari de Lluc, Pl. Pelegrins s/n* ☎ *971/871525* *www.lluc.net/eng/ahostatg.html* *136 rooms* *In-room: no a/c, kitchen (some), no TV. In-hotel: 3 restaurants, bar* *V.*

MINORCA

Minorca, the northernmost of the Balearics, is a knobby, cliff-bound plateau with some 200 kilometers of coastline and a single central hill—El Toro—from whose 1,100-foot summit you can see the whole island. Prehistoric monuments—*taulas* (huge stone T-shapes), *talayots* (spiral stone cones), and *navetes* (stone structures shaped like overturned boats)—left by the first Neolithic settlers are everywhere on the island.

Tourism came late to Minorca, which aligned with the Republic in the Civil War; Franco punished the island by discouraging the investment in infrastructure that fueled the Balearic boom on Mallorca and Ibiza. Minorca has avoided many of the problems of overdevelopment: there are still very few high-rise hotels, and the herringbone road system, with a single central highway, means that each resort is small and separate. There's less to see and do on Minorca, and more unspoiled countryside—the island has been a designated Biosphere Reserve since 1993—than on the other Balearics; it's where Spaniards and Catalans tend to take their families on holiday.

GETTING HERE AND AROUND

To get to Minorca from Barcelona take the overnight ferry, fast hydrofoil (about three hours), or a 40-minute flight. It's a six-hour ferry from Palma.

Several buses a day run the length of Minorca between Mahón and Ciutadella, stopping at Alaior, Mercadal, and Ferreries en route. The bus line Autos Fornells serves the northeast; Transportes Minorca connects Mahón with Ciutadella and with the major beaches and *calas* around the island. From smaller towns there are daily buses to Mahón and connections, though often indirect, to Ciutadella. In summer, regular bus service from the west end of Ciutadella's Plaça Explanada shuttles beachgoers between town and the resorts to the south and west; from Mahón, excursions to Minorca's most remote beaches leave daily from the jetty next to the Nuevo Muelle Comercial, in the harbor.

If you want to beach hop in Minorca, it's best to have your own transportation, but most of the island's historic sights are in Mahón or Ciutadella, and once you're in town everything is within walking distance.

You can see the island's archaeological remains in a day's drive, so you may want to rent a car for just that part of your visit.

Horseback riding, breeding, and dressage have been traditions on the island for hundreds of years, and the magnificent black Menorcan horses play an important role, not only as work animals and for sport, but in shows and colorful local festivals. There are some 17 riding clubs on island, a number of which offer excursions on the rural lanes of the unspoiled Minorcan countryside. The Camí de Cavalls is a riding route in 20 stages that completely circumnavigates the island. Cavalls Son Angel in Ciutadella, Centre Equestre Equimar in Es Castell, Menorca a Cavall in Ferreries, and Picadero Menorca in Alaior organize excursions for adults and children. Son Martorellet, on the road to the beach at Cala Galdana is a ranch where you can visit the stables and watch dressage training exhibitions; there's an equestrian show in traditional costume every Tuesday and Thursday evening at 8:30, from May to October.

ESSENTIALS

Bus Contacts **Autos Fornells** (*www.autosfornells.com*). **Transportes Minorca** (*www.tmsa.es*). **Torres Alles Autocares** (*www.e-torres.net*).

Horseback Riding Contacts **Cavalls Son Angel** (*609/833902* *cavalls-sonangel.com*). **Centre Equestre Equimar** (*667/009532*). **Menorca a Cavall** (*971/374637* *www.menorcaacavall.com*). **Picadero Menorca** (*660/286176*). **Son Martorellet** (*639/156851 or 971/377115* *www.sonmartorellet.com*).

MAHÓN (MAÓ)

Established as the island's capital in 1722, when the British began their nearly 80-year occupation, Mahón still bears the stamp of its former rulers. The streets nearest the port are lined with four-story Georgian town houses; the Mahónese drink gin and admire Chippendale furniture; English is widely spoken. The city is quiet for much of the year, but between June and September the waterfront pubs and restaurants swell with foreigners.

GETTING HERE AND AROUND

Within Mahón, Torres Alles Autocares has three bus lines around the city and to the airport.

ESSENTIALS

Bike Rental **Velo Rent Bike** (*S'Arraval 97, Mahón* *971/353798*).

Bus Contact **Torres Alles Autocares** (*www.e-torres.net*).

Bus Station **Estació Autobuses** (*Carrer Josep Anselm Clavé 2* *971/360457*).

Taxi Contact Minorca **Radio-Taxi** (*Mahón* *971/367111*).

Visitor Information **Aeropuerto de Minorca** (*Ctra. de San Clemente s/n Mahón* *971/157115*). **Mahón** (*Moll de Llevant 2* *971/355952*).

EXPLORING

A leisurely walk through the city might begin at the Plaza de Esplanada. From there, take the Carrer de Sa Rovellada de Dalt to the right, turn left on Carrer de ses Moreres, then right on Carrer Bastió to where it becomes Carrer Costa Deià, and—if it's open—have a look at the **Teatre Principal** (✉ *Carrer Costa Deià 40* ☎ *971/355776* 🌐 *www.teatremao.com*). The theater was built in 1824 as an opera house, with five tiers of boxes, red plush seats, and gilded woodwork—a La Scala in miniature. Fully restored in 2005, the Principal still hosts a brief opera season; if you're visiting in the first week of December or June, get tickets at all costs.

Carrer Costa Deià descends to the Plaça Reial (a bit grandiosely named, for an unimposing little rectangle), where it becomes the Carrer sa Ravaleta. Ahead is the church of **La Verge del Carme** (✉ *Pl. del Carme* ☎ *971/362402*), which has a fine painted and gilded altarpiece. Adjoining the church are the cloisters, now a **market**, with stalls selling fresh produce and a variety of local specialties such as cheeses and sausages. The central courtyard is a venue for a variety of cultural events throughout the year.

A few steps north from the Cloister del Carme bring you to the church of **Santa María** (✉ *Pl. de la Constitució* ☎ *971/363949*), which dates

Mahon's harbor at Es Castell, called Cales Font, is close to the main square and lined with restaurants: perfect for a summer evening.

from the 13th century but was rebuilt during the British occupation and restored after being sacked during the civil war. The church's pride is its 3,200-pipe baroque organ, imported from Austria in 1810. There are midday concerts (€4) here Monday through Saturday, 11:30–12:30, from May to October.

Behind the church of Santa María is the **Plaça de la Conquesta**, with a statue of Alfons III of Aragón, who wrested the island from the Moors in 1287. From here, walk up Carrer Alfons III and turn right at the **Ajuntament** (✉ *Pl. de la Constitució 1* ☎ *971/369800*) to Carrer Isabel II, a street lined with many Georgian homes. Turn west from Carrer Isabel II on Carrer Rector Mort, and at the far end of the street is the massive gate of **Puerta de San Roque**, the only surviving portion of the 14th-century city walls, rebuilt in 1587 to protect Mahón from the pirate Barbarossa (Redbeard).

WHERE TO EAT

$$$–$$$$ SEAFOOD ✕ **El Jàgaro.** Named for a mussel-like bivalve that has a tail to propel itself across the ocean floor, this simple waterfront restaurant is a local favorite. The eager lunchtime crowd comes for the platter of lightly fried mixed fish with potatoes, while in the evening you can enjoy grilled *pescado de roca* (rockfish), *sepia* (cuttlefish), or *Menorcan mussels.* The menu takes a quantum leap in price for the €71 spiny lobster, a delicacy in its various forms. The *ortigues* (sea anemones) are a house specialty not to be missed. The prix-fixe lunch is a good value. ✉ *Moll de Llevant 334–35* ☎ *971/362390* ▭ *AE, MC, V* ⏲ *Closed Mon. and Sun. evening Nov.–Mar.*

$$–$$$$ SPANISH Fodor's Choice ★ **Es Moli de Foc.** Originally a flour mill—*de foc* means "of fire," signifying that the mill was operated by internal combustion rather than wind—this is the oldest building in the village of Sant Climent, about 3 km (2 mi) from the airport. Es Moli may not look like much, but the food is exceptional. Don't miss the prawn carpaccio with cured Mahón cheese and artichoke oil or the black paella with monkfish and squid. Order off the menu for the *carrilleras de ternera* (boiled beef cheeks) with potato purée—or ask for the separate menu of arrozes (rice dishes)—the best on the island and (with apologies to Valencia) arguably the best in Spain. End with Minorcan cheese ice cream and figs. In summer, book a table on the terrace. *Carrer Sant Llorenç 65, Sant Climent 971/153222 MC, V Closed Jan. and Mon. Oct.–May. No dinner Sun.*

$$–$$$ ECLECTIC **Itake.** Itake is an amiable clutter of 12 tables, a chalkboard listing specials of the day, paper place mats, and frosted-glass lamps. This is arguably the best place in Mahón for an inexpensive, informal meal with a different touch. Where neighboring eateries pride themselves on fresh fish, Itake serves warm goat cheese, burgers, kangaroo steaks in mushroom sauce, and ostrich breast with strawberry coulis. That said, nothing here is made with any real elaboration: orders come out of the kitchen at nearly the rate of fast food. *Moll de Llevant 317 971/354570 AE, DC, MC, V Closed Mon. No dinner Sun. Sept.–June.*

$$$–$$$$ SPANISH ★ **Marivent.** Mahónese generally agree this is the best kitchen in town, with a seasonal menu that always features fresh fish and Minorcan free-range beef. The sea bream with black-rice risotto and Mahón cheese is wonderful, as is the beef tenderloin with foie gras and morels. There is a second-floor patio for dining alfresco; the third-floor main room, with a harbor view, is done in understated elegance. The staff is attentive, and the wine list has some 200 Spanish and French labels. *Moll de Llevant 314 971/369801 or 699/062117 Reservations essential in August AE, MC, V Closed Tues. and Christmas–3rd wk of Jan. No dinner Mon., Wed., and Sun. Feb.–May,*

WHERE TO STAY

$$$–$$$$ Fodor's Choice ★ **Biniarroca Boutique Hotel.** Antique embroidered bed linens, shelves with knickknacks, and comfy chairs: this is an English vision of a secluded rural retreat, a haven of quiet at reasonable rates. The glory of Biniarroca is its Alice in Wonderland garden of irises, lavender, and flowering trees. The hotel's fine little restaurant ($$$–$$$$), open to the public only at dinner, features Continental classics like duck in orange and Grand Marnier sauce and innovative dishes like coconut tempura langoustines. **Pros:** friendly personal service; outbuilding suites have private terraces. **Cons:** bit of a drive to the nearest good beach; rooms at the ends of the main building have low ceilings; not child-friendly. *Cami Vell 57, Sant Lluis 971/150059 or 619/460942 www.biniarroca.com 17 rooms, 1 suite In-room: safe, DVD (some), Wi-Fi. In-hotel: restaurant, room service, bar, pools, bicycles, laundry service, Internet terminal, Wi-Fi hotspot, parking (free), some pets allowed, no kids under 16 MC, V Closed Nov.–Mar.*

9

$$$ **Casa Albertí**. The most central of the Mahón hotels, the Casa Alberti was built in 1740 as a private home, during the British occupation, and is registered as a *patrimonio historico-cultural*. The house had been empty some 15 years when a group of young Catalan entrepreneurs bought it and turned it into a friendly, comfortable boutique hotel in 2004. The house has 15-foot ceilings, the original marble staircases, and tile floors; the rooms are furnished in rustic style from local and Barcelona antiques shops. In July and August the restaurant is open to the public for dinners of traditional Japanese cuisine ($$$) prepared by an expert from Barcelona. Rates include breakfast. **Pros:** good-natured; anything-to-help hospitality; just-right location for exploring Mahón. **Cons:** a bit pricey for the dearth of amenities; no elevator. ✉ *Carrer Isabel II 9* ☎ *971/354210 or 686/393569* 🌐 *www.casalberti.com* *4 rooms, 2 suites* *In-room: safe, refrigerator, Wi-Fi. In-hotel: Wi-Fi hotspot, some pets allowed* *MC, V.*

$$$$ **Sant Joan de Binissaida**. Approach this lovely restored farmhouse, some 15 km (9 mi) from Mahón, on an avenue lined with chinaberry and fig trees. There's an excellent restaurant ($$$–$$$$), with meals on the deck in good weather; a row of adjoining stables has been converted to additional guest accommodations, with individual terraces. The family property of opera aficionados, all the rooms at Sant Joan are named for composers. The decor is mainly antique, including a wonderful upstairs common room with deep leather chairs, a baize-topped card table—and an oratory; the public spaces on the first floor, redesigned in 2009 in modern style with blonde wood furnishings and floors, are open and relaxing. **Pros:** vistas clear to the port of Mahón; huge pool, child-friendly. **Cons:** bit of a drive to the nearest beaches; rooms in the annex lack privacy. ✉ *Camí de Binissaida 108, Es Castell* ☎ *971/355598 or 618/874381* 🌐 *www.binissaida.com* *10 rooms, 2 suites* *In-room: safe, refrigerator, DVD (some), Wi-Fi. In-hotel: restaurant, room service, bar, pool, laundry service, Internet terminal, Wi-Fi hotspot, parking (free)* *MC, V* *Closed Jan.–Mar.*

NIGHTLIFE

Akelarre (✉ *Anden de Poniente 43* ☎ *971/368520*) is a smart drinking venue near the port with live concerts (jazz and blues) on Thursday and Friday nights. Catch live jazz Tuesday (May–September) at the **Casino** (✉ *Sant Jaume 4, Sant Climent* ☎ *971/153418* *€10*) bar and restaurant (closed Wednesday). Sant Climent is 4 km (2½ mi) southwest of Mahón.The hottest spot in relatively staid Minorca is the **Cova d'en Xoroi** (✉ C. *Cova s/n* ☎ *971/377236* *€6*), in the beach resort of Cala en Porter, about a 20-minute drive from Mahón. The setting is a series of caves in a cliff high above the sea that, according to local legend, was once the refuge of a castaway Moorish pirate. By day (11–7) it's a tourist attraction, with bars and café terraces; by night, it's a dance-until-dawn disco. In Mahón itself, the bars opposite the ferry terminal fill with locals and visitors. The longtime favorite **Mambo** (✉ *Moll de Llevant 209* ☎ *971/356782*) has rustic stone walls and tasty cocktails.

SPORTS AND THE OUTDOORS

DIVING The clear Mediterranean waters here are ideal for diving. Equipment and lessons are available at Cala En Bosc, Son Parc, Fornells, and Cala Tirant.

GOLF Minorca's sole golf course is **Golf Son Parc** (✉ *Urb. Son Parc s/n* ☎ *971/188875* 🌐 *www.golfsonparc.com*), 9 km (6 mi) east of Mercadal.

WALKING In the south, each cove is approached by a *barranca* (ravine or gully), often from several miles inland. The head of **Barranca Algendar** is down a small, unmarked road immediately on the right of the Ferreries–Cala Galdana Road; the barranca ends at the local beach resort, and from there you have a lovely walk north along the sea to an unspoiled half moon of sand at **Cala Macarella.** Extend your walk north, if time allows, through the forest along the riding trail to **Cala Turqueta,** where you'll find some of the island's most impressive sea grottoes.

WINDSURFING AND SAILING Charter a yacht from **Nautica Tecnimar** (✉ *Ctra. de Cal'n Blanes s/n, Ciutadella* ☎ *971/384469* 🌐 *www.nauticatecnimar.com*) Monday–Saturday. For charters and trips around the island, contact **Blue Mediterraneum** (✉ *Moll de Llevant s/n, Mahón* ☎ *655/753808* 🌐 *www.chartermenorca.com*) Tuesday–Sunday.

SHOPPING

Minorca is known for shoes and leather wear, as well as cheese, gin, and, recently, wine. In Mahón, buy leather goods at **Marks** (✉ *Sa Ravaleta 18* ☎ *971/362660*). Inland, the showroom of **Pons Quintana** (✉ *Calle San Antonio 120, Alaior* ☎ *971/371050*) has a full-length window overlooking the factory where its ultrachic women's shoes are made. It's closed weekends. The company also has a shop in Mahón, at Sa Ravaleta 21, that stays open on Saturday. The showroom of **Jaime Mascaro** (✉ *Poligon Industrial s/n, Ferreries* ☎ *971/374500*), on the main highway from Alaior to Cuitadella, features not only shoes and bags but fine leather coats and belts for men and women. Mascaro also has a shop in Mahón, at Carrer ses Moreres.

A good place to buy the tangy, Parmesan-like Mahón cheese is **Hort de Sant Patrici** (✉ *Camí Ruma-Sant Patrici s/n, Ferreries* ☎ *971/373702* 🌐 *www.santpatrici.com*). You can't visit the dairy itself, but Sant Patrici has a shop, beautiful grounds with a small vineyard and botanical garden, and a display of traditional cheese-making techniques and tools.

In the 18th century, wine was an important part of the Minorcan economy: the British, who knew a good place to grow grapes when they saw one, planted the island thick with vines. Viticulture was simply abandoned when Minorca returned to the embrace of Spain, and it has emerged again only in the past few years. The most promising of the small handful of new Minorcan wineries is **Bodegas Binifadet** (✉ *Ses Barraques s/n, Sant Lluis* ☎ *971/150715* 🌐 *www.binifadet.com*) ; the robust young Binifadet reds and whites are on the shelves all over Minorca, and the owners have recently expanded their product line into cavas, olive oil, and wine-based jams and conserves. The winery is open for tastings May–October, Monday–Saturday 10–2 and 4–8, and well worth a visit.

The other gastronomic legacy of the British occupation was gin. Visit the **Xoriguer distillery** (✉ *Anden de Poniente 91* ☎ *971/362197*), on Mahón's quayside near the ferry terminal, where you can take a guided tour, sample various types of gin, and buy some to take home.

SIDE TRIP TO TORRALBA

Puzzle over Minorca's prehistoric past at **Torralba**. Driving west from Mahón, you turn south at Alaior on the road to Cala en Porter. Torralba, a megalithic site with a number of stone constructions, is 2 km (1 mi) ahead at a bend in the road, marked by an information kiosk on the left. The massive *taula* (table; a T-shape stone monument) is through an opening to the right. Behind it, from the top of a stone wall, you can see, in a nearby field, the monolith **Fus de Sa Geganta.**

SIDE TRIP TO TORRE D'EN GAUMÉS

Torre d'en Gaumés, 16 km (9½ mi) west of Mahón, is a far more complex set of stone constructions than Torralba. Fortifications, monuments, deep pits of ruined dwellings, huge vertical slabs, and *taulas* mark the site. Turn south toward Son Bou on the west side of Alaior. After about 1 km (½ mi), the first fork left will lead you to the ruins.

CIUTADELLA

44 km (27 mi) west of Mahón.

Ciutadella was Minorca's capital before the British settled in Mahón, and its history is richer. As you arrive via the ME1, the main artery across the island from Mahón, turn left at the second roundabout and follow the ring road to the Passeig Marítim; at the end, near the **Castell de Sant Nicolau** watchtower (June–October, daily 10–1 and 5–10) is a **monument to David Glasgow Farragut,** the first admiral of the U.S. Navy, whose father emigrated from Ciutadella to the United States. From here, take Passeig de Sant Nicolau to the **Plaça de s'Esplanada** and park near the Plaça d'es Born.

GETTING HERE AND AROUND

Autocares Torres has a single bus line serving Ciutadella and the beaches and *calas* near the city.

ESSENTIALS

Bike Rentals Bike Minorca (✉ *Av. Fransesc Femenias 4, Ciutadella* ☎ *971/487827*).

Bus Contact Torres Alles Autocares (🌐 *www.e-torres.net*).

Bus Station Ciutadella (✉ *Pl. de S'Esplanada, across from tourist office*).

Taxi Contact Minorca Parada de Taxis de Ciutadella (☎ *971/381197*).

Visitor Information Ciutadella (✉ *Pl. de la Catedral 5* ☎ *971/382693*).

EXPLORING

From a passage on the left side of Ciutadella's columned and crenellated **Ajuntament** (✉ *Pl. d'es Born*), on the west side of the Born, steps lead up to the **Mirador d'es Port,** a lookout from which you can survey the harbor. The local **Museu Municipal** houses artifacts of Minorca's prehistoric, Roman, and medieval past, including records of land grants made by Alfons III to the local nobility after defeating the Moors. It's in an ancient defense tower, the Bastió de Sa Font (Bastion of the Fountain), at the east end of the harbor. ☎ *971/380297* 🌐 *www.ciutadella.org/museu* 🎫 *€2.25, free Wed.* ⏲ *Oct.–Apr., Tues.–Sat. 10–2; May–Sept., Tues–Sat. 10–2 and 6–9.*

The monument in Plaça d'es Born commemorates the citizens' resistance of a Turkish invasion in 1588. South from the plaza along the east side of the Born is the block-long 19th-century **Palau Torresaura** (✉ *Carrer Major del Born 8*), built by the Baron of Torresaura, one of the noble families from Aragón and Catalonia that repopulated Minorca after it was captured from the Moors in the 13th century. The interesting facade faces the plaza, though the entrance is on the side street (it is not open to the public).The **Palau Salort**, on the opposite side of the Carrer Major, is the only noble home regularly open to the public. The coats of arms on the ceiling are those of the families Salort (a salt pit and a garden: *sal* and *ort,* or *huerta*) and Martorell (a marten). ✉ *Carrer Major des Born* 🎫 *€2* ⏲ *May–Oct., Mon.–Sat. 10–2.*

The Carrer Major leads to the Gothic **cathedral** (✉ *Pl. de la Catedral at Pl. Píus XII*), which has some beautifully carved choir stalls. The side chapel has round Moorish arches, remnants of the mosque that once stood on this site; the bell tower is a converted minaret.

Follow the arcade of Carrer de Quadrado north from the cathedral and turn right on Carrer del Seminari, lined on the west side with some of the city's most impressive historic buildings. Among them is the **Seminary of the 17th-century Convent and Eglésia del Socors** (✉ *Carrer del Seminari at Carrer Obispo Vila*), which hosts Ciutadella's summer festival of classical music.

Ciutadella's **port** is accessible from steps that lead down from Carrer Sant Sebastià. The waterfront here is lined with seafood restaurants, some of which burrow into caverns far under the Born.

WHERE TO EAT AND STAY

$$$–$$$$ SEAFOOD ✕ **Cafe Balear.** Seafood doesn't get much fresher than here, as the owners' boat docks nearby every day except Sunday and the restaurant fish tank is seldom empty. The relaxed atmosphere welcomes either a quick bite or a full dining experience. The house special, *arroz caldoso de langosta* (lobster and rice stew), is a masterpiece, as are *pulpo a la gallega* (octopus in paprika and olive oil), *cigalas* (crayfish), lobster with onion, and grilled *navajas* (razor clams). ✉ *Paseo San Juan 15* ☎ *971/380005* 💳 *AE, DC, MC, V* ⏲ *Open Mon.–Sat. July–Sept., Tues.–Sun. Oct. and Dec.-June. Closed Nov.*

$$$$ ★ 🏨 **Hotel Rural Sant Ignasi.** The town of Ciutadella itself is not especially well endowed with hotels, but 10 minutes by car from the central square, in the countryside, is this comfortable and relatively reasonably priced delight. The main building is a manor house dating to 1777; the original barn now accommodates five large suites. Rooms have stone arches, cupboard closets, and English and Minorcan antiques. Ask for a ground-floor double with a private garden terrace. Es Loc, the hotel's excellent restaurant ($$$–$$$$), specializes in Minorcan seafood; in summer, meals are served on the tree-shaded poolside terrace.

The Sant Ignasi is a favorite with young Spanish families. **Pros:** great value for price; friendly staff. **Cons:** kids in the pool all day, short season. ✉ *Ctra. Cala Morell, Ronda Puerto s/n, Ciutadella* ☎ *971/385575* 🌐 *www.santignasi.com* *16 doubles, 9 suites* *In-room: safe, refrigerator, Wi-Fi (some). In-hotel: restaurant, room service, bar, tennis court, pools, bicycles, laundry service, Internet terminal, Wi-Fi hotspot, parking (free), some pets allowed* ▭ *MC, V* ⏱ *Closed Oct.–Mar.*

SHOPPING

Gin, shoes, leather, costume jewelry, and cheese are the items to shop for here; try the Ses Voltes area, the Es Rodol zone near Plaça Artrutx and Ses Voltes, and along the Camí de Maó between Plaça Palmeras and Plaça d'es Born. **Nadia Rabosio** (✉ *Carrer Santissim 4* ☎ *971/384080*) is an inventive designer with an original selection of jewelry and hand-painted silks. **Maria Juanico** (✉ *Carrer Seminari 38* ☎ *971/480879* ⏱ *Weekdays 10:30–2 and 5:30–8, Sat. 10:30–2*) has an atelier in the back of the shop, where she makes her interesting plated and anodized silver jewelry and accessories.The industrial complex *(polígono industrial)* on the right as you enter Ciutadella has shoe factories, each with a shop. Prices may be the same as in stores, but the selection is wider. In Plaça d'es Born, a market is held on Friday and Saturday. Visit **ARTEME** (*Artesanos de Minorca* ✉ *Carrer Comerciants 9* ☎ *971/381550*) for the town's only *alferería* (pottery maker).

EL TORO

24 km (15 mi) northwest of Mahón.

Follow signs in Es Mercadal (the crossroads at the island's center) to the peak of El Toro, Minorca's highest point, at all of 1,555 feet. From the monastery on top you can see the whole island and across the sea to Majorca.

WHERE TO EAT

$$ SPANISH ✕ **Molí d'es Reco**. A great place to stop for lunch, this restaurant is in an old windmill just off the highway, at the west end of Es Mercadal; it has fortress-thick whitewashed stone walls and low vaulted ceilings, and a constant air of cheerful bustle. On warm summer days there are tables on the terrace. Minorcan specialties here include squid stuffed with anglerfish and shrimp and chicken with *centollo* (spider crab). The thick vegetable soup, called *sopas menorquinas,* is excellent. ✉ *Carrer Major 53, Mercadal* ☎ *971/375392* ▭ *AE, DC, MC, V.*

FORNELLS

35 km (21 mi) northwest of Mahón.

A little village (full-time population: 500) of whitewashed houses with red tile roofs, Fornells comes alive in the summer high season, when Spanish and Catalan families arrive in droves to open their holiday chalets at the edge of town and in the nearby beach resorts. The bay—Minorca's second largest and deepest—offers ideal conditions for windsurfing, sailing, and scuba diving. The first fortifications built here to defend the Bay of Fornells from pirates date to 1625.

WHERE TO EAT

$$$–$$$$ SEAFOOD ✕ **Es Pla**. The modest wooden exterior of this waterside restaurant in Fornells's harbor, on the north coast, is misleading. King Juan Carlos is said to make regular detours here during Balearic jaunts to indulge in the *caldereta de langosta* (lobster stew)—which, at market price/weight, skews an otherwise reasonably priced menu. Excellent fish dishes include scallops "Gallega" style, anglerfish with *maresco* (seafood) sauce, and grilled scorpion fish—a local specialty. ✉ *Pasaje Es Pla, Puerto de Fornells* ☎ *971/376655* ▭ *AE, DC, MC, V.*

WINDSURFING AND SAILING

Several miles long and a mile wide but with a narrow entrance to the sea and virtually no waves, the Bay of Fornells gives the beginner a feeling of security and the expert plenty of excitement.

Wind Fornells (✉ *Carrer Nou 33, Es Mercadal* ☎ *971/188150 or 659/577760* 🌐 *www.windfornells.com*) rents boards, dinghies, and catamarans and gives lessons; it's open May–October.

COVA DES COLOMS

40 km (24 mi) west of Mahón.

The massive Cova Des Coloms (Cave of Pigeons), also known as the Cathedral, is the most spectacular cave on Minorca. Eerie rock formations rise up to a 77-foot-high ceiling. To reach the cave, take the Ferreries road at San Cristóbal and turn up to the primary school; beyond the school the paved road continues for about 3 km (2 mi) toward Binigaus Nou. Leave the car in the designated parking area, climb over the stile, and take the path that follows the right-hand side of the *barranca* (ravine or gully) toward the sea; you'll come to a well-trodden path bearing down into the bottom of the barranca and up the other side. The entrance to the cave is around an elbow, camouflaged by a tree. A flashlight helps.

IBIZA

Settled by the Carthaginians in the 5th century BC, Ibiza has seen successive waves of invasion and occupation—the latest of which began in the 1960s, when it became a tourist destination. With a full-time population of barely 140,000, it now gets some 2 million visitors a year. Blessed with beaches—50 of them, by one count—it also has the world's largest disco, Privilege, with a capacity of 10,000. About 25% of the people who live on Ibiza year-round are foreigners.

From October to April, the pace of life here is decidedly slow, and many of the island's hotels and restaurants are closed. In the 1960s and early 1970s Ibiza was discovered by sun-seeking hippies, eventually emerging as an icon of counterculture chic. Ibizans were—and still are—friendly and tolerant of their eccentric visitors. In the late 1980s and 1990s, club culture took over. Young ravers flocked here from all over the world to dance all night and pack the sands of built-up beach resorts like Sant Antoni. That party-hearty Ibiza is still alive and well, but a new wave of luxury rural hotels, offering oases of peace and privacy, with spas and gourmet restaurants, marks the most recent transformation of the island into a venue for "quality tourism."

GETTING HERE AND AROUND

Ibiza is a 40-minute flight or a nine-hour ferry ride from Barcelona.

Eivissabus serves the island. Buses run every half hour from the new CETIS Intermodal Transportation Services Center in Carrer Canarias in Eivissa to Sant Antoni and Playa d'en Bossa, roughly hourly to Santa Eulalia. Buses from Ibiza to other parts of the island are less frequent, as is the cross-island bus between Sant Antoni and Santa Eulalia. The schedule is published in newspapers.

On Ibiza, a six-lane divided highway connects the capital with the airport and Sant Antoni. Roundabouts and one-way streets make it a bit confusing to get in and out of Eivissa, but out in the countryside driving is easy and remains the only feasible way of getting to some of the island's smaller coves and beaches.

ESSENTIALS

Bus Contact Eivissabus (🌐 *www.eivissabus.info*).

Taxi Contacts Radio-Taxi (✉ *Eivissa* ☎ *971/398483*). **Cooperativa Limitada de Taxis de Sant Antoni** (✉ *Sant Antoni* ☎ *971/340074 or 971/346026*).

Visitor Information Aeropuerto de Ibiza (✉ *Ctra. al Aeropuerto s/n, Sant Josep* ☎ *971/809118*). **Santa Eularia des Riu** (✉ *Carrer Mariano Riquer Wallis 4* ☎ *971/330728*). **Sant Antoni** (✉ *Passeig de Ses Fonts s/n* ☎ *971/343363*).

IBIZA TOWN (EIVISSA)

★ Hedonistic and historic, Eivissa (Ibiza, in Castilian) is a city jam-packed with cafés, nightspots, and trendy shops; looming over it are the massive stone walls of **Dalt Vila**—the medieval city declared a UNESCO World Heritage site in 1999—and its Gothic cathedral. Squeezed between the north walls of the old city and the harbor is **Sa Penya,** a long labyrinth of stone-paved streets that offer some of the city's best offbeat shopping, snacking, and exploring.

ESSENTIALS

Visitor Information Eivissa (✉ *Paseo Vara de Rey 1* ☎ *971/301900*).

EXPLORING

Enter Sa Penya from the west end of Passeig Vara de Rey. Across from the Hotel Montesol, take **Carrer Rimbau** and turn on Carrer Guillem Montgri to the **Plaça de la Constitució;** the little Hellenic-looking building in the square is the town's open-air produce market. Beyond it, a ramp leads up to the **Portal de Ses Taules,** the main gate of **Dalt Vila,** the walled upper town.

Inside Dalt Vila, the ramp continues to the right between the outer and inner walls and opens into Sa Carroza, a long, narrow plaza lined with boutiques and sidewalk cafés. A little way up, a sign points left toward the **Museu d'Art Contemporani**, above the gateway arch. ✉ *Ronda Pintor Narcis Putget s/n* ☎ *971/302723* 🎫 *€2, Sun. free* ⏲ *Oct.–Apr.,*

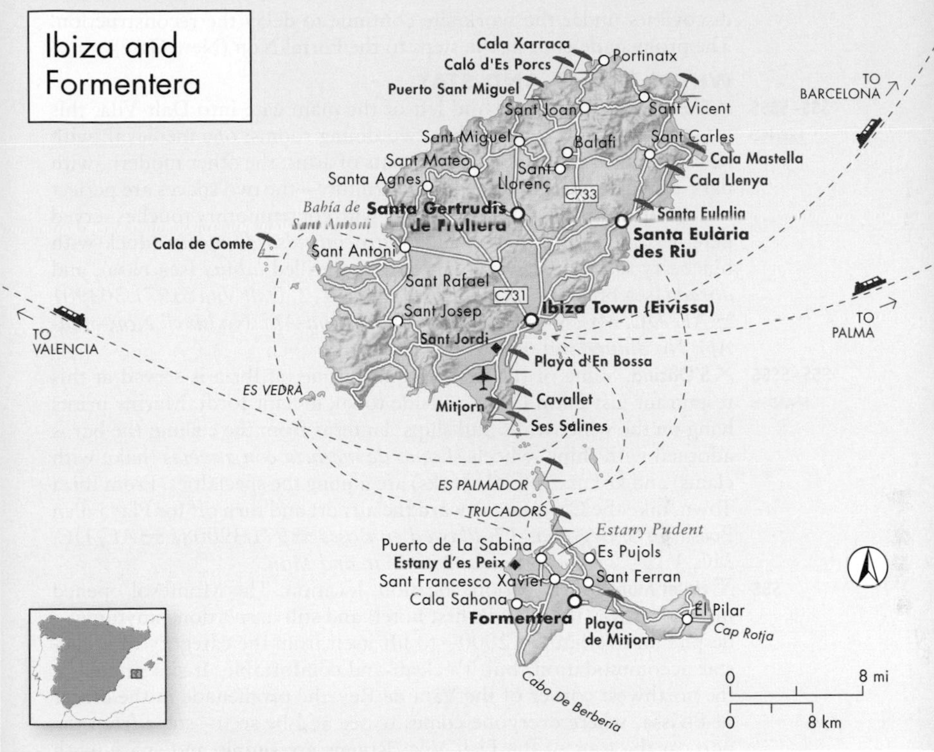

Tues.–Fri. 10–1:30 and 4–6, weekends 10–1:30; May–Sept., Tues.–Fri. 10–1:30 and 5–8, weekends 10–1:30.

Uphill from the museum, on the left, the wide **Bastió de Santa Llúcia** (Bastion of Ste. Lucia) has a panoramic view.

Wind your way up past the 16th-century church of **Sant Domingo** (✉ *Carrer de Balanzat*), its roof an irregular landscape of tile domes, and turn right in front of the *ajuntament* (town hall), housed in the church's former monastery. From the church of Sant Domingo, follow any of the streets or steps leading uphill to Carrer Obispo Torres (Carrer Major). (Don't worry about losing your way: aim uphill for the cathedral, downhill for the gate.) The **cathedral** is on the site of religious structures from each of the cultures that have ruled Ibiza since the Phoenicians. Built in the 13th and 14th centuries and renovated in the 18th century, it has a Gothic tower and a baroque nave. ✉ *Carrer Major* ☎ *971/312774* ⏲ *Weekdays 10–1, Sun. 10:30–noon.*

Behind the cathedral, from the **Bastió de Sant Bernat** *(Bastion of St. Bernard)*, a promenade with sea views runs west to the bastions of Sant Jordi and Sant Jaume, past the **Castell**—a fortress formerly used as an army barracks, turned over to the city of Ibiza in 1973. In 2007 work began to transform it into a 70-room luxury parador, but archaeological discoveries under the work site continue to delay the reconstruction. The promenade ends at the steps to the **Portal Nou** (New Gate).

WHERE TO EAT AND STAY

$$$–$$$$ FRENCH ✕ **El Portalón**. Just inside and left of the main gate into Dalt Vila, this intimate French restaurant has two dining rooms; one medieval, with heavy beams, antiques, oils, and coats of arms; the other modern, with dark-orange walls and sleek black furniture—the two spaces are perfect metaphors for the traditional cuisine with contemporary touches served here. Excellent offerings include *pato con salsa de moras* (duck with blueberry sauce), *solomillo* (sirloin) and grilled *lubina* (sea bass), and *dorada* (sea bream). ✉ *Pl. Desamparados 1–2, Dalt Vila* ☎ *971/303901* ▭ *AE, DC, MC, V* ⏲ *Closed Sun. Nov.–mid-Apr. No lunch Nov.–mid-Apr. No dinner Sun. mid-Apr.–Oct.*

$$$–$$$$ SPANISH ✕ **S'Oficina**. Some of the best Basque cuisine on Ibiza is served at this restaurant just 2 km (1 mi) outside town, in Sant Jordi. Marine prints hang on the white walls and ships' lanterns from the ceiling; the bar is adorned with ships' wheels. *Lomo de merluza con almejas* (hake with clams) and *kokotxas* (cod cheeks) are among the specialties. From Ibiza Town, take the Carretera toward the airport and turn off for Playa d'en Bossa. ✉ *C. Begonias 17, Playa d'en Bossa* ☎ *971/390081* ▭ *AE, DC, MC, V* ⏲ *Closed weekends Oct.–Mar. and Mon.*

$$$ **Hotel Montesol**. Location, location, location. The Montesol opened in 1934 (it was the island's first hotel) and still hasn't done anything—despite an overhaul in 2000—to lift itself from the category of a one-star accommodation, but it's clean and comfortable. It sits smack on the northwest corner of the Vara de Rey, the promenade in the center of Eivissa, where everyone comes to see and be seen—steps from the port, at the foot of the Dalt Vila. Rooms are simple and spare, with bare, white tile floors and flower-print bedspreads mismatched to plaid drapes. Only four rooms have double beds: the rest are twins and singles. Fashion photographers love the balconies facing the promenade. **Pros:** value for price; convenient; good for meeting people. **Cons:** noisy; small rooms; minimal amenities. ✉ *Paseo Vara de Rey 2* ☎ *971/310161* 🌐 *www.hotelmontesol.com* *55 rooms* *In-room: safe. In-hotel: restaurant* ▭ *MC, V* *BP.*

$$$ **La Ventana**. Inside the medieval walls, this intimate hillside hotel is within a 10-minute stroll of the port. Rooms are painted in soothing pastel blues and yellows; all have beds draped in white canopies. The little roof terrace offers a chill-out space with Moroccan-style sofas; rooms on the third floor have fine views of the old town and the harbor. **Pros:** historic setting is charming; good value. **Cons:** rooms are small; lots of stairs to climb; surroundings can be noisy until the wee hours. ✉ *Sa Carrossa 13* ☎ *971/390857* 🌐 *www.laventanaibiza.com* *2 suites, 12 rooms* *In-room: safe, refrigerator, Wi-Fi. In-hotel: restaurant, room service, laundry service, Internet terminal, Wi-Fi hotspot, some pets allowed* ▭ *AE, MC, V.*

NIGHTLIFE

Fodor's Choice ★ **Ibiza's discos** are famous throughout Europe. Keep your eyes open during the day for free invitations handed out on the street—these can save you expensive entry fees. Also note that a handy, all-night "Discobus"

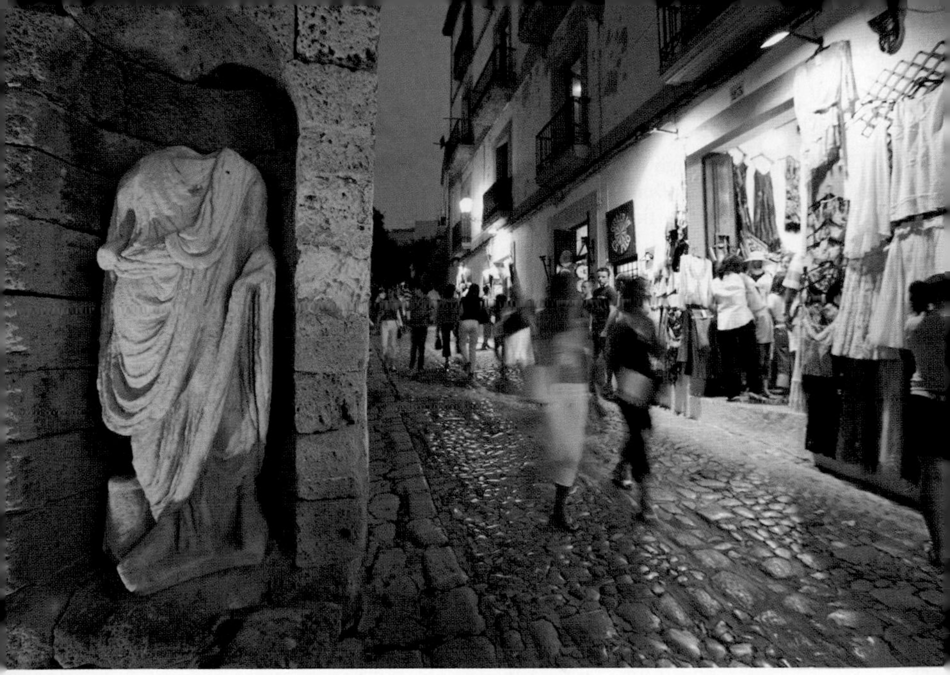

An evening stroll among the shops in Ibiza town.

service (☎ *971/192456*) runs June–September between Eivissa, Sant Antoni, Santa Eulalia, and the major party venues (midnight–7; €3 one-way, €12 for a five-trip ticket). As a rule, the clubs open in mid-June and close in late September, though some have special parties on New Year's Eve.

Down in the town, the trendy place to start the evening is **Keeper** (✉ *Paseo Marítimo s/n, Ibiza Nueva* ☎ *971/310509*), where you can sip your drink sitting on a carousel horse. A lively, very young scene rocks **El Divino Café** (✉ *Carrer Lluís Turi Palau 10* ☎ *971/311016*). In summer, boats depart between 1 AM and 4 AM from in front of El Divino Café for the marina and **El Divino Disco** (✉ *Puerto Deportivo, Ibiza Nueva* ☎ *971/318338* 🌐 *www.eldivino-ibiza.com*), which is a typical Ibiza disco with throbbing dance music (and spectacular views of Ibiza Town). The "in" place for older nighthawks is the stylish bar in the foyer of the former **Teatre Pereira** (✉ *Carrer Roselló 3* ☎ *971/191468*). A young, international crowd dances to techno at **Pacha** (✉ *Av. 8 de Agosto s/n* ☎ *971/313612* 🌐 *www.pacha.com*). The popular **Amnesia San Rafael** (✉ *Ctra. Sant Antoni, opposite Km 5 marker* ☎ *971/198041*) has several ample dance floors that throb to house and funk. **Privilege** (✉ *Ctra. Ibiza–Sant Antoni, Km 7, San Rafael* ☎ *971/198086*) is the grande dame of Ibiza's nightlife, with a giant dance floor, a swimming pool, and more than a dozen bars. **Space** (✉ *Playa d'en Bossa s/n* ☎ *971/396793* 🌐 *www.space-ibiza.es*) is where the serious clubbers come to dance "after hours."

The **Casino de Ibiza** is a small gaming club with roulette tables, blackjack, and slots. You need your passport to enter. ✉ *Paseo de Juan Carlos I s/n*

☎ *971/313312* 🌐 *www.casinoibiza.com* 🎫 *€5 1st visit, free subsequent visits* ⏲ *Weekdays 6 PM–5 AM, weekends 6 PM–6 AM.*

Gay nightlife converges on **Carrer de la Verge**, in **Sa Penya**. The popular gay bar **Dome** (✉ *Carrer Alfonso XII* ☎ *971/317456*) has a leafy terrace that overflows with revelers in summer.

SPORTS AND THE OUTDOORS

For information on sports on Ibiza and Formentera, obtain a free copy of the magazine **Touribisport**, available locally.

BOATING Explore Ibiza by sea with **Coral Yachting** (✉ *Marina Botafoc, Eivissa* ☎ *971/313926* 🌐 *www.coralyachting.com*). **Ibiza Azul** (✉ *Ctra. Sant Joan, Km 8* ☎ *971/325264* 🌐 *www.ibizazul.com*) has motorboats and Jet Skis for rent, as well as a 12-meter live-aboard sailboat for weekend or week-long charters.

CYCLING **Extra Rent** (✉ *Av. Santa Eulalia 25–27/ Estación Marítimo* ☎ *971/191717*) has mountain bikes and scooters for rent.

GOLF Ibiza's only 18-hole course is **Golf de Ibiza** (✉ *Ctra. Jesús–Cala Llonga, Km 6, Santa Eulària* ☎ *971/196118*). Greens fees are €90 a day.

HIKING ETC. **Ecoibiza** (✉ *Av. de Juan Carlos I, Edificio Transat, Local 10, Ibiza Ciutat* ☎ *971/302347* 🌐 *www.ecoibiza.com*) while primarily a realty agency, can arrange a variety of ecologically friendly countryside hikes as well as horseback riding, sailing, and sea fishing.

HORSEBACK RIDING **Can Mayans** (✉ *Ctra. Santa Gertrudis a Sant Lorenç, Km 3* ☎ *971/187388*) has horses for hire for rides along the coast and inland.

SCUBA DIVING Year-round a team with a decompression chamber is on standby at the **Policlínica de Nuestra Señora del Rosario** (✉ *Via Romana s/n* ☎ *971/301916*).

Go scuba diving in Sant Antoní with **Centro de Buceo Sirena** (✉ *Balanzat 21 bajo, Sant Antoní* ☎ *971/342966*). Dive in Sant Joan with **Centro Subfari** (✉ *Cala Portinatx, San Joan* ☎ *689/253001*). **Diving Center San Miguel** (✉ *Apartado 17, Puerto de San Miguel* ☎ *971/334539* 🌐 *www.divingcenter-sanmiguel.com*) also offers diving. **Active Generation** (✉ *Edifici Faro II, Local 10, Pasea Marítimo, San Antoní* ☎ *971/341344* 🌐 *www.active-generation.com*) offers instruction and guided dives, as well as kayaking, parasailing, and boat rentals. Rent scuba gear in Eivissa at **Vellmari** (✉ *Marina Botafoc, Local 10* ☎ *971/192884* 🌐 *www.vellmari.com*).

TENNIS **Ibiza Club de Campo** (✉ *Ctra. Sant Josep, Km 2.5* ☎ *971/300088* 🌐 *www.ibizaclubdecampo.org*), with six clay and two composition courts, is the largest tennis club on the island. Nonmembers can play here for €6.40 per hour. There are public tennis courts at **Port Sant Miquel**.

SHOPPING

Although the Sa Penya area of Eivissa still has a few designer boutiques, much of the area is now home to the so-called hippie market, with stalls selling clothing and craftwork of all sorts May to October from 5 PM to well past midnight. For trendy casual gear, sandals, belts, and bags, try **Ibiza Republic** (✉ *Carrer Antoni Mar 15* ☎ *971/314175*). For wines and spirits, visit **Enotecum** (✉ *Av. d'Isidoro Macabich 43* ☎ *971/399167*).

SANTA EULÀRIA DES RIU

15 km (9 mi) northeast of Ibiza.

At the edge of this town on the island's eastern coast, to the right below the road, a Roman bridge crosses what is claimed to be the only permanent river in the Balearics (hence "des Riu," or "of the River"). The town itself follows the curve of a long sandy beach, a few blocks deep with restaurants, shops, and holiday apartments. From here it's a 10-minute drive to Sant Carles and the open-air hippie market held there every Saturday morning.

ESSENTIALS

Bike Rentals Kandani (✉ *Ctra. Es Canar 109, Santa Eulària des Riu* ☎ *971/339264*).

WHERE TO EAT AND STAY

$$ ITALIAN ✕ **Mezzanotte.** This charming little portside restaurant has just 12 tables inside, softly lit with candles and track lighting; in summer, seating expands to an interior patio and tables on the sidewalk. The kitchen prides itself on hard-to-find fresh ingredients flown in from Italy. The linguine with jumbo shrimp, saffron, and zucchini or with *bottarga* (dried and salted mullet roe from Sardinia) is wonderful. Value for price here is excellent; the prix-fixe menu, served at dinner in summer and lunch in winter, is an absolute bargain. ✉ *Paseo de s'Alamera 22, Santa Eulària* ☎ *971/319498* ▭ *AE, MC, V* ⊗ *Closed Jan., Feb., and Mon. No lunch June–Aug.*

$$$$ Fodor's Choice ★ **Can Curreu.** The traditional Ibizan architecture here feels a lot like a Greek-island village: a cluster of low buildings with thick whitewashed walls, the edges and corners gently rounded off. Each accommodation at Can Curreu has one of these buildings to itself, with a private patio, artfully separated from its neighbors. Rooms have comfortable, deep sofas, upholstered in orange-red and yellow, built-in pine cupboard closets, and red-brown tile floors: the overall effect is supremely soothing. Suites have fireplaces and Jacuzzi tubs. The hotel has its own stables and orange and lemon groves. The Can Curreu restaurant ($$$–$$$$) (closed Monday in winter) serves an excellent five-course tasting menu. Mick Jagger and his family stayed here. No satisfaction? Hard to believe. **Pros:** superbly designed for privacy; friendly, efficient staff; horses; airport pick up. **Cons:** restaurant is pricey. ✉ *Ctra. de Sant Carles, Km 12, Santa Eulària* ☎ *971/335280* 🌐 *www.cancurreu.com* *4 rooms, 13 suites* *In-room: safe, kitchen (some), refrigerator, DVD(some), Wi-Fi. In-hotel: restaurant, room service, bar, 3 pools, gym, spa, bicycles, laundry service, Wi-Fi hotspot, parking (free)* ▭ *AE, MC, V* 🍽 *BP.*

$$$$ ★ **Can Gall.** In 2001 owner Santi Marí Ferrer remodeled his family *finca* (farmhouse)—with its massive stone walls and native *savina* wood beams—into one of the friendliest and most comfortable *agroturisme* country inns on the island. Rooms are huge; original stone arches separate sleeping from bathing areas. Oranges, lemons, olives, fresh produce, meat, and eggs all come from the family farm. The 25-meter pool has an access ramp for guests with disabilities. Relax in the pergola at sunset with a view of the mountains and nurse a glass of Santi's

9

homemade five-year-old *ierbas* (herb liqueur). **Pros:** family-friendly; espresso maker in the room; big, fluffy terry-cloth robes. **Cons:** 15-minute drive to nearest good beaches. ✉ *Crta. Sant Joan Km 17.2, Sant Lorenç* ☎ *971/337031 or 670/876054* 🌐 *www.agrocangall.com* *2 rooms, 7 suites* *In-room: safe (some), refrigerator, DVD (some), Internet, Wi-Fi. In-hotel: restaurant, room service, bar, pool, spa, bicycles, laundry service, Internet terminal, Wi-Fi hotspot, parking (free)* *DC, MC, V* *BP.*

SANTA GERTRUDIS DE FRUITERA

15 km (9 mi) north of Eivissa.

Blink and you miss it: that's true of most of the small towns in the island's interior and especially so of Santa Gertrudis, not much more than a bend in the road. But don't blink: Santa Gertrudis is strategic, and it's cute. The town square was renovated in 2008, paved with brick and closed to vehicle traffic—perfect for the sidewalk cafés. From here, you are only a few minutes' drive from some of the island's flat-out best resort hotels and spas and the most beautiful secluded north coves and beaches: **S'Illa des Bosc, Benirrás** (where they have drum circles to salute the setting sun), **S'Illot des Renclí, Portinatx, and Caló d'En Serra.** Artists and expats like it here: they've given the town an appeal that now makes for listings of half a million dollars or more for a modest two-bedroom chalet.

WHERE TO EAT AND STAY

$$$ SPANISH ✕ **Can Caus.** Ibiza might pride itself on its seafood, but there comes a time for meat and potatoes. When it arrives, take the 20-minute drive to the outskirts of Santa Gertrudis to this informal, family-style roadside restaurant and feast on skewers of barbecued *sobrasada* (soft pork sausage), goat chops, lamb kebabs, or grilled sweetbreads with red peppers, onions, and eggplant. Most people eat at the long wooden tables on the terrace. ✉ *Ctra. Sant Miquel, Km 3.5, Santa Gertrudis* ☎ *971/197516* *AE, MC, V* *Closed Mon. Sept.–June.*

$$$$ ★ **Cas Gasí.** With splendid views of Ibiza's one and only mountain, the 1,567-foot Sa Talaiassa, this lovely late-19th-century manor house is surrounded by hills of olive trees, redolent of Tuscany. Privacy—the sort that draws people like Richard Gere and Claudia Schiffer—is key here: there's a monitored gate at the driveway, and the restaurant and spa are exclusively for guests. Airy, rustic rooms with wood-beam ceilings are gracefully furnished; bathrooms have Moroccan-style tiling. One hitch: a minimum five-night stay is required in July and August. **Pros:** attentive personal service; peace and quiet' sailing charters arranged. **Cons:** 15-minute drive to the nearest good beaches; not particularly geared to families. ✉ *Cami Vell a Sant Mateu s/n, Santa Gertrudis* ☎ *971/197700* 🌐 *www.casgasi.com* *9 double rooms, 1 suite* *In-room: safe, kitchen (some), refrigerator, DVD, Wi-Fi. In-hotel: restaurant, room service, bar, 2 pools, gym, spa, bicycles, laundry service, Internet terminal, Wi-Fi hotspot, parking (free), some pets allowed* *AE, DC, MC, V* *BP.*

QUICK BITES

Bar Costa (✉ *Pl. de la Iglesia s/n, Santa Gertrudis* ☎ *971/197021*) **is just the right place to sit out under the awning with a coffee and croissant or a** ***bocadillo*** **(sandwich) and contemplate your next move. Inclement weather? The back room has a fireplace, and the walls are covered with funny, irreverent modern art from the owner's collection.**

SHOPPING

te Cuero (✉ *Pl. de la Iglesia s/n, Santa Gertrudis* ☎ *971/197100* ⏲ *Mon.–Sat. 11–1:30 and 5–8*) specializes in hand-tooled leather bags and belts with great designer buckles.

FORMENTERA

Much of Formentera is strictly protected from the rampant development that plagues the other islands, so it's a calm respite from Ibiza's dance-'til-you-drop madness. Though it does get crowded in the summer, the island's long white-sand beaches are among the finest in the Mediterranean; inland, you can explore quiet country roads by bicycle in relative solitude.

From the port at La Sabina, it's only 3 km (2 mi) to Formentera's capital, **Sant Françesc Xavier,** a few yards off the main road. There's an active hippie market in the small plaza in front of the church. At the main road, turn right toward Sant Ferran, 2 km (1 mi) away. Beyond Sant Ferran the road travels 7 km (4 mi) along a narrow isthmus, staying slightly closer to the rougher northern side, where the waves and rocks keep yachts—and thus much of the tourist trade—away.

The plateau on the island's east side ends at the lighthouse **Faro de la Mola.** Nearby is a **monument to Jules Verne,** who set part of his novel *Journey Through the Solar System* in Formentera. The rocks around the lighthouse are carpeted with purple thyme and sea holly in spring and fall.

Back on the main road, turn right at Sant Ferran toward Es Pujols. The few hotels here are the closest Formentera comes to beach resorts, even if the beach is not the best. Beyond Es Pujols the road skirts **Estany Pudent,** one of two lagoons that almost enclose La Sabina. Salt was once extracted from Pudent, hence its name, which means "stinking pond," although the pond now smells fine. At the northern tip of Pudent, a road to the right leads to a footpath that runs the length of **Trucadors,** a narrow sand spit. The long, windswept beaches here are excellent.

GETTING HERE AND AROUND

Formentera is a one-hour ferry ride from Ibiza, or 25 minutes on the jet ferry. Both Balearia and Iscomar operate ferry services to Formentera from Ibiza and Denia, the nearest landfall on the Spanish mainland.

On Ibiza, Santa Eulalia and Sant Antoni also run ferries to Formentera's La Sabina (one hour, €23) as well as numerous ferries to the coves and *calas* on the east and west coasts of Ibiza. Day-trippers can go to Formentera for lunch and a few hours in the sun before heading back to Ibiza to plug into the nightlife. If you plan to picnic, buy supplies in Ibiza. La Sabina has several car-, bicycle-, and moped-rental agencies.

A very limited bus service connects Formentera's villages, shrinking to one bus each way between San Francisco and Pilar on Saturday and disappearing altogether on Sunday and holidays.

ESSENTIALS

Ferry Contacts Balearia (*www.balearia.com*). **Iscomar** (*www.iscomar.com*).

Taxi Information Parada de Taxis La Sabina (*La Sabina 971/322002 Es Pujols 971/332016*).

Visitor Information Formentera (*Carrer Calpe s/n, Port de La Sabina 971/322057*).

WHERE TO EAT AND STAY

$$–$$$ SEAFOOD **Sa Palmera.** On the beachfront in Es Pujols, Sa Palmera is known for its rice dishes and the extremely fresh fish served in the garden or on the terrace overlooking the beach. Specialties include the grilled *dorada* (gilthead bream) and *lubina* (sea bass), while the *frito de sepia* (fried cuttlefish) and the *parrillada,* a mixed grill of three types of fish cooked over coals (depending on the catch of the day) served with potatoes and a salad are house favorites. *Calle Aguadulce 15–31, Es Pujols 971/328356 MC, V Closed Mon. and last Fri. of Oct.–1st Fri. of Mar.*

SHOPPING

El Pilar is the chief crafts village here. Stores and workshops sell handmade items, including bags, ceramics, jewelry, and leather goods. El Pilar's crafts market draws shoppers on Sunday afternoon, May–September, and also Wednesday from June through August. From May through September, crafts are sold in the morning at the San Françesc Xavier market and in the evening in Es Pujols.

SPORTS AND THE OUTDOORS

You can rent bikes and motorcycles at the port in La Sabina at **Moto Rent Mitjorn** (*971/322306 or 696/014292*).

DIVING You can take diving courses at **Vell Marí** (*Puerto Deportivo Marina de Formentera, Local 14–16, La Sabina 971/322105*).

Andalusia

10

WORD OF MOUTH

"Sevilla: A maze of history and neighborhoods that date back more than 2000 years . . . Giant palm trees, the smell of orange blossoms through the air and the warm sun blanket this enchanting place. Life's road is too short and the world to small to say I will be back soon but a piece of Sevilla will always be with us."

—johnb

Join, Ask, Share. www.fodors.com/community/

WELCOME TO ANDALUSIA

TOP REASONS TO GO

★ **Arabian romance:** Soak in the history and drama of Granada's exquisite Alhambra.

★ **Flamenco:** Olé deep into the night at a heel-clicking flamenco performance in Jerez de la Frontera, the "cradle of flamenco."

★ **Priceless paintings:** Bask in the golden age of Spanish art at Seville's Museo de Bellas Artes.

★ **Exquisite architecture:** Marvel at the marble, granite, and onyx of Córdoba's Mezquita.

★ **Tempting tapas:** Try a little bit of everything on an evening tapas crawl.

★ **Tumultuous fiestas:** Celebrate Semana Santa (Holy Week) with rich festivities in Granada, Cordóba, or Seville.

★ **Ancient glory:** Explore Cádiz, believed to be the oldest port in Europe, resplendent with its sumptuous architecture and a magnificent cathedral.

★ **White villages:** Enjoy the simple beauty of a bygone age by exploring the gleaming white *pueblos blancos*.

1 Seville. Long Spain's chief riverine port, the captivating town of Seville sits astride the Guadalquivir River, which launched Christopher Columbus to the New World and Ferdinand Magellan around the globe. South of the capital is fertile farmland; in the north are highland villages. Don't miss stunning, mountaintop Ronda, nearby, which has plenty of atmosphere and memorable sights.

2 Huelva. Famed as live oak–forested grazing grounds for the treasured *cerdo ibérico* (Iberian pig), Huelva's Sierra de Aracena is a fresh and leafy mountain getaway on the border of Portugal. The province's Doñana National Park is one of Spain's greatest national treasures.

GETTING ORIENTED

Andalusia is infinitely varied and diverse within its apparent unity. Seville and Granada are like feuding sisters, one vivaciously flirting, the other darkly brooding; Córdoba and Cádiz are estranged cousins, one landlocked, the other virtually under sail; Huelva is a verdant Atlantic Arcadia; and Jaén is an upland country bumpkin—albeit one with Renaissance palaces—compared with the steamy cosmopolitan seaport of Málaga, all of which, along with the southern Andalusian cities and towns of Marbella, and Ronda, are covered in the Costas chapter.

3 Cádiz Province and Jerez de la Frontera. Almost completely surrounded by water, the city of Cádiz is Western Europe's oldest continually inhabited city, a dazzling bastion at the edge of the Atlantic. Jerez de la Frontera is known for its sherry, flamenco, and equestrian culture.

4 Córdoba. A center of world science and philosophy in the 9th and 10th centuries, Córdoba is a living monument to its past glory. Its prized building is the Mezquita (Mosque). In the countryside, acorns and olives thrive.

5 Jaén. Andalusia's northwesternmost province is a striking contrast of olive groves, pristine wilderness, and Renaissance towns with elegant palaces and churches.

6 Granada. Christian and Moorish cultures are dramatically counterposed in Granada, especially in the graceful enclave of the Alhambra.

ANDALUSIA PLANNER

When to Go

The best months to go to Andalusia are October and November and April and May. It's blisteringly hot in the summer, so, if that's your only chance to come, plan time in the Sierra de Aracena in Huelva, the Pedroches of northern Córdoba province, Granada's Sierra Nevada and Alpujarras highlands, or the Sierra de Cazorla in Jaén to beat the heat. Autumn catches the cities going about their business, the temperatures are moderate, and you will rarely see a line form.

December through March tends to be cool, uncrowded, and quiet, but come spring, it's fiesta time, with Seville's Semana Santa (Holy Week, between Palm Sunday and Easter) the most moving and multitudinous. April showcases whitewashed Andalusia at its floral best, every patio and facade covered with flowers from bougainvillea to honeysuckle.

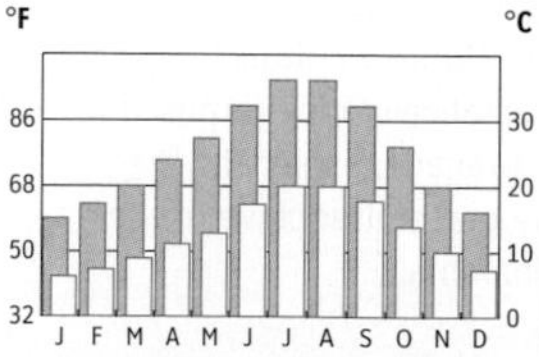

Fiesta Fun

Carnival, on the days leading up to Ash Wednesday, and **Semana Santa** (Holy Week, between Palm Sunday and Easter) are big celebrations, especially in Córdoba, Seville, and Cádiz

Córdoba's **Festival de los Patios** (Patio Festival) during the second week of May is fun to take part in; the **Concurso Nacional de Flamenco** (National Flamenco Competition) is also during the second week of May, but only every third year. The city's annual **Feria de Mayo** is the city's main street party, held during the last week of May.

In Seville, the secular **Feria de Abril**, focuses on horses and bullfights.

May is Córdoba's **Cruces de Mayo** (Festival of Crosses) and its floral patio competition.

Early June in Huelva means the gypsy favorite, the **Romería del Rocío** festival, a pilgrimage on horseback and carriage to the hermitage of la Virgen del Rocío (Our Lady of the Dew).

From mid-June to mid-July is Granada's **Festival Internacional de Música y Danza de Granada** (🌐 *www.granadafestival.org*), with some events in the Alhambra itself.

The **International Guitar Festival** brings major artists to Córdoba in early July.

Early August showcases **horse races** on the beaches of Sanlúcar de Barrameda.

May and September are the most exciting times to visit Jerez: for the **Feria del Caballo** (Horse Fair), in early May, carriages and riders fill the streets, and purebreds from the School of Equestrian Art compete in races and dressage displays. September brings the **Fiesta de Otoño** (Autumn Festival), when the first of the grape harvest is blessed on the steps of the cathedral.

Jaén celebrates the **olive harvest** in the second week of October.

November is the time for Granada's **Festival Internacional de Jazz de Granada** (🌐 *www.jazzgranada.net*).

Early December means Granada's **Encuentro Flamenco** festival, which attracts some of the country's best performers.

About the Restaurants and Hotels

Many restaurants are closed Sunday night; some close for all of August.

Seville has grand old hotels, such as the Alfonso XIII, and a number of former palaces converted into sumptuous hostelries.

The Parador de Granada, next to the Alhambra, is a magnificent way to enjoy Granada. Hotels on the Alhambra hill, especially the parador, must be reserved long in advance. Lodging establishments in Granada's city center, around the Puerta Real and Acera del Darro, can be unbelievably noisy, so if you're staying there, ask for a room toward the back. Though Granada has plenty of hotels, it can be difficult to find lodging during peak tourist season (Easter to late October).

In Córdoba, several pleasant hotels occupy houses in the old quarter, close to the mosque. Other than during Holy Week and the May Patio Festival, it's easy to find a room in Córdoba, even without a prior reservation.

WHAT IT COSTS (IN EUROS)

	¢	$	$$	$$$	$$$$
Restaurants	under €8	€8–€12	€13–€17	€18–€22	over €22
Hotels	under €60	€60–€90	€91–€125	€126–€180	over €180

Prices are per person for a main course at dinner, and for two people in a standard double room in high season, excluding tax.

Planning Your Time

A week in Andalusia should include visits to Córdoba, Seville, and Granada to see, respectively, the Mezquita, the cathedral and its Giralda minaret, and the Alhambra. Two days in each city nearly fills the week, though the extra day would be best spent in Seville, Andalusia's most vibrant concentration of art, architecture, culture, and excitement.

Indeed, a week or more in Seville alone would be ideal, especially during the Semana Santa celebration, when the city becomes a giant street party. With more time on your hands, Cádiz, Jerez de la Frontera, and Sanlúcar de Barrameda form a three- or four-day jaunt through flamenco, sherry, Andalusian equestrian culture, and tapas emporiums.

A three-day trip through the Sierra de Aracena will introduce you to a lovely Atlantic upland, filled with Mediterranean black pigs deliciously fattened on acorns, while the Alpujarras, the mountain range east of Granada, is famed for its *pueblos blancos* (villages of whitewashed houses). In this region you can find anywhere from three days to a week of hiking and trekking opportunities in some of the country's highest and wildest reaches. For nature enthusiasts, the highland Cazorla National Park and the wetland Doñana National Park are Andalusia's highest and lowest outdoor treasures.

10

GETTING HERE AND AROUND

By Air

Andalusia's regional airports can be reached via Spain's domestic flights or from major European hubs. Málaga Airport (*see the Costa del Sol and Costa de Almería chapter*) is one of Spain's major hubs and a good access point for exploring this part of Andalusia.

The region's second-largest airport, after Málaga, is in Seville. The smaller Aeropuerto de Jerez is 7 km (4 mi) northeast of Jerez on the road to Seville; there's no public transport into Jerez so you have to take a taxi (approximately €22).

By Taxi

Taxis are plentiful throughout Andalusia and may be hailed on the street or from specified taxi stands. Fares are reasonable, and meters are strictly used; the minimum fare is about €4. You are not required to tip taxi drivers, although rounding off the amount is appreciated.

In Seville or Granada, expect to pay around €20-€25 for cab fare from the airport to the city center.

Sports Tours

Rustic Blue organizes walking and riding excursions in Andalusia and is a good resource for villa rentals in the area.

Rustic Blue (✉ *Barrio de la Ermita, Bubión* ☎ *958/763381* 🌐 *www.rusticblue.com*).

Based in the Alpujarras, **Nevadensis** (✉ *Pl. de la Libertad, Pampaneira* ☎ *958/763127* 🌐 *www.nevadensis.com*) leads guided tours of the Alpujarras region on bike, foot, and horseback.

In Granada, **Sólo Aventura** (✉ *Pl. de la Romanilla 1, Centro, Granada* ☎ *958/804937* 🌐 *www.soloaventura.com*) offers one-to-seven-day outdoor sports—trekking, mountaineering, climbing, mountain biking, and other activities—around the Alpujarras, Sierra Nevada, and the rest of the province.

Kayak Sur (✉ *Calle Arabial, Urbanizació Parque del Genil, Edificio Topacio, Sur, Granada* ☎ *958/523118* 🌐 *www.kayaksur.com*) organizes kayaking and canoeing trips to the Guadalfeo River. **Granada Romántica/ Grupo Al Andalus** (✉ *Calle Santa Ana 16, Granada* ☎ *958/805481* 🌐 *www.grupoalandalus.com*) takes up to five people in balloon trips above the city of Granada.

Excursiones Bujarkay (☎ *953/721111* 🌐 *www.guiasnativos.com*) leads guided hikes as well as horseback and four-wheel-drive tours in the Sierra de Cazorla.

In Zuheros, the **Alúa** (✉ *Calle Horno 3, Zuheros* ☎ *957/694527* 🌐 *www.aluactiva.com*) can help you with planning and getting the equipment for hiking, rock climbing, mountain biking, caving, and other active sports. **Cabalgar Rutas Alternativas** (✉ *Calle Bubión, Bubión, Alpujarras* ☎ *958/763135* 🌐 *www.ridingandalucia.com*) is an established Alpujarras equestrian agency. **Dallas Love** (✉ *Ctra. de la Sierra, Bubión, Alpujarras* ☎ *958/763038* 🌐 *www.spain-horse-riding.com*) offers trail rides for up to 10 days in the Alpujarras. The price includes overnight stays and most meals.

By Car

If you're planning to explore beyond Seville, Granada, and Córdoba, a car makes travel convenient.

The main road from Madrid is the A4/E5 through Córdoba to Seville, a four-lane *autovía* (highway). From Granada or Málaga, head for Antequera, then take A92 *autovía* by way of Osuna to Seville. Road trips from Seville to Córdoba, Granada, and the Costa del Sol (by way of Ronda) are slow but scenic. Driving in western Andalusia is easy—the terrain is mostly flat land or slightly hilly, and the roads are straight. From Seville to Jerez and Cádiz, the A4/E5 toll road gets you to Cádiz in under an hour. The only way to access Doñana National Park by road is to take the A49/E1 Seville–Huelva highway, exit for Almonte/Bollullos par del Condado, then follow the signs for El Rocío and Matalascañas. The A49/E1 west of Seville will also lead you to the freeway to Portugal and the Algarve. There are some beautiful scenic drives here about which the respective tourist offices can advise you. The A369 (also known as C341), heading southwest from Ronda to Gaucín, passes through stunning whitewashed villages.

With the exception of parts of the Alpujarras, most roads in this region are smooth, and touring by car is one of the most enjoyable ways to see the countryside. Local tourist offices can advise about scenic drives. One good route heads northwest from Seville on the N433 passing through stunning scenery; turn northeast on the N435 to Santa Olalla de Cala to the village of Zufre, dramatically set at the edge of a gorge. Backtrack and continue on to Aracena. Return via the Minas de Riotinto (signposted from Aracena), which will bring you back to the N433 heading east to Seville.

Rental contacts Autopro (✉ *Málaga* ☎ *952/176030* 🌐 *www.autopro.es*). **Crown Car Hire** (☎ *952/176486* 🌐 *www.crowncarhire.com*).

By Boat and Ferry

From Cádiz, Trasmediterránea operates ferry services to the Canary Islands with stops at Las Palmas de Gran Canaria (39 hours) and connecting ferries on to La Palma (8 hours) and Santa Cruz de Tenerife (6½ hours). There are no direct ferries from Seville.

Contact Acciona Trasmediterránea (✉ *Estación Marítima* ☎ *956/227421 or 902/454645* 🌐 *www.trasmediterranea.es*).

By Train

From Madrid, the best approach to Andalusia is via the high-speed AVE. In just 2½ hours, the spectacular ride winds through olive groves and rolling fields of Castile to Córdoba and on to Seville.

Seville, Córdoba, Jerez, and Cádiz all lie on the main rail line from Madrid to southern Spain. Trains leave Madrid for Seville (via Córdoba) almost hourly; two of the non-AVE trains continue to Jerez and Cádiz. Travel time from Seville to Cádiz is 1½ to 2 hours. Trains also depart regularly for Barcelona (three daily, 11 hours), Cáceres (one daily, 6 hours), and Huelva (four daily, 1½ hours). From Granada, Málaga, Ronda, and Algeciras, trains go to Seville via Bobadilla. A daily train connects Málaga and Ronda; travel time is about two hours.

By Bus

The best way to get around Andalusia, if you're not driving, is by bus. Buses serve most small towns and villages and are faster and more frequent than trains. Alsina Gräells is the major regional bus company, but there are also others.

Bus Line Alsina Gräells (☎ *950/238197 in Almería, 957/278100 in Córdoba, 958/185480 in Granada, 953/255014 in Jaén, 95/441–8811 in Seville* 🌐 *www.alsinagraells.net*).

10

EATING AND DRINKING WELL IN ANDALUSIA

Andalusian cuisine, as diverse as the geography of seacoast, farmland, and mountains, is held together by its Moorish aromas. Cumin seed and other Arabian spices, along with sweet-salt combinations, are ubiquitous.

Top left: A cool bowl of gazpacho, with accompaniments to be added as desired. Top right: Crispy fried fish are an Andalusia delicacy. Bottom left: Fried calamari with lemon.

The eight Andalusian provinces cover a wide geographical and culinary spectrum. Superb seafood is at center stage in Cádiz, Puerto de Santa María, and Sanlúcar de Barrameda. *Jamon ibérico de bellota* (Iberian acorn-fed ham) and other Iberico pork products rule from the Sierra de Aracena in Huelva to the Pedroches mountains north of Sevilla. In Sevilla look for products from the Guadalquivir estuary, the Sierra, and the rich Campiña farmland all prepared with great creativity. In Córdoba try *salmorejo cordobés* (a thick gazpacho), *rabo de toro* (oxtail stew), or representatives of the salt-sweet legacy from Córdoba's Moorish heritage such as *cordero con miel* (lamb with honey). Spicy *crema de almendras* (almond soup) is a Granada favorite along with *habas con jamón de Trevélez* (broad beans with ham) from the Alpujarran village of Trevélez.

SHERRY

Dry sherry from Jerez de la Frontera (known as *fino*) and *manzanilla*, sherry from Sanlúcar de Barrameda, share honors as favorite tapas accompaniment. Manzanilla, the generally preferred choice, is fresher and more delicate, with a slight marine tang.

COLD VEGETABLE SOUPS

Spain's most popular contribution to world gastronomy after paella may well be gazpacho, a simple peasant soup served cold and filled with scraps and garden ingredients. Tomatoes, garlic, oil, bread, and chopped peppers are the ingredients, and side plates of chopped onion, peppers, garlic, tomatoes, and croutons accompany, to be added to taste. *Salmorejo cordobés,* a thicker cold vegetable soup with the same ingredients but a different consistency, is used to accompany tapas.

MOORISH FLAVORS

Andalusia's 781-year sojourn at the heart of Al-Andalus, the Moorish empire on the Iberian Peninsula, left as many tastes and aromas as mosques and fortresses. Cumin-laced *adobo de boquerón* (herring) or the salt-sweet *cordero a la miel* (lamb with honey) are two examples, along with coriander-spiked *espinacas con garbanzos* (spinach with garbanzo beans) and *perdiz con dátiles y almendras* (partridge stewed with dates and almonds). Desserts especially reflect the Moorish legacy in morsels such as *pestiños,* cylinders or twists of fried dough in anise-honey syrup.

FRIED FISH

Andalucía is famous for its fried fish, from *pescaito frito* (fried whitebait) to *calamares fritos* (fried squid rings). Masters of deep-frying techniques using very hot olive and vegetable oils that produce

peerlessly crisp, dry *frituras* (fried seafood), much of Andalusia's finest tapas repertory is known for being served up piping hot and crunchy. Look for *tortilla de camarones,* a delicate lacework of tiny fried shrimp.

STEWS

Guisos are combinations of vegetables, with or without meat, cooked slowly over low heat. *Rabo de toro* (bull or oxtail stew) is a favorite throughout Andalusia, though Córdoba claims the origin of this dark and delicious stew made from the tail of a fighting bull. The segments of tail are cleaned, browned, and set aside before leeks, onions, carrots, garlic, and laurel are stewed in the same pan. Cloves, salt, pepper, a liter of wine and a half liter of beef broth are added to the stew with the meat, and it's all simmered for two to three hours until the meat is falling off the bone and thoroughly tenderized. *Alboronía,* also known as *pisto andaluz* is a traditional stew of eggplant, bell peppers, and zucchini traced back to 9th-century Baghdad and brought to Córdoba by the Umayyad dynasty.

ANDALUSIA'S WHITE VILLAGES

Looking a bit like sugar cubes spilled onto a green tablecloth, Andalusia's *pueblos blancos* (white villages) are usually found nestled on densely wooded hills, clinging to the edges of deep gorges, or perched precariously on hilltops.

Top left: The white houses, with their red-tile roofs, are quintessential Andalusia. Top right: The winding streets of Frigiliana can be confusing. Bottom left: Gaucín is an easy trip from Ronda.

The picturesque locations of the *pueblos blancos* usually have more to do with defense than anything else, and many have crumbling walls and fortifications that show their use as defensive structures along the frontier between the Christian and Moorish realms. In a few, the remains of magnificent Moorish castles can be spied. The suffix *de la frontera*, literally meaning "on the frontier," tacked onto a town's name relates to this historical border position. A visit to the white villages gives a glimpse into a simpler time when the economy was based on agriculture, architecture was built to withstand the climate, and life moved at more of a donkey-plod pace. Little wonder that foreign residents are starting to move to these rural communities in a bid to discover a more tranquil life, far from the crowds and clamor of the coast.

PICASSO'S CUBES

It's been suggested that Picasso, who was born in Málaga, was inspired to create Cubism by the *pueblos blancos* of his youth. The story may be apocryphal, but it's nonetheless easy to imagine—there *is* something wondrous and inspiring about Andalusia's whitewashed villages, with their houses that seem to tumble down the mountain slopes like giant dice.

ANDALUSIA'S WHITE VILLAGES

VEJER DE LA FRONTERA
This dazzling white town is perched high on a hill, perfectly positioned to protect its citizens from the threat of marauding pirates. Today it is one of the most charming pueblos blancos on the Cádiz coast, known for its meandering cobbled lanes, narrow arches, and large number of atmospheric bars and restaurants. More recently, Vejer has been popular with an artsy crowd that has brought contemporary art galleries, crafts shops, and low-key music venues.

FRIGILIANA
This impossibly pretty whitewashed village is 7 km (5 mi) north of the well-known resort of Nerja. Despite the encroachment of modern apartment buildings, the old center has remained relatively unchanged. Pots of crimson geraniums decorate the narrow streets, while the bars proudly serve the local sweet wine. Frigiliana is a good place for seeking out ceramics made by the town's craftspeople. Hikers can enjoy the 3-km (2-mi) hike from the old town to the hilltop El Fuerte, site of a 1569 skirmish between the Moors and the Christians *(see Chapter 11)*.

GAUCÍN
The countryside surrounding Ronda is stunning, especially in the spring when the ground is carpeted with wild flowers, including exquisite purple orchids. Not surprisingly, the Serranía de Ronda (as this area is known) is famous for its superb walking. Gaucín is a lovely village crowned by a ruined Moorish castle. It is popular with artists who open their studios to the public each year over a couple of weekends in October. The town also has several excellent restaurants and a couple of sophisticated boutique hotels.

PITRES AND LA TAHA
Granada's Alpujarras mountains are home to some of Andalusia's most unspoiled white villages. Two of the best known are Bubión and Capileira, while Pitres and La Taha villages of Mecina, Mecinilla, Fondales, Ferreirola, and Atalbéitar are lovely hamlets separated by rough tracks that wind through orchards and woodland and set in a valley that attracts few visitors.

GRAZALEMA
About half an hour from Ronda is Grazalema, the prettiest—and the whitest—of the white towns. It's a lovely, small town, worth some time wandering, and well situated for a visit to the mountains of the Sierra de Grazalema Natural Park.

Gypsies, flamenco, horses, bulls—Andalusia is the Spain of story and song, simultaneously the least and most surprising part of the country: least surprising because it lives up to the hype and stereotype that long confused all of Spain with the Andalusian version, and most surprising because it is, at the same time, so much more.

To begin with, five of the eight Andalusian provinces are maritime, with colorful fishing fleets and a wealth of seafood usually associated with the north. Second, there are snowcapped mountains and ski resorts in Andalusia, the kind of high sierra resources normally associated with the Alps, or even the Pyrenees, yet the Sierra Nevada, with Granada at the foothills, is within sight of North Africa. Third, there are wildlife-filled wetlands and highland pine and oak forests rich with game and trout streams, not to mention free-range Iberian pigs. And last, there are cities like Seville that somehow manage to combine all of this with the creativity and cosmopolitanism of London or Barcelona.

Andalusia—for 781 years (711–1492) a Moorish empire and named for Al-Andalus (Arabic for "Land of the West")—is where the authentic history and character of the Iberian Peninsula and Spanish culture are most palpably, visibly, audibly, and aromatically apparent.

An exploration of Andalusia must begin with the cities of Seville, Córdoba, and Granada as the fundamental triangle of interest and identity. All the romantic images of Andalusia, and Spain in general, spring vividly to life in Seville: Spain's fourth-largest city is a cliché of matadors, flamenco, tapas bars, gypsies, geraniums, and strolling guitarists, but there's so much more than these urban treasures. A more thorough Andalusian experience includes such unforgettable natural settings as Huelva's Sierra de Aracena and Doñana wetlands, Jaén's Parque Natural de Cazorla, Cádiz's *pueblos blancos* (white villages), and Granada's Alpujarras mountains.

SEVILLE

550 km (340 mi) southwest of Madrid.

Seville's whitewashed houses bright with bougainvillea, ocher-color palaces, and baroque facades have long enchanted both Sevillanos and travelers. Lord Byron's well known line, "Seville is a pleasant city famous for oranges and women," may be true, but is far too tame a comment: yes, the orange trees are pretty enough, but the fruit is too bitter to eat except as Scottish-made marmalade. And as for the women, stroll down the swankier pedestrian shopping streets and you can't fail to notice just how good-looking everyone is. Aside from being blessed with even features and flashing dark eyes, Sevillanos exude a cool sophistication that seems more Catalan than Andalusian.

This bustling city of more than 700,000 does have some downsides: traffic-choked streets, high unemployment, a notorious petty-crime rate, and at times the kind of impersonal treatment you won't find in the smaller cities of Granada and Córdoba.

GETTING HERE AND AROUND

Seville's airport is about 7 km (4.3 mi) east of the city. There's a bus from the airport to the center of town every half hour on weekdays (6:30 AM–8 PM; €2.30 one-way) and every hour on weekends and holidays. Taxi fare from the airport to the city center is about €24. A number of private companies, including J. González, operate private airport shuttle services.

Train connections include the high-speed AVE service from Madrid, with a journey time of less than 2½ hours.

Getting in and out of Seville by car isn't difficult, thanks to the SE30 ring road, but getting around in the city by car is problematic. We advise leaving your car at your hotel or in a lot while you're here.

Seville has two intercity bus stations: Estación del Prado de San Sebastián, serving the west and northwest, and the Estación Plaza de Armas, which serves central and eastern Spain.

Seville's urban bus service is efficient and covers the greater city area. Buses C1, C2, C3, and C4 run circular routes linking the main transportation terminals with the city center. The C1 goes east in a clockwise direction, from the Santa Justa train station via Avenida de Carlos V, Avenida de María Luisa, Triana, the Isla de la Cartuja, and Calle de Resolana. The C2 follows the same route in reverse. The C3 runs from the Avenida Menéndez Pelayo to the Puerta de Jerez, Triana, Plaza de Armas, and Calle de Recaredo. The C4 does that route counterclockwise. Buses do not run within the Barrio de Santa Cruz because the streets are too narrow, though they amply serve convenient access points around the periphery of this popular tourist area.

City buses operate limited night service between midnight and 2 AM, with no service between 2 and 4 AM. Single rides cost €1.25, but it is more economical to buy a ticket for 10 rides, which costs €5.90, for use on any bus. Special tourist passes (Tarjeta Turística) valid for one or three days of unlimited bus travel cost (respectively) €3.50 and €7.75.

Tickets are sold at newspaper kiosks and at the main bus station, Prado de San Sebastián.

Seville is perfect for bike travel, and there are several bike rental companies within the city, including those listed below. Seville also operates a free bike rental service with pickup and drop-off points throughout the city. For further details, contact the tourist office.

In Seville, the **Asociación Provincial de Informadores Turísticos, Guidetour,** and **ITA** can hook you up with a qualified English-speaking guide. **Sevilla Walking Tours** offers a choice of three walking tours in English, leaving Plaza Nueva (statue of San Fernando) at 10:30 AM, Monday–Saturday: the Alcázar (€6) the Cathedral Tour (€6), or the city tour (€12). The tourist office (⇨ Visitor Information) has information on open-bus city tours run by Servirama, Hispalense de Tranvias, and others; buses leave every half hour from the Torre del Oro, with stops at Parque María Luisa and the Isla Mágica theme park. You can hop on and off at any stop; the complete tour lasts about 90 minutes.

ESSENTIALS

Airport Transfers J. González (☎ *958/490164* www.autocaresjosegonzalez.com/).

Bike Contacts Rent and Tours (✉ *Calle General Castaños 33, Seville* ☎ *954/229883* 🌐 *www.bici4city.com*). **Cyclotour/Telebike** (✉ *Residencial Virgen de Rocío 3, 4th fl., A, Mairena del Aljarafe, Seville* ☎ *605/252–8312* 🌐 *www.cyclotouristic.com*).

Bus Stations Estación del Prado de San Sebastián (✉ *Prado de San Sebastián s/n*). **Estación Plaza de Armas** (✉ *Calle Cristo de la Expiración*).

Taxi Contact Radio Teléfono Giralda (☎ *95/467–5555*).

Tour Contacts Sevilla Walking Tours (☎ *902/158226 or 616/501100* 🌐 *www.sevillawalkingtours.com*). **Sevirama** (✉ *Paseo de las Delicias, Edifico Cristina, 2nd fl., Arenal, Seville* ☎ *95/456–0693* 🌐 www.busturistico.com). **SevillaTour** (✉ *Calle Jaén 2* ☎ *95/450–2099* 🌐 *www.citysightseeing-spain.com*). **Sevilla Visión** (✉ *Pl. Cristo de Burgos 9, Santa Catalina, Seville* ☎ *95/422–4641*).

Train Station Estación Santa Justa (✉ *Av. Kansas City*).

Visitor Information City of Seville (✉ *Av. de la Constitución 21, Arenal* ☎ *95/422–1404* 🌐 *www.sevilla.org* ✉ *Costurero de la Reina, Paseo de las Delicias 9, Arenal* ☎ *95/423–4465*). **Province of Seville** (✉ *Pl. de Triunfo 1–3, by cathedral, Santa Cruz* ☎ *95/421–0005* 🌐 *www.turismosevilla.org*).

EXPLORING

The layout of the historic center of Seville makes exploring easy. The central zone—**Centro**—around the cathedral, the Alcázar, Calle Sierpes, and Plaza Nueva is splendid and monumental, but it's not where you'll find Seville's greatest charm. **El Arenal,** home of the Maestranza bullring, the Teatro de la Maestranza concert hall, and a concentration of picturesque taverns, still buzzes the way it must have when stevedores loaded and unloaded ships from the New World. Just southeast of Centro, the medieval Jewish quarter, **Barrio de Santa Cruz,** is a lovely, whitewashed tangle of alleys. The **Barrio de la Macarena** to the northeast

Seville's grand Alcazar is a World Heritage site and an absolute must-see.

is rich in sights and authentic Seville atmosphere. The fifth and final neighborhood to explore, on the far side of the river Guadalquiviris, is in many ways, the best of all—**Triana,** the traditional habitat for sailors, bullfighters, and flamenco artists, as well as the main workshop for Seville's renowned ceramicists.

CENTRO

3 Fodor's Choice ★ **Alcázar**. The Plaza Triunfo forms the entrance to the Mudejar palace built by Pedro I (1350–69) on the site of Seville's former Moorish *alcázar* (fortress). Don't mistake the Alcázar for a genuine Moorish palace like Granada's Alhambra—it may look like one, and it was designed and built by Moorish workers brought in from Granada, but it was commissioned and paid for by a Christian king more than 100 years after the reconquest of Seville. The palace is the official residence of the king and queen when they're in town.

Entering the Alcázar through the Puerta del León (Lion's Gate) and the high, fortified walls, you'll first find yourself in a garden courtyard, the **Patio del León** (Courtyard of the Lion). Off to the left are the oldest parts of the building, the 14th-century **Sala de Justicia** (Hall of Justice) and, next to it, the intimate **Patio del Yeso** (Courtyard of Plaster), the only part of the original 12th-century Almohad Alcázar. Cross the **Patio de la Montería** (Courtyard of the Hunt) to Pedro's Mudejar palace, arranged around the beautiful **Patio de las Doncellas** (Court of the Damsels), resplendent with delicately carved stucco. Opening off this patio, the **Salón de Embajadores** (Hall of the Ambassadors), with its cedar cupola of green, red, and gold, is the most sumptuous hall in the palace.

Other royal rooms include the three baths of Pedro's powerful and influential mistress, María de Padilla. María's hold on her royal lover—and his courtiers—was so great that legend says they all lined up to drink her bathwater. The **Patio de las Muñecas** (Court of the Dolls) takes its name from two tiny faces carved on the inside of one of its arches, no doubt as a joke on the part of its Moorish creators. Here Pedro reputedly had his half brother, Don Fadrique, slain in 1358; and here, too, he murdered guest Abu Said of Granada for his jewels—one of which, a huge ruby, is now among England's crown jewels. (Pedro gave it to the Black Prince, Edward, Prince of Wales [1330–76], for helping during the revolt of his illegitimate brother in 1367.)

WHERE'S COLUMBUS?

Christopher Columbus knew both triumph and disgrace, yet he found no repose—he died, bitterly disillusioned, in Valladolid in 1506. No one knows for certain where he's buried; he was reportedly laid to rest for the first time in the Dominican Republic and then moved over the years to other locations. A portion of his remains can be found in Seville's Cathedral.

The Renaissance **Palacio de Carlos V** (Palace of Carlos V) is endowed with a rich collection of Flemish tapestries depicting Carlos's victories at Tunis. Look for the map of Spain: it shows the Iberian Peninsula upside down, as was the custom in Arab mapmaking. There are more goodies—rare clocks, antique furniture, paintings, and tapestries—on the upper floor, in the **Estancias Reales** (Royal Chambers).

In the **gardens,** inhale the fragrances of jasmine and myrtle, wander among terraces and baths, and peer into the well-stocked goldfish pond. From here, a passageway leads to the **Patio de las Banderas** (Court of the Flags), which has a classic view of the Giralda.

Tours depart in the morning only, every half hour in summer and every hour in winter. ✉ *Pl. del Triunfo, Santa Cruz* ☎ *95/450–2324* 🌐 *www.patronato-alcazarsevilla.es* 🎫 *€7.50* ⏲ *Tues.–Sun. 9:30–7.*

19 **Ayuntamiento** *(City Hall)*. This Diego de Riaño original, built between 1527 and 1564, is in the heart of Seville's commercial center. A 19th-century plateresque facade overlooks the Plaza Nueva. The other side, on the Plaza de San Francisco, is Riaño's work. ✉ *Pl. Nueva 1, Centro* ☎ *95/459–0101* 🎫 *Free* ⏲ *Tours Tues.–Thurs. at 5:30.*

20 **Calle Sierpes.** This is Seville's classy main shopping street. Near the southern end, at No. 85, a plaque marks the spot where the Cárcel Real (Royal Prison) once stood. Miguel de Cervantes began writing *Don Quixote* in one of its cells.

1 ★ **Cathedral.** Seville's cathedral can be described only in superlatives: it's the largest and highest cathedral in Spain, the largest Gothic building in the world, and the world's third-largest church, after St. Peter's in Rome and St. Paul's in London. After Ferdinand III captured Seville from the Moors in 1248, the great mosque begun by Yusuf II in 1171 was reconsecrated to the Virgin Mary and used as a Christian cathedral. In 1401 the people of Seville decided to erect a new cathedral, one that would equal the glory of their great city. They pulled down the old mosque,

leaving only its minaret and outer courtyard, and built the existing building in just over a century—a remarkable feat for the time.

The cathedral's dimly illuminated interior, aside from the well-lighted high altar, can be disappointing: Gothic purity has been largely submerged in ornate baroque decoration. In the central nave rises the **Capilla Mayor** (Main Chapel). Its magnificent *retablo* (altarpiece) is the largest in Christendom (65 feet by 43 feet). It depicts some 36 scenes from the life of Christ, with pillars carved with more than 200 figures.

On the south side of the cathedral is the **monument to Christopher Columbus**: his coffin is borne aloft by the four kings representing the medieval kingdoms of Spain: Castile, León, Aragón, and Navarra. Columbus's son Fernando Colón (1488–1539) is also interred here; his tombstone is inscribed with the words A CASTILLA Y A LEÓN, MUNDO NUEVO DIO COLÓN (To Castile and León, Columbus gave a new world).

In the **Sacristía de los Cálices** (Sacristy of the Chalices) look for Juan Martínez Montañés's wood carving *Crucifixion, Merciful Christ*; Juan de Valdés Leal's *St. Peter Freed by an Angel*; Francisco de Zurbarán's *Virgin and Child*; and Francisco José de Goya y Lucientes's *St. Justa and St. Rufina*. The **Sacristía Mayor** (Main Sacristy) holds the keys to the city, which Seville's Moors and Jews presented to their conqueror, Ferdinand III. Finally, in the dome of the **Sala Capitular** (Chapter House), in the cathedral's southeastern corner, is Bartolomé Estéban Murillo's *Immaculate Conception,* painted in 1668.

One of the cathedral's highlights, the **Capilla Real** (Royal Chapel), is concealed behind a ponderous curtain, but you can duck in if you're quick, quiet, and properly dressed (no shorts or sleeveless tops): enter from the Puerta de los Palos, on Plaza Virgen de los Reyes (signposted ENTRADA PARA CULTO—entrance for worship). Along the sides of the chapel are the tombs of the Beatrix of Swabia, wife of the 13th century's Ferdinand III, and their son Alfonso X, called the Wise; in a silver urn before the high altar rest the relics of Ferdinand III himself, Seville's liberator. Canonized in 1671, he was said to have died from excessive fasting.

Don't forget the **Patio de los Naranjos** (Courtyard of Orange Trees), on the church's northern side, where the fountain in the center was used for ablutions before people entered the original mosque. Near the Puerta del Lagarto (Lizard's Gate), in the corner near the Giralda, try to find the wooden crocodile—thought to have been a gift from the emir of Egypt in 1260 as he sought the hand of the daughter of Alfonso the Wise—and the elephant tusk, found in the ruins of Itálica.

The Christians could not bring themselves to destroy the tower when they tore down the mosque, so they incorporated it into their new cathedral. In 1565–68 they added a lantern and belfry to the old minaret and installed 24 bells, one for each of Seville's 24 parishes and the 24 Christian knights who fought with Ferdinand III in the reconquest. They also added the bronze statue of Faith, which turned as a weather vane—*el giraldillo,* or "something that turns," thus the whole tower became known as the **Giralda**. With its baroque additions, the slender Giralda rises 322 feet. Inside, instead of steps, 35 sloping ramps—wide enough for two horsemen to pass abreast—climb to a viewing platform 230 feet up. It is said that Ferdinand III rode his horse to the top to admire the city he had conquered. ✉ *Pl. Virgen de los Reyes, Centro* ☎ *95/421–4971* 🎟 *Cathedral and Giralda €8* ⏲ *Cathedral July and Aug., Mon.–Sat. 9.30–4, Sun. 2.30–6; Sept.–June, Mon.–Sat. 11:15–5, Sun. 2.30–6.*

A CRAZY CHURCH?

In building Seville's cathedral, the clergy renounced their incomes for the cause, and a member of the chapter is said to have proclaimed, "Let us build a church so large that we shall be held to be insane."

22 **Iglesia del Salvador.** Built between 1671 and 1712, the Church of the Savior stands on the site of Seville's first great mosque, of which remains can be seen in its Courtyard of the Orange Trees.

Also of note are the sculptures of *Jesús de la Pasión* and St. Christopher by Martínez Montañés. In 2003 archaeologists discovered an 18th-century burial site here; walkways have been installed to facilitate visits. ✉ *Pl. del Salvador, Centro* ☎ *95/421–1679* 🎟 *€3 with guide* ⏲ *Mon.–Sat. 8:45–10 and 6:30–9, Sun. 10:30–2 and 7–8:45.*

21 **Palacio de la Condesa de Lebrija.** This lovely palace has three ornate patios, including a spectacular courtyard graced by a Roman mosaic taken from the ruins in Itálica, surrounded by Moorish arches and fine azulejos. The side rooms house a collection of archaeological items. ✉ *Calle Cuna 8, Centro* ☎ *95/422–7802* 🎟 *€8, €4 for ground floor only* ⏲ *July and Aug., weekdays 9–3, Sat. 10–2; Sept.–June, weekdays 10:30–7:30, Sat. 10–2.*

BARRIO DE SANTA CRUZ

2 **Archivo de las Indias** *(Archives of the Indies).* Opened in 1785 in the former Lonja (Merchants' Exchange), this dignified Renaissance buildingstores archives of more than 40,000 documents, including drawings, trade documents, plans of South American towns, and even the autographs of Columbus, Magellan, and Cortés. ✉ *Av. de la Constitución, Santa Cruz* ☎ *95/421–1234* 🎟 *Free* ⏲ *Mon.–Sat. 10–4, Sun. 10–2.*

★ The twisting alleyways and traditional whitewashed houses add to the tourist charm of this barrio, the old **Jewish Quarter**. On some streets, bars alternate with antiques stores and souvenir shops, but most of the quarter is quiet and residential. On the Plaza Alianza, pause to enjoy the antiques shops and outdoor cafés. In the Plaza de Doña Elvira, with its fountain and azulejo (painted tile) benches, young Sevillanos gather to play guitars. Just around the corner from the hospital, at Callejón del Agua and Jope de Rueda, Gioacchino Rossini's Figaro serenaded Rosina on her Plaza Alfaro balcony. Adjoining the Plaza Alfaro, in the Plaza Santa Cruz, flowers and orange trees surround a 17th-century filigree iron cross, which marks the site of the erstwhile church of Santa Cruz, destroyed by Napoléon's General Jean-de-Dieu Soult.

23 ★ **Casa de Pilatos.** This palace was built in the first half of the 16th century by the dukes of Tarifa, ancestors of the present owner, the duke of Medinaceli. It's known as Pilate's House because Don Fadrique, first marquis of Tarifa, allegedly modeled it on Pontius Pilate's house in Jerusalem,

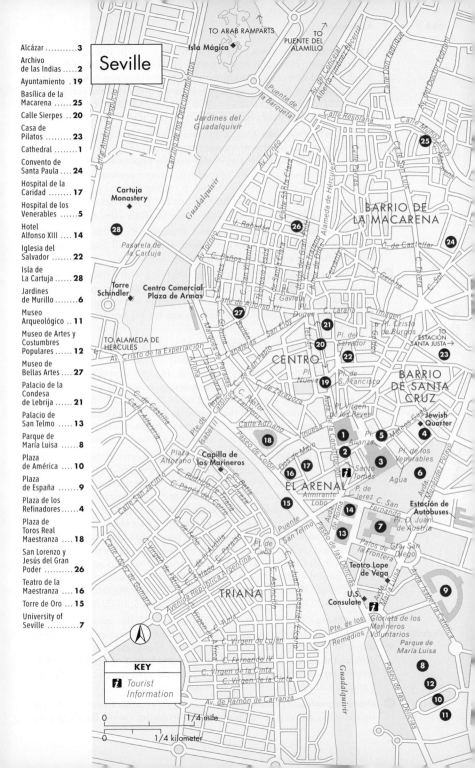

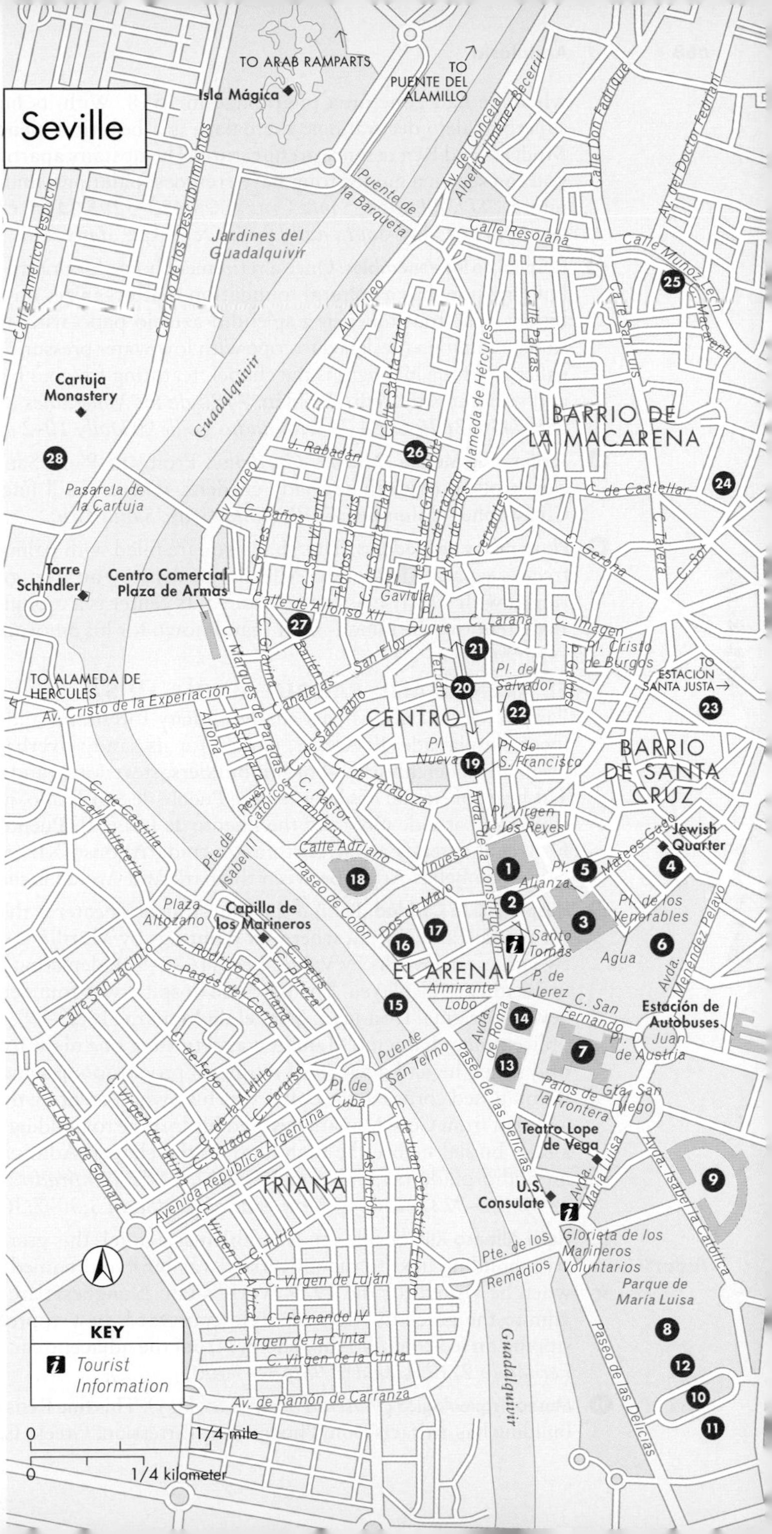

Seville
TO ARAB RAMPARTS
TO PUENTE DEL ALAMILLO
Isla Mágica
Jardines del Guadalquivir
Cartuja Monastery
Pasarela de la Cartuja
Torre Schindler
Centro Comercial Plaza de Armas
TO ALAMEDA DE HERCULES
Av. Cristo de la Experiación
Puente de la Barqueta
Calle Resolana
BARRIO DE LA MACARENA
C. de Castellar
CENTRO
BARRIO DE SANTA CRUZ
Jewish Quarter
TO ESTACIÓN SANTA JUSTA
Capilla de los Marineros
EL ARENAL
Estación de Autobuses
Teatro Lope de Vega
U.S. Consulate
TRIANA
Glorieta de los Marineros Voluntarios
Parque de María Luisa
Guadalquivir
KEY
Tourist Information
1/4 mile
1/4 kilometer

where he had gone on a pilgrimage in 1518. With its fine patio and superb azulejo decorations, the palace is a beautiful blend of Spanish Mudejar and Renaissance architecture. The upstairs apartments, which you can see on a guided tour, have frescoes, paintings, and antique furniture. ✉ *Pl. Pilatos 1, Santa Cruz* ☎ *95/422–5298* 💰 *€8, €5 for ground floor only* ⏲ *May–Sept., daily 9–7; Oct.–Apr., daily 9–6.*

5 **Hospital de los Venerables.** Once a retirement home for priests, this baroque building now has a cultural foundation that organizes on-site art exhibitions. The tour takes in a splendid azulejo patio with an interesting sunken fountain (designed to cope with low water pressure) and upstairs gallery, but the highlight is the chapel, featuring frescoes by Valdés Leal and sculptures by Pedro Roldán. ✉ *Pl. de los Venerables 8, Santa Cruz* ☎ *95/456–2696* 💰 *€4.75 with audio guide* ⏲ *Daily 10–2 and 4–7.*

6 **Jardines de Murillo** *(Murillo Gardens).* From the Plaza Santa Cruz you can stroll through these shady gardens, where you'll find a statue of Christopher Columbus. ✉ *Pl. Santa Cruz, Santa Cruz.*

4 **Plaza de los Refinadores.** This shady square filled with palms and orange trees is separated from the Murillo gardens by an iron grillwork and ringed with stately glass balconies. At its center is a monument to Don Juan Tenorio, the famous Don Juan known for his amorous conquests. ✉ *Santa Cruz.*

EL ARENAL AND PARQUE MARÍA LUISA

Parque María Luisa is part shady midcity forestland and part monumental esplanade. El Arenal, named for its sandy riverbank soil, was originally a neighborhood of shipbuilders, stevedores, and warehouses. The heart of Arenal lies between the Puente de San Telmo, just upstream from the Torre de Oro, and the Puente de Isabel II (Puente de Triana). El Arenal extends as far north as Avenida Alfonso XII to include the Museo de Bellas Artes. Between the park and Arenal is the university.

17 **Hospital de la Caridad.** Behind the Maestranza Theater is this almshouse for the sick and elderly, where six paintings by Murillo (1617–82) and two gruesome works by Valdés Leal (1622–90), depicting the Triumph of Death, are displayed. The baroque hospital was founded in 1674 by Seville's original Don Juan, Miguel de Mañara (1626–79). A nobleman of licentious character, Mañara was returning one night from a riotous orgy when he had a vision of a funeral procession in which the partly decomposed corpse in the coffin was his own. Accepting the apparition as a sign from God, Mañara devoted his fortune to building this hospital and is buried before the high altar in the chapel. Admission includes an audio guide (available in English). ✉ *C. Temprado 3, El Arenal* ☎ *95/422–3232* 💰 *€5* ⏲ *Mon.–Sat. 9–1:30 and 3:30–7:30, Sun. 9–1.*

14 Fodor's Choice ★ **Hotel Alfonso XIII.** Seville's most emblematic hotel, this grand, Mudejar-style building next to the university was built and named for the king when he visited for the 1929 World's fair. Nonguests are welcome to admire the gracious Moorish-style courtyard, best appreciated while sipping an ice-cold *fino* (dry sherry) from the adjacent bar. ✉ *Calle San Fernando 2, El Arenal* ☎ *95/491–7000.*

11 **Museo Arqueológico** *(Museum of Archaeology).* This fine Renaissance-style building has artifacts from Phoenician, Tartessian, Greek, Carthaginian,

Iberian, Roman, and medieval times. Displays include marble statues and mosaics from the Roman excavations at Itálica and a faithful replica of the fabulous Carambolo treasure found on a hillside outside Seville in 1958: 21 pieces of jewelry, all 24-karat gold, dating from the 7th and 6th centuries BC. ✉ *Pl. de América, El Arenal/Porvenir* ☎ *95/423–2401* 🎫 *€1.50* ⏲ *Tues. 2:30–8:30, Wed.–Sat. 9–8:30, Sun. 9–2:30.*

12 **Museo de Artes y Costumbres Populares** *(Museum of Folklore)*. The Mudejar pavilion opposite the Museum of Archaeology is the site of this museum of mainly 19th- and 20th-century Spanish folklore. The first floor has re-creations of a forge, a bakery, a wine press, a tanner's shop, and a pottery studio. Upstairs, exhibits include 18th- and 19th-century court dress, stunning regional folk costumes, carriages, and musical instruments. ✉ *Pl. de América 3, El Arenal/Porvenir* ☎ *95/423–2576* 🎫 *€1.50* ⏲ *Tues. 3–8, Wed.–Sat. 9–8, Sun. 9–2.*

27 **Museo de Bellas Artes** *(Museum of Fine Arts)*. This museum is second only to Madrid's Prado for Spanish art. It's in the former convent of La Merced Calzada, most of which dates from the 17th century. The collection includes works by Murillo and the 17th-century Seville school, as well as by Zurbarán, Diego Velázquez, Alonso Cano, Valdés Leal, and El Greco; outstanding examples of Sevillian Gothic art; and baroque religious sculptures in wood (a quintessentially Andalusian art form). In the rooms dedicated to Sevillian art of the 19th and 20th centuries, look for Gonzalo Bilbao's *Las Cigarreras*, a group portrait of Seville's famous cigar makers. ✉ *Pl. del Museo 9, El Arenal/Porvenir* ☎ *95/478–6482* 🌐 *www.museosdeandalucia.es* 🎫 *€1.50* ⏲ *Tues. 2:30–8:15, Wed.–Sat. 9–8:15, Sun. 9–2:15.*

Fodor's Choice ★

13 **Palacio de San Telmo**. This splendid baroque palace is largely the work of architect Leonardo de Figueroa. Built between 1682 and 1796, it was first a naval academy and then the residence of the Bourbon dukes of Montpensier, during which time it outshone Madrid's royal court for sheer brilliance. The palace gardens are now the Parque de María Luisa, and the building itself is the seat of the Andalusian government. The main portal, vintage 1734, is a superb example of the fanciful Churrigueresque style. ■ **TIP→ Call in advance if you want to arrange a visit.** ✉ *Av. de Roma, El Arenal* ☎ *95/503–5500.*

8 **Parque de María Luisa**. Formerly the garden of the Palacio de San Telmo, this park blends formal design and wild vegetation. In the burst of development that gripped Seville in the 1920s, it was redesigned for the 1929 Exhibition, and the impressive villas you see now are the fair's remaining pavilions, many of them consulates or schools. Note the **statue of El Cid** by Rodrigo Díaz de Vivar (1043–99), who fought both for and against the Muslim rulers during the Reconquest. ✉ *Main entrance: Glorieta San Diego, El Arenal.*

Fodor's Choice ★

10 **Plaza de América**. Walk to the south end of the Parque de María Luisa, past the Isla de los Patos (Island of Ducks), to find this plaza designed by Aníbal González and typically carpeted with a congregation of white doves (children can buy grain from a kiosk here to feed them). It's a blaze of color, with flowers, shrubs, ornamental stairways, and fountains tiled in yellow, blue, and ocher. The three impressive buildings

Seville's cathedral is the largest and highest cathedral in Spain, the largest Gothic building in the world, and the third-largest church in the world, after St. Peter's in Rome and St. Paul's in London.

surrounding the square—in neo-Mudejar, Gothic, and Renaissance styles—were built by González for the 1929 fair. Two of them now house Seville's museums of archaeology and folklore.

9 **Plaza de España**. This grandiose half-moon of buildings on the eastern edge of the Parque de María Luisa was Spain's centerpiece pavilion at the 1929 Exhibition. The brightly colored azulejo pictures represent the provinces of Spain, while the four bridges symbolize the medieval kingdoms of the Iberian Peninsula. In summer you can rent small boats to row along the arc-shaped canal.

18 **Plaza de Toros Real Maestranza** *(Royal Maestranza Bullring)*. Sevillanos have spent many a thrilling Sunday afternoon in this bullring, built between 1760 and 1763. Painted a deep ocher, the stadium is the one of the oldest and loveliest *plazas de toros* in Spain. The 20-minute tour takes in the empty arena, a museum with elaborate costumes and prints, and the chapel where matadors pray before the fight. ✉ *Paseo de Colón 12, El Arenal* ☎ *95/422–4577* 🎟 *Plaza and bullfighting museum €6 with English-speaking guide* ⏲ *May–Oct., daily 9:30–8; Nov.–Apr., daily 9:30–7 (bullfighting days 9:30–3).*

15 **Torre de Oro** (Tower of Gold). Built by the Moors in 1220 to complete the city's ramparts, this 12-sided tower on the banks of the Guadalquivir served to close off the harbor when a chain was stretched across the river from its base to a tower on the opposite bank. In 1248, Admiral Ramón de Bonifaz broke through the barrier, and Ferdinand III captured Seville. The tower houses a small naval museum. ✉ *Paseo Alcalde Marqués de Contadero s/n, El Arenal* ☎ *95/422–2419* 🎟 *€2* ⏲ *Tues.–Fri. 10–2, weekends 11–2.*

7 **University of Seville.** At the far end of the Jardines de Murillo, opposite Calle San Fernando, stands what used to be the **Real Fábrica de Tabacos** (Royal Tobacco Factory). Built in the mid-1700s, the factory employed some 3,000 *cigarreras* (female cigar makers) less than a century later, including Bizet's opera heroine Carmen, who reputedly rolled her cigars on her thighs. ✉ *C. San Fernando s/n, Parque María Luisa* ☎ *95/455–1000* 🎫 *Free* ⏲ *Weekdays 9–8:30.*

BARRIO DE LA MACARENA

This immense neighborhood covers the entire northern half of historic Seville and deserves to be walked many times. Most of the best churches, convents, markets, and squares are concentrated around the center in an area delimited by the Arab ramparts to the north, the Alameda de Hercules to the west, the Santa Catalina church to the south, and the Convento de Santa Paula to the east. The area between the Alameda de Hercules and the Guadalquivir is known to locals as the Barrio de San Lorenzo, a section that's ideal for an evening of tapas grazing.

25 **Basílica de la Macarena.** This church holds Seville's most revered image, the Virgin of Hope—better known as La Macarena. Bedecked with candles and carnations, her cheeks streaming with glass tears, the Macarena steals the show at the procession on Holy Thursday, the highlight of Seville's Holy Week pageant. The patron of gypsies and the protector of the matador, her charms are so great that young Sevillian bullfighter Joselito spent half his personal fortune buying her emeralds. When he was killed in the ring in 1920, the Macarena was dressed in widow's weeds for a month. There's a small adjacent museum devoted to her costumes and jewels, but it's closed for refurbishment until late 2010; check at the tourist office for an update. ✉ *C. Bécquer 1, La Macarena* ☎ *95/490–1800* 🎫 *Free* ⏲ *Basilica daily 9:30–2 and 5–9.*

24 **Convento de Santa Paula.** This 15th-century Gothic convent has a fine facade and portico, with ceramic decoration by Nicolaso Pisano. The chapel has some beautiful azulejos and sculptures by Martínez Montañés. It also contains a small museum and a shop selling delicious cakes and jams made by the nuns. ✉ *C. Santa Paula 11, La Macarena* ☎ *95/453–6330* 🎫 *€3* ⏲ *Tues.–Sun. 10–1.*

Fodor's Choice ★

26 **San Lorenzo y Jesús del Gran Poder.** This 17th-century church has many fine works by such artists as Martínez Montañés and Francisco Pacheco, but its outstanding piece is Juan de Mesa y Velasco's *Jesús del Gran Poder* (Christ Omnipotent). ✉ *C. Jesús del Gran Poder, La Macarena* ☎ *95/438–4558* 🎫 *Free* ⏲ *Daily 8–1:30 and 6–9.*

TRIANA

Across the Guadalquivir from central Seville, Triana used to be the gypsy quarter. Today it has a tranquil, neighborly feel by day, and its atmospheric clubs and flamenco bars throb at night. Enter Triana by the **Puente Isabel II** (better known as the Puente de Triana), built in 1852, the first bridge to connect the city's two sections. Walk across Plaza Altozano up Calle Jacinto and turn right at **Calle Alfarería** (Pottery Street) to see a slew of pottery shops. Return to Plaza Altozano and walk down Calle Pureza as far as the small **Capilla de los Marineros** (Seamen's Chapel), home to a venerated statue of Mary called the Esperanza de

DON JUAN: LOVER OF LEGENDS

Originally brought to literary life by the Spanish Golden Age playwright Fray Gabriel Téllez (better known as Tirso de Molina) in 1630, the figure of Don Juan has been portrayed in countless variations through the years, usually changing to reflect the moral climate of the times. As interpreted by such notables as Molière, Wolfgang Amadeus Mozart, Carlo Goldoni, George Gordon Lord Byron, and George Bernard Shaw, Don Juan has ranged from voluptuous hedonist to helpless victim, from fiery lover to coldhearted snake.

The plaques around his effigy in Plaza de los Refinadores translate as: "Here is Don Juan Tenorio, and no man is his equal. From haughty princess to a humble fisherwoman, there is no female he doesn't desire, nor affair of gold or riches he will not pursue. Seek him ye rivals; surround him players all; may whoever values himself attempt to stop him or be his better at gambling, combat, or love."

Triana. Head back toward the river and **Calle Betis** for some of the city's most colorful bars, clubs, and restaurants.

28 **Isla de La Cartuja**. Named after its 14th-century Carthusian monastery, this island in the Guadalquivir River across from northern Seville was the site of the decennial Universal Exposition (Expo) in 1992. The island has the Teatro Central, used for concerts and plays; Parque del Alamillo, Seville's largest least-known park; and the Estadio Olímpico, a 60,000-seat covered stadium. The best way to get to La Cartuja is by walking across one or both (one each way) of the superb Santiago Calatrava bridges spanning the river. The Puente de la Barqueta crosses to La Cartuja, and downstream the Puente del Alamillo connects La Isla Mágica with Seville. Buses C1 and C2 also serve La Cartuja.

The eastern shore holds the **Isla Mágica** (*902/161716 www.islamagica.es Apr. and May €25, June–Oct. €28 Apr. and May, weekends 11 AM–midnight; June–Oct., daily 11 AM–midnight*) with 14 attractions, including the hair-raising Jaguar roller coaster.

The 14th-century **Monasterio de Santa María de las Cuevas** (*Monasterio de La Cartuja Isla de la Cartuja*) was regularly visited by Christopher Columbus, who was buried here for a few years. Part of the building houses the Centro Andaluz de Arte Contemporáneo, which has an absorbing collection of contemporary art. *Av. Americo Vespucci 2, La Cartuja.*

WHERE TO EAT AND STAY

Use the coordinate (B2) at the end of each listing to locate a site on the corresponding map.

TAPAS BARS

Bar Giralda. This old Moorish bathhouse across from the Giralda has been a tapas bar since 1934. The outdoor seating area has cathedral views. One specialty is *patatas a la importancia* (fried potatoes stuffed with ham and cheese). ✉ *Calle Mateos Gago 1, Santa Cruz* ☎ *95/422–7435* ✥ *C3.*

Bar Gran Tino. Named for the giant wooden wine cask that once dominated the bar, this busy spot with outside seating on the funky Plaza Alfalfa serves an array of tapas, including *calamares fritos* (fried squid) and wedges of crumbly Manchego cheese. ✉ *Pl. Alfalfa 2, Centro* ☎ *95/421–0883* ✥ *C2.*

★ **Bar Rincón San Eloy.** This place is always heaving with a happy mix of shoppers and students. You can buy stacked mini-sandwiches, as well as tapas and sherry from the barrel. If no tables are left, grab a pew on the tiled steps. ✉ *Calle San Eloy 2, Centro* ☎ *95/421–8079* ✥ *B2.*

FIESTA TIME!

Seville's color and vivacity are most intense during Semana Santa, when lacerated Christs and bejeweled, weeping Mary statues are paraded through town on floats borne by often barefoot penitents. A week later, Sevillanos throw April Fair, featuring midday horse parades with men in broad-brim hats and Andalusian riding gear astride prancing steeds, and women in ruffled dresses riding sidesaddle behind them. Bullfights, fireworks, and all-night singing and dancing complete the spectacle.

El Rinconcillo. Founded in 1670, this lovely spot serves a classic selection of dishes, such as the *caldereta de venado* (venison stew), a superb *salmorejo* (gazpacho-style soup), and *espinacas con garbanzos* (creamed spinach with chickpeas). The views of the Iglesia de Santa Catalina out the front window are unbeatable, and your bill is chalked up on the wooden counters as you go. ✉ *C. Gerona 40, La Macarena* ☎ *95/422–3183* ⏲ *Closed Wed* ✥ *C2.*

WHERE TO EAT

$$$ SPANISH

✕ Becerrita. The affable Jesús Becerra runs this cozy—verging on cramped—establishment decorated with traditional columns, tiles, and colorful paintings of Seville. Diligent service and tasty modern treatments of such classic Spanish dishes as *lomo de cordero a la miel* (loin of lamb in a honey sauce) and *rape con gambas y ajo* (monkfish with garlic and prawns) have won the favor of Sevillanos, as have the signature oxtail croquettes. Smaller appetites can try such tasty tapas as stuffed calamari and garlic-spiked prawns. ✉ *Calle Recaredo 9, Santa Cruz/Santa Catalina* ☎ *95/441–2057* 🌐 *www.becerrita.com* ⚠ *Reservations essential* 💳 *AE, MC, V* ⏲ *No dinner Sun. and Aug.* ✥ *D2.*

$ MEDITERRANEAN Fodor's Choice ★

✕ Borear. Near Plaza de Armas, behind a disarmingly bland-looking facade, this restaurant hits the mark for innovative cuisine. Dishes are often culinary works of art, and there are vegetarian options like *mosaico de verduras atemperadas con caramelo de vino do jerez* (lightly grilled vegetables in a caramelized sherry sauce) and *espárragos con berenjenas al pesto* (asparagus and eggplant in a pesto sauce). Other choices include a *wok de pollo* (chicken)—a stir fry is pretty unusual around here—and *verdures* (vegetables). The interior is decorated in slick black and white, and the waitstaff is zippy and young. ✉ *Pl. Puerta Real 6, El Arenal* ☎ *954/916334* 💳 *MC, V* ⏲ *Closed Mon.* ✥ *A2.*

CLOSE UP

Seville's Long and Noble History

Conquered in 205 BC by the Romans, Seville gave the world two great emperors, Trajan and Hadrian. The Moors held Seville for more than 500 years and left it one of their greatest works of architecture—the iconic Giralda tower that served as the minaret over the main city mosque. Saint Ferdinand III (King Fernando III) lies enshrined in the glorious cathedral, and his rather less saintly descendant, Pedro the Cruel, builder of the Alcázar, is buried here as well.

Seville is justly proud of its literary and artistic associations. The painters Diego Rodríguez de Silva Velázquez (1599–1660) and Bartolomé Estéban Murillo (1617–82) were sons of Seville, as were the poets Gustavo Adolfo Bécquer (1836–70), Antonio Machado (1875–1939), and Nobel Prize–winner Vicente Aleixandre (1898–1984). The tale of the ingenious knight of La Mancha was begun in a Seville debtors' prison, where Don Quixote's creator, Miguel de Cervantes, once languished. Tirso de Molina's Don Juan seduced his lovers in Seville's mansions; Rossini's barber, Figaro, was married in the Barrio de Santa Cruz; and Bizet's sultry Carmen first met Don José in the former tobacco factory that now houses the university.

$$$$ SPANISH ★

✕ **Egaña-Oriza.** Owner José Mari Egaña is Basque, but he's considered one of the fathers of modern Andalusian cooking. His restaurant, on the edge of the Murillo Gardens opposite the university, has an atrium-style dining room with high ceilings and wall-to-wall windows; in warm weather, you can eat on the terrace under the orange trees. The menu might include *lomos de lubina con salsa de erizos de mar* (sea bass with sea urchin sauce) or *solomillo con foie natural y salsa de ciruelas* (fillet steak with foie gras and plum sauce). On the downside, the service can be slow, but you can always drop into the adjoining Bar España for tapas such as stuffed mussels with béchamel sauce. ⊠ *San Fernando 41, Santa Cruz Jardines de Murillo* ☎ *95/422–7211* ▭ *AE, DC, MC, V* ⊗ *Closed Sun. and Aug. No lunch Sat.* ✣ *C4.*

$$–$$$ SPANISH Fodor's Choice ★

✕ **Enrique Becerra.** Excellent tapas and a lively bar await at this restaurant run by the fifth generation of a family of celebrated restaurateurs (Enrique's brother Jesús owns Becerrita). The menu focuses on traditional, home-cooked Andalusian dishes, such as *pez espada al amontillado* (swordfish cooked in dark sherry) and *cordero a la miel con espinacas* (honey-glazed lamb stuffed with spinach and pine nuts). Don't miss the cumin seed–laced *espinacas con garbanzos* (spinach with chickpeas) or the extensive wine list. ⊠ *Calle Gamazo 2, El Arenal* ☎ *95/421–3049* ▭ *AE, DC, MC, V* ⊗ *Closed Sun. and last 2 wks of July* ✣ *B3.*

$$ SPANISH

✕ **Mesón Don Raimundo.** Tucked into an alleyway off Calle Argote de Molina near the cathedral, this former 17th-century convent with its dark wood furniture and eclectic decor of religious artifacts tends to attract the tour buses. Still, it's worth the trip for the generous portions of traditional fare, including Mozarab-style wild duck (braised in sherry), solomillo *a la castellana* (Castilian-style steak), and the refreshingly straightforward

The half-moon of Plaza de España

cazuela de pescados y mariscos al brandy (fish and seafood casserole with brandy). Start with the crisp *tortillitas de camarones* (batter-fried shrimp pancakes) or stuffed peppers. The wine list is excellent, as is the house wine, which is well-priced for the quality. ✉ *Argote de Molina 26, Santa Cruz* ☎ *95/422–3355* 💳 *AE, DC, MC, V* ✥ *C3.*

$$$ MEDITERRANEAN ★ ✕ **San Marco.** In a 17th-century palace on one of the most charming pedestrian streets in the shopping district, this elegant restaurant has original frescoes, stately columns, and a gracious patio flanked by cascading ivy, and the menu combines Italian, French, and Andalusian cuisine. Pasta dishes, such as ravioli stuffed with shrimp and pesto sauce, are notable. The restaurant has two satellites, including one in the heart of the Santa Cruz district in a similarly historic building—an original Arab bathhouse. This one has the edge, however, as far as culinary skill is concerned. ✉ *Calle Cuna 6, Centro* ☎ *95/421–2440* ✍ *Reservations essential* 💳 *AE, DC, MC, V* ✥ *B2.*

10

$$ SPANISH ✕ **Taberna de Alabardero.** In a magnificent manor house, this restaurant's upstairs dining rooms are set around a central arcade with tables arranged under the tinkling crystal of chandeliers. Exquisite paintings and a pale green and yellow color scheme add to the charm. The cuisine is innovative and sophisticated, with dishes like crayfish with trout caviar and chickpeas with thistles and prawns. More affordable fare is available at the ground-level bistro. ✉ *C. Zaragoza 20, Arenal* ☎ *954/502721* 💳 *MC, V* ✥ *B3.*

$ SPANISH ✕ **Vineria San Telmo.** As you enter the dimly lighted dining room, prepare to spend some time perusing a menu that is full of surprises. The tapas are superb and sophisticated, especially the foie gras with lychees and the black pudding on toast topped with slivers of creamy goat's milk

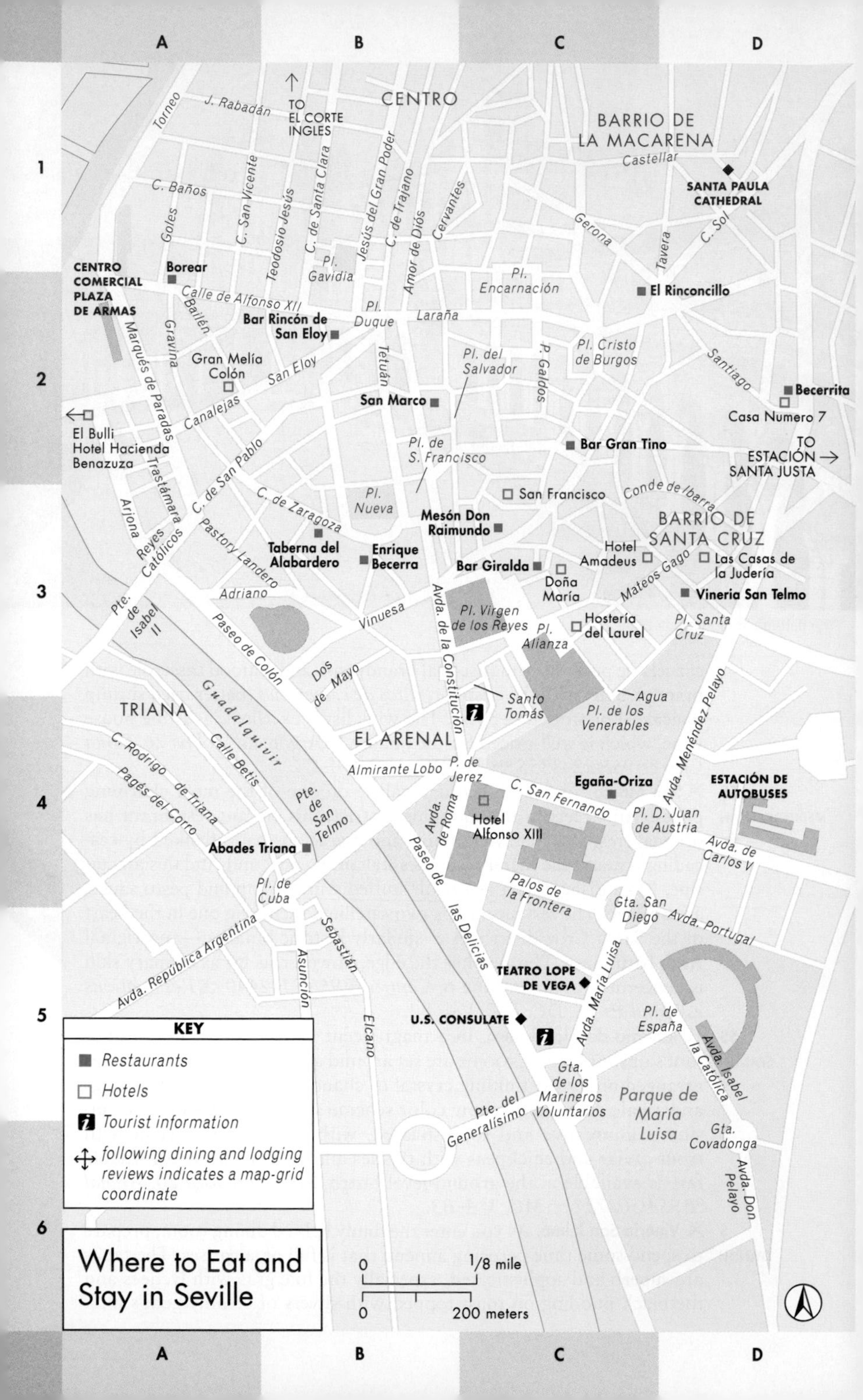

A
B
C
D
1
2
3
4
5
6
CENTRO
BARRIO DE LA MACARENA
TO EL CORTE INGLES
Torneo
J. Rabadán
C. Baños
Goles
C. San Vicente
Teodosio Jesús
C. de Santa Clara
Jesús del Gran Poder
C. de Trajano
Amor de Diós
Cervantes
Castellar
SANTA PAULA CATHEDRAL
Gerona
Tavera
C. Sol
Pl. Gavidia
Pl. Encarnación
El Rinconcillo
CENTRO COMERCIAL PLAZA DE ARMAS
Borear
Calle de Alfonso XII
Bailén
Gravina
Marqués de Paradas
Bar Rincón de San Eloy
Pl. Duque
Laraña
Tetuán
Pl. del Salvador
P. Galdos
Pl. Cristo de Burgos
Santiago
Gran Melía Colón
San Eloy
Canalejas
San Marco
Becerrita
Casa Numero 7
El Bulli Hotel Hacienda Benazuza
Trastámara
Pl. de S. Francisco
Bar Gran Tino
TO ESTACIÓN SANTA JUSTA
C. de San Pablo
C. de Zaragoza
Pl. Nueva
San Francisco
Conde de Ibarra
Arjona
Reyes Católicos
Pastor y Landero
Mesón Don Raimundo
BARRIO DE SANTA CRUZ
Taberna del Alabardero
Enrique Becerra
Bar Giralda
Doña María
Hotel Amadeus
Mateos Gago
Las Casas de la Judería
Vineria San Telmo
Adriano
Pte. de Isabel II
Paseo de Colón
Vinuesa
Avda. de la Constitución
Pl. Virgen de los Reyes
Pl. Alianza
Hostería del Laurel
Pl. Santa Cruz
Dos de Mayo
Santo Tomás
Agua
Pl. de los Venerables
TRIANA
Guadalquivir
EL ARENAL
Avda. Menéndez Pelayo
C. Rodrigo de Triana
Calle Betis
Pagés del Corro
Almirante Lobo
P. de Jerez
Egaña-Oriza
ESTACIÓN DE AUTOBUSES
Pte. de San Telmo
Avda. de Roma
Hotel Alfonso XIII
C. San Fernando
Pl. D. Juan de Austria
Avda. de Carlos V
Abades Triana
Paseo de las Delicias
Palos de la Frontera
Pl. de Cuba
Gta. San Diego
Avda. Portugal
Sebastián
Asunción
Avda. República Argentina
TEATRO LOPE DE VEGA
Avda. María Luisa
U.S. CONSULATE
Elcano
Pl. de España
Avda. Isabel la Católica
KEY
Restaurants
Hotels
Tourist information
following dining and lodging reviews indicates a map-grid coordinate
Gta. de los Marineros Voluntarios
Pte. del Generalísimo
Parque de María Luisa
Gta. Covadonga
Avda. Don Pelayo
Where to Eat and Stay in Seville
0
1/8 mile
0
200 meters

cheese. For a main course, try the black spaghetti with scallops. The Argentinean-owned restaurant's vast glass-fronted wine cellar includes some exciting South American labels as well as an extensive choice of Spanish vinos. It's near the touristy Alcazar, but there's barely a french fry or burger in sight. ✉ *Pl. Catalina de Ribera 4, Santa Cruz* ☎ *954/410600* ▭ *MC, V* ✣ *D3.*

WHERE TO STAY

Use the coordinate (✣ B2) at the end of each listing to locate a site on the corresponding map.

$$$$ Fodor's Choice ★ **Casa Numero 7.** Dating from 1847, this converted town house retains a homey, lived-in feel with family photographs, original oil paintings, and plush furnishings throughout. The owner is a director of González Byass, a major sherry producer, who apparently spent three years restoring the house, the result being that each room is individually decorated with tasteful artwork and antiques. The elegant salon has a fireplace and comfy chairs. The roof terrace has views of the Giralda, and breakfast is excellent, with fluffy scrambled eggs an agreeable option. **Pros:** the personal touch of a B&B; delightfully different. **Cons:** some rooms on interior patios have no natural light. ✉ *C. Virgenes 7, Santa Cruz* ☎ *95/422–1581* 🌐 *www.casanumero7.com* *6 rooms* *In-room: a/c, no TV, Wi-Fi. In-hotel: bar* ▭ *AE, V* *BP* ✣ *D2.*

$$$$ Fodor's Choice ★ **El Bulli Hotel Hacienda Benazuza.** This luxury hotel is in a rambling 10th-century country palace near Sanlúcar la Mayor, 15 km (9 mi) outside Seville. Surrounded by olive and orange trees and in a courtyard with towering palms, the building incorporates an 18th-century church. The interior has clay-tile floors and ocher walls. The acclaimed Michelin-starred restaurant, La Alquería, serves Spanish and international dishes. **Pros:** nonpareil beauty and taste; polished service. **Cons:** far from Seville; expensive. ✉ *C. Virgen de las Nieves, Sanlúcar la Mayor* ☎ *95/570–3344* 🌐 *www.elbullihotel.com* *26 rooms, 18 suites* *In-room: a/c, Wi-Fi. In-hotel: 2 restaurants, bar, tennis court, pool, Internet terminal, parking (free), some pets allowed* ▭ *AE, DC, MC, V* *Closed Nov.–Mar.* ✣ *A2.*

$$$$ **Gran Meliá Colón.** Much of this classic hotel's original decor remains, including a marble staircase leading up to the central lobby, which is crowned by a magnificent stained-glass dome and crystal candelabra. The hotel was originally built for 1929's Ibero-American Exposition, and each floor celebrates a different Spanish artist, with reproduction paintings set against an artful combination of period and contemporary design. Downstairs is the toreador-themed El Burladero bar and restaurant, which is packed midday with local business executives. The luxurious spa on the seventh floor offers a range of treatments. **Pros:** good central location; excellent restaurant; some great views. **Cons:** some rooms overlook airshaft; busy and noisy street. ✉ *Calle Canalejas 1, El Arenal/San Vicente* ☎ *95/450–5599* 🌐 *www.granmeliacolon.com* *162 rooms, 25 suites* *In-room: a/c, Wi-Fi. In-hotel: restaurant, bar, spa, Internet terminal, Wi-Fi hotspot* ▭ *AE, DC, MC, V* *BP* ✣ *A2.*

$$$$ ★ **Hotel Alfonso XIII.** Inaugurated by King Alfonso XIII in 1929, this grand hotel is a splendid, historic Mudejar-style palace, built around a central patio and surrounded by ornate brick arches. Public rooms have

marble floors, wood-panel ceilings, heavy Moorish lamps, stained glass, and ceramic tiles in typical Seville colors. The hotel houses both a Spanish and a Japanese restaurant and an elegant bar. If you can't afford a room, you can still enjoy the sumptuous surroundings: sip a glass of *fino* (sherry) while overlooking the fabulous central courtyard and appearing appropriately superior (and rich). **Pros:** both stately and hip; impeccable service. **Cons:** a tourist colony; colossally expensive. ✉ *San Fernando 2, El Arenal* ☎ *95/491–7000* 🌐 *www.westin.com/hotelalfonso* *127 rooms, 19 suites* *In-room: a/c, Wi-Fi. In-hotel: 2 restaurants, bar, pool, parking (paid)* ▭ *AE, DC, MC, V* ✥ *C4.*

$$ Fodor's Choice ★ **Hotel Amadeus.** With pianos in some of the soundproof rooms, a music room off the central patio, and classical concerts regularly held, this acoustic oasis is ideal for touring professional musicians and music fans in general. Each room is named for a different composer, and the 18th-century manor house has been equipped with such modern amenities as Wi-Fi and a small glass-wall elevator that moves quietly up and down a corner of the central patio. You can enjoy breakfast (an extra €8) on the roof terrace overlooking the Judería and Giralda. **Pros:** small but charming rooms; roof terrace. **Cons:** certain rooms are noisy; staff not always that helpful. ✉ *Calle Farnesio 6, Santa Cruz* ☎ *95/450–1443* 🌐 *www.hotelamadeussevilla.com* *14 rooms* *In-room: a/c, Wi-Fi. In-hotel: restaurant, parking (paid)* ▭ *AE, DC, MC, V* ✥ *C3.*

$$$ **Las Casas de la Judería.** This labyrinthine hotel tucked into a passageway off the Plaza Santa María occupies three of the barrio's old palaces, each arranged around an inner courtyard with fountains, traditional tile work, and plenty of greenery. The spacious guest rooms are painted in subdued pastels and decorated with prints of Seville; most have four-poster beds and wood beams. Breakfast is generous and includes champagne; the staff will also pack you a picnic if you have to depart early in the morning. **Pros:** lovely buildings; charming rooms. **Cons:** cobbled patios can be slippery; some rooms get little natural light. ✉ *Callejón de Dos Hermanas 7, Santa Cruz* ☎ *95/441–5150* 🌐 *www.casasypalacios.com* *103 rooms, 3 suites* *In-room: a/c, Wi-Fi. In-hotel: restaurant, bar, parking (paid)* ▭ *AE, D, DC, MC, V* *BP* ✥ *D3.*

$ **Posada del Lucero.** The country's only 16th-century building being used as a posada has architecture that combines Mudejar-style flourishes with cutting-edge modern design. Original columns and three interior patios (including the former carriage house) add to the period charm. A tastefully tiled fountain provides a soothing backdrop of running water reminiscent of the traditional Moorish gardens. In contrast, the rooms are decorated in a minimalist style with ocher-, brown-, and cream-color textiles and sleek walnut furniture. The bathrooms are of dramatic black slate. **Pros:** lots of historic atmosphere; excellent central position. **Cons:** no restaurant. ✉ *Almirante Apodaca 7, Centro* ☎ *95/450–2480 www.hotelposadadellucero.com 40 rooms In-room: a/c, Wi-Fi. In-hotel: bar, laundry service, Wi-Fi hotspot* ▭ *AE, MC, V* ✥ *C1.*

$ **San Francisco.** An 18th-century town house near the main shopping street houses this modest hotel. A cool patio enlivens the entrance, and the simple rooms have traditional dark wood furniture, tiled floors, and small en suite marble bathrooms. The upstairs terrace is a major perk, with its five-star cathedral views; the rooms up here are the best, if you can get one. The friendly owner speaks some English. **Pros:** attentive management; excellent value; fine location. **Cons:** noisy neighborhood; rooms small and drab. ✉ *Calle Álvarez Quintero 38, Santa Cruz* ☎ *95/450–1541* 🌐 *www.sanfranciscoh.com* *17 rooms* *In-room: a/c, Wi-Fi. In-hotel: bar, parking (paid)* *AE, DC, MC, V* ⏲ *Closed Aug.* ✥ *C3.*

NIGHTLIFE AND THE ARTS

Seville has lively nightlife and plenty of cultural activity. The free monthly magazine *El Giraldillo* (🌐 *www.elgiraldillo.es*) lists classical and jazz concerts, plays, dance performances, art exhibits, and films in Seville and all major Andalusian cities. (For American films in English, look for the designation *v.o.*, for *versión original.*)

NIGHTLIFE

FLAMENCO CLUBS

Seville has a handful of commercial *tablaos* (flamenco clubs), patronized more by tourists than locals. They generally offer somewhat mechanical flamenco at high prices, with mediocre cuisine. Check local listings and ask at your hotel for performances by top artists. Spontaneous flamenco is often found for free in *peñas flamencas* (flamenco clubs) and flamenco bars in Triana.

In the heart of Triana, **Casa Anselma** is an unmarked bar on the corner of Antillano Campos where Anselma and her friends sing and dance for the pure joy and catharsis that are at the heart of flamenco. ✉ *Calle Pagés del Corro 49, Triana* ☎ *No phone* *Free* ⏲ *Shows Mon.–Sat. at 11.*

★ **Casa de la Memoria de Al-Andaluz**, in an 18th-century palace, has a nightly show plus classes for the intrepid. ✉ *Calle Ximenez de Enciso 28, Santa Cruz* ☎ *95/456–0670* 🌐 *www.casadelamemoria.es* *€15* ⏲ *Shows nightly at 9.*

El Tamboril is a late-night bar in the heart of the Barrio de Santa Cruz, noted for its great glass case in which the Virgin of Rocío sits in splendor. At 11 each night, locals pack in to sing the *Salve Rociera,* an emotive prayer to her. Afterward, everything from flamenco to salsa continues until the early hours. ✉ *Pl. Santa Cruz, Santa Cruz* *Free.*

★ **La Carbonería**, a rambling former coal yard, is usually packed on Thursday when the flamenco is spontaneous. There's no entry charge, and it's open the rest of the week, too, except Sunday. ✉ *C. Levíes 18, Santa Cruz* ☎ *95/421–4460* ⏲ *1st show at 11* PM, *2nd at 1* AM.

La Madrugá collects Triana fans and flamenco faithful hoping to catch a spontaneous outburst of dance. ✉ *Calle Salado, at Calle Virgen de las Huertas, Triana* ☎ *No phone* *Free* ⏲ *Shows nightly after 11.*

Los Gallos is an intimate club in the heart of the Barrio de Santa Cruz. Performances are entertaining and reasonably authentic. ✉ *Pl. Santa Cruz 11, Santa Cruz* ☎ *95/421–6981* 🌐 *www.tablaolosgallos.com* *€30 with 1 drink* ⏲ *Shows nightly at 8 and 10:30. Closed Jan.*

Continued on page 686

FLAMENCO

THE HEARTBEAT OF SPAIN

Palmas, the staccato clapping of flamenco.

Rule one about flamenco: You don't see it. You feel it. There's no soap-opera emoting here. The pain and yearning on the dancers' faces and the eerie voices—typically communicating grief over a lost love or family member—are real. If the dancers manage to summon the supernatural *duende* and allow this inner demon to overcome them, then they have done their jobs well.

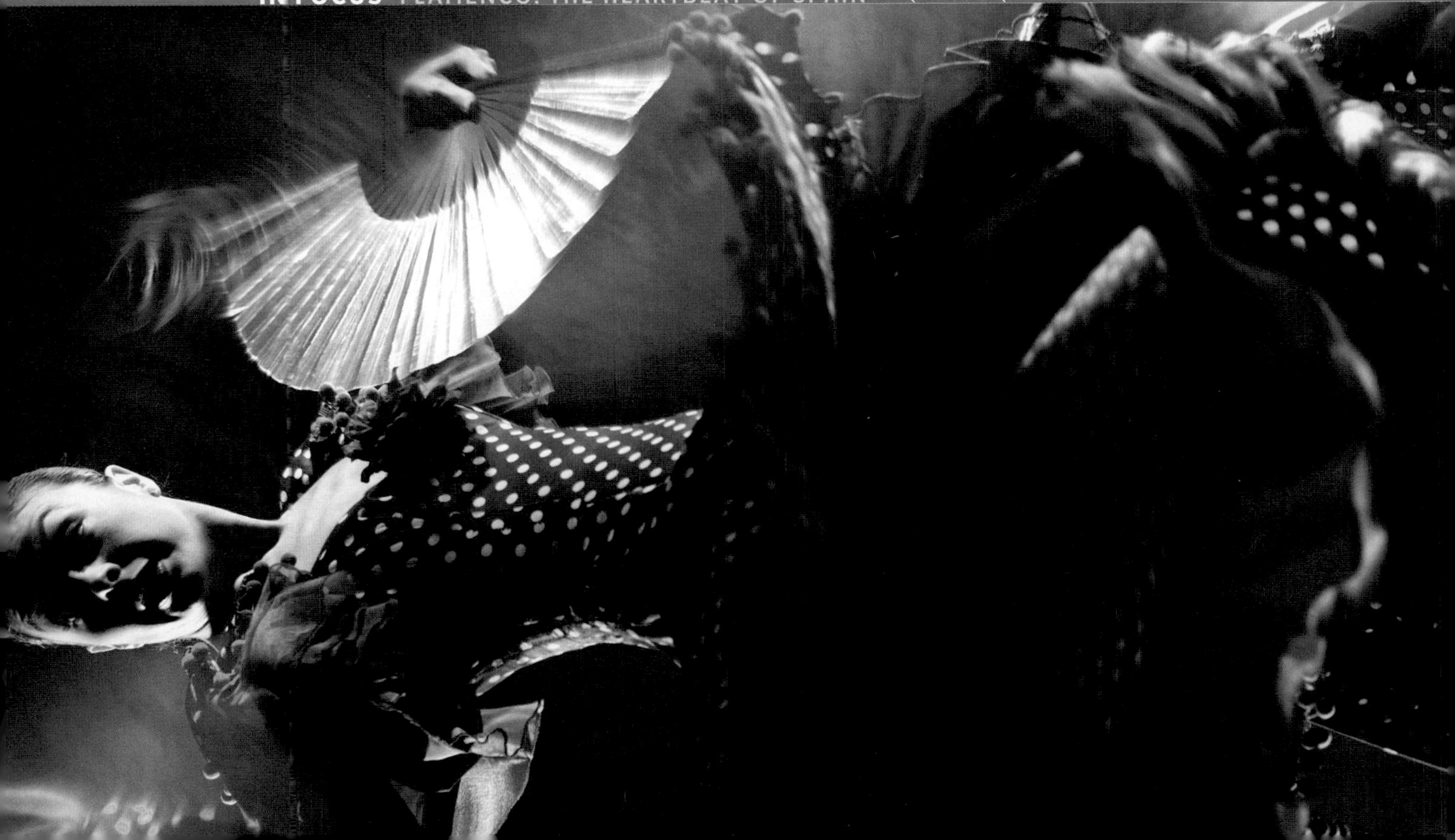

DUENDE HEAD TO TOE

FACE

Facial expression is considered another tool for the dancer, and it's never plastered on but projected from some deeper place. For women, the hair is usually pulled back in touring flamenco performances in order to give the back row a chance to see more clearly the passionate expressions. In smaller settings like *tablaos*, hair is usually let down and is supposed to better reveal the beauty of the female form overall.

LEGS

The knees are always slightly bent to absorb the shock of repeated rapid-fire stomping. Flamenco dancers have legs that rival marathon runners' for their lean, muscular form.

HANDS

Wrists rotate while hands move, articulating each finger individually, curling in and out. The trick is to have it appear like an effortless flourish, instead of a spinning helicopter blade.

CARRIAGE

Upright and proud. The chest is out; shoulders back. Despite this position, the body should never carry tension—it needs to remain pliable and fluid.

FEET

With professional dancers, the feet can move so quickly, they blur like humming bird wings in action. When they move slowly, you can watch the different ways a foot can strike the floor. A *planta* is when the whole foot strikes the floor, as opposed to when the ball of the foot or the heel (*taco*) hits. Each one must be a "clean" strike or the sound will be off. This percussion is the dancers' musical contribution to the song; if a step is off, it can throw the whole song out of whack.

FLAMENCO 101

All the elements of flamenco working in harmony.

ORIGINS

The music is largely Arabic in its beginnings, but you'll detect echoes of Greek dirges and Jewish chants, with healthy doses of Flemish and traditional Castillian thrown in. Hindu sways, Roman mimes, and other movement informs the dance, but we may never know the specific origins of flamenco.

The dance, along with the nomadic Gypsies, spread throughout Andalusia and within a few centuries had developed into many variations and styles, some of them named after the city where they were born (such as Malagueñas, Sevillanas) and others taking on the names after people, emotions, or bands. In all, there are over 50 different styles (or *palos*) of flamenco, four of which are the stylistic pillars others branch off from—differing mainly in rhythm and mood: *Toná*, *Soleá*, *Fandango*, and *Seguiriya*.

CLAPPING AND CASTANETS

The sum of its parts are awe-inspiring, but if you boil it down, flamenco is a combination of music, singing, and dance. Staccato hand-clapping almost sneaks in as a fourth part—the sounds made from all the participants' palms, or *palmas* is part of the *duende*—but this element remains more of a

continued on following page

THE FLAMENCO HOOK-UP

When *duende* leads to love.

That cheek-to-cheek chemistry that exists between dance partners isn't missing in flamenco—it's simply repositioned between the dancer and the musicians. In fact, when you watch flamenco, you may feel what seems like an electric wire connecting the dancer to the musicians. In each *palo* (style) of music there are certain *letras* (lyrics) inherent within the song that tip off dancers and spark a change in rhythm. If the cues are off, the dancer may falter or simply come off flat. At its best, the dancer and the guitarist are like an old married couple that can musically finish each other's sentences. This interconnectedness has been known to lead into the bedroom, and it's not unusual for dancers and musicians to hook up offstage. Two famous couples include dancer Eva La Yerbabuena with guitarist Paco Jarano and dancer Manuela Carrasco with guitarist Joaquín Amador.

connector that all in the performance take part in when their hands are free.

Hand-clapping was likely flamenco's original key instrument before the guitar, *cajón* (wooden box used for percussion), and other instruments arrived on the scene. Perhaps the simplest way to augment the clapping is to add a uniquely designed six-string guitar, in which case you've got yourself a *tablao*, or people seated around a singer and clapping. Dance undoubtedly augments the experience, but isn't necessary for a *tablao*. These exist all throughout Andalusia and are usually private affairs with people who love flamenco. One needn't be a Gypsy in order to take part in it. But it doesn't hurt.

Castanets (or *palillos*) were absorbed by the Phoenician culture and adopted by the Spanish, now part of their own folklore. They accompany other traditional folk dances in Spain and are used pervasively throughout flamenco (though not always present in some forms of dance). Castanets can be secured in any number of ways. The most important thing is that they are securely fastened to the hand (by thumb or any combination of fingers) so that the wrist can snap it quickly and make the sound.

FLAMENCO NOW

Flamenco's enormous international resurgence has been building for the past few decades. Much of this revival can be attributed to pioneers like legendary singer Camarón de la Isla, guitarist Paco de Lucía, or even outsiders like Miles Davis fusing flamenco with other genres like jazz and rock. This melding brought forth flamenco pop—which flourished in the '80s and continues today—as well as disparate fusions with almost every genre imaginable, including heavy metal and hip-hop. Today the most popular flamenco fusion artists include Ojos de Brujo and Chambao—all of which have found an audience outside of Spain.

IT'S A MAN'S WORLD

Joaquín Cortés

In the U.S., our image of a flamenco dancer is usually a woman in a red dress. So you may be surprised to learn that male dancers dominate flamenco and always have. In its beginnings, men did all the footwork and only since the '40s and '50s have women started to match men step-for-step and star in performances. And in the tabloids, men usually get the sex symbol status more than women (as seen through Farruquito and Cortés). Suits are the traditional garb for male dancers, and recent trends have seen female dancers wearing them as well—presumably rebelling against the staid gender roles that continue to rule Spain. Today, male dancers tend to wear a simple pair of black trousers and a white button-down shirt. The sex appeal comes from unbuttoning the shirt to flash a little chest and having the pants tailor-made to a tightness that can't be found in any store. In traditional *tablaos*, male dancers perform without accessories, but in touring performances—upping the razzle dazzle—anything goes: canes, hats, tuxedos, or even shirtless (much to the delight of female fans).

DANCING WITH THE STARS

SEX, MANSLAUGHTER, EVEN MONOGAMY

Farruquito was born into a flamenco dynasty. He started dancing when he was 8 years old and rose very high in the flamenco and celebrity world (*People* magazine named him one of the 50 most beautiful people in the world) until September 2003 when he ran two lights in an unlicensed, uninsured BMW, hitting and killing a pedestrian.

FARRUQUITO,
The Wild Child

EVA LA YERBABUENA,
The Pro

This young dancer from Granada has won numerous prizes, including the coveted Flamenco Hoy's Best Dancer award in 2000. In 2006, she took her tour around Asia and New Zealand. She tends to stay away from the tabloids because she doesn't run red lights and enjoys a stable relationship with flamenco guitarist Paco Jarano.

Stateside, we're still swooning over her Oscar-nominated sister, Penélope, but in Spain, Mónica also captures the spotlight. With the same dark hair and pillowy lips as her sibling, Mónica works as a flamenco dancer and actress. Most recently she starred in a soap opera in Spain called *Paso Adelante*, a Spanish version of *Fame*.

MÓNICA CRUZ,
The Bombshell

JOAQUÍN CORTÉS,
The Lady's Man

He's considered a visionary dancer, easily the most famous worldwide for the past 15 years. Despite this, he's often in the press for the hotties he's dated rather than his talent; former flames include Oscar-winner Mira Sorvino and supermodel Naomi Campbell. Even *Sports Illustrated* cover girl Elle MacPherson labeled him "pure sex."

Outdoor restaurants in Seville's Santa Cruz quarter

THE ARTS

Long prominent in the opera world, Seville is proud of its opera house, the **Teatro de la Maestranza** (✉ *Paseo de Colón 22, El Arenal* ☎ *95/422–3344* 🌐 *www.teatromaestranza.com*). Classical music and ballet are performed at the **Teatro Lope de Vega** (✉ *Av. María Luisa s/n, Parque de María Luisa* ☎ *95/459–0853*). The modern **Teatro Central** (✉ *José de Gálvez s/n, Isla de la Cartuja* ☎ *95/503–7200* 🌐 *www.teatrocentral.com*) stages theater, dance, and classical and contemporary music.

BULLFIGHTING Bullfighting season is Easter through Columbus Day; most *corridas* (bullfights) are held on Sunday. The highlight is the April Fair, with Spain's leading toreros; other key dates are Corpus Christi (about seven weeks after Easter), Assumption (August 15), and the last weekend in September. Bullfights take place at the **Maestranza Bullring** (✉ *Paseo de Colón 12, Arenal* ☎ *95/422–4577*). Tickets are expensive; buy them in advance alongside the bullring from the official ticket office, the **despacho de entradas** (✉ *Calle Adriano 37, El Arenal* ☎ *95/450–1382*). Unofficial despachos sell tickets on Calle Sierpes but charge a 20% commission.

SHOPPING

Seville is the region's main shopping area and the place for archetypal Andalusian souvenirs, most of which are sold in the Barrio de Santa Cruz and around the cathedral and Giralda, especially on Calle Alemanes. The shopping street for locals is Calle Sierpes, along with neighboring Cuna, Tetuan, Velázquez, Plaza Magdalena, and Plaza Duque—boutiques abound here. **El Postigo** (✉ *Calle Arfe s/n, El Arenal* ☎ *95/456–0013*) is a permanent arts-and-crafts market, open every day except Sunday, near the cathedral. Near the Puente del Cachorro bridge, the old Estación de Córdoba train station has been converted into a stylish shopping center, the **Centro Comercial Plaza de Armas** (✉ *Enter on Pl. de la Legión, El Arenal*), with boutiques, bars, fast-food joints, a nightclub, and a cinema complex. The main branch of the pan-Spanish department store **El Corte Inglés** (✉ *Pl. Duque 8, Centro* ☎ *95/422–0931*) has everything from high fashion to local wine. It does not close for siesta.

ANTIQUES

For antiques, try Mateos Gago, opposite the Giralda, and in the Barrio de Santa Cruz on Jamerdana and Rodrigo Caro, off Plaza Alianza.

BOOKS

A large assortment of books in English, Spanish, French, and Italian can be found near the cathedral at the American-owned **Librería Vértice** (✉ *San Fernando 33–35, Santa Cruz* ☎ *95/421–1654*).

CERAMICS

In the Barrio de Santa Cruz, browse along Mateos Gago; on Romero Murube, between Plaza Triunfo and Plaza Alianza, on the edge of the barrio; and between Plaza Doña Elvira and Plaza de los Venerables. Look for traditional azulejo tiles and other ceramics in the Triana **potters' district**, on Calle Alfarería and Calle Antillano Campos. **Cerámica Montalván** (✉ *Calle Alfarería 23, El Zurraque* ☎ *95/434–4608*) is the only ceramics store in Triana that doubles as a workshop. If you ask nicely, you may be able to watch the craftsmen at work. In central Seville, **Martian Ceramics** (✉ *Calle Sierpes 74, Centro* ☎ *95/421–3413*) has high-quality dishes, especially the finely painted flowers-on-white patterns native to Seville.

FANS

Casa Rubio (✉ *Sierpes 56, Centro* ☎ *95/422–6872*) is Seville's premier fan store—no mean distinction.

FLAMENCO WEAR

Flamenco wear can be expensive; local women will gladly spend a month's grocery money, or more, on their frills, with dresses ranging from €100 to €400 and up.

Lola Azahare (✉ *Calle Cuna 31, Centro* ☎ *95/422–6287*) is a highly recommended local shop. **Molina** (✉ *Sierpes 11, Centro* ☎ *95/422–9254*) sells flamenco dresses as well as traditional foot-tapping shoes. For privately fitted and custom-made flamenco dresses, try **Taller de Diseño** (✉ *Calle Luchana 6, Centro* ☎ *95/422–7186*).

PASTRIES

Seville's most celebrated pastry outlet is **La Campana** (✉ *Sierpes 1, Centro* ☎ *95/422–3570*), founded in 1885. Under the gilt-edged ceiling you can enjoy the flanlike *tocino de cielo*, or "heavenly bacon." Andalusia's convents are known for their homemade pastries, and you can sample sweets from several convents at **El Torno** (✉ *Pl. del Cabildo s/n, Santa Cruz* ☎ *95/421–9190*), named after the revolving tray the nuns use to display their wares.

PORCELAIN

La Cartuja china, originally crafted at La Cartuja Monastery but now made outside Seville, is sold at **La Alacena** (✉ *Calle Alfonso XII 25, San Vicente* ☎ *95/422–8021*).

STREET MARKETS

A few blocks north of Plaza Nueva, **Plaza del Duque** has a crafts market on Friday and Saturday. The flea market **El Jueves** is held on Calle Feria in the Barrio de la Macarena on Thursday morning.

TEXTILES

You can find blankets, shawls, and embroidered tablecloths woven by local artisans at the three shops of **Artesanía Textil** (✉ *Calle García de Vinuesa 33, El Arenal* ☎ *95/456–2840* ✉ *Sierpes 70, Centro* ☎ *95/422–0125* ✉ *Pl. de Doña Elvira 4, Santa Cruz* ☎ *95/421–4748*).

AROUND SEVILLE

CARMONA

32 km (20 mi) east of Seville off NIV.

Wander the ancient, narrow streets of here and you'll feel like you've been transported back in time. Claiming to be one of the oldest inhabited places in Spain (both Phoenicians and Carthaginians had settlements here), Carmona, on a steep, fortified hill, became an important town under the Romans and the Moors. There are many Mudejar and Renaissance churches, medieval gateways, and simple whitewashed houses of clear Moorish influence, punctuated here and there by a baroque palace. Local fiestas are held in mid-September.

ESSENTIALS

Visitor Information Carmona (✉ *Arco de la Puerta de Sevilla* ☎ *95/419–0955* 🌐 *www.turismo.carmona.org*).

EXPLORING

Park your car near the Puerta de Sevilla in the imposing **Alcázar de Abajo** (Lower Fortress), a Moorish fortification built on Roman foundations. Maps are available at the tourist office, in the tower beside the gate. Across the road from the Alcázar de Abajo is the church of **San Pedro** (✉ *Calle San Pedro*), begun in 1466. Its interior is an unbroken mass of sculptures and gilded surfaces, and its baroque tower, erected in 1704, unabashedly imitates Seville's Giralda. Up Calle Prim is the **Plaza San Fernando**, in the heart of the old town; its 17th-century houses have Moorish overtones.

The Gothic church of **Santa María** (✉ *Calle Martín*) was built between 1424 and 1518 on the site of Carmona's former Great Mosque and retains its beautiful Moorish courtyard, studded with orange trees. It's open Monday–Saturday, and entrance is €3.

Behind Santa María is the **Museo de la Ciudad**, with exhibits on Carmona's history. There's plenty for children, and the interactive exhibits are labeled in English and Spanish. ✉ *Calle San Ildefonso 1* ☎ *954/140128* 🎫 *€2* ⏲ *Mon. 11–2, Tues.–Sun. 11–7.*

Stroll down to the **Puerta de Córdoba** (Córdoba Gate) on the eastern edge of town. This old gateway was first built by the Romans around AD 175, then altered by Moorish and Renaissance additions.

The Moorish **Alcázar de Arriba** (Upper Fortress) was built on Roman foundations and converted by King Pedro the Cruel into a Mudejar palace. Pedro's summer residence was destroyed by a 1504 earthquake, but the parador amid its ruins has a breathtaking view.

★ The **Roman Necropolis** lies at the western edge of town in underground chambers where 900 tombs were placed between the 2nd and 4th centuries BC. The walls, decorated with leaf and bird motifs, have niches for burial urns and tombs such as the **Elephant Vault** and the **Servilia Tomb**, a complete Roman villa with colonnaded arches and vaulted side galleries. ✉ *C. Enmedio* ☎ *95/562–4615* 🎫 *2€* ⏲ *Mid-Sept.–mid-June, Tues.–Fri. 9–4:45, weekends 10–1:45; mid-June–mid-Sept., Tues.–Fri. 8:30–1:45, Sat. 10–2.*

WHERE TO EAT AND STAY

$$–$$$ SPANISH ✕ **San Fernando**. You enter from a side street, but this second-floor restaurant in an 18th-century palace looks out onto the Plaza de San Fernando. The beige dining room is quietly elegant in its simplicity, and the kitchen serves Spanish dishes with flair—as in cream of green apple soup or lightly fried potato slivers shaped into a bird's nest. Game, including partridge, is a perennial favorite. Larger appetites can opt for the special menu with five tasting dishes—a steal at under €30. ✉ *Calle Sacramento 3* ☎ *95/414–3556* 💳 *AE, DC, MC, V* ⏲ *Closed Mon. and Aug. No dinner Sun.*

$$$ Fodor's Choice ★ 🏨 **Parador Alcázar del Rey Don Pedro**. This parador has superb views from its hilltop position among the ruins of Pedro the Cruel's summer palace. The public rooms surround a central, Moorish-style patio, and the vaulted dining hall and adjacent bar open onto an outdoor terrace overlooking the sloping garden. The spacious guest rooms have rugs and dark furniture. All but six, which face onto the front courtyard, look south over the valley; the best rooms are on the top floor. **Pros:** unbeatable views over the fields; great sense of history. **Cons:** feels slightly lifeless after Seville. ✉ *Calle del Alcázar s/n* ☎ *95/414–1010* 🌐 *www.parador.es* 🛏 *63 rooms* 🛎 *In-room: a/c, Wi-Fi. In-hotel: restaurant, bar, pool, Internet terminal* 💳 *AE, DC, MC, V.*

ITÁLICA

12 km (7 mi) north of Seville, 1 km (½ mi) beyond Santiponce.

Fodor's Choice ★ One of Roman Iberia's most important cities in the 2nd century, with a population of more than 10,000, Itálica today is a monument of Roman ruins, complete with admission charge. Founded by Scipio Africanus in 205 BC as a home for veteran soldiers, Itálica gave the Roman world two great emperors: Trajan (52–117) and Hadrian (76–138). You can find traces of city streets, cisterns, and the floor plans of several villas, some with mosaic floors, though all the best mosaics and statues have been removed to Seville's Museum of Archaeology. Itálica was abandoned and plundered as a quarry by the Visigoths, who preferred Seville. It fell into decay around AD 700. The remains include the huge, elliptical **amphitheater**, which held 40,000 spectators, a **Roman theater**, and **Roman baths.** ☎ *95/599–7376 or 95/599–6583* ✉ *€1.50* ⏲ *Tues.–Sat. 9–5:30, Sun. 10–4.*

RONDA

Fodor's Choice ★ *147 km (91 mi) southeast of Seville, 61 km (38 mi) northwest of Marbella.*

Ronda, one of the oldest towns in Spain, is known for its spectacular position and views. Secure in its mountain fastness on a rock high over the Río Guadalevín, the town was a stronghold for the legendary Andalusian bandits who held court here from the 18th to early 20th centuries. Ronda's most dramatic element is its ravine (360 feet deep and 210 feet across)—known as **El Tajo**—which divides La Ciudad, the old Moorish town, from El Mercadillo, the "new town," which sprang up after the Christian Reconquest of 1485. Tour buses roll in daily with sightseers from the coast 49 km (30 mi) away, and on weekends affluent Sevillanos flock to their second homes here. Stay overnight midweek to see this noble town's true colors.

The most attractive approach is from the south. The winding but well-maintained A376 from San Pedro de Alcántara travels north up through the mountains of the Serranía de Ronda. Take the first turnoff to Ronda from A376. Entering the lowest part of town, known as El Barrio, you can see parts of the old walls, including the 13th-century Puerta de Almocobar and the 16th-century Puerta de Carlos V gates. The road climbs past the Iglesia del Espíritu Santo (Church of the Holy Spirit) and up into the heart of town.

GETTING HERE AND AROUND

At least three daily buses run here from Marbella (via San Pedro de Alcántara), the same number from Antequera, and six from Málaga (via Grazalema).

ESSENTIALS

Visitor Information Ronda (✉ *Pl. de España 1* ☎ *952/871272*). **Ronda** (✉ *Paseo de Bas Infante s/n* ☎ *952/187119*).

EXPLORING

Begin in El Mercadillo, where the **tourist office** *(see Essentials, above)* in the Plaza de España can supply you with a map.

Immediately south of the Plaza de España is Ronda's most famous bridge, the **Juan Peña El Lebrijano** (also known as the Puente Nuevo or New Bridge), an architectural marvel built between 1755 and 1793. The bridge's lantern-lit parapet offers dizzying views of the awesome gorge. Just how many people have met their ends here nobody knows, but the architect of the Puente Nuevo fell to his death while inspecting work on the bridge. During the civil war, hundreds of victims were hurled from it.

Cross the Puente Nuevo into **La Ciudad**, the old Moorish town, and wander the twisting streets of white houses with birdcage balconies.

The excavated remains of the **Baños Arabes** (Arab Baths) date from Ronda's tenure as capital of a Moorish *taifa* (kingdom). The star-shape vents in the roof are an inferior imitation of the ceiling of the beautiful bathhouse in Granada's Alhambra. The baths are beneath the Puente Arabe (Arab Bridge) in a ravine below the Palacio del Marqués de Salvatierra. *€3 Weekdays 10–6, weekends 10–3.*

The collegiate church of **Santa María la Mayor**, which serves as Ronda's cathedral, has roots in Moorish times: originally the Great Mosque of Ronda, the tower and adjacent galleries, built for viewing festivities in the square, retain their Islamic design. After the mosque was destroyed (when the Moors were overthrown), it was rebuilt as a church and dedicated to the Virgen de la Encarnación after the Reconquest. The naves are late Gothic, and the main altar is heavy with baroque gold leaf. The church is around the corner from the remains of a mosque, Minarete Arabe (Moorish Minaret) at the end of the Marqués de Salvatierra. ✉ *Pl. Duquesa de Parcent €4 May–Sept., daily 10–8; Oct.–Apr., daily 10–6.*

A stone palace with twin Mudejar towers, the **Palacio de Mondragón** (Palace of Mondragón) was probably the residence of Ronda's Moorish kings. Ferdinand and Isabella appropriated it after their victory in 1485. Today you can wander through the patios, with their brick arches and delicate Mudejar-stucco tracery, and admire the mosaics and *artesonado* (coffered) ceiling. The second floor holds a small museum with archaeological items found near Ronda, plus the reproduction of a dolmen, a prehistoric stone monument. ✉ *Pl. Mondragón ☎ 952/878450 €3 Apr.–Oct., weekdays 10–6, weekends 10–3; May–Sept., weekdays 10–8, weekends 10–3.*

The main sight in Ronda's commercial center, El Mercadillo, is the **Plaza de Toros**. Pedro Romero (1754–1839), the father of modern bullfighting and Ronda's most famous native son, is said to have killed 5,600 bulls here during his long career. In the museum beneath the plaza you can see posters for Ronda's very first bullfights, held here in 1785. The plaza was once owned by the late bullfighter Antonio Ordóñez, on whose nearby ranch Orson Welles's ashes were scattered (as directed in his will)—indeed, the ring has become a favorite of filmmakers. Every September, the bullring is the scene of Ronda's *corridas goyescas,* named after Francisco Goya, whose bullfight sketches (*tauromaquias*) were inspired by Romero's skill and art. The participants and the dignitaries in the audience don the costumes of Goya's time for the occasion. Seats for these fights cost a small fortune and are booked far in advance. Other than that, the plaza is rarely used for fights except during Ronda's May festival. ☎ *952/874132 €6 Oct.–Apr., daily 10–6; May–Sept., daily 10–8.*

10

OFF THE BEATEN PATH

Beyond the bullring in El Mercadillo, you can relax in the shady **Alameda del Tajo** gardens, one of the loveliest spots in Ronda. At the end of the gardens, a balcony protrudes from the face of the cliff, offering a vertigo-inducing view of the valley below. Stroll along the cliff-top walk to the Reina Victoria hotel, built by British settlers from Gibraltar at the turn of the 20th century as a fashionable rest stop on the Algeciras–Bobadilla rail line.

WHERE TO EAT AND STAY

$–$$$ SPANISH ✕ **Almocábar.** Tucked agreeably away from the main tourist hub, this unpretentious tapas bar and restaurant on a lovely plaza offers great value and inventive cuisine. Dishes include unusual and tasty starters, like duck paté with goat cheese, and several salad choices, including one of pear, pine nuts, and walnuts on mixed greens. Get here early if you want to sample the tapas, as the narrow bar gets packed with the local crowd on their *tapear* bar crawl. The delicious *patatas alioli* (cooked potatoes in a creamily pungent garlic sauce) are great for sharing. ✉ *Calle Ruedo Alameda 5* ☎ *952/875977* ▭ *No credit cards* ⊙ *Closed Tues.*

$$ SPANISH ✕ **Pedro Romero.** Named for the father of modern bullfighting, this restaurant opposite the bullring is packed with bullfight paraphernalia. Mounted bulls' heads peer down at you as you tuck into *sopa de la casa* (soup with ham, rice, bread, and eggs) or *conejo a la Rondeña* (rabbit in onion sauce) and, for dessert, *leche frita con salsa de mandarina* (fried custard with orange sauce). Previous diners include Ernest Hemingway and Orson Welles, whose photos are displayed. ✉ *Virgen de la Paz 18* ☎ *952/871110* ▭ *AE, DC, MC, V.*

$$$$ ECLECTIC ★ ✕ **Tragabuches.** Argentinean chef Walter Geist is famed for his innovative menu, and the best way to sample it is to choose the *menú de degustación,* a taster's menu of five courses and a dessert (€59.90). It includes imaginative choices such as *ajoblanco* (creamy cold soup with almonds, smoked mackerel, caviar, and mushrooms) and white-garlic ice cream with pine nuts (delicious, despite how it sounds). Traditional and modern furnishings blend in the two dining rooms. This Michelin-star restaurant is around the corner from Ronda's parador. You can also purchase a cookbook that contains some of the restaurant's best-loved dishes. Be wary when ordering bottled water as there have been complaints that unnecessarily expensive imports are presented, which can hike up the price. ✉ *José Aparicio 1* ☎ *952/190291* ▭ *AE, DC, MC, V* ⊙ *Closed Mon. No dinner Sun.*

$$ ★ 🏨 **Alavera de los Baños.** This small, German-run hotel was used as a backdrop for the film classic *Carmen.* Fittingly, given its location next to the Moorish baths, there's an Arab-influenced theme throughout, with terra-cotta tiles, graceful arches, and pastel-color washes on the walls. The two rooms on the first floor have their own terraces and open onto the split-level garden—well worth the extra €10. The dinner-only restaurant ($) specializes in Moroccan cuisine using predominantly organic foods. Breakfast includes homemade jams and breads, plus local cheeses. **Pros:** very atmospheric and historic; owners speak several languages. **Cons:** rooms vary in size; no lunch available. ✉ *Hoya San Miguel s/n* ☎ *952/879143* 🌐 *www.andalucia.com/alavera* ⇆ *9 rooms* ♨ *In-room: no a/c. In-hotel: restaurant, bar, pool, Wi-Fi hotspot* ▭ *MC, V* 🍽 *BP.*

$$$ 🏨 **Ancinipo.** The artistic legacy of its former owners, Ronda artist Téllez Loriguillo and acclaimed Japanese watercolor painter Miki Haruta, is

The stunningly perched hilltop town of Ronda

evidenced throughout this boutique hotel. The interior has exposed stone panels, steel-and-glass fittings, mosaic-tile bathrooms, and many murals and paintings. The more expensive rooms have small sitting areas and bathrooms with hydromassage tubs. Most rooms have dramatic mountain views. The Atrium restaurant ($$) dishes up such traditional favorites as *migas* (fried bread crumbs with sausage and spices) and oxtail stew, followed by chestnuts with brandy and cream. **Pros:** very central position; cutting-edge design. **Cons:** a few rooms lack panoramic view; starting to look a tad shabby. ✉ *José Aparicio 7* ☎ *952/161002* 🌐 *www.hotelacinipo.com* *16 rooms* *In-room: Wi-Fi. In-hotel: restaurant, bar, parking* ▭ *AE, DC, MC, V.*

10

$$–$$$ **El Molino del Santo**. In a converted olive mill next to a rushing stream near Benaoján, 10 km (7 mi) from Ronda, this British-run establishment was one of Andalusia's first country hotels. Guest rooms are arranged around a pleasant patio and come in different sizes, some with a terrace. This is a good base for walks in the mountains, and the hotel also rents mountain bikes. It's eco-conscious, too, and uses solar panels for hot water and to heat the pool. The restaurant ($–$$) serves excellent meals. **Pros:** superb for hikers; friendly owners. **Cons:** you won't hear much Spanish spoken (most guests are British); a car is essential if you want to explore further afield. ✉ *Estación de Benaoján s/n, Benaoján* ☎ *952/167151* 🌐 *www.andalucia.com/molino* *18 rooms* *In-room: no TV. In-hotel: restaurant, pool, bicycles* ▭ *AE, DC, MC, V* ⊙ *Closed mid-Nov.–mid-Feb.* 🍴 *BP.*

$$ **Finca la Guzmana**. This traditional Andalusian *corijo* (cottage) 4 km (2½ mi) east of Ronda has been lovingly restored with bright, fresh decor to complement the original beams, wood-burning stoves, and

sublime setting—the cottage is surrounded by olive trees and grapevines. Walkers, bird-watchers, and painters are frequent guests. The owners also organize trips (guided or unguided) through the surrounding villages, and you can borrow bicycles. Breakfast is more generous here than many other places, with homemade bread, preserves, and local cheeses, and there are tea- and coffee-making facilities in the rooms. **Pros:** surrounded by beautiful countryside; English-speaking owners. **Cons:** it's a hike to Ronda and the shops; no restaurant. ✉ *Aptdo de Correos 408* ☎ *600/006305* 🌐 *www.laguzmana.com* *5 rooms* *In-room: Wi-Fi. In-hotel: pool* *No credit cards* *CP.*

$$ ★ **San Gabriel.** In the oldest part of Ronda, this hotel is run by a family who converted their 18th-century home into an enchanting, informal hotel (they still live in part of the building). The common areas, furnished with antiques, are warm and cozy and include a DVD screening room with autographed photos of actors (John Lithgow, Isabella Rossellini, and Bob Hoskins, in town to film the 2000 television movie version of *Don Quixote,* were among the hotel's first guests). Some guest rooms have small sitting areas and Jacuzzi bathtubs; all are sumptuously furnished with four-poster beds and antiques. Breakfast includes organic pâtés, cheese, and preserves. **Pros:** traditional Andalusian house; excellent Internet deals. **Cons:** some rooms are rather dark; no panoramic views. ✉ *Marqués de Moctezuma 19* ☎ *952/190392* 🌐 *www.hotelsangabriel.com* *20 rooms, 1 suite* *In-room: a/c. In-hotel: restaurant, Internet terminal, Wi-Fi hotspot, parking (paid)* *AE, MC, V.*

AROUND RONDA: CAVES, ROMANS, AND PUEBLOS BLANCOS

This area of spectacular gorges, remote mountain villages, and ancient caves is fascinating to explore and a dramatic contrast with the clamor and crowds of the coast.

About 20 km (12 mi) west of Ronda toward Seville is the prehistoric **Cueva de la Pileta** *(Pileta Cave).* Take the left exit for the village of Benaoján—from here the caves are well signposted. A Spanish guide (who speaks some English) will hand you a paraffin lamp and lead you on a roughly 90-minute walk that reveals prehistoric wall paintings of bison, deer, and horses outlined in black, red, and ocher. One highlight is the Cámara del Pescado (Chamber of the Fish), whose drawing of a huge fish is thought to be 15,000 years old. Tours take place hourly with a maximum of 25 people per group. ☎ *952/167343* *€8* *Nov.–Apr., daily 10–1 and 4–6; May–Oct., daily 10–1 and 4–5.*

Ronda la Vieja (Old Ronda), 20 km (12 mi) north of Ronda, is the site of the old Roman settlement of **Acinipo**. A thriving town in the 1st century AD, Acinipo was abandoned for reasons that still baffle historians. Today it's a windswept hillside with piles of stones, the foundations of a few Roman houses, and what remains of a theater. Excavations are often under way at the site, during which times it's closed to the public. Call to check before visiting. ✉ *Take A376 toward Algodonales; turnoff for ruins is 9 km (5 mi) from Ronda on MA449* ☎ *952/187119 1* *Free* *Weekdays 10–2:30 and 5–8, weekends noon–2 and 5–8.*

Setenil de las Bodegas, 8 km (5 mi) north of Acinipo, is a small city in a cleft in the rock cut by the Guadalporcín River. The streets resemble long, narrow caves, and on many houses the roof is formed by a projecting ledge of heavy rock.

WORD OF MOUTH

"Ronda is amazing, and so are the White Villages. Not to be missed! We loved Zahara and Grazalema. We had lunch in both places. In Zahara, we climbed up to the top of the moorish fort with its incredible views over the town, mountains, lakes and countryside." —RalphR

In **Olvera**, 13 km (8 mi) north of Setenil, two imposing silhouettes dominate the crest of the hill: the 11th-century castle Vallehermoso, a legacy of the Moors, and the neoclassical church of La Encarnación, reconstructed in the 19th century on the foundations of the old mosque.

A solitary watchtower dominates a crag above the village of **Zahara de la Sierra**, its outline visible for miles around. The tower is all that remains of a Moorish castle where King Alfonso X once fought the emir of Morocco; the building remained a Moorish stronghold until it fell to the Christians in 1470. Along the streets you can see door knockers fashioned like the hand of Fatima: the fingers represent the five laws of the Koran and are meant to ward off evil. ✉ *From Olvera, drive 21 km (13 mi) southwest to village of Algodonales then south on A376 to Zahara de la Sierra 5 km (3 mi).*

GRAZALEMA AND THE SIERRA DE GRAZALEMA

Village of Grazalema: 28 km (17 mi) northwest of Ronda.

The village of **Grazalema** is the prettiest of the *pueblos blancos*. Its cobblestone streets of houses with pink-and-ocher roofs wind up the hillside, red geraniums splash white walls, and black wrought-iron lanterns and grilles cling to the housefronts.

The Sierra de Grazalema Natural Park encompasses a series of mountain ranges known as the Sierra de Grazalema, which straddle the provinces of Málaga and Cádiz. These mountains trap the rain clouds that roll in from the Atlantic, and the area has the distinction of being the wettest place in Spain, with an average annual rainfall of 88 inches. Because of the park's altitude and prevailing humidity, it's one of the last habitats for the rare fir tree *Abies pinsapo*; it's also home to ibex, vultures, and birds of prey. Parts of the park are restricted, accessible only on foot and when accompanied by an official guide. The village of Grazalema itself is quite small.

10

ESSENTIALS

Visitor Information Grazalema (✉ *Pl. de España* ☎ *956/132073*).

EXPLORING

From Grazalema, the A374 takes you to **Ubrique**, on the slopes of the Saltadero Mountains and known for its leather tanning and embossing industry. Look for the **Convento de los Capuchinos** (Capuchin Convent), the church of **San Pedro,** and, 4 km (2½ mi) away, the ruins of the Moorish castle **El Castillo de Fátima.**

Another excursion from Grazalema takes you through the heart of the protected reserve. Follow the A344 west through dramatic mountain scenery, past Benamahoma, to **El Bosque**, home to a trout stream and information center.

WHERE TO STAY

$ **La Mejorana.** This is the spot to find rural simplicity: though a mere 20 years old, the house has been cleverly designed and built to resemble an old-fashioned village home, complete with beams, tiled floors, and thick whitewashed walls. The rooms are essentially small suites, each with a sitting area. All have small terraces and stunning mountain views. There is a tranquil flower-filled garden for sunny days, and when temperatures drop, there's a cozy fireplace in the communal sitting room. **Pros:** in the center of the village; tastefully furnished. **Cons:** no TV; owners speak no English. ✉ *C. Santa Clara 6, Grazalema* ☎ *956/132327* 🌐 *www.lamejorana.net* *5 rooms* *In-room: no TV. In-hotel: pool* *CP.*

WESTERN ANDALUSIA'S GREAT OUTDOORS: PROVINCE OF HUELVA

When you've had enough of Seville's urban bustle, nature awaits in Huelva. From the Parque Nacional de Doñana to the oak forests of the Sierra de Aracena, nothing is much more than an hour's drive from Seville. If you prefer history, hop on the miners' train at Riotinto or visit Aracena's spectacular caves. Columbus's voyage to the New World was sparked near here, at the monastery of La Rábida and in Palos de la Frontera. The visitor center at La Rocina has Doñana information.

Once a thriving Roman port, the city of Huelva, an hour east of Faro, Portugal, was largely destroyed by the 1755 Lisbon earthquake. As a result, it claims the dubious honor of being the least distinguished city in Andalusia. If you do end up here, **Taberna el Condado** is the place to go for tapas and beer.

ESSENTIALS

Bus Station Huelva (✉ *Av. Doctor Rubio s/n* ☎ *959/256900*).

Taxi Contact Tele Taxi (☎ *959/250022*).

Train Station Huelva (✉ *Av. de Italia* ☎ *959/246666*).

DOÑANA NATIONAL PARK

100 km (62 mi) southwest of Seville.

Fodor's Choice ★ One of Europe's most important swaths of unspoiled wilderness, these wetlands spread out along the west side of the Guadalquivir estuary. The site was named for Doña Ana, wife of a 16th-century duke, who, prone to bouts of depression, one day crossed the river and wandered into the wetlands, never to be seen alive again. The 188,000-acre park sits on the migratory route from Africa to Europe and is the winter home and breeding ground for as many as 150 species of rare birds. Habitats range from beaches and shifting sand dunes to marshes, dense brushwood, and sandy hillsides of pine and cork oak. Two of Europe's most endangered species, the imperial eagle and the lynx, make their homes here, and kestrels, kites, buzzards, egrets, storks, and spoonbills breed among the cork oaks.

At the Doñana **La Rocina Visitor Center** (☎ *959/442340*), less than 2 km (1 mi) from El Rocío, you can peer at the park's many bird species from a 3½-km (2-mi) footpath. It's open daily 9–7. Five kilometers (3 mi) away, an exhibit at the **Palacio de Acebrón** (✉ *Ctra. de la Rocina s/n* ☎ *959/448711*) explains the park's ecosystems. It's open daily 9–6:30; last entrance is one hour before closing.

> **DOÑANA TOURS**
>
> Jeep tours of Doñana National Park depart twice daily at 8 and 3 (from May to September there is a 5 PM tour as well) from the park's Acebuche reception center, 2 km (1 mi) from Matalascanas. Tours take four hours, cost €25 and cover a 70-km (43-mi) route through beaches, sand dunes, marshes, and scrub. They should be booked well in advance. Passengers can arrange to be picked up from hotels in Matalascañas. Contact **Parque Nacional de Doñana** (✉ *Av. Canaliega s/n, El Rocío-Huelva* ☎ *959/442474* 🌐 *www.donanareservas.com*).

Two kilometers (1 mi) before Matalascañas is **Acebuche** (✉ *El Acebuche s/n* ☎ *959/448640* 🌐 *www.parquenacionaldonana.com*), the park's main interpretation center and the departure point for jeep tours. The center is open June–September, daily 8 AM–9 PM, and October–May, daily 9–7. There's also a visitor center for the park in Cádiz, at Sanlúcar de Barrameda *(see below)*.

WHERE TO STAY

$$ **El Cortijo de Los Mimbrales.** On the Rocío–Matalascañas road, this convivial Andalusian farmhouse is perched on the park's edge, a mere 1 km (½ mi) from the visitor center at La Rocina. It's a lovely place to spend a relaxed evening with fellow nature lovers in comfy chairs by the fireplace in the large common lounge. Pick a colorfully decorated room or a bungalow that sleeps two to four with a kitchenette and small private garden. Some rooms and bungalows have fireplaces. There are stables on the premises, and the hotel can arrange horseback rides on the fringes of the park. **Pros:** great views of Doñana; rustic retreat. **Cons:** mosquitoes, gnats, and sand fleas; heat in midsummer. ✉ *Ctra. del Rocío a Matalascañas (A483), Km 30* ☎ *959/442237* 🌐 *www.cortijomimbrales.com* *24 rooms, 2 suites, 5 bungalows* *In-room: no a/c. In-hotel: restaurant, bar, pool, Wi-Fi hotspot, some pets allowed* *AE, DC, MC, V* *BP.*

MAZAGÓN

19 km (12 mi) south of Huelva.

There isn't much to see or do in this coastal town, but the parador makes a good base for touring La Rábida, Palos de la Frontera, and

10

Moguer. Mazagón's sweeping sandy beach, sheltered by steep cliffs, is among the region's nicest.

ESSENTIALS

Visitor Information Mazagón (✉ *Av. de los Conquistadores s/n* ☎ *959/376300*).

WHERE TO STAY

$$$ **Parador de Mazagón.** This peaceful modern parador stands on a cliff surrounded by pine groves, overlooking a sandy beach 3 km (2 mi) southeast of Mazagón. Most of the spacious and comfortable rooms have balconies overlooking the garden, and the restaurant serves Andalusian dishes and local seafood specialties, such as stuffed baby squid and hake medallions. **Pros:** good base for bird-watching, views, and biking through the wetlands. **Cons:** mediocre dining; functional but drab rooms. ✉ *Pl. de Mazagón* ☎ *959/536300* 🌐 *www.parador.es* *63 rooms* *In-room: a/c, Wi-Fi. In-hotel: restaurant, bar, tennis courts, pools, bicycles, parking (free)* *AE, DC, MC, V.*

LA RÁBIDA

8 km (5 mi) northwest of Mazagón.

La Rábida's monastery is worth a stop if you're a history buff: it's nicknamed "the birthplace of America" because in 1485 Columbus came from Portugal with his son Diego to stay in theMudejar-style Franciscan monastery, where he discussed his theories with friars Antonio de Marchena and Juan Pérez, who interceded on his behalf with Queen Isabella who had originally rejected his planned expedition.

ESSENTIALS

Visitor Information La Rábida (✉ *Paraje de la Rábida s/n* ☎ *959/531137*).

The Mudejar-style Franciscan monastery of **Santa María de La Rábida** church has a much-venerated 14th-century statue of the **Virgen de los Milagros** (Virgin of Miracles). There are relics from the discovery of America displayed in the museum and the **frescoes** in the gatehouse were painted by Daniel Vázquez Díaz in 1930. ✉ *Camino del Monasterio, Ctra. de Huelva* ☎ *959/350411* 🌐 *www.monasteriodelarabida.com* *€3.50 with audio guide, €3 without* *Tues.–Sun. 10–1 and 4–7.*

Two kilometers (1 mi) from the monastery, on the seashore, is the **Muelle de las Carabelas** (Caravels' Wharf), a reproduction of a 15th-century port. The star exhibits here are the full-size models of Columbus's flotilla, the *Niña, Pinta,* and *Santa María,* built using the same techniques as in Columbus's day. You can go aboard each and learn more about the discovery of the New World in the adjoining museum. ✉ *Paraje de la Rábida* ☎ *959/530597 or 959/530312* *€3.50* *Tues.–Sun. 10–7.*

ARACENA

105 km (65 mi) northeast of Huelva, 100 km (62 mi) northwest of Seville.

Stretching north of the provinces of Huelva and Seville is the 460,000-acre Sierra de Aracena nature park, an expanse of hills cloaked in cork

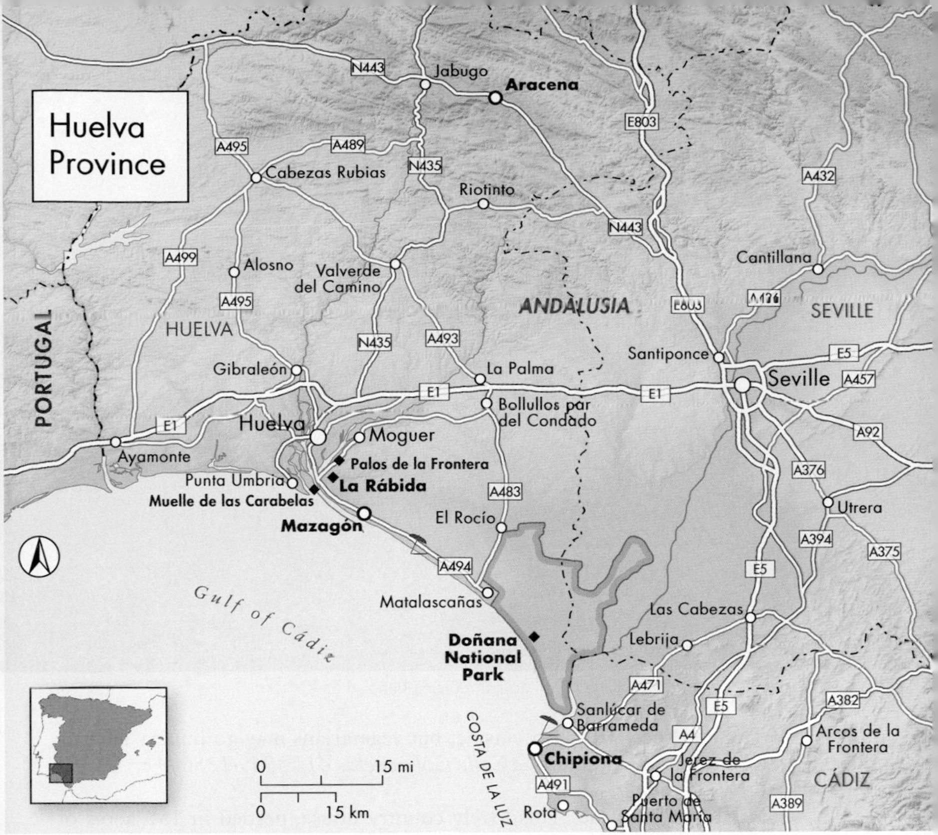

and holm oak. This region is known for its cured Ibérico hams, which come from the prized free-ranging Iberian pigs that gorge on acorns in the autumn months before slaughter; the hams are buried in salt and then hung in cellars to dry-cure for at least two years. The best Ibérico hams have traditionally come from the village of **Jabugo.**

ESSENTIALS

Visitor Information Aracena (✉ *Pl. de San Pedro s/n* ☎ *959/128825*).

The capital of the region is Aracena, whose main attraction is the spectacular cave known as the **Gruta de las Maravillas** *(Cave of Marvels)*. Its 12 caverns contain long corridors, stalactites and stalagmites arranged in wonderful patterns, and stunning underground lagoons. ✉ *Pl. Pozo de Nieves, Pozo de Nieves* ☎ *959/128355* *€9* ⏲ *Guided tours, if sufficient numbers, weekdays hourly 10:30–3 and 4–6; weekends hourly 10:30–1:30 and 3–6.*

WHERE TO EAT AND STAY

$$ SPANISH ✕ **Casas.** There's not much wall space left in the intimate beamed dining room of this typical Sierra Morena restaurant: plates, pots, pans, mirrors, and religious pictures cover every inch. Specializing in the region's famous ham and pork, the honest, home-style cooking is at its best with dishes prepared according to what is in season, including wild asparagus grilled with oyster mushrooms and garlic. The owner

Wild Andalusian horses near the village of El Rocío, in Donana National Park

is an expert on sierra cuisine, but vegetarians may go hungry as little is not meat-oriented. ✉ *Calle Colmenetas 41* ☎ *959/128044* 💳 *MC, V* ⏲ *No dinner.*

$$$ Fodor's Choice ★ **Finca Buenvino.** This lovely country house, nestled in 150 acres of woods, is run by a charming British couple, Sam and Jeannie Chesterton. The room price includes a big breakfast; dinner, available for a small fee, uses vegetables and herbs from the garden and eggs from the owners' chickens. Jeannie also conducts Spanish cookery courses for groups of up to six people. Three woodland self-catering cottages are available, converted from former stables and workers' cottages. The house is 6 km (4 mi) from Aracena. **Pros:** intimate and personal; friendly hosts. **Cons:** somewhat removed from village life. ✉ *N433, Km 95, Los Marines* ☎ *959/124034* 🌐 *www.fincabuenvino.com* *4 rooms, 3 cottages* *In-room: no a/c, no phone, kitchen (some), no TV, Wi-Fi. In-hotel: restaurant, bar, pools* 💳 *MC, V* ⏲ *Closed mid-July–mid-Sept.* 🍽 *MAP.*

$$ ★ **Finca de la Silladilla.** In a wild Iberian pig–infested oak forest, this ranch offers a chance to see Spain's most prized products priming themselves for your palate. The rooms and small stone houses are impeccably decorated in heavy slabs of beautifully finished wood, and the

COLUMBUS SETS SAIL

On August 2, 1492, the *Niña*, the *Pinta*, and the *Santa María* set sail from the town of Palos de la Frontera. At the door of the church of **San Jorge** (1473), the royal letter ordering the levy of the ships' crew and equipment was read aloud, and the voyagers took their water supplies from the fountain known as La Fontanilla at the town's entrance.

bathrooms have unusual ceramic-and-copper washbasins. Communal areas combine warm tones with whites, ochers, and terra-cottas. The staff can organize tours of the Sierra de Aracena, equestrian outings, and visits to nearby Jabugo, famed for its *jamón ibérico de bellota* (acorn-fed Ibérico ham). **Pros:** rustic chic; pig sightings. **Cons:** far from nearest village; no restaurant. ✉ *Ctra. Los Romeros, Los Romeros, Jabugo* ☎ *959/501350* *2 rooms, 2 suites, 4 houses* *In-room: a/c, kitchen. In-hotel: pool, some pets allowed* *AE, DC, MC, V* *BP.*

THE LAND OF SHERRY: CÁDIZ PROVINCE AND JEREZ DE LA FRONTERA

A trip through this province is a trip back in time. Winding roads take you through scenes ranging from flat and barren plains to seemingly endless vineyards, and the rolling countryside is carpeted with blindingly white soil known as *albariza*—unique to this area and the secret to the grapes used in sherry. In Jerez de La Frontera, you can savor the town's internationally known sherry or delight in the skills and forms of purebred Carthusian horses.

Throughout the province, the *pueblos blancos* (white villages) provide striking contrasts with the terrain, especially at Arcos de la Frontera, where the village sits dramatically on a crag overlooking the gorge of the Guadalete River. In the city of Cádiz you can absorb about 3,000 years of history in what is generally considered the oldest continuously inhabited city in the Western world.

JEREZ DE LA FRONTERA

★ *97 km (60 mi) south of Seville.*

Jerez, world headquarters for sherry, is surrounded by vineyards of chalky soil, whose Palomino grapes have funded a host of churches and noble mansions. Names such as González Byass, Domecq, Harvey, and Sandeman are inextricably linked with Jerez. The word "sherry," first used in Great Britain in 1608, is an English corruption of the town's old Moorish name, Xeres. Both sherry and horses are the domain of Jerez's Anglo-Spanish aristocracy, whose Catholic ancestors came here from England centuries ago. At any given time, more than half a million barrels of sherry are maturing in Jerez's vast aboveground cellars.

ESSENTIALS

Bus Station Jerez de la Frontera (✉ *Calle de la Cartuja* ☎ *956/345207*).

Taxi Contact Tele Taxi (✉ *Jerez de la Frontera* ☎ *956/344860*).

Train Station Jerez de la Frontera (✉ *Pl. de la Estación s/n, off Calle Diego Fernández Herrera* ☎ *956/342319*).

Visitor Information Jerez de la Frontera (✉ *Alameda Cristina s/n* ☎ *956/341711* 🌐 *www.turismojerez.com*).

10

EXPLORING

The 12th-century **Alcázar** was once the residence of the caliph of Seville, and its small, octagonal **mosque** and **baths** were built for the Moorish governor's private use. The baths have three sections: the *sala fria* (cold room), the larger *sala templada* (warm room), and the *sala caliente* (hot room) for steam baths. In the midst of it all is the 17th-century **Palacio de Villavicencio**, built on the site of the original Moorish palace. A camera obscura, a lens-and-mirrors device that projects the outdoors onto a large indoor screen, offers a 360-degree view of Jerez. ✉ *Alameda Vieja* ☎ *956/350129* 🎫 *€3, €5.40 including camera obscura* ⏲ *Mid-Sept.–Apr., daily 10–6; May–mid-Sept., daily 10–8.*

Across from the Alcázar and around the corner from the González Byass winery, the **Catedral de Jerez** (✉ *Pl. de la Encarnación* ⏲ *Weekdays 11–1 and 6–8, Sat. 11–2 and 6–8, Sun. 11–2*) has an octagonal cupola and a separate bell tower, as well as Zurbarán's canvas *La Virgen Niña* (The Virgin as a Young Girl).

One block from the Plaza del Arenal, near the Alcázar, stands **San Miguel** (✉ *Pl. de San Miguel* ☎ *956/343347*). The interior of this church, built over the 15th and 16th centuries, illustrates the evolution of Gothic architecture, with various styles mixed into the design. Visits are by appointment only. On the **Plaza de la Asunción**, one of Jerez's most intimate squares, you can find the Mudejar church of **San Dionisio** and the ornate **cabildo municipal** (city hall), whose lovely plateresque facade dates from 1575.

Diving into the maze of streets that form the scruffy San Mateo neighborhood east of the town center, you come to the **Museo Arqueológico**, one of Andalusia's best archaeological museums. The collection is strongest on the pre-Roman period and the star item, found near Jerez, is a Greek helmet dating from the 7th century BC. ✉ *Pl. del Mercado s/n* ☎ *956/341350* 🎫 *€3.50* ⏲ *Sept.–mid-June, Tues.–Fri. 10–2 and 4–7, Sat. 10–2:30; mid-June–Aug., Tues.–Sun. 10–2:30.*

QUICK BITES

The award-winning Bar Juanito (✉ *Pescadería Vieja 8 and 10* ☎ *956/334838*) is known for its flowery patio. Jolly Faustino Rodríguez and his family serve 50 different tapas and larger-portion *raciones*.

Just west of the town center, the **Parque Zoológico** is set in lush botanical gardens where you can usually spy up to 33 storks' nests. Primarily a place for the rehabilitation of injured or endangered animals native to the region, the zoo also houses white tigers, elephants, and a giant red panda. ✉ *C. Taxdirt* ☎ *956/153164* 🌐 *www.zoobotanicojerez.com* 🎫 *€9* ⏲ *June–Sept., Tues.–Sun. 10–8; Oct.–May, Tues.–Sun. 10–6.*

Fodor's Choice ★

The **Real Escuela Andaluza del Arte Ecuestre** *(Royal Andalusian School of Equestrian Art)* operates on the grounds of the Recreo de las Cadenas, a 19th-century palace. This prestigious school was masterminded by Alvaro Domecq in the 1970s, and every Thursday (and at various other times throughout the year) the Cartujana horses—a cross between the native Andalusian workhorse and the Arabian—and skilled riders in 18th-century riding costume demonstrate intricate dressage techniques and jumping in the spectacular show "Cómo Bailan los Caballos

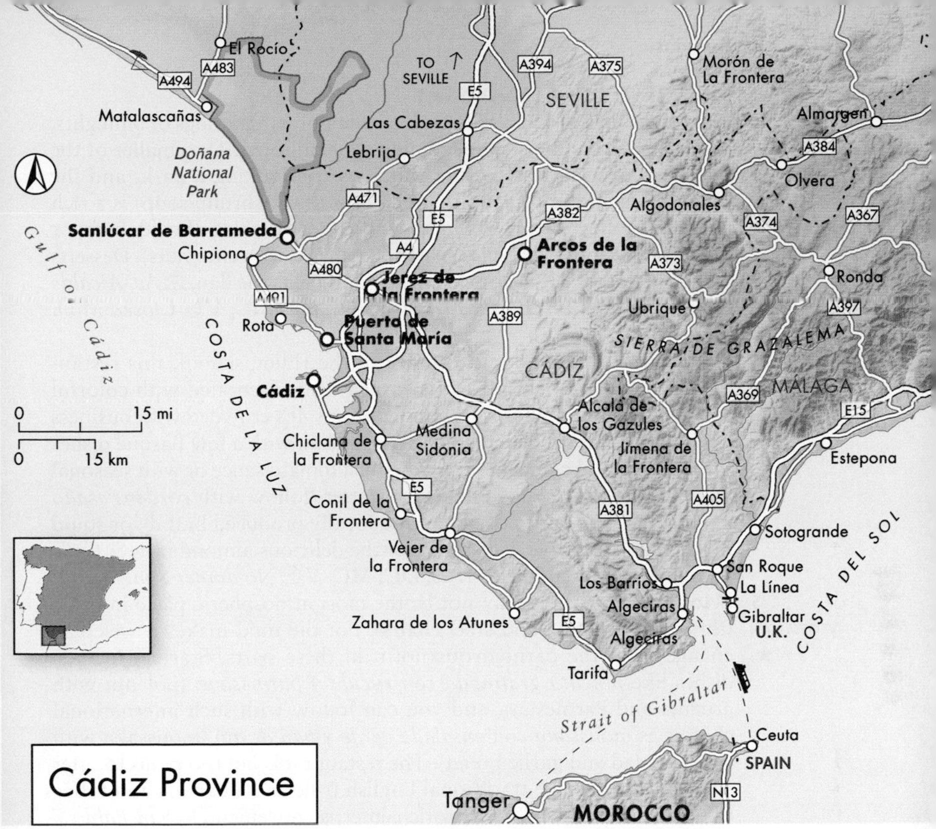

Andaluces" (roughly, "The Dancing Horses of Andalusia"). Reservations are essential. Admission price depends on how close to the arena you sit; the first two rows are the priciest. The rest of the week, you can visit the stables and tack room, watch the horses being schooled, and see rehearsals. ✉ *Av. Duque de Abrantes s/n* ☎ *956/319635* 🌐 *www.realescuela.org* 🎫 *€18–€25, €10 for rehearsals* ⏲ *Shows Mar.–mid-Dec., Tues. and Thurs. at noon (also Fri. at noon in Aug.); mid-Dec.–Feb., Thurs. at noon.*

Just outside Jerez de la Frontera, **Yeguada de la Cartuja** is a farm specializing in Carthusian horses. In the 15th century, a Carthusian monastery on this site started the breed for which Jerez and the rest of Spain are now famous. Every Saturday at 11 AM a full tour and show begin. Book ahead. ✉ *Finca Fuente El Suero, Ctra. Medina–El Portal, Km 6.5* ☎ *956/162809* 🌐 *www.yeguadacartuja.com* 🎫 *€13.50–€18.50, according to seating* ⏲ *Show Sat. at 11 AM.*

Jerez's **bullring** is on Calle Circo, northeast of the city center. Tickets are sold at the official ticket office on Calle Porvera, though only about five bullfights are held each year, in May and October. Six blocks from the bullring is the **Museo Taurino**, a bullfighting museum where admission includes a drink. ✉ *Calle Pozo del Olivar 6* ☎ *956/319000* 🎫 *€5* ⏲ *Daily 9:30–2.*

WHERE TO EAT AND STAY

$–$$ SPANISH
✕ **El Bosque.** In a modern villa with contemporary paintings of bullfights, this is one of the most stylish dining spots in town. The smaller of the two dining rooms has picture windows overlooking a park, and the food is contemporary Spanish. *Sopa de galeras* (shrimp soup) is a rich appetizer; follow up with *confit de pato de laguna* (leg of wild duck) or *perdiz estofado con castañas* (partridge stewed with chestnuts). Desserts are less exciting but include a creamy and delicious flan. ✉ *Av. Alcalde Alvaro Domecq 26* ☎ *956/307030* ▭ *AE, DC, MC, V* ⊙ *Closed Mon. No dinner Aug.*

$–$$ SPANISH
✕ **Gaitán.** Within walking distance of the riding school, this restaurant has brick arches and whitewashed walls decorated with colorful ceramic plates and photos of famous guests. It's crowded with business executives at lunch. The menu is Andalusian, with a few Basque dishes thrown in. Local clams, served either in a tomato sauce or with seasonal wild mushrooms, make a delicious starter; follow with *cordero asado* (roast lamb) in a sauce of honey and locally produced brandy or squid in its own ink. Finish with a slice of the delicious almond tart. ✉ *Calle Gaitán 3* ☎ *956/168021* ▭ *AE, DC, MC, V* ⊙ *No dinner Sun.*

$ VEGETARIAN ★
✕ **La Alternativa.** This may not be the most atmospheric place in town (think bright lights and steel chairs), but the food makes a welcome change from the carnivorous norm in these parts. Starters include dishes like *polenta gratinada con rúcula y parmesano* (polenta with arugula and Parmesan), and you can follow with such international choices as *moussaka con ensalada verde y pan de ajo* (moussaka with a green salad and garlic bread). The restaurant is not too pious to offer calorific desserts like traditional English trifle and a banana and toffee cake. The location in the historic center is convenient. ✉ *San Pablo 7* ☎ *956/343961* ▭ *MC, V* ⊙ *Closed Sun.*

$$ SPANISH
✕ **La Carboná.** In a former bodega, this eatery has a rustic atmosphere with arches, beams, and a fireplace for winter nights. In summer you can often enjoy live music, and sometimes flamenco dancing, while you dine. The chef has worked at several top restaurants, and his menu includes traditional grilled meats as well as innovative twists on classic dishes, such as *pechuguitas de cordorniz rellenas de pétalos de rosa y foié* (quail stuffed with rose petals and liver pâté). For an unusual dessert, go for cinnamon cake with licorice ice cream. Both the tapas menu and the wine list are excellent. ✉ *C. San Francisco de Paula 2* ☎ *956/347475* ▭ *AE, DC, MC, V* ⊙ *Closed Tues.*

$–$$ SPANISH ★
✕ **La Mesa Redonda.** Owner José Antonio Valdespino spent years researching the classic recipes once served in aristocratic Jerez homes, and now his son, José, presents them in this small, friendly restaurant off Avenida Alcalde Alvaro Domecq, around the corner from the Hotel Avenida Jerez. Don't be put off by the bland exterior—within, the eight tables are surrounded by watercolors and shelves lined with cookbooks; the round table at the end of the room gave the restaurant its name. The menu typically includes wild game dishes like boar and rabbit. ✉ *Calle Manuel de la Quintana 3* ☎ *956/340069* ▭ *AE, DC, MC, V* ⊙ *Closed Sun. and mid-July–mid-Aug.*

A TOAST TO JEREZ: WINERY TOURS

On a **bodega** (winery) visit, you'll learn about the *solera* method of blending old wine with new, and the importance of the *flor* (yeast that forms on the wine as it ages) in determining the kind of sherry.

Phone ahead for an appointment to make sure you join a group that speaks your language. Cellars usually charge an admission fee of €10 (€15 with wine and tapas tasting). Tours, which last about an hour, go through the aging cellars, with their endless rows of casks. (You won't see the actual fermenting and bottling, which take place in more modern, less romantic plants outside town.) Finally, you'll be invited to sample generous amounts of pale, dry *fino*; nutty *amontillado*; or rich, deep *oloroso*, and, of course, to purchase a few robustly priced bottles in the winery shop.

If you have time for only one bodega, tour the **González Byass** (✉ *Calle Manuel María González* ☎ *956/357000* 🌐 *www.gonzalezbyass.com*), home of the famous Tío Pepe. This tour is well organized and includes La Concha, an open-air aging cellar designed by Gustave Eiffel. Jerez's oldest bodega is **Domecq** (✉ *Calle San Ildefonso 3* ☎ *956/151500* 🌐 *www.bodegasfundadorpedrodomecq.com*), founded in 1730. Aside from sherry, Domecq makes the world's best-selling brandy, Fundador. **Harveys** (✉ *Calle Pintor Muñoz Cebrián s/n* ☎ *956/319650* 🌐 *www.harveys-usa.com*) is the source of Harveys Bristol Cream. **Sandeman** (✉ *Calle Pizarro 10* ☎ *956/301100* 🌐 *www.sandeman.com*) is known for its dashing man-in-a-cape logo.

$$–$$$ SPANISH

✕ **Sabores.** The walled garden at this eatery is a cool spot on a warm night. The staff's enthusiasm and culinary knowledge will help guide your choice. Consider kick-starting your meal with the creative *pica pica* (a variety of small portions, which you can "pick at"), which includes peach gazpacho with prawns, roast peppers, black olives, and spicy black sausage with garlic mayonnaise. For main dishes, the oxtail with apple purée receives rave reviews from readers, as does the tuna on a bed of creamed leeks. ✉ *Chancilleria Hotel, Calle Chancilleria 21,* ☎ *956/329835* ✍ *Reservations essential* ▭ *MC, V* ⊙ *No dinner Sun.*

$–$$ SEAFOOD

✕ **Venta Antonio.** Crowds come to this roadside inn for superb, fresh seafood cooked in top-quality olive oil. You enter through the busy bar, where lobsters await their fate in a tank. Try the specialties of the Bay of Cádiz, such as *sopa de mariscos* (shellfish soup) followed by succulent *bogavantes de Sanlúcar* (local lobster). Be prepared for large, noisy Spanish families dining here on the weekends, particularly during the winter months. ✉ *Ctra. de Jerez–Sanlúcar, Km 5* ☎ *956/140535* ▭ *AE, DC, MC, V* ⊙ *Closed Mon.*

$$$–$$$$ Fodor's Choice ★

🏨 **Hotel Palacio Garvey.** Dating from 1850, this luxurious hotel was once the home of the prestigious Garvey family. The original neoclassical architecture and decor has been exquisitely restored, and parts of the ancient city wall are visible from the gardens. Tastefully minimalist rooms have shiny parquet floors and sleek furniture. The artwork throughout the hotel is edgy and modern, and the restaurant's

10

Riders fill the streets during Jerez's Feria del Caballo (Horse Fair), in early May.

red lacquered chairs provide a suitably innovative impact to match the modern Mediterranean cuisine. **Pros:** near the center of town; fashionable and contemporary feel. **Cons:** small pool. ✉ *Calle Tornería 24* ☎ *956/326700* 🌐 *www.sferahoteles.net* 🛏 *16 rooms* 👍 *In-room: a/c, DVD, Internet, Wi-Fi. In-hotel: restaurant, room service, pool, laundry service, Wi-Fi hotspot, parking (free)* 💳 *AE, D, DC, MC, V* 🍴 *BP.*

¢ **Hotel San Andrés.** This charming low-rise hotel has an inviting traditional entrance patio and rooms set around a courtyard filled with plants, local tile work, and graceful arches. The rooms are modestly decorated with pine furniture set against dazzling white walls. There is also a less expensive *hostal* within the same building, with similar quality rooms but shared bathrooms. **Pros:** charming owners; easy on-street parking. **Cons:** small rooms; no frills. ✉ *Calle Morenos 12* ☎ *956/341983* 🌐 *www.hotelsanandres.es* 🛏 *38 hotel rooms, 18 hostal rooms* 👍 *In-room: a/c, no TV (some)* 💳 *MC, V.*

$$$ **Hotel Villa Jerez.** This tastefully furnished hacienda-style hotel offers luxury on the outskirts of town. The gardens surround a traditional courtyard and are lushly landscaped with palm trees and a dazzling array of colorful plants. Facilities include an elegant restaurant with terrace, a saltwater swimming pool, and a gym. The bedrooms are individually decorated, plush, and well equipped, and the staff is friendly and efficient. **Pros:** elegant surroundings; noble architecture. **Cons:** outside of town; small pool. ✉ *Av. de la Cruz Roja 7* ☎ *956/153100* 🌐 *www.villajerez.com* 🛏 *14 rooms, 4 suites* 👍 *In-room: a/c, Internet. In-hotel: restaurant, bar, pool, Wi-Fi hotspot* 💳 *AE, DC, MC, V.*

¢ **Las Palomas.** This inexpensive hotel also happens to be one of the oldest in town. Thanks to the enthusiasm of the latest owners, it has been

Just about the whole city turns out for the horse festival, and traditional Andalusian costumes are a common sight.

given a new lease on life with sunny yellow paint, wrought-iron beds, wood shutters, and ocher floor tiles. The rooms are set around a charming tiled patio. The owners speak English and can advise on local restaurants, sights, and activities. **Pros:** simple and homey rooms; friendly owners. **Cons:** no restaurant or bar; small rooms. ✉ *Calle Higueras 17* ☎ *956/343773* 🌐 *www.hostal-las-palomas.com* *35 rooms* *In-room: a/c, no TV. In hotel: Wi-Fi hotspot* ▭ *MC, V.*

SPORTS

Formula One Grand Prix races—including the Spanish motorcycle Gran Prix on the first weekend in May—are held at Jerez's racetrack, the **Circuito Permanente de Velocidad** (✉ *Ctra. Arcos, Km 10* ☎ *956/151100* 🌐 *www.circuitodejerez.com*).

10

SHOPPING

Calle Corredera and **Calle Bodegas** are the places to go if you want to browse for wicker and ceramics. **Duarte** (✉ *Calle Lancería 15* ☎ *956/342751*) is the best-known saddle shop in town. It sends its beautifully wrought leather all over the world, including to the British royal family.

ARCOS DE LA FRONTERA

★ *31 km (19 mi) east of Jerez.*

Its narrow and steep cobblestone streets, whitewashed houses, and finely crafted wrought-iron window grilles make Arcos the quintessential Andalusian *pueblo blanco* (white village). Make your way to the main square, the Plaza de España, the highest point in the village; one side of the square is open, and a balcony at the edge of the cliff offers views of the Guadalete Valley. On the opposite end is the church of **Santa María de la Asunción**, a fascinating blend of architectural styles: Romanesque, Gothic, and Mudejar, with a plateresque doorway, a Renaissance *retablo*, and a 17th-century baroque choir. The *ayuntamiento* (town hall) stands at the foot of the old castle walls on the northern side of the square; across is the Casa del Corregidor, onetime residence of the governor and now a parador. Arcos is the most western of the 19 pueblos blancos dotted around the Sierra de Cádiz.

ESSENTIALS

Visitor Information Arcos de la Frontera (✉ *Pl. del Cabildo s/n* ☎ *956/702264* 🌐 *www.arcosdelafrontera.es*).

WHERE TO EAT AND STAY

$ SPANISH ✕ **Taberna de Boabdil.** The restaurant encompasses a series of rambling caves colorfully decorated in quasi-Moorish style by charming owner Francisco Saborido. The handwritten menu includes an array of tapas reflecting Moorish, Andalusian, and Jewish influences. House-made wine is available, as is a set *menu del día* (daily special) that features whatever is fresh in the market that day, such as vegetable couscous or creamy ajo blanco (cold soup with almonds and garlic). ✉ *Paseo de los Boliches 35* ☎ *956/705191* ▭ *MC, V.*

$ Fodor's Choice ★ **El Convento.** Perched atop the cliff behind the town parador, this tiny hotel in a former 17th-century convent shares the amazing view of its swish neighbor (La Casa Grande), though the rooms are much smaller and cheaper. Some rooms have private terraces, and all are furnished tastefully with period artwork and sculptures. In addition guests have the use of a large rooftop terrace on the edge of the cliff. There is no restaurant, but breakfast is available. **Pros:** location; intimacy. **Cons:** small spaces. ✉ *Calle Maldonado 2* ☎ *956/702333* 🌐 *www.hotelelconvento.es* *13 rooms* *In-room: a/c. In-hotel: some Wi-Fi, Internet terminal* ▭ *AE, DC, MC, V* ⊗ *Closed Jan.*

$ ★ **La Casa Grande.** Built in 1729, this extraordinary 18th-century mansion encircles a lushly vegetated central patio and is perched on the edge of the 400-foot cliff to which Arcos de la Frontera clings. Catalan owners Elena Posa and Ferran Grau have restored each room, and the artwork, casually elegant design of the living quarters, and inventive bathrooms are all a delight. The breakfast terrace allows you to look down on falcons circling hundreds of feet above the riverbed below. The rooftop rooms El Palomar (the Pigeon Roost) and El Soberao (the Attic) are the best. **Pros:** attentive owners; impeccable aesthetics. **Cons:** inconvenient parking; long climb to the top floor. ✉ *Calle Maldonado 10* ☎ *956/703930* 🌐 *www.lacasagrande.net* *8 rooms* *In-room: a/c, Wi-Fi (some). In-hotel: Internet terminal, Wi-Fi hotspot* ▭ *AE, DC, MC, V* *BP.*

$$$ ★ **Parador Casa del Corregidor.** Expect a spectacular view from the terrace, as the parador clings to the cliff side, overlooking the rolling valley of the Guadalete River. Public rooms include a popular bar and restaurant that opens onto the terrace and an enclosed patio. Spacious guest rooms are furnished with dark Castilian furniture, reed rugs, and abundant tiles. The best are rooms 15–18, which overlook the valley. At the restaurant, try a local dish such as *berenjenas arcenses*

(spicy eggplant with ham and chorizo) or sample 10 regional specialties with the tasting menu. **Pros:** gorgeous views from certain rooms; elegant decor. **Cons:** blindingly bright; populous public rooms. ✉ *Pl. del Cabildo* ☎ *956/700500* 🌐 *www.parador.es* *24 rooms* *In-room: a/c, Internet, Wi-Fi. In-hotel: restaurant, bar, Internet terminal* ▭ *AE, DC, MC, V.*

SANLÚCAR DE BARRAMEDA

24 km (15 mi) northwest of Jerez.

This fishing town has a crumbling charm and is best known for its langostinos (jumbo shrimp) and Manzanilla, an exceptionally dry sherry, though it's also known because Columbus sailed from this harbor on his third voyage to the Americas, in 1498, and 20 years later Ferdinand Magellan began his circumnavigation of the globe from here. The most popular restaurants are in the **Bajo de Guía** neighborhood, on the banks of the Guadalquivir. Here, too, is a visitor center for Doñana National Park.

Boat trips can take you up the river, stopping at various points in the park; the **Real Fernando**, with bar and café, does a four-hour cruise up the Guadalquivir to the Coto de Doñana. ✉ *Bajo de Guía, Sanlúcar de Barrameda* ☎ *956/363813* 🌐 *www.visitasdonana.com* *€18* ⏲ *Cruises Apr., May, and Oct., daily at 10 AM and 4 PM; Nov.–Mar., daily at 10 AM; June–Sept., daily at 10 AM and 5 PM.*

WHERE TO EAT AND STAY

$$–$$$ SEAFOOD ✕ **Casa Bigote.** Colorful and informal, this spot near the beach is known for its fried *acedias* (a type of small sole) and langostinos, which come from these very waters. The seafood paella is also catch-of-the-day fresh. To get here head down the Bajo de Guía; the restaurant is toward the end. Reservations are essential in summer as the place gets packed with holidaymakers and locals. ✉ *Bajo de Guía* ☎ *956/362696* ▭ *AE, DC, MC, V* ⏲ *Closed Sun. and Nov.–Feb.*

$$ SEAFOOD ✕ **Mirador de Doñana.** This Bajo de Guía landmark overlooking the water serves delicious shrimp, *chocos* (crayfish), and *mi barca mirador* (white fish in a tomato sauce), the signature dish. The menu also includes delicious *langostinos de Sanlúcar* (locally caught lobster), which is particularly recommended when washed down with a glass of locally produced Manzanilla sherry. The dining area overlooks the large, busy tapas bar. ✉ *Bajo de Guía* ☎ *956/364205* ▭ *MC, V* ⏲ *Closed Jan.*

¢–$ ★ **Los Helechos.** Named for the ferns *(los helechos)* that dominate the public spaces, this former private mansion has rooms set around two delightful courtyards, with traditional stone fountains and leafy plants and palms. The spacious rooms are painted in cool pastels and have cozy drapes and wooden floors. A lovely rooftop terrace has the distinct advantage of being out of earshot but within stumbling distance of the Plaza del Cabildo. **Pros:** ideal location; top value. **Cons:** not easy to find; plain rooms. ✉ *Pl. Madre de Dios 9* ☎ *956/361349* 🌐 *www.hotelloshelechos.com* *56 rooms* *In-room: a/c, Wi-Fi. In-hotel: restaurant, bar, parking (paid)* ▭ *AE, DC, MC, V.*

PUERTO DE SANTA MARÍA

12 km (7 mi) southwest of Jerez, 17 km (11 mi) north of Cádiz.

This attractive if somewhat dilapidated little fishing port on the northern shores of the Bay of Cádiz, with lovely beaches nearby, has white houses with peeling facades and vast green grilles covering the doors and windows. The town is dominated by the Terry and Osborne sherry and brandy bodegas. Columbus once lived in a house on the square that bears his name (Cristóbal Colón), and Washington Irving spent the autumn of 1828 at Calle Palacios 57. The marisco bars along the Ribera del Marisco (Seafood Way) are Puerto de Santa María's main claim to fame. Casa Luis, Romerijo, La Guachi, and Paco Ceballos are among the most popular, along with El Beti, at Misericordia 7. The tourist office has a list of six tapas routes that take in 39 tapas bars in total.

ESSENTIALS

Visitor Information Puerto de Santa María (✉ *Calle Luna 22* ☎ *956/542413* 🌐 *www.elpuertosm.es*).

EXPLORING

The **Castillo de San Marcos** was built in the 13th century on the site of a mosque. Created by Alfonso X, it was later home to the duke of Medinaceli. Among the guests were Christopher Columbus—who tried unsuccessfully to persuade the duke to finance his voyage west—and Juan de la Cosa, who, within these walls, drew up the first map ever to include the Americas. The red lettering on the walls is a 19th-century addition. ✉ *Pl. del Castillo* ☎ *965/851751* 🎟 *€5.50, free Tues.* ⏲ *Tues.–Sat. 10–2.*

This stunning neo-Mudejar **Plaza de Toros** was built in 1880 thanks to a donation from the winemaker Thomas Osborne. It originally had seating for exactly 12,816 people, the entire population of Puerto at that time. ✉ *Los Moros* 🎟 *Free* ⏲ *Apr.–Oct., Thurs.–Tues. 11–1:30 and 6–7:30; Nov.–Mar., Thurs.–Tues. 11–1:30 and 5:30–7. Closed bullfight days plus 1 day before and after each bullfight.*

WHERE TO EAT AND STAY

$$$–$$$$ SPANISH ✕ **Aponiente.** Internationally acclaimed chef Angel Leon opened this elegant restaurant to showcase his creative seafood dishes. The edgy decor is a dramatic interplay of black and white with some crimson highlights. Expect such gastronomic inventions and "deconstructions" as fried fish served as breadsticks and lobster baked in bricks of sand. Another winner is the shrimp served in a rolled up frittata. Leon avoids species of fish that have become scarce, championing lesser-known species that are more abundant. ✉ *Calle Puerto Escondido 6* ☎ *956/851870* 🌐 *www.aponiente.com* ✍ *Reservations essential* 💳 *AE, MC, V* ⏲ *Closed Mon. No dinner Sun.*

$$–$$$ SPANISH ✕ **El Faro del Puerto.** In a villa outside town, the "Lighthouse in the Port" is run by the same family that established the classic El Faro in Cádiz. Like its predecessor, it serves excellent fish and seafood like lobster carpaccio, as well as such meat dishes as bull's cheek in a mushroom puree with mashed potatoes. Vegetarian options include *canalones de puerros rellenos de calabaza con jugo de setas* (pasta with leeks and zucchini

in an oyster mushroom sauce). Finish with the heavenly chocolate soufflé. ✉ *Ctra. Fuentebravia–Rota, Km 0.5* ☎ *956/870952* 🌐 *www.elfarodelpuerto.com* ▭ *AE, DC, MC, V* ⊗ *No dinner Sun. Sept.–July.*

$$$–$$$$ Fodor's Choice ★ **Monasterio San Miguel.** Dating from 1733, this monastery is a few blocks from the harbor. There's nothing spartan about the former cells; they're now plush suites with all the trappings. The restaurant is in a large, vaulted hall (formerly the nuns' laundry), the baroque church is now a concert hall, and the cloister's gardens provide a peaceful refuge. Beam ceilings, polished marble floors, and huge brass lamps enhance the 18th-century feel. **Pros:** supremely elegant; efficient service. **Cons:** air-conditioning erratic; authoritarian hotel staff. ✉ *C. Virgen de los Milagros 27* ☎ *956/540440* 🌐 *www.monasteriosanmiguel.com* *141 rooms, 24 suites* *In-room: a/c, Wi-Fi. In-hotel: restaurant, bar, pool, Internet terminal, parking (paid)* ▭ *AE, DC, MC, V.*

CÁDIZ

★ *32 km (20 mi) southwest of Jerez, 149 km (93 mi) southwest of Seville.*

Surrounded by the Atlantic Ocean on three sides, Cádiz is a bustling town that's been shaped by a variety of cultures, and has the varied architecture to prove it. Founded as Gadir by Phoenician traders in 1100 BC, Cádiz claims to be the oldest continuously inhabited city in the Western world. Hannibal lived in Cádiz for a time, Julius Caesar first held public office here, and Columbus set out from here on his second voyage, after which the city became the home base of the Spanish fleet. In the 18th century, when the Guadalquivir silted up, Cádiz monopolized New World trade and became the wealthiest port in Western Europe. Most of its buildings—including the cathedral, built in part with gold and silver from the New World—date from this period. The old city is African in appearance and immensely intriguing—a cluster of narrow streets opening onto charming small squares. The golden cupola of the cathedral looms above low white houses, and the whole place has a slightly dilapidated air. Spaniards flock here in February to revel in the carnival celebrations, but in general it's not very touristy.

GETTING HERE AND AROUND

Cadíz is easy to get to and navigate by car; the old city is easily explored by foot.

The city has two bus stations: Comes, which serves most destinations in Andalusia, and Los Amarillos, which serves Jerez, Seville, Córdoba, Puerto de Santa María, Sanlúcar de Barrameda, and Chipiona.

Every day, a dozen or more local trains connect Cádiz with Seville, Puerto de Santa María, and Jerez, though there are no trains to Doñana National Park, Sanlúcar de Barrameda, or Arcos de la Frontera or between Cádiz and the Costa del Sol.

ESSENTIALS

Bus Station Cádiz–Estación de Autobuses Comes (✉ *Pl. de la Hispanidad 1* ☎ *956/342174*).

Taxi Contact Unitaxi (✉ *Cádiz* ☎ *956/212121*).

10

Puerto de Santa María is a wonderful tapas and sherry-tasting destination.

Train Station Cádiz (✉ *Pl. de Sevilla s/n* ☎ *956/251010*).

Visitor Information Regional Tourist Office (✉ *Av. Ramón de Carranza s/n* ☎ *956/258646* 🌐 *www.cadizturismo.com*). **Provincial Tourist Office** (✉ *Pl. de San Antonio 3, 2nd fl.* ☎ *956/807061*). **Local Tourist Office** (✉ *Pl. San Juan de Dios 11* ☎ *956/241001* 🌐 *www.cadizturismo.com*).

EXPLORING

Begin your explorations in the Plaza de Mina, a large, leafy square with palm trees and plenty of benches. The tourist office is in the northwestern corner.

On the east side of the Plaza de Mina is the **Museo de Cádiz** *(Provincial Museum)*. Notable pieces include works by Murillo and Alonso Cano as well as the *Four Evangelists* and a set of saints by Zurbarán. The archaeological section contains Phoenician sarcophagi from the time of this ancient city's birth. ✉ *Pl. de Mina* ☎ *956/212281* 🎫 €2 ⏲ *Tues. 2:30–8:30, Wed.–Sat. 9–8, Sun. 9:30–2:30.*

A few blocks east of the Plaza de Mina, next door to the Iglesia del Rosario, is the **Oratorio de la Santa Cueva**, an oval 18th-century chapel with three frescoes by Goya. ✉ *C. Rosario 10* ☎ *956/222262* 🎫 €3 ⏲ *Tues.–Fri. 10–1 and 4:30–7:30, weekends 10–1.*

Farther up Calle San José from the Plaza de la Mina is the **Oratorio de San Felipe Neri**. Spain's first liberal constitution was declared at this church in 1812, and the Cortes (Parliament) of Cádiz met here when the rest of Spain was subjected to the rule of Napoléon's brother, Joseph Bonaparte (more popularly known as Pepe Botella, for his love of the bottle). On the main altar is an *Immaculate Conception* by Murillo, the great Sevillian artist who in 1682 fell to his death from a scaffold while working on his *Mystic Marriage of St. Catherine* in Cádiz's Chapel of Santa Catalina. ✉ *Calle Santa Inés 38* ☎ *956/211612* 🎫 *€3* ⏲ *Mon.–Sat. 10–1:30.*

Next door to the Oratorio de San Felipe Neri, the small but pleasant **Museo de las Cortes** has a 19th-century mural depicting the establishment of the Constitution of 1812. Its real showpiece, however, is a 1779 ivory-and-mahogany model of Cádiz, with all of the city's streets and buildings in minute detail, looking much as they do now. ✉ *Santa Inés 9* ☎ *956/221788* 🎫 *Free* ⏲ *Oct.–May, Tues.–Fri. 9–1 and 4–7, weekends 9–1; June–Sept., Tues.–Fri. 9–1 and 5–8, weekends 9–1.*

Four blocks west of Santa Inés is the Plaza Manuel de Falla, overlooked by an amazing neo-Mudejar redbrick building, the **Gran Teatro Manuel de Falla**. The classic interior is impressive as well; try to attend a performance. ✉ *Pl. Manuel de Falla* ☎ *956/220828.*

Fodor's Choice ★

At 150 feet, the **Torre Tavira** is the highest point in the old city. More than a hundred such watchtowers were used by Cádiz ship owners to spot their arriving fleets. A camera obscura gives a good overview of the city and its monuments; the last show is a half hour before closing time. ✉ *Calle Marqués del Real Tesoro 10* ☎ *956/212910* 🎫 *€4* ⏲ *Mid-June–mid-Sept., daily 10–8; mid-Sept.–mid-June, daily 10–6.*

Five blocks southeast of the Torre Tavira are the gold dome and baroque facade of Cádiz's **cathedral**, begun in 1722, when the city was at the height of its power. The Cádiz-born composer Manuel de Falla, who died in 1946 at the age of 70, is buried in the **crypt.** The cathedral **museum,** on Calle Acero, displays gold, silver, and jewels from the New World, as well as Enrique de Arfe's processional cross, which is carried in the annual Corpus Christi parades. The cathedral is known as the New Cathedral because it supplanted the original 13th-century structure next door, which was destroyed by the British in 1592, rebuilt, and rechristened the church of **Santa Cruz** when the New Cathedral came along. The entrance price includes the crypt, museum, and church of Santa Cruz. ✉ *Pl. Catedral* ☎ *956/259812* 🎫 *€5* ⏲ *Mass Sun. at noon; museum Tues.–Fri. 10–2 and 4:30–7:30, Sat. 10–1.*

Next door to the church of Santa Cruz are the remains of a 1st-century BC **Roman theater** (✉ *Campo del Sur s/n, Barrio del Pópulo* 🎫 *Free* ⏲ *Daily 10–2*), which is still under excavation.

The impressive **ayuntamiento** (*City hall* ✉ *Pl. de San Juan de Dios s/n*) overlooks the Plaza San Juan de Diós, one of Cádiz's liveliest hubs. The building is attractively illuminated at night.The **Plaza San Francisco**, near the *ayuntamiento*, is a pretty square surrounded by white-and-yellow houses and filled with orange trees and elegant streetlamps. It's especially lively during the evening *paseo* (promenade).

WHERE TO EAT AND STAY

$–$$ SPANISH Fodor's Choice ★

✕ **Casa Manteca.** Cádiz's most quintessentially Andalusian tavern is in the neighborhood of La Viña (named for the vineyard that once grew here). *Chacina* (Iberian ham or sausage) served on waxed paper and Manzanilla (sherry from Sanlúcar de Barrameda) are standard fare at this low wooden counter that has served bullfighters and flamenco

10

singers, as well as dignitaries from around the world, since 1953. The walls are covered with colorful posters and other memorabilia from the annual carnival, flamenco shows, and ferias. ✉ *Corralón de los Carros 66* ☎ *956/213603* ▭ *AE, DC, MC, V* ⊙ *Closed Mon. No lunch Sun.*

$$–$$$ SPANISH Fodor's Choice ★ ✕ **El Faro.** This famous fishing-quarter restaurant near Playa de la Caleta is deservedly known as the best in the province. From the outside, it's one of many whitewashed houses with bright-blue flowerpots; inside it's warm and inviting, with half-tile walls, glass lanterns, oil paintings, and photos of old Cádiz. Fish dishes dominate the menu, of course, but alternatives include *cebón al queso de cabrales* (venison in blue-cheese sauce). If you don't want to go for the full splurge (either gastronomically or financially), there's an excellent tapas bar. ✉ *Calle San Felix 15* ☎ *956/211068* ▭ *AE, DC, MC, V.*

$$ SPANISH ✕ **El Ventorrillo del Chato.** Standing on its own on the sandy isthmus, this former inn was founded in 1780 by a man ironically nicknamed "El Chato" (small-nosed) for his prominent proboscis. Run by a scion of El Faro's Gonzalo Córdoba, the restaurant serves tasty regional specialties in charming Andalusian surroundings. Seafood is a favorite, but meat, stews, and rice dishes are also well represented on the menu, and the wine list is very good. ✉ *Vía Augusta Julia s/n* ☎ *956/250025* ▭ *AE, DC, MC, V* ⊙ *No dinner Sun.*

$$ **Las Cortes de Cádiz.** At this colonial-style lodging, four floors of rooms are clustered around a delightful light-filled atrium. From the glossy marble-and-tile reception area to the rooms washed in pale pastel shades, the hotel has an attractive and stylish appeal. Modern comforts include a small well-equipped gym and a rooftop terrace with sweeping views. **Pros:** tastefully renovated building; excellent service. **Cons:** few staffers speak English. ✉ *Calle San Francisco 9,* ☎ *956/212668* 🌐 *www.hotellascortes.com* *36 rooms* *In-room: a/c. In-hotel: restaurant, gym, Wi-Fi hotspot, parking (paid)* ▭ *AE, MC, V.*

$$$ **Parador de Cádiz.** Cádiz's modern Parador Atlántico has a privileged position overlooking the bay. The spacious public rooms have marble floors, and tables and chairs surround a fountain on the small patio. The cheerful, bright-green bar, decorated with ceramic tiles and bullfighting posters, is a popular meeting place for Cádiz society. Most rooms have small balconies facing the sea. The pool also has ocean views and is surrounded by a lush green lawn. **Pros:** panoramic views; central location; bright and cheerful. **Cons:** characterless modern building. ✉ *Av. Duque de Nájera 9* ☎ *956/226905* 🌐 *www.parador.es* *143 rooms, 6 suites* *In-room: a/c, Internet, Wi-Fi. In-hotel: restaurant, bar, pool, gym, parking (free), some pets allowed* ▭ *AE, DC, MC, V* *BP.*

CÓRDOBA

166 km (103 mi) northwest of Granada, 407 km (250 mi) southwest of Madrid, 239 km (143 mi) northeast of Cádiz, 143 km (86 mi) northeast of Seville.

Strategically located on the north bank of the Guadalquivir River, Córdoba was the Roman and Moorish capital of Spain, and its old quarter, clustered around its famous Mezquita (mosque), remains one of

Cádiz's majestic cathedral, as seen from the Plaza de la Catedral

the country's grandest and yet most intimate examples of its Moorish heritage. Once a medieval city famed for the peaceful and prosperous coexistence of its three religious cultures—Islamic, Jewish, and Christian—Córdoba is also a perfect analogue for the cultural history of the Iberian Peninsula.

The Romans invaded in 206 BC, later making it the capital of Rome's section of Spain. Nearly 800 years later, the Visigoth king Leovigildus took control. The tribe was soon supplanted by the Moors, whose emirs and caliphs held court here from the 8th century to the early 11th century. At that point Córdoba was one of the greatest centers of art, culture, and learning in the Western world; one of its libraries had a staggering 400,000 volumes. Moors, Christians, and Jews lived together in harmony within Córdoba's walls. In that era, it was considered second in importance only to Constantinople, but in 1009 Prince Muhammad II and Omeyan led a rebellion that broke up the caliphate, leading to power flowing to separate Moorish kingdoms.

Córdoba remained in Moorish hands until it was conquered by King Ferdinand in 1236 and repopulated from the north of Spain. Later, the Catholic Monarchs used the city as a base from which to plan the conquest of Granada. In Columbus's time, the Guadalquivir was navigable as far upstream as Córdoba, and great galleons sailed its waters. Today, the river's muddy water and marshy banks evoke little of Córdoba's glorious past, but an old Arab waterfall and the city's bridge—of Roman origin, though much restored by the Arabs and successive generations—recall a far grander era.

Córdoba today, with its modest population of just more than 300,000, offers a cultural depth and intensity—a direct legacy from the great emirs, caliphs, philosophers, physicians, poets, and engineers of the days of the caliphate—that far outstrips the city's current commercial and political power. Its artistic and historical treasures begin with the *mezquita-catedral* (mosque-cathedral), as it is ever-more-frequently called, and continue through the winding, whitewashed streets of the Judería (the medieval Jewish quarter); the jasmine-, geranium-, and orange blossom–filled patios; the Renaissance palaces; and the two dozen churches, convents, and hermitages, built by Moorish artisans directly over former mosques.

GETTING HERE AND AROUND

Córdoba is easily accessible by bus, train, or car. If you opt for the latter, note that the city's one-way system can be something of a nightmare to navigate.

Córdoba has an extensive public bus network with frequent service. Buses usually start running at 6:30 or 7 AM and stop around midnight. You can buy 10-trip passes at newsstands and the bus office in Plaza de Colón. A single-trip fare is €1.10.

The city's modern train station is the hub for a comprehensive network of regional trains, with regular service to Seville, Málaga, Madrid, and Barcelona. Trains for Granada change at Bobadilla.

Córdoba has a number of organized open-top bus tours of the city that can be booked via the tourist office or by contacting the company directly.

ESSENTIALS

Bus Station Córdoba (✉ *Glorieta de las Tres Culturas, Córdoba* ☎ *957/404040*).

Taxi Contact Radio Taxi (✉ *Córdoba* ☎ *957/764444*).

Tour Contacts Córdoba Visión (✉ *Av. de Doctor Fleming, Centro, Córdoba* ☎ *957/760241*). **GranaVisión** (✉ *Calle Reyes Católicos 47–49, Centro, Córdoba* ☎ *958/535875*).

Train Contacts Train Station (✉ *Glorieta de las Tres Culturas s/n* ☎ *957/403480*).

Visitor Information Provincial Tourist Office (✉ *Palacio de Exposiciones, Calle Torrijos 10, opposite mosque, Judería* ☎ *957/471235* 🌐 *www.andalucia.org/cordoba*). **Local Tourist Office** (✉ *Pl. Juda Levi, Judería* ☎ *957/200522 wwww.turismodecordoba.org*).

EXPLORING

Córdoba is an easily navigable city, with twisting alleyways that hold surprises around every corner. The main city subdivisions used in this book are the **Judería** (which includes the Mezquita); **Sector Sur,** around the **Torre de la Calahorra** across the river; the area around the **Plaza de la Corredera,** a historic gathering place for everything from horse races to bullfights, and the **Centro Comercial,** from the area around Plaza de las Tendillas to the Iglesia de Santa Marina and the Torre de la Malmuerta. Incidentally, the last neighborhood is much more than a succession of shops and stores. The town's real life, the everyday hustle and bustle, takes place here, and the general ambience is very different from that of the tourist center around the Mezquita, with its plethora of souvenir shops. Some of the city's finest Mudejar churches and best taverns, as well as the Palacio de los Marqueses de Viana, are in this pivotal part of town well back from the Guadalquivir waterfront.

Some of the most characteristic and rewarding places to explore in Córdoba are the parish churches and the taverns that inevitably accompany them, where you can taste *finos de Moriles,* a dry, sherrylike wine from the Montilla-Moriles district, and *tentempies* (tapas—literally, "keep you on your feet"). The *iglesias fernandinas* (so-called for their construction after Fernando III's conquest of Córdoba) are nearly always built over mosques with stunning horseshoe arch doorways and Mudejar towers, and taverns tended to spring up around these populous hubs of city life. Examples are the Taberna de San Miguel (aka Casa el Pisto) next to the church of the same name, and the Bar Santa Marina (aka Casa Obispo) next to the Santa Marina Church.

■TIP→ Córdoba's officials frequently change the hours of the city's sights; before visiting an attraction, confirm hours with the tourist office or the sight itself.

❶ **Alcázar de los Reyes Cristianos** *(Fortress of the Christian Monarchs).* Built by Alfonso XI in 1328, the Alcázar is a Mudejar-style palace with splendid gardens. (The original Moorish Alcázar stood beside the Mezquita, on the site of the present Bishop's Palace.) This is where, in the 15th century, the Catholic Monarchs held court and launched their conquest of Granada. Boabdil was imprisoned here in 1483, and for nearly 300 years the Alcázar served as the Inquisition's base. The most important sights here are the Hall of the Mosaics and a Roman stone sarcophagus from the 2nd or 3rd century. ✉ *Pl. Campo Santo de los Mártires, Judería* ☎ *957/420151* 💶 *€4* ⏲ *May–Sept., Tues.–Sat. 10–2 and 6–8, Sun. 9:30–3; Oct.–Apr., Tues.–Sat. 10–2 and 4:30–6:30, Sun. 9:30–2:30.*

⓯ **Calleja de las Flores.** You'd be hard pressed to find prettier patios than those along this tiny street, a few yards off the northeastern corner of the Mezquita. Patios, many with ceramics, foliage, and iron grilles, are key to Córdoba's architecture, at least in the old quarter, where life is lived behind sturdy white walls—a legacy of the Moors, who honored both the sanctity of the home and the need to shut out the fierce summer sun. Between the second and the third week of May, right after the early May **Cruces de Mayo** (Crosses of May) competition, when neighborhoods compete at setting up elaborate crosses decorated with flowers and plants, Córdoba throws a **Patio Festival,** during which private patios are filled with flowers, opened to the public, and judged in a municipal competition. Córdoba's council publishes a map with an itinerary of the best patios in town—note that most are open only in the late afternoon during the week but all day on weekends.

❼ ★ **Iglesia de San Miguel.** Complete with Romanesque doors built around Mudejar horseshoe arches, the San Miguel Church, the square and café terraces around it, and its excellent tavern, Taberna San Miguel–Casa El Pisto, form one of the city's finest combinations of art, history, and gastronomy. ✉ *Pl. San Miguel, Centro.*

16 Fodor's Choice ★ **Mezquita** *(Mosque)*. Built between the 8th and 10th centuries, Córdoba's mosque is one of the earliest and most transportingly beautiful examples of Spanish Muslim architecture. The plain, crenellated walls of the outside do little to prepare you for the sublime beauty of the interior. As you enter through the **Puerta de las Palmas** (Door of the Palms), some 850 columns rise before you in a forest of jasper, marble, granite, and onyx. The pillars are topped by ornate capitals taken from the Visigothic church that was razed to make way for the mosque. Crowning these, red-and-white-stripe arches curve away into the dimness, and the ceiling is carved of delicately tinted cedar. The Mezquita has served as a cathedral since 1236, but its origins as a mosque are clear. Built in four stages, it was founded in 785 by Abd ar-Rahman I (756–88) on a site he bought from the Visigoth Christians. He pulled down their church and replaced it with a mosque, one-third the size of the present one, into which he incorporated marble pillars from earlier Roman and Visigothic shrines. Under Abd ar-Rahman II (822–52), the Mezquita held an original copy of the Koran and a bone from the arm of the prophet Mohammed and became a Muslim pilgrimage site second only to Mecca in importance.

CÓRDOBA ON TWO WHEELS

Never designed to support cars, Córdoba's medieval layout is ideal for bicycles. **Todo Bici** (✉ *Calle Sereria 5* ☎ *957/485766* 🌐 *www.todobici.net*) rents bikes at reasonable rates (€2 per hour/€10 per day).

Al Hakam II (961–76) built the beautiful **mihrab** (prayer niche), the Mezquita's greatest jewel. Make your way over to the **qiblah,** the south-facing wall in which this sacred prayer niche was hollowed out. (Muslim law decrees that a mihrab face east, toward Mecca, and that worshippers do likewise when they pray. Because of an error in calculation, this one faces more south than east. Al Hakam II spent hours agonizing over a means of correcting such a serious mistake, but he was persuaded to let it be.) In front of the mihrab is the **maksoureh,** a kind of anteroom for the caliph and his court; its mosaics and plasterwork make it a masterpiece of Islamic art. A last addition to the mosque as such, the maksoureh was completed around 987 by Al Mansur, who more than doubled its size.

After the Reconquest, the Christians left the Mezquita largely undisturbed, dedicating it to the Virgin Mary and using it as a place of Christian worship. The clerics did erect a wall closing off the mosque from its courtyard, which helped dim the interior and thus separate the house of worship from the world outside. In the 13th century, Christians had the **Capilla de Villaviciosa** built by Moorish craftsmen, its Mudejar architecture blending with the lines of the mosque. Not so the heavy, incongruous baroque structure of the **cathedral,** sanctioned in the very heart of the mosque by Carlos V in the 1520s. To the emperor's credit, he was supposedly horrified when he came to inspect the new construction, exclaiming to the architects, "To build something ordinary, you have destroyed something that was unique in the world" (not that this sentiment stopped him from tampering with the Alhambra to build

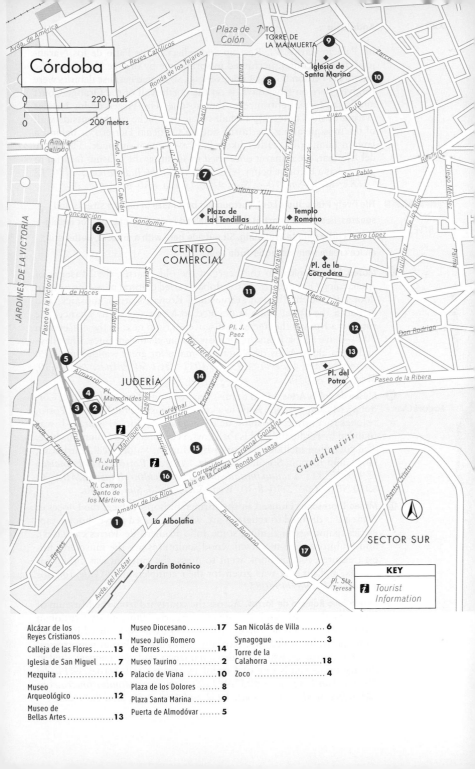

Alcázar de los Reyes Cristianos **1**	Museo Diocesano **17**	San Nicolás de Villa **6**
Calleja de las Flores **15**	Museo Julio Romero de Torres **14**	Synagogue **3**
Iglesia de San Miguel **7**	Museo Taurino **2**	Torre de la Calahorra **18**
Mezquita **16**	Palacio de Viana **10**	Zoco **4**
Museo Arqueológico **12**	Plaza de los Dolores **8**	
Museo de Bellas Artes **13**	Plaza Santa Marina **9**	
	Puerta de Almodóvar **5**	

his Palacio Carlos V). Rest up and reflect in the **Patio de los Naranjos** (Orange Court), perfumed in springtime by orange blossoms. The **Puerta del Perdón** (Gate of Forgiveness), so named because debtors were forgiven here on feast days, is on the north wall of the Orange Court and is the formal entrance to the mosque. The **Virgen de los Faroles** (Virgin of the Lanterns), a small statue in a niche on the outside wall of the mosque along the north side on Cardenal Herrero, is behind a lantern-hung grille, rather like a lady awaiting a serenade. The **Torre del Alminar,** the minaret once used to summon the Muslim faithful to prayer, has a baroque belfry. ✉ *C. de Torrijos s/n, Judería* ☎ *957/470512* 🎫 *€8* ⏲ *Mon.–Sat. 10–6, Sun. 9–10:45 and 1:30–6:30.*

QUICK BITES

The lively Plaza Juda Levi, surrounded by a maze of narrow streets and squares, lies at the heart of the Judería and makes a great spot for indulging in a little people-watching. Sit outside here with a drink or, better still, an ice cream from Helados Juda Levi.

⓬ **Museo Arqueológico.** In the heart of the old quarter, the Museum of Archaeology has finds from Córdoba's varied cultural past. The ground floor has ancient Iberian statues and Roman statues, mosaics, and artifacts; the upper floor is devoted to Moorish art. By chance, the ruins of a Roman theater were discovered right next to the museum in 2000—have a look from the window just inside the entrance. The alleys and steps along Altos de Santa Ana make for great wandering. ✉ *Pl. Jerónimo Paez, Judería* ☎ *957/474011* 🎫 *€1.50* ⏲ *Tues. 2:30–8:30, Wed.–Sat. 9–8:30.*

⓭ **Museo de Bellas Artes.** Hard to miss because of its deep-pink facade, Córdoba's Museum of Fine Arts, in a courtyard just off the Plaza del Potro, belongs to a former Hospital de la Caridad (Charity Hospital). It was founded by Ferdinand and Isabella, who twice received Columbus here. The collection includes paintings by Murillo, Valdés Leal, Zurbarán, Goya, and Joaquín Sorolla y Bastida. ✉ *Pl. del Potro 1, San Francisco* ☎ *957/473345* 🌐 *www.juntadeandalucia.es/cultura/museos/MBACO* 🎫 *€1.50* ⏲ *Tues. 2:30–8:30, Wed.–Sat. 9–8:30, Sun. 9–2:30.*

Fodor's Choice ★

⓱ **Museo Diocesano.** Housed in the former Bishop's Palace, the Diocesan Museum is devoted to religious art, with illustrated prayer books, tapestries, paintings (including some Julio Romero de Torres canvases), and sculpture. The medieval wood sculptures are the museum's finest treasures. As this book went to press, the museum was closed for repairs, and no date was given for their completion. ✉ *Calle Torrijos 12, Judería* ☎ *957/496085.*

⓮ ★ **Museo Julio Romero de Torres.** Across the courtyard from the Museum of Fine Arts, this museum is devoted to the early-20th-century Córdoban artist Julio Romero de Torres (1874–1930), who specialized in mildly erotic portraits of demure, partially dressed Andalusian temptresses. Romero de Torres, who was also a flamenco *cantador* (singer), died at the age of 56 and is one of Córdoba's greatest folk heroes. ✉ *Pl. del Potro 1, San Francisco* ☎ *957/491909* 🌐 *www.museojulioromero.com* 🎫 *€4, free Wed.* ⏲ *Tues.–Sat. 10–2 and 4:30–6:30, Sun. 9:30–2:30.*

2 **Museo Taurino** *(Museum of Bullfighting).* Two adjoining mansions on the Plaza Maimónides (or Plaza de las Bulas) house this museum, and it's worth a visit, as much for the chance to see a restored mansion as for the posters, Art Nouveau paintings, bull's heads, suits of lights (bullfighting outfits), and memorabilia of famous Córdoban bullfighters, including the most famous of all, Manolete. To the surprise of the nation, Manolete, who was considered immortal, was killed by a bull in the ring at Linares in 1947. As this book went to press, the renovated museum was scheduled to reopen in late 2010. ✉ *Pl. Maimónides, Judería* ☎ *957/201056.*

10 **Palacio de Viana.** This 17th-century palace is one of Córdoba's most splendid aristocratic homes. Also known as the **Museo de los Patios,** it contains 12 interior patios, each one different; the patios and gardens are planted with cypresses, orange trees, and myrtles. Inside the building are a carriage museum, a library, embossed leather wall hangings, filigree silver, and grand galleries and staircases. As you enter, note that the corner column of the first patio has been removed to allow the entrance of horse-drawn carriages. ✉ *Pl. Don Gomé, Centro* ☎ *957/496741* *Patios €3, patios and interior €6* ⏲ *May–Sept., Mon.–Sat. 9–2; Oct.–Apr., Mon.–Sat. 10–1 and 4–6.*

8 **Plaza de los Dolores.** The 17th-century Convento de Capuchinos surrounds this small square north of Plaza San Miguel. The square is where you feel most deeply the city's languid pace. In its center, a statue of **Cristo de los Faroles** (Christ of the Lanterns) stands amid eight lanterns hanging from twisted wrought-iron brackets. ✉ *Centro.*

9 **Plaza Santa Marina.** At the edge of the **Barrio de los Toreros,** a quarter where many of Córdoba's famous bullfighters were born and raised, stands a statue of the famous bullfighter Manolete (1917–47) opposite the lovely *fernandina* church of Santa Marina de Aguas Santas (St. Marina of Holy Waters). Not far from here, on the Plaza de la Lagunilla, is a bust of Manolete. ✉ *Pl. Conde Priego, Centro.*

5 **Puerta de Almodóvar.** Outside this old Moorish gate at the northern entrance of the Judería is a statue of **Seneca,** the Córdoba-born philosopher who rose to prominence in Nero's court in Rome and was forced to commit suicide at his emperor's command. The gate stands at the top of the narrow and colorful Calle San Felipe.

6 **San Nicolás de Villa.** This classically dark Spanish church displays the Mudejar style of Islamic decoration and art forms. Córdoba's well-kept city park, the pleasant **Jardínes de la Victoria,** with tile benches and manicured bushes, is a block west. ✉ *C. San Felipe, Centro.*

3 **Synagogue.** The only Jewish temple in Andalusia to survive the expulsion and inquisition of the Jews in 1492, Córdoba's synagogue is also one of only three ancient synagogues left in all of Spain (the other two are in Toledo). Though it no longer functions as a place of worship, it's a treasured symbol for Spain's modern Jewish communities. The outside is plain, but the inside, measuring 23 feet by 21 feet, contains some exquisite Mudejar stucco tracery. Look for the fine plant motifs and the Hebrew inscription saying that the synagogue was built in 1315. The women's gallery, not open for visits, still stands, and in the east wall is

DID YOU KNOW?

One of the most notable aspects of Córdoba's Mezquita, or mosque, is that it's been used as a cathedral since the 13th century: as elsewhere, when the Christians reconquered the city, they didn't bother to build a church but converted what was already there, adding an altar in the middle.

the ark where the sacred scrolls of the Torah were kept. ✉ *C. Judíos, Judería* ☎ *957/202928* 🎫 *€1* ⏲ *Tues.–Sat. 9:30–2 and 3:30–5:30, Sun. 9:30–1:30.*

18 **Torre de la Calahorra.** The tower on the far side of the Puente Romano (Roman Bridge) was built in 1369 to guard the entrance to Córdoba. It now houses the **Museo Vivo de Al-Andalus** (Arabic for "Land of the West"), with films and audiovisual guides (in English) on Córdoba's history. Climb the narrow staircase to the top of the tower for the view of the Roman bridge and city on the other side of the Guadalquivir. ✉ *Av. de la Confederación, Sector Sur* ☎ *957/293929* 🌐 *www.torrecalahorra.com* 🎫 *€4.50 including audio guide, €1.20 extra for slide show* ⏲ *Daily 10–6.*

4 **Zoco.** *Zoco* is the Spanish word for the Arab souk, the onetime function of this courtyard near the synagogue. It's now the site of a daily crafts market, where you can see artisans at work, and evening flamenco in summer. ✉ *Calle Judíos 5, Judería* ☎ *957/204033* 🎫 *Free.*

NEED A BREAK?

Wander over to the Plaza de las Tendillas, which is halfway between the Mezquita and Plaza Colón. The terraces of Café Boston and Café Siena are both enjoyable places to relax with a coffee when the weather is warm.

WHERE TO EAT

¢–$ VEGETARIAN

✕ **Amaltea.** Satisfying both vegetarians and their meat-eating friends, this organic restaurant includes some meat and fish dishes on the menu. There's a healthy mix of Mexican, Asian, Spanish, and Italian-influenced dishes, including pasta with artichokes, vegetable curry with mango, and several inventive dishes with *bacalau* (cod). The decor is warm and inviting, and diners are treated to a soothing musical backdrop of jazz, blues, and chill-out music. ✉ *Ronda de Isasa 10, Centro* ☎ *957/491968* 💳 *MC, V* ⏲ *Closed Mon. No dinner Sun.*

¢ SPANISH Fodor's Choice ★

✕ **Bar Santos.** This very small, quintessentially Spanish bar, with no seats and numerous photos of matadors and flamenco dancers, seems out of place surrounded by the tourist shops and overshadowed by the Mezquita, but its appearance—and its prices—are part of its charm. Tapas such as *morcillo ibérico* (Iberian blood sausage) and *bocadillos* (sandwiches that are literally "little mouthfuls") are excellent in quality and value, while the *tortilla de patata* (potato omelet) is renowned and celebrated both for its taste and its heroic thickness. ✉ *Calle Magistral González Francés 3, Judería* ☎ *957/479360* 💳 *MC, V.*

$$–$$$ SPANISH Fodor's Choice ★

✕ **Bodegas Campos.** A block east of the Plaza del Potro, this traditional old wine cellar is the epitome of all that's great about Andalusian cuisine. The dining rooms are in barrel-heavy rustic rooms and leafy traditional patios (take a look at some of the signed barrels—you may recognize a name or two, such as the former UK prime minister Tony Blair. Magnificent vintage flamenco posters decorate the walls. Regional dishes include *ensalada de bacalao y naranja* (salad of salt cod and orange with olive oil) and *solomillo con salsa de setas* (sirloin with a wild mushroom sauce). There's also an excellent tapas bar. ✉ *Calle Los Lineros 32, San Pedro* ☎ *957/497643* 💳 *AE, MC, V* ⏲ *No dinner Sun.*

$$–$$$ SPANISH ✕ **Casa Pepe de la Judería.** Antiques and some wonderful old oil paintings fill this three-floor labyrinth of rooms just around the corner from the mosque, near the Judería. The restaurant is always packed, noisy, and fun. May through October, the rooftop opens for barbecues, and there is live Spanish guitar music most nights. A full selection of tapas and house specialties includes *presa de paletilla ibérica con salsa de trufa* (pork shoulder fillet with a truffle sauce) and the solidly traditional *rabo de toro* (oxtail stew). ✉ *Calle Romero 1, off Deanes, Judería* ☎ *957/200744* ▭ *AE, DC, MC, V.*

$$–$$$ SPANISH ✕ **El Blasón.** One block west of Avenida Gran Capitán, El Blasón has a Moorish-style entrance bar leading onto a patio enclosed by ivy-covered walls. Downstairs is a lounge with a red-tile ceiling and old polished clay plates on the walls. Upstairs are two elegant dining rooms where blue walls, white silk curtains, and candelabras evoke early-19th-century luxury. The menu includes *salmón fresco al cava* (fresh salmon in sparkling wine) and *muslos de pato al vino dulce* (leg of duck in sweet wine sauce). ✉ *José Zorrilla 11, Centro* ☎ *957/480625* ▭ *AE, DC, MC, V.*

$$$–$$$$ SPANISH **Fodor's Choice** ★ ✕ **El Caballo Rojo.** This is one of the most famous traditional restaurants in Andalusia, frequented by royalty and society folk. The interior resembles a cool, leafy Andalusian patio, and the dining room is furnished with stained glass, dark wood, and gleaming marble; the upstairs terrace overlooks the Mezquita. The menu mixes traditional specialties, such as *rabo de toro* (oxtail stew) and *salmorejo* (a thick version of gazpacho), with dishes inspired by Córdoba's Moorish and Jewish heritage, such as *alboronia* (a cold salad of stewed vegetables flavored with honey, saffron, and aniseed), *cordero a la miel* (lamb roasted with honey), and *rape mozárabe* (grilled monkfish with Moorish spices). ✉ *Calle Cardenal Herrero 28, Judería* ☎ *957/475375* 🌐 *www.elcaballorojo.com* ▭ *AE, DC, MC, V.*

$$$ SPANISH ✕ **El Choco.** The city's most exciting restaurant, El Choco has award-winning chef Kisko Garcia at the helm whipping up innovative starters like scallops in a foie gras and truffle sauce and a frothy tortilla served in a glass. Outstanding main courses include fish dishes like *bacalao confitado con guiso de sus callos* (cod candied with its own juices), sea bass with arugula, and sumptuous roast suckling pig. The desserts, such as the fabulous layered lemon pudding, are decadent, and the decor is minimalist, with charcoal-color walls and glossy parquet floors. ✉ *Compositor Serrano Lucena 14, Centro* ☎ *957/264863* ▭ *MC, V* ⏲ *Closed Mon. No dinner Sun.*

$$–$$$ SPANISH ★ ✕ **El Churrasco.** The name suggests grilled meat, but this restaurant in the heart of the Judería serves much more than that. In the colorful bar try tapas such as the *berenjenas crujientes con salmorejo* (crispy fried eggplant slices with thick gazpacho). In the restaurant, the grilled fish is supremely fresh, and the steak is the best in town, particularly the namesake *churrasco* (grilled meat, served here in a spicy tomato-based sauce). On the inner patio, there's alfresco dining when it's warm outside, also the season to try another specialty: *gazpacho blanco de piñones* (a white gazpacho made with pine nuts). Save some room for the creamy fried ice cream. ✉ *Calle Romero 16, Judería* ☎ *957/290819* ▭ *AE, DC, MC, V* ⏲ *Closed Aug.*

$ MIDDLE EASTERN ★ **Medina Califal.** Above Córdoba's Arab hammam baths, this eatery has many vegetarian and vegan choices, like the *ensalada de sultan* starter with pine nuts, raisins, and dried fruits in an orange-and-almond dressing. Traditional *moutabal* (baba ghanoush) and hummus are tempting dips served with freshly made, warm pita bread. You can follow with a choice of couscous, including meat or vegetables, or more conventional mains, like roasted lamb in a honey-based sauce. Adjourn to the *tetería* (tea shop) after dinner for an herb tea or a *batido* (fruit smoothie)—the yogurt-date-banana version is delicious. You can combine a visit to the baths with a meal in the restaurant. ✉ *Calle Corregidor Luís de la Cerda 5, Judería* ☎ *957/484746* ▭ *MC, V.*

TOP 3 TAPAS BARS IN CÓRDOBA

You can find delicious tapas at most of the restaurants we list, but if you're just looking for a tapas destination before you embark on dinner, try one of these spots.

Plateros de San Francisco, *Calle San Francisco 6* Taberna Plateros, *Calle Maria Auxilliadora 25* Taberna San Miguel, *Plaza San Miguel 1*

$ MEDITERRANEAN **Pizarro.** Owner Luis Pizarro offers a diverse menu of traditional and international dishes at his bright modern restaurant with peach-color walls, exposed brick, and pine furniture. Starters include eggplant crepes with prawns and salmon and *madrileño*-style garlic soup topped with a poached egg. Meaty mains include Magret duck and roasted lamb with rosemary and garlic, while fish lovers can opt for a seafood menu that includes grilled prawns and *pil-pil* (cod baked in a spicy chili-based sauce). There is a reasonable three-course lunch special (€14) and a more extensive dinner special (€25). ✉ *Calle Deanes 10, Judería* ☎ *957/422047* ▭ *MC, V* ⊙ *No dinner Sun.*

¢–$$ SPANISH **Taberna Plateros.** On a narrow side street, this delightful spot dates from the 17th century. One of the city's most historic inns, it has a large patio that leads to more rooms and the traditional marble bar where blue-collar types and business executives meet. Photographs of iconic local bullfighter Manolete line the walls, and the patio is decorated with giddily patterned tiles and bricks. The food is solid home-style cooking, with choices including fried green peppers, Spanish potato omelet, and hearty oxtail stew. Go easy on the starters, which are meals in themselves. ✉ *San Francisco 6, Plaza de la Corredera* ☎ *957/470042* ▭ *MC, V* ⊙ *Closed Sun. and Mon.*

WHERE TO STAY

$$$–$$$$ ★ **Amistad Córdoba.** Two 18th-century mansions overlooking Plaza de Maimónides in the heart of the Judería have been melded into a stylish hotel. (You can also enter through the old Moorish walls on Calle Cairuán.) There's a cobblestone Mudejar courtyard, carved-wood ceilings, and a plush lounge; the newer wing across the street is done in blues and grays and Norwegian wood. Guest rooms are large and comfortable. **Pros:** cool design; pleasant and efficient service. **Cons:** parking is difficult. ✉ *Pl. de Maimónides 3, Judería* ☎ *957/420335* 🌐 *www.*

nh-hoteles.com ⇨ *84 rooms* ☝ *In-room: a/c, Wi-Fi. In-hotel: restaurant, room service, bar, laundry service, parking (paid)* ▭ *AE, DC, MC, V.*

$$ Fodor's Choice ★ **Casa de los Azulejos.** This 17th-century house still has original details like the majestic vaulted ceilings. Decorated with colorful tiles, it mixes Andalusian and Latin American influences. All rooms are painted in warm pastels, filled with antiques, and open onto the tropical central patio with banana trees, lofty palms, and frilly ferns. The floors in the rooms are tiled with stunning original azulejos (hence the name). There's an excellent Mexican cantina called La Guadalupana and a generous breakfast buffet. **Pros:** interesting architecture; friendly staff. **Cons:** hyper-busy decor; limited privacy. ✉ *Calle Fernando Colón 5, Centro* ☎ *957/470000* 🌐 *www.casadelosazulejos.com* ⇨ *7 rooms, 1 suite* ☝ *In-room: a/c, Wi-Fi. In-hotel: restaurant, Internet terminal* ▭ *MC, V.*

¢–$ ★ **Gonzalez.** A few minutes from the Mezquita, the Gonzalez was originally built as a 16th-century palace for the son of the famous local artist Julio Romero de Torres. The building has been since been converted into a small hotel with an elegant marble entrance, sumptuous decor, and a typical flower-filled patio. The rooms are small and plainly decorated but have comparatively large bathrooms with tubs. **Pros:** top value; central location. **Cons:** minimal amenities; exterior rooms noisy. ✉ *Calle Manrique 3, Judería* ☎ *957/479819* 🌐 *www.hotel-gonzalez.com* ⇨ *17 rooms* ☝ *In room: a/c, Wi-Fi* ▭ *AE, DC, MC, V.*

$$$$ Fodor's Choice ★ **Hospes Palacio del Bailío.** This tastefully renovated 17th-century mansion built over the ruins of a Roman house in the historic center of town is one of the city's top lodging options. Archaeological remains combine with contemporary features, as in Roman ruins visible beneath the glass floor of one of the patios and the dining room. Clever lighting and a relaxing spa complete the mélange of contemporary and antique. The spacious rooms have parquet floors, exposed brick walls, and many original architectural features. **Pros:** dazzling decor; impeccable comforts. **Cons:** not easy to reach by car. ✉ *Calle Ramírez de las Casas Deza 10–12, Plaza de La Corredera* ☎ *957/498993* 🌐 *www.hospes.es* ⇨ *53 rooms* ☝ *In-room: a/c, Internet, Wi-Fi. In-hotel: restaurant, bar, pools, spa, bicycles, laundry facilities, Internet terminal* ▭ *MC, V.*

¢ **Hotel Maestre.** Around the corner from the Plaza del Potro, this affordable hotel has rooms overlooking a gracious inner courtyard framed by arches. The Castilian-style furniture, gleaming marble, and high-quality oil paintings add elegance to excellent value. The management also runs an even cheaper lodging a few doors away, the Hostal Maestre, and two types of apartments down the street; the best apartments are large and clean and a great deal. **Pros:** good location; great value. **Cons:** flimsy beds; ancient plumbing. ✉ *Calle Romero Barros 4–6, San Pedro* ☎ *957/472410* 🌐 *www.hotelmaestre.com* ⇨ *26 rooms* ☝ *In-room: a/c, Wi-Fi. In-hotel: parking (paid)* ▭ *AE, MC, V.*

$$ **Lola.** The eponymous owner has decorated the rooms (each is named after an Arab princess) in this former 19th-century palace with flair and attention to detail. There are original beams, woven rugs, antique wardrobes and telephones, and Art Deco accents throughout. The bathrooms are airy, modern, and marbled. Tucked down a side street, Lola is far

A typical Córdoba patio, filled with flowers

enough away from the tour groups but within walking distance of all the big-city sights. Breakfast is served on the roof terrace, which has views of the Mezquita tower. There's parking on nearby Plaza Vallinas. **Pros:** good value for the money; lively decor. **Cons:** cramped shower; decor is too twee. ✉ *Calle Romero 3, Judería* ☎ *957/200305* 🌐 *www.hotelconencantolola.com* ↪ *8 rooms* 👍 *In-room: a/c, Wi-Fi. In-hotel: laundry service* 💳 *AE, MC, V* 🍴 *CP.*

$$$ **Parador de Córdoba.** A peaceful garden surrounds this modern parador on the slopes of the Sierra de Córdoba, 5 km (3 mi) north of town on the site of Abd ar-Rahman I's 8th-century summer palace. Rooms are sunny, with wood or wicker furnishings, and the pricier ones have balconies overlooking the lush green garden or facing Córdoba. **Pros:** wonderful views from south-facing rooms; sleek decor; quality traditional cuisine. **Cons:** characterless modern building; far from main sights. ✉ *Av. de la Arruzafa, El Brillante* ☎ *957/275900* 🌐 *www.parador.es* ↪ *89 rooms, 5 suites* 👍 *In-room: a/c, Internet, Wi-Fi. In-hotel: restaurant, room service, tennis court, pool, parking (free)* 💳 *AE, DC, MC, V.*

NIGHTLIFE AND THE ARTS

NIGHTLIFE

Córdoba locals hang out mostly in the areas of Ciudad Jardín (the old university area), Plaza de las Tendillas, and the Avenida Gran Capitán.

For some traditional tipple, check out atmospheric **Bodega Guzman** (✉ *Calle de los Judios 6, Judería* ☎ *No phone*) near the old synagogue. Its sherries are served straight from the barrel in a room that doubles as a bullfighting museum. **Café Málaga** (✉ *Calle Málaga 3, Centro* ☎ *957/476298*), a block from Plaza de las Tendillas, is a laid-back hangout for jazz and blues aficionados. **Salón de Té** (✉ *Calle del Buen Pastor 13, Judería* ☎ *No phone*), a few blocks from the Mezquita, is a beautiful place for tea, with a courtyard, side rooms filled with cushions, and a shop selling Moroccan clothing. It closes at midnight. The two locations of **Sojo** (✉ *Calle Benito Pérez Galdós 3, off Av. Gran Capitán, Centro* ☎ *957/487211* ✉ *José Martorell 12, Judería*) attract a trendy crowd. The branch in the Judería has DJs on weekends.

FLAMENCO Córdoba's most popular flamenco club, the year-round **Tablao Cardenal** (✉ *Calle Torrijos 10, Judería* ☎ *957/483320* 🌐 *www.tablaocardenal.com*) is worth the trip just to see the courtyard of the 16th-century building, which was Córdoba's first hospital. Admission is €20.

SHOPPING

Córdoba's main shopping district is around Avenida Gran Capitán, Ronda de los Tejares, and the streets leading away from Plaza Tendillas. **Artesanía Andaluza** (✉ *Calle Tomás Conde 3, Judería* ☎ *957/203781*), near the Museo Taurino, sells Córdoban crafts, including fine embossed leather (a legacy of the Moors) and jewelry made of filigree silver from the mines of the Sierra Morena. Córdoba's artisans sell their crafts in the **Zoco** (✉ *C. Judíos, opposite synagogue, Judería* ☎ *957/204033*), though many stalls are open May–September only. **Meryan** (✉ *Calleja de las Flores 2 and Encarnación 12* ☎ *957/475902* 🌐 *www.meryancor.com*) is one of Córdoba's best workshops for embossed leather.

EN ROUTE **Medina Azahara** (sometimes written as Madinat Al-Zahra) was built in the foothills of the Sierra Morena—about 8 km (5 mi) west of Córdoba on C431—by Abd ar-Rahman III for his favorite concubine, az-Zahra (the Flower). Construction on this once-splendid summer pleasure palace began in 936; historians say it took 10,000 men, 2,600 mules, and 400 camels 25 years to erect this fantasy of 4,300 columns in dazzling pink, green, and white marble and jasper brought from Carthage. On three terraces stood a palace, a mosque, luxurious baths, fragrant gardens, fish ponds, an aviary, and a zoo. In 1013 the place was sacked and destroyed by Berber mercenaries. In 1944 the Royal Apartments were rediscovered, and the throne room carefully reconstructed. The outline of the mosque has also been excavated. The only covered part of the site is the Salon de Abd ar-Rahman III; the rest is a sprawl of foundations and arches that hint at the splendor of the original city-palace. No public transport comes here, but there is a daily tourist bus; check with the tourist office. ✉ *Off C431; follow signs en route to Almodóvar del Río* ☎ *957/355506* *€3* ⏲ *Tues.–Sat. 10–8:30, Sun. 10–2.*

SIDE TRIPS FROM CÓRDOBA

If you have time to go beyond Córdoba and have already seen the Medina Azahara palace ruins, head south to the wine country around Montilla, olive oil–rich Baena, and the Subbética mountain range, a cluster of small towns virtually unknown to travelers.

The enitre Subbética region is protected as a natural park, and the mountains, canyons, and wooded valleys are stunning. You'll need a car to explore, though, and in some parts, the roads are rather rough. To reach these meriting-a-visit towns in *la campiña* (the countryside), take the low road (N331) through Montilla, cutting north to Baena via Zuheros, or take the high road (N432) through Espejo and Baena, cutting south through Cabra. For park information or hiking advice, contact the **Mancomunidad de la Subbética** (✉ *Ctra. Carcabuey–Zagrilla, Km 5.75, Carcabuey* ☎ *957/704106* 🌐 *www.subbetica.org*). You can also pick up information, including a pack of maps titled *Rutas Senderistas de la Subbética,* from any local tourist office. The handy cards detail 10 walks with sketched maps.

Southern Córdoba is also the province's main olive-producing region, with the town of **Lucena** at its center. If you follow the Ruta del Aceite (olive oil route), you'll pass some of the province's most picturesque villages. In Lucena is the Torre del Moral, where Granada's last Nasrid ruler, Boabdil, was imprisoned in 1483 after launching an unsuccessful attack on the Christians; and the Parroquia de San Mateo, a small but remarkable Renaissance–Gothic cathedral. The town makes furniture and brass and copper pots. Southeast of Lucena, C334 crosses the **Embalse de Iznájar** (Iznájar Reservoir) amid spectacular scenery. On C334, halfway between Lucena and the reservoir, in **Rute,** you can sample the potent *anís* (anise) liqueur for which this small, whitewashed town is famous.

MONTILLA

46 km (28 mi) south of Córdoba.

Heading south from Córdoba toward Malaga, you'll pass through hills ablaze with sunflowers in early summer before you reach the Montilla–Morilés vineyards. Every fall, 47,000 acres' worth of Pedro Ximénez grapes are crushed here to produce the region's rich Montilla wines, which are similar to sherry. Recently, Montilla has started developing a young white wine similar to Portugal's Vinho Verde.

ESSENTIALS

Visitor Information Montilla (✉ *Capitán Alonso de Vargas 3* ☎ *957/652462*).

EXPLORING

Bodegas Alvear. Founded in 1729, this bodega in the center of town is Montilla's oldest. Besides being informative, the fun tour and wine tasting gives you the chance to buy a bottle or two of Alvear's tasty version of the sweet Pedro Ximenez aged sherry. Tours must be booked in advance and must include at least seven people. ✉ *Calle María Auxiliadora 1* ☎ *957/652939* 🌐 *www.alvear.es* 🎫 *Tour €3.95, with wine tasting €4–€5.50* ⏲ *Guided tour and wine tasting weekdays 12:30; shop Mon. 4:30–6:30, Tues.–Fri. 10–2 and 4:30–6:30, Sat. 11–1:30.*

WHERE TO EAT AND STAY

$$ SPANISH ★ ✕ **Las Camachas.** The best-known restaurant in southern Córdoba Province is in an Andalusian-style hacienda outside Montilla—near the main road toward Málaga. Start with tapas in the attractive bar, then

move on to one of the six dining rooms. Regional specialties include *alcachofas al Montilla* (artichokes braised in Montilla wine), *salmorejo* (a thick, garlicky gazpacho), *perdiz campiña* (country-style partridge), and *cordero a la miel* (lamb with honey). You can also try local wines here. ✉ *Av. Europa 3* ☎ *957/650004* 💳 *AE, DC, MC, V.*

SWEET WINE

Montilla's grapes contain so much sugar (transformed into alcohol during fermentation) that they are not fortified with the addition of extra alcohol. For this reason, the locals claim that Montilla wines do not give you a hangover.

$ **Don Gonzalo.** Just 3 km (2 mi) southwest of Montilla is one of Andalusia's better roadside hotels. The wood-beam-covered common areas have a mixture of decorative elements: note the elephant tusks flanking the TV in the lounge. The clay-tile rooms are large and comfortable; some look onto the road, others onto the garden and pool. Ask to see the wine cellar; it's a beauty. The hotel also has a highly regarded and elegant restaurant. **Pros:** easy to get to; refreshing pool. **Cons:** outside of town; heavy truck traffic on highway. ✉ *Ctra. Córdoba–Málaga, Km 47* ☎ *957/650658* 🌐 *www.hoteldongonzalo.com* *35 rooms, 1 suite* *In-room: a/c, Wi-Fi. In-hotel: restaurant, bar, tennis court, pool, spa* 💳 *AE, DC, MC, V.*

SHOPPING

On the outskirts of town, coopers' shops produce barrels of various sizes, some small enough to serve as creative souvenirs. On Montilla's main road, **Tonelería J. L. Rodríguez** (✉ *Ctra. Córdoba–Málaga, Km 43.3* ☎ *957/650563* 🌐 *www.toneleriajlrodriguez.com*) is worth a stop not just to buy barrels and local wines, but also to pop in the back and see the former being made.

BAENA

66 km (43 mi) southeast of Córdoba, 42 km (26 mi) east of Montilla.

Outside the boundaries of Subbética and surrounded by chalk fields producing top-quality olives, Baena is an old town of narrow streets, whitewashed houses, ancient mansions, and churches clustered beneath Moorish battlements.

The **Museo del Olivar y el Aceite** is housed in the old olive mill owned and operated by Don José Alcalá Santaella until 1959. The machinery on display dates from the middle of the 19th century, when the mill was capable of processing up to 3 tons of olives a day. The museum aims to demonstrate the way of life of workers in this important industry. You can taste and buy olive oil at the shop. ✉ *Calle Cañada 7* ☎ *957/691641* 🌐 *www.museoaceite.com* *€2* *May–Sept., Tues.–Sat. 11–2 and 6–8, Sun. 11–2; Oct.–Apr., Tues.–Fri. 11–2 and 4–6, Sun. 11–2.*

WHERE TO STAY

$ **Fuente las Piedras.** This stylish hotel is on the edge of the Parque Natural Sierra Subbética, 25 km (15 mi) northeast of Baena in the town of Cabra on the A316 road to Jaén. The rooms are elegantly modern and generous in size, and a large pool is surrounded by exquisitely

10

landscaped gardens. **Pros:** good stop midway between Córdoba and Granada; park access. **Cons:** pool is open to the public weekends. ✉ *Av. Fuente de las Piedras s/n, Cabra* ☎ *957/529740* 🌐 *www.mshoteles.com* *61 rooms* *In-room: a/c, Wi-Fi. In-hotel: restaurant, bar, pool, laundry facilities, laundry service, parking (free)* ▭ *MC, V.*

$$ ★ **La Casa Grande.** In the center of town just a few steps from the famous Nuñez de Prado olive oil mill, this is the top hotel in Baena and for miles around. The reception hall has elegant high ceilings, the restaurant is a good reason to stop in for a meal, and the professional and friendly staff is always helpful. The public rooms are sumptuous to an almost over-the-top degree with antiques, chandeliers, suits of armor, and old-fashioned paintings, and the rooms are only slightly more muted, so if you like modern minimalism, this hotel is probably not for you. **Pros:** classical elegance; walking distance from everything. **Cons:** more formal than relaxed. ✉ *Av. De Cervantes 35* ☎ *957/671905* 🌐 *www.lacasagrande.es* *38 rooms* *In-room: a/c, Wi-Fi. In-hotel: restaurant, bar, pool, laundry facilities, laundry service, parking (free)* ▭ *AE, DC, MC, V.*

ZUHEROS

80 km (50 mi) southeast of Córdoba, 10 km (6 mi) south of Baena.

Zuheros, at the northern edge of the Subbética mountain range and at an altitude of 2,040 feet, is one of the most attractive villages in the province of Córdoba. From the road up, it's hidden behind a dominating rock face topped off by the dramatic ruins of a castle built by the Moors over a Roman castle. The view from here back over the valley is expansive. Next to the castle is the Iglesia de Santa María, built over a mosque. The base of the minaret is the foundation for the bell tower.

WHAT TO SEE

The **Museo Histórico-Arqueológico Municipal** displays archaeological remains found in local caves and elsewhere; some date back to the Middle Paleolithic period some 35,000 years ago. You can also visit the remains of the Renaissance rooms in the castle, across the road. Call ahead for tour times. ✉ *Pl. de la Paz 2* ☎ *957/694545* *€2* *Apr.–Sept., Tues.–Fri. 10–2 and 5–7; weekends 10–7; Oct.–Mar., Tues.–Fri. 10–2 and 4–6; weekends 10–6.*

Housed in an impressive square mansion from 1912, the **Museo de Costumbres y Artes Populares Juan Fernandez Cruz** is at the edge of the village. Exhibits detail local customs and traditions. ✉ *Calle Santo s/n* ☎ *957/694690* *€2* *Tues.–Sun. 11–2 and 4–7.*

Some 4 km (2½ mi) above Zuheros along a windy, twisty road, the **Cueva de los Murciélagos** *(Cave of the Bats)* runs for about 2 km (1¼ mi), although only about half of that expanse is open to the public. The main attractions are the wall paintings dating from the Neolithic Age (6000–3000 BC) and Chalcolithic Age (3000–2000 BC), but excavations have indicated that the cave was inhabited as far back as 35,000 years ago. Items from the Copper and Bronze ages as well as from the Roman period and the Middle Ages have also been found here. Note that, due to ongoing restoration work, visits are limited to 20 people at a time.

✉ *Information and reservations: Calle Nueva 1* ☎ *957/694545 weekdays 10–2 and 5–7* 🌐 *www.cuevadelosmurcielagos.com* 🎫 *€5* ⏲ *By appointment only: weekdays 10–2 and 4–6.*

WHERE TO EAT AND STAY

$–$$ SPANISH ✕ **Los Palancos**. Built into the cliff face of the towering mountain, this small restaurant and tavern has a fair bit of charm. Expect mountain-style cuisine featuring roast young goat, rabbit, partridge, and acorn-fed suckling pig, and choose from many items of local produce to take home with you. Vegetarians can opt for the restaurant's renowned goat cheese salad. Soccer player David Beckham likes the food here, and there's a photo on the wall to prove it. ✉ *Calle Llana 43* ☎ *957/694538* 💳 *MC, V.*

$$–$$$ Fodor's Choice ★ 🏨 **Hacienda Minerva**. This stylish hotel was created out of a country estate dating from the late 19th century. The original features, including the historic oil mill, have been preserved, while the rooms are typical farmhouse style. The parlor has a large fireplace flanked by panoramic windows framing a gorgeous landscape. The restaurant serves creative dishes such as wild boar in a red currant sauce and cannelloni stuffed with partridge. **Pros:** tranquil surroundings; superb restaurant. **Cons:** outside of town; no pool. ✉ *Carretera Zuheros, Doña Mencia*

☎ 957/090951 ⊕ *www.haciendaminerva.com* ↩ *10 rooms* ♿ *In-room: a/c, Wi-Fi. In-hotel: restaurant* ≡ *AE, MC, V* ⎮◯⎮ *BP.*

$ ⊞ **Zuhayra.** This small hotel on a narrow street has comfortable rooms painted a sunny yellow with views over the village rooftops to the valley below, plus a cozy bar and dining room with original beams and an open fireplace. During the summer months diners can sit outside on the attractive cobbled patio. **Pros:** cozy public spaces; stunning vistas. **Cons:** a bit far from the center of town; plain decor. ⊠ *C. Mirador 10* ☎ *957/694693* ⊕ *www.zercahoteles.com* ↩ *18 rooms* ♿ *In-room: a/c, Wi-Fi (some). In-hotel: restaurant, bar, Wi-Fi hotspot* ≡ *AE, DC, MC, V.*

PRIEGO DE CÓRDOBA

★ *103 km (64 mi) southeast of Córdoba, 25 km (15 mi) southeast of Zuheros, and 37 km (23 mi) east of Lucena via A339.*

The jewel of Córdoba's countryside is Priego de Córdoba, a town of 14,000 inhabitants at the foot of Mt. Tinosa. Wander down Calle del Río, opposite the town hall, to see 18th-century mansions, once the homes of silk merchants. At the end of the street is the Fuente del Rey (King's Fountain), with some 130 water jets, built in 1803. Don't miss the lavish baroque churches of La Asunción and La Aurora or the Barrio de la Villa, an old Moorish quarter with a maze of narrow streets of white-walled buildings.

WHERE TO EAT AND STAY

$ ✗ **La Paloma.** About 30 km (18 mi) south of Priego de Córdoba, this restaurant overlooks the rolling hills of the Subbética. It's run by an Italian-Spanish couple; husband Felippo Lapini hails from Tuscany and honed his culinary skills in one of Marbella's more exclusive restaurants before opting for the Córdoba countryside. The menu has plenty of Italian influence, including dishes like freshly made ravioli with fresh mint and veal wrapped in ham with a fragrant rosemary sauce. Most of the vegetables are from the couple's organic garden. ⊠ *Carretera Salinas-Iznajar, Km 63, Villanueva de Tapia* ☎ *952/750409* ≡ *MC, V.*

MEDITERRANEAN

$$$$ ⊞ **Barceló La Bobadilla.** On its own 1,000-acre estate amid olive and oak
★ trees, this complex 42 km (24 mi) west of Priego de Córdoba resembles a Moorish village. The buildings have white walls, tile roofs, and patios, and there are fountains and an artificial lake on the property. Guest buildings center on a 16th-century-style chapel that houses a 1,595-pipe organ. Each room has a balcony, a terrace, or a garden. One of the restaurants, El Mirador, concentrates on dishes prepared from locally grown ingredients. A spa rounds out the list of nice extras. The hotel is just south of the La Subbética region, technically in Granada Province. **Pros:** spacious, comfortable rooms; lovely setting; many activities. **Cons:** expensive extras. ⊠ *Finca La Bobadilla, Apdo 144 E, Loja* ☎ *958/321861* ⊕ *www.barcelolabobadilla.com* ↩ *52 rooms, 10 suites* ♿ *In-room: a/c, Wi-Fi. In-hotel: 3 restaurants, bars, tennis courts, pools, gym, spa, Wi-Fi hotspot, some pets allowed* ≡ *AE, DC, MC, V.*

$ ⊞ **Villa Turística de Priego.** Clustered to form an Andalusian pueblo, the semidetached units of this gleaming-white complex sleep from two to six people each and are surrounded by colorful gardens and a patio. Some have a terrace or balcony. The property is in the heart of the Subbética nature park—near Zagrilla, 6 km (4 mi) from Priego de Córdoba, and the hotel management can arrange activities including horse riding and guided walks. **Pros:** family-friendly vibe; quiet retreat. **Cons:** far from town. ✉ *Aldea de Zagrilla* ☎ *957/703503* 🌐 *www.villadepriego.com* *47 apartments/villas, 5 rooms* *In-room: a/c. In- hotel: restaurant, bar, pool, Internet terminal, Wi-Fi hotspot* *AE, DC, MC, V* *Closed Jan.*

LAND OF OLIVES: JAÉN PROVINCE

Jaén is dominated by its *alcázar* (fortress). To the northeast are the olive-producing towns of Baeza and Úbeda. Cazorla, the gateway to the Parque Natural Sierra de Cazorla Segura y Las Villas, lies beyond.

JAÉN

107 km (64 mi) southeast of Córdoba, 93 km (58 mi) north of Granada.

Nestled in the foothills of the Sierra de Jabalcuz, Jaén is surrounded by towering peaks and olive-clad hills. The modern part of town holds little interest for travlers these days, but the old town is an atmospheric jumble of narrow cobblestone streets hugging the mountainside. Jaén's grand parador, in the city's hilltop castle, is a great reason to stop here.

The Arabs called Jaén Geen (Route of the Caravans) because it formed a crossroad between Castile and Andalusia. Captured from the Moors by Fernand III in 1246, Jaén became a frontier province, the site of many a skirmish and battle over the next 200 years between the Moors of Granada and Christians from the north and west.

ESSENTIALS

Visitor Information Jaén (✉ *C. Maestra, 13-Bajo* ☎ *953/190455*).

★ The **Castillo de Santa Catalina**, perched on a rocky crag 400 yards above the center of town, is Jaén's star monument. The castle may have originated as a tower built by Hannibal, but whatever its start, the site was fortified continuously over the centuries. The Nasrid king Alhamar, builder of Granada's Alhambra, constructed an *alcázar* here, but Ferdinand III captured it from him in 1246 on the feast day of Santa Catalina (St. Catherine). Catalina consequently became Jaén's patron saint, so when the Christians built a castle and chapel here, they dedicated both to her. ✉ *Ctra. del Castillo de Santa Catalina* ☎ *953/120733* 🌐 *www.castillosnet.org* *€3* *June–Sept., Thurs.–Tues. 10–2 and 4:30–7; Oct.–May, Thurs.–Tues. 10–2 and 3:30–6.*

Jaén's **cathedral** is a hulk that looms above the modest buildings around it. Begun in 1492 on the site of a former mosque, it took almost 300 years to build. Its chief architect was Andrés de Vandelvira (1509–75)—many more of his buildings can be seen in Úbeda and Baeza. The ornate facade was sculpted by Pedro Roldán, and the figures on top of the columns include San Fernando (Ferdinand III) and the four evangelists.

10

The cathedral's most treasured relic is the **Santo Rostro** (Holy Face), the cloth with which, according to tradition, St. Veronica cleansed Christ's face on the way to Calvary, leaving his image imprinted on the fabric. The *rostro* (face) is displayed every Friday. In the underground **museum,** look for the paintings *San Lorenzo,* by Martínez Montañés; the *Immaculate Conception,* by Alonso Cano; and a Calvary scene by Jácobo Florentino. ✉ *Pl. Santa María* ☎ *953/234233* 🎫 *Cathedral free, museum €3* ⏲ *Cathedral Mon.–Sat. 8:30–1 and 5–8, Sun. 9–1 and 6–8; museum Tues.–Sat. 10–1 and 5–8.*

Explore the narrow alleys of old Jaén as you walk from the cathedral to the **Baños Árabes** (Arab Baths), which once belonged to Ali, a Moorish king of Jaén, and probably date from the 11th century. In 1592, Fernando de Torres y Portugal, a viceroy of Peru, built himself a mansion, the **Palacio de Villardompardo,** right over the baths, so it took years of painstaking excavation to restore them to their original form. The palace contains a fascinating, albeit small, museum of folk crafts and a larger museum devoted to native art. Guided tours of the baths, some of the largest and best conserved in Spain, start every 30 minutes. ✉ *Palacio de Villardompardo, Pl. Luisa de Marillac* ☎ *953/248068* 🎫 *Free* ⏲ *Tues.–Fri. 9–8, weekends 9:30–2:30.*

★ Jaén's **Museo Provincial** has one of the best collections of Iberian (pre-Roman) artifacts in Spain. The newest wing has 20 life-size Iberian sculptures discovered by chance near the village of Porcuna in 1975. The museum proper is in a 1547 mansion and has a patio with the facade of the erstwhile Church of San Miguel. The fine-arts section has a roomful of Goya lithographs. ✉ *Paseo de la Estación 29* ☎ *953/313339* 🎫 *€1.50* ⏲ *Tues. 3–8, Wed.–Sat. 9–8:30, Sun. 9–2:30.*

WHERE TO EAT AND STAY

$$–$$$ SPANISH ✕ **Casa Antonio.** Exquisite Andalusian food with a contemporary twist is served at this somber yet elegant restaurant with three small dining rooms, all with cherry-paneled walls and dramatic contemporary artwork. Try the *foie y queso en milhojas de manzana verde caramelizada en aceite de pistacho* (goose or duck liver and cheese with julienned green apples caramelized in pistachio oil) or *salmonetes de roca en caldo tibio de molusco y aceite de vainilla* (red mullet in a warm mollusk broth and vanilla oil). ✉ *Calle Fermín Palma 3* ☎ *953/270262* 💳 *AE, DC, MC, V* ⏲ *Closed Aug. and Mon. No dinner Sun.*

$$–$$$ SPANISH ✕ **Casa Vicente.** Locals typically pack this family-run restaurant around the corner from the cathedral. You can have drinks and tapas in the colorful tavern, then move to the cozy dining room or outside patio. The traditional local dishes—*pastel de carne de caza* (wild game potpie), *espinacas jienenses* (spinach cooked with garlic, red peppers, and laurel), and *cordero Mozárabe* (roast lamb with a sweet-and-sour sauce)—are especially good. End your meal with *manjar blanco*, a delicious milky dessert spiked with cinnamon. ✉ *Calle Francisco Martín Mora 1* ☎ *953/232816* 💳 *AE, MC, V* ⏲ *Closed Aug. No dinner Sun.*

$$$ Fodor's Choice ★ 🏨 **Parador de Jaén.** Built amid the mountaintop towers of the Castillo de Santa Catalina, this 13th-century castle is one of the showpieces of the Parador chain and a good reason to visit Jaén. The parador's grandiose exterior echoes the Santa Catalina fortress next door, as do the massive

Olive groves near Priedo de Córdoba

vaulted halls, tapestries, baronial shields, and suits of armor inside. Comfortable bedrooms with lofty ceilings, Islamic tilework, and canopy beds have balconies overlooking fields stretching toward a dramatic mountain backdrop. **Pros:** architectural grandeur; panoramic views. **Cons:** outside Jaén. ✉ *Calle Castillo de Santa Catalina* ☎ *953/230000* 🌐 *www.parador.es* *45 rooms* *In-room: a/c, Wi-Fi. In-hotel: restaurant, pool, Wi-Fi hotspot* 💳 *AE, DC, MC, V.*

ALCALÁ LA REAL

75 km (46.5 mi) south of Jaén on N432 and A316.

Alcalá la Real's hilltop fortress, the Fortaleza de la Mota, was installed by the Moors in 727 and sits imperiously at an elevation of 3,389 feet, dominating not only the town but the whole area for miles around. Spectacular views of the peaks of the Sierra Nevada are visible on the southern horizon.

This ancient city, known to the Iberians and Romans, grew to prominence under the Moors who ruled here for more than 600 years. It was they who gave it the first part of its name, Alcalá, which originated from a word meaning "fortified settlement."

During the 12th century the city changed hands frequently as the Moors fought to maintain control of the area. Finally, in 1341, Alfonso XI conquered the town for good, adding Real (Royal) to its name. It remained of strategic importance until the Catholic Monarchs took Granada in 1492—indeed, it was from here that they rode out to accept the keys

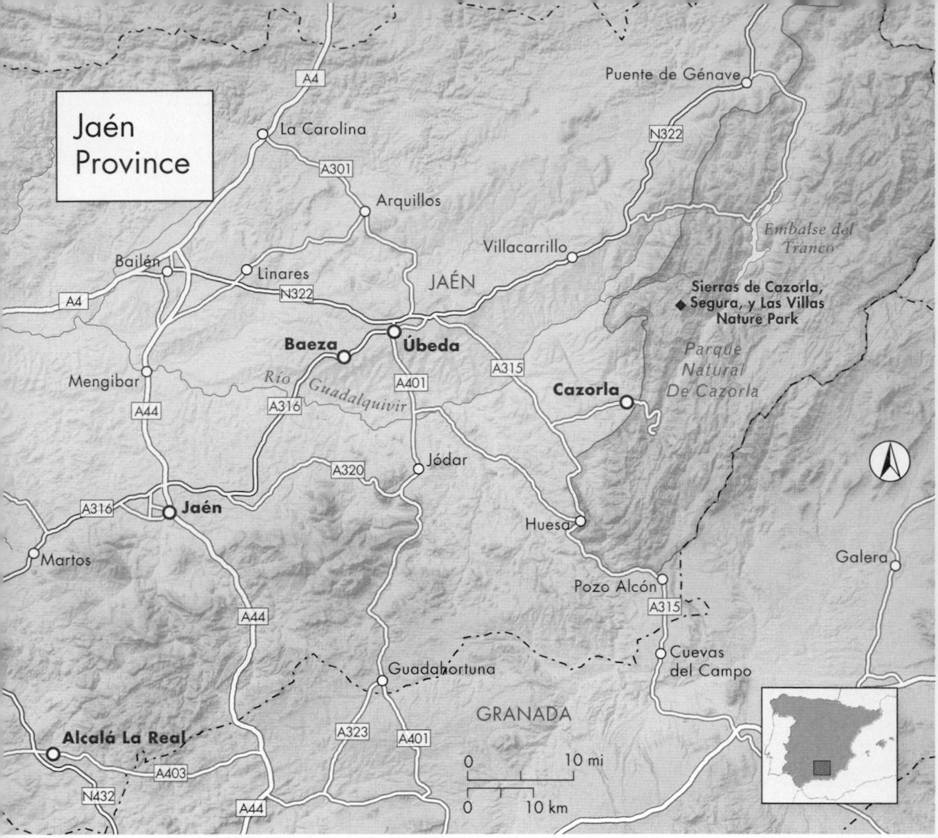

of the city and the surrender. Hundreds of years later, French forces left the town in ruins after their retreat in the early 19th century.

The town of Alcala la Real itself was gradually rebuilt, but the **Hilltop Fortress,** consisting of the *alcazaba* (citadel) and the abbey church that Alfonso XI built, was more or less ignored. Up until the late 1990s, exposed skeletons were visible in some open tombs on the floor of the church. Today visitors can wander around the ruins and visit the small archaeological museum. *€1.50* *June–Sept., daily 10:30–1:30 and 5–8; Oct.–May, daily 10:30–1:30 and 3:30–6:30.*

WHERE TO STAY

$ **Hospedería Zacatín.** This smallish hideaway in the center of town is an inexpensive and cozy way station for visitors to Alcalá la Real. Rooms are simply furnished with pine furniture but equipped with modern touches, including Wi-Fi. The more expensive rooms are slightly larger, with wrought-iron beds and warm peach walls. The restaurant is rustic and comfortable. **Pros:** roof terrace for barbecues; Andalusian cuisine. **Cons:** no frills; street-side rooms can be noisy on weekends. *Calle Pradillo 2* *953/580568* *www.hospederiazacatin.com* *15 rooms* *In-room: Wi-Fi. In-hotel: restaurant, bar, parking (free)* *AE, DC, MC, V.*

BAEZA

Fodor's Choice ★

48 km (30 mi) northeast of Jaén on N321.

The historic town of Baeza, nestled between hills and olive groves, is one of the best-preserved old towns in Spain. Founded by the Romans, it later housed the Visigoths and became the capital of a Moorish *taifa*, one of some two dozen mini-kingdoms formed after the Ummayad Caliphate was subdivided in 1031. Ferdinand III captured Baeza in 1227, and for the next 200 years it stood on the frontier of the Moorish kingdom of Granada. In the 16th and 17th centuries, local nobles gave the city a wealth of Renaissance palaces.

ESSENTIALS

Visitor Information Baeza (✉ *Pl. del Pópulo* ☎ *953/740444*).

EXPLORING

The **Casa del Pópulo**, in the central paseo—where the Plaza del Pópulo (or Plaza de los Leones) and Plaza de la Constitución (or Plaza del Mercado Viejo) merge to form a cobblestone square—is a graceful town house built around 1530. The first Mass of the Reconquest was supposedly celebrated on its curved balcony; it now houses Baeza's tourist office.

In the center of the town square is an ancient Iberian-Roman statue thought to depict Imilce, wife of Hannibal; at the foot of her column is the **Fuente de los Leones** (Fountain of the Lions).

Baeza's **cathedral** was originally begun by Ferdinand III on the site of a former mosque. The structure was largely rebuilt by Andrés de Vandelvira, architect of Jaén's cathedral, between 1570 and 1593, though the west front has architectural influences from an earlier period. A fine 14th-century rose window crowns the 13th-century Puerta de la Luna (Moon Door). Don't miss the baroque silver monstrance (a vessel in which the consecrated Host is exposed for the adoration of the faithful), which is carried in Baeza's Corpus Christi processions—the piece is kept in a concealed niche behind a painting, but you can see it in all its splendor by putting a coin in a slot to reveal the hiding place. Next to the monstrance is the entrance to the clock tower, where a small donation and a narrow spiral staircase take you to one of the best views of Baeza. The remains of the original mosque are in the cathedral's Gothic cloisters. ✉ *Pl. de Santa María* ☎ *953/744157* 🎫 *Cathedral free, cloister and museum €2* ⏲ *May–Sept., daily 10–1 and 5–7; Oct.–Apr., daily 10:30–1 and 4–6.*

Plaza de Santa María. The main square of the medieval city is surrounded by palaces as well as the cathedral. The highlight is the fountain, built in 1564 and resembling a triumphal arch.

Iglesia de Santa Cruz. This rather plain church dates from the early 13th century. One of the first built here after the Reconquest, it's also one of the earliest Christian churches in all of Andalusia. It has two Romanesque portals and a curved stone altar. ✉ *Pl. de Santa Cruz s/n* 🎫 *Free* ⏲ *Mon.–Sat. 11–1:30 and 4–6, Sun. noon–2.*

Casa Museo de Vera Cruz. Immediately behind the Santa Cruz church, this building dating from 1540 holds religious artifacts from the 16th, 17th, 18th, and 19th centuries. There's also a small shop selling souvenirs, such as local honey and Virgin Mary key rings. ✉ *Pl. de Santa Cruz s/n* *Free* ⏲ *Daily 11–1 and 4–6.*

Palacio de Jabalquinto. Built between the 15th and 16th centuries by Juan Alfonso de Benavides as a palatial home, this palace has a flamboyant Gothic facade and a charming marble colonnaded Renaissance patio. It is now part of the International University of Andalucía, and you can wander in and view the patio for free. ✉ *Pl. de Santa Cruz s/n* ⏲ *Weekdays 9–2 and 4–6.*

The ancient student custom of inscribing names and graduation dates in bull's blood (as in Salamanca) is still evident on the walls of the seminary of **San Felipe Neri** (✉ *Cuesta de San Felipe*), opposite the cathedral and built in 1660.

Baeza's **ayuntamiento** (*Town hall*✉ *Pl. Cardenal Benavides, just north of Pl. del Pópulo*) was designed by cathedral master Andrés de Vandelvira. The facade is ornately plateresque; look between the balconies for the coats of arms of Felipe II, the city of Baeza, and the magistrate Juan de Borja. Arrange for a visit to the *salón de plenos,* a meeting hall with painted, carved woodwork.A few blocks west, the 16th-century **Convento de San Francisco** (✉ *C. de San Francisco*) is one of Vandelvira's architectural religious masterpieces.The building was spoiled by the French army and partially destroyed by a light earthquake in the early 1800s, but you can see its restored remains.

WHERE TO EAT AND STAY

$$–$$$ SPANISH ✕ **Vandelvira.** How often do you get the chance to eat in a 16th-century convent? This restaurant, in two galleries on the first floor of the Convento de San Francisco, has lots of character and magnificent antiques. Specialties include *pâté de perdiz con aceite de oliva virgen* (partridge pâté with olive oil), *solomillo al carbon* (grilled steak), and *manitas de cerdo rellenas de perdiz y espinacas* (pig's knuckles filled with partridge and spinach). A summer terrace doubles as a tavern. ✉ *C. de San Francisco 14* ☎ *953/748172* ▭ *AE, DC, MC, V* ⏲ *Closed Mon. No dinner Sun.*

¢ ★ **Juanito.** Rooms in this small, unpretentious hotel are simple and comfortable. The proprietor is a champion of Andalusian food, and the chef has revived such regional specialties as *ensalada de perdiz* (partridge salad) and *cordero con habas* (lamb and broad beans). The hotel is next to a gas station on the edge of town, toward Úbeda. **Pros:** fine in-house dining; friendly staff. **Cons:** on a busy road; undistinguished building. ✉ *Paseo Arca del Agua* ☎ *953/740040* 🌐 *www.juanitobaeza.com* *33 rooms, 2 suites* *In-room: a/c, Wi-Fi. In-hotel: restaurant, tennis court, pool* ▭ *AE, DC, MC, V* ⏲ *No dinner Sun. and Mon.*

ÚBEDA

Fodor's Choice ★

9 km (5½ mi) northeast of Baeza on N321.

Úbeda's *casco antiguo* (old town) is one of the most outstanding enclaves of 16th-century architecture in Spain. It's a stunning surprise in the heart of Jaén's olive groves, set in the shadow of the wild Sierra de Cazorla mountain range. For crafts enthusiasts, this is Andalusia's capital for everything from ceramics to leather. Follow signs to the Zona Monumental (Monumental Zone), where there are countless Renaissance palaces and stately mansions, though most are closed to the public.

ESSENTIALS

Visitor Information Úbeda (✉ *Palacio Marqués del Contadero, C. Baja del Marqués 4* ☎ *953/750897*).

EXPLORING

The Plaza del Ayuntamiento is crowned by the privately owned **Palacio de Vela de los Cobos**, designed by the architect Andrés de Vandelvira (1505–75), a key figure in the Spanish Renaissance era, for Úbeda's magistrate, Francisco de Vela de los Cobos. The corner balcony has a central white marble column that's echoed in the gallery above.

Vandelvira's 16th-century Palacio Juan Vázquez de Molina is better known as the **Palacio de las Cadenas** (House of Chains) because decorative iron chains were once affixed to the columns of its main doorway. It's now the town hall and has entrances on both Plaza Vázquez de Molina and Plaza Ayuntamiento. Molina was a nephew of Francisco de los Cobos, and both served as secretaries to Emperor Carlos V and King Felipe II.

The Plaza Vázquez de Molina, in the heart of the old town, is the site of the **Sacra Capilla de El Salvador**. This building is photographed so often that it's become the city's unofficial symbol. Sacra Capilla was built by Vandelvira, but he based his design on some 1536 plans by Diego de Siloé, architect of Granada's cathedral. Considered one of the masterpieces of Spanish Renaissance religious art, the chapel was sacked in the frenzy of church burnings at the outbreak of the civil war, but it retains its ornate western facade and altarpiece, which has a rare Berruguete sculpture. ✉ *Pl. Vázquez de Molina* ☎ *953/758150* 🎫 *€3* ⏲ *Mon.–Sat. 10–2 and 4:30–7, Sun. 10:45–2 and 4:30–7.*

The **Ayuntamiento Antiguo** (Old Town Hall), begun in the early 16th century but restored as a beautiful arcaded baroque palace in 1680, is now a conservatory of music. From the hall's upper balcony, the town council watched celebrations and *autos-da-fé* ("acts of faith"—executions of heretics sentenced by the Inquisition) in the square below. You can't enter the town hall, but on the north side you can visit the 13th-century church of San Pablo, with an Isabelline south portal. ✉ *Pl. Primero de Mayo, off C. María de Molina* 🎫 *Free* ⏲ *1-hr tour at 7 PM.*

The **Hospital de Santiago**, sometimes jokingly called the Escorial of Andalusia (in allusion to Felipe II's monolithic palace and monastery outside Madrid), is a huge, angular building in the modern section of town, and yet another one of Vandelvira's masterpieces in Úbeda. The plain facade is adorned with ceramic medallions, and over the main entrance is a carving of Santiago Matamoros (St. James the Moorslayer) in his traditional horseback pose. Inside are an arcaded patio and a grand staircase. Now a cultural center, it holds some of the events at the International Spring Dance and Music Festival. ✉ *Av. Cristo Rey* ☎ *953/750842* *Free* ⏲ *Daily 8–3 and 4–10.*

Casa Museo Arte Andalusi. The town's latest museum is in an attractive building with a traditional patio and displays a former private collection of period antiques including Moorish, Mudejar, and Mozarabic pieces. Flamenco shows take place here on Saturday from 10 PM. ✉ *Calle Narvaez 11* ☎ *619/076132* *Free* ⏲ *Daily 10:30–2:30 and 4–8:30.*

WHERE TO EAT AND STAY

$$ SPANISH ✕ **Asador de Santiago.** At this adventurous restaurant just off the main street, chef Anselmo Juarez creates innovative dishes like confit of salt cod on a bed of creamy leeks and lamb sweetbreads with crisp slices of potatoes and artichokes. Vegetarian choices are more limited but include black truffle and mushroom risotto. The candle-filled interior is more traditional than the menu and has terra-cotta tiles, dark wood furnishings, and crisp white linens. ✉ *Av. Cristo Rey 4, Úbeda* ☎ *953/750463* *Reservations essential* ▭ *MC, V* ⏲ *No dinner Sun.*

$–$$ SPANISH ✕ **La Posada de Úbeda.** This inn and restaurant on a back street doubles as a modest little agricultural museum. It's known for its charm, folklore, and authentic no-fuss regional cuisine. M*igas* (bread crumbs, sausage, bacon, and garlic) is a typical dish, as is the *andrajos* (a stew of fish, pasta, and vegetables). You can gaze at the various agricultural artifacts while you dine. ✉ *Calle de San Cristóbal 17* ☎ *953/790473* ▭ *AE, DC, MC, V.*

$–$$ SPANISH ✕ **Mesón Gabino.** A stalwart defender of Úbeda's culinary traditions, this cavelike restaurant serves such standards as *andrajos de Úbeda* (fish, pasta, and vegetable stew). It's on the edge of town near the Puerta del Losal, but it's well worth the walk from Plaza 1 de Mayo. Beef, lamb, and fish cooked over coals are always delicious, while the wine list offers an ample range of Rioja and Ribera de Duero selections. You can have tapas at the bar. ✉ *Calle Fuente Seca s/n* ☎ *953/757553* ▭ *AE, DC, MC, V* ⏲ *Closed Sun.*

$ **HusaRosaleda de Don Pedro.** This beautiful 16th-century mansion, in the city's *Zona Monumental*, blends the best of the old with many of the comforts a modern traveler would want, including king-size beds. Recently taken over by the prestigious Spanish Husa chain, its rooms and public areas are tastefully furnished and spacious. The pool (a rarity in this town) offers relief from the summer heat. The restaurant serves good traditional cuisine. **Pros:** easy parking; good food. **Cons:** hard to find; less than effusive reception. ✉ *Calle Obispo Toral 2* ☎ *953/795147* 🌐 *www.rosaledadedonpedro.com* *45 rooms* *In-room: a/c, Wi-Fi. In-hotel: restaurant, bar, pool, Internet terminal, parking (paid)* ▭ *AE, DC, MC, V.*

$$ **Palacio de la Rambla.** In old Úbeda, this beautiful 16th-century mansion has been in the same family since it was built, and it still hosts the Marquesa de la Rambla when she's in town. Eight of the rooms are open to overnighters; each is unique, but all are large and furnished with

original antiques, tapestries, and works of art, and some have chandeliers and four-poster beds. The palace is arranged on two levels, around a cool, ivy-covered patio. **Pros:** central location; elegant decor. **Cons:** public space limited; little parking. ✉ *Pl. del Marqués 1* ☎ *953/750196* 🌐 *www.palaciodelarambla.com* *6 rooms, 2 suites* *In room: a/c, Wi-Fi (some). In-hotel: parking (paid), Wi-Fi hotspot* *AE, DC, MC, V* *Closed 3 wks in Jan. and mid-July–early Aug.*

$$$ Fodor's Choice ★ **Parador de Úbeda.** This splendid parador is in a 16th-century ducal palace in a prime location on the Plaza Vázquez de Molina, next to the Capilla del Salvador. A grand stairway decked with tapestries and suits of armor leads up to the guest rooms, which have tile floors, lofty ceilings, Castilian-style furniture, four-poster beds, and large bathtubs. The dining room, specializing in regional dishes, serves some of the best food in Úbeda; try the typical local favorite *perdiz* (partridge) with *habas* (broad beans). There's a bar in the vaulted basement. **Pros:** elegant surroundings; perfect location. **Cons:** parking is difficult; church bells in the morning. ✉ *Pl. Vázquez de Molina s/n* ☎ *953/750345* 🌐 *www.parador.es* *35 rooms, 1 suite* *In-room: a/c, Wi-Fi. In-hotel: restaurant, bar* *AE, DC, MC, V.*

SHOPPING

Little Úbeda is the crafts capital of Andalusia, with workshops devoted to carpentry, basket weaving, stone carving, wrought iron, stained glass, and, above all, the city's distinctive green-glaze pottery. Calle Valencia is the traditional potters' row, running from the bottom of town to Úbeda's general crafts center, northwest of the old quarter (follow signs to Calle Valencia or Barrio de Alfareros).

Úbeda's most famous potter was Pablo Tito, whose craft is carried on at three different workshops run by two of his sons, Paco and Juan, and a son-in-law, Melchor, each of whom claims to be the sole true heir to the art. The extrovert **Juan Tito** (✉ *Pl. del Ayuntamiento 12* ☎ *953/751302*) can often be found at the potter's wheel in his rambling shop, which is packed with ceramics of every size and shape. **Melchor Tito** (✉ *Calle Valencia 44* ☎ *953/753365*) focuses on classic green-glaze items. **Paco Tito** (✉ *Calle Valencia 22* ☎ *953/751496*) devotes himself to clay sculptures of characters from *Don Quixote,* which he fires in an old Moorish-style kiln. His shop has a small museum as well as a studio.

All kinds of ceramics are sold at **Alfarería Góngora** (✉ *Calle Cuesta de la Merced 32* ☎ *953/754605*). **Antonio Almazara** (✉ *Calle Valencia 34* ☎ *953/753692* ✉ *Calle Fuenteseca 17* ☎ *953/753365*) is one of several shops specializing in Úbeda's green-glaze pottery. For handmade *esparto*-grass ware, such as rugs, mats, and baskets, go to **Artesanía Blanco** (✉ *Calle Real 47* ☎ *953/750456*), supplied by its own local factory.

CAZORLA

48 km (35 mi) southeast of Úbeda.

Unspoiled and remote, the village of Cazorla is at the east end of Jaén province. The pine-clad slopes and towering peaks of the Cazorla and

The picturesque city of Cazorla, in Jaén province

Segura sierras rise above the village, and below it stretch endless miles of olive groves. In spring, purple jacaranda trees blossom in the plazas.

EXPLORING

For a break from human-made sights, drink in the scenery or watch for wildlife in the **Parque Natural Sierra de Cazorla, Segura y Las Villas** (Cazorla, Segura and Las Villas Nature Park). Deer, wild boar, and mountain goats roam the slopes of this carefully protected patch of mountain wilderness 80 km (50 mi) long and 30 km (19 mi) wide, and hawks, eagles, and vultures soar over the 6,000-foot peaks. Within the park, at **Cañada de las Fuentes** (Fountains' Ravine), is the source of Andalusia's great river, the Guadalquivir. The road through the park follows the river to the shores of **Lago Tranco de Beas.** Alpine meadows, pine forests, springs, waterfalls, and gorges make Cazorla a perfect place to hike. Past Lago Tranco and the village of Hornos, a road goes to the **Sierra de Segura** mountain range, the park's least crowded area. At 3,600 feet, the spectacular village of **Segura de la Sierra,** on top of the mountain, is crowned by an almost perfect castle with impressive defense walls, a Moorish bath, and a nearly rectangular bullring.

A short film shown in the **Centro de Interpretación Torre del Vinagre** (*✉ Ctra. del Tranco, Km 37.8 ☎ 953/713040 ⏲ Daily 11–2 and 4–6*), in Torre de Vinagre, introduces the park's main sights. Displays explain the park's plants and geology, and the staff **can advise you on camping, fishing, and hiking trails.** There's also a **hunting museum,** with random attractions such as the interlocked antlers of bucks who clashed in autumn rutting season, became helplessly trapped, and died of starvation. Nearby are a **botanical garden** and a **game reserve.**

Early spring is the ideal time to visit; try to avoid the summer and late spring months, when the park teems with tourists and locals. It's often difficult, though by no means impossible, to find accommodations in fall, especially on weekends during hunting season (between September and February). Between June and October the park maintains seven well-equipped campsites. For information on hiking, camping, canoeing, horseback riding, or guided excursions, contact the **Agencia de Medio Ambiente** (✉ *Tejares Altos, Cazorla* ☎ *953/720125*), or the park visitor center. For hunting or fishing permits, apply to the Jaén office well in advance.

Déjate Guiar-Excursiones organizes four-wheel-drive trips into restricted areas of the park to observe the flora and fauna and photograph the larger animals. ✉ *Paseo del Santo Cristo 17, Bajo, Edificio Parque* ☎ *953/721351* 🌐 *www.turisnat.org.*

EN ROUTE

Leave Cazorla Nature Park by an alternative route—drive along the spectacular **gorge** carved by the Guadalquivir River, a rushing torrent beloved by kayak enthusiasts. At the El Tranco Dam, follow signs to Villanueva del Arzobispo, where N322 takes you back to Úbeda, Baeza, and Jaén.

WHERE TO EAT AND STAY

$ SPANISH ✕ **La Sarga.** Although the dining rooms are a tad too brightly lit, fresh flowers, tasteful artwork and attentive service provide the essential backdrop for a meal at La Sarga. The pretty-as-a-picture dishes include classics like *setas en salsa de almendras* (oyster mushrooms in an almond sauce) and *alcachofas en salsa de romero* (artichokes with rosemary). More adventurous eaters can opt for the *mousse de foie gras de conejo con pan de centeno* (rabbit mousse with seed-crusted bread). The generous €18 menu del día includes a bottle of house wine. ✉ *Pl. del Mercado s/n* ☎ *953/721507* ▭ *MC, V* ⊙ *Closed Tues.*

$ 🏨 **Coto del Valle.** This delightful hotel in Cazorla's foothills is easily recognized by the huge fountain outside. Surrounded by pine trees, the modern hotel has been built using a traditional highland stone architectural style, with wooden beams and terra-cotta tiles. The rooms have a simple rustic decor, and the large restaurant has a fireplace and mounted game ranging from mountain goats to red leg partridges. **Pros:** nature lover's paradise; perfect hiker's base camp. **Cons:** undistinguished restaurant; 10-minute drive from town. ✉ *Ctra. del Tranco, Km 34.3* ☎ *953/124067* 🌐 *www.hotelcotodelvalle.com* *59 rooms* *In-room: a/c. In-hotel: restaurant, bar, pool, Wi-Fi hotspot, parking (free)* ▭ *AE, DC, MC, V* ⊙ *Closed Dec.*

$$–$$$ 🏨 **Parador de Cazorla.** You'll find this modern parador with its red-tile roof isolated in a valley at the edge of the nature reserve, 26 km (16 mi) above Cazorla village. Despite the disappointing exterior, the setting is bucolic, amid a pine forest on a hillside. It's a quiet place, popular with hunters and anglers. The restaurant serves regional dishes such as *pipirrana* (a salad of finely diced peppers, onions, and tomatoes). **Pros:** lovely views from the pool; mountain cooking. **Cons:** not all rooms have views; slow going in bad weather. ✉ *Calle Sierra de Cazorla* ☎ *953/727075* 🌐 *www.parador.es* *34 rooms* *In-room: a/c, Wi-Fi.*

10

In-hotel: restaurant, pool, parking (free) ▭ *AE, DC, MC, V* ⊗ *Closed Dec. 19–Feb. 6.*

$–$$ **Villa Turística de Cazorla.** On a hill with superb views of the village of Cazorla, this leisure complex rents semidetached apartments that sleep four to six guests. Each has a balcony or terrace as well as a kitchenette—some have a full kitchen—and fireplace. The restaurant specializes in trout, lamb, and, in particular, game, with dishes like wild boar in a honey-based sauce. **Pros:** self-catering option. **Cons:** noisy families; decor functional but plain. ✉ *Ladera de San Isicio s/n* ☎ *953/710100* 🌐 *www.villacazorla.com* *32 apartments* *In-room: a/c, kitchen, Wi-Fi. In-hotel: restaurant, bar, pool* ▭ *MC, V.*

GRANADA

430 km (265 mi) south of Madrid, 261 km (162 mi) east of Seville, and 160 km (100 mi) southeast of Córdoba.

The Alhambra and the tomb of the Catholic Monarchs are the pride of Granada. The city rises majestically from a plain onto three hills, dwarfed—on a clear day—by the Sierra Nevada. Atop one of these hills perches the reddish-gold Alhambra palace, whose stunning view takes in the sprawling medieval Moorish quarter, the caves of the Sacromonte, and, in the distance, the fertile *vega* (plain), rich in orchards, tobacco fields, and poplar groves.

Split by internal squabbles, Granada's Moorish Nasrid dynasty gave Ferdinand of Aragón an opportunity in 1491; spurred by Isabella's religious fanaticism, he laid siege to the city for seven months, and on January 2, 1492, Boabdil, the "Rey Chico" (Boy King), was forced to surrender the keys of the city. As Boabdil fled the Alhambra via the Puerta de los Siete Suelos (Gate of the Seven Floors), he asked that the gate be sealed forever.

GETTING HERE AND AROUND

In Granada, **J. González** buses (€3.10) run between the center of town and the airport, leaving every 30 minutes from the Palacio de Congresos and making a few other stops along the way to the airport. Times are listed at the bus stop; service is reduced in winter. **Line 14**, a municipal bus service (€1), also operates between the airport and the city center, with buses every 30 minutes.

Granada's main bus station is at Carretera de Jaén, 3 km northwest of the center of town beyond the end of Avenida de Madrid. Most buses operate from here, except for buses to nearby destinations such as Fuentevaqueros, Viznar, and some buses to Sierra Nevada, which leave from the city center's Plaza del Triunfo near the RENFE station. Luggage lockers (*la consigna*) at the main bus station cost €2.

Autocares Bonal operates buses between Granada and the Sierra Nevada. **Alsina Gräells** buses run to Las Alpujarras, Córdoba (8 times daily), Seville (10 times daily), Málaga (14 times daily), and Jaén, Baeza, Úbeda, Cazorla, Almeria, Almuñécar, and Nerja several times daily.

There are regular trains to Seville and Almeria, but service to Málaga and Córdoba is less convenient, necessitating a change at Bobadilla.

A new fast track is currently under construction, however, which will reduce these journey times considerably. There are a couple of daily trains to Madrid, Valencia, and Barcelona from Granada.

Granada has an extensive public bus network within the city. You can buy 6- and 21-trip discount passes on the buses and 10-trip passes at newsstands. The single-trip fare is €1.20.

In Granada, **CitySightseeing Granada** bus tours include informative commentary on major sights. Tickets, which cost €10 and are valid for 24 hours (€18 for 48 hours), allow you to hop on and off both the large open-topped bus that takes in the sights in the lower city and the minibus that winds up to the Alhambra and through the narrow streets of Albaicín.

ESSENTIALS

Airport Contact **Aeropuerto de Granada** (☎ *958/245200*) (Aeropuerto Federico García Lorca).

Bus Station **Granada** (✉ *Ctra. Jaén, Granada* ☎ *958/185480*).

Taxi Contacts **Asociació de RadioTaxi** (✉ *Granada* ☎ *958/132323*). **Tele Radio Taxi** (✉ *Granada* ☎ *958/280654*).

Tour Contact **CitySightseeing Granada** (✉ *Gran Vía de Colón s/n, Granada* ☎ *902/101081* 🌐 *www.city-sightseeing.com*).

Train Contacts **Station** (✉ *Av. de los Andaluces s/n* ☎ *958/271272*).

Visitor Information **Provincial Tourist Office** (✉ *Pl. Mariana Pineda 10, Centro* ☎ *958/247146* 🌐 *www.turismodegranada.org*).

EXPLORING

Granada can be characterized by its major neighborhoods: East of the Darro River and up the hill is **La Alhambra.** South of it and around a square and a popular hangout area, Campo del Príncipe, is **Realejo.** To the west of the Darro and going from north to south are the two popular neighborhoods, **Sacromonte** and **Albayzín** (also spelled Albaicín). The latter is the young and trendy part of Granada, full of color, flavor, charming old architecture, and narrow, hilly streets. On either side of Gran Vía de Colón and the streets that border the cathedral (Reyes Católicos and Recogidas—the major shopping areas) is the area generally referred to as **Centro,** the city center. These days much of the Alhambra and Albayzín areas are closed to cars, but starting from the Plaza Nueva there are now minibuses—numbers 30, 31, 32, and 34—that run frequently to these areas.

LA ALHAMBRA

Fodor's Choice ★ **Alhambra.** With more than 2 million visitors a year, the Alhambra is Spain's most popular attraction. The complex has three main parts: the Alcazaba, the Palacios Nazaríes (Nasrid Palaces), and the Generalife, the ancient summer palace. The Museo de la Alhambra is in the Alhambra building, too. *See the Alhambra In-Focus feature for more details.*

17 **Carmen de los Mártires.** Up the hill from the Hotel Alhambra Palace, this turn-of-the-20th-century *carmen* (private villa) and its gardens—the only area open to tourists—are like a Generalife in miniature. ✉ *Paseo*

de los Mártires, Alhambra ☎ *958/227953* 🎫 *Free* ⏲ *Apr.–Oct., weekdays 10–2 and 5–7, weekends 10–7; Nov.–Mar., weekdays 10–2 and 4–6, weekends 10–6.*

18 **Casa-Museo de Manuel de Falla.** The composer Manuel de Falla (1876–1946) lived and worked for many years in this rustic house tucked into a charming hillside lane with lovely views of the Alpujarra Mountains. In 1986 Granada paid homage to him by naming its new concert hall (down the street from the Carmen de los Mártires) the Auditorio Manuel de Falla—from this institution, fittingly, you have a view of his little white house. Note the bust in the small garden: It's placed where the composer once sat to enjoy the sweeping vista. ✉ *C. Antequeruela Alta 11, Alhambra* ☎ *958/228318* 🌐 *www.museomanueldefalla.com* 🎫 *€2* ⏲ *Tues.–Sun. 10–2.*

REALEJO

19 **Fundación Rodríguez-Acosta/Instituto Gómez Moreno.** A few yards from the impressive Alhambra Hotel, this nonprofit organization was founded at the bequest of the painter José Marí Rodríguez-Acosta. Inside a typical *carmen* (private villa), it houses works of art, archaeological findings, and a library collected by the Granada-born scholar Manuel Gómez-Moreno Martínez. Other exhibits include valuable and unique objects from Asian cultures and the prehistoric and classical eras. Call ahead, as advance reservations are required. ✉ *Callejón Niños del Rollo 8, Realejo* ☎ *958/227497* 🌐 *www.fundacionrodriguezacosta.com* 🎫 *€4* ⏲ *Weekdays 10–2.*

12 **Museo de Artes y Costumbres Populares–Casa de los Tiros.** This 16th-century palace, adorned with the coat of arms of the Grana Venegas family who owned it, was named House of the Shots for the musket barrels that protrude from its facade. The stairs to the upper-floor displays are flanked by portraits of miserable-looking Spanish royals, from Ferdinand and Isabella to Felipe IV. The highlight is the carved wooden ceiling in the Cuadra Dorada (Hall of Gold), adorned with gilded lettering and portraits of royals and knights. Old lithographs, engravings, and photographs show life in Granada in the 19th and early 20th centuries. ✉ *Calle Pavaneras s/n, Realejo* ☎ *958/221072* 🌐 *www.juntadeandalucia.es/cultura/museos/MCTGR* 🎫 *€1.50* ⏲ *Tues. 2:30–8:30, Wed.–Sat. 9–8:30, Sun. 9–2:30.*

SACROMONTE

The third of Granada's three hills, the Sacromonte rises behind the Albayzín. The hill is covered with prickly pear cacti and riddled with caverns. The Sacromonte has long been notorious as a domain of Granada's gypsies and, thus, a den of thieves and scam artists, but its reputation is largely undeserved. The quarter is more like a quiet Andalusian *pueblo* (village) than a rough neighborhood. Many of the quarter's colorful *cuevas* (caves) have been restored as middle-class homes, and some of the old spirit lives on in a handful of *zambras* (flamenco performances in caves, which are garishly decorated with brass plates and cooking utensils). These shows differ from formal flamenco shows in that the performers mingle with you, usually dragging one or two onlookers onto the floor for an improvised dance lesson. Ask

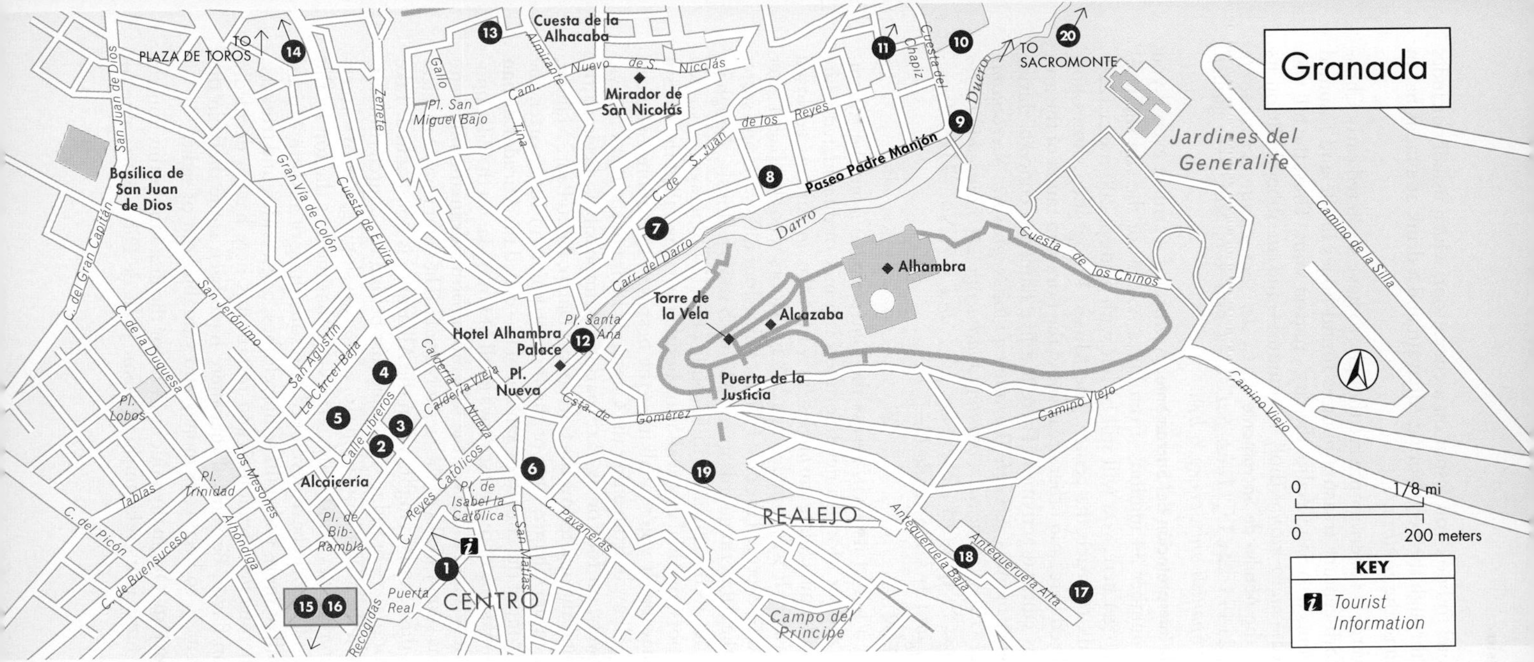

Abadia de Sacromonte	**20**
Capilla Real	**4**
Carmen de los Mártires	**17**
Casa de Castril	**8**
Casa de los Pisa	**12**
Casa del Chapíz	**10**
Casa-Museo de Manuel de Falla	**18**
Casa-Museo Federico García Lorca	**16**
Cathedral	**5**
Centro de Interpretación del Sacromonte	**11**
Centro José Guerrero	**2**
Corral del Carbón	**1**
Dar al-Horra	**13**
El Bañuelo	**7**
Fundación Rodríguez-Acosta/ Instituto Gómez Moreno	**19**
Monasterio de La Cartuja	**14**
Museo de Artes y Costumbres Populares— Casa de los Tiros	**6**
Palacio de los Córdova	**9**
Palacio Madraza	**3**
Parque de las Ciencias	**15**

your hotel to book you a spot on a cueva tour, which usually includes a walk through the neighboring Albayzín and a drink at a tapas bar in addition to the *zambra*.

20 The caverns on Sacromonte are thought to have sheltered early Christians; 15th-century treasure hunters found bones inside and assumed they belonged to San Cecilio, the city's patron saint. Thus, the hill was sanctified—*sacro monte* (holy mountain)—and an abbey built on its summit, the **Abadía de Sacromonte** (✉ *C. del Sacromonte, Sacromonte* ☎ *958/221445* 💶 *€3* ⏲ *Tues.–Sat. 11–1 and 4–6, Sun. 4–6; guided tours, in Spanish only, every ½ hr*).

11 **Centro de Interpretación del Sacromonte.** A word of warning: even if you take the number 34 minibus (from Plaza Nueva) or the city sightseeing bus to get here, you will still be left with a steep, 200-meter (219-yard) walk to reach the center. The Museo Etnográfico shows how people lived here, and other areas show the flora and fauna of the area as well as cultural activities. There are live flamenco concerts during the summer months. ✉ *Calle Barranco de los Negros s/n, Sacromonte* ☎ *958/215120* 🌐 *www.sacromontegranada.com* 💶 *€5 museum, €1 for other areas* ⏲ *Apr.–Oct., Tues.–Fri. 10–2 and 5–9; Nov.–Mar., Tues.–Fri. 10–2 and 4–7, weekends 11–7.*

ALBAYZÍN

Fodor's Choice ★ Covering a hill of its own, across the Darro ravine from the Alhambra, this ancient Moorish neighborhood is a mix of dilapidated white houses and immaculate *carmenes* (private villas in gardens enclosed by high walls). It was founded in 1228 by Moors who fled Baeza after Ferdinand III captured the city. Full of cobblestone alleyways and secret corners, the Albayzín guards its old Moorish roots jealously, though its 30 mosques were converted to baroque churches long ago. A stretch of the Moors' original city wall runs beside the ridge called the **Cuesta de la Alhacaba**. If you're walking—the best way to explore—you can enter the Albayzín from either the Cuesta de Elvira or the Plaza Nueva. Alternatively, on foot or by taxi (parking is impossible), begin in the Plaza Santa Ana and follow the Carrera del Darro, Paseo Padre Manjón, and Cuesta del Chapíz. One of the highest points in the quarter, the plaza in front of the church of San Nicolás—called the **Mirador de San Nicolás**—has one of the finest views in all of Granada: on the hill opposite, the turrets and towers of the Alhambra form a dramatic silhouette against the snowy peaks of the Sierra Nevada. The sight is most magical at dawn, dusk, and on nights when the Alhambra is floodlighted. Take note of Granada's brand new mosque just behind the church. Interestingly, given the area's Moorish history, the two sloping, narrow streets of Calderería Nueva and Calderería Vieja that meet at the top by the Iglesia San Gregorio have developed into something of a North African bazaar, full of shops and stalls selling clothes, bags, crafts, and trinkets. The numerous little teahouses and restaurants here have a decidedly Moroccan flavor. Be warned that there have been some thefts in the Albayzín area, so keep your money and valuables out of sight.

12 **Casa de los Pisa.** Originally built in 1494 for the Pisa family, this house's claim to fame is its relationship to San Juan de Dios, who came to

A GOOD WALK: GRANADA

Save a full day for the Alhambra and the Alhambra hill sights: the **Alcazaba, Generalife, Alhambra Museum, Fundación Rodríguez Acosta/Instituto Gomez Moreno** ⓳, **Casa-Museo de Manuel de Falla** ⓲, and **Carmen de los Mártires** ⓱. This walk covers the other major Granada sights.

Begin at Plaza Isabel la Católica (corner of Gran Vía and Calle Reyes Católicos), with its statue of Columbus presenting the Queen with his New World maps. Walk south on Calle Reyes Católicos and turn left into the **Corral del Carbón** ❶—the oldest building in Granada.

Cross back over Calle Reyes Católicos to the **Alcaicería,** once the Moorish silk market and now a maze of alleys with souvenir shops and restaurants. Behind it is Plaza Bib-Rambla, with its flower stalls and historic Gran Café Bib-Rambla, famous for hot chocolate and *churros.* Calle Oficios is also home to the fascinating Centro José Guerrero ❷ and leads to **Palacio Madraza** ❸ and the **Capilla Real** ❹, next to the **cathedral** ❺.

Off the cathedral's west side is the 16th-century Escuela de las Niñas Nobles, with its plateresque facade. Next to the cathedral, just off Calle Libreros, are the Curia Eclesiástica, an Imperial College until 1769; the Palacio del Arzobispo; and the 18th-century Iglesia del Sagrario. Behind the cathedral is the Gran Vía de Colón. Detour to the **Museo de Artes y Costumbres Populares-Casa de los Tiros** ❻ (on Calle Pavaneras) before heading to Plaza Isabel la Católica. Follow Reyes Católicos to Plaza Nueva and the ornate 16th-century Real Cancillería (Royal Chancery), now the Tribunal Superior de Justicia (High Court). Just north are Plaza Santa Ana and the church of Santa Ana.

Walk through Plaza Santa Ana to Carrera del Darro—which flanks the river and is lined with shops, hotels, bars, and restaurants—and you come to the 11th-century Arab bathhouse, **El Bañuelo** ❼, and the 16th-century **Casa de Castril** ❽, site of Granada's Archaeological Museum.

Follow the river along the Paseo del Padre Manjón (Paseo de los Tristes)—to the **Palacio de los Córdoba** ❾. Climb Cuesta del Chapíz to the Morisco **Casa del Chapíz** ❿. To the east are the caves of Sacromonte and the **Centro de Interpretación del Sacromonte (Cuevas)** ⓫. Turn west into the streets of the Albayzín, with the **Casa de los Pisa** ⓬ and **Dar al-Horra** ⓭ nearby. Best reached by taxi are the 16th-century **Monasterio de La Cartuja** ⓮, the interactive science museum **Parque de las Ciencias** ⓯, and **Casa-Museo Federico García Lorca** ⓰.

10

Granada in 1538 and founded a charity hospital to take care of the poor. Befriended by the Pisa family, he was taken into their home when he fell ill in February 1550. A month later, he died there, at the age of 55. Since that time, devotees of the saint have traveled from around the world to this house with a stone Gothic facade, now run by the Hospital Order of St. John. Inside are numerous pieces of jewelry, furniture, priceless religious works of art, and an extensive collection of paintings and sculptures depicting St. John. ✉ *Calle Convalecencia 1,*

Albayzín ☎ 958/222144 €2.50 ⏲ Mon.–Sat. 10–1.

8 **Casa de Castril.** Bernardo Zafra, secretary to Queen Isabella, once owned this richly decorated 16th-century palace. Before you enter, notice the exquisite portal and the facade carvings depicting scallop shells and a phoenix. Inside is the **Museo Arqueológico** (Archaeological Museum), where you can find artifacts from provincial caves and from Moorish times, Phoenician burial urns from the coastal town of Almuñécar, and a copy of the *Dama de Baza* (Lady of Baza), a large Iberian sculpture discovered in northern Granada Province in 1971 (the original is in Madrid). ✉ *Carrera del Darro 41, Albayzín ☎ 958/225640 €1.50 ⏲ Tues. 2:30–8, Wed.–Sat. 9–8:30, Sun. 9–2:30.*

BICYCLING IN GRANADA

At the foot of the Iberian Peninsula's tallest mountain—the 11,427-foot Mulhacén peak—Granada offers challenging mountain-biking opportunities, and spinning through the hairpin turns of the Alpujarras east of Granada is both scenic and hair-raising. For more information about cycling tours around Granada (and Andalusia), contact **Cycling Country** (✉ *C. Salmerones 18, Alhama de Granada ☎ 958/360655 🌐 www.cyclingcountry.com*), run by husband-and-wife team Geoff Norris and Maggi Jones in a town about 55 km (33 mi) away.

10 **Casa del Chapíz.** There's a delightful garden in this fine 16th-century Morisco house (built by Moorish craftsmen under Christian rule). It houses the School of Arabic Studies and is not generally open to the public, but if you knock the caretaker might show you around. ✉ *C. Cuesta del Chapíz at C. del Sacromonte, Albayzín.*

13 **Dar al-Horra.** Hidden in the back of the upper Albayzín, this semisecret gem was built in the 15th century for the mother of Boabdil, last Nasrid ruler of Granada. After the 1492 conquest of Granada, Dar al-Horra (House of the Honest Woman) was ceded to royal secretary Don Hernando de Zafra. Isabel la Católica later founded the Convent of Santa Isabel la Real here, which operated until the 20th century. Typical of Nasrid art, the interior resembles that of the Alhambra. The north side is the most interesting, with two floors and a tower. The bottom floor has an exquisite flat wooden ceiling decorated with geometric figures. ✉ *Callejón de las Monjas s/n, Albayzín ☎ 958/027800 Free ⏲ Weekdays 10–2.*

7 **El Bañuelo** *(Little Bath House)*. These 11th-century Arab steam baths might be a little dark and dank now, but try to imagine them some 900 years ago, filled with Moorish beauties. Back then, the dull brick walls were backed by bright ceramic tiles, tapestries, and rugs. Light comes in through star-shape vents in the ceiling, à la the bathhouse in the Alhambra. ✉ *Carrera del Darro 31, Albayzín ☎ 958/027800 Free ⏲ Tues.–Sat. 10–2.*

QUICK BITES

Along the Darro River, Paseo Padre Manjón is also known as the Paseo de los Tristes (Promenade of the Sadnesses) because funeral processions once passed this way. The cafés and bars here are a good place for a coffee

Continued on page 761

ALHAMBRA: PALACE-FORTRESS

Floating mirage-like on its promontory overlooking Granada, the mighty and mysterious Alhambra shimmers vermilion in the clear mountain air, with the white peaks of the Sierra Nevada rising behind it. This sprawling palace-fortress, named from the Arabic for "red citadel" *(al-Qal'ah al-Hamra)*, was the last bastion of the 800-year Moorish presence on the Iberian Peninsula. Composed of royal residential quarters, court chambers, baths, and gardens, surrounded by defense towers and massive walls, the Alhambra is an architectural gem where Moorish kings worked and played—and murdered their enemies.

LOOK UP

Among the stylistic elements you can see in the Alhambra are **Arabesque** geometrical designs, and elaborate **Mocárabe** arches.

Built of perishable materials, the Alhambra was meant to be forever replenished and replaced by succeeding generations. Currently, it is the Patio de los Leones's (above) season for restoration.

INSIDE THE FORTRESS

More than 2 million annual visitors come to the Alhambra today, making it Spain's top attraction. Vistors revel in the palace's architectural wonders, most of which had to be restored after the alterations made after the Christian reconquest of southern Spain in 1492 and the damage from an 1821 earthquake. Incidentally, Napoléon's troops commandeered the site in 1812 with intent to level it but their attempts were foiled.

The courtyards, patios, and halls offer an ethereal maze of Moorish arches, columns, and domes containing intricate stucco carvings and patterned ceramic tiling. The intimate arcades, fountains, and light reflecting pools throughout are identified in the ornamental inscriptions as physical renderings of paradise taken from the Koran and Islamic poetry. The contemporary visitor to this dreamlike space feels the fleeting embrace of a culture that brought its light to a world emerging from medieval darkness.

ARCHITECTURAL TERMS

Arabesque: An ornament or decorative style that employs flower, foliage, or fruit, and sometimes geometrical, animal, and figural outlines to produce an intricate pattern of interlaced lines.

Mocárabe: A decorative element of carved wood or plaster based on juxtaposed and hanging prisms resembling stalactites. Sometimes called *muquarna* (honeycomb vaulting), the impression is similar to a beehive and the "honey" has been described as light.

Mozárabe: Sometimes confused with Mocárabe, the term Mozárabe refers to Christians living in Moorish Spain. Thus, Christian artistic styles or recourses in Moorish architecture (such as the paintings in the Sala de los Reyes) are also identified as *mozárabe*, or, in English, mozarabic.

Mudéjar: This word refers to Moors living in Christian Spain. Moorish artistic elements in Christian architecture, such as horseshoe arches in a church, also are referred to as Mudéjar.

ALHAMBRA'S ARCHITECTURAL HIGHLIGHTS

The **columns** used in the construction of the Alhambra are unique, with extraordinarily slender cylindrical shafts, concave base moldings, and carved rings decorating the upper extremities. The capitals have simple cylindrical bases under prism-shaped heads decorated in a variety of vegetal motifs. Nearly all of these columns support false arches constructed purely for decorative purposes. The 124 columns surrounding the Patio de los Leones (Court of the Lions) are the best examples.

Court of the Lions

Cursive epigraphy is used to quote the Koran and Arabic poems. Considered the finest example of this are the Ibn-Zamrak verses that decorate the walls of the Sala de las Dos Hermanas.

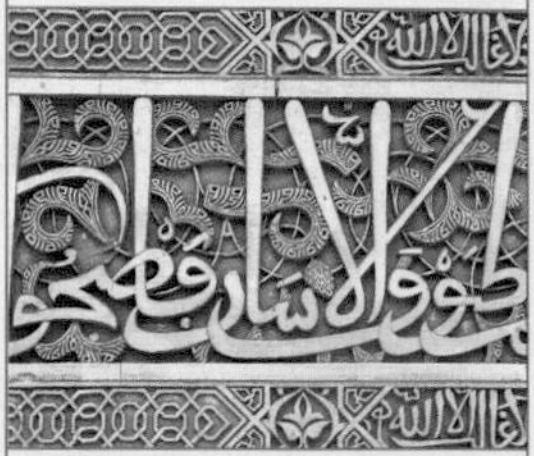

Cursive epigraphy

Glazed ceramic tiles covered with geometrical patterns in primary colors cover the walls of the Alhambra with a profusion of styles and shapes. Red, blue, and yellow are the colors of magic in Sufi tradition, while green is the life-giving color of Islam.

Ceramic tiles

The **horseshoe arch**, widening before rounding off with lower ends extending around the circle until they begin to converge, was the quintessential Moorish architectural innovation, used not only for aesthetic and decorative purposes but because it allowed greater height than the classical, semicircular arch inherited from the Greeks and Romans. The horseshoe arch also had a mystical significance in recalling the shape of the *mihrab*, the prayer niche in the *qibla* wall of a mosque indicating the direction of prayer and suggesting a door to Mecca or to paradise. Horseshoe arches and arcades are found throughout the Alhambra.

Gate of Justice

The Koran describes paradise as "gardens underneath which rivers flow," and **water** is used as a practical and ornamental architectural element throughout the Alhambra. Whether used musically, as in the canals in the Patio de los Leones or visually, as in the reflecting pool of the Patio de los Arrayanes, water is used to enhance light, enlarge spaces, or provide musical background for a desert culture in love with the beauty and oasis-like properties of hydraulics in all its forms.

Alhambra fountains

The Alcazaba was built chiefly by Nasrid kings in the 1300s.

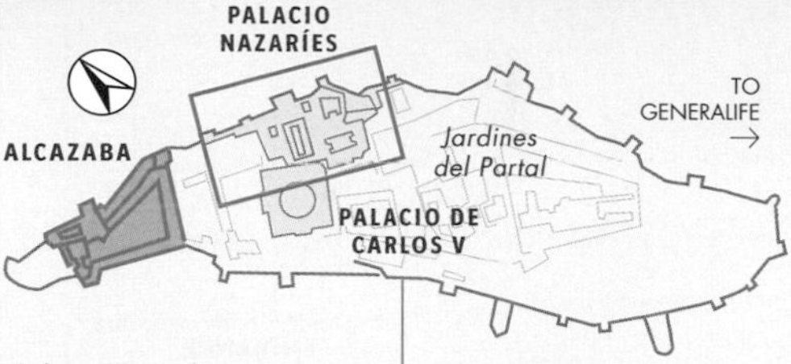

LAY OF THE LAND

The complex has three main parts: the Alcazaba, the Palacio Nazaríes (Nasrid Royal Palace), and the Generalife. Across from the main entrance is the original fortress, the **Alcazaba**. Here, the watchtower's great bell was once used to announce the opening and closing of the irrigation system on Granada's great plain.

A wisteria-covered walkway leads to the heart of the Alhambra, the **Palacios Nazaríes**. Here, delicate apartments, lazy fountains, and tranquil pools contrast vividly with the hulking fortifications outside. It is divided into three sections: the *mexuar,* where business, government, and palace administration were headquartered; the *serrallo,* a series of state rooms where the sultans held court and entertained their ambassadors; and the *harem*, which in its time was entered only by the sultan, his family, and their most trusted servants, most of them eunuchs. Nearby is the Renaissance **Palacio de Carlos V** (Palace of Charles V), featuring a perfectly square exterior but a circular interior courtyard. Designed by Pedro Machuca, a pupil of Michelangelo, it is where the sultan's private apartments once stood. Part of the building houses the free **Museo de la Alhambra**, devoted to Islamic art. Upstairs is the more modest **Museo de Bellas Artes.**

Over on Cerro del Sol (Hill of the Sun) is **Generalife**, the ancient summer palace of the Nasrid kings.

TIMELINE

1238 First Nasrid king, Ibn el-Ahmar, begins Alhambra.

1391 Nasrid Palaces is completed.

1492 Boabdil surrenders Granada to Ferdinand and Isabella, parents of King Henry VIII's first wife, Catherine of Aragon.

1524 Carlos V begins Renaissance Palace.

1812 Napoléonic troops arrive with plans to destroy Alhambra.

1814 The Duke of Wellington sojourns here to escape the pressures of the Peninsular War.

1829 Washington Irving lives on the premises and writes *Tales of the Alhambra,* reviving interest in the crumbling palace.

1862 Granada municipality begins Alhambra restoration that continues to this day.

2006 The Patio de los Leones undergoes a multiyear restoration.

ALHAMBRA'S PASSAGES OF TIME

From Columbus's commissioning to a bloody murder, historic events as well as everyday affairs happened between these walls.

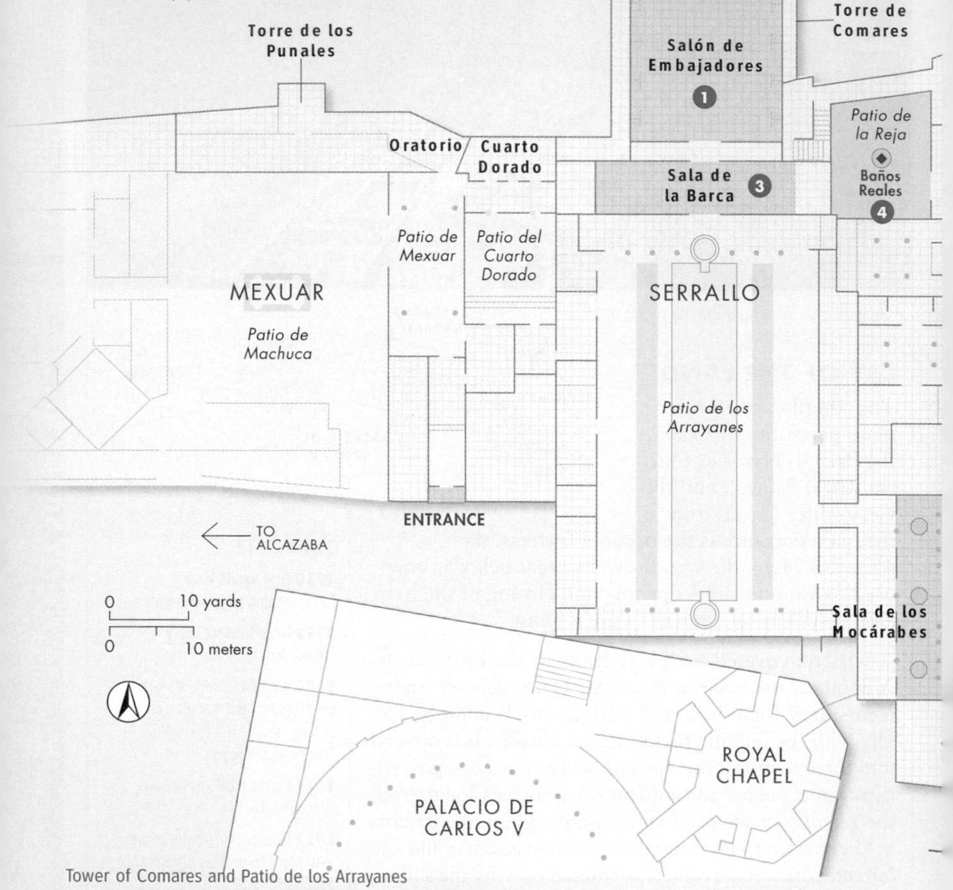

Tower of Comares and Patio de los Arrayanes

❶ In **El Salón de Embajadores**, Boabdil drew up his terms of surrender, and Christopher Columbus secured royal support for his historic voyage in 1492. The carved wooden ceiling is a portrayal of the seven Islamic heavens, with six rows of stars topped by a seventh-heaven cupulino or micro-cupola.

❷ **Torre de Comares**, a lookout in the corner of this hall is where Carlos V uttered his famous line, "Ill-fated the man who lost all this."

❸ Mistakenly named from the Arabic word *baraka* (divine blessing), **Sala de la Barca** has a carved wooden ceiling often described as an inverted boat.

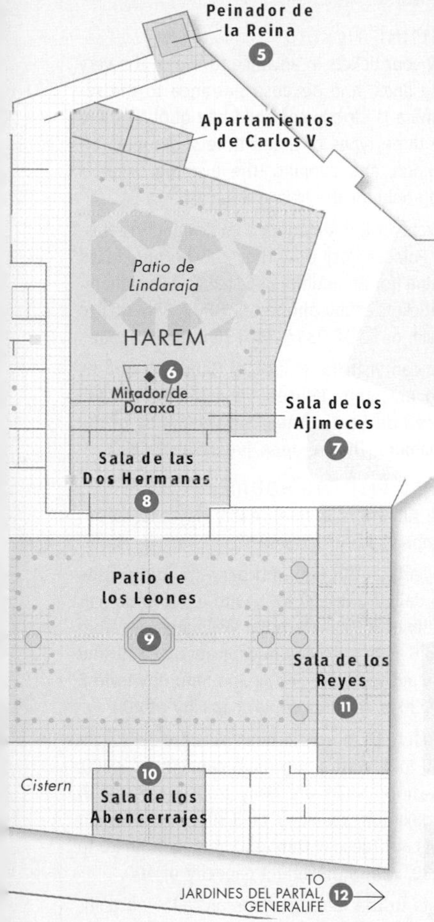

4 The **Baños Reales** is where the sultan's favorites luxuriated in brightly tiled pools beneath star-shape pinpoints of light from the ceiling above. It is open to visitors on certain days. An up-to-date timetable can be obtained from the tourist office.

5 **El Peinador de la Reina**, a nine-foot-square room atop a small tower was the Sultana's boudoir. The perforated marble slab was used to infiltrate perfumes while the queen performed her toilette. Washington Irving wrote his *Tales of the Alhambra* in this romantic tree-house-like perch.

Sala de los Reyes

6 Sultana Zoraya often found refuge in this charming little balcony (**Mirador de Daraxa**) overlooking the Lindaraja garden.

7 Shhh, don't tell a secret here. In the **Sala de los Ajimeces**, a whisper in one corner can be clearly heard from the opposite corner.

8 In the **Sala de las Dos Hermanas**, twin slabs of marble embedded in the floor are the "sisters," though Washington Irving preferred the story of a pair of captive Moorish beauties.

9 In the **Patio de Los Leones** (Court of the Lions), a dozen crudely crafted lions support the fountain at the center of this elegant courtyard, representing the signs of the zodiac sending water to the four corners.

10 In the **Sala de los Abencerrajes**, Muley Hacen (father of Boabdil) murdered the male members of the Abencerraje family in revenge for their chief's seduction of his daughter Zoraya. The rusty stains in the fountain are said to be bloodstains left by the pile of Abencerraje heads.

The star-shaped cupola, reflected in the pool, is considered the Alhambra's most beautiful example of stalactite or honeycomb vaulting. The octagonal dome over the room is best viewed at sunset when the 16 small windows atop the dome admit sharp, low sunlight that refracts kaleidoscopically through the beehive-like prisms.

11 In the **Sala de los Reyes**, the ceiling painting depicts the first 10 Nasrid rulers. It was painted by a Christian artist since Islamic artists were not allowed to usurp divine power by creating human or animal figures.

The overhead painting of the knight rescuing his lady from a savage man portrays chivalry, a concept introduced to Europe by Arabic poets.

12 The terraces of **Generalife** grant incomparable views of the city.

Generalife gardens

PLANNING YOUR VISIT

The acoustics in the Palace of Charles V are ideal for the summer symphony concerts at the Alhambra.

GETTING HERE

Getting to the Alhambra on foot requires a 1-km uphill climb, so we recommend taking a taxi or bus from Plaza Nueva. Buses 30 and 32 make several stops in the Alhambra complex, including the ticket office (Entrance Pavilion). If you're driving, don't park on the street (it leaves your car vulnerable to a break-in). Instead, use the Alhambra parking lot or park underground on Calle San Agustín, just north of the cathedral, and take a taxi or the minibus from Plaza Nueva.

BEST ROUTES IN THE ALHAMBRA

There are three recommended options for visiting the Alhambra, and you can only see the Nasrid Palaces during the time slot on your ticket.

A: Alcazaba-Nasrid Palaces-Generalife

B: Nasrid Palaces-Alcazaba-Generalife

C: Generalife-Alcazaba-Nasrid Palaces

WHEN TO GO

Winter's low, slanting sunlight is best for seeing the Alhambra, and the temperatures are ideal for walking. Spring brings lush floral colors to the gardens. Fall is also sharp, cooler, and clear. July and August are crowded and hot.

The **Festival Internacional de Música y Danza de Granada** (☎ 34 958/276241 🌐 www.granadafestival.org) held annually from mid-June to mid-July offers visitors an opportunity to hear a concert in the Alhambra or watch a ballet in the Generalife amphitheater.

GETTING TICKETS

Buy your tickets in advance to avoice the very long lines, and because entrance to the Alhambra is strictly controlled by quotas. There are three types of timed tickets: morning, afternoon, and evening (the evening ticket is valid only for the Nasrid Palaces).

Tickets for the Alhambra complex and the Nasrid Palaces cost €12. They can be purchased online (for an additional €1) at 🌐 www.alhambratickets.es, by phone at ☎ 902/888–001 in Spain, or ☎ 34 934/923–750 outside Spain.

You can visit the Palace of Charles V and its two museums (Museo de la Alhambra and Museo de Bellos Artes) independently of the Alhambra. They're open Tues.–Sat. 9–2:30.

TIMED VISITING HOURS

The Alhambra is open every day except December 25 and January 1.

November through February, morning visits are daily from 8:30 to 2, with a maximum capacity of 3,300; afternoon visits are daily from 2 to 6, with a maximum capacity of 2,100; and evening visits are Friday and Saturday from 8 to 9:30, with a maximum capacity of 400.

March to October, morning visits are daily from 8:30 to 2, with a maximum capacity of 3,300; afternoon visits are daily from 2 to 8, with a maximum capacity of 3,300; and evening visits are Tuesday through Saturday from 10 to 11:30, with a maximum capacity of 400.

Visits to the main gardens are allowed daily, from 8:30 to 6 year-round; from March through October access is until 8.

CONTACT INFORMATION

Patronato de la Alhambra ☎ 34 902/441–221 ✉ informacion.alhambra.pag@juntadeandalucia.es 🌐 www.alhambra-patronato.es.

break. The park on the paseo, dappled with fountains and stone walkways, has a stunning view of the Alhambra's northern side.

9 **Palacio de los Córdoba.** At the end of the Paseo Padre Manjón, this 17th-century noble house today holds Granada's municipal archives and is used for municipal functions and art exhibits. You're free to wander about the large garden. ✉ *Cuesta del Chapiz 4, Albayzín.*

CENTRO

4 **Capilla Real** *(Royal Chapel).* Catholic Monarchs Isabella of Castile and Ferdinand of Aragón are buried at this shrine. The couple originally planned to be buried in Toledo's San Juan de los Reyes, but Isabella changed her mind when the pair conquered Granada in 1492. When she died in 1504, her body was first laid to rest in the Convent of San Francisco (now a parador), on the Alhambra hill. The architect Enrique Egas began work on the Royal Chapel in 1506 and completed it 15 years later, creating a masterpiece of the ornate Gothic style now known in Spain as Isabelline. In 1521 Isabella's body was transferred to a simple lead coffin in the Royal Chapel crypt, where it was joined by that of her husband, Ferdinand, and later her unfortunate daughter, Juana la Loca (Joanna the Mad), and son-in-law, Felipe el Hermoso (Philip the Handsome). Felipe died young, and Juana had his casket borne about the peninsula with her for years, opening the lid each night to kiss her embalmed spouse good night. A small coffin to the right contains the remains of Prince Felipe of Asturias, a grandson of the Catholic Monarchs and nephew of Juana la Loca who died in his infancy. The **crypt** containing the five lead coffins is quite simple, but it's topped by elaborate marble **tombs** showing Ferdinand and Isabella lying side by side (commissioned by their grandson Carlos V and sculpted by Domenico Fancelli). The **altarpiece,** by Felipe Vigarini (1522), comprises 34 carved panels depicting religious and historical scenes; the bottom row shows Boabdil surrendering the keys of the city to its conquerors and the forced baptism of the defeated Moors. The **sacristy** holds Ferdinand's sword, Isabella's crown and scepter, and a fine collection of Flemish paintings once owned by Isabella. ✉ *Calle Oficios, Centro* ☎ *958/229239* 🌐 *www.capillarealgranada.com* 🎟 *€3.50* ⏲ *Mon.–Sat. 10:15–1:30 and 4–7.30, Sun. 11–1.30 and 3:30–7:30.*

10

5 **Cathedral.** Granada's cathedral was commissioned in 1521 by Carlos V, who considered the Royal Chapel "too small for so much glory" and wanted to house his illustrious late grandparents someplace worthier. Carlos undoubtedly had great intentions, as the cathedral was created by some of the finest architects of its time: Enrique Egas, Diego de Siloé, Alonso Cano, and sculptor Juan de Mena. Alas, his ambitions came to little, for the cathedral is a grand and gloomy monument, not completed until 1714 and never used as the crypt for his grandparents (or parents). Enter through a small door at the back, off the Gran Vía. Old hymnals are displayed throughout, and there's a museum, which includes a 14th-century gold-and-silver monstrance (used for communion) given to the city by Queen Isabella. Audio guides are available for an extra €3.50. ✉ *Gran Vía s/n, Centro* ☎ *958/222959* 🎟 *€3.50*

Apr.–Oct., Mon.–Sat. 10:30–1:30 and 4–8, Sun. 4–8; Nov.–Mar., Mon.–Sat. 10:45–1:30 and 4–7, Sun. 4–7.

2 **Centro José Guerrero.** Just across a lane from the Cathedral and Capilla Real, this building houses colorful modern paintings by José Guerrero. Born in Granada in 1914, Guerrero traveled throughout Europe and lived in New York in the 1950s before returning to Spain. The center also runs excellent temporary contemporary art shows. *Calle Oficios 8, Centro 958/225185 www.centroguerrero.org Free Tues.–Sat. 11–2 and 5–9, Sun. 11–2.*

1 **Corral del Carbón** *(Coal House)*. This building was used to store coal in the 19th century, but its history goes further back. Dating from the 14th century, it was used by Moorish merchants as a lodging house, and then by Christians as a theater. It's one of the oldest Moorish buildings in the city and the only Arab structure of its kind in Spain. *Pl. Mariana Pineda s/n, Centro 958/221118 Free Weekdays 10–1:30 and 5–8, weekends 10:30–2.*

3 **Palacio Madraza.** This building conceals the Islamic seminary built in 1349 by Yusuf I. The intriguing baroque facade is elaborate; inside, across from the entrance, an octagonal room is crowned by a Moorish dome. It hosts occasional free art and cultural exhibitions. *C. Zacatín s/n, Centro 958/223447.*

OUTSKIRTS OF TOWN

16 **Casa-Museo Federico García Lorca.** Granada's most famous native son, the poet Federico García Lorca, gets his due here, in the middle of a park devoted to him on the southern fringe of the city. Lorca's onetime summer home, **La Huerta de San Vicente,** is now a museum—run by his niece Laura García Lorca—with such artifacts as his beloved piano and changing exhibits on specific aspects of his life. *Parque García Lorca, Virgen Blanca s/n, Arabial 958/258466 www.huertadesanvicente.com €3, free Wed. July and Aug., Tues.–Sun. 10–2:30; Apr.–June and Sept., Tues.–Sun. 10–12:30 and 5–7:30; Oct.–Mar., Tues.–Sun. 10-12:30 and 4–6:30. Guided tours every 45 min until 30 min before closing.*

14 **Monasterio de La Cartuja.** This Carthusian monastery in northern Granada (2 km [1 mi] from the center of town and reached by the No. 8 bus) was begun in 1506 and moved to its present site in 1516, though construction continued for the next 300 years. The exterior is sober and monolithic, but inside are twisted, multicolor marble columns; a profusion of gold, silver, tortoiseshell, and ivory; intricate stucco; and the extravagant sacristy—it's easy to see why it has been called the Christian answer to the Alhambra. Among its wonders are the trompe l'oeil spikes, shadows and all, in the Sanchez Cotan cross over the *Last Supper* painting at the west end of the refectory. If you're lucky you may see small birds attempting to land on these faux perches. *C. de Alfacar, Cartuja 958/161932 €4 Apr.–Oct., Mon.–Sat. 10–1 and 4–8, Sun. 10–noon and 4–8; Nov.–Mar., daily 10–1 and 3:30–6.*

15 **Parque de las Ciencias** *(Science Park)*. Across from Granada's convention center and easily reached on either a No. 1 or 5 bus, this museum (the most visited in Andalusia) has a planetarium and interactive

demonstrations of scientific experiments. The 165-foot observation tower has views to the south and west. ✉ *Av. del Mediterráneo, Zaidín* ☎ *958/131900* 🌐 *www.parqueciencias.com* 🎟 *Park €6, planetarium €2.50* ⏲ *Tues.–Sat. 10–7, Sun. and holidays 10–3. Closed Sept. 15–30.*

WHERE TO EAT AND STAY

TAPAS BARS

Poke around the streets between the Carrera del Darro and the Mirador de San Nicolás, particularly around the bustling Plaza San Miguel Bajo, for Granada's most colorful twilight hangouts. Also try the bars and restaurants in the arches underneath the Plaza de Toros (Bullfighting Ring), on the west side of the city, a bit farther from the city center.

For a change, check out some Moroccan-style tea shops, known as *teterías*—these first emerged in Granada and are now also popular in Seville and Málaga, particularly among students. Tea at such places can be expensive, so be sure to check the price of your brew before you order. The highest concentration of *teterías* is in the Albayzín, particularly around Calle Caldereria Nueva where, within a few doors from each other, you find Kasbah Tetería, Tetería Oriental, and El Jardín de los Sueños.

La Brujidera (✉ *Monjas del Carmen 2, Centro* ☎ *958/222595*) has innovative tapas like marinated pork loin and attracts a buzzy student crowd. The popular **Bodegas Castañeda** (✉ *Elvira 6, Centro* ☎ *958/226362*) serves classic tapas, as well as baked potatoes with a choice of fillings. Southeast of Granada's cathedral, **Café Botánico** (✉ *Calle Málaga 3, Centro* ☎ *958/271598*) is a modern hot spot with a diverse menu that serves twists on traditional cuisine for a young, trendy crowd.

Off Calle Navas in Plaza Campillo is **Chikito** (✉ *Pl. del Campillo 9, Puerta Real* ☎ *958/223364*), best known for its sit-down meals, but the bar is an excellent place for tapas. It's usually packed, so additional tables are set up on the square in summer. **El Pilar del Toro** (✉ *C. Hospital de Santa Ana 12, Albayzín* ☎ *958/225470*) is a bar and restaurant with a beautiful patio. **Taberna Salinas** (✉ *Elvira 13, Centro* ☎ *958/221411*) has brick-and-beam decor and great wine to accompany its delicious tapas. There's another branch at Calle Almireceros 5 near Plaza Nueva. More filling fare is also available.

WHERE TO EAT

$$–$$$ LA NUEVA COCINA

✕ **Azafrán.** A charming surprise nestled at the foot of the Albayzín by the Darro River, this sleek contemporary space in the shadow of the Alhambra offers a selection of specialties. The menu is interesting and diverse and includes dishes like spinach crepes with shrimp, raisins, and pine nuts; lamb couscous; and several salads including mango and goat cheese salad with fresh spinach leaves, basil, and sweet raspberry vinegar. Steel furniture and black and red decor contribute to the air of sophistication. ✉ *Paseo de los Tristes 1, Albayzín* ☎ *958/226882* 💳 *AE, DC, MC, V.*

$$ SPANISH ★ **Bodegas Castañeda.** A block from the cathedral across Gran Vía, this is a delightfully typical Granadino bodega with low ceilings and dark wood furniture. In addition to the wines, specialties here are *jamón ibérico de bellota* (acorn-fed ham) and *embutidos* (sausages). The extensive list of tapas includes *queso viejo en aceite* (cured cheese in olive oil), bacon with Roquefort cheese, and *jamón de Trevélez* (ham from the village of Trevélez). If you like garlic, don't miss the Spanish tortilla with creamy *alioli* (garlic-spiked mayonnaise). ✉ *Calle Almireceros 1–3, Centro* ☎ *958/223222* ▭ *MC, V.*

$$–$$$ SPANISH ★ **Cunini.** Around the corner from the cathedral is, arguably, Granada's best fish restaurant. Catch-of-the-day fish and seafood, fresh from the boats at Motril, are displayed in the window at the front of the tapas bar, adjacent to the cozy wood-paneled dining room. Both the *frito* (fried) and the *parrillada* (grilled) fish are good choices. If it's chilly, you can warm up with *caldereta de arroz, pescado y marisco* (rice, fish, and seafood stew). There are tables outdoors overlooking a pretty plaza in warm weather. ✉ *Calle Pescadería 14, Centro* ☎ *958/250777* ▭ *AE, DC, MC, V* ⊙ *Closed Mon. No dinner Sun.*

$–$$ MOROCCAN **Kasbah Tetería.** On a sloping pedestrian street lined with Moroccan teashops, Moroccan bakeries, Moroccan souvenir shops, and Moroccan restaurants, stepping out is just like being in Morocco. Kasbah Tetería is primarily a teashop but also has a short menu of dishes that include couscous with chicken, lamb, and vegetables as well as tasty *pasteles árabes* (pastries), exotic teas, and milkshakes in flavors like honey and date or almond pistachio. ✉ *Calle Calderería Nueva 4, Centro* ☎ *958/227936* ▭ *MC, V.*

$$$–$$$$ SPANISH **La Ermita en la Plaza de Toros.** Whether for tapas or a meal, this restaurant, built under the vaults supporting the Granada bullring, is a carnivore's delight. Its specialties are meats ranging from *solomillo de buey sobre salsa de hongos* (filet mignon in a wild mushroom sauce) to *jamón ibérico de bellota* (acorn-fattened ham). Fish lovers have a modest selection of choices that includes Galician-style octopus and Biscay-style cod. The exposed brick walls are decorated with mounted fighting bulls' heads and bullfight posters. ✉ *Calle Dr. Olóriz 25, Centro* ☎ *958/290257* ▭ *MC, V.*

$–$$ SPANISH **Mesón Blas Casa.** In the choicest square in the Albayzín, which is covered with tables and chairs in the summer, this restaurant serves solidly traditional cuisine that includes *rabo de toro* (oxtail), *habas con jamón* (ham with broad beans), and swordfish Mozarab (grilled with a Moorish-inspired combination of dried fruits, grapes, and nuts). There's a cheap and filling *menú del día* (daily menu), and the fireplace will warm your toes when there's snow on the Sierras. ✉ *Pl. San Miguel Bajo 15, Albayzín* ☎ *958/273111* ▭ *MC, V* ⊙ *Closed Mon.*

$$–$$$ SPANISH ★ **Mirador de Morayma.** Buried in the Albayzín, this hard-to-find restaurant might appear to be closed, so ring the doorbell. Once inside, you'll have unbeatable views across the gorge to the Alhambra, particularly from the wisteria-laden outdoor terrace. In colder weather you can enjoy the open fireplace and attractive dining space inside. The menu has some surprises, such as smoked *esturión* (sturgeon) from Riofrío, served cold with cured ham and a vegetable dip, and

the *ensalada de remojón granadino,* a salad of cod, orange, and olives. Actress Gwyneth Paltrow likes this place—it was one of the few restaurants she selected in Granada for inclusion in her popular television series *Spain–On the Road Again.* ✉ *Calle Pianista García Carrillo 2, Albayzín* ☎ *958/228290* ▭ *AE, MC, V* ⊙ *No dinner Sun.*

$–$$ SPANISH ✕ **Puerta del Carmen.** This bustling bar and restaurant occupies an elegant town house and exudes a whiff of tradition with its dark-wood furnishings, lofty ceilings, and tasteful decor. A congenial staff and a reliably good menu add to the appeal. It's popular with the business community and ladies who lunch, and there are plenty of plates to share, including king prawns with hearts of palm. Main courses include marinated octopus carpaccio and baked wild sea bass. The wine list is superb. ✉ *Plaza Carmen 1, Centro* ☎ *958/223737* ▭ *MC, V.*

$$$–$$$$ SPANISH ★ ✕ **Ruta del Veleta.** It's worth the short drive 5 km (3 mi) out of town to this restaurant, which serves some of the region's best food. Menu items are innovative twists on Spanish recipes using seasonal ingredients—the restaurant grows many of its own vegetables. Innovative options include *librito de mango y esturión sobre espejo de picual con huevos de trucha asalmonada* (a layered stack of mango and sturgeon, topped with salmon trout eggs) and *solomillo de jabalí con frutos de otoño y salsa de vinagre* (wild boar with autumn fruits in a vinegar-and-honey sauce). Dessert might be *natillas ligeras de caramelo con bizcocho de nueces y miel y helado de chirimoya* (light caramel custard with a nut and honey biscuit and custard apple ice cream). ✉ *Ctra. de la Sierra 136, on road to Sierra Nevada, Cenes de la Vega* ☎ *958/486134* ▭ *AE, DC, MC, V* ⊙ *No dinner Sun.*

$$–$$$ SPANISH ★ ✕ **San Nicolás.** Near the Mirador San Nicolás, this elegant restaurant has panoramic views of the Alhambra from the upstairs Green Room and outside terrace. Renowned chef Enrique Martín from Córdoba has introduced such attractive dishes as crunchy mango and *foie* gras ravioli with herb bread and a yogurt sauce and sautéed baby calamari with vegetable risotto but also offers a more traditional menu of oxtail stew, grilled sea bass, and lobster and rice. The second dining room, the Red Room, has traditional black-and-white tiles and warm ocher paintwork. Service is exemplary. ✉ *San Nicolás 3, Albayzín* ☎ *958/804262* ▭ *AE, DC, MC, V* ⊙ *Closed Mon. No dinner Sun.*

10

$$–$$$ SPANISH ★ ✕ **Sevilla.** Open since 1930, this two-story restaurant has fed the likes of composer Manuel de Falla and poet Federico García Lorca. There are four colorful dining rooms and a small but superb tapas bar, all furnished traditionally with lots of dark wood and decorative plates and pictures on the walls. On sunny days opt for the outdoor terrace overlooking the Royal Chapel and cathedral. The dinner menu includes Granada favorites such as *sopa sevillana* (soup with fish and shellfish), fresh whitebait stuffed with black pudding, and, for braver diners, *tortilla al Sacromonte* (with bull's brains and testicles). ✉ *Calle Oficios 12, Centro* ☎ *958/221223* ▭ *AE, DC, MC, V* ⊙ *No dinner Sun.*

¢–$ SPANISH ✕ **Tot Taberna Tofe.** Despite the odd name, this is not a restaurant geared to small children with a sweet tooth. One of an energetic stretch of similarly appealing traditional and contemporary bars and restaurants, it's a good choice for tapas or more substantial fare like roasted chicken.

Part of the holy week procession in Granada

The *surtido de tapas* is a platter of tasty selections that includes *patatas bravas* (fried potatoes in a spicy chili-spiked tomato sauce), grilled mushrooms with garlic, and wedges of tortilla. A jug of sangria makes a good accompaniment. The interior is an attractive well-lighted space with pine furniture, plus there is an outside terrace for alfresco dining. ✉ *Campo del Principe 18, Centro* ☎ *958/226207* ▭ *MC, V.*

WHERE TO STAY

Staying in the immediate vicinity of the Alhambra tends to be pricier than the city center. The latter is a good choice if you want to combine your Alhambra visit with enjoying the vibrant commercial center with its excellent shops, restaurants, and magnificent cathedral. The Albayzín is also a good place to stay for sheer atmosphere: this historic Arab quarter still has a tangible Moorish feel with its pint-sized plazas and winding pedestrian streets.

$$$ **Carmen.** This hotel has a prized city-center location on a busy shopping street. The rooms are spacious and have a mix of modern and classic decor; standard ones are carpeted, and superior ones have glossy parquet floors. The rooftop terrace and pool have stunning views of the city. For entertainment there's an English-style pub with live music nightly. **Pros:** downtown location; rooftop pool. **Cons:** air-conditioning erratic. ✉ *Acera del Darro 62, Centro* ☎ *958/258300* 🌐 *www.hotelcarmen.com* *270 rooms, 13 suites* *In-room: a/c, Wi-Fi. In-hotel: restaurant, bar, pool, parking (paid)* ▭ *AE, DC, MC, V.*

$$$ **Carmen de la Alcubilla del Caracol.** In a traditional Granadino villa on the slopes of the Alhambra, this is one of Granada's most stylish hotels. The rooms are bright, airy, and furnished with antiques; most also

have private verandas with views over the city and the Sierra Nevada. The terraced garden, with watering troughs fed by an irrigation system from the Alhambra, is a peaceful oasis. Try to book the room in the *torre* (tower). **Pros:** great views; personal service; impeccable taste. **Cons:** tough climb in hot weather. ✉ *Calle Aire Alta 12, Alhambra* ☎ *958/215551* 🌐 *www.alcubilladelcaracol.com* *7 rooms* *In-room: a/c, Wi-Fi. In-hotel: restaurant, bar, parking (free)* ▭ *AE, DC, MC, V* *Closed Aug.*

$$–$$$ ★ **Casa Morisca.** The architect who owns this 15th-century building transformed it into a hotel so distinctive that he received a National Restoration Award. The three-floor brick building has many original architectural elements, including a central courtyard with a small pond. The rooms aren't large, but they have a heady Moorish feel as a result of their wonderful antiques and views of the Alhambra and Albayzín. Even if you don't stay in it, ask for a look at the bridal suite, with its intricately carved and painted wooden ceiling. **Pros:** handy to Albayzín; easy parking. **Cons:** mediocre breakfast; stuffy interior rooms. ✉ *Cuesta de la Victoria 9, Albayzín* ☎ *958/221100* 🌐 *www.hotelcasamorisca.com* *12 rooms, 2 suites* *In-room: a/c, Wi-Fi. In-hotel: parking (free)* ▭ *AE, DC, MC, V.*

$$$ ★ **Palacio de los Navas.** In the center of the city, this palace was built by aristocrat Francisco Navas in the 16th century and later became the Casa de Moneda (the Mint). Original architectural features blend well with modern ones. Rooms, set around a traditional columned inner patio, are decorated with understated elegance. Enjoy breakfast on warm days on the outside terrace. **Pros:** great location; peaceful oasis. **Cons:** can be noisy at night. ✉ *Calle Navas 1, Centro* ☎ *958/215760* 🌐 *www.palaciodelosnavas.com* *19 rooms* *In-room: a/c. In-hotel: Wi-Fi hotspot, parking (paid)* ▭ *AE, DC, MC, V.*

$$$$ ★ **Palacio de los Patos.** This beautifully restored palace is unmissable, as it sits proudly on its own in the middle of one of Granada's busiest shopping streets. While retaining its 19th-century classical architecture, the hotel also includes all the most up-to-date luxuries, including a highly praised restaurant and a luxurious spa. The rooms are spacious and have a minimalist vibe, with dazzling white decor and shiny parquet floors. **Pros:** central location; historic setting. **Cons:** slow restaurant service; noisy street. ✉ *Calle Solarillo de Gracia 1, Centro* ☎ *958/536516* 🌐 *www.hospes.es* *42 rooms* *In-room: a/c, Wi-Fi. In-hotel: restaurant, bar, pool, spa, parking (paid)* ▭ *AE, DC, MC, V.*

$$–$$$ **Palacio de Santa Inés.** It's not often you get to stay in a 16th-century palace, and this one has a stunning location in the heart of the Albayzín. Each room is magnificently decorated with antiques and modern art; some have balconies with Alhambra views, and others boast original carved wooden ceilings. Rooms on the two upper floors center around a courtyard with frescoes painted by a disciple of Raphael. **Pros:** perfect location for exploring the Albayzín; gorgeous decor. **Cons:** can't get there by car; service slow and sloppy. ✉ *Cuesta de Santa Inés 9, Albayzín* ☎ *958/222362* 🌐 *www.palaciosantaines.com* *15 rooms, 20 suites* *In-room: a/c, Wi-Fi. In-hotel: restaurant, parking (paid)* ▭ *AE, DC, MC, V.*

$$$$ Fodor's Choice ★ **Parador de Granada**. This is Spain's most expensive and popular parador, and it's right in the Alhambra neighborhood. The building, a former Franciscan monastery built in the 15th century by the Catholic Monarchs after they captured Granada, is soul-stirringly gorgeous. Try to get a room in the old section, which has beautiful antiques, woven curtains, and bedspreads. Rooms in the newer wing are also charming but more simply decorated. **Pros:** good location; lovely decor; garden restaurant. **Cons:** no views; removed from city life. ✉ *Calle Real de la Alhambra s/n, Alhambra* ☎ *958/221440* 🌐 *www.parador.es* *34 rooms, 2 suites* *In-room: Internet, Wi-Fi. In-hotel: a/c, restaurant, bar, parking (free)* *AE, DC, MC, V.*

NIGHTLIFE AND THE ARTS

FLAMENCO

Flamenco can be enjoyed throughout the city, especially in the gypsy *cuevas* (caves) of the Albayzín and Sacromonte, where *zambra* shows—informal performances by gypsies—take place almost daily year round. The most popular *cuevas* are along the Camino de Sacromonte, the major street in the neighborhood of the same name. Be warned that this area has become very tourist oriented and prepare to part with lots of money (€18–€20 is average) for any show. In August free shows are held at the delightful El Corral del Carbón square—home of the tourist office.

If you do not want to show up randomly at the flamenco clubs, join a tour through a travel agent or your hotel or contact **Los Tarantos** (✉ *Calle del Sacromonte 9, Sacromonte* ☎ *958/224525*), which has lively nightly shows with midnight performances on Friday and Saturday. **Sala Alhambra** (✉ *Parque Empresarial Olinda, Edif. 12* ☎ *958/412269 or 958/412287*) runs well-organized performances. **La Rocío** (✉ *Calle del Sacromonte 70, Albayzín* ☎ *958/227129*) is a good spot for authentic flamenco shows. **María La Canastera** (✉ *Calle del Sacromonte 89, Sacromonte* ☎ *958/121183*) is one of the *cuevas* on Camino de Sacromonte with unscheduled *zambra* shows.

NIGHTLIFE

Granada's ample student population makes for a lively bar scene. Some of the trendiest bars are in converted houses in the Albayzín and Sacromonte and in the area between Plaza Nueva and Paseo de los Tristes. Calle Elvira, Caldereria Vieja, and Caldereria Nueva are crowded with laid-back coffee and pastry shops. In the modern part of town, Pedro Antonio de Alarcón and Martinez de la Rosa have larger but less glamorous offerings. Another nighttime gathering place is the Campo del Príncipe, a large plaza surrounded by typical Andalusian taverns.

El Eshavira (✉ *Calle Postigo de la Cuna 2, Albayzín* ☎ *958/290829*) is a smoky, dimly lighted club where you can hear sultry jazz and occasional flamenco. **Fondo Reservado** (✉ *Calle Santa Inés 4, Albayzín* ☎ *958/222375*) is a hip hangout mainly for students and has late-night dance music. **Granada 10** (✉ *Calle Carcel Baja 10, Centro* ☎ *958/224001*), with an upscale crowd, is a discotheque in a former theater. **La Industrial Copera** (✉ *Calle de la Paz 7, Ctra. de la Armilla*

☎ *958/258449*) is a popular disco, especially on Friday night. **Planta Baja** (✉ *C. Horno de Abad 11, Centro* ☎ *958/207607*) is a funky late-night club that hosts bands playing everything from exotic pop to garage and soul. **Zoo** (✉ *C. Mora 2, Puerta Real* ☎ *No phone*) is one of the longest-established and largest discos in town.

SHOPPING

A Moorish aesthetic pervades Granada's ceramics, marquetry (especially the *taraceas*, wooden boxes with inlaid tiles on their lids), woven textiles, and silver-, brass-, and copper-ware. The main shopping streets, centering on the Puerta Real, are the Gran Vía de Colón, Reyes Católicos, Zacatín, Ángel Ganivet, and Recogidas. Most antiques stores are on Cuesta de Elvira and Alcaicería—off Reyes Católicos. Cuesta de Gomérez, on the way up to the Alhambra, also has many handicraft shops. **Cerámica Fabre** (✉ *Pl. Pescadería 10, Centro*), near the cathedral, has typical Granada ceramics: blue-and-green patterns on white, with a pomegranate in the center.For wicker baskets and *esparto*-grass mats and rugs, head off the Plaza Pescadería to **Espartería San José** (✉ *C. Jaudenes 22, Centro* ☎ 958/26715).

SIDE TRIPS FROM GRANADA

The fabled province of Granada spans the Sierra Nevada mountains, with the beautifully rugged Alpujarras and the highest peaks on mainland Spain—Mulhacén at 11,407 feet and Veleta at 11,125 feet. This is where you can find some of the prettiest, most ancient villages, and it's one of the foremost destinations for Andalusia's increasingly popular rural tourism. Granada's *vega* (plain), covered with orchards and tobacco and poplar groves, is blanketed in snow half the year.

EN ROUTE

Eight miles (12 km) south of Granada on N323, the road reaches a spot known as the **Suspiro del Moro** *(*Moor's Sigh*)*. Pause here a moment and look back at the city, just as Granada's departing "Boy King," Boabdil, did 500 years ago. As he wept over the city he'd surrendered to the Catholic Monarchs, his scornful mother pronounced her now legendary rebuke: "You weep like a woman for the city you could not defend as a man."

SANTA FE

8 km (5 mi) west of Granada just south of N342.

Santa Fe was founded in winter 1491 as a campground for Ferdinand and Isabella's 150,000 troops as they prepared for the siege of Granada. It was here, in April 1492, that Isabella and Columbus signed the agreements that financed his historic voyage, and thus the town has been called the Cradle of America. Santa Fe was originally laid out in the shape of a cross, with a gate at each of its four ends, inscribed with Ferdinand and Isabella's initials. The town has long since transcended those boundaries, but the gates remain—to see them all at once, stand in the square next to the church at the center of the old town.

FUENTEVAQUEROS

10 km (6 mi) northwest of Santa Fe.

Federico García Lorca was born in the village of Fuentevaqueros on June 5, 1898, and lived here until age six. The **Museo Casa Natal Federico García Lorca**, the poet's childhood home, opened as a museum in 1986, when Spain commemorated the 50th anniversary of his assassination (he was shot without trial by Nationalists at the start of the civil war in August 1936) and celebrated his reinstatement as a national figure after 40 years of nonrecognition during the Francisco Franco regime. The house has been restored with original furnishings, and the former granary, barn, and stables have been converted into exhibition spaces, with temporary art shows and a permanent display of photographs, clippings, and other memorabilia. A two-minute video shows the only existing footage of Lorca. Tour hours vary; call ahead. ✉ *Calle del Poeta García Lorca 4* ☎ *958/516453* 🌐 *www.museogarcialorca.org* 🎫 *€3* 🕒 *Closed Mon.*

THE SIERRA NEVADA

The drive southeast from Granada to Pradollano along the N420/A395—Europe's highest road, by way of Cenes de la Vega—takes about 45 minutes. It's wise to carry snow chains from mid-November to as late as April or even May. The mountains here make for an easy and worthwhile excursion, especially for those keen on trekking.

The **Pico de Veleta**, peninsular Spain's second-highest mountain, is 11,125 feet high. The view from its summit across the Alpujarras range to the sea at distant Motril is stunning; on a very clear day you can see the coast of North Africa. In July and August you can drive or take a minibus to within hundreds of yards of the summit—a trail takes you to the top. ■ **TIP→ It's cold up here, so bring a warm jacket and scarf, even if Granada is sizzling hot.** To the east, the mighty **Mulhacén**, the highest peak in mainland Spain, soars to 11,427 feet. Legend has it that it came by its name when Boabdil, the last Moorish king of Granada, deposed his father, Muly Abdul Hassan, and had the body buried at the summit of the mountain so that it couldn't be desecrated. For more information on trails to the two summits, call the **Natural Parks Service office** (☎ *958/763127* 🌐 *www.nevadensis.com*) in Pampaneira.

SKIING

The **Estación de Esquí Sierra Nevada** is Europe's southernmost ski resort and one of its best equipped. At the Pradollano and Borreguiles stations there's good skiing from December through May; each has a special snowboarding circuit, floodlighted night slopes, a children's ski school, and après-ski sun and swimming in the Mediterranean less than an hour away. In winter, **buses** (✉ *Autocares Bonal* ☎ *958/465022*) to Pradollano leave Granada's bus station three times a day on weekdays and four times on weekends and holidays. Tickets are €6 round-trip. As for Borreguiles, you can get there only on skis. There's an **information center** (☎ *958/249100* 🌐 *www.cetursa.es*) at Plaza de Andalucía 4.

WHERE TO STAY

$$$$ **El Lodge.** A fantastic slope-side location and friendly, professional service add up to the best hotel in the Sierra Nevada. The lodge is built of Finnish wood—unusual for southern Spain but appropriate in this alpine area. Rooms are luxurious yet cozy, and the en suite bathrooms have hydromassage tubs: perfect for the après-ski soak. The lodge also has an excellent restaurant specializing in Basque cuisine. The hotel is geared toward families and has a purpose-designed playroom for the tots. **Pros:** next to ski lift; cozy and comfortable. **Cons:** some small rooms. ✉ *C. Maribel 8* ☎ *958/480600* 🌐 *www.ellodge.com* *16 rooms, 4 suites* *In-room: Wi-Fi. In-hotel: restaurant, bar, gym* *AE, DC, MC, V* *BP* *Closed May–Oct.*

THE ALPUJARRAS

★ *Village of Lanjarón: 46 km (29 mi) south of Granada.*

A trip to the Alpujarras, on the southern slopes of the Sierra Nevada, takes you to one of Andalusia's highest, most remote, and most scenic areas, home for decades to painters, writers, and a considerable foreign population. The Alpujarras region was originally populated by Moors fleeing the Christian Reconquest (from Seville after its fall in 1248, then from Granada after 1492). It was also the final fiefdom of the unfortunate Boabdil, conceded to him by the Catholic Monarchs after he surrendered Granada. In 1568 rebellious Moors made their last stand against the Christian overlords, a revolt ruthlessly suppressed by Philip II and followed by the forced conversion of all Moors to Christianity and their resettlement farther inland and up Spain's eastern coast. The villages were then repopulated with Christian soldiers from Galicia, who were granted land in return for their service. To this day the Galicians' descendants continue the Moorish custom of weaving rugs and blankets in the traditional Alpujarran colors of red, green, black, and white, and they sell their crafts in many of the villages. Be on the lookout for handmade basketry and pottery as well.

Houses here are squat and square; they spill down the southern slopes of the Sierra Nevada, bearing a strong resemblance to the Berber homes in the Rif Mountains, just across the sea in Morocco. If you're driving, the road as far as Lanjarón and Orgiva is smooth sailing; after that come steep, twisting mountain roads with few gas stations. Beyond sightseeing, the area is a haven for outdoor activities such as hiking and horseback riding. Inquire at the **Information Point** at Plaza de la Libertad s/n, at Pampaneira.

EN ROUTE

Lanjarón, the western entrance to the Alpujarras some 46 km (29 mi) from Granada, is a spa town famous for its mineral water collected from the melting snows of the Sierra Nevada and drunk throughout Spain. **Orgiva,** the next and largest town in the Alpujarras, has a 17th-century castle. Here you can leave C348 and follow signs for the villages of the Alpujarras Altas (High Alpujarras), including **Pampaneira, Capileira,** and especially **Trevélez,** which lies on the slopes of the Mulhacén at 4,840 feet above sea level. Reward yourself with a plate of the locally produced *jamón serrano* (cured ham). Trevélez has three levels, the Barrio Alto, Barrio Medio, and Barrio Bajo; the butchers are concentrated in the lowest section (Bajo). The higher levels have narrow cobblestone streets, whitewashed houses, and shops.

WHERE TO STAY

$ Fodor's Choice ★ **Alquería de Morayma.** Close to the banks of the Guadalfeo River, the buildings in this charming complex have been remodeled in the old Alpujarreño style, including some rooms in an old chapel. The setting is quite lovely, surrounded by 40 hectares of organically cultivated vineyards and woodland with almond, fig, olive, and fruit trees, and an old bodega and nearby farm supply the hotel. The two dining rooms, one more formal and the other with an inviting fireplace, serve traditional Spanish food. The management can arrange walking and trekking activities. **Pros:** tranquil location; lots of activities. **Cons:** need a car to get around; no nearby restaurants. ✉ *Ctra. A348, Km 50, Cádiar* ☎ *958/343221* 🌐 *www.alqueriamorayma.com* *13 rooms, 10 apartments* *In-hotel: restaurant, pool, parking (free)* ▭ *MC, V.*

$ **Taray Botánico.** This hotel has its own farm and is a perfect base for exploring the Alpujarras. Public areas and guest rooms are in a low, typical Alpujarran building. The sunny quarters are decorated with Alpujarran handwoven bedspreads and curtains; three rooms have rooftop terraces, and there's a pleasant common terrace. Most of the restaurant's food comes from the estate, including trout and lamb; in season, you can even pick your own raspberries or oranges for breakfast. This exceedingly child-friendly place also has a small farm with animals and a delightful turtle pond. **Pros:** fun for families; great organic food. **Cons:** somewhat isolated; livestock attract abundant flies. ✉ *Ctra. Tablate–Albuñol, Km 18, Órgiva* ☎ *958/784525* 🌐 *www.hoteltaray.com* *15 private bungalows* *In-room: Wi-Fi. In-hotel: restaurant, pool* ▭ *AE, DC, MC, V.*

GUADIX

47 km (30 mi) east of Granada on A92.

Today, Guadix—and the neighboring village of Purullena—is best known for its cave communities, though this was an important mining town as far back as 2,000 years ago and has its fair share of monuments, including a cathedral (built 1594–1706) and a 9th-century Moorish *alcazaba* (citadel). Around 2,000 caves were carved out of the soft, sandstone mountains, and most are still inhabited. Far from being troglodytic holes in the wall, they are well furnished and comfortable, with a pleasant year-round temperature; a few serve as hotels. A small cave museum, **Cueva Museo,** is in Guadix's cave district. Toward the town center, the **Cueva la Alcazaba** has a ceramics workshop. A number of private caves have signs welcoming you to inspect the premises, though a tip is expected if you do. Purullena, 6 km (4 mi) from Guadix, is also known for ceramics.

Costa del Sol and Costa de Almería

WORD OF MOUTH

"Marbella old town is absolutely gorgeous with orange trees, narrow winding streets and quaint restaurants. The modern town is nice too, though, surprisingly untacky for the area with beautiful beaches, nice restaurants & bars. Puerto Banus is where the wild nights and seriously monied are and everything is extortionate! . . . Marbella is lovely!"

—carolemg

WELCOME TO THE COSTA DEL SOL AND COSTA DE ALMERÍA

TOP REASONS TO GO

★ **Sun and Sand:** Relax at any of the many beaches; they're all free, though in summer there isn't much towel space on the sand.

★ **Lovely Strolls:** Spend a morning in Marbella's old town, stopping for a drink at Plaza de los Naranjos before the shops shut for the afternoon siesta.

★ **Puerto Banús:** Wine, dine, and celebrity watch at the Costa's most luxurious and sophisticated port.

★ **Sensational Seafood:** Tuck into a dish of delicious *fritura malagueño* (fried fish, anchovies, and squid) at one of La Carihuela–area restaurants in Torremolinos.

★ **Cabo de Gato Nature Reserve:** This protected natural reserve is one of the wildest and most beautiful stretches of coast in Spain.

★ **Souvenir Shopping:** Check out the weekly market in one of the Costa resorts to pick up bargain-price souvenirs, like ceramics or Spanish music CDs.

1 The Costa de Almería. This Costa region is hot and sunny virtually year-round and is famed for its spectacular beaches, unspoiled countryside, miles of golf courses, and (less appealingly) plastic greenhouse agriculture. Just west of the Murcia Coast, Almería, a handsome, underrated city, boasts a fascinating historic center with narrow pedestrian streets flanked by sunbaked ocher buildings and tapas bars.

2 The Costa Tropical. Less developed than the Costa del Sol, this stretch of coastline is distinctive for its attractive seaside towns, rocky coves, excellent water sports, and mountainous interior.

3 Málaga Province. Don't miss the capital of the province: Málaga is an increasingly sophisticated city yet retains a traditional Andalusian feel; better known are the coastal resorts due west with their sweeping beaches and excellent tourist facilities.

GETTING ORIENTED

The towns and resorts along the southeastern Spanish coastline vary considerably according to whether they lie to the east or to the west of Málaga. To the east are the Costa de Almería and Costa Tropical, less developed stretches of coastline. Towns like Nerja also act as a gateway to the dramatic mountainous region of La Axarquía. West from Málaga along the Costa del Sol proper, the strip between Torremolinos and Marbella is the most densely populated. Seamless though it may appear, as one resort merges into the next, each town has a distinctive character, with its own sights, charms, and activities.

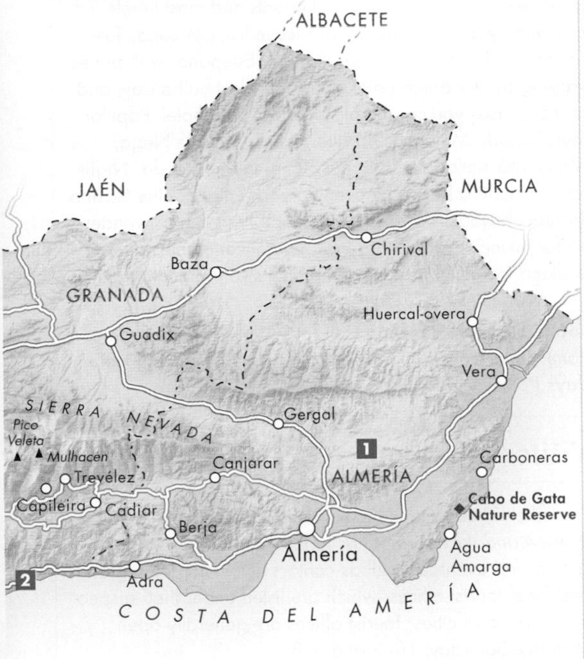

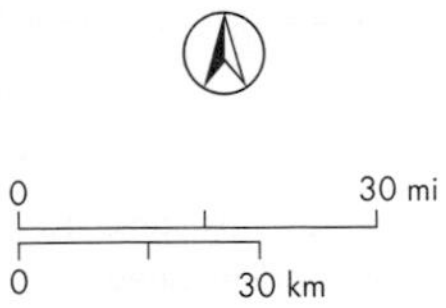

4 Gibraltar. The "Rock" is an extraordinary combination of Spain and Britain and has a fascinating history. There are also some fine restaurants here, as well as traditional olde English pubs.

THE COSTA DEL SOL AND COSTA DE ALMERÍA PLANNER

When to Go

Fall and spring, especially May, June, and September, are the best times to visit this coastal area, when there's plenty of sunshine but fewer tourists than in the hottest season of July and August. Winter can have bright sunny days, but you may feel the chill: many hotels in the lower price bracket have heat for only a few hours a day; you can also expect several days of rain. Holy Week, the week before Easter Sunday, is a fun time to visit.

Fairs and Fiestas

Málaga's **Semana Santa** (Holy Week) processions are dramatic. Nerja and Estepona celebrate **San Isidro** (May 15) with typically Andalusian *ferias* with plenty of flamenco and *fino* (sherry). The feast of **San Juan** (June 23 and 24) is marked by midnight bonfires on beaches along the coast. Coastal communities honor the **Virgen del Carmen,** the patron saint of fishermen, on her feast day (July 16). The annual **ferias** (more general and usually lengthier celebrations than fiestas) in Málaga (early August) and Fuengirola (early October) are among the best for sheer exuberance.

Tour Options

Many one- and two-day excursions from Costa del Sol resorts are run by the national company Julia Travel and by smaller firms. All local travel agents and most hotels can book you a tour; excursions leave from Málaga, Torremolinos, Fuengirola, Marbella, and Estepona, with prices varying by departure point. Most tours last half a day, and in most cases you can be picked up at your hotel. Popular tours include Málaga, Gibraltar, the Cuevas de Nerja, Mijas, Marbella, Puerto Banús, Tangier, and Ronda. Night tours include a barbecue evening and a night at the Casino Torrequebrada. The varied landscape here is also wonderful for hiking and walking, and several companies offer walking tours. All provide comprehensive information on their Web sites.

Tour Operators Bicycling Holidays (🌐 *www.sierracycling.com*). **Julia Travel** (🌐 *www.juliatravel.com*). **Walking Holidays** (🌐 *www.walksinspain.com*).

Visitor Information

The official Web site of the Andalusian government is 🌐 *www.andalucia.org*; it has further information on sightseeing and events as well as contact details for the regional and local tourist offices, which are listed under their respective towns and cities. Tourist offices are generally open Monday–Saturday, 10–2 and 5–8.

Golf in the Sun

Nicknamed the Costa del Golf, the Sun Coast has some 40 golf courses within putting distance of the Mediterranean, making it a prime golfing destination. Most of the courses are between Rincón de la Victoria (east of Málaga) and Gibraltar, and the best time for golfing is October to June; greens fees are lower in high summer. Check out the comprehensive Web site 🌐 *www.spainguides.com/costagolf.html* for up-to-date information.

About the Hotels

Most hotels on the developed stretch between Torremolinos and Fuengirola offer large, functional rooms near the sea at competitive rates, but the area's popularity as a budget destination means that most such hotels are booked in high season by package-tour operators. Finding a room at Easter, in July and August, or over holiday weekends can be difficult if you haven't reserved in advance. Málaga is an increasingly attractive base for visitors to this corner of Andalusia and has some good hotels. Marbella, meanwhile, has more than its fair share of grand lodgings, including some of Spain's most expensive accommodations. Rooms in Gibraltar's handful of hotels tend to be more expensive than most comparable lodgings in Spain. There are also apartments and villas for short- or long-term stays, ranging from traditional Andalusian farmhouses to luxury villas. An excellent source for apartment and villa rentals is *www.andalucia.com*. You can also try **Gilmar** (*952/861341* *www.gilmar.es*) or **Viajes Rural Andalus** (*952/276229* *www.ruralandalus.es*).

WHAT IT COSTS (IN EUROS)

	¢	$	$$	$$$	$$$$
Restaurants	under €8	€8–€12	€13–€17	€18–€22	over €22
Hotels	under €60	€60–€90	€91–€125	€126–€180	over €180

Prices are per person for a main course at dinner, and for two people in a standard double room in high season, excluding tax.

WHAT IT COSTS (IN GIBRALTAR POUNDS)

	¢	$	$$	$$$	$$$$
Restaurants	under £5	£5–£12	£13–£18	£19–£25	over £25
Hotels	under £30	£30–£80	£81–£120	£121–£165	over £165

Prices are per person for a main course at dinner, and for two people in a standard double room in high season, excluding tax.

Planning Your Time

Travelers with their own wheels who want a real taste of the area in just a few days could start by exploring the relatively unspoiled villages of the Costa Tropical: wander around quaint Salobreña, then hit the larger coastal resort of Nerja and head inland for a look around pretty Frigiliana.

Move on to Málaga next; it has lots to offer, including museums, excellent restaurants, and some of the best tapas bars in the province. It's also easy to get to stunning, mountaintop Ronda (see Chapter 10) (also on a bus route).

Hit the coast at Marbella, the Costa del Sol's swankiest resort, then take a leisurely stroll around Puerto Banús. Next, head west to Gibraltar for a day of shopping and sightseeing before returning to the coast and Torremolinos for a night on the town.

Choose your base carefully, as the various areas here make for different experiences. Málaga is a vibrant Spanish city, virtually untainted by tourism, while Torremolinos is a budget destination catering mostly to the mass market. Fuengirola is quieter, with a large, and notably middle-aged, foreign resident population; farther west, the Marbella–San Pedro de Alcántara area is more exclusive and expensive.

GETTING HERE AND AROUND

By Bus

Until the high-speed AVE train line opens in 2011, buses are the best way to reach the Costa del Sol from Granada, and, aside from the train service from Málaga to Fuengirola, the best way to get around once you're here. During holidays it's wise to reserve your seat in advance for long-distance travel.

On the Costa del Sol, bus service connects Málaga with Cádiz (4 daily), Córdoba (5 daily), Granada (18 daily), and Seville (12 daily). In Fuengirola you can catch buses for Mijas, Marbella, Estepona, and Algeciras. The Portillo bus company serves most of the Costa del Sol. Alsina Gräells serves Granada, Córdoba, Seville, and Nerja. Los Amarillos serves Cádiz, Jerez, Ronda, and Seville. Málaga's tourist office has details on other bus lines.

By Air

Delta Airlines has weekly service from JFK (New York) to Málaga. All other flights from the United States connect in Madrid. Iberia and British Airways fly once daily from London to Málaga, and numerous British budget airlines, such as Easyjet and Monarch, also link the two cities. There are direct flights to Málaga from most other major European cities on Iberia or other national airlines. Iberia has up to eight flights daily from Madrid (flying time is 1 hour), three flights a day from Barcelona (1½ hours), and regular flights from other Spanish cities.

Málaga's Pablo Picasso airport is 10 km (6 mi) west of town. A long-awaited third terminal opened in March 2010. Trains from the airport into town run every half hour (6:49 AM–11:49 PM, journey time 12 minutes, €1.45) and from the airport to Fuengirola every half hour (5:34 AM–10:45 PM, journey time 25 minutes, €2), stopping at several resorts en route, including Torremolinos and Benalmádena.

From the airport there's also bus service to Málaga every half hour from 6:30 AM to 11:30 PM (€1.10). Ten daily buses (more July–September) run between the airport and Marbella (journey time 1 hour, €4). Taxi fares from the airport to Málaga, Torremolinos, and other resorts are posted inside the terminal: from the airport to Marbella is about €45, to Torremolinos €16, and to Fuengirola €28. Many of the better hotels and all tour companies will arrange for pickup at the airport.

By Taxi

Taxis are plentiful throughout the Costa del Sol and may be hailed on the street or from specified taxi ranks marked TAXI. Restaurants are usually obliging and will call you a taxi, if you request it. Fares are reasonable, and meters are strictly used. You are not required to tip taxi drivers, though rounding off the amount will be appreciated.

By Car

A car allows you to explore Andalusia's mountain villages. Mountain driving can be hair-raising but is getting better as highways are improved.

Málaga is 580 km (360 mi) from Madrid, taking the NIV to Córdoba, then N331 to Antequera and the N321; 182 km (114 mi) from Córdoba via Antequera; 214 km (134 mi) from Seville; and 129 km (81 mi) from Granada by the shortest route of N342 to Loja, then N321 to Málaga.

There are some beautiful scenic drives here about which the respective tourist offices can advise you. The N334 from Churriana to Coín, via Alhaurín de la Torre and Alhaurín el Grande. From here, take the N337 toward Marbella, which travels via the villages of Monda and Ojén, finally ending at the coast just north of Marbella.

To take a car into Gibraltar you need, in theory, an insurance certificate and a logbook (a certificate of vehicle ownership). In practice, all you need is your passport. Head for the well-signposted multistory car park, as street parking on the Rock is scarce.

National Car-Rental Agencies Autopro (☎ *34/952–176–030* 🌐 *www.autopro.es*).

By Bike

The Costa del Sol is famous for its sun and sand, but many people supplement their beach time with mountain-bike forays into the hilly interior, particularly around Ojén, near Marbella, and along the mountain roads around Ronda. A popular route, which affords sweeping vistas, is via the mountain road from Ojén west to Istán. The Costa del Sol's temperate climate is ideal for biking, though it's best not to exert yourself on the trails in July and August, when temperatures soar. There are numerous bike-rental shops in the area, particularly in Marbella, Ronda, and Ojén; many shops also arrange bike excursions. The cost to rent a mountain bike for the day ranges between €15 and €20. Guided bike excursions, which include bikes, support staff, and cars, generally start at about €62 a day.

Contact Spanish Cycling Federation (☎ *91/542–0421* 🌐 *www.rfec.com*).

By Train

Málaga is the main rail terminus in the area, with three high-speed trains a day from Madrid (2½ hours), plus five slower trains (via Córdoba, 4½ hours). In January 2009, a new high-speed train was introduced linking Málaga with Barcelona (3 daily, 5 hours and 40 minutes). Five daily trains also link Seville with Málaga in less than 2 hours.

From Granada to Málaga (3–3½ hours), you must change at Bobadilla, making buses more efficient from here (a high-speed AVE line is currently under construction from Granada to Málaga, due for completion in late 2011). Málaga's train station is a 15-minute walk from the city center, across the river.

RENFE connects Málaga, Torremolinos, and Fuengirola, stopping at the airport and all resorts along the way. The train leaves Málaga every half hour between 5:19 AM and 10:19 PM and Fuengirola every half hour from 6:35 AM to 11:17 PM. For the city center get off at the last stop: Málaga María Zambrano, which is also the main train station, a 15-minute walk from the city center. A daily train connects Málaga and Ronda via the dramatic Chorro gorge. Travel time is about two hours.

EATING AND DRINKING WELL ALONG SPAIN'S SOUTHERN COAST

Spain's southern coast is known for fresh fish and seafood, grilled or quickly fried in olive oil. Sardines roasted on spits are popular along the Málaga coast, while upland towns offer more robust mountain fare, especially in Almería.

Top left: Beachside dining on the Costa del Sol. Top right: Sardines being roasted over hot coals. Bottom left: A classic potato-based stew.

Sardines at *chiringuitos*, small shanty shacks along the beaches, are summer-only Costa de Sol restaurants that serve fish fresh off the boats. Málaga is known for seafood restaurants serving *fritura malagueña de pescaito*, fried fish. In the mountain towns you'll find superb *rabo de toro* (bull or oxtail), goat and sheep cheeses, wild mushrooms, and game dishes. Almería shares Moorish aromas of cumin and cardamom with its Andalusian sisters to the east but also turns the corner toward its northern neighbor, Murcia, where delicacies such as salt dried tuna (*mojama*) and *hueva de maruca* (ling roe) have been favorites since Phoenician times. Almería's wealth of vegetables and legumes combine with pork and game products for a rougher, more powerful culinary canon of thick stews and soups.

TO DRINK

Málaga has long been famous for the sweet muscatel wine that Russian Empress Catherine the Great loved so much she imported it to Saint Petersburg duty free in 1792. Muscatel was sold medicinally in pharmacies in the 18th century for its curative powers and is still widely produced and often served as accompaniment to dessert or tapas.

COLD ALMOND AND GARLIC SOUP

Ajoblanco, summer staple in Andalusia, is a refreshing salt-sweet combination served cold. Exquisitely light and sharp, the almond and garlic soup has a surprisingly dark yet fresh taste. Almonds, garlic, hard white bread, olive oil, water, sherry vinegar, and moscatel grapes on top are the standard ingredients.

FRIED FISH MÁLAGA-STYLE

A popular dish along the Costa del Sol and the Costa de Almería, *fritura malagueña de pescaito* is basically any sort of very small fish—such as anchovies, cuttlefish, baby squid, whitebait, and red mullet—fried in oil so hot that the fish end up crisp and light as a feather. The fish are lightly dusted in white flour, crisped quickly, and drained briefly before arriving piping hot and bone-dry on your plate. For an additional Moorish aroma, fritura masters add powdered cumin to the flour.

ALMERÍA STEWS

Almería is known for heartier fare than neighboring Málaga. *Puchero de trigo* (wheat and pork stew) *is* a fortifying winter comfort stew of whole, boiled grains of wheat cooked with chickpeas, pork, black sausage, fatback, potatoes, saffron, cumin, and fennel. *Ajo colorao,* another popular stew that's also known as *atascaburras,* consists of potatoes, dried peppers, vegetables, and fish that are simmered into a thick ochre-color stew *de cuchara* (eaten with a spoon). Laced with cumin and garlic and served with thick country bread, it's a stick-to-your-ribs mariner's soup.

ROASTED SARDINES

Known as *moraga de sardinas,* or *espetones de sardinas,* this method of cooking sardines is popular in the summer along the Pedregalejo and La Carihuela beaches east and west of Málaga: the sardines are skewered and extended over coals at an angle so that the fish oils run back down the skewers instead of falling into the coals and igniting a conflagration. Fresh fish and cold white wine or beer make this a beautiful and relaxing sunset beach dinner.

A THOUSAND AND ONE EGGS

Something about the spontaneous nature of Spain's southern latitudes seems to lend itself to the widespread use of eggs to bind ingredients together. In Andalusia and especially along the Costa del Sol, *huevos a la flamenca* (eggs flamenco style) is a time-tested dish combining peppers, potatoes, ham, and peas with an egg broken over the top and baked sizzling hot in the oven. A *revuelto de setas y gambas* (scrambled eggs with wild mushrooms and shrimp) is a counterpoint between the familar egg, the mushrooms, and the shrimp. And, of course, there is the universal Iberian potato omelet, the *tortilla de patata.*

BEST BEACHES OF THE SOUTHERN COAST

The resorts of the Costa del Sol have been attracting tourists since the 1950s with their magical combination of brochure-blue sea, miles of beaches, reliable sun-bronzing weather.

Top left: One of the many resorts in Torremolinos. Top right: Tarifa is known for its wind: great for windsurfing and kite-flying. Bottom left: Crashing waves at Cabo de Gata.

The beaches here range from shingle in Almuñecar, Nerja, and Málaga to fine, gritty sand from Torremolinos westward. The best—and most crowded—beaches are east of Málaga and those flanking the most popular resorts of Nerja, Torremolinos, Fuengirola, and Marbella. For more secluded beaches, head west of Estepona and past Gibraltar to Tarifa and the Cádiz coast. The beaches change when you hit the Atlantic, becoming appealingly wide with fine golden sand. The winds are usually quite strong here, which means that although you can't read a newspaper while lying out, the conditions for wind- and kite-surfing are near perfect.

Beaches are free and busiest in July, August, and on Sundays from May through October when Malagueno families arrive for a day on the beach and lunch at a seafood *chiringuito* (seaside restaurant or bar).

OVER THE TOP-LESS

In Spain, as in many parts of Europe, it is perfectly acceptable for women to go topless on the beach, although covering up is the norm at beach bars. There are several nude beaches on the Costas; look for the *playa naturista* sign. The most popular are in Maro (near Nerja), Benalmádena Costa, and near Tarifa.

BEST BEACHES

LA CARIHUELA, TORREMOLINOS

This former fishing district of Torremolinos has a wide stretch of beach. The *chiringuitos* here are some of the best on the Costa, and the promenade, which continues until Benalmádena port with its striking Asian-inspired architecture and great choice of restaurants and bars, is delightful for strolling.

CARVAJAL, FUENGIROLA

The unspoiled beach here has a refreshing low-key feel and is backed by low-rise buildings and greenery. East of Fuengirola center, the Carvajal beach bars have a young vibe with regular live music in summer. It's also an easily accessible beach on the Málaga–Fuengirola train with a stop easy walking distance from the sand.

PLAYA LOS LANCES, TARIFA

This white sandy beach is one of the least spoiled in Andalusia. Backed by lush vegetation, lagoons, and the occasional campsite and boho-chic hotel (see listing for the Hurricane Hotel), Tarifa's main beach is famed throughout Europe for its wind- and kite-surfing, so expect some real winds: *levante* from the east and *poniente* from the west.

CABO DE GATA, ALMERÍA

Backed by natural parkland, with volcanic rock formations creating dramatic cliffs and secluded bays, Almería's stunning Cabo de Gata coastline includes superb beaches and coves within the protected Unesco Biosphere Reserve. The fact that most of the beaches here are only accessible via marked footpaths adds to their off-the-beaten-track appeal.

PUERTO BANÚS, MARBELLA

Looking for action? The world-famous luxurious port city is flanked by some great beach scenes. Pedro's Beach is known for its excellent, laid-back Caribbean seafood restaurants, good music, and hip good-looking crowd. Another superb sandy choice is the famous Buddha Beach, one of the first so-called boutique beaches with a club area and massages available, as well as an attractive beach and tempting shallow waters.

EL SALADILLO, ESTEPONA

Between Marbella and Estepona (take the Cancelada exit from the N340), this relaxed and inviting beach is not as well known as its glitzier neighbors as it's harder to find and, therefore, mainly frequented by locals in the know. There are two popular seafood restaurants here, including Pepe's Beach (dating from the 1970s), plus a volleyball net, showers, and sun beds and parasols for hire.

With an average of 320 days of sunshine a year, the Costa del Sol well deserves its name, "the Sunshine Coast." It's no wonder much of the coast has become built up with resorts and high-rise hotels. Don't despair, though; you can still find some classic Spanish experiences, whether it be the old city of Marbella or one of the smaller villages like Casares. And despite the hubbub during high season, visitors can unwind here, basking or strolling on mile after mile of sandy beach.

Technically, the stretch of Andalusian shore known as the Costa del Sol runs west from the Costa Tropical, near Granada, to the tip of Tarifa, the southernmost point in Europe, just beyond Gibraltar. For most of the Europeans who have flocked here over the past 40 years, though, the Sunshine Coast has been largely restricted to the 70-km (43-mi) sprawl of hotels, vacation villas, golf courses, marinas, and nightclubs between Torremolinos, just west of Málaga, and Estepona, down toward Gibraltar. Since the late 1950s this area has mushroomed from a group of impoverished fishing villages into an overdeveloped seaside playground and retirement haven. The city of Almería and its coastline, the Costa de Almería, is southwest of Granada's Las Alpujarras region, and due west of the Costa Tropical (around 147 km [93 mi] from Almuñecar).

THE COSTA DE ALMERÍA

West of Spain's Murcia Coast lie the shores of Andalusia, beginning with the Costa de Almería. Several of the coastal towns here, like Cabo de Gata and Agua Amarga, have a laid-back charm, with miles of sandy beaches and a refreshing lack of high-rise developments. The mineral riches of the surrounding mountains gave rise to Iberia's first true civilization, whose capital can still be glimpsed in the 4,700-year-old ruins of Los Millares, near the village of Santa Fe de Mondújar. The small towns of Níjar and Sorbas maintain an age-old tradition

CLOSE UP

Bird-Watching in Andalusia

A bird-watcher's paradise, Andalusia attracts ornithologists throughout the year, but the variety of birds increases in spring, when you can see many wintering species along with those arriving for the summer months.

The Straits of Gibraltar are a key point of passage for birds migrating between Africa and Europe. Soaring birds, such as raptors and storks, cross here because they rely on thermals and updrafts, which occur only over narrower expanses of water. One of the most impressive sights over the Straits is a crossing of flocks of storks, from August to October—numbers sometimes reach up to 3,000.

Overall, northern migrations take place between mid-February and June, while birds heading south will set off between late July and early November, when there's a westerly wind. Gibraltar itself is generally good for bird-watchers, although when there isn't much wind the Tarifa region on the Atlantic coast can be better.

There are also some 13 resident raptor species in Andalusia, and several that migrate here annually from Africa. The hillier inland parts of the Costa del Sol are the best places to see them circling high in the sky.

For more information about bird-watching in Andalusia, contact Centro Ornitológio del Estrecho de Gibraltar (*Parque Natural Los Alcornocales, Carretera Nacional* 🌐 *www.alcornocales.org*), or the *www.andalucia.com/rural/birdwatching.htm* Web site.

of pottery-making and other crafts, and the western coast of Almería has tapped unexpected wealth from a parched land, thanks to modern (if unaesthetic) farming techniques, with produce grown in plastic greenhouses. In contrast to the inhospitable landscape of the mountain-fringed Andarax Valley, the area east of Granada's Las Alpujarras, near Alhama, has a cool climate and gentle landscape, both conducive to making fine wines.

AGUA AMARGA

22 km (14 mi) north of San José and 55 km (30 mi) east of Almería.

★ Agua Amarga is perhaps the most pleasant village on the Cabo de Gata coast. Like other coastal hamlets, it started out in the 18th century as a tuna-fishing port. Today it has a boho-chic appeal that attracts more visitors, although it thankfully remains less developed than San José. One of the coast's best beaches is just to the north: the dramatically named **Playa de los Muertos** (Beach of the Dead), a long stretch of fine sand bookended with volcanic outcrops.

GETTING HERE AND AROUND

If you're driving here from Almería, follow signs to the airport, then continue north on the A7; Agua Amarga is signposted just north of the Parque Natural Cabo de Gato. Once here, the village is small enough to explore on foot.

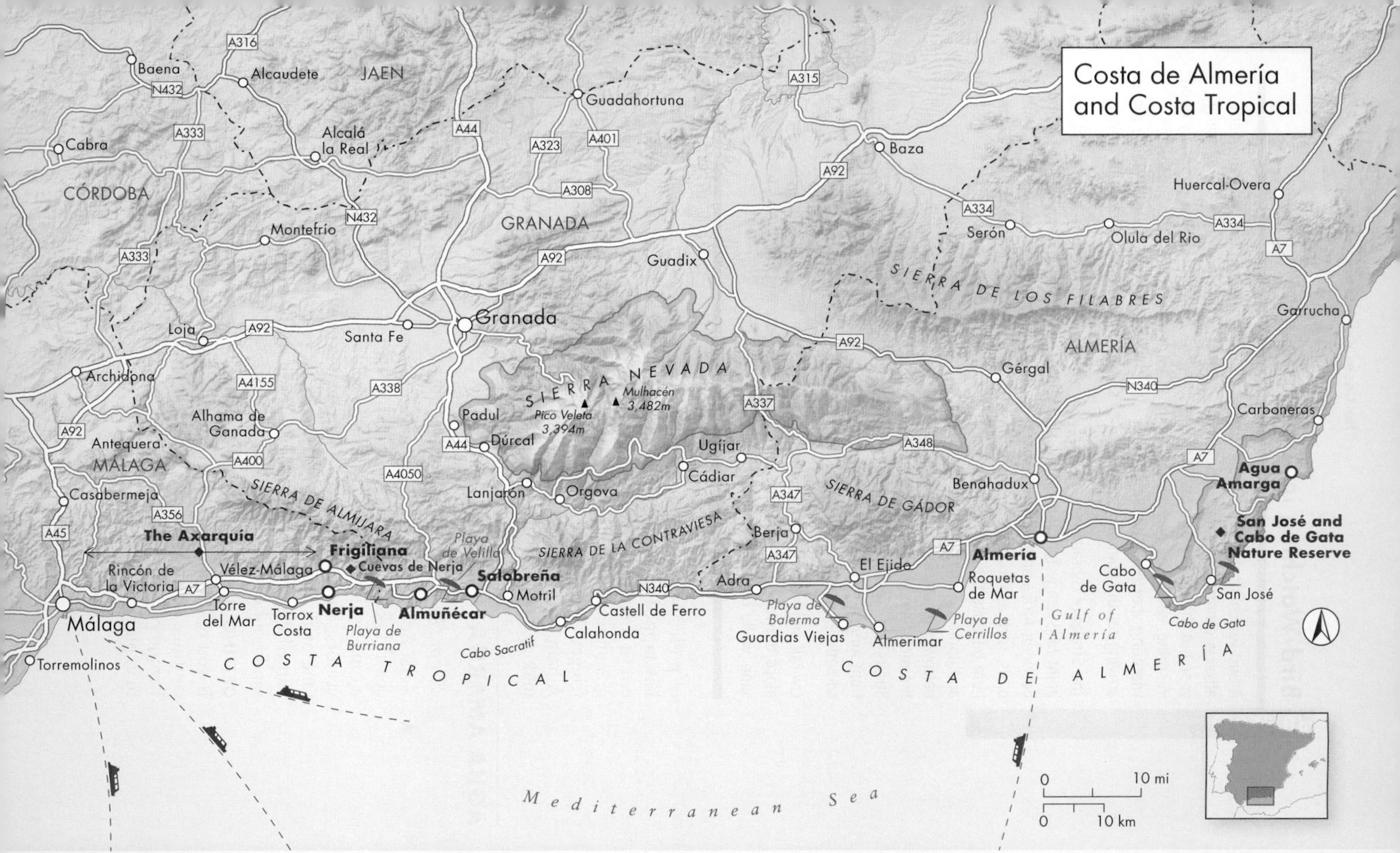
Costa de Almería and Costa Tropical
Baena
Alcaudete
JAEN
Guadahortuna
Cabra
Alcalá la Real
CÓRDOBA
Montefrío
GRANADA
Baza
Huercal-Overa
Serón
Olula del Rio
Guadix
SIERRA DE LOS FILABRES
Granada
Loja
Santa Fe
Garrucha
ALMERÍA
Archidona
Gérgal
SIERRA NEVADA
Mulhacén 3,482m
Pico Veleta 3,394m
Padul
Alhama de Ganada
Antequera
Dúrcal
Ugíjar
Carboneras
MÁLAGA
Cádiar
Benahadux
Agua Amarga
Casabermeja
SIERRA DE ALMIJARA
Lanjarón
Orgova
SIERRA DE GÁDOR
The Axarquia
SIERRA DE LA CONTRAVIESA
Berja
San José and Cabo de Gata Nature Reserve
Frigiliana
Cuevas de Nerja
Playa de Velilla
Almería
Rincón de la Victoria
Vélez-Málaga
Salobreña
El Ejido
Roquetas de Mar
Cabo de Gata
San José
Motril
Adra
Torre del Mar
Torrox Costa
Nerja
Almuñécar
Castell de Ferro
Málaga
Playa de Burriana
Calahonda
Playa de Balerma
Guardias Viejas
Almerimar
Playa de Cerrillos
Gulf of Almería
Cabo de Gata
Cabo Sacratif
Torremolinos
COSTA TROPICAL
COSTA DE ALMERÍA
Mediterranean Sea
0 10 mi
0 10 km
A316
N432
A333
A44
A323
A401
A315
A308
A92
N432
A334
A7
A92
A4155
A338
A337
N340
A348
A400
A4050
A44
A347
A356
A45
A7
N340

WHERE TO EAT AND STAY

$$–$$$ CONTEMPORARY ★ **La Chumbera.** This stylish restaurant, in a villa off the coastal road just north of Agua Amarga, is one of the province's finest dining spots. It has only a handful of tables, so reservations are strongly recommended. Try to come for sunset and enjoy stunning sea views from the terrace, though the dining room has intimate charm with its arches, terra-cotta tile work, and dazzle of fresh flowers. The menu changes regularly, and an Italian chef means some interesting Mediterranean dishes with a healthy dose of fresh Italian flavors and influence, like risotto with wild *setas* (oyster mushrooms) and creamy tiramisu. The presentation and service are superb and the atmosphere one of relaxed elegance. ✉ *Los Ventorrillos* ☎ *950/168321* ▭ *MC, V* ⊗ *Closed Dec.–Mar. No lunch July and Aug.*

$$$ **MiKasa.** The MiKasa has recently expanded and now encompasses the original small smart hotel, plus MiKasa Suites and Luz de Agua—the latter comprising seven smart town houses. All the accommodations have the same design-conscious look with cubist Moorish-style architecture and chic modern rooms. Rooms are named after places, like Bali and Cadaques (of Salvador Dali fame), and the themes are reflected in the decor. Perks include Jacuzzi bathtubs and a highly regarded restaurant, La Villa, which prepares innovative international dishes. **Pros:** wonderful breakfasts; heated pool; romantic hideaway feel. **Cons:** could be too quiet for some; not suitable for young children or late-night partying ✉ *Ctra. de Carboneras s/n* ☎ *950/138073* 🌐 *www.mikasasuites.com* *20 rooms, 12 suites, 7 town houses* *In-room: no phone. In-hotel: restaurant, tennis court, pools, gym, Wi-Fi hotspot* ▭ *AE, MC, V* ⊗ *Closed Jan.–Mar.*

SAN JOSÉ AND THE CABO DE GATA NATURE RESERVE

40 km (25 mi) east of Almería, 86 km (53 mi) south of Mojácar.

San José is the largest village in the southern part of the Cabo de Gata Nature Reserve and has a pleasant bay, though these days the village has rather outgrown itself and can be quite busy in summer. Those preferring smaller, quieter destinations should look farther north at places such as Agua Amarga and the often-deserted nearby beaches.

GETTING HERE AND AROUND

You really need your own wheels to explore the nature reserve and surrounding villages, including San José.

EXPLORING

Just south of San José is the **Parque Natural Marítimo y Terrestre Cabo de Gata–Níjar** (✉ *Road from Almería to Cabo de Gata, Km 6*). Birds are the main attraction at this nature reserve; it's home to several species native to Africa, including the *camachuelo trompetero* (large-beaked bullfinch), which is not found anywhere else outside Africa. Check out the **Centro Las Amuladeras visitor center** (☎ *950/160435* 🌐 *www.cabodegata-nijar.com*) at the park entrance, which has an exhibit and information on the region.

For beach time, follow signs south to the **Playa Los Genoveses** and **Playa Monsul.** A rough road follows the coast around the spectacular cape, eventually linking up with the N332 to Almería. Alternatively, follow the signs north for the towns of Níjar (approximately 20 km north) and Sorbas (32 km northeast of Níjar); both towns are famed for their distinctive green-glazed pottery, which you can buy directly from the workshops.

WHERE TO STAY

$ **La Isleta**. This small hotel with the same name as the village tucked around a charming bay nestles right up against the blue waters of the Mediterranean. A low-rise white blocky building with blue trim, it's nothing fancy. What you're paying for is the location, within a stone's throw of the beach, with superb sea views. The rooms are plain but clean and comfortable, and the downstairs restaurant is noted for its excellent seafood. On the downside, fodors.com readers have complained that the reception service can be offhand. **Pros:** fabulous location. **Cons:** no frills; can be noisy with families in summer. ✉ *C. Isleta del Moro* ☎ *950/389713* 🖷 *950/389764* *10 rooms* *In-hotel: restaurant* ▭ *MC, V* *BP.*

ALMERÍA

183 km (114 mi) east of Málaga.

Warmed by the sunniest climate in Andalusia, Almería is a youthful Mediterranean city, basking in sweeping views of the sea from its coastal perch. It's also a capital of the grape industry, thanks to its wonderfully mild climate in spring and fall. Rimmed by tree-lined boulevards and some landscaped squares, the city's core is a maze of narrow, winding alleys formed by flat-roof, distinctly Mudejar houses. Though now surrounded by modern apartment blocks, these dazzling-white older homes give Almería an Andalusian flavor.

GETTING HERE AND AROUND

The No. 20 bus runs roughly every half hour from the airport to the center of town (Calle del Doctor Gregorio Marañón).

The city center is compact, and most of the main sights are within easy strolling distance of each other. The beach is roughly 1 km (0.6 mi) away.

ESSENTIALS

Visitor Information Almería (✉ *Parque Nicolás Salmerón s/n* ☎ *950/274355*).

EXPLORING

Dominating the city is its **alcazaba** (fortress) built by Caliph Abd ar-Rahman I and given a bell tower by Carlos III. From here you have sweeping views of the port and city. Among the ruins of the fortress, damaged by earthquakes in 1522 and 1560, are landscaped gardens of rock flowers and cacti. ✉ *C. Almanzor* ☎ *950/175500* *€1.50* *Apr.–Oct., Tues.–Sun. 10–7:30; Nov.–Mar., Tues.–Sun. 9–6:30.*

Below the *alcazaba* stands the **cathedral**, whose buttressed towers make it look like a castle. It's Gothic in design but with some classical touches around the doors. *€3* *Weekdays 10–2 and 4–6, Sat. 10–2.*

Dramaric views of the coastline from Cabo de Gata national park

WHERE TO EAT AND STAY

$–$$$ SPANISH ✕ **La Encina.** This justly popular restaurant is housed in an 1860s building that also incorporates an 11th-century Moorish well. Time may have stood still with the setting, but the cuisine reflects a modern twist on traditional dishes, including seafood mains like *pastel de merluz hojaldrado con crujiente de espinacas* (hake in puff pastry with crunchy spinach) or *solomillo de cerdo Ibérico con queso Idiazabal y vino de Oporto* (pork medallions accompanied by traditional Basque Idiazabal cheese and port). The restaurant is fronted by a popular tapas bar that is generally full with a boisterous business crowd. ✉ *Calle Marín 3, Almería* ☎ *950/273429* ▭ *MC, V* ⏲ *Closed Sun. and Mon.*

$$ SPANISH ✕ **Valentín.** This popular, central spot serves fine regional specialties, such as *cazuela de rape* (monkfish baked in a sauce of almonds and pine nuts), *arroz negro* (rice flavored with squid ink), and the deliciously simple *pescado en adobe* (dog fish baked in clay with garlic, oregano, and paprika). If you're considering serious credit-card overdrive, go for the lobster. The surroundings are rustic-yet-elegant Andalusian: lime-washed white walls, dark wood, and exposed brick. Come on the early side (around 9) to get a table. The generous *menú degustación* is €42. ✉ *Tenor Iribarne 7* ☎ *950/264475* ▭ *AE, MC, V* ⏲ *Closed Mon. No dinner Sun.*

$–$$ **AC Almería.** All creams, beiges, and browns, this hotel has a modern corporate feel, yet reflects a comforting attention to detail. Those little features make all the difference, from angled reading lamps on the head of the bed to personal climate control in all rooms. The hotel's contemporary gloss peaks in the reception area with the metallic staircase that spirals up to the rooms. There are two restaurants to choose from: the avant-garde La Cata and the more traditional (think grilled meat) El Asador. **Pros:** at the center of town; great for people-watching on the plaza. **Cons:** can be crowded with business and tour groups; service can feel impersonal. ✉ *Plaza de las Flores, Almería]* ☎ *950/234999* 🌐 *www.ac-hoteles.com* *97 rooms* *In-room: Wi-Fi. In-hotel: 2 restaurants, room service, bar, pool, gym, laundry service, Wi-Fi hotspot, parking (paid)* ▭ *MC, V* *BP.*

$ **Hotel Sevilla.** Looking for inexpensive comfort? This is the place. In the labyrinth of the old town, the Sevilla has unassuming decor, with cream-colored walls and light wood furnishings. Rooms vary: those on the street side have small terraces; those on the quiet interior look out over courtyards and rooftops. **Pros:** friendly and traditional. **Cons:** small rooms; poor TV reception. ✉ *Granada 25* ☎ *950/230009* 🌐 *www.hotelsevillaalmeria.es* *37 rooms* *In-room: a/c* ▭ *MC, V.*

$ **Torreluz III.** Value is the overriding attraction of this comfortable yet elegant modern hotel. Guest rooms are slick and bright, with the kind of amenities for which you'd expect to pay more. The restaurant, Torreluz Mediterráneo ($$), is famous among locals for innovative cuisine and brisk lunchtime service; the menu is an excellent cross section of southeastern fare—try the *zarzuela de marisco a la marinera* (mixed seafood in a zesty red marinade). The cheaper Torreluz Hotel, with just 24 rooms ($) next door (they share a phone number) is also good value, as are the nearby apartments, which offer more space for the same price as the main hotel. **Pros:** great central location; parking. **Cons:** no pool. ✉ *Pl. Flores 3* ☎ *950/234399* 🌐 *www.torreluz.com* *94 rooms* *In-room: a/c. In-hotel: 2 restaurants, bar, Wi-Fi hotspot, parking (paid)* ▭ *AE, DC, MC, V.*

OFF THE BEATEN PATH

The archaeological site of **Los Millares** (☎ *677/903404* *Free* *Tues.–Sat. 9:30–4*) is 2.3 km (1½ mi) southwest from the village of Santa Fe de Mondújar and 19 km (12 mi) from Almería. This collection of ruins scattered on a windswept hilltop was the birthplace of civilization in Spain nearly 5,000 years ago. Large, dome-shaped tombs show that the community had an advanced society, and the existence of formidable defense walls indicates it had something to protect. A series of concentric fortifications shows that the settlement increased in size, eventually holding some 2,000 people. The town was inhabited from 2700 to 1800 BC and came to dominate the entire region. From the reception center at the edge of the site, a guide will take you on a tour of the ruins. Phone in advance for all visits.

NIGHTLIFE

Nocturnal action in Almería centers on **Plaza Flores,** moving down to the beach in summer. In town, try the small **Cajón de Sastre** (✉ *Pl. Marques de Heredia 8* ☎ *No phone*) for typical *copas* (libations) and a mainly Spanish crowd.For foot-stomping live flamenco, check out the excellent **Peña El Taranto** (✉ *C. Tenor Iribame 20* ☎ *950/235057*) with nightly performances.

THE COSTA TROPICAL

East of Málaga and west of Almería lies the Costa Tropical. It's escaped the worst excesses of the property developers, and its tourist onslaught has been mild. A flourishing farming center, the area earns its keep from tropical fruit, including avocados, mangoes, and papaws (also known as custard apples). Housing developments are generally inspired by Andalusian village architecture rather than bland high-rise design. You may find packed beaches and traffic-choked roads at the height of the season, but for most of the year the Costa Tropical is relatively free of tourists, if not also devoid of expatriates.

SALOBREÑA

102 km (63 mi) east of Málaga.

This unspoiled village of near-perpendicular streets and old white houses on a steep hill beneath a Moorish fortress is a true Andalusian *pueblo,* separated from the beachfront restaurants and bars in the newer part of town. You can reach Salobreña by descending through the mountains from Granada or by continuing west from Almería on N340.

ALMUÑÉCAR

85 km (53 mi) east of Málaga.

Almuñécar is a small-time resort with a shingle beach, popular with Spanish and northern-European vacationers. It's been a fishing village since Phoenician times, 3,000 years ago, when it was called Sexi; later, the Moors built a castle here for the treasures of Granada's kings. The road west from Motril and Salobreña passes through what was the empire of the sugar barons, who brought prosperity to Málaga's province in the 19th century: the cane fields now give way to lychees, limes, mangoes, papaws, and olives.

The village is actually two, separated by the dramatic rocky headland of Punta de la Mona. To the east is Almuñécar proper, and to the west is **La Herradura,** a quiet fishing community. Between the two is the Marina del Este yacht harbor, which, along with La Herradura, is a popular diving center.

GETTING HERE AND AROUND

The N340 highway runs north of town. There is an efficient bus service to surrounding towns and cities, including Málaga, Granada, Nerja, and, closer afield, La Herradura. Almuñecar's town center is well laid out for strolling, and the local tourist office has information on bicycle and scooter rental.

ESSENTIALS

Visitor Information Almuñécar (✉ *Calle Alta del Mar 8* ☎ *958/634007*).

EXPLORING

Crowning Almuñécar is the **Castillo de San Miguel** *(St. Michael's Castle).* A Roman fortress once stood here, later enlarged by the Moors, but the castle's present aspect owes more to 16th-century additions. The

A religious procession in Almuñécar

building was bombed during the Peninsular War in the 19th century and what was left was used as a cemetery until the 1990s. You can wander the ramparts and peer into the dungeon; the skeleton at the bottom is a reproduction of human remains discovered on the spot. €2, *includes admission to Cueva de Siete Palacios July and Aug., Tues.–Sat. 10:30–1:30 and 6–9, Sun. 10–2; Sept.–June, Tues.–Sat. 10:30–1:30 and 4–6:30, Sun. 10:30–2.*

Beneath the Castillo de San Miguel is a large, vaulted stone cellar of Roman origin, the **Cueva de Siete Palacios** (Cave of Seven Palaces), now Almuñecar's archaeological museum. The collection is small but interesting, with Phoenician, Roman, and Moorish artifacts. €2, *includes admission to Castillo de San Miguel July and Aug., Tues.–Sat. 10:30–1:30 and 6–9, Sun. 10–2; Sept.–June, Tues.–Sat. 10:30–1:30 and 4–6:30, Sun. 10:30–2.*

WHERE TO EAT AND STAY

$$ FRENCH ★ **Jacquy-Cotobro.** One of the finest French restaurants on Spain's southern coast, Jacquy-Cotobro is cozy, with brick walls and green wicker chairs; a beachfront terrace is open in summer. Try the *menú gourmet* (€36), with four courses plus dessert and wine; it might include fresh pasta topped with oyster mushrooms and prawns, lobster salad with truffle oil or duck in orange sauce, then a calorific delight such as the strawberry mousse with kirsch. Service is excellent. *Edificio Río, Paseo Cotobro 10 958/631802 MC, V Closed Mon.*

$ **Casablanca.** There's something quaint about this family-run hotel with its pink-and-white neo-Moorish facade and arches, and the location is choice, next to the beach (Playa de San Cristóbal) and near the botanical park. The rooms, which are all different, have modern fittings juxtaposed with antiques and the occasional four-poster bed. All have private balconies or large picture windows with superb views. The restaurant ($) specializes in traditional cuisine, such as *migas* (bread crumbs fried with sausage and spices), grilled meats, and paella. **Pros:** family-run; atmospheric. **Cons:** rooms vary, with some on the small side. *✉ Pl. San Cristóbal 4 ☏ 958/635575 ⊕ www.hotelcasablancaalmunecar.com ⇨ 35 rooms ☞ In-room: a/c. In-hotel: restaurant, bar, Internet terminal, parking ▬ D, MC, V ⓘ BP.*

NERJA

52 km (32 mi) east of Málaga, 22 km (14 mi) west of Almuñécar.

Nerja—the name comes from the Moorish word *narixa,* meaning "abundant springs"—has a large foreign resident community living mainly outside town in *urbanizaciones* ("village" developments). The old village is on a headland above small beaches and rocky coves, which offer reasonable swimming despite the gray, gritty sand. In July and August, Nerja is packed with tourists, but the rest of the year it's a pleasure to wander the old town's narrow streets.

GETTING HERE AND AROUND

Nerja is a speedy hour's drive northeast from Málaga on the A7. If you're driving, park in the underground car park just west of the Balcón de Europa (it's signposted) off Calle La Cruz. The town is small enough to explore on foot.

ESSENTIALS

Visitor Information **Nerja** (*✉ Puerta del Mar ☏ 952/521531 ⊕ www.nerja.org*).

EXPLORING

☺ ★ The highlight of the town is the **Balcón de Europa**, a tree-lined promenade with magnificent views, on a promontory just off the central square.

The **Cuevas de Nerja** (Nerja Caves) lie between Almuñécar and Nerja on a road surrounded by giant cliffs and dramatic seascapes. Signs point to the cave entrance above the village of Maro, 4 km (2½ mi) east of Nerja. Its spires and turrets created by millennia of dripping water are now floodlit for better views. One suspended pinnacle, 200 feet long, is the world's largest known stalactite. The awesome subterranean chambers create an evocative setting for concerts and ballets during the Nerja Festival of Music and Dance, held annually during the second and third weeks of July. *☏ 952/529520 ⊕ www.cuevanerja.com* ▭ €7 *⊙ Oct.–Apr., daily 10–2 and 4–6:30; May–Sept., daily 10–2 and 4–8.*

WHERE TO EAT AND STAY

$$ SPANISH ✕ **Casa Luque.** One of Nerja's most authentic Spanish restaurants, Casa Luque is in an old Andalusian house in a lovely square just off the Balcón de Europa. A large and picturesque terrace affords sweeping views of the coast. The innovative menu offers an haute culinary twist to traditional dishes from northern Spain, often of Basque or Navarrese origin, with an emphasis on meat and game. Examples of dishes are chicken liver paté with *pacharan* (liquor) sauce, curried chicken with dates, and pork fillet with Rioja. The restaurant is noted for its excellent

and extensive tapas menu, two or three of which can easily equal a relatively inexpensive and filling meal. ✉ *Pl. Cavana 2* ☎ *952/521004* ▭ *AE, DC, MC, V* ⊙ *Closed Wed. No dinner Sun.*

$–$$ SPANISH ✕ **El Mesón de Julio**. Check the blackboard outside this long-standing and reliably good restaurant for the day's specialties and the long list of tapas. There's comfortable seating outside on the terrace or in an attractive pine-clad interior with bare brick columns, wood beams, and an inviting bar. The menu includes familiar Andalusian meat, like leg of lamb, roast pork, and fish dishes, along with more international options, including baked Camembert with strawberry preserves and goat cheese salad. Julio's is popular with the local business community at midday, so get here early if you want a table for lunch. ✉ *Calle Cristo 7* ☎ *952/521190* ▭ *MC, V.*

$$–$$$ ★ **Hotel Carabeo**. Tucked away down a side street near the center of town and the sea, this British-owned boutique hotel has shelves of books, antiques, and cozy overstuffed sofas in the downstairs sitting room. Hung throughout are colorful oil paintings by local artist David Broadhead. In the main building there are seven rooms, five with sea views, and a private terrace overlooking the sea. A newer annex has six more rooms, plus a small gym and game room. The restaurant is reliably good and serves a fusion of contemporary and traditional cuisines. **Pros:** friendly owners; great location. **Cons:** rooms in the annex lack character; winter closure. ✉ *C. Hernando de Carabeo 34* ☎ *952/525444* 🌐 *www.hotelcarabeo.com* *13 rooms* *In-room: a/c. In-hotel: restaurant, bar, pool, gym, Internet terminal* ▭ *MC, V* *CP* ⊙ *Closed late Oct.–mid-Mar.*

NIGHTLIFE AND THE ARTS

El Colono (✉ *Granada 6* ☎ *952/521826*) is a flamenco club in the town center. Although the show is geared toward tourists, the club has an authentic *olé* atmosphere. The food is good, and local specialties, including paella, are served. Dinner shows begin at 9 PM on Wednesday and Friday from February until the end of October.

FRIGILIANA

58 km (36 mi) east of Málaga.

The village of Frigiliana, on a mountain ridge overlooking the sea, has spectacular views and an old quarter of narrow, cobbled streets and dazzling white houses decorated with pots of geraniums. It was the site of one of the last battles between the Christians and the Moors.

Frigiliana is a short drive from the highway to the village; if you don't have a car, you can take a bus here from Nerja.

ESSENTIALS

Visitor Information Frigiliana (✉ *Pl. del Ingenio* ☎ *952/534261*).

Views of the Mediterranean Sea, with the mountains in the background

THE AXARQUÍA

Vélez-Málaga: 36 km (22 mi) east of Málaga.

The Axarquía region stretches from Nerja to Málaga, and the area's charm lies in its mountainous interior, peppered with pueblos, vineyards, and tiny farms. Its coast consists of narrow, pebbly beaches and drab fishing villages on either side of the high-rise resort town of Torre del Mar.

GETTING HERE AND AROUND

Although the bus routes are fairly comprehensive throughout the Axarquía, reaching the smaller villages may involve long delays; renting a car is convenient and lets you get off the beaten track and experience some of the beautiful unspoiled hinterland in this little-known area. The four-lane E15 highway speeds across the region a few miles in from the coast; traffic on the old coastal road (N340) is slower.

ESSENTIALS

Visitor Information Cómpeta (✉ *Avenida de la Constitucion* ☎ *952/553685*).

EXPLORING

Vélez-Málaga is the capital of the Axarquía: it's a pleasant agricultural town of white houses, strawberry fields, and vineyards. Worth quick visits are the **Thursday market,** the ruins of a **Moorish castle,** and the church of **Santa María la Mayor,** built in the Mudejar style on the site of a mosque that was destroyed when the town fell to the Christians in 1487.

If you have a car and an up-to-date road map, explore the Axarquía's inland villages: You can follow the **Ruta del Vino** *(Wine Route)* 22 km (14 mi) from the coast, stopping at villages that produce the sweet, earthy local wine, particularly Cómpeta. Alternatively you can take the **Ruta de la Pasa** *(Raisin Route)* through Moclinejo, El Borge, and Comares. Both are signposted locally.

Comares perches like an eagle's nest atop one of La Serrazuela's highest mountains and dates back to Moorish times. This area is especially spectacular during the late-summer grape-harvest season or in late autumn, when the leaves of the vines turn gold. A short detour to Macharaviaya (7 km [4 mi] north of Rincón de la Victoria) might lead you to ponder the past glory of this now sleepy village: In 1776 one of its sons, Bernardo de Gálvez, became Spanish governor of Louisiana and later fought in the American Revolution (Galveston, Texas, takes its name from him). Macharaviaya prospered under his heirs and for many years enjoyed a lucrative monopoly on the manufacture of playing cards for South America.

WHERE TO EAT AND STAY

¢–$$ ★ **El Molino de los Abuelos.** Under a canopy of jasmine and bougainvillea, this former olive mill in Comares has a cobbled courtyard where you can enjoy a glass of *fino* (sherry) at sundown while ogling the stunning views. The rooms are all different, varying from small and simple with shared bath to a sumptuous suite with a hot tub. The restaurant has fabulous views, and the Dutch-Colombian owners organize terrific themed entertainment (like tango and flamenco nights). **Pros:** full of traditional Andalusian character; great views. **Cons:** rooms are plain; several bathrooms are old-fashioned (including their plumbing); mediocre food. ✉ *Pl. Balcón De La Axarquía, 2, Comares* ☎ *952/509309* 🌐 *www.hotelmolinodelosabuelos.com* *6 rooms* *In-room: a/c, no TV (some). In-hotel: restaurant* ▭ *AE, MC, V.*

MÁLAGA PROVINCE

The city of Málaga and the provincial towns of the upland hills and valleys to the north create the kind of contrast that makes travel in Spain so tantalizing. The region's Moorish legacy—tiny streets honeycombing the steamy depths of Málaga, rocky cliffs and gorges, the layout of the farms, and the crops themselves, including olives, grapes, oranges, and lemons—is a unifying visual theme. Ronda and the whitewashed villages of Andalusia behind the Costa del Sol comprise one of Spain's most scenic and emblematic driving routes.

To the west of Málaga, along the coast, the sprawling outskirts of Torremolinos signal that you're leaving the "real" Spain and entering, well, the "real" Costa del Sol, with its beaches, high-rise hotels, and serious tourist activity. On the far west, you can still discern Estepona's fishing village and Moorish old quarter amid its booming coastal development. Just inland, Casares piles whitewashed houses over the bright-blue Mediterranean below.

Málaga and Inland

MÁLAGA

175 km (109 mi) southeast of Córdoba.

With about 550,000 residents, the city of Málaga is technically the capital of the Costa del Sol, though most travelers head straight for the beaches west of the city. Approaching Málaga from the airport, you'll be greeted by huge 1970s high-rises that march determinedly toward Torremolinos but don't despair: in its center and eastern suburbs, Málaga is a pleasant port city, with ancient streets and lovely villas amid exotic foliage. Blessed with a subtropical climate, it's covered in lush vegetation and averages some 324 days of sunshine a year.

Málaga has been spruced up with tastefully restored historic buildings and the steady emergence of increasingly sophisticated shops, bars, and restaurants. The opening of the prestigious Museo Carmen Thyssen Bornemisza in late 2010 will doubtless further boost tourism to this Costa capital, although there are still far fewer visitors here than in the other grand-slam Andalusian cities of Seville, Córdoba, and Granada. ☞ *Note that more tourists usually means more pickpockets, so stay alert, particularly around the historic city center.*

Arriving from Nerja, you'll enter Málaga through the suburbs of El Palo and Pedregalejo, once traditional fishing villages. Here you can eat fresh

Alcazaba 4
Cathedral 6
Centro de Arte Contemporáneo de Málaga 12
Fundación Picasso 2
Gibralfaro 3
La Concepción ...1
Mercado de Atarazanas 11
Museo Carmen Thyssen Bornemisza 9
Museo de Artes Populares...... 10
Museo Picasso...5
Palacio Episcopal 7
Pasaje Chinitas ..8

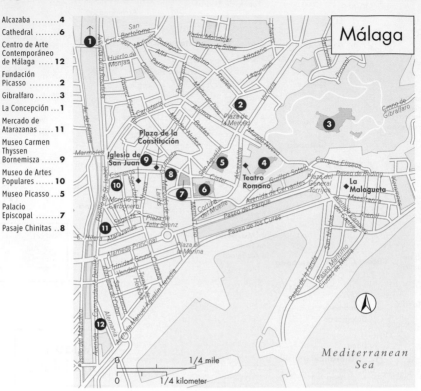

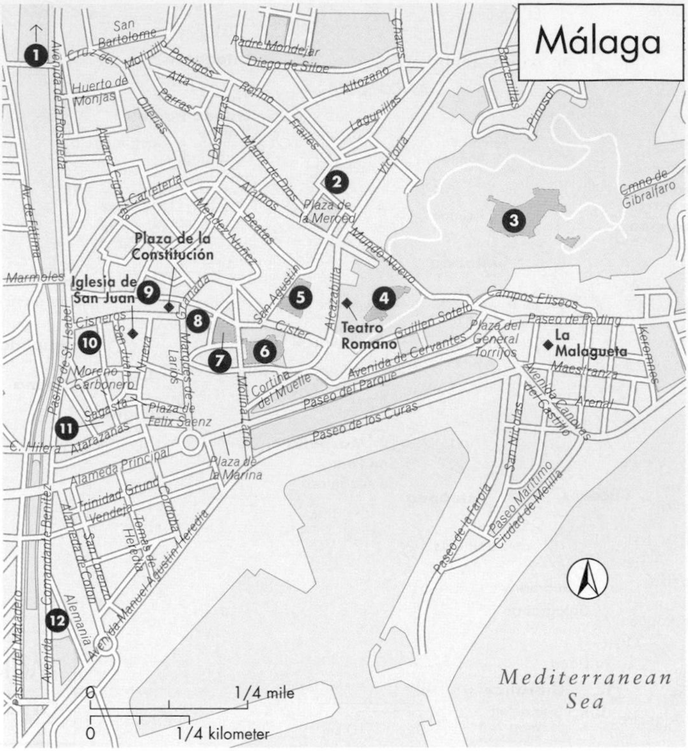

fish in the numerous *chiringuitos* (beachside bars) and stroll Pedregalejos's seafront promenade or the tree-lined streets of El Limonar. At sunset, walk along the **Paseo Marítimo** and watch the lighthouse start its nightly vigil. A few blocks inland is Málaga's bullring, **La Malagueta,** built in 1874. Continuing west you'll soon reach the city center and the inviting **Plaza de la Marina;** with cafés and an illuminated fountain overlooking the port, it's a pleasant place for a drink. From here, stroll through the shady, palm-lined gardens of the **Paseo del Parque** or browse on **Calle Marqués de Larios,** the elegant pedestrian-only main shopping street.

GETTING HERE AND AROUND

If you're staying at one of the coastal resorts between Málaga and Fuengirola, the easiest way to reach Málaga is via the half-hourly train. Otherwise, there are several new, well-signposted underground car parks, and it's not a daunting place to negotiate by automobile. The best way to explore Málaga is on foot, but you could also hop on an open-top sightseeing bus or rent a bike. There is a comprehensive bus network, too, and the tourist office can advise on routes and schedules. The city is in the throes of introducing a metro but, given the inevitability of delays caused by archaeological discoveries, the completion date is, as yet, undetermined.

The colorful, open-top Málaga Tour City Sightseeing Bus is a good way to see the city's attractions in a day. The bus stops at all the major sights in town, including the Gibralfaro and the cathedral.

ESSENTIALS

Airport Contact Aeropuerto de Málaga (AGP) (*Pablo Picasso Airport ☎ 952/048804 🌐 www.ccoo-agp.com*).

Bike Rental Contact Cyclo Point (*✉ Av. Juan Sebastian Elcano 50, Málaga ☎ 952/297324 🌐 www.cyclo-point.com*).

Bus Contact Málaga bus station (*✉ Paseo de los Tilos ☎ 952/350061*).

Car Rental Contacts Crown Car Hire (*✉ Málaga Airport 🌐 www.crowncarhire.com*). **Niza Cars** (*✉ Málaga Airport 🌐 www.nizacars.com*).

Taxi Company Morales Rodriguez–Málaga (*☎ 952/430077*).

Tour Information Málaga Tour City Sightseeing Bus (*🌐 www.citysightseeing-spain.com*).

Train Information Málaga train station (*✉ Explanada de la Estación ☎ 952/360202*).

Visitor Information Málaga (*✉ Av. Cervantes 1, Paseo del Parque ☎ 952/604410*).

EXPLORING

4 Just beyond the ruins of a Roman theater on Calle Alcazabilla, the Moorish **Alcazaba** is Málaga's greatest monument. This fortress was begun in the 8th century, when Málaga was the principal port of the Moorish kingdom, though most of the present structure dates from the 11th century. The inner palace was built between 1057 and 1063, when the Moorish emirs took up residence; Ferdinand and Isabella lived here for a while after conquering the city in 1487. The ruins are dappled with orange trees and bougainvillea and include a small museum; from the highest point you can see over the park and port. *✉ Entrance on Alcazabilla 🎫 €2.10, €3.45 combined entry with Gibralfaro ⏲ Nov.–Mar., Tues.–Sun. 8:30–7; Apr.–Oct., Tues.–Sun. 9:30–8.*

6 Málaga's **cathedral**, built between 1528 and 1782, is a triumph, although a generally unappreciated one, having been left unfinished when funds ran out. Because it lacks one of its two towers, the building is nicknamed *La Manquita* (the One-Armed Lady). The enclosed choir, which miraculously survived the burnings of the civil war, is the work of 17th-century artist Pedro de Mena, who carved the wood wafer-thin in some places to express the fold of a robe or shape of a finger. The choir also has a pair of massive 18th-century pipe organs, one of which is still used for the occasional concert. Adjoining the cathedral is a small museum of religious art and artifacts. A walk around the cathedral on Calle Cister will take you to the magnificent Gothic Puerta del Sagrario. *✉ C. de Molina Larios ☎ 952/215917 🎫 €4 ⏲ Weekdays 10–6, Sat. 10–5:45.*

12 **Centro de Arte Contemporáneo** *(Contemporary Arts Center)*. This museum includes photographic studies and paintings, some of them immense. With 7,900 square feet of bright exhibition hall, the museum aims to showcase ultramodern artistic trends in four exhibitions—a changing

DID YOU KNOW?

As seems appropriate for the city of Picasso's birth, Málaga's Picasso museum is a considered a family affair: the works on view here are the ones that the master kept for himself or gave to family members.

show from the permanent collection, two temporary shows, and one show dedicated to up-and-coming Spanish artists. The gallery attracts world-class modern artists like the United Kingdom's Tracy Emin, whose famously controversial "unmade bed" was included in a two-month exhibition here in early 2009. ✉ *Alemania s/n* ☎ *952/120055* 🌐 *www.cacmalaga.org* 🎟 *Free* 🕑 *Tues.–Sun. 10–8.*

2 The childhood home of Málaga's most famous native son, Pablo Picasso, born here in 1881, is on the Plaza de la Merced. Now the **Fundación Picasso**, the building has been painted and furnished in the style of the era and houses a permanent exhibition of the artist's early sketches and sculptures, as well as memorabilia, including his christening robe and family photos. ✉ *Pl. de la Merced 15* ☎ *952/600215* 🌐 *www.fundacionpicasso.malaga.eu* 🎟 *€1* 🕑 *Mon.–Sat. 9:30–8, Sun. 10–2.*

3 Surrounded by magnificent vistas, Málaga's **Gibralfaro** (castle), is floodlit at night. The fortifications were built for Yusuf I in the 14th century; the Moors called them Jebelfaro, from the Arab word for "mount" and the Greek word for "lighthouse," after a beacon that stood here to guide ships into the harbor and warn of pirates, which has been succeeded by a small parador *(see Where to Stay)*. You can drive here by way of Calle Victoria or take a minibus that leaves 10 times a day, between 11 and 7, roughly every hour, from the bus stop in the park near the Plaza de la Marina. ✉ *Gibralfaro Mountain* ☎ *952/220043* 🎟 *€2.10, €3.45 combined entry with Alcazaba* 🕑 *Nov.–Mar., daily 9–5:45; Apr.–Oct., daily 9–7:45.*

1 A 150-year-old botanical garden, **La Concepción** was created by the daughter of the British consul, who married a Spanish shipping magnate—the captains of the Spaniard's fleet had standing orders to bring back seedlings and cuttings from every "exotic" port of call. The garden is just off the exit road to Granada—too far to walk, but well worth the cab fare from the city center. ✉ *Ctra. de las Pedrizas, Km 216* ☎ *952/252148* 🎟 *€4.20* 🕑 *Tues.–Sun. 9:30–5:30.*

11 From the Plaza Felix Saenz, at the southern end of Calle Nueva, turn onto Sagasta to reach the **Mercado de Atarazanas**. The typical 19th-century iron structure incorporates the original **Puerta de Atarazanas,** the exquisitely crafted 14th-century Moorish gate that once connected the city with the port. The actual market stalls have been moved to a purpose-built building on the corner of nearby Calle Agujero and Paseo Santa Isabel while the interior is being refurbished (completion estimated mid-2010).

QUICK BITES

The Antigua Casa de Guardia (✉ *Alameda 18* ☎ *952/214680*), around the corner from the Mercado de Atarazanas, is Málaga's oldest bar, founded in 1840. Andalusian wines and finos (sherries) flow straight from the barrel, the walls are lined with sepia-photos of old Málaga—including some of Picasso, who was evidently a frequent customer here—and the floor is ankle-deep in discarded shrimp shells.

9 Visitors who've been to Madrid will be familiar with that city's Museo Thyssen Bornemisza, and in late 2010 a further 358 works from the

private collection of Baroness Thyssen are to go on show at Málaga's very own **Museo Carmen Thyssen Bornemisza**, housed in a renovated 16th-century palace. The collection is set to include paintings by some of Spain's greatest artists, like Joaquín Sorolla y Bastida and Francisco de Zurbarán. At this writing, opening hours and admission costs were not set in stone; check with the tourist office (☎ *952/213445*) before visiting. ✉ *C. Compañía* ☎ *Unavailable at time of publication* 🎫 *€6* ⏲ *Tues.–Sun. 10–7.*

10 In the old Mesón de la Victoria, a 17th-century inn, is the **Museo de Artes Populares** (Arts and Crafts Museum). On display are horse-drawn carriages and carts, old agricultural implements, folk costumes, a forge, a bakery, an ancient grape press, and Malagueño-painted clay figures and ceramics. ✉ *Pasillo de Santa Isabel 10* ☎ *952/217137* 🌐 *www.museoartespopulares.com* 🎫 *€2* ⏲ *Oct.–May, weekdays 10–1:30 and 4–7, Sat. 10–1:30; June–Sept., weekdays 10–1:30 and 5–8, Sat. 10–1:30.*

5 Fodor's Choice ★ Part of the charm of the **Museo Picasso**, one of the city's most prestigious museums, is that it's such a family affair. These are the works that Pablo Picasso kept for himself or gave to his family and include the heartfelt *Paulo con gorro blanco* (Paulo with a White Cap), a portrait of his first-born son painted in the early 1920s, and *Olga Kokhlova con mantilla* (Olga Kokhlova with Mantilla), a 1917 portrait of his certifiably insane first wife. The holdings were largely donated by two family members—Christine and Bernard Ruiz-Picasso, the artist's daughter-in-law and her son. The works are displayed in chronological order according to the periods that marked Picasso's development as an artist, from Blue and Rose to Cubism and beyond. The museum is housed in a former palace where, during restoration work, Roman and Moorish remains were discovered. These are now on display, together with the permanent collection of Picassos and temporary exhibitions. ✉ *C. de San Agustín* ☎ *952/602731* 🌐 *www.museopicassomalaga.org* 🎫 *Permanent exhibition €6, combined permanent and temporary exhibition €8, last Sun. of every month free* ⏲ *Tues.–Thurs. 10–8, Fri. and Sat. 10–9.*

7 **Palacio Episcopa** *(Bishop's Palace)*, which faces the cathedral's main entrance, has one of the most stunning facades in the city. It's now a venue for temporary art exhibitions. ✉ *Pl. Obispo 6* ☎ *952/602722* 🎫 *Free* ⏲ *Tues.–Sun. 10–2 and 6–9.*

8 The narrow streets and alleys on each side of Calle Marqués de Larios have charms of their own. Wander the warren of passageways around **Pasaje Chinitas**, off Plaza de la Constitución, and peep into the dark, vaulted bodegas where old men down glasses of *seco añejo* or *Málaga Virgen,* local wines made from Málaga's muscatel grapes. Silversmiths and vendors of religious books and statues ply their trades in shops that have changed little since the early 1900s. Backtrack across Larios, and, in the streets leading to Calle Nueva, you can see shoeshine boys, lottery-ticket vendors, Gypsy guitarists, and tapas bars serving wine from huge barrels.

WHERE TO EAT

SOMETHING SWEET

For coffee and sweets, malagueños favor Lepanto, the classy shop at Calle Marqués de Larios 7, where uniform-clad servers serve a variety of pastries, cakes, and other sweets.

$ SPANISH **El Trillo.** A long-standing favorite for traditional Andalusian cuisine, El Trillo could fit in happily in Madrid with its hams over the bar, well-worn tiles, and dark wood furniture. Alcoves add to the intimate feel, while outside tables overlook the smart shopping street Marques de Larios. The menu includes regional specialties like Córdoba-style oxtail and medallions of monkfish, as well as more unusual dishes such as a starter of artichokes filled with baby broad beans and goose liver paté. Desserts are nothing special; instead nip across the road to Lepanto, the city's most famous café and patisserie. ✉ *C. Don Juan Diaz 4* ☎ *952/603920* ▭ *MC, V.*

$$–$$$ SPANISH **La Ménsula.** If you're looking to sample traditional Andalusian cuisine in an elegant yet cozy atmosphere, this is the place, on a fairly anonymous side street between the port and the city center. The setting is warm and woody, with arches, beams, and a barrel-vaulted ceiling, and the service is appropriately hospitable and efficient. Stone-cooked steak, warm fish salad, and king prawns with *setas* (oyster mushrooms) are just some of the menu options, and the adjacent bar offers a range of tapas. ✉ *C. Trinidad Grund 28* ☎ *952/221314* ▭ *DC, MC, V* ⊙ *Closed Sun.*

¢–$ SPANISH Fodor's Choice ★ **Logueno.** This traditional tapas bar has two dining spaces: the original well-loved bar, shoehorned into a deceptively small space on a side street near Calle Larios, and a more recent expansion across the street. The original is especially appealing, with its L-shape wooden bar crammed with a choice of more than 75 tantalizing tapas, including many Logueno originals such as grilled oyster mushrooms with garlic, parsley, and goat cheese. There's an excellent selection of Rioja wines, and the service is fast and good, despite the lack of elbow room. ✉ *Marin Garcia s/n* ☎ *No phone* ▭ *No credit cards* ⊙ *Closed Sun.*

$ SPANISH **Tintero.** Come to this sprawling, noisy restaurant for the experience rather than the food, which is fine but not spectacular. There's no menu—waiters circle the restaurant carrying various dishes (tapas and main courses) and you choose whatever looks good. The bill is totaled up according to the number and size of the plates on the table at the end of the meal. On the El Palo seafront, Tintero specializes in catch-of-the-day seafood, such as *boquerones* (fresh anchovies), *sepia* (cuttlefish), and the all-time familiar classic, *gambas* (grilled prawns). Be warned that it's packed on Sunday with the local expat community and boisterous Spanish families (i.e., not the place for a romantic lunch for two). ✉ *Pl. del Dedo, El Palo* ☎ *952/204464* ▭ *No credit cards* ⊙ *No dinner.*

$$–$$$ ECLECTIC **Vino Mio.** This Dutch-owned restaurant is well placed, just off Plaza de la Merced, and the menu is diverse and interesting, including dishes like *cocodrilo Dundee* (crocodile steaks with red pepper chutney, potatoes, and seasonal vegetables) that have fast made this one of the city's most fashionable see-and-be-seen dining spots. Slightly more conservative dishes include *pollo Indonesia* (chicken prepared in a peanut sauce),

pasta Lili (rigatoni with oyster mushrooms, walnuts, and zucchini), and seven salad choices, such as the *Marrakesh* (couscous with vegetables, raisins, and herbs). The atmosphere is contemporary chic with regular art exhibitions and live music nightly, ranging from flamenco to jazz. ✉ *Calle Alamos 11* ☎ *952/609093* ▭ *MC, V.*

WHERE TO STAY

$ **Castilla**. This gracious hotel in a butter-colored building is between the city center and the port. Rooms are excellent value, if small, with attractive fabrics, primrose-yellow walls, and curtains to help block out any late-night street revelry. The adjacent cafeteria is handy for a typical *desayuno* (breakfast) of *café con leche* and *tostada con tomate* (toast with fresh tomatoes and olive oil) or an early evening aperitif before going out on the town. The owners are helpful and friendly but speak only Spanish. **Pros:** central location; parking. **Cons:** rooms are small; only Spanish TV. ✉ *C. Córdoba 7* ☎ *952/218635* *37 rooms* *In-hotel: Wi-Fi hotspot* ▭ *MC, V.*

$$ Fodor's Choice ★ **Humaina**. In this small hotel 16 km (10 mi) north of the city, the rooms are painted a sunny yellow and have terra-cotta tile floors. Balconies overlook a thickly forested park of olive, pine, and oak trees. Solar energy, an organic garden, and serious recycling are part of the eco-friendly package. Horseback riding, bird-watching, and hiking excursions can be arranged. The restaurant dishes up healthy, tasty dishes, and vegetarians are happily accommodated—a rarity in these parts. **Pros:** environmentally friendly; bucolic countryside surroundings. **Cons:** a car is essential for exploring the coast and inland; room views vary. ✉ *Parque Natural Montes de Málaga, Ctra. del Colmenar s/n* ☎ *952/641025* 🌐 *www.hotelhumaina.es* *10 rooms, 4 suites* *In-hotel: restaurant, pool* ▭ *MC, V* *BP.*

$$$ Fodor's Choice ★ **Parador de Málaga–Gibralfaro**. Surrounded by pine trees and crowning the Gibralfaro hill, 3 km (2 mi) above the city, this cozy, gray-stone parador has spectacular views of Málaga and the bay. Rooms are attractive—with blue curtains and bedspreads and woven rugs on bare tile floors—and some of the best in Málaga, so reserve well in advance. All have terraces with panoramic views. The restaurant ($–$$$) excels at such classic Mediterranean dishes as calamari and fried green peppers. **Pros:** some of the best views on the Costa; excellent service. **Cons:** a bit of a hike into town; books up quickly. ✉ *Monte de Gibralfaro s/n, Monte* ☎ *952/221902* 🌐 *www.parador.es* *38 rooms* *In-room: a/c, Internet. In-hotel: restaurant, bar, pool, Wi-Fi hotspot, parking (free)* ▭ *AE, DC, MC, V.*

$–$$ **Petit Palace Plaza Malaga.** The sumptuous historic exterior belies the modern decor within the Petit Palace, one of Málaga's most exciting new hotels. A member of Spain's High Tech hotel chain, it has an edgy contemporary interior from the bold black-and-orange color scheme in the downstairs breakfast room to the rooms with their minimalist decor, punchy modern colors, parquet floors, and in-room notebook computers and Wi-Fi. Some rooms have stunning views of the cathedral spires with the hilltop Alcazaba beyond. Other perks include free bicycle rental and a 24-hour coffee and tea lounge. **Pros:** superb central location; great for business travel. **Cons:** may be too corporate and modern for some; no bar. ✉ C. Nicasio 5 ☎ 952/222132 🌐 www.hthoteles.com ⇨ 66 rooms ♨ In-room: Wi-Fi. In-hotel: restaurant, room service, laundry service, Internet terminal ▭ AE, D, DC, MC, V.

$–$$ **Room Mate Larios.** On the central Plaza de la Constitución, this lodging is in a 19th-century building that's been elegantly restored and was taken over by a national hotel chain in 2009. Rooms are luxuriously furnished with carpeting throughout and king-size beds (unusual in Spain). Several have balconies overlooking the sophisticated strut of shops and boutiques along Calle Marqués de Larios, while the black-and-white marble bathrooms are spacious and elegant. The roof terrace bar is separately owned but easily accessible, with stunning views of the cathedral, while the restaurant has a sophisticated choice of dishes, including crispy duck. The choice of 11 bottled waters from all over the world makes for entertaining reading. **Pros:** stylish; efficiently run. **Cons:** on busy shopping street that can be noisy in daytime; some rooms on the small side. ✉ *Marqués de Larios 2* ☎ *952/222200* 🌐 *www.room-matehotels.com* ⇨ *34 rooms, 6 suites* ♨ *In-room: Wi-Fi. In-hotel: restaurant, bar* ▭ *AE, DC, MC, V* 🍽 *BP.*

NIGHTLIFE AND THE ARTS

Málaga's main nightlife districts are Maestranza, between the bullring and the Paseo Marítimo, and the beachfront in the suburb of Pedregalejos. Central Málaga also has a lively bar scene around Plaza Uncibay.

ANTEQUERA

64 km (40 mi) northwest of Málaga, 108 km (67 mi) northeast of Ronda, via Pizarra.

Antequera became a stronghold of the Moors after their defeat at Córdoba and Seville in the 13th century. Its fall to the Christians in 1410 paved the way for the reconquest of Granada—the Moors retreated, leaving a fortress on the town heights.

GETTING HERE AND AROUND

There are several daily buses from Málaga and Ronda to Antequera. Drivers should head for the underground car park on Calle Diego Ponce in the center of town, which is well signposted.

ESSENTIALS

Visitor Information Antequera (✉ *Pl. de San Sebastian 7* ☎ *952/702505* 🌐 *www.antequera.es*).

EXPLORING

Next to the town fortress is the former church of **Santa María la Mayor,** one of 27 churches, convents, and monasteries in Antequera. Built of sandstone in the 16th century, it has a ribbed vault that is now a concert hall. The church of **San Sebastián** has a brick baroque Mudejar tower topped by a winged figure called the Angelote (Big angel), the symbol of Antequera. The church of **Nuestra Señora del Carmen** (Our Lady of Carmen) has an extraordinary baroque altarpiece that towers to the ceiling.

Antequera's pride and joy is *Efebo*, a beautiful bronze statue of a boy that dates back to Roman times. Standing almost 5 feet high, it's on display in the **Museo Municipal**. ✉ *Pl. Coso Viejo* ☎ *952/704051* 🎫 *€3* ⏲ *Tues.–Fri. 10–1:30 and 4:30–6:30, Sat. 10–1:30, Sun. 11–1:30.*

The mysterious prehistoric **dolmens** are megalithic burial chambers just outside Antequera, built some 4,000 years ago out of massive slabs of stone weighing more than 100 tons each. The best-preserved dolmen is La Menga. ✉ *Signposted off Málaga exit rd.* 🎫 *Free* ⏲ *Tues.–Sat. 9–6, Sun. 9:30–2:30.*

Europe's major nesting area for the greater flamingo is **Fuente de Piedra**, a shallow saltwater lagoon. In February and March, these birds arrive from Africa by the thousands to breed, returning to Africa in August when the water dries up. The visitor center has information on wildlife. Bring binoculars if you have them. ✉ *10 km (6 mi) northwest of Antequera, off A92 to Seville* ☎ *952/111715* 🎫 *Free* ⏲ *May–Sept., Wed.–Sun. 10–2 and 4–6; Oct.–Apr., Wed.–Sun. 10–2 and 6–8.*

East of Antequera, along N342, is the dramatic silhouette of the **Peña de los Enamorados** *(Lovers' Rock)*, an Andalusian landmark. Legend has it that a Moorish princess and a Christian shepherd boy eloped here one night and cast themselves to their deaths from the peak the next morning. The rock's outline is often likened to the profile of the Cordobés bullfighter Manolete.

About 8 km (5 mi) from Antequera's Lovers' Rock, the village of **Archidona** winds its way up a steep mountain slope beneath the ruins of a Moorish castle. This unspoiled village is worth a detour for its **Plaza Ochavada,** a magnificent 17th-century square resplendent with contrasting red and ocher stone. ✉ *8 km (5 mi) beyond Peña de los Enamorados, along N342, Antequera.*

Fodor's Choice ★ Well-marked walking trails (stay on them) guide you at the **Parque Natural del Torcal de Antequera** *(El Torcal Nature Park)*, where you can walk among eerie pillars of pink limestone sculpted by aeons of wind and rain. Guides can be arranged for longer hikes. The visitor center has a small museum. ✉ *Centro de Visitantes, Ctra. C3310, 10 km (6 mi) south of Antequera* ☎ *649/472688* 🎫 *Free* ⏲ *Daily 10–5.*

WHERE TO EAT AND STAY

$ SPANISH ✕ **Caserío San Benito.** If it weren't for the cell-phone transmission tower looming next to this country restaurant 11 km (7 mi) north of Antequera, you might think you'd stumbled into an 18th-century scene. Popular dishes include *porra antequerana* (a thick gazpacho topped with diced ham) and *migas* (fried bread crumbs with sausage and spices). There are more innovative dishes here as well, like pork loin risotto with asparagus and fried cabbage with onions and prawns. It's a popular Sunday lunch spot for hungry *malagueños* in the winter months (in summer they head for the beach). ✉ *Ctra. Málaga–Córdoba, Km 108* ☎ *952/111103* 💳 *AE, MC, V* ⏲ *Closed Mon. and 1st 2 wks in July. No dinner Tues.–Thurs.*

$–$$ SPANISH ✕ **Coso San Francisco.** This delightful restaurant in the hotel of the same name is an evocative 17th-century building complete with low ceilings, uneven floors, ancient beams, and an intimate dining room, which a hefty wood-burning stove makes cozy in winter. The menu uses fresh ingredients (most of the vegetables are grown organically by the owner) and includes some interesting twists on traditional dishes, like the *porrilla de espárragos* (asparagus soup with fried bread and an egg). Egg, meat, and fish dishes are accompanied by crisp wide-cut fries and salads. There's live chamber music on Thursday evenings, April to October. ✉ *Calle Calzada 27–29* ☎ *952/840014* 🌐 *www.cososanfrancisco.com* 💳 *MC, V.*

$$ SPANISH Fodor's Choice ★ ✕ **El Angelote.** Across the square from the Museo Municipal, El Angelote is one of Antequera's most popular, well-established restaurants. Kick-start your appetite with a glass of *fino* (sherry) at the traditional L-shape bar, then head to one of the two wood-beam dining rooms in back, which fill up fast at lunchtime. The menu is solidly traditional and includes local specialties like *porrilla de setas* (wild mushrooms in an almond-and-wine sauce) or *perdiz hortelana* (stewed partridge). Antequera's typical dessert is *bienmesabe* (literally, "tastes good to me"), a delicious concoction of almonds, chocolate, and apple custard. ✉ *Pl. Coso Viejo* ☎ *952/703465* 💳 *DC, MC, V* ⏲ *Closed Mon. No dinner Sun.*

$ 🏨 **Coso San Francisco.** Surrounded by shops, bars, and cafés, this charming hotel and restaurant *(see above)* is in a lovely 17th-century building, complete with a first-floor gallery that overlooks the central courtyard dining room. The 10 rooms are all appropriately furnished in a rustic manner with dark wood, and several still have features from the original building, such as niches, low beams, and original timber doors. It's worth the extra cost for breakfast, as the downstairs restaurant is excellent. **Pros:** atmospheric historic building; great restaurant. **Cons:** rooms are rather spartan for some; right in town so can be noisy. ✉ *Calle Calzada 27–29* ☎ *952/840014* 🌐 *www.cososanfrancisco.com* *10 rooms* *In-room: refrigerator. In-hotel: restaurant, bar, parking (free)* 💳 *AE, DC, MC, V* *BP.*

THE GUADALHORCE VALLEY

About 5 km (3 mi) from Antequera, via the El Torcal exit (turn right onto A343).

From the village of Alora, follow the small road north to the awe-inspiring **Garganta del Chorro** (Gorge of the Stream), a deep limestone chasm where the Guadalhorce River churns and snakes its way some 600 feet below the road. The railroad track that worms in and out of tunnels in the cleft is, amazingly, the main line heading north from Málaga for Bobadilla junction and, eventually, Madrid.Clinging to the cliff side is the **Caminito del Rey** (King's Walk), a suspended catwalk built for a visit by King Alfonso XIII at the beginning of the 19th century, although it's been closed for construction and renovations since 1992, and there's still no word on completion.

North of the gorge, the Guadalhorce has been dammed to form a series of scenic reservoirs surrounded by piney hills, which constitute the **Parque de Ardales** nature area. Informal, open-air restaurants overlook the lakes and a number of picnic spots. Driving along the southern shore of the lake, you reach Ardales and, turning onto A357, the old spa town of **Carratraca**. Once a favorite watering hole for both Spanish and foreign aristocracy, it has a Moorish-style *ayuntamiento* (town hall) and an unusual **polygonal bullring.** Today it has been renovated into a luxury Ritz-Carlton spa hotel. The splendid Roman-style marble-and-tile **bathhouse** has benefited from extensive restoration.

TORREMOLINOS

11 km (7 mi) west of Málaga, 16 km (10 mi) northeast of Fuengirola, 43 km (27 mi) east of Marbella.

Torremolinos is all about fun in the sun. It may be more subdued than it was in the action-packed 1960s and 1970s, but scantily attired northern Europeans of all ages still jam the streets in season, shopping for bargains on Calle San Miguel, downing sangria in the bars of La Nogalera, and congregating in the karaoke bars and English pubs. By day, the sunseekers flock to the El Bajondillo and La Carihuela beaches, where, in high summer, it's hard to find towel space on the sand.

ESSENTIALS

Bike Rental Contact Moto Mercado (✉ *Pl. de los Comunidades, Torremolinos* ☎ *952/052671* 🌐 *www.rentabike.org*).

Bus Contact Bus Station (✉ *Calle Hoyo* ☎ *952/382419*).

Taxi Contact Radio Taxi Torremolinos (☎ *952/380600*).

Visitor Information Torremolinos (✉ *Pl. Blas Infante 1* ☎ *952/379512*).

EXPLORING

Torremolinos has two sections. The first, **Central Torremolinos**, is built around the Plaza Costa del Sol; Calle San Miguel, the main shopping street; and the brash Nogalera Plaza, which is full of overpriced bars and restaurants. The Pueblo Blanco area, off Calle Casablanca, is more pleasant; and the Cuesta del Tajo, at the far end of Calle San Miguel, winds down a steep slope to Bajondillo Beach. Here, crumbling walls, bougainvillea-clad patios, and old cottages hint at the quiet fishing village of bygone years. The second, much nicer, section of Torremolinos is **La Carihuela**. To get here, head west out of town on Avenida Carlota Alessandri and turn left following the signs. Far more authentically Spanish, the Carihuela still has a few fishermen's cottages and excellent seafood restaurants. The traffic-free esplanade is pleasant for strolling, especially on a summer evening or Sunday at lunchtime, when it's packed with Spanish families.

WHERE TO EAT AND STAY

$$–$$$ SEAFOOD ✕ **Casa Juan**. An institution among *malagueño* families, who flock here on weekends for the legendary fresh seafood, this restaurant has been steadily increasing its girth, and there are now several Casa Juans surrounding an attractive square, one line back from the seafront. Try for a table overlooking the mermaid fountain. This is a good place to indulge in *fritura malagueña* (fried seafood) or *arroz marinera* (seafood with rice), one of 10 different rice dishes prepared here; others include lobster rice, vegetable rice, and black rice flavored with squid ink. ✉ *Pl. San Gines, La Carihuela* ☎ *952/373512* ▭ *MC, V* ⏲ *Closed Mon.*

Colorful beach umbrellas at Torremolinos beach

$$$$ SPANISH **La Consula**. Just north of Torremolinos (toward Coín), this cooking school is well worth the detour. The main building dates from 1856—in the 1850s it was the residence of an American family, and Ernest Hemingway was a frequent visitor—and is surrounded by tropical gardens. Today, diners can enjoy excellent and innovative cuisine prepared by the students. Typical dishes include artichoke soup served with a cuttlefish and mushroom ragout, lightly steamed sea bass with coriander vinegar and boletus mushrooms, and desserts like the irresistible passion fruit creme Catalan with coconut sorbet and a stick of raspberry licorice. The restaurant is very popular with businessmen from Málaga, so reserve in advance. *Finca La Consula, Churriana* *952/262–2562* *www.laconsula.com* *MC, V* *Closed weekends. Lunch only.*

$$$ SPANISH **Yate El Cordobes.** Ask the locals which beachfront *chiringuito* they prefer and El Yate will almost doubtless be the answer. Run and owned by an affable Cordobes family, the menu holds few surprises, but seafood is freshly caught, and meat and vegetables freshly sourced. Go for the classic Córdoba salmorejo soup (deliciously thick and garlicky gazpacho, topped with diced egg and ham) as a starter. You may be tempted by the barbecued sardines or choose a freshly grilled fish like dorada (gilthead) or lubina (sea bass) for your entrée. The back terrace with its sea and sand views fills up fast. Alternatively, the dining room is large and light with picture windows. The service is friendly and fast, although little or no English is spoken. Desserts are the usual limited choice of crème caramel, rice pudding, and similar, but at least they're made in house. *Paseo Marítimo Playamar s/n, Torremolinos* *952/384956* *MC, V* *Closed Tues. Nov.–Mar.*

$$ **Don Pedro.** Extremely comfortable and well maintained, this three-story, traditional Andalusian-style hotel is part of the reliable Spanish Sol Melia chain. Rooms are spacious and have balconies; sea views get snapped up fast. The bodega-style bar is popular at happy hour, and nightly entertainment here includes flamenco shows. The hearty breakfast buffet should set you up for the day; lunch is more mediocre. Note that the views vary considerably, so ask for a sea view when you book or you could find yourself overlooking the parking lot. **Pros:** across from the beach; good deals via the Web site. **Cons:** popular with tour groups; pool area gets crowded and noisy in peak season. ✉ *Av. del Lido* ☎ *952/386844* 🌐 *www.solmelia.com* *524 rooms* *In-room: a/c. In-hotel: restaurant, pools, beachfront, Wi-Fi hotspot* ▭ *AE, DC, MC, V* 🍽 *BP.*

$$ **Miami.** Something of a find, this small hotel dates from 1950, when it was designed by Manolo Blascos, Picasso's cousin, for flamenco Gypsy dancer Lola Medina. Rooms are individually furnished, if a little dated, and there's a sitting area with a TV, cozy fireplace, and small library. The inn is surrounded by a shady garden west of the Carihuela, making a stay here like visiting a private Spanish home. Many guests return year after year. Reserve ahead. **Pros:** plenty of character; close to the beach. **Cons:** rooms could use some updating; inconvenient for public transportation. ✉ *Aladino 14, at C. Miami* ☎ *952/385255* 🌐 *www.residencia-miami.com* *26 rooms* *In-room: a/c. In-hotel: bar, pool, Wi-Fi hotspot, some pets allowed* ▭ *MC, V* 🍽 *CP.*

$–$$ **Tropicana.** On the beach at the far end of the Carihuela, in one of the most pleasant parts of Torremolinos, this low-rise resort hotel has its own beach club. A tropical theme runs throughout, from the purple passionflower climbers covering the brickwork to the common areas with exotic plants and bamboo furniture to the rooms, with their warm color schemes and dazzling white fabrics. The hotel has a friendly, homey feel that has earned the hotel a loyal following. **Pros:** great for families; surrounded by bars and restaurants. **Cons:** can be noisy; a half-hour walk to the center of Torremolinos. ✉ *Trópico 6, La Carihuela* ☎ *952/386600* 🌐 *www.hoteltropicana.es* *84 rooms* *In-room: a/c, refrigerator. In-hotel: restaurant, bar, pool, beachfront, Wi-Fi hotspot* ▭ *AE, DC, MC, V* 🍽 *BP.*

NIGHTLIFE AND THE ARTS

Most nocturnal action is in the center of town. Many of the better hotels stage flamenco shows, but you may also want to check out the **Taberna Flamenca Pepe López** (✉ *Pl. de la Gamba Alegre* ☎ *952/381284*), which has nightly shows at 10 from April to October. The rest of the year shows are weekends only.

BENALMÁDENA

9 km (5½ mi) west of Torremolinos, 9 km (5½ mi) east of Mijas.

ESSENTIALS

Visitor Information Benalmádena Costa (✉ *Av. Antonio Machado 14* ☎ *952/379512*).

EXPLORING

★ **Benalmádena-Pueblo**, the village proper, is on the mountainside 7 km (4 mi) from the coast. It's surprisingly unspoiled and offers a glimpse of the old Andalusia. **Benalmádena-Costa**, the beach resort, is practically an extension of Torremolinos; it's run almost exclusively by package-tour operators, although the marina does have shops, restaurants, and bars aimed at a more sophisticated clientele that may appeal to the independent traveler.

In Benalmádena-Costa's marina, **Sea Life Benalmádena** is an above-average aquarium with fish from local waters, including rays, sharks, and sunfish; there's also a turtle reef where you can watch rare green turtles and learn about various conservation projects. Adjacent is a pirate-theme miniature golf course. ✉ *Puerto Marina Benalmádena* ☎ *952/560150* 🌐 *www.sealife.es* 🎟 *€13.50 mini golf €7* 🕐 *May–Sept., daily 10–midnight; Oct.–Apr., daily 10–6.*

The Costa del Sol's leading amusement park is **Tivoli World**, with rides, Wild West shows, and 40-odd restaurants and snack bars. A 4,000-seat, open-air auditorium showcases international stars alongside can-can, flamenco, and Spanish ballet performances. You can take a cable car to the top of Calamorro Mountain for hiking trails and a birds of prey show. ✉ *Av. Tivoli s/n, Arroyo de la Miel* ☎ *952/577016* 🌐 *www.tivoli.es* 🎟 *€7* 🕐 *May–Sept., daily 1 PM–1 AM; Oct.–Apr., weekends noon–8.*

WHERE TO EAT AND STAY

$–$$ CONTINENTAL ✕ **Casa Fidel.** This Benalmádena-Pueblo restaurant is in a typical Andalusian house complete with arches, terra-cotta tiles, a large fireplace, and a small leafy patio. For a starter, try *crema fría de aguacate con salmón marinado* (cold avocado soup with marinated salmon) or *ensalada templada de setas y gambas* (warm salad with shrimp and wild mushrooms). Main courses include *langostinos con chalotas y puré de garbanzos* (king prawns with shallots and garbanzos) and some retro dishes, like chicken Kiev with rice. Parking is near impossible in the surrounding narrow streets; instead, head for the car park at the base of the elevator near the Iglesia Santo Domingo church. ✉ *Maestra Ayala 1* ☎ *952/449165* 💳 *AE, DC, MC, V* 🕐 *Closed Tues. and Aug. 1–15. No lunch Wed.*

$–$$ SPANISH ✕ **El Higueron.** If you've done any traveling on the Costa's main A7 highway, you've doubtless spotted this place, perched high in the pine-clad hills above the village, and the views from the dining room stretch all the way to Africa on a clear day. Chef Nacho Romero trained at two-Michelin-starred La Broche in Madrid and believes in simple dishes made with the freshest ingredients, and the restaurant is popular with a sophisticated Spanish clientele. Highlights include the *gazpacho de aguacate* (cold gazpacho soup based on avocado), seafood salad, and delicious tuna steak prepared with a chili-spiked tomato sauce. ✉ *Carretera Benalmádena-Mijas, Km 3.1* ☎ *952/119163* ✍ *Reservations essential* 💳 *MC, V.*

$$$$ 🏨 **Riu Marina Hotel.** This dazzling white hotel fits in well with the surrounding quasi-Oriental architecture of the Puerto Deportivo. Rooms are spacious and smart, with bold fabrics contrasting with pastel

paintwork and arty prints. Most of the balconies have sea views. There is nightly entertainment ranging from flamenco to magic shows, and the breakfast buffet has been applauded by guests for its wide choice of hot and cold choices. The hotel is also ideally placed for La Carihuela's famed seafood restaurants and the international dining choices to be found in the port. **Pros:** part of the prestigious and quality Riu hotel chain; superb location. **Cons:** can be noisy from nearby late-night clubs and bars; lunch buffet a little bland. ✉ *Av. del Puerto Deportivo* ☎ *952/961696* 🌐 *www.riu.es* *272 rooms* *In-room: safe, Wi-Fi. In-hotel: restaurant, room service, bar, pool, gym, bicycles, laundry facilities, laundry service, parking (paid)* ▭ *AE, D, DC, MC, V* *BP.*

¢–$$ **Sunset Beach Club.** It's big and brash, but this hotel has a lot going for it, not least the price: you can get great deals out of season and by booking online. Accommodations are in apartments with attractive decor and furnishings. Kitchens are well-equipped so that, after preparing a cocktail, you can adjourn to your generous-sized terrace and enjoy the sunset over the sea. Included in the myriad activities offered are a cabaret theater with live nightly shows and an introduction to diving. Half the apartments are owned on a time-share basis. **Pros:** excellent facilities for families; well located for shops and beach. **Cons:** beach towels on a hire basis; most apartments just have twin beds. ✉ *Av. del Sol 5, Benalmádena-Costa* ☎ *952/579400* 🌐 *www.sunsetbeachclub.com* 53 rooms *In-room: kitchen. In-hotel: 2 restaurants, bars, pools, gym, spa, beachfront, diving, children's programs (ages 6–12), laundry service, Internet terminal, Wi-Fi hotspot, parking (free)* ▭ *AE, D, DC, MC, V* *BP.*

NIGHTLIFE

For discos, piano bars, and karaoke, head for the port. The **Fortuna Nightclub** in the **Casino Torrequebrada** (✉ *Av. del Sol s/n* ☎ *952/446000* 🌐 *www.torrequebrada.com*) has flamenco and an international dance show with a live orchestra, starting at 10:30 PM. A passport, jacket, and tie are required in the casino, open daily 9–4.

FUENGIROLA

16 km (10 mi) west of Torremolinos, 27 km (17 mi) east of Marbella.

Fuengirola is less frenetic than Torremolinos. Many of its waterfront high-rises are vacation apartments that cater to budget-minded sunseekers from northern Europe and, in summer, a large contingent from Córdoba and other parts of Spain. The town is also a haven for British retirees (with plenty of English and Irish pubs to serve them) and a shopping and business center for the rest of the Costa del Sol. The Tuesday market here is the largest on the coast and a major tourist attraction.

GETTING HERE AND AROUND

Fuengirola is the last stop on the train line from Málaga. There are also regular buses that leave from Málaga's main bus station.

ESSENTIALS

Bike Rental Contact Moto Mercado (✉ *Av. Niro Padre Jesús Cautivo 27, Los Boliches* ☎ *952/052671* 🌐 *www.rentabike.org*).

Bus Contact Bus Station (✉ *Av. Alfonso X 111* ☎ *952/475066*).

Taxi Contact Radio Taxi Fuengirola (☎ *952/471000*).

Visitor Information Fuengirola (✉ *Av. Jesús Santos Rein 6* ☎ *952/467625*).

EXPLORING

The most prominent landmark in Fuengirola is **Castillo de Sohail.** The original structure dates from the 12th century, but the castle served as a military fortress until the early 19th century. Just west of town, the castle makes a dramatic performance venue for the annual summer season of music and dance. *€1.50* ⏲ *Tues.–Sun. 10–3.*

The American company Rain Forest operates the cageless **Fuengirola Zoo.** Four different habitats have been created, providing natural environments for the animals, which include chimpanzees, big cats, and dolphins. The company is heavily involved with worldwide conservation programs. ✉ *Av. José Cela 6* ☎ *952/666301* 🌐 *www.zoofuengirola.com* *€15.50* ⏲ *Daily 10–dusk.*

WHERE TO EAT AND STAY

¢–$ MEDITERRANEAN ✕ **Terra Sana.** Excellent innovative and healthy food is what you'll find on the menu at centrally located Terra Sana (there are eight branches of the restaurant on the Costa del Sol, with five in Marbella). Casual and family-friendly, it's a particularly good spot for lunch. Selections like the Thai Break salad (spicy chicken, red peppers, zucchini, bean sprouts, cucumber, carrots, coriander, and nuts with a spicy lime dressing) are perfect for a light meal, while larger appetites may prefer the Al Andalus Wrap filled with Serrano ham, Manchego cheese, tomatoes, olives, spinach, and caramelized red onions. ✉ *C. Emancipación 13* ☎ *952/663937* 🌐 *www.terrasana.net* ▭ *MC, V.*

$$ FRENCH ✕ **Patrick Bausier.** Impeccable service and innovative French Mediterranean cuisine make this restaurant a definite class act. Chef and owner Patrick Bausier studied French cuisine in Paris, and it's evident in such dishes as sea bass in a fresh herb sauce, a beautifully prepared roast rack of lamb, and decadent desserts such as a chocolate marquise with shavings of nougat. Excellent touches include complimentary sparkling wine upon arrival and delicious homemade bread and rolls. ✉ *Paseo Maritimo, Bajos del Hotel Yaramar* ☎ *691/483321* *Reservations essential* ▭ *MC, V* ⏲ *No lunch Mon.–Sat., no dinner Sun.*

¢–$ VEGETARIAN ✕ **Vegetalia.** This attractive, long-established restaurant has a large, pleasant dining space decorated with plants and giant prints of (surprise, surprise) vegetables. It's best known for its excellent, and vast, lunchtime buffet that includes salads and hot dishes like lentil burgers and seitan cutlets, and is increasingly popular with the expatriate "ladies who lunch." The dinner menu includes curries, vegetable kebabs, pasta dishes, and stir-fries. Leave room for the blueberry pie, homemade by the Finnish owner Katya's mother. Biodynamic wines are available as well as more mainstream Spanish varieties. ✉ *C. Santa Isabel 8, Los Boliches* ☎ *952/586031* ▭ *MC, V* ⏲ *Closed July and Aug., Sun. and Mon. year-round.*

$$–$$$ **Florida.** Fuengirola's latest accommodation option has a sophisticated edge on its high-rise-hotel neighbors. Expanses of glossy marble in the

Horsemen in Fuengirola's El Real de la Feria

lobby are crowned by a dramatic stained-glass dome, and glass elevators give dramatic views of the coast and mountains en route to your room. The rooms themselves are light and airy, with pale parquet floors, tasteful floral fabrics, tea- and coffee-making facilities, and private terraces overlooking the port and surrounding beach. The spa has a good range of treatments, including the irresistible sounding chocolate body wrap. **Pros:** great location; in-house spa. **Cons:** not all rooms have a sea view; can be an overload of business travelers. ✉ *C. Galvez Ginachero,* ☎ *952/922700* 🌐 *www.hotel-florida.es* *184 rooms* *In-hotel: restaurant, room service, bar, gym, spa, beachfront, laundry service, Internet terminal, Wi-Fi hotspot, parking (paid)* *AE, DC, MC, V* *BP.*

$ **Hostal Italia.** Right off the main plaza and near the beach, this small, family-run hotel is deservedly popular, and guests come here year after year, particularly during the October feria. Rooms are small but full of light and very comfortable, and most have small balconies. There's a larger sun terrace for catching rays. The hostal is surrounded by restaurants and bars, so finding a *desayuno* (breakfast) destination is no problem. If you're here during Easter, the owners display one of the most impressive *belenes* (model nativity scenes) in town. **Pros:** friendly owners; spotless rooms. **Cons:** very little English spoken; rooms are small. ✉ *C. de la Cruz 1* ☎ *952/474193* 🌐 *www.hostal-italia.com* *40 rooms* *In-room: a/c* *MC, V.*

NIGHTLIFE AND THE ARTS

Amateur local troupes regularly stage plays and musicals in English at the **Salón de Variétés Theater** (✉ *Emancipación 30* ☎ *952/474542*). For concerts—from classical to rock to jazz—check out the modern

Palacio de la Paz (✉ *Recinto Ferial, Av. Jesús Santo Rein* ☎ *952/589349*) between Los Boliches and the town center.

MIJAS

★ *8 km (5 mi) north of Fuengirola, 18 km (11 mi) west of Torremolinos.*

Mijas is in the foothills of the sierra just north of the coast. The pretty whitewashed pueblo (town) was discovered long ago by foreign retirees, and, though the large, touristy square may look like an extension of the Costa, beyond it are hilly residential streets with time-worn homes. Try to visit late in the afternoon, after the tour buses have left.

GETTING HERE AND AROUND

Buses leave Fuengirola every half hour for the 20-minute drive through hills peppered with villas. If you have a car and don't mind a mildly hair-raising drive, take the more dramatic approach from Benalmádena-Pueblo, a winding mountain road with splendid views. You can park in the underground parking garage signposted on the approach to the village.

ESSENTIALS

Visitor Information Mijas (✉ *Pl. Virgen de la Peña* ☎ *958/589034*).

EXPLORING

The **Museo Mijas** occupies the former town hall. Themed rooms, including an old-fashioned bakery and bodega, surround a patio, and regular art exhibitions are mounted in the upstairs gallery. ✉ *Pl. de la Libertad* ☎ *952/590380* 🎫 *Free* ⏲ *Daily 10–2 and 5–8.*

Bullfights take place year-round, usually on Sunday at 4:30, at Mijas's tiny **bullring**. One of the few square bullrings in Spain, it's off the Plaza Constitución—Mijas's old village square—and up the slope beside the Mirlo Blanco restaurant. ✉ *Pl. Constitución* ☎ *952/485248* 🎫 *Museum €3* ⏲ *June–Sept., daily 10–10; Oct.–Feb., daily 9:30–7; Mar., daily 10–7:30; Apr. and May, daily 10–8:30.*

Worth a visit is the delightful village church **Iglesia Parroquial de la Inmaculada Concepción** *(Immaculate Conception)*. It's impeccably decorated, especially at Easter, and the terrace and spacious gardens have a splendid panoramic view. The church is up the hill from the bullring. ✉ *Pl. Constitución.*

QUICK BITES

The Bar Porras on Plaza de la Libertad (at the base of Calle San Sebastián—the most photographed street in the village) attracts a regular crowd of locals with its good-value, tasty tapas.

Mijas extends down to the coast, and the coastal strip between Fuengirola and Marbella is officially called **Mijas-Costa**. This area has several hotels, restaurants, and golf courses.

WHERE TO EAT AND STAY

$–$$ SPANISH ✕ **La Alcazaba.** The views of the coastline here are stunning and about the best you will get anywhere in this mountaintop village, so it's a real bonus that a new chef has improved the food has improved enormously of late. Starters may include crisp slices of eggplant with local honey or goose pâté with green peppers; main courses might be salmon with raisins and orange aroma or shoulder of lamb with thyme. ✉ *Pl. de la Constitución* ☎ *952/590253* ▭ *MC, V* ⊙ *Closed Mon.*

$$$ SPANISH ✕ **Mirlo Blanco.** In an old house on the pleasant Plaza de la Constitución, with a terrace for outdoor dining, this restaurant is run by a Basque family that's been in the Costa del Sol restaurant business for decades. The interior is welcoming and intimate, with original noteworthy artwork interspersed among the arches, hanging plants, and traditional white paintwork. Good choices here are Basque specialties such as *txangurro* (spider crab) and *kokotxas de bacalau* (cod cheeks). And don't miss the sensational Grand Marnier soufflé for dessert. There's an outside terrace for alfresco summer dining and a permanent exhibition of paintings by local foreign artists. ✉ *Pl. de la Constitución 2* ☎ *952/485700* ▭ *AE, MC, V* ⊙ *Closed Jan.*

$$–$$$ CONTINENTAL ✕ **Valparaíso.** Halfway up the road from Fuengirola on the way to Mijas, this sprawling villa stands in its own garden, complete with swimming pool. There's live music nightly, ranging from flamenco to opera and jazz. This is a favorite among local (mainly British) expatriates, some of whom come in full evening dress to celebrate birthdays or other events. In winter, logs burn in a cozy fireplace. The *pato a la naranja* (duck in orange sauce) is popular, but there's also an emphasis on Italian cuisine with pasta choices that include linguine with seafood, tortellini with smoked salmon and caviar, and penne with tomatoes, porcini mushrooms, and chilies. ✉ *Ctra. de Mijas–Fuengirola, Km 4* ☎ *952/485996* ▭ *AE, DC, MC, V* ⊙ *No dinner Sun. No lunch Oct.–June.*

$$$ Fodor's Choice ★ **Beach House.** The epitome of cool Mediterranean-inspired decor, the Beach House seems not so much a hotel but a sumptuous villa owned by a hospitable (and wealthy) friend. From the pleasing bougainvillea-draped bar, the pool seems to merge seamlessly with the sea, while the interior of the hotel is all clean lines, sparkling marble, and minimalist good taste. There's a stylish lounge with a fireplace for relaxing on cooler evenings. The town and restaurants of Fuengirola are 10 minutes away. **Pros:** exclusive feel; gracious, efficient service. **Cons:** lack of nearby shops or entertainment. ✉ *Urbanización El Chaparral, CN340, Km 203* ☎ *952/494540* 🌐 *www.beachhouse.nu* *10 rooms* *In-room: Internet, Wi-Fi (some). In-hotel: pool, no kids under 12* ▭ *MC, V* *CP.*

$$$$ ★ **Gran Hotel Guadalpin.** On the edge of Mijas's golf course (closer to Fuengirola than to Mijas), in a huge garden of palms, cypresses, and fountains, this is one of the most exclusive hotels on the Costa del Sol. It's primarily a spa known for its thalassotherapy—a skin treatment using seawater and seaweed, applied in a Roman-like temple of cool, white-and-blue marble tiles. Three outstanding restaurants ($$$–$$$$) serve savory regional and international dishes. You can often get great deals by booking through the hotel's Web site. **Pros:** luxurious, large rooms. **Cons:** not much in the way of views; can seem rather sterile. ✉ *Urbanización Mijas-Golf, Mijas-Costa* ☎ *952/473050* 🌐 *www.granhotelguadalpin.com* *109 rooms, 35 suites* *In-room: a/c, Internet. In-hotel: 3 restaurants, bars, golf courses, tennis courts, pools,*

gym, spa, Internet terminal, Wi-Fi hotspot, some pets allowed ☐ *AE, DC, MC, V* ⏣ *BP.*

11

$$$ ☷ **TRH Mijas.** It's easy to unwind here, thanks to the poolside restauran-tand bar and the gardens with views of the hillsides stretching down to Fuengirola and the sea. The tasteful decor is marked by marble floors throughout, wrought-iron window grilles, and wooden shutters. The lobby is large and airy, and there's an attractive glass-roof terrace. All rooms are comfortably furnished, with wood fittings and marble floors. TRH Mijas is at the entrance to Mijas village. The management can advise on activities that may be enjoyed in the surrounding countryside, including horse riding and golf. **Pros:** superb panoramic views; traditional Andalusian atmosphere. **Cons:** inconvenient for the beach; touristy village. ✉ *Urbanización Tamisa* ☎ *952/485800* ⊕ *www.hoteltrhmijas.com* ⤳ *204 rooms, 2 suites* ♿ *In-room: a/c, Internet. In-hotel: restaurant, bar, tennis court, pool, gym, Wi-Fi hotspot* ☐ *AE, DC, MC, V.*

MARBELLA

27 km (17 mi) west of Fuengirola, 28 km (17 mi) east of Estepona, 50 km (31 mi) southeast of Ronda.

Playground of the rich and home of movie stars, rock musicians, and dispossessed royal families, Marbella has attained the top rung on Europe's social ladder. Dip into any Spanish gossip magazine and chances are the glittering parties that fill its pages are set in Marbella. Much of this action takes place on the fringes—grand hotels and luxury restaurants line the waterfront for 20 km (12 mi) on each side of the town center. In the town itself, you may well wonder how Marbella became so famous. The main thoroughfare, Avenida Ricardo Soriano, is distinctly charmless, and the Paseo Marítimo, though pleasant, with a mix of seafood restaurants and pizzerias overlooking an ordinary beach, is far from spectacular. About 4 mi west lies **Puerto Banús**, comprising a marina with some of the most expensive yachts you will see this side of Dubai, fringed by restaurants, bars, and designer boutiques.

GETTING HERE AND AROUND

There are regular buses departing from the bus station to the surrounding resorts and towns, including Fuengirola, Estepona, and Málaga.

ESSENTIALS

Bus Contact Bus Station (✉ *Av. Trapiche* ☎ *952/764400*).

Visitor Information Marbella (✉ *Glorieta de la Fontanilla* ☎ *952/822818*) can provide a map of town and monthly calendar of exhibits and events.

EXPLORING

Marbella's appeal lies in the heart of the **old village**, which remains surprisingly intact. Here, a block or two back from the main highway, narrow alleys of whitewashed houses cluster around the central **Plaza de los Naranjos** (Orange Square), where colorful, albeit pricey, restaurants vie for space under the orange trees. Climb onto what remains of the old fortifications and stroll along the Calle Virgen de los Dolores to the Plaza de Santo Cristo.

The **Museo del Grabado Español Contemporáneo**, in a restored 16th-century palace in the heart of the old town, has contemporary Spanish prints and temporary exhibitions. ✉ *Hospital Bazán* ☎ *952/765741* 🎟 *€2.50* ⏲ *Tues.–Fri. 9–9, Mon. and Sat. 9–2.*

In a modern building just east of Marbella's old quarter, the **Museo de Bonsai** has a collection of miniature trees, including a 300-year-old olive tree from China. ✉ *Parque Arroyo de la Repesa, Av. Dr. Maiz Viñal* ☎ *952/862926* 🎟 *€4* ⏲ *June–Sept., daily 10:30–1:30 and 5–8:30; Oct.–May, daily 10:30–1:30 and 4–7.*

QUICK BITES

Enjoy a glass of wine and a transplanted Basque delight at La Taberna del Pintxo (✉ *Av. Miguel Cano 7* ☎ *952/829321*). A *pintxo* is a little morsel served on a slice of bread or with a toothpick. This restaurant serves platter after platter of creative examples, from shellfish to slices of omelet to mushrooms baked in garlic to vegetables in vinaigrette.

Marbella's wealth glitters most brightly along the Golden Mile, a tiara of star-studded clubs, restaurants, and hotels west of town stretching from Marbella to **Puerto Banús**. A mosque, an Arab bank, and the former residence of Saudi Arabia's late King Fahd betray the influence of oil money in this wealthy enclave. About 7 km (4½ mi) west of central Marbella (between Km 175 and Km 174), a sign indicates the turnoff leading down to Puerto Banús. Though now hemmed in by a belt of high-rises, Marbella's plush marina, with 915 berths, is a gem of ostentatious wealth, a Spanish answer to St. Tropez. Huge, flashy yachts, beautiful people, and countless expensive stores and restaurants make up the glittering parade that marches long into the night. The backdrop is an Andalusian pueblo—built in the 1960s to resemble the fishing villages that once lined this coast.

WHERE TO EAT

$$ ITALIAN

✕ **Amore e Fantasía.** Without knowing better, you could mistakenly take this for an antique and decor shop rather than a restaurant, what with the Buddha statues, gilt mirrors, Moorish lights, and Pompeii-themed frieze. It was one of the first restaurants to open in the port, back in the 1980s, and the menu is vast, with traditional and deliciously prepared Italian choices like *risotto al funghi porcini* (with porcini mushrooms), more sophisticated dishes including *cannelloni al foie gras,* and a well-priced daily three-course menu del día (€13.50). Opt for the superbly moist dark chocolate soufflé served with vanilla ice cream if it's available. One of the original partners is from Naples, a fact reflected in the superb crisp pizzas prepared in a traditional wood-burning oven. ✉ *Muelle Benabolá 5–6, Puerto Banús* ☎ *952/813464* 💳 *AE, DC, MC, V.*

$$$$ MEDITERRANEAN

✕ **Calima.** Avant-garde celebrity chef Dani Garcia uses scientific techniques to transform traditional ingredients into innovatively textured, flavored, and visually stunning dishes at his much-lauded Michelin-star restaurant. Liquid nitrogen, for instance, is used to freeze ingredients without the use of water, maximizing the flavors in Sherry Mary oysters with crushed tomato sorbet. Other signature offerings include foie gras with a creamy slice of Ronda goat cheese and a miniature baked potato served with edible silver foil. The space manages to be Zen minimalist, yet warm and intimate, with beautiful panoramic sea views. ✉ *Grand Melia Don Pepe, C. José Melia, Marbella* ☎ *952/764252* ✍ *Reservations essential* ▭ *AE, V, MC.*

$$ SPANISH ✕ **El Balcón de la Virgen.** A special treat here is to dine on the traditional Andalusian patio, which is overlooked by a 300-year-old statue of the Virgin (hence the name) surrounded by a colorful dazzle of plants. The menu includes hearty options like meat and fish dishes, including roast pork and marinated swordfish, as well as lighter bites like fresh salads, fluffy omelets, and gazpacho. One of the house specialties is paella, with four choices to select from, including vegetable, fish and seafood, and traditional Valenciana with chicken and rabbit. After your meal, you can stroll round the corner for a coffee in lovely Plaza de los Naranjos. ✉ *C. Virgen de los Dolores 2* ☎ *952/776092* ▭ *AE, DC, MC, V* ⏲ *Closed Tues.*

$ SPANISH ✕ **Sol y Sombre.** One of the real good-value restaurants on the (frequently) overpriced Marbella dining scene, this family owned freiduria, serving mainly fried fish, has been attracting a loyal clientele for 45 years for the no-frills, wonderfully fresh fried fish and seafood. Among the choices are red mullet, clams, Málaga prawns, swordfish, sardines, and squid. ✉ *C. Tetuán 7, Marbella Closed Mon.*

¢–$ MEDITERRANEAN ✕ **Terra Sana.** All of the outposts of Terra Sana, including the five in Marbella, serve excellent innovative and healthy food. All serve similar cuisine, with selections like the Thai Break salad (spicy chicken, red peppers, zucchini, bean sprouts, cucumber, carrots, coriander, and nuts with a spicy lime dressing) or the Al Andalus Wrap filled with Serrano ham, Manchego cheese, tomatoes, olives, spinach, and caramelized red onions. ✉ *Antonio Belon 1, Marbella* ☎ *952/901274* 🌐 *www.terrasana.net* ▭ *MC, V.*

$$–$$$ MEDITERRANEAN Fodor's Choice ★ ✕ **Zozoi.** Tucked into the corner of one of the town's squares, upbeat, Belgian-owned Zozoi consistently receives rave reviews. The fashionably Mediterranean menu makes little distinction between starters and mains, as all the portions are generous, and shows imaginative use of ingredients in such dishes as grilled fillet of sea bass with saffron fettuccini and green asparagus and roasted duck breast with black cherries and pepper. For dessert, try the red forest fruits with mille-feuille or lemon sorbet spiked with vodka. The large courtyard terrace has a cozy traditional feel with its brightly tiled walls and terra-cotta–tiled floor. ✉ *Pl. Altamirano 1* ☎ *952/858868* ✍ *Reservations essential* ▭ *MC, V* ⏲ *Closed Sun. No lunch.*

WHERE TO STAY

$$$$ 🏨 **Claude.** This stylish boutique hotel is in a sumptuous 17th-century mansion, the former summer home of Napoléon's third wife. While all the original architectural features and finishes have been preserved, the overall look is chic and sophisticated with plush furnishings and fabrics, crystal chandeliers, gorgeous claw-foot antique bathtubs, and original beams, alcoves, arches, and columns. There is a fairytale-like rooftop terrace on several levels, with intimate corners and stunning views of the mosaic-tiled steeple of the adjacent Santa Cristo church and beyond. **Pros:** fabulous breakfast; owners can arrange gourmet tours of Andalusia. **Cons:** pricey given the lack of facilities; no on-site parking.

DID YOU KNOW?

A long leisurely lunch at an outdoor café is one of summer's quintessential enjoyments throughout Spain.

✉ *C. San Francisco 5* ☎ *952/900840* 🌐 *www.hotelclaudemarbella.com* *7 rooms* *In-room: Wi-Fi. In-hotel: restaurant, room service* ▭ *AE, MC, V* 🍴 *BP.*

$–$$ **La Morada Mas Hermosa.** Situated on one of Marbella's prettiest plant-filled pedestrian streets, this small hotel has a warm, homey feel with its traditional courtyard and low ceilings. The lobby welcomes with turquoise-and-blue tiling, and bright, Andalusian-themed paintings hang throughout the property. Rooms are thoroughly enjoyable, with wood beams, terra-cotta tiles, wrought-iron headboards, and exquisitely tiled bathrooms in warm earth tones. Breakfast is taken in the cozy dining room, after which the boutiques and beach of Marbella are just a short stroll away. **Pros:** a hotel with real character; quiet street, yet near the action. **Cons:** bedrooms are small; owner speaks little English. ✉ *C. Montenebros 16A* ☎ *952/924467* 🌐 *www.lamoradamashermosa.com* *7 rooms* ▭ *MC, V* 🍴 *BP.*

$–$$ **Lima.** This midrange option is in downtown Marbella, two blocks from the beach and conveniently across the street from a branch of Terra Sana. The tastefully decorated rooms are a bit generic, with dark wood furniture, bright floral bedspreads, and balconies; corner rooms are the largest. **Pros:** location good for town and beach; towels are provided for the beach so you don't have to sneak the fluffy white ones out from the bathroom. **Cons:** room sizes vary considerably. ✉ *Av. Antonio Belón 2* ☎ *952/770500* 🌐 *www.hotellimamarbella.com* *64 rooms* *In-room: a/c. In-hotel: restaurant, bicycles, laundry service, Wi-Fi hotspot, parking (paid)* ▭ *AE, DC, MC, V.*

$$$$ Fodor's Choice ★ **Marbella Club.** The grande dame of Marbella hotels was a creation of the late Alfonso von Hohenlohe, a Mexican-Austrian aristocrat who helped turn the town into a playground for the rich and famous. The exquisite grounds have lofty palm trees, dazzling flower beds, and a beachside tropical pool area. The bungalow-rooms vary in size; some have private pools. The main restaurant ($$$) has a classy, eclectic menu of modern Mediterranean cuisine. If you can't afford to stay here, at least stop by for afternoon tea, served daily in summer from 4 to 6:30. **Pros:** classic hotel; superb service and facilities. **Cons:** a drive from Marbella's restaurants and nightlife; slightly stuffy atmosphere. ✉ *Blvd. Principe Alfonso von Hohenlohe at Ctra. de Cádiz, Km 178, 3 km (2 mi) west of Marbella* ☎ *952/822211* 🌐 *www.marbellaclub.com* *84 rooms, 37 suites, 16 bungalows* *In-room: a/c, DVD, Wi-Fi. In-hotel: 3 restaurants, golf course, pools, gym, beachfront, Internet terminal, parking (free)* ▭ *AE, DC, MC, V* 🍴 *BP.*

$$$ Fodor's Choice ★ **The Town House.** In a choice location in one of old town Marbella's prettiest squares, this former family home has been exquisitely transformed into a boutique hotel. A combination of antiques and modern fittings make for luxurious rooms, which have accents in earthy colors and white linen. The spacious bathrooms are decked out in shiny marble. There is an attractive bar and plenty of restaurants nearby, plus you are within easy strolling distance of the Puente Romano Beach Club, where day beds can be rented for €16 a day. **Pros:** upbeat design; great central location. **Cons:** small rooms; street noise on weekends. ✉ *C. Alderete 7, Plaza Tetuan* ☎ *952/901791* 🌐 *www.townhouse.nu* *9 rooms* *In-hotel: bar* ▭ *MC, V.*

NIGHTLIFE AND THE ARTS

Art exhibits are held in private galleries and in several of Marbella's leading hotels, notably the Puente Romano.

Fodor's Choice ★ Much of the nighttime action revolves around the **Puerto Banús**, in such bars as Sinatra's and Joy's Bar. Marbella's most famous nightspot is the **Olivia Valére disco** (✉ *Ctra. de Istán, Km 0.8* ☎ *952/828861*), decorated to resemble a Moorish palace; head inland from the town's mosque (it's easy to spot).

The trendy **Dreamers** (✉ *CN 340 km, Puerto Banús* ☎ *952/812080*) attracts a young, streetwise crowd with its live bands, international DJs, and massive dance space. The **Casino Nueva Andalucía** (✉ *Bajos Hotel Andalucía Pl., N340* ☎ *952/814000*), open 8 PM–6 AM May–October (until 5 AM November–April), is a chic gambling spot in the Hotel Andalucía Plaza, just west of Puerto Banús. Jacket and tie are required for men and passports for all. In the center of Marbella, **Ana María** (✉ *Pl. de Santo Cristo 5* ☎ *952/775646*) is a popular flamenco venue but open only from May to September.

OJÉN

10 km (6 mi) north of Marbella.

For a contrast to the glamour of the coast, drive up to Ojén, in the hills above Marbella. Take note of the beautiful pottery and, if you're here the first week in August, don't miss the **Fiesta de Flamenco,** which attracts some of Spain's most respected flamenco names, including the Juan Peña El Lebrijano, Chiquetete, and El Cabrero. Four kilometers (2½ mi) from Ojén is the **Refugio del Juanar,** a former hunting lodge in the heart of the Sierra Blanca, at the southern edge of the Serranía de Ronda, a mountainous wilderness. A bumpy trail takes you a mile from the Refugio to the **Mirador** (lookout), with a sweeping view of the Costa del Sol and the coast of North Africa.

GETTING HERE AND AROUND

Approximately a dozen buses that leave from the Marbella main bus station for Ojén.

ESSENTIALS

Bike Rental Contact Monte Aventura (✉ *Pl. de Andalucía 1, Ojén* ☎ *952/881519* 🌐 *www.monteaventura.com*).

WHERE TO STAY

$$ **Castillo de Monda**. Designed to resemble a castle, this hotel incorporates the ruins of Monda's Moorish fortress, some of which date back to the 8th century. The interior is decorated with ceramic tiles, elaborate arches, and extensive use of Moorish-style stucco bas-relief. Guest rooms are sumptuous and fun, with four-poster beds, heated marble bathroom floors, and colorful fabrics. Several have a private Jacuzzi and sauna. The main restaurant ($$–$$$), which resembles a medieval banquet hall, has terrific views of the countryside, while the library with fireplace is wonderfully inviting in cooler months. **Pros:** theatrical feel; pretty village. **Cons:** inconvenient for the beach; rather formal. ✉ *El Castillo s/n,Monda* ☎ *952/457142* 🌐 *www.mondacastle.*

com 17 *rooms, 6 suites* *In-room: a/c, DVD, Internet. In-hotel: restaurant, bar, pool, Wi-Fi hotspot, parking (free)* *AE, MC, V.*

$\$–\$\$\$ **Refugio del Juanar.** Once an aristocratic hunting lodge (King Alfonso XIII came here), this secluded hotel and restaurant was sold to its staff in 1984 for the symbolic sum of 1 peseta. The hunting theme prevails, both in the common areas—where a log fire roars in winter—and on the restaurant menu ($–$$), where game is emphasized. The rooms are simply decorated, and six (including the three suites) have a fireplace. Good deals can usually be found, out of season, on the Web site. **Pros:** superb for hikers; traditional Andalusian decor. **Cons:** can seem very cut off; a long way from the coast. *Sierra Blanca s/n* *952/881000* *www.juanar.com* *23 rooms, 3 suites* *In-room: a/c. In-hotel: restaurant, tennis court, pool, Internet terminal* *AE, DC, MC, V.*

ESTEPONA

17 km (11 mi) west of San Pedro de Alcántara, 22 km (13 mi) west of Marbella.

Estepona is a pleasant and relatively tranquil seaside resort, despite being surrounded by an ever-increasing number of urban developments. The beach, more than 1 km (½ mi) long, has better-quality sand than the Costa norm, and the promenade is lined with well-kept, aromatic flower gardens. The gleaming white **Puerto Deportivo** is lively and packed with bars and restaurants, serving everything from fresh fish to Chinese food. Back from the main Avenida de España, the old quarter of cobbled narrow streets and squares is surprisingly unspoiled.

GETTING HERE AND AROUND

Buses run every half hour from 6:40 AM to 10:40 PM from Marbella to Estepona. The town is compact enough to make most places accessible via foot.

ESSENTIALS

Bus Contact **Bus Station** (*Av. de España* *952/800249*).

Visitor Information **Estepona** (*Av. San Lorenzo* *952/802002*).

WHERE TO EAT AND STAY

$\$–\$\$\$ SPANISH **Alcaría de Ramos.** José Ramos, a winner of Spain's National Gastronomy Prize, opened this restaurant in the El Paraíso complex, between Estepona and San Pedro de Alcántara, and has watched it garner an enthusiastic following as his two sons followed in his culinary footsteps. Try the ensalada *de lentejas con salmón ahumado* (salad with lentils and smoked salmon) followed by *el pato asado con pure de manzana y col roja* (grilled duck with red cabbage and apple puree), but leave room for the exemplary crepes Suzette or the equally irresistible fried ice cream with raspberry sauce. *Urbanización El Paraíso, Ctra. N340, Km 167* *952/886178* *MC, V* *Closed Sun. No lunch.*

$–$$ MEDITERRANEAN **Puro Beach.** This luxurious beach club and restaurant has all the trendy trappings: white canopied beach beds, exotic Oriental-themed decor, a glossy marbled spa, hip young waitstaff, and de rigueur chill-out music. The restaurant menu offers seafood dishes and meatier fare, including the popular Puro burger. Lighter options include a sashimi platter and an Asian beef salad with Thai noodles. Desserts range from the familiar (brownies and cheesecake) to more interesting options like bourbon panacotta with tropical fruit. Cocktails are a specialty and the classic Puro pina colada is a deliciously decadent frothy concoction. ✉ *Laguna Village, Pl. El Padrón* ☎ *951/316699* 🌐 *www.purobeach.com* ▭ *MC, V* ⊙ *Closed Nov.–Apr.*

$$$ ★ **Albero Lodge.** Owner Myriam Perez Torres's love for travel infuses this boutique hotel, where each room is named after a well-known city, with decor to match. Exotic Fez has rich fabrics and colors; European rooms, such as Florence and Berlin, are elegantly decorated with antiques; the New York room is dramatic, with a black-and-white theme. There are private terraces, and a sandy path leads to the beach. Myriam can arrange hiking, horseback riding, and boat trips, as well as therapeutic massages. **Pros:** funky decor; friendly owner. **Cons:** breakfast is €10 extra; no bar or restaurant. ✉ *Urb. Finca La Cancelada, Calle Támesis 16* ☎ *952/880700* 🌐 *www.alberolodge.com* *9 rooms* *In-hotel: pool* ▭ *AE, DC, MC, V.*

$$$–$$$$ **Kempinski.** This luxury resort between the coastal highway and the beach looks like a cross between a Moroccan casbah and the Hanging Gardens of Babylon: tropical gardens, with a succession of large swimming pools, meander down to the beach. The rooms are spacious, modern, and luxurious, with faux–North African furnishings and balconies overlooking the Mediterranean. Nightly live music can be enjoyed during the summer at the hotel's La Brisa Italian restaurant. **Pros:** great beachside location, excellent facilities. **Cons:** no shops or nightlife within walking distance. ✉ *Pl. El Padrón, Ctra. N340, Km 159* ☎ *952/809500* 🌐 *www.kempinski-spain.com* *132 rooms, 15 suites* *In-room: a/c, Internet, Wi-Fi. In-hotel: 4 restaurants, pools, gym, children's programs (ages 5–12), laundry service, parking (free), some pets allowed* ▭ *AE, DC, MC, V* *BP.*

CASARES

20 km (12 mi) northwest of Estepona.

The mountain village of Casares lies high above Estepona in the Sierra Bermeja, with streets of ancient white houses piled one on top of the other perch on the slopes beneath a ruined but impressive Moorish castle. The heights afford stunning views over orchards, olive groves, and cork woods to the Mediterranean, sparkling in the distance.

WHERE TO EAT

$ SPANISH **Venta Molina.** Hearty home-cooked and inexpensive food is the theme at Venta, where congenial owner Cathy intersperses the traditional menu with tasty surprises like a hot gazpacho soup with artichokes, beans, tomatoes, and egg or goat stew. The vegetables and eggs come from her small farmstead. In a simple whitewashed building, the dining room is pleasantly rustic with dark beams, simply painted furniture, and, in the winter, an open fire. ✉ *Ctra.Casares-Manilva* ☎ *952/894151* ⊙ *Closed Mon.*

CLOSE UP

Olive Oil, the Golden Nectar

Inland from the Costa de Sol's clamor and crowds, the landscape is stunning. Far in the distance, tiny villages cling precariously to the mountainside like a tumble of sugar cubes, while in the foreground, brilliant red poppies and a blaze of yellow mimosa are set against a rippling quilt of cool-green olive trees and burnt-ocher soil.

Up close, most of the trees have dark twisted branches and gnarled trunks, which denote a lifetime that can span more than a century. It's believed that many of the olive trees here are born from seeds of the original crop brought to the Mediterranean shores in the 7th century BC by Greek and Phoenician traders. Since that time, the oil produced has been used for innumerable purposes, ranging from monetary to medicinal.

These days, the benefits of olive oil are well known, but the locals don't need convincing. Olive oil has long been an integral part of the traditional cuisine and is used lavishly in every meal, including breakfast—when the country bars fill up with old men wearing flat caps, starting their day with coffee, brandy, and black tobacco along with slabs of toasted white bread generously laden with olive oil, garlic, and salt.

Spain's most southerly province produces a copious 653 metric tons of olive oil each year, or 90% of the entire country's output. The area currently exports to more than 95 countries, with the main buyers of bulk oil being Italy, France, Germany, Portugal, and the United Kingdom. The type and grade of oil varies according to the destination. Some oils taste sweet and smooth; others have great body and character and varying intensities of bitterness. North Americans like their oil to be light, with little distinctive taste, while Mexicans prefer olive oil that is dark and strong.

It has been years since medical journals revealed that people living in the southern Mediterranean countries had the lowest incidence of heart disease in the Western world, which led to increased use of olive oil throughout the West, not only for salad dressing but also as a healthy and tasty substitute for butter and vegetable oil in almost every aspect of cooking—except, that is, as a spread for toast; it may take several decades more before olive oil becomes standard breakfast fare anywhere else but in rural Andalusia!

TARIFA

Fodor's Choice ★ *35 km (21 mi) west of San Roque.*

Tarifa, on the Straits of Gibraltar at the southernmost tip of mainland Europe—where the Mediterranean and the Atlantic meet—has become Europe's biggest wind- and kite-surfing center. One of the earliest Moorish settlements in Spain, strong winds kept it off the tourist maps for years but have ultimately proven a source of wealth: the vast wind farm on the surrounding hills creates electricity, and the wide, white-sand beaches stretching north of the town have become a huge attraction. As a result, the town has continued to grow and prosper. Downtown cafés, which not that long ago were filled with men playing dominoes and drinking *anís*, now serve croissants with their *café con leche* and make fancy tapas for a cosmopolitan crowd.

Tarifa's 10th-century **castle** is famous for the siege of 1292, when the defender Guzmán el Bueno refused to surrender even though the attacking Moors threatened to kill his captive son. In defiance, he flung his own dagger down to them, shouting, "Here, use this," or something to that effect (they did indeed kill his son). The Spanish military turned the castle over to the town in the mid-1990s, and it now has a **museum** on Guzmán and the sacrifice of his son. ☒ €1.50 ⊘ Tues.–Sun. 10–2 and 4–6.

Ten kilometers (6 mi) north of Tarifa on the Atlantic coast are the Roman ruins of **Baelo Claudia**, once a thriving production center of *garum*, a salty fish paste appreciated in Rome. ☎ 956/688530 ☒ Free ⊘ July–mid-Sept., Tues.–Sat. 10–6, Sun. 10–2; mid-Sept.–June, Tues.–Sat. 10–5, Sun. 10–2.

WHERE TO STAY

$ 🏨 **Convento de San Francisco.** The rooms here are comfortable and attractive, with exposed stone walls and arches, but the main draw is the setting: a restored 17th-century convent in the spectacular village of Vejer, just west of Tarifa, overlooking the coast. The original cloisters are quite lovely, lined with plants and bench seating for those in a reflective mood. Breakfast is served in the former refectory, now a restaurant specializing in traditional Andalusian cuisine. **Pros:** great location in the center of the village; friendly owners. **Cons:** rooms rather bare; it's a long way from the beach. ☒ La Plazuela ☎ 956/451001 ⊕ www.tugasa.com ♨ 25 rooms ⚷ In-hotel: restaurant, Wi-Fi hotspot ☰ MC, V.

$$$ 🏨 **Hurricane Hotel.** One of the best loved hip hotels on this stretch of coastline, the Hurricane is surrounded by lush subtropical gardens and fronts on the beach. It's famous for its Club Mistral wind- and kite-surfing school, and its horse-riding center. Rooms are light and simply furnished in upbeat rustic style with lots of white, cream, and natural terra-cotta tiling. The restaurant gets rave reviews. **Pros:** hip and sophisticated atmosphere; excellent restaurant. **Cons:** 6 km from Tarifa proper; rooms quite plain. ☒ Ctra. 340, Km 78, Tarifa ☎ 956/684919 ⊕ www.hotelhurricane.com ♨ 28 rooms, 5 suites ⚷ In-hotel: restaurant, bar, pools, gym, beachfront, water sports, bicycles, laundry service, Wi-Fi hotspot, parking (free), some pets allowed ☰ AE, D, DC, MC, V ⭤ BP.

GIBRALTAR

20 km (12 mi) east of Algeciras, 77 km (48 mi) southwest of Marbella.

The Rock is like Britain with a suntan. There are double-decker buses, policemen in helmets, and red mailboxes. Millions of dollars have been spent in developing its tourist potential, and a steady flow of expat Brits comes here from Spain to shop at Morrisons supermarket and High Street shops. The tiny British colony—nicknamed Gib, or simply the Rock—whose impressive silhouette dominates the strait between Spain and Morocco, was one of the two Pillars of Hercules in ancient times, marking the western limits of the known world. Gibraltar today is a

DID YOU KNOW?

Casares is one of the most astmospheric of the pueblos blancos, and is becoming more and more of a tourist destination.

Windsurfing at Tarifa

bizarre anomaly of Moorish, Spanish, and British influences in a prime position commanding the narrow pathway between the Mediterranean Sea and the Atlantic Ocean.

The Moors, headed by Tariq ibn Ziyad, seized the peninsula in 711 preliminary to the conquest of Spain. The Spaniards recaptured Tariq's Rock in 1462. The English, heading an Anglo-Dutch fleet in the War of the Spanish Succession, gained control in 1704, and, after several years of local skirmishes, Gibraltar was finally ceded to Great Britain in 1713 by the Treaty of Utrecht. Spain has been trying to get it back ever since. In 1779 a combined French and Spanish force laid siege to the Rock for three years to no avail. During the Napoléonic Wars, Gibraltar served as Admiral Horatio Nelson's base for the decisive naval Battle of Trafalgar, and during the two World Wars, it served the Allies well as a naval and air base. In 1967 Franco closed the land border with Spain to strengthen his claims over the colony, and it remained closed until 1985.

Britain and Spain have been talking about joint Anglo-Spanish sovereignty, much to the ire of the majority of Gibraltarians, who remain fiercely patriotic to the crown.

GETTING HERE AND AROUND

Andalus Lineas Aereas has daily flights from Madrid to Gibraltar.

There are frequent day tours organized from the Costa del Sol resorts, either via your hotel or any reputable travel agency.

ESSENTIALS

Airline Information Andalus Lineas Aerias (🌐 *www.andalus.es*).

CLOSE UP

A Rocky History

Plenty of places in Spain are culturally a country apart, but Gibraltar is literally so. A little piece of Britain at the bottom of Spain, Gibraltar has an amusing mix of tea-and-biscuits culture paired with the baking sun of its Mediterranean surroundings. This strategic spot, a quick skip into Africa and a perfect point of departure around the base of Europe, has inspired a number of turf wars, ultimately placing it in the hands of the British. Today the relationship is amicable, but in the beginning it was anything but.

Although the Romans ruled the area from 500 BC to AD 475, it was left to the Moors to establish the first settlement here in 1160. The Duke of Medina Sidonia then recaptured the Rock for Spain in 1462. In 1501 Isabella the Catholic declared Gibraltar a crown property, and the following year it received the Royal Warrant that bestowed on it a coat of arms consisting of a castle and a key. In 1704 an Anglo-Dutch force eventually captured Gibraltar, which led to Spain's ceding it to England in 1713.

In 1779, combined Spanish and French forces totaling more than 50,000 troops laid the final Great Siege against a mere 5,000 defenders. The attack highlighted all the unusual problems involved in defending Gibraltar: the great north face of the Rock guarded the entrance, but it seemed impossible to mount guns on it. The answer: tunnels. Of course, the solution had one major problem: cannons are designed to fire up, not down. This problem was circumvented by digging tunnels that sloped downward. Later, in World War II, tunnels were used again to defend Gibraltar. General Dwight D. Eisenhower conducted the Allied invasion of North Africa from one of the tunnels, and all of them remain under military control today.

From 1963 to 1964, Gibraltar's future was debated at the United Nations, but in a referendum on September 10, 1967, which has now become Gibraltar's National Day, 99.9% of Gibraltarians voted to remain part of England. In 1969 this resulted in a new constitution granting self-government. These events severely provoked General Franco, and he closed the coastal border that same year. It stayed closed until February 5, 1985, and Spain occasionally decided to make the crossing more difficult. In 2002, the UK and Spanish governments reached an agreement in principle on joint sovereignty. Another referendum resulted in 99% of Gibraltar's population voting against the idea. Nevertheless, it led to the creation of a tripartite forum that included the Gibraltar government, which is a positive move toward obtaining greater cooperation and recognition between Spain and Gibraltar.

Visitor Information Gibraltar (✉ *Duke of Kent House, Cathedral Sq.* ☎ *200/74950*).

There are likely few places in the world that you enter by walking or driving across an airport runway, but that's what happens in Gibraltar. First you show your passport; then you make your way out onto the narrow strip of land linking Spain's La Linea with Britain's Rock. Unless you have a good reason to take your car—such as loading up on cheap gas or duty-free goodies—you're best off leaving it in a guarded parking area in La Linea, the Spanish border town. Don't bother hanging around here; it's a seedy place. In Gibraltar you can hop on buses and take taxis that expertly maneuver the narrow, congested streets. The Official Rock Tour—conducted either by minibus or, at a greater cost, taxi—takes about 90 minutes and includes all the major sights, allowing you to choose where to come back and linger later. When you call Gibraltar from Spain or another country, prefix the seven-digit telephone number with 00–350. If you're calling from within Gibraltar, note that the former five-digit number is now prefixed by 200. Prices in this section are given in British pounds.

EXPLORING

8 The famous Barbary Apes are a breed of cinnamon-color, tailless monkeys (not apes, despite their name) native to Morocco's Atlas Mountains. Legend holds that as long as they remain in Gibraltar, the British will keep the Rock; Winston Churchill went so far as to issue an order for their preservation when their numbers began to dwindle during World War II. They are publicly fed twice daily, at 8 and 4, at **Apes' Den**, a rocky area down Old Queens Road near the Wall of Carlos V. Among the monkeys' mischievous talents are their grabbing of food, purses, and cameras.

9 ★ You can reach St. Michael's Cave—or ride all the way to the top of Gibraltar—on a **cable car**. The car doesn't go high off the ground, but the views of Spain and Africa from the Rock's pinnacle are superb. It leaves from a station at the southern end of Main Street. *Cable car £8 round-trip* *Daily 9:30–5:45.*

1 **Casemates Square**, in the northern part of town, is Gibraltar's social hub. It has been pedestrianized, and there are plenty of places to sit with a drink and watch the world go by. There's a **tourist office** (*200/50762* *Weekdays 9–5:30, weekends 10–4*) branch here, as well as the **Gibraltar Crystal** company, where you can watch the glassblowers at work.

4 **Catalan Bay**, a fishing village founded by Genoese settlers, is now a resort on the eastern shores. The massive water catchments once supplied the colony's drinking water. *From Rock's eastern side, go left down Devil's Tower Rd. as you enter Gibraltar.*

13 From **Europa Point**, have a look across the straits to Morocco, 23 km (14 mi) away. You're now standing on one of the two ancient Pillars of Hercules. In front of you, the lighthouse has dominated the meeting place of the Atlantic and the Mediterranean since 1841; sailors can see its light from a distance of 27 km (17 mi). Construction is under way here for a new commercial complex with restaurants and bars. *Continue along coast road to Rock's southern tip.*

5 The dignified Regency architecture of Great Britain blends well with the shutters, balconies, and patios of southern Spain in colorful, congested **Gibraltar town**. Shops, restaurants, and pubs beckon on Main Street; at the Governor's Residence, the ceremonial Changing of the Guard takes place six times a year and the Ceremony of the Keys takes place twice a year. Make sure you see the Law Courts, where the famous case of the sailing ship *Mary Celeste* was heard in 1872; the Anglican

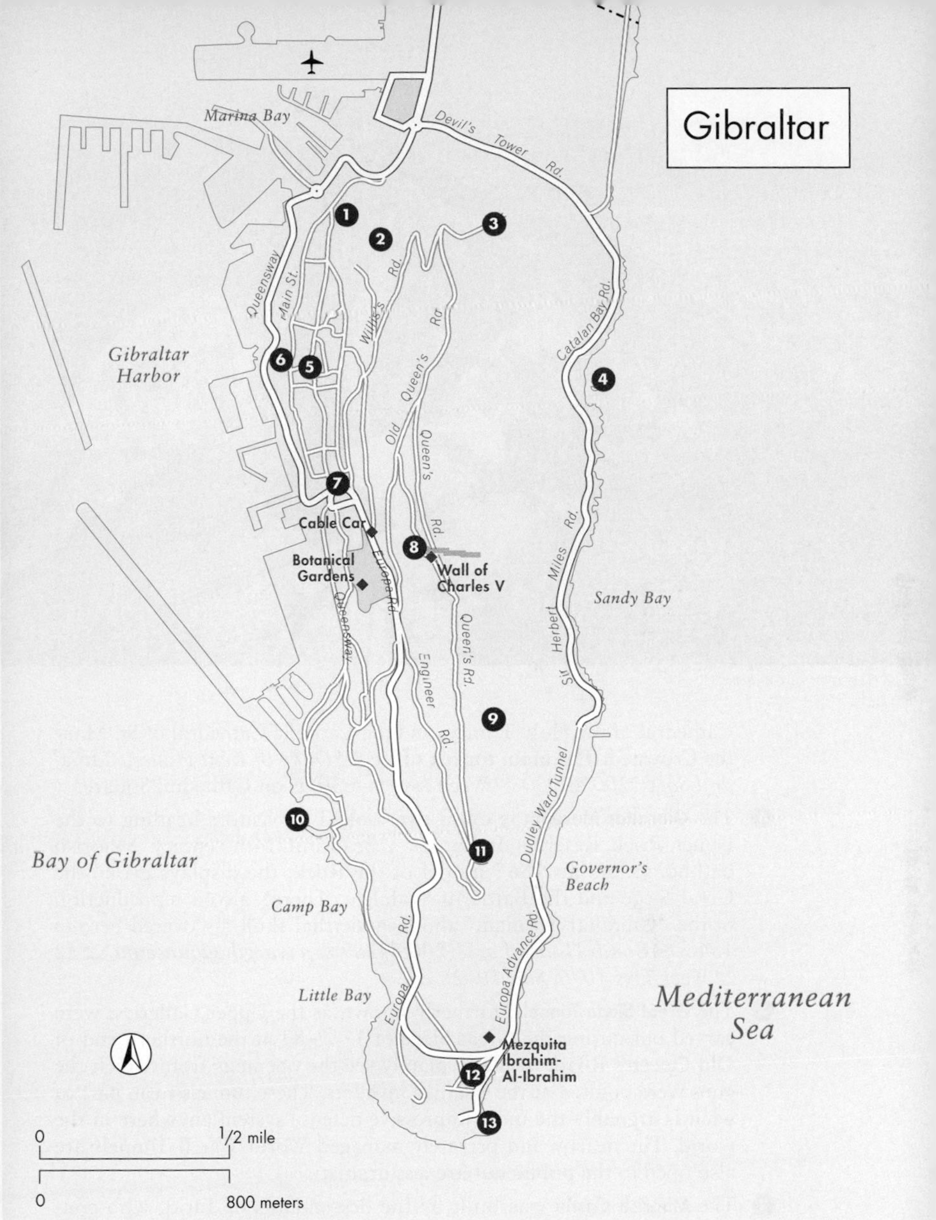

Apes' Den **8**
Casemates Square **1**
Catalan Bay **4**
Europa Point **13**
Gibraltar Museum **6**
Gibraltar Town **5**
Great Siege Tunnels **3**
Moorish Castle 2
Nefusot Yehuda Synagogue **7**
Rosia Bay **10**
Shrine of Our Lady of Europe **12**
St. Michael's Cave **9**
Upper Rock Nature Reserve 11

The rock of Gibraltar

Cathedral of the Holy Trinity; and the Catholic Cathedral of St. Mary the Crowned. The **main tourist office** (✉ *Duke of Kent House, Cathedral Sq.* ☎ *200/45000* ⏲ *Weekdays 9–5:30*) is on Cathedral Square.

❻ The **Gibraltar Museum** is often overlooked by visitors heading to the Upper Rock Reserve. It houses a beautiful 14th-century Moorish bathhouse and an 1865 model of the Rock; the displays evoke the Great Siege and the Battle of Trafalgar. There's also a reproduction of the "Gibraltar Woman," the Neanderthal skull discovered here in 1848. ✉ *Bomb House La.* ☎ *200/74289* 🌐 *www.gib.gi/museum* 🎫 *£2* ⏲ *Weekdays 10–6, Sat. 10–2.*

❸ The **Great Siege Tunnels**, formerly known as the Upper Galleries, were carved out during the Great Siege of 1779–82 at the northern end of Old Queen's Road. You can plainly see the openings from which the guns were pointed at the Spanish invaders. These tunnels form part of what is arguably the most impressive defense system anywhere in the world. The nearby and privately managed World War II Tunnels are also open to the public but are less dramatic.

❷ The **Moorish Castle** was built by the descendants of Tariq, who conquered the Rock in 711. The present Tower of Homage dates from 1333, and its besieged walls bear the scars of stones from medieval catapults (and, later, cannonballs). Admiral George Rooke hoisted the British flag from its summit when he captured the Rock in 1704, and it has flown here ever since. The castle is on Willis's Road but may be viewed from outside only.

7 The 18th-century **Nefusot Yehuda Synagogue**, on Line Wall Road, is one of the oldest synagogues on the Iberian Peninsula, dating back to 1724. There are guided tours twice a day at 12:30 and 2:30, accompanied by a short history of the Gibraltar Jewish community. ☎ *200/78804*.

10 There are fine views to be had if you drive up above **Rosia Bay**. The bay was where Nelson's flagship, HMS *Victory*, was towed after the Battle of Trafalgar in 1805. On board were the dead, who were buried in Trafalgar Cemetery on the southern edge of town—except for Admiral Nelson, whose body was returned to England, preserved in a barrel of rum. ✉ *From Europa Flats, follow Queensway back along Rock's western slopes.*

12 To the north of the lighthouse is the **Shrine of Our Lady of Europe**, venerated by seafarers since 1462. Once a mosque, the small Catholic chapel has a small museum with a 1462 statue of the Virgin and some documents. ✉ *Just north of Europa Point and lighthouse, along Rock's southern tip* *Free* *Weekdays 10–7.*

9 **St. Michael's Cave** is the largest of Gibraltar's 150 caves. A series of underground chambers full of stalactites and stalagmites, it's an ideal performing-arts venue. The skull of a Neanderthal woman (now in the British Museum) was found at nearby Forbes Quarry eight years before the world-famous discovery in Germany's Neander Valley in 1856; nobody paid much attention to it at the time, which is why the prehistoric race is called Neanderthals rather than *Homo calpensis* (literally, "Gibraltar Man," after the Romans' name for the Rock, *Calpe*). ✉ *Queen's Rd.*

11 The **Upper Rock Nature Preserve**, accessible from Jews' Gate, includes St. Michael's Cave, the Apes' Den, the Great Siege Tunnels, the Moorish Castle, and the Military Heritage Center, which chronicles the British regiments who have served on the Rock. ✉ *From Rosia Bay, drive along Queensway and Europa Rd. as far as Casino, above Alameda Gardens. Makesharp right here, up Engineer Rd. to Jews' Gate, a lookout over docks and Bay of Gibraltar toward Algeciras* *£8, includes all attractions, plus £1.50 per vehicle* *Daily 9–6:15.*

WHERE TO EAT AND STAY

$ BRITISH ✕ **Sacarello's**. Right off Main Street, this dining spot is as well known for its excellent coffee and cakes as it is for the rest of its food. There's a lavish salad buffet, as well as filled baked potatoes; panfried noodles with broccoli, mussels, and chicken; and rack of lamb with wine and fine herbs. Top your meal off with a specialty coffee with cream and vanilla. The restaurant has several warmly decorated rooms with cozy corners, dark-wood furnishings, and low-beamed ceilings. The whole place has an old-fashioned English feel. ✉ *57 Irish Town* ☎ *200/70625* *MC, V* *No dinner Sun.*

$–$$ MEDITERRANEAN ✕ **14 On the Quay.** One of the Rock's more sophisticated new restaurants, 14 On the Quay is appropriately located in Queensway Quay, which is less brash than nearby, newer Ocean Village. The menu changes with the seasons, but starters like lemon risotto with seared scallops and mains among the likes of roasted loin of wild boar with the classic British bubble and squeak are all served on locally produced exquisite crystal plates. Desserts such as the creamy malt-flavored mousse with a chocolate crust and shortbread are sublime. ✉ *Queensway, Quay Marina* ☎ *200/43731* 🌐 *MC, V.*

$$ **Bristol.** This stately, colonial-style hotel in the heart of town has splendid views of the bay and the cathedral. The public spaces are spacious and comfortable, especially the downstairs lounge, which exudes an air of faded elegance with graceful chandeliers and soft sofas. The rooms are carpeted throughout, and the overall color scheme is a warm burgundy and cream, which might feel a bit stifling in midsummer; luckily, the tropical garden is a cool haven. **Pros:** superb location near restaurants, shops, and nightlife; comfortable carpeted rooms. **Cons:** hotel exterior dingy; interior needs updating. ✉ *10 Cathedral Sq.* ☎ *200/76800* 🌐 *www.bristolhotel.gi* *60 rooms* *In-room: a/c. In-hotel: bar, pool, parking (free), Wi-Fi hotspot* *AE, DC, MC, V.*

$$$$ **O'Callaghan Eliott.** If you want to stay at the slickest and most modern of the Rock's hotels, try this one right in the center of the town. Ask for a room at the top of the hotel, with a view over the Bay of Gibraltar; failing that, check out the rooftop pool. The bar hosts live jazz Thursday evenings. **Pros:** views of either marina or the Rock; well located for pubs and restaurants. **Cons:** very business-traveler oriented; fee for Wi-Fi. ✉ *2 Governor's Parade* ☎ *200/70500* 🌐 *www.ocallaghanhotels.com* *106 rooms, 8 suites* *In-room: a/c, Internet, Wi-Fi. In-hotel: 2 restaurants, bars, pool, gym* *AE, DC, MC, V* *BP.*

$$$$ **The Rock.** This hotel overlooking the straits first opened in 1932, and although furnishings in the rooms and restaurants are elegant and colorful, they still preserve something of the English colonial style: bamboo, ceiling fans, and a terrace bar covered with wisteria. There are various whimsical touches, like plastic ducks in the bath and toy-monkey key rings, plus more thoughtful touches, like complimentary tea, coffee, and biscuits. The buffet breakfast is lavish, including the typical English fry-up of eggs, bacon, sausages, mushrooms, tomatoes, and baked beans. **Pros:** old-fashioned excellent service; magnificent Gibraltar bay views. **Cons:** inconvenient for High Street shopping; conservative decor. ✉ *3 Europa Rd.* ☎ *200/73000* 🌐 *www.rockhotelgibraltar.com* *101 rooms, 2 suites* *In-room: a/c, Internet, Wi-Fi. In-hotel: restaurant, bar, pool* *AE, DC, MC, V* *BP.*

NIGHTLIFE

Lord Nelson (✉ *Casemates Square* ☎ *200/50009*), a restaurant during the day but a lively bar at night, has live bands—ranging from jazz and blues to rock—on Friday and Saturday, starting at about 10 PM.

SPORTS AND THE OUTDOORS

Bird- and dolphin-watching, diving, and fishing are popular activities on the Rock. For details on tours and outfitters, visit the Gibraltar government Web site's "On Holiday" page (🌐 *www.gibraltar.gov.uk*) or call the local tourist office (☎ *200/745000*).

VOCABULARY

ENGLISH	SPANISH	PRONUNCIATION

BASICS

Hello	Hola	**oh**-la
Yes/no	Sí/no	see/no
Please	Por favor	pohr fah-**vohr**
May I?	¿Me permite?	meh pehr-**mee**-teh
Thank you (very much)	(Muchas) gracias	(**moo**-chas) **grah**-see-as
You're welcome	De nada	deh **nah**-dah
Excuse me	Con permiso/perdón	con pehr-**mee**-so/ pehr-**dohn**
Pardon me/ what did you say?	¿Perdón?/Mande?	pehr-**dohn/mahn**-deh
Could you tell me . . . ?	¿Podría decirme . . . ?	po-**dree**-ah deh-**seer**-meh
I'm sorry	Lo siento	lo see-**en**-to
Good morning!	¡Buenos días!	**bway**-nohs **dee**-ahs
Good afternoon!	¡Buenas tardes!	**bway**-nahs **tar**-dess
Good evening!	¡Buenas noches!	**bway**-nahs **no**-chess
Goodbye!	¡Adiós!/ ¡Hasta luego!	ah-dee-**ohss/ ah**-stah-**lwe**-go
Mr./Mrs.	Señor/Señora	sen-**yor**/sen-**yohr**-ah
Miss	Señorita	sen-yo-**ree**-tah
Pleased to meet you	Mucho gusto	**moo**-cho **goose**-to
How are you?	¿Cómo está usted?	**ko**-mo es-**tah** oo-**sted**
Very well, thank you.	Muy bien, gracias.	**moo**-ee bee-**en, grah**-see-as
And you?	¿Y usted?	ee oos-**ted**
Hello (on the phone)	Diga	**dee**-gah

DAYS OF THE WEEK

Sunday	domingo	doh-**meen**-goh
Monday	lunes	**loo**-ness
Tuesday	martes	**mahr**-tess
Wednesday	miércoles	me-**air**-koh-less
Thursday	jueves	hoo-**ev**-ess
Friday	viernes	vee-**air**-ness

Saturday	sábado	**sah**-bah-doh

NUMBERS

1	un, uno	oon, **oo**-no
2	dos	dohs
3	tres	tress
4	cuatro	**kwah**-tro
5	cinco	**sink**-oh
6	seis	saice
7	siete	see-**et**-eh
8	ocho	**o**-cho
9	nueve	new-**eh**-veh
10	diez	dee-**es**
11	once	**ohn**-seh
12	doce	**doh**-seh
13	trece	**treh**-seh
14	catorce	ka-**tohr**-seh
15	quince	**keen**-seh
16	dieciséis	dee-**es**-ee-**saice**
17	diecisiete	dee-**es**-ee-see-**et**-eh
18	dieciocho	dee-**es**-ee-**o**-cho
19	diecinueve	dee-**es**-ee-new-**ev**-eh
20	veinte	**vain**-teh
21	veinte y uno/ veintiuno	**vain**-te-oo-noh
30	treinta	**train**-tah
32	treinta y dos	train-tay-**dohs**
40	cuarenta	kwah-**ren**-tah
50	cincuenta	seen-**kwen**-tah
60	sesenta	sess-**en**-tah
70	setenta	set-**en**-tah
80	ochenta	oh-**chen**-tah
90	noventa	no-**ven**-tah
100	cien	see-**en**
200	doscientos	doh-see-**en**-tohss
500	quinientos	keen-**yen**-tohss
1,000	mil	meel
2,000	dos mil	dohs meel

USEFUL PHRASES

Do you speak English?	¿Habla usted inglés?	**ah**-blah oos-**ted** in-**glehs**
I don't speak Spanish	No hablo español	no **ah**-bloh es-pahn-**yol**
I don't understand (you)	No entiendo	no en-tee-**en**-doh
I understand (you)	Entiendo	en-tee-**en**-doh
I don't know	No sé	no seh
I am American/ British	Soy americano (americana)/ inglés(a)	soy ah-meh-ree-**kah**-no (ah-meh-ree-**kah**-nah)/in-**glehs**(ah)
My name is . . .	Me llamo . . .	meh **yah**-moh
Yes, please/ No, thank you	Sí, por favor/ No, gracias	**see** pohr fah-**vor**/ no **grah**-see-ahs
Yesterday/today/ tomorrow	Ayer/hoy/mañana	ah-**yehr**/oy/mahn-**yah**-nah
This morning/ afternoon	Esta mañana/tarde	**es**-tah mahn-**yah**-nah/**tar**-deh
Tonight	Esta noche	**es**-tah **no**-cheh
This/Next week	Esta semana/ la semana que entra	**es**-tah seh-**mah**-nah/lah seh-**mah**-nah keh **en**-trah
This/Next month	Este mes/el próximo mes	**es**-teh mehs/el **prok**-see-moh mehs
How?	¿Cómo?	**koh**-mo
When?	¿Cuándo?	**kwahn**-doh
What?	¿Qué?	keh
What is this?	¿Qué es esto?	keh es **es**-toh
Why?	¿Por qué?	por **keh**
Who?	¿Quién?	kee-**yen**
Where is . . . ?	¿Dónde está . . . ?	**dohn**-deh es-**tah**
the train station?	la estación del tren?	la es-tah-see-**on** del **train**
the subway station?	la estación del metro?	la es-ta-see-**on** del **meh**-tro
the bus stop?	la parada del autobus?	la pah-**rah**-dah del oh-toh-**boos**
the bank?	el banco?	el **bahn**-koh
the hotel?	el hotel?	el oh-**tel**
the post office?	la oficina de correos?	la oh-fee-**see**-nah deh-koh-**reh**-os
the museum?	el museo?	el moo-**seh**-oh
the hospital?	el hospital?	el ohss-pee-**tal**
the bathroom?	el baño?	el **bahn**-yoh

Here/there	Aquí/allá	ah-**key**/ah-**yah**
Open/closed	Abierto/cerrado	ah-bee-**er**-toh/ ser-**ah**-doh
Left/right	Izquierda/derecha	iss-key-**er**-dah/ dare-**eh**-chah
Straight ahead	Todo recto	**toh**-doh-**rec**-toh
Is it near/far?	¿Está cerca/lejos?	es-**tah sehr**-kah/ **leh**-hoss
I'd like . . . a room the key a newspaper a stamp	Quisiera . . . una habitación la llave un periódico un sello	kee-see-**ehr**-ah **oo**-nah ah-bee-tah-see-**on** lah **yah**-veh oon pehr-ee-**oh**-dee-koh **say**-oh
How much is this?	¿Cuánto cuesta?	**kwahn**-toh **kwes**-tah
A little/a lot	Un poquito/ mucho	oon poh-**kee**-toh/ **moo**-choh
More/less	Más/menos	mahss/**men**-ohss
I am ill	Estoy enfermo(a)	es-**toy** en-**fehr**-moh(mah)
Please call a doctor	Por favor llame un médico	pohr fah-**vor ya**-meh oon **med**-ee-koh
Help!	¡Ayuda!	ah-**yoo**-dah

ON THE ROAD

Avenue	Avenida	ah-ven-**ee**-dah
Broad, tree-lined boulevard	Paseo	pah-**seh**-oh
Highway	Carretera	car-reh-**ter**-ah
Port; mountain pass	Puerto	poo-**ehr**-toh
Street	Calle	**cah**-yeh
Waterfront promenade	Paseo marítimo	pah-**seh**-oh mahr-**ee**-tee-moh

IN TOWN

Cathedral	Catedral	cah-teh-**dral**
Church	Iglesia	**tem**-plo/ee-**glehs**-see-ah
City hall, town hall	Ayuntamiento	ah-yoon-tah-me-**yen**-toh
Door, gate	Puerta	poo-**ehr**-tah
Main square	Plaza Mayor	plah-thah mah-**yohr**
Market	Mercado	mer-**kah**-doh

Neighborhood	Barrio	**bahr**-ree-o
Tavern, rustic restaurant	Mesón	meh-**sohn**
Traffic circle, roundabout	Glorieta	glor-ee-**eh**-tah
Wine cellar, wine bar, wine shop	Bodega	boh-**deh**-gah

DINING OUT

A bottle of . . .	Una botella de . . .	**oo**-nah bo-**teh**-yah deh
A glass of . . .	Un vaso de . . .	oon **vah**-so deh
Bill/check	La cuenta	lah **kwen**-tah
Breakfast	El desayuno	el deh-sah-**yoon**-oh
Dinner	La cena	lah **seh**-nah
Menu of the day	Menú del día	meh-**noo** del **dee**-ah
Fork	El tenedor	ehl ten-eh-**dor**
Is the tip included?	¿Está incluida la propina?	es-**tah** in-cloo-**ee**-dah lah pro-**pee**-nah
Knife	El cuchillo	el koo-**chee**-yo
Large portion of tapas	Ración	rah-see-**ohn**
Lunch	La comida	lah koh-**mee**-dah
Menu	La carta, el menú	lah **cart**-ah, el meh-**noo**
Napkin	La servilleta	lah sehr-vee-**yet**-ah
Please give me . . .	Por favor déme . . .	pohr fah-**vor deh**-meh
Spoon	Una cuchara	**oo**-nah koo-**chah**-rah

MENU GUIDE

STARTERS

aguacate con gambas avocado and prawns
caldo thick soup
champiñones al ajillo mushrooms in garlic
consomé clear soup
gazpacho chilled soup made with tomatoes, onions, peppers, cucumbers, and oil
huevos flamencos eggs with spicy sausage and tomato
judías con tomate/jamón green beans with tomato/ham
sopa soup
sopa de ajo garlic soup
sopa de garbanzos chickpea soup
sopa de lentejas lentil soup
sopa de mariscos shellfish soup
sopa sevillana soup made with mayonnaise, shellfish, asparagus, and peas

OMELETS (TORTILLAS)

tortilla de champiñones mushroom omelet
tortilla de gambas prawn omelet
tortilla de mariscos seafood omelet
tortilla de patatas, tortilla española Spanish potato omelet
tortilla francesa plain omelet
tortilla sacromonte (in Granada) omelet with ham, sausage, and peas

MEATS (CARNES)

beicón bacon
bistec steak
cerdo pork
lomo de cerdo pork tenderloin
cabrito roasted kid
chorizo seasoned sausage
chuleta chop, cutlet
cochinillo suckling pig
cordero lamb
filete steak
jamón ham
jamón de York cooked ham
jamón serrano cured raw ham
morcilla blood sausage
salchicha sausage
salchichón Spanish salami (cured pork sausage)
solomillo de ternera fillet of beef
ternera veal

POULTRY (AVES) AND GAME (CAZA)

conejo rabbit
cordonices quail
faisán pheasant
jabalí wild boar
oca, ganso goose
pato duck
pato salvaje wild duck
pavo turkey
perdiz partridge
pollo chicken

ORGAN MEATS

callos tripe
criadillas bull's testicles (shown on Spanish menus as "unmentionables")
hígado liver
lengua tongue
mollejas sweetbreads
riñones kidneys
sesos brains

FISH (PESCADOS)

ahumados smoked fish (i.e. trout, eel, salmon)
anchoas anchovies
anguila eel
angulas baby eel
atún, bonito tuna
bacalao salt cod
besugo sea bream
boquerones fresh anchovies
lenguado sole
lubina sea bass
merluza hake, whitefish
mero grouper fish
pez espada, emperador swordfish
rape angler fish
raya skate
salmón salmon
salmonete red mullet
sardina sardine
trucha trout

SHELLFISH AND SEAFOOD (MARISCOS)

almeja clam
calamares squid
cangrejo crab
centolla spider crab
chipirones, chopitos small squid
cigalas crayfish
concha scallops
gambas prawns, shrimp
langosta lobster
langostino prawn
mejillones mussels
ostra oyster
percebes barnacles
pulpo octopus
sepia cuttlefish
vieiras scallop (in Galicia)
zarzuela de mariscos shellfish casserole

VEGETABLES (VERDURAS)

aceituna olive
aguacate avocado
ajo garlic
alcachofa artichoke
apio celery
berenjena eggplant
berza green cabbage
brécol/bróculi broccoli
calabacín zucchini
cebollo onion
calabaza pumpkin
champiñon mushroom
col cabbage
coliflor cauliflower
endivia endive
escarola chicory
ensalada salad
ensaladilla rusa potato salad
espárragos asparagus
espinacas spinach
espinacas a la catalana spinach with garlic, rasins, and pine nuts
garbanzos chickpeas
guisantes peas
habas broad beans
judías dried beans
judías verdes green beans
lechuga lettuce
lenteja lentil
palmitos palm hearts
patata potato
pepinillo gherkin
pepino cucumber
pimientos green/red peppers
puerro leek
seta chanterelle
tomate tomato
verduras green vegetables
zanahoria carrot

FRUIT (FRUTAS)

albaricoque apricot
ananás, piña pineapple
cereza cherry
chirimoya custard apple
ciruela plum
frambuesa raspberry
fresa strawberry
fresón large strawberry
grosella negra black currant
limón lemon
manzana apple
melocotón peach
melón melon
naranja orange
pera pear
plátano banana
sandía watermelon
uvas grapes
zarzamora blackberry

DESSERTS (POSTRES)

bizcocho, galleta biscuit
bizocho de chocolate chocolate cake
buñuelos warm, sugared, deep-fried doughnuts, sometimes cream-filled
con nata with cream
cuajada thick yogurt with honey
ensalada de frutas, macedonia fruit salad
flan caramel custard
fresas con nata strawberries and cream
helado de vainilla, fresa, café, chocolate vanilla, strawberry, coffee, chocolate ice cream
melocotón en almibar canned peaches
pastel cake
pera en almibar canned pears
pijama ice cream with fruit and syrup
piña en almibar canned pineapple

postre de músico dessert of dried fruit and nuts
la tarta de queso cheesecake
tarta helada ice-cream cake
la tartaleta de frutas fruit cake
yogur yogurt

MISCELLANEOUS

a la brasa barbequed
a la parrilla grilled
a la plancha grilled
aceite de oliva olive oil
al horno roasted, baked
arroz rice
asado roast
azúcar sugar
carbonade pot roasted
churros: baton-shaped donuts for dipping in hot chocolate, typically eaten at breakfast.
crudo raw
espaguettis spaghetti
fideos noodles
frito fried
guisado stewed
huevo egg
mahonesa mayonnaise
mantequilla butter
mermelada jam
miel honey
mostaza mustard
pan bread
patatas fritas french fries
perejil parsley
poché poached
queso cheese
relleno filled, stuffed
sal salt
salsa sauce
salsa de tomate catsup
vinagre vinegar

DRINKS (BEBIDAS)

agua water
agua con gas carbonated mineral water
agua sin gas still mineral water
blanco y negro cold black coffee with vanilla ice cream
café con leche coffee with cream
café solo black coffee (espresso)
caliente hot
caña small draught beer
cava, champán sparkling wine, champagne
cerveza beer
chocolate hot chocolate
cuba libre rum and coke
fino very dry sherry
frío/fría cold
gaseosa soda
granizado de limón (de café) lemon (or coffee) on crushed ice
hielo ice
horchata cold summer drink made from ground nuts
jerez sherry
jugo fruit juice
leche milk
limonada lemonade
manzanilla very dry sherry or camomile tea
sidra cider
té tea
con limón with lemon
con leche with milk
vaso glass
un vaso de agua a glass of water
vermut vermouth
vino wine
vino añejo vintage wine
vino blanco white wine
vino dulce sweet wine
vino espumoso sparkling wine
vino rosado rosé
vino seco dry wine
vino tinto red wine
zumo de naranja orange juice

Travel Smart Spain

WORD OF MOUTH

"The AVE is a wonderful thing. Both the trip between Seville and Madrid and Toledo and Madrid were flawless and on time. The trains are comfortable and Atocha station is a marvel (I commute out of North Station in Boston, so if you're familiar with that you'll know that I am green with envy over Atocha!)."

—amyb

"I agree with those who recommend you read through the trip reports in this forum [fodors.com]. They were invaluable in helping plan our recent 10 day trip to Spain."

—screen_name_taken

www.fodors.com/community

GETTING HERE AND AROUND

BY AIR

Flying time from New York to Madrid is about seven hours; from London, it's just over two hours.

Regular nonstop flights serve Spain from many major cities in the eastern United States; flying from other North American cities usually involves a stop. If you're coming from North America and want to land in a city other than Madrid or Barcelona, consider flying a European carrier.

There are a few solid package flight options for travel to and within Spain. If you buy a round-trip transatlantic ticket on Iberia, you might want to purchase an Iberiabono Spain air pass, valid for economy-class travel to 35 destinations across Spain; the period of use corresponds to the time for which your international ticket is valid. The pass must be purchased before you arrive in Spain, and all flights must be booked in advance; the cost starts at €60 per ticket, with a minimum purchase of two. On certain days of the week Iberia also offers *minitarifas* (minifares), which can save you up to 40% on domestic flights. Tickets must be purchased at least two days in advance, and you must stay over Saturday night. Another option is to join the Iberia Plus Internet club, which can offer exceptionally low fares.

The Europe By Air Flight Pass is a unique flat-rate ticket. For $99 or $129 per flight within Europe, and with no minimum purchase, you get access to more than 170 destinations on 20-plus airlines. There are no blackout dates, no charges for reservation charges, and no fare zones, but be aware that these passes are nonrefundable and sold only to non-EU residents.

Air Europa offers a special called "Talonair 20," which allows travelers to choose nonstop flights in coach on any of its domestic routes (except to the Canary Islands, which requires two coupons).

FODORS.COM CONNECTION

Before your trip, be sure to check out what other travelers are saying in the forums on www.fodors.com.

In the past few years there has been a sharp rise in the number of cheap flights from the United Kingdom to Spain on carriers such as Monarch (🌐 *www.flymonarch.com*) and bmi (🌐 *www.flybmi.com*). They provide competition to the market's main players, easyJet (🌐 *www.easyjet.com*) and Ryanair (🌐 *www.ryanair.com*). All these carriers offer frequent flights, cover small cities as well as large ones, and have very competitive fares. Attitude Travel (🌐 *www.attitudetravel.com/lowcostairlines*), Skyscanner (🌐 *www.skyscanner.net*), and Wegolo (🌐 *www.wegolo.com*) are comprehensive search sites for low-cost airlines worldwide.

Contacts Air Europa (☎ *800/238–7672 in U.S., 902/401501 in Spain* 🌐 *www.air-europa.com*). **FlightPass** (☎ *888/321–4737* 🌐 *www.europebyair.com*). **Iberia** (☎ *800/772–4642, 902/400500 in Spain* 🌐 *www.iberia.com*).

Transportation Security Administration (🌐 *www.tsa.gov*) has answers for almost every question that might come up.

AIRPORTS

Most flights from North America land in, or pass through, Madrid's Barajas (MAD). The other major gateway is Barcelona's El Prat de Llobregat (BCN). From England and elsewhere in Europe, regular flights also touch down in Málaga (AGP), Alicante (ALC), Palma de Mallorca (PMI), and many other smaller cities. Many budget airlines flying from the United Kingdom to Barcelona land at the increasingly busy Girona airport, 90 minutes north of Barcelona. Sagalés runs a shuttle bus service between Girona's airport and Barcelona timed for arrivals and departures of Ryanair flights.

Airport Information Madrid–Barajas (☎ *91/305–8343* 🌐 *www.aena.es*). **Barcelona–El Prat de Llobregat** (☎ *902/404704* 🌐 *www.aena.es*). **Girona** (☎ *972/186600*). **Sagalés Buses** (☎ *902/130014* 🌐 *www.sagales.com*).

FLIGHTS

From North America, Air Europa and Spanair fly to Madrid; American, Continental, Delta, Iberia, and USAirways fly to Madrid and Barcelona—some of these airlines use shared facilities and do not operate their own flights. Within Spain, Iberia is the main domestic airline, but Air Europa and Spanair fly most domestic routes at lower prices. The budget airline Vueling heavily promotes its Internet bookings, which are often the country's cheapest domestic flight prices. The further from your travel date you purchase the ticket, the more bargains you're likely to find. Air Europa and Spanair also travel both within Spain and to the rest of Europe.

Iberia runs a shuttle, the *Puente Aereo*, offering flights just over an hour long between Madrid and Barcelona, every 30 minutes (more often during peak travel times) from 7 AM to 11 PM. You don't need to reserve ahead; you can buy your tickets at the airport ticket counter upon arriving or book online at Iberia.com. Passengers can also use the newly installed self-service check-in counters to avoid queues. Puente Aereo departs from Terminal T1 in Barcelona; in Madrid, the shuttle departs from Terminal 4.

Airline Contacts Air Europa (☎ *888/238–7672 in U.S., 902/401501 or 807/505050 in Spain* 🌐 *www.air-europa.com*). **American Airlines** (☎ *800/4337300* 🌐 *www.aa.com*). **Continental Airlines** (☎ *800/523–3273 for U.S. reservations, 800/231–0856 for international reservations* 🌐 *www.continental.com*). **Delta Airlines** (☎ *800/221–1212 for U.S. reservations, 800/241–4141 for international reservations* 🌐 *www.delta.com*). **Iberia** (☎ *800/772–4642* 🌐 *www.iberia.com*). **Northwest Airlines** (☎ *800/225–2525* 🌐 *www.nwa.com*). **Spanair** (☎ *888/545–5757, 902/131415 in Spain* 🌐 *www.spanair.com*). **United Airlines** (☎ *800/864–8331 for U.S. reservations, 900/813996 in Spain* 🌐 *www.united.com*). **USAirways** (☎ *800/428–4322 for U.S. and Canada reservations, 800/622–1015 for international reservations* 🌐 *www.usairways.com*).

Within Spain Air Europa (☎ *902/401501 or 807/505050* 🌐 *www.air-europa.com*). **Iberia** (☎ *902/400500 or 807/123456* 🌐 *www.iberia.com*). **Spanair** (☎ *902/131415 or 807/5051052* 🌐 *www.spanair.com*). **Vueling** (☎ *902/104296 or 807/001717* 🌐 *www.vueling.com*).

BY BIKE

Taking bikes on Spanish intercity trains is restricted to overnight trains (on which bikes go under your bunk). Short-range daytime trains normally accept bicycles, though the conductor may decide that the train's too crowded and bump you and your bike. The very expensive alternative is to courier them. Cycling on freeways is against the law. For bike rentals, contact local tourist offices or check with rural hotels; we list some in individual cities.

BY BOAT

Regular car ferries connect the United Kingdom with northern Spain. Brittany Ferries sails from Plymouth and Portsmouth to Santander; P&O European Ferries sails from Portsmouth to Bilbao. Trasmediterránea and Balearia connect mainland Spain to the Balearic and Canary islands.

Direct ferries from Spain to Tangier leave daily from Tarifa on FRS and from Algeciras on Trasmediterránea. Otherwise, you can take your car either to Ceuta (via Algeciras, on Balearia) or Melilla (via Malaga, on Trasmediterránea), two Spanish enclaves on the North African coast, and then move on to Morocco.

INFORMATION

Balearia (☎ *902/160180* 🌐 *www.balearia.com*).**Brittany Ferries** (☎ *0870/907–6103 in U.K., 94/236–0611 in Spain* 🌐 *www.brittany-ferries.com*). **FRS** (☎ *956/681830* 🌐 *www.frs.es*). **P&O European Ferries** (☎ *0871/664–8005 in U.K., 902/020461 in Spain* 🌐 *www.poferries.com*). **Trasmediterránea** (☎ *902/454645* 🌐 *www.trasmediterranea.com*).

BY BUS

Within Spain, a mix of private companies provides bus service ranging from knee-crunchingly basic to luxurious. Fares are almost always lower than the corresponding train fares, and service covers more towns. Smaller towns don't usually have a central bus depot, so ask the tourist office where to wait for the bus. Note that service is less frequent on weekends. Spain's major national long-haul bus line is Alsa-Enatcar.

For longer trips, you can travel to Spain by modern buses (Eurolines/National EXpress, for example) from European destinations such as London, Paris, Rome, Frankfurt, Prague, and other major European cities. Although it may once have been the case that international bus travel was significantly cheaper than air travel, new budget airlines have changed the equation. For perhaps a little more money and a large savings of travel hours, flying is increasingly the better option.

Most of Spain's larger companies have buses with comfortable seats and adequate legroom; on longer journeys (two hours or more), a movie is shown on board, and earphones are provided. Except on smaller, regional lines, all buses have bathrooms on board; most long-haul buses also usually stop at least once every two to three hours for a snack and bathroom break. Smoking is prohibited on board.

Alsa-Enatcar has two luxury classes in addition to its regular seating. Supra Clase includes roomy leather seats and onboard meals; also, you have the option of *asientos individuales,* individual seats (with no other seat on either side) that line one side of the bus. The next class is the Eurobus, with comfortable seats and plenty of legroom. The Supra Clase and Eurobus usually cost, respectively, up to one-third and one-fourth more than the regular seats.

If you plan to return to your initial destination, you can save by buying a round-trip ticket. Also, some of Spain's smaller, regional bus lines offer multitrip passes, which are worthwhile if you plan to move back and forth between two fixed destinations within the region. Generally, these tickets offer a savings of 20% per journey; you can buy them at the station. The general rule for children is that if they occupy a seat, they pay full fare. Check the bus Web sites for *ofertas* (special offers).

At bus station ticket counters, most major credit cards (except American Express) are accepted. If you buy your ticket on the bus, it's cash only. Big lines such as Enatcar are now encouraging online purchasing. Once your ticket is booked, there's no need to go to the terminal sales desk—it's simply a matter of showing up at the bus with your ticket number and ID. The smaller regional services are increasingly providing online purchasing but will often require that your ticket be picked up at the terminal sales desk.

During peak travel times (Easter, August, and Christmas), it's a good idea to make a reservation at least a week in advance.

INFORMATION

Alsa-Enatcar (☎ *902/422242* 🌐 *www.enatcar.com*). **Eurolines/National Express** (☎ *0871/781–8181* 🌐 *www.eurolines.co.uk*).

Eurolines Spain (☎ *902/405040* 🌐 *www.eurolines.es*).

BY CAR

RENTAL CARS

Alamo, Avis, Budget, Europcar, Hertz, and National (partnered in Spain with the Spanish agency Atesa) have branches at major Spanish airports and in large cities.

Smaller, regional companies and wholesalers offer lower rates. The online outfit Pepe Car has been a big hit with travelers; in general, the earlier you book, the less you pay. Rates run as low as €20 a day, taxes included—but note that pickups at their center-city locations are considerably cheaper than at the airports. All agencies have a range of models, but virtually all cars in Spain have a manual transmission. **TIP→ If you don't want a stick shift, reserve weeks in advance and specify automatic transmission, then call to reconfirm your automatic car before you leave for Spain.** Rates in Madrid begin at the equivalents of U.S. $65 a day and $300 a week for an economy car with air-conditioning, manual transmission, and unlimited mileage plus 16% tax. A small car, aside from saving you money, is prudent for the tiny roads and parking spaces in many parts of Spain.

Anyone over 18 with a valid license can drive in Spain, but some rental agencies will not rent cars to drivers under 21.

Major Agencies Alamo (☎ *877/222–9075* 🌐 *www.alamo.com*). **Avis** (☎ *800/331–1084, 902/135531 in Spain* 🌐 *www.avis.com*). **Budget** (☎ *800/472–3325, 901/201212 in Spain* 🌐 *www.budget.com*). **Europcar** (☎ *902/105030 in Spain* 🌐 *www.europcar.es*). **Hertz** (☎ *800/654–3001, 902/402405 in Spain* 🌐 *www.hertz.com*). **National Car Rental/Atesa** (☎ *800/227–7368, 902/100101 in Spain* 🌐 *www.atesa.es*). **Pepe Car** (☎ *807/414243 in Spain* 🌐 *www.pepecar.com*).

Your own driver's license is valid in Spain, but U.S. citizens are highly encouraged to obtain an International Driving Permit (IDP). The IDP may facilitate car rental and help you avoid traffic fines—it translates your state-issued driver's license into 10 languages so officials can easily interpret the information on it. Permits are available from the American Automobile Association.

Driving is the best way to see Spain's rural areas. The main cities are connected by a network of excellent four-lane divided highways (*autovías* and *autopistas),* which are designated with the letter A and have speed limits—depending on the area—of between 80 KPH (50 MPH) to 120 KPH (74 MPH). If the artery is a tollway ("toll" is *peaje*) it is designated AP. The letter N indicates a *carretera nacional*: a national or intercity route, with local traffic, which may have four or two lanes. Smaller towns and villages are connected by a network of secondary roads maintained by regional, provincial, and local governments, with an alphabet soup of different letter designations.

Spain's network of roads and highways is essentially well maintained and well marked, but bears a lot of traffic, especially during the vacation season and long holiday weekends. Crackdown campaigns on speeding have reduced what used to be a ghastly annual death toll on the roads—but you still need to drive defensively. Be prepared, too, for heavy truck traffic on national routes, which, in the case of two-lane roads, can have you creeping along for hours.

GASOLINE

Gas stations are plentiful, and most on major routes and in big cities are open 24 hours. On less-traveled routes, gas stations are usually open 7 AM–11 PM. Most stations are self-service, though prices are the same as those at full-service stations. At night, however, you must pay before you fill up. Most pumps offer a choice of gas, including unleaded (*gasolina sin plomo*), high octane, and diesel, so be careful to pick the right one for your car. Prices vary little among stations and were at this writing €1.06 a liter for unleaded. A good site to monitor prices is 🌐 *www.aaroadwatch.ie/eupetrolprices*. Credit cards are widely accepted.

PARKING

Parking is, almost without exception, a nightmare in Spanish cities. Don't park where the curb is painted yellow or where there is a yellow line painted a few inches from the curb. No-parking signs are also fairly easy to recognize.

In most cities, there are street-parking spaces marked by blue lines. Look for a nearby machine with a blue-and-white "P" sign to purchase a parking ticket, which you leave inside your car, on the dashboard, before you lock up. Sometimes an attendant will be nearby to answer questions. Parking time limits, fees, and fines vary. Parking lots are available, often underground, but spaces are at a premium. The rule of thumb is to leave your car at your hotel unless absolutely necessary.

ROAD CONDITIONS

Spain's highway system includes some 6,000 km (3,600 mi) of beautifully maintained superhighways. Still, you'll find some stretches of major national highways that are only two lanes wide, where traffic often backs up behind trucks. *Autopista* tolls are steep, but as a result these highways are often less crowded than the free ones. If you're driving down through Catalonia, be aware that there are more tolls here than anywhere else in Spain. This can result in a quicker journey but at a sizable cost. If you spring for the autopistas, you'll find that many of the rest stops are nicely landscaped and have cafeterias with decent but overpriced food.

Most Spanish cities have notoriously long morning and evening rush hours. Traffic jams are especially bad in and around Barcelona and Madrid. If possible, avoid the morning rush, which can last until noon, and the evening rush, which lasts from 7 to 9. Also be aware that at the beginning, middle, and end of July and August, the country suffers its worst traffic jams (delays of six to eight hours are common) as millions of Spaniards embark on, or return from, their annual vacations.

ROADSIDE EMERGENCIES

The rental agencies Hertz and Avis have 24-hour breakdown service. If you belong to AAA, you can get emergency assistance from the Spanish counterpart, RACE.

Emergency Service RACE (✉ *Isaac Newton 4, Parque Tecnológico de Madrid* ☎ *902/404545 for info, 902/300505 for assistance* 🌐 *www.race.es*).

RULES OF THE ROAD

Spaniards drive on the right and pass on the left, so stay in the right-hand lane when not passing. Children under 12 may not ride in the front seat, and seat belts are compulsory for both front- and backseat riders. Speed limits are 50 KPH (31 MPH) in cities, 100 KPH (62 MPH) on national highways, 120 kph (74 MPH) on the *autopista* or *autovía*. The use of mobile phones, even on the side of the road, is illegal, except with completely hands-free devices.

Severe fines are enforced throughout Spain for driving under the influence of alcohol. Spot Breathalyzer checks are often carried out, and you will be cited if the level of alcohol in your bloodstream is found to be 0.05% or above.

Spanish highway police are increasingly vigilant about speeding and illegal passing. Police are empowered to demand payment from non-Spanish drivers on the spot. Rental-car drivers are disproportionately targeted by police for speeding and illegal passing, so play it safe.

BY CRUISE SHIP

Barcelona is the busiest cruise port in Spain and Europe. Other popular ports of call in the country are Málaga, Alicante, and Palma de Mallorca. Nearby Gibraltar is also a popular stop. Although cruise lines such as Silversea and Costa traditionally offer cruises that take in parts of Spain and other Mediterranean countries such as Italy and Greece, it is becoming increasingly common to find package tours wholly within Spain. Two popular routes consist of island-hopping in the Balearics or around the Canary Islands. Among the many cruise lines that call on Spain are Royal Caribbean, Holland America Line, Norwegian Cruise Line, and Princess Cruises.

BY TRAIN

TRAIN TRAVEL TIMES	
Madrid to Barcelona: From €109.50 to €198.70.	AVE rapid trains make the trip in 2 hours 52 minutes.
Madrid to Seville: From €80.70 to €146.20.	Fastest AVE trains take 2 hours 30 minutes.
Madrid to Granada: From €66.80 to €104.20.	Running time about 4 hours 25 minutes.
Madrid to Valencia. From €47.10 to €77.80.	Fastest AVE trains take 3 hours 35 minutes.
Madrid to Santiago de Compostela. From €66.80 to €104.20.	Fastest time about 7 hours.
Barcelona to Bilbao. From €62.30 to €83.10.	Running time about 6 hours 15 minutes.
Barcelona to Valencia. From €42.70 to €70.80.	Fastest time 2 hours 55 minutes.
Seville to Granada. From 07:00 to 17:40. €23.90.	Running time about 3 hours.

International overnight trains run from Madrid to Lisbon (9 hours), Barcelona to Paris (12 hours), and Madrid to Paris (13½ hours). An overnight train also runs from Barcelona to Geneva (10 hours) and Zurich (14½ hours).

Spain's wonderful high-speed train, the 290-KPH (180-MPH) AVE, travels between Madrid and Seville (with a stop in Córdoba) in 2½ hours; prices start at about €80 each way. They also serve the Madrid–Barcelona route, cutting travel time to just under 3 hours. From Madrid you can also reach Lleida, Huesca, Málaga, and Valladolid.

The fast Talgo service is also efficient, but other elements of the state-run rail system—known as RENFE—are still a bit below par by European standards and some long-distance trips with multiple stops can be tediously slow. Although some overnight trains have comfortable sleeper cars, first-class fares that include a sleeping compartment are comparable to, or more expensive than, airfares.

The chart below has information about popular train routes (see the Experience chapter for a map of the country, with train routes). Prices are for one-way fares (depending on seating and where purchased) and subject to change.

Most Spaniards buy train tickets in advance at the train station's *taquilla* (ticket office). The lines can be long, so give yourself plenty of time. For popular train routes, you will need to reserve tickets more than a few days in advance and pick them up at least a day before traveling. The ticket clerks at the stations rarely speak English, so if you need help or advice in planning a more complex train journey, you may be better off going to a travel agency that displays the blue-and-yellow RENFE sign. A small commission should be expected. For shorter, regional train trips, you can often buy your tickets from machines in the train station.

You can buy train tickets with a major credit card at most city train stations. In the smaller towns and villages, it may be cash only. Seat reservations are required on most long-distance and some other trains, particularly high-speed trains, and are wise on any train that might be crowded. You'll also need a reservation if you want a sleeping berth.

The easiest way to make reservations is to go to the English version of the RENFE Web site (choose English from the drop-down menu under "seleccione su idioma") and click on the asterisk logo in the upper right corner—though be aware that the site can often be wonky with unpredictable broken links. Input your destination(s) and date(s), and the site will indicate seat availability; book earlier if you're traveling in Holy Week, on long holiday weekends, or in July–August. (The site allows you to make reservations up to 62 days in advance, which is important in qualifying for online purchase discounts: see below.) When you've completed your reservation, you can print out a pdf version of your ticket, with the car and seat assignment; you will also get a confirmation by e-mail with a *localizador* (Locator Number)—which you can use, in case you can't access the pdf file, to pick up the tickets at any RENFE station (most major airports have a RENFE booth, so you can retrieve your tickets as soon as you get off the plane and arrive in Spain); central stations in most major cities have automated check-in machines. You'll need your passport and the credit card you used for the reservation. You can review your pending reservations online at any time.

Caveats: You cannot buy tickets online for certain regional lines or for commuter lines (*cercanias*). Station agents cannot alter your reservations: You must do this yourself online. The RENFE Web site may not work with all browsers, and won't (as of this writing) accept AmEx.

DISCOUNTS

If you purchase a ticket on the RENFE Web site for the AVE or any of the Grandes Lineas (the faster, long-distance trains, including the Talgo) you can get a discount of anywhere from 20% to 60%, depending on how far ahead you book and how you travel: discounts on one-way tickets, for some reason, are higher than on round-trips. Discount availabilities disappear fast: get online at the earliest opportunity: 62 days in advance. If you're holding an international airline ticket and want to take the AVE within 48 hours of your arrival but haven't booked online, you can still get a 25% discount on the AVE ticket. On regional trains, you receive a 10% discount on round-trip tickets.

RAIL PASSES

If you're coming from the U.S. and are planning extensive train travel throughout Europe, check Rail Europe for Eurail passes. Whichever pass you choose, remember that you must buy it before you leave for Europe.

Spain is one of 20 European countries in which you can use the Eurail Global Pass, which buys you unlimited first-class rail travel in all participating countries for the duration of the pass. If you plan to rack up the miles, your best bet might be a Select Pass, which allows you to travel on as many as 15 days of your choice within a two-month period, and among up to five bordering countries. Prices (for passengers 26 or older) range from $455 to $1,009, depending on the number of travel days and countries you select.

If Spain is your only destination, a Eurail Spain Pass allows three days of unlimited train travel in Spain within a two-month period for $275 (first class) and $219 (second class); for 10 days of unlimited travel within two months, the passes are $565 and $449, respectively. The Eurail Spain Rail 'n Drive Pass combines three days of unlimited train travel with two days of car rentals. There are also combination passes for those visiting Spain and Portugal, Spain and France, and Spain and Italy.

Many travelers assume that rail passes guarantee them seats on the trains they wish to ride: not so. Reserve seats in advance even if you're using a rail pass.

Contacts Eurail (*www.eurail.com*). **Rail Europe** (*800/622–8600 in the U.S. or 800/361–7245 in Canada* *www.raileurope.com*). **RENFE** (*902/243402* *www.renfe.es*).

ESSENTIALS

ACCOMMODATIONS

By law, hotel prices in Spain must be posted at the reception desk and should indicate whether or not the value-added tax (I.V.A.; 8%) is included. Note that high-season rates prevail not only in summer but also during Holy Week and local fiestas. In much of Spain, breakfast is normally *not* included.

TIP→ See each chapter's Planner section for price charts.

Most hotels and other lodgings require you to give your credit-card details before they will confirm your reservation. If you don't feel comfortable e-mailing this information, ask if you can fax it (some places even prefer faxes). However you book, get confirmation in writing and have a copy of it when you check in.

Be sure you understand the hotel's cancellation policy. Some places allow you to cancel without any kind of penalty—even if you prepaid to secure a discounted rate—if you cancel at least 24 hours in advance. Others require you to cancel a week in advance or penalize you the cost of one night. Small inns and bed-and-breakfasts are most likely to require you to cancel far in advance.

TIP→ Assume that hotels operate on the European Plan (EP, no meals) unless we specify that they use the Breakfast Plan (BP, with full breakfast), Continental Plan (CP, continental breakfast), Full American Plan (FAP, all meals), or Modified American Plan (MAP, breakfast and dinner).

APARTMENT AND HOUSE RENTALS

If you are interested in a single-destination vacation, or are staying in one place and using it as a base for exploring the local area, renting an apartment or a house can be a good idea. However, it is not always possible to ensure the quality beforehand, and you may be responsible for supplying your own bed linens, towels, etc.

WORD OF MOUTH

Did the resort look as good in real life as it did in the photos? Did you sleep like a baby, or were the walls paper thin? Did you get your money's worth? Rate hotels and write your own reviews in Travel Ratings, or start a discussion about your favorite places in Travel Talk on www.fodors.com. Your comments might even appear in our books. Yes, you, too, can be a correspondent!

Contacts Barclay International Group (☎ *516/364–0064 or 800/845–6636* 🌐 *www.barclayweb.com*). **Homes Away** (☎ *416/920–1873 or 800/374–6637* 🌐 *www.homesaway.com*). **Interhome** (☎ *954/791–8282 or 800/882–6864* 🌐 *www.interhome.us*). **Villas and Apartments Abroad** (☎ *212/213–6435 or 800/433–3020* 🌐 *www.vaanyc.com*). **Villas International** (☎ *415/499–9490 or 800/221–2260* 🌐 *www.villasintl.com*).

HOSTELS

Youth hostels (*albergues juveniles*) in Spain are usually large and impersonal (but clean) with dorm-style beds. Most are geared to students, though many have a few private rooms suitable for families and couples. These rooms fill up quickly, so book at least a month in advance. Other budget options are the university student dorms *(residencia estudiantil)*, some of which offer accommodation in summer, when students are away.

TIP→ Note that in Spain *hostals* are not the same as the dorm-style youth hostels common elsewhere in Europe—hostals are inexpensive hotels with individual rooms, not communal quarters.

Information Hostelling International—USA (☎ *301/495–1240* 🌐 *www.hiusa.org*).

HOTELS AND BED-AND-BREAKFASTS

The Spanish government classifies hotels with one to five stars, with an additional rating of five-star GL (Gran Luxo) indicating the highest quality. Although quality is a factor, **the rating is technically only an indication of how many facilities the hotel offers.** For example, a three-star hotel may be just as comfortable as a four-star hotel but lack a swimming pool. Similarly, Fodor's price categories (¢–$$$$) indicate room rates only, so you might find a well-kept $$$ inn more charming than the famous $$$$ property down the street.

All hotel entrances are marked with a blue plaque bearing the letter H and the number of stars. The letter R (standing for *residencia*) after the letter H indicates an establishment with no meal service, with the possible exception of breakfast. The designations *fonda* (F), *pensión* (P), *casa de huéspedes* (CH), and *hostal* (Hs) indicate budget accommodations. In most cases, especially in smaller villages, rooms in such buildings will be basic but clean; in large cities, these rooms can be downright dreary.

When inquiring in Spanish about whether a hotel has a private bath, ask if it's an *habitación con baño*. Although a single room (*habitación sencilla*) is usually available, singles are often on the small side. Solo travelers might prefer to pay a bit extra for single occupancy of a double room (*habitación doble uso individual*). Make sure you request a double bed (*matrimonial*) if you want one—if you don't ask, you may end up with two singles.

There's a growing trend in Spain toward small country hotels and agrotourism. Estancias de España is an association of more than 40 independently owned hotels in restored palaces, monasteries, mills, and estates, generally in rural Spain. Similar associations serve individual regions, and tourist offices also provide lists of establishments. In Galicia, *pozos* are beautiful, old, often stately homes converted into small luxury hotels; Pozos de Galicia is the main organization for them. In Cantabria, *casonas* are small to large country houses, but as they don't have individual Web sites, it is necessary to check the regional tourist office Web sites.

A number of *casas rurales* (country houses similar to B&Bs) offer pastoral lodging either in guest rooms or in self-catering cottages. You may also come across the term *finca,* for country estate house. Many *agroturismo* accommodations are *fincas* converted to upscale B&Bs.

PARADORS

The Spanish government runs almost 100 paradors—upmarket hotels in historic buildings or near significant sites. Rates are reasonable, considering that most paradors have four- or five-star amenities, and the premises are invariably immaculate and tastefully furnished, often with antiques or reproductions. Each parador has a restaurant serving regional specialties, and you can stop in for a meal without spending the night. Paradors are popular with foreigners and Spaniards alike, so make reservations well in advance. (⇨ *See the* Paradors: A Night with History *feature, in the Experience chapter, for more details.*)

Contact Paradores de España (🌐 *www.parador.es*).

COMMUNICATIONS

INTERNET

Internet cafés are most common in tourist and student precincts. If you can't find one easily, ask at either the tourist office or a hotel's front desk. The most you're likely to pay for Internet access is about €3 an hour.

Migration to the country's bigger cities means the demand has skyrocketed for *locutorios* (cheap international phone centers), which double as places to get on the Internet.

Internet access in Spanish hotels is now fairly widespread, even in less expensive accommodations. In-room dial-up connections are graduallly getting phased out, in favor of Wi-Fi; some hotels will still have a computer console somewhere in the lobby for the use of guests (either free or with a fee), but Wi-Fi hotspots are already more common.

Contacts Cybercafes (🌐 *www.cybercafes.com*) lists more than 4,000 Internet cafés worldwide. **Gonuts4free** (🌐 www.gonuts4free.com/yellow/internetcafes/index.htm).

PHONES

The good news is that you can now make a direct-dial telephone call from virtually any point on earth. The bad news? You can't always do so cheaply. Calling from a hotel is almost always the most expensive option; hotels usually add huge surcharges to all calls, particularly international ones. In some countries you can phone from call centers or even the post office. Calling cards usually keep costs to a minimum, but only if you purchase them locally. And then there are mobile phones, which are sometimes more prevalent—particularly in the developing world—than land- lines; as expensive as mobile phone calls can be, they are still usually a much cheaper option than calling from your hotel.

Spain's phone system is efficient but can be expensive. Most travelers buy phone cards, which for €5 or €6 allow for about three hours of calls nationally and internationally. Phone cards can be used with any hotel, bar, or public telephone. There are many cards that work for only certain regions of the country, but the all-encompassing Fantastic card works for anywhere in the world. Phone cards can be bought at any tobacco shop or at most Internet cafés.

Note that only cell phones conforming to the European GSM standard will work in Spain. If you're going to be traveling in Spain for an extended period, buying a phone often turns out to be a money-saver. Using a local cell phone means avoiding the hefty long-distance charges accrued when using your own cell phone. Prices fluctuate, but offers start as low as €20 for a phone with €10 worth of calls.

The country code for Spain is 34. The country code is 1 for the United States and Canada.

CALLING WITHIN SPAIN

For general information in Spain, dial 1003. International operators, who generally speak English, are at 025.

All area codes begin with a 9. To call within Spain—even locally—dial the area code first. Numbers preceded by a 900 code are toll-free in Spain, however, 90x numbers are not (e.g., 901, 902, etc.). Phone numbers starting with a 6 belong to cellular phones. Note that when calling a cell phone, you do not need to dial the area code first; also, calls to cell phones are significantly more expensive than calls to regular phones.

You'll find pay phones in individual booths, in local telephone offices (*locutorios*), and in many bars and restaurants. Most have a digital readout so you can see your money ticking away. If you're calling with coins, you need at least €0.15 to call locally and €0.45 to call another province. Simply insert the coins and wait for a dial tone. Note that rates are reduced on weekends and after 8 PM during the week.

CALLING OUTSIDE SPAIN

International calls are awkward from coin-operated pay phones and can be expensive from hotels. Your best bet is to use a public phone that accepts phone cards or go to the *locutorios*. Those near the center of town are generally more expensive; farther from the center, the rates are sometimes as much as one third less. You converse in a quiet, private booth and are charged according to the meter.

To make an international call, dial 00, then the country code, then the area code and number.

The country code for the United States is 1.

LOCAL DO'S AND TABOOS

GREETINGS

When addressing Spaniards with whom you are not well acquainted or who are elderly, use the formal *usted* rather than the familiar *tu.*

DRESS

Some town councils are cracking down on people wearing swimsuits in public spaces. Use your common sense—it's unlikely you'd be allowed entry in a bar or restaurant wearing swimming attire back home, so don't do it when overseas. Be respectful when visiting churches: casual dress is fine if it's not too revealing. Spaniards object to men going bare-chested anywhere other than the beach or poolside.

OUT ON THE TOWN

These days, the Spanish are generally very informal, and casual-smart dress is accepted in most places.

DOING BUSINESS

Spanish office hours can be confusing to the uninitiated. Some offices stay open more or less continuously from 9 to 3, with a very short lunch break. Others open in the morning, break up the day with a long lunch break of two to three hours, then reopen at 4 or 5 until 7 or 8. Spaniards enjoy a certain notoriety for their lack of punctuality, but this has changed dramatically in recent years, and you are expected to show up for meetings on time. Smart dress is the norm.

Spaniards in international fields tend to conduct business with foreigners in English. If you speak Spanish, address new colleagues with the formal *usted* and the corresponding verb conjugations, then follow their lead in switching to the familiar *tu* once a working relationship has been established.

LANGUAGE

One of the best ways to avoid being an Ugly American is to learn a little of the local language. You need not strive for fluency; even mastering a few basic words and terms is bound to make chatting with the locals more rewarding.

Although Spaniards exported their language to all of Central and South America, Spanish is not the principal language in all of Spain. Outside their big cities, the Basques speak Euskera. In Catalonia, you'll hear Catalan throughout the region, just as you'll hear Gallego in Galicia and Valenciano in València (the latter, Mallorquín in Majorca, and Menorquín in Menorca are considered Catalan dialects). Although almost everyone in these regions also speaks and understands Spanish, local radio and television stations may broadcast in their respective languages, and road signs may be printed (or spray-painted over) with the preferred regional language. Spanish is referred to as Castellano, or Castilian.

Fortunately, Spanish is fairly easy to pick up, and your efforts to speak it will be graciously received. Learn at least the following basic phrases: *buenos días* (hello—until 2 PM), *buenas tardes* (good afternoon—until 8 PM), *buenas noches* (hello—after dark), *por favor* (please), *gracias* (thank you), *adiós* (good-bye), *sí* (yes), *no* (no), *los servicios* (the toilets), *la cuenta* (bill/check), *habla inglés?* (do you speak English?), and *no comprendo* (I don't understand). If your Spanish breaks down, you should have no trouble finding people who speak English in major cities and coastal resorts, but you won't necessarily be able to count on the bus driver or the passerby on the street. It's much more likely that you'll find an English-language speaker if you approach people under age 30.

General Information AT&T (☎ *800/222-0300*). **MCI WorldCom** (☎ *800/444-3333*). **Sprint** (☎ *800/793-1153*).

CALLING CARDS

Pay phones require phone cards (*tarjetas telefónicas*), which you can buy in various denominations at any tobacco shop or newsstand. Some phones also accept credit cards, but phone cards are more reliable.

MOBILE PHONES

If you have a multiband phone (some countries use different frequencies than what's used in the United States) and your service provider uses the world-standard GSM network (as do T-Mobile, AT&T, and Verizon), you can probably use your phone abroad. Roaming fees can be steep, however: 99¢ a minute is considered reasonable. Overseas you normally pay the toll charges for incoming calls. It's almost always cheaper to send a text message than to make a call, as text messages have a very low set fee (often less than 5¢).

If you just want to make local calls, consider buying a new SIM card (note that your provider may have to unlock your phone) and a prepaid service plan in the destination. You'll then have a local number and can make local calls at local rates. If your trip is extensive, you could also simply buy a new cell phone in your destination, as the initial cost will be offset over time.

■TIP→ **If you travel internationally frequently, save one of your old mobile phones or buy a cheap one on the Internet; ask your cell phone company to unlock it for you and take it with you as a travel phone, buying a new SIM card with pay-as-you-go service in each destination.**

Contacts Cellular Abroad (☎ *800/287-5072* 🌐 *www.cellularabroad.com*) rents and sells GMS phones and sells SIM cards that work in many countries. **Mobal** (☎ *888/888-9162* 🌐 *www.mobalrental.com*) rents mobiles and sells GSM phones (starting at $49) that will operate in 140 countries. Per-call rates vary throughout the world. **Planet Fone** (☎ *888/988-4777* 🌐 *www.planetfone.com*) rents cell phones at $40 a week, but discounts can cut that fee almost in half.

EATING OUT

Sitting around a table eating and talking is a huge part of Spanish culture, defining much of people's daily routines. Sitting in the middle of a typical bustling restaurant here goes a long way toward building understanding of how fundamental food can be to Spanish lives.

Although Spain has always had an extraordinary range of regional cuisine, in the past decade or so its restaurants have won it international recognition at the highest levels. A new generation of Spanish chefs—led by the revolutionary Ferran Adrià—has transformed classic dishes to suit contemporary tastes, drawing on some of the freshest ingredients in Europe and bringing an astonishing range of new technologies into the kitchen.

Larger restaurants are obliged to provide a no-smoking section. Smaller ones retain the option for the time being to permit smoking across the board or to ban it altogether. With a few exceptions, the proprietors of these establishments have maintained the status quo, presumably because of the fact that one in three Spaniards smokes, and they are fearful of losing clients. All eating and drinking establishments are obliged to inform clients by posting a sign at the entrance. *Se permite fumar* means you can smoke, *no se permite fumar* means you can't, and *sala habilitada para no fumadores* means a no-smoking section is available.

MEALS AND MEALTIMES

Outside major hotels, which serve morning buffets, breakfast (*desayuno*) is usually limited to coffee and toast or a roll. Lunch (*comida* or *almuerzo*) traditionally consists of an appetizer, a main course, and dessert, followed by coffee and perhaps a liqueur. Between lunch and dinner the best way to snack is to sample some tapas (appetizers) at a bar; normally you can choose from quite a variety. Dinner (*cena*) is somewhat lighter, with perhaps only one course. In addition to à la carte selections, most restaurants offer a daily fixed-price menu (*menú del día*), consisting of a starter, main plate, beverage, and dessert. Restaurants in many of the larger tourist areas will have the menú del día posted outside. The menú del día is traditionally offered only at lunch, but increasingly it's also offered at dinner in popular tourist destinations. If your waiter does not suggest it when you're seated, ask for it—"*Hay menú del día, por favor?*"

Mealtimes in Spain are later than elsewhere in Europe, and later still in Madrid and the southern region of Andalusia. Lunch starts around 2 or 2:30 (closer to 3 in Madrid) and dinner after 9 (as late as 11 or midnight in Madrid). Weekend eating times, especially dinner, can begin upward of an hour later. In areas with heavy tourist traffic, some restaurants open a bit earlier.

Unless otherwise noted, the restaurants listed in this guide are open daily for lunch and dinner.

PAYING

Credit cards are widely accepted in Spanish restaurants, but some smaller establishments do not take them. If you pay by credit card and you want to leave a small tip above and beyond the service charge, leave the tip in cash.

For guidelines see Tipping.

RESERVATIONS AND DRESS

Regardless of where you are, it's a good idea to make a reservation if you can. In some places, it's expected. We only mention them specifically when reservations are essential (there's no other way you'll ever get a table) or when they are not accepted. For popular restaurants, book as far ahead as you can (often 30 days), and reconfirm as soon as you arrive. (Large parties should always call ahead to check the reservations policy.) We mention dress only when men are required to wear a jacket or a jacket and tie.

WINES, BEER, AND SPIRITS

Apart from its famous wines, Spain produces many brands of lager, the most popular of which are San Miguel, Moritz, Cruzcampo, Aguila, Voll Damm, Mahou, and Estrella. Jerez de la Frontera is Europe's largest producer of brandy and is a major source of sherry. Catalonia produces the world's best *cava* (sparkling wine). Spanish law prohibits the sale of alcohol to people under 18.

ELECTRICITY

Spain's electrical current is 220–240 volts, 50 cycles alternating current (AC); wall outlets take Continental-type plugs, with two round prongs.

Consider making a small investment in a universal adapter, which has several types of plugs in one lightweight, compact unit. Most laptops and mobile phone chargers are dual voltage (i.e., they operate equally well on 110 and 220 volts) and require only an adapter. These days the same is true of small appliances such as hair dryers. Always check labels and manufacturer instructions to be sure. Don't use 110-volt outlets marked FOR SHAVERS ONLY for high-wattage appliances such as hair dryers.

EMERGENCIES

The pan-European emergency phone number (☎ *112*) is operative in some parts of Spain but not all. If it doesn't work, dial the emergency numbers below

for the national police, local police, fire department, or medical services. On the road, there are emergency phones marked SOS at regular intervals on *autovías* (freeways) and *autopistas* (toll highways). If your documents are stolen, contact both the local police and your embassy. If you lose a credit card, phone the issuer immediately.

Foreign Embassies U.S. Embassy (✉ *Calle Serrano 75, Madrid* ☎ *91/587–2200* 🌐 *www.embusa.es*).

General Emergency Contacts National police (☎ *091*). **Local police** (☎ *092*). **Fire department** (☎ *080*). **Medical service** (☎ *061*).

HEALTH

The most common types of illnesses are caused by contaminated food and water. Make sure food has been thoroughly cooked and is served to you fresh and hot; avoid vegetables and fruits that you haven't washed (in bottled or purified water) or peeled yourself. If you have problems, mild cases of traveler's diarrhea may respond to Imodium (known generically as loperamide) or Pepto-Bismol. Be sure to drink plenty of fluids; if you can't keep fluids down, seek medical help immediately.

Infectious diseases can be airborne or passed via mosquitoes and ticks and through direct or indirect physical contact with animals or people. Some, including Norwalk-like viruses that affect your digestive tract, can be passed along through contaminated food. Condoms can help prevent most sexually transmitted diseases, but they aren't absolutely reliable and their quality varies from country to country. Speak with your physician and/or check the CDC or World Health Organization Web sites for health alerts, particularly if you're pregnant, traveling with children, or have a chronic illness.

SPECIFIC ISSUES IN SPAIN

Medical care is good in Spain, but nursing can be perfunctory, as relatives are expected to stop by and look after patients' needs. In some popular destinations, such as the Costa del Sol, there are volunteer English interpreters on hand at hospitals and clinics.

In the summer, sunburn and sunstroke are real risks in Spain. Even if you're not normally bothered by strong sun you should cover yourself up, slather on sunblock, drink plenty of fluids, and limit sun time for the first few days. If you require medical attention for any problem, ask your hotel's front desk for assistance or go to the nearest public **Centro de Salud** (day hospital); in serious cases, you'll be referred to the regional hospital.

OVER-THE-COUNTER REMEDIES

Over-the-counter remedies are available at any *farmacia* (pharmacy), recognizable by the large green crosses outside. Some will look familiar, such as *aspirina* (aspirin), and other medications are sold under various brand names. If you get traveler's diarrhea, ask for an *antidiarréico* (antidiarrheal medicine); Fortasec is a well-known brand. Mild cases may respond to Imodium (known generically as loperamide) or Pepto-Bismol. To keep from getting dehydrated, drink plenty of purified water or herbal tea. In severe cases, rehydrate yourself with a salt-sugar solution—½ teaspoon salt (*sal*) and 4 tablespoons sugar (*azúcar*) per quart of water, or pick up a package of oral rehydration salts at any local farmacia.

If you regularly take a nonprescription medicine, take a sample box or bottle with you, and the Spanish pharmacist will provide you with its local equivalent.

HOURS OF OPERATION

The ritual of a long afternoon siesta is no longer as ubiquitous as it once was. However, the tradition does remain, and many people take a postlunch nap before returning to work or continuing on with their

day. The two-to-three-hour lunch makes it possible to eat and then snooze. Midday breaks generally begin at 1 or 2 and end between 4 and 5, depending on the city and the sort of business. The midafternoon siesta—often a half-hour power nap in front of the TV—fits naturally into the workday cycle, since Spaniards tend to work until 7 or 8 PM.

Traditionally, Spain's climate created the siesta as a time to preserve energy while afternoon temperatures spiked. After the sun began to set, they went back to working, shopping, and taking their leisurely *paseo* (stroll). In the big cities—particularly with the advent of air-conditioning—the heat has less of an effect on the population; in the small towns in the south of Spain, however, many still use a siesta as a way to wait out the weather.

Until a decade or so ago, it was common for many businesses to close for a month in the July/August period. When open, they often run on a summer schedule, which can mean a longer-than-usual siesta (sometimes up to four hours), a shorter working day (until 3 PM only), and no Saturday-afternoon trading.

Banks are generally open weekdays from 8:30 or 9 until 2 or 2:30. From October to May the major banks open on Saturday from 8:30 or 9 until 2 or 2:30, and savings banks are also open Thursday 4:30 to 8. Currency exchanges at airports, train stations, and in the city center stay open later; you can also cash traveler's checks at El Corte Inglés department stores until 10 PM (some branches close at 9 PM or 9:30 PM). Most government offices are open weekdays 9–2.

Most museums are open from 9:30 to 2 and 4 to 7 or 8 six days a week, every day but Monday. Schedules are subject to change, particularly between the high and low seasons, so confirm opening hours before you make plans. A few large museums, such as Madrid's Prado and Reina Sofía and Barcelona's Picasso Museum, stay open all day, without a siesta.

Pharmacies keep normal business hours (9–1:30 and 5–8), but every midsize town (or city neighborhood) has a duty pharmacy that stays open 24 hours. The location of the duty pharmacy is usually posted on the front door of all pharmacies.

When planning a shopping trip, remember that almost all shops in Spain close from 1 or 2 PM for at least two hours. The only exceptions are large supermarkets and the department-store chain El Corte Inglés. Most shops are closed on Sunday, and in Madrid and several other places they're also closed Saturday afternoon. Larger shops in tourist areas may stay open Sunday in summer and during the Christmas holiday.

HOLIDAYS

Spain's national holidays are New Year's Day on January 1 (*Año Nuevo*), Three Kings Day on January 6 (*Día de los Tres Reyes*), Father's Day on March 19 (*San José*), Good Friday (*Viernes Santo*), Easter Sunday (*Día de Pascua*), Labor Day on May 1 (*Día del Trabajo*), St. John's Day on June 24 (*San Juan*; the bonfire celebrations are the night before), *Corpus Christi* (June), St. Peter/St. Paul Day on June 29 (*San Pedro y San Pablo*), St. James Day on July 25 (*Santiago*), Assumption on August 15 (*Asunción*), Columbus Day on October 12 (*Día de la Hispanidad*), All Saints Day on November 1 (*Todos los Santos*), Constitution Day on December 6 (*Día de la Constitución*), Immaculate Conception on December 8 (*Immaculada Concepción*), and Christmas Day on December 25 (*Navidad*). In addition, each region, city, and town has its own holidays honoring political events and patron saints.

Many stores close during *Semana Santa* (Holy Week—also sometimes translated as Easter Week), the week that precedes Easter.

If a public holiday falls on a Tuesday or Thursday, remember that many businesses also close on the nearest Monday or Friday for a long weekend, called a *puente*

(bridge). If a major holiday falls on a Sunday, businesses close on Monday.

MAIL

Spain's postal system, or *correos,* does work, but delivery times vary widely. An airmail letter to the U.S. may take from four days to two weeks; delivery to other destinations is equally unpredictable. Sending your letters by priority mail (*urgente*) or the cheaper registered mail (*certificado*) ensures speedier and safer arrival.

Airmail letters to the United States cost €0.78 up to 20 grams. Letters within Spain are €0.31. Postcards carry the same rates as letters. You can buy stamps at post offices and at licensed tobacco shops.

Because mail delivery in Spain can often be slow and unreliable, it's best to have your mail held at a Spanish post office; have it addressed to LISTA DE CORREOS (the equivalent of *poste restante*) in a town you'll be visiting. Postal addresses should include the name of the province in parentheses, for example, Marbella (Málaga).

SHIPPING PACKAGES

When time is of the essence, or when you're sending valuable items or documents overseas, you can use a courier (*mensajero*). The major international agencies, such as FedEx, UPS, and DHL, have representatives in Spain; the biggest Spanish courier service is Seur. MRW is another local courier that provides express delivery worldwide.

Express Services Correos (☎ *902/197197* 🌐 *www.correos.es*). **DHL** (☎ *902/122424 for air, 902/123030 for ground* 🌐 *www.dhl.es*). **FedEx** (☎ *902/100871* 🌐 *www.fedex.com/es_english*). **MRW** (☎ *900/300400* 🌐 *www.mrw-transporte.com*). **Seur** (☎ *902/101010* 🌐 *www.seur.com*). **UPS** (☎ *902/888820* 🌐 *www.ups.es*).

MONEY

Spain is no longer a budget destination, even less so in the expensive cities of Barcelona, San Sebastián, and Madrid. However, prices still compare slightly favorably with those elsewhere in Europe.

Prices throughout this guide are given for adults. Substantially reduced fees are almost always available for children, students, and senior citizens.

TIP→ Banks never have every foreign currency on hand, and it may take as long as a week to order. If you're planning to exchange funds before leaving home, don't wait until the last minute.

ATMS AND BANKS

Your bank will probably charge a fee for using ATMs abroad; the foreign bank you use may also charge a fee. Nevertheless, you'll usually get a better rate of exchange at an ATM than you will at a currency-exchange office or even when changing money in a bank, and extracting funds as you need them is a safer option than carrying around a large amount of cash.

TIP→ PINs with more than four digits are not recognized at ATMs in Spain. If yours has five or more, remember to change it before you leave.

You'll find ATMs in every major city in Spain, as well as in most smaller towns. ATMs will be part of the Cirrus and/or Plus networks and will allow you to withdraw euros with your credit or debit card, provided you have a valid PIN.

Spanish banks tend to maintain an astonishing number of branch offices, especially in the cities and major tourist destinations, and the majority have an ATM.

CREDIT CARDS

Throughout this guide, the following abbreviations are used: **AE,** American Express; **D,** Discover; **DC,** Diners Club; **MC,** MasterCard; and **V,** Visa.

It's a good idea to inform your credit-card company before you travel, especially if you're going abroad and don't travel internationally very often. Otherwise, it might put a hold on your card owing to unusual activity—not a good thing halfway through your trip. Record all your credit-card numbers—as well as the phone numbers to call if your cards are lost or stolen—in a safe place, so you're prepared should something go wrong. Both MasterCard and Visa have general numbers you can call (collect if you're abroad) if your card is lost, but you're better off calling the number of your issuing bank, since MasterCard and Visa usually just transfer you to your bank; your bank's number is usually printed on your card.

If you plan to use your credit card for cash advances, you'll need to apply for a PIN at least two weeks before your trip. Although it's usually cheaper (and safer) to use a credit card abroad for large purchases (so you can cancel payments or be reimbursed if there's a problem), note that some credit-card companies *and* the banks that issue them add substantial percentages to all foreign transactions, whether they're in a foreign currency or not. Check on these fees before leaving home, so there won't be any surprises when you get the bill.

■ **TIP→** Before you charge something, ask the merchant whether he or she plans to do a dynamic currency conversion (DCC). In such a transaction the shop, restaurant, or hotel (not Visa or MasterCard) converts the currency and charges you in dollars. In most cases you'll pay the merchant a 3% fee for this service in addition to any credit-card company and issuing-bank foreign-transaction surcharges.

DCC programs are becoming increasingly widespread. Merchants who participate in them are supposed to ask whether you want to be charged in dollars or the local currency, but they don't always. And even if they do offer you a choice, they may well avoid mentioning the additional surcharges. The good news is that you *do* have a choice. And if this practice really gets your goat, you can avoid it entirely thanks to American Express; with its cards, DCC simply isn't an option.

Reporting Lost Cards American Express (☎ *800/528–4800 in U.S., 336/393–1111 collect from abroad* 🌐 *www.americanexpress.com*). **Diners Club** (☎ *800/234–6377 in U.S., 303/799–1504 collect from abroad* 🌐 *www.dinersclub.com*). **MasterCard** (☎ *800/627–8372 in U.S., 636/722–7111 collect from abroad* 🌐 *www.mastercard.com*). **Visa** (☎ *800/847–2911 in U.S.* 🌐 *www.visa.com*).

Use these toll-free numbers in Spain. **American Express** (☎ *917/437000*). **Diners Club** (☎ *901/101011*). **MasterCard** (☎ *900/971231*). **Visa** (☎ *900/991124*).

CURRENCY AND EXCHANGE

Since 2002, Spain has used the European monetary unit, the euro (€). Euro notes come in denominations of 5, 10, 20, 50, 100, 200, and 500; coins are worth 1 cent of a euro, 2 cents, 5 cents, 10 cents, 20 cents, 50 cents, 1 euro, and 2 euros. Forgery is quite commonplace in parts of Spain, especially with 50-euro notes. You can generally tell a forgery by the feel of the paper: counterfeits tend to be smoother than the legal notes, and the metallic line down the middle is darker than those in real bills.

At this writing the euro has yet to regain the strength it lost in 2008 and 2009 against the U.S. dollar and other currencies: it stands at €1.38 to the U.S. dollar.

■ **TIP→** Even if a currency-exchange booth has a sign promising no commission, rest assured that there's some kind of huge, hidden fee. (Oh . . . that's right. The sign didn't say no *fee*.) And as for rates, you're almost always better off getting foreign currency at an ATM or exchanging money at a bank.

PASSPORTS AND VISAS

Visitors from the United States need a passport valid for a minimum of six months to enter Spain.

■ **TIP→** Before your trip, make two copies of your passport's data page (one for someone at home and another for you to carry separately). Or scan the page and e-mail it to someone at home and/or yourself.

VISAS

Visas are not necessary for those with U.S. passports valid for a minimum of six months and who plan to stay in Spain for tourist or business purposes for up to 90 days. Should you need a visa to stay longer than this, contact the Spanish consulate office nearest to you in the U.S. to apply for the appropriate documents.

RESTROOMS

Spain has some public restrooms (*servicios*), including, in larger cities, small coin-operated booths, but they are few and far between. Your best option is to use the facilities in a bar or cafeteria, remembering that at the discretion of the establishment you may have to order something. Gas stations have restrooms (you usually have to request the key to use them), but they are more often than not in terrible condition.

The Bathroom Diaries (🌐 *www.thebathroomdiaries.com*) is flush with unsanitized info on restrooms the world over—each one located, reviewed, and rated.

SAFETY

Petty crime is a huge problem in Spain's most popular tourist destinations. The most frequent offenses are pickpocketing (particularly in Madrid and Barcelona) and theft from cars (all over the country). Never leave anything valuable in a parked car, no matter how friendly the area feels, how quickly you'll return, or how invisible the item seems once you lock it in the trunk. Thieves can spot rental cars a mile away, and they work very efficiently. In airports, laptop computers are choice prey.

Distribute your cash and any valuables (including your credit cards and passport) between a deep front pocket or an inside jacket or vest pocket. Don't wear a money belt or a waist pack, both of which peg you as a tourist. When walking the streets, particularly in large cities, carry as little cash as possible. Men should carry their wallets in their front pocket; women who need to carry purses should strap them across the front of their bodies. Leave the rest of your valuables in the safe at your hotel. On the beach, in cafés and restaurants, and in Internet centers, always keep an eye on your belongings.

Be cautious of any odd or unnecessary human contact, verbal or physical, whether it's a tap on the shoulder, someone asking you for a light, someone spilling a drink at your table, and so on. Thieves often work in twos, so while one is distracts your attention, the other swipes your wallet.

TAXES

Value-added tax, similar to sales tax, is called I.V.A. in Spain (pronounced "*ee*-vah," for *impuesto sobre el valor añadido*). It's levied on both products and services, such as hotel rooms and restaurant meals. When in doubt about whether tax is included, ask, "*Está incluido el I.V.A.?*" As of July 2010, the I.V.A. rate for hotels and restaurants is 8%, regardless of their number of stars. A special tax law for the Canary Islands allows hotels and restaurants there to charge 4% I.V.A. Menus will generally say at the bottom whether tax is included (*I.V.A. incluido*) or not (*más 8% I.V.A.*).

Although food, pharmaceuticals, and household items are taxed at the lowest rate, most consumer goods are now taxed at 18%. A number of shops participate in Global Refund (formerly Europe Tax-Free Shopping), a V.A.T. refund service that makes getting your money back relatively hassle-free. You cannot get a refund on the V.A.T. for such items as meals or services such as hotel accommodation or taxi fares.

When making a purchase that qualifies for Global Refund, find out whether the merchant gives refunds—not all stores do, nor are they required to—and ask for a V.A.T. refund form. Have the form stamped like any customs form by customs officials when you leave the country or, if you're visiting several European Union countries, when you leave the EU. After you're through passport control, take the form to a refund-service counter for an on-the-spot refund (which is usually the quickest and easiest option), or mail it to the address on the form (or the envelope with it) after you arrive home. You receive the total refund stated on the form, but the processing time can be long, especially if you request a credit-card adjustment.

Global Refund is a Europe-wide service with 225,000 affiliated stores and more than 700 refund counters at major airports and border crossings. The refund form, called a Tax Free Check or Refund Cheque, is the most common across the European continent. The service issues refunds in the form of cash, check, or credit-card adjustment.

V.A.T. Refunds Global Refund (☎ *800/566-9828* 🌐 *www.globalrefund.com*).

TIME

Spain is on Central European Time, six hours ahead of Eastern Standard Time. Like the rest of the European Union, Spain switches to daylight saving time on the last weekend in March and switches back on the last weekend in October.

Time Zones Timeanddate.com (🌐 *www.timeanddate.com/worldclock*) can help you figure out the correct time anywhere.

TIPPING

Restaurant checks do not list a service charge on the bill but consider the tip included. If you want to leave a small tip in addition to the bill, do not tip more than 10% of the bill, and leave less if you eat tapas or sandwiches at a bar—just enough to round out the bill to the nearest €1. Tip cocktail servers €0.30–€0.50 a drink, depending on the bar.

Tip taxi drivers about 10% of the total fare, plus a supplement to help with luggage. Note that rides from airports carry an official surcharge plus a small handling fee for each piece of luggage.

Tip hotel porters €0.50 a bag and the bearer of room service €0.50. A doorman who calls a taxi for you gets €0.50. If you stay in a hotel for more than two nights, tip the maid about €0.50 per night.

Tour guides should be tipped about €2, ushers in theaters or at bullfights €0.15 to €0.20, barbers €0.50 to €1, and women's hairdressers at least €1 for a wash and style. Restroom attendants are tipped €0.15.

TOURS

SPECIAL-INTEREST TOURS

Madrid and Beyond (☎ *91/758–0063* 🌐 *www.madridandbeyond.com*) offers an array of customized private luxury tours, focusing on culinary, cultural, and sports-related themes.

ART

In the U.S., **Atlas Cruises and Tours** (☎ *800/942–3301* 🌐 *www.escortedspaintours.com*) offers a range of tours with accents on art, cultural history, and the outdoors.

Ole Spain Tours (☎ *91/551–5294* 🌐 *www.olespaintours.com*) also offers art and historical tours to Spain.

Based in New York, **Heritage Tours** (☎ *800/378–4555* 🌐 *www.heritagetoursonline.com*) helps arrange customized cultural tours based on your interests and budget. Guides are drawn from a network of curators, gallery owners, and art critics.

BIRD-WATCHING

In the Coto Doñana National Park in Andalucía, **Discovering Doñana** (☎ *959/442466* 🌐 *www.discoveringdonana.com*) offers some of the best guided bird-watching tours and expeditions in Spain.

CULINARY AND WINE

Artisans of Leisure (☎ *800/214–8144* 🌐 *www.artisansofleisure.com*) offers personalized food-and-wine and cultural tours to Spain. Based in Madrid, **Cellar Tours** (☎ *91/1829790* 🌐 *www.cellartours.com*) offers a wide array of wine and cooking tours to Spain.

GOLF

The following Spain-based companies offer golf tours and information. **Golf Spain** (☎ *913/512415* 🌐 *www.golfspain.com*). **Golf in Spain** (☎ *952/474848* 🌐 *www.golfinspain.com*).

HIKING

For a company that offers all kinds of adventure tours check out **Spain Adventures** (☎ *877/717–7246* 🌐 *www.spainadventures.com*).

LANGUAGE PROGRAMS

One of the best resources for language schools in Spain is **Go Abroad** (☎ *720/570–1702* 🌐 *www.goabroad.com*).

VOLUNTEER PROGRAMS

The best resource for volunteering and finding paid internships in Spain is **Go Abroad** (☎ *720/570–1702* 🌐 *www.goabroad.com*).

ONLINE TRAVEL TOOLS

ALL ABOUT SPAIN

For more information on Spain, visit the Tourist Office of Spain at 🌐 *www.spain.info* or 🌐 *www.okspain.org*. Also check out the sites 🌐 *www.in-spain.info*, 🌐 *www.red2000.com/spain*, and 🌐 *www.idealspain.com*; the latter focuses more on living, working, or buying property in Spain. A useful Craigslist-type site listing everything from vacation rentals to language lessons is 🌐 *www.loquo.com/en_us*. For a virtual brochure on Spain's *paradors* and online booking, go to 🌐 *www.parador.es*.

INDEX

I

J

PHOTO CREDITS

1, Hidalgo & Lopesino / age fotostock. 2 (top left), mellocello, Fodors.com member. 2 (bottom left and bottom right), Bob_Estremera1, Fodors.com member. 2 (top right), ciaony, Fodors.com member. 2 (center right), Ann Forcier, Fodors.com member. 5, JLImages / Alamy. Chapter 1: Experience Spain: 10-11, Carsten Leuzinger / age fotostock. 12, Minerva Bloom, Fodors.com member. 13 (left), Sandra Balboa, Fodors.com member. 13 (right), J.D. Dallet/age fotostock. 14, Nicki Geigert, Fodors.com member. 15 (left), larondel, Fodors.com member. 15 (right), Wojtek Buss/age fotostock. 17, Factoria Singular/age fotostock. 20, Robert DiPietro, Fodors.com member. 21 (left), Juan Manuel Silva/age fotostock. 21 (right), Rafael Campillo/age fotostock. 22, Peter Forde, Fodors.com member. 23, jitna Bhagani, Fodors.com member. 24 (left), Brian Maudsley/Shutterstock. 24 (top center), Javier Larrea/age fotostock. 24 (bottom center), Foucras G./age fotostock. . 24 (right), Javier Larrea/age fotostock. 25 (top left), Atlantide S.N.C./age fotostock. 25 (bottom left), Victor Kotler/age fotostock. 25 (bottom center), Paco Gómez García/age footstock. 25 (right), José Fuste Raga/age fotostock. 26, EllenS, Fodors.com member. 27 (left), love2explore, Fodors.com member. 27 (right), J.D. Dallet/age fotostock. 28, dalbera/ Flickr. 29, ezio bocci/age fotostock. 30, Matt Trommer/Shutterstock. 31, Alan Copson/age fotostock. 36, Howard/age fotostock. 37 (left), Juan Manuel Silva/age fotostock. 37 (right), Ken Welsh/age fotostock. 38, Pedro Salaverría/age fotostock. 39 (left), J.D. Dallet/age fotostock. 39 (right), Alberto Paredes/ age fotostock. 42, Carlos Nieto/age fotostock. 43, Javier Larrea/age fotostock. 44 (top), Pictorial Press Ltd / Alamy. 44 (bottom), The Print Collector / Alamy. 45 (top), Paradores de Turismo de España, S.A.. 45 (bottom), Jean Dominique DALLET / Alamy. 46, Fernando Fernandez/age fotostock. Chapter 2: Madrid: 47, Factoria Singular/age fotostock. 48, Duncan P Walker/iStockphoto. 49 (left), E.M. Promoción de Madrid, S.A.(Paolo Giocoso). 49 (right), VICTOR PELAEZ TORRES/iStockphoto. 51, Luis Sandoval Mandujano/iStockphoto. 54, Peter Doomen/Shutterstock. 55 left),jlstras/wikipedia.org. 55 (right), Mª Angeles Tomás/iStockphoto. 56, Graham Heywood/iStockphoto. 61, Alan Copson / age fotostock. 64, Doco Dalfiano / age fotostock. 69, Alberto Paredes / age fotostock. 72, Sergio Pitamitz / age fotostock. 77, José Fuste Raga / age fotostock. 80, Peter Barritt / Alamy. 81, David R. Frazier Photolibrary, Inc. / Alamy. 82 (top), Factoria Singular/age fotostock. 82 (bottom), REUTERS/Susana Vera/ Newscom. 84, HUGHES Hervé / age fotostock. 85, rubiphoto/Shutterstock. 86 (top), Mary Evans Picture Library / Alamy. 86 (center and bottom), Public Domain. 87 (all), Public Domain. 88 (top), Public Domain. 88 (2nd from top), Peter Barritt / Alamy. 88 (3rd from top), A. H. C./age fotostock. 88 (bottom), Tramonto/age fotostock. 95, E.M. Promoción de Madrid, S.A.(Paolo Giocoso). 104, Paul D. Van Hoy II / age fotostock. 111, La Terraza del Casino. 118 (top), Derby Hotels Collection. 118 (bottom left), Hostel Adriano. 118 (bottom right), Palacio del Retiro. 127, Berchery/age fotostock. 128, imagebroker / Alamy. 129, G.Haling/age fotostock. 130 (center), Charles Sturge / Alamy. 130 (top), Paco Ayala. 130 (bottom), Jean Du Boisberranger / Hemis.fr / Aurora Photos. 131, Vinicius Tupinamba/Shutterstock. 135, Chris Seba / age fotostock. 140, E.M. Promoción de Madrid, S.A.(Carlos Cazurro). Chapter 3: Toledo and Trips from Madrid: 147, José Fuste Raga/age fotostock. 148, J.D. Dallet/age fotostock. 149, Juan Carlos Muñoz/age fotostock. 152 (left), Carlos Nieto/age fotostock. 152 (right), Aguililla & Marín/age footstock. 154, Mª Angeles Tomás/iStockphoto. 155 (left), zordor/Flickr. 155 (right), Boca Dorada/wikipedia.org. 156, jms122881, Fodors.com member. 162, José Antonio Moreno/age fotostock. 165, Ivern Photo / age fotostock. 170, Jose Fuste Raga / age fotostock. 179, Josep Curto / age fotostock. 182, PHB.cz (Richard Semik)/Shutterstock. 188, Jeronimo Alba / age fotostock. 191, Alan Copson / age fotostock. 193, Ioseba Egibar/age fotostock. 194, Javier Larrea/age fotostock. 196 (top left), Daniel P. Acevedo/age fotostock. 196 (bottom left), Sam Bloomberg-Rissman/ age fotostock. 196 (right), Javier Larrea/age fotostock. 197, J.D. Dallet/age fotostock. 198 (top), PHB. cz (Richard Semik)/Shutterstock. 198 (2nd from top), Javier Larrea/age fotostock, 198 (3rd from top), Jakub Pavlinec/Shutterstock, 198 (4th from top), J.D. Dallet/age fotostock. 198 (5th from top), Fresnel/ Shutterstock. 198 (6th from top), J.D. Dallet/age fotostock. 198 (bottom), Marta Menéndez /Shutterstock. 199 (top left), Mauro Winery. 199 (top 2nd from left), Cephas Picture Library/Alamy. 199 (top 3rd from left), Alvaro Palacios Winery. 199 (top right), Mas Martinet Winery. 199 (bottom), Mike Randolph/age fotostock. 209, Kevin George / age fotostock. 214, M. A. Otsoa de Alda / age fotostock. 219, José Antonio Moreno/age fotostock. 225, Richard Semik / age fotostock. 228, José Fuste Raga/age fotostock. Chapter 4: Galicia and Asturias: 231, Francisco Turnes/Shutterstock. 232, Alberto Paredes/ age fotostock. 233 (left), plazas i subiros/Shutterstock. 233 (right), Alan Copson/age fotostock. 235, plazas i subiros/Shutterstock. 236, Aguililla & Marín/age fotostock. 237, Juan Carlos Muñoz / age fotostock. 238, Alberto Paredes/age fotostock. 239 (left), scaredy_kat/Flickr. 239 (right), Mª Angeles Tomás/iStockphoto. 240, lheitman, Fodors.com member. 247, José Carlos Pires Pereira/iStockphoto. 253, imagebroker / Alamy. 254, Schütze Rodemann/age footstock. 255 (left), Visual Arts Library (London) / Alamy. 255 (right), John Warburton-Lee Photography / Alamy. 256 (top), Javier Larrea/age fotostock. 256 (bottom), R. Matina/age fotostock. 257, J.D. Dallet/age fotostock. 258 (left), Toño Labra/age fotostock. 258 (center), Anthony Collins / Alamy. 258 (right), Ian Dagnall / Alamy. 259 (left), Javier Larrea/age fotostock. 259 (right), Miguel Angel Munoz Pellicer / Alamy. 264, SOMATUSCANI/ iStockphoto. 271, Phooey/iStockphoto. 272, Javier Larrea / age fotostock. 279, Cantabria tradicional / age fotostock. 280, Ivern Photo / age fotostock. 286, Aguililla & Marín/age fotostock. 291, Alberto Paredes / age fotostock. 292, Javier Larrea / age fotostock. Chapter 5: Bilbao and the Basque Country: 295, Jeronimo Alba / age fotostock. 296, Javier Larrea/age fotostock. 297 (top), Juan Carlos Muñoz/ age fotostock. 297 (bottom), Javier Larrea/age fotostock. 300, Gonzalo Azumendi/age fotostock. 301, Adriaan Thomas Snaaijer/Shutterstock. 302, OSOMEDIA / age fotostock. 303 (left), Patty Orly/Shutterstock. 303 (right), Núria Pueyo/wikipedia.org. 304, Javier Gil/Shutterstock. 308, Gonzalo Azumendi / age fotostock. 313, Atlantide S.N.C./age fotostock. 316, John Miller / age fotostock. 321, BERNAGER E./age fotostock. 322 (left and right), Javier Larrea/age fotostock. 323 (left), Le Naviose/ age fotostock, .323 (right), Mark Baynes / Alamy. 323 (top), Robert Fried / Alamy. 323 (bottom), Mark Baynes / Alamy. 324, Mark Baynes / Alamy. 333, Iñaki Caperochipi / age fotostock. 338, Toño Labra / age fotostock. 342-43, FSG / age fotostock. 342 (bottom), Jon Arnold Images / Alamy. 344 (top), Tim Hill / Alamy. 344 (2nd from top), mediacolor's / Alamy. 344 (3rd from top), Ramon grosso dolarca/ Shutterstock. 344 (bottom), Peter Cassidy/age fotostock. 345 (left), Kathleen Melis/Shutterstock. 345 (top right), Mark Baynes / Alamy. 345 (2nd from top right), Alex Segre / Alamy. 345 (3rd from top right), Peter Cassidy/age fotostock. 345 (bottom right), Frank Heuer/laif/Aurora Photos. 353, Graham Lawrence / age fotostock. 357, Wojtek Buss / age fotostock. 362, Brigitte Merz / age fotostock. Chapter 6: The Pyrenees: 367, GUY Christian/age fotostock. 368, Bryan Brooks, Fodors.com member. 369 (left), Jule_Berlin/wikipedia.org. 369 (right), Matyas Arvai/Shutterstock. 372, Gustavo Naharro/wikipedia.org. 373, Matyas Arvai/Shutterstock. 374, Gonzalo Azumendi / age fotostock. 375 (left), Leser / age fotostock. 375 (right), Toniher/wikipedia.org. 376, Gustavo Naharro/wikipedia.org. 383, Gonzalo Azumendi/age fotostock. 388, Alfred Abad / age fotostock. 397, P. Narayan / age fotostock. 402, Tolo Balaguer/age fotostock. 405, Javier Larrea/age fotostock. 408, horrapics/Wikimedia Commons. 412, Hugo Alonso / age fotostock. 421, Marco Cristofori / age fotostock. Chapter 7: Barcelona: 423, Rafael Campillo / age fotostock. 430, Peter Holmes / age fotostock. 431 (left), Tamorlan/wikipedia.org. 431 (right), diluvi/wikipedia.org. 432, Mikhail Zahranichny/Shutterstock. 433 (left), Philip Lange/ Shutterstock. 433 (right), Regien Paassen/Shutterstock. 434, Vinicius Tupinamba/Shutterstock. 439, BORGESE Maurizio / age fotostock. 444, Ken Welsh / age fotostock. 447, Ruben Olavo / age fotostock. 452, Petr Svarc / age fotostock. 458, Oso Media/Alamy. 459, Sandra Baker/Alamy. 460 (top left), Public Domain. 460 (bottom left), Alfonso de Tomás/Shutterstock. 460 (top right), Zina Seletskaya/Shutterstock. 460 (center right), Amy Nichole Harris/Shutterstock. 460 (bottom right), Luis M. Seco/ Shutterstock. 461 (left), Iwona Grodzka/Shutterstock. 461 (top right), zvonkomaja/Shutterstock. 461 (center right), Public Domain. 461 (bottom right), Smackfu/wikipedia.org. 462 (top left), synes/Flickr. 462 (bottom left), rubiphoto/Shutterstock. 462 (right), Solodovnikova Elena/Shutterstock. 463 (top), Quim Roser/age fotostock. 463 (bottom), Jan van der Hoeven/Shutterstock. 469, Factoria Singular / age fotostock. 473, Jordi Puig / age fotostock. 476, OSOMEDIA / age fotostock. 487, Elan Fleisher / age fotostock. 500 (top), Duquesa de Cardona. 500 (center left), Claris Hotel/leonardo.com. 500 (bottom left), Hotel Sant Agustí. 500 (center right), Condes de Barcelona Hotel /leonardo.com. 500 (bottom right), Starwood Hotels & Resorts. 501 (top), The Leading Hotels of the World. 501 (bottom left), Rafael Vargas. 501 (bottom right), Hotel Majestic Barcelona. 510, alterna2/Flickr. 521, Isidoro Ruiz Haro / age fotostock. Chapter 8: Catalonia, Valencia, and the Costa Blanca: 523, Hermes/age fotostock. 524, VRoig/Flickr. 525, Helio San Miguel. 529, Bjorn Svensson/age fotostock. 530, Patty Orly/Shutterstock. 531 (left), Ana Abadía/ age fotostock. 531 (right), Mauricio Pellegrinetti/Flickr. 532, Helio San Miguel. 536, Oscar García Bayerri / age fotostock. 541, Carlos S. Pereyra / age fotostock. 544, B&Y Photography Inc. / age fotostock. 547, Oscar García Bayerri / age fotostock. 550, José Fuste Raga / age fotostock. 557, Helio San Miguel. 559 (top left and bottom left), Francesc Guillamet. 559 (right), Restaurante Arzak. 560 (top row), Francesc Guillamet. 560 (center and bottom), Maribel Ruíz de Erenchun. 561 (top left), Peter Arnold, Inc./Alamy. 561 (top center), Kari Marttila/Alamy. 561 (top right), Sol Melia Hotels & Resorts. 561 (bottom left and right), Francesc Guillamet. 562 (top left and right), Restaurante Arzak. 562 (bottom), vittorio sciosia/age fotostock. 563 (top and bottom), Javier Espinosa. 566, Alberto Paredes / age fotostock. 574, Nils-Johan Norenlind/age fotostock. 579, Igor Gonzalo Sanz / age fotostock. 585, Charles Bowman / age fotostock. 588, Hidalgo & Lopesino/age fotostock. 592, Alan Copson/age fotostock. Chapter 9: The Balearic Islands: 595, Stuart Pearce / age fotostock. 596 (left), Factoria Singular/age fotostock. 596 (right), Casteran/age fotostock. 597 (top), M.Szymaniak/iStockphoto. 597 (bottom), mayla, Fodors.com member. 598, Joan Mercadal/age fotostock. 602, Bartomeu Amengual / age fotostock. 603 (left), Rafael Campillo / age fotostock. 603 (right),

Laurie Geffert Phelps, Fodors.com member. 604, GARDEL Bertrand / age fotostock. 605 (left), Anibal Trejo/Shutterstock. 605 (right), Salvador & lvaro Nebot/age fotostock. 606, Karolina Ksiazek/Shutterstock. 611, Skowron/Shutterstock. 614, Katja Kreder / age fotostock. 619, Hubertus Blume / age fotostock. 624, Martin Siepmann/age fotostock. 627, snap fotodesign / age fotostock. 632, Gonzalo Azumendi / age fotostock. 643, Stuart Pearce/age fotostock. Chapter 10: Andalusia: 649, José Fuste Raga/age fotostock. 650, Hayal, Fodors.com member. 651, Mariana Sacramento, Fodors.com member. 653, bxb52, Fodors.com member. 656, Seiffe / age footstock. 657 (left), ampFotoStudio/Shutterstock. 657 (right), Carmen Martínez Banús/iStockphoto. 658, riverside, Fodors.com member. 659 (left), csp/Shutterstock. 659 (right), José Francisco Ruiz/age footstock. 660, Christine B. Patronick, Fodors.com member. 663, MOIRENC Camille / age footstock. 670, José Antonio Moreno / age fotostock. 675, Johnny Stockshooter/age fotostock. 680, Marina Spironetti / Alamy. 681, Kimball Hall / Alamy. 682, Profimedia International s.r.o. / Alamy. 683 (top), amjad el-geoushi / Alamy. 683 (left), Felipe Trueba / Alamy. 683 (right), Redferns Music Picture Library / Alamy. 684, christina wilson / Alamy. 685 (top left), Marco Brindicci/Reuters/Corbis. 685 (bottom left), AFP/Getty Images. 685 (top right), Ted Pink/Alamy. 685 (bottom right), Christina Wilson/Alamy. 686, ©Doug Scott/age footstock. 693, lbuchanan, Fodors.com member. 700, Alessandra Sarti / age fotostock. 706, S Tauqueur / age fotostock. 707, Travel Pix Collection / age fotostock. 712, Francisco Barba / age fotostock. 715, Ken Welsh/age fotostock. 722-23, Sylvain Grandadam. 728, Lucas Vallecillos / age fotostock. 737, Thomas Dressler / age fotostock. 744, Juergen Richter / age fotostock. 753 (top), JLImages / Alamy. 753 (bottom), Vladimir Korostyshevskiy/Shutterstock. 754, Peter Horree / Alamy. 755, Jeronimo Alba/age fotostock. 756 (top), Werner Otto/age fotostock. 756 (2nd from top), Sylvain Grandadam/age fotostock. 756 (3rd from top), Tony Wright/earthscapes / Alamy. 756 (4th from top), Ken Welsh/age fotostock. 756 (bottom), Victor Kotler/age fotostock. 757, Javier Larrea/age fotostock. 758, Hideo Kurihara / Alamy. 759 (top and bottom), Javier Larrea/age fotostock. 760, Jeronimo Alba/age fotostock. 766, Paco Ayala/age fotostock. Chapter 11: Costa del Sol and Costa de Almería: 773, Jordi Puig/age fotostock. 774, andyandjill, Fodors.com member. 775 (top), Terri Rea, Fodors.com member. 775 (bottom) and 778, Judi, Fodors.com member. 780, Jochem Wijnands / age fotostock. 781 (left), J.D. Dallet / age fotostock. 781 (right), gildemax/wikipedia.org. 782, J.D. Dallet/age fotostock. 783 (left), Claus Mikosch/iStockphoto. 783 (right), sunshinecity/Flickr. 784, Freefly/iStockphoto. 789, Daniela Sachsenheimer/Shutterstock. 792, Herbert Scholpp / age fotostock. 795, Judi, Fodors.com member. 800, Ken Welsh / age fotostock. 809, RENAULT Philippe/age fotostock. 814, Jeronimo Alba/age fotostock. 820, J.D. Dallet / age fotostock. 827, Taka/age fotostock. 828, J.D. Dallet/age fotostock. 832, Freefly/iStockphoto

NOTES

NOTES